BRITISH WRITERS

BRITISH WRITERS

JAY PARINI
Editor

SUPPLEMENT XII

CHARLES SCRIBNER'S SONS
An imprint of Thomson Gale, a part of The Thomson Corporation

THOMSON
★
GALE

Detroit • New York • San Francisco • New Haven, Conn. • Waterville, Maine • London • Munich

British Writers Supplement XII
Jay Parini, Editor in Chief

Project Editor
Michelle Kazensky

Copyeditors
Gretchen Gordon, Robert E. Jones, Linda Sanders

Proofreader
Susan Barnett, Tara Marion

Indexer
Wendy Allex

Permissions Researcher
Laura Myers

Permissions
Carolyn Evans, Lisa Kincade, Kim Smilay

Composition Specialist
Gary Leach

Buyer
Rhonda A. Dover

Publisher
Frank Menchaca

Product Manager
Peg Bessette

LIBRARY OF CONGRESS CATALOGING-IN-PUBLICATION DATA

British Writers Supplement XII / Jay Parini, editor.
   p. cm.
Includes bibliographical references and index.
   ISBN 0-684-31511-4 (alk. paper)
   1. English literature–History and criticism. 2. English literature–Bio-bibliography. 3. Commonwealth literature (English)–History and criticism. 4. Commonwealth literature (English)–Bio-bibliography. 5. Authors, English–Biography 6 . Authors, Commonwealth–Biography. I. Parini, Jay.
   PR85 .B688 Suppl. 12
   820.9'001–dc22
                                  2006020939

Printed in the United States of America
10 9 8 7 6 5 4 3 2 1

Acknowledgments

Acknowledgment is gratefully made to those publishers and individuals
who permitted the use of the following materials in copyright:

FLEUR ADCOCK. Adcock, Fleur. From *Poems 1960 - 2000*. Bloodaxe Books, 2000. Copyright © 2000 Bloodaxe Books. Reproduced by permission. From *The Incident Book*. Oxford University Press, 1986. Copyright © 1986 Fleur Adcock. Reproduced by permission of Oxford University Press. Primas, Aurelianensisr Hugh. From "Poem 23," in *Hugh Primas and the Archpoet*. Edited by Fleur Adcock. Cambridge University Press, 1994. Copyright © 1994 Cambridge University Press. Reprinted with the permission of Cambridge University Press. From *Tigers*. Oxford University Press, 1967. Reproduced by permission of Oxford University Press. From *Inner Harbour*. Oxford University Press, 1979. Reproduced by permission of Oxford University Press. From *Time Zones*. Oxford University Press, 1991. Reproduced by permission of Oxford University Press. From *Looking Back*. Oxford University Press, 1997. Reproduced by permission of Oxford University Press.

KAMAU (EDWARD) BRATHWAITE. Brathwaite, Edward. From *The Arrivants: A New World Trilogy*. Oxford University Press, 1973. Copyright © Edward Brathwaite 1967, 1968, 1969, 1973. Reproduced by permission of Oxford University Press.

G. F. DUTTON. Dutton, G. F. From *Squaring the Waves*. Bloodaxe Books Ltd., 1986. © G. F. Dutton, 1986. Reproduced by permission. From *The Bare Abundance: Selected Poems 1975 - 2001*. Bloodaxe Books, 2002. Copyright © G. F. Dutton 1978, 1986, 1991, 2002. Reproduced by permission. From *Swimming Free: On and Below the Surface of Lake, River and Sea*. St. Martin's Press, 1972. Copyright © 1972 G. J. F. Dutton. All rights reserved. Reproduced by permission of the author.

PETER FALLON. Fallon, Peter. From *The Speaking Stones*. The Gallery Press, 1978. © Peter Fallon 1978. Reproduced by permission. From *Winter Work*. The Gallery Press, 1983. © Peter Fallon 1983. Reproduced by permission. From *The News and Weather*. The Gallery Press, 1987. © Peter Fallon 1987. Reproduced by permission. From *Eye To Eye*. The Gallery Press, 1992. © Peter Fallon 1992. Reproduced by permission. From *News of the World: Selected and New Poems*. The Gallery Press, 1998. © Peter Fallon 1998.

Reproduced by permission. Sacks, Peter M. From *The English Elegy: Studies in the Genre from Spenser to Yeats*. Johns Hopkins University Press, 1985. Copyright © 1985 The Johns Hopkins University Press. All rights reserved. Reproduced by permission.

JANICE GALLOWAY. Norquay, Glenda. From "Fraudulent Mooching," in *Contemporary Scottish Women Writers*. Edited by Aileen Christianson and Alison Lumsden. Edinburgh University Press, 2000. Reproduced by permission of Edinburgh University Press. www.eup.ed.ac.uk. Eliass, Dorte, "Reflections On Clara," http://www.galloway.1to1.org, 2003. Reproduced by permission of A. P. Watt on behalf of Janice Galloway. Kernan, Aoife, "Interview with Janice Galloway," http://www.galloway.1to1.org, 2003. Originally published in *Trinity News*. Trinity College, Dublin, Ireland. Reproduced by permission.

PHILIP KERR. *Publishers Weekly*, April 8, 1996. Copyright © 1996 by Reed Publishing USA. Reproduced from Publishers Weekly, published by the Bowker Magazine Group of Cahners Publishing Co., a division of Reed Publishing USA, by permission. *Sunday Times*, Junc 16, 1996 for "A Plan to Thrill" by Eddie Gibb. Copyright © 1996 Times Newspapers Ltd. Reproduced by permission of the author. *New Statesman*, May 22, 2002. Copyright (c) 2002 New Statesman, Ltd. Reproduced by permission.

HUGH MACDIARMID. MacDiarmid, Hugh. From "A Drunk Man Looks At The Thistle," in *Complete Poems 1920—1976, volume 1*. Edited by Michael Grieve and W. R. Aitken. Martin Brian & O'Keefe Ltd, 1978. © Copyright Christopher Murray Grieve 1978. Reproduced by permission of Carcanet Press Limited. From "To Circumjack Cencrastus," in *Complete Poems 1920—1976, volume 1*. Edited by Michael Grieve and W. R. Aitken. Martin Brian & O'Keefe Ltd., 1978. © Copyright Christopher Murray Grieve 1978. Reproduced by permission of Carcanet Press Limited. From "First Hymn To Lenin," in *Complete Poems 1920—1976, volume 1*. Edited by Michael Grieve and W. R. Aitken. Martin Brian & O'Keefe Ltd., 1978. © Copyright Christopher Murray Grieve 1978. Reproduced by permission of Carcanet Press Limited. From "The Seamless Garment," in *Complete*

ACKNOWLEDGMENTS

Poems 1920—1976, volume 1. Edited by Michael Grieve and W. R. Aitken. Martin Brian & O'Keefe Ltd., 1978. © Copyright Christopher Murray Grieve 1978. Reproduced by permission of Carcanet Press Limited. From "Water Music," in *Complete Poems 1920—1976, volume 1.* Edited by Michael Grieve and W. R. Aitken. Martin Brian & O'Keefe Ltd., 1978. © Copyright Christopher Murray Grieve 1978. Reproduced by permission of Carcanet Press Limited. From "The Skeleton of the Future (At Lenin's Tomb)," in *Complete Poems 1920—1976, volume 1.* Edited by Michael Grieve and W. R. Aitken. Martin Brian & O'Keefe Ltd., 1978. © Copyright Christopher Murray Grieve 1978. Reproduced by permission of Carcanet Press Limited. From "On A Raised Beach," in *Complete Poems 1920—1976, volume 1.* Edited by Michael Grieve and W. R. Aitken. Martin Brian & O'Keefe Ltd., 1978. © Copyright Christopher Murray Grieve 1978. Reproduced by permission of Carcanet Press Limited. From "Perfect," in *Complete Poems 1920—1976, volume 1.* Edited by Michael Grieve and W. R. Aitken. Martin Brian & O'Keeffe Ltd, 1978. © Copyright Christopher Murray Grieve 1978. Reproduced by permission of Carcanet Press Limited. From "The Bonnie Broukit Bairn," in *Complete Poems 1920—1976, volume 1.* Edited by Michael Grieve and W. R. Aitken. Martin Brian & O'Keeffe Ltd, 1978. © Copyright Christopher Murray Grieve 1978. Reproduced by permission of Carcanet Press Limited. From "The Watergaw," in *Complete Poems 1920—1976, volume 1.* Edited by Michael Grieve and W. R. Aitken. Martin Brian & O'Keefe Ltd, 1978. © Copyright Christopher Murray Grieve 1978. Reproduced by permission of Carcanet Press Limited. From "The Eemis Stane," in *Complete Poems 1920 - 1976, volume 1.* Edited by Michael Grieve and W. R. Aitken. Martin Brian & O'Keefe Ltd., 1978. © Copyright Christopher Murray Grieve 1978. Reproduced by permission of Carcanet Press Limited. From "Empty Vessel," in *Complete Poems 1920—1976, volume 1.* Edited by Michael Grieve and W. R. Aitken. Martin Brian & O'Keefe Ltd., 1978. © Copyright Christopher Murray Grieve 1978. Reproduced by permission of Carcanet Press Limited. From "In Memoriam James Joyce," in *The Complete Poems of Hugh MacDiarmid, volume 2.* Edited by Alan Riach. Carcanet, 1994. Copyright © Christopher Murray Grieve, 1978. Copyright © Valda Grieve, 1985. All rights reserved. Reproduced by permission of Carcanet Press Limited.

DAVID MALOUF. Malouf, David. From *The Year of The Foxes and Other Poems.* George Braziller Inc., 1979. Copyright © 1979 by David Malouf. All rights reserved. Reproduced by permission.

MARTIN MCDONAGH. McDonagh, Martin. From *Pillowman.* Faber and Faber, 2003. © Martin McDonagh, 2003. Reproduced by permission of The Rod Hall Agency.

R. S. THOMAS. Thomas, Ronald Stuart. From *Frequencies.* Macmillan London Ltd., 1978. Copyright © Kunjana Thomas 2001. All rights reserved. Reproduced by permission of the Literary Estate of Ronald Stuart Thomas. From *Counterpoint.* Bloodaxe Books, Ltd., 1990. Copyright © R. S. Thomas 1995. Reproduced by permission. From *Mass for Hard Times.* Bloodaxe Books, 1992. Copyright © R. S. Thomas. Reproduced by permission. From *Collected Poems 1945 - 1990.* Copyright © 1993 R. S. Thomas. All rights reserved. Reproduced by permission of J. M. Dent and Sons, a division of The Orion Publishing Group. From *Collected Later Poems 1988—2000.* Bloodaxe Books, 2004. Reproduced by permission. From *No Truce with the Furies.* Bloodaxe Books, Ltd., 1995. Bloodaxe Books, Ltd., 1995. Copyright © R. S. Thomas 1995. Reproduced by permission.

Contents

Contents ....*vii*

Introduction ....*ix*

Chronology ....*xi*

List of Contributors ....*liii*

Subjects in Supplement XI

FLEUR ADCOCK / Abby Mims 1

GEORGE BORROW / Fred Bilson 17

KAMAU (EDWARD) BRATHWAITE / Amor Kohli 33

PETER CAREY / Ian Bickford 49

LOUIS DE BERNIÈRES / Deborah Seddon 65

G. F. DUTTON / Gerry Cambridge 81

PETER FALLON / Richard Rankin Russell 101

JANICE GALLOWAY / Claire Keyes 117

ELIZA HAYWOOD / Scott R. MacKenzie 133

JULIAN OF NORWICH / Jane Beal 149

MARGERY KEMPE / Jane Beal 167

PHILIP KERR / Patrick A. Smith 185

HUGH MacDIARMID / Les Wilkinson 201

DAVID MALOUF / Brian Henry 217

MARTIN McDONAGH / Kimberly Lewis 233

PATRICK O'BRIAN / John Lennard 247

FLORA ANNIE STEEL / Phillip Mallett 265

R. S. THOMAS / William V. Davis 279

MASTER INDEX to Volumes I–VII, Supplements I–XII, Retrospective Supplements I–II 295

INTRODUCTION

these writers has yet enjoyed sustained critical attention, and a beginning is attempted with these articles.

Several writers from the distant past are treated here, having been passed over in earlier volumes for no good reason. Two of these, Julian of Norwich and Margery Kempe, were religious writers of considerable power and significance in the contemplative tradition, and their lives and work deserve close inspection and appreciation. Flora Annie Steel lived part of her life in India during the Raj, and was a gifted novelist and historian of the empire. Eliza Haywood was an eighteenth century novelist, actress, poet, and playwright of considerable distinction, and she has not been sufficiently studied before. Among nineteenth century travel writers, George Borrow ranks high, and his work is also given its due in these pages.

Martin McDonagh is a young Irish playwright whose concentrated work has made a vivid impression on stages from Ireland and Britain to the U.S. His drama continues to evolve and grow, and he will surely continue to attract criticism for years to come, but this sketch of his life and work to date marks a beginning.

As ever, our purpose in presenting these critical and biographical essays is to bring readers back to the texts discussed, and to assist those who have been struck by an author and want to know more about his or her work. This is biographical criticism in the best sense, examining the work in the context of an evolving life, and reading from the work to the life, while not trying to read the life into the work—as is sometimes done, to the diminishment of the work. These articles should, in theory, assist those who wish to understand an author's work in a more systematic fashion. They should also increase the reader's pleasure in the texts themselves.

—JAY PARINI

Chronology

ca. 1342 Birth of John Trevisa and **Julian of Norwich**

1348 The Black Death (further outbreaks in 1361 and 1369)

ca. 1350 Boccaccio's *Decameron*
Langland's *Piers Plowman*

1351 The Statute of Laborers pegs laborers' wages at rates in effect preceding the plague

1356 The Battle of Poitiers

1360 The Treaty of Brétigny: end of the first phase of the Hundred Years' War

1362 Pleadings in the law courts conducted in English
Parliaments opened by speeches in English

1369 Chaucer's *The Book of the Duchess*, an elegy to Blanche of Lancaster, wife of John of Gaunt

1369–1377 Victorious French campaigns under du Guesclin

ca. 1370 John Lydgate born

1371 Sir John Mandeville's *Travels*

1372 Chaucer travels to Italy

1372–1382 Wycliffe active in Oxford

1373–1393 William of Wykeham founds Winchester College and New College, Oxford

ca. 1373 **Margery Kempe born**

ca. 1375–1400 *Sir Gawain and the Green Knight*

1376 Death of Edward the Black Prince

1377–1399 Reign of Richard II

ca. 1379 Gower's *Vox clamantis*

ca. 1380 Chaucer's *Troilus and Criseyde*

1381 The Peasants' Revolt

1386 Chaucer's *Canterbury Tales* begun
Chaucer sits in Parliament
Gower's *Confessio amantis*

1399–1413 Reign of Henry IV

ca. 1400 Death of William Langland

1400 Death of Geoffrey Chaucer

1408 Death of John Gower

1412–1420 Lydgate's *Troy Book*

1413–1422 Reign of Henry V

1415 The Battle of Agincourt

ca. 1416 Death of **Julian of Norwich**

1420–1422 Lydgate's *Siege of Thebes*

1422–1461 Reign of Henry VI

1431 François Villon born
Joan of Arc burned at Rouen

ca. 1439 **Death of Margery Kempe**

1440–1441 Henry VI founds Eton College and King's College, Cambridge

1444 Truce of Tours

1450 Jack Cade's rebellion

ca. 1451 Death of John Lydgate

1453 End of the Hundred Years' War
The fall of Constantinople

1455–1485 The Wars of the Roses

ca. 1460 Births of William Dunbar and John Skelton

1461–1470 Reign of Edward IV

1470–1471 Reign of Henry VI

1471 Death of Sir Thomas Malory

1471–1483 Reign of Edward IV

1476–1483 Caxton's press set up: *The Canterbury Tales*, *Morte d'Arthur*, and *The Golden Legend* printed

1483–1485 Reign of Richard III

1485 The Battle of Bosworth Field; end of the Wars of the Roses

1485–1509 Reign of Henry VII

1486 Marriage of Henry VII and Elizabeth of York unites the rival houses of Lancaster and York
Bartholomew Diaz rounds the Cape of Good Hope

1492 Columbus' first voyage to the New World

1493 Pope Alexander VI divides undiscovered territories between Spain and Portugal

1497–1498 John Cabot's voyages to Newfoundland and Labrador

1497–1499 Vasco da Gama's voyage to India

CHRONOLOGY

1499   Amerigo Vespucci's first voyage to America

Erasmus' first visit to England

1503   Thomas Wyatt born

1505   John Colet appointed dean of St. Paul's: founds St. Paul's School

1509–1547   Reign of Henry VIII

1509   The king marries Catherine of Aragon

1511   Erasmus' *Praise of Folly* published

1513   Invasion by the Scots defeated at Flodden Field

1515   Wolsey appointed lord chancellor

1516   Sir Thomas More's *Utopia*

1517   Martin Luther's theses against indulgences published at Wittenberg

Henry Howard (earl of Surrey) born

1519   Charles V of Spain becomes Holy Roman Emperor

1519–1521   Magellan's voyage around the world

1525   Cardinal College, the forerunner of Christ Church, founded at Oxford

1526   Tyndale's English translation of the New Testament imported from Holland

1529   Fall of Cardinal Wolsey

Death of John Skelton

1529–1536   The "Reformation" Parliament

1531   Sir Thomas Elyot's *The Governour* published

1532   Thomas Cranmer appointed archbishop of Canterbury

Machiavelli's *The Prince*

1533   The king secretly marries Anne Boleyn

Cranmer pronounces the king's marriage with Catherine "against divine law"

1534   The Act of Supremacy constitutes the king as head of the Church of England

1535   Sir Thomas More executed

Thomas Cromwell appointed vicar general of the Church of England

1536   The Pilgrimage of Grace: risings against the king's religious, social, and economic reforms

Anne Boleyn executed

The king marries Jane Seymour

1537   The dissolution of the monasteries: confiscation of ecclesiastical properties and assets; increase in royal revenues

Jane Seymour dies

1538   First complete English Bible published and placed in all churches

1540   The king marries Anne of Cleves

Marriage dissolved

The king marries Catherine Howard

Fall and execution of Thomas Cromwell

1542   Catherine Howard executed

Death of Sir Thomas Wyatt

1543   The king marries Catherine Parr

Copernicus' *De revolutionibus orbium coelestium*

1546   Trinity College, Cambridge, refounded

1547   The earl of Surrey executed

1547–1553   Reign of Edward VI

1548–1552   Hall's *Chronicle*

1552   The second Book of Common Prayer

ca. 1552   Edmund Spenser born

1553   Lady Jane Grey proclaimed queen

1553–1558   Reign of Mary I (Mary Tudor)

ca. 1554   Births of Walter Raleigh, Richard Hooker, John Lyly, and Fulke Greville

1554   Lady Jane Grey executed

Mary I marries Philip II of Spain

Bandello's *Novelle*

Philip Sidney born

ca. 1556   George Peele born

1557   Tottel's *Miscellany*, including the poems of Wyatt and Surrey, published

ca. 1558   Thomas Kyd born

1558   Calais, the last English possession in France, is lost

Birth of Robert Greene

Mary I dies

1558–1603   Reign of Elizabeth I

1559   John Knox arrives in Scotland

Rebellion against the French regent

ca. 1559   George Chapman born

1561   Mary Queen of Scots (Mary Stuart) arrives in Edinburgh

CHRONOLOGY

Thomas Hoby's translation of Castiglione's *The Courtier Gorboduc*, the first English play in blank verse
Francis Bacon born

1562 Civil war in France
English expedition sent to support the Huguenots

1562–1568 Sir John Hawkins' voyages to Africa

1564 Births of Christopher Marlowe and William Shakespeare

1565 Mary Queen of Scots marries Lord Darnley

1566 William Painter's *Palace of Pleasure*, a miscellany of prose stories, the source of many dramatists' plots

1567 Darnley murdered at Kirk o' Field
Mary Queen of Scots marries the earl of Bothwell

1569 Rebellion of the English northern earls suppressed

1570 Roger Ascham's *The Schoolmaster*

1571 Defeat of the Turkish fleet at Lepanto

ca. 1572 Ben Jonson born

1572 St. Bartholomew's Day massacre
John Donne born

1574 The earl of Leicester's theater company formed

1576 The Theater, the first permanent theater building in London, opened
The first Blackfriars Theater opened with performances by the Children of St. Paul's
John Marston born

1576–1578 Martin Frobisher's voyages to Labrador and the northwest

1577–1580 Sir Francis Drake sails around the world

1577 Holinshed's *Chronicles of England, Scotlande, and Irelande*

1579 John Lyly's *Euphues: The Anatomy of Wit*
Thomas North's translation of *Plutarch's Lives*

1581 The Levant Company founded
Seneca's *Ten Tragedies* translated

1582 Richard Hakluyt's *Divers Voyages Touching the Discoverie of America*

1583 Philip Massinger born

1584–1585 Sir John Davis' first voyage to Greenland

1585 First English settlement in America, the "Lost Colony" comprising 108 men under Ralph Lane, founded at Roanoke Island, off the coast of North Carolina

1586 Kyd's *Spanish Tragedy*
Marlowe's *Tamburlaine*
William Camden's *Britannia*
The Babington conspiracy against Queen Elizabeth
Death of Sir Philip Sidney

1587 Mary Queen of Scots executed
Birth of Virginia Dare, first English child born in America, at Roanoke Island

1588 Defeat of the Spanish Armada
Marlowe's *Dr. Faustus*

1590 Spenser's *The Faerie Queen*, Cantos 1–3
Richard Brome born

1592 Outbreak of plague in London; the theaters closed
Henry King born

1593 Death of Christopher Marlowe

1594 The Lord Chamberlain's Men, the company to which Shakespeare belonged, founded
The Swan Theater opened
Death of Thomas Kyd

1595 Ralegh's expedition to Guiana
Sidney's *Apology for Poetry*

1596 The earl of Essex's expedition captures Cadiz
The second Blackfriars Theater opened

ca. 1597 Death of George Peele

1597 Bacon's first collection of *Essays*

1598 Jonson's *Every Man in His Humor*

1598–1600 Richard Hakluyt's *Principal Navigations, Voyages, Traffics, and Discoveries of the English Nation*

1599 The Globe Theater opened
Death of Edmund Spenser

1600 Death of Richard Hooker

1601 Rebellion and execution of the earl of Essex

1602 The East India Company founded
The Bodleian Library reopened at Oxford

1603–1625 Reign of James I

1603 John Florio's translation of Montaigne's *Essays*

CHRONOLOGY

Cervantes' *Don Quixote* (Part 1)
The Gunpowder Plot
Thomas Browne born
1604 Shakespeare's *Othello*
ca. 1605 Shakespears's *King Lear*
Tourneur's *The Revenger's Tragedy*
1605 Bacon's *Advancement of Learning*
1606 Shakespeare's *Macbeth*
Jonson's *Volpone*
Death of John Lyly
Edmund Waller born
1607 The first permanent English colony established at Jamestown, Virginia
1608 John Milton born
1609 Kepler's *Astronomia nova*
John Suckling born
1610 Galileo's *Sidereus nuncius*
1611 The Authorized Version of the Bible
Shakespeare's *The Tempest*
1612 Death of Prince Henry, King James's eldest son
Webster's *The White Devil*
Bacon's second collection of *Essays*
ca. 1613 Richard Crashaw born
1613 The Globe Theatre destroyed by fire
Webster's *The Duchess of Malfi*
1614 Ralegh's *History of the World*
1616 George Chapman's translation of Homer's *Odyssey*
Deaths of William Shakespeare, Francis Beaumont, and Miguel Cervantes
ca. 1618 Richard Lovelace born
1618 The Thirty Years' War begins
Sir Walter Ralegh executed
Abraham Cowley born
1619 The General Assembly, the first legislative assembly on American soil, meets in Virginia
Slavery introduced at Jamestown
1620 The Pilgrims land in Massachusetts
John Evelyn born
1621 Francis Bacon impeached and fined
Robert Burton's *Anatomy of Melancholy*
Andrew Marvell born
1622 Middleton's *The Changeling*
Henry Vaughan born
1623 The First Folio of Shakespeare's plays

Visit of Prince Charles and the duke of Buckingham to Spain; failure of attempts to negotiate a Spanish marriage
1624 War against Spain
1625–1649 Reign of Charles I
1625 Death of John Fletcher
Bacon's last collection of *Essays*
1626 Bacon's *New Atlantis*, appended to *Sylva sylvarum*
Dutch found New Amsterdam
Death of Cyril Tourneur
Death of Francis Bacon
1627 Ford's *'Tis Pity She's a Whore*
Cardinal Richelieu establishes the Company of New France with monopoly over trade and land in Canada
Buckingham's expedition to the Isle of Ré to relieve La Rochelle
Death of Thomas Middleton
1627–1628 Revolt and siege of La Rochelle, the principal Huguenot city of France
1628 Buckingham assassinated
Surrender of La Rochelle
William Harvey's treatise on the circulation of the blood (*De motu cordis et sanguinis*)
John Bunyan born
Death of Fulke Greville
1629 Ford's *The Broken Heart*
King Charles dismisses his third Parliament, imprisons nine members, and proceeds to rule for eleven years without Parliament
The Massachusetts Bay Company formed
1629–1630 Peace treaties with France and Spain
1631 John Dryden born
Death of John Donne
1633 William Laud appointed archbishop of Canterbury
Death of George Herbert
Samuel Pepys born
1634 Deaths of George Chapman and John Marston
1635 The Académie Française founded
George Etherege born
1636 Pierre Corneille's *Le Cid*
Harvard College founded

CHRONOLOGY

ca. 1637   Thomas Traherne born
1637   Milton's "Lycidas"
Descartes's *Discours de la méthode*
King Charles's levy of ship money challenged in the courts by John Hampden
The introduction of the new English Book of Common Prayer strongly opposed in Scotland
Death of Ben Jonson
ca. 1638   Death of John Webster
1638   The Scots draw up a National Covenant to defend their religion
ca. 1639   Death of John Ford
1639   Parliament reassembled to raise taxes
Death of Thomas Carew
Charles Sedley born
1639–1640   The two Bishops' Wars with Scotland
1640   The Long Parliament assembled
The king's advisers, Archbishop Laud and the earl of Strafford, impeached
Aphra Behn born
Death of Philip Massinger
1641   Strafford executed
Acts passed abolishing extraparliamentary taxation, the king's extraordinary courts, and his power to order a dissolution without parliamentary consent
The Grand Remonstrance censuring royal policy passed by eleven votes
William Wycherley born
1642   Parliament submits the nineteen Propositions, which King Charles rejects as annihilating the royal power
The Civil War begins
The theaters close
Royalist victory at Edgehill; King Charles established at Oxford
Death of Sir John Suckling
1643   Parliament concludes the Solemn League and Covenant with the Scots
Louis XIV becomes king of France
Charles Sackville, earl of Dorset, born
1644   Parliamentary victory at Marston Moor

The New Model army raised
Milton's *Areopagitica*
1645   Parliamentary victory under Fairfax and Cromwell at Naseby
Fairfax captures Bristol
Archbishop Laud executed
1646   Fairfax besieges King Charles at Oxford
King Charles takes refuge in Scotland; end of the First Civil War
King Charles attempts negotiations with the Scots
Parliament's proposals sent to the king and rejected
1647   Conflict between Parliament and the army
A general council of the army established that discusses representational government within the army
The Agreement of the People drawn up by the Levelers; its proposals include manhood suffrage
King Charles concludes an agreement with the Scots
George Fox begins to preach
John Wilmot, earl of Rochester, born
1648   Cromwell dismisses the general council of the army
The Second Civil War begins
Fairfax defeats the Kentish royalists at Maidstone
Cromwell defeats the Scots at Preston
The Thirty Years' War ended by the treaty of Westphalia
Parliament purged by the army
1649–1660   Commonwealth
1649   King Charles I tried and executed
The monarchy and the House of Lords abolished
The Commonwealth proclaimed
Cromwell invades Ireland and defeats the royalist Catholic forces
Death of Richard Crashaw
1650   Cromwell defeats the Scots at Dunbar
1651   Charles II crowned king of the Scots, at Scone
Charles II invades England, is defeated at Worcester, escapes to France

CHRONOLOGY

Thomas Hobbes's *Leviathan*
1652 War with Holland
Death of Richard Brome
1653 The Rump Parliament dissolved by the army
A new Parliament and council of state nominated; Cromwell becomes Lord Protector
Walton's *The Compleat Angler*
1654 Peace concluded with Holland
War against Spain
1655 Parliament attempts to reduce the army and is dissolved
Rule of the major-generals
1656 Sir William Davenant produces *The Siege of Rhodes*, one of the first English operas
1657 Second Parliament of the Protectorate
Cromwell is offered and declines the throne
Death of Richard Lovelace
1658 Death of Oliver Cromwell
Richard Cromwell succeeds as Protector
1659 Conflict between Parliament and the army
1660 General Monck negotiates with Charles II
Charles II offers the conciliatory Declaration of Breda and accepts Parliament's invitation to return
Will's Coffee House established
Sir William Davenant and Thomas Killigrew licensed to set up two companies of players, the Duke of York's and the King's Servants, including actors and actresses
Pepys's *Diary* begun
1660–1685 Reign of Charles II
1661 Parliament passes the Act of Uniformity, enjoining the use of the Book of Common Prayer; many Puritan and dissenting clergy leave their livings
Anne Finch born
1662 Peace Treaty with Spain
King Charles II marries Catherine of Braganza
The Royal Society incorporated (founded in 1660)

1664 War against Holland
New Amsterdam captured and becomes New York
John Vanbrugh born
1665 The Great Plague
Newton discovers the binomial theorem and invents the integral and differential calculus, at Cambridge
1666 The Great Fire of London
Bunyan's *Grace Abounding*
London Gazette founded
1667 The Dutch fleet sails up the Medway and burns English ships
The war with Holland ended by the Treaty of Breda
Milton's *Paradise Lost*
Thomas Sprat's *History of the Royal Society*
Death of Abraham Cowley
1668 Sir Christopher Wren begins to rebuild St. Paul's Cathedral
Triple Alliance formed with Holland and Sweden against France
Dryden's *Essay of Dramatick Poesy*
1670 Alliance formed with France through the secret Treaty of Dover
Pascal's *Pensées*
The Hudson's Bay Company founded
William Congreve born
1671 Milton's *Samson Agonistes* and *Paradise Regained*
1672 War against Holland
Wycherley's *The Country Wife*
King Charles issues the Declaration of Indulgence, suspending penal laws against Nonconformists and Catholics
1673 Parliament passes the Test Act, making acceptance of the doctrines of the Church of England a condition for holding public office
1674 War with Holland ended by the Treaty of Westminster
Deaths of John Milton, Robert Herrick, and Thomas Traherne
1676 Etherege's *The Man of Mode*
1677 Baruch Spinoza's *Ethics*
Jean Racine's *Phèdre*

CHRONOLOGY

King Charles's niece, Mary, marries her cousin William of Orange

1678 Fabrication of the so-called popish plot by Titus Oates
Bunyan's *Pilgrim's Progress*
Dryden's *All for Love*
Death of Andrew Marvell
George Farquhar born

1679 Parliament passes the Habeas Corpus Act
Rochester's *A Satire Against Mankind*

1680 Death of John Wilmot, earl of Rochester

1681 Dryden's *Absalom and Achitophel* (Part 1)

1682 Dryden's *Absalom and Achitophel* (Part 2)
Thomas Otway's *Venice Preserv'd*
Philadelphia founded
Death of Sir Thomas Browne

1683 The Ashmolean Museum, the world's first public museum, opens at Oxford
Death of Izaak Walton

1685–1688 Reign of James II

1685 Rebellion and execution of James Scott, duke of Monmouth
John Gay born

1686 The first book of Newton's *Principia De motu corporum*, containing his theory of gravitation presented to the Royal Society

1687 James II issues the Declaration of Indulgence
Dryden's *The Hind and the Panther*
Death of Edmund Waller

1688 James II reissues the Declaration of Indulgence, renewing freedom of worship and suspending the provisions of the Test Act
Acquittal of the seven bishops imprisoned for protesting against the Declaration
William of Orange lands at Torbay, Devon
James II takes refuge in France
Death of John Bunyan
Alexander Pope born

1689–1702 Reign of William III

1689 Parliament formulates the Declaration of Rights

William and Mary accept the Declaration and the crown
The Grand Alliance concluded between the Holy Roman Empire, England, Holland, and Spain
War declared against France
King William's War, 1689–1697 (the first of the French and Indian wars)
Samuel Richardson born

1690 James II lands in Ireland with French support, but is defeated at the battle of the Boyne
John Locke's *Essay Concerning Human Understanding*

1692 Salem witchcraft trials
Death of Sir George Etherege

ca. 1693 **Eliza Haywood born**

1694 George Fox's *Journal*
Voltaire (François Marie Arouet) born
Death of Mary II

1695 Congreve's *Love for Love*
Death of Henry Vaughan

1697 War with France ended by the Treaty of Ryswick
Vanbrugh's *The Relapse*

1698 Jeremy Collier's *A Short View of the Immorality and Profaneness of the English Stage*

1699 Fénelon's *Les Aventures de Télémaque*

1700 Congreve's *The Way of the World*
Defoe's *The True-Born Englishman*
Death of John Dryden
James Thomson born

1701 War of the Spanish Succession, 1701–1714 (Queen Anne's War in America, 1702–1713)
Death of Sir Charles Sedley

1702–1714 Reign of Queen Anne

1702 Clarendon's *History of the Rebellion* (1702–1704)
Defoe's *The Shortest Way with the Dissenters*

1703 Defoe is arrested, fined, and pilloried for writing *The Shortest Way*
Death of Samuel Pepys

1704 John Churchill, duke of Marlborough, and Prince Eugene of Savoy defeat the French at Blenheim
Capture of Gibraltar

CHRONOLOGY

Swift's *A Tale of a Tub* and *The Battle of the Books*
The Review founded (1704–1713)

1706 Farquhar's *The Recruiting Officer*
Deaths of John Evelyn and Charles Sackville, earl of Dorset

1707 Farquhar's *The Beaux' Stratagem*
Act of Union joining England and Scotland
Death of George Farquhar
Henry Fielding born

1709 The *Tatler* founded (1709–1711)
Nicholas Rowe's edition of Shakespeare
Samuel Johnson born
Marlborough defeats the French at Malplaquet
Charles XII of Sweden defeated at Poltava

1710 South Sea Company founded
First copyright act

1711 Swift's *The Conduct of the Allies*
The *Spectator* founded (1711–1712; 1714)
Marlborough dismissed
David Hume born

1712 Pope's *The Rape of the Lock* (Cantos 1–2)
Jean Jacques Rousseau born

1713 War with France ended by the Treaty of Utrecht
The *Guardian* founded
Swift becomes dean of St. Patrick's, Dublin
Addison's *Cato*
Laurence Sterne born

1714–1727 Reign of George I

1714 Pope's expended version of *The Rape of the Lock* (Cantos 1–5)

1715 The Jacobite rebellion in Scotland
Pope's translation of Homer's *Iliad* (1715–1720)
Death of Louis XIV

1716 Death of William Wycherley
Thomas Gray born

1717 Pope's *Eloisa to Abelard*
David Garrick born
Horace Walpole born

1718 Quadruple Alliance (Britain, France, the Netherlands, the German Empire) in war against Spain

1719 Defoe's *Robinson Crusoe*

Death of Joseph Addison

1720 Inoculation against smallpox introduced in Boston
War against Spain
The South Sea Bubble
Gilbert White born
Defoe's *Captain Singleton* and *Memoirs of a Cavalier*

1721 Tobias Smollett born
William Collins born

1722 Defoe's *Moll Flanders, Journal of the Plague Year,* and *Colonel Jack*

1724 Defoe's *Roxana*
Swift's *The Drapier's Letters*

1725 Pope's translation of Homer's *Odyssey* (1725–1726)

1726 Swift's *Gulliver's Travels*
Voltaire in England (1726–1729)
Death of Sir John Vanbrugh

1727–1760 Reign of George II

1728 Gay's *The Beggar's Opera*
Pope's *The Dunciad* (Books 1–2)
Oliver Goldsmith born

1729 Swift's *A Modest Proposal*
Edmund Burke born
Deaths of William Congreve and Sir Richard Steele

1731 Navigation improved by introduction of the quadrant
Pope's *Moral Essays* (1731–1735)
Death of Daniel Defoe
William Cowper born

1732 Death of John Gay

1733 Pope's *Essay on Man* (1733–1734)
Lewis Theobald's edition of Shakespeare

1734 Voltaire's *Lettres philosophiques*

1736 James Macpherson born

1737 Edward Gibbon born

1738 Johnson's *London*

1740 War of the Austrian Succession, 1740–1748 (King George's War in America, 1744–1748)
George Anson begins his circumnavigation of the world (1740–1744)
Frederick the Great becomes king of Prussia (1740–1786)
Richardson's *Pamela* (1740–1741)
James Boswell born

1742 Fielding's *Joseph Andrews*

CHRONOLOGY

Edward Young's *Night Thoughts* (1742–1745)

Pope's *The New Dunciad* (Book 4)

1744 Johnson's *Life of Mr. Richard Savage*

Death of Alexander Pope

1745 Second Jacobite rebellion, led by Charles Edward, the Young Pretender

Death of Jonathan Swift

1746 The Young Pretender defeated at Culloden

Collins' *Odes on Several Descriptive and Allegorical Subjects*

1747 Richardson's *Clarissa Harlowe* (1747–1748)

Franklin's experiments with electricity announced

Voltaire's *Essai sur les moeurs*

1748 War of the Austrian Succession ended by the Peace of Aix-la-Chapelle

Smollett's *Adventures of Roderick Random*

David Hume's *Enquiry Concerning Human Understanding*

Montesquieu's *L'Esprit des lois*

1749 Fielding's *Tom Jones*

Johnson's *The Vanity of Human Wishes*

Bolingbroke's *Idea of a Patriot King*

1750 The *Rambler* founded (1750–1752)

1751 Gray's *Elegy Written in a Country Churchyard*

Fielding's *Amelia*

Smollett's *Adventures of Peregrine Pickle*

Denis Diderot and Jean le Rond d'Alembert begin to publish the *Encyclopédie* (1751–1765)

Richard Brinsley Sheridan born

1752 Frances Burney and Thomas Chatterton born

1753 Richardson's *History of Sir Charles Grandison* (1753–1754)

Smollett's *The Adventures of Ferdinand Count Fathom*

1754 Hume's *History of England* (1754–1762)

Death of Henry Fielding

George Crabbe born

1755 Lisbon destroyed by earthquake

Fielding's *Journal of a Voyage to Lisbon* published posthumously

Johnson's *Dictionary of the English Language*

1756 The Seven Years' War against France, 1756–1763 (the French and Indian War in America, 1755–1760)

William Pitt the elder becomes prime minister

Johnson's proposal for an edition of Shakespeare

Death of Eliza Haywood

1757 Robert Clive wins the battle of Plassey, in India

Gray's "The Progress of Poesy" and "The Bard"

Burke's *Philosophical Enquiry into the Origin of Our Ideas of the Sublime and Beautiful*

Hume's *Natural History of Religion*

William Blake born

1758 The *Idler* founded (1758–1760)

1759 Capture of Quebec by General James Wolfe

Johnson's *History of Rasselas, Prince of Abyssinia*

Voltaire's *Candide*

The British Museum opens

Sterne's *The Life and Opinions of Tristram Shandy* (1759–1767)

Death of William Collins

Mary Wollstonecraft born

Robert Burns born

1760–1820 Reign of George III

1760 James Macpherson's *Fragments of Ancient Poetry Collected in the Highlands of Scotland*

William Beckford born

1761 Jean-Jacques Rousseau's *Julie, ou la nouvelle Héloïse*

Death of Samuel Richardson

1762 Rousseau's *Du Contrat social* and *Émile*

Catherine the Great becomes czarina of Russia (1762–1796)

1763 The Seven Years' War ended by the Peace of Paris

Smart's *A Song to David*

CHRONOLOGY

1764 James Hargreaves invents the spinning jenny

1765 Parliament passes the Stamp Act to tax the American colonies
Johnson's edition of Shakespeare
Walpole's *The Castle of Otranto*
Thomas Percy's *Reliques of Ancient English Poetry*
Blackstone's *Commentaries on the Laws of England* (1765–1769)

1766 The Stamp Act repealed
Swift's *Journal to Stella* first published in a collection of his letters
Goldsmith's *The Vicar of Wakefield*
Smollett's *Travels Through France and Italy*
Lessing's *Laokoon*
Rousseau in England (1766–1767)

1768 Sterne's *A Sentimental Journey Through France and Italy*
The Royal Academy founded by George III
First edition of the *Encyclopaedia Britannica*
Maria Edgeworth born
Death of Laurence Sterne

1769 David Garrick organizes the Shakespeare Jubilee at Stratford-upon-Avon
Sir Joshua Reynolds' *Discourses* (1769–1790)
Richard Arkwright invents the spinning water frame

1770 Boston Massacre
Burke's *Thoughts on the Cause of the Present Discontents*
Oliver Goldsmith's *The Deserted Village*
Death of Thomas Chatterton
William Wordsworth born
James Hogg born

1771 Arkwright's first spinning mill founded
Deaths of Thomas Gray and Tobias Smollett
Walter Scott born

1772 Samuel Taylor Coleridge born

1773 Boston Tea Party
Goldsmith's *She Stoops to Conquer*
Johann Wolfgang von Goethe's *Götz von Berlichingen*

1774 The first Continental Congress meets in Philadelphia
Goethe's *Sorrows of Young Werther*
Death of Oliver Goldsmith
Robert Southey born

1775 Burke's speech on American taxation
American War of Independence begins with the battles of Lexington and Concord
Samuel Johnson's *Journey to the Western Islands of Scotland*
Richard Brinsley Sheridan's *The Rivals* and *The Duenna*
Beaumarchais's *Le Barbier de Séville*
James Watt and Matthew Boulton begin building steam engines in England
Births of Jane Austen, Charles Lamb, Walter Savage Landor, and Matthew Lewis

1776 American Declaration of Independence
Edward Gibbon's *Decline and Fall of the Roman Empire* (1776–1788)
Adam Smith's *Inquiry into the Nature & Causes of the Wealth of Nations*
Thomas Paine's *Common Sense*
Death of David Hume

1777 Maurice Morgann's *Essay on the Dramatic Character of Sir John Falstaff*
Sheridan's *The School for Scandal* first performed (published 1780)
General Burgoyne surrenders at Saratoga

1778 The American colonies allied with France
Britain and France at war
Captain James Cook discovers Hawaii
Death of William Pitt, first earl of Chatham
Deaths of Jean Jacques Rousseau and Voltaire
William Hazlitt born

1779 Johnson's *Prefaces to the Works of the English Poets* (1779–1781); reissued in 1781 as *The Lives of the Most Eminent English Poets*

CHRONOLOGY

Sheridan's *The Critic*
Samuel Crompton invents the spinning mule
Death of David Garrick

1780 The Gordon Riots in London
Charles Robert Maturin born

1781 Charles Cornwallis surrenders at Yorktown
Immanuel Kant's *Critique of Pure Reason*
Friedrich von Schiller's *Die Räuber*

1782 William Cowper's "The Journey of John Gilpin" published in the *Public Advertiser*
Choderlos de Laclos's *Les Liaisons dangereuses*
Rousseau's *Confessions* published posthumously

1783 American War of Independence ended by the Definitive Treaty of Peace, signed at Paris
William Blake's *Poetical Sketches*
George Crabbe's *The Village*
William Pitt the younger becomes prime minister
Henri Beyle (Stendhal) born

1784 Beaumarchais's *Le Mariage de Figaro* first performed (published 1785)
Death of Samuel Johnson

1785 Warren Hastings returns to England from India
James Boswell's *The Journey of a Tour of the Hebrides, with Samuel Johnson, LL.D.*
Cowper's *The Task*
Edmund Cartwright invents the power loom
Thomas De Quincey born
Thomas Love Peacock born

1786 William Beckford's *Vathek* published in English (originally written in French in 1782)
Robert Burns's *Poems Chiefly in the Scottish Dialect*
Wolfgang Amadeus Mozart's *The Marriage of Figaro*
Death of Frederick the Great

1787 The Committee for the Abolition of the Slave Trade founded in England

The Constitutional Convention meets at Philadelphia; the Constitution is signed

1788 The trial of Hastings begins on charges of corruption of the government in India
The Estates-General of France summoned
U.S. Constitution is ratified
George Washington elected president of the United States
Giovanni Casanova's *Histoire de ma fuite* (first manuscript of his memoirs)
The *Daily Universal Register* becomes the *Times* (London)
George Gordon, Lord Byron born

1789 The Estates-General meets at Versailles
The National Assembly (Assemblée Nationale) convened
The fall of the Bastille marks the beginning of the French Revolution
The National Assembly draws up the Declaration of Rights of Man and of the Citizen
First U.S. Congress meets in New York
Blake's *Songs of Innocence*
Jeremy Bentham's *Introduction to the Principles of Morals and Legislation* introduces the theory of utilitarianism
Gilbert White's *Natural History of Selborne*

1790 Congress sets permanent capital city site on the Potomac River
First U.S. Census
Burke's *Reflections on the Revolution in France*
Blake's *The Marriage of Heaven and Hell*
Edmund Malone's edition of Shakespeare
Wollstonecraft's *A Vindication of the Rights of Man*
Death of Benjamin Franklin

1791 French royal family's flight from Paris and capture at Varennes; imprisonment in the Tuileries

CHRONOLOGY

Bill of Rights is ratified
Paine's *The Rights of Man* (1791–1792)
Boswell's *The Life of Johnson*
Burns's *Tam o'Shanter*
The *Observer* founded

1792 The Prussians invade France and are repulsed at Valmy September massacres
The National Convention declares royalty abolished in France
Washington reelected president of the United States
New York Stock Exchange opens
Mary Wollstonecraft's *Vindication of the Rights of Woman*
William Bligh's voyage to the South Sea in H.M.S. *Bounty*
Percy Bysshe Shelley born

1793 Trial and execution of Louis XVI and Marie-Antoinette
France declares war against England
The Committee of Public Safety (Comité de Salut Public) established
Eli Whitney devises the cotton gin
William Godwin's *An Enquiry Concerning Political Justice*
Blake's *Visions of the Daughters of Albion and America*
Wordsworth's *An Evening Walk* and *Descriptive Sketches*
John Clare born

1794 Execution of Georges Danton and Maximilien de Robespierre
Paine's *The Age of Reason* (1794–1796)
Blake's *Songs of Experience*
Ann Radcliffe's *The Mysteries of Udolpho*
Death of Edward Gibbon

1795 The government of the Directory established (1795–1799)
Hastings acquitted
Landor's *Poems*
Death of James Boswell
John Keats born
Thomas Carlyle born

1796 Napoleon Bonaparte takes command in Italy
Matthew Lewis' *The Monk*

John Adams elected president of the United States
Death of Robert Burns

1797 The peace of Campo Formio: extinction of the Venetian Republic
XYZ Affair
Mutinies in the Royal Navy at Spithead and the Nore
Blake's *Vala, Or the Four Zoas* (first version)
Mary Shelley born
Deaths of Edmund Burke, Mary Wollstonecraft, and Horace Walpole

1798 Napoleon invades Egypt
Horatio Nelson wins the battle of the Nile
Wordsworth's and Coleridge's *Lyrical Ballads*
Landor's *Gebir*
Thomas Malthus' *Essay on the Principle of Population*

1799 Napoleon becomes first consul
Pitt introduces first income tax in Great Britain
Sheridan's *Pizarro*
Honoré de Balzac born
Thomas Hood born
Alexander Pushkin born

1800 Thomas Jefferson elected president of the United States
Alessandro Volta produces electricity from a cell
Library of Congress established
Death of William Cowper
Thomas Babington Macaulay born

1801 First census taken in England

1802 The Treaty of Amiens marks the end of the French Revolutionary War
The *Edinburgh Review* founded

1803 England's war with France renewed
The Louisiana Purchase
Robert Fulton propels a boat by steam power on the Seine
Birth of Thomas Lovell Beddoes and **George Borrow**

1804 Napoleon crowned emperor of the French
Jefferson reelected president of the United States
Blake's *Milton* (1804–1808) and *Jerusalem*

CHRONOLOGY

The Code Napoleon promulgated in France
Beethoven's *Eroica* Symphony
Schiller's *Wilhelm Tell*
Benjamin Disraeli born

1805   Napoleon plans the invasion of England
Battle of Trafalgar
Battle of Austerlitz
Beethoven's *Fidelio* first produced
Scott's *Lay of the Last Minstrel*

1806   Scott's *Marmion*
Death of William Pitt
Death of Charles James Fox
Elizabeth Barrett born

1807   France invades Portugal
Aaron Burr tried for treason and acquitted
Byron's *Hours of Idleness*
Charles and Mary Lamb's *Tales from Shakespeare*
Thomas Moore's *Irish Melodies*
Wordsworth's *Ode on the Intimations of Immortality*

1808   National uprising in Spain against the French invasion
The Peninsular War begins
James Madison elected president of the United States
Covent Garden theater burned down
Goethe's *Faust* (Part 1)
Beethoven's Fifth Symphony completed
Lamb's *Specimens of English Dramatic Poets*

1809   Drury Lane theater burned down and rebuilt
The *Quarterly Review* founded
Byron's *English Bards and Scotch Reviewers*
Byron sails for the Mediterranean
Goya's *Los Desastres de la guerra* (1809–1814)
Alfred Tennyson born
Edward Fitzgerald born

1810   Crabbe's *The Borough*
Scott's *The Lady of the Lake*
Elizabeth Gaskell born

1811–1820   Regency of George IV

1811   Luddite Riots begin
Coleridge's *Lectures on Shakespeare* (1811–1814)

Jane Austen's *Sense and Sensibility*
Shelley's *The Necessity of Atheism*
John Constable's *Dedham Vale*
William Makepeace Thackeray born

1812   Napoleon invades Russia; captures and retreats from Moscow
United States declares war against England
Henry Bell's steamship *Comet* is launched on the Clyde river
Madison reelected president of the United States
Byron's *Childe Harold* (Cantos 1–2)
The Brothers Grimm's *Fairy Tales* (1812–1815)
Hegel's *Science of Logic*
Robert Browning born
Charles Dickens born

1813   Wellington wins the battle of Vitoria and enters France
Jane Austen's *Pride and Prejudice*
Byron's *The Giaour* and *The Bride of Abydos*
Shelley's *Queen Mab*
Southey's *Life of Nelson*

1814   Napoleon abdicates and is exiled to Elba; Bourbon restoration with Louis XVIII
Treaty of Ghent ends the war between Britain and the United States
Jane Austen's *Mansfield Park*
Byron's *The Corsair* and *Lara*
Scott's *Waverley*
Wordsworth's *The Excursion*

1815   Napoleon returns to France (the Hundred Days); is defeated at Waterloo and exiled to St. Helena
U.S.S. *Fulton*, the first steam warship, built
Scott's *Guy Mannering*
Schlegel's *Lectures on Dramatic Art and Literature* translated
Wordsworth's *The White Doe of Rylstone*
Anthony Trollope born

1816   Byron leaves England permanently
The Elgin Marbles exhibited in the British Museum
James Monroe elected president of the United States
Jane Austen's *Emma*

CHRONOLOGY

Byron's *Childe Harold* (Canto 3)
Coleridge's *Christabel, Kubla Khan: A Vision, The Pains of Sleep*
Benjamin Constant's *Adolphe*
Goethe's *Italienische Reise*
Peacock's *Headlong Hall*
Scott's *The Antiquary*
Shelley's *Alastor*
Rossini's *Il Barbiere di Siviglia*
Death of Richard Brinsley Sheridan
Charlotte Brontë born

1817 *Blackwood's Edinburgh* magazine founded
Jane Austen's *Northanger Abbey* and *Persuasion*
Byron's *Manfred*
Coleridge's *Biographia Literaria*
Hazlitt's *The Characters of Shakespeare's Plays* and *The Round Table*
Keats's *Poems*
Peacock's *Melincourt*
David Ricardo's *Principles of Political Economy and Taxation*
Death of Jane Austen
Death of Mme de Staël
Branwell Brontë born
Henry David Thoreau born

1818 Byron's *Childe Harold* (Canto 4), and *Beppo*
Hazlitt's *Lectures on the English Poets*
Keats's *Endymion*
Peacock's *Nightmare Abbey*
Scott's *Rob Roy* and *The Heart of Mid-Lothian*
Mary Shelley's *Frankenstein*
Percy Shelley's *The Revolt of Islam*
Emily Brontë born
Karl Marx born
Ivan Sergeyevich Turgenev born

1819 The *Savannah* becomes the first steamship to cross the Atlantic (in 26 days)
Peterloo massacre in Manchester
Byron's *Don Juan* (1819–1824) and *Mazeppa*
Crabbe's *Tales of the Hall*
Géricault's *Raft of the Medusa*
Hazlitt's *Lectures on the English Comic Writers*

Arthur Schopenhauer's *Die Welt als Wille und Vorstellung (The World as Will and Idea)*
Scott's *The Bride of Lammermoor* and *A Legend of Montrose*
Shelley's *The Cenci*, "The Masque of Anarchy," and "Ode to the West Wind"
Wordsworth's *Peter Bell*
Queen Victoria born
George Eliot born

1820–1830 Reign of George IV
1820 Trial of Queen Caroline
Cato Street Conspiracy suppressed; Arthur Thistlewood hanged
Monroe reelected president of the United States
Missouri Compromise
The *London* magazine founded
Keats's *Lamia, Isabella, The Eve of St. Agnes, and Other Poems*
Hazlitt's *Lectures Chiefly on the Dramatic Literature of the Age of Elizabeth*
Charles Maturin's *Melmoth the Wanderer*
Scott's *Ivanhoe* and *The Monastery*
Shelley's *Prometheus Unbound*
Anne Brontë born

1821 Greek War of Independence begins
Liberia founded as a colony for freed slaves
Byron's *Cain, Marino Faliero, The Two Foscari*, and *Sardanapalus*
Hazlitt's *Table Talk* (1821–1822)
Scott's *Kenilworth*
Shelley's *Adonais* and *Epipsychidion*
Death of John Keats
Death of Napoleon
Charles Baudelaire born
Feodor Dostoyevsky born
Gustave Flaubert born

1822 The Massacres of Chios (Greeks rebel against Turkish rule)
Byron's *The Vision of Judgment*
De Quincey's *Confessions of an English Opium-Eater*
Peacock's *Maid Marian*
Scott's *Peveril of the Peak*
Shelley's *Hellas*

CHRONOLOGY

Death of Percy Bysshe Shelley
Matthew Arnold born
1823 Monroe Doctrine proclaimed
Byron's *The Age of Bronze* and *The Island*
Lamb's *Essays of Elia*
Scott's *Quentin Durward*
1824 The National Gallery opened in London
John Quincy Adams elected president of the United States
The *Westminster Review* founded
Beethoven's Ninth Symphony first performed
William (Wilkie) Collins born
James Hogg's *The Private Memoirs and Confessions of a Justified Sinner*
Landor's *Imaginary Conversations* (1824–1829)
Scott's *Redgauntlet*
Death of George Gordon, Lord Byron
1825 Inauguration of steam-powered passenger and freight service on the Stockton and Darlington railway
Bolivia and Brazil become independent Alessandro Manzoni's *I Promessi Sposi* (1825–1826)
1826 André-Marie Ampère's *Mémoire sur la théorie mathématique des phénomènes électrodynamiques*
James Fenimore Cooper's *The Last of the Mohicans*
Disraeli's *Vivian Grey* (1826–1827)
Scott's *Woodstock*
1827 The battle of Navarino ensures the independence of Greece
Josef Ressel obtains patent for the screw propeller for steamships
Heinrich Heine's *Buch der Lieder*
Death of William Blake
1828 Andrew Jackson elected president of the United States
Births of Henrik Ibsen, George Meredith, Margaret Oliphant, Dante Gabriel Rossetti, and Leo Tolstoy
1829 The Catholic Emancipation Act
Robert Peel establishes the metropolitan police force
Greek independence recognized by Turkey

Balzac begins *La Comédie humaine* (1829–1848)
Peacock's *The Misfortunes of Elphin*
J. M. W. Turner's *Ulysses Deriding Polyphemus*
1830–1837 Reign of William IV
1830 Charles X of France abdicates and is succeeded by Louis-Philippe
The Liverpool-Manchester railway opened
Tennyson's *Poems, Chiefly Lyrical*
Death of William Hazlitt
Christina Rossetti born
1831 Michael Faraday discovers electromagnetic induction
Charles Darwin's voyage on H.M.S. *Beagle* begins (1831–1836)
The Barbizon school of artists' first exhibition
Nat Turner slave revolt crushed in Virginia
Peacock's *Crotchet Castle*
Stendhal's *Le Rouge et le noir*
Edward Trelawny's *The Adventures of a Younger Son*
Isabella Bird born
1832 The first Reform Bill
Samuel Morse invents the telegraph
Jackson reelected president of the United States
Disraeli's *Contarini Fleming*
Goethe's *Faust* (Part 2)
Tennyson's *Poems, Chiefly Lyrical*, including "The Lotus-Eaters" and "The Lady of Shalott"
Death of Johann Wolfgang von Goethe
Death of Sir Walter Scott
Lewis Carroll born
1833 Robert Browning's *Pauline*
John Keble launches the Oxford Movement
American Anti-Slavery Society founded
Lamb's *Last Essays of Elia*
Carlyle's *Sartor Resartus* (1833–1834)
Pushkin's *Eugene Onegin*
Mendelssohn's *Italian Symphony* first performed

CHRONOLOGY

1834   Abolition of slavery in the British Empire
Louis Braille's alphabet for the blind
Balzac's *Le Père Goriot*
Nikolai Gogol's *Dead Souls* (Part 1, 1834–1842)
Death of Samuel Taylor Coleridge
Death of Charles Lamb
William Morris born

1835   Hans Christian Andersen's *Fairy Tales* (1st ser.)
Robert Browning's *Paracelsus*
Births of Samuel Butler and Mary Elizabeth Braddon
Alexis de Tocqueville's *De la Democratie en Amerique* (1835–1840)
Death of James Hogg

1836   Martin Van Buren elected president of the United States
Dickens' *Sketches by Boz* (1836–1837)
Landor's *Pericles and Aspasia*

1837–1901   Reign of Queen Victoria

1837   Carlyle's *The French Revolution*
Dickens' *Oliver Twist* (1837–1838) and *Pickwick Papers*
Disraeli's *Venetia* and *Henrietta Temple*

1838   Chartist movement in England
National Gallery in London opened
Elizabeth Barrett Browning's *The Seraphim and Other Poems*
Dickens' *Nicholas Nickleby* (1838–1839)

1839   Louis Daguerre perfects process for producing an image on a silver-coated copper plate Faraday's *Experimental Researches in Electricity* (1839–1855)
First Chartist riots
Opium War between Great Britain and China
Carlyle's *Chartism*

1840   Canadian Act of Union
Queen Victoria marries Prince Albert
Charles Barry begins construction of the Houses of Parliament (1840–1852)
William Henry Harrison elected president of the United States
Robert Browning's *Sordello*
Thomas Hardy born

1841   New Zealand proclaimed a British colony
James Clark Ross discovers the Antarctic continent
Punch founded
John Tyler succeeds to the presidency after the death of Harrison
Carlyle's *Heroes and Hero-Worship*
Dickens' *The Old Curiosity Shop*

1842   Chartist riots
Income tax revived in Great Britain
The Mines Act, forbidding work underground by women or by children under the age of ten
Charles Edward Mudie's Lending Library founded in London
Dickens visits America
Robert Browning's *Dramatic Lyrics*
Macaulay's *Lays of Ancient Rome*
Tennyson's *Poems*, including "Morte d'Arthur," "St. Simeon Stylites," and "Ulysses"
Wordsworth's *Poems*

1843   Marc Isambard Brunel's Thames tunnel opened
The Economist founded
Carlyle's *Past and Present*
Dickens' *A Christmas Carol*
John Stuart Mill's *Logic*
Macaulay's *Critical and Historical Essays*
John Ruskin's *Modern Painters* (1843–1860)

1844   Rochdale Society of Equitable Pioneers, one of the first consumers' cooperatives, founded by twenty-eight Lancashire weavers
James K. Polk elected president of the United States
Elizabeth Barrett Browning's *Poems*, including "The Cry of the Children"
Dickens' *Martin Chuzzlewit*
Disraeli's *Coningsby*
Turner's *Rain, Steam and Speed*
Gerard Manley Hopkins born

CHRONOLOGY

1845 The great potato famine in Ireland
begins (1845–1849)
Disraeli's *Sybil*

1846 Repeal of the Corn Laws
The *Daily News* founded (edited by
Dickens the first three weeks)
Standard-gauge railway introduced
in Britain
The Brontës' pseudonymous *Poems
by Currer, Ellis and Action Bell*
Lear's *Book of Nonsense*

1847 The Ten Hours Factory Act
James Simpson uses chloroform as
an anesthetic
Anne Brontë's *Agnes Grey*
Charlotte Brontë's *Jane Eyre*
Emily Brontë's *Wuthering Heights*
Bram Stoker and **Flora Annie Steel**
born
Tennyson's *The Princess*

1848 The year of revolutions in France,
Germany, Italy, Hungary, Poland
Marx and Engels issue *The Com-
munist Manifesto*
The Chartist Petition
The Pre-Raphaelite Brotherhood
founded
Zachary Taylor elected president of
the United States
Anne Brontë's *The Tenant of Wild-
fell Hall*
Dickens' *Dombey and Son*
Elizabeth Gaskell's *Mary Barton*
Macaulay's *History of England*
(1848–1861)
Mill's *Principles of Political
Economy*
Thackeray's *Vanity Fair*
Death of Emily Brontë

1849 Bedford College for women
founded
Arnold's *The Strayed Reveller*
Charlotte Brontë's *Shirley*
Ruskin's *The Seven Lamps of Archi-
tecture*
Death of Anne Brontë
Death of Thomas Lovell Beddoes

1850 The Public Libraries Act
First submarine telegraph cable laid
between Dover and Calais
Millard Fillmore succeeds to the
presidency after the death of Taylor

Elizabeth Barrett Browning's *Son-
nets from the Portuguese*
Carlyle's *Latter-Day Pamphlets*
Dickens' *Household Words* (1850–
1859) and *David Copperfield*
Charles Kingsley's *Alton Locke*
The Pre-Raphaelites publish the
Germ
Tennyson's *In Memoriam*
Thackeray's *The History of Penden-
nis*
Wordsworth's *The Prelude* is pub-
lished posthumously

1851 The Great Exhibition opens at the
Crystal Palace in Hyde Park
Louis Napoleon seizes power in
France
Gold strike in Victoria incites Aus-
tralian gold rush
Elizabeth Gaskell's *Cranford*
(1851–1853)
Meredith's *Poems*
Ruskin's *The Stones of Venice*
(1851–1853)

1852 The Second Empire proclaimed
with Napoleon III as emperor
David Livingstone begins to ex-
plore the Zambezi (1852–1856)
Franklin Pierce elected president of
the United States
Arnold's *Empedocles on Etna*
Thackeray's *The History of Henry
Esmond, Esq.*

1853 Crimean War (1853–1856)
Arnold's *Poems*, including "The
Scholar Gypsy" and "Sohrab and
Rustum"
Charlotte Brontë's *Villette*
Elizabeth Gaskell's *Crawford and
Ruth*

1854 Frederick D. Maurice's Working
Men's College founded in London
with more than 130 pupils
Battle of Balaklava
Dickens' *Hard Times*
James George Frazer born
Theodor Mommsen's *History of
Rome* (1854–1856)
Tennyson's "The Charge of the
Light Brigade"
Florence Nightingale in the Crimea
(1854–1856)

Oscar Wilde born

1855 David Livingstone discovers the Victoria Falls

Robert Browning's *Men and Women*

Elizabeth Gaskell's *North and South*

Olive Schreiner born

Tennyson's *Maud*

Thackeray's *The Newcomes*

Trollope's *The Warden*

Death of Charlotte Brontë

1856 The Treaty of Paris ends the Crimean War

Henry Bessemer's steel process invented

James Buchanan elected president of the United States

H. Rider Haggard born

1857 The Indian Mutiny begins; crushed in 1858

The Matrimonial Causes Act

Charlotte Brontë's *The Professor*

Elizabeth Barrett Browning's *Aurora Leigh*

Dickens' *Little Dorritt*

Elizabeth Gaskell's *The Life of Charlotte Brontë*

Thomas Hughes's *Tom Brown's School Days*

Trollope's *Barchester Towers*

1858 Carlyle's *History of Frederick the Great* (1858–1865)

George Eliot's *Scenes of Clerical Life*

Morris' *The Defense of Guinevere*

Trollope's *Dr. Thorne*

1859 Charles Darwin's *The Origin of Species*

Dickens' *A Tale of Two Cities*

Arthur Conan Doyle born

George Eliot's *Adam Bede*

Fitzgerald's *The Rubaiyat of Omar Khayyám*

Meredith's *The Ordeal of Richard Feverel*

Mill's *On Liberty*

Samuel Smiles's *Self-Help*

Tennyson's *Idylls of the King*

1860 Abraham Lincoln elected president of the United States

The *Cornhill* magazine founded with Thackeray as editor

James M. Barrie born

William Wilkie Collins' *The Woman in White*

George Eliot's *The Mill on the Floss*

1861 American Civil War begins

Louis Pasteur presents the germ theory of disease

Arnold's *Lectures on Translating Homer*

Dickens' *Great Expectations*

George Eliot's *Silas Marner*

Meredith's *Evan Harrington*

Francis Turner Palgrave's *The Golden Treasury*

Trollope's *Framley Parsonage*

Peacock's *Gryll Grange*

Death of Prince Albert

1862 George Eliot's *Romola*

Meredith's *Modern Love*

Christina Rossetti's *Goblin Market*

Ruskin's *Unto This Last*

Trollope's *Orley Farm*

1863 Thomas Huxley's *Man's Place in Nature*

1864 The Geneva Red Cross Convention signed by twelve nations

Lincoln reelected president of the United States

Robert Browning's *Dramatis Personae*

John Henry Newman's *Apologia pro vita sua*

Tennyson's *Enoch Arden*

Trollope's *The Small House at Allington*

Death of John Clare

1865 Assassination of Lincoln; Andrew Johnson succeeds to the presidency

Arnold's *Essays in Criticism* (1st ser.)

Carroll's *Alice's Adventures in Wonderland*

Dickens' *Our Mutual Friend*

Meredith's *Rhoda Fleming*

A. C. Swinburne's *Atalanta in Calydon*

1866 First successful transatlantic telegraph cable laid

George Eliot's *Felix Holt, the Radical*

Elizabeth Gaskell's *Wives and Daughters*

CHRONOLOGY

Beatrix Potter born
Swinburne's *Poems and Ballads*

1867 The second Reform Bill
Arnold's *New Poems*
Bagehot's *The English Constitution*
Carlyle's *Shooting Niagara*
Marx's *Das Kapital* (vol. 1)
Trollope's *The Last Chronicle of Barset*
George William Russell (AE) born

1868 Gladstone becomes prime minister (1868–1874)
Johnson impeached by House of Representatives; acquitted by Senate
Ulysses S. Grant elected president of the United States
Robert Browning's *The Ring and the Book* (1868–1869)
Collins' *The Moonstone*

1869 The Suez Canal opened
Girton College, Cambridge, founded
Arnold's *Culture and Anarchy*
Mill's *The Subjection of Women*
Trollope's *Phineas Finn*

1870 The Elementary Education Act establishes schools under the aegis of local boards
Dickens' *Edwin Drood*
Disraeli's *Lothair*
Morris' *The Earthly Paradise*
Dante Gabriel Rossetti's *Poems*
Saki [Hector Hugh Munro] born

1871 Trade unions legalized
Newnham College, Cambridge, founded for women students
Carroll's *Through the Looking Glass*
Darwin's *The Descent of Man*
Meredith's *The Adventures of Harry Richmond*
Swinburne's *Songs Before Sunrise*
William H. Davies born

1872 Max Beerbohm born
Samuel Butler's *Erewhon*
George Eliot's *Middlemarch*
Grant reelected president of the United States
Hardy's *Under the Greenwood Tree*

1873 Arnold's *Literature and Dogma*
Mill's *Autobiography*

Pater's *Studies in the History of the Renaissance*
Trollope's *The Eustace Diamonds*

1874 Disraeli becomes prime minister
Hardy's *Far from the Madding Crowd*
James Thomson's *The City of Dreadful Night*

1875 Britain buys Suez Canal shares
Trollope's *The Way We Live Now*
T. F. Powys born

1876 F. H. Bradley's *Ethical Studies*
George Eliot's *Daniel Deronda*
Henry James's *Roderick Hudson*
Meredith's *Beauchamp's Career*
Morris' *Sigurd the Volsung*
Trollope's *The Prime Minister*

1877 Rutherford B. Hayes elected president of the United States after Electoral Commission awards him disputed votes
Henry James's *The American*

1878 Electric street lighting introduced in London
Hardy's *The Return of the Native*
Swinburne's *Poems and Ballads* (2d ser.)
Births of A. E. Coppard and Edward Thomas

1879 Somerville College and Lady Margaret Hall opened at Oxford for women
The London telephone exchange built
Gladstone's Midlothian campaign (1879–1880)
Browning's *Dramatic Idyls*
Meredith's *The Egoist*

1880 Gladstone's second term as prime minister (1880–1885)
James A. Garfield elected president of the United States
Browning's *Dramatic Idyls Second Series*
Disraeli's *Endymion*
Radclyffe Hall born
Hardy's *The Trumpet-Major*
Lytton Strachey born

1881 Garfield assassinated; Chester A. Arthur succeeds to the presidency
Henry James's *The Portrait of a Lady* and *Washington Square*

CHRONOLOGY

D. G. Rossetti's *Ballads and Sonnets*

P. G. Wodehouse born

Death of George Borrow

1882 Triple Alliance formed between German empire, Austrian empire, and Italy

Leslie Stephen begins to edit the *Dictionary of National Biography*

Married Women's Property Act passed in Britain

Britain occupies Egypt and the Sudan

1883 Uprising of the Mahdi: Britain evacuates the Sudan

Royal College of Music opens

T. H. Green's *Ethics*

T. E. Hulme born

Stevenson's *Treasure Island*

1884 The Mahdi captures Omdurman: General Gordon appointed to command the garrison of Khartoum

Grover Cleveland elected president of the United States

The *Oxford English Dictionary* begins publishing

The Fabian Society founded

Hiram Maxim's recoil-operated machine gun invented

1885 The Mahdi captures Khartoum: General Gordon killed

Haggard's *King Solomon's Mines*

Marx's *Das Kapital* (vol. 2)

Meredith's *Diana of the Crossways*

Pater's *Marius the Epicurean*

1886 The Canadian Pacific Railway completed

Gold discovered in the Transvaal

Births of Frances Cornford, Ronald Firbank, and Charles Stansby Walter Williams

Henry James's *The Bostonians* and *The Princess Casamassima*

Stevenson's *The Strange Case of Dr. Jekyll and Mr. Hyde*

1887 Queen Victoria's Golden Jubilee

Rupert Brooke born

Haggard's *Allan Quatermain* and *She*

Hardy's *The Woodlanders*

Edwin Muir born

1888 Benjamin Harrison elected president of the United States

Henry James's *The Aspern Papers*

Kipling's *Plain Tales from the Hills*

T. E. Lawrence born

1889 Yeats's *The Wanderings of Oisin*

Death of Robert Browning

1890 Morris founds the Kelmscott Press

Agatha Christie born

Frazer's *The Golden Bough* (1st ed.)

Henry James's *The Tragic Muse*

Morris' *News From Nowhere*

Jean Rhys born

1891 Gissing's *New Grub Street*

Hardy's *Tess of the d'Urbervilles*

Wilde's *The Picture of Dorian Gray*

1892 Grover Cleveland elected president of the United States

Conan Doyle's *The Adventures of Sherlock Holmes*

Shaw's *Widower's Houses*

J. R. R. Tolkien born

Rebecca West and **Hugh MacDiarmid** born

Wilde's *Lady Windermere's Fan*

1893 Wilde's *A Woman of No Importance* and *Salomé*

Vera Brittain born

1894 Kipling's *The Jungle Book*

Moore's *Esther Waters*

Marx's *Das Kapital* (vol. 3)

Audrey Beardsley's *The Yellow Book* begins to appear quarterly

Shaw's *Arms and the Man*

1895 Trial and imprisonment of Oscar Wilde

William Ramsay announces discovery of helium

The National Trust founded

Conrad's *Almayer's Folly*

Hardy's *Jude the Obscure*

Wells's *The Time Machine*

Wilde's *The Importance of Being Earnest*

Yeats's *Poems*

1896 William McKinley elected president of the United States

Failure of the Jameson Raid on the Transvaal

Housman's *A Shropshire Lad*

CHRONOLOGY

Edmund Blunden born

1897 Queen Victoria's Diamond Jubilee
Conrad's *The Nigger of the Narcissus*
Havelock Ellis' *Studies in the Psychology of Sex* begins publication
Henry James's *The Spoils of Poynton* and *What Maisie Knew*
Kipling's *Captains Courageous*
Shaw's *Candida*
Stoker's *Dracula*
Wells's *The Invisible Man*
Death of Margaret Oliphant

1898 Kitchener defeats the Mahdist forces at Omdurman: the Sudan reoccupied
Hardy's *Wessex Poems*
Henry James's *The Turn of the Screw*
C. S. Lewis born
Shaw's *Caesar and Cleopatra* and *You Never Can Tell*
Alec Waugh born
Wells's *The War of the Worlds*
Wilde's *The Ballad of Reading Gaol*

1899 The Boer War begins
Elizabeth Bowen born
Noël Coward born
Elgar's *Enigma Variations*
Kipling's *Stalky and Co.*

1900 McKinley reelected president of the United States
British Labour party founded
Boxer Rebellion in China
Reginald A. Fessenden transmits speech by wireless
First Zeppelin trial flight
Max Planck presents his first paper on the quantum theory
Conrad's *Lord Jim*
Elgar's *The Dream of Gerontius*
Sigmund Freud's *The Interpretation of Dreams*
V. S. Pritchett born
William Butler Yeats's *The Shadowy Waters*

1901–1910 Reign of King Edward VII

1901 William McKinley assassinated; Theodore Roosevelt succeeds to the presidency
First transatlantic wireless telegraph signal transmitted

Chekhov's *Three Sisters*
Freud's *Psychopathology of Everyday Life*
Rudyard Kipling's *Kim*
Thomas Mann's *Buddenbrooks*
Potter's *The Tale of Peter Rabbit*
Shaw's *Captain Brassbound's Conversion*
August Strindberg's *The Dance of Death*

1902 Barrie's *The Admirable Crichton*
Arnold Bennett's *Anna of the Five Towns*
Cézanne's *Le Lac D'Annecy*
Conrad's *Heart of Darkness*
Henry James's *The Wings of the Dove*
William James's *The Varieties of Religious Experience*
Kipling's *Just So Stories*
Maugham's *Mrs. Cradock*
Stevie Smith born
Times Literary Supplement begins publishing

1903 At its London congress the Russian Social Democratic Party divides into Mensheviks, led by Plekhanov, and Bolsheviks, led by Lenin
The treaty of Panama places the Canal Zone in U.S. hands for a nominal rent
Motor cars regulated in Britain to a 20-mile-per-hour limit
The Wright brothers make a successful flight in the United States
Burlington magazine founded
Samuel Butler's *The Way of All Flesh* published posthumously
Cyril Connolly born
George Gissing's *The Private Papers of Henry Ryecroft*
Thomas Hardy's *The Dynasts*
Henry James's *The Ambassadors*
Alan Paton born
Shaw's *Man and Superman*
Synge's *Riders to the Sea* produced in Dublin
Yeats's *In the Seven Woods* and *On Baile's Strand*
William Plomer born

1904 Roosevelt elected president of the United States

CHRONOLOGY

Russo-Japanese war (1904–1905)
Construction of the Panama Canal begins
The ultraviolet lamp invented
The engineering firm of Rolls Royce founded
Barrie's *Peter Pan* first performed
Births of Cecil Day Lewis and Nancy Mitford
Chekhov's *The Cherry Orchard*
Conrad's *Nostromo*
Henry James's *The Golden Bowl*
Kipling's *Traffics and Discoveries*
Georges Rouault's *Head of a Tragic Clown*
G. M. Trevelyan's *England Under the Stuarts*
Puccini's *Madame Butterfly*
First Shaw-Granville Barker season at the Royal Court Theatre
The Abbey Theatre founded in Dublin
Death of Isabella Bird

1905 Russian sailors on the battleship Potemkin mutiny
After riots and a general strike the czar concedes demands by the Duma for legislative powers, a wider franchise, and civil liberties
Albert Einstein publishes his first theory of relativity
The Austin Motor Company founded
Bennett's *Tales of the Five Towns*
Claude Debussy's *La Mer*
E. M. Forster's *Where Angels Fear to Tread*
Richard Strauss's *Salome*
H. G. Wells's *Kipps*
Oscar Wilde's *De Profundis*
Births of Norman Cameron, Henry Green, and Mary Renault

1906 Liberals win a landslide victory in the British general election
The Trades Disputes Act legitimizes peaceful picketing in Britain
Captain Dreyfus rehabilitated in France
J. J. Thomson begins research on gamma rays
The U.S. Pure Food and Drug Act passed

Churchill's *Lord Randolph Churchill*
William Empson born
Galsworthy's *The Man of Property*
Kipling's *Puck of Pook's Hill*
Shaw's *The Doctor's Dilemma*
Yeats's *Poems* 1899–1905

1907 Exhibition of cubist paintings in Paris
Henry Adams' *The Education of Henry Adams*
Henri Bergson's *Creative Evolution*
Conrad's *The Secret Agent*
Births of Barbara Comyns, Daphne du Maurier, and Christopher Fry
Forster's *The Longest Journey*
André Gide's *La Porte étroite*
Shaw's *John Bull's Other Island* and *Major Barbara*
Synge's *The Playboy of the Western World*
Trevelyan's *Garibaldi's Defence of the Roman Republic*
Christopher Caudwell (Christopher St. John Sprigg) born

1908 Herbert Asquith becomes prime minister
David Lloyd George becomes chancellor of the exchequer
William Howard Taft elected president of the United States
The Young Turks seize power in Istanbul
Henry Ford's Model T car produced
Bennett's *The Old Wives' Tale*
Pierre Bonnard's *Nude Against the Light*
Georges Braque's *House at L'Estaque*
Chesterton's *The Man Who Was Thursday*
Jacob Epstein's *Figures* erected in London
Forster's *A Room with a View*
Anatole France's *L'Ile des Pingouins*
Henri Matisse's *Bonheur de Vivre*
Elgar's First Symphony
Ford Madox Ford founds the *English Review*

1909 The Young Turks depose Sultan Abdul Hamid

CHRONOLOGY

The Anglo-Persian Oil Company formed

Louis Bleriot crosses the English Channel from France by monoplane

Admiral Robert Peary reaches the North Pole

Freud lectures at Clark University (Worcester, Mass.) on psychoanalysis

Serge Diaghilev's Ballets Russes opens in Paris

Galsworthy's *Strife*

Hardy's *Time's Laughingstocks*

Malcolm Lowry born

Claude Monet's *Water Lilies*

Stephen Spender born

Trevelyan's *Garibaldi and the Thousand*

Wells's *Tono-Bungay* first published (book form, 1909)

1910–1936	Reign of King George V
1910	The Liberals win the British general election

Marie Curie's *Treatise on Radiography*

Arthur Evans excavates Knossos

Edouard Manet and the first post-impressionist exhibition in London

Filippo Marinetti publishes "Manifesto of the Futurist Painters"

Norman Angell's *The Great Illusion*

Bennett's *Clayhanger*

Forster's *Howards End*

Galsworthy's *Justice* and *The Silver Box*

Kipling's *Rewards and Fairies*

Norman MacCaig born

Rimsky-Korsakov's *Le Coq d'or*

Stravinsky's *The Firebird*

Vaughan Williams' *A Sea Symphony*

Wells's *The History of Mr. Polly*

Wells's *The New Machiavelli* first published (in book form, 1911)

1911	Lloyd George introduces National Health Insurance Bill

Suffragette riots in Whitehall

Roald Amundsen reaches the South Pole

Bennett's *The Card*

Chagall's *Self Portrait with Seven Fingers*

Conrad's *Under Western Eyes*

D. H. Lawrence's *The White Peacock*

Katherine Mansfield's *In a German Pension*

Edward Marsh edits *Georgian Poetry*

Moore's *Hail and Farewell* (1911–1914)

Flann O'Brien born

Strauss's *Der Rosenkavalier*

Stravinsky's *Petrouchka*

Trevelyan's *Garibaldi and the Making of Italy*

Wells's *The New Machiavelli*

Mahler's *Das Lied von der Erde*

1912	Woodrow Wilson elected president of the United States

SS *Titanic* sinks on its maiden voyage

Five million Americans go to the movies daily; London has four hundred movie theaters

Second post-impressionist exhibition in London

Bennett's and Edward Knoblock's *Milestones*

Constantin Brancusi's *Maiastra*

Wassily Kandinsky's *Black Lines*

D. H. Lawrence's *The Trespasser*

1913	Second Balkan War begins

Henry Ford pioneers factory assembly technique through conveyor belts

Epstein's *Tomb of Oscar Wilde*

New York Armory Show introduces modern art to the world

Alain Fournier's *Le Grand Meaulnes*

Freud's *Totem and Tabu*

D. H. Lawrence's *Sons and Lovers*

Mann's *Death in Venice*

Proust's *Du Côté de chez Swann* (first volume of *À la recherche du temps perdu*, 1913–1922)

Barbara Pym born

Ravel's *Daphnis and Chloé*

R.S. Thomas born

1914	The Panama Canal opens (formal dedication on 12 July 1920)

CHRONOLOGY

Irish Home Rule Bill passed in the House of Commons
Archduke Franz Ferdinand assassinated at Sarajevo
World War I begins
Battles of the Marne, Masurian Lakes, and Falkland Islands
Joyce's *Dubliners*
Norman Nicholson born
Shaw's *Pygmalion* and *Androcles and the Lion*
Yeats's *Responsibilities*
Wyndham Lewis publishes *Blast* magazine and *The Vorticist Manifesto*
C. H. Sisson born and **Patrick O'Brian**

1915 The Dardanelles campaign begins
Britain and Germany begin naval and submarine blockades
The *Lusitania* is sunk
Hugo Junkers manufactures the first fighter aircraft
First Zeppelin raid in London
Brooke's *1914: Five Sonnets*
Norman Douglas' *Old Calabria*
D. W. Griffith's *The Birth of a Nation*
Gustav Holst's *The Planets*
D. H. Lawrence's *The Rainbow*
Wyndham Lewis's *The Crowd*
Maugham's *Of Human Bondage*
Pablo Picasso's *Harlequin*
Sibelius' Fifth Symphony
Denton Welch born

1916 Evacuation of Gallipoli and the Dardanelles
Battles of the Somme, Jutland, and Verdun
Britain introduces conscription
The Easter Rebellion in Dublin
Asquith resigns and David Lloyd George becomes prime minister
The Sykes-Picot agreement on the partition of Turkey
First military tanks used
Wilson reelected president president of the United States
Henri Barbusse's *Le Feu*
Griffith's *Intolerance*
Joyce's *Portrait of the Artist as a Young Man*

Jung's *Psychology of the Unconscious*
Moore's *The Brook Kerith*
Edith Sitwell edits *Wheels* (1916–1921)
Wells's *Mr. Britling Sees It Through*

1917 United States enters World War I
Czar Nicholas II abdicates
The Balfour Declaration on a Jewish national home in Palestine
The Bolshevik Revolution
Georges Clemenceau elected prime minister of France
Lenin appointed chief commissar; Trotsky appointed minister of foreign affairs
Conrad's *The Shadow-Line*
Douglas' *South Wind*
Eliot's *Prufrock and Other Observations*
Modigliani's *Nude with Necklace*
Sassoon's *The Old Huntsman*
Prokofiev's *Classical Symphony*
Yeats's *The Wild Swans at Coole*

1918 Wilson puts forward Fourteen Points for World Peace
Central Powers and Russia sign the Treaty of Brest-Litovsk
Execution of Czar Nicholas II and his family
Kaiser Wilhelm II abdicates
The Armistice signed
Women granted the vote at age thirty in Britain
Rupert Brooke's *Collected Poems*
Gerard Manley Hopkins' *Poems*
Joyce's *Exiles*
Lewis's *Tarr*
Sassoon's *Counter-Attack*
Oswald Spengler's *The Decline of the West*
Strachey's *Eminent Victorians*
Béla Bartók's *Bluebeard's Castle*
Charlie Chaplin's *Shoulder Arms*

1919 The Versailles Peace Treaty signed
J. W. Alcock and A. W. Brown make first transatlantic flight
Ross Smith flies from London to Australia
National Socialist party founded in Germany

CHRONOLOGY

Benito Mussolini founds the Fascist party in Italy
Sinn Fein Congress adopts declaration of independence in Dublin
Eamon De Valera elected president of Sinn Fein party
Communist Third International founded
Lady Astor elected first woman Member of Parliament
Prohibition in the United States
John Maynard Keynes's *The Economic Consequences of the Peace*
Eliot's *Poems*
Maugham's *The Moon and Sixpence*
Shaw's *Heartbreak House*
The Bauhaus school of design, building, and crafts founded by Walter Gropius
Amedeo Modigliani's *Self-Portrait*

1920 The League of Nations established
Warren G. Harding elected president of the United States
Senate votes against joining the League and rejects the Treaty of Versailles
The Nineteenth Amendment gives women the right to vote
White Russian forces of Denikin and Kolchak defeated by the Bolsheviks
Karel Ĉapek's *R.U.R.*
Galsworthy's *In Chancery* and *The Skin Game*
Sinclair Lewis' *Main Street*
Katherine Mansfield's *Bliss*
Matisse's *Odalisques* (1920–1925)
Ezra Pound's *Hugh Selwyn Mauberly*
Paul Valéry's *Le Cimetière Marin*
Yeats's *Michael Robartes and the Dancer*
Edwin Morgan born

1921 Britain signs peace with Ireland
First medium-wave radio broadcast in the United States
The British Broadcasting Corporation founded
Braque's *Still Life with Guitar*
Chaplin's *The Kid*
Aldous Huxley's *Crome Yellow*

Paul Klee's *The Fish*
D. H. Lawrence's *Women in Love*
John McTaggart's *The Nature of Existence* (vol. 1)
Moore's *Héloïse and Abélard*
Eugene O'Neill's *The Emperor Jones*
Luigi Pirandello's *Six Characters in Search of an Author*
Shaw's *Back to Methuselah*
Strachey's *Queen Victoria*
Births of George Mackay Brown and Brian Moore

1922 Lloyd George's Coalition government succeeded by Bonar Law's Conservative government
Benito Mussolini marches on Rome and forms a government
William Cosgrave elected president of the Irish Free State
The BBC begins broadcasting in London
Lord Carnarvon and Howard Carter discover Tutankhamen's tomb
The PEN club founded in London
The *Criterion* founded with T. S. Eliot as editor
Kingsley Amis born
Eliot's *The Waste Land*
A. E. Housman's *Last Poems*
Joyce's *Ulysses*
D. H. Lawrence's *Aaron's Rod* and *England, My England*
Sinclair Lewis's *Babbitt*
O'Neill's *Anna Christie*
Pirandello's *Henry IV*
Edith Sitwell's *Façade*
Virginia Woolf's *Jacob's Room*
Yeats's *The Trembling of the Veil*
Donald Davie born

1923 The Union of Soviet Socialist Republics established
French and Belgian troops occupy the Ruhr in consequence of Germany's failure to pay reparations
Mustafa Kemal (Ataturk) proclaims Turkey a republic and is elected president
Warren G. Harding dies; Calvin Coolidge becomes president
Stanley Baldwin succeeds Bonar Law as prime minister

CHRONOLOGY

Adolf Hitler's attempted coup in Munich fails
Time magazine begins publishing
E. N. da C. Andrade's *The Structure of the Atom*
Brendan Behan born
Bennett's *Riceyman Steps*
Churchill's *The World Crisis* (1923–1927)
J. E. Flecker's *Hassan* produced
Nadine Gordimer born
Paul Klee's *Magic Theatre*
Lawrence's *Kangaroo*
Rainer Maria Rilke's *Duino Elegies* and *Sonnets to Orpheus*
Sibelius' *Sixth Symphony*
Picasso's *Seated Woman*
William Walton's *Façade*
Elizabeth Jane Howard born

1924 Ramsay MacDonald forms first Labour government, loses general election, and is succeeded by Stanley Baldwin
Calvin Coolidge elected president of the United States
Noël Coward's *The Vortex*
Forster's *A Passage to India*
Mann's *The Magic Mountain*
Shaw's *St. Joan*
G. F. Dutton born

1925 Reza Khan becomes shah of Iran
First surrealist exhibition held in Paris
Alban Berg's *Wozzeck*
Chaplin's *The Gold Rush*
John Dos Passos' *Manhattan Transfer*
Theodore Dreiser's *An American Tragedy*
Sergei Eisenstein's *Battleship Potemkin*
F. Scott Fitzgerald's *The Great Gatsby*
André Gide's *Les Faux Monnayeurs*
Hardy's *Human Shows and Far Phantasies*
Huxley's *Those Barren Leaves*
Kafka's *The Trial*
O'Casey's *Juno and the Paycock*
Virginia Woolf's *Mrs. Dalloway* and *The Common Reader*

Brancusi's *Bird in Space*
Shostakovich's *First Symphony*
Sibelius' *Tapiola*

1926 Ford's *A Man Could Stand Up*
Gide's *Si le grain ne meurt*
Hemingway's *The Sun also Rises*
Kafka's *The Castle*
D. H. Lawrence's *The Plumed Serpent*
T. E. Lawrence's *Seven Pillars of Wisdom* privately circulated
Maugham's *The Casuarina Tree*
O'Casey's *The Plough and the Stars*
Puccini's *Turandot*
Jan Morris born

1927 General Chiang Kai-shek becomes prime minister in China
Trotsky expelled by the Communist party as a deviationist; Stalin becomes leader of the party and dictator of the Soviet Union
Charles Lindbergh flies from New York to Paris
J. W. Dunne's *An Experiment with Time*
Freud's *Autobiography* translated into English
Albert Giacometti's *Observing Head*
Ernest Hemingway's *Men Without Women*
Fritz Lang's *Metropolis*
Wyndham Lewis' *Time and Western Man*
F. W. Murnau's *Sunrise*
Proust's *Le Temps retrouvé* posthumously published
Stravinsky's *Oedipus Rex*
Virginia Woolf's *To the Lighthouse*

1928 The Kellogg-Briand Pact, outlawing war and providing for peaceful settlement of disputes, signed in Paris by sixty-two nations, including the Soviet Union
Herbert Hoover elected president of the United States
Women's suffrage granted at age twenty-one in Britain
Alexander Fleming discovers penicillin
Bertolt Brecht and Kurt Weill's *The Three-Penny Opera*

Eisenstein's *October*
Huxley's *Point Counter Point*
Christopher Isherwood's *All the Conspirators*
D. H. Lawrence's *Lady Chatterley's Lover*
Wyndham Lewis' *The Childermass*
Matisse's *Seated Odalisque*
Munch's *Girl on a Sofa*
Shaw's *Intelligent Woman's Guide to Socialism*
Virginia Woolf's *Orlando*
Yeats's *The Tower*
Iain Chrichton Smith born

1929 The Labour party wins British general election
Trotsky expelled from the Soviet Union
Museum of Modern Art opens in New York
Collapse of U.S. stock exchange begins world economic crisis
Robert Bridges's *The Testament of Beauty*
William Faulkner's *The Sound and the Fury*
Robert Graves's *Goodbye to All That*
Hemingway's *A Farewell to Arms*
Ernst Junger's *The Storm of Steel*
Hugo von Hoffmansthal's *Poems*
Henry Moore's *Reclining Figure*
J. B. Priestley's *The Good Companions*
Erich Maria Remarque's *All Quiet on the Western Front*
Shaw's *The Applecart*
R. C. Sheriff's *Journey's End*
Edith Sitwell's *Gold Coast Customs*
Thomas Wolfe's *Look Homeward, Angel*
Virginia Woolf's *A Room of One's Own*
Yeats's *The Winding Stair*
Second surrealist manifesto; Salvador
Dali joins the surrealists
Epstein's *Night and Day*
Mondrian's *Composition with Yellow Blue*

Death of Flora Annie Steel

1930 Allied occupation of the Rhineland ends
Mohandas Gandhi opens civil disobedience campaign in India
The *Daily Worker*, journal of the British Communist party, begins publishing
J. W. Reppe makes artificial fabrics from an acetylene base
John Arden born
Auden's *Poems*
Coward's *Private Lives*
Eliot's *Ash Wednesday*
Wyndham Lewis's *The Apes of God*
Maugham's *Cakes and Ale*
Ezra Pound's *XXX Cantos*
Evelyn Waugh's *Vile Bodies*
Birth of **Kamau (Edward) Brathwaite** and Ruth Rendell

1931 The failure of the Credit Anstalt in Austria starts a financial collapse in Central Europe
Britain abandons the gold standard; the pound falls by twenty-five percent
Mutiny in the Royal Navy at Invergordon over pay cuts
Ramsay MacDonald resigns, splits the Cabinet, and is expelled by the Labour party; in the general election the National Government wins by a majority of five hundred seats
The Statute of Westminster defines dominion status
Ninette de Valois founds the Vic-Wells Ballet (eventually the Royal Ballet)
Coward's *Cavalcade*
Dali's The *Persistence of Memory*
John le Carré born
O'Neill's *Mourning Becomes Electra*
Anthony Powell's *Afternoon Men*
Antoine de Saint-Exupéry's *Vol de nuit*
Walton's *Belshazzar's Feast*
Virginia Woolf's *The Waves*
Caroline Blackwood born

CHRONOLOGY

1932 Franklin D. Roosevelt elected president of the United States
Paul von Hindenburg elected president of Germany; Franz von Papen elected chancellor
Sir Oswald Mosley founds British Union of Fascists
The BBC takes over development of television from J. L. Baird's company
Basic English of 850 words designed as a prospective international language
The Folger Library opens in Washington, D.C.
The Shakespeare Memorial Theatre opens in Stratford-upon-Avon
Faulkner's *Light in August*
Huxley's *Brave New World*
F. R. Leavis' *New Bearings in English Poetry*
Boris Pasternak's *Second Birth*
Ravel's *Concerto for Left Hand*
Peter Redgrove born
Rouault's *Christ Mocked by Soldiers*
Waugh's *Black Mischief*
Yeats's *Words for Music Perhaps*

1933 Roosevelt inaugurates the New Deal
Hitler becomes chancellor of Germany
The Reichstag set on fire
Hitler suspends civil liberties and freedom of the press; German trade unions suppressed
George Balanchine and Lincoln Kirstein found the School of American Ballet
Beryl Bainbridge born
Lowry's *Ultramarine*
André Malraux's *La Condition humaine*
Orwell's *Down and Out in Paris and London*
Gertrude Stein's *The Autobiography of Alice B. Toklas*
Anne Stevenson born

1934 The League Disarmament Conference ends in failure
The Soviet Union admitted to the League
Hitler becomes Führer
Civil war in Austria; Engelbert Dollfuss assassinated in attempted Nazi coup
Frédéric Joliot and Irene Joliot-Curie discover artificial (induced) radioactivity
Einstein's *My Philosophy*
Fitzgerald's *Tender Is the Night*
Graves's *I, Claudius* and *Claudius the God*
Toynbee's *A Study of History* begins publication (1934–1954)
Waugh's *A Handful of Dust*
Births of **Fleur Adcock,** Alan Bennett, Christopher Wallace-Crabbe, and Alasdair Gray

1935 Grigori Zinoviev and other Soviet leaders convicted of treason
Stanley Baldwin becomes prime minister in National Government; National Government wins general election in Britain
Italy invades Abyssinia
Germany repudiates disarmament clauses of Treaty of Versailles
Germany reintroduces compulsory military service and outlaws the Jews
Robert Watson-Watt builds first practical radar equipment
Karl Jaspers' *Suffering and Existence*
Births of André Brink, Dennis Potter, Keith Roberts, and Jon Stallworthy
Ivy Compton-Burnett's *A House and Its Head*
Eliot's *Murder in the Cathedral*
Barbara Hepworth's *Three Forms*
George Gershwin's *Porgy and Bess*
Greene's *England Made Me*
Isherwood's *Mr. Norris Changes Trains*
Malraux's *Le Temps du mépris*
Yeats's *Dramatis Personae*
Klee's *Child Consecrated to Suffering*
Benedict Nicholson's *White Relief*

1936 Edward VII accedes to the throne in January; abdicates in December
1936–1952 Reign of George VI

xxxviii

CHRONOLOGY

1936   German troops occupy the Rhineland
Ninety-nine percent of German electorate vote for Nazi candidates
The Popular Front wins general election in France; Léon Blum becomes prime minister
Roosevelt reelected president of the United States
The Popular Front wins general election in Spain
Spanish Civil War begins
Italian troops occupy Addis Ababa; Abyssinia annexed by Italy
BBC begins television service from Alexandra Palace
Auden's *Look, Stranger!*
Auden and Isherwood's *The Ascent of F-6*
A. J. Ayer's *Language, Truth and Logic*
Chaplin's *Modern Times*
Greene's *A Gun for Sale*
Huxley's *Eyeless in Gaza*
Keynes's *General Theory of Employment*
F. R. Leavis' *Revaluation*
Mondrian's *Composition in Red and Blue*
Dylan Thomas' *Twenty-five Poems*
Wells's *The Shape of Things to Come* filmed
Reginald Hill born

1937   Trial of Karl Radek and other Soviet leaders
Neville Chamberlain succeeds Stanley Baldwin as prime minister
China and Japan at war
Frank Whittle designs jet engine
Picasso's *Guernica*
Shostakovich's Fifth Symphony
Magritte's *La Reproduction interdite*
Hemingway's *To Have and Have Not*
Malraux's *L'Espoir*
Orwell's *The Road to Wigan Pier*
Priestley's *Time and the Conways*
Virginia Woolf's *The Years*
Emma Tennant born
Death of Christopher Caudwell (Christopher St. John Sprigg)

1938   Trial of Nikolai Bukharin and other Soviet political leaders
Austria occupied by German troops and declared part of the Reich
Hitler states his determination to annex Sudetenland from Czechoslovakia
Britain, France, Germany, and Italy sign the Munich agreement
German troops occupy Sudetenland
Edward Hulton founds *Picture Post*
Cyril Connolly's *Enemies of Promise*
du Maurier's *Rebecca*
Faulkner's *The Unvanquished*
Graham Greene's *Brighton Rock*
Hindemith's *Mathis der Maler*
Jean Renoir's *La Grande Illusion*
Jean-Paul Sartre's *La Nausée*
Yeats's *New Poems*
Anthony Asquith's *Pygmalion* and Walt Disney's *Snow White*
Ngũgĩ wa Thiong'o born

1939   German troops occupy Bohemia and Moravia; Czechoslovakia incorporated into Third Reich
Madrid surrenders to General Franco; the Spanish Civil War ends
Italy invades Albania
Spain joins Germany, Italy, and Japan in anti-Comintern Pact
Britain and France pledge support to Poland, Romania, and Greece
The Soviet Union proposes defensive alliance with Britain; British military mission visits Moscow
The Soviet Union and Germany sign nonaggression treaty, secretly providing for partition of Poland between them
Germany invades Poland; Britain, France, and Germany at war
The Soviet Union invades Finland
New York World's Fair opens
Eliot's *The Family Reunion*
Births of Ayi Kwei Armah, Seamus Heaney, Michael Longley and Robert Nye
Isherwood's *Good-bye to Berlin*
Joyce's *Finnegans Wake* (1922–1939)
MacNeice's *Autumn Journal*

CHRONOLOGY

Powell's *What's Become of Waring?*
Ayi Kwei Armah born

1940 Churchill becomes prime minister
Italy declares war on France, Britain, and Greece
General de Gaulle founds Free French Movement
The Battle of Britain and the bombing of London
Roosevelt reelected president of the United States for third term
Betjeman's *Old Lights for New Chancels*
Angela Carter born
Chaplin's *The Great Dictator*
Bruce Chatwin born
Death of William H. Davies
J. M. Coetzee born
Disney's *Fantasia*
Greene's *The Power and the Glory*
Hemingway's *For Whom the Bell Tolls*
C. P. Snow's *Strangers and Brothers* (retitled *George Passant* in 1970, when entire sequence of ten novels, published 1940–1970, was entitled *Strangers and Brothers*)

1941 German forces occupy Yugoslavia, Greece, and Crete, and invade the Soviet Union
Lend-Lease agreement between the United States and Britain
President Roosevelt and Winston Churchill sign the Atlantic Charter
Japanese forces attack Pearl Harbor; United States declares war on Japan, Germany, Italy; Britain on Japan
Auden's *New Year Letter*
James Burnham's *The Managerial Revolution*
F. Scott Fitzgerald's *The Last Tycoon*
Huxley's *Grey Eminence*
Shostakovich's *Seventh Symphony*
Tippett's *A Child of Our Time*
Orson Welles's *Citizen Kane*
Virginia Woolf's *Between the Acts*

1942 Japanese forces capture Singapore, Hong Kong, Bataan, Manila
German forces capture Tobruk

U.S. fleet defeats the Japanese in the Coral Sea, captures Guadalcanal
Battle of El Alamein
Allied forces land in French North Africa
Atom first split at University of Chicago
William Beveridge's *Social Insurance and Allied Services*
Albert Camus's *L'Étranger*
Joyce Cary's *To Be a Pilgrim*
Edith Sitwell's *Street Songs*
Waugh's *Put Out More Flags*
Births of Douglas Dunn, and Jonathan Raban

1943 German forces surrender at Stalingrad
German and Italian forces surrender in North Africa
Italy surrenders to Allies and declares war on Germany
Cairo conference between Roosevelt, Churchill, Chiang Kaishek
Teheran conference between Roosevelt, Churchill, Stalin
Eliot's *Four Quartets*
Henry Moore's *Madonna and Child*
Sartre's *Les Mouches*
Vaughan Williams' *Fifth Symphony*
Peter Carey and David Malouf born

1944 Allied forces land in Normandy and southern France
Allied forces enter Rome
Attempted assassination of Hitler fails
Liberation of Paris
U.S. forces land in Philippines
German offensive in the Ardennes halted
Roosevelt reelected president of the United States for fourth term
Education Act passed in Britain
Pay-as-You-Earn income tax introduced
Beveridge's *Full Employment in a Free Society*
Cary's *The Horse's Mouth*
Huxley's *Time Must Have a Stop*

CHRONOLOGY

Maugham's *The Razor's Edge*
Sartre's *Huis Clos*
Edith Sitwell's *Green Song and Other Poems*
Graham Sutherland's *Christ on the Cross*
Trevelyan's *English Social History*
W. G. Sebald born

1945 British and Indian forces open offensive in Burma
Yalta conference between Roosevelt, Churchill, Stalin
Mussolini executed by Italian partisans
Roosevelt dies; Harry S. Truman becomes president
Hitler commits suicide; German forces surrender
The Potsdam Peace Conference
The United Nations Charter ratified in San Francisco
The Labour Party wins British General Election
Atomic bombs dropped on Hiroshima and Nagasaki
Surrender of Japanese forces ends World War II
Trial of Nazi war criminals opens at Nuremberg
All-India Congress demands British withdrawal from India
De Gaulle elected president of French Provisional Government; resigns the next year
Betjeman's *New Bats in Old Belfries*
Britten's *Peter Grimes*
Orwell's *Animal Farm*
Russell's *History of Western Philosophy*
Sartre's *The Age of Reason*
Edith Sitwell's *The Song of the Cold*
Waugh's *Brideshead Revisited*
Births of Wendy Cope and Peter Reading

1946 Bills to nationalize railways, coal mines, and the Bank of England passed in Britain
Nuremberg Trials concluded

United Nations General Assembly meets in New York as its permanent headquarters
The Arab Council inaugurated in Britain
Frederick Ashton's *Symphonic Variations*
Britten's *The Rape of Lucretia*
David Lean's *Great Expectations*
O'Neill's *The Iceman Cometh*
Roberto Rosselini's *Paisà*
Dylan Thomas' *Deaths and Entrances*

1947 President Truman announces program of aid to Greece and Turkey and outlines the "Truman Doctrine"
Independence of India proclaimed; partition between India and Pakistan, and communal strife between Hindus and Moslems follows
General Marshall calls for a European recovery program
First supersonic air flight
Britain's first atomic pile at Harwell comes into operation
Edinburgh festival established
Discovery of the Dead Sea Scrolls in Palestine
Princess Elizabeth marries Philip Mountbatten, duke of Edinburgh
Auden's *Age of Anxiety*
Camus's *La Peste*
Chaplin's *Monsieur Verdoux*
Lowry's *Under the Volcano*
Priestley's *An Inspector Calls*
Edith Sitwell's *The Shadow of Cain*
Waugh's *Scott-King's Modern Europe*
Births of Dermot Healy, and Redmond O'Hanlon

1948 Gandhi assassinated
Czech Communist Party seizes power
Pan-European movement (1948–1958) begins with the formation of the permanent Organization for European Economic Cooperation (OEEC)

CHRONOLOGY

Berlin airlift begins as the Soviet Union halts road and rail traffic to the city
British mandate in Palestine ends; Israeli provisional government formed
Yugoslavia expelled from Soviet bloc
Columbia Records introduces the long-playing record
Truman elected of the United States for second term
Greene's *The Heart of the Matter*
Huxley's *Ape and Essence*
Leavis' *The Great Tradition*
Pound's *Cantos*
Priestley's *The Linden Tree*
Waugh's *The Loved One*
Death of Denton Welch

1949   North Atlantic Treaty Organization established with headquarters in Brussels
Berlin blockade lifted
German Federal Republic recognized; capital established at Bonn
Konrad Adenauer becomes German chancellor
Mao Tse-tung becomes chairman of the People's Republic of China following Communist victory over the Nationalists
Peter Ackroyd born
Simone de Beauvoir's *The Second Sex*
Cary's *A Fearful Joy*
Arthur Miller's *Death of a Salesman*
Orwell's *Nineteen Eighty-four*

1950   Korean War breaks out
Nobel Prize for literature awarded to Bertrand Russell
R. H. S. Crossman's *The God That Failed*
T. S. Eliot's *The Cocktail Party*
Fry's *Venus Observed*
Doris Lessing's *The Grass Is Singing*
C. S. Lewis' *The Chronicles of Narnia* (1950–1956)
Wyndham Lewis' *Rude Assignment*

George Orwell's *Shooting an Elephant*
Carol Reed's *The Third Man*
Dylan Thomas' *Twenty-six Poems*
Births of Sara Maitland, and A. N. Wilson

1951   Guy Burgess and Donald Maclean defect from Britain to the Soviet Union
The Conservative party under Winston Churchill wins British general election
The Festival of Britain celebrates both the centenary of the Crystal Palace Exhibition and British postwar recovery
Electric power is produced by atomic energy at Arcon, Idaho
W. H. Auden's *Nones*
Samuel Beckett's *Molloy* and *Malone Dies*
Benjamin Britten's *Billy Budd*
Greene's *The End of the Affair*
Akira Kurosawa's *Rashomon*
Wyndham Lewis' *Rotting Hill*
Anthony Powell's *A Question of Upbringing* (first volume of *A Dance to the Music of Time*, 1951–1975)
J. D. Salinger's *The Catcher in the Rye*
C. P. Snow's *The Masters*
Igor Stravinsky's *The Rake's Progress*
Peter Fallon born

1952– Reign of Elizabeth II
At Eniwetok Atoll the United States detonates the first hydrogen bomb
The European Coal and Steel Community comes into being
Radiocarbon dating introduced to archaeology
Michael Ventris deciphers Linear B script
Dwight D. Eisenhower elected president of the United States
Beckett's *Waiting for Godot*
Charles Chaplin's *Limelight*
Ernest Hemingway's *The Old Man and the Sea*
Arthur Koestler's *Arrow in the Blue*

CHRONOLOGY

F. R. Leavis' *The Common Pursuit*
Lessing's *Martha Quest* (first volume of *The Children of Violence*, 1952–1965)
C. S. Lewis' *Mere Christianity*
Thomas' *Collected Poems*
Evelyn Waugh's *Men at Arms* (first volume of *Sword of Honour*, 1952–1961)
Angus Wilson's *Hemlock and After*
Births of Rohinton Mistry and Vikram Seth

1953 Constitution for a European political community drafted
Julius and Ethel Rosenberg executed for passing U.S. secrets to the Soviet Union
Cease-fire declared in Korea
Edmund Hillary and his Sherpa guide, Tenzing Norkay, scale Mt. Everest
Nobel Prize for literature awarded to Winston Churchill
General Mohammed Naguib proclaims Egypt a republic
Beckett's *Watt*
Joyce Cary's *Except the Lord*
Robert Graves's *Poems 1953*
Death of Norman Cameron

1954 First atomic submarine, *Nautilus,* is launched by the United States
Dien Bien Phu captured by the Vietminh
Geneva Conference ends French dominion over Indochina
U.S. Supreme Court declares racial segregation in schools unconstitutional
Nasser becomes president of Egypt
Nobel Prize for literature awarded to Ernest Hemingway
Kingsley Amis' *Lucky Jim*
John Betjeman's *A Few Late Chrysanthemums*
William Golding's *Lord of the Flies*
Christopher Isherwood's *The World in the Evening*
Koestler's *The Invisible Writing*
Iris Murdoch's *Under the Net*
C. P. Snow's *The New Men*

Thomas' *Under Milk Wood* published posthumously
Births of Iain Banks, **Louise De Bernières,** Romesh Gunesekera, Kevin Hart, Alan Hollinghurst, and Hanif Kureishi

1955 Warsaw Pact signed
West Germany enters NATO as Allied occupation ends
The Conservative party under Anthony Eden wins British general election
Cary's *Not Honour More*
Greene's *The Quiet American*
Philip Larkin's *The Less Deceived*
F. R. Leavis' *D. H. Lawrence, Novelist*
Vladimir Nabokov's *Lolita*
Patrick White's *The Tree of Man*
Patrick McCabe born

1956 Nasser's nationalization of the Suez Canal leads to Israeli, British, and French armed intervention
Uprising in Hungary suppressed by Soviet troops
Khrushchev denounces Stalin at Twentieth Communist Party Congress
Eisenhower reelected president of the United States
Anthony Burgess' *Time for a Tiger*
Golding's *Pincher Martin*
Murdoch's *Flight from the Enchanter*
John Osborne's *Look Back in Anger*
Snow's *Homecomings*
Edmund Wilson's *Anglo-Saxon Attitudes*
Janice Galloway and Philip Kerr born

1957 The Soviet Union launches the first artificial earth satellite, *Sputnik I*
Eden succeeded by Harold Macmillan
Suez Canal reopened
Eisenhower Doctrine formulated
Parliament receives the Wolfenden Report on Homosexuality and Prostitution
Nobel Prize for literature awarded to Albert Camus

CHRONOLOGY

Beckett's *Endgame* and *All That Fall*
Lawrence Durrell's *Justine* (first volume of *The Alexandria Quartet*, 1957–1960)
Ted Hughes's *The Hawk in the Rain*
Murdoch's *The Sandcastle*
V. S. Naipaul's *The Mystic Masseur*
Eugene O'Neill's *Long Day's Journey into Night*
Osborne's *The Entertainer*
Muriel Spark's *The Comforters*
White's *Voss*

1958 European Economic Community established
Khrushchev succeeds Bulganin as Soviet premier
Charles de Gaulle becomes head of France's newly constituted Fifth Republic
The United Arab Republic formed by Egypt and Syria
The United States sends troops into Lebanon
First U.S. satellite, *Explorer 1,* launched
Nobel Prize for literature awarded to Boris Pasternak
Beckett's *Krapp's Last Tape*
John Kenneth Galbraith's *The Affluent Society*
Greene's *Our Man in Havana*
Murdoch's *The Bell*
Pasternak's *Dr. Zhivago*
Snow's *The Conscience of the Rich*

1959 Fidel Castro assumes power in Cuba
St. Lawrence Seaway opens
The European Free Trade Association founded
Alaska and Hawaii become the forty-ninth and fiftieth states
The Conservative party under Harold Macmillan wins British general election
Brendan Behan's *The Hostage*
Golding's *Free Fall*
Graves's *Collected Poems*
Koestler's *The Sleepwalkers*
Harold Pinter's *The Birthday Party*
Snow's *The Two Cultures and the Scientific Revolution*

Spark's *Memento Mori*
Robert Crawford born

1960 South Africa bans the African National Congress and Pan-African Congress
The Congo achieves independence
John F. Kennedy elected president of the United States
The U.S. bathyscaphe *Trieste* descends to 35,800 feet
Publication of the unexpurgated *Lady Chatterley's Lover* permitted by court
Auden's *Hommage to Clio*
Betjeman's *Summoned by Bells*
Pinter's *The Caretaker*
Snow's *The Affair*
David Storey's *This Sporting Life*
Ian Rankin born

1961 South Africa leaves the British Commonwealth
Sierra Leone and Tanganyika achieve independence
The Berlin Wall erected
The New English Bible published
Beckett's *How It Is*
Greene's *A Burnt-Out Case*
Koestler's *The Lotus and the Robot*
Murdoch's *A Severed Head*
Naipaul's *A House for Mr Biswas*
Osborne's *Luther*
Spark's *The Prime of Miss Jean Brodie*
White's *Riders in the Chariot*

1962 John Glenn becomes first U.S. astronaut to orbit earth
The United States launches the spacecraft *Mariner* to explore Venus
Algeria achieves independence
Cuban missile crisis ends in withdrawal of Soviet missiles from Cuba
Adolf Eichmann executed in Israel for Nazi war crimes
Second Vatican Council convened by Pope John XXIII
Nobel Prize for literature awarded to John Steinbeck
Edward Albee's *Who's Afraid of Virginia Woolf?*
Beckett's *Happy Days*

CHRONOLOGY

Anthony Burgess' *A Clockwork Orange* and *The Wanting Seed*
Aldous Huxley's *Island*
Isherwood's *Down There on a Visit*
Lessing's *The Golden Notebook*
Nabokov's *Pale Fire*
Aleksandr Solzhenitsyn's *One Day in the Life of Ivan Denisovich*

1963   Britain, the United States, and the Soviet Union sign a test-ban treaty
Birth of Simon Armitage
Britain refused entry to the European Economic Community
The Soviet Union puts into orbit the first woman astronaut, Valentina Tereshkova
Paul VI becomes pope
President Kennedy assassinated; Lyndon B. Johnson assumes office
Nobel Prize for literature awarded to George Seferis
Britten's *War Requiem*
John Fowles's *The Collector*
Murdoch's *The Unicorn*
Spark's *The Girls of Slender Means*
Storey's *Radcliffe*
John Updike's *The Centaur*

1964   Tonkin Gulf incident leads to retaliatory strikes by U.S. aircraft against North Vietnam
Greece and Turkey contend for control of Cyprus
Britain grants licenses to drill for oil in the North Sea
The Shakespeare Quatercentenary celebrated
Lyndon Johnson elected president of the United States
The Labour party under Harold Wilson wins British general election
Nobel Prize for literature awarded to Jean-Paul Sartre
Saul Bellow's *Herzog*
Burgess' *Nothing Like the Sun*
Golding's *The Spire*
Isherwood's *A Single Man*
Stanley Kubrick's *Dr. Strangelove*
Larkin's *The Whitsun Weddings*
Naipaul's *An Area of Darkness*
Peter Shaffer's *The Royal Hunt of the Sun*

Snow's *Corridors of Power*
Alan Warner born

1965   The first U.S. combat forces land in Vietnam
The U.S. spacecraft Mariner transmits photographs of Mars
British Petroleum Company finds oil in the North Sea
War breaks out between India and Pakistan
Rhodesia declares its independence
Ontario power failure blacks out the Canadian and U.S. east coasts
Nobel Prize for literature awarded to Mikhail Sholokhov
Robert Lowell's *For the Union Dead*
Norman Mailer's *An American Dream*
Osborne's *Inadmissible Evidence*
Pinter's *The Homecoming*
Spark's *The Mandelbaum Gate*

1966   The Labour party under Harold Wilson wins British general election
The Archbishop of Canterbury visits Pope Paul VI
Florence, Italy, severely damaged by floods
Paris exhibition celebrates Picasso's eighty-fifth birthday
Fowles's *The Magus*
Greene's *The Comedians*
Osborne's *A Patriot for Me*
Paul Scott's *The Jewel in the Crown* (first volume of *The Raj Quartet*, 1966–1975)
White's *The Solid Mandala*

1967   Thurgood Marshall becomes first black U.S. Supreme Court justice
Six-Day War pits Israel against Egypt and Syria
Biafra's secession from Nigeria leads to civil war
Francis Chichester completes solo circumnavigation of the globe
Dr. Christiaan Barnard performs first heart transplant operation, in South Africa
China explodes its first hydrogen bomb
Golding's *The Pyramid*

CHRONOLOGY

Nobel Prize for literature awarded to Derek Walcott

1993 Czechoslovakia divides into the Czech Republic and Slovakia; playwright Vaclav Havel elected president of the Czech Republic

Britain ratifies Treaty on European Union (the "Maastricht Treaty")

U.S. troops provide humanitarian aid amid famine in Somalia

United States, Canada, and Mexico sign North American Free Trade Agreement

Nobel Prize for literature awarded to Toni Morrison

1994 Nelson Mandela elected president in South Africa's first post-apartheid election

Jean-Baptiste Aristide restored to presidency of Haiti

Clinton health care reforms rejected by Congress

Civil war in Rwanda

Republicans win control of both houses of Congress for first time in forty years

Prime Minister Albert Reynolds of Ireland meets with Gerry Adams, president of Sinn Fein

Nobel Prize for literature awarded to Kenzaburo Õe

Amis's *You Can't Do Both*

Naipaul's *A Way in the World*

Death of Dennis Potter

1995 Britain and Irish Republican Army engage in diplomatic talks

Barings Bank forced into bankruptcy as a result of a maverick bond trader's losses

United States restores full diplomatic relations with Vietnam

NATO initiates air strikes in Bosnia

Death of Stephen Spender

Israeli Prime Minister Yitzhak Rabin assassinated

Nobel Prize for literature awarded to Seamus Heaney

1996 IRA breaks cease-fire; Sein Fein representatives barred from Northern Ireland peace talks

Prince and Princess of Wales divorce

Cease-fire agreement in Chechnia; Russian forces begin to withdraw

Boris Yeltsin reelected president of Russia

Bill Clinton reelected president of the United States

Nobel Prize for literature awarded to Wislawa Szymborska

Death of Caroline Blackwood

1996 British government destroys around 100,000 cows suspected of infection with Creutzfeldt-Jakob, or "mad cow" disease

1997 Diana, Princess of Wales, dies in an automobile accident

Unveiling of first fully-cloned adult animal, a sheep named Dolly

Booker McConnell Prize for fiction awarded to Arundhati Roy

1998 United States renews bombing of Bagdad, Iraq

Independent legislature and Parliaments return to Scotland and Wales

Booker McConnell Prize for fiction awarded to Ian McEwan

Nobel Prize for literature awarded to Jose Saramago

1999 King Hussein of Jordan dies

United Nations responds militarily to Serbian President Slobodan Milosevic's escalation of crisis in Kosovo

Booker McConnell Prize for fiction awarded to J. M. Coetzee

Nobel Prize for literature awarded to Günter Grass

Deaths of Ted Hughes, Brian Moore, and Iain Chrichton Smith

2000 Penelope Fitzgerald dies

J. K. Rowling's *Harry Potter and the Goblet of Fire* sells more than 300,000 copies in its first day

Oil blockades by fuel haulers protesting high oil taxes bring much of Britain to a standstill

Slobodan Milosevic loses Serbian general election to Vojislav Kostunica

Death of Scotland's First Minister, Donald Dewar

Nobel Prize for literature awarded to Gao Xingjian

CHRONOLOGY

Booker McConnell Prize for fiction awarded to Margaret Atwood

George W. Bush, son of former president George Bush, becomes president of the United States after Supreme Court halts recount of closest election in history

Death of former Canadian Prime Minister Pierre Elliot Trudeau

Human Genome Project researchers announce that they have a complete map of the genetic code of a human chromosome

Vladimir Putin succeeds Boris Yeltsin as president of Russia

British Prime Minister Tony Blair's son Leo is born, making him the first child born to a sitting prime minister in 152 years

Death of **Patrick O'Brian** Keith Roberts and **R.S. Thomas**

2001 In Britain, the House of Lords passes legislation that legalizes the creation of cloned human embryos

British Prime Minister Tony Blair wins second term

Margaret Atwood's *The Blind Assassin* wins Booker McConnell Prize for fiction

Kazuo Ishiguro's *When We Were Orphans*

Trezza Azzopardi's *The Hiding Place*

Terrorists attack World Trade Center and Pentagon with hijacked airplanes, resulting in the collapse of the World Trade Center towers and the deaths of thousands. Passengers of a third hijacked plane thwart hijackers, resulting in a crash landing in Pennsylvania. The attacks are thought to be organized by Osama bin Laden, the leader of an international terrorist network known as al Qaeda

Ian McEwan's *An Atonement*

Salman Rushdie's *Fury*

Peter Carey's *True History of the Kelly Gang*

Deaths of Eudora Welty and W. G. Sebald

2002 Former U.S. President Jimmy Carter awarded the Nobel Peace Prize

Europe experiences its worst floods in 100 years as floodwaters force thousands of people out of their homes

Wall Street Journal reporter Daniel Pearl kidnapped and killed in Karachi, Pakistan while researching a story about Pakistani militants and suspected shoe bomber Richard Reid. British-born Islamic militant Ahmad Omar Saeed Sheikh sentenced to death for the crime. Three accomplices receive life sentences.

Slobodan Milosevic goes on trial at the U.N. war crimes tribunal in The Hague on charges of masterminding ethnic cleansing in the former Yugoslavia.

Yann Martel's *Life of Pi* wins Booker McConnell Prize for fiction

Nobel Prize for literature awarded to Imre Kertész

2003 Ariel Sharon elected as Israeli prime minister

Venezuelan President Hugo Chavez forced to leave office after a nine week general strike calling for his resignation ends

U.S. presents to the United Nations its Iraq war rationale, citing its Weapons of Mass Destruction as imminent threat to world security

U.S. and Britain launch war against Iraq

Baghdad falls to U.S. troops

Official end to combat operations in Iraq is declared by the U.S.

Aung San Suu Kyi, Burmese opposition leader, placed under house arrest by military regime

NATO assumes control of peacekeeping force in Afghanistan

American troops capture Saddam Hussein

J.K. Rowling's *Harry Potter and the Order of the Phoenix*, the fifth installment in the wildly popular series, hit the shelves and rocketed up the best-seller lists

Nobel Prize for literature awarded to J. M. Coetzee

Death of C. H. Sisson

2004 NATO admits seven new members—Bulgaria, Estonia, Latvia, Lithuania, Romania, Slovakia, and Slovenia

Terrorists bomb commuter trains in Spain—al–Qaeda claims responsibility

Ten new states join the European Union, expanding it to twenty–five members states total

Muslim terrorists attack a school in Beslan, Russia, resulting in over 300 civilian deaths, many of them schoolchildren

George W. Bush is re–elected president of the United States

Allegations of corruption in the election of Ukraine's Viktor Yanukovych result in the "Orange Revolution" and Parliament's decision to nullify the first election results—the secondary run–off election is closley monitored and

favors Viktor Yushchenko for president

A massive 9.0 earthquake rocks the Indian Ocean, resulting in a catastrophic tsunami, devastating southern Asia and eastern Africa and killing tens of thousands of people

Alan Hollinghurst's *The Line of Beauty* wins Man Booker Prize for fiction

2005 Terrorists bomb three subway stations in London, killing 52 and injuring more than 700

Pope John Paul II dies, marking the end of an era for the Roman Catholic Church. He is succeeded by Pope Benedict XVI

Hurricane Katrina hits the U.S. Golf Coast, devastating cities in Louisianna and Mississippi, and killing over 1,000 people.

J.K. Rowling's *Harry Potter and the Half-Blood Prince* sells over 6.9 billion copies on the first day of release in the U.S. alone

Nobel Prize for literature awarded to Harold Pinter

Deaths of Saul Bellow and Arthur Miller

List of Contributors

JANE BEAL. Jane Beal is a visiting assistant professor of English at Wheaton College in Illinois. She earned her doctorate from the University of California, Davis in English Literature with specializations in medieval literature, classical mythology, and the literature of the Bible. Her publications frequently concern the life, works, and reception of John Trevisa, a fourteenth-century translator. Her most recent article, "Why Authority: Trevisa, Translation, and the Audience of the English Polychronicon," appears in the *Medieval Authorship*, ed. Stephen Partridge (University of British Columbia Press, 2006). **Julian of Norwich, Margery Kempe**

IAN BICKFORD. Ian Bickford lives and teaches in New York City. His poetry and other writing has appeared in *Agni, Asheville Poetry Review, Colorado Review, CutBank, LIT, Oxford Encyclopedia of American Literature, Post Road, Smartish Pace, Spork,* and elsewhere. **Peter Carey**

FRED BILSON. Fred Bilson holds a bachelor's degree in English and a master's degree in science. He has lectured in English, linguistics, and computer systems and works as a support tutor to university students with dyslexia. **George Borrow**

GERRY CAMBRIDGE Scots-Irish poet and editor. His books of verse include *The Shell House* (Scottish Cultural Press, 1995), *Nothing but Heather!: Scottish Nature in Poems, Photographs and Prose* (Luath Press, 1999), illustrated with his own natural history photography, and *Madame Fi Fi's Farewell and Other Poems* (Luath Press, 2003). He edits the Scottish-American poetry magazine, *The Dark Horse,* and was the 1997–1999 Brownsbank Writing Fellow, based at Hugh MacDiarmid's former home, Brownsbank Cottage, near Biggar in Scotland. His website is at: www.gerrycambridge.com. **G. F. Dutton**

WILLIAM V. DAVIS. William V. Davis is a poet and literary critic. His book of poetry *One Way to*

Reconstruct the Scene (1980) won the Yale Series of Younger Poets Award. *The Dark Hours* (1984) won the Calliope Press Chapbook Prize. Along with his work on R. S. Thomas and scores of critical essays on writers from the ancient Greeks to the most contemporary, Davis has published several scholarly books, including *Understanding Robert Bly* and *Robert Bly: The Poet and His Critics.* He is a professor of English and writer-in-residence at Baylor University in Waco, Texas. **R. S. Thomas**

BRIAN HENRY. Brian Henry is associate professor of English at the University of Georgia and a former Fulbright scholar in Australia. He is the author of three books of poetry—*Astronaut* (2000), *American Incident* (2002), and *Graft* (2003)—and editor of *On James Tate* (2004). His criticism appears in the *New York Times Book Review, Times Literary Supplement, Yale Review, Virginia Quarterly Review,* and many other publications. **David Malouf**

CLAIRE KEYES. Professor emerita at Salem State College in Massachusetts, Claire Keyes served as chair of the English Department and coordinator of the Graduate English Programs. She is the author of *The Aesthetics of Power: The Poetry of Adrienne Rich,* as well as numerous articles and reviews. Her poems have appeared in *Spoon River Poetry Review, Zone 3,* and *Blueline,* among others. Her chapbook, winner of the Foothills Poetry Competition, is titled *Rising and Falling.* She has been the recipient of grants from the Massachusetts Council of the Arts and the Wurlitzer Foundation. **Janice Galloway**

AMOR KOHLI. Amor Kohli is assistant professor in the African and Black Diaspora Studies Program at DePaul University in Chicago. He received his Ph.D. in English from Tufts University. He has published on the poetry of the African-American Beat poet Bob Kaufman and is currently writing

LIST OF CONTRIBUTORS

on the poetry of Amiri Baraka, Kamau Brathwaite, and Linton Kwesi Johnson. **Kamau (Edward) Brathwaite**

JOHN LENNARD. John Lennard teaches at Cambridge University in England and has written a number of books and articles about modern literature. He has also published a well-known introduction to poetry. **Patrick O'Brian**

KIMBERLY LEWIS. Kimberly Lewis is currently working on a Ph.D. dissertation in comparative literature at the University of Chicago. She also contributed an article on Hart Crane to the Scribner's *American Writers* series. **Martin McDonagh**

SCOTT R. MACKENZIE. Scott R. MacKenzie has published articles and reviews on topics relating to eighteenth-century and Romantic era British literature in several scholarly journals, most recently "An Englishwoman's Workhouse is Her Castle: Poor Management and Gothic Fiction in the 1790s" in *ELH*. He is completing a book-length study on the relationship between domesticity and nationality in eighteenth- and early-nineteenth-century British literature and culture. **Eliza Haywood**

PHILLIP MALLETT. Phillip Mallett is senior lecturer in English at the University of St. Andrews. In addition to collections of essays on Kipling and on European satire, he has edited four volumes of essays on Thomas Hardy, most recently *Advances in Thomas Hardy Studies* for Palgrave Macmillan, and is the author of *Rudyard Kipling: A Literary Biography*, published in 2003. His most recent work is the Norton Critical edition of Hardy's *The Return of the Native*, published in January 2006. **Flora Annie Steel**

ABBY MIMS. Abby Mims has an M.F.A. from University of California, Irvine. Her stories have appeared in several literary journals and anthologies, including *Swink, The Santa Monica Review, Other Voices* and *Women On The Edge: L. A. Women Writers*. She is presently at work on a collection of stories and a memoir. **Fleur Adcock**

RICHARD RANKIN RUSSELL. Richard Rankin Russell is assistant professor of English at Baylor University. His essays on Irish and British writers have appeared in *Modern Drama, Journal of Modern Literature, Colby Quarterly,* and *New Hibernia Review,* among other journals. He has recently finished a manuscript, "Michael Longley, Seamus Heaney, and the Devolution of Northern Irish Literature," which explores their contributions to the emergence of a regional Northern Irish literature and the subsequent implications for reconciliation in the province. **Peter Fallon**

DEBORAH SEDDON. Lecturer in English at Rhodes University, in Grahamstown, South Africa, Deborah Seddon recently completed a doctorate at Clare College, Cambridge University, and has published articles based on her research on the first translations of Shakespeare into an African language. Her poems have appeared in *Ariel* and *Writing from Here*. **Louis De Bernières**

PATRICK A. SMITH. Patrick A. Smith holds a B.A. in English from Penn State University and a Ph.D. in American Literature from Ohio University. He is assistant professor of English at Bainbridge College, Georgia. Smith's books include *The True Bones of My Life: Essays on the Fiction of Jim Harrison, Tim O'Brien: A Critical Companion,* and *Thematic Guide to Popular Short Stories*. His criticism, fiction, articles, interviews, and reviews have appeared in *Quarter After Eight,* Scribner's *American Writers, Aethlon: The Journal of Sport Literature, Studies in Short Fiction, Sports Afield,* and *Notes on Contemporary Literature,* among other publications. Smith lives with his family in Tallahassee, Florida. **Philip Kerr**

LES WILKINSON. Les Wilkinson is senior master at Nottingham High School, England, where he has taught English for twenty nine years and where he has directed a number of major dramatic productions. His interest in Scottish Literature was awoken at St Andrews University where he studied in the early seventies. **Hugh McDiarmid**

BRITISH WRITERS

FLEUR ADCOCK

(1934—)

Abby Mims

FLEUR ADCOCK OCCUPIES an interesting position in the poetic world, one of auspicious dual identity: she is at once one of the most popular poets in Great Britain while also garnering critical acclaim in New Zealand, the country of her birth. Both countries lay claim to Adcock and her poetry, yet it is difficult to say to which country she can be most closely tied. She is classified as both an immigrant and an expatriate, having spent fragmented portions of her childhood in New Zealand while making England her home for over thirty years. She maintains an uneasy relationship with New Zealand: its landscape appears in her work as the backdrop of her untamed youth, a place full of extended family and friends, yet it is ultimately portrayed it as a place Adcock escaped. England, on the other hand, seems to be the country she considers her true home, whether she is writing of the countryside and its wildlife or the politics of its urban centers. Regardless, the geographical split between these two countries shapes much of Adcock's poetry, leaving her forever emotionally divided in her search for national and personal identity.

Her work is appreciated by critics and general readers alike and is often noted for its irony, wit, and finely crafted lyrics, coupled with its accessibility. In the *Times Literary Supplement,* John Greening wrote, "Adcock is an insouciant elegist, celebrator of life's sweet symmetry and its lewd gargoyles, one whose native senses flower because they are so deeply rooted in her dreams of elsewhere" (p. 25). The sentiment that Adcock has a particularly fine ear for the poignant moments of the everyday is shared by many and is reflected in the many honors Adcock has received from Britain and New Zealand. They began after her first publication, for which she won the Festival of Wellington Poetry Award (1961) and went on to include the New Zealand

State Literary Fund Award (1964), Buckland Award (1968, 1979), Jesse Mackey Prize (1968, 1972), New Zealand National Book Award (1984), and an Arts Council Writer's Award (1988). In 1996 she was awarded the esteemed OBE (officer of the Order of the British Empire) and was also considered for the post of poet laureate of Great Britain after Ted Hughes's death in 1998.

It is difficult to generalize in terms of Adcock's subject matter, shifting and evolving as it does with each new piece of work. She is said to have created her own genre of love poetry from her earliest collection, *The Eye of the Hurricane* (1964), because her verses lack sentimentality or rhetorical romantic sensibility and are instead detached, often casting a chilly view of desire and the impulses it brings. While she has enjoyed several romantic relationships with men and likes the feeling of intimacy, she is clear that sex is sex and love is a slippery and ephemeral concept at best. Despite what might be deemed a calloused view of romance, her work is often tender underneath its unimpassioned surface, vulnerable and sensitive to the nuances of intimate relationships. She also concerns herself with the essential concrete moments of the everyday, the details of which unfold to create the full bloom of life, yet this does not stop her from experimenting with the mythical or the fantastical as well as the space between dreams and reality. The rift in her national identity often causes her to focus on the present, leading to intense description and startling imagery, while also relying on an outsider's point of view, creating narrators who simultaneously identify with and withdraw from the emotional and physical world that surrounds them. Her later work explores the ecological and the political world, with particular attention to gender concerns. Often labeled a feminist poet because of these forays (and despite a feminist bent to much of her work), Adcock does not see a reason to be labeled a "female poet," for although she may write about women's concerns, addressing her work to women exclusively might well alienate the male portion of her potential audience.

Adcock is formally trained in the classics and is praised for a restrained voice and straightforward prose style that is influenced by the Group and the Movement poets. She does not enjoy the academicism, fragmentation, or esoteric symbolism that characterize the neoromantic or modernist poet, and she strives to be accessible to the reader in both language and thought process. She has, however, experimented with free verse from the beginning of her career while also employing crafted, complex sentence structure and more traditional lyrical form. This range and flexibility has granted her acceptance into the more conservative realms of the British literary establishment while concurrently gaining respect and admiration from her peers and nonspecialist readers.

Although Adcock's work has been well received, some critics find her preoccupation with the details of the everyday to be more mundane than interesting and note that these observations often do not amount to more than the sum of their parts or arise from a compelling need. Others relegate her success in the domestic realm to those pieces addressed to animals and small children or fault her later work for its preoccupation with wit and political currency over substance and form.

Whatever the critical response, Adcock has made forays for women in the world of modern British poetry while leaving behind a literary legacy that will stand the test of time. In addition to ten volumes of her own poetry, she has translated several volumes of Latin and Romanian verses and composed the lyrics for two operas. She has also edited several anthologies, including *The Faber Book of Twentieth-Century Women's Poetry* and is a frequent literary critic in publications such as the *Times of London* and the *New Statesman*. She has held writing fellowships at Charlotte Mason College of Education at Amble-

side and the universities of Newcastle upon Tyne, Durham, East Anglia, and Adelaide, Australia. A retrospective, *Poems 1960–2000* (2000), reads as if it were an epigraph, but it should be noted that well into her seventies, she continues to teach and write and it therefore would be premature to assume more work is not forthcoming.

LIFE

Adcock was born in Auckland, New Zealand, on February 10, 1934, to Cyril and Irene Adcock. A sister, Marilyn, followed two years later. The family was mobile from the time Adcock was very young, moving from one township to the next as her father taught in various country schools. In 1939 her father decided to pursue his Ph.D. in psychology at the University of London, and the family set sail in September of that year. While they were en route World War II broke out, and it was too late for the ship to return to New Zealand. Once settled in Britain, both Adcock's parents worked for the Civil Ambulance Service and her father traveled extensively giving lectures for the WEA (Workers' Educational Association). These activities delayed his university education and also separated him from the immediate family for long periods of time. Their father's (and sometimes mother's) absence coupled with the threat of bombings made it necessary for Adcock and her sister to live with relatives in the English countryside, and given this set of circumstances Adcock attended eleven schools in seven-and-a-half years. Ever the new girl, she was constantly in the position of attempting to fit in, and the chaos of her young life permanently left her feeling on the outside of things. As might be expected, much of her work reflects this isolation and a sense that she has never belonged to any one particular place or nation. Despite the trauma she sustained as a result of her tumultuous childhood, Adcock feels that these various relocations sharpened her senses of perception and provided her with a foundation of images and emotions from which to write. Her work is infused with the various landscapes she avidly studied as a child, from the wildflowers and animals of the English countryside to the beaches and green hills of New Zealand.

From an early age, writing was Adcock's refuge from the world. At age six she began scribbling down poems while hiding in an abandoned shed from bullies after school. Many of her poems chronicle the difficult years of her youth, with an entire section in *The Incident Book* (1986) simply titled "Schools." There is no doubt she was a precocious child or that her rebellious nature got an early start, as is captured in "Loving Hitler," from *The Incident Book*. Here a six-year-old Adcock attempts to get her parents' attention away from the radio by claiming that she loves Hitler and holds out for several minutes as "a mini-proto neo Nazi" while the adults buzz around shocked, aghast at her declaration. In a child's voice, Adcock explains to the reader that at school everyone loved someone, and while she had tried to love Albert, a fellow classmate, he had only laughed at her, and you could be sure of one thing: Hitler didn't laugh at people. This is representative of Adcock's irony and dry wit, using as she does the actions of a frustrated child to provide a moment of levity during a time of war, going so far as to invoke one of the world's most notorious dictators as a potential love interest.

The family continued to live in England until 1947, when Cyril Adcock was offered a position back in New Zealand at the University of Wellington. Adcock and her sister were resistant to returning and once there were overwhelmed by the close presence of their relatives in their native country, having become accustomed to their independent nuclear family. Adcock eventually adjusted and began to flourish in school, learning German, French, and Latin and scoring high enough marks to be admitted into Victoria University. She went on to learn Greek and major in classics while developing a passion for linguistics and continuing to write poetry. It was also at Victoria that she encountered her first live poets, including James Baxter, Louis Johnson, Denis Glover, and Alistair Campbell. Access to this literary circle resulted in a romantic liaison for Adcock; she and Campbell were married in

1952, six months after they met. Adcock was just eighteen years old and Campbell twenty–five. Two years later she gave birth to their first son, Gregory, and three years later their son Andrew was born. She was writing less during this time, immersed as she was in being a mother and wife, although she also managed to earn her M.A. degree from Victoria in 1956 and publish her first poem in *Landfall,* a New Zealand literary magazine, that same year. By then, however, her marriage was falling apart and Campbell was in love with another woman. Despite that fact, they ended things fairly amicably, and wanting to avoid a custody battle, decided that Andrew should stay with Adcock and Gregory with Campbell, an unusual arrangement for the time. In retrospect Adcock deeply regrets that she missed most of Gregory's childhood and that her sons were not able to grow up together. It remains a painful topic that she does not readily discuss or easily write about, although there are allusions to it in her work.

After her separation from Campbell, Adcock moved to Dunedin, a city in the south of New Zealand, where she became a junior lecturer in classics at the University of Otago. The next three years were crucial in her apprenticeship as a writer, as she had more time to write and also fell in with a group of poets headed by Charles Brasch, the founder of *Landfall*. Adcock feels she began to truly understand how to write poetry during those years; Brasch obviously agreed and began steadily publishing more of her work, which officially launched her career. Despite this auspicious start, she was sidelined slightly in 1962 when she met Barry Crump, a fellow New Zealander and author of best-selling picaresque, anecdotal sagas. A month later he was her second husband, but this union was not to endure either. Among other problems, Crump physically abused Adcock, and the marriage was dissolved after less than a year. Given that she was married twice at such a young age, it is not surprising that vestiges of her romantic troubles have haunted much of Adcock's prose, and indeed, her observations of relationships often take on the tone of a world-weary realist who has decided to put her energies elsewhere, namely into familial bonds and close friendships. She often makes her ex-husbands and lovers part of her subject matter and has no qualms about naming names, using "To Alistair Campbell" to chronicle her unusual post-divorce friendship with Campbell while painting a much less flattering picture of an abuser in "Batterer," a piece that appears to be addressed directly to Crump.

Adcock was desperate to make a fresh start for herself and her son after her divorce from Crump and in 1963 decided to leave New Zealand for England. Ironically, it was only a year later that her first collection, *The Eye of the Hurricane,* was printed in New Zealand, making her a celebrated published poet in her native country, a place she would never again consider her home (she would not even return for a visit for the next thirteen years). Adcock arrived in London an unemployed single mother during the coldest winter in nearly twenty years. Adcock quickly secured a job as a librarian at the Foreign Office Library and would remain there for fifteen years. Not long after, she began to circulate in London literary society and became a member of the Group, an influential circle of poets in Britain that included George MacBeth, Peter Porter, Anthony Thwaite, and Edward Lucie-Smith. These contacts led to publication in British literary magazines and the release of her second collection, *Tigers,* in 1967. With the changing social and political atmosphere of the 1960s, Adcock was recognized as a brave new voice in modern British poetics, and her career has only ascended from there.

EARLY WORK

From the publication of *Tigers* which also included the poems previously published in *The Eye of the Hurricane,* Adcock's work was known for its unsentimental approach to romantic relationships as well as an underlying tenderness and exploration of the psychological scars such encounters can entail. She drew praise for her ability to record the small moments in intimate relationships, those between lovers or parents and their children, in a way that was emotionally honest without becoming confessional. Adcock

earned a reputation for looking upon life and relationships with a cold, keen eye, demonstrating an ability to stay detached from her subject matter. In this way she stood out among her contemporaries, such as Anne Sexton and Sylvia Plath, who were categorized as confessional female poets.

Given her style and subject matter, she was grouped with the Movement poets early on and concedes that her work was inclined toward that of Philip Larkin and his contemporaries, but she also counts Robert Graves, W. H. Auden, and Ezra Pound among her influences. Her early poems certainly follow some of the traditions of the Movement in that they are straightforward and accessible, make an effort to stay true to the experiences of life, and are often sly and ironic in tone, yet she also often experiments with free-form verse and infuses her prose with the erotic and hedonistic. Commenting on the source and inspiration for her work, Adcock states that it comes largely from what she has directly experienced, whether that be relationships, places, or people. The resulting images or ideas in her poems are constructed from these things both consciously and subconsciously.

Perhaps it can be said then that in her early work, Adcock attempts to strike a balance between the emotional and the rational when exploring her life experiences, often employing startling imagery to provide a brief window into the poet's psyche, carefully calibrated to allow only as much as she wants the reader to see. This kind of tempered approach can be seen throughout *Tigers,* particularly in "Knife-Play," which recounts the physical wounds the narrator has inflicted upon herself as a response to the less tangible emotional wounds her lover has left on her psyche. At first she blames him for all of her pain, but it is slowly revealed that she now has the upper hand in the relationship, having been well schooled in emotional cruelty by her partner. These newfound skills leave her free to stab and retreat at will, as it were, but she has realized this is a hollow victory at best and makes the decision to stop their dance:

No: I would make an end of fighting
and, bleeding as I am from old wounds,

die like a bee upon a sting.

(p. 19)

While there is an element of raw emotion and bitterness in these last lines, the final image rings more of a tired wisdom than rage or contempt.

These first volumes have a feminist bent to them at times, although Adcock notes that the female roles in them were few aside from fictionalized versions of herself. She instead often wrote from the point of view of men or children, and as for feminism Adcock comments, "I think I was a very late developer as a feminist. It took me a long time to realize I wasn't just a man in some basic sense. The poets I modeled myself on were men and I earned my living and I got a mortgage and I did all the things men do. And then it leaked through almost accidentally" (O'Brien, p. 148). But leak through it did, particularly in poems like "Advice to a Discarded Lover" where the narrator compares the self-pity of a rejected suitor to maggots eating away at a dead bird; she advises him not to return to her until his bones are wiped clean. The power of the female over the male is even more striking in "Instructions to Vampires," wherein the narrator enacts her revenge on her male counterpart by advising the vampires to not simply drain him of blood, as is customary, but instead

use acid or flame
secretly, to brand or cauterise
and on the soft globes of his mortal eyes
etch my name.

(p. 19)

Responses to Adcockian images such as these have been mixed: one critic called the poem funny, alarming, and perversely sexy, while another commented that it was frightening, even hateful. Despite sometimes unfavorable reactions, Adcock is never one to shy away from turning the power dynamics between the sexes upside down, often invoking myth or allegory to make her point.

When she is not exploring the enigma of male-female relationships in *Tigers,* Adcock turns her attention to the domestic pastoral, motherhood in particular. "For Andrew" leaves Adcock with the difficult task of answering her son's impossible question, "Will I die?" Knowing that her "yes," no matter how it is couched, will not be an answer he can absorb, she chooses for a moment to share in his childish optimism that if he eats his vegetables and looks both ways before crossing the street he will live forever; both are comforted by this false assurance of the future. A darker interaction happens in "For a Five-Year-Old" as Adcock's son saves a snail from his bedroom, delivering it back outside because this is what his mother has taught him to do. The irony of the blind faith that occurs between mother and child is revealed in the second stanza, where Adcock ponders her own past cruelties and betrayals before wryly concluding "But that is how things are: I am your mother / And we are kind to snails" (p. 21).

High Tide in the Garden (1971) also reflects domestic concerns, with poems about a newly purchased house in East Finchley as well as several about Adcock's son Gregory and her previous life in New Zealand. One of her most famous pieces, "Against Coupling," appears in this volume, a poem well known for its wit and political overtones. Although Adcock claims not to write political poems, the very subject of the poem is political because the female is opting out of the mutual sexual act of her own accord. It goes on to proclaim the inherent pleasure of masturbation and its efficiency over the mess and complications of sexual intercourse:

I write in praise of the solitary act:
of not feeling a trespassing tongue
forced into one's mouth.
. . .
No need to set the scene,
dress up (or undress), make speeches.
Five minutes of solitude are
enough–in the bath, or to fill
that gap between the Sunday papers and lunch.

(p. 26)

The backdrop of the 1960s and its elevation of the mutual sexual experience to near religious heights certainly plays a role in this poem, yet the voice seems almost bored by the topic before it can be brought up, lending to the poem's overall subversive nature.

With the publication of *The Scenic Route* (1974), Adcock begins to delve more deeply into a lifelong obsession with her immigrant status and national identity, recounting a visit to the Ireland of her mother's relatives. In "Please Identify Yourself" she finds it difficult to claim either her British citizenship or her New Zealand heritage and when asked remains steadfastly in a gray area. She is forced to choose sides in Belfast, however, a place where neutrality is no longer an option. In a city inflamed with religious tensions and faced with a bigoted Protestant preacher, Adcock has no choice but to align herself with Catholicism. Given that this is not the religion she would normally choose to defend, she appears to be making fun of her own inability to remain indifferent, at the civilized person's response to prejudice. Other pieces in the collection, such as "Richey," "The Voyage Out," and "Moa Point" explore the experiences of people who have emigrated to New Zealand, recording the fractured lives of those who have left their homelands to live there. An additional pamphlet, *Below Loughrigg,* was published by Bloodaxe Books in 1979 and recounts Adcock's year spent in the Lake District of England.

With these first five volumes, then, the reader can see the development of Adcock's already assured poetic voice and the exploration of a wide range of subject matter. Also firmly established are the major themes Adcock will continue to explore for the duration of her career: love, loss, familial bonds, ancestry, and the essential questions of identity.

THE INNER HARBOUR

Although her early volumes of poetry established Adcock's career, many consider the poems included in *The Inner Harbour* (1979) to be among her best. Self-knowledge without illusion is apparent in her previous work, but this collection develops it into a fine art. Adcock wrote *The Inner Harbour* after she traveled to New Zealand for the first time in thirteen years, a difficult journey that left her with mixed feelings at best about her nationality. Despite a warm reception from friends and family, she felt like a foreigner in her mother country—a foreigner who missed England terribly, no less. The visit also appears to have propelled an obsession with the issues of personal and national identity to new heights; it is not surprising then that this volume deals heavily with the themes of family origin, love, relationships, and loss, coupled with the struggles of the immigrant throughout time.

Adcock divides the work into four sections: "Beginnings," "Endings," "The Thing Itself," and "To and Fro." In "Beginnings" several poems that muse about the writing process, none so apt as "Future Work," Adcock's ironic response to an editor who has rejected a poem yet encourages her to send more. Playing on the difficulties of creating this so-called future work, Adcock assures the editor that she will send it along just as soon as she finishes the tasks she has set for herself this summer—building a brick wall in the garden, writing the third novel of a trilogy, translating Persian creation myths, and last but not least, competing for the Ping-Pong championships in Manila. Despite its playful tone and her obvious exaggeration of activities, Adcock closes the poem with a line that captures the endless challenge of a writer's life, that of mustering the courage and resolve to sit down and write:

And poems? Yes, there will certainly be poems:
they sing in my head, they tingle along my nerves.
It is all magnificently about to begin.

(p. 84)

In "Things," Adcock deftly brings us into the world of her anxieties while simultaneously causing us, in only six lines, to catalog our own regrets and missteps:

There are worse things than having behaved foolishly
  in public.
There are worse things than these miniature betrayals,
committed or endured or suspected; there are worse
  things
than not being able to sleep for thinking about them.
It is 5 A.M. All the worse things come stalking in
and stand icily about the bed looking worse and worse
  and worse.

(p. 87)

Although Adcock never deviates from generalities, the readers are meant to feel as though she is confessing a great deal; this is a tactic she often employs, which makes a poem achingly personal while at the same time revealing more about the reader than it does about her.

In "Endings," Adcock moves to the realm of the fantastic, opening the section with what is perhaps her most critically acclaimed poem, "The Ex-Queen Among the Astronomers." Often viewed as a rant against patriarchy, the ex-queen is seen to represent all women, oppressed by the dominating male, used only for sexual exploits and discarded once the novelty has worn off. The male scientists appear self-important, and the poem suggests that their inquiries are less about science than about material gain and power, the kind that would result in a world of ordered control and controlled and ordered women. Adcock does not claim to have written the poem as a stance against the male establishment, and although she allows that the ex-queen represents a type of woman who was raised to please men, she was mainly fascinated with the phrase that became the poem's title. While it may be easy to reduce the poem to issues of patriarchy and oppression, it can also be said that the world Adcock creates here is one of the duality between the rational, scientific plane on which the astronomers reside and the emotional, earthbound realm of the ex-queen. Although she is stripped of her powers in the first few stanzas, and her actions thereafter appear to be only ephemerally rebellious, certain phrases raise questions as to the ex–queen's complete submission to the male. If she truly conforms to the idioms of male sexuality, what is made of her desire to seek "terrestrial bodies to bestride" (p. 93)? Another question is whether her encounters with these men are involuntary or willful, and at the close of the poem, lovemaking occurs with no specific man, just one that she has "plucked" from the group of scientists. While the two are joined, the ex–queen momentarily blends with the expanse of the universe:

her hair
crackles, her eyes are comet–sparks
She brings the distant briefly close

above his dreamy abstract stare.

(p. 93)

This union of the ex-queen with the skies that the astronomer wishes to claim as his own could be viewed as an act of residual power on her part, a way of encompassing a world beyond the one he currently controls. Whatever the interpretations, the poem asks more questions than it answers. As Sean O'Brien observes, "The blend of the general and the circumstantial seems to give the poem the status of a myth, in which we can recognize, though not resolve, our own conditions—except into art" (p. 153).

Adcock leaves behind the mythical in "The Thing Itself," turning instead to landscapes of New Zealand, England, and Africa while also exploring the bonds of family and the devastation of terminal illness. One of her most poignant poems, "The Soho Hospital for Women," highlights Adcock's ability to present a clear-sighted view of life while expressing compassion for its inherent fragility. She shows a reticent courage toward the cancer she is being treated for: "Doctor, I am not afraid of a word / But neither do I wish to embrace that visitor" (p. 101). In a dark parody, she likens the surgeon to a lover: "I have admitted the gloved hands and the speculum / and must open my ordinary legs to the surgeon's knife." This unwanted intimacy is underscored by the surgeon's practiced smile and inability to offer true comfort to his patient. There are also portraits of the other women in the ward; the woman who smokes only outside yet drags in the smell of cigarettes behind her, the woman who puts on her best brooch before radiation, the woman who religiously takes in her skirt as she grows thinner and thinner. These are in essence the moments of hope seen among the sick. But Adcock will not let the reader be distracted from death for long, pointing to Mrs. Golding, the woman who never smiles. To this Adcock answers, "And why should she?" Her question serves as another example of the writer's ability to force the reader to look at the hard truth, rather than look away.

Fittingly, the last section of the collection is "To and Fro," which captures the back-and-forth between continents that characterized Adcock's childhood and the constant shuffling of identity that confronts her on a daily basis. Appropriately titled poems such as "Settlers," "Going Back," "Immigrant," and "Londoner" are included here, yet the one that perhaps captures Adcock's dilemma most eloquently is "Instead of an Interview." It opens with Adcock detailing the vagaries of landscape (hills, water, clear air, rivers) for the journalists who ask her to describe the feelings surrounding her first journey back to New Zealand in over a decade. She refuses to yield to more in-depth probing in the hope of simplifying a very complicated question, attempting to answer it for herself in the remaining stanzas. She chronicles her journey through the country that appears to offer everything she needs—a lover, friends, family, galleries, gardens, passion fruit, and lemons growing wild, yet "not a town or city I could live in" (p. 115). Although she brings a suitcase full of bark, stones, and shells back with her to England and spreads them around her study, this seems to be as close as she wants her mother country to be. The poem closes with the alienation and loss this choice has left her with, as she queries whether the act of going back after thirteen years has indeed turned her into the exile that she has long been labeled. This question haunts the volume from start to finish, as does the space between hope and despair, reality and fantasy, and innocence and disillusionment.

After the publication of *The Inner Harbour*, Adcock was able to leave her job as a librarian and write full time. The next decade would greatly expand her career as she continued to publish her own work while exploring other areas of poetic practice, including the translation of Latin and Romanian poetry and the crafting of two operatic librettos. This essay therefore will explore her volumes after *The Inner Harbour* more briefly while delving into her skills as a translator and lyricist in an effort to sketch out the full breadth of her career.

THE INCIDENT BOOK

The 1980s brought the publication of Adcock's first collected works, *Selected Poems* (1983), *The Incident Book* (1986), and another pamphlet from Bloodaxe Books, *Meeting the Comet* (1988). *Selected Poems* contains such famous pieces as "The Prize-Winning Poem," which compiles a list of the necessary ingredients that would indeed win one first prize in a poetry competition. In the end these are impossible to define beyond the obvious (the poet must be able to spell) and the ludicrous (the poet will not include a photo of himself), so Adcock narrows it down to this: "it's got to be good" (p. 137). In "Revision" she explores the ax that all writers must grind if their work is to be successful. Her love of the art is evident here as she compares the constant relearning inherent in rewriting to the taste of wine at first communion and floating on one's back in seawater. This affirmation is reflected in her emphatic last line, "So yes: teach it to me again" (p. 133).

"Across the Moor" is much more serious in tone and demonstrates Adcock's understated narrative ability. She puts herself inside the mind of a man who is ominously following a woman at night and is suddenly interrupted by another man and his dogs. This causes the would-be stalker to see something in the woman's face that makes him decide to let her go, although what exactly it is he sees is not quite clear. As he stands on a bridge, he reflects on the natural landscape of the wind and the stream of traffic below, reconciling internally where the impulse to leave her unharmed might have come from. Never one to spare the male ego, it is interesting that Adcock creates an empathetic portrait of the male predator's state of mind in a situation that would seem call for outrage on the author's part. The poem is characteristic of the way Adcock maintains her composure by keeping the focus firmly on the subject, earning authority with the reader through the boldness of her imagination.

The most significant work Adcock produced in this decade was *The Incident Book,* which chronicles the England of her roving childhood while also exploring a modern-day Britain fraught with social tension, consumerism, and individualism. Response to *The Incident Book* was mixed, and the book is frequently viewed as a turning point in Adcock's career because the overall voice appears more focused on being clever and witty than on engaging the reader emotionally, leaving it less intimate and vulnerable than her previous works. That said, Adcock branches out in this volume by exploring realms that are not strictly autobiographical while also demonstrating a sophisticated, diverse voice that encompasses a wide range of subject matter, landscapes in particular. "Loving Hitler" and "For Heidi with Blue Hair" are lighthearted forays into the follies and rebellions of youth, whereas "On the School Bus," "Earlswood," and "Chippenham" delve into areas of intimidation by schoolmates and schoolmasters, events that confirmed Adcock's status as permanent outsider. Some of her most elegiac works regarding friendships and familial bonds appear in this collection as well, including "The Keepsake," written in memory of a close friend whose last act was to loan her a book with this title, and "The Chiffonier," a premature elegy to her mother as Adcock prepares for her inevitable death.

"Drowning," which describes the thoughts of a woman condemned to death by drowning for the murder of her husband, is often recognized for its feminist streak and strength of voice. It opens with the narrator stating that death by drowning drowns the soul, yet the woman offers no remorse in these stanzas. On the contrary, she is defiant toward her husband until her last breath:

Then let the fishes feast on us
and slurp our blood after we're finished
they'll find no souls to suck from us.

(p. 28)

Another moving and notable poem is "Accidents," which manages to capture the haunting, nagging conception within the collective unconscious that the most terrible things that could befall us are simply too horrific to conceive. The poem summons images of sleeping babies and mothers who would not dare think of crib death; a driver on a slick road who has not yet crashed; a rescue party who cannot believe the tunnel has collapsed. Adcock does provide us with a small modicum of comfort however, leaving us with a few children drinking hot cocoa at their aunt's house, a momentary safe haven in an otherwise unstable world.

As for "Thatcherland," a section of more pointedly political poems, it is apparent that Adcock's view of England has shifted from one of a country that answers the deficiencies of New Zealand to a more troubled place rife with political and social unease. Wryly humorous pieces like "Post Office" and "Demonstration" observe a Britain moving into the future: a country that once did not need to raise its voice that now shouts above the construction of a six-lane road that has desecrated trees and meeting spots, "Come with us into the nineties!" (p. 188). Despite her overall reluctance to engage in nostalgia and her ability to remain detached from her subject matter, throughout this volume Adcock longs for the England she was introduced to as a child: a safer, quieter place where nature reigned over industry.

In 1986, the same year *The Incident Book* was published, Adcock collaborated with the composer Gillian Whitehead and produced *Hotspur,* an operatic ballad to accompany Whitehead's music. The opera focuses on Henry Percy, known as Hotspur, who was the eldest son of the first earl of Northumberland, a family of Norman descent who controlled the north of England for several centuries. Accounts of his life also appear in fictionalized form in Shakespeare's *Richard II* and *Henry IV, Part 1.* Adcock was drawn to this character, a study in contradiction who was legendary both for his courage and devotion to the ideals of chivalry and for his brutality and the pleasure he took in warfare. He changed alliances at will, which led to his death at the Battle of Shrewsbury during an uprising against Henry IV, whom Hotspur himself conspired to put on the throne. The ballad is written in the voice of Hotspur's wife, Elizabeth Mortimer, as, upon hearing of her husband's violent death, she reflects upon their life together. Adcock has also collaborated with Whitehead on a full-length opera about Eleanor of Aquitaine.

ADCOCK AS TRANSLATOR

The 1980s and early 1990s were a prolific time for Adcock as she began publishing translations of Latin and Romanian poetry alongside her own collections. Her interest in linguistics began at

Victoria University, where she seized the opportunity to learn Latin and Greek while developing her understanding of the English language. If it can be said that a successful translation cannot consist simply of dictionary equivalents but must instead incorporate the essence of a language from the inside out, this is a lofty goal Adcock achieves time and again with each poem she translates.

It speaks to the level of Adcock's intellectual curiosity that she began *The Virgin and the Nightingale: Medieval Latin Lyrics* (1983) as a project of personal satisfaction, translating medieval Latin poems taken from the *Carmina Burana* during her fellowships at Newcastle upon Tyne and Durham. Never one to shy away from the controversial or the sexual, Adcock chose several erotic works by Peter of Blois, a scholar, diplomat, and political secretary for Henry II, who turned to religion in his later years and disclaimed the explicit verses that Adcock translates. The volume includes his Latin texts as well as poems by monks and clerics that are often focused on young women and birds, and Adcock uses her classical training and technical skill to create lively translations that deftly reproduce the form and rhyme schemes of the originals. She initially explored the texts in the university libraries, twisting the intricate meters and rhyme schemes into English and working on them for the love of a challenge, not for the purpose of publication. As it happened, her friend Neil Astley acquired the manuscript in 1979 and went on to found Bloodaxe Books, a press that by 1983 was one of the most prominent publishers of poetry in Great Britain.

Her next translation project, *Hugh Primas and the Archpoet,* was even more daunting and complex and would not be published until 1994. With this volume she again turned her hand to Latin with the works of all the known poems of Hugh Primas of Orleans and the Archpoet, two of the most famous poets of the twelfth century. Given the many interpretations of their identities and respective works, Adcock relied on the historian Peter Dronke's scholarship to provide the context for historical and textual questions; it is within his framework that the poems are translated. She was faced with a unique problem with these verses in that by the twelfth century, rhythmical verse forms had become more common than quantitative verse, and both poets were masters of the art. Rhyme is quite different in Latin and in English, English being a more homogeneous language, making it a struggle to preserve both the rhyme scheme and the meaning of the original Latin text. This issue challenged Adcock to the point of defeat several times, and she resolved it in part by settling for "half-rhymes," which displeased her to some extent but satisfied critics and readers. An example of her rhyming solution from one of Primas' best known poems:

I was rich and people loved me;
There was none they set above me
Now decrepitude has bent me
And old age has quite undone me
So I'm poor and they neglect me;
Even down and outs reject me.

(p. 51)

In her own poems Adcock plays with such half-rhymes and sound effects, skills that lent themselves very successfully to this project. The resulting volume is a nearly flawless translation of these works, which allows for an increased readership among Latinists and general readers. Given its touches of satire and coarse realism captured so eloquently by Adcock, the edition is a welcome addition to the few English volumes of translated medieval Latin texts.

Adcock's other foray into translation began after she visited Romania in 1984; she would return to the country several times before and after the revolution. The country impacted her own poetry as well, particularly in *Time-Zones* (1991), as she recorded her observations of an impoverished country before the fall of communism and the surreal experiences that occurred after this historic political change. "On the Way to the Castle" shows her view from the safety of a tour bus as rain falls on the parched landscape outside; an editor of a prominent magazine is guiding a group of writers through the countryside. Watching the peasants scrounge for potatoes "the size of bullets" she notes the cocoon from which she and her group observe this foraging; the guide would not want them to focus on the fact that the rain is perhaps months too late and that the harvest is scorched and nearly unsalvageable. "Romania" explores the chaos immediately following the ousting of Nicolae Ceausescu as Adcock, back in England, desperately tries to contact her friends there and, unable to, plays a tape she had secretly recorded with one of them. As they sip "blood-pink" beverages they muse in two languages about what the peasants of the country might drink, sarcastically noting that the question itself is irrelevant, for according to Ceausescu's regime the peasants themselves do not exist. Then there is a phone call, a breaking through, the question "Did it really happen?" and the resounding yes that follows. Adcock lets the reader in to the violence and oppression of the country with a sideways glance, handing it over in manageable bits of potato and drinks the color of watered-down blood, all laced with her impeccable sense of the ironic.

Over the years she learned Romanian and befriended two prominent female poets, Grete Tartler and Daniela Crasnaru, eventually translating their work. For all the obstacles Adcock encountered while working with Latin texts, she says that the Romanian texts proved even more of a challenge. While the Latin translations were mainly a showcase for her technical skills, with Tartler's and Crasnaru's works she was obligated to present the poetry of these women as straightforwardly as possible, while keeping her own voice from overshadowing the originals. Given her talents as a translator, Adcock was able to achieve both of these goals with surefooted skill and her inherent agility with language.

Her translation of Tartler's *Orient Express* appeared in 1989 to positive reviews, but it was her translation of Crasnaru's work, *Letters from Darkness (1991),* that garnered national attention and was nominated for the best book of Great Britain that year. Crasnaru is a poet and a political activist who was outspoken against the Ceausescu regime, and *Letters from Darkness* is a collection of subversive poems exposing the oppression of prerevolutionary Romania. Artists and writers there were strictly controlled under

Ceausescu and encouraged to treat him with nothing but praise in their work, although some subversive types of literature did escape complete censure. Crasnaru hid her most dangerous work in a box of onions kept in her aunt's cellar in Bucharest, as Crasnaru's own flat was likely to be searched at any time. It was only after the revolution that Crasnaru wrote to Adcock stating that she was now finally free to send the author these works, her "real" poems. Despite Crasnaru's political background, her work is not simply a vehicle for political expression and is praised for its sympathetic portrayal of the hardships of ordinary people, individuals so accustomed to their harsh reality that it would never occur to them to give up, despite their feelings of helplessness. She often mixes the ridiculous with vivid realism to achieve this convincing portrait of the human condition. Adcock acknowledges this universality found in the work of female Romanian poets in her introduction to *Silent Voices: An Anthology of Romanian Women Poets* (1986), which also includes Tartler and Crasnaru. She notes that while the poems' images may reflect these women's specific nationality, the more inner-focused moments in their verses make it clear they have insights to share with women the world over.

WORKS 1990–2000

This decade allowed for Adcock's exploration into more ecological and political concerns with *Time-Zones* and a broader portrait of her ancestors in *Looking Back* (1997), while her *New Poems* were included in the retrospective volume *Poems 1960–2000* (2000). By the publication of *Time-Zones* Adcock's work is markedly more relaxed in terms of tone, moving from a more formal voice to a relaxed, colloquial style. Adcock herself attributes this shift to her increased agility with poetry, noting that with any art form artists must first learn the finer technical points of their craft and once that is mastered decide when to employ these standards and when to break away from tradition. The collection's title comes from the division of hemispheres and also refers to the pervasive undercurrent of memory that can be felt in the everyday. These qualities are registered in a work that is at once preoccupied with the death of Adcock's father while deftly moving from the Communist regime in Romania to the poet's concerns about the effects of chemical pollution on the environment.

With "The Greenhouse Effect," "The Last Moa," and "Wildlife," Adcock points to the global shifts in climate and its lasting repercussions on an animal kingdom now replete with endangered and vanished species. We are then brought to the constant battle between memory and nostalgia in "My Father" as she captures the shock and grief of death and the illusive nature of the desires it engenders in those left behind. She muses about uncovering his family origins as a way of keeping him alive:

When I got up that morning I had no father.
. . .
I didn't see it; he went so suddenly,
. . .
I'll go look for where they were born and bred
I'll go next month; we'll both go, I and my sister.
We'll tell him about it, when he stops being dead.

(p. 195)

Adcock includes several poems in which she confronts the idealized nostalgia that can accompany even the most painful of memories, mainly those of childhood. In "House-martins" she imagines a mock corner of suburbia in Margaret Thatcher's Britain, a veritable theme park of false comforts. In fifty years, she says, the children now living on "Shakespeare Close" (Adcock's wry name for the street) will be "sick with nostalgia" (p. 201) for this inauthentic landscape, mourning the loss of their plasticized youth. "Creosote" plays with one of the most powerful triggers of memory, that of smell. The narrator recalls the smell of her uncle's farm, oils and animal waste and tin, an odor that brings a tingling to the tongue, a smell that one might assume to be quite unpleasant. But the memory is so beloved by the narrator that she longs for the scents to be bottled somewhere: "it's a tin at the back of the shed: open it / snort it! You can't: the lid's stuck on" (p. 206). By sealing off our access

to the past in this way, Adcock reminds us how often we are victims of our own revisionist history.

Not all the poems are without a sense of humor, and "Smokers for Celibacy" is one of Adcock's more famous. Here she captures the irony of an age in which sex is conceivably more dangerous than smoking, and the smokers narrating the poem list various sexually transmitted diseases and cancers of the reproductive track as their "evidence" that we all should start lighting up and forgo sex altogether. This is not to mention the perk that cigarettes (unlike lovers) are never moody and do not keep you up all night discussing their mothers or their first wives. Only Adcock could tackle the subject of death and sex in quite this way, making the gravest of topics palatable, even funny.

Looking Back is divided into two parts, the first of which deals with Adcock's family history and genealogy from the mill hands of Manchester in the 1890s to men who were members of the court of Edward II in the early fourteenth century. Her lineage is presented as part truth, part poetic play, demonstrating that history, like memory, is a kind of fiction; even if one comes up with the proper documentation, there is no way to be certain of what really transpired. She shows a particular empathy for her female ancestors in these poems, throwing light on women who were disregarded in their time. Adcock does this subtly in "Framed," where she shows us her grandfather's photo, silver-framed and hanging proudly while her grandmother's has gone forever unframed, wrapped instead in tissue paper and tucked away in a drawer. She also presents a range of colloquial voices—subversive, rebellious, offbeat—that privilege the females of her family.

Although some authors might be eager to display their extensive research, Adcock instead chooses not to take herself too seriously, relfecting what a silly business tracing back one's ancestry can be. In "Ancestor to Devotee," one of her relatives chides her for the excitement she feels upon finding a document with a signature on it, asking "what is it that makes you hold your breath— / what reverent, half-perverted thrill?"

(p. 247). Her deflating humor is present in "At Great Hampden" as she attempts with a vicar to find a burial plaque of Griffith Hampden and his wife Ann Cave. Together on their hands and knees, they roll back the carpet together while Adcock dismisses certain plaques engraved with cherubs or intricate curlicues because she is sure her relatives would have had better taste. At long last she finds them at the opposite end of the hall, but now she and the vicar are covered in fluff, and buttons are popping off her overcoat, a testament to the messy and unglamorous work involved in this undertaking.

Adcock also demonstrates a particular talent for bringing these distant relatives to life with something that goes beyond mere curiosity and begins to resemble a kind of love as she allows them to speak for themselves. In "Frances," Frances Weale of Arlesey bequeaths a half-dozen silver spoons to her son, and Adcock takes this gesture back in time, spinning the story of this woman's life around the silverware as it is passed from one person to the next. This kind of care is echoed in "Ancestor to Devotee," in which Adcock recognizes the delicacy and impermanence of what she is trying to capture when the ancestor says

What's left of me, if you gathered it up
is a faggot of bones, some ink-scrawled paper,
flown-away cells of skin and hair.
. . .
But I'm combustible now. Watch out:
you'll burn me up with that blow-torch flame.

(p. 248)

Another pitch-perfect rendering occurs in "Peter Wentworth in Heaven," Adcock's imagining of a man who was imprisoned in the Tower of London several times by Elizabeth I for demanding that Parliament be allowed to discuss the succession and various other matters without censure. In the tradition of Jane Austen, Adcock creates the epitome of an Englishman:

My Pithie Exhoration still exists–
go and read it in your British Library.
I have discussed it here with your father

he was always a supporter of free speech.

(p. 255)

The second half of the volume is more personal and autobiographical, as Adcock guides the reader through the living generations of her family. "The Video" features Adcock's ninety-year-old mother and is a vignette of sibling rivalry among her granddaughters; "Giggling" chronicles her similarities to her Aunt Lizzie, as Adcock revels in the fun of old age. "A Political Kiss" details a dream of Adcock's in which she has a liaison with John Prescott, a member of Parliament; the poem garnered her and Prescott a fair amount of press in Britain. "Pilgrim Fathers" takes a shot at the world of literary criticism, the title being taken from one of Adcock's earliest poems, crafted at age nine and read aloud in class. In a different kind of "looking back" she wistfully recounts the innocence and purity of this act, spoofing questions that might be posed by would–be critics regarding the poem's patriarchal title or its childish tendencies.

With New Poems, which appears at the end of Poems 1960–2000, Adcock could well be answering some of those critics, for these verses seem to have been written solely for the purpose of pleasing herself, a fitting gesture on the poet's part. Among these poems are tributes to long friendships, ruminations on being a grandmother, and the compulsory fears one generation always has for the next. Adcock even tackles the computer age in "It's Done This!," listing all the errors and glitches she experiences while trying to write, yet she is still up all night with the page, and in the end neither she nor the software is shutting down. The last sequence is "Kensington Gardens," a series of very short vignettes that chronicles a summer in the life of the poet, one filled with writing, a friend's cancer, migrating butterflies, and a polypectomy. The range of these moments is pure Adcock, at once serious and ironic, painful and true, all a fitting tribute to the way her work mirrors life.

CONCLUSION

Looking at the arc of Adcock's body of work, it has remained firmly rooted in the autobiographi-

13

cal, with special attention to women's issues, whether they be relationships, family life, women's histories, health, or social concerns. And while there is a consistent preoccupation with the domestic, over time Adcock has encompassed a more a global consciousness, from politics and war to chemical pollution and its effects on the environment. Also observed is her initial preoccupation with the inner workings and ultimate failings of her own romantic relationships has morphed into a particular appreciation for friendships and bonds that are formed beyond the realm of sexual attraction. This maturation can be traced as well from her personal struggles with national identity and various identifications with both New Zealand and England to a wider view of the immigrant struggle throughout the centuries, including the extensive research of her own bloodlines and ancestry. This concern for history goes beyond the personal and her own poetry at times, as witnessed by the several volumes of translation she has published in the hope of preserving these ancient and politically important texts.

Although Adcock's body of work is impressive in and of itself, it is all the more remarkable given the era in which her career began. In the late 1950s and 1960s Adcock was a single working mother striving to publish in a literary world dominated by men, with only a handful of female poets to serve as models: Sylvia Plath, Anne Sexton, Stevie Smith, Patricia Beer, Marianne Moore, and Elizabeth Jennings. To have established herself as quickly and notably as she did was no small feat, and much of Adcock's initial success came from the fact that she set herself apart from those few female poets, writing about men and women in a way that seemed to erase centuries of insincere rhetoric that passed for love poetry. It speaks to Adcock's talent that she was able to write pointedly about the concerns of women in a style that appealed to both sexes, one that was conversationally confrontational and subversive without causing the alienation of either sex.

Adcock's contribution to the world of poetry, in short, has been the way she is able to combine her acerbic wit and sharp, direct observations of the world into psychologically deft moments that evoke genuine emotion. She has never been afraid to speak her mind, to resist easy labels and the status quo, but with all she reveals she manages to preserve an air both mischievous and ironic, hinting that there is much more to uncover in her work that has not yet been realized. What can be made of this dichotomy, of a poet who appears to confess a great deal about her own life yet has never been labeled "confessional"? How her often classical and deceptively simple verses can contain worlds of understanding? While Adcock herself provides no definitive answers, it could be that the portrait on the cover of *Poems 1960–2000,* titled *Lady with a Squirrel and Starling* by Hans Holbein the Younger, offers a few clues to the essence of Adcock's work. The woman painted here appears plain and serene, gazing introspectively beyond the boundaries of the canvas, flocked by a dark blue sky while a starling rests on a tree branch behind her and a squirrel eats quietly in her lap. It is only by looking more closely that the expression on her face is seen slightly disturbed and the squirrel is chained to her wrist and pulled closely into her chest, giving us the sense that perhaps neither of them sits there of her own accord. This is much the way Adcock draws the reader into her verses, presenting a pragmatic, seemingly calm view of reality which in turn contains moments of shock and revelation that leap out when the reader least expects them.

While it seems Adcock never tires of this type of interaction with her readers, the publication of this retrospective has led to much speculation about her continued contributions to the world of poetry. This conjecture is fueled as much by the volume's contents as by Adcock's own declarations that she has lost interest in poetry and has turned instead to writing prose. While one can never be entirely sure what Adcock will do or say next, many point to the final poem in the collection as prophetic in terms of her future work. It comes at the end of a series on a summer spent in Kensington Gardens:

Goodbye, summer. Poetry goes to bed.
The scruffy blue tits by the Long Water are fed

for the last time from my palm—with cheese, not
 bread
(more sustaining). The chestnut blossoms are dead.
The gates close early. What wanted to be said is said.

(*Goodbye*, p. 279)

Selected Bibliography

WORKS OF FLEUR ADCOCK

POETRY

The Eye of the Hurricane. New Zealand: Reed, 1964.

Tigers. London and New York : Oxford University Press, 1967.

High Tide in the Garden. London and New York: Oxford University Press, 1971.

The Scenic Route. London and New York: Oxford University Press, 1974.

The Inner Harbour. Oxford and New York: Oxford University Press, 1979.

Below Loughrigg. Newcastle upon Tyne, U.K.: Bloodaxe, 1979.

Selected Poems. Oxford and New York: Oxford University Press, 1983.

The Incident Book. Oxford University Press, 1986.

Meeting the Comet. Newcastle upon Tyne, U.K.: Bloodaxe, 1988.

Time–Zones. Oxford and New York: Oxford University Press, 1991.

Looking Back. Oxford and New York: Oxford University Press, 1997.

Poems 1960–2000. Newcastle upon Tyne, U.K.: Bloodaxe, 2000.

TRANSLATIONS

The Virgin and the Nightingale: Medieval Latin Lyrics. Newcastle upon Tyne, U.K.: Bloodaxe, 1983.

Orient Express. By Grete Tartler. Oxford and New York: Oxford University Press, 1989.

Letters from Darkness. By Daniela Crasnaru. New York: Oxford University Press, 1991.

Hugh Primas and the Archpoet. Cambridge, U.K., and New York: Cambridge University Press, 1994.

AS EDITOR

New Poetry Four. With Anthony Thwaite. London: Hutchinson, 1978.

The Oxford Book of Contemporary New Zealand Poetry. New York: Oxford University Press, 1982.

The Faber Book of Twentieth Century Women's Poetry. London and Boston: Faber, 1987.

ARTICLES, INTRODUCTIONS, AND ANTHOLOGIES

Contemporary Authors Online. Autobiographical essay by Adcock: Detroit: Gale, 2000.

4–Pack 1: Four from Northern Women. With Maura Dooley, S. J. Litherland, and Jill Maugham. Newcastle upon Tyne, U.K.: Bloodaxe, 1986.

Silent Voices: An Anthology of Romanian Women Poets. Translated by Andrea Deletant and Brenda Walker with an introduction by Fleur Adcock. London: Forest Books, 1986.

The Poet's Voice and Craft. Edited by C. B. Cully. Manchester, U.K.: Carcanet, 1994.

OTHER WORKS

Hotspur: A Ballad for Music (libretto). Music by Gillian Whitehead. Newcastle upon Tyne, U.K.: Bloodaxe, 1986.

The Oxford Book of Creatures. With Jacqueline Simms. New York: Oxford University Press, 1995, 1998.

CRITICAL AND BIOGRAPHICAL STUDIES

Greening, John. "Simply Daring." *Times Literary Supplement,* July 21, 2000, p. 25.

Couzyn, Jeni. *The Bloodaxe Book of Contemporary Women Poets: Eleven British Writers*. Newcastle upon Tyne, U.K.: Bloodaxe, 1985.

Davis, Robert Murray. "Romanian Writing Redivius." *World Literature Today,* March 22, 2002.

Hulse, Michael. "Fleur Adcock: A Poet with Bite." *Quadrant* 28:52–53 (January–February 1984).

Kester–Shelton, Pamela, ed. *Feminist Writers*. Detroit: St. James Press, 1996.

O'Brien, Sean. *The Deregulated Muse*. Newcastle upon Tyne, U.K.: Bloodaxe, 1998.

Pascal, Paul. "Hugh Primas and the Archpoet." *Medieval Review,* July 6, 1996.

Robinson, Lillian S., ed. *Modern Women Writers*. Vol. 1. New York: Continuum, 1996.

Robinson, Roger, and Nelson Wattie, eds. *The Oxford Companion to New Zealand Literature*. Oxford and Melbourne: Oxford University Press, 1998.

Shelton, Pamela L., ed. *Contemporary Women Poets*. Detroit: St. James Press, 1997.

Stannard, Julian. *Fleur Adcock in Context: From Movement to Martians*. Lewiston, N.Y.: Mellen Press, 1997.

Tromp, Ian. "Fleur Adcock: Poems 1960–2000." *Poetry,* August 2001, p. 293.

FLEUR ADCOCK

INTERVIEWS

Edmond, Lauris. Interview with Adcock. *Landfall: A New Zealand Literary Magazine* 36:320–326 (1982).

Stannard, Julian. "An Interview with Fleur Adcock." *Thumbscrew* 17 (winter 2000/2001).

Vincent, Sally. "Final Touch." *Guardian,* July 29, 2000.

GEORGE BORROW

(1803–1881)

Fred Bilson

GEORGE HENRY BORROW was born July 5, 1803, in East Dereham, Norfolk, the second of two sons of Thomas Borrow and Ann Perfrement Borrow. His father was a professional soldier who was compelled to move around the country with his family and finally settled in Norwich after the Napoleonic wars. By origin, Borrow's father was Cornish (Celtic rather than English) and his mother was a descendant of Protestant refugees from France. They were Church of England Protestant Episcopalians and quietly devout. Borrow himself added to this a partisanship for the Church that gave him an animus against members of other religions, especially Catholicism, that most modern readers will find unattractive.

After high school Borrow started out to train as a lawyer (1818–1823), but when his father died in 1824, he abandoned the law for financial reasons and became a working writer in London for a few months. From 1825 to 1832 he led a vagabond life, often living with the Roma (Gypsies) who were to feature so much in his work.

About 1832 Borrow met Mary Skepper Clarke, the widow of a naval officer. Through her he found work with the British and Foreign Bible Society, where his employers recognized his talent for picking up languages and his total commitment to a Protestant Christianity. He became a translator and colporteur—that is, a traveling salesman in Protestant Bibles. Unlike Catholic Bibles, these contain no notes or commentary; readers are expected to interpret them for themselves. A tour of Russia (1833–1835) was followed by a tour of Spain, Portugal, and Morocco (1835–1839). In 1840 he married Mary Clarke and joined her and her daughter Henrietta in her house in Suffolk.

Borrow was a bluff, cheerful man, a swimmer, boxer, runner, wrestler, and athlete. At six-foot-three inches tall, Borrow's height made him easily recognizable; in addition his hair, originally a typical Cornish black, had turned gray by the time he was in his twenties.

He died on July 26, 1881; his wife had died before him. Gossip has it that he died forgotten and neglected, but this is unlikely. Henrietta was in touch with him and had been staying with him in April.

WORK

Borrow is one of the best and most prolific of English travel writers. He wrote four works in the genre. *The Bible in Spain* (1842) is an account of the years he spent in Portugal, Spain, and Morocco from 1835 to 1839; *Lavengro* (1851) tells the story of his life from infancy to 1825 and describes how he got to know the Roma and how he came to learn a wide variety of languages; the story is continued in *Romany Rye* (1857). *Wild Wales* (1862) looks back on a walking tour of Wales he made between July and November 1854.

His interests are not those of a standard tourist; he has little interest in either scenery or architecture. He suffered from ophthalmia in Spain and was probably nearsighted in any case; he regularly reports seeing people at a distance and only recognizing them when they come closer to him. He describes well what might be called the kinesthetics of travel, the feeling of being there and moving through it, of being involved in an adventure. For example, in *The Bible in Spain* he conveys what it is like to ride all day through the badlands in the chill of November, to arrive at nightfall at an inn crowded with mule-drivers and bushwhackers and sit before a roaring fire on which a whole olive tree or cork tree is burning, and then to eat a very non–English supper consisting of

> one [rabbit] fried, the gravy of which was delicious, and afterwards a roasted one, which was brought up on a dish entire; the hostess, having first washed her hands, proceeded to tear the animal to pieces, which having accomplished, she poured over the fragments a sweet sauce. . . Excellent figs, from the Algarves, and apples. . . which we ate in a little side room with a mud floor, which sent such a piercing chill into my system, as prevented me from deriving that pleasure from my fare and my agreeable companions that I should have otherwise experienced.
>
> (p. 25)

His second achievement is to create an empathy with the people he meets. It is not simply that he speaks a variety of languages, but he is also someone other people trust and tend to open up to. He always takes care to blend in with his company, as he describes his practice in political matters, for example: "I am invariably of the politics of the people at whose table I sit, or beneath whose roof I sleep . . . by pursuing which system I have more than once escaped a bloody pillow, and having the wine I drank spiced with [poison]" (p. 237). As a result, Roma take him for a Romany chal (fellow); a German takes him for another German, Welshmen take him for a Welshman from another area of Wales. He visits the English College in Lisbon (a Catholic seminary) and the fathers take him for a Catholic. Those he meets are allowed to speak for themselves, and this makes for a creative tension between the hegemonic Protestant values that he regularly signals to the reader and the voices of those he meets. Speaking with Antonio, a Romany, he voices the fatalism of that people. "I have no fears; every man must accomplish his destiny: what befalls my body or soul was written . . . a thousand years before the foundation of the world" (p. 106). To voice that fatalism is, for a moment, to adopt it. In this way other views of the world than his own regularly find their expression in Borrow's writing.

THE BIBLE IN SPAIN (1842)

In November 1835 Borrow arrived in Lisbon, Portugal, on the start of a working journey through Portugal, Spain, and Morocco. The Bible Society had sent him to carry out a feasibility study. He was to investigate whether the standard of literacy was high enough to justify the belief that the Portuguese would be able to read the Bible or if education was such that it might increase literacy; secondly he must see whether storekeepers could be recruited to stock and sell the Portuguese Bible. After that Borrow was to go on to Spain and attempt to set up a press to print a Spanish Bible in Madrid.

This was a period in which civil wars in both Portugal and Spain had virtually destroyed the social fabric. Anticlerical governments had reduced the power of the Catholic Church; monasteries and convents had been closed and their communities forced to live life as lay people. Much of the Church's wealth had been confiscated.

For any traveler this would have been dangerous time, with bushwhackers robbing and killing travelers on the roads and widespread disorder. It was doubly difficult for Borrow because his religious agenda might bring harassment from both the authorities and from ordinary people. Though no longer fiercely pro-Catholic, they had not become pro-Protestant.

The book opens on November 10, 1835, on the ship that is bringing Borrow to Lisbon. He has made friends with a young sailor, who is distressed that morning because he has had a dream that he will be drowned. In fact, he falls into the sea from the rigging and a boat is launched to save him.

> ...but the rudder was unfortunately not at hand, and only two oars could be procured, with which the men could make but little progress in so rough a sea. They did their best, however, and had arrived within ten yards of the man, who still struggled for his life, when I lost sight of him; and the men on their return, said that they saw him below the water, at glimpses, sinking deeper and deeper, his arms stretched out and his body apparently stiff, but that

they found it impossible to save him.

(p. 2)

It is almost impossible not to read this opening as a metaphor that represents the danger of the journey and the possibility of sudden calamity. For those of Borrow's Protestant mindset it is also metaphoric of the possibility of the loss of salvation and metaphoric of Spain, about to be lost if the Bible cannot be introduced quickly enough. The state of the boat is crucial here; they thought it was ready, but it was not.

Lisbon is a poverty-stricken capital, still bearing the signs of the earthquake of 1755, and the war has exacerbated this poverty. The human cost is sometimes dreary rather than dramatic. Early on Borrow goes to see a school in a Portuguese town called Mafra. He meets "a short stout man, between sixty and seventy years of age, dressed in a blue jerkin and grey trousers, without shirt or waistcoat" who is too proud to admit to being the schoolmaster. "[W]hoever told me he was a schoolmaster lied, for that he was a friar of the convent, and nothing else. 'It is not, then, true,' said I, 'that all the convents have been broken up and the monks dismissed?' 'Yes, yes,' said he with a sigh, 'it is true' . . . his better nature overcoming his angry feelings, he produced a snuff-box and offered it to me." Borrow comments that the sharing of snuff is a gesture of courtesy that is the "olive branch of the Portuguese," and despite all his rancor against the Catholics he says, "I felt for the poor man who had been driven out of his home in the noble convent close by, and from a state of affluence and comfort reduced in his old age to indigence and misery, for his present dwelling scarcely seemed to contain an article of furniture" (pp. 13–14). Borrow finds unfailing courtesy all over Spain and Portugal; it is both offered and demanded in return. He calls this courtesy an "olive branch" because it reflects the desire to assert peace in the midst of war.

Borrow also spends some time in the company of a group of Romany, who invite him to marry one of their number. They describe their visits across to Morocco, and he becomes particularly close to Antonio, with whom he has the discussion about fate quoted above. But one night the police capture the Romany; as thieves, many of them face death. Borrow has been separated from them and escapes, showing the police chief his passport signed by Lord Palmerston and allowing him to keep it for an hour or two. The last thing the policeman asks him is to be allowed to see the famous signature again. The capture of the Romany and Borrow's lucky escape are equal accidents of fate. Borrow moves on without mourning over his Romany friends. What else is there to do?

In November 1836 Borrow returned to Spain after a brief trip to London to meet with his employers. This time, as the ship approaches Finisterre it appears that it will not be only one sailor that is lost. During a storm, Borrow questions a member of the crew:

[The steersman] replied, "Sir, it is a bad affair; no boat could live for a minute in this sea, and in less than an hour the ship will have her broadside on Finisterre, where the strongest man-of-war ever built must go to shivers instantly. None of us will see the morning." The captain, likewise, informed the other passengers in the cabin to the same effect, telling them to prepare themselves ... The lightning enveloped us as with a mantle, the thunders were louder than the roar of a million cannon and in the midst of all this turmoil, the wind, without the slightest intimation, *veered right about,* and pushed us from the horrible coast faster than it had previously driven us towards it.

The oldest sailors on board acknowledged that they had never witnessed so providential an escape. I said, from the bottom of my heart, "Our Father–hallowed be thy name." (p. 211)

This incident is potentially more disastrous than the loss of the single sailor the year before, so the society he finds is even more under strain than before. The civil war is in stalemate; the Carlist insurgents are winning victories in the countryside but cannot take a major town. Borrow stays with a family whose son is a *nacional* soldier, fighting for the government against the Carlists. It is an easy life—the soldier takes his guitar on parade so his comrades can have a song afterward; he is unfit for any other life. One day, a group of these soldiers goes off to lynch a politician. When they return, they order coffee at a bar, produce a handkerchief, and take from it the fingers of the dead man with which they stir the coffee. Though the Victorian reader would have had access to other literature that conveyed the horror of war, this is an early instance of writing that highlights how casual that horror is when normal human decency has disappeared because death is always present.

Having established the details of life in Spain, in the later part of the book Borrow steps back and takes a more strategic approach. In the effort to obtain permission to print and sell his Bibles he works patiently through the political system, explaining that the difficulty of getting a decision is not that the Spanish officials are perverse or bureaucratic but that they are simply overworked, and finally is able to spend two hours standing in a Madrid street simply looking at the elegant bookshop he has set up to sell his Bibles to the public. It was not all smooth sailing. His relationship with the Romany attracted suspicion and was eventually used as an excuse to imprison him. His description of life in the prison and the other prisoners he met make a magnificent series of set pieces.

In the end he is expelled from Spain, taking his Bibles with him, or rather, the Bibles are expelled and he has to go with them. The reason is that he has published a translation of the New Testament in Spanish Romany; a magazine is started by some of the Catholics specifically to attack him, and he is accused of plotting with gypsy thieves and fortune-tellers to destroy Spain. He travels via Gibraltar to Morocco, and there the book stops. It doesn't end; the implication seems to be that the work of spreading the gospelwill go on, but now someone else must do it.

LAVENGRO: THE SCHOLAR, THE GYPSY, THE PRIEST *(1851) AND* ROMANY RYE *(1857)*

"Lavengro" (stressed on the second syllable, La-VEN-gro) and "Romany Rye" were two of the names Borrow was given by his Romany adoptive brother, who appears in the books as Jasper Petulengro; in real life his given name was Ambrose and he used the English translation of Petulengro (Smith) as his surname. Lavengro means

"The Language Man" and Romany Rye means "The Romany Gentleman." The two books constitute a sequence giving an account of Borrow's travels of exploration in Britain from childhood on, as he moved round with his family, with spells in Ireland and Scotland as well as England. He includes his explorations of other languages and cultures than the English, most especially those of three of the United Kingdom's language minorities, the Romany, the Irish, and the Welsh. Though not a conventional account of the development of a writer, the books are full of psychological interest.

At the opening of *Lavengro,* Borrow describes his childhood. "By nature slow of speech I took no pleasure in conversation....When people addressed me I not infrequently...turned away my head from them, and if they persisted in their notice burst into tears" (p. 7). This sounds like a mild autism, a condition that includes a partial inability to attend to the immediate stimulus. Even in adolescence, working in a lawyer's office, Borrow depicts himself as absorbed in reading Welsh poetry during office hours and unable to distinguish which of the callers are important and which are not because he only looks at faces, never at the clues in clothes and shoes that indicate the wealth of a caller.

At age six his brother's godmother leaves him a parcel that he opens when he is left alone, though he is not sure that he should do so. He reasons it is all right, because the parcel is simply wrapped in paper, not sealed or tied with string. The moral debate that surrounds this decision foreshadows a regular device he uses: in the gradual approach to a new experience, he teases both himself and the reader, who is challenged to guess the outcome. "What cared I for books? . . . yet something within me told me that my fate was connected with the book that had been last brought" (p. 17). Two of the books in the parcel he puts aside, but the third is illustrated with pictures of a man caught in a wild sea. "'He must be drowned! he must be drowned!' I almost shrieked, and dropped the book."

And then he comes in his book to the illustration of a footprint on the shore. "Reader, is it necessary to name the book. . . it was a book that has . . . an influence certainly greater than any other of modern times [for Englishmen]. . . England has better bards than either Greece or Rome, yet I could spare them easier far than De Foe" (p. 19).

Only then does the reader notice the only touch of artfulness in the account. Borrow claims that when the visitor brought the books, he did not clearly hear what she said they were in her conversation with his mother. So he comes upon *Robinson Crusoe* without any previous hint, discovers it for himself, and immerses himself in it, disappearing on his first journey of exploration.

Very early in life Borrow discovered a talent that would be important later. He reports that at the age of three he picked up and handled a venomous snake, a viper, which accepted him but turned on his brother. He compares this to the talent of the "horse whisperer" which he later turned out to share (pp. 9–10). Chapter 4 of *Lavengro* describes an encounter while the family is in a town where French prisoners of war are being held in terrible conditions. Borrow, now seven or eight years old, meets a man who is catching vipers; he is literally a snake-oil man, who makes medicine from their fat. The boy and the old man become friends, and when the old man moves on he leaves the boy a tame viper as a pet. At one point the old man tells the tale of how he once took a good haul of snakes only to see a huge viper coming straight for him—it was the king of the vipers, come to help the vipers in the bag. At the last minute the king viper is scared off by a distant noise. Well, says the boy, suppose the King of the French should come to Norman Cross to help the French prisoners? "He can't come, child . . . the water lies between. The French don't like the water; neither vipers nor Frenchmen take kindly to the water" (pp. 26–28).

This chapter is interesting at several levels. First, it is an account of a country custom that is passing; the snake-catcher and his kind are hunting the vipers to the edge of extinction, but Borrow's account looks back forty years to an age where almost every meadow had its vipers. Secondly, it is a vivid picture of an encounter between an inquisitive child and an adult prepared to talk to him, rather unusual for that time, and

of the way in which child reasoning meets adult reasoning, as in the discussion of the French King, where the boy absorbs the old man's contempt for the French. And there is also the portrait of the pert young Borrow at their first encounter:

> "What do you think of that, my boy. . . what do you think of catching such a thing as that with the naked hand?"
>
> "What do I think? . . . Why, that I could do as much myself. "
>
> ". . . Lord, how the young people in these days are given to conceit. . . "
>
> (p. 25)

The tone of this encounter is one the reader will meet regularly in Borrow: the uncompromising lack of modesty, the putting forward of a claim that he will later substantiate.

The snake plays a part in the next encounter that results in one of the most significant relationships of his life. Walking along a green lane, he comes upon an encampment, where a man and woman are busy by a campfire. His silent approach alarms them and they rush him. He finds them wild and threatening but stands his ground, noticing that their manner of speech is peculiar-not quite English but not quite foreign. They threaten to drown him, but he responds:

> "What's all this about? was it because I saw you with your hands full of straw plait? and my mother there . . . " "Yes," said the woman; "what was I about?" [She had been polishing metal with a white powder.]
>
> Myself: How should I know? Making bad money perhaps!
>
> (p. 30)

Borrow addresses himself to the man, who is about to attack him with a ladle, and speaks in what is virtually verse: "my father lies concealed within my tepid breast, and if to me you offer any harm or wrong, I'll call him forth to help me with his forked tongue." With this he exposes the viper, and the man and woman draw back. Changing their approach, they talk rapidly in a foreign language and then offer him a seat by the fire. They would like him to join them and take up the Romany life. The man says, "[Y]ou might still be our God Almighty, or at any rate our clergyman." As Borrow is to discover later, the Romany are not Christians.

Their son Jasper, some four years older than Borrow, returns to the camp and at first thinks Borrow rather puny, but when he learns he is a "sap-engro" (a man who can charm snakes) he is impressed and decides they will be brothers. Finally the camp is broken up by the arrival of Nat, who has come to collect the counterfeit money and take it north. Jasper and his family leave. "A strange set of people," thinks the boy, "I wonder who they can be" (p. 37).

It is of course his first encounter with the Roma. (Only Nat, when he curses them for being slow, gives a clue to this when he calls them "Romans.") They are a people who live in seclusion on the edge of English society, secretive and suspicious of strangers. Borrow would never have been admitted to their company, he suggests, if he had not been a sap-engro, one who had the power of charming snakes. He also seems to show some power of reading the future. He refers to Mrs. Smith as "my mother," and by the end of the day she is exactly that, as the mother of his new brother. He speaks in the elevated poetic diction of a prophet. He guesses that they are engaged in counterfeiting coins but is clearly not a spy sent to track them down. And Borrow gives the reader one ghastly clue suggesting they will meet again, as he describes watching the execution of Nat at Newgate Prison some fifteen years later. He and Jasper do meet again, though it is noticeable that the Roma contact him, he does not find them.

In Ireland, at age ten, Borrow learns Irish from one of his schoolmates and pays him with a pack of cards. So he acquires the language that to him was "the stepping-stone to other languages" (p. 67) because it was a spoken language, not a book language. He had long been in love with the sound of it, wanting to know what the country people were saying to each other. He wants the ability to use the language to share their society when he chooses, and that implies understanding their culture (especially their poetry) as well.

Habitually, he does not tell Irish, Roma, or Welsh people that he can speak their language until it suits him. Borrow found learning languages easy, and his fluency never left him—he would still be able to speak Irish forty years later. But it is clear that his enthusiasm for a language and those who speak it could wane. He writes, looking back at his learning Irish, "though I find myself . . . turning up my nose at Irish when I hear it in the street; yet I still have a kind of regard for it," and the regard shows itself by his quoting without translating a line from an old poem calling Irish "the language that Patrick spoke in Inisfail" (p. 68).

He is never sentimental in his approach to the Irish, the Roma or the Welsh, but he lets them tell the tale themselves and in the course of this may experience something out of the ordinary. Here he is, now age thirteen or so, dealing with an Irish smith; though he finds the smith dirty and avaricious, he calls him a "fairy smith" because of his power over horses and because in folklore magic smiths (like Wayland Smith) have immense power. Borrow demonstrates a technical mastery of one feature of narrative, when it is necessary to handle in English a conversation that took place in another language. Notice how Borrow doesn't always translate the Irish, but usually indicates what each of the phrases means, and how the conversation takes on the speech rhythms of the Irish. This is what learning a foreign language is like when one lets the context carry one along rather than translating into English all the time. He has taken his horse into a smithy because it has lost a shoe.

> "Shoe this horse and do it quickly, a gough [smith]."
>
> *"Arrigod yuit?"* said the fellow.
>
> "Yes, I have money . . . and of the best;" and I pulled out an English shilling.
>
> *"Tabhair chugam,"* said the smith stretching out his grimy hand.
>
> "No, I sha'n't," said I; "some people are glad to get their money when the work is done."
>
> (p. 30)

The boy and the smith have a boasting context. It's a vicious horse, says the smith. It's your handling of him that does it then, says Borrow, and proceeds to pass under the horse between his hind legs.

"And is that all you can do, *agrah*?" [my love]

"No . . . I can ride him. . . . I can leap him over a six foot wall." . . .

"Can you do this, *agrah*?" and he uttered a word which I had never heard before . . . a strange thrill ran through me; but [the cob] . . . became like one mad, and reared and kicked with the utmost desperation.

"Go between his legs, *agrah*. . . ."

"I dare not . . . he would kill me . . . something tells me so."

"And it tells ye truth, *agrah*; but it's a fine beast and it's a pity to see him in such a state: *Is agam an't leigeas*"—and here he uttered another word . . . the animal lost all its fury and became at once calm and gentle. The smith went up to it, coaxed and patted it . . . then turning to me . . . said "And now ye will be giving me the Sassenach tenpence, *agrah*?"

(pp. 82–83)

There are two further contacts with Jasper in Book I of *Lavengro* that focus on Borrow's increasing closeness with the Romany. First he meets Jasper at a horse fair. Jasper's parents have been transported, and he is now king of his family. He is rich—he has both horses and gold, and he is concerned that Borrow cannot "shift for himself"; Jasper thinks he wants two things, "mother sense and gentle Rommany." Jasper's wife's mother, Mrs. Herne, tells Borrow what a precious gift the language is. "Would you teach it me?" Borrow asks Jasper. "None sooner." "Suppose we begin now." "Suppose we do, brother."

But Mrs. Herne objects, "Not whilst I am here." She visualizes Borrow as a Gorgio (a non-Romany) who will be able warn the farmers when the Romany are practicing some trick. " [Borrow] looks over–gorgious. An ill day to the Romans when he masters Rommany; and when I says that I pens a true dukkerin [I tell a true fortune]." So incensed is Mrs. Herne that she splits ways with Jasper; she will go north to Yorkshire, let him go south to London. "Ye are no longer Rommany. To gain a bad brother, ye have

lost a good mother" (pp 103–108).

The other contact is the most famous passage Borrow ever wrote. In chapter 25 he describes two occasions on which he heard a Methodist preacher discoursing on the hope of everlasting life after death. Still rapt, Borrow encounters Jasper in the sunset.

"That's not you, Jasper?"

"Indeed, brother."

"I've not seen you for years. . . . Any news since we parted?"

"Two deaths, brother." [His parents had died while being transported to Botany Bay.] . . .

"What is your opinion of death, Mr Petulengro?"

" . . . When a man dies, he is cast into the earth, and his wife and child sorrow over him. If he has neither wife nor child, then his mother and father, I suppose . . . and there is an end of the matter . . . more's the pity."

"Why do you say so?"

"Life is sweet, brother. . . . There's night and day, brother, both sweet things; sun, moon and stars, brother, all sweet things; there's likewise the wind on the heath. Life is very sweet, brother; who would wish to die?"

"I would wish to die—"

"You talk like a gorgio—which is the same as talking like a fool. . . . A Rommany Chal would wish to live for ever."

" . . . In blindness, Jasper?"

"There's the wind on the heath, brother; if I could only feel that, I would gladly live for ever. Dosta [enough] . . . [we'll] put on the [boxing] gloves: and I'll try to make you feel what a sweet thing it is to be alive."

(pp. 163–165)

In the context of the Methodist preaching, Jasper's certainty that death is the end chills Borrow. This conversation with Jasper is a great moment of encounter with pagan belief. Borrow points it up by quoting two contrasting poems; a hymn by John Wesley—"For thou shalt surely raise me up / To glorious life and endless joy"— and the Romany "Cana marel o manus chivios andé puv, / Ta rovel pa leste o chavo to romi" (When a man dies, he is cast into the earth, / And

book was stolen, and they are fences like the apple-seller had been.)

Cheating isn't against the law. When the police move the thimble-rig men on, it's because their games lead to fighting and near-riots, not because they are cheating their punters. The Romany world and the world of the cheat overlap. Though the thimble-rig man is Jewish, he understands at once when Borrow warns him in pure Romany that the police are coming.

So Borrow has been offered a job with a man who is not quite honest; the job entails being a bodyguard (which is honest work) and helping to set up the suckers (which is not honest, but not quite criminal). If you stand on the edges of crime, you can get sucked in.

Borrow's attempts to earn money honestly have centered on writing, but he has only managed to place the six volumes describing trials. Finally he achieves some success. He responds to an advertisement in a bookseller's window asking for novels (booksellers were quite often their own publishers as well). He writes very rapidly a novel that earns him twenty pounds (one hundred dollars) for a few days' work. Though he is offered the chance of placing more, he turns it down and leaves London. He decides that since he came to London from the northeast, he'll leave by the southwest. His last experience of London is another swindle. A coach driver offers him a lift and when he is aboard demands a fare. So Borrow arrives in Wiltshire, where he begins a period of wandering the roads without any definite plan.

He records a series of encounters beginning with a shepherd at Stonehenge. He spends a few days with a successful author and a few hours with a returned transport who is perhaps the son of the apple–woman. Then he encounters a tinker (not a Romany) who travels the country in a donkey cart, mending kettles and doing some work as a smith. The man is being terrified by a Romany tinker called the Flaming Tinman and gladly sells Borrow his cart and tools for five pounds ten (twenty-seven dollars and fifty cents).

Now Borrow becomes a traveling tinker. He knows the work and the customs of the trade; he knows that he has to lend his customer a kettle while he takes hers away to mend it.

One night he encounters a girl, Leonora, who is clearly Romany. She has recognized him. She brings him a cake from her grandmother that poisons him; the grandmother is Mrs. Herne, his old enemy. But as Mrs. Herne triumphs over his paralyzed body, she realizes in a flash of second sight that he is not going to die and goes off in a dudgeon. Peter and Winifred Williams, a traveling Welsh Methodist preacher and his wife, happen along and give Borrow an oil that is an antidote. (Snake oil? One wonders.) Borrow travels back toward Wales with the Williamses; he is attracted by their religious enthusiasm but cannot share it and cannot bring himself to attend his own church either.

He will not cross over into Wales with them, and Peter Williams gives him his Welsh Bible. Borrow meets Jasper again as he and the Williamses part. Jasper tells him that Mrs. Herne is dead. Unusual for a Romany, she has committed suicide; now that Borrow has been allowed into the knowledge of the Romany world, she believes it will be destroyed.

Alone again, Borrow camps in a dingle (a small wooded creek) and the Flying Tinman catches up with him, accompanied by his wife and another girl, Isopel Berners, known as Belle. There is a fight; Borrow wins and the Romany and his wife leave, but Belle remains behind.

It's clear that as the book closes, Borrow is in the grip of a major depressive crisis. He has abandoned the career in writing at which he has finally made a start and taken to the road as a vagrant, trying to make a living as a smith. He has no emotion, not even for Belle, no religious life (though he feels sometimes he should). His only energy goes into rants against Catholicism. Then a groom he meets knocks away the last prop. Looking at how Borrow has shod his donkey, he tells him he is no blacksmith: "[N]o blacksmith would have made shoes in that manner . . . a real blacksmith would have thrown off three or four sets of donkey shoes in one morning, but you . . . have been hammering at these for days" (p. 523).

It is impossible to tell how much of the material in this part of the book is based on fact. Borrow claims to have written a book called *The Life and Adventures of Joseph Sell;* no book with that title has ever been traced. He really did have a Welsh Bible inscribed "Peter Williams"—is that proof of the episode with the Methodist preacher? But the veracity hardly matters. These encounters in the second part of *Lavengro* represent Borrow's visions of alternative lives he might have led. He might have been a criminal transported to Botany Bay and then returning to a life of poverty. He might have been a rich and successful author, if only, he implies, he could have written in a comic mode. He might have been a Methodist.

But above all, of course, he gave the book a Romany title, because the most likely alternative was to adopt the Romany way of life. He rejects it in the end, as it rejects him; literally, it poisons him. It is un-Christian and unsettled. So he does not sentimentalize his Romany. They are a quarrelsome, pugnacious lot, vindictive in the case of Mrs. Herne. They are underskilled; Borrow learned his blacksmithing from Jasper and describes his work at the forge using the Romany terms. But Jasper, as a wandering Romany, had never served an apprenticeship; if a horse shed a shoe Jasper's work would do to save a few pennies for a real blacksmith, but the work is shoddy, and this creates bad feeling among the settled people with whom they deal as they travel around the country. They also move in and out of the world of crime, their society further destabilized by the loss of those who are hanged or, like Jasper's parents, transported.

Romany Rye begins the morning after *Lavengro* ends. Much of the book is given over to tidying up the loose ends in *Lavengro*. Borrow proposes to Belle, but she rejects him; he gives away his cart and tools to a newly married Romany couple. Small points are explained too; the reader learns why Mrs. Smith was polishing coins when Borrow first met her. Gold coins can have part of their surface gold stripped away by an acid called aquafortis; the gold can be recovered but the coins look black and arouse suspicion. Mrs Smith had been polishing the coins to make them look better so that they can be passed more easily. She was part of a criminal gang. As a boy, Borrow had suspected her of being involved in coining, but the full explanation only came later in life.

The central narrative is built around a horse. Jasper insists on Borrow taking fifty guineas from him to buy the horse, and Borrow then decides to take it to Horncastle Horse Fair in Lincolnshire (180 miles away) to sell it. On the journey he has encounters with people who foreshadow his future—a man from Hungary (a country he was to visit) and another man who has been paralyzed by grief on the death of his young wife. The only thing to arouse his curiosity is the Chinese words written on a collection of crockery. He sets out to learn to read Chinese and has first to learn French, because all the books that describe Chinese are in French. (The first job Borrow had with the Bible Society was supervising a Chinese translation of the Bible.)

Ulick Ralph Burke, who provided notes for the later John Murray editions, was quite shocked by all this. Citing the fact that Jasper Petulengro had reminded Borrow in 1842 that he had lent him the money to buy the horse and that Borrow sold it "three days after," he suggests Borrow was never in Horncastle at all and that the meeting with the Hungarian is "drawn from his experiences [there] in 1844." Burke concludes, "It is a pity that [Borrow] did not adhere to the chronological facts of his life in *Romany Rye* as strictly as he did in *Lavengro*. Truth and literature would have gained by it" (p. 386). Perhaps not. Borrow represents the two books as containing a series of visions, and they include visions of the future shape of Borrow's life.

The book ends with Borrow meeting a recruiting officer signing up men for the army of the East India Company, which enforced British rule in India. The few Hindustani words he uses sound like Romany to Borrow, who says to himself, "I think I'll go there" (p. 301). The depression is over; a new life as a philologist will begin soon. It did not, in fact, take him to India, but it did take him around Europe and give him a reputation as a philologist and as a novelist. Increasingly his skill with languages would give him a rewarding career.

WILD WALES *(1862)*

In 1854 Borrow, his wife, and stepdaughter decided on a holiday. Borrow persuaded them to accept his plan to spend some time in Wales, which they agreed was "a very nice picturesque country, where. . . they should get on very well, more especially as I [spoke] Welsh" (*Wild Wales,* p. 6).

The family traveled by train to Chester in northwest England, and then the ladies went on to Llangollen, in North Wales, by train to rent a house for the summer. Borrow would walk to Llangollen the following day. It is about twenty miles west of Chester and about ten miles into Wales and was then a small market town. Between July and November Borrow would walk right across Wales from east to west and from Holyhead in the far northwest to Chepstow in the far southeast.

He had chosen Llangollen because that was where Lloyd came from. When Borrow was working in the lawyer's office in Norwich, his employer spoke a little Welsh and Borrow began to add Welsh to the Romany, Latin, Greek, and Irish he already knew. But his main teacher was a local groom, called Lloyd. Lloyd was a figure of fun to the other clerks, who jeered at his strange ways. Lloyd (Borrow spells it in the Welsh fashion, Lluyd) is introduced unpromisingly: "A queer [stable] groom he was . . . about forty–seven years of age and about five foot eight in height . . . neck he had none . . . his eyes grey and deeply sunken . . . an expression . . . partly sullen and partly irascible" (p. 6). The oddness of his appearance attracts the mockery of Borrow's fellow clerks, who next learn that he is a Welshman, so the mockery increases. But Borrow wins the groom's friendship and persuades him to teach Borrow conversational Welsh. Borrow describes the difference in Lloyd's appearance when he comes to Borrow's home on Sundays for the lessons. Borrow describes him as "very respectably dressed, in a beaver hat, blue surtout, whitish waistcoat, black trousers and Wellingtons [that is Wellington boots]." Lloyd will not come to the office, " a nest of porcupines."

Borrow reports that "he told me in confidence that on the morning of the very day I first began to conciliate him he had come to the resolution of . . . [either hanging himself] . . . or giving [notice] . . . both of which he should have been unwilling to do, more particularly as he had a wife and family" (p. 8). There's something very Welsh about Lloyd's story here—the dramatic coincidence; the bathos of the choice between hanging himself or giving notice, the circumstantial detail of the wife and family that adds the air of verisimilitude. And there's something very English in Borrow taking it at face value.

This is an early example of Borrow's failure to totally understand the Welsh. The Welsh like to dramatize a story when we tell it; the English prefer understatement, and therefore tend to take Welsh exaggeration literally.

After Lloyd inherited a farm near Llangollen and returned there with his family, Borrow lost touch with him. It would be thirty years before Borrow himself visited Wales.

As in the earlier works, Borrow relies on chance for the meetings he has, but now generally they are relaxed, good-humored encounters in a good–humored book by someone who loves Wales and the Welsh, but on his own terms. He intersperses the account of the journey with digressions on the history and legends of Wales and on the Welsh literature that he prefers, especially that of Dafydd Ap Gwilym (c. 1315–c. 1360) and Ellis Wynne (1671–1734). Borrow had long set a high value on Wynne's *Bardd Cwsg* (in English, *Visions of the Bard While Asleep*). It is a religious work, a prose allegory, and difficult for all its merits. Borrow's devotion to the earlier poets of Wales tended to blind him to what was being written in his own day.

Borrow has another blind spot that matches his blind spot over literature. He deplores Methodism and constantly tells the reader that what Wales needs is better ministers in the Church of England to lure people back from the Methodist chapels. He won't even read the Methodist daily newspaper *Yr Amserau* (the *Times*), sticking to *Y Cymro* (the *Welshman*), which supports the

"English Church." Borrow uses that phrase without irony, without realizing that "English" is as foreign here as the "Roman" he attaches to "Catholic." When he went to Spain as a young man, he went informed; he read the English newspapers and knew more about the political situation than the Spanish. But this is not the case in Wales.

Many of the Welsh at the time felt they were facing a crisis of colonialism. Though they were not suffering more exploitation than the people of any other area of the United Kingdom they increasingly felt they were paying an additional price. If they were to succeed in the new commercial and industrial environment, they needed to be bilingual or even give up Welsh altogether; an English hegemony was being imposed on them. The fact that many of them readily gave up the Welsh language did not make the situation easier to accept. This explains the move to Methodism. The local chapel was the organization through which small communities could organize themselves and protect their identity. This is what Borrow missed. And there was a fierce debate, with pamphlets and plays in print, centering on a government report on education in Wales published in 1847 that recommended the suppression of the Welsh language.

So from the first, there was a qualification in the Welsh reception of *Wild Wales*. Usually a travel book of this sort provoked little reaction from the people it described, who generally could not read it, but the Welsh were a literate people and overwhelmingly English-speaking as well. Many of the people Borrow encountered read the book and recognized themselves in his description, even where he disguised their names, and even today there are families (sometimes still living in the same homes as Borrow visited) who preserve family legends of the encounter, which do not always fit with Borrow's.

But the book, after all, is about a holiday, and the mood is relaxed, as shown in an early chapter describing a typical day in Llangollen.

Borrow sets off to climb a hill called Dinas Bran (Crow's Castle); he is followed by a number of children, mostly girls, who hope "you will give us something." He tells them he will not, but they still follow him, singing as they go. He meets a man mowing hay and hears that he usually works in the flannel factory, but work there is slack, so he is working at mowing even though he was not bred to farming work. Learning the man is Welsh, Borrow asks what books he has read.

> ...the Bible, sir, and one or two other books.
>
> Did you ever read the *Bardd Cwsg*? said I.
>
> No. . . . I have seen it, but it was far too deep Welsh for me. . . .
>
> And how is it," said he, "that you can read Welsh without being a Welshman?
>
> . . . even as you learned to mow without being bred up to farming work.

Borrow says he had never been able to learn to use a scythe.

> "Will your honour take mine now, and try again?" said he.
>
> "No. . . for if I take your scythe in hand I must give you a shilling, you know, by mower's law."
>
> He gave a broad grin. . . .
>
> (pp. 37–38)

Borrow walks on, down the hill, along the canal, meeting a boatman and discussing the trip along the canal to London; next there is a blacksmith and his men loading a boat; then a cottager leaning on his gate with whom he has a chat about local legends and religion, and so home to a dinner of salmon and roast mutton—the best in the world, he tells us—then out after dinner for a stroll before bed.

Borrow does not seem to follow through on the conversations he has. He doesn't ask the mower what the other books are that he has read. The mower hasn't read the *Bardd Cwsg*, but he has tried it. Why does he say it was "deep Welsh"? Has he read any of the modern Welsh poets Borrow ignores, such as the religious poets William Williams of Pantycelyn (1717–1791) or Anne Griffiths (1776–1805), whose works were then becoming known to all Welsh Methodists as hymns?

How good was Borrow's Welsh? Clearly he could hold a conversation with someone who speaks no English, but often only on topics in the immediate context ("What is that hill called?" "Is this the road to Llangollen?"). Given that he learned his Welsh from a man from Llangollen, it is noticeable that some people there assume he is from South Wales. Borrow's Welsh, it seems, was slightly odd; overcorrect and slightly bookish perhaps.

He fails the one test that the North Welsh still set for the visitor, which is to invite him to explain some word or tell them some local piece of history, while pretending they don't know the answer. A lady who has a cottage by the ruined abbey above Llangollen talks to Borrow about the Welsh language and its literature. She brings him a portrait of a writer called Twm o'r Nant, a playwright and actor whom she calls the "Welsh Shakespeare." It has an inscription on it in Welsh.

". . .Was he not a great poet?"

"I dare say he was," said I, "for the pieces which he wrote, and which he called Interludes, had a great run and he got a great deal of money by them. . . ."

"What do the lines [under the picture] mean? . . . they are Welsh . . . but . . . far beyond my understanding."

A brief look at the lines may help us see the problem. They read,

Llun Gwr yw llawn gwir Awen
Y Byd a lanwodd o'i Ben.

They are in the strict Welsh poetic form. There are seven syllables to each line, with a marked break after syllable four. There is also a classic pattern of alliteration in the first line; the first four consonants are exactly repeated in the second four (*ll n g r – ll n g r – n*).

Because Borrow spots this right away, he assumes that the lady cannot understand the words, because the complex form gets in the way. But they are in fact quite clear and close to spoken Welsh. They mean "The picture of a man who is full of true inspiration / The World he filled out of his head." Borrow resumes,

"They may be thus translated," said I:

"God in his head the Muse instill'd / And from his head the world he fill'd."

"Thank you, sir. . . . I never found any one before who could translate them."

(pp. 66–67)

Though florid, Borrow's translation is accurate enough. It is not clear he understands that the lady can translate the verse, or that she understands it. The woman is being ironic in the sense that Socrates was ironic; she is pretending ignorance. Of course she understands the Welsh and can translate it, and knows that Borrow has translated them correctly. Otherwise she could not make the comment, "I never found any one before who could translate [the lines]". What is it in Borrow's attitude that she wishes to expose?

Unconsciously, Borrow appears to suggest that the Welsh text only has meaning if it is translated into English; that is what is implied by the question "What does it mean?" And Borrow himself, as the expert translator is the gatekeeper, letting such texts as he approves of through. Like many with the colonialist mind-set, he loves both the culture and the people he is implicitly colonising (as Kipling loved India). But he intends to take control of them.

There is one more voice that represents the principality writing back, and that is a carter in a tavern in South Wales where Borrow stays the night. In the morning in the washroom, Borrow prepares to go on his way, but the carter seizes the clothes brush and insists on grooming Borrow. The previous night all the regulars had been drinking in the kitchen together and Borrow had been a star performer, with his talk and a ghost story. The carter won't talk to Borrow as he brushes his coat and hat; won't answer any questions. Finally he grins and says "Nice gentleman–will do anything for him but answer questions, and let him hear my discourse. . . . Know what he comes about. Wants to hear discourse of poor man . . . poor man's little ways and invirmities [sic] and mark them down in one small, little book to serve for fun to Lord Palmerston and other great gentlefolks in London" (p. 570). It pins Borrow down, as though he could hear the carter saying, We know you, who else could you be but the author of *The Bible in Spain,* and we know why you have come to Wales; you're like the boys in Norwich who mocked Lloyd. It is a mark of Borrow's honesty that he includes this tale against himself, as he had included Jasper's thoughts on death in *Lavengro.*

In the end, Wales goes a bit sour on Borrow— literally, in fact. He visits Bala in Merioneth during the summer and calls at the White Lion, where Tom Jenkins serves him a beer he had brewed himself. "The ale was indeed admirable, equal to the best I had ever before drunk–rich and mellow" (p. 290). At the end of October, he is at the White Lion again and complains to the maid at dinner, "This is very bad ale . . . very different from what I drank in the summer." "It is the same ale, sir," she replies, "but the last in the cask; and we shan't have any more for six months when [Tom Jenkins] will come again to brew for the summer" (p. 409).

The book ends with Borrow on a train from Chepstow to London listening to the noise of a party of sailors returning from Admiral Napier's expedition to the Baltic, a campaign in the war against Russia that was raging that year. Napier's expedition was not a success; was Borrow's? *The Bible in Spain* is so immediate to its historical context that is has become a historical document. Because *Wild Wales* is more superficial in its treatment of the pressures of Welsh life, it is less of a historical document and remains a book on the Welsh character that is challenging in its accuracy. A hundred and fifty years have passed since his journey, a period that has seen at least three great social upheavals in Wales, but the surface remains the same. Bala is still overwhelmingly Welsh–speaking, and the White Lion is still there in the building Borrow knew.

REPUTATION

Only *The Bible in Spain* was a success on first publication, but Borrow's reputation grew in the years that followed. He had two extrinsic appeals to the generations that followed him. One was that you could educate yourself; like Borrow you could buy a Danish Bible and teach yourself Danish. The other was the promise that the world had not been homogenized by commerce and industrialization; you might set off down a country road one morning and by evening have had an adventure or at least found a cool, clean pub with a pint of good beer. Sentimental and whimsical this might be, but for any writer who started his career between 1890 and 1939, say, Borrow was likely to be a beneficent influence, as in the case of Edward Thomas (1878–1917), who was from a Welsh background and had two years (his last) as an innovative poet; earlier he had written a book on Borrow.

Selected Bibliography

WORKS OF GEORGE BORROW

TRAVEL WRITING

The Bible in Spain; or, The Journeys, Adventures, and Imprisonments of an Englishman in an Attempt to Circulate the Scriptures on the Peninsula. London: Ward, Lock, 1842; London: John Murray, 1843. Reprinted, London: John Murray, 1905.

Lavengro: The Scholar, the Gipsy, the Priest. London: John Murray, 1851; New York: Harper & Bros., 1851. Reprinted, London: John Murray, 1931.

The Romany Rye; A Sequel to "Lavengro". London: John Murray, 1857; New York: Harper & Bros., 1857. Reprinted, London, John Murray, 1903.

Wild Wales: Its People, Language, and Scenery. London: John Murray, 1862. Reprinted, London: Dent, Everyman's Library, 1907.

MEMOIRS OF FAMOUS CRIMINALS

Celebrated Trials, and Remarkable Cases of Criminal Jurisprudence from the Earliest Records to the Year 1825. 6 vols. London: Knight and Lacey, 1825.

Celebrated Trials and Remarkable Cases . . . Dealing with the Report of the Trial of Elizabeth Canning. London: 1825.

ROMANY LIFE AND LANGUAGE

The Zincali; or, An Account of the Gypsies of Spain. London: John Murray, 1841; New York: Wiley and Putnam, 1842.

Romano Lavo–Lil: Word–Book of the Romany; or, English Gypsy Language. London: John Murray, 1874.

COLLECTED WORKS

The Works of George Borrow. Edited by Clement Shorter. Norwich edition. 16 vols. London: Constable, 1923- 1924; New York: Gabriel Wells, 1923- 1924.

There is a wealth of papers, including fiction in manuscript, and letters held at various universities. For a listing consult the University of London Library at http://www.aim25.ac.uk/cgi–ndash;bin/frames/.

CRITICAL AND BIOGRAPHICAL STUDIES

Davies, John. "George Borrow's Wales." *Planet* (Aberystwyth, Wales) 134 (April–May 1999).

Thomas, Edward. *George Borrow: The Man and His Books.* London: Chapman and Hall, 1912.

Watts–Dunton, Theodore. "Talk About 'Wild Wales'." Introduction to *Wild Wales.* London: Dent, Everyman's Library, 1906.

Williams, David. *A World of His Own: The Double Life of George Borrow.* Oxford: Oxford University Press, 1982.

The George Borrow Society publishes a bulletin and has a website (www.clough5.fsnet.co.uk/gb.html).

KAMAU (EDWARD) BRATHWAITE

(1930—)

Amor Kohli

IN 1998 THE literary critic Laurence Breiner argued that the publication of Kamau Brathwaite's 1973 trilogy *The Arrivants* was the "single most *consequential* event in the history of West Indian poetry to date" (p. 177). While some critics have debated the specific merits of Brathwaite's work, the consequence of it is agreed upon. So significant has his presence and voice been that along with his contemporary and fellow West Indian Derek Walcott, Brathwaite has come to signify the poetry of the Caribbean for many critics and readers. As cultural critic, historian, poet, archivist, and organizer, Brathwaite has exhibited a tireless commitment to the study and development of Caribbean literature and culture. His contributions to cultural and literary discussions over the last half-century are such that it can be argued that all subsequent West Indian writing—divergent from as well as convergent with his views—must in some way engage with the legacies of his work and ideas.

Brathwaite's long career has been distinguished by a search for an alternative to European literary tradition, an alternative that he would locate in the voices and rhythms of "the folk" rather than in the forms and cadences of "high culture." Brathwaite has set an example for poets who share his concerns: the potential for cultural resistance in language, the role of orality in poetics, the trajectory of black diasporic music, the presence of Africa in the Americas, and the epic qualities of black history. While Walcott's receipt of the Nobel Prize in literature cemented his status as poetic powerhouse for academics and the literati, Brathwaite has emerged for many as the poet of the "common people" as well as a figure respected in progressive and avant–garde

poetic circles. While the two poets share more general concerns, Walcott's vexed allegiance to a more canonical poetic tradition has set him apart from Brathwaite.

Brathwaite's poetic career might be profitably read as the journey through four stages: three different trilogies followed by a break of sorts, a departure into new formal innovations. The first trilogy, *The Arrivants,* which was published in 1973, consists of *Rights of Passage* (1967), *Masks* (1968), and *Islands* (1969). His second trilogy, *Ancestors,* finally published in 2001 in a considerably revised and expanded form, is made up of the volumes *Mother Poem* (1977), *Sun Poem* (1982), and *X/Self* (1987). Although it has never been published as a single collection, the three volumes documenting a particularly harrowing period in Brathwaite's life that he has called his "time of salt" may be considered a third trilogy. It was after having emerged from this dark time that he began the experiments with typography through the manipulation of computer fonts to create what he calls his "Sycorax video-style," which moved his emphasis from the oral and aural properties of his poetry to an equal emphasis on the visuality of poetic manuscripts.

Throughout all of these stages, his concern with the continuities and disjunctions of which black New World history consists has remained constant. The types of questions with which he began his poetic journey—How did black people get into the Caribbean? What is the nature of their presence there? How have they translated the particulars of their lived experience into cultural productions?—consist of the multiple strands that continue to amplify his work. As much as Brathwaite is committed to the Caribbean as a major point of reference, his work is also infused with global cultural and political concerns. The legacies of colonial education, the reach and influence of black American culture, the residues of imperialism, and the search for a "usable past" for peoples of African descent in the New World all but necessitate the type of interplay between the local and the global readers find in Brathwaite. The pivotal question asked in *Rights of Passage:* "Where then is the nigger's / home?" is a question that is asked throughout much of his work. Articulating a "home" or at the very least a sense of related space and belonging is the goal of much of Brathwaite's poetry. The travels and movement that defined his life for so long—the West Indies through Britain and Africa, back to the West Indies and then on to the United States—have provided him with particular insight into the demands of exile and home.

LIFE

Brathwaite was born Lawson Edward Brathwaite in Bridgetown, Barbados, on May 11, 1930 to Hilton and Beryl Gill Brathwaite. The family was solidly in the black Barbadian middle class, and as such Brathwaite had access to the type of colonial education available to children of the middle and upper classes on the island. However, as Brathwaite has told it, he was fortunate to form relationships and friendships with children whose families were less privileged. On the one hand this afforded him an acquaintance with values other than those of the West Indian middle class and on the other hand kept him from making any "serious investment in West Indian middle class values" ("Timehri," p. 37). Although he would not recognize that he was becoming aware of any alternative value system other than that of one thoroughly informed by colonialism until later in life, the interest in unearthing a value system in those of the lower and working classes in the Caribbean (those he would refer to as "the folk") would serve as a major impetus for much of his later creative and intellectual work.

Nonetheless, his education was one that fit soundly into the parameters of the social position of his family. Educated at Harrison College, he won a Barbados scholarship to read history at Pembroke College, University of Cambridge. He read at Cambridge between 1950 and 1953 and then stayed on for one final year to obtain a certificate of education. From there he faced a crossroads. For a West Indian educated in the metropole, there was no sense that there was anything for him "at home." Of course this was the reason so many bright young students in the West Indies left to be educated in London or Paris in the first place.

He accepted a postition in 1955 as education officer in Ghana's Ministry of Education, a position he held until 1962. During those eight years in Ghana he was deeply affected by Ghana's move toward independence, a process that came to fruition in 1957 under the guidance and vision of Kwame Nkrumah. As the first independent postcolonial African nation, Ghana held a special place in the imaginations of black people all over the world. Ghana's liberation intensified feelings of connection across the African diaspora. Brathwaite's presence in Ghana during this heady period encouraged him to explore the possibilities in these connections, possibilities he would subsequently engage as poet and as historian. On the other hand, his time in Africa awakened him to just how much he, as a native to the Caribbean and not to Africa, was often in a contradictory relationship to Africa.

In 1962 he returned to the Caribbean. For one year he held the position of resident tutor in the Department of Extra-Mural Studies at the University of the West Indies (UWI) at St. Lucia, after which he was offered a lectureship in history at UWI's main campus at Mona, Jamaica. The three years he spent in the West Indies after his African experience were years in which he was able to examine more concretely the continuities between African and West Indian culture that he had begun to notice while in Africa. Now as someone with actual experiential knowledge of Africa, he began to contemplate the Caribbean. It was during this time that the first volume in the *Arrivants* trilogy, *Rights of Passage,* began to enter its final manifestation before being published in 1967. Although Brathwaite had been publishing poetry since 1950 when his poem "Shadow Suite" was published in the influential West Indian literary journal *Bim,* by the time he left for England again—this time in 1965 for a research fellowship at the University of Sussex— his poetic direction, if not his path, was much clearer.

While in England for the second go-around, Brathwaite threw a significant portion of his energies into the founding of the Caribbean Artists Movement (CAM). Along with his wife Doris (whom he married in 1960), John La Rose, and Andrew Salkey, Brathwaite embraced the considerable task of putting into dialogue a group of West Indian writers and artists living in England. Perhaps because of the relative isolation of Sussex from the literary and cultural happenings of London, Brathwaite was eager to create links between creative intellectuals from all of the islands of the English, French, and Spanish-speaking Caribbean as well as with other British and Commonwealth artists. CAM's function was initially as a writers' and artists' group whose members would discuss issues related to West Indian literature and art. It became, ultimately, a hothouse for all sorts of debates including the possibility and nature of a West Indian aesthetic, the responsibility of the artist to his or her community, and the role of art and artists in the burgeoning black radical politics of the later 1960s. Under Brathwaite's leadership and prodding, CAM made quite an impact on the West Indian community in London through public readings, lectures, and art shows, but at bottom, arguably its most significant contribution was its synthesis of a West Indian artistic community in England that had been haphazardly in contact at best.

Somewhere among all that was occurring with CAM and his own poetry, Brathwaite compiled the historical research that would earn him a Ph.D. degree at Sussex. His dissertation would subsequently be published in 1971 as *The Development of Creole Society in Jamaica, 1770-1820.* Before that, in 1968 he returned to the Caribbean to his post in the Department of History at UWI-Mona, a campus that was then in the midst of the type of political and cultural upheaval that was occurring among black and other colonized peoples all over the world. Brathwaite details the impact of these events in his 1976 essay "The Love Axe/l." Versions of that essay have been published by Brathwaite as the beginning of a larger examination of the relationship between the politics of the late 1960s and a Caribbean aesthetic. His experiences in Ghana and the political atmosphere when he returned to the Caribbean prompted in him a surer sense of the responsibility that an artist has to his or her society. This question, which had been roundly debated during the CAM meetings in England now, in a very different, more volatile political climate, left the realm of theorizing and entered the realm of praxis.

Brathwaite remained at UWI-Mona for two decades after his return to Jamaica. He was awarded numerous fellowships that allowed him to travel, but Jamaica remained his base. He received a Guggenheim Fellowship in 1972, but it was during a short short fellowship in the City of Nairobi in 1971 that he participated in a naming ceremony in which the grandmother of the Kenyan novelist Ngũgĩ wa Thiong'o (who had himself been renamed from James Ngũgĩ) gave Brathwaite the name "Kamau," which in Kikuyu means "quiet warrior." Naming is inseparable from identity for Brathwaite, and the act of naming oneself is particularly important for formerly colonized and enslaved peoples who have been named—and therefore defined—by others. During this period Brathwaite joined a number of black creative intellectuals around the globe in engaging this question of naming, which fed into a broader desire for the power of self-determination and self-fashioning.

In 1991 Brathwaite joined Ngugi in New York University's Department of Comparative Literature, which has remained his institutional base since. The move to the United States followed the traumatic years in Jamaica that would form the basis for the unofficial third, unnamed trilogy. *SHAR* (1990), the first in that series, deals with the hurricane in 1988 that not only demolished his house in the hills of Jamaica but also effectively wiped out his vast library collection. For years Brathwaite had been collecting artifacts, pamphlets, manuscripts, and recordings that in essence told a fuller, richer story of the literature and culture in the Caribbean than had any to date. The destruction of this trove has been compared to the destruction of the library at Alexandria, an irreparable loss. The death of Brathwaite's wife, Doris, of cancer in 1986 is the subject of *The Zea Mexican Diary* which was published in 1993. Aside from being his partner in marriage, Doris was a partner in his work. She was instrumental in encouraging his efforts toward preserving and documenting West Indian culture. Written in diary form during the three months between Doris' diagnosis and her death, *The Zea Mexican* (Doris's nickname) *Diary* is both a tribute to her and a ritual portrait of the depths of grief. The final images of Brathwaite's traumatic few years here are presented in 1994's *Trench Town Rock.* In 1990, in an episode that Brathwaite describes as his "murder," two gunmen broke into the residence he had taken up in Kingston, Jamaica, after the hurricane. After having bound and gagged Brathwaite and ransacking the place, his assailants mock-executed him by shooting him in the base of his skull. Although the chamber of the gun was not loaded, this "ghost bullet" (as Brathwaite has called it) took an enormous psychological toll on him. Aside from this toll, this particular event made it horrifically clear to Brathwaite not only the increasing brutality of the society at large but also of the political circumstances that gave rise to this situation. Prominent among these are the legacies of colonialism and the dashed hopes of the postcolonial society. In true Brathwaite fashion, however, he cast his recovery from this trauma into a rebirth, rebuilding his spirit and his poetics. Out of this came what he has discussed as a poetic break, a new way of seeing that results in the "Sycorax video-style" that has characterized his work ever since.

THE ARRIVANTS

The world first became aware of Brathwaite's range with the publication of the three volumes that make up *The Arrivants: A New World Trilogy.* These volumes, published by Oxford University Press, announced Brathwaite as a poet of panoramic vision. Each volume's release seemed an occasion for celebration but also for an intensification of the debates in which Brathwaite often found himself and his work. *The Arrivants* may be the center of many of the discussions that were occurring during the period in which all of its volumes were being conceived and written. The nature of West Indian poetry, the relation of black people in the African diaspora to Africa, the search for an West Indian aesthetic based in folk culture, the fractured conception of black New World history, the force of cross-cultural and transnational connections-all of these emerge in one form or another throughout the whole of *The Arrivants.* Brathwaite has expressed exasperation that the majority of the critical attention paid to his work makes it seem as if he has not published since the late 1960s. This is partly due to the fortuitous manner in which this trilogy takes up themes and concerns that continue to be potent. The critical focus on this text also may be attributed to the effect its publication had on literature in the West Indies. Brathwaite's later work is gaining more attention, but the critical imbalance and the importance of *The Arrivants* necessitate its extended treatment in this essay.

Four sections make up the basic structure of the first volume, *Rights of Passage*: "Work Song and Blues," "The Spades," "Islands and Exiles," and "The Return." *Rights* takes a largely panoramic view of the African diaspora and its inhabitants. The "Prelude" that opens the work offers a breathless, compacted view of the movement and migration of the African. Traveling through drought, desert, and death; building, moving, and rebuilding, the people journey across the African continent to the ocean on the western coast where in the second poem of the volume, "New World A'Comin'," they meet modernity and their historical rupture in the guise of the European and his weapons:

Click lock
your fire–
lock fore–
arm fire–
arm flashed

fire and our firm
fleshed, flame
warm, fly
bitten warriors
fell.

(p. 9)

The rest of *Rights* takes place in various locations and situations in the New World. Brathwaite casts a figure named Tom as the voice and center of the rest of the volume. Tom, whose name is a reference to Harriet Beecher Stowe's main character in *Uncle Tom's Cabin,* is a conflicted presence who retains the memories of Africa and its cultural heritage while attempting to forge some way in this strange new place. He is isolated from his home and alienated from his descendants who mock him and his choices:

They call me Uncle
Tom and mock me

these my children
mock me

they hate the hat
in hand

the one–
roomed God

I praise

(p. 17)

Tom can offer them nothing but memories. These recollections are useless; he cannot pass them on and his descendants do not want them. He grieves over the choices and directions of his children but is unable to guide or aid them. Brathwaite's Tom is an impotent, sad figure who seems to be simply "timid Tom / father / founder / flounderer" (p. 15). In "Didn't He Ramble," we see a brief flash of a different Tom before he dies. We see Tom's deference and timidity as a tactic he has used for survival:

I finally come
hope in my belly
hate smothered down
to the bone
to suit the part

I am playing.

(p. 22)

The part Tom plays while suppressing the hate he feels is followed by a series of portraits of his descendants who also play parts but have accepted tactics that are quite different from Tom's. The next two sections of *Rights of Passage,* "The Spades" and "Islands and Exiles," present these roles that Tom's children play as responses to the situations of black people in the African diaspora. Rather than deference, these roles are characterized by Brathwaite as often nihilistic, escapist, defiant, or resigned. Through these portraits he comments on the weight of stereotypes and the manner in which people can inhabit them.

Rights of Passage's last section, "The Return," narrows the panoramic focus of the previous sections onto the lived realities of the Caribbean. The centerpiece of the section is "The Dust." This poem has been acclaimed as one of Brathwaite's major achievements in this early work. It is the first time the reader encounters female voices in any substantial manner in the volume, but its significance lies in the sustained use of language specific to the Caribbean. Brathwaite's use of dialect, which he will rename "nation language" (and which will be discussed in a separate section), reaches its heights here. In "The Dust" a group of women meet in a shop and their conversation is overheard. They begin with pleasantries and small talk:

No man, you even lookin'
more hearty!

A'ready?
Then all uh kin say
an' uh say it agen:
we got to thank God
fuh small mercies.

Amen,
Eveie, chile.
Amen,
Eveie, chile.

(pp. 62–63)

Soon they begin to discuss the recent volcanic eruptions on a neighboring island and the effects the volcanic ash has had on their island. "The Dust" presents ordinary people as engaged with not only the mundane but also the weightier questions of existence. As they try to make sense of the vagaries of life and history through their attempts to understand and explain the volcanic effects, the voices of the poem end on a note that the most learned poets and philosophers have echoed:

an' suddenly so, without rhyme,

without reason, all you hope gone
ev'rything look like it comin' out wrong.
Why is that? What it mean?

(pp. 68–69)

Through the use of these colloquial rhythms, Brathwaite provides fragments of the submerged history of the ordinary people of the Caribbean. He returns the text back to Tom, whose now empty cabin, standing neglected and falling apart, is "all / that's left of hopes, of hurt, / of history" (p. 71). The history of the people is one that, although neglected, is for Brathwaite as significant as the one that will be acknowledged, written, and studied. Tom's life is one that can be read in the house, in the grounds—the hopes of Tom "whose life here, look / how snapped, how / broken, will not be / recorded on our cenotaphs or / books" (p. 72). Histories of people like Tom are inscribed in their material culture and, Brathwaite would also argue, in their spoken language. Many critics recognized the success with which Brathwaite employed the spoken language and praised its formal innovations. The effect was sharpened by the widespread notion that this was a text that demanded to be performed. It was well known by now that Brathwaite was a powerful performer, and the release of a recording of *Rights of Passage* in 1969 cemented that reputation. That recording was followed by releases of the poet performing the two following texts in the trilogy, *Masks* and *Islands,* in 1972 and 1973, respectively.

The volume ends with a reprise of the opening prologue but introduces a new character, "old Negro Noah," who enters a new world. *Rights of Passage* thus concludes with a wandering figure and with a question and answer:

Should you

shatter the door
and walk
in the morning
fully aware

of the future
to come?
There is no
turning back.

(p. 85)

It is therefore more intriguing that the next volume in the trilogy seems to "turn back." The twenty-three poems of *Masks* are often seen as a poetic "return" to Africa. While that interpretation is correct at face-value, what complicates that return is the evidence that proves the sentiment with which the previous volume ends. In its six sections, *Masks* makes use of much of the material and observations that Brathwaite collected during his stay in Africa. The first three sections of the text continue *Rights of Passage's* emphasis on migration; however, these sections recount a history that journeys through the historical kingdoms and tribes that make up the history of the African continent. Brathwaite's poems in this section trace African cultural practices and rituals. The poem "Making of the Drum" recounts the making of that and other instruments while inhabiting the space and time of that ritual. Half of the poem "Atumpan" is written in Akan, the language of the peoples that make up what is now Ghana. The rituals and practices are shown in the first section, while the second section takes the voice of the cultural historian, or griot, the traditional figure who sings the history of his people. The set of poems in this section travels across the continent, telling histories of peoples and the land, mirroring the migration of the people from East to West Africa.

Although the next half of *Masks* begins with a section called "The Return," it cannot be characterized as a triumphant return. The narrator of the poem is landing for the first time on the shores of West Africa. However, the people who greet him welcome him as "you who have come / back a stranger / after three hundred years" (p. 124). He returns only to be face to face with his lack of memory, fear, mistrust, and at best a sense of disequilibrium. Brathwaite's tone in these poems is rather bleak, not what one might expect from a return to the "motherland." Throughout the poems in *Masks* the speaker is repeatedly confronted by the gaps between his experience and the experiences of Africans. In the poem "The Golden Stool"—which refers back to Tom's treasured memory in *Rights of Passage*—the speaker has a vision in which the glorious origin of the Golden Stool is recounted.

The bleakness that characterizes much of *Masks* runs throughout this poem as the speaker sees his own people, "wailing like flutes / whipped for their weakness" brought to this town as slaves. In the next poem, "Sunsum," which begins the last section of *Masks*, Tom's vision is by now recognized to be a slave's vision, seen through the eyes of his master. It is not his history, neither is it seen through his eyes:

. . .I wear this

past I borrowed; his–
tory bleeds
behind my hollowed eyes.

(p. 148)

Thus the African ancestry and the ancestry in the Americas are both versions of the masks of the volume's title. All that is left is for the speaker to unmask himself and look clearly at the history he did not borrow. After having traveled with Nana Tano, the god of the river, the dancer rises, lifted up by the god and the rhythms of the drummer. Supported by these cultural roots, the speaker rises from the rhythms as a tree from the ground.

The final poem of *Masks*, "The Awakening," brings the major threads of the volume together. The drummer of "Atumpan" and the dancer of "Tano" coalesce in the speaker's newly emerging sense of self. The dancer and the drummer, as conduits for the earth's rhythmic energy, are now connected to the spirit of the speaker. In spite of all he has seen and all that he has learned, he asserts

so slowly slowly
ever so slowly

I will rise
and stand on my feet.

(p. 156)

He has come to the realization that the ground upon which his feet must rest and the history his own eyes must see are not those of Africa. Rather, it is of the Caribbean, of the islands, of home.

The last volume of *The Arrivants* is called, therefore, *Islands*. *Masks*'s painful but necessary coming to terms with the realities of a nonidealized African experience and of the speaker's tenuous connection to Africa has provided valuable lessons. However, while the connection may be tenuous, Brathwaite will not seek to deny it absolutely. To illustrate this he begins *Islands* with an emphatically diasporic image: "Nairobi's male elephants uncurl / their trumpets to heaven / Toot-Toot takes it up / in Havana / in Harlem" (p. 162). In this context "Nairobi's male elephants" refers to the Kenyan freedom fighters who had become known as the Mau Mau fighters. "Toot-Toot" refers to the jazz trumpeter Dizzy Gillespie. Brathwaite thus presents in this image a compact but dizzying trip across the African diaspora. Liberation politics is explicitly connected to the cultural forms of the New World that resonate in the United States and the Caribbean.

The poet links his tasks with those images. His contribution must correspond to those various tale-tellers throughout the volume: the drummer, the jazz musician, and finally, the griot who sings the cultural history of his people. *Islands* is written in the voice of someone who has returned home and sees with new vision, not with the "hollowed eyes" of *Masks*'s speaker. As the speaker returns to the New World, he begins to see, as in the opening image of the volume described above, how the culture in the Americas echoes that of Africa. That it is an echo is significant in that Brathwaite recognizes that the initial African cultural "call" is reconfigured in the cultural "response" of the Americas. As an echo, however, it is not the same. This is the crucial point Brathwaite makes in *Islands*. Looking anew at the culture of the Caribbean, the speaker sees the connections to Africa as well as the innovations that are native to the Caribbean. African deities such as Legba, Ananse, and Ogun are still present but in profoundly altered or disguised forms in the Caribbean, and the speaker detects their presence. With new eyes he sees and with new ears he hears.

Along with the continuities of African culture, Brathwaite's major focus in *Islands* is on the indigenous culture developed by the people of the Caribbean. Brathwaite's historical research connects with this. The idea of a Creole society in the Caribbean runs throughout *Islands* and was the subject of his dissertation. Creolization as a new formation in the Caribbean, the meeting and blending of different cultural forces, gives rise to the indigenous rituals with which Brathwaite is fascinated. Religious innovations such as Pocomania and Rastafarianism, as well as the popular diversions of limbo, carnival, and cricket are shown as almost equivalent forms in *Islands*.

The poem "Rites" illustrates some of the major themes here. Revisiting the form of the "The Dust" from *Rights of Passage,* "Rites" is written entirely in a West Indian patois, itself a Creole form. The poem is told in the voice of a tailor in his shop as he recounts a cricket match. The tone of his account is quite dramatic, recalling perhaps an early epic poet or a preacher. Imbuing the events of the match with this sort of weightiness gives the cricket match the grandeur of a great battle. The title "Rites" both recalls the earlier "Rights" in *Rights of Passage* and makes a specific connection between the cultural practices of sport and religion. Both forms are significant for Brathwaite because of the manner in which the people of the islands have adapted the nonnative forms of cricket and Christianity to suit their own needs. In the poem, the tailor asserts "Boy, dis is cricket!" in a pun on the phrase the British often use to describe something untoward or awry, "That isn't cricket." Cricket, then, is played in the colonies, but a style and manner that makes it something other than cricket in England. Just as with African cultures, the colonizing culture is present but transformed as well.

The fact that *Islands* often vacillates between the mundane and the otherworldly, such as sports and religion, is important as well. For instance,

the speaker begins to see the iron forging related to the African god Ogun in the woodworking of his own uncle. One of the critical controversies surrounding this trilogy may be seen in this example. Are we to read these instances as the resurgence of African gods in the Caribbean or as the cultural innovations of humans who feel as though they have been abandoned by those very gods? Resolution of this conflict may very well lie in the way in which one reads the emphasis on Africa in the trilogy.

Perhaps the end of *Islands* (and thus, of the *Arrivants* trilogy) is telling. Brathwaite ends the text with a section he ntitles "Beginning." In the final image of the trilogy, he imagines creation out of the cultural fragments found in the Caribbean. As his use of the language and rhythms of the people in the Caribbean has shown, his goal is to make the people aware of the existence of a West Indian culture, which together the people and the poet can shape. *The Arrivants* ends on a note of hope and possibility: that together they may—on what the poet has described as "this broken ground" (p. 266)—make

with their

rhythms some–
thing torn

and new.

(p. 270)

The Arrivants remains Brathwaite's best-known work. Through the three volumes that make up the trilogy, the maturing of a poetic vision and style is shown: the experimentation with different modes of spoken language and the attempt to rectify the (at best) critical and literary inattention to Africa and the (at worst) complete dismissal of Africa and its cultural products; and the attention to the culture of the ordinary people of the Caribbean.

ANCESTORS

One of Brathwaite's favorite images is that of a stone being skipped across the water. He uses this metaphor first as a child's activity, then expands it into an alternative creation story for the Caribbean in which the islands are created through the action of a god's skipping a stone across the ocean. This metaphor first arises in the poem "Calypso" from *Rights of Passage*: "The stone had skidded arc'd and bloomed into islands" (p. 48).

People in search of a connection to their home place, to their local geography, becomes increasingly central to Brathwaite's poetry after *The Arrivants*. *Mother Poem,* the first book of Brathwaite's second trilogy, which would be revised and collected as *Ancestors* (2001), deals with his attempt to rediscover the specificity of the place of Barbados, a search connected to the poem's focus on women. Knowledge of the mother is paralleled with the rediscovery of the physical setting of Barbados. "My Mother-Barbados" is the poem's setting. The phrase also describes the main character of the poem, who is shown through her interactions with different men: her husband, teacher, parson. These men are central to her life, yet her connections with them are shown to be in some way fractured. The fragmentation of the language, the human connections, are all mirrored in the fragmentary nature of the social conditions that Brathwaite condemns as a legacy of colonialism. Most of *Mother Poem* consists of illustrations of her various relations with these broken men and the tactics and strength she must use to survive. Thus, within the condemnation of the present conditions and the past that has created to these conditions, *Mother Poem* praises the strength of the mother. It ends on an optimistically creative and procreative note. The main character is transformed from a natural to a mythic force. The mother's words of the volume fill the dried "waterbeds." The flow of her language becomes the water.

Sun Poem's scope inhabits a similarly mythic frame. Brathwaite moves from the feminine landscape of the preceding volume to a masculine conception of history. The father sun's daily life cycle—its rising over the island provides the place with light and warmth, its setting abandons the island—is linked to the similarly transitory masculine cycle in the movement from child (son/sun) to father to grandfather. The volume's narrative action focuses on a boy named Adam, a choice that clearly indicates the mythic dimensions upon which Brathwaite means for this to operate. Adam's journey, charting a movement from the west coast of Barbados to the east, reversing the actual movement of the sun, is shown by Brathwaite as a journey back to origins—or least a consciousness of origins—since *The Arrivants* had shown that a return to origins was not possible or ultimately fruitful. Although the narrative movement is from coast to coast, the text ends instead at the center of the island as Adam's grandfather is being buried. The grandfather's funeral causes the boy to enter into awareness of the male life cycle that is central to the text. As the fragmentary nature of a language and society that are products of colonial imposition is shown by the use of "stammering world," *Sun Poem* returns to a similar sentiment that ends *The Arrivants* of new creation out of the available fragments.

X/Self, the last book of the trilogy, moves the center of the trilogy's poetic activity away from the Caribbean and casts its gaze on "Rome" and Europe in general as signs of empire. Brathwaite places Mont Blanc as the definitive figure of Europe—as its central image and metaphor. The oblique reference to the Percy Shelley poem does not seem accidental; it is the very image of power and sublimity that Brathwaite wishes to recall with the allusion. Mount Kilimanjaro, however, is placed as the African opposing figure to Mont Blanc. Mont Blanc is the driving force of the industrial explosion of the West and its consequent association with slavery and empire. Kilimanjaro is resonant of the agrarian economies that lay in its shadow. From this seminal opposition, *X/Self* displays some of the oppositions that have emerged, especially the masculinist, phallic missile and the feminine circular target. *X/Self* follows the oppositions of the two previous volumes, the feminine *Mother Poem* and the masculine *Sun Poem*. Thus *X/Self* is situated both at and as the crossing point of the two. The poet's position between the two forces symbolized by the mountains, of Europe and Africa and of past and present, is what *X/Self* explores. The title of the volume may also be read as a return to Brathwaite's emphasis on the relationship between name and identity. The "X," which was most famously taken up by Malcolm X, was used in order to signify the loss of the power of naming, as well as of the name itself, as a result of the enslavement of Africans in the New World. The name's separation from the identity—the "X" from the "Self"-resonates with the poet's attempt to ground himself between these two forces. On the whole, in *X/Self* the reader is shown the manifestation of the relationships between opposite historical forces. Rather than following the traditional conception of the dialectic, Brathwaite concentrates here on another relationship, the back-and-forth of opposing processes that he will call, as more befitting the experience of the Caribbean, "tidalectics." These oppositions are related; identity is neither one nor the other but a back-and-forth between the two, which is best symbolized for Brathwaite in the rise and fall of the tides.

The 2001 release of the three texts as one volume, the trilogy *Ancestors,* provided the world with a significantly revised text. As opposed to *The Arrivants,* which was released with very little deviation from the original texts, *Ancestors* is a volume in which new poems have been added and others omitted. The entire text is rewritten in Brathwaite's new Sycorax video-style. *Ancestors* is a poem that has been altered rhythmically as well as emotionally. Perhaps reflective of the great trials Brathwaite endured in his personal life, along with a growing sense of disillusionment with the society at large, the trilogy is now resonant with an anger that is less evident in the three texts as they were first released. A case in point is the inclusion of the poem "Pixie" in *Mother Poem.* "Pixie" enters the narrative of *Mother Poem* with harrowing force, thus significantly altering the original's flow and emotional register. "Pixie" is the story of a thirteen-year-old girl and her journey through drugs and prostitution. It is not unusual for Pixie to disappear from home for a few days, but this time she is gone longer than that and her mother calls the police to file a missing persons report. The narrative Brathwaite provides in the poem (some of which is taken from newspaper accounts) shows a life of violence and misdirection. The mother of *Mother Poem* is recast as someone who has lost all control of her child. "Heartbreak Hotel," which continues the Pixie story, is told in Pixie's voice—Brathwaite indicates that it is transcribed from a radio program in November 1997—and shows a lost young woman who seeks only "love," "attention," and "somebody to care & to direct my life and tell me what to do" (p. 69). Random sexual encounters, robbery, and drug and alcohol use provide Pixie with fleeting connections that she does not receive from anyone else, least of all from her mother. The tone of the poet, however, neither exempts her nor places all of the blame on the colonial legacies that have contributed to this situation. They are both at fault, and the anger at that fact and slow leak of hope from the story are more palpable in *Ancestors* than in what Brathwaite had originally written.

"ALTER/NATIVE"

The search in indigenous traditions for an alternative to European literary traditions and value judgments can be seen through Brathwaite's formal innovations as well as subject matter. This search does not imply a complete break from that tradition. Rather it suggests discomfort with an uncritical acceptance by West Indian writers of that tradition as a pure heritage. Brathwaite would acknowledge the presence and continuing effects of that English tradition, but the significance here resides in his subtle alignment with the projects of T. S. Eliot, Ezra Pound, and James Joyce. Certainly his invocation of those modernist figures as compatriots in a "colonial" project has something to do with their experiments with language. However, understanding them as "colonials" of a sort, Brathwaite connects with other parts of their legacies. Eliot has been acknowledged by Brathwaite as a significant influence on his own work. However, the Eliot with whom Brathwaite most identifies is the expatriate who wed the St. Louis, Missouri, rhythms of his spoken voice with the diction and cadences of High Anglicanism. We may recognize Pound as

KAMAU (EDWARD) BRATHWAITE

the poetic iconoclast who reminded us that breaking the pentameter "was the first heave." Echoing Pound, Brathwaite describes the incongruity of traditional metrical patterns for a Caribbean aesthetic and the experience out of which it arises when he notes that "the hurricane does not roar in pentameter" (*Roots,* p. 265). Joyce may well be an underacknowledged precursor to Brathwaite, yet the Joyce with whom Brathwaite might most identify is Joyce the national writer, whose use of fragmentation and interest in the epic qualities of the quotidian rhythms and experiences of "ordinary" people mirrors Brathwaite's goal of an alternative Caribbean aesthetic that not only acknowledges the significance of the ordinary but emerges out of that native experience. He would punningly describe this as his search for an "alter/native" form that can be discerned through attention to the culture and practices of the folk that he saw as forming a "Little Tradition" as opposed to the "Great Tradition" of European cultural forms. The alternative to the Great Tradition of European literary and cultural forms and ideas could, for Brathwaite, be found in the Little Tradition of the folk or the "natives" of the West Indies. Brathwaite understood their culture—folktales, oral traditions, musical innovations—as having a hidden African core. This would become a point of heated contention, but for this purpose it is useful to note that Brathwaite's often-stated goal was not to deny the impact on the Great Tradition but to unearth the qualities and forms of the Little Tradition that might help connect the West Indian writer to his or her society.

BRATHWAITE AND MUSIC

Poetry and music share many qualities that are readily evident, for instance a concern with sound and with rhythm. Given this it may not seem like much of a stretch to suggest that a certain poet is a "musical poet." Certainly the historical connections between music, poetry, and song may be said to extend back as far as the earliest of the oral poets. However, the music of the black diaspora has for Brathwaite not only formal but far-reaching thematic and ideological

implications. His reputation as a thoughtful and knowledgeable critic of music and literature had been established for a West Indian audience during the years he was in Africa, via consistent publication in the journal *BIM*. One of the earliest, most developed expositions of his attempts to explicate a Caribbean aesthetic is the essay "Jazz and the West Indian Novel." This essay, published in *BIM* in three parts through 1967 and 1968 but first presented at one of the early CAM meetings, indicates Brathwaite's shift from a discussion in earlier essays of trends in Caribbean literature—the theme of exile in "Sir Galahad and the Islands" (1957), the effects of the physical landscape of a country on the artists it has produced in "The Controversial Tree of Time" (1960), and the relationship between the West Indian artist's psychic exile and the physical experience of migration in "Roots" (1963)—into a sustained attempt to distinguish and elaborate the qualities of a cultural aesthetic that is somehow indigenous to the Caribbean. Brathwaite's tentative vehicle for unearthing these qualities is jazz.

Brathwaite's interest in jazz had been evident since his days at Barbados' Harrison College. There he cultivated a taste for the radical jazz innovations of the 1940s that came to be known as bebop and wrote a jazz column for the student paper. Bebop's dissonance soon landed him in a bit of trouble when he caused a ruckus by playing recordings by Charlie Parker, Dizzy Gillespie, and Stan Kenton, among others, during a college radio show. The station received numerous angry phone calls, many of which decried the barbarity of this music or argued that the sound coming out of their radios was not music at all. Some twenty or so years later, when he wrote "Jazz and the West Indian Novel," he still recognized jazz as an oppositional cultural form, an alternative born of the black New World experience that would assist in the elaboration of a new poetic form. Crucially jazz signified the music of the "emancipated Negro," that is, of "the rootless . . . truly expatriate Negro" (*Roots,* pp. 55-56). As a model for creative movement, jazz erases the distance separating artist, audience, and the artist's society. The same question of the gap between poet and people informs his thinking at this time, as seen during the discussion of *The Arrivants,* particularly in the way Brathwaite ends that text.

The essay is also important for Brathwaite's assertion that there is "no West Indian jazz," no art form indigenous to the Caribbean that achieves the same results as jazz. Caribbean musical forms are for Brathwaite essentially only collective, simply dance music that denies any individualism. On the other hand, jazz best exemplifies the relationship of the "individual-in-the-group and group–individual improvisation" that reflects the writer's relationship to West Indian society (*Roots,* p. 57). Although at this time Brathwaite does not see any model for writing in the Caribbean that contains the same potential as jazz, he will later recognize it in the Caribbean in calypso and reggae, especially as the latter began to emerge as a substantial musical and political vehicle in the 1970s. In the essay he also finds this potential reflected in the rhythms, patterns, and variations in the language of the few jazz novels he discusses. Although he discusses aspects of a jazz aesthetic in some novels, it is only in Roger Mais's novel *Brother Man* (1954) that he finds a sustained jazz expression. That Brathwaite can only present one novel that displays this aesthetic caused some critics to find his argument less than compelling. However, Brathwaite makes clear that he is using jazz as a heuristic model, as he calls it, "a way of seeing; a critical tool" (*Roots,* p. 107).

Black music, jazz especially early on in Brathwaite's poetry, appears as a cultural reference as well. Many of the poems contain references to song titles such as "Didn't He Ramble," after a New Orleans funeral march, and "Wings of a Dove," which was a popular ska tune. Some are references to particular musicians as cultural icons: "Trane," "Miles," "Bird," and "Jah's reference to "Toot-Toot" (Dizzy Gillespie) are only a few mentions. Just as often, however, Brathwaite has attempted to use black musicians as formal inspirations, such as "Clock (for Albert Ayler)," in which Brathwaite responds to Ayler's own fracturing of traditional harmonics with his own splintering of the poem's sense of space and time.

Brathwaite also takes formal inspiration from the sounds of the Caribbean. In the poem "Negus," which he later dedicated to the Rastafarian drummer Count Ossie, he channels the rhythms of the drums into a verbal language struggling to be reborn:

It
it
it
it is not
. . .
it is not
it is not
it is not enough
it is not enough to be free
of the whips, principalities and powers
where is your kingdom of the Word?

(*Arrivants,* p. 222)

In black musical forms, Brathwaite hears the resonances of the Little Tradition and grabs hold of the rhythms peculiar to black music and speech as a guide into a "kingdom of the Word" that is specific to the experience of the black New World in general and West Indian experience in particular.

NATION LANGUAGE

It should be no surprise that, as a poet, and as one who is concerned with the accurate representation of West Indian experience and expression, Brathwaite has a deep interest in the actuality of language. How, then, does poetic form represent the embedded features and characteristics of an experience that it seeks to plumb and elaborate? Brathwaite carries this question further: How, also, does the very language people use express certain histories and experiences? Experience here does not for Brathwaite only refer to cultural or social experience, though those are significant. How, he will also ask, can we rhythmically approach the natural experience, the experience of the actual physical environment and landscape of a place?

In his 1981 essay "History of the Voice" he discusses this very problem, wondering how, given the hegemony of formal models such as the pentameter, which is the product of a very different experience, West Indian writers can develop a system to allow them to more closely express their own place: "In other words, we haven't got the syllables, the syllabic intelligence, to describe the hurricane, which is our own experience" (*Roots,* p. 263). At the very bottom of Brathwaite's goal to break with formal colonial models and the cultural meanings and assumptions embedded in them is a fundamental concern with language. In "History of the Voice" he sets out on a sustained discussion of what he refuses to call "dialect" but instead calls "nation language." Discarding the pejorative connotations of the term "dialect" he argues that nation language must not be understood as "bad" English. On the contrary, it is expression that carries within it a "submerged, surrealist experience and sensibility" that comes out through rhythm, inflections that approximate more closely a Caribbean experience. Brathwaite's theory ideally results not only in a subversion or inversion of "traditional" forms but ultimately in a complete break from them. Thus nation language is a new sense of English but also "sometimes not English at all, but *language*" (*Roots,* p. 259). It is the language of the slaves and indentured laborers. Nation language, because it is not the standard but an underground language, still differs from the standard even as it recalls it. When heard, nation language may be recognized as English more or less, based on vocabulary or phonetics; however, Brathwaite argues that it is not English in rhythm, inflection, or even syntax. This point introduces another major aspect of nation language. Since it does not represent the language of the standard, the establishment, or of education, Brathwaite argues that it cannot be fully accessed by reading. It is part of what he calls "total expression," in which the importance of the oral tradition is paramount. Based on sound and song, emanating from the historical experiences of people who were not (or could not be) reliant on books but instead on their own verbal and sonic patterns, a true expression of their experience could not deny the oral tradition. Instead, orality is the key to and the conduit for that expression. Nation language allows Brathwaite to theorize

about the formal experimentation with language in his poetry since poems like "The Dust" in *Rights of Passage* or *Islands'* "Rites."

It is once again worthwhile to remember that, as in *The Arrivants* and *Ancestors,* Brathwaite does not totally deny the presence or the impact of those European formal models. Rather, he seeks to explore that "submerged," hidden, or simply ignored presence of the other tradition, that which reflects the African presence in the Caribbean. Nation language "may be in English, but often it is in an English which is like a howl, or a shout, or a machine-gun, or the wind, or a wave. . . . And sometimes it is English and African at the same time" (*Roots,* p. 266). However, since nation language carries within it the African experience in the Caribbean, it is necessary for Brathwaite an oppositional model. The unearthing and recognition of this emergent language may provide the West Indian writer with the alternative for which he had been searching.

SYCORAX VIDEO-STYLE

Brathwaite's next move toward a break from European models and their concurrent assumptions was the development of what he calls his "Sycorax video-style." After his development of nation language, the dilemma he faced was clear: how to most accurately represent a language that has a rhythm and syntax of its own but remains tied to an orthography that does not represent the experience out of which it arises. Sycorax video-style addresses this dilemma as the natural extension of nation language. Whereas nation language remained tied to an approximation of the phonetic differences between a standard and nation language within a traditional orthographic system, Sycorax video-style attempts a break from even traditional orthography in order to bring poetry even closer to orality.

With the still developing video-style Brathwaite means to suggest as closely as possible in print the vocal inflections and the physical gestures that the written poem often only remotely implies. With the aid of a personal computer, Brathwaite creates his video-style by employing icons and various typefaces and sizes along with the range of stylistic devices the computer makes available to him. He seeks to present the poem as a project involving variations of seeing and hearing, reading, writing, and sounding. The poem thus becomes a sort of multisensory collage. The design of the words changes to permit the music of the poem to be translated into a visual shape.

Many of Brathwaite's experiments with the Sycorax video-style have involved rewriting or revising, or re-envisioning, his earlier works. *Ancestors,* for instance, is not only a collection of the three books *Mother Poem, Sun Poem,* and *X/Self* but also an attempt to add the shades of meaning, nuance, and inflection via the Sycorax style that were missing from the original texts. His 1999 book *ConVERSations with Nathaniel Mackey* is a Sycorax revision of a 1993 interview with Mackey that includes revisions of other poetic works, letters, and newspaper articles. The way in which the title *ConVERSations* appears in this essay points to one of the problems and criticisms of Brathwaite's innovation. The title cannot be replicated here in the exact manner in which it appears in his work. Visually, although the capitalization of "VERS" does make it appear larger than the rest of the word, the word "Conversations" in the original resembles a sort of enlarged dot-matrix printing. A criticism lodged against Brathwaite's style is that it renders the text inaccessible to many readers (and publishers). However, this visual obstruction may be thought of as part of the point. The visual element opens up new meanings for his "old" poems and for Brathwaite makes it as culturally specific as, perhaps, the dense allusions that one may find in the work of an Eliot or Joyce. Moreover, by returning for a moment to *Sun Poem's* notion of the "stammering world," the reader can connect the project of the Sycorax style to an attempt to overcome the stammering of the language itself. It does not always hold. Brathwaite's work still stutters even with the use of this visual style, as for instance in "X/Self xth letter / from the thirteenth provinces" that first appears in the 1987 version of *X/Self.* It is a poem that Brathwaite has revised numerous times in print, most recently in *Ancestors.* The poem retains its stam-

mer, even as it delights in the opportunities available in this technology.

Brathwaite's use of video-style is a further manifestation of the issues and ideas he has been working with since the 1960s. In his essay "Timehri" he discusses the Guyanese visual artist Aubrey Williams, whose point of reference extends farther back into the submerged aspect of the Caribbean, except in this case, of the Amerindian. Williams makes use of the ancient art of the Warraou Indians, "timehri" that Brathwaite describes as "rock signs, paintings, petroglyphs; glimpses of a language, glitters of a vision of a world, scattered utterals of a remote *gestalt* but still there, near, potentially communicative" ("Timehri," p. 43). It is worth reading Brathwaite's own earlier description since the fragments and stutters of communication are to be found throughout his work. After having gone through nation language, some twenty–five years later with the aid of the personal computer he is able via the Sycorax video-style to create–or re-ndash;create—a form of "timehri." Brathwaite foreshadows this type of move in his discussion of Williams' work in this 1970 essay: "What we are confronted with in Williams, is a modern artist working in an ancient form; or—and this is the paradox of the statement—an ancient artist working in a modern form. . . . Form, content, technique, vision-all make a seamless garment for the mind and senses" (p. 43). We can see Brathwaite's own later experiments in just this light. The multisensory nature of the Sycorax style and Brathwaite's own use of modern technology assists him in getting closer to what he sees and hears as the ancient sounds and rhythms that resonate through the language and motions of West Indians. As with many of Brathwaite's experiments and strides, it is in a continual process of reinvention. His re-creations of his earlier poems in Sycorax style recall his final point on Aubrey Williams' paintings: "Everyone [sic] of his paintings is a variation on a central theme; his source's central vision" (p. 43).

CONCLUSION

It is the fearlessness of Brathwaite's central vision that signals his continuing relevance. His work is necessarily conflicted. It has been formed within a conflicted situation brought forth by imperialism, yet it still attempts to free itself of its restraints. He continually reinvents both the form and function of poetry, while also presenting a challenge to the ideological structures that surround and help dictate that very form and function. His innovations demand that readers of his poetry extend themselves and their frames of reference and approach farther outward. Throughout his career, he has never let go of his sense of the responsibility of an artist to his or her society. Often this results in the celebration of Brathwaite for his role as a poet of "the people." While there is truth to this, more problematic for some is fully grappling with the legacies of his formal innovations. What is constant, however, is that Brathwaite's career has been one of experimentalism, the penchant for looking ahead at possibility rather than behind at nostalgia or bitterness.

Selected Bibliography

WORKS OF KAMAU (EDWARD) BRATHWAITE

POETRY

Rights of Passage. London and New York: Oxford University Press, 1967.

Masks. London and New York: Oxford University Press, 1968.

Islands. London and New York: Oxford University Press, 1969.

The Arrivants: A New World Trilogy. London and New York: Oxford University Press, 19731973. (Includes *Rights of Passage, Masks,* and *Islands.*).

Other Exiles. London and New York: Oxford University Press, 1975.

Black + Blues. Havana, Cuba: Casa de las Americas, 1976; New York: New Directions, 1995.

Mother Poem. Oxford and New York: Oxford University Press, 1977.

Sun Poem. Oxford and New York: Oxford University Press, 1982.

Third World Poems. London: Longman, 1983.

Jah Music. Kingston, Jamaica: Savacou, 1986.

X/Self. Oxford and New York: Oxford University Press, 1987.

SHAR: Hurricane Poem. Kingston, Jamaica: Savacou, 1990.

Middle Passages. Newcastle upon Tyne, UK: Bloodaxe, 1992; New York: New Directions, 1993.

Ancestors. New York: New Directions, 2001. (Contains *Mother Poem, Sun Poem,* and *X/Self* in revised form.)

Words Need Love Too. Cambridge, UK: Salt Publishing Ltd, 2004.

Born to Slow Horses. Middletown, Conn.: Wesleyan University Press, 2005.

MEMOIR AND FICTION

The Zea Mexican Diary, 7 Sept. 1926–7 Sept. 1986. Madison: University of Wisconsin Press, 1993.

Barabajan Poems 1492-1992. Kingston, Jamaica, and New York: Savacou North, 1994.

DreamStories. Harlow, UK: Longman, 1994.

Trench Town Rock. Providence, R.I.: Lost Roads, 1994.

HISTORICAL WRITINGS

Folk Culture of the Slaves in Jamaica. London: New Beacon Books, 1970. Revised, 1980.

The Development of Creole Society in Jamaica, 1770-1820. Oxford: Clarendon, 1971.

"Caribbean Man in Space and Time." *Savacou* 11-12:1-11, 1975. Also included in *Carifesta Forum: An Anthology of 20 Caribbean Voices.* Edited by John Hearne. Kingston, Jamaica: Carifesta 76, 1976.

"Caliban, Ariel, and Unprospero in the Conflict of Creolization: A Study of the Slave Revolt in Jamaica in 1831-1832." In *Caribbean Slavery in the Atlantic World.* Edited by Verene Shepherd and Hilary McD. Beckles. Princeton, N.J.: Marcus Weiner, 2000, pp. 879–895.

LITERARY AND CULTURAL CRITICISM

"The Controversial Tree of Time." *Bim* 8, no. 30:104-114, 1960. "Timehri." *Savacou* 2:35-44, 1970. Reprinted in *Is Massa Day Dead? Black Moods in the Caribbean.* Edited by Orde Coombs. Garden City, N.Y.: Doubleday, 1974.

Contradictory Omens: Cultural Diversity and Integration in the Caribbean. Kingston, Jamaica: Savacou, 1974.

Roots. Ann Arbor: University of Michigan Press, 1993 (Contains the essays "Sir Galahad and the Islands," 1957/1963; "Roots," 1963; "Jazz and the West Indian Novel," 1967-1968; "Caribbean Critics," 1969; "Creative Literature of the British West Indies During the Period of Slavery," 1970; "Brother Mais," 1974; "The African Presence in Caribbean Literature," 1970/1973; "History of the Voice," 1979/1981.)

"The Love Axe/(l): Developing a Caribbean Aesthetic 1962-1974." In *Reading Black: Essays in the Criticism of African, Caribbean, and Black American Literature.* Edited by Houston A. Baker Jr. Ithaca, N.Y.: Cornell University Press, 1976. Pp. 20–36. (An expanded version of this essay was first published in three parts in the journal *Bim.* Part 1 in *Bim* 16, no. 61:53-65, 1977; part 2 in *Bim* 16, no. 62:101-106, 1977; part 3 in *Bim* 16, no. 63:181-192, 1978.

ConVERSations with Nathaniel Mackey. Staten Island, N.Y.: WE Press; Minneapolis: Xcp: Cross–Cultural Poetics, 1999. (A joint publication; expands on another Mackey interview and includes new work and revisions of earlier work.)

AUDIO RECORDINGS

Rights of Passage. London: Argo Records, DA 101, 102, 1969 (issued as PLP 1110/1 in 1972).

Masks. London: Argo Records, PLP 1183, 1972.

Islands. London: Argo Records, PLP 1184/5, 1973.

Edward Kamau Brathwaite Reading His Poems. U.S. Library of Congress, Archive of Recorded Poetry and Literature, 1982.

BIBLIOGRAPHIES

Brathwaite, Doris Monica. *E. K. B: His Published Prose and Poetry, 1948-1996, A Checklist.* Kingston, Jamaica: Savacou Cooperative, 1986.

———. *A Descriptive and Chronological Bibliography (1950-1982) of the Work of Edward Kamau Brathwaite.* London and Port of Spain, Trinidad: New Beacon, 1988.

CRITICAL AND BIOGRAPHICAL STUDIES.

Breiner, Laurence A. *An Introduction to West Indian Poetry.* Cambridge, UK, and New York: Cambridge University Press, 1998.

Brown, Stewart, ed. *The Art of Kamau Brathwaite.* Bridgend, Wales: Seren, 1995.

Reiss, Timothy J., ed. *For the Geography of a Soul: Emerging Perspectives on Kamau Brathwaite.* Trenton, N.J.: Africa World Press, 2001.

Rohlehr, Gordon. *Pathfinder: Black Awakening in The Arrivants of Edward Kamau Brathwaite.* Tunapuna, Trinidad: self–published, 1981. (Reprinted 1992.) *World Literature Today* 68, no. 4 (Autumn 1994). (A special issue of the journal completely dedicated to Brathwaite.)

INTERVIEWS

Brown, Stewart. "Interview with Edward Kamau Brathwaite." *Kyk–over–al* 40:84-93 (December 1989).

Dawes, Kwame. "Kamau Brathwaite." In *Talk Yuh Talk: Interviews with Anglophone Caribbean Poets.* Edited by Kwame Dawes. Charlottesville: University of Virginia Press, 2001.

Mackey, Nathaniel. "An Interview with Edward Kamau Brathwaite." *Hambone* 9:42-59 (winter 1991). Reprinted as "An Interview with Kamau Brathwaite." In *The Art of Kamau Brathwaite.* Edited by Stewart Brown. Bridgend, Wales: Seren, 1995.

Smilowitz, Erika. "Interview with Edward Kamau Brathwaite." *Caribbean Writer* 5:73-78 (1991).

PETER CAREY

(1943—)

Ian Bickford

GIVEN HIS HUMOR, his instinct for side-door justice, his set-piece aesthetic, and not least his many orphans, there is nothing undue in the fact that critics often describe Peter Carey as Dickensian. Indeed when Carey's sixth novel, *Jack Maggs,* appeared in 1997, cropping, enlarging, and finally revising a portion of Charles Dickens's *Great Expectations* (1861) in order to explore the torments of the notorious outcast Abel Magwitch, it once and for all solidified the comparison. Although the formidable collection of novels and stories that Carey has produced over the past three decades certainly casts back to Dickens and other European forebears, the project of placing him within canonical ranks unleashes at least as many critical departures as liaisons.

Twice a recipient of the prestigious Booker Prize, first in 1988 for *Oscar and Lucinda* and again in 2001 for *True History of the Kelly Gang* (his second published novel, *Illywhacker,* was short-listed for the honor in 1985), Carey has been irrevocably initiated into the greater constellation of British literary stars. As an Australian writer, however, he veers between a quizzical and an excoriating stance toward the mechanics of cultural regulation set forth in the course of colonial history. Then, to complicate matters, Carey has resided in New York City since the late 1980s. Although "the Americans" are stock villains in a number of his early stories, largely owing to what he, along with many others, understands to be the neo-imperialist role adopted by the United States toward Australian politics in the mid-1970s, there is a perceptible American influence in his later writing. In the parlance of the twentieth century, he has been discussed as a fabulist, a postmodernist, and a postcolonialist. Besides Dickens, he has been compared to John Barth, John Fowles, Jorge Luis Borges, Gabriel García Márquez, Salman Rushdie, and, at least for his short stories, Franz Kafka. From a standpoint of genre, he moves with seeming ease among science fiction, mystery, and historical realism. Perhaps the most fair—and certainly the most thorough—account belongs to Bruce Woodcock, who in his book-length critical study titled *Peter Carey* (1996) deems the meandering author a "hybrid" of all these forces, movements, influences, and styles.

Still, if a single line threads all or almost all of Carey's work, it is surely his enthrallment with the importance and the ultimate fragility of concepts of place, whether geographical, political, industrial, natural, national, local, public, private, global, or otherwise. The borders of his imagination tend to fall along literal borders, and many of his characters in the course of their development come to equal or meld with or stand in for the places they live. Therefore, to Carey, characters frequently resemble landscapes, and the land itself almost always participates as an active character. It is for this quality—often leading to an undisguised political critique—that Carey has acquired the reputation of a postcolonial writer, and of all his costumes, if only for its consistency, this is probably the one that suits him best.

Carey has been by turns celebrated and criticized for his treatment of Australian history and politics, often for the same material. Many of his readers balked at the suggestion in *True History of the Kelly Gang* (2000) that Ned Kelly, the legendary outlaw and folk hero, is an Australian equivalent of Thomas Jefferson, but just as many applauded the comparison. Likewise, he was both booed and cheered for his attempt in *Illywhacker* (1985) to profess a national literature, unrecognized yet vibrant, buried in an ethos of lying and self-delusion. Much of the antipathy he has earned for alleged attacks against the integrity of his homeland would seem, to his supporters, to stem from a misreading of Carey's purpose. Though it's true that at one of his Booker Prize dinners he avowed Australia to be, as Bruce Woodcock reports, "hedonistic and intrinsically corrupt" and said that it "probably always has been" (p. 123), in a mysterious way, for Carey such spleen manages to amass into an immovably sympathetic attitude—sympathetic because it is, above all, judicious.

This is perhaps most obvious in his memoir *30 Days in Sydney: A Wildly Distorted Account* (2000), written as part of an occasional series published by Bloomsbury in which writers tell of the city they know most intimately. Recounting his visit home, Carey paints himself as always at loggerheads with his friends over how he has portrayed them, their city, their country, and their culture in his fiction. When one friend tells what is intended to be a story of companionship and loyalty, Carey hears hints of police corruption. When another friend sees in the expansion of the city an exciting pastiche of popular culture, Carey wonders how anyone can justify the industrial devouring of a beautiful harbor.

He combs history for moments of political fraud, economic deception, and colonial hubris, and upon finding these moments he offers them up relentlessly. But by the end of *30 Days in Sydney,* Carey's hard-nosed dissection of Australian eccentricities has begun to seem less sourness than a persistent appreciation for his home. He appears a little like the firebrand protagonist of *Illywhacker,* albeit a more retiring version, whose often misunderstood rants about the deficiencies of Australian character actually exhibit a deeply—almost obsessively—patriotic mind. The same is true in other ways of Carey's Ned Kelly, for whom an Australian identity rests within his Irish ancestry, thereby forming a kind of doubled British colonial condition. Kelly's rebellion, physical and verbal, against governmental corruption is essentially optimistic as he seeks to describe the private borders of a home and family within the strict, encroaching borders of the law.

Carey's judgments become unequivocally brutal only when dealing with issues of race in Australian history. In his most direct treatment of the ruin wrought upon indigenous peoples in the wake of colonial ambition, *Oscar and Lucinda* (1988), he describes the delivery of a lovely, strange, inspired, yet ultimately impractical glass church across a land unmapped and unknown to Europeans. Late in the novel he narrates the slaughter of a tribe of natives who may or may not stand in the way of the expedition's success. This scene traps us within our own sympathies, which have grown fixed upon Oscar's mission of love, risk, and faith. In the end Oscar likewise becomes trapped inside the church as it plunges into a river. The sinking of his dream and the loss of his life supply an allegorical equivalent to the drowning of reckless colonial intentions within the currents of historical reality. The problems of the novel abruptly turn from romance to empire, leading in Carey's imagination to catastrophe both for the black inhabitants of the land and for the group of white travelers who wish, for various reasons, to triumph over the land.

Concerns of place and belonging exert themselves in Carey's work as an uncanny, ubiquitous force, larger than any individual and pressing down upon everyone, producing a bizarre world, often nightmarish, just as often exquisitely beautiful, whose players are lost to the circumstances they occupy. Sometimes hugging the margins of the absurd, sometimes taking the opposite tack to play upon principles of nineteenth-century realism, Carey steers his fiction through extraordinary scenarios, not to invent new versions of human experience but to prove something astonishing (if terrible) about *this* version—as Woodcock explains, quoting André Breton, "effecting 'the prosecution of the real world' through estrangement" (p. 1).

BIOGRAPHY

Peter Philip Carey was born in Bacchus Marsh, Victoria, Australia, on 7 May 1943. His parents, Percival Stanley Carey and Helen Jean Warriner Carey, owned an automotive dealership, Carey's Motors, representing first Ford and later General Motors. The dealership was passed along to

Carey's older brother and sister, who ran it until they retired, after which the building was sold. Although Carey did not join the family business, the customs and ethics of salesmanship would develop into a running theme in his fiction, showing up first in *Illywhacker,* then in *The Tax Inspector* (1991), and making further appearances among major and minor characters throughout his career. Additionally Carey would find rich material in the image of small-town Australian salespeople subservient to overseas corporate interests, in particular American interests, and he would use this image in his ongoing critique of economic globalization as a kind of neo-colonialism.

Having attended Bacchus Marsh State School until the age of ten, Carey then was sent to the exclusive Geelong Grammar School, a boarding school considered to be the Eton of Australia and, by all accounts, a miniature stage for the intricacies of class and wealth in midcentury Australia. Carey has described this move as dislocating, and perhaps the reader can take it as the first of many dislocations by which he grew, very slowly, toward his eventual narrative craft. An article titled "Fiction's Great Outlaw," which appeared in the *Guardian* on 8 January 2001, a week before the release of *True History of the Kelly Gang,* quotes Carey linking his experience in boarding school with the fact that his writing is dominated by orphans: "I first thought it was because I was lazy and it is so much easier not having to fill in the family. But now I think there is something more going on." He implies that his life and his work share the search for a home, both actual and allegorical, and that the search, for him as well as for his characters, is probably lifelong.

However, Carey is not a writer for whom we can easily transpose autobiography and fiction, the action in most of his stories and novels being too inventive and fabulous to arouse suspicions of self-portraiture. His personal history, important to his books less in its events than in its settings, provides a succession of backdrops to flavor and inform the imagined lives of his characters. After having left Geelong in 1960 he embarked on a series of projects, adventures, and lifestyles that

would lay the grounds for the grand, strange, delicious landscapes and communities of his fiction.

Carey likes to say that he read almost no literature in his youth, though at least one of his former teachers has taken issue with that contention. He tends to dismiss evocations of influence more readily than he will lay claim to them, and from one perspective his portrayal of himself as a literary outsider, unique, blithely infiltrating the dusty bookish set, is not disingenuous. In 1961 he began work on a degree in chemistry and zoology at Monash University in Melbourne, but after a serious car accident he flubbed his first year exams (he has hinted that these events were a fortunate way out of a career track that he did not really want, his interest in science being more fanciful than rigorous) and left school for good. His next step, a job at National Advertising Services in Melbourne, inadvertently but fortuitously adopted Carey into a literary culture via contact with the writers-cum-ad-men Barry Oakley and Morris Lurie. Under their tutelage Carey began reading Jack Kerouac, Samuel Beckett, William Faulkner, Saul Bellow, Vladimir Nabokov, and other twentieth-century experimentalists. He was nineteen years old, and the platform was finally in place for him to begin writing.

Not only did Carey stick with the advertising business while he cut his teeth as a writer, but he became quite successful in it. He worked for various agencies in different capacities for many years, going so far as to start his own advertising agency in 1980 with business partner Bani McSpedden. With the encouragement of Oakley and Lurie he brazenly launched into writing. Right out of the gate, as it were, in 1964 he decided to write a novel. The result, *Contacts,* went unpublished, but it brought him to the finalist round of a competitive Stanford University writing contest and was excerpted—his first publication—in an anthology titled *Under Twenty-five* (1966). He then rewrote the book, retitled it (with some irony) *The Futility Machine,* and this time it was accepted for publication by Sun Books. Despite this hopeful accomplishment, however, and for reasons that remain vague, the publication never occurred.

During the same period Carey was producing the spare, intense short stories that are the real achievement of his early literary efforts. Two more novels would remain unpublished, but Carey's collections of stories, *The Fat Man in History* (1974) and *War Crimes* (1979), are prodigious enough to erase any doubt about his early narrative acumen. Outside the context of his later career, these stories are perhaps most easily understood as science fiction, describing not-too-distant futures in which something—it is rarely clear what—has gone terribly wrong, forcing humankind to deal emotionally and technologically with the aftermath. But as Carey began to spin out his later successful novels, few if any of which assume a futuristic conceit—though *Bliss* (1981) and *The Unusual Life of Tristan Smith* (1994) are deliberately unforthcoming as to place and time—the project in the first stories merged into a much more idiosyncratic trajectory than science fiction alone could encompass.

The stories participate with the novels in critiquing American economic dominance, satirizing the human trust of cultural systems in the midst of complete social collapse, and predicting, as Carey put it in a 1977 interview in *Science Fiction: A Review of Speculative Literature,* "What will happen to us if we keep on living like we do now. . . ." They were well received, War Crimes winning the New South Wales Premier's Award in 1980. Also in 1980 a selection of stories from Carey's first two volumes was published by large trade houses in New York and London, to high acclaim, under the title *The Fat Man in History and Other Stories.*

Alongside his prolific, fast-moving new career as a nationally and then internationally recognized literary figure, Carey's personal life throughout the sixties and seventies continued to move in complex directions. He married his first wife, Leigh Weetman, in 1964. Around that time the political air in Melbourne was somewhat unforgiving of people whose ideas veered from the norm, and although Carey has in retrospect described himself in youth as conservative, his stories indicate that his political ideas were by no

means mainstream. Appalled at Australia's involvement in the Vietnam War, a cause into which some of his friends were conscripted, he left for Europe and lived in London from 1968 to 1970. Finding the social and political situation among young people very different there than in Melbourne, he was drawn to the antiwar ideas of the radical left and to an increasingly unfettered hippie lifestyle. He worked periodically as an advertising copywriter and set his attention toward a novel titled *Wog,* another of the unpublished four.

Initially Carey had sworn that he was done with Australia, fed up with the repressive situation there, but in 1970 he broke down and returned to his life in Melbourne where he continued to write and to support himself with part-time advertising work. For a second time he was short-listed for, but failed to receive, a writing fellowship from Stanford University. He completed the last of his stillborn novels, *Adventures Aboard the Marie Celeste,* which the Outback Press accepted for publication but Carey then withheld in anticipation of releasing *The Fat Man in History* —probably a wise move given the groundbreaking brilliance of the stories in that collection.

In 1973 he separated from Leigh Weetman, then in 1974 followed a job with the Grey advertising agency to Sydney. Living in Balmain, a bohemian suburb described at length in *30 Days in Sydney,* he cut an unusual figure in his to-and-fro between avant-garde artistic circles and the more bourgeois world of business. But this sort of contradiction is characteristic of Carey. Politically progressive on the one hand, he maintains an enthusiastic if incredulous appreciation for the workings of modern culture, stopping short of the idea that society should turn back on itself or that the dominant system remains irreconcilable to radical proposals for reform. Called by some a socialist novelist—true enough, in one sense—he treats the challenges of capitalism as something not plainly to discard, but instead to rewrite.

The debate lurking beneath Carey's double lifestyle in the seventies emerges unreduced (if yet with uncertain conclusions) in his first published novel, *Bliss,* which describes an oblivious advertising executive in the wake of a near-death experience who becomes seduced by the half-baked but idealistic values of a back-to-the-land alternative community. Carey too made such a leap of lifestyle, joining a community in 1977 in a rainforest at Yandina similar to the one portrayed in *Bliss*. He lived in a cabin, commuted into Sydney where he continued to work for Grey's, and threw himself ever more vigorously into writing. As Woodcock points out, the upheavals of the late sixties and early seventies were in certain ways fortunate for a writer like Carey, who so thoroughly evades categorization. In part owing to the commotion surrounding Vietnam, a new Labour Party government was elected in 1972, which led in turn to unprecedented public funding for literary production in the form of the Literature Board of the Australia Council for the Arts. The availability of these funds helped the Queensland University Press to create the Paperback Prose series—a publishing list of largely experimental authors—through which Carey's first book was released. Just as the readers can recognize some of the circumstances of the times in the concerns of Carey's fiction, so did those circumstances allow for his fiction to first see the light of day.

In 1981 Carey moved from Yandina to Glennifer, near Bellingen, a bohemian neighborhood outside Sydney in New South Wales. *Bliss* was published that year in Australia, London, and New York and in 1982 was awarded the New South Wales Premier's Award, the Miles Franklin Award, and the National Book Council Award. He met Alison Summers in 1984 and married her a year later in 1985, the same year as the publication of his massive second novel, *Illywhacker.* While *Bliss* and the volumes of stories had been highly admired, *Illywhacker* was Carey's first out-and-out popular success. As well as being short-listed for the Booker Prize, it received numerous major awards for fiction, including the Age Book of the Year Award and the National Book Council Award for Australian Literature, the country's top literary prize.

Also in 1985 *Bliss* was produced as a major motion picture, cowritten by Carey and the director Ray Lawrence, winning awards from the Australian Film Institute for best picture, best director, and—most notably for Carey—best screenplay. As a theater professional, Alison has no doubt influenced Carey's work; in any case his interests turned somewhat toward drama in the following years. After the successful *Bliss* script, he collaborated with performance artist Mike Mullins on a musical titled *Illusion* that used rock-and-roll to address ecological and political themes. Later he wrote the screenplay for Wim Wenders's *Until the End of the World* (1991), and of course dramatic theater features heavily in his most fanciful novel, *The Unusual Life of Tristan Smith.*

Oscar and Lucinda, Carey's best-known book in part because of its revival in the 1997 Hollywood film starring Ralph Fiennes and Cate Blanchett, beat Salman Rushdie's *Satanic Verses* for the 1988 Booker Prize and catapulted Carey well beyond his previous fame. Carey and his wife and their first son, Sam, born in 1986, moved to Greenwich Village in New York City where he began his ongoing residence teaching creative writing at New York University. Charles, the couple's second son, was born shortly thereafter in 1990.

Still critical of global Americanization, Carey persistently separated his admiration for New York and New Yorkers from his political feelings about the United States itself. However, an anecdote he has shared publicly about his elder son underscores some of his ambivalence in regard to these issues. Talking with Sam about politics, Carey noticed the fourteen-year-old using the phrase "When we bombed Iraq," and corrected him: "No—when they bombed Iraq." Sam rejoined, "No. We." In an open letter to the London *Observer* written a week or so after the 11 September 2001 catastrophes, Carey remarks, "It put a chill in me. I was very happy for him to be a New Yorker, but I wasn't sure I wished him to be American." Nonetheless it reminded him that his family's collective sense of place and belonging might be different from his own—an emotional intricacy projected against a global backdrop, and just the sort of thing with which Carey has long grappled in his fiction.

Since his move to New York, Carey has published five novels: *The Tax Inspector, The Unusual Life of Tristan Smith, Jack Maggs, True History of the Kelly Gang,* and *My Life as a Fake* (2003). His *Collected Stories* appeared in 1995. He has also written a children's book, *The Big Bazoohley* (1995), and two memoirs, *30 Days in Sydney* and *Wrong About Japan: A Father's Journey with His Son* (2004).

THE STORIES

It seems clear why Carey left behind short stories for novels. His imagination simply outgrew the bounds of a condensed form. As the astonishing abundance of his early career attests, so much of it unpublished, Carey was spilling over from the start. So in a way he simply settled his ideas in a form appropriate to their size. Yet even as the stories that make up *The Fat Man in History and War Crimes* forecast everything else Carey would eventually write, they are also wonderfully unique within his repertoire.

Generally the characters in the stories are not as distinctive and therefore not as memorable as, for instance, Oscar Hopkins or Jack Maggs or even the somewhat historical version of Ned Kelly, all of whose obsessions and loves and quirks of personality are painstakingly cast against the intricate circumstances of their lives. But although a well-honed sense of character became one of Carey's best-known attributes, in the early stories any focus on individual people seems somehow irrelevant. Despite a narrative stage smaller than in the novels, in many ways the venture playing upon it appears large enough to eclipse the concerns of individual players.

This may or may not be simply excuse-making for a young Carey who, after all, came relatively late to his craft and was still learning his way while writing his first two published books. His first characters may seem flat simply because he did not know how to make them round. Whatever the cause, the effect is the same: stories such as "The Chance," "American Dreams," "Do You Love Me?" "The Fat Man in History," and even "War Crimes" (a relatively late piece in which characters begin to take on the kind of superla-

tive personalities so populous in many of the novels), share an uneasy sense that global events have passed beyond the moment when humanity can do anything to control them, and that therefore individual desires betoken a much greater distress. Personalities disappear, in other words, into a world gone terribly wrong.

At the same time, if the individual characters are not noteworthy, we are made to care deeply for the groups of characters living through Carey's imagined out-of-control scenarios. Even as they vanish before us, or perhaps because of their vanishing, we as readers stretch to grasp the terror of their struggle—and we find in the more successful stories that we don't have to stretch far. If readers agree with the early trend and regard these pieces essentially as science fiction, they nonetheless must admit that they are science fiction of a singular kind, not engaged in improbable far-off futures but instead envisioning highly probable futures—some real, some allegorical—whose potential eminence cannot but cause a bona fide anxiety for those of us witnessing them from beyond the page.

In "The Chance," a society is in disarray after a series of economic invasions, first by the Americans, a lurking historical factor in many of the stories, and then by "the Fastalogians," alien swindlers whose technology allows people to inhabit random new bodies and thereby, so goes the sales pitch, renegotiate the conditions of their lives. Though the conceit is far-fetched, the story is designed to provoke a real response: readers uneasily ask themselves whether they, given the opportunity, would "take a chance" on a new body.

Similarly, in "War Crimes" the reader can recognize a foundation based wholly in contemporary problems and, more hauntingly, contemporary dreams in the extravagance of a new world order. Corporations resort to the most hardfisted strategies, and the phrase "violent takeover" becomes literal. Via the narrator's reflections on the physical style of his business partner, Barto, Carey scathingly evaluates the relationship between entrepreneurial aggression, consumer idealism, and pop-cultural aesthetic: "He looked like a prince of darkness, standing at the gate in a purple T-shirt, a fur coat, the fingers of his gun-hand painted in green and blue. I smiled and watched him, thinking that capitalism had surely entered its most picturesque phase" (*The Fat Man in History and Other Stories,* p. 162). The problem with this image is its attractiveness. It draws on rock-and-roll, calling up visions of Mick Jagger (who, oddly, played Ned Kelly in a 1970 biopic unrelated to Carey's much later Kelly resurrection), Bob Dylan (the song "Stuck Inside of Mobile with the Memphis Blues Again" is quoted in the story), and the way in which the cotton-shirt romanticism of the sixties swerved into the velvet-and-leather excesses of the seventies. It draws on Hollywood myths of the American Wild West, where capitalist dreams are enforced with gunslinging bravado. And it anticipates MTV, the visual affectations of the eighties and nineties codified in a sweeping corporate plan.

As does the Fastalogians' "genetic lottery," these stories pinpoint genuine human desires and then dismantle them in the dreadful situations they cause. But Carey does not aim puritanically to undo desire. Because it is impossible to separate the pleasure of these stories from their inherent alarm, the "picturesque phase" of capitalism is submitted at least somewhat without irony. Whether due to Carey's relentless imagination, forever working overtime, or his conviction that assessment of postcolonial society must be as much self-directed as otherwise, the disasters around which his stories fold are almost always unsettlingly, authentically, stunningly handsome.

It would be possible to illustrate these observations in regard to nearly any of Carey's short works: "The Puzzling Nature of Blue" incorporates elements of Carey's own conflicting movements between business and anti-establishment agitation; "Exotic Pleasures" joins "The Chance" in positing what would happen if humanity's most indulgent fantasies were intensified by unknown extraterrestrial factors; and "American Dreams," not so much science fiction as Hitchcockian embellishment mixed with Baudrillardian postmodernism, and a touch of Gabriel García Márquez's postcolonial tragicomedy thrown in, depicting small-town people disappearing into their own simulated counterparts as global tourism closes in on them.

In the story that takes the amalgam of these problems to its extreme, "Do You Love Me?", a culture that places all its value in a process of counting, mapping, and describing its belongings and its terrain begins to disappear piecemeal: one person, one building, one region at a time. Even the Cartographers, the elite group responsible for maintaining the society's obsessive surveying and census-taking, begin to disappear. The narrator's Cartographer father believes the disintegration has to do with lack of love. Anything or anyone uncared for is unnecessary and therefore—the pun goes unstated in the story—immaterial. Others blame Cartography itself, wondering whether "Those who filled out their census forms incorrectly would lose those items they had neglected to describe" (p. 49). Whatever the reason, this story provides the sum to which the others contribute. Things beyond human control, yet probably stemming from human actions, threaten everything from culture to nature to the very chance for life to continue on the planet.

BLISS *AND* ILLYWHACKER

Wildly different in form and feeling from Carey's first two novels, "Do You Love Me?" feeds in interesting ways into some of the innovations of *Bliss* and *Illywhacker* which in turn do not resemble each other but as a pair reveal a consistency of concerns amidst changeable techniques. A description in "Do You Love Me?" of the experience of disappearing prefigures a parallel description of near-death in the first pages of *Bliss,* as well as (in a different way) a process of voluntary disappearing in *Illywhacker.* The aftermath of the disappearance of the I.C.I building in "Do You Love Me?" finds a surviving groundskeeper "look[ing] almost translucent. In the days that followed he made some name for himself as a mystic, claiming that he had been able to see other worlds, layer upon layer, through the fabric of the here and now" (p. 47). *Bliss,* opening with the brief death of Harry Joy on his front lawn, uses much the same language to disclose "many different worlds, layer upon layer, as thin as filo pastry." Harry "touched walls like membranes, which shivered with pain, and a sound, as insistent as a pneumatic drill, promised meaningless tortures as terrible as the Christian stories of his youth" (p. 12).

In *Illywhacker,* Herbert Badgery is taught as a child by a surrogate father named Goon Tse Ying to harness his existential terror and thereby disappear at will: "I disappeared and the world disappeared from me. I did not escape from fear, but went to the place where fear lives. I existed like waves from a tuning fork in chloroformed air. I could not see Goon Tse Ying. I was nowhere" (p. 220). Such thematic reliability between dissimilar texts proves that Carey's trajectory as a writer is no helter-skelter set of random fancies, despite his formal departures, but is a single developing, metamorphosing creature. The terror in all these instances of vanishing speaks indirectly, too, to Carey's postcolonial fretting: In the absence of regional or national borders adequate to the job of defining a person's identity, where does identity sit? Is it permanent? What exists beyond it?

Bliss takes a second cue from "Do You Love Me?" in its narrative strategy. Both texts assume the guise of children telling their parents' stories. In "Do You Love Me?" this is overt, a son exploring his contentious relationship with his father and eventually narrating his father's disappearance. *Bliss,* on the other hand, deliberately obscures the narrator's identity until the very last sentence, when "the children of Honey Barbara and Harry Joy" finally reveal themselves to be the owners of the collective voice we've been following for nearly three hundred pages. The novel gives more obvious attention to the issue of children adopting and retelling inherited stories in Harry's own rote parroting of his father's adventure yarns, at first without comprehension but later instilling them with new relevance.

Illywhacker reverses the model, its language issuing from the pen and mouth of a supposedly 139-year-old narrator (confusions of date and plot throw deliberate doubt on this number) telling his own story alongside the stories of his children and grandchildren, most of whom he has outlived. But a surprise ending akin to, indeed even surpassing, the revelation at the end of *Bliss* imbues *Illywhacker* with a disturbing uncertainty as to who is responsible for telling the story. The novel closes on Herbert's grandson, Hissao, having imprisoned his family and other "typical" Australians in the Best Pet Shop in the World—founded by Hissao's father and Herbert's son, Charles. The image is foremost a piece in Carey's postcolonial mosaic, reminiscent of the story "American Dreams" in its sad deference to the power and depravity of tourism as a global force. But furthermore, as it becomes suddenly clear that Herbert's very long autobiography is spoken to a paying clientele from his bed in the pet shop, the degree to which the story has been compromised under Hissao's tyrannical oversight is impossible to decipher. To make matters more complicated, Herbert has been hilariously forthright from the beginning that the story is full of lies—we simply assume that the lies are his own. How much of the story is the father's? How much the son's? How much the grandson's?

Some of these problems cast back to Carey's own childhood and his relationship to his father's business. Carey has said that he respects his father for never adopting a subservient attitude toward Ford or General Motors, and we have no reason to doubt this assertion. Yet in *Illywhacker* he reconstructs many of the symbols and markers of his early years to expose certain personal ethical dilemmas stemming from conditions of global trade. Herbert Badgery, a staunch Australian patriot, rails at every chance against the national habit of passivity in the marketplace (Australia needs its own motorcar, he says, its own airplane, and so forth), but he also continually returns out of economic necessity to the salesmanship passed inadvertently to him by his estranged father. He sells Model T Fords, all the while condemning the practice but admitting, "I have a salesman's sense of history" (p. 343).

Packed into this little acknowledgment are all Carey's feelings about the corrupt, interlocked, fascinating, inescapable characteristics of globalization and of the billions of lives occurring within it. Herbert Badgery spends measureless energy defaming American business, yet he is drawn to the ease of franchise. Peter Carey spends his early career stocking his stories and novels with American entrepreneurial villains, yet his obsession with the relationship of Australia to America, and with his father's relationship to American corporations, is more complex than mere censure will allow, as is evident in his eventually settling in New York. Of course neither of Carey's sons were yet born when *Illywhacker* was published, but additional echoes are present between Carey and Herbert in their role as fathers. Herbert expresses distaste at the way Charles and Hissao increasingly ally themselves with the American marketplace, while Carey suffers his own upset, in the anecdote recounted earlier, at Sam's grammatical solidarity with the United States via the pronoun "we." Children may inherit stories from their parents, but Carey keenly perceives the way the child's perspective then amends, recasts, and relocates those stories. These issues arise again and again for Carey, most notably in *Oscar and Lucinda* and in *True History of the Kelly Gang*.

Returning to "Do You Love Me?" and that haunting line, "Those who filled out their census forms incorrectly would lose those items they had neglected to describe." The inclination of children to tell their parents' stories and of parents to tell of their deceased children, is always at least in part an expression of loss. The telling seems at points almost compulsive, as if that which goes unrecorded will disappear—a spine-tingling actualization of the allegorical disappearances in "Do You Love Me?" This evokes yet another regular theme of Carey's, one he has continued to explore throughout his career: that of nonwriters becoming writers out of necessity, the authorial urge growing not from artistic ambition but from the desire or requirement for a lasting record. Many of the frames by which Carey shapes his novels and stories are based on this detail—indeed the occasions that his work has been referred to as metafiction (fiction about fiction) emerge from it. It is of course interesting to note this in terms of the image Carey has promoted of himself as a writer outside the established literary field—a writer who is actually an advertiser, or a scientist, or a salesman, or whatever. This is the link by which he seems to connect most intimately with his characters.

Bliss ends with Harry Joy inhabiting a kind of utopian existence, highly respected as a village storyteller in an alternative rainforest community. The tableau clearly derives in part from the facts and wishes of Carey's own self-image and his time living at Yandina. The novel begins quite differently, however, in a riff on a different part of Carey's life. Harry is a successful advertising executive, a "good bloke" whom everybody likes and who, to the degree allowed in his limited emotional capacity, genuinely loves his family. But when he dies for nine minutes on his front lawn, everything changes. During his recovery he comes to believe that he is actually in hell and that the people around him, save for a few fellow sufferers, have been replaced by "actors." To him is revealed a world of corporate greed, corruption, poisonous foods, and cancer.

Carey has been criticized as naive for providing Harry with a way out of this human mess via the utopian vision of Bog Onion Road and the love of the rather puritanical Honey Barbara, but in fairness neither the romance nor the community really come across as particularly pure; and, on the other hand, the advertising business Harry abandons doesn't seem all that evil in the end. Some of the most reprehensible, stupid actions in the book are performed by the Bog Onion people, while some of the most spectacularly genuine moments have to do with Harry's wife, Bettina, and her uncut, artistic love of advertising. Harry's real revival has to do with his relationship to telling stories. His father, a dominant figure in his life, was an endless source of stories that Harry tries to reproduce for his own family, but the heart and meaning of them elude him. It is not leaving behind the urban for the rural that saves Harry from hell, but finally learning how to participate in and contribute to his father's narrative legacy—not necessarily a less naive conclusion than the one pinned on Carey by his critics but at least less didactic in its assumptions.

Illywhacker also features a narrator who comes late to authorship—in fact for much of the book he is illiterate—but Herbert Badgery is not such a hesitant storyteller as Harry Joy. Instead he is fantastically inventive and funny and deeply self-aware in regard to both traits: "I am a terrible liar and I have always been a liar. I say that early to set things straight" (p. 11). Lying is a kind of ethical imperative for Herbert, woven with his patriotism and his salesmanship and finally his scholar's intellect into, weirdly, something capable of more historical honesty than the straightforward truth, in all its codified fraudulence, could ever be. This book directly addresses the problematic heritage of Australia, pointing to the original legal lie on which the European version of the place was founded: that although the continent was inhabited it was not cultivated, allowing under British statute for it to be claimed by the crown. One can sense that when Herbert speaks of his children midway through the book, he joins Carey in a larger concern for an Australian birthright based in crime and falsehood: "Spawned by lies, suckled on dreams, infested with dragons, my children could never have been normal, only extraordinary" (p. 359).

OSCAR AND LUCINDA

Oscar and Lucinda was an immediate international success. While very popular, *Illywhacker* had been plagued with accusations of overreaching and dullness—although given its ecstatic humor and sweeping imaginative edge, "dull" seems an unfit adjective. *Bliss* too received a great deal of attention, at least for a first novel, but was misunderstood by many as didactic and naive. Perhaps because its historical realism gives a kind of grounding to Carey's flights of fancy or perhaps simply because Carey had passed beyond the category of new writer, *Oscar and Lucinda* was taken more seriously. Still, it is difficult to imagine the depth of character, the generous backstories, and the formal innovations of *Oscar and Lucinda* without the foregoing novels having first set the stage. Like *Bliss,* for instance, *Oscar and Lucinda* features an unnamed narrator who turns out to be a descendant of the novel's characters. Made clear from the start rather than

surfacing as an abrupt surprise at the end, the relationship is simply more explicit in *Oscar and Lucinda.*

In *Bliss* Carey clearly acknowledges his debt to the Columbian writer Gabriel García Márquez, going so far as to borrow the first line of *One Hundred Years of Solitude* (1967) to narrate Harry Joy's eldest son's adventures in South America. García Márquez: "Many years later, as he faced the firing squad, Colonel Aureliano Buendía was to remember that distant afternoon when his father took him to discover ice." Carey: "When he was about to die in a foreign country, years later, Harry's son would tell his captors that he had been born in an electrical storm. . . . David Joy remembered the night his father took him to see lightning" (pp. 29–30). García Márquez's famous line grammatically collapses the past and future, initiating the complex organization of time and lineage that guides the novel. Cribbing this scheme in *Bliss* and then *Illywhacker,* Carey sustains it and finally establishes it as his own in *Oscar and Lucinda.* It is almost impossible in *One Hundred Years of Solitude* to keep track of the branching Buendiá family tree: Who is the parent of whom, who is a sibling, who is a cousin?

Carey delights in *Oscar and Lucinda* in leading the reader through the complexities, the gaps, the deceptive alliances, and the impossible romances offered to us by a partisan narrator in order to skew our basic sense of continuity. Early details make it clear that although Oscar is the great-grandparent of the narrator, Lucinda cannot be the great-grandmother. Still, the strength of their tale of love makes it more and more difficult to admit this inevitability. We crave the quixotic ending of *Bliss,* wherein Honey Barbara and Harry Joy spin off new generations to tell their story—the Adam and Eve of the narrative line. *Oscar and Lucinda* more loyally adheres to the influence of García Márquez in its unwillingness to allow pat resolution to the desires of either the characters or the readers. Certain genealogical lines are shattered, others are infiltrated by outside factors, and the children left to wear the storyteller's mantle are representatives of only half the story, a hodge-podge, a "hybrid" of influences, as Bruce Woodcock says of Carey.

Two themes evenly split *Oscar and Lucinda:* gambling and religion. Carey neatly parlays these binary elements, so different from each other at surface, into an enthralling, endless interplay between two more closely partnered notions: luck and faith. As a child Oscar Hopkins confuses the evangelical convictions of his father, Theophilus, with an impression that every event is a miraculous communication with God. He imagines divinity in mere accidents. One day, angry with his father for a confrontation involving a Christmas pudding, Oscar prays that God "smite" him—whereupon Theophilus, collecting specimens in the sea for scientific research, happens to fall in. The event ultimately causes Oscar to renounce the Plymouth Brethren for an Anglican education and ministry.

At university he discovers gambling, and it dangerously fits his religious assumptions: if every outcome of every race or coin toss or card game is a divine communication, then every bet is an act not of chance but of faith. These tangled enthusiasms propel Oscar, a strange, skinny, poorly socialized fellow, from England to Australia, to ruin, and then to Lucinda—an equally avid gambler, but "compulsive" rather than "obsessive."

The remarkable glass church represents the marriage of Lucinda's passions with Oscar's. Her secular dream of a house made entirely of glass combined with his confidence in religious transparency launches each metaphor, with the fervor and unreason of any romance, into reality. But faith, for both, is really a principle of luck. The bet intended to seal their love leads with terrible inexorability to Lucinda's financial devastation and Oscar's death, and, as a side note that would be almost comic but for the pain it causes, to the conception and birth of Oscar's child, the narrator's grandparent, by somebody who not only is not Lucinda, but is more or less subsidiary to the rest of the novel.

The conclusion of *Oscar and Lucinda* has been called tired, incomplete, unsatisfying for all its sudden withdrawals and turnarounds, yet if we read it in terms of the novel's primary metaphor it can be understood as nothing but completely accurate. Prince Rupert's Drops are the byproducts of glass manufacturing that first inspire Lucinda in her lifelong fixation on glass. Teardrop shaped, as Carey describes them, they can withstand any pressure, any blow, but merely clipping the small end will cause them to explode into infinitesimal bits. Carey's novel, so well formed until the end, likewise explodes—not without warning, but troublingly nonetheless. Some of the characters blow away to unresolved ends, like Oscar's friend Wardley-Fish whose search for Oscar will never, we imagine, conclude. Others settle loosely over the novel's remainder, the illusion destroyed that their faith is indestructible or that it was ever anything more than a gamble.

THE TAX INSPECTOR

By far Carey's most unforgiving work, *The Tax Inspector* (1991) tells the story of a family ruined by child molestation. The entire narrative occurs against the backdrop of a four-day tax audit. The Catchprices are the proprietors of Catchprice Motors (an obvious allusion to Carey's own childhood), a car dealership and repair shop on the outskirts of Sydney that comes to the attention of the Taxation Office for run-of-the-mill violations. Maria Takis, the eight months pregnant tax inspector assigned to the investigation, considers the kind of shakedown required for such trifling offenses to be at odds with her idiosyncratic idealism, her moral code whereby taxation ought to be used for righting social wrongs. But the Catchprices' financial problems veil more deeply seeded family demons, and their hilarious attempts to hide the business ledgers from Maria amass as a symbolic double for their repression of a history of father-son sexual abuse.

Benny, the younger son of Mort, is the vessel for all the family's pain. It is perhaps the single sharpest example of Carey's ongoing assessment of Australia that Benny, who as many critics have pointed out metaphorically embodies Australian problems and eccentricities, is both chief victim and chief villain in *The Tax Inspector.* The book opens with his having been fired from his job in the spare parts department of Catchprice Motors by his own aunt, Cathy, and her husband, Howie.

The sympathy we experience for him at that moment (not unlike our sympathetic hopes for Oscar in his fool's errand) is not diminished but is only complicated by his later transformation into an "angel" of vengeance and harm. After all, he has been traumatized by his disturbed father, with whom he and his brother, Vish (now a Hare Krishna), were left alone after their mother walked in on Mort molesting Benny, accidentally shot her three-year-old son with a .22 rifle, and fled, so when Benny kidnaps and tortures Sarkis, a new employee of Catchprice Motors, or when he begins to harass Maria in some truly creepy ways, it is impossible (not to mention irresponsible) to convert initial compassion for him into pure censure. Similarly Mort himself is not excused for destroying his son's emotional wellbeing by the fact that he had been abused by his father, but Carey strives to make us understand that the cycle of abuse is indeed a cycle—the guilt is individual, yes, but also shared.

In the distinctive Carey style, the honesty of the treatment ameliorates the crudeness of likening cycles of child abuse to cycles of public corruption. As in *30 Days in Sydney,* the human element of the story both motivates and mollifies the public element, and Carey's relentless prosecution of a corrupt world seems not stern or presumptuous but drawn from a deep reservoir of custodial empathy.

THE UNUSUAL LIFE OF TRISTAN SMITH

Carey's most ambitious work, and in many ways his most thrilling, has also been his least commercially successful. *The Unusual Life of Tristan Smith* (1995) is a story of deformation, drama, popular culture, international politics, and a mythic hero named Bruder Mouse, all set in a not entirely made-up world. Carey draws on his entire repertoire of writerly skills to eradicate any trace of fabrication in this fictional milieu-science fiction, political critique, detailed description, endless character development—opting to explain almost nothing of the rules by which we

are meant to live for the duration of the novel but instead allowing us to pick them up piecemeal while we read. Therefore the novel is difficult, infuriating, and finally rewarding in a way that most fiction, uptight by comparison, can never be.

The reader begins to understand the different dialects at work in the book as Carey's invented words, gibberish at first, trickle into their definitions via context (never mind the glossary of "Efican" and "Voorstand" English at the end of the book, which serves to clarify some issues, though most often is a bit of a killjoy). The reader follows lines of thought recognizable from our own world, such as persistent French and Dutch influences, or the recurring celebration of Shakespeare, into unfamiliar, disorienting realms. The "Sirkus," "an entertainment born of the belief that animals should not be held captive by humans" (p. 422), seems to be an exaggerated riff on American popular culture, its symbols emerging from a mythology of giant talking animals not entirely unlike the real-world Disney menagerie.

This pop mentality spreading outward from the colonial nation of Voorstand to the more provincial, quieter Efica (not entirely believable in its quaintness as a stand-in for Australia) is at least partly a commentary on cultural globalization. Tristan Smith, the physically misshapen son of a beautiful, famous Efican actress, is the hero and narrator of the novel—another in Carey's growing catalog of unlikely storytellers. His eventual embracing of the guise of Bruder Mouse is a wonderful critique of the way the culture trade can be at the same time oppressive and liberating.

JACK MAGGS *AND* MY LIFE AS A FAKE

Two of Carey's later books, *Jack Maggs* (1997) and *My Life as a Fake* (2003), were not published consecutively (*True History of the Kelly Gang* came out between them in 2000), but together they show a stylistic departure for Carey which, to many readers, comes as a surprise in the continuing development of his authorial methods.

True enough, *Jack Maggs* confirms the frequent comparison of Carey to Charles Dickens, lifting the story of the convict Abel Magwitch from *Great Expectations* and testing it against certain postcolonial themes lurking in the original text. More than that, Carey latches onto the fact that Dickens often used real-life people as models for his characters; instead of simply redrafting a Dickensian character, Carey in a sense preempts that character, conceiving of Maggs as the inspiration for Magwitch rather than vice versa. His character Tobias Oates is a thinly veiled portrait of a young Dickens, obsessed, as was the real writer, with mesmerism. Oates and Maggs meet when Maggs returns from his prosperous life in Australia, á la *Great Expectations*, to reconnect with his secret protégé. As much as describing Maggs's obsession with the Pip character, whose name in Carey's version is Henry Phipps, Carey fixes on Oates's obsession with Maggs, thus redirecting the story to themes of authorship and of the author's naturally coercive rapport with the world and with the people around him.

This may be exactly what sets *Jack Maggs,* and with it *My Life as a Fake,* apart from Carey's other writing. Whereas most of Carey's work involves people stumbling accidentally into authorial roles (*True History of the Kelly Gang* takes that premise to its furthest extent), these two books address with extreme deliberation the act of writing on purpose, writing with only the goal of writing, and, more problematically, living one's life with only the goal of writing. For a Peter Carey, long past any credible claim to his old position as a literary insurgent, by now solidly established as a professional writer, these issues are immensely personal. Does literary work change when it is a goal rather than a byproduct—when, in other words, it is the thing the glassworks was built to produce rather than the Prince Rupert's Drops scattered accidentally around?

My Life as a Fake finds its narrator, Sarah Wode-Douglass, a critic and editor, investigating these very issues. Following the poet John Slater from London to Malaysia in the hopes of discovering his long-unspoken knowledge of her mother's suicide, she finds herself obsessed with another mystery—a literary one involving an old

hoax coming quite physically to life. If *Jack Maggs* draws its frame from Dickens, *My Life as a Fake* likewise excavates its key constructions from Mary Wollstonecraft Shelley's *Frankenstein* (1818). Christopher Chubb, the schemer behind the fake poet Bob McCorkle, does not quite live up to the legacy of Victor Frankenstein—jealous instead of ambitious, wheedling instead of remorseful—but his initial reactions are similar to Frankenstein's when McCorkle comes, apparently, to life. It should be noted that McCorkle weirdly resembles Jack Maggs in build and temperament.

The fact that this is an incomplete narrative, Sarah Wode-Douglass appearing no closer to solving the mystery of McCorkle at the end than at the beginning of the book, though she does come to believe wholeheartedly in his genius, is perhaps a concession on Carey's part to the ineffability of literary heritage. Submerged deeper with each successive book in a centuries-spanning community of authors, the tangles of source and influence become for Carey not more but indeed exponentially less possible to trace.

TRUE HISTORY OF THE KELLY GANG

Not unlike the Canadian poet and novelist Michael Ondaatje's *Collected Works of Billy the Kid* (1970) in its objectives, *True History of the Kelly Gang* seeks to lend an authorial voice to a deeply problematic and culturally charged figure. Ned Kelly, an alleged outlaw, in Carey's telling takes an unlikely stand against an oppressive legal and cultural system. Just as William H. Bonney (a.k.a. Billy the Kid), he is killed in the process, in part due to a Judas-like betrayal. And as Billy the Kid has come to epitomize both the cruelty and the romance in legends of the American Wild West, so Kelly occupies a double place in Australian storytelling: from one perspective he is a point of shame, from another he is a heroic symbol. But the legends of the Kelly Gang go beyond the corresponding legends of Billy the Kid's cohort in their moral complexity. If Billy the Kid represents the lamentable loss of innocence and promise in the corrupt expansion of national interests (his story, too, is in ways a colonial one), he could never be reasonably construed, like Ned Kelly, as a Robin Hood type of redeemer. Kelly and his little band of not-so-merry men rob only the rich, and sure enough they give much of what they steal to the poor.

It is to the disgusted voice of the schoolteacher Thomas Curnow, who finally betrays Kelly, that Carey entrusts all the ambivalence and, behind it, all the wonder he has maintained in his feelings toward Australia through each of his works: "What is it about we Australians, eh? he demanded. What is wrong with us? Do we not have a Jefferson? A Disraeli? Might we not find someone better to admire than a horse-thief and a murderer? Must we always make such an embarrassing spectacle of ourselves?" (p. 364).

Despite his criticism, it is the same Thomas Curnow who "continued to labour obsessively" (p. 365) over Kelly's messy autobiographical manuscript, the text which composes most of *True History of the Kelly Gang.* This is another detail that might well have been lifted straight from Billy the Kid's story: it was a book by Pat Garrett, the friend turned sheriff who supposedly killed Billy, that stood for a long time as the premier account of the hapless outlaw's life. While in interviews Carey has expressed nothing but admiration for Ned Kelly's struggle, which he regards as a truly demonstrative moment in Australian history, we can also recognize something of Curnow's thinking in him.

In a country founded on the ethically untenable assumptions of imperialism, developed largely as a penal colony and receptacle for undesirables, then advanced in a history of vice and fraud (laid out in detail in *30 Days in Sydney*), is it not revealing that even the heroes have something of the scoundrel in them and, if so, is this something to laud or to condemn? It is, as ever, the old postcolonial debate explored everywhere in Carey's fiction: in the degrading cycles of public and private abuse described in *The Tax Inspector;* in the irresponsible idealism of *Oscar and Lucinda;* in the bipolar desires of the characters in *Bliss* and *Illywhacker;* in the clash of gratification and subjugation forged amidst the cultural imperialism of *The Unusual Life of Tristan Smith.*

The sustained broken vernacular in which Carey assembles *True History of the Kelly Gang* is among his most remarkable feats. It testifies to his skill at developing characters to the point that they can live on their own, seamlessly, believably—carried as far into being as possible without actually materializing like Bob McCorkle. Indeed, although *True History of the Kelly Gang* and *My Life as a Fake* are astoundingly different books to have been written in such close sequence (only three years separate their publication dates), this is a place where they cross paths. Carey's account of the Kelly Gang is a kind of literary hoax of its own, albeit a transparent one, professing to have gathered together a series of documents written by Ned Kelly to his daughter, whom he never meets, in order to set straight the record of his life.

As the narrative progresses and as it becomes unlikely that he will survive the political maelstrom that he has provoked, his writing becomes more and more urgent. He grows increasingly obsessed with it. In many ways Ned Kelly is Carey's ultimate inadvertent author, brought to writing out of necessity rather than choice. He also, like Herbert Badgery, reverses the pattern by now so familiar in Carey's work of younger generations recording the stories of the old: this is Kelly casting his story forward, offering it to the future, putting it in the hands of his daughter so that she can eventually tell it, but Carey's sense of history does not allow for perfect endings. It will not be Ned Kelly's kin who preserves his autobiography, but his enemy, the man who in life betrays him.

For *True History of the Kelly Gang* Peter Carey became a two-time winner of the Booker Prize in 2001. He and J. M. Coetzee of South Africa are, to date, the only authors to have achieved that distinction.

Selected Bibliography

WORKS OF PETER CAREY

NOVELS AND SHORT STORIES
The Fat Man in History: Short Stories. St. Lucia: University of Queensland Press, 1974.

War Crimes. St. Lucia: University of Queensland Press, 1979.

The Fat Man in History and Other Stories. London: Faber, 1980; New York: Random House, 1980. Reprint under the title *Exotic Pleasures,* London: Picador, 1981. (This volume reprints ten of the stories from *The Fat Man in History: Short Stories and War Crimes.* The present essay quotes the Random edition.)

Bliss. St. Lucia: University of Queensland Press, 1981; London: Faber, 1981; New York: Harper, 1981; New York: Vintage, 1996. (The present essay quotes from the Vintage edition.)

Illywhacker. London: Faber, 1985; New York: Harper, 1985; St. Lucia: University of Queensland Press, 1985; New York: Vintage, 1996. (The present essay quotes from the Vintage edition.)

Oscar and Lucinda. St. Lucia: University of Queensland Press, 1988; London: Faber, 1988; New York: Harper, 1988.

The Tax Inspector. St. Lucia: University of Queensland Press, 1991; London: Faber, 1991; New York: Knopf, 1991.

The Unusual Life of Tristan Smith. St. Lucia: University of Queensland Press, 1994; London: Faber, 1994; New York: Knopf, 1995.

Collected Stories. London: Faber and Faber, 1995.

The Big Bazoohley. Illustrated by Abira Ali. New York: Henry Holt, 1995; London: Faber, 1995; St. Lucia: University of Queensland Press, 1995. (Children's fiction.)

Jack Maggs. St. Lucia: University of Queensland Press, 1997; London: Faber, 1997; New York: Knopf, 1998.

True History of the Kelly Gang. St. Lucia: University of Queensland Press, 2000; New York: Knopf, 2000; London: Faber, 2001; New York: Vintage, 2002. (The present essay quotes from the Vintage edition.)

My Life as a Fake. New York: Knopf, 2003; London: Faber, 2003; Milson's Point, New South Wales: Random House Australia, 2003.

OTHER WORKS

Bliss: The Screenplay. Cowritten by Ray Lawrence. St. Lucia: University of Queensland Press, 1985. (Screenplay for Bliss. Directed by Ray Lawrence. Sydney: Window III Productions and New South Wales Film Corporation, 1985.)

Until the End of the World. Cowritten by Wim Wenders. North Hollywood, Calif.: Hollywood Scripts, 1991. (Screenplay for Until the End of the World. Directed by Wim Wenders. Australian Film Finance Corporation, Road Movies Filmproduktion, and Argos Films, 1991.)

30 Days in Sydney: A Wildly Distorted Account. The Writer and the City. London: Bloomsbury, 2001; New York: Bloomsbury, 2001. (Memoir.)

Wrong About Japan: A Father's Journey with His Son. Sydney: Random House Australia, 2004; New York: Knopf, 2005. (Travel memoir.)

UNCOLLECTED WORKS

"Contacts." In *Under Twenty-five: An Anthology.* Edited by Anne O'Donovan, Jayne Sanderson, and Shane Porteous. Brisbane: Jacaranda Press, 1966, pp. 34–36.

"The Cosmic Pragmatist." *Nation Review,* 8–14 September 1977, pp. 14–15.

"We Close Our Eyes and Say a Prayer." *Observer,* 23 September 23 September 2001, Special Reports. (Letter to the literary editor, Robert McCrum.)

CRITICAL AND BIOGRAPHICAL STUDIES

Daniel, Helen. "Lies for Sale: Peter Carey." In her *Liars: Australian New Novelists.* Ringwood, Victoria: Penguin, 1988. pp. 145–184.

———. "Peter Carey: The Rivalries of the Fictions." In *International Literature in English: Essays on the Major Writers.* Edited by Robert L. Ross. New York: Garland, 1991. pp. 405–415.

Hassall, Anthony J. *Dancing on Hot Macadam: Peter Carey's Fiction.* St. Lucia: University of Queensland Press, 1994.

Huggan, Graham. "Is the (Günther) Grass Greener on the Other Side? Oskar and Lucinde in the New World." *World Literature Written in English* 30, no. 1 (1990): 1–10.

———. *Peter Carey.* Melbourne: Oxford University Press, 1996.

Ikin, Van. "Peter Carey." In *Contemporary Novelists.* 6th ed. Edited by Susan Windisch Brown. Detroit: St. James Press, 1996. pp. 180–181.

———. "Peter Carey: The Stories." *Science Fiction: A Review of Speculative Literature* (Syndey) 1, no. 1 (1977):19–29.

Kane, Paul. "Postcolonial/Postmodern: Australian Literature and Peter Carey." *World Literature Today* 67, no. 3 (1993): 519–522.

Lamb, Karen. *Peter Carey: The Genesis of Fame.* Pymble, New South Wales: Angus & Robertson, 1992.

Mellors, John. "Moral Imperatives: The Fiction of Peter Carey." *London Magazine* 31, nos. 7/8 (1991): 89–94.

Ommundsen, Wenche. "Narrative Navel–gazing; or, How to Recognize a Metafiction When You See One." *Southern Review* (Adelaide) 22, no. 3 (1989): 264–274.

Thwaites, Tony. "More Tramps at Home: Seeing Australia First." *Meanjin* 46, no. 3 (1987):400–409.

Turner, Graeme. "American Dreaming: The Fictions of Peter Carey." *Australian Literary Studies* 12, no. 4 (1986): 431–441.

———. "Nationalizing the Author: The Celebrity of Peter Carey." *Australian Literary Studies* 16, no. 2 (1993):131–139.

Woodcock, Bruce. *Peter Carey.* Manchester: Manchester University Press, 1996. Exp. ed., 2003. (The 2003 edition includes studies of *Jack Maggs* and *True History of the Kelly Gang.*)

Wroe, Nicholas. "Fiction's Great Outlaw." *Guardian,* 8 January 2001, Books.

LOUIS DE BERNIÈRES

(1954—)

Deborah Seddon

LOUIS DE BERNIÈRES IS best known as the author of *Captain Corelli's Mandolin* (published in the United States as *Corelli's Mandolin*), which tells the story of the wartime love affair between Pelagia, the daughter of a Greek doctor, and Antonio Corelli, the Italian artillery captain of the army occupying the small Greek island of Cephallonia during the Second World War. Published in 1994, the novel has received both popular and critical acclaim. It won De Bernières the Commonwealth Writers' Prize for best book in the same year and was short-listed for the *Sunday Express* Book of the Year. It has been translated into eleven languages, and a film adaptation, directed by John Madden and starring Nicolas Cage, Penélope Cruz, and John Hurt, was released in 2001. In 2003 the novel was included in the Top 21 of the BBC's *Big Read,* in which viewers voted for their 100 favorite books in the English language. The novel did not, however, start out as a best-seller; the phenomenal success of the text was the result of the concomitant development of reading groups and book clubs on both sides of the Atlantic in the early 1990s. The novel's popularity with reading groups ensured a steady yearly pattern of sales, which then attracted the boost of widespread media attention.

With the success of *Captain Corelli's Mandolin,* De Bernières has become something of a household name, but by the time it was published he was already the author of three less well-known novels forming a trilogy set in a fictional South American country. The first, *The War of Don Emmanuel's Nether Parts* (1990), explores the history of abduction and torture that has haunted the continent and won the Commonwealth Writers' Prize (best first book, Eurasia region) in 1991. The sequel, *Señor Vivo and the Coca Lord* (1991), examines the South American drug trade. It was awarded the Commonwealth Writers' Prize (best book, Eurasia region) in the following year. The third of his South American novels, *The Troublesome Offspring of Cardinal Guzman* (1992), returns to the same setting to scrutinize religious fanaticism. In 1993 De Bernières was selected as one of the twenty "Best Young British Novelists" by the British literary magazine *Granta.*

De Bernières initially intended to produce five Latin American novels, including one about a dictator. In a 2001 interview he said that his change of setting from South America to Greece in his fourth novel was motivated by his expectation that with Latin American democratization the novel "would have become an anachronism" (Reynolds and Noakes, p. 9). At the same time, he had traveled to Greece on holiday and encountered the story of the 1953 earthquake on Cephallonia. During his stay on the island, he said, "the story of Captain Corelli just fell into my lap" (Reynolds and Noakes, p. 10).

A great deal of De Bernières' writing stems directly from his travel to other countries. If *Captain Corelli's Mandolin* was inspired by a vacation to Cephallonia, the style and setting of his three Latin American novels drew on his experience of living in Colombia in his youth. In 1998 De Bernières attended a literary festival in Perth, and a chance encounter with the bronze statue of a sheepdog in the small western Australian mining town of Karratha prompted a return visit and weeks of research, during which he drove around collecting stories about the adventures of this legendary kelpie. These he transformed into *Red Dog* (2001), a collection of short stories for older children. De Bernières' next novel, *Birds Without Wings* (2004), also began with a holiday, this time to the southwestern coast of Turkey. The book traces the story of a small town in the Ottoman Empire, in southwest Anatolia, in which Christians and Muslims had peaceably coexisted for centuries until the forces of war and the nationalist aspiration for clearly defined ethnic and religious identities put an end to this way of life. In an interview with the *Observer,* De Bernières described how in Turkey he discovered a ghost town that "used to be a mixed community, as described in the book more or less, and they obviously had a wonderful way of life, quite sophisticated. The town was finally destroyed by an earthquake in the 1950s, but it really started to die when the Christian population was deported. It was walking around that very special place that gave me the idea" (Bedell, 2004).

De Bernières has also published a number of short stories in magazines, many of which counter the common perception that all of his fiction is set outside of Britain. In 1993 he published *Labels,* a comic novella about a man obsessed with collecting cat food labels. He has also written two radio plays. The first, *A Mad British Pervert Has a Sexual Fantasy About the 10th Street Bridge in Calgary,* he read on radio for the Canadian Broadcasting Corporation in 1996 while he was Markin-Flanagan Distinguished Visiting Writer at the University of Calgary, Alberta. The second, *Sunday Morning at the Centre of the World,* was commissioned by and performed on BBC Radio 4 in 1998 and published in 2001. It was inspired by Dylan Thomas' *Under Milk Wood* and is based on the ten years De Bernières spent living above a small shop on Garrat Lane in Earlsfield, southwest London. In the foreword he describes the play as his "farewell embrace to the polymorphous people of Earlsfield" (p. xiii). In the play, De Bernières explores notions of belonging, community, and the question of anyone being a foreigner in London. It attempts to convey the history of a multiethnic, working-class community directly through the voices of characters such as Mr. Wong, Mr. Rajiv, Posh Katy, Emphysemic Eric, Thrombotic Bert, the French and English Dead, and the London sparrows.

BIOGRAPHY

De Bernières was born in London as Louis de Bernière-Smart on December 8, 1954. He characterizes his family as typically British middle-class, informed by traditional values, "one of those where you either go into the clergy or the military" (Reynolds and Noakes, p. 17). His father, Reginald Piers Alexander de Bernière-Smart, was an army officer who had spent time overseas; his mother, Jean (maiden name Ashton) was a homemaker. De Bernières spent most of his early life in the rural community of Hambledon, Surrey, where as an adolescent he attended Bradfield College. His father's military background meant that De Bernières was expected to follow in his footsteps and join his father's regiment. Thus, when he left school at eighteen De Bernières entered Sandhurst, the British military academy, in 1973. However, after four months he realized that the army life of taking and giving orders was incompatible with his own personality, and he left. The decision caused him great difficulty, angering and disappointing his parents: "it was a bit of a catastrophe for my father" (Reynolds and Noakes, p. 17). Needing to escape the hostile atmosphere at home, he decided to leave, and when offered a job on a ranch in South America, he took the opportunity. After a year in Colombia working as a private tutor teaching English and working on a livestock farm he returned to attend university in England, graduating in 1977 with a B.A. in philosophy from the University of Manchester. He earned a postgraduate certificate in education at Leicester Polytechnic in 1981 and earned an M.A. at the University of London in 1985.

In the 1980s De Bernières began publishing short stories in British literary magazines such as *Granta.* He lived for almost ten years in the impoverished Earlsfield area in southwest London, the setting for his radio play. He was employed in various odd jobs, including work as a landscape gardener, motorcycle messenger, and car mechanic. He also worked as a supply teacher. A motorcycle accident in 1982 finally led De Bernières to his career as a novelist. He initially took up writing to cope with the temporary immobility caused by a broken leg and spent this time looking over his old short stories, one of which became his first novel.

Despite his rejection of the army, De Bernières now concedes that his four months of military training was useful hands-on experience of the practicalities of modern warfare. His own knowledge of the reality of digging trenches and handling machine guns and hand grenades, as well as the camaraderie developed between men in adverse circumstances, would all become grist to the mill of his fiction. He also notes the valuable input of other people's experiences, particularly that provided by his father, into the experience of conflict depicted in his novels.

MAJOR CONCERNS

De Bernières has been described as an author who "writes with alternating savagery and sentimentality" (*Observer*, 1994). Part of the popular appeal of his work is the vast canvas on which his stories of love, loss, conflict, and tenderness are played out. He notes that his year in South America had a direct and lasting impact on his concerns as a writer: "whilst in Colombia I was living on a ranch, and mainly with peasants, so I didn't have the chance to develop into the sort of north London type of writer who just writes about themselves and their friends having dinner parties. I like to include everybody, and by that I mean including animals and old people and children and all sorts, because they are all part of our lives" (Reynolds and Noakes, pp. 16–17). A major theme in his work is what may be described as the impossibility of history, because history is written by the victors and never by the unfortunate nobodies whose simple lives are disrupted and destroyed by historical events. In an interview with the *Observer*, De Bernières commented: "Setting up a community and seeing what happens to it when the megalomaniacs get busy: that's my main preoccupation" (Bedell, 2004).

De Bernières' distinctive style of telling is to weave together a number of stories in one novel, alternating the narrative from one chapter to the next. Implicit in such a design is a demonstration of the way in which larger historical events have far-reaching consequences for the lives of peasants, merchants, fishermen, and craftsmen in small, isolated towns. In all of his fiction there is an underlying nostalgia for the simplicity of human life in such communities. Within such places prejudice and violence do occur, but these events are shown to have human solutions, which are not possible or applicable when political events conspire to bring entire nations and peoples to war. The villains of De Bernières' fiction are the authoritarians and the zealots. As he explains, his writing offers harsh criticism of nationalist, xenophobic, or religious ideologies, which "permit people not to think for themselves":

> To follow an absolutist ideology gives them some sort of moral pretext for doing things that they would never otherwise have done. So you can kill someone in the name of your country, you can kill someone in the name of your faith, or your political ideal. Even if you are the kind of person who, walking down a street, would never dream of killing anybody. You're given permission to be bad.
>
> (*Reynolds and Noakes*, p. 26)

All of De Bernières' novels contain graphic scenes of conflict and violence. He is concerned with demonstrating the devastating psychological consequences of war on the ordinary soldier and the way it often manifests as violence against women. De Bernières sees the ordinary soldier as a victim as much as a perpetrator, the pawn of power-hungry and misguided authorities. In his depiction of conflict, his soldiers suffer not only violence but also the incompetence of their superiors. They walk through snow or desert with their feet wrapped in rotting rags, wracked by starvation, dysentery, and often madness. In this way his fiction continues to defend his own early decision to reject the military.

One unusual feature of De Bernières' fiction is the importance given to the relationship of humans with animals. The Australian kelpie named Red Dog is the central character of his collection of stories for children, but in all his novels, the relationship of humans with animals serves as an important illustration of character. This relationship is also deployed to broaden the reader's sense of the widespread effect of political and social events. Many of the heroes of De

Bernières' fiction—Dr. Iannis, Dionisio Vivo, General Carlo Maria Fuerte, Rustem Bey, and Abdulhamid Hodja—develop a bond with a particular animal, which is shown to broaden their humanity. Their appreciation of this creature intimates an acceptance of otherness in the wider political and social sphere. In contrast, the villains of his fiction, the Italian fascist dictator Benito Mussolini in *Captain Corelli's Mandolin* or the serial rapist and murderer Captain Rodrigo Jose Figueras of *The War of Don Emmanuel's Nether Parts,* are shown to have a pathological aversion to animals. Both have a repugnance for domestic cats that borders on paranoia. De Bernières often mentions his own Burmese cat, Toby, in interviews, and in his fiction cats are a positive image. The three Latin American novels feature the rural community of Cochadebajo de los Gatos, "the city of cats beneath a lake" (*Don Emmanuel,* p. 353). The freedom and independence of spirit of its people are demonstrated on a symbolic level by means of the city's relationship with a group of magical black jaguars. The jaguars are immune to bullets, eat only for enjoyment, and behave in the manner of domestic cats.

In Captain Corelli's Mandolin the generosity of spirit that characterizes Dr. Iannis is demonstrated not only by his progressive attitude to his daughter's education and his lighthearted dealings with his patients but in his medical care for and adoption of Psipsina, the pine marten, "a funny kind of cat" discovered impaled on a barbed-wire fence by the little girl Lemoni (p. 44). The same generosity is seen in the relationship between Abdulhamid Hodja, the imam of Eskibahçe, and his beautiful horse Nilufer in *Birds Without Wings.* The imam's capacity for wisdom and love—his intervention for instance, when Rustem Bey's wife Tamara is stoned for adultery by the townsfolk—is emphasized by his devotion to his horse. When the Turkish troops arrive in his small town and, in the face of his desperate protests, requisition Nilufer for the war effort, the imam himself begins to die. The breaking of their relationship by war and the imam's painful demise is suggestively deployed to illustrate the erosion of the way of life of the town of Eskibahçe itself. Nilufer's loss, like Psipsi-

na's, occurs because of war and marks the passing away of the joy of the ordinary, the capacity for love in all its different manifestations—war is bereft of such elemental interactions.

In one of the most affecting scenes of *Captain Corelli's Mandolin,* the dying Mandras, a man "warped and ruined" by war, walks down to the seaside and calls by name to the three dolphins with whom, in his youth, he had swum as his fished:

> He recalled that there had been three wild and exuberant creatures who had loved and trusted him. Creatures who in their grace and simplicity were unruffled about dowries and inconstancy, unconcerned about changing the world, creatures with love but without complications. . . . The fisherman who recovered the bloated body reported that when he had found it, there had been three dolphins taking it in turns to nudge it towards the shore. But there had been stories like that from ancient times, and in truth no one knew any more whether it was merely a romantic figure or a fact of life.
>
> (p. 369)

Mandras represents the corrupted innocent, one of many characters in De Bernières' fiction whose life is irrevocably damaged by an absolutist ideology. Mandras, like Ibrahim and Karatavuk of *Birds Without Wings,* is emblematic of a young man whose ideals and being are affected by the deep personal shock of warfare.

The above passage is typical of De Bernières' fiction, a moment that may be read as both a factual and a magical occurrence. Much of the critical response to the South American trilogy has noted the strong influence of the tradition of magic realism, particularly the work of Gabriel García Márquez, a preoccupation De Bernières himself admits by describing himself as a "Márquez parasite" (Bedell, June 20, 2004). Although after the South American trilogy De Bernières' fiction becomes more realist; the use of symbolism, unique coincidences, and bizarre happenings adds to the semi-mythic quality of his works. *Captain Corelli's Mandolin* draws successfully on the ancient mythical heritage of Cephallonia. As with *Birds Without Wings,* the daily comfort given to ordinary people through the power ascribed to saints, icons, and rituals is an important aspect of the story. De Bernières notes "I am very interested in magic," and he argues that his attraction to magic is in the idea "that reality may be other than we suppose, and you might be able to make a difference in our everyday reality by using this other reality which is hidden behind appearances." He also notes that "there is something magical about fiction" as well as about music (Reynolds and Noakes, p. 24). His central characters are often musicians or magicians, and his fiction explores the human capacity to mythologize and to endow life, people, and events with meaning.

De Bernières' concern with the particularity of human experience is carried through on a linguistic level as he attempts to convey something of the flavor, tone, and style of his settings by a generous use of foreign-language terms. Thus the South American trilogy is liberally sprinkled with Spanish and Portuguese words and curses to illustrate the patois used by the central characters in the village, the brothel, and the forest—a colorful discourse as mixed as their fusion of indigenous and Christian rituals. *Captain Corelli's Mandolin* and *Birds Without Wings* similarly utilize Italian, Greek, Turkish, and Arabic. *Red Dog* includes a glossary of the Australianisms used by the characters. De Bernières' style is also characterized by a deliberate use of unusual English words. This has not always impressed reviewers. Christopher Tayler, quoting phrases such as "mommixity and foofaraw," "but little bequalmed," and "inexplicably disculpated" from *Birds Without Wings,* suggests that De Bernières' "characteristic mode reads like García Márquez translated by Dr Johnson" (*London Review of Books,* 2004).

THE SOUTH AMERICAN NOVELS

At the center of De Bernières' South American trilogy is the utopian community of Cochadebajo de los Gatos. The founders of this mountain city are the main characters of the three novels. They are the villagers of Chiriguana, two landowners, a Marxist priest, and a collection of "campesinos, whores and guerrilleros" (peasants, prostitutes, and guerrilla fighters) who decide toward the end

of the first novel to escape the persecution of the National Army and travel into the Andes to begin a new life in the safety of isolation. They are led on their journey by one of the central characters of the trilogy, Aurelio, an Aymara Indian and a great brujo, or medicine man, who can take the form of an eagle. He gives the name to the city, which is uncovered by an earthquake during the group's perilous journey. The earthquake is presented as a miracle, one that simultaneously buries their old village of Chiriguana in the valley below and reveals an "intact Inca city still half-buried in alluvial mud" (*Don Emmanuel,* p. 353). The city had for centuries been concealed beneath a lake, and thus Cochadebajo de los Gatos appears on no maps. This is an important metaphor, suggesting that it is only when free from the interference of central authorities, with their hunger for power, that any community will be able to exist as human beings are intended to. Within the existing structures of the ancient Inca city, the founders of Cochadebajo de los Gatos "inaugurate a better world and a new way of life amongst the stained stones of a civilization long immersed beneath the waters" (*Cardinal Guzman,* p. 28).

Over the course of the three novels De Bernières uses events in the life of this ideal community to explore different facets of South American history. The city throws into sharp relief the sociopolitical mismanagement of the fictional South American country in which the novels are set. In Cochadebajo de los Gatos, life and love in all its particularity and variety is allowed to flourish without judgment or censure. Education, relationships, religion, and politics are explored in the city, which is a significant thought experiment on the good life. In "that wonderful city with its proliferation of tame black jaguars, its Inca buildings and its population who practise the most enlightened and congenial religion" is De Bernières' vision of successful and happy human existence (*Cardinal Guzman,* p. 12). Over time the townspeople dig out their homes, gradually revealing the ancient Inca structures. They establish new methods of collective farming, educate their young people with spectacular teaching aids, and labor hard in their fertile plateau of crops and fruit trees, but they always stop for love and for the afternoon siesta. Organized by a group of men and women who are leaders by consent, the town benefits from an unspoken law of hard work and cooperation for the benefit of all. Its only written law is a flexible and often bizarre constitution in which everyone has an input. This is a life alive with fiestas, invention, and sexual ardor. According to General Carlo Maria Fuerte, who becomes the city's self-appointed anthropologist, two facets of these people mark them off from others: their capacity for merriment and their thirst for knowledge.

De Bernières' argument builds as the city itself develops, from the dream of a different existence in the first novel to the fruition of human cooperation in the third. In the lands beneath the semimythical city, the lives of the people are afflicted with poverty, violence, drug addiction, and oppression. Each of the novels concentrates on a different facet of this destabilization, thus examining some of the major sociopolitical events that have affected South America.

The critical verdict on the South American novels is mixed. While the novels were esteemed for their humor and inventiveness, critics such as Susan Lowell, writing in the *New York Times,* argued that "the characters tend to be types: clever peasants, wise whores, haughty dames transformed by love, knights-errant" (1992). *Señor Vivo and the Coca Lord* is generally considered the best of the trilogy, and illustrative of what Geraldine Bedell of the *Observer* called De Bernières' "extraordinary facility for sudden switches between gentle comedy and sadistic bloodshed" (2004).

THE WAR OF DON EMMANUEL'S NETHER PARTS *(1990)*

Focusing on the iniquity of an army licensed to make war on its own people, *The War of Don Emmanuel's Nether Parts* has at its heart an unflinching representation of South America's history of torture and disappearance. The fictional South American country in which the trilogy is set is run by President Enciso Veracruz, who is more interested in providing shopping trips for his young wife, a former stripper from a club in Panama, than in the problems affecting his country. The corruption and nepotism of South American political life is exposed through a series of such satirical cameos, a method De Bernières continues to utilize in his fiction. The foreign secretary of the country is the ex-manager of the Panama strip club, a man who at the expense of his ministry publishes a number of books on the occult, which he believes have been dictated to him by the archangel Gabriel. The club's former doormen have been appointed minister for agriculture and minister for public health.

De Bernières' characterization of President Veracruz is suggestive of his attitude toward South American politics as a whole. This self-involved and ineffectual leader feels incapacitated by two forces: his own powerful military and the pervasive influence of the United States. He describes his country as "a beggar in rags sitting on a pile of gold," as control of the country's mineral resources is in the hands of foreign corporations who have the available investment capital (p. 335). Veracruz is aware that any attempt at nationalization or economic reform would lead to intervention from the United States: "he remembered what had happened to Salvador Allende and how the USA had reacted when Castro had thrown out the American tycoons, and he realized it would be the same thing as inviting the CIA to depose him" (p. 335). The constant threat of a military coup also prevents Veracruz from taking any steps to curtail the power of his armed forces. As a result, all real political clout lies in the hands of General Ramirez, Admiral Fleta, and Air Chief Marshal Sanchis, heads of the National Army, Navy, and Air Force respectively and collectively responsible for setting up the torture chambers designed to rid the country of "subversivos" (subversives).

The novel examines how such misuse of military power leads to armed resistance. It strives toward a psychological understanding of the heart of the guerrilla fighter by demonstrating that revolutionaries are created, not born. In the opening pages of the novel the adolescent Federico witnesses the rape and pillage of Chiriguana by Captain Rodrigo Jose Figueras and his army of conscripts, who are ostensibly seeking out Communist guerrillas. Federico steals his father's gun and leaves for the mountains to join the insurgents, people driven by their hatred of "the army, the state and the United States who propped it up" (p. 19). Throughout the novel the pervasive influence of the United States on South American politics is subject to criticism. For instance, Figueras has been "trained in Panama by the United States Army, at their own expense" and learned from them the art of doctoring reports so as to justify and celebrate the worst atrocities of the army (p. 2).

Federico's encounter with a group of guerrilla fighters called the People's Vanguard introduces the characters who appear throughout the trilogy and operate as touchstones of wisdom. Despite De Bernières' well-publicized hostility to communism, the life led by the guerrillas comes under high praise and sophisticated commentary. The leader of the People's Vanguard is Remedios, an austere and highly ethical young woman who was raped as a schoolgirl during a military raid on her village during La Violencia. A Communist who has turned to armed resistance, she feels that "all the poor people of the earth" are her family and heads a group of guerrilla fighters who have joined the resistance because they have all, in one way or another, been directly victimized by the military (p. 39). Allied with the guerrillas are the leaders of the villagers of Chiriguana: Hectoro, a proud horseman and descendant of the Arahuacax Indians; Professor Luis the schoolteacher; Dolores and Consuelo, prostitutes whose bravery matches the men of the village; and Pedro, a hunter and shaman. There is also Aurelio, the Aymara Indian of the Sierra. Through Aurelio, De Bernières illustrates the decimation of indigenous South American tribes by colonialism, environmental despoliation, and corrupt business practices. He also portrays the strength of indigenous cultures: the spirituality, magic, and wisdom at the heart of their communities. South America is shown as a diverse society, and its colonial history is constantly woven into De Bernières' narrative.

The society he depicts is composed of mountain and jungle Indians, mestizos, and mulattos descended from African slaves. The peasant classes and the petite bourgeoisie are often in conflict with the oligarchy of rich landowners who are descended from the Spanish conquistadors. The novel also recalls the history of La Violencia, the armed conflict between liberal and conservative parties, which has left the continent ravaged by a legacy of brutality and corruption.

However, for all the seriousness of the subject matter, the tone and style of De Bernières' representation of South America is often irrepressibly lighthearted, verging at times on the bizarre and the ridiculous. Remedios and her People's Vanguard kidnap Doña Constanza, a landowner whose plan to redirect a river in order to fill her swimming pool brings the intervention of Don Emmanuel, a stock farmer who has lived in South America since he was left behind while on a field trip as a botany student with the University of Cambridge. The novel's title derives from the ludicrous confrontation between Don Emmanuel and Doña Constanza and his declared wish to bathe his nether parts in the river she wishes to divert.

The kidnapping of Doña Constanza is told in tragicomic style. The bridge at which the People's Vanguard plan to exchange their captive for cash is blown up by a rival group. This brings the army into the area again and leaves the guerrillas with no choice but to continue to hold Doña Constanza until, through her own free will, she decides to join them. She is inspired more by her lust for the young guerrilla fighter Gonzago than by the convictions of the group. Nevertheless, her transformation from lonely, spoiled housewife to contributing member of a community with a shared purpose is the first step toward the eventual founding of Cochadebajo de los Gatos. The guerrillas are also responsible for the transformation of General Carlo Maria Fuerte, whom they capture while he is on leave from the army researching butterflies. He is subjected to a trial during which he learns that the brutal acts against villagers that are always blamed on guerrilla activity are the work of his own armed forces. Fuerte had always regarded this idea as idle propaganda, but his conversion and subsequent defection from the army is one of the most important aspects of this many-storied novel. This change is wrought in him through great physical suffering and much that is magical and inexplicable. Fuerte's realization that as a general he is complicit "because I have not done enough" leads to a disorientating depression (p. 124). Mistaken for a wandering vagrant, he is captured by the National Army and imprisoned and tortured at the Security Wing of the Army School of Electrical and Mechanical Engineering, the main site for the worst of the army's atrocities financed by Ramirez, Fleta, and Sanchis. Fuerte's own suffering at the hands of the torturers awakens him to reality and to the necessity for intervention.

The novel is an early example of De Bernières' uncanny ability to intertwine the lyrical and brutal. Juxtaposed with vile details of the torture chambers, the lives of ordinary South Americans are shown as exuberant and vigorous. The People's Vanguard and the villagers of Chiriguana overcome Figueras and his army through a war fought with magic, cunning, and stealth. They are then themselves beset by extraordinary events, first "a plague of laughter" and then "a plague of cats," instigated as Fuerte's donkey, Maria, gives birth to four unusually large black kittens (p. 233). The patterns of imagery in the novel suggest that the plague of cats is the result of the reunion in the spirit world of the lovers Federico and Parlanchina, the daughter of the Indian brujo Aurelio. Both young people are killed violently, Parlanchina and her pet cat by army mines and Federico by a jaguar, an important animal in indigenous mythology. In the magical jaguars that are born and then adopt the town of Chiriguana, the union of the two young lovers after death is made manifest. The arrival of the cats (*gatos*) also collectively suggests the entry into the lives of the villagers of all that is beneficent. The novel closes, however, with a recognition shared by the inhabitants of Chiriguana and the members of the People's Vanguard that after their defeat of the National Army they will never again know peace and isolation. They leave, with their cats, to begin a new life. They are joined by General Fuerte who, after his defeat of the three men at the center of the torture ring, fakes his own death. High in the Andes they establish the mythical city, which will remain the touchstone of all activity in De Bernières' South American fiction.

SEÑOR VIVO AND THE COCA LORD *(1991)*

De Bernières' second novel is set seven years after the conclusion of the first. This novel concentrates on one central character, Dionisio Vivo, a philosophy lecturer whose frequent letters to the newspaper *La Prensa* about the destructive effects on his country of the coca trade elicit the anger of the drug lord Pablo Ecobandobo, or El Jerarca. There may be an autobiographical element to De Bernières' characterization of Vivo, who is described as a gentle man besotted with cats. Although his father is a soldier, he himself is an intellectual, a pacifist, and a musician. Vivo's seemingly miraculous luck in evading the assassination attempts of El Jerarca's men, and the superhuman strength he develops when attacked, lead to his reputation as a brujo, one enhanced by his alliance with Aurelio, the medicine man of Cochadebajo de los Gatos, who brings him two pet jaguars for his protection.

In Vivo's story De Bernières' attention shifts overtly to the devastation of South America by drugs. This is done in two mutually supportive ways: through realist depiction on the one hand and on the other through the mythical story of Lazaro, a forest dweller who falls ill with a mysterious affliction. The welts on his skin and the internal growths that disfigure his face are the objective correlative of the defacement of a country—where gold mines cause deforestation and the rural economy has collapsed as a result of addiction to *basuco,* a derivative of coca adulterated with lead and sulfuric acid, ultimately lethal when smoked.

It is to such horrors that Vivo's letters are directed, and he becomes the unofficial spokesperson for the ordinary and the oppressed. Students from all disciplines cram into his philosophy lectures, where he tells them to reject European philosophy but first to understand it, because it is the shaky premise on which the entire Western world is based. As well as using his character to question the basis of Western thought, the mythologizing of Vivo by his local community allows De Bernières to playfully explore the fusions of Christian and indigenous religion that make up South American society. This is a superstitious country where "it is possible to believe every religion at once" (p. 67). In the spiritual mythologizing of Dionisio Vivo,

> there was a general consensus that he was a white man with a beard and long brown hair with the gentle eyes of a doe and the hint of nimbus about his head. There developed a fashion for portraying him with a scarlet heart for a breast that bled for his country, and so he became a kind of crossbreed between Jesus Christ and the Blessed Virgin.
>
> (p. 68)

This mythologizing is intensified in the indigenous religions of the mountains. At the festival of Santeria at Cochadebajo de los Gatos, Vivo is depicted as the Deliverer, and as the inhabitants commune with the indigenous gods he is granted many powers: the gift of healing, the ability to trick the Lord of Death, the relentless power of a volcano, and the love of the female sex. The novel remains deliberately ambiguous as to his actual possession of such gifts. Quite without his instigation, women arrive in his town of Ipasueño, setting up camp and calling themselves his disciples. Their courage and ingenuity is the major source of support in Vivo's campaign.

Nevertheless, Vivo's stand requires sacrifices. He loses both his lover Anica and his best friend, Ramón, a policeman. Both are killed by the coca lords in retaliation for his activities. The brutal murder and disfigurement of Anica in an abandoned carnation warehouse is an unforgettable scene in the novel. The horrific incident drew letters from many readers and prompted De Bernières to respond that he had been deeply affected by the writing of this chapter but saw it as his duty to tell the truth about the coca trade.

As Vivo triumphs at last over El Jerarca, De Bernières characteristically asserts the power of myth in the lives of the ordinary. The women in the camps are finally "the only ones who were right about him which was because they were the only ones who had not been rational about the whole affair" (p. 152). Vivo fathers many children with them. The boys are called Dionisio and carry the scars of his adventures; the girls are named for Anica. His legacy also extends to a piece of music he writes for Anica and Ramón, *Requiem Angelico,* which becomes world famous.

The novel contains an ambiguous ending, however. A farmer, Fernando, inquires at the local office of the Department of Agricultural Progress and Reform about the new policies whereby those farmers who had previously grown coca are eligible for a grant to enable them to plant coffee instead. But Fernando has never farmed coca, and thus by the perverse logic of government bureaucracy he would need destroy his coffee plants and plant a coca crop first. This anecdote serves to qualify the mythic triumphalism of Vivo's success over El Jerarca, indicating both the willingness of societies to change and the practical difficulties of doing so.

THE TROUBLESOME OFFSPRING OF CARDINAL GUZMAN *(1992)*

Perhaps of all the South American novels, the third takes most strongly as its theme the contrast between the city of the mountains and the suffering in the rest of the country. The absurd theologies, bizarre relationships, and extraordinary beliefs found in the "blessed city" of Cochadebajo de los Gatos are set against the insanity of religious persecution (p. 28).

Religious persecution is the focus of this novel, specifically as it manifests in the atrocities of the "New Albigensian Crusade." The original Albigensians were heretics in thirteenth-century southern France who were suppressed by the Roman Catholic Church. De Bernières links the inquisition in his novel, with its attendant beatings, burnings, and torture, to such a historical precedent in order to suggest the heresy implicit in religious fanaticism itself. Blinded by certainty, the zealots of the new crusade use statements made by the military to sanction a brutal campaign that acts not only against their communities but also against all religious doctrine. De Bernières contextualizes the nation's widespread suffering as rooted in political negligence. While the leader of the new crusade, Don Rechin Anquilar, and his band of mercenaries move like a destructive wave through the countryside, President Veracruz travels to the United States for an operation to improve his sexual prowess.

Also at fault, as De Bernières is clear to point out, is the hypocrisy and self-interest of the Catholic clergy. His satire falls on one man, Cardinal Guzman, who is haunted by a pantheon of demons. The characterization of Guzman is complex. His painful hallucinations are brought on by his "offspring," a twin incorporated into his own stomach while he developed in the womb, a being that may or may not have a soul. But Guzman is certain the demons are punishment for his sexual guilt. He has broken his vow of chastity with his housekeeper, Concepción. Such ironic or allusive naming is typical of De Bernières, who notes that he often chooses the names of his characters for their underlying meanings. The novel repeatedly suggests that Guzman's guilt is misplaced, for his relationship with Concepción, and his secret delight in their little son Cristóbal, is the best element of his character.

Neither Guzman nor Veracruz is inherently evil but rather weakened by personal conflicts and preoccupations. Guzman is unaware of the new crusade and unable to prevent what his own mishandling of the church has instigated. In a paradoxical rewriting of the Christ story, Guzman, while beset with hallucinations, kills his own son. He mistakes the boy for a demon and throws him from a window. Cristóbal returns as a hummingbird, his delicate beauty set against the horrors of the church's fanatical members, who order the killing of *los olvidados,* the forgotten ones, in the *favelas* (slums) that stretch beyond Guzman's window in the capital city.

Within the novel De Bernières explores the history of liberation theology, common in the 1960s in South America, whereby the clergy aligned itself with the poor, seeking to maintain and sustain communities and actively work to combat injustice. However, he champions no version of theology so much as the human capacity to create religions that are personal, beautiful, and diverse. Cochadebajo de los Gatos exhibits this capacity most fully, and thus the searchlights of the new zealots fix on the city as a source of evil. In their final battle, the inhabitants have to turn from their happy lives to war against the fiend of religious absolutism.

This vivid account of the zealots' attempt to stamp the world in the image of themselves is given additional commentary in the prologue, in which the most successful soft-drink company in the world attempts to project its logo onto the snows of the Arctic. The logo is then painted onto the moon. With the passage of time, the specially formulated paint begins to break up, "until it appeared that the face of the moon was smeared with blood. People would look up at the night sky and shudder" (p. 2). On the day Guzman arrives in Cochadebajo de los Gatos, with Concepción and their little hummingbird, to live a life that is his own, the final traces of red paint disappear from the surface of the moon.

CAPTAIN CORELLI'S MANDOLIN *(1994)*

De Bernières' novel about the love affair between Pelagia and the mandolin-playing Captain Antonio Corelli, leader of the occupying Italian force on the Greek island Cephallonia, is his best-known work. It catapulted De Bernières to the top of the best-seller lists in England for 240 weeks and prompted the English novelist A. S. Byatt to compare De Bernières' style to that of Charles Dickens. This novel has a broad canvas of characters so that the history with which it deals is told in a number of styles: the first-person musings of the Italian dictator Benito Mussolini and his Greek counterpart Ioannis Metaxas, love letters, diary entries, and the narrator's third-person accounts.

As Mussolini attempted to prove his military prowess in his alliance with Hitler, he invaded Albania and then Greece. The history of the disastrous Italian campaign against the Greeks in 1940–1941 is told through the diary of Carlo Piero Guercio, a homosexual Italian soldier who joins the army for the purity of love he discovers is possible for his fellow soldiers in adversity. Carlo comments:

> History is the propaganda of the victors. . . . I know that the Duce [Mussolini] has made it clear that the Greek campaign was a resounding victory for Italy. But he was not there. He does not know what happened. He does not know that the ultimate truth is that history ought to consist only of the anecdotes of the little people who are caught up in it.
>
> (p. 33)

De Bernières' choice of Cephallonia for the setting of his tale ensures a focus on "the little people." The island is where Carlo's story intertwines with that of the other major characters, Captain Antonio Corelli, whom Carlo comes to serve under; Dr. Iannis and his daughter Pelagia; the priest Father Arsenios; the strong man Velisarios; and the goatherds, merchants, and fishermen of Cephallonia. Despite her gentle humility, Pelagia is something of an anachronism on the island: an educated woman without the companionship to answer her own potential. Her mother's early death and her father's insistence that she learn to read and write means that she is to some degree both isolated and curtailed by Cephallonian life. Dr. Iannis is resistant to Pelagia's betrothal to Mandras, knowing that the handsome fisherman will not make a suitable husband for the daughter he hopes will become a doctor. Mandras is illiterate. Thus, when he leaves to join the campaign against the Italians, he can neither understand nor answer Pelagia's frequent letters. As a result, her youthful infatuation turns to lonely disillusion. Like the Penelope of Greek myth waiting for Odysseus, Pelagia waits for her lover's return while sewing and unpicking her wedding blanket. Despite her patience, the blanket remains as shapeless, knotted, and unraveled as their fraught relationship. These complications increase as Mandras, traumatized by the Greek-Italian War, joins the Communist partisans on the Greek mainland. Mandras finds a purpose in Communist ideology that rivals all human commitments, including his love for Pelagia.

In contrast, through Antonio Corelli, De Bernières characterizes the ambivalent position of the Italian army in the Second World War. Pelagia's initial resistance to the invasion of her home by the leader of an occupying army begins to wane as she encounters an intelligent man who plays the mandolin, identifies culturally and emotionally with the people he is sent to occupy, and is less interested in politics and war than in music and love. Each finding an intellectual and spiritual match in the other, their relationship, despite the barriers of nationality and war, inevitably begins to flower.

Corelli's name echoes that of the Italian composer Arcangelo Corelli. His sane priorities and ability to relate to others as individuals are repeatedly stressed, often through the symbolism of music. His mandolin, called Antonia, represents the anima of his personality. Corelli's irreverence for the hierarchies of army life can be seen in his formation of an opera club, La Scala, in his regiment, into which he invites "the good Nazi" Günter Weber, from the German garrison. Weber cannot sing a note but is nevertheless assigned by Corelli the "rank" of "dotted semiquaver rest" (p. 203). But their friendship is engulfed by the events of September 1943.

In 1943, when Italy declared an armistice with the Allies, Italian troops on Cephallonia refused to surrender to the Germans and fought desperately for ten days. More than nine thousand Italian soldiers were killed on Hitler's orders or drowned as they were deported by ship. These events are echoed in the novel, as Weber is ordered to execute the Italian soldiers who once befriended him. As they face the German firing squad, Carlo, who has always secretly loved Corelli, saves him from certain death. Carlo uses his own titanic frame to protect Corelli's body from the bullets. Corelli is then secreted off the island. His reunion with Pelagia, however, is deferred until much later in the characters' lives. The cyclic movement of the novel is echoed in Pelagia's name. It is derived from the Greek word for "sea," and as De Bernières has explained, "the pelagic current is one that goes in a huge circle and comes back to where it starts, that's why I chose the name for her" (Reynolds and Noakes, p. 13).

The conflict between individual and national history is a strong theme in the novel, which sets the voice of Mussolini in an opening chapter against the attempts of Dr. Iannis to write a history of his island:

> "The New History of Cephallonia" was proving a problem; it seemed impossible to write it without the intrusion of his own feelings and prejudices. Objectivity seemed quite unattainable, and he felt his false starts must have wasted more paper than was normally used on the island in the space of a year. The voice that emerged in his account was intractably his own; it was never historical. It lacked grandeur and impartiality. It was not Olympian.
>
> (p. 4)

Dr. Iannis' first attempts are eaten by his daughter's pet goat, and his frustrated efforts are only made possible when he renames "The New History" as "A Personal History": "Now he could forget about leaving out the loaded adjectives and the ancient historical grudges, now he could be vitriolic" (p. 5).

It is ironic, considering this awareness in the novel of the hazards of historical writing, that some critics consider De Bernières' own personal version of Greek history, particularly his controversial anti-Communist bias in the novel, to be not only vitriolic but seriously factually flawed. His presentation of the Greek Communist resistance, particularly in the characters of Mandras and Hector as sadistic ideologues whose "liberation of the masses" consists of rapine and brutality, has led to some of the most severe critiques of the novel. In an article that presents the novel as more "Greek myth" than Greek history, Seumas Milne notes the novel's ideological bias, describing De Bernières' portrayal of the Greek Communists, who led the resistance against the Italian and German occupations and later fought British- and American-backed forces in the civil war of the late 1940s, as "crude and unremittingly hostile." He also criticizes the "notably sympathetic portrait of the pre-war Greek dictator Metaxas—a man responsible for the torture, imprisonment and murder of thousands of left-wing political opponents" and notes, moreover,

the irony of the fact that "Mussolini's occupation army, fresh from its genocidal sweeps through Ethiopia and Libya, is presented as a collection of harmless, fun-loving rogues" (*Guardian,* 2000).

The controversy over the novel first surfaced in Britain in 1999, when Andrew Murray, writing in the British Communist newspaper the *Morning Star,* accused De Bernières of "the most crude and brazen anti-communism" and of being an "apologist for the excesses of the right in Greece" (*Guardian,* 2000). As Seumas Milne notes, in Greece itself, particularly for many of the older generation who lived through the events described in De Bernières' book, his story "was viewed as a slur on the record of the Greek resistance to the Nazis." Milne also records that many Greek and Italian readers wince at what they see as "condescending national stereotyping," taking exception to the scenes of communal defecation and leisurely mandolin playing or opera singing under conditions of military occupation. The controversy resulted in De Bernières excising certain passages from the Greek edition on the advice of his publisher (*Guardian,* 2000). While Cephallonians welcomed the tourism boom that accompanied the film adaptation of the novel, they also required public assurances that the filmmakers would not repeat what they saw as De Bernières' defamation of the Greek resistance movement. They were somewhat heartened that the choice of scriptwriter was Shawn Slovo, the daughter of the anti-apartheid activist Ruth First and of Joe Slovo, the leader of the South African Communist party. Shawn Slovo publicly dismissed the novel's portrayal of the Greek resistance as "offensive and inaccurate" (Milne, *Guardian,* 2001). De Bernières first reacted to the attack in the *Morning Star* with defiance, thus bringing further publicity to the controversy. In 2001, however, he was quoted as saying: "it became clear to me that many people were offended by the portrayal of the communist resistance, or thought that it was inaccurate, I haven't changed my mind about what I think is the truth, but I had to bear in mind the possibility that I might be wrong" (*Guardian,* 2001).

LOUIS DE BERNIÈRES

RED DOG *(2001)*

Set in the desert-mining region of Western Australia, *Red Dog* is the semifictionalized biography of the adventures of a Red Cloud kelpie, a breed of Australian sheepdog. Red Dog "isn't just any old dog" but a nomadic character who spends his time hitching rides in the outback, traveling wherever he wishes (p. 31). He is not a pet, nor a working dog, but an independent spirit, welcoming food and friendship where he finds it and "happy to have lots of names" (p. 23). A bus driver named John, of the Hammersley Iron Transport section, is "the only person to whom he ever belonged," but because of his tendency to "go bush," Red Dog belongs to everyone and no one (p. 23). In the prologue De Bernières notes that the historical Red Dog was born in 1971 and the stories in the book are based on fact. All the human characters, except John, are inventions. Red Dog's famous walkabouts in and around the town of Dampier demonstrate his hardy spirit of adventure, which is admired and celebrated by the miners and truckers who befriend him.

Interviewed in the *Age* (Melbourne), De Bernières noted that until he encountered the facts about Red Dog he had "always had it in mind to write a children's book but I'd never had a decent story before" (Wyndham, 2001). The book's most notable quality is the evocation of the Australian landscape, an aspect praised by reviewers who drew attention to De Bernières' ability to "make the outback sing" (*Observer,* 2001). Likewise, Sandra Howard in the *Spectator* praised the book's brilliant evocation of "the red heat of Australian summer"(2001). But Paul Bravmann, in the *New York Times* (2001), felt that "unlike De Bernières's previous work, *Red Dog* is terribly thin, suitable only for uncritical Australophiles and dog lovers, or as bedtime stories en route to an unruffled sleep."

BIRDS WITHOUT WINGS *(2004)*

Essentially the story of the disappearance of a small, multicultural community, *Birds Without Wings* is set against the background of the collapsing Ottoman Empire, the First World War, and the subsequent conflict between the Greeks and the Turks that led to the emergence of Turkey as a nation-state. At the heart of the story is Eskibahçe, a small town within the Ottoman Empire inhabited by Christians and Muslims who both speak only Turkish but write it in Greek script. Their fusion of cultures and religions is emphasized at the outset of the novel where the birth of a girl, Philothei, to a Christian family is celebrated with rituals from both religions. Before labor, her mother Polyxeni eats paper inscribed by the imam with verses from the Koran, provided by his wife Ayse and believed to ensure an easy birth. Philothei is loved throughout her life by the Muslim boy Ibrahim, who devotedly follows the beautiful little girl everywhere. Despite the differing religions of the young people, the prospect of their marriage is happily accepted by the community as inevitable.

But like so much in Eskibahçe, such inevitabilities are shattered by the larger events of history. As Iskander the Potter, one of the novel's many narrative voices, notes in the opening sentence, few understand why it is that Ibrahim went mad. Ibrahim's story remains a thumbnail sketch in this multivocal historical novel. As the novel slowly elaborates the cause of Ibrahim's madness, Iskander ascribes this, and many of the terrible human events that beset his community, to the actions of "the great world" (p. 3). The destruction of Eskibahçe through war, and the eventual deportation of the Christians in the community to Greece, is interspersed with twenty-two short chapters, all written in the present tense, that plot the rise to political power of Mustafa Kemal, later called Atatürk, the creator of Turkey as a nation.

In contrast, the story of the people of Eskibahçe is told, quite deliberately, in the past tense. The symbolic weight of the narrative, of human beings as birds without wings, is taken by a group of young Christian and Muslim friends: Ibrahim, Philothei, her best friend Drosoula, Philothei's brother Nico, and his best friend Abdul, son of Iskander the Potter. Abdul and Nico are known to all by their nicknames, Karatavuk and Mehmetçik, the blackbird and the robin, which derive from the clay bird whistles Iskander makes for them as children. Their lifelong friendship, like the love affair between Philothei and Ibrahim, is also disrupted by the war. Karatavuk is sent to face the horror of the conflict at Gallipoli against the Franks, but Mehmetçik cannot defend his homeland because he is now seen as an enemy Christian. Ibrahim, the joyful boy who could imitate the characteristic bleats of his goats, is mentally destroyed as he is forced to participate in the atrocities of war. The forced removal of the Christians from Eskibahçe is a chaotic and tragic day. Philothei, pursued by Ibrahim, falls from a cliff to her death. Drosoula and her lover Gerasimos witness her fall as they prepare to escape the forced march by leaving by boat for the island of Cephallonia. In the character of Drosoula, De Bernières presents a typical intertextual link between his novels. She is the mother of the Greek fisherman Mandras in *Captain Corelli's Mandolin,* but in *Birds Without Wings* the reader encounters Drosoula in the first-person narrative of an exiled old woman who still dreams in her Turkish mother tongue.

Although life in Eskibahçe is by no means utopian, relations among the townsfolk demonstrate both the tenderness and limitations of human community. In the novel, De Bernières stresses that such personal bonds are eroded by ideologies. At a significant moment in the novel, the wealthy merchant of Eskibahçe, Rustem Bey, travels to multicultural Istanbul in search of a Circassian mistress. He encounters Jewish, Italian, Greek, French, and Bedouin traders, and the cultural complexity of the city is set against the grand narratives developing in his lifetime that would divide people according to their religion and race. Rustem Bey finally learns that his mistress, Leyla Hanim, the woman he believes to be Circassian, is herself a Greek.

Appearing in print a full ten years after *Captain Corelli's Mandolin, Birds Without Wings* was eagerly anticipated by the public and critics alike. Before publication the *Guardian*feted the novel as promising an epic akin to Tolstoy's *War and Peace,* but the subsequent critical response registered some disappointment. The reviews are worth noting in some detail as they represent a distinct shift in the appraisal of De Bernières' work. The description of the conflict at Gallipoli was seen by many reviewers as what Amy Kroin described as the novel's "most illuminating section" (*New York Times,* 2004). But the critical consensus was articulated by Nicholas Gage, who argued that despite "several brilliant set pieces," the novel does "not hang together well enough to be the master work the author intended" (*Washington Post,* 2004). Reviewers also noted the similarity of Eskibahçe to the small Cephallonian community in the previous novel and criticized the opportunistic repetition of a recognizably winning formula: a small town, chiming with goat bells and scents of rosemary, torn apart by war. Michael Cain, writing in the *Times Literary Supplement,* described *Birds Without Wings* as "Louis de Bernières's most serious and ambitious achievement to date" but argued that the novel is "wearyingly symbolic" and has "something polemic about it" (2004). He suggested that only a few characters "survive the eloquently clashing rocks of impassioned history lessons and the sentimental symbolism." Christopher Tayler, of the *London Review of Books,* concurred. He complained that "mini-lectures stud the narrative" (2004). Both Cain and Tayler echoed earlier criticism of De Bernières' radio play and his South American trilogy in their comments on his lasting tendency to create one-dimensional figures with names such as Iskander the Potter, Levon the Sly, and Yusuf the Tall. Tayler criticized the novel's reduction of the Turk to a liberal in "curly slippers . . . at heart a decent chap, often hard to distinguish from a certain kind of Englishman."

CONCLUSION

De Bernières has developed a distinctive form of storytelling, involving marginal communities set on large historical stages in a number of geographical and cultural locations. Overall this has ensured both popular and critical acclaim and made De Bernières a notable presence within contemporary British writing. His writing has not always avoided criticism, however, as regards his chosen approach toward cultural and historical subject matter. In an interview given shortly before the publication of *Birds Without Wings*, De Bernières briefly sketched the plans for his next project. He described it as a "big book," again in the historical vein but set closer to his home. It will begin in 1892 and end around 1990, with the first third set in Britain (*Bedell*, June 20, 2004).

Selected Bibliography

WORKS OF LOUIS DE BERNIÈRES

NOVELS

The War of Don Emmanuel's Nether Parts. London: Secker & Warburg, 1990; New York: Morrow, 1991.

Señor Vivo and the Coca Lord. London: Secker & Warburg, 1991; New York: Morrow, 1991.

The Troublesome Offspring of Cardinal Guzman. London: Secker & Warburg, 1992; New York: Morrow, 1994.

Captain Corelli's Mandolin. London: Secker & Warburg, 1994. Published in the United States as *Corelli's Mandolin.* New York: Pantheon, 1994.

Birds Without Wings. London: Secker & Warburg, 2004; New York: Knopf, 2004.

SHORT STORIES AND NOVELLAS

"The Brass Bar." *Granta* 43:23–31 (spring 1993).

Labels. Illustrated by Christopher Wormald. London: One Horse Press, 1993. (A novella that originally appeared in a limited edition of 2,000 numbered and signed copies. Republished by One Horse Press in 1997).

"The Death of Miss Agatha Feakes." In *Shorts: New Writing from Granta Books.* London: Granta, 1998.

"Feathers in Our Knickers." In *Does the Sun Rise Over Dagenham? and Other Stories: New Writing from London.* Foreword by Mark Lawson. London: Fourth Estate, 1998.

"Our Lady of Beauty." *Paris Review,* fall 1998, pp. 67–79.

"A Conditional Being." *Sunday Telegraph,* 1999.

A Day Out for Mehmet Erbil. Illustrated by Eileen Hogan. London: Belmont Press, 1999.

"*The Turks Are So Wonderful with Children.*" *Guardian,* 2000.

Günter Weber's Confession. London: Tartarus, 2001. (Published in a limited edition of 350 copies. This short work forms a sequel or additional chapter to *Captain Corelli's Mandolin* in which the German officer Günter Weber returns to Dr. Iannis' house after the massacre of the Italian soldiers on Cephallonia.)

Red Dog. Illustrated by Alan Baker. London: Secker & Warburg, 2001; New York: Pantheon, 2001.

A Night Off for Prudente de Moraes. (A short story published in a limited edition on May 28, 2004 by Hay Festival Press).

PLAYS AND PRODUCED SCRIPTS

Sunday Morning at the Centre of the World. (Commissioned by the BBC and first broadcast on BBC Radio 4 in 1998. Performed at the Dylan Thomas Centre, Swansea, Wales in 1999 and 2000.) Published as *Sunday Morning at the Centre of The World: A Play for Voices.* London: Vintage, 2001.

A Mad British Pervert Has a Sexual Fantasy About the 10th Street Bridge in Calgary. Canadian Broadcasting Corporation, 1996.

OTHER WORKS

Introduction to *Philosopher or Dog?* by Joachim Machado de Assis. Translated by Clotilde Wilson. London: Bloomsbury, 1997.

Introduction to *The Book of Job: Authorised King James Version.* Pocket Canon Series. Edinburgh: Canongate, 1998; New York: Grove, 1999.

Introduction to *Bricks Without Mortar: A Selection of Poems from Hartley Coleridge.* Edited by Lisa Gee. London: Picador, 2000.

CRITICAL STUDIES

McDermott, Emily A. "Every Man's an Odysseus: An Analysis of the Nostos Theme in *Corelli's Mandolin.*" *Classical and Modern Literature: A Quarterly* 20, no. 2:21–37 (winter 2000).

Reynolds, Margaret, and Johnathan Noakes. *Louis de Bernières: The Essential Guide, Vintage Living Texts Essential Guide to Contemporary Literature.* London: Vintage, 2002. (Contains an interview with De Bernières and reading guides for *Captain Corelli's Mandolin, The War of Don Emmanuel's Nether Parts, Señor Vivo and the Coca Lord,* and *The Troublesome Offspring of Cardinal Guzman,* as well as a few excerpts from newspaper reviews and a glossary of literary terms used in the text).

Sheppard, Richard. "Savagery, Salvage, Salves, and Salvation: The Historico–Theological Debate of *Captain Corelli's Mandolin.*" *Journal of European Studies* 32:51–61 (March 2002).

Talmor, Sascha. "An Englishman in Latin America: *The War of Don Emmanuel's Nether Parts* by Louis de Bernières." *History of European Ideas* 17:73–94 (January 1993).

LOUIS DE BERNIÈRES

REVIEWS

Arroyo, Jose. "Paradise Lust." *Sight and Sound* 2, no. 5:16–18 (May 2001).

Bravmann, Paul. "Red Dog." *New York Times,* October 7, 2001.

Cain, Michael. "Why Ibrahim Went Mad." *Times Literary Supplement,* July 9, 2004.

Farrell, Nicholas. "False Note on Il Duce." *Spectator,* March 27, 1999, pp. 20–21.

Flett, Kathryn. "Traveller's Tail." *Observer,* September 30, 2001.

Gage, Nicholas. "Of Love and War." *Washington Post,* October 17, 2004, p. T06.

Gibbons, Fiachra. "Taking Sting out of Captain Corelli." *Guardian,* April 20, 2001.

Grant, Richard. "Players in a Theater of War." *Washington Post,* September 18, 1994, p. WBK6.

Henneberger, Melinda. "Corelli's Greek Isle Feels Burned and Bewildered by Instant Celebrity." *New York Times,* August 21, 2001.

Holland, Tom. "Best-Seller." *New Statesman,* December 4, 1998.

Howard, Sandra. "Dog Days in the Boondocks." *Spectator,* October 13, 2001.

"In Brief: De Bernières Admits Corelli Film Disappointment." *Guardian,* August 23, 2002.

Jackson, Harold. "Listening Brief: *Sunday Morning at the Centre of the World,* BBC Radio 4." *Guardian,* March 22, 1999.

Karpf, Anne. "Teeming with Warmth, but a Flat and Homogenising Effect: *Sunday Morning at the Centre of the World,* BBC Radio 4." *Guardian,* March 24, 1999.

Kroin, Amy. "The Winds of War." *New York Times,* October 31, 2004, p. 22.

Lowell, Susan. " *The War of Don Emmanuel's Nether Parts.* " *New York Times,* March 1, 1992, p. BK11.

Milne, Seumas. "Communists Go to War with Captain Corelli." *Guardian,* July 30, 1999.

———. "Novel Damned by Captain Corelli's Model." *Guardian,* July 29, 2000.

———. "Greek Myth." *Guardian,* July 29, 2000.

———. "Corelli's Curiosity." *Guardian,* April 25, 2001.

Polk, James. "Between Pathos and Slapstick." *Washington Post,* February 2, 1992, p. WBK1.

———. "In the Mold of García Márquez: Dark Magic from South America's Mystical Minefield." *Washington Post,* August 17, 1992, p. D2.

Smith, David. "The Nation's Love Affair with Stories of Childhood (The Big Read Top 21 Revealed: Britain's Favourite Novels—As Voted by the Public—and Their Celebrity Supporters)." *Observer,* October 19, 2003.

Tayler, Christopher. "But Little Bequalmed." *London Review of Books,* August 26, 2004.

Whitehouse, Anne. "Señor Vivo and the Coca Lord." *New York Times,* September 13, 1992, p. 24.

Willan, Philip. "The Real Captain Corelli." *Guardian,* April 11, 2001.

Yardley, Jonathan. "War: The Reality That Defies Fiction." *Washington Post,* August 17, 1992, p. D2.

INTERVIEWS

Bedell, Geraldine. "I Know I'm Not Tolstoy, but I Try." *Observer,* June 20, 2004.

De Bertodano, Helena. "The Real Captain Corelli." *Daily Telegraph,* September 14, 1996.

Gerrard, Nicci. "A Soldier and His Musical Instruments." *Observer,* April 3, 1994.

Reynolds, Margaret, and Johnathan Noakes. "Interview with Louis De Bernières." In their *Louis de Bernières: The Essential Guide, Vintage Living Texts Essential Guide to Contemporary Literature.* London: Vintage, 2002.

Wyndham, Susan. "From the Red Heart." *Age,* October 20, 2001.

FILMS AND TEXTS BASED ON THE WORKS OF LOUIS DE BERNIÈRES

Captain Corelli's Mandolin. Screenplay by Shawn Slovo. Directed by John Madden, 2001.

Clark, Steve. *Captain Corelli's Mandolin: The Illustrated Film Companion.* Introduction by De Bernières. London: Headline, 2001.

Harris, Andy. *Captain Corelli's Island: Cephallonia.* Photographs by Terry Harris. London: Pavilion, 1999.

Slovo, Shawn. *Captain Corelli's Mandolin: Screenplay.* London: Vintage, 2001.

G. F. DUTTON

(1924—)

Gerry Cambridge

G. F. DUTTON—NOT to be mistaken for his Australian namesake, Geoffrey Dutton (1922–1998), the poet and publisher—is a modern Anglo-Scottish polymath who, in a long life, has achieved distinction in several fields. While the Scottish poet Hugh MacDiarmid in his proselytizing way advocated that poets integrate science with poetry, Dutton is the real thing, an experimental researcher of international reputation in biochemistry who, like the late Miroslav Holub, the Czech immunologist with whom he has been compared, belongs in the rare category of genuine scientist-poets. Dutton is renowned also in horticultural circles for what he has called his "ecological dialogue" with the "marginal garden" he has guided for almost a half-century around his exposed mountainside house in Scotland. In addition he has practiced mountaineering and "wild water swimming," unusually energetic activities for a Scottish literary figure. These diverse aspects of his life manifest themselves markedly in Dutton's work as a poet of singular and individual achievement. The verse forms an examination of whatever binds all these together in his own life and in our present culture of city and countryside. He has called his life an exploration of the reality of metaphor.

LIFE

Geoffrey John Fraser Dutton—"G. F" for literary work, "G. J." for scientific papers, "G. J. F." for horticultural, forestry, and similar writings, and "Geoffrey Fraser Dutton" for his book on wild-water swimming—was born in the Cheshire town of Chester, England, within its Roman walls, on December 30, 1924. Chester was then a quiet administrative and agricultural center of forty thousand people, two miles from what is now the Welsh border. Dutton was an only child. His father, Norman Nicholas Dutton, of a very old Cheshire family, was a native of Chester and a well-known pharmacist (which perhaps explains the poet's early aptitude for things experimental). His mother, connecting him significantly to his "Scottishness," was Jean Stevenson Simpson, a native of Melrose in Scotland. Through her and her mother—Dutton's Scottish maternal grandparents had recently moved south to Cheshire—the boy was nurtured in the songs, ballads and stories of what he calls "the local Scottish diaspora," a socially active and commercially influential group. This connected in turn to "a host of relations throughout the Scottish Border," of whom Dutton later observed: "all seemed on a different plane to the Cheshire relatives and more in my line of being," though he eventually, with no ill-feeling, lost touch with both lines. As early as the age of five the poet-to-be discovered, on family excursions into the Welsh hills, a passion for wild country and open spaces that would illuminate the rest of his life.

Dutton seemed to be a headstrong youngster of obvious intelligence. After attending what he called, in an unpublished autobiographical account, "a pretty dreadful local preparatory school," he gained a scholarship to the King's School in Chester, founded in 1541. In its library he could investigate freely: "it laid out, unassumingly, one single culture from a plurality of approaches," as he later noted—a lesson the poet would bring forward into his own life, in which he claimed to see a continuous spectrum of experience running through art and science.

Dutton's relationship with his father seems to have been unaffectedly straightforward. That with his mother appears to have been more problematic. Efficiently setting up a shop that sold tobacco and fancy goods, she could display stark switches of mood, obviously alcohol-induced; her son would later consider them almost a form of possession. Otherwise, she was a delight to the little boy, the object of her intense affection. Dutton would later consider the experience as influencing much of what he wrote. His mother now seems to him emblematic of the spirit of Scotland in her disconcerting duality, one not uncommon in the Scottish psyche as evidenced by such works in the nation's literature as James Hogg's *Private Memoirs and Confessions of a Justified Sinner* (1824) and Robert Louis Stevenson's *The Strange Case of Dr. Jekyll and Mr. Hyde* (1886). One might suggest that Dutton's involvement in experimental science and its intellectual clarities, the appeal that the natural world's saving indifference has for him, and the compassionate distancing in much of his verse was enhanced by this childhood experience.

Despite it, much else was happening. He discovered the pleasures of swimming, scrambling, rowing, and cycling, awakening "the physical intimacy with those other natural forces which has so enriched my life," and later likening such initial explorations to the excitement of "the first line of an unexpected poem." Further, when Dutton was in his mid-teens, the Second World War broke out. He joined the AFS, the fire service, as a cycle-messenger through the raids. Its camaraderie introduced him to a new and different social reality—a useful lesson. He would remain, throughout his life, open to such initiations—later, most notably, in mountaineering. Meanwhile, a gifted student, he sailed through his exams and, flummoxing the expectations of his school that he would choose Oxford or Cambridge on a scholarship—"I had had enough," he later wrote, "of Gothic quadrangles and clerical kneebreeches and the suffocating English gentility within mediaeval walls"—he opted for Edinburgh, following his Scottish bent. Accepted, he nonetheless stayed at school to take further exams, but in winter 1942 decided, with uncharacteristic impetuosity—and maybe because his mother was by then suffering a terminal illness—to join the army. He was selected for officer training at Manchester University and then in various parts of Scotland and England. During

this, his mother died one night in late 1943, when Dutton was en route by crowded train to cadet barracks in the Scottish border town of Lanark. She was only fifty-two years old. In an unpublished autobiographical account produced in response to the present writer's request for biographical information, he wrote this:

> I went to the corridor window and gazed out at a moonlit Scotland I had not seen since the War began. On either side, processing past, were huge rounded hills, welcoming and mammary, whitened increasingly with early snow. They ushered in, if you like, a Revelation. I was alone with my maternal Scotland. The rest of it died that night.

If, originally, he had joined up partly to escape the turmoil and confusion caused by his mother's illness, then by late 1944, with the war apparently ending in Europe and rumors of posting to the Indian Army, he looked for a way to reenlist in his scientific field, where he could be of greater use. Eventually, demobilized in 1945, though still part of the Civil War Reserve—liable to recall if required—he resumed his early Edinburgh plans.

Dutton's years as an undergraduate at Edinburgh were notable not only for his B.S. with honors in biochemistry in 1949 but for his experiencing the vibrant renascence of Scottish art, letters, and the separatist politics of that time. Always keen to cover his "spectrum," he climbed in Scotland and abroad with the university mountaineering club and the Junior Mountaineering Club of Scotland, with its motley collection of eccentrics and individualists. Many would later feature as characters in his celebrated mountaineering tales collected as *The Complete Doctor Stories* (1997). After having graduated, Dutton was offered a temporary teaching postition in Edinburgh's then-prestigious Department of Biochemistry for three years, "theoretically," as he put it, "under part-time supervision for a Ph.D, but practically on my own." He was awarded a full-time personal grant by the Medical Research Council when his Ph.D. funding expired and earned his Ph.D., with the Gunning Prize, in 1954 at the age of thirty. The minutiae of Dutton's scientific career are beyond the scope of this overview, but his research proved groundbreaking, discovering a molecular mechanism, as he has written, "concerned with transport of biologically powerful molecules such as hormones . . . about the body to their target organs or for their eventual safe excretion; and for targetting 'foreign,' often carcinogenic, molecules absorbed from the surrounding industrial and biological environment, rendering them harmless and ushering them out similarly." The work was socially important in that this mechanism was found to be rudimentary or absent in babies and the late fetus, increasing the risk of their contamination by pollutants and other substances, including numerous drugs previously considered safe. Offered fellowships and jobs in the United States and London, to the consternation of international colleagues he applied for a tenured lectureship at Queen's College in Dundee, then a part of St. Andrews University. It was a typically canny decision: with his research prowess he could obtain grants wherever he worked, but importantly for him, Dundee, on the Tay Estuary of Scotland's east coast, was a center of a local urban and rural folk art revival and also gave easy access to the wild hinterlands that already formed such a substantial part of his life and early poetry. He bought a cheap two-room factory-side tenement flat in the city in 1954 and, as he had since 1945, continued to spend most weekends on the hills after each workaholic week of rigorous research.

In 1957 he married Elizabeth Caird at her small isolated church in the Perthshire Glens. She was a local veterinarian then working at the Dundee Medical School. Like Dutton's mother, his wife is of long Scottish descent and can be thought of again as a symbol of his enduring need for spiritual connection with that country. The marriage has been most happy.

The following twenty-five years—Dutton retired officially in 1983—saw his life, career, and art blossoming. In 1959 his wife, after the birth of their first child, Alasdair, gave up her job and went to live in a cottage previously rented by her family in Perthshire's then remote Glen Shee, with Dutton joining them on weekends. When the couple found a site ideal for them lower down that same glen, just at the tree line, they were virtually given several rocky acres from a like-minded local family and designed a simple house built from British Columbian red cedar by a local Polish ex-serviceman (its roof was still sound in 2004). Dutton then began the planting of the sheltering "marginal garden" that would achieve celebrity in gardening circles, as proved by the reception of his horticultural volume *Some Branch Against the Sky* (1997). Here, another son, Rory, and a daughter, Kirsty, were born in 1961 and 1962 respectively.

Meanwhile his literary presence also began to be established. In 1972 Dutton published his book *Swimming Free: On and Below the Surface of Lake, River, and Sea,* which details his experiences as a wild-water swimmer since the 1950s. At about this time he met the Anglo-American poet Anne Stevenson, writer-in-residence at Dundee University between 1972 and 1975. She became a considerable advocate of Dutton's sparse minimalist poetry and encouraged him to publish it in numerous periodicals. Although familiar with the Edinburgh literary scene at the time, the poet avoided being drawn toward a conventional literary career: he had no desire for "celebrity," having already experienced the distractions of this, after a fashion, in his scientific career. After initial public readings in the 1970s he largely discontinued them, finding them a temptation to the composing of easy, audience-pleasing rhetoric. Despite his lack of public profile—surprisingly, even a Scottish literary reference book such as *The Mainstream Companion to Scottish Literature,* published in 1993, omits him—his work has been greatly admired. His first two full collections of verse received Scottish Arts Council Literary Prizes, and both his third book, *The Concrete Garden* (1991), and his 2002 volume *The Bare Abundance* received Poetry Book Society recommendations from London's Poetry Society.

His scientific distinctions, meanwhile, were numerous. He was awarded a doctorate of science from Dundee in 1968 and elected a fellow of the Royal Society of Edinburgh in 1973. Given the chair in pharmacological biochemistry at Dundee University in 1976 (his early work there helped make Dundee University an international center for such research), he published over 100 scientific papers and traveled the world lecturing and discussing at scientific conferences as well as hosting numerous eminent scientists: he would later note that his wife had "baked bread for more than one Nobel Laureate" in his modest Perthshire house. Awarded honorary doctorates from universities in France, Finland, and Scotland, in 1983, however, he retired, partly to allow tenure to young outstanding researchers in his department. He moved to Perthshire, busy with writing, publishing, "being," and tree planting: by the 1990s the original landowner had allowed the Duttons to increase their land to some nine acres—a dramatically diverse landscape including crags, caves, and mountain river—its only access still a narrow rocky footpath. Later visitors to his home would find the poet and his wife living frugally though fully, book-, tape- and record-surrounded among the marginal garden they have created, without TV and with only a small radio. Dutton is characteristically individualistic concerning these examples of the modern media, dismissing them as existing primarily to earn their perpetrators profit and disliking having his own schedule dictated by theirs.

Some writers show little apparent relationship between their everyday lives and their art. Wallace Stevens, an insurance executive by day and a poet writing elaborate philosophical verse by night, would be an obvious example. G. F. Dutton, by contrast, belongs with those writers who display little disjunction between their lived life and their writing.

THE EXPLORATORY PROSE: SWIMMING FREE AND HARVESTING THE EDGE

An engaging stylist, Dutton writes documentary prose that significantly provides a context for his verse. *Swimming Free: On and Below the Surface of Lake, River and Sea* was published in 1972, five years before his first pamphlet of poetry is absorbing and at times rather droll account of "wild-water swimming" with only mask, snorkel, and flippers—to which he added latterly a neoprene wetsuit—in various locations around Britain, mainly in Scotland, and worldwide. He details sometimes forensically the effect of the underwater environment: his accounts of swim-

ming in lochs and the sea are especially engaging; rivers prove to be less amenable to his explorations. *Swimming Free* is less an instructional book than a pleasingly idiosyncratic memoir and spiritual investigation of how, "when one is easy in the water," the "curious exaltation" one experiences "can be likened to the effect of great mountains, or music or verse, or religious revelation." (p. 9) It is clear that for Dutton swimming in such environments was a physical version of his experiences in writing poetry. The various accounts are buttressed by the clarity of his description and talent for metaphor. Here he describes swimming above a sandy seabed:

> Nearer shore, in schools of sand ghosts, black-eyed and invisible, shrimps and prawns flick and scatter, burrow and stare at you, crowding in behind as you pass, like the shades peering at Orpheus; and there are colonies of worms and molluscs, with small feathery feelers or mouths, tubed and fanned, pushed brazenly or hopefully above the sand; as you approach, waves of retraction precede you.
>
> (p. 23)

While *Swimming Free* charts Dutton's submarine explorations, *harvesting the edge: some personal explorations from a marginal garden* (1994), is a meditative essay eighty-seven pages long about Dutton's hillside "garden," now almost fifty years old. The book interlinks autobiography, practical plant lore, general observations on the creatures inhabiting the area, and philosophical asides. It is loosely based on the seasonal round, and intersperses poems among the prose, less illustrative than impressionist. Whereas Dutton's *Some Branch Against the Sky: Gardening in the Wild* (1997) is a specialist horticultural text widely admired in gardening circles, outside the scope of this overview, *harvesting the edge* is a literary work in that one does not require specialist knowledge to appreciate it. Intrinsically interesting for its individuality of style, it also helps—like *Swimming Free*—to provide a context for his verse. As ever, Dutton stresses connections between verse and his other activities:

> I could . . . argue that making this garden is writing a poem, and walking the paths, reading it. And like

a poem, only partly composed by oneself . . .

(p. 81)

Dutton frequently emphasizes this importance of inspiration beyond the conscious control of the poet in the composition of a poem. It is a measure of his artistic modesty.

The book also contains numerous mordant asides and witty mini-essays embedded in the main text. Discussing idiosyncratic voles, for instance, who have begun a habit of stacking the buds of a particular flower "at burrow entrances for neighbours to admire," the author continues:

> Some local entrepreneur is responsible; his companions become addicted; bereaved stems sob helplessly around them. If I trap the activists at once, the habit does not spread, and vole tradition is spared that particularly self-destructive individual talent.

(p. 46)

This is the paced and measured prose of a poet, as for example in the three successive and logically unfolding clauses of the first sentence quoted, disciplined by their semicolons; unexpected but apt adjectives and verbs—"bereaved" and "sob," for instance—further enliven the writing. For good measure, Dutton finishes with a witty allusion to T. S. Eliot's essay "Tradition and the Individual Talent"—the voles too, extending Dutton's metaphor of gardening as a form of poetry, are involved in their own variety of literary criticism.

THE COMPLETE DOCTOR STORIES: THE RIDICULOUS MOUNTAINS *AND* NOTHING SO SIMPLE AS CLIMBING

Gathered together in a single volume of forty-one stories in 1997, *The Complete Doctor Stories* were originally issued in two individual volumes in 1984 and 1993 respectively. They allow free reign to the drollery present as a sparkle elsewhere in Dutton's prose. Richly anecdotal, the stories are based upon his mountaineering experiences over decades, beginning around 1945. They detail in a variety of adventures what Dutton has called the "hilariously disputatious clanjamf-rie"—a "clanjamfrie" being a motley gathering—primarily of the Scottish mountaineering community. The tales feature three main characters: the Doctor, a general practitioner of considerable vintage and wide climbing experience, given to insouciant understatement, inhuman enthusiasm, and relentless and comic optimism; the relatively modest, unassuming, and unextravagant narrator; and the ironically called Apprentice, a skilled, sardonic, and youthful climber. The stories contain some specialist references but are generally lucid enough to nonspecialists. A great deal of the stories' amusement—they are at times laugh-out-loud hilarious—comes from the dynamic between the three main characters. The Doctor is an extravagant overreacher somewhat in the manner of, for example, the character Meserve in Robert Frost's narrative poem "Snow." He is forever proposing new adventures, modestly presented, to his suspicious but perennially gullible climbing companions. The humor in the stories is knockabout and slapstick, wonderfully conveyed by Dutton's tongue-in-cheek understatement, which ironically counterpoints the sheer exaggeration of the action and characters. The three go skiing or potholing—cave exploration which may involve climbing or swimming; they are plagued by flies or, those horrors of the Scottish Highlands, midges; they plan sorties from "Daddy Mackay's," an Edinburgh bar. This was in fact Milne's Bar in Hanover Street, Edinburgh—the renowned poet's pub where, as well as meeting Hugh MacDiarmid, Norman MacCaig, Sydney Goodsir Smith, George Mackay Brown, and other Scottish poets in the 1950s, Dutton also caroused with a variety of mountaineering characters and other practical types. They were "overflowing," as he wrote in a letter, "with wit and practical knowledge of people and places out to the far stony limits of the country." *The Complete Doctor Stories* adds another facet to Dutton's oeuvre, a frank exuberance he has largely kept out of his verse. They contradict the simplistic presumption by some reviewers that the bareness of tone in the poetry passively reflects the author's personality rather than being part of a deliberated aesthetic.

G. F. DUTTON

DUTTON AS POET: AN OVERVIEW

The first thing the reader new to Dutton's poetry will note is the idiosyncrasy of his style. He is a minimalist—most of his poems are less than a page long, and frequently half a page—and characteristically writes in a methodical free verse that often employs rhyme and meter for sonal and conceptual emphasis. The movement of his poems, with their enjambments and at times uneven line lengths, seems in fact the lineal equivalent of a mountaineer's questing ascent of a cliff face to a—hopefully—revelatory conclusion. Typographically, if a poem doesn't capitalize initial letters in sentences, the poet intends this to indicate a monotonal, "flat" delivery when the poem is read out loud; more conventional punctuation indicates natural speech. Dutton also has a tendency to begin a poem unexpectedly; the reader can be left searching for context another poet would supply. This increases the compression of the verse, though it also gives the work on occasion a gnomic, riddling quality.

The second main thing is his subject matter. The reader will find here no intimate revelations about the poet's private life, nothing chatty, anecdotal, or conventionally humorous (Dutton reserves his considerable humor for his prose). As he has written in an unpublished overview of his poetic intentions:

> Wholly subjective, "confessional" poems, currently popular, I find too limited an exploration: other influences visit us besides that of obsessive self-regard—animal, mineral and vegetable, not to mention what we call spiritual—enlarging, not diminishing, the spread of our humanity.

In a personality-obsessed culture some critics have felt this absence as a lack; the work, however, reflects what Dutton has called "the passionate austerities" of Scotland, and predominantly a winter or autumn Scotland at that. It is seldom bountiful summer in a Dutton poem. He is a poet who finds abundance in bareness; many of the poems celebrate it. Also, while some individual poems stand out, the effect of his work is cumulative; in many respects, to expect what Ted Hughes called, in his early poem "Famous

Poet," the "old heroic bang" from a Dutton poem is to assume an impulse for bravura performance that the poet has no interest in. He has stated that the verse is written primarily as a form of spiritual exploration for himself; on occasion his poems explicitly criticize the principle of competition of which, perhaps, the notion of overt displays of verbal fireworks forms a part. (It is not surprising, then, that in his musical tastes he dislikes the histrionics of opera, for instance, preferring the bleaker, bare classicism of the Gaelic pipe music known as pibroch, which he himself has played.) In his essay "Mountaineering Poetry: The Metaphorical Imperative," comparing climbing with the writing of poems, he writes:

> There need be no absolute criterion of "greatness" in either climb or verse; the fact of creation, not its degree, is what counts. For both explorations, success has memorialised for you an "epiphany"—one of Pater's "privileged moments of existence."
>
> (p. 2)

Confirming this, the poems tend in tone to be quietly meditative and unshowy.

THE EARLY POETRY

Dutton is a relentless rewriter, and much of his earlier verse has been reworked for the gathering of poems in his fourth volume, *The Bare Abundance: Selected Poems, 1975–2001* (2002). The poet regards its versions as definitive, and it is to this volume that most of this essay's discussion will be devoted. For Dutton's rewrites—unlike those of many poets, of whom John Crowe Ransom provides a most striking example—are frequently textual improvements, therefore tending to make less relevant the previous "draft" (though observing the evolution of a Dutton poem can be intriguing). To an extent, then, the validity of his individual collections *as entities* has been overtaken by the appearance of this *Selected,* which gathers over 60 percent of his collected published work, 112 poems from a total of 172.

Dutton's publishing history, verse-wise, is a relatively sparse one. His first publication of poems, the twenty-page pamphlet *31 Poems,* appeared in 1977 when the poet was fifty-three years old. It was published privately by Anne Stevenson and produced by Neil Astley, who the following year would found Bloodaxe Books, now one of Britain's foremost poetry publishing imprints. (Bloodaxe has since issued all of Dutton's verse with the exception of his first full collection, *Camp One,* published in 1978.) Twenty-two of *31 Poems'* pieces survived into *Camp One;* the remainder Dutton has never republished, perhaps because they didn't fit into a particular ordering. Dutton seldom prints an entirely negligible poem, though possibly because some of his poems give up their meanings gradually, and may never be entirely paraphrasable, it can be difficult at initial readings to distinguish his "successes" from his "failures." Among the more unusual pieces uncollected after *31 Poems* is "daughter of the house," a poem of overt praise, rare in Dutton's oeuvre, addressed to a young island woman. It begins, with a warm irony, "how dare you sit there smiling," as if the narrator is already sufficiently startled by the woman's beauty without the added burden of her expression, and closes:

you sit there smiling, your brow
white as the breakers off Mealasta—
and the land trembles in gratitude.

(p. 12)

Mealasta is a small uninhabited island off the west coast of the Hebridean island of Lewis. In this metaphor, the girl is the sea. That wave-shaken land trembling "with gratitude" can be seen by extension as the narrator in his response to the young woman. It need not be a coincidence that Mealasta is uninhabited. There may too be an ambiguity in "breakers" with what it implies of a happily destructive energy.

Another poem, "interview," has its narrator being queried by an anonymous questioner: "why do you never / write about people, / author?" The two individuals are sitting before a fire. The narrator replies:

because they are
always too near me, close by the window

close by the door
stirring between us
ashes
as if they had just been there.

(p. 19)

Like "daughter of the house," this poem is interesting, if one reads it as a partial explication of Dutton's aesthetic, for its relative rareness in his oeuvre—he seldom justifies his aesthetic practice in his work. Structurally it is bare, containing no adjective to qualify any of the eight nouns in its forty-one words. Its literal meaning is perfectly plain, yet the poem compounds rather than solves an enigma. Who, for example, are these "people," and why do they have this effect on the narrator? One can posit, if one takes the narrative voice to be Dutton's own, that they are dead members of his family, infringing on the present, "stirring between us"—the "us" being either the narrator and his interviewer, or the narrator and these "people"—"ashes": a fitting noun as the two people sit in the poem's present, before a living fire. What is certain is that these shadowy presences affect both the narrator's perception or viewpoint—they are close by the "window"—and his points of exit and entry—they are "close by the door." Meaning tends to be foregrounded in Dutton's work because his poems are never constructed simply as melodious artifacts: structure is subordinated to content, rather than an end in itself. W. H. Auden, in an essay on Robert Frost, and alluding to Shakespeare's last play, *The Tempest,* made the distinction between an "Ariel poem" and a "Prospero poem," a work which is either beautiful, or true, respectively. While there are infinite graduations, of course, between these two extremes, Dutton's work tends toward the latter type.

CAMP ONE

It was with the Edinburgh-published *Camp One,* which appeared the year after *31 Poems,* in 1978, that Dutton established a poetic presence, at least in Scotland. A prefatory note indicates that this gathering of seventy-one poems had been arranged, irrespective of chronology, "with some regard for grouping and progression so that it might be considered as constituting a single poem"—an impulse toward ordering his oeuvre that would return, overtly, with his *Selected Poems*. Among the twenty-eight poems from *Camp One* uncollected in his *Selected* volume, the eight-line "flora" demonstrates the functionality of his aesthetic.

This can be read as a statement of Dutton's poetic as well as a statement about fruit trees. He is a poet who generally, metaphorically speaking, eschews blossom—though he can write with a graceful lyricism when he chooses—in favor of fruit. It is not that he is on the side of the stripping wind but that it can be seen as analogous to his own critical faculty, prizing most that which cannot be scattered and which will feed the future. The lyric register of that "white scattering / stilled at the root" can be seen as mimetic of those "gestures" which the last eleven monosyllabic words of the closing two lines counteracts and grounds. The strong full rhyme between "root" and "fruit" further emphasizes the functionality.

Fifteen of the twenty-eight poems uncollected in the out-of-print *Camp One* Dutton has stated privately are worth preserving though effectively "in limbo." Even to a close reader, the poet's preferences here can seem somewhat subjective. The best of the poems, however, like landscapes lived in over time, gradually reveal their nuances. A piece such as "against the sun," for instance— later collected in *The Bare Abundance*—begins: "a clatter of stained glass." and continues by describing a pheasant taking flight. With the exception of the "window," mentioned in the poem, Dutton seems to address a straightforward account of a hunter shooting—or trying to shoot—a pheasant. The opening metaphor about stained glass, with its religious, church association, is both unexpected and apt, and links to the poem's close. The "clatter" is the sound of the pheasant's wing beating as it erupts, as pheasants do, into flight; the "stained glass" refers to its brilliantly colored feathers. The metaphor can be read as granting the bird an element of sanctity; to extend it, the wood becomes a sort of church. The hunter has "broken a window," with all this implies of a change of perception, either by disturbing the pheasant or by killing it. (It's unclear whether the pheasant dies.) The poem's narrator doesn't moralize, however: to break such a window may be either good or bad, though there is a hint of shame in the hunter when he leaves, not looking upward. The poem's title can be taken either visually or conceptually: if the sun's main effect is creation, the hunter is "against the sun" in shooting or attempting to shoot the pheasant. Bounded by a line at either end about a window being broken, the lines enclosed between them present what the "broken" window reveals. Structurally the poem is mimetic of the jarring of perception that its content enacts. Like many of Dutton's pieces, the poem seems poised delicately between the explicit and the mysterious.

SQUARING THE WAVES

Dutton is a judicious selector of his own work. Thirty-three of the forty-nine poems of *Squaring the Waves* (1986) he later collected and re-ordered in *The Bare Abundance*. Though *Squaring the Waves* began utilizing Dutton's experiences as a wild-water swimmer and mountaineer, the sixteen omitted poems include "trim," ostensibly about the trimming of a birch tree "to make it fit / under your sun, sit / in your hedge, / inhabit / your street" (p. 32) in comparison with the wild tree. Via this metaphor the poem examines the potential for individual violence emanating from repression and categorization of one by another, through a birch trimmed so "it begins to match / how you'd describe it." The verse somewhat negatively compares a gardening procedure with repression, unusual for Dutton in not being in some way about aesthetics. Another poem, "dragon class," is on a related theme, while confirming the maritime note of the volume. The narrator is steering a "dragon class" yacht—sleekly and elegantly designed for speed—"in the garbage of a harbour" before reaching the open sea. The yacht is a symbol of freedom and of the hauteur of something fitted to a wild environment which the narrator has to ease "through the soiled / goodfellowship of farewell" (p. 43). As often with Dutton, the notion of goodfellowship is not without its price, here the harbor garbage, "oildrums," and "black fucoidae"—the latter being seaweeds of the genus Fucus. At times the work manifests a Frostian or Jeffers-reminiscent independence of spirit that can display a certain degree of reductionist impatience. (In a later poem, "Recycling," for instance, he can compare a book of Scottish history to a "shovelful of debris / off the floor / of this particular cage / of Godstained monkeys . . . ." (*The Bare Abundance*, p. 121)

THE CONCRETE GARDEN

That independence is exemplified by "Carmen Mortis," one of the most unusual of the fifteen poems omitted from *The Bare Abundance* out of the fifty-two pieces of *The Concrete Garden* (1991). Here, Death shares his wisdom:

Wha gangs alane,
gangs free.

Wha's for companie,
gangs wi me.

(p. 46)

Dutton has rewritten "alane" as "his lane" since the poem's publication, though this doesn't fundamentally change the meaning; it does, however, provide a gender. Translated from its Scots in this rewritten version, the verse reads: "Who travels by himself, / travels free. // Who seeks out company, / travels with me." It is an engaging mouthful of epigram, though the truth of its central point is debatable. For of course we travel with death—our own—even without the company of others. Yet solitariness is regarded as freedom. To have companions trammels through the possibility of their deaths. The poem is unique in Dutton's oeuvre in being written in Scots.

By the time *The Concrete Garden* was published Dutton's reputation was considerable—though the only reference to Geoffrey Dutton in Ian Hamilton's *Oxford Companion to Twentieth-Century Poetry* (1994) was to Dutton's Australian namesake. Anne Stevenson, however, confirmed her view in a jacket comment that the Anglo-Scottish writer was "one of the finest poets of

our time," and the Scottish poet-critic Robert Crawford called him "a poet of genuine accomplishment."

THE BARE ABUNDANCE

Something of that accomplishment can be seen in Dutton's major collection. It contains 131 poems, 112 of them published in his previous books; 19 are new or previously uncollected. It has a striking cover, combining two NASA photographs: one, that of the earth from space against a black backdrop, bright as a blue-and-white pearl; the other, as a foreground, the surface of the moon. The book is organized in four sections, with the poems ordered as the poet felt appropriate. The scene is set by two prefatory poems, "The Bare Abundance"—a praise poem for "the One Delight," of "some simple bright / coherence," "a reassurance" that reveals Dutton's imagination as fundamentally Platonic—and "The Miraculous Issue." If the first piece is a rare paean, the narrator in the latter poem, by means of a hillside spring, contrasts and reconciles a measurable scientific truth with the equal truth of imagination: the spring's year-round temperature is a steady four degrees Celsius as gauged by a thermometer; its temperature is felt as warmer or cooler to an individual's plunged hand in winter or summer respectively because of the different air temperatures at each season. The poem reconciles science with imagination: only together, Dutton implies, do they constitute the human truth.

The Bare Abundance freshly served to demonstrate Dutton's individuality in contemporary British poetry. He is quite separate from its socio-domestic or political strain as exemplified by Tony Harrison or some of Philip Larkin, and his verse has nothing of the hieratic energies of Ted Hughes or Peter Redgrove. Rhythmically it can bear comparison to the earlier verse of R. S. Thomas, though Dutton is probably closer to American poets—he has a longtime enthusiasm for American poetry—such as Robert Frost and Wallace Stevens, or Robinson Jeffers in the temporal sweep of his work, if lacking Jeffers' preachiness, Freudian cast of mind, sheer textual bulk, or narrative drive. Explicit sexuality is absent; even implicit sexuality is relatively uncommon.

His "Introductory Note" lays out almost programmatically the overlapping boundaries of each of the book's four sections. The opening one, "City: The Grasp of the Hand" celebrates "the struggle in a flux of artifact from prehistory to, one hopes, a tomorrow." Broadly, it considers the development of humanity as a tool-using animal. It opens with "minimal," a bare nine-line verse in three three-line stanzas. The first depicts a fence post that is leaning over in the snow; the second, the narrator who comes to set it upright again with a blow. The first and last stanzas contain the same words as end rhymes; stanza two, rhyming with the stanza on either side, has the effect of emphasizing the flurry of human intervention in this leveling universe, the cost of which is not only "a single blow" but the pristine appearance of the natural scene. If, in Robert Frost's poem "The Wood-pile," the second law of thermodynamics, which predicts the gloomy winding down of everything to a final stasis, is implicitly depicted in its narrator's vision of a frozen woodpile abandoned in the woods, Dutton's poem sparsely celebrates the potential for human action and for setting a boundary, as symbolized by the post. In another Frost poem, "Mending Wall," a boundary becomes a divisive symbol of territory. In Dutton, by contrast, to be able to set boundaries is a frail but valid affirmation against chaos. The linguistic bareness of "minimal" mimics the bareness of the scene. It is a verse designed to give little of that aesthetic pleasure readers may expect if they view contemporary poetry as little more than entertainment. Metrically the first two stanzas employ an anapestic bounce mimetic of the action; the final stanza, in particular its last two lines, which portray the effect and the "cost" of the action, slow everything down. The penultimate line is three syllables, each carrying a strong stress; the last line reverses the poem's predominant anapestic pattern by beginning with a trochee. Rhythmically both lines reinforce their content.

The facing poem, "neolithic," has a Neolithic narrator. He is being watched by animals that are "crossing themselves"—an intriguing phrase in that to "cross yourself" is an informal Catholic term for making the sign of the Cross—though here describing, presumably, how they cross and recross their own tracks as they huddle closer to observe the narrator. He is fashioning

axes arrowheads
   bold succession
   of irreparable windows

(p. 17)

Though in its original form the poem finished with the lines quoted, Dutton added a stanza to the final version, with humans taking "that glittering walk / towards the volcanoes"—a closure implying future or incipient volatility and human violence, a violence found elsewhere in this opening section. That "glitter" is perhaps the broken glass of those "windows." The original closure, however, shows his capacity for memorable phrasemaking within his austere compass. The fashioning of weapons is a form of new vision (those "windows," a metaphor that recurs in several poems) yet also one with its cost, as the qualifier "irreparable," indicating a degree of damage, makes clear. As usual in Dutton, there is a balancing of costs. In a related poem, "Barbarians," set in a Pictish Scotland, the outsider "barbarians," the Picts, narrate their pleasure in the "empire / of grasses and air, far / from the engines of Caesar"; they choose to "follow the wind / with iron" of their own (p. 20). The poem has a relevance that transcends its temporal setting, speaking for an independence of spirit the poet shares. One can read the poem as emblematic too of these elements—wildness versus discipline—in the human psyche, as well as in poetry itself.

If stone as weapon features in "neolithic," it recurs as symbol strongly elsewhere in the first section. In "Angle" a tall ruined corner of masonry found in the wood is "such chiselled power" that the narrator experiences "the dizzying thrill / of Ascendancy" (p. 22) but recognizes, at the poem's closure, that this discovered transience is his and his fellows' too. In "east window," a poem of seven three-line stanzas, Dutton intriguingly figures, in a metaphor that reverses what is implied in "against the sun," the granite of a church as being "every tree / renounced to stone, a / chastity." It is a complex poem resistant to straightforward paraphrase. The church is a renunciation of nature; it is "chaste," pure and nonsexual, and therefore out of the organic order; at night its floor "flowers" not botanically but "with candles," their flames arguably a symbol of the spirit. After a stanza describing the stillness of this forest substitute, with its motionless "granite branches," the poem closes:

> only the sun
> lighting its wheel
> recollects confusion;
>
> it makes a great sky
> that choirs the wall,
> and rising together
>
> glass people
> torture to colour
> stone's lucidity.

> (p. 36)

The sun still possesses the power to "recollect"—a verb that can be read in two senses, of remembering and of regathering—the "confusion" of the organic wood. Shining through a stained-glass window depicting saints, presumably, but more reductively called here "glass people" as if to emphasize their fragile artificiality, it projects their image onto the stone wall. If the stone is "lucid," the "glass people" represent, arguably, in that torturing to color, some of the organic chaos—as well as their own spiritual struggle—the church as a structure has avoided. Its stone is "lucidity," though that comes at the price of never having been alive. The poet seems to take no polarized view of this: "choirs the wall" seems an affirmation, though the use of the verb "torture" is highly ambiguous. It is worth noting that, if the sun is rising, as the poem's title "east window" would imply, then the "glass people" will in fact be sinking together rather than ascending. Their ascension implies that they and the sun in some way "overcome" this paradoxically lucid stone; if they were descending, the implication would be the opposite.

On the page facing "east window," in the eight-line "the high flats at Craigston," another purpose of stone is represented, this time physical shelter against the changing elements. The poem belongs with Dutton's urban verse in a contemporary setting. Built on the outskirts of Dundee, against the backdrop of the Sidlaw Hills, the flats represent the destruction of an established community and its inhabitants' resettlement, a pattern repeated all over urban Scotland. The flats are "rawboned in a raw land"; washed and shadowed by the changing weathers, they are brash by day—like, by implication, their inhabitants—but at night reveal their vulnerability when they "cling together and tremble with light." The poem sets the flats as representative of their inhabitants against the massive backdrop of natural forces in Scotland. The buildings are ultimately frail, gestural defenses against those forces, yet as affirming as the man's setting upright of the fence post in "minimal." The poem is obscurely touching.

Elsewhere, in poems such as "Exact Fare Please," the theme of urban man's activities against the larger natural backdrop is continued. Its title comments sardonically on Scottish buses requiring the "exact fare," for no change is given. One conforms to this, if one is able, for the brief privilege of shelter and transport, but without "the right kind of coin / you have to walk home." The cost of safety or ease is precision and conformity. "Exact fare please" vividly depicts the brash vivacity of urban buses in wild weather, in twenty-four lines; the poem closes, flatly:

> When all are gone the dark and the rain
> move in with their own
> more practised conclusion.

> (p. 41)

Despite all the show and color of the preceding lines, the final word is given to the larger environment; what is now the elements' "more practised conclusion" was, in its first published version, "minor conclusion"—an interesting rewriting that demonstrates Dutton's desire to set the urban scene in its larger and more ancient environment.

Dutton never forgets that larger environment and the temporal change it implies. His poems are constantly underpinned with the awareness of transience. (He was born after all among Roman ruins; he now lives among Scottish ones.) Sometimes, indeed, he celebrates in spite or because of it, as in "bond," a commemoration of an expertly constructed masonry wall. The poem's narrator refuses to regret the wall's eventual demise whether by political upheaval or climate change, implying instead that the important thing is the skill in its making—a celebration of process as much as product which the poet's awareness of change sharpens.

In "stone," meanwhile, he celebrates one of the fundamental building blocks of life as well as of masonry. It begins with the bare, one-word sentence "stone."—a pure noun and verbal representation of the object. The poem's narrator recalls a large example that had to be dug out "years ago" when his house was being built. The stone is left

just where we pass,

grey and silent,
gathering cracks;
eyes, eggs
seething beneath it,

moss and ivy
eager beside it, already
lichen has tried it, it is marked
for life.

(p. 44)

The temporal people pass while the stone remains. There seems an ambiguity in that "just"—with so precise a writer as Dutton one can feel certain that a word is seldom present only as rhythmical "padding." The word can mean "precisely," but it also conjures the notion of the stone sitting in judgment and being "just," that is, fair. It supplies a site for the sheltering and propagation of life in the small creatures below it; lichen has already begun the process of wearing it down; it is "marked / for life" not only in the colloquial meaning of "for the duration of its existence" but in the sense of being "marked out for" life, that is, to help produce it. The poem closes:

I remember it yellow, unblemished,
a growing refusal in the sunlight.
and us kneeling before it
sweating, dismantling its earth.

(p. 44)

Digging out the stone, the narrator and his helpers "kneel" before it in a worshipful attitude nonetheless linked to labor; the stone is yellow, a flower color, and the positive organic adjective accompanying the negative of the stone's "refusal" continues this conceit ironically. The diggers can only dismantle "its earth," not it. It also is possible to read "stone" to some degree as a metaphor for the writing of a poem. In the end, the earth that conceals it is "dismantled," much as finishing a poem may involve discarding irrelevancies.

"Sea: The Pull of the Tide" charts another of Dutton's explorations, to some extent dealing with the wild-water swimming he engaged in between 1950 and the mid-1980s and wrote about in his prose book *Swimming Free*. Dutton's note to the section says that it covers the "physical flux," and a central sequence is "How Calm the Wild Water," a dozen poems of considerable complexity synthesizing Dutton's swimming experiences. There is a sensual and physically implicated note in most of the poems. The sequence begins with "whatever sea," a delineation of the cyclical physical processes that, finally, "will drown you / as if you were glad of it." The poem begins:

call it the blood,
salt in darkness
fathoming bones;
any tide
at any stones.

(p. 60)

It has a ritual tone, repeating three times the invocation (half a suggestion) to "call"—to name or categorize. The first word in each of the first four lines quoted is either a strong stress or begins with one, which helps to emphasize rhythmically the ineluctable physical processes the poem is partly concerned with. There is a deliberate ambiguity in "fathoming," which can mean to "to sink, as under fathoms" but which also conjures a wisp of the verb's British colloquial meaning, "to work out, to understand." The poem has four stanzas. The first three look at this symbolic sea from various angles; among other things, it may be the "ache / to cave hearts," or "the calm glass / behind the eyes, / quietener of ships." At the poem's close the attempt at categorization is abandoned; "whatever sea" it is, whether symbolic or actual, it will drown the reader as if he were "glad" to be drowned.

Another poem in the sequence, "Dive," can be read as continuing Dutton's characteristic analogies between physical activity and the poetic process. It describes how, on the sea floor, "a square / of your own measure,"

will greet you

hug you with rarities,
sandgrain and stone
clutch of white shells. Then
dismiss you again

back to the surface to pour
shell stone and sand
out through your hand
into indifferent water. Nor

anything more. That was your dive.
That was belief.
Being achieved
for the price of a breath.

(p. 65)

The emphasis is again on process rather than the end result: what is important here is "being," not the characteristically poor objects brought back which, on the sea floor, seemed "rarities." The poem explicates, in creativity as in a dive, the element of faith, the "belief" that precedes the activity.

The sequence's final poem, "After the Swim," charts the sense of disorientation experienced by the swimmer—or artist returning from having created something, having been immersed in the creative element—and returning anonymously to the shore and its previously familiar scenes and people. It is, at the poem's close

Time

to pocket stone,

put on boots of iron,
tramp across and join them.

(p. 71)

After the weightlessness of the swimming experience, the swimmer's clothes are heavy: he is returned to the world of gravity, and to the bewilderingly obvious world of the everyday that he has to rejoin. He is the token adventurer, a shaman who returns with his knowledge to his society.

The section finishes with the twelve-line poem "the waves have gone back,"—also its opening line—which Anne Stevenson noted in an essay on Dutton's work was the first poem of his she read that made her believe him to be "a writer of the first order." She speculated that the poem was "about" the Christian day of judgment. It pictures a scene after the retreat of some great incursion of sea, when

even the drowned
do not roll eyeless

about the coast
but assemble, talking dispassionately
in some great gathering ground.
the unborn are not lost.

(p. 72)

It is possible also to read it as a simple affirmation after some great natural disaster, and the paradoxical lines about the "drowned" "talking dispassionately" as an affirmation of faith. Or, by extension, it could be about any situation in which some cathartic event has led to a restoration of equilibrium and a sense of a new beginning with all the optimism such an event engenders. As often the case with Dutton, the literal sense is obvious (though his syntax can frequently be complex); yet the poem harbors an enigma, retaining an irreducible shimmer.

The section "Forest: The Thrust of the Seed" carries a note by Dutton that it "meets the biological flux, our own kin among metropolitan blocks, rocks and asteroids." Much of the section emanates from his work in his marginal garden. Its opening poem, "cutting trail," while ostensibly about cutting a trail "through young pine" is also emblematic of Dutton's own exploration via verse which, as, he wrote in an unpublished essay, "was a conscious avoidance of already-breathed air, the second-hand, the exploited. . . . I tried to exclude from verse all but personal experiences, and what I made of them."

The poem "cutting trail" stands as precursor to what follows. Its narrator is "axeing darkness / here below" on a journey, like the pines, "to the sun." He is, however,

peering ahead
where no one has been,
either side
where no one will go.

(p. 74)

"axeing darkness / here below" is paradoxical in that darkness is a state as well as a substance. The pines, by contrast, don't consider, they are purely instinctive; they climb up "past" the narrator. Meanwhile he is "peering ahead," that is, trying to discern. He is "cutting trail" too through his own unique experience, a pioneer of sorts. Arguably the closure strikes an elegiac note: verse is an exploration limited in linear terms; there are whole areas of consciousness on either side "where no one will go."

Pruning of a more brutal sort features in the poem "Joy," one of three pieces in the section featuring birds. (Another, strategically placed on its facing page, is "against the sun" discussed earlier: the poems present contrasting views.) The narrator of "Joy"—whom Dutton changed from the first-person singular in earlier versions to the third person, as if to further distance himself—recounts how bullfinches, a beautiful British finch, the male of which has a carmine pink breast, visited his "cherry trees / from Japan." The bird is, however, notorious for its pillaging of cherry blossom:

not for food

but for the delight
of ripping them out
and throwing them down, . . .

(p. 102)

Seeing this, the narrator shoots twenty-seven of the birds in a week, because "There was some-thing about them / misusing the sun / for private joy / that offended his sense / of our common inheritance." The "joy" of the poem's title may be taken, as much as the bullfinches' in their apparent vandalism, as that of the narrator in dispatching them. The title is deeply comprehensive. Joy is thought through for its consequences. One creature's joy is another's destruction; the conflict of joys leads to violence and death. The poem finishes:

Twenty-seven bullfinches
In one week of sun. The best,
almost, with that particular gun.

(p. 102)

There are other guns or their equivalents, of course, as well as other equivalents of bullfinches and of this narrator. "Joy" expands from its "particular gun" and situation to a much wider relevance.

While many of the poems in this section are preoccupied with arboriculture and gardening, they can also be read on various levels. In some respects one can make an analogy between Dutton's gardening and ordering against the unpredictable and the poetic tension between craft and inspiration. It is a theme he alludes to in the punningly-titled "Culture" in which "Just to choose / a corner of the wilderness / is to enclose / it with intent." Art is an inevitable ordering, analogous to gardening in that one has to "decide / what wild flower / that once had led you there / is now a weed." Other poems here examine this tension.

One such, the intriguing "Weed Species," looks at

the trees
that grow straight, seed
of knowledge, planted, fed,
tended line by line to be

felled in a gale
of sawdust and petrol

(p. 86)

These trees are compared with the species just over the fence, "strays / swarming with eyes and evasion / pests and diseases." The poet admires the untended birch and aspen across the fence:

they are "wry" and paradoxically described at the poem's close as "Beautiful / weed species," with Dutton's line break emphasizing the paradox. Ostensibly about trees, the poem can also be read as contrasting a cultivated civility with an undisciplined and random beauty, as of a poetry produced by the unpredictabilities of inspiration rather than deliberation, not "tended line by line." The poet, however, draws no explicit moral; he simply presents the situation.

In "pleasaunce," Dutton gives a justification for his work in his garden. Here, hardship and the thrawnness of living things are what keep him engaged:

were it not for the frost,
rocks, teeth, rasping tongue,
the living virulence I live among
I would throw down
spade and pen,
cry off this slapped rump of a mountain.
go back to earnest discussion.
take a room in town.

(p. 96)

Action is a counterpoint to "earnest discussion." The urban—that "room in town"—is seen as a sort of giving up, a failure to meet the realities of marginal living—and gardening—on its own terms. The "living virulence" encourages him rather than the opposite. He retains the discipline needed to control it, in order to produce the exotic flowers that "reward" his "toil / sparsely, . . . lost / in deprecating leaves." Notably Dutton conjoins "spade and pen"; this can be read too as a poem about poetry.

Other poems here also draw analogies from botanical experience. Dutton's fine piece "On Passing," regarding the annual "sky-blue-bloomed" berries of juniper, begins with a relevance to more than berries:

No it is not repeat
repeat, it is once
only and enough.

(p. 110)

The poem's narrator notices the beautiful berries of juniper on their branch in the snow, "their green / one-year-behind // successors crowding about them." The poem is an unusually lyrical one for Dutton, celebrating transience, "The prize the primacy of it," and with a final stanza added from its first appearance in book form, praising

Your own passing and theirs
together, stars
in the eternal glitter.

(pp. 110–111)

It is notable that in Dutton's scheme of things the biological process berries and reader share relates them, beyond hierarchy; the "passing,"—not, noticeably, the mere "being," which would not indicate transitoriness— both of the juniper berries and of one's self are, equally "stars," manifestations of light and energy in darkness—in "the eternal glitter" which is the universe whether created or grandly accidental. And the price of being such "stars" is to be transitory.

"Forest: the Thrust of the Seed" seems to utilize Dutton's insights as marginal gardener. The book's closing section, "Rock: Facing up to the Stars," foregrounds his experience as a mountaineer. It begins with two poems, "fault," and "of only a single poem," which celebrate through a mountaineering metaphor the pioneering exploratory spirit, a celebration confirmed by later poems in the sequence. As often the case in Dutton's work, they can be read as blueprints for his practice of poetry. The poem "fault" (originally titled "raining outside"), which Dutton has rewritten substantially since its first collected appearance in *Camp One,* is related to "interview," his uncollected poem from his first pamphlet. One can read "fault" as a defense of his poetic in the face of an unnamed critic who complains (ironically "at the window") that his verse "does not reflect / the human situation." It begins with characteristic brevity and a reliance on the strength of unadorned nouns:

city, sea
and forest. all
rooted on rock.

(p. 114)

Similarly Dutton's poetry is founded on rock, not on its myriad manifestations. He is writing about

G. F. DUTTON

fundamentals. The mountaineers who pit themselves against massive natural forces, whose "each logical grip" is "a grope towards luck," are at the very forefront of human endeavor, existential pioneers of the spirit. Another piece, "of only a single poem," also valorizes the human pioneering spirit and its poetic equivalent, offering a vigorous defense of such activities. The poem opens:

above the plains
mountains flourish,
white, distracting eyes
from lower compulsions.

(p. 115)

Until the clarification of line four, there is an initial ambiguity in line three, which appears as a complete syntactic unit with "distracting" as an adjective rather than an active verb, and the faintly surreal though intriguing comparison of mountains to "white, distracting eyes"; line four suddenly focuses the meaning. In its first published version, this line read: "at intersections." The poet's revision removes the idea of the mountains being, ironically, distractors from possible uncertainty—those "intersections." Instead it brings out something of the <u>hauteur</u> and likably proud disdain that the rest of the poem buttresses. It is more direct, a touch more proselytizing. After presenting in a crisp stanza the less conventionally appealing qualities of mountains, the poem closes:

then why climb them?
ask your constituents
ask the headbellies ask
the paunchbrains. not knowing

what it is to represent them
what it is to be the guest
dirty unapologetic

of even a minor pinnacle.

(p. 115)

This peremptory response is as much a defense of the urge to write poems, and poems not about "lower compulsions" at that, as it is to climb mountains. The narrator contrasts the purity of "being a guest" of "even a minor pinnacle" with

the incomprehension of the "headbellies" and "paunchbrains," two roundly rebarbative terms that wink at those "lower compulsions." He ends, despite that, by dubiously giving such uncomprehending critics the benefit of the doubt: they have no knowledge of the mountaineering or poetic experience. If they had, the question would become irrelevant. Dutton foregrounds the spiritual quest itself, for all the arrogance here, with a certain amount of humility: one is a "guest" only, of pinnacle or poem, a point that recalls Robert Frost's remark that there could be no such thing as a "master poet"—though there could be a master versifier—because such mastery implies complete control over one's materials, and genuine poetry is as much a result of luck and good fortune as deliberation. In that "dirty" is also the recognition by Dutton of the sheer messiness of creativity, for poet as for mountaineer. Taken farther, the mountain/poem metaphor intriguingly suggests that for Dutton, poem, like peak, has an existence predating the narrator's writing it; like a mountain, it is not so much created as discovered.

"Rock: Facing up to the Stars" is arguably the most powerful section of *The Bare Abundance*, as if Dutton there finds his fundamental themes most starkly visible. "Belief" is a remarkable, ambiguous poem, spoken in defense of the wild unregulated quality of mountains in the ironic persona of a kind of bureaucrat who criticizes and then patronizingly disparages mountaineers—or, by extension, believers of any variety—for not wishing to have their mountain regulated. The mountain is "A trodden disgrace"—there is a hint of sardonic humor in the hyperbole of that "disgrace"—which nonetheless this disorganized bunch would defend, and not "forgive // their elevation / interfered with, // made safe." "Elevation" is both the mountain's height and their own raising by it. "They put weight / on the doubt"—a typically witty and paradoxical idea. Risk is part of the point of the exercise, an extravagance of spirit, a wandering beyond accepted bounds, if not in a spirit of competition as "goal," which another poem here makes clear. Through the picture of a child playing with a ball in the poem titled "goal," Dutton contrasts the child's natural tendency to enjoy the process of play with society's preoccupation with outcome, as manifest in the child having been taught "to lodge [the ball] in some net." Previously the child was able to score "every foot of the way." Dutton's own verses are similarly as much about process; in an environment of flux themselves, they largely resist the too-resonant closure or "goal." "Time," for instance, is a cannily simple poem that examines that flux via "a roofless house" in ruins; the supersession of one culture by another is a frequent theme in Dutton. The former dwelling in its current state is portrayed as something almost ornamental: its "decorations"—presumably wildflowers and saplings growing from the ruin—are stripped by autumn and pinned up again by spring. The poem closes:

Each summer
however
the walls stand lower.

Something
is spoiling the picture.
Not keeping time.

(p. 141)

It takes considerable skill to write at a level as bare as this and maintain interest. With a bold title that risks windy portentousness, this delphic mouthful reveals some of the most characteristic qualities of Dutton's poetry. What is "spoiling the picture" by, presumably, "Not keeping time"? In one reading, of course, it is the house itself. It disintegrates as summer flourishes: it is outwith the natural rhythms, and in this sense not keeping time; nor is it keeping time in the sense of "hoarding" time, as the house and its occupants, by living, could be said to have done. It has relinquished time and, though part of the natural processes, disintegrates irrespective of the circularity of the seasons. The most they can do is "decorate" its ruin. Interestingly, winter is the only season not mentioned explicitly; the season of disintegration and death, it could also be read as the "something," as symbolized by the roof-

less ruin, that "spoils" the picture. This ten-line poem shimmers with ambiguities.

Two other short poems, "passage" and "as so often in Scotland," examining Scotland from different perspectives, also demonstrate the compression of Dutton's verse. The first cleverly mingles the aerial view of the country from an airplane with a compressed historical perspective:

it faced the north with a roar, then
ran snivelling southward, long
green dribbles into the sun
where cattle were happy . . .

(p. 123)

This can arguably be read both as the track of a plane and a sardonic note on Scottish history and the debatable obsequiousness of the country and its subjugation by the dominant neighbor to the south, England, which may be the place witheringly described as "where cattle were happy." Scotland, meanwhile, "now . . . / empties under our wingtips, / five minutes of wrinkles, // a dusting of snow." The following poem, "as so often in Scotland," mingles a natural effect, a traveling beam of light across the Scottish landscape, which ends "on one brown summit" before flaring "its moment, too" and vanishing, with the emergence and passing of eminence or genius in Scotland. Almost everything in Dutton's verse can be read as metaphor; his summits are more than themselves. Mountains are, as he wrote in his mountaineering essay, "Metaphorical Gymnasia."

"Fracture," also in this section, is atypical for its obvious human-centered approach in its investigation of a love affair by the poem's narrator. Originally published as disparate poems in *The Concrete Garden,* it is in five sections, all of which, with the exception of section four, spoken primarily in the third person, are narrated in the first-person singular or plural. Section one, "fracture," describes the beginning of the attraction; section two, "Family Break," is set on "the first full day of summer" and may be spoken either by a narrator missing a lover or with "his" lover (from the descriptions the speaker appears to be male) and melancholic over his family situation; the "Break" of the section's title is ambiguous. Section three, "Weekend," appears to depict the lovers spending a weekend together—they have "travelled how far, / as if to get nearer." In the penultimate section, "Forecast," against the background of the "grey, / indicative east," a man leaves a woman—perhaps, judging by the final section, his wife—to go "over the moor / back to beyond." In the final section, "Open Cast"—the title functioning as a metaphor for the wound caused by a love triangle—a narrator addresses a "my dear," probably a child, ironically reassuring him or her that "It will all be put back / just as it was before" and that "you will love her as much as your mother," implying that the affair has proved to be the beginning of a new relationship for the adult speaker. As often with Dutton, "Fracture" takes a part of its power from its obliqueness and artifice, though impatient readers may find its riddling quality irksome and somewhat coy. Overly literal or obvious poems, however, Dutton tends to disown later, perhaps because they lack the range of suggestion and resistance to paraphrase he sees everywhere else.

If "Fracture" marked something of a departure for Dutton, two of this section's finest poems, "Bulletin" and "in memoriam George Forrest," return to the theme of human endeavor in a challenging universe. In the former, "The glaciers have come down / dead white / at the end of the street," a huge natural force which is nonetheless defied by the "great lights" of the machines "tossing back darkness." The engineers, who "have promised to save us," represent a tentative hope; the poem finishes by describing how

already upstairs
they are teaching their children
to sing like the ice.

(p. 150)

The closure is a complex image: power can only be opposed by power; the engineers, and what they can teach their children, partake of the power of nature too. But the close of Dutton's poem could also imply that the children, rebelliously, will come to "act out" with a force analogous to that of those glaciers; that the engineers are "teaching their children" not

deliberately but unwittingly. The poem intriguingly marries human temperament with larger realities. Humanity in Dutton is never separate from nature, even in urban environments.

Meanwhile, "in memoriam George Forrest" is a praise poem for a botanical pioneer—one of the mountaineering spirits Dutton often praises. It is easy to see why Dutton, an explorer in these various ways, should praise such a figure. Forrest was from Falkirk in Scotland, a remarkable autodidact made a fellow of the Royal Botanical Society. Born in 1873, he died suddenly from a massive heart attack at the age of fifty-nine in 1932 while abroad. In all he made seven expeditions to the Chinese Himalaya and discovered twelve hundred species of plants, despite being caught up in political violence on the first trip to Yunnan province that saw him barely escape with his life and a supporter of his work, a local missionary named Père Dubernard, brutally killed. Dutton's poem repeats the phrase "here" in incantatory fashion before delineating the various events that took place: a beautiful description of the flowers discovered leads to a savage account of the death of Dubernard and how the "so-precious" seeds were sent from there by Forrest: beauty, violence, utility, and faith are contrasted and conjoined. The poem finishes:

here

the snow plume flies
night and day
over the last white stations,
over the buried disarray,
bursting icefall, twisted alloy,
fossils and fragments, cylinders, ropes,
fluttering shreds
of the expedition tents.

(p. 154)

The dominant "snow plume" that "flies" forms, in its syntactic simplicity, a dramatic contrast to all the doomed human endeavor described, with its adjectives, active verbs, and hectic listing, divided by commas, of expedition objects. With overwhelming simplicity, elemental Nature reclaims the evidence of human struggle: the snow plume effortlessly "flies," while the shreds of the tents can only flutter, like trapped birds. Nonetheless, they witness an abundant heroism.

CONCLUSION

For all its apparent austerity, Dutton's verse is of extraordinary depth and range, which makes it all the more surprising that serious critics have seldom as yet considered his oeuvre. Anne Stevenson, in one of the few attempts at deeper engagement with Dutton's poetry, has written that "he is writing about the human predicament." (p. 206) Finally, this seems true. His verse deals, ultimately, with ultimate things—transience, death, regeneration, and people facing up to existential realities in a harsh environment against the massive backdrop of space and time. These seem undatable concerns. Dutton has noted them assiduously, yet the verse is seldom allowed to fall into easy paraphrasable meaning. Written largely from the historical edge of contemporary life, which enables Dutton to see pattern below apparent confusion, he refuses, in the last poem in his *Selected Poems*, "Finale," any single vote, either "against the asteroid" or for "the Cross." Instead his work surveys an austere unifying reality with honesty and courage. Reflecting the role of the two introductory poems of the book, the second part of "Finale" flings a real stone into a real pool; the impact of this everyday asteroid disturbs a sudden "white bird" toward the "untouched, disappearing, westward." Dutton has written a body of poetry unique in tone, worth reading for its artistic integrity, its deceptive complexity, and for his broad perspective—not least on humanity—from a distant past to, as he himself has written, "one hopes, a future."

Selected Bibliography

WORKS OF G. F. DUTTON

POETRY

31 Poems. Oxford: Anne Stevenson, 1977.

Camp One. Loanhead, Scotland: M. McDonald, 1978.

Squaring the Waves. Newcastle upon Tyne, UK: Bloodaxe, 1986.

The Concrete Garden. Newcastle upon Tyne, UK: Bloodaxe, 1991.

The Bare Abundance: Selected Poems, 1975–2001 Tarset, UK: Bloodaxe, 2002.

NONFICTION

Swimming Free: On and Below the Surface of Lake, River and Sea. London: Heinemann, 1972; New York: St. Martin's, 1972.

harvesting the edge: some personal explorations from a marginal garden. London: Menard, 1994.

Some Branch Against the Sky: Gardening in the Wild. Newton Abbot, UK: David & Charles, 1997; Portland, Ore.: Timber Press, 1997.

"Mountaineering Poetry: The Metaphorical Imperative." *Loose Scree* 12:6–11 (March 2003).

STORIES

The Ridiculous Mountains. London: Diadem, 1984.

Nothing So Simple as Climbing. London: Diadem, 1993.

The Complete Doctor Stories. Illustrated by Albert Rusling. London: Bâton Wicks, 1997; reprinted 1999. (Combines the two earlier volumes.)

CRITICAL STUDIES AND REVIEWS

Franks, Bradley. *Scottish Literary Journal* 15, no. 1 (spring 1988). Review Supplement 28:34–36.

Relich, Mario. "A Landscape of Stones." *Lines Review* 104:41–43 (March 1988).

———. "Diamond-Hard Exactitude: The Poetry of G. F. Dutton." *Dark Horse* 15:81–86 (summer 2003).

Stevenson, Anne. "The Poetry of G. F. Dutton." *Ploughshares* 4, no. 3:204–208 (1978).

Young, Augustus. "The Timely Weed." *Chapman* 104:129–130 (2004).

PETER FALLON

(1951—)

Richard Rankin Russell

PETER FALLON HAS been the leading publisher of Irish poetry for well over two decades through the auspices of his Gallery Press. He is also an accomplished poet but has garnered little critical acclaim: while there is a short introduction to his poetry and several of his poems are included in the third volume of the monumental *Field Day Anthology of Irish Writing,* he is not included in the seemingly comprehensive bibliography of Irish poets at the end of the *Cambridge Companion to Contemporary Irish Poetry* published in 2003. Fallon's main influences have been the Irish poet Patrick Kavanagh and the American poets Robert Frost and Wendell Berry. In their introduction to their popular anthology *The Penguin Book of Contemporary Irish Poetry,* Fallon and his co-editor Derek Mahon approvingly note the authoritative status Patrick Kavanagh has assumed in the view of the current generation of Irish writers: "Kavanagh may be seen as the true origin of much Irish poetry today. One poem, the sonnet 'Epic,' gave single-handed permission for Irish poets to trust and cultivate their native ground and experience" (p. xvii).

Fallon has taken Kavanagh's advice in the latter's essay "The Parish and the Universe" to cultivate parochialism since its specificity and knowledge of local details lends it an artistic integrity that provincialism, which always mimics the city, does not attain. Fallon repeatedly and intimately explores his own parish, the townland of Loughcrew in County Meath. His familiarity with his surroundings lends him poetic sustenance; as he notes in an interview with Eileen Battersby, "it sustains me, it's my natural habitat" (p. 10).

If Kavanagh gave contemporary Irish poets such as Fallon permission "to trust and cultivate their native ground and experience," the American Robert Frost likewise gave Fallon a transat-

lantic example of an outstanding poet with the courage to base a body of work upon a local landscape, redolent with the unhurried movements of farm animals. Jerry Lincecum has argued that Fallon's "preference for simple diction, colloquial speech patterns, fixed verse forms, and what he calls 'mischief' or a teasing playfulness all have antecedents in Frost" (p. 54). Additionally, Fallon's reading of the American neo-agrarian author and thinker Wendell Berry has confirmed his desire to write locally grounded, specific poetry and fully engage in rural, communal life. After a series of undistinguished poems largely set in an urban locale in his first two-and-a-half volumes, starting with the poems of the latter half of *The First Affair* (1974) Fallon began writing poems that attested to the world he had known growing up in County Meath. His best poems are pastoral elegies for the animals of the sheep farm he would move to later in his career. Whereas the traditional pastoral is a conventional expression of the urban poet's nostalgic view of the rural life, Fallon's pastoral poetry rejects idyllic misconceptions of agricultural living for a grittily realistic setting populated by human beings committed to helping others through their embrace of communal values.

LIFE

Peter Fallon was born in Germany to Irish parents on February 26, 1951, and his family moved to a farm in County Meath, Ireland, in 1957. His attachment to the rhythms of rural life was formed through his exposure to it at this time. He was educated at St. Gerard's School in Bray, County Wicklow, and at Ampleforth. He left Ampleforth at age sixteen and started the Meath Poetry Group with a reading in Navan in 1968. This group published a pamphlet titled *Twenty-One Poems* and later started a magazine called *Capella.* Fallon studied at Trinity College, Dublin, and went on to found two presses, Tara Telephone and later Gallery Press. Gallery Press was started at Fallon's new home in Dublin in 1970 and in 1988 was moved to a stone cottage by his home near the megalithic burial grounds of Loughcrew, in Oldcastle, County Meath. Fallon finally earned an honors degree from Trinity in 1975. In 1976 he was appointed as poet-in-residence at Deerfield Academy in Massachusetts. Lincecum has argued that this year spent in Massachusetts "reinforced his already strong liking for Robert Frost's work. He remembers that knowing Frost's poems gave him the advantage of feeling comfortable with the New England landscape right away" (p. 54). In 1981 Fallon won an Irish Arts Council bursary for poetry, and in 1987 he won the Meath Merit Award for Arts and Culture. Fallon taught at the School of Irish Studies in Dublin from 1985 until its close in 1990 and had a sabbatical year from running Gallery Press at Deerfield Academy during the 1996–1997 academic year. Fallon was the first holder of the Charles A. Heimbold Chair of Irish Studies at Villanova University. He continues to write poetry, run Gallery Press, and operate his sheep farm near Loughcrew, where he lives with his family.

EARLY WORK

Fallon's first three volumes generally lack the surety and precision of subsequent volumes. Fallon often rambles and the poems are too expansive, especially in comparison with the compressed verse of later work. Fallon published his first volume, *Among the Walls,* in 1971. This volume canvasses an imagined otherworld populated with dinosaurs, rainbows, and two-headed creatures in poems such as "The Dinosaur," "Babes," and "The Two-Headed Beast" and juxtaposes them with poems about a lover. The poet seems adrift in the city of Dublin, not securely anchored to a place as his later poems, written after the move back to County Meath, attest. Already the rural landscape exerts a strong attraction on the poet, however; it intrudes in

poems such as "Until Eternal Music Ends," "Snow White's Journey to the City," and "My Christ Is No Statue." The volume *Co-Incidence of Flesh,* (1972) published a year later, also features many poems addressed to a lover, and an element of the fantastic persists, especially in the poems about merman and a maiden named Springrin. These potentially interesting poems are marred by repetitious diction and vague imagery. Throughout the volume, lyrical phrases are often submerged beneath flat free verse. The title poem is one of the most interesting and deals with the fragile nature of the speaker's relationship with his lover. Her "skilled fingers" are shown "bandaging the frayed ends of my needs" (p. 28), and he decides to only touch her that night as he lies beside her despite his deep need for her. A survey of the poems in this volume demonstrates Fallon's growing preference for shorter poems, although the voice here is still too garrulous.

Victor Luftig argues that the turning point in Fallon's poetic career "comes with the second half of the third book, *The First Affair* (1974), which addresses the realities of winter and rough weather—his constant themes thereafter" (p. 422). It would be more accurate to state instead that Fallon's usual themes, first adumbrated here, include the grinding realities of farmwork regardless of season or weather. Several poems that conclude the first half of the volume suggest Fallon's growing desire to return to the County Meath countryside. Many of the poems of the shorter, first half of the volume certainly are of a piece with those many forgettable poems about different lovers in the first two volumes, but the penultimate stanza of "Love-silly and Jubilant" offers evidence of what would become the focus of Fallon's more mature poems:

The one thing certain hugs the moment,
the human ties, the animal,
they're one to make a necessary Eden.

(p. 15)

His recognition of the human and animal interdependence common to rural areas will blossom later into fuller explorations of the origins and underpinnings of such communities, even as he jettisons the idyllic naïveté of the younger speaker in this poem who apparently believes that an Eden is possible. The last two poems of the first half of this volume, "If She's Your Lover Now" and "The Lightening Hours," show the poet growing more attuned to the cycle of the seasons, another sign of his yearning to return to the County Meath countryside where he had lived as a boy. In the first poem the speaker locates the body of his former lover in autumn and terms it "a ripe fruit" (p. 16). The latter poem is also set in autumn and features lovers who see parks with leaves being burned in them.

Many of the poems of part two of *The First Affair* were written in Suffolk, England and in County Meath. In these poems Fallon deftly incorporates folk wisdom and snatches of Irish dialect. He seems to be an observer, yet one who is familiar enough with the landscapes and animals to intimately render their individual characteristics. The first poem of this section, "Legend," suggests the inexplicable quality of various features of the Irish landscape:

At Fore the water flows uphill,
won't boil and wood won't burn.
No living men could raise that lintel
and God knows how the abbey stands at all—
fast on a scra
no known architecture proves its stay.

(p. 38)

Even though scra is glossed at the bottom of the page as "a tuft of roots, whatever, in marshland; a fastness," it lends the poem an air of mystery that accords with the strange actions of the water, the immobility of the lintel, and the permanence of the abbey mentioned in the first stanza. In its last stanza the poem also celebrates the syncretistic worldview still prevalent in some areas of Ireland:

Before the first god there was some god.
Who'd tear a rosary of faith
and not a rumoured gain.

(p. 23)

Immediately after these lines the speaker concludes, "The man is wise who'll not ask why, / who'll not explain" (p. 23). These seemingly simple lines blend the local preference for reticence—a quality lauded in many later Fallon poems about rural life—with the inexplicable, timeless mysteries of the landscape evoked in the first two stanzas. Later poems in this section chart the joys of rural life and suggest the potential for happiness if man is connected with nature. Fallon's rural landscape is not idyllic, however, as "A Hungry Eye" shows. Here the harvesters are "haggard" (p. 27) and make less money every year.

A suite of poems later in this section explores the vagaries of waterfalls, lakes, and rivers. Although several phrases stand out, such as the stanza from "Waterfall"—"Slow hums remind / that water falls into itself, / a ragged rope of roaring / wind and miles diminish" (p. 15)—these poems are too cryptic, partly through their purposeful Hopkinsesque omissions, to properly convey their messages. A series of poems largely about specific animals closes the volume. Sprinkled with biblical allusions and pagan references, these poems again evoke the syncretistic religious milieu of Irish rural life. For example, "Dragonfly" compares the titular insect's eyes to the geometric shape of the pregnant Eve in Genesis—"Round as Eve's belly / the eyes"—yet concludes by suggesting the pagan connotations of the creature: "Jewelled eyes fly everywhere / to guard their treasures in / a purse the devil sews" (p. 36). The poem recalls Gerard Manley Hopkins' "As Kingfishers Catch Fire," which opens with an image of dragonfly wings lit with the fire of sunlight; Fallon's poem opens similarly: "Bribed by light / The wings unmoisten" (p. 36). But while Hopkins's poem celebrates an array of creatures in nature as they display their God-created inner identity, or inscape, Fallon's poem is a snapshot of one creature with both Christian and demonic associations in accord with a syncretistic Irish worldview that was common in the *Gaeltacht,* or Irish-speaking areas of Ireland, for many years.

LATER WORK

Beginning with the second half of *The First Affair,* Fallon's poetry increasingly focuses on rural life and particularly on domestic and wild animals. The only other contemporary Irish poet who has focused to such a degree on animal poetry is Michael Longley. While Longley's poetry suggests the continuity between the fragility of the natural world and the human world of war-torn Belfast, Fallon's nature poetry ushers the reader into a world removed from the concerns of the city and immerses them in the life of the country with its pleasures and suffering. Many of the poems from his next three volumes, *A Gentler Birth* (1976), *Victims* (1977), and *Finding the Dead* (1978) appear in the 1978 volume *The Speaking Stones* along with some new poems. They are mostly autobiographical poems set on the sheep farm in Loughcrew, County Meath, to which Fallon had recently moved.

The Speaking Stones are near Loughcrew. Their titular presence in this volume suggests the continuing influence of the Irish past upon Fallon's work and his feeling of connection to it. In the title poem the speaker recalls the slow decay of four stones, all of which once stood upright. The stones are associated with local legend and supposedly would speak on condition that they be asked a question but once. Upon being asked to speak more than once they refused to speak anymore. The stones still exert a presence despite their silence. Once when a local man tried to break them, he "learned his child had drowned / in the lower meadow southward" (p. 39). The poem concludes by noting that "still in the richest field around / are the stones tongue-tied / in the townland they've given their name" (p. 39). This poem amply demonstrates how, in Fallon's Ireland, the past constantly encroaches upon the present, shaping and influencing it. His role in poems such as these is that of poet-anthropologist, dedicated to discovering and preserving local traditions. In this regard Fallon's anthropological poems share the concerns of those of the Northern Irish poet Seamus Heaney, who dedicated many of his poems of the 1960s and 1970s to recording declining crafts such as thatching in County Derry.

Other poems in *The Speaking Stones* explore the harshness of rural farm life as animals struggle for survival. For example, in "One," a poem reprinted from *A Gentler Birth,* the speaker takes some solace in the opening stanza from finding signs of a merciful death after having seen the remnants of a more horrific one earlier that day:

an egg among feathers and bone,
immediate death
and a gentler birth
than a lamb's whose eyes
the crows had picked this morning
before its two feet touched the ground
as a ewe wondered
what labour happened
to herald that doom behind her left shoulder.

(p. 11)

The lamb whose eyes had been plucked out that fateful morning in "One" is recalled by the concluding incident in the poem "Victim," reprinted from *Victims*. The poem opens positively as the passing sheep are compared to salmon swimming through the brush. The speaker, however, quickly recalls the stupidity of the animals, previously having seen them starved to death in a field full of good pasturage. He concludes with his memory of seeing a dead sheep in a ditch with a worm gnawing at its eye, a moment that puts the reader in mind of the dead lamb whose eyes were pecked out by the crows in "One."

Perhaps the most satisfying poem of the collection and the one that best expresses Fallon's realistic but optimistic worldview is "The Positive Season," a poem that recalls the way in which the speaker and another person have tended the domestic animals on a farm. Calling themselves "surgeons, saviours, / sorrowers" (p. 46), the speaker remembers having saved a ewe with an infected head only to find her drowned in a stream later in the week. The seeming futility of their medical intervention almost becomes absurd in light of the animal's death. Other memories stream through the speaker's mind, images of suffering and pain that he likens to the stations of the cross in the Catholic ritual: "all, all the pitiful stations" (p. 46). Despite the pain he has seen and even inflicted in his quest to heal these animals, the speaker remains relatively sanguine, realizing that life will continue:

But this is the positive season,
Though loss is expected,
A part of the whole,
The breeches, abortions
Accepted, it's minor,
The primary pulse is new.

(p. 46)

He follows this affirmation of new life in the midst of death and slaughter by depicting a ewe about to give birth for the first time. Even though she is naive, she is instinctively an expert at this process, and soon the newborn lambs flock to her full udders. After some moments of chaos, the lambs totter out to the fields, and the speaker, even while knowing that they too will be killed someday, approvingly sees them as part of "the larger, enduring herd" (p. 47).

Other poems in the volume feature animals such as domestic collie dogs, a possum, rabbits, and a badger. The badger is featured in a poem titled "A Dream of Heaven," which is both a naturalistic study of the animal and a reclamation of all the timid nocturnal and underground animals such as the mole featured in another poem. As he watches the badger, the speaker has a dream of heaven in which all nocturnal creatures emerge into the daylight moving proudly and boldly.

While the majority of these poems feature animal life, Fallon is also attentive to the life of the community and is especially keen to portray the recreational activities of the locals during their rare free moments away from the bone-grinding weariness of their farms. Even in these poems, however, death intrudes. For example, in "Cards," a man named Pat Mullion slumps over and dies while playing; the shocked players laugh, then are ashamed. Card playing eventually becomes a metaphor for living, as the speaker relates in the concluding stanza. He observes that sometimes they do not play by the rules and that they take terrible risks in order to love and to live. Occasionally they play hands they are not dealt, and when they are given bad hands they blame it on the dealer. At the same time, their persistence in playing the game of life is encouraging. In the inexplicably named "El Dorado," Fallon, in his role as anthropologist, captures all the intimacies and nuances of a country dance with the locals dressed up and a lively band playing.

Even in such a tight community there are outsiders, and in one of the most heart-searing poems in the volume, "Child of God," Fallon portrays a local who is mentally retarded and teased by many in the village. Drawing on the card games that unite the villagers in their downtime, the speaker uses terms from this pastime to show both the man's deftness with animals and his function as laughingstock of the community. He notes that "The shuffled herds that strayed / he dealt as if by instinct" and then states, "In any pub's pack he was joker" (p. 44). Finally, the speaker indicts himself too for having teased him before but compassionately and tenderly offers the poem as a paean to the young man, even though he knows he cannot read it. He reminds the others to be kind as Larry, the young man, is kind. Flashes of tenderness like these, interspersed with moments of cruelty and death, create a tonally diverse volume of poetry that suggests Fallon had found his voice as recorder of rural life's rhythms, its heartaches and its joys.

As Fallon has immersed himself in the rural life of County Meath, he has been particularly drawn to agrarian theories about the interrelationships among the people, the animals, and the land. He shares with the American poet and farmer Wendell Berry a respect for the land and a desire to maintain ecological balance with it. As Fallon notes in his acknowledgments at the end of his volume *Eye to Eye* (1992), "Wendell's supreme example remains a guiding light" (p. 62). Fallon's commitment to farming is pervasive and ongoing and underscores the importance of community in his life and poetry. Berry himself, a champion of community living, has declared his approval of the worldview found in Fallon's poetry. On the back cover of Fallon's *News of the World: Selected Poems* (1993), Berry appreciatively notes, "here is a book of poems as whole hearted and readable as a good tale. Its characters and voices are deftly shaped within their moments of revelation."

PETER FALLON

Berry's approbation of Fallon's "voices" is revelatory. Just as Berry has seamlessly integrated the dialect of his rural Henry County, Kentucky, into his work, Fallon has skillfully integrated Irish words and phrases into his poetry. As Richard Wilbur has remarked about Fallon's use of rural Irish dialect: "On the whole, Fallon's words move artfully within the lexicon of the rural town; their poetry is in the rightness of naming and describing, the exact ear for the beat and savor of country speech, the honest tuning of the poet's feelings toward his chosen place" (back cover of *News of the World*).

Fallon's title poem from his 1983 volume *Winter Work* illustrates the aptness of Wilbur's appraisal. For example, Fallon employs the Irish word *meitheal* in line thirteen. In his appendix to *News of the World: Selected Poems,* he glosses the word as "a co-operative work force. I remember especially the congregations of friends and neighbours to help with the threshing. And I've learned since then of Amish barn-raising or "frolics" and, in New England, of sewing and quilting bees" (p. 79). The incorporation of this Irish word into the title poem suggests how he views his individual life as a farmer within the broader community:

I warm to winter work, its rituals
and routines, and find--indoors . . . alone
or going out to work with neighbours, a *meitheal* still.

(p. 48)

Fallon's embrace of a communal worldview is puzzling for many of those who have long since succumbed to a virulent form of modernism, especially its American manifestation, which values independence and can reject help as a sign of weakness.

Many of the poems in *Winter Work* are, like the title poem, evocations of the home in Loughcrew that Fallon finally felt he had found. In this concluding poem to the volume he notes, "All I approve persists, / is here, at home" (p. 48), and in the opening poem, appropriately titled "Home," he confidently pits his knowledge of local people and places against his cosmopolitan brother's boasting. In an inversion of the old saw about the grass being greener on the other side of the fence,

he opens "Home" by stating, "The faraway hills are green but these / are greener" (p. 11). He quickly recalls his brother's smugness and his own reply:

My brother roamed the world
and seemed to know everything. He boasted it
until I burst, "Well you don't know John Joe Farrell,"
the butcher's son, my friend."

(p. 11)

This retort exemplifies Kavanagh's conception of parochialism by displaying Fallon's intimacy with his local community, as does a later line in the poem that recalls the Irish name for a hill as "the hag's mountain," while the speaker quickly and self-deprecatingly adds, "but that's the way it is for lowlanders will call // a small incline a mountain and mountain-men mention a hill and point to Everest" (p. 11).

The third poem, "Loughcrew," names Fallon's home and situates him within this landscape: "I'm living in the townland of Loughcrew, / *loch na craoibhe,* lake of the limb / of the oak on the island" (p. 13). He straightforwardly admits, "I wasn't born here but I came / to be at home near my home place" (p. 13). In "The Lost Field," Fallon again inscribes himself into the countryside, noting that "When I came home from Dublin / I found my place" (p. 18). He goes on to muse about what can be done with land and the lost field of the title.

Think of all that lasts. Think of land.
The things you could do with a field.
Plough, pasture or re-claim. The stones
You'd pick, the house you'd build. . .
I'm out to find that field, to make it mine.

(pp. 18–19)

As the Irish poet Eamon Grennan has remarked, "Everything about these lines suggests purposeful action, putting something to use. In its palpable but restrained enthusiasm, too, the tone contains something of that moral energy to be found in the response to any clearly understood vocation" (p. 174). Fallon's land reclamation project is thus intensely personal. Having been gone from County Meath for some time, he desired to fit in with the local community when he returned—not just for personal but also vocational reasons. The lost field that belonged to his family is on "outlying land," befitting his own outsider status. If he could successfully reclaim his place in the community, notwithstanding his search for the field, he truly would be home again.

Fallon's desired home is much more than a place; it connotes an entire system of relationships. His home shares a salient characteristic with the Irish conception of home in general. As the Irish cultural and political critic Fintan O'Toole has pointed out, "One of the things that culture reminds us of is that home is much more than a name we give to a dwelling place. It is also a whole set of connections and affections, the web of mutual recognition that we spin around ourselves and that gives us a place in the world" (p. 167). This "web of mutual recognition" is abundantly evident in the poems of *Winter Work* and is even suggested in the volume's title: the harsh season and the continued necessity of outdoor work can only be dealt with effectively through a communal effort based on respect, trust, and affection.

Also necessary to understanding this community is Fallon's respect and awe for the land itself. His clear appreciation for the land is suggested by another line from "The Lost Field" that suggests he will reintegrate himself into this world: "My part in this is reverence" (p. 18). Revering the land he had come back to stands Fallon in good stead, as does his taciturnity. In "Loughcrew" he admits the community's view of him with a trace of pride: "They say that I say little, / say I fish in deeper waters" (p. 13). Just as Seamus Heaney's early poems such as "The Forge" show the rural community's appreciation of silent craftsmen, poems such as "Loughcrew" acknowledge this rural tradition of reticence and demonstrate how the quiet poet is thus well received by the relatively closed community to which he has returned.

Another way in which the poet became part of the townland of Loughcrew is through his reclamation of memories growing up in nearby Lennoxbrook. In the opening stanza of "Acts of Restoration," the speaker recalls his envy at the ease with which his cousins worked and handled tools when he watched them upon his return from boarding school and university. As he turns away from this memory into the barn, he starts

an act of restoration
and matched again
the implements to the man
or beast who wielded them . . .

(pp. 20–21)

Through these acts a vanished world comes into focus, a world replete with playful neighbors in the midst of bone-wearying work. Looking back on his childhood, the speaker wistfully recalls, "We were at home, / we knew our place between comings and goings" (p. 22). This important poem functions as a metaphor for the other poems in the volume, suggesting that they too are not only acts of reclamation, as in "The Lost Field," but also acts of restoration. While the now mature speaker knows he cannot fully recover his long-ago boyhood, his childlike wonder nevertheless enables him to enjoy the rituals and rhythms of the rural life he had left behind so long ago.

Fallon's deliberate choice to return to the area of County Meath near where he was raised was, as Grennan has remarked, purposeful in respect to his vocations as farmer and poet: "One of this place's most important features, I believe, is the fact of its being a *chosen* place, a place deliberately selected to be commensurate with a life. That chosen place will be a lifetime's vocation" (p. 173). Indeed Fallon's vocation as sheep farmer in his chosen place has provided him a range of subjects for his poetry. One of the many ritualistic tasks Fallon found himself doing on his return involved his role as a midwife of sorts for his sheep. It is in the context of this role that some of his best poems are written. For example, in "Fostering," Fallon draws on the biblical story of Jacob and Esau as he tricks a foster ewe into accepting a lamb that is not her own:

I took the stillborn lamb and cleft
with axe on chopping-block its head,
four legs, and worked the skin apart with deft
skill and rough strength. I dressed the living lamb
in it. It stumbled with the weight, all pluck,
towards the ewe who sniffed and smelled and licked

raiment she recognized. Then she gave suck-
and he was Esau's brother and I Isaac's wife
working kind betrayals in a field blessed for life.

(p. 23)

Fallon's adaptation of a buckled Shakespearean
sonnet form with the concluding end rhyme of
that sonnet and his variable rhyme scheme, as
the writer has noted elsewhere, "enable him to
give form and shape to his feelings on the death
of one lamb and fostering of another." Further,
"Its terseness is a perfect vehicle to adequately
convey the harsh reality of life on a sheep farm,
while its allusion to the story of Jacob and Esau
in Genesis 27 and use of archaic words such as
'raiment' lend a religious significance and
transcendence to what has transpired" (Russell,
p. 349). While the tragedy of the first lamb cannot be entirely mitigated, its death enables the
second lamb to be saved as it claims its "birthright," the first lamb's mother's milk. "Fostering"
is typical of Fallon in its gritty evocation of the
grim tragedies of farm life and in its attempts to
find something life affirming in the midst of
sorrow. As Grennan has pointed out, this poem
displays a "zest for life" displayed by the poet's
own intervening actions (p. 178).

Fallon clearly admires the determination of the
animals on his farm and tenderly cares for them.
In "Ewes" he traces the seasonal patterns of the
sheep as they migrate throughout the year to ed-
ible pasturage. He concludes by approvingly noting about the ewes, "Gathered / like midges, they
brace to brave all weathers / and settle down to
gimmering, to being mothers" (p. 37). Somewhat
like the shepherd in Christ's parable about the
man who had all but one of his hundred sheep
and searched diligently for that last one, the
speaker in "Sabbath" seeks a lost ewe and finds
her near-frozen in some mud. She is his favorite
at the time and he recalls her lambing and the
stumbling attempts at walking of her first lamb.
Now the mother lies awkwardly, unable even to
stand, but he believes with proper care she will
recover. "Sabbath" portrays the shepherd working on a traditional day of rest yet working in
such a merciful manner as to render moot any
thoughts of criticism. His clear reverence for the
animals that surround him knits him into creation

with a respect for life that is salutary. Home
again, Fallon will increasingly explore the bounds
of his parish in subsequent volumes.

While the poems of *The News and Weather*
(1987) continue in this parochial vein, there is an
increasing awareness of a wider world. Nowhere
is this awareness more clearly signaled than in
the opening poem, "My Care." As the speaker
talks of watching *Hill Street Blues* in Phil's pub,
indicating the increasing influence of American
culture on Ireland, that pastime is shunted aside
in favor of viewing the news, which features
examples of atrocities being committed in
Northern Ireland: "A kidnap, check-points,
searches, / killers on the run" (p. 11). Shaken, the
speaker wonders what his role is in the midst of
such terrible violence, admitting in a term borrowed from terrorist jargon, "All I ever wanted
was / to make a safe house in the midlands" (p.
11). The domestic serenity of Fallon's adopted
home that was achieved in *Winter Work* has been
shattered by the news from the North. When he
returns home, even the fire has taken on ominously explosive qualities: "Soon I'm sitting by a
riot / of kindling, the soft explosions of seasoned
logs. / They have shaken the roots of that familiar
quiet" (p. 11). The poet who was wide-eyed and
reverent toward the land in *Winter Work* as assumed his vocations of farmer, poet, and publisher now contemplates whether he should add
another role—that of interventionist—to stop the
violence issuing from Northern Ireland. He
wonders in the middle of the poem, "Should I do
more? Is it enough / to keep a weather eye and
talk to friends?" (p. 11).

Keeping a "weather eye," more wary now than
before, enables him to develop a wider vision in
this volume than in previous ones. Alongside Fallon's developing political vision resides another
type of vision he found in his recovered community in Meath. In the second poem of the
volume Fallon recalls a wild corner of the
property on which he grew up called "The
Witches' Corner." This place gives the poem its
title and suggests its aura of mysteriousness. He
recalls the dry floor of this area of brush as "A
hiding-place. A refuge. A retreat" (p. 12), suggesting how important it is for him to recover

this hiding place suffused with memories, perhaps as an escape from the explosiveness of the situation in Northern Ireland. But the Witches' Corner also functions as a site of airy imaginings when he recalls climbing a giant cedar. This lofty perch enabled him to survey panoramically his known world, "every roof, the yard, / the back yard and the haggard" (p. 12), a world that was comforting in its solidity: "That day I knew / that in the compass of our view // was all I wanted or would want" (p. 13). And yet, his immersion in the air from the top of the tree also enabled him to realize "There was weather there that wasn't / on the ground. The sway of the branches. / That thin air" (p. 13). The last lines of the poem recall the adult Fallon's "weather eye" in the previous poem but suggest how, as a child, he was more open to the wide world than he has been until recently bombarded with news of the violence in Northern Ireland:

I stayed there
a long time, weathering a storm.
I kept everything
in my wide eye and didn't miss a thing.

(p. 13)

The Wordsworthian receptivity and wonder of the little boy proves enabling for the adult poet as he ponders his response to the "Troubles."

His reply comes in a remarkable poem entitled "The Heartland" much later in the volume. Acknowledging that Meath has never been as removed from danger as he might have thought in "My Care," Fallon notes that he lives

An hour's drive from Orange halls, apocrypha
of fife and drums,
the hole-in-the-wall of South Armagh-
we never had to wait and wonder
if outside worlds might queer
this pastoral.

(p. 24)

These lines indicate Fallon knows his pastoral world is not hermetically sealed, nor should it be. Like a radio antenna, he attunes himself to hear the latest news, which he will weather like other incidents, suggesting the relevance of the volume's title. He hears of the Kerry babies'

investigation in which unwanted babies were dumped by their mothers in southwestern Ireland and of more troubles on the border with Northern Ireland. Recalling his recent conversation with a college student from Minnesota who fearfully attacks him for being "too contented" and not caring enough about world events such as the repercussions of Vietnam, he replies quietly but forthrightly (p. 24). His response is altogether fitting for a wordsmith committed to his local community:

It's true I chose another course, talk
in small communities, a hope to sway
by carry-on people I understand
and love. I came on a place and had to stay
that I might find my feet, repair
the mark of human hand, and repossess
a corner of my country. I write to her:
our lives are rafts; risk happiness.

(p. 25)

He thus concludes in language borrowed from Robert Frost, noting, "It's true I chose another course," suggesting the road he has taken—one of reclamation and reintegration into a community. He also reclaims, as an agent of change, the power of dialogue among those he knows, an affirmation of local government against the girl's desire to effect change through petitioning the federal government of the United States. The poem itself is finally transformed into a sort of linguistic rescue device Fallon has sent out to the girl on a tide of hope that may enable her to adopt a realistic but more sanguine worldview.

In the process of affirming the role he has chosen to play in his particular community while increasingly confronted with sectarian violence, Fallon also turns his attention to the bloodshed endemic to his own farm. One of his most powerful elegies about lambs, along with "Fostering" from *Winter Work,* is "Caesarean" from *The News and Weather,* in which a "humpbacked, worn out" pregnant ewe is slaughtered by Fallon and his coworker so that her offspring can survive (p. 20). After they shoot her and cut her open,

She opened like a bloom
beneath the red script of the scalpel's nib
and we found twins, abandoned, perfectly formed in

the warm nest of her womb.

(p. 20)

The flower simile powerfully implies the possibility of her lambs' survival, as does the maternal connotation of the "warm nest of her womb." But the men have chosen to spare the wrong animals, since the lambs are premature and

lay like kindlings dazed by daylight,
the tips of their tongues, their front feet pressed
to dive as one into the waters
of the world.

(pp. 20–21)

The lambs will soon be drowned by the chilly realities of the cold world outside their mother's womb. The poem concludes with Fallon despairing that

they'd never know their gifts,
the everyday miracles of which they were part.
They were part instead of that sacrifice of the whole.

(p. 21)

Fallon's tender role as shepherd is heightened by his lament for these lambs and also undercut by his actions since he kills the mother, who almost certainly would have lived. His typical reticence is on full display in the concluding terse sentences: "We had done what we could. Now there / were other things to do. We said nothing for a while" (p. 21). This pragmatic acceptance of the lambs' death forms part of a necessary survival strategy for the poet/farmer himself: if he becomes too involved with his animals' lives, he himself could descend to the depths of despair.

In a further development of Fallon's religious worldview, which had previously been slanted toward the syncretistic element in local Meath culture, several poems in *The News and Weather* move toward a worship of the natural world, as already seen intimated in "Caesarean." In the lovely "Spring Song," the poet writes of the "chestnut / candelabra" and the various other blossoms bursting into life during spring (p. 14). After having surveyed the burgeoning animal and plant life around him, he concludes by stating simply, "And this is heaven: / sunrise through a

copper beech" (p. 15). "Country Music," on the other hand, offers a realistic, glimpse of the rituals attending the care of livestock, which resemble those of the Catholic Church:

They worship at an altar
of a trailer with the tailboard off,
up to their knees in a muck moraine.
They swish the thuribles of their tails, slap
incense breath on the silage psalter,
grain, torn cud; a smothered cough.

(p. 28)

It is finally the continuity of this natural world in poems such as "Spring Song" and "Country Music" that enables Fallon to keep going in the midst of heartache. As the writer has argued elsewhere, pastoral elegies such as "Caesarean" "portray Fallon's intense sense of loss in the midst of the pastoral plenum that surrounds him as a kind of secondary irony and sustenance" (Russell, p. 349).

Fallon's 1992 volume *Eye to Eye* continues to explore the inner workings of his adopted community and to record the heartaches of rural life. But this volume also marks a departure from earlier ones, as it is the most intensely personal one the poet has written. Dedicated to the memory of his son, John Fallon, who lived only from December 7 to December 8, 1990, the volume continues the vision metaphor first adumbrated in *The News and Weather* in its insistence on rightly seeing his son's death in its communal and familial context. If Fallon had gazed tenderly upon the deaths of sheep in previous works, he would gaze achingly and sorrowfully upon his infant son, even as he would again celebrate life—this time in the arrival of a new baby daughter—soon after his son's death.

The harsh weather is another theme carried over into this volume from the previous one. While *The News and Weather* featured the poet attuned to new political realities and responding to these in his role of village poet, this volume portrays him trudging through an extremely cold winter, seemingly unprepared for the personal tragedy about to befall him. Literal winds swirl around him, bringing change but also hope in the form of windfalls. In "Windfalls" the poet discusses the continuing violence in Northern

Ireland with a fellow farmer whose stoicism is tinged with optimism. Despite the gale-force winds that slice through them, the poet realizes the older farmer will "saw and split the windfalls when the wind dies down," using them for much-needed fuel to give warmth against that same cold wind (p. 19). Harvesting some good from the bad thus is introduced in this poem as a major theme of the volume. The wind will also blow some good toward the lonely ewe and lamb featured in the next poem, "Gravities: West." These animals are able to forage upon "wild, western commonage / windfalls that depend // on whatever way that wind blows" (p. 20).

The tempered optimism of these two poems is shattered by the stark piece "The State of the Nation," a devastatingly frank discussion of the atrocities ongoing in Northern Ireland. Various means of killing and dismembering are discussed in this poem including the way in which bolt-cutters are used to slice off fingers from victims' hands. Fallon sweepingly indicts all those who provide aid to the men of terror, such as those who acted as drivers or sold the Irish Republican Army rag *An Phoblacht,* and grimly observes, "If their day comes / the country's fucked" (p. 23). In a blow to the reticence he and his community and others like it have always valued, he concludes with a short dialogue that also condemns those who know the identities of those involved in paramilitaries but do not expose them: "And you mean to say / no one knows who they are? / I mean to say no one's saying" (p. 23). In these lines there is more than an echo of Seamus Heaney's famous poem "Whatever You Say, Say Nothing" from his 1976 volume *North*. Fallon, like Heaney before him, laments the silence that enables atrocities to continue.

In other poems in the volume Fallon also criticizes the ongoing violence in Northern Ireland and shows its impact upon families. "A Handful of Air" recalls the images of dismembered body parts in "The State of the Nation" as Fallon meets a series of friends with fingers missing from different accidents and quickly conflates their missing digits with the body parts that were severed through sectarian atrocities in the North. The chilling last stanza objectively indicts those

on both sides of the conflict as all the hands and fingers that have been separated reunite and point at each other: "Hands hold hands, / fingers are crossed, and the fingers point" (p. 31).

Although Fallon was upset about the continuing violence in the North, he was devastated by the passing of his day-old son. His seven brief elegies about John Fallon, "A Part of Ourselves," are wrung from the depths of his despair and movingly mourn the child and chart the effects of his death upon Fallon, his family, and the community. "A Part of Ourselves" ultimately inscribes his dead son into the collective memory of the local community. These deeply moving elegies gained a wide audience for this volume, as Victor Luftig has observed: "*Eye to Eye* received attention for its treatment of the death of a child; even forums not usually attentive to poetry, such as an afternoon talk show on a Midlands radio station, discussed the book" (p. 422).

"The World of Women" introduces the occasion that prompted the aforementioned elegies. In it, the poet must fight off the urge to stroke his wife's breast, which ironically soon will fill with milk for the dead child:

> Resist the will
> to caress her breast.
> It will fill
> into a fortune of milk
> for the baby who died
> on Saturday.
>
> (p. 53)

The "fortune of milk" signifies the death of the Fallon baby and the hope of another child in the future. The silence and tenderness of this poem stand in stark contrast to the elegies that follow, in which the poet and his wife loudly bewail the loss of their baby.

The first lyric in "A Part of Ourselves" reveals that the poet and his wife were "Forewarned but not forearmed— / no, not for this" (p. 54). The awkward tone of the first stanza is heightened by the view in the second stanza of the sonogram that depicts their child; this image implies how far away the baby already is with its unfocused, distant quality: "The scanned screen slips out of focus, / a lunar scene, granite shapes, shifting" (lines 8–9). The juxtaposition of sentences and fragments—the first two lines of the second stanza are fragments, while the final four lines are complete—implies the baby's premature status and lost chance at wholeness.

Subsequent lyrics portray the family slowly moving through the grieving process. The final line of each of the seven lyrics is set off from the rest of the poem, signifying the continuing separation of the infant from his family. The second lyric concludes optimistically: "There are things worse than death" (p. 55), as though the poet is trying to convince himself of this assertion. A motif of breathing marks the third lyric, which pictures a man tenuously surviving in an oxygen tent and emphasizes the permanent loss of breath by the Fallon baby.

The fourth lyric depicts the actions of Fallon and his wife while their son is dying. This lyric wearily emphasizes their waiting, heightened by the repetition in line five: "as I waited, waited, for the given end" (p. 57). The morning, usually associated with hope and new beginnings instead starts dully with the blaring of the telephone: "Then, at dawn, the telephone. / It seems I've been sleepwalking / since" (p. 57). The isolation of "since" marks off this event as a discrete unit of time in the Fallons' lives—everything that occurs after this event will be "since," colored by what has happened.

In the fifth elegy the Fallons "broached the sorrow hoard / of women" (p. 58) who tell them "about unwanted pregnancies, abortions, miscarriages,"

as his remains, a fingerful of hair,
a photograph, his cold kiss called, "Remember me,"
and I stood with them at the lip
of graves.

(p. 58)

These lines enable John Fallon's death to become part of a litany of sorrowful stories the community has experienced. At the same time, the incorporation of his death into these other narratives elides the particularity of his story.

The final elegy features the attempts of Fallon and his family to integrate the child not just into the community but more especially into their family:

He'll die again at Christmas every year.
We felt the need grow all night
to give him a name, to assert him
as a member of our care, to say he was
alive.

(p. 60)

The parents leave the child a name, "to assert him / as a *member* of our care . . ." (p. 60). This bodily imagery tries to incorporate the dead child into the living family. Their efforts to figuratively embrace the baby are heightened in lines eight and nine: "In a hospital corridor / I held him in my arms. I held him tight." While John Fallon has died, the very act of his naming lends him a continuing life in the family's memory.

The final poem of this sequence did not appear until the publication of *News of the World: Selected Poems* in 1993. "A Human Harvest" begins after John Fallon's passing and soon offers a fleshly replacement of sorts for him:

Our wishes quicken into flesh
and yield a human harvest.
Remembered, revived—
the parts of a family
flock home to nest.
His sister, our daughter—
we clutch her as a text
of faith. He needs to know,
Will she still be here in the morning?
Yes, love, tomorrow, and the next.

(p. 78)

The spare lines of this poem display the family's loss and their closeness. They "clutch" the newborn child "as a text of faith," and to some degree their grief over the death of John Fallon is leavened with happiness. The poem's shape suggests the outstretched arms of the family welcoming the new infant. Fallon then redeploys the typical rhetorical question asked in elegies and uses it as an actual, vocalized question that, when answered, gives the remaining child great hope.

Reading "A Part of Ourselves" in tandem with the preliminary poem, "A Fortune," and the poem that serves as an epilogue, "A Human Harvest," reveals that these works constitute three successive parts of one lengthy poem. These divisions correspond to the traditional three sections of the elegy: lament, praise, and consolation. "A Fortune," then, mourns the day-old child, whereas the entire sequence "A Part of Ourselves," while composed of many lamentations, should be read as an encomium that inscribes John Fallon into living memory. Finally, "A Human Harvest" provides a human consolation in the form of a new baby as a sort of replacement for the dead child.

As the writer has argued elsewhere, Fallon's pastoral elegies, including "A Part of Ourselves," represent a remarkable achievement because of both their originality and their emotional depth:

> His pastoral elegies constitute a unique contribution to twentieth-century Irish pastoral poetry in both their expanded subject matter and in their inversion of many traditional conventions of this genre. Whereas Yeats would idealize the bucolic western counties of Ireland in his early poetry and Kavanagh (in *The Great Hunger*) and Heaney (in "Death of a Naturalist") would invert this optimistic view of rural Ireland with their anti-pastorals, Fallon recognizes losses which haunt the Irish countryside but then reconfigures these sorrows as sites of human and cultural potential. Fallon's pastoral elegies proclaim the value of all life in a deeply searching manner that refuses to descend into saccharine sentiment.
>
> (Russell, p. 355)

While there is always loss in Fallon's world, there is likewise nearly always gain. Life goes on, just as it has to, but not in the soul-numbing way that it does in say, Philip Larkin's bleakly nihilistic "Aubade." Human agency, Fallon suggests, can make a difference in obviating tragedy and finding good in the created world.

Fallon's accomplishments in the elegy are remarkable, especially given society's prevailing views of death, which have been elucidated by Peter Sacks:

> Recent attitudes toward death have made it increasingly difficult to write a conventional elegy. Sociologists and psychologists, as well as literary and cultural historians, consistently demonstrate the ways in which death has tended to become obscene, meaningless, impersonal—an event either stupefyingly colossal in cases of large-scale war or genocide, or clinically concealed somewhere behind the technology of the hospital and the techniques of the funeral home.
>
> (p. 299)

Fallon's successful pastoral elegies enable their animal and human subjects room to be themselves, not over-idealized as they were in the traditional pastoral elegy or reduced in form or function as they would be in an urban locale, but fully real, recognizable in their very ordinariness.

LATER WORK/NEW DIRECTIONS

Fallon's 1997 sequence *The Deerfield Series: Strength of Heart,* written to commemorate the bicentennial of Deerfield Academy in Massachusetts that year, confirms his status not just as an outstanding Irish poet but also as a fine transatlantic one, capable of attuning himself to the intricacies of American colonial history and responding thoughtfully to a series of tragedies that occurred where Deerfield stands today. This volume also strengthens Fallon's conception of community as a web of loving individuals.

The similarities between "the pale," the area of Ireland around Dublin beyond which there was no English control, and England's similar area in New England, the boundary of which was marked by Deerfield in western Massachusetts, resonate in this volume. As an Irishman, Fallon would have been acutely aware of the imperial significance of the pale in both countries and yet writes sympathetically of the slaughters of the English that took place in and around Deerfield, such as the Bloody Brook massacre in 1675, in which English settlers were slaughtered by a coalition of Native Americans, and the Leap Day slaughter, which subsequently forced the march of English captives by the French and Native Americans to Canada in 1704. The natural world around the Deerfield community is lovingly described in the long poem "Beaver Ridge," which opens the sequence, and is given prelapsarian qualities in the third section of the poem: "Here was the promise of plenty. / Here was plenty". The betrayal of the earth by the gathered humans begins in the fourth section, which recalls the environmental concerns of Hopkins' "God's Grandeur" with its fiscal and physical images of a "spent" earth: "They spent the earth / as if it were / an endless currency" (p. 88). And in return for shedding the "beaver's blood, they "received / the gift of government, / of plagues and poxes." The last section of "Beaver Ridge" concludes with radiant hints of the earth's renewal, somewhat akin to the conclusion of "God's Grandeur" but without Hopkins' supernatural invocation of the Holy Spirit:

Morning, and the sun begins to shine.
The beaver of Pocumtuck stirs.
In the lodge of perpetuity
it is but sleeping.

(p. 89)

Other poems in the volume survey the relations between the colonizing English and the Native Americans, including the aforementioned atrocities. One cannot help but feel reminded of the U.S. government's forced march of Cherokee Indians during the early nineteenth century in reading "29 February, 1704"—except in this case, the Native Americans are the brutal captors. Fallon's condemnation of the violence committed by Native Americans resonates with his poems about Northern Ireland; in their joint critique of any human beings who perpetrate atrocities. The harsh winter weather met with in earlier volumes reappears here in an even grimmer guise in the second section of this poem as "frost grew in suppurating wounds, / heart weak in the bewildered ways."

The volume concludes with "Strength of Heart," a poem that examines the role of suffering in the lives of the reader. Suffering, Fallon implies, both enables one to live in a place and grow strong in that place. As he points out in his notes to these poems at the end of *News of the World: New and Selected Poems,* "It demands that communities, and families, try to be, as Hemingway wrote of a character, 'strong in the broken places'" (p. 138). As if to show us how to be strong, two "uncarved commandments" conclude

the poem: "Be worthy of this life. And, Love the world." One can sense the ripening of Fallon's consistent themes of suffering and potential in these carefully balanced poems.

News of the World: Selected and New Poems (1998), Fallon's latest collection, consists of three parts. Part one reprints selected poems from *The Speaking Stones, Winter Work, The News and Weather,* and *Eye to Eye.* Part two reprints the entirety of *The Deerfield Series: Strength of Heart,* while part 3, titled "The Heart's Home," features new poems. The shining potential glimpsed at the end of the elegies about John Fallon in *Eye to Eye* appears again in "The Heart's Home." For example, "Our Lives Now" wonders what future generations will make of the debris left behind by the current generation but plainly states, "We don't regret. We treasure all that's bred / to pass away, like fingerprints / on water" (p. 115). The last line suggests the family's heavenly hope for the deceased John Fallon: "And he is still with us, the bundle of the boy / who, in the order of things, will not be dead" (p. 115).

The imagined resurrection of John Fallon is heightened by the almost supernatural appearance of the spring in "Easter Prayer." Surrounded by blossoms, the poet simply notes, "I love my children / and my wife. / Rise all again and again" (p. 117). This natural prayerful profusion is heightened in the title poem, another veritable litany of wild vegetation and flowers that recalls similar listing poems about flowers by Michael Longley such as "The Ice Cream Man." The poet encourages the growth of the vegetation and celebrates its utter variety. He asks, "Let it be a healing place, / where the heart releases care" (p. 133). The poem concludes with an invitation: "Let's reunite there, love, / where refuge clings like mistletoe, / where the heart's home." (p. 134).

One of the most resonant poems in the series is "Gate," which affirms the decision made long ago and dramatized by the poet in "The Lost Field." The field there symbolized the poet's vocation and place in the rural community that he was reclaiming by returning to County Meath. In "Gate," an iron gate stands in the middle of a field and signifies the future. In the conclusion, Fallon muses on the relationship between the field and the gate:

Say for a moment
The field is your
Life and you come
To a gate at the centre
Of it. What then?
Then you pause. And open it. And enter.

(p. 124)

Fallon's rootedness in the field of his current life and his willingness to step confidently into the future and welcome what may come are salutary. He has become a truly parochial poet in Kavanagh's terms, intimate with the particular contours of his corner of Ireland and its plant and animal life. That early reverence toward the land he proclaimed in "The Lost Field" has stood him in good stead as he approaches his life and his poetry with a sense of awe at the plenum surrounding and sustaining him.

Selected Bibliography

WORKS OF PETER FALLON

POETRY
Among the Walls. Dublin: Tara Telephone, 1971.

Co-Incidence of Flesh. Dublin: Gallery Press, 1972.

The First Affair. Dublin: Gallery Press, 1974.

A Gentler Birth. Deerfield, Mass.: Deerfield Press, 1976.

Victims. Deerfield, Mass.: Deerfield Press, 1977.

Finding the Dead. Deerfield, Mass.: Deerfield Press, 1978.

The Speaking Stones. Dublin: Gallery Press, 1978.

Winter Work. Dublin: Gallery Press, 1983.

The News and Weather. Dublin: Gallery Press, 1987.

Eye to Eye. Loughcrew, Ireland: Gallery Press, 1992.

News of the World: Selected Poems. Winston-Salem, N.C.: Wake Forest University Press, 1993.

The Deerfield Series: Strength of Heart. Deerfield, Mass.: Deerfield Press, 1997.

News of the World: Selected and New Poems. Loughcrew, Ireland: Gallery Press, 1998.

PLAY
Tarry Flynn: A Play in Three Acts Based on the Novel by Patrick Kavanagh. Loughcrew, Ireland: Gallery Press, 2005.

AS EDITOR
Emily Lawless: Poems. Dublin: Dolmen Press, 1965.

The First Ten Years: Dublin Arts Festival Poetry. With Dennis O'Driscoll. Dublin: Dublin Arts Festival, 1979.

Soft Day: A Miscellany of Contemporary Irish Writing. With Sean Golden. Dublin Wolfhound, 1979; South Bend, Ind.: University of Notre Dame Press, 1980.

The Writers: A Sense of Ireland. With Andrew Carpenter. Dublin: The O'Brien Press, 1980; NY: Braziller, 1980.

The Penguin Book of Contemporary Irish Poetry. Introduced and edited with Derek Mahon. London and New York: Penguin, 1990.

MEMOIR
Fallon, Peter. "Notes on a History of Publishing Poetry." *Princeton University Library Chronicle* 59, no. 3:547–558, spring, 1998.

TRANSLATIONS
Fallon, Peter. *The Georgies at Virgil.* Loughcrew, Ireland: Galley Press, 2004.

ARCHIVE MATERIAL
The Gallery Press Collection includes drafts of Fallon's own poems and many drafts of the work of the Irish poets, dramatists, and fiction writers he has published over the years. It is housed at the Robert W. Woodruff Library, Special Collections, Emory University, Atlanta.

CRITICAL AND BIOGRAPHICAL STUDIES

Grennan, Eamon. "Chosen Home: The Poetry of Peter Fallon." *Eire-Ireland* 29, no. 2:173–187 (summer 1994).

Heaney, Seamus. *Death of a Naturalist.* London: Faber, 1966.

Heaney, Seamus, et al. "Tributes to Peter Fallon: 25 Years of Gallery Press." *Irish Literary Supplement,* fall 1995, p. 6.

Johnston, Dillon. *Irish Poetry After Joyce.* 2nd ed. Syracuse University Press, 1997.

Lincecum, Jerry B. "Peter Fallon: Contemporary Irish Poet, Editor, and Publisher." *Notes on Modern Irish Literature* 3:52–58 (1991).

Luftig, Victor. "Peter Fallon." *In Dictionary of Irish Literature.* Rev. and exp. ed. Edited by Robert Hogan. Westport, Conn.: Greenwood Press, 1996. pp. 421–423.

O'Toole, Fintan. "No Place Like Home." In his *The Lie of the Land: Irish Identities.* New York: 1997. pp. 160–172.

Russell, Richard Rankin. "Loss and Recovery in Peter Fallon's Pastoral Elegies." *Colby Quarterly* 37, no. 4:343–356 (December 2001).

Sacks, Peter. *The English Elegy: Studies in the Genre from Spenser to Yeats.* Baltimore: Johns Hopkins University Press, 1985.

INTERVIEWS AND PROFILES

Battersby, Eileen. "The View from Gallery—25 Years On." Irish Times, February 7, 1995, p. 10.

Johnston, Dillon. "My Feet on the Ground: An Interview with Peter Fallon." Irish Literary Supplement, fall 1995, pp. 4–5.

JANICE GALLOWAY

(1956—)

Claire Keyes

WITH THE PUBLICATION of *The Trick is to Keep Breathing* (1989), her first novel, Glasgow-based Janice Galloway joined James Kelman, Alasdair Gray, and the poet Tom Leonard as exemplars of "the new Glasgow writing" The "newness" appears in an unashamed embracing of Scottish themes and language patterns. Although Galloway earned her early reputation primarily in Scotland, the quality of her fiction and the reach of her themes have captured the interest of readers in Europe, the United States, and beyond. In her short stories (*Blood,* 1991, and *Where You Find It,* 1996) she continued to employ Scottish settings, mainly urban, but locale is trumped by the striking intensity of her fiction and the muscularity of her style. *Foreign Parts* (1994), her second novel, is set in France, but Galloway retains her Scottish characters. Their conflicts over issues of family and relationships know no nationality. *Clara,* her 2002 novel, marks Galloway's departure from Scottishness while also drawing upon her interest in music and musicians. As a subject, Clara, the wife of the German Romantic composer Robert Schumann, allowed Galloway to deepen her study of women, male/female relations, and the conflicts therein.

In addition to fiction, Galloway has developed expertise in other genres and collaborative work. Sally Beamish, the Scottish composer, invited her to develop text for her opera *Monster,* based on Mary Shelley's *Frankenstein.* It premiered at the Scottish Opera in October 2002. Galloway's interest in women deeply imbues all her work and led to another collaboration, *Rosengarten* (2004) with the sculptor Anne Bevan. The sculptures exploring obstetric equipment and the history and mythology of birthing, accompanied by Galloway's text, were exhibited at the Hunterian Museum in Glasgow. This collaboration turned into a book, as did an earlier collabora-

tion, also with Bevan, called *Pipelines,* (2000) a work about water and the underground network of pipes that carry it. Galloway has also published *Boy book see* (2002), a chapbook of "pieces and poems," which includes the text of *Pipelines.* In the acknowledgments to her chapbook Galloway says that doing the collaborations reminded her of why she became a writer: not only dealing with "real places and real objects and the transcendence of the everyday" but also engaging in "the battle against forms, walls, restrictions, etc." With her collaborative ventures, her editing work on several volumes of *New Scottish Writing,* and her forays into other genres besides fiction, Janice Galloway is a significant literary figure. Ultimately, however, Galloway is valued for her fiction and for her renderings of the lives of people who have few, if any, opportunities of breaking into the higher freedoms: to imagine, to re-invent themselves, to break free of social and religious constraints. As she said to interviewer Kirsti Wishart, "My work is all about joy-finding it where you can even in the most bleak of surroundings."

BIOGRAPHY

Janice Galloway comes from a working-class family. Both parents, James Galloway and Janet Clark McBride, worked before their marriage for Scottish Motor Transport, he as a driver, she as a ticket collector or "clippie." They lived in Saltcoats on the Ayrshire coast, and their first child, a son, was stillborn. Nora, Galloway's older sister, was born in 1938. She died in 2000. Janice, born in 1956, was the third and youngest child, referred to by her mother as "a mistake." As, such family life was not particularly happy. Galloway's father was an alcoholic; he and her mother separated when Janice was four-years old. He died when she was six, and she admits to having few memories of him.

In a piece she wrote for the Edinburgh International Book Fair publication and republished in *A Scottish Childhood,* an anthology that collects stories from a variety of Scots, Galloway describes her early childhood and her evolution as a writer. She could read by the time she entered primary school. To conform, she pretended to participate in reading lessons with the others in her class. This conformist instinct didn't last. At the local library, attempts to read books above her grade level were discouraged; she read them anyway. Her sister read books, but not by women: "Women canny write," Nora would say, meaning women can't write. Just as she defied the librarian by reading the books that interested her, Galloway bristled at this rule as well. The main thing she learned from other people's reactions to her precociousness was that "Enjoying words was an occupation fraught with pain, full of traps, bombs and codes." She describes how she "accidentally wrote a novel" when she was ten. Upon finding Janice's opus, Mrs. Galloway burned it as trash. Janice Galloway was not the coddled child or one nurtured for her brilliance. Told that women can't write, she became a writer. This trait of defying categories, of refusing assent to the rules of what is acceptable, is also a hallmark of her work in fiction.

Fortunately the upper grades of the local school system were richer experiences—at least musically—and Janice flourished. She learned how to read music and play an instrument. She joined the school orchestras and sang in the choirs. Kenneth Hetherington, the teacher she credits for bringing music into her life, also provided the necessary pressure on her mother to allow her to go to the university. Glasgow University being close by and the only one she had even heard of, she enrolled there. It disappointed her, chiefly because there was no emphasis on what she calls "making"—as in making music. In addition, male professors dominated, and reading lists ignored both women and Scottish writers. She took a year off to get her bearings and worked for the Welfare Department before returning to finish her degree.

Fittingly her none-too-helpful academic adviser gave her the impetus to complete her studies by saying, "Girls often give up, it's nothing to be ashamed of." In 1978, at the age of twenty-two, Janice earned her M.A. degree. While dropping out was a disorienting experience in which she questioned her desire for higher education, the interlude in the Welfare Department provided some of the experiences and insights that fed into her early short stories and first novel.

She didn't return to such work after graduation and was unemployed for awhile until her mother pressured her to get a job. Galloway became a teacher and stayed with the profession for ten years. Typically, she was rebellious and turned up in trousers on the first day, only to be sent home to change. She must conform. Examining the reading list for seniors, she counted only thirteen women among the sixty writers listed. She says in *A Scottish Childhood* that the constraints "started something on a slow simmer" in her brain. Over this decade, the simmer in her brain "melted down all the bloody nonsense I'd been led to believe about AUTHORSHIP, WOMEN, SCOTLAND, CLASS AND ART (her emphasis)0sqb;. . . . I could connect reading lists with straitjackets, the university with Saltcoats Library, and my sister with Hitler."

Nowhere in this major awakening does Galloway mention the influence of the women's movement, a powerful force for women at this time. Instead she portrays herself as the lonely outsider. Her rejection of categories for herself, among them "feminist," is apparently absolute. She states clearly to the interviewer Dorte Eliass, "I don't regard myself as a 'feminist' writer. I regard myself, if at all, as a writer trying hard to get things, states of mind, as clear as I can make them" (p. 7). Even so, she expressed herself in words any feminist would applaud when she told Christie Leigh March that "I want to write as though having a female perspective is normal" (p. 1).

Galloway's contribution to *A Scottish Childhood* ends with a bracing, passionate list of the three things she had learned before she started writing:

a) the words ART, GOOD and REAL are bigger than a lot of folk would have us believe;

b) I didn't have to believe everything I was told; and

c) anything starting with *women canny* stunk like a month-old kipper

In her early thirties, she wrote a short story that was accepted for publication at the *Edinburgh Review.* She describes it as the first story she wrote, evidently not counting her novel writing at age ten. Her career as a writer had officially begun.

THE TRICK IS TO KEEP BREATHING

To become a writer, for Janice Galloway, meant embracing her own language, its idiosyncracies, its beauties. Being a Scot has been both boon and bane for her. As the twentieth century drew to a close, there was a hunger among Scots themselves to hear their own voices and experiences validated by writers like James Kelman, A. L. Kennedy, and Galloway, among others, in works often labeled "urban and gritty." Galloway rejects any pigeonholing of her work, and this labeling, she tells Kirsti Wishart, was simply "shorthand for 'Scottish' at one time" and she deeply resents it. Her first novel, *The Trick Is to Keep Breathing* (1989), is "Scottish" in a good sense. Galloway knows the particulars of her place and the way her characters speak and think. In this novel her tone is dark but not bitter. Her wit and her empathy for her characters leaven the heaviness of her theme: human suffering and the enormous effort it takes to overcome it.

In *Trick,* Galloway plunges the reader directly into the consciousness of her main character, Joy Stone, though the reader doesn't learn her name for quite awhile. Surely her name is ironic; surely it isn't. Galloway keeps the reader guessing and interested by interweaving flashbacks with the present of this young woman who appears terribly alone and in desperate straits. What happened to her lover? Why did he drown himself while on a holiday with her? Was his death her fault? She thinks it must be and suffers torments

trying to continue her own life. The reader gets to know Joy in a personal waymdash;only more deeply because the reader is privy to the motion of her thoughts. Like the great literary modernists of the early twentieth century—James Joyce, Virginia Woolf—Galloway employs the stream-of-consciousness technique; her subject, however, is a Scot, a woman, a teacher, and not the bearer of any large symbolic significance except her own desperate situation: How ordinary she is; how excruciating her struggle with a descent into madness and self-loathing; how unheroic the "tricks" she discovers to keep her life going. As Galloway states to March, "I was astonished by her keeping going, by the fact that people do. . . . That great works of art get made is remarkable, but more remarkable than that is that there is so much bloody misery in the world, so much effort and demand and folk keep at it, trying to construct, make it better" (p. 8).

Despite the brilliance of *Trick,* it's a difficult novel to read because of Joy's desperation and Galloway's commitment to deal with subject matter that is often perverse. Nicholas Royle in *The Uncanny* describes the novel as a "first person [narrative] concerned with hunger and madness, with someone who does not or will not eat and whose disturbed state of mind is disturbing to others, not least the reader" (p. 215). Galloway explores all the dimensions of Joy's "disturbed state" from anxious attempts at normality to her scattered efforts at diverting herself with women's magazines to bulimic episodes. Desperate to act normally, Joy begins to fix lunch for herself. She finds a can of soup in her cupboard, opens it, and then gets more involved with it: "The next thing I knew, I'd pushed my hand right inside the can. The semi-solid mush seethed and slumped over the sides and onto the worktop as my nails tipped the bottom and the torn rim scored the skin." As she cleans up the mess, she makes a significant discovery: "it had never dawned on me till I stood here, bug-eyed at the sink, congealing soup up to my wrists. I didn't need to eat." She repeats the sentence: "I didn't need to eat" (p. 38). As the depiction of someone whose self-loathing has turned to revulsion toward the physical nature of food, this passage is both riveting and convincing.

The bleakness of Galloway's novel is leavened by her dark wit. When Joy commits herself to a mental hospital because she recognizes that she's not getting better on her own, she expects professional help. She has encounters with various men in the medical profession whom she labels Dr. One, Dr. Two and Dr. Three because they don't bother to introduce themselves. The encounters are presented as minidramas or scenes in a play with Joy in the role of Patient:

Patient: I've been here nearly a week.

Dr. Three: Yes. So what can I do for you?

Patient: [Confused. Has forgotten and is trying to remember.] Treatment. I want to know about treatment.

Dr. Three: [Leans back with an ominous creak] I don't know what sort of thing you expected. There's no set procedure for these things. . . . Any other questions?

(p. 126).

This ludicrous exchange ends with the doctor assuming she wants a pass to leave the hospital grounds. He tells her she can go out any time she likes. Dr. Three doesn't have a clue how to "treat" Joy Stone, nor does he seem concerned about her well-being. What's absurd is that Joy thought she might be helped. The droll naming of the doctor, Joy's befuddlement at how inept the professionals are, the deadpan "stage directions" all add up to the satirical humor characteristic of Galloway's art.

In addition to dialogue scenes like the above, *Trick* contains postcards written to and from Joy, self-help lists, the lyrics of pop songs, and snippets from advice columns Joy reads in women's magazines: "Perfect Pasta in Minutes / Nononsense Looks for the Working Mum" (p. 39). *Trick*, unlike most novels—even those by modernists such as Woolf and Joyce—would not work well as an audio experience or as a "Book on Tape." It requires a textual reading. As Mary McGlynn points out in *The Poor Mouth*, "*Trick* has a body. . . . [It] demands that the reader approach it as an object" (p. 190). Words bleed into the margins; italics and capitalization play a large part in the text (as they do in Galloway's interviews and essays). McGlynn states that "these features work in the context of a book about anorexia to assert the physicality of the text" (p. 190). Thus Galloway's novel can be healthy even if her main character is distinctly not healthy.

Joy is looking for something, and even as she looks she understands it is "No good. But then it's all no good" (p. 39). Her search is messy and she's looking for help in the wrong places. But where are the right places? And who is to judge? Galloway comes down hard on popular culture in this novel, but she doesn't use a sledgehammer. Her approach is satirical, not didactic, and gets the point that there's not much in social services or women's magazines to help anyone. Joy must locate whatever reason she finds to keep living within herself. Galloway espouses an existential point of view. There is no meaning outside the self for Joy to discover. Whatever meaning she finds lies within her own bereaved heart and befuddled mind. The ending of the novel, as Nicholas Royle points out, is "redemptive" (p. 216). Alone, Joy imagines that a friend may visit—or she may visit a friend. She thinks about learning to swim ("I read somewhere the trick is to keep breathing. . . . They say it comes with practice") and possibly reading some "light fiction." She listens to tapes on her headphones and hears a voice, her own, saying: "I forgive you. . . . Nobody needs to know I said it. Nobody needs to know" (p. 235). Royle reads this ending as a cop-out because Joy is still coaching herself with what she reads in popular magazines: "They say" and "I read somewhere." Royle is too harsh. The voice that Joy hears is her own and not an advice columnist's. In addition, she is protective about her self-forgiveness. It's not for public consumption; it's her truth.

BLOOD

Galloway's *Blood,* a collection of short stories, appeared in 1991, but the stories had been written both before and during the writing of *Trick.* They share some of the same concerns, characters who live in Scotland, use language with Scottish idioms, and so on. Galloway is not to be mistaken, however, as a local colorist, as Josiane Paccaud Huguet reminds us in "Breaking Through Cracked Mirrors: The Short Stories of Janice Galloway," an extensive and dense essay on *Blood.* "Galloway's stories," Huguet insists, "are symbolic centres rather than slices of Scottish life or womanly experience" (p. 16). By "symbolic centres" she means the way the narratives derive their energy from symbols and, in particular, Galloway's reliance on metonymy to develop her meanings, writing what Huguet calls "poetic prose." Huguet sees Galloway as a modernist whose narratives give us a sense of the "reality of fragmentation" both as a "motif and a structuring principle" (p. 11). Similar to T. S. Eliot in *The Waste Land,* Galloway depicts a fragmented world (the "cracked mirror") and a loss of wholeness, both interior and exterior.

If wholeness or unity does exist, it has been lost; instead of wholeness, decomposition abounds in the stories contained in *Blood.* Perhaps the most graphic instance of decomposition/loss of wholeness occurs in "The Meat," a narrative about a butcher who hangs a carcass on a hook in his shop. The "meat" gives off a terrible odor that gets worse as the days pass. Customers avoid it. Galloway describes the process of its decay: "By the tenth day, the fat on its surface turned leathery and translucent like the rind of an old cheese. Flies landed in the curves of the neck and he did not brush them away. The deep-set ball of bone sunk in the shoulder turned pale blue" (p. 109). Finally the butcher takes it out back of the shop for the animals to pick at. As appalling as the "meat" is, Galloway describes it with an intense fascination. More appalling are the implications of the narrative's ending, which simply relates how the butcher "salvaged" the remains "and sealed [them] in a plain wooden box beneath the marital bed. A wee minding" (p. 109). Evidently the "meat" was the butcher's wife. Ultimately Galloway's narrative depicts the end result of the decomposition of wholeness in the marital relation and, by extension, between man and woman.

Here the man is portrayed as brutal and commonplace, the woman as victim.

"The Meat" is, perhaps, the grimmest tale in *Blood* and the most grotesque. Several interviewers and critics have called attention to Galloway's use of the grotesque (rotting corpses, copious flows of blood, an intense physicality). Galloway ascribes this interest to her Scottishness and tells Eliass: "Grotesquerie is merely another method. Scottish writing has long been steeped in the telling of dark tales—from Border Ballads. . . to Scott and Stevenson to Alasdair Gray and Muriel Spark—that perspective is part of our culture and something we're at home with. It's a way of seeing from this dark landscape, perhaps . . ." (p. 8).

Other stories treating male/female relations in *Blood* evolve into outcomes a shade less dark than in "The Meat." Take, for example, "Fearless," a story named after an eccentric and terrifying old man who torments the villagers who have learned to ignore his belligerence and obscenities. He makes the mistake of harassing the narrator's mother: "A lot of loud, jaggy words came out the black hole of his mouth. I didn't know the meanings but I felt their pressure. I knew they were bad. And I knew they were aimed at my mother." She finds courage within herself not only to face him (her mother's back is turned) but to plant a kick. The result is that the tormentor leaves, "clutching the ankle with his free hand" but still swearing. Because the narrator tells this story of her childhood encounter from the remove of age, she is able to put it into perspective. She says she can still hear the sound of "Fearless" (though he must be dead by now, as is her mother): "the chink and drag from the close mouth in the dark . . . with every other woman . . . I hear it, still trying to lay down the rules. It's more insistent now because we're less ready to comply, look away and know our place. . . . The outrage is still strong and I kick like a mule" (p. 115). For anyone who has asserted the right not to be trampled, the story and its conclusion are powerful. For a subjugated woman, of course, the story is a manifesto.

Perhaps the most painful aspect of "Fearless" is not the dreadful man and his angry encounters but the reaction of the narrator's mother to the well-placed kick. She does not see it as liberating but berates her daughter and warns her she will "be found dead strangled up a close one day and never to do anything like that again" (p. 114). The heroic child (also "Fearless") has a timid, fearful mother who does not appreciate her. This is just one indication of what Huguet means when she characterizes the "voice" in these stories as "speaking from the dislocations of womanhood" (p. 1). Both mother and daughter find themselves located in an environment where hostility toward women is commonplace. Acting on the natural bond she feels for her mother, the daughter earns only her disapproval. She cannot locate herself in her mother's affection or esteem. Dislocation is anxiety-producing and perplexing and leads, necessarily, to fragmentation. You are not part of a whole, but unattached. While this situation leads to personal freedom, it's not conducive to unity or wholeness.

To use Huguet's term, the "symbolic centre" of "Fearless" would be the "black hole" of the old man's mouth, a phrase Galloway repeats with a variation in the conclusion, describing a terrifying sound coming from "the close-mouth in the dark." This "black hole" stands for anything that can engulf or consume an individual, in other words, oppression. It is terrifying, but it must be withstood or else the self will be annihilated.

That same sense of oppression also operates in Galloway's title story, aptly named "Blood." Overtly it deals with a young girl's experience with having a tooth pulled and the bleeding that results. Her dentist does not use modern methods but sheer physical force: "He put his knee up on her chest getting ready to pull, tilting the pliers" (p. 1). Choosing not to close her eyes, the girl can see, close-up, the man's features, "his cheeks a kind of mauve colour, twisting at something inside her mouth." She prefers to keep her eyes open because it is even worse to imagine what he is doing. Instead she "focus[es] past the blur of knuckles to the cracked ceiling. She was trying to see a pattern, make the lines into something she could recognize." While the male dentist is clearly in a power position, the girl still has volition and she uses it. Provided with a sanitary

napkin—a "crass offering" according to Margery Metzstein (p. 143)—to catch the flow of blood from the extraction, the girl leaves the office to return to school. On the way she feels the beginning of her menstrual period and retreats to a practice room to find something "clear" and "clean" as a relief from her body. The story is intensely physical—bordering on the grotesque—and the reader experiences a visceral response to the ending when the girl opens her mouth to tell an inquiring male student that the piece she is playing is Mozart not Haydn and the blood in her mouth comes "spilling over the white keys and dripping onto the clean tile floor." Metzstein refers to the blood in this story as "a powerful symbol . . . for those aspects of the female which cannot be contained and which cause fear" (p. 144). The boy is appalled and sees the pulled tooth, with its "claw roots," saved in a piece of tissue. The girl is equally appalled, "sitting dumb on the piano stool, not able to move, not able to breathe" (p. 9).

The intense physicality of Galloway's writing in passages such as this is one of the defining characteristics of her style. Galloway's fascination with physicality—or the fact of being—deeply informs the concluding story in Blood and the longest, "A Week with Uncle Felix." The story focuses on Senga, a girl around the same age as the pianist in "Blood." Traveling with her Aunt Grace and her Uncle Duncan, Senga is visiting Grace's brother Felix, her dead father's brother. Like the pianist, Senga has great trouble speaking; she is abnormally shy. She overhears the adults talking about her, saying "She's bound to be funny, a bit withdrawn" (p. 48). They attribute this to Senga's mother, described as "bitter." The reader pieces together the information much as Senga does. In one scene Felix encourages her to ask him about her dead father, Jock. She can't think of anything to ask until it is too late, "then she knew. She knew what she should have asked all along. What was his spit? This thing she was, just his spit. And forming the question, she suddenly suspected the answer. It was something too terrible to know about, something nobody would say to you even if you asked, even if they understood" (p. 170). This is also something quite different from "spitting image," which would mean she simply resembles her father.

She has been told she is her father's "spit" as the reader later learns when Senga looks at a photograph of herself that Felix has placed in his guest room. On the photo is written "Senga, Jock's girl." Senga thinks about the identification she has been given, the fact of her being "Jock's girl." Her mother never even said his name. Just your father; just his spit, his bloody spit" (p. 173). The "spit" is semen, her father's sperm or seed. So that is all she is, at least in the eyes of her mother. The evening before the guests leave to go back to Saltcoats, Felix comes to Senga's room, slightly drunk, and asks her for a kiss. He tells her: "Wouldn't believe I had a niece so pretty, your age. Surprise, your coming so late. Your dad said you were a mistake. Mistake. But just fun, just fun" (p. 176). The casual reference to her being a "mistake" compounds the insult of her being her dad's "spit." How could she be the "normal lassie" her relatives would like? She never had a decent relationship with her father, and her mother bears a grudge against him that she takes out on Senga.

As Senga gradually puts the pieces together to create a semicoherent picture of who she is, the reader performs a similar function by being attentive to Galloway's handling of metonymy. The key is "spit" and the way she repeats it, then repeats it again with a twist—perhaps revenge—in the strand of pearls Felix gives to Senga: "Your Aunt June's, long time ago. Pearls, love. Just seed, but pearls all right" (p. 174). She does not want them but has to accept them, has to say something nice: "Lovely. They're lovely." She does not find them beautiful but "terrifying" because they come from the lecherous old man and are an attempt to buy her affection. She leaves them behind when getting ready to go home, but Grace spots them and scolds her for forgetting them. Senga's refusal to take the beads is her revenge, and the box slips from her hand: "Three of four beads pattered onto the rug, pinholes staring up like tiny eyes" (p. 178). Grace retrieves them, but Senga has made her point: she is not going to take any more "seeds," any

more "spit." Once the reader becomes aware of Galloway's technique in these stories, the experience of reading them becomes deeply satisfying. Senga may not be able to speak what she feels, but she can act and her actions speak for her.

With all its obvious merits, *Blood* was shortlisted for the *Guardian* Fiction Prize and the Saltire Society Scottish Book of the Year Award and was a *New York Times* Notable Book of the Year. Acclaimed at home in Scotland and abroad, Janice Galloway was in full stride and began her second novel, *Foreign Parts* (1994). In this book, winner of the McVitie's Prize, she moved away from a distinctly Scottish locale. When asked by Aoife Kernan whether this move was "conscious" and an attempt to remove herself from inclusion in some sort of generic "Scottish" writing, Galloway responded:

> I write about what interests me. . . . It's not a "choice" in any conventional sense. Having said that, whilst carrying out the work, I often found it was a relief not to have to openly embroil myself in the expectation that I was fascinated by my own geographical origin. . . . The focusing on "whither Scottishness" is horrible—a kind of throwback to not having any real belief in your country's right to exist.
>
> (p. 2).

FOREIGN PARTS

Central to understanding what Janice Galloway has achieved in *Foreign Parts* is what she reveals in "Tongue in My Ear: On Writing and Not Writing *Foreign Parts*." She began the novel and then stopped after having composed fifty pages. She had set her novel about Cassie and Rona, two women friends, in France, a place she admits not knowing much about. They can't speak the language well nor do they communicate particularly well with each other. She was stuck on this problem for a year, during which time she had a baby, a son. Giving birth and then caring for her child helped her to establish her priorities around what were the "ESSENTIALS" (her emphasis). Returning to the novel, she understood more clearly what it wanted to be about: "multiple isolations, unspoken feelings, repressions, restrictions and all."

Galloway attributes her interest in these themes to her Scottish background. "It's hardly contentious to say," she explains, "that a significant number of Scottish novels are more notable for this preoccupation for what is not said rather than what is; with the struggle to find a 'voice'" (p. 1). Galloway writes of the "psychological damage" that has been done to Scots because of "centuries of contempt for Scottish accents, syntax and expression." Scots themselves have participated in this denigration, she says, "keen to internalize ruling-class contempt and pass it on to our children." This pathology is not unique to Scots but extends to all "disempowered, artificially silenced or marginalised groups." Perhaps having a child and thinking of what she would pass on to him provoked these thoughts. Galloway identifies herself as a "woman writer from a working-class Scottish background." As such, she finds herself "trebly familiar" with issues of marginalization and finding a voice: 1) as woman, 2) as working-class, and 3) as a Scot. Knowing herself and her own concerns allowed her to return to Cassie and Rona not as a problem but as "home ground; complexly simple products of Scottish female experience." Galloway concludes her piece on writing *Foreign Parts* by saying, "[Cassie and Rona] taught me a lot about how I work, what I feel to be important."

What Galloway deems important keeps circling back to her own life story: the absent then dead father, the bitter mother, a dysfunctional family. *Foreign Parts* opens with chapter "none" delineated as page 000. In it a young girl is running home and being chased by her mother who tells her, "Your daddy's died." The girl doesn't understand who this "daddy" is; the mother tells her it is "the man you visit at Aunty Nora's" and then "you've no daddy any more." The girl can't comprehend this death, only the physical reality of "the sound of the sea," always a presence where she lives. She thinks of the bridge crossing a portion of the sea and of the "chill noise of the waves washing up against the metal girders." Galloway announces her themes in a poetic fashion through her images. This novel will be about going home, but not to the traditional family, such a failure in this girl's (Cassie's) case. As the novel begins at the edge of the sea, so will it end, only on a more positive note.

Early on in the novel Cassie and Rona encounter the word "BRICOLAGE" (Galloway's emphasis) on a French billboard. Neither of them seems to know what it means. As Glenda Norquay explains in "Fraudulent Mooching," her essay on *Foreign Parts,* "in its everyday usage . . . 'bricolage' carries connotations of 'fragments' and 'construction' " (p. 1). For Norquay these two meanings underlie the structure and intent of Galloway's novel. As in *Trick* and *Blood,* Galloway deals with issues of fragmentation and dislocation, on the most literal level placing her characters in an unfamiliar place needing to find their own way. Their guidebook, *Potted France,* snippets of which appear throughout the novel, is useless. Cassie is particularly annoyed by the guidebook's reference to the war cemeteries: "When you think what happened out there and this thing sticks in something that misses the point" (p. 19). Rona does not respond to Cassie's outrage. Since Cassie never learned how to drive, Rona attends to the road. "'Look,' she said. 'Cows'" (p. 20).

Rona's lack of response, her deflection of the subject, is typical of exchanges in the novel. They may be traveling together but they are not seeing the same world. For Cassie the flatness of the terrain is a gut-wrenching reminder of the war, when northern France was "bombed to hell." Rona sees cows. The fragmentation aspect of "bricolage" is prominent and easy to see. Norquay sums up the theme and technique: Galloway "works with broken narratives and syntax, breaks in chronology and unfinished sentences. . . . The past . . . breaks into the present through memories and photographs. . . . Foreign voices break into the narrative, the guidebook excerpts structure the women's journey, they read letters from Rona's grandfather (killed in France in the First World War) to his wife" (p. 1).

While noticing the fragments in the text, the reader should also keep in mind the other aspect of "bricolage"-construction. Like *Trick, Foreign Parts* moves toward a positive outcome, and

Norquay terms both novels "reconstructive fictions" (p. 3). Galloway's technique is to refashion something new from the bits and pieces of her text. Norquay says that "things are put back together but in a new way. In the hopeful ending to the narrative we are allowed a glimpse of new possibilities, of a way of living which might not be determined by all the old discourses" (p. 3).

Primary among the "old discourses" are male/female relations, specifically Cassie's ten-year relationship with her former boyfriend Chris. Both Cassie and Rona are single and neither has, at present, a significant male lover in her life. Rona proposes the trip and Cassie goes along for lack of anything better to do. They have taken previous trips together—as have Cassie and Chris. Horst Pillager points out that "the flashbacks that tell the story of her holidays, and her life, with Chris and other men, are presented in the form of Cassie showing . . . snapshots to somebody. . . . By sorting out her past she is trying to achieve a perspective for her future" (p. 129). As is typical of the novel's "bricolage" technique, the "photos" are glossed by Cassie and appear as snippets in the text and only gradually accrue a meaning. About an early photo, Cassie says, "This was meant to be one of me but I'm not in it. A bit of Nelson's column and two pigeons." She also tells us about Chris, the taker of the shot: "He used to kid folk on it was an Art shot but it wasn't. He just slipped when he was pressing the shutter release" (p. 22). In this casual description Cassie reveals something about who was calling the shots (Chris) and who got erased (Cassie). While joking, Cassie also reveals something about Chris's pretensions.

In a photo taken of her toward the end of her relationship with Chris, more significant issues concerning Chris's pretensions emerge. Taken in Turkey, the photo causes Cassie to remark on her "colour": "I look like a peeled scab." She is sunburned, obviously a foreigner, and with Chris, who enjoys the locals practicing their English with him. Cassie mentions how he "loved all that, talking in a drawl about the House of Parliament and London Our Capital. It's Edinburgh his bloody capital only he didn't want to risk saying that and have them think he was less important

than they thought" (p. 179). Cassie was poised to tell the truth, only he stopped her. "Come on Cassie, for christsake lighten up we're on our holidays, smiling like he was going to bite" (p. 179). Chris is the embodiment of Galloway's statement about Scots "internalizing ruling-class contempt," and Cassie eventually leaves him when she can't stand his lack of authenticity any longer.

As Cassie sorts out her past relationships with Chris and other men, she begins a new configuration centered upon her friendship with Rona, difficult and exasperating as it is most of the time. Mary McGlynn in "The Poor Mouth" sums up the import of the ending by stating that Cassie and Rona

> turn away from conventional notions of family, creating their own family unit in a relationship that cannot be filed under any existing stereotype. they seem somewhat like crabby old maids facing the remainder of their lives together, but a warm physicality combined with the hint of sexual promise, not an out-and-out lesbian theme, asserts a new form of interaction.
>
> (p. 218).

Significantly, the last chapter of *Foreign Parts* begins with another snapshot and gloss by Cassie, this time a photo of Rona. Her photo and a second photo of Joan of Arc's statue in Rouen signify a change for Cassie. Rona's ongoing presence in Cassie's life is the hoped-for new reality. Cassie is also critical of how Joan of Arc is rendered, the burning pyre "not causing undue concern." For Cassie, the statue lies: "The skin can't keep its distance from that much reality. Suffering is not made nobler by being unobtrusive," she says, to recapitulate the novel's interest in bringing forth the unexpressed.

From Rouen they head to the coast for the return ferry, Galloway referring to them always with a double naming and reversal: "Rona and Cassie / Cassie and Rona" to emphasize they are equal partners, neither one the main figure of the couple. Cassie, however, is the focalizer, the one through whose eyes we "see" the events of the novel. As the novel opens with a scene by the sea in Cassie's hometown, so it ends, this time on a much happier note on the French coast. The two women meet an Algerian student and they strike up a conversation, most of it in French, halting on the part of Rona and Cassie, "but he doesn't mind. He comes with us." This friendly dark-skinned man with whom they converse comfortably takes some of the edge off the harsh pronouncements of the previous chapter, Cassie's railing about men's "emotional dishonesty," their "laziness and evasion." The Algerian man wishes them "au revoir" and gives his name, Aki, "his face. . . luminous with pleasure." He looks closely at both women and asks Cassie if Rona is "votre soeur." Cassie replies, "Oui, ma soeur." He then takes their photo, the last in the text: "Me and Rona on the beach at Veulettes"(p. 259). It is clear, then, that Galloway intends this ending to suggest a new kind of family for Cassie and Rona, one not dependent upon what McGlynn calls "concessions to blood relations, advocating instead the ideal of family as constructed by choice, not biology" (p. 207).

WHERE YOU FIND IT

Galloway's 1995 collection of short stories, *Where You Find It,* allows her to pursue the theme of love without getting into the trickier waters of constructing a new form of family. Galloway needs the range and variety of the short story form in order to explore imaginatively many diverse kinds of human loving—or not loving, as the case may be. Graham Dickson's review of *Where You Find It* calls attention to the central theme of love "in all its forms." He rightly points out that "perfect romantic love is noticeable by its absence." What the reader finds instead is "Love as reality. Love despite knowing better," even "absence of love." In this last category are some of Galloway's most poignant stories.

In "babysitting", for example, a young boy babysits his toddler brother. No adults care for them and the children fend for themselves. In a grotesque touch, the last scene depicts the living room where their dead father sits before the television, the stench of his body nearly overwhelming. In "someone had to," an adult man abuses a little girl, her mother a passive enabler. While Galloway detests the label "urban

and gritty," the adjectives seem appropriate for these stories in which she imaginatively enters the tawdry experiences of those for whom love is nothing but a gaping hole in their experience. Galloway's courage as a writer is daunting.

Of course, readers can find love stories in the tabloids and in romance novels. What Galloway brings to the dance is what Dickson terms her "muscular writing that yanks straight out the nerves of her subjects. Writing that is playful, sensual, sexual and prone to diving off at sudden angles." The title story, "where you find it," begins with the blunt topic sentence "Nobody kisses like Derek" and then proceeds to describe from the recipient's point of view the unique qualities of Derek's talents. While the narrator is supposedly wowed by Derek's performance, even awestruck at the capaciousness of his lips and tongue, there is an undercurrent of doubt about whether it's so wonderful to be kissed by him, for the narrator says, "They're our thing [the kisses], how he keeps me in line." Derek's kisses are a form of subjugation.

Fiona in "the bridge" is looking for love on a visit she makes to London where she hooks up with an acquaintance from Glasgow, a young artist named Charlie. The story swerves, or as Dickson would say, dives off at sudden angles away from their relationship when Fiona spots a beggar sleeping on the steps to the bridge, a sign reading "I need money" propped beside him. Charlie does not notice but Fiona stops to give him what she has. As Fiona and Charlie talk about Glasgow, Fiona says, somewhat ruefully, "I'm stuck with Glasgow," but then admits that she is fond of the place. Charlie, more rootless than she, disdains any attachment and says, "I don't think I want to belong to anything. Except Art maybe, my work" (p. 148). Fiona speaks up to him and articulates what appears to be the thematic center of all these stories. Daring to sound ridiculous, she tells him what life is: "Talking and interchanging, the raising of weans. Getting by. Behaving decently towards other people. Love, I suppose." Older than she is and a man, Charlie feels he can put her down: "That's where women always fuck up," he says. "Sentimentality" (p. 153). When Fiona seeks to patch things up between them, she asks for a kiss and he refuses. Moving off the bridge they see that "A piece of scarf, a rag of cloth was tied on the rail on the way down but the man was gone." Fiona notices but Charlie does not. The appearance of the beggar at the beginning and end of the story is slightly contrived, but Fiona's actions toward him ground her philosophizing about life in something specific. Without her act of charity, she would appear simply to be mouthing some fine sentiments. This young woman puts her money where her mouth is—and is believed.

Like "the bridge" and many of the stories in *Where You Find It,* the story entitled "sonata form" has a woman focalizer. The events of this post-concert evening are seen through the eyes of Mona, the pregnant girlfriend of a talented and celebrated pianist, Danny. Drawing upon her musical training, Galloway structures this story in sonata form, not in any rigid way but employing a sonata's three main sections: exposition (preceded by a slow introduction), development, and recapitulation (followed by a coda). This attempt to marry music and fiction is a precursor to Galloway's *Clara,* in which she employs a more ambitious musical organization. Mona is quite aware of the women who will be surrounding Danny at the reception; she has been through many similar events. The women perceive Danny's glamour; Mona knows about "Danny in his room all the time with the bloody piano, crashing away till midnight . . . her trying to write at the kitchen table" (p. 29).

The story swerves away from its concentration upon Mona and Danny's admirers to introduce a strange encounter with an older man who babbles away about the money it takes to run an orchestra and then barks out that "what's wrong with the whole country" is that there is "no servant class." To Mona he seems bizarre, and she tells him (Galloway's women can be verbally bold): "My mother was a servant." The man admits that his mother was also. Then he taunts Mona by challenging her to tell him "the Koechel number of [the] concerto" Danny played that evening. She doesn't know. The man then questions Danny's knowledge as well and Mona almost loses her temper, but she restrains herself. There is a dif-

ferent tone in this section of the story, cranky and odd. It indicates how Galloway is working with a two-part tonal structure characteristic of the sonata form.

After having endured the women fawning over Danny and the man insulting her and him, Mona finally gets to be with Danny. She pulls him toward her and makes a plea: "Tell me our child will not have to play the piano for a living, Danny. Tell me" (p. 33). He thinks her request is "daft," but at least he is affectionate: "He smiled like the sun coming out, kissed her cheek and started walking."

The story ends as it begins with an image of Danny's black dress tails with the "crimson lining." In this "coda," Mona is carrying the tails, "the hanger . . . biting into her fingers. It was so bloody heavy." She follows Danny to a take-out place and thinks how "She hadn't even told him how good he'd been, how proud she was of him." Then she speaks and tells him, "I love you, Danny." Mona's love for Danny is complex, both a burden and a joy. In "sonata form" Galloway presents a nuanced example of the collection's main theme: love is where you find it.

CLARA

"The sea in a blue bowl, a face staring up from the surface." So the novel *Clara* begins with a three-page preamble depicting Clara Schumann after her husband Robert's death. At novel's end Galloway will return to this same scene with Clara now imagining roads "ravelling out to the sea." In *Clara's* opening image, the sea is contained and Clara is looking at her own reflection in the water: "Touch and it breaks. For all this it's not fragile. Watch and what scatters on the water's surface comes whole again" (p. 5). From her opening pages, Galloway presents Clara Schumann as a survivor, a woman to be admired, and not, as some would have it, an impediment to her genius husband.

Galloway's novel was sparked by an off-the-cuff remark made by her son's father, a concert pianist who was "a Chopin-Schumann specialist." One day he referred to Clara Schumann as "this dreadful bitch [Schumann] was married to"

(Richards, p. 9). Galloway recalls questioning whether this was an accurate picture of Clara and started looking into the lives of the composer and his wife. With Galloway's own musical background and interest in women, the subject of her novel seems a natural. Even so, she insists to Kernan that "It's not a music book, not a biography or something for a specialist. . . . It's a story about a woman first and foremost. . . ." In fact, she says, "the book is not really 'about' Clara Schumann as an individual. I think it's about creativity and love, silence and sound—and these through the lens of that one life and the lives that surrounded it" (p. 1). Even so, the musical texture of the novel deeply informs its themes.

Clara, which won the 2004 IMPAC Dublin Literary Award, is dedicated to the memory of Kenneth Hetherington, Galloway's Saltcoats music teacher, and structured in eight chapters according to the titles of Robert Schumann's eight-part song cycle *Frauenliebe und-leben, OP. 42* (Woman's life and love). As Galloway tells Dorte Eliass, "*Clara* has eight chapters to mirror the eight songs, but allows the eight song titles to mean very different things" (p. 1). Settling upon this structure enabled Galloway to fix the parameters of her material. Written by Schumann for Clara during their courtship and early married years, these songs and others are specifically mentioned in the novel, for example the "Kreiseriana," part of OP. 42 and cited in chapter four. This song, Robert wants her to know, is his wedding gift to her since "[Clara], only she, is the theme and core it all. None of these pieces exist without her, she is the heart of everything . . ."(p. 157).

Clara lived from 1819 to 1896, yet the book ends shortly after Robert Schumann's death in 1856. Though some readers and critics fault the novelist for stopping there, telling the whole story of Clara's life was not Galloway's intent, as she explains above. After the three-page preamble the novel moves chronologically with brief quotes from the song cycle as chapter headings. An analysis of chapter four will help clarify Galloway's structure and its intent. Titled "Der Ring" this section focuses on Clara and Robert's path toward marriage, the wedding ring serving as its key symbol. Clara Wieck is eighteen, Schumann ten years older and madly in love with the daughter of his former piano teacher. Clara's father, who has disciplined her as a child prodigy and developed her career as a concert pianist, is firmly against the marriage. Although quite young, Clara has been performing for years and making discoveries about herself: "Before now, it never occurred to her to wonder *why* one played, one simply did. One still does, of course, but now she learns something new. It lends power, this thing she can do. People *admire* it" (p. 144). Robert has offered her a ring and marriage. Writing to him back home in Leipzig, Clara responds in a practical manner: "We'll need enough money, and money of our own. We can do nothing without money. . . . A ring is an object, no more. Make your promise and mean it, that's all" (p. 146). With her no-nonsense attitude toward finances and her refusal to romanticize a ring, Clara comes across as eminently practical.

Continuing her tour, Clara is acclaimed in Vienna, where "They sell Clara-cakes in the cafés" (p. 151). Schumann writes her love letters, tells her of the music he is composing, songs inspired by her. Both of them dream of their life together, but her father is a tremendous impediment, for he thinks he has the right to own Clara. Didn't he shape her, develop her talent, push her to the forefront? He fills her with guilt—or tries to: "You will never be able to repay me for all I have done for you" (p. 158). Clara's choice is clear and excruciating, either her father or a life with Robert. Her father slanders Robert in the newspapers; Robert sues and wins. The chapter ends with the wedding and the image of Clara that evening standing and looking out a window, "the spread of her fingers on the pane." Robert joins her and she sees both of them reflected in the glass and, "On the window clasp, her wedding ring, glittering like a blade" (p. 189). A ring is a symbol of marriage, of the union of two souls into one. A ring "glittering like a blade" is something else. The connotations are darker, perhaps threatening. This marriage of Clara and Robert Schumann threatens him because Clara is no stay-at-home wife but a woman who has learned her own power. He was "A man who had his pride . . . and wanted a true wife at his side, not one who earned the family income" (p. 169). The marriage threatens Clara, who would now be asked to subsume her own identity. Galloway's image of the ring focuses the chapter and is both provocative and telling. Similar patterns may be observed in other chapters.

Male/female relations have occupied Galloway's interest since the beginning of her literary career, so Clara cannot be called "a radical departure from her previous work" as stated in the IMPAC Dublin Literary Award. Galloway notes additional links in her interview with Eliass: "I have always written about intense states of mind, and about loneliness and how creative the human head can be in its attempt to survive. I think *Clara* is a development, and that the other novels were attempts in the same direction" (p. 8). What is radical is a different voice in the novel, not a Scottish voice. As Lavinia Greenlaw points out in the *New Statesman*, "the book is written in an interior but indirect version of [Clara's] voice, so that the impact of everything on her is felt but, like her, cannot evade or assert anything in response" (p. 1). The passage about seeing her and Robert's reflections in the window is typical. Clara does not speak, so what we get is that "interior" voice. Her letters and diary entries provide other instances of her voice, and Galloway had access to as many records as she required. As she points out to Eliass, "Any diary fragments quoted . . . are genuine. . . . I made none up, though some are heavily condensed" (p. 4).

The difficulty Galloway encountered in her rendering of Clara's character was, as she puts it, to make "gripping" what she perceived as "Clara's quiet, very unfashionable heroism" (p. 4). Married to a mentally unstable musical genius, bearing child after child (eight) because she did not know about contraception or feared to suggest it to her husband, feeling her own musical dreams squashed, Clara not only endured but prevailed. She was a good woman with "steadfast and womanly notions of family duty and love" (p. 4). That the reader is gripped by

the story of this good, "unfashionable" woman is a testament to Galloway's power as a writer.

Unlike a central character such as Joy Stone in *Trick* or Cassie in *Foreign Parts,* Clara, as Galloway points out, "had no access to or enthusiasm for irony, snide asides, smart put-downs. [Galloway] had to 'vulnerablise' the twenty-first century voice [she] was more used to writing in and be prepared to open the character up in a more terrifyingly direct way" (p. 4). What Galloway means by this can be illustrated at almost any point in the text. Take, for example, her portrayal of Clara performing her wifely duty of transcribing Robert's travel notes from their trip to Russia into their marriage diary. In one instance Robert wrote, "My suffering was barely endurable—and Clara's dreadful conduct!" Clara doesn't know what he is referring to, but copies the words because "that was her task and she stuck with it. Duty was duty" (p. 271).

While she performs her duty she can't help feeling terrible to think she has done something to cause him pain. Here Galloway opens up Clara's interior life: "The mix of feelings as she read these words, something bitter and sharp at once, held also a tinge of fear. Certainly fear. She told herself she would speak to him tomorrow, the day after, maybe, find out what he meant. For now, she was tired. She picked up the pen and wrote what she could" (p. 271). Where Cassie in *Foreign Parts* might have felt "something bitter and sharp," it would probably advance to a comic put-down, say, of her lover Chris and his pretensions. Clara's nature is more deeply informed by her nineteenth-century sense of wifely duty. Instead of criticizing Robert, she keeps copying. What is this "fear" Clara experiences? Her note in the diary, her own thoughts, not Robert's, provides a clue: "I can't think what this means, but I notice while reading these notes that I seem often to have made Robert angry enough to speak ill of me. Whatever I did was surely not meant. I am slow, perhaps, not tactful. I sometimes fail" (p. 171). Clara fears that she has lapsed in her wifely allegiance to Robert. Something she did or said was less than loving. Whatever fault there may be, she ascribes to herself.

Is this gripping? Is Clara's goodness dramatic? Yes, because the reader is well aware by this point that Robert is mentally and emotionally unstable. He imagines "dreadful conduct" where there is none. Before his marriage to Clara, it is possible that Schumann contracted syphilis, but this cannot be proven. His health degenerated, he attempted to drown himself in the Rhine, and he was finally incarcerated in an insane asylum, only to die at age forty-six. Clara has much more to fear that she can possibly imagine.

In the twenty-first century serious diseases like syphilis can be treated with antibiotics and wifely duty has gone out of style with the hoop skirt, yet much of *Clara* has resonance for contemporary readers. Clara Schumann attempts to have it all: marriage, motherhood, a brilliant career. The forces that tear at her are familiar to many women today. Robert is not particularly enlightened about "the woman question," but in a letter to Clara he expresses the following insight about his refusal to accompany her on a tour:

> It really was the most stupid thing I ever did to let you go. God bring you home. Should I have neglected my own work to be your companion on this trip? Should you have left yours unused when you are at the peak of your powers? No—we are a Modern Couple and hit on a way out, that was all.
> (p. 233).

He goes on to tell her that the situation won't happen again. His solution? They will travel in America, make money touring, and then return home: "Two years would earn us enough to live on and then we might live as we choose" (p. 234). Thinking over what he has written, he has his doubts about the plan and then writes, "Drinking too much. Stupid ass" (p. 235). Schumann was not "stupid" at all about their situation; Clara and Robert were a "Modern Couple" struggling to find a way to make their lives work for both partners. Even in the twenty-first century we struggle with much the same issues.

A happy solution was not to be the Schumanns'. Instead, as A. Manette Ansay says in her *Washington Post* review, "Soul-grinding sorrow is the novel's overwhelming theme." Robert descends into madness and his doctors force Clara to stay away from him. By focusing

on these two people, their musical careers and domestic tragedy, Janice Galloway helps to deepen the understanding about "timeless common things: about the inescapable influences of childhood, about creativity and married life, about communication and silence, about how art is made and how art, in turn, may erode or save the life that nourishes it" (IMPAC 2004 Award). Galloway's *Clara* is a stunning achievement.

CONCLUSION

While Janice Galloway's five major works are diverse in scope and intent, many elements connect them, both thematically and technically. Whether writing a short story or a novel, Galloway admits that she has "always written about . . . loneliness." This is as true for Joy Stone's painful alienation after her lover's death as it is for Cassie in *Foreign Parts* struggling to come to a new definition of family. Being with someone (Cassie and Rona / Rona and Cassie) is no guarantee for overcoming isolation, a truth learned by Clara Schumann as well. The "reality of fragmentation" is another theme that connects Galloway's diverse fictions. Mirrored in her style, this theme is conveyed brilliantly by Galloway in her collage technique or in "bricolage," as in *Foreign Parts*. Whatever she writes, Galloway develops keep insights into male/female relations and she often employs a female focalizer in her short stories and novels.

A feisty writer who insists upon the "normality" of the female perspective, Galloway is labeled by some as a feminist. She defies this categorization and invests her work with the truth as she sees it. If the result is an assertion of female power rather than victimhood, so be it. Passionate about her characters and themes and courageous in her forays into the darker recesses of the human condition, Janice Galloway has drawn upon the riches of Scottish literary tradition (granting a role to the grotesque, acknowledging the power of the repressed thought or emotion, allowing room for a dark wit, and so forth) to forge stories and novels that resonate with universal themes. Familiar with life on the margins as a Scot, a member of the working class, and a woman, she refuses to believe in notions of predetermined inferiority. She has consistently broken down boundaries on what is acceptable in fiction, and her work is rightly acknowledged as experimental in form and in content. In her poetic prose, this teller of dark tales does not succumb to gloom but finds joy in the way ordinary people insist upon their right to shape their own lives, their own solutions.

Selected Bibliography

WORKS OF JANICE GALLOWAY

NOVELS AND SHORT STORIES

The Trick Is to Keep Breathing. Edinburgh: Polygon, 1989; Normal, Ill.: Dalkey, 1994.

Blood. London: Secker and Warburg, 1991; New York: Random House, 1992.

Foreign Parts. London: Jonathan Cape, 1994; Normal, Ill.: Dalkey, 1995.

Where You Find It. London: Jonathan Cape, 1996; New York: Simon & Schuster, 2002.

Clara. London: Jonathan Cape, 2002; New York: Simon & Schuster, 2003.

OTHER WORKS

Chute (play). Paris: Editions Solaires Intempestifs, 1998.

Pipelines (collaboration with Anne Bevan, sculptor). Edinburgh: Fruitmarket Gallery, 2000.

Boy book see (poetry). Glasgow: Mariscat Press, 2002.

Monster (opera libretto, collaboration with Sally Beamish). Glasgow: Scottish Music Information Center, 2002. (Premiered by Scottish Opera, February 28, 2002.)

Rosengarten (collaboration with Anne Bevan). Edinburgh: Platform Projects, 2004. (Premiered at Hunterian Museum, Glasgow, 2004.)

NONFICTION

"Tongue in My Ear: On Writing and Not Writing *Foreign Parts*." *Review of Contemporary Fiction.* Chicago: Dalkey Archive Press, 1995. Available online (http://www.galloway.1to1.org/ear.html).

"Objective Truth and the Grinding Machine." Republished in *A Scottish Childhood: 70 Famous Scots Remember.* Compiled and edited by Anthony Kamm and Anne Lean.

London: Trafalgar Square, 1999. Available online (http://www.galloway.1to1.org/HowIstarted.html).

"Balancing the Books: Regarding Writers' Earnings." *Scotsman,* spring 2000. Available online (http://www.galloway.1to1.org/Balancing.html).

CRITICAL STUDIES AND REVIEWS

Ansay, A. Manette. "Sad Song: *Clara.* by Janice Galloway." *Washington Post,* March 9, 2003, p. BW09.

Dickson, Graham. "Review of *Where You Find It. .*" *Richmond Review,* 1996. Available online (http://www.richmondreview.co.uk/books/whereyou/html).

Greenlaw, Lavinia. "*Clara by Janice Galloway.*" *New Statesman,* July 8, 2002.

Huguet, Josiane Paccaud. "Breaking Through Cracked Mirrors: The Short Stories of Janice Galloway." *Etudes Ecossaises.* 2:5–29 (1993). Available online (http://www.galloway.1to1.org/Mirrors.html). IMPAC Dublin Literary Award (http://www.impacdublinaward.ie/2004 20Award/Titles/Galloway.htm).

McGlynn, Mary Margaret. "The Poor Mouth: Versions of the Vernacular in 20th Century Narratives." Ph.D. dissertation. Columbia University, 2000.

———. "Janice Galloway." *Review of Contemporary Fiction.* (summer 2001). Metzstein, Margery. "Of Myths and Men: Aspects of Gender in the Fiction of Janice Galloway." *The Scottish Novel Since the Seventies: New Visions, Old Dreams.* Edited by Gavin Wallace and Randall Stevenson. Edinburgh: Edinburgh University Press, 1993. Pp. 136–146.

Norquay, Glenda. "Fraudulent Mooching." In *Contemporary Scottish Women Writers.* Edited by Aileen Christianson and Alison Lumsden. Edinburgh: Edinburgh University Press, 2000. Available online (http://www.galloway.1to1.org/Norquay.html).

Prillinger, Horst. *Family and the Scottish Working-Class Novel, 1984–1994.* Frankfurt am Main and New York: Peter Lang, 2000.

Royle, Nicholas. *The Uncanny.* London and New York: Routledge, 2003.

INTERVIEWS

Eliass, Dorte. "Reflections on *Clara.*" *Buchkultur.* . Vienna, 2003. Available online (http://www.galloway.1to1.org/Buchkultur.html).

Kernan, Aoife. *Trinity News.* Dublin. February, 2003. Available online (http://www.galloway.1to1.org/Trinity.html).

March, Christie Leigh. "Exchanges" *Edinburgh Review.* 101 (March 1999). Available online (http://www.galloway.1to1.org/Leighmarch.html).

Richards, Linda. "January Interview: Janice Galloway." *January Magazine.* June 2003. Available online (http://www.januarymagazine.com/profiles/jgalloway.html).

Wishart, Kirsti. "Collaboration: *Pipelines.*" *Red Wheelbar-
   row,* 2000. Available online (http://www.galloway.1to1.
   org/Wheelbarrow.html).

ELIZA HAYWOOD

(c. 1693 –1756)

Scott R. Mackenzie

ALTHOUGH ELIZA HAYWOOD has not featured prominently in most major discussions of eighteenth-century British fiction and its evolution, such discussions are now under revision. The period of Haywood's career was also that of the rise of capitalism in England and the professionalization of authorship. Haywood was a pioneer in the new literary industry, and a successful one: her first book, *Love in Excess* (1719–1720) was one of the three best-selling works of fiction of the early eighteenth century (the others were *Robinson Crusoe* and *Gulliver's Travels*). She was also a celebrity, a stage actress, and a member of more than one important literary coterie. What has kept her from receiving adequate recognition seems to be her gender and, paradoxically, her commercial ambition. Literary history has treated many women writers unjustly, but Haywood must be among the most harshly treated of all. She had the misfortune to fall foul of the great satirists Alexander Pope and Jonathan Swift, the dominant bullies in a period when literary rivalries and battles were an important part of literature itself. Pope's *The Dunciad* (1728), for instance, is one of the greatest satirical poems in English, and much of its invective is directed at writers that Pope despised, including Haywood. In a famous passage of the poem, he describes Haywood as a "Juno of majestic size, / With cowlike udders" and two illegitimate children, and he makes her the prize in a contest between two booksellers over who can produce the greatest stream of urine (p. 120).

The very force of Pope's raillery, however, indicates that Haywood ranked as a significant target, able to compete with him for public notice and affection. The joke about her immense fertility in *The Dunciad* passage must refer at least in part to her prolific literary output. Her name is attached to more than seventy plays, pamphlets, periodicals, translations, satires, and works of fiction. Poetry is one of the few fields of literary endeavor in which Haywood appears to have taken little or no part. She even spent a decade or so struggling to establish herself as a publisher and bookseller (enterprises that often went hand in hand at the time). She is a remarkable figure, by turns popular and scandalous, often commercially successful and ultimately unable to make ends meet. Most of her works are hybrid in one way or another; they usually draw upon established genres, themes, and social values but turn those qualities to new, commercial, and often salacious purposes. Frequently Haywood's writings thrilled and shocked their audiences by emphasizing women's participation in thoughts and actions that were traditionally restricted to men. In her works of fiction Haywood regularly granted to female characters the kinds of desires and sexual exploits that had hitherto been largely the domain of male characters. Along with a few other writers, including Aphra Behn, Delarivier Manley, and Lady Mary Wortley Montagu, Haywood helped to introduce English culture to ways of understanding women as possessors of intellects and desires not fundamentally different from or inferior to those of men. Resistance to those ideas, of course, persisted long after the end of Haywood's career—and the renewal of interest in her is a further step in overcoming those resistances.

LIFE AND CAREER

Virginia Woolf once lamented that we know little about Eliza Haywood other than that "she married a clergyman and ran away" (p. 23). As a result of work published in the 1990s by Christine Blouch, we now know a good deal more about

Haywood, including that she certainly did not, contrary to Woolf's opinion, marry the Reverend Valentine Haywood. The story, which suited Haywood's reputation for transgression, had emerged from hasty conclusions drawn by George Frisbie Whicher in his 1915 book *The Life and Romances of Mrs. Eliza Haywood*. The Reverend Haywood of Norfolk did indeed have a spouse named Eliza, who fled the marriage, but Blouch has proven that that Eliza's maiden name was Foord, whereas our Eliza was born Eliza Fowler. In fact our knowledge of Haywood's life before she published *Love in Excess* is rather inexact. There are three possible scenarios for the birth and family of Eliza Fowler Haywood, and though we know she married and that the marriage had almost certainly ended by 1719, we do not know whom she married nor how it ended. The three candidates for Haywood's origin are these: she is the daughter of Robert and Elizabeth Fowler of Cornhill, London, born January 21, 1689; she is the daughter of Francis and Elizabeth Fowler of St. Sepulchre parish, London, born October 14, 1693; or she is the sister of the baronet Sir Richard Fowler of Harnage Grange, Shropshire, christened January 12, 1692 or 1693. As Blouch admits, the critical preference for dating Haywood's birth to 1693 seems to rest more upon averages than positive assurance. Likewise the tradition that she is the daughter of London merchants continues to inspire adherents even though Haywood herself claimed in a letter to be "nearly related to Sir Richard of the Grange." Whichever family she came from, it is clear that she grew up in comfortable circumstances and had access to a more wide-ranging education than most women could expect at the time.

The earliest undisputed public record of the Eliza Haywood who would publish *Love in Excess* comes in 1715, when she acted the part of Chloe in a Dublin production of the play *The History of Timon of Athens; or, The Man-Hater,* an adaptation from Shakespeare by Thomas Shadwell. Although she remained involved with professional theater well into the 1730s, it appears that Haywood found authorship a more effective means of supporting herself and two children. The two careers were, nonetheless, closely connected. In the early eighteenth century no author could survive on the proceeds of publication alone; patronage was essential to any artistic career. In other words, authors would seek the approval and support of wealthy—usually aristocratic—patrons whom they would exalt in dedications and other kinds of literary praise. In return a patron would provide financial support, often in the form of a nominal public office with a steady salary. Haywood's theatrical experience was a considerable help to her in this respect. She was a member of the artistic circle surrounding Aaron Hill, a successful playwright and theater manager. In this group she met both Richard Savage, a poet with whom she had an intimate and probably sexual relationship for a year or so, and William Hatchett, her lover and playwrighting collaborator through much of the 1730s. This group of friends and rivals also provided Haywood with her experience of another crucial part of eighteenth-century literary culture, the coterie. Since the era of John Dryden in the last third of the seventeenth century, coteries had been the elite realm of artistic endeavor. They provided a forum for critical exchange, social advancement, and the circulation of works. It is the coterie culture that Alexander Pope defends against the commercial ambitions of "Hacks," who seek to turn literature into a marketplace of indiscriminate taste and little learning. In a figure like Haywood, Pope saw someone who not only debased the values of art and aristocratic privilege but also, particularly because she was a woman, showed unacceptable social aspirations. In a footnote to *The Dunciad* he decried "the profligate licentiousness of those shameless scribblers (for the most part of that sex, which ought least to be capable of such malice or impudence) who in libellous memoirs and novels, reveal the faults and misfortunes of both sexes, to the ruin or disturbance of publick fame or private happiness" (p. 119).

But Pope's complaints are extraordinarily disingenuous. He was one of the few writers of the era who was even more successful than Haywood at negotiating the tricky divide between coterie and marketplace. He enriched himself both through patron-client relationships and through publishing contracts. His vicious attacks on Haywood and other writers are as much a means of diverting attention away from his own social and commercial ambitions as they are a defense of aesthetic values. Indeed Pope and Haywood shared remarkably similar political perspectives. They were both Tories, which is to say they believed that political power was vested by God in the monarchy and a landholding aristocracy, and they were both bitterly opposed to the parliamentary reign of Robert Walpole and his Whig party. Choosing one's enemies and battles was in many respects as important as acquiring and maintaining friendships in this period. Through the 1720s Haywood maintained her profile with great skill. In this decade she published well over half of her career output—more than forty works, including a pair of four-volume collected works, translations, satires, novels, and several plays. In 1724 alone she published twelve books: *Poems on Several Occasions, A Spy Upon the Conjurer, The Masqueraders, The Fatal Secret, The Surprise, The Arragonian Queen, La Belle Assemblée* (a translation), *Bath-Intrigues, Fantomina, The Force of Nature, Memoirs of the Baron de Brosse,* and the first volume of *Memoirs of a Certain Island adjacent to the Kingdom of Utopia.* Many of these works were scandalous tales of sexual intrigue, earning their author the title the "Great Arbitress of Passion"—and a very wide audience.

From 1729 on, however, Haywood's output dropped considerably. During the 1730s her only published work of fiction was a satire of the Walpole Whigs entitled *The Adventures of Eovaai* (1736). Until the early 1990s most critics accepted the theory that Haywood withdrew from the world of letters because of the hurt inflicted by Pope in his *The Dunciad* attack. More recent critics have found little reason to accept that idea and tend to argue that Haywood diverted her career back toward the theater. She wrote and performed in plays and also published seven editions (the last in 1756) of a critical catalog, *The Dramatic Historiographer; or, The British Theatre Delineated,* which was later retitled *The Companion to the Theatre.* In this voluminous work she offered "a view of our most celebrated

dramatic pieces: in which the plan, characters, and incidents of each are particularly explained. Interspersed with remarks historical, critical, and moral" (title page). Also during the 1730s Haywood had considerable professional contact with another major literary figure, Henry Fielding. Fielding is best known for his novels, especially *Tom Jones* (1751), but at this earlier time he was a celebrated writer of satirical plays. Most of Haywood's stage work in this part of her career was with Fielding's company at the Little Theatre Haymarket. Fielding was also a Tory and, like Pope, he satirized Haywood. He based the character Mrs. Novel in his play *The Author's Farce* on her. Fielding's assault on Haywood seems to have been much less venomous than Pope's, however; many critics believe that Haywood acted the part of Mrs. Novel at least once. In return Haywood made fun of Fielding and his theater in *The History of Miss Betsy Thoughtless* (1751) when she wrote of "F_____g's scandal shop," which served two purposes: "the one to get money . . . from such as delighted in low humour . . . and the other, in the hope of having some post given him by those whom he had abused, in order to silence his dramatic talent" (pp. 66–67). In spite of this evident antipathy, Haywood was the recipient of a benefit performance by Fielding's company on May 23, 1737.

Haywood's benefit performance took place on a momentous date. The following day Robert Walpole introduced a bill to Parliament that became the Licensing Act, a law that enabled the government to suppress any theatrical performance that it found objectionable. Henry Fielding is generally seen as the direct target of this legislation and as a result he turned his hand to novels. Haywood also returned to fiction. Within four years a bookseller named Samuel Richardson had published a novel called *Pamela,* a book that could hardly have been better designed to arouse Tory ire. It tells the story, in the words of the title character, of a young servant girl whose rakish gentleman master becomes besotted with her. By her persistent and obstinate virtue and modesty, Pamela reforms him and they marry. The novel became the greatest publishing sensation that England had ever seen. A storm of debate swirled around it. Fielding published two satires of it, *Shamela* (1741) and *Joseph Andrews* (1742), and Haywood published one entitled *Anti-Pamela; or, Feign'd Innocence Detected* (1741). The *Pamela* controversy was a watershed in the development of the novel in English. Thereafter novels were inextricably associated with themes of individualism, self-determination, and the social roles of women. That Haywood had in many ways already made these themes her own is an important reason for the current revival in her critical fortunes. In the minds of novelists then and many critics today, however, Haywood's earlier fiction belonged to a genre that was deemed romance and dismissed because of its incorporation of aristocratic and chivalric codes of conduct and its association with continental Europe, especially France. In his 1714 poem *The Rape of the Lock,* for instance, Alexander Pope speaks contemptuously of "vast French Romances, neatly gilt" (p. 161).

As we have already seen, however, Haywood's literary career was much more complex than that of a hack romancer. In many respects she embodies the rise of middle-class aspiration, and her later works do so too. She spent much of the 1740s engaged in a frustrated attempt to establish herself as a bookseller and produced or contributed to three different periodicals, the first of which was the *Female Spectator.* This journal was almost entirely Haywood's own work and lasted over two years, appearing monthly. Its title alluded to the *Spectator,* the most famous of the early-eighteenth-century English periodicals. Both the *Spectator* and the *Female Spectator* consisted of essays, observations, and letters addressed to affluent urban readers. Haywood's journal was explicitly aimed at women and tended to focus more on domestic issues, but it is in other respects very much a counterpart to the original *Spectator.* The other works that Haywood published after *Anti-Pamela* include some half-dozen novels, several translations, and some books of conduct advice mostly directed at women. The later novels show the impact of the *Pamela* controversy. They treat their characters (especially the women) with greater psychological depth, focus more on domestic and private

experience, and tend to be more overtly instructive with regard to morality. Oddly enough one of them, *The Virtuous Villager* (1742), is an imitation, not a parody, of *Pamela.* The best-known of the late works is *The History of Miss Betsy Thoughtless* (1751), a four-volume fiction that follows the amorous adventures of a naive orphan "of good fortune and family" through many courtships and a poorly chosen marriage to a final happy marriage.

The difference between Haywood's early fictions and her later ones, however, is not as striking as one might imagine. Her first work of fiction also featured a main character who starts out with little understanding of the intrigues of love and sex, falls into an unfortunate marriage, and then escapes it to achieve a happy concluding marriage. In a sense what changed was as much the social, commercial, and political circumstances within which Haywood wrote as Haywood's themes and techniques themselves. She was throughout her career an adaptable and inventive artist. Often she was oppressed by social and financial circumstances that were exacerbated by her gender. The insoluble contradictions of her art must be explained at least in part by the volatile environment in which she wrote. Her collected works seem both scandalous and moralistic, carefully crafted and commercially oriented, principled and mercenary—often all at once. Her last published work was an installment of her periodical the *Young Lady,* which ends with an apology to her patrons and readers, hoping that "if Providence, in his goodness should restore her to health, to endeavor at making them amends by employing her time in something that may more immediately merit their protection and encouragement" (p. 42). These words were written in January 1756. On February 25, Haywood died.

EARLY FICTION

One of the enduring debates of English literary criticism concerns the modern novel, how it differs from earlier forms of fiction, and who should receive credit for its invention. There is a broad, though not universal, critical consensus that what we now think of as novels began appearing in English during the first half of the eighteenth century. Some critics believe that Daniel Defoe was the first genuine novelist, some that it was Samuel Richardson or Henry Fielding, or even the two of them in an unintended partnership. Eliza Haywood has never been promoted as a major progenitor of the novel, but more and more discussion is growing around the important part that she played in its development. Many criteria have been used to distinguish modern novels from earlier forms of prose fiction, and many of them remain disputed. Among those criteria is realism, which incorporates careful and linear tracing of time, representations of place and space that are specific or actual, action that is plausible and explicable, and characters that are individuals rather than stereotypes, which meant abandonment of elaborate allegorical meanings. Other criteria include a preference for domestic and private relationships and conflicts over national or political ones; plots that follow a gradually developed arc rather than a series of loosely related episodes; rejection of chivalric codes of love and honor; greater psychological depth, most notably in women characters; characters who change and develop; and a general concentration on characters who are not of the highest birth, even a tendency to denigrate the aristocracy. Haywood's fiction, particularly that from the first decade of her career, fits each of these definitions at some times and defies them at others. Her stories often feature noble men and women caught up in conflicts over honor. There are grandiose and implausible situations and passions and characters who are hardly three-dimensional. But the aristocratic values invoked tend to be questioned and undermined. The events of the stories are generally set in motion by personal desires; they do not have larger allegorical meanings, and some characters do show distinct growth and change.

One way to think about how striking and scandalous *Love in Excess* must have seemed to its original audience is to consider the standard beliefs about literature at the time. Taking scripture as the supreme model, readers expected literature to be the bearer of some higher meaning. Certainly it was acceptable for fiction also to provide enjoyment (to "delight" was the contemporary term), but to offer enjoyment alone was virtually unheard of. William Warner writes in his article "Formulating Fiction": "If an earlier, reverential practice of reading was grounded in the claim that books represented (some kind of) truth, Haywood's novels seemed ready to deliver nothing more than pleasure" (p. 285). Haywood herself admits in a preface that she has been accused of trying to "divert more than improve the minds of my readers" (*The Injur'd Husband and Lasselia,* p. 105). *Love in Excess* was not scandalous simply because it had sexual content but because it was fun. Fictions that were even more frank about sexuality had already been published by Aphra Behn and Delarivier Manley. Behn's *Love Letters Between a Nobleman and His Sister* (1684) follows a love affair between Sylvia and her brother-in-law Philander, a relationship that would have been legally defined as incest. Manley's *The New Atalantis* (1709) is a set of tales of sexual intrigue that includes actual brother-sister incest. Unlike *Love in Excess* both of these works subordinate their salacious content to allegorical themes. Behn's, written in the aftermath of the Duke of Monmouth's attempt to capture the throne of England, compares seducing a woman with usurping a throne. *The New Atalantis,* which is often called a scandal romance, satirizes the Duke of Marlborough and the Whigs who held parliamentary power. Manley was actually arrested by the government, but the grounds for her arrest were political rather than moral.

Love in Excess is not completely without themes or moral lessons, but it is certainly not an allegory in the sense that the works of Behn and Manley are. It is set in France immediately after the War of the Spanish Succession (1701–1713), and its central character is Count D'elmont, a hero of the war whose military honor, charm, and dazzling physical beauty make him irresistible: "whilst those of his own [sex] strove which should gain the largest share of his friendship; the other vented fruitless wishes, and in secret, cursed that custom which forbids women to make a declaration of their thoughts" (p. 37). But D'elmont is naive in romantic matters, "having never experienced the force of love" (p. 40), and he becomes ensnared in a triangle, created by his misinterpretation of an anonymous love note, with the innocent Amena and the worldly Alovisa. Alovisa's cunning easily overcomes D'elmont's affection for Amena, who flees to a monastery while Alovisa and D'elmont marry. This triangle, though, is only the first. In the second volume D'elmont finds that he still has not truly experienced love when he meets and falls for the "matchless Melliora," a young woman who becomes his ward. More intrigues are set off by the Baron D'espernay and Melantha, Melliora's coquettish rival. The baron persuades D'elmont to pursue Melliora but also plots to have Alovisa discover her husband's infidelity. Melliora loves D'elmont but resists his advances. Her desire, however, almost overcomes her virtue more than once, but the mischievous Melantha interrupts them just as he is "preparing to take from the resistless Melliora, the last and only remaining proof that she was all his own" (p. 124). Later Melantha fools D'elmont into sleeping with her in the belief that she is Melliora, and both the baron and Alovisa, in another nighttime intrigue, end up mistakenly stabbed to death. A third volume of the novel features yet more triangles. Here we encounter a pair of withered aristocratic siblings, Ciamarra and Citolini, Melliora's brother Frankville, and the tragic Violetta who, denied the love of D'elmont, denies herself life. Finally, after experiencing a myriad of love's rivalries, agonies, and triumphs, D'elmont and Melliora are able to achieve conjugal bliss, and desire is satisfied.

Desire is in many ways the key to *Love in Excess*. It is the force that generates the excess of the title, growing too powerful for the bounds of good sense and social stricture. For instance, the narrator describes Melliora's reaction to D'elmont's overtures: "Desire, with watchful diligence repelled, returns with greater violence in unguarded sleep, and overthrows the vain efforts of day" (p. 116). In her sleep she cries out, "Oh D'elmont, cease, cease to charm, to such a height—Life cannot bear these raptures. . . . O! too, too lovely Count—extatick ruiner!" (p. 116). D'elmont's feelings are just as uncontrollable:

"Friendship? . . . that term is too mean to express a zeal like mine . . . one great unutterable! Comprehensive meaning, is mine!" (p. 89). They are literally too much for each other. Not only do these two characters have too much desire, but their excessive attractiveness ensures that they have too many admirers as well. Conflict and intrigue arise where these volatile energies run up against each other or against social prohibitions, which include honor, virtue, ambition, and fathers' plans for their daughters. Most of the action of the novel consists of tricks and plots that are meant to circumvent the obstructions created by these prohibitions and rivalries. Alovisa, for instance, pretends to support the distraught Amena while simultaneously clearing the way for her own attempt to seduce D'elmont. The characters keep up so many secrets and falsehoods that no one (except the attentive reader) knows all of the intrigues at any one moment. Few intrigues, though, succeed as planned. Accidents and the intrigues of other characters continually interfere, as when Melantha interrupts D'elmont's seduction of Melliora, frustrating D'espernay. The narrative reaches its conclusion by eliminating its excesses, sending one character to a convent, killing off several others, and finding mutual partnerships of love for those who remain; there are actually three marriages at the end of volume 3. Closure comes when there is exactly enough love and enough lovers to share it.

We must note that Haywood is by no means the first author to portray love triumphing over adversity. It is the kind of adversity and the means of triumphing that are notable. *Love in Excess* depicts desire as a force that causes internal conflict but also as a justification for the pursuit of personal goals even at the cost of one's place in society and one's moral virtue: "Why," D'elmont asks, "should what we can't avoid be called a crime? Be witness for me Heaven! How much I have struggled with this rising passion, even to madness struggled!" (p. 124). Young women defy their fathers, D'elmont rejects lover after lover (including one he has married), Melantha tricks D'elmont into sex, and Melliora is continually at the point of surrendering herself to

D'elmont: "I no longer can withstand the too powerful magick of your eyes, nor deny any thing that charming tongue can ask" (p. 123). But desire is also a force capable of transforming people. At the beginning of the book D'elmont is a soldier and a nobleman far more than a lover: "ambition was certainly the reigning passion in his soul, and Alovisa's quality and vast possessions, promising a full gratification of that, he ne'er so much as wished to know a farther happiness in marriage" (p. 76). Haywood shows love undermining aristocratic values. From ambition, the reigning passion of a soldier and lord, D'elmont passes to lust. His willingness to hear D'espernay's advice that he "enjoy" Melliora without regard to the consequences shows, however, that his development is incomplete. Finally Violetta's dying admission that she has loved D'elmont helps him to become a lover in the full sense that Haywood intends: "'What is it that I hear, madam?' cried the Count . . . 'can it be possible that the admired Violetta could forsake her father,—country,—friends,—forgoe her sexes pride,—the pomp of beauty,—gay dresses, and all the equipage of state, and grandeur, to follow in a mean disguise, a man unworthy of her thoughts?'" (p. 264). Love, he learns, must not take account of family, class, society, wealth, or beauty. It must consist only in the desire of two people for one another.

William Warner has noted the parallel between this theme of love for its own sake and the way *Love in Excess* seems to offer pleasure for its own sake. He argues that Haywood's early fictions "teach readers, men as well as women, to articulate their desire and 'put the self first,' in the same way their characters do" (p. 284). This promotion of the idea that individuals can act freely and choose to determine their own fates implicates Haywood in the loosening of the rigid British system of social status and also argues for her place in the developing tradition of the modern novel. It would be a mistake, however, to see her as revolutionary. Her commercial activities obviously indicate a sympathy with the urge to determine one's own prosperity, but her fiction does not endorse genuine class mobility the way a novel like *Pamela* seems to do. Most

critics have now settled for the term "amatory fiction" to describe Haywood's novels, a term that fits somewhere between romance and the modern novel and that also acknowledges their deep preoccupation with love and sexual desire. More radical than the implications of individualism in Haywood's early fiction is the extension of that individualism to female characters. If being an individual means having personal desires that are independent of (and often opposed to) social rules and expectations, then Haywood distinguishes very little between men and women in that respect. When D'elmont and Melliora first appear, eighteenth-century readers would have recognized them as quite typical examples of the haughty nobleman and the cold beauty. But each of them is transformed by the potent forces in their hearts. Melliora begins as the kind of woman usually found in tales of chivalry and courtly love: "she urged the arguments she brought against giving way to love, and the danger of all softning amusements, with such a becoming fierceness, as made every body of the opinion that she was born only to create desire, not to be susceptible of it herself" (p. 107). But after locking herself away from D'elmont, she discovers something surprising:

> Melliora thought she had done a very heroick action, and sat her self down on the bed-side in a pleased contemplation of the conquest, she believed her virtue had gained over her passion. But alas! How little did she know the true state of her own heart? She no sooner heard a little noise at the door . . . but she thought it was the Count, and began to tremble, not with fear, but desire.
>
> (p. 130)

What is more, Haywood does not condemn Melliora for her failure to remain a passive object of desire.

Even though she breaches rules of decorum and virtue, especially "that custom which forbids women to make declaration of their thoughts" (p. 37), Melliora's wishes are answered. "Do I not bear at least an equal share in all your agonies?" she asks D'elmont. "Hast thou no charms—Or have I not a heart?—A most susceptible and tender heart?—Yes, you may feel it throb, it beats against my breast, like an imprisoned bird, and fain would burst its cage! To fly to you, the aim of all its wishes" (p. 124). More than one hundred years later, audiences would still find controversy in the protest voiced by Charlotte Brontë's Jane Eyre:

> women feel just as men feel; they need exercise for their faculties, and a field for their efforts as much as their brothers do; they suffer from too rigid a restraint, too absolute a stagnation, precisely as men would suffer. . . . It is thoughtless to condemn them, or laugh at them, if they seek to do more or learn more than custom has pronounced necessary for their sex.
>
> (p. 109)

Unlike Jane Eyre, Haywood's female characters do not actually move beyond the expression of desire to effectively change the course of their lives. Women like Alovisa and Melantha who act upon their desires fail to achieve their goals; indeed "fate" punishes them. Haywood's 1722 novel *The Injur'd Husband* centers on Baroness de Tortillée, a sexually adventurous woman who betrays her husband and numerous lovers, including Beauclair, the beloved of the virtuous Montamour. The Baroness ends up committing suicide in prison and Montamour marries Beauclair, but it is Montamour's refusal to actively oppose the Baroness that makes her success possible.

In *The Rash Resolve* (1723) the heroine, Emanuella, tries to escape an unwanted marriage by making an eloquent appeal to the King of Spain: "Permit me then, great King! To unfold a story must make my vile accuser's heart grow cold within him" (p. 29). But only the reader of the book believes her appeal and Emanuella's sufferings continue and grow worse. Haywood's early fiction explores over and over women's experiences of powerful passions, the ways that they react to those passions, and the effects of their actions or refusal to act. Virtually all of her women suffer, often extravagantly, and the depiction of the emotions and sufferings is affected surprisingly little by whether or not the woman concerned is virtuous. Nothing is kept back. In her dedication to *Lasselia* (1723) Haywood writes,

> My design in writing this little novel (as well as those I have formerly publish'd) being only to remind the unthinking part of the world, how dangerous it is to give way to passion, will, I hope, excuse the too great warmth, which may perhaps appear in some particular pages; for without the expression being invigorated in some measure proportionate to the subject, 'twou'd be impossible for a reader to be sensible how far it touches him.
>
> (p. 105)

Although Haywood urges her readers to restrain themselves, she herself does not do so in her prose.

SATIRES AND PERIODICALS

Eliza Haywood's lifetime coincided not only with the rise of the novel but with the first flowering of English periodical culture and the greatest era in British satire. Her contributions to these two genres are not so prolific or significant as her fiction, but they certainly merit examination. The eighteenth-century vogue for satire had begun in the latter part of the previous century when writers had become interested in reviving classical Greek and Roman literary styles. The most prominent of these writers was John Dryden. He was followed by Alexander Pope, whose *The Dunciad* has already been mentioned here, and Jonathan Swift, perhaps the greatest of all British satirists. Swift is best known for the mock exploration narrative *Gulliver's Travels;* the essay "A Modest Proposal," which draws attention to the poverty of the Irish people by advocating that the English eat Irish children who would otherwise starve; and *A Tale of a Tub,* an allegorical satire on church politics. Other important satirists of the era include Henry Fielding, who has also been mentioned here; Lady Mary Wortley Montagu, who sparred with Swift and Pope in verse; and John Gay, author of *The Beggar's Opera,* which pokes fun at the similarities between London's political establishment and its criminal underclass. Most of the well-known satirists were Tories like Haywood, and most of them devoted at least some of their writing to attacking Robert Walpole, whose domination of

Parliament lasted almost twenty-one years from 1721 on. Haywood was among them. Her musical drama *The Opera of Operas* (1733), which she cowrote with William Hatchett, is an adaptation of *The Tragedy of Tragedies; or, The Life and Death of Tom Thumb the Great* (1731), one of Henry Fielding's satirical stabs at Walpole. Her other assault on Walpole is the satirical fiction *The Adventures of Eovaai,* which will be discussed further below.

In the 1720s Haywood also produced two scandal romances comparable to Delarivier Manley's *The New Atalantis.* They were *Memoirs of a Certain Island Adjacent to the Kingdom of Utopia* (1724–1725) and *The Secret History of the Present Intrigues of the Court of Caramania* (1726). These two works are not fully fledged Tory satire insofar as they do not deal extensively with political questions but rather Haywood's moral reflections and personal disputes. They make fun of fellow writers and figures in and around the court. *The Memoirs* is narrated by Cupid in a highly allegorized style. It features a variety of sexual encounters (including rapes) and rivalries and portrays a nation in the grip of corruption that has its source in greed and lust. As in her amatory fiction, Haywood shows innocent young women seduced and betrayed by self-serving courtiers. In keeping with Tory ideology, she offers the countryside as a realm of innocence and refuge from the depredations of city and court. Among the specific targets of satire are the mother and mistress of Haywood's supposed former lover, Richard Savage. Haywood and Savage had clearly fallen out, and Savage took revenge by insulting her in his book An *Author to be Lett* (1729). *The Secret History* is more formally unified than the *Memoirs.* It deals also with sexual excesses at court. This time the primary target is King George II and many of his well-known affairs. He is represented as Prince Theodore and Queen Caroline as Queen Hyanthe. Hyanthe's patient suffering seems to indicate the primary lesson of the book: infidelity places women in a double bind: if they protest, they risk abandonment and possibly destitution; if they do not protest, they must suffer in silence. "To accuse the prince," Hyanthe thinks to herself, "would but provoke him to avow his crime, and by that means lay her under the necessity of . . . coming to an open rupture. . . . She chose therefore not to seem to know what, acknowledging to know, she must resent, but had not the power of redressing" (pp. 303–304).

In 1735 an unexpurgated version of *Gulliver's Travels* was published for the first time. When Swift first published the book in 1726, associates, possibly including Alexander Pope, had toned down the attacks on particular public figures for fear that Swift would be arrested. The Whig regime was notoriously heavy-handed in its responses to published criticism, as Delarivier Manley's earlier experience attests. Hence most attacks on the Whigs were framed in allegorical terms, often published under pseudonyms, and sometimes presented as found manuscripts. The severity of the political climate, then, contributed considerable, if unintended, impetus to this great flowering of satire. A year after Swift's unexpurgated *Gulliver* and a year before Walpole effectively terminated Henry Fielding's theatrical career, Haywood made her major contribution to the anti-Walpole cause. *The Adventures of Eovaai, Princess of Ijaveo* (1736), like *Gulliver,* is set in distant lands. It is also set in distant times: "I presume to present your Grace with a small sketch of the world before Adam," writes the "translator" in the dedication, which is addressed to the Duchess of Marlborough (p. 45). The translator, according to a note on the frontispiece, is "the son of a Mandarin, residing in London," and he has translated it from Chinese into which it had earlier been translated from "the language of Nature" by "a cabal of seventy philosophers" (frontispiece). The elaborate distancing tactics work very much in the mode established by Swift to redouble the irony of the reader's recognition of the public figures and events depicted. The more absurd or unlikely an event or figure appears the better. In a preface to *Gulliver's Travels,* for instance, the supposed publisher writes, "the author was so distinguished for his veracity, that it became a sort of proverb among his neighbours . . . when anyone affirmed a thing, to say, it was as true as if Mr. Gulliver had spoke it" (p. viii).

Princess Eovaai, daughter of King Eojaeu, becomes ruler of Ijaveo at the age of fifteen when her father dies, having "done everything in his power to form her mind for governing in such a manner as shou'd render her reign glorious for herself, and fortunate for her subjects" (p. 54) and having given her a jewel "of more worth than ten thousand empires" that will "defend you, and the nations under you, in all the dangers with which you are threatned" (p. 55). The beautiful and virtuous princess immediately loses the jewel and falls victim to factions that contend for her affection and her throne. She is captured by the wicked magician Ochihatou, prime minister of Hypotofa, a man "born of a mean extraction, and so deformed in his own person that not even his own parents cou'd look on him with satisfaction" (p. 62). Ochihatou, who had learned "to cast such a delusion before the eyes of all who saw him, that he appeared to them such as he wished to be, a most comely and graceful man" (p. 62), is obviously the figure who represents Walpole. Amid great luxury and beauty, Ochihatou convinces Eovaai that "everything [is] virtue in the great, and vice confined to those in low life" (p. 77), and she swears to "renounce all rules but those prescribed by my own will—all law but inclination" (p. 78). In other words, Eovaai embraces Ochihatou/Walpole's style of tyrannical, absolute rule. Only interruption by a political emergency prevents Ochihatou from completing her "ruin." A guardian spirit rescues her, and she makes a journey during which she encounters allegories of governance including the spirit of republicanism, who almost persuades Eovaai that no monarch can be a good monarch. But Eovaai is a monarch herself and the narrative ultimately justifies her response:

> in those monarchies, where power is limited by laws . . . [the monarch] is indeed the head of a large family; for whose happiness he is perpetually contriving, who watches for their repose, labours for their ease, exposes himself for their safety, and has no other recompence for all his cares than that homage, that grandeur, which he ought not to be envied.
>
> (p. 115)

Recaptured by Ochihatou, she manages to break his wand and is rescued by Adelhu, who happens to be heir to the throne of Hypotofa and to have in his possession the jewel that Eovaai had lost. Ochihatou kills himself; Eovaai and Adelhu marry; and the united kingdoms of Ijaveo and Hypotofa enter an era of happiness and prosperity.

The breaking of Ochihatou's wand and the return of Eovaai's jewel are two of the bluntest examples of the parallels that Haywood draws in this text between sexuality and politics. The association of sexual license with political corruption and tyranny is typical of Tory politics, and of eighteenth-century political debate in general. *The Adventures of Eovaai* is interesting because it allows its heroine to recover her virtue, and symbolically her virginity, having surrendered herself to sexual experience. To the established Tory ideal of the monarch who subordinates his will to the law and well-being of his nation, Haywood adds the image of a female monarch able to comprehend the appeals of sexuality and corruption but restrain those urges, and by extension a woman able to be both sexually aware and virtuous. The book condemns Walpole's alliance of the wealthy and greedy, under whose rule "private luxury" causes "publick misery" (p. 95), and the decay of a nation where "each grew above his honest labour, forsook his home, to wait at the levees of the great, and preferr'd slavery, accompanied with splendour, to the plain and simple freedom of his ancestor" (p. 95). Haywood also loads the text with complex parallel stories, references to historical events, and footnotes that indicate disputes over the authority of the "translation." This latter feature of the text in particular calls on the reader to mistrust any voice whose claims to truth are strictly its own word and eloquence. Authority and truth, and therefore rightful governance, must emerge from a monarch established and constrained by an enlightened system of law, parliament, and a public dedicated to the greater good. The greater good, Haywood implies, also includes the need for a literary culture that can produce dissenting voices: "it was the business of true patriots," Eovaai is told, "to humble the pride of crowns, not wear them" (p. 97); one may dissent and satirize, but no one may set him- or herself up as the absolute source of rule and right.

In the periodicals she wrote in the 1740s and 1750s, Haywood's focus is very much more domestic than in the satires. Critics have identified them as partly in the tradition of early periodicals and partly—because they are explicitly by and for women—in the tradition of conduct books, which are works written to instruct women of means about etiquette, marriage, and household duties. The *Female Spectator* was published in twenty-four monthly "books" from April 1744 to May 1746. Haywood's other periodicals were the *Parrot,* which was published weekly from August 2 to October 4, 1746, and the *Young Lady,* of which there were seven weekly installments ending February 17, 1756, eight days before Haywood's death. The *Female Spectator* has always been treated as the most important of Haywood's periodicals. Although readership is hard to calculate, it seems to have had a wide audience. It explicitly models itself as a women's version of the *Spectator,* an enormously successful daily periodical produced by Joseph Addison and Richard Steele between 1711 and 1714. Addison and Steele's paper, since it appeared so much more often than Haywood's monthly, was limited to a single page for each issue. The *Female Spectator* was much longer, each issue comprising a small book. The original *Spectator* was an instant and lasting success, being reprinted in selected and collected editions throughout the eighteenth century and indeed ever since. Its voice was that of a persona, Mr. Spectator, who introduces himself and his mission in the first issue:

> I live in the world, rather as a spectator of mankind, than as one of the species; by which means I have made my self a speculative statesman, soldier, merchant and artizan. . . . I am very well versed in the theory of an husband, or a father, and can discern the errors in the oeconomy, business and diversion of others better than those who are engaged in them . . . and since I have neither time nor inclination to communicate the fulness of my heart in speech, I am resolved to do it in writing; and to print myself out, if possible, before I die.
>
> (p. 199)

He also draws upon the collective wisdom of his club, which includes a landed gentleman, Sir Roger de Coverley; an unnamed lawyer; and a merchant, Sir Andrew Feeport. The 635 numbers of the *Spectator* include observations on politics, home life, manners, the role of women, fashion, city and country life, literary criticism, economics, and many other topics. Many issues include and respond to letters, either actual or invented.

The *Female Spectator* adapts most aspects of that format. In the first issue, the unnamed authorial persona offers "in imitation of my learned brother of ever precious memory, [to] give some account of what I am, and those concerned with me in this undertaking" (p. 7). She is a woman who has had her share of society: "I have run through as many scenes of vanity and folly as the greatest coquet of them all" and "with this experience, added to a genius tolerably extensive, and an education more liberal than is ordinarily allowed to persons of my sex, I flattered myself that it might be in my power to be in some measure both useful and entertaining to the public" (pp. 8–9). The female spectator's club consists of three women:

> The first . . . I shall distinguish by the name of Mira, a lady descended from a family to which wit seems hereditary, married to a gentleman every way worthy of so excellent a wife. . . . The next is a widow of quality, who not having buried her vivacity in the tomb of her lord, continues to make one in all the modish diversions of the times. . . . The third is the daughter of a wealthy merchant, charming as an angel, but endued with so many accomplishments, that to those who know her truly, her beauty is the least distinguished part of her.
>
> (pp. 9–10)

These four, along with their "spies . . . placed not only in all the places of resort in and about this great Metropolis [London], but at Bath, Tunbridge, and the Spaw," conspire to offer a variety of topics:

> To confine myself to any one subject, I knew, could please but one kind of taste, and my ambition was to be as universally read as possible: from my observations of human nature, I found that curiosity had, more or less, a share in every breast; and my business, therefore, was to hit this reigning humour in such a manner, as that the gratification it should receive from being made acquainted with other

people's affairs, should at the same time teach every one to regulate their own.

(p. 9)

The range of topics in Haywood's magazine is by no means as wide as that in the *Spectator*. In the fourteenth issue she rephrases her goal, wondering "whether these monthly essays answer the great end proposed by them, of conducing in some measure to the rectification of manners which this age stands so much in need of" (p. 155). A very high proportion of issues feature discussions relating to courtship and marriage. The *Female Spectator* also includes more narrative than its antecedent did and develops its stories at greater length. Here we tend to find shorter and more obviously instructive versions of Haywood's amatory fictions from the 1720s. Sexual indiscretions still occur, though the tone of their description is more intrusively moralistic than in Haywood's early works. The first issue, for instance, tells the story of Martesia, who marries her very first suitor because her parents are too restrictive. She soon falls in love with and becomes pregnant by Clitander, the man she truly loves but cannot marry. Number 2 is largely taken up with the story of an arranged marriage between Celinda and Aristobulus, which leads only to misery because Aristobulus refuses to consummate the union, despite Celinda's beauty and adoration, since he is not inclined to marry. The characters' names are conventional, vaguely classical, names of the kind used at that time mostly in parody of romantic love poems and stories. The themes tend to follow Haywood's favored patterns; the stories demonstrate the constrictions within which middle– and upper–class women live and advise on the best means to find happiness and contentment within those constrictions. Like the *Spectator,* this magazine frequently includes letters that purport to be from readers. Number 8, for instance, responds to a letter from John Careful on the dangers of tea drinking. Tea is represented as a kind of gateway drug: "The three objections which Mr. Careful makes, or indeed that any body can make against the tea–table, are first, the loss of time and hindrance to business;—secondly, the expence;—and, lastly, the consequences, often arising from

it, dram–drinking and ill–health" (p. 88). Typically adventurous, inventive, and commercially astute, the *Female Spectator* helps give shape to the domestic settings in which most of Haywood's later fictions take place.

LATER FICTION

Another shift in critical perceptions of Haywood concerns the differences between her early and later fiction. In 1785 the English novelist Clara Reeve published a critical work called *The Progress of Romance* which contains the suggestion that Haywood "repented of her faults, and employed the latter part of her life in expiating the offences of the former" (*Love in Excess,* p. 285). Following that assertion, critics long viewed Haywood's fiction of the 1740s and 1750s as more morally upright than her earlier libertine works. Many critics saw this shift more as a response to commercial imperatives than the kind of atonement that Reeve describes. In any case, since the early 1990s Haywood's readers have begun to ask whether the virtuous/vicious distinction really applies to the two periods of her career, regardless of what might have motivated it. These readers have argued that the same openness about sexuality that marked *Love in Excess* appears also in the later works. In her article for *The Passionate Fictions of Eliza Haywood,* for instance, Paula Backscheider quotes from *The Invisible Spy* (1754): "he pulled me to him," reports Alinda of her teacher, Le Bris, "and making me sit upon his knee,—'You are very pretty, my dear miss, said he, and have no defect in your shape, but being a little too flat before;'—with these words he thrust one of his hands within my stays, telling me that handling my breasts would make them grow" (p. 25). There is no dispute that the later novels are, as a rule, longer. In its 2000 edition the text of *Love in Excess* fills 230 pages, while the 1998 edition of *The History of Miss Betsy Thoughtless* runs to over 600 pages. Haywood has introduced chapter divisions and, in the style of Henry Fielding, places a brief synopsis at the head of each chapter. At first the synopses actually describe what happens in the chapter, such as volume 1, chapter 2: "Shews Miss Betsy in a new scene of life, and the frequent opportunities she had of putting in practice those lessons she was beginning to receive from her young instructress at the boarding–school" (p. 31); but they quickly become ironic prefatory comments, also in the manner of Fielding. In volume 1, chapter 18, we are informed: "Treats on no fresh matters, but serves to heighten those already mentioned" (p. 142), and volume 2, chapter 7, is simply, "the better for being short" (p. 219). The later novels also, as has been noted, tend to take place more within English middle–class domestic settings. Their themes, however, are in general the familiar examinations of the difficulties and pain that women suffer in matters of love, sex, and marriage.

The History of Miss Betsy Thoughtless, published in 1751, is easily the best known of the late novels. Others include *Dalinda; or, The Double Marriage* (1749), *The History of Jemmy and Jenny Jessamy* (1753), and the posthumous *The History of Leonora Meadowson* (1788). As was stated above, the story of *Betsy Thoughtless* is structurally quite similar to *Love in Excess* with the gender of the central character changed. Betsy is an orphan with a substantial inheritance and considerable charm who comes to live with Mr. Goodman, a wealthy merchant in London. Mr. Goodman has married Lady Mellasin, widow of a baronet, with a daughter of Betsy's age named Flora. The social life at the Goodman household is busy: "Never did the mistress of a private family indulge herself, and those about her, with such a continual round of publick diversions. The court, the play, the ball, and opera, with giving and receiving visits, engrossed all the time could be spared from the toilet" (p. 36). Little wonder that Betsy "should have her head turned with the promiscuous enjoyment, and the very power of reflection lost amidst the giddy whirl, nor that it should be so long before she could recover it enough, to see the little true felicity of such a course of life" (p. 37). Naturally Betsy attracts lovers quickly and often. As a result, she becomes a coquette, learning that the fashionable way to treat a lover is to be cruel: "she exulted,—she plumed herself,—she used

him ill and well by turns, taking an equal pleasure in raising, or depressing, his hopes" (p. 37). She herself is not afflicted by love, just as D'elmont in *Love in Excess* does not know the emotion until he meets Melliora.

So Betsy proceeds from suitor to suitor, never passing beyond flirtation and rejecting all alike. Along the way she makes a rival of Flora; hears the sad story of her old schoolmate, Miss Forward, who has been raped by a suitor and rejected by her father; and falls victim to a scurrilous rumor that she has had an illegitimate child. "What can make the generality of women so fond of marrying?" she wonders at one point. "It looks to me like an infatuation.—Just as if it were not a greater pleasure to be courted, complimented, admired and addressed by a number, than be confined to one who from a slave becomes a master, and perhaps uses his authority in a manner disagreeable enough" (p. 488). One suitor, though, a Mr. Trueworth, leaves some impression. After she has allowed him to give up his suit, Betsy happens to hear a street singer perform these lines:

Young Philander woo'd me long,
I was peevish, and forbad him;
I would not hear his charming song,
But now I wish, I wish I had him.

(p. 289)

The song "beat an alarm upon her heart.—It reminded her how inconsiderate she had been, and showed the folly of not knowing how to place a just value on any thing, till it was lost" (pp. 289–290). Nonetheless she allows Trueworth to slip away. Her first marriage comes, at last, because her brothers insist upon it and she consents, understanding already that Trueworth would have been a better match. The man she marries is Mr. Munden, and he quickly turns out to be a dreadful husband. He commits adultery, steals her money, expects Betsy to help advance his career by sleeping with his aristocratic patron, and even kills her pet squirrel. Betsy leaves Munden, with the support of her friends, an event almost unheard of in eighteenth–century English fiction. Divorce, however, will destroy Betsy's social standing, so she is fortunate that Munden dies soon after she leaves him. Widowhood is a relatively secure and respectable position for a woman, enabling her to own property and live independently. Nevertheless, when Trueworth returns and the two make up their differences, Betsy chooses to marry him.

It is her choice upon which the emphasis should fall. Haywood presents a case here, and in much of her fiction, for what critics have come to call the companionate marriage. This kind of marriage is distinguished not just by the mutual love that the two partners feel but by the companionship that endures after they marry, breaking down the slave–and–master relationship of which Betsy complains above. The companionate marriage allows greater recognition of the woman's intellect and desires than the aristocratic style of marriage that Betsy experiences with Munden: "It is not the place of nativity, nor the birth, nor the estate,—but the person, and the temper of the man, can make me truly happy," Betsy tells her adviser, Lady Trusty. "If I ever become a wife again, love, an infinity of love, shall be the chief inducement." "On whose side?" asks Lady Trusty. "On both, I hope, madam," replies Betsy (pp. 629–630). Although Haywood professed herself an enemy to Samuel Richardson when she published *Anti–Pamela,* they are in some ways both engaged in the same process—leading the attack on the aristocratic conditions of marriage, which put the emphasis entirely on male lineage and the passing on of estates. Within that system the wife is little more than property, something that Betsy realizes after she has married for the first time: "Is not all I am the property of Mr. Munden?" (p. 557). Changing the institution of marriage was an important goal for the rising commercial classes in Britain. It enabled new mobility in property and class status. If a woman is as entitled as a man to assess the worth of her partner based on his personal qualities rather than his heritage, then personal merit must allow deserving people to rise in status and gain substantial property. Here is one of the reasons why women's intellects, desires, and passions became such a matter of public interest in the eighteenth century, and Eliza Haywood's fiction provided a great deal of matter for the public to consider.

As has been observed here, Haywood remains an ambivalent figure in this debate. Her Tory politics mean that she would not wholly endorse the idea of free class mobility and the republican possibilities of a totally commercial society. As we see in *The Adventures of Eovaai,* Haywood holds onto the concept of monarchic rule within an established system. In this queenly version of the marriage plot, Eovaai makes herself symbolically subservient to her people and also to her husband; the male line still holds sway in this system. At the end of *Eovaai* the couple visit Adelhu's father, Oeros, where we learn that "the satisfaction of Oeros, in embracing a son, whom he had so long thought dead, or that of the people, in seeing their prince with his beautiful consort, would fill a volume" (p. 166). Eovaai is objectified as the "beautiful consort" rather than the fellow monarch. But at the same time, Haywood was a woman without a husband engaged in a profession that seems to have been her main means of support. The motif that she uses so frequently of a woman who is all but fully initiated into sexuality but retains or regains her virtue is Haywood's strongest expression of an idea about women's education that Mary Astell outlines in *Some Reflections Upon Marriage* (1700):

> if a woman were duly principled and taught to know the world, especially the true sentiments that men have of her, and the traps they lay for her under so many gilded compliments, and such a seemingly great respect, that disgrace would be prevented which is brought upon too many families; women would marry more discreetly, and demean themselves better in the married state than some people say they do.
>
> (p. 85)

Not necessarily a feminist in the sense that is frequently applied to her near contemporaries Astell and Mary Wollstonecraft, Haywood is nonetheless no longer to be neglected among innovators both male and female in gender and class politics, literary form, and the profession of authorship.

Selected Bibliography

WORKS OF ELIZA HAYWOOD

FICTION

The Young Lady. London: T. Gardner, 1756.

Memoirs of a Certain Island Adjacent to the Kingdom of Utopia. Edited by Michael Shugrue. New York and London: Garland, 1972.

The Secret History of the Present Intrigues of the Court of Caramania. Edited by Michael Shugrue. New York and London: Garland, 1972.

The Agreeable Caledonian. Edited by Michael Shugrue. New York and London: Garland, 1973.

The Mercenary Lover. Edited by Michael Shugrue. New York: Garland, 1973.

The Rash Resolve; or, The Untimely Discovery. Edited by Michael Shugrue. New York: Garland, 1973.

The Fortunate Foundlings. New York: Garland, 1974.

The History of Jemmy and Jenny Jessamy. New York: Garland, 1974.

Anti-Pamela; or, Feign'd Innocence Detected, 1742. New York: Garland, 1975.

Four Novels of Eliza Haywood. Delmar, N.Y.: Scholars' Facsimiles & Reprints, 1983. (Includes *The Force of Nature, Lasselia, The Injur'd Husband,* and *The Perplex'd Duchess.*)

Masquerade Novels of Eliza Haywood. Delmar, N.Y.: Scholars' Facsimiles & Reprints, 1986. (Includes *The Masqueraders, Fantomina, The Fatal Secret,* and *Idalia.*)

Bath-Intrigues: In Four Letters to a Friend in London. New York: AMS Press, 1992.

The Distressed Orphan, The City Jilt, and *The Double Marriage.* In *Three Novellas.* Edited by Earla A. Wilputte. East Lansing, Mich.: Colleagues Press, 1995.

Fantomina and *The British Recluse.* In *Popular Fiction by Women, 1660–1730: An Anthology.* Edited by Paula R. Backscheider and John J. Richetti. Oxford: Clarendon, 1996.

The History of Miss Betsy Thoughtless. Edited by Christine Blouch. Peterborough, Ont.: Broadview Press, 1998.

The Adventures of Eovaai, Princess of Ijaveo. Edited by Earla Wilputte. Peterborough, Ont.: Broadview Press, 1999.

The Injur'd Husband; or, The Mistaken Resentment, and Lasselia; or, The Self-Abandoned. Edited by Jerry C. Beasley. Lexington: University Press of Kentucky, 1999.

Love in Excess; or, The Fatal Enquiry. Edited by David Oakleaf. 2nd ed. Peterborough, Ont.: Broadview Press, 2000.

COLLECTIONS OF OTHER WORKS

The Dramatic Historiographer; or, The British Theatre Delineated. 7 vols. London, 1735-1756. (Last volume retitled *The Companion to the Theatre.*)

The Plays of Eliza Haywood. Edited by Valerie C. Rudolph. New York: Garland, 1983.

Selected Fiction and Drama of Eliza Haywood. Edited by Paula R. Backscheider. New York: Oxford University Press, 1999.

Selections from "The Female Spectator." Edited by Patricia Meyer Spacks. New York: Oxford University Press, 1999.

BIBLIOGRAPHIES

Backscheider, Paula, Felicity Nussbaum, and Philip B. Anderson. "Eliza Haywood." In *An Annotated Bibliography of Twentieth-Century Critical Studies of Women and Literature, 1660–1800.* New York and London: Garland, 1977. pp. 159–161.

Barash, Carol L. "Eliza Fowler Haywood." In *An Encyclopedia of British Women Writers.* Edited by Paul Schlueter and June Schlueter. New York: Garland, 1988. pp. 223 225.

Blouch, Christine. "Eliza Haywood." In *Eighteenth-Century Anglo-American Women Novelists: A Reference Guide.* Edited by Doreen Saar and Mary Anne Schofield. New York: Macmillan, 1996. pp. 263–265.

RELATED WORKS

Astell, Mary. *Some Reflections upon Marriage.* New York: Source Book Press, 1970.

Behn, Aphra. *Love Letters Between a Nobleman and His Sister.* In *The Works of Aphra Behn.* Vol. 2. Edited by Janet Todd. Columbus: Ohio State University Press, 1993.

Brontë, Charlotte. *Jane Eyre.* Edited by Margaret Smith. Oxford: Oxford University Press, 2000.

Fielding, Henry. *The Author's Farce.* Edited by Charles B. Woods. Lincoln: University of Nebraska Press, 1966.

————*The Tragedy of Tragedies.* In *Complete Works of Henry Fielding.* Vol. 9. New York: Barnes & Noble, 1967. pp. 5-72.

————*Joseph Andrews and Shamela.* Edited by Douglas Brooks-Davies and Martin C. Battestin. Oxford: Oxford University Press, 1970.

Manley, Delarivier. *The New Atalantis.* Edited by Ros Ballaster. London: Penguin, 1992.

Pope, Alexander. *The Rape of the Lock.* Edited by Cynthia Wall. Boston: Bedford Books, 1998.

————.*The Dunciad.* In *The Poems of Alexander Pope.* Vol. 5. Edited by James Sutherland. 2nd ed. London: Methuen, 1953.

Reeve, Clara. *The Progress of Romance.* New York: Facsimile Text Society, 1930.

Richardson, Samuel. *Pamela*. Edited by Peter Sabor. London: Penguin, 1985.

Savage, Richard. *An Author to be Lett*. London: Edmund Curll, 1729.

Steele, Richard, and Joseph Addison. *Selections from* The Tatler *and* The Spectator. Edited by Angus Ross. London: Penguin, 1982.

Swift, Jonathan. *Gulliver's Travels*. Edited by Robert A. Greenberg. New York: Norton, 1961.

CRITICAL AND BIOGRAPHICAL STUDIES

Backscheider, Paula R. "The Shadow of an Author: Eliza Haywood." *Eighteenth–Century Fiction* 11:79–100 (October 1998).

Ballaster, Ros. *Seductive Forms: Women's Amatory Fiction from 1684 to 1740*. Oxford: Clarendon Press, 1992.

Black, Scott. "Trading Sex for Secrets in Haywood's *Love in Excess*." *Eighteenth–Century Fiction* 15, no. 2:207–226 (January 2003).

Blouch, Christine. "Eliza Haywood and the Romance of Obscurity." *Studies in English Literature* 31:535–552 (1991).

Carnell, Rachel. "It's Not Easy Being Green: Gender and Friendships in Eliza Haywood's Political Periodicals." *Eighteenth–Century Studies* 32:199–214 (1998–1999).

Ellis, L. B. "Engendering the *Bildungsroman*: The *Bildung* of Betsy Thoughtless." *Genre* 28, no. 3:279–302 (autumn 1995).

Hollis, Karen. "Eliza Haywood and the Gender of Print." *Eighteenth Century: Theory & Interpretation* 38:43–62 (spring 1997).

Ingrassia, Catherine. "Fashioning Female Authorship in Eliza Haywood's *The Tea Table*." *Journal of Narrative Technique* 28, no. 3:287–304 (fall 1998).

King, Kathryn R. "Spying upon the Conjurer: Haywood, Curiosity, and 'The Novel' in the 1720s." *Studies in the Novel* 30, no. 2:178–193 (summer 1998).

Nestor, Deborah J. "Virtue Rarely Rewarded: Ideological Subversion and Narrative Form in Haywood's Later Fiction." *Studies in English Literature* 34:579–598 (summer 1994).

Oakleaf, David. "The Eloquence of Blood in Eliza Haywood's *Lasselia*." *Studies in English Literature 1500–1900* 39, no. 3:483–498 (summer 1999).

Potter, Tiffany. "The Language of Feminised Sexuality: Gendered Voice in Eliza Haywood's *Love in Excess* and *Fantomina*." *Women's Writing* 10, no. 1:169–186 (spring 2003).

Richetti, John J. "Voice and Gender in Eighteenth–Century Fiction: Haywood to Burney." *Studies in the Novel* 19, no. 3:263–272 (fall 1987).

———. *Popular Fiction Before Richardson: Narrative Patterns 1700–1739*. Oxford: Clarendon Press, 1969.

Saxton, Kirsten T., and Rebecca P. Bocchicchio, eds. *The Passionate Fictions of Eliza Haywood: Essays on Her Life and Work*. Lexington: University Press of Kentucky, 2000.

Schofield, Mary Anne. *Quiet Rebellion: The Fictional Heroines of Eliza Fowler Haywood*. Washington, D.C.: University Press of America, 1982.

———. *Eliza Haywood*. Boston: Twayne, 1985.

Stuart, Shea. "Subversive Didacticism in Eliza Haywood's *Betsy Thoughtless*." *Studies in English Literature* 42, no. 3:559–575 (summer 2002).

Warner, William B. "Formulating Fiction: Romancing the General Reader in Early Modern Britain." In *Cultural Institutions of the Novel*. Edited by Deirdre Lynch and William B. Warner. Durham, N.C.: Duke University Press, 1996. pp. 279–305.

Whicher, George Frisbie. *The Life and Romances of Mrs. Eliza Haywood*. New York: Columbia University Press, 1915.

Wilputte, Earla A. "The Textual Architecture of Eliza Haywood's *Adventures of Eovaai*." *Essays in Literature* 22:31–44 (spring 1995).

Woolf, Virginia. "A Scribbling Dame." In *The Essays of Virginia Woolf*. Edited by Andrew McNeillie. Vol. 2, *1912–1918*. San Diego, Calif.: Harcourt, Brace, Jovanovitch, 1987. pp. 22–26.

JULIAN OF NORWICH

(c. 1342 – c. 1416)

Jane Beal

JULIAN OF NORWICH probably derived her name from association with her anchorhold at the Church of St. Julian and St. Edward at Conisford, Norwich, in England. It was not uncommon for medieval anchorites to take (or receive) the name of the patron saint of the church to which they were bound. It may be significant that Julian of Norwich chose the Church of St. Julian—and thus, in effect, the name by which she came to be so well known—because the legends of Saint Julian relate to the most famous episode in the life of Julian of Norwich: the near-fatal illness she experienced at the age of thirty that inspired her visions and meditations on the crucified Christ.

There were in fact at least two saints named Julian in the early Christian centuries, and the church in Norwich may be dedicated to either one. The first lived in the third century and was the first bishop of Le Mans, France. According to the *Legenda aurea (Golden Legend),* a popular collection of saints' legends written by Jacobus de Voragine in the thirteenth century, this Julian raised three dead persons back to life and was renowned for his virtues. A second Julian lived in the ninth century and was the victim of fate.

According to medieval legend, the young Julian was hunting in the woods one day when he came upon a stag who turned and spoke to him, prophesying that he would kill his own parents. Fearing this, Julian ran away from home, became a knight in the service of a prince, and married a rich widow. His parents, meanwhile, went looking for him and came to his castle, where his wife let them sleep in his bed. When Julian saw two people in his bed, he mistook them for his wife and a man he thought was her lover, and he killed them both. Horrified to discover the two people were his own parents, Julian went on a penitential pilgrimage with his wife. At a wild river the saint and his wife established a hospice to care for travelers, and they transported poor people across the water at no charge. One night a leper came to the hospice, and Julian cared for him by putting him in his own bed. Shortly thereafter the leper arose transformed into midair and declared that the Lord had accepted Julian's penance, then disappeared. Because of this episode, the latter Saint Julian often appears in medieval art carrying a leper across a river.

Both saints could have inspired Julian of Norwich to become their namesake since the first raised people from the dead, just as Julian felt she was raised from the dead after the severity of her illness had passed, and the second cared for those who were gravely ill, just as Julian felt she was cared for during the suffering brought on by her illness. Julian makes no explicit statement about the origins or significance of her name, but the connections between her name and her church, and between her church and the two saints called Julian, are worth noting because they were meaningful to Julian herself. Furthermore, people who knew Julian in the fourteenth and fifteenth centuries would have known the stories of the saints who shared her name and would have associated her with their sanctity.

DATES AND DOCUMENTS, 1342–1416/1429

Like her name, the dates of Julian's life are not completely certain. Generally Julian of Norwich is believed to have been born in 1342 and to have died sometime after 1416. Her birth year can be derived from her assertion, found in her *Revelation of Love,* that she experienced her visions on 13 May 1373 when she was thirty and a half years old. This assertion is precise, and can be granted as true and accurate from Julian's perspective, but some scholarly consideration ought to be given to the fact that Julian's assertion of her age at the time of her visions coincides with Christ's age at the beginning of his public ministry as recorded in the four canonical Gospels. It could, therefore, have symbolic significance as well as (or instead of) being literally or historically accurate.

Julian's date of death is less easy to establish since no record has been found of it. In a will of 1416, Isabel Ufforde, countess of Suffolk, bequeathed twenty shillings to Julian, when the anchoress would have been in her seventies. Marion Glasscoe, a scholar well versed in Julian's life and work, has suggested that Julian might have been alive as late as 1429 when a Robert Baxster left three shillings and four pence to the anchorite (perhaps Julian) in the churchyard of St. Julian's Conisford in Norwich.

Only a few events in Julian's life between 1342 and 1416 can be known with any certainty. In general these are recorded in her major work, *A Revelation of Love;* deduced from information contained therein, or found in contemporary documents, including Norwich wills. Margery Kempe, a contemporary of Julian, left a record of her encounter with Julian in her autobiographical *Book of Margery Kempe.* Julian's *Revelation of Love* gives a limited amount of biographical information about its author. It makes plain that Julian, at thirty and a half years of age in the year 1373, had visions of the crucified Christ during a "bodily sickness" and was visited by a number of people, including her mother, a priest, and a child, when she was near death. The longer of the two versions of Julian's work states that she meditated on her visionary experience for twenty years, which places the composition of the longer version around 1393. It reveals the depth and sincerity of Julian's faith in God and her intense understanding of the love of God as revealed through the passion of the Christ. However, the work makes no statement about Julian's religious position, social class, or marital status before, during, or after the revelations.

Contemporary documents, especially Norwich wills, help fill in the picture a little bit more. In 1394, for example, Roger Reed, rector of St. Michael Coslany, Norwich, bequeathed two shillings to Julian, "anchorite," which indicates she had entered her anchorhold at the Church of St. Julian and St. Edward by that date, if not earlier. In 1404 another will names her as anchoress, and in 1413 the scribe of the shorter version of her visions calls her "a devout woman and her name is Julian that is recluse at Norwich and is yet on life." This testament that Julian is "a devout woman" suggests that her reputation for holiness was being acknowledged by this date and seems further confirmed by a visit from Margery Kempe, which took place at about the same time. (See Glasscoe, p. vii.)

The purpose of the visit, according to *The Book of Margery Kempe,* was to discuss revelations which Margery herself had received from God and to determine if any deceit was in them. Margery believed that the Lord had bidden her to make the visit to Julian, "for the anchoress was expert in such things and good counsel could give." The conversation, according to Margery's account, went well. Julian advised Margery to be obedient to God's will and reminded her that the Holy Spirit encouraged charity, chastity, and steadfastness. The anchoress asserted that the devil has no power over a human soul, but that the soul of a righteous person is the seat of God. She prayed for Margery and emphasized the importance of patience, of waiting and suffering, as a means of guarding and keeping her own soul. According to Margery's book, they enjoyed each other's fellowship in the love of Jesus for many days.

In addition to the scant information supplied by Julian, by contemporary records, and by Margery Kempe, scholars have made educated guesses and suppositions about Julian's life. Some, for example, have thought that she might have been a nun who entered a convent in her youth, a widow who lost her husband and possibly a child to the plague, or a well-to-do woman who received her visions in her own household among relatives and servants. However, historical documentation is insufficient to confirm such suppositions. Titles like "Mother," "Lady," and "Dame," might seem to support the notion that

JULIAN OF NORWICH

Julian was a Benedictine nun, but in fact such titles could be applied to both nuns and anchoresses. Since Julian was certainly an anchoress, a more fruitful approach to garnering information about her life is to recall what it meant to be an anchoress in the fourteenth and fifteenth centuries.

JULIAN THE ANCHORESS

The terms "anchorite," "anchoress," "anchorage," and "anchorhold" all derive from a Greek root, anachorein, which means "to retire, retreat, withdraw." Choosing to become an anchoress meant consciously and willfully withdrawing from the world. The practice was well known and widely practiced in the later medieval period. Anchorholds might be attached to churches, monasteries, convents, or castles. In England between 1259 and 1415, documents show that recluses lived in Winchester, Lincoln, London, York, Beverley, Stafford, Hampole, Leek, Newcastle, Gainsborough, Southwell, Stamford, Dartford, Shrewsbury, Kirby Wath, Kexby Wighton, and of course, Norwich.

Ann Warren, a scholar of anchoritism in England, notes that most of those enclosed in later medieval England were lay women. The approximate ratio of female to male recluses in the fourteenth century was 5:2 and in the fifteenth century, 5:3. The number of anchoresses could be explained by a variety of factors: a woman's desire to escape the expectations of secular society (marriage, childbirth, traditional female roles), her search for empowerment through solitary communion with God (by private worship, prayer, and fasting), or her wish to contribute to the spiritual well-being of her community (by praying for others, advising them spiritually, and encouraging them emotionally). Other explanations might be that the woman was without a husband because she was a widow or without a suitable partner; that there was no place for her in the nearby convent; or, as in Julian's case, that a dramatic personal experience with God motivated her to devote her life wholly to God's service in contemplative life.

The development of the anchoritic movement in England was encouraged and governed by thirteen rules written between the eleventh and fourteenth centuries. Beginning with the *Liber confortatorius* (ca. 1080) of Goscelin, a Benedictine monk, and perhaps concluding with Walter Hilton's *Epistola ad quendam solitarium* (ca. 1350–1400), these rules were frequently written by men for women who had chosen the enclosed life. The rules emphasized withdrawing from the world in order to devote oneself fully to God, and they advised recluses about how to conduct their daily lives materially and spiritually within their enclosures. The *Ancrene Wisse* (ca. 1215–1224) was one such well known, often copied, and updated rule. Richard Rolle's *Form of Living* (ca. 1348) and Walter Hilton's *Scale of Perfection* (before 1397) are two other rules for enclosed living that are contemporary with the life of Julian of Norwich.

The cultural response in medieval England to the anchoritic movement was, on the whole, positive. The prevalence of enclosed persons, the testimony of wills that bequeathed money to them, the rules written to govern their way of life, the literature they themselves produced, and other factors all suggest that anchorites were valued in the late medieval world. Ordinary people in surrounding areas could appreciate the presence of anchorholds and the people within them who prayed on their behalf. Anchorites were often considered to be holy men and women. This view of them relates to the manner in which they entered and maintained their lives apart from the world.

Those who felt called to take a vow of withdrawal and lead a contemplative life first informed the Church of their intentions. Each case would be investigated by an archdeacon or abbot appointed by a bishop. The investigation included consideration of how the would-be anchorites intended to support her- or himself after enclosure. Once the investigators were satisfied, the ceremony of enclosure could take place.

The medieval Church honored and solemnized the vows of those who chose to withdraw from the world and live contemplative lives. A bishop celebrated mass, either the Mass of the Dead or the Mass of the Holy Spirit, to mark the significance of the occasion. Within that mass the anchoress professed her calling and took her vows. She was clothed for her new life. When the mass ended, the anchoress processed from the church to her cell, the place where she would be enclosed, with the congregation singing psalms. The bishop would bless the cell and its new occupant, sprinkling the anchoress with holy water and censing her cell. Once the anchoress entered the cell, it became, in effect, a symbolic tomb. The anchoress could then truly feel the import of the words of the Apostle Paul in his Letter to the Colossians: "For you died, and your life is now hidden with Christ in God" (3:3). Some records suggest that the bishop performed the burial liturgy at this point, and once the bishop emerged from the cell, the entrance was shut up. The anchoress was now enclosed and committed to remaining so until her death.

Within the cell, the anchoress lived a life disciplined by prayer. Prayer might be according to a Holy Rule, such as that of Saint Benedict, or a rule set out by the bishop. Enclosed priests could say the Mass, and laypersons could assist with it. Whether Julian of Norwich followed the Benedictine Rule or some other rule to guide her daily devotions, she would have prayed multiple times throughout the day at set hours.

Though the vows of withdrawal and the ceremony of enclosure were thorough, anchorites rarely lived in total isolation. They might engage in activities to provide subsistence for themselves. Anchoresses might spin, embroider, or do needlework. They could also teach girls and on occasion boys. Anchorites might write or illuminate or make crafts. Both men and women could act as spiritual advisors from within their enclosures to visitors who sought them out. In addition to communion with God, anchorites could expect to interact with priests, servants, and visitors. Priests would administer the sacraments to them. Servants would deliver food and other necessities to the cell. Anchorites were not required to take vows of poverty, and Julian of Norwich is known to have had at least two servants, Sara and Alice, who facilitated her ability to keep her vow of withdrawal, as such servants did for other enclosed persons. Visitors could come to the cell and receive spiritual advice from the anchorite. Certainly the record of Margery Kempe's visit suggests that Julian was sought out by others in need of spiritual advice. Perhaps her visitors included those who later bequeathed money to her in their wills, such as Roger Reed, rector of St. Michael Coslany, Norwich, and Isabel Ufforde, Countess of Suffolk; and perhaps Robert Baxter.

The design of the anchorhold, also known as a cell or enclosure, facilitated visitation. It could be a single room or as big as two or three. Sometimes it included a garden. The cell could have two or three windows. If attached to a church, the enclosure would have a window that opened on the sanctuary so that the anchoress could hear the mass and receive the Eucharist. A second window might be reserved for a servant to pass things in and take things out of the anchoress's cell. A final window, the "world-side window," would be where the anchoress could meet and talk with visitors, answering their questions, praying for them, and giving them spiritual advice. This might be done from behind a curtain. Julian of Norwich had such a window in her enclosure.

While regulated contact with the outside world was permitted, to protect the enclosed person, windows were small, sometimes only twenty-one inches square. These windows were often kept closed or, when opened, kept curtained. At least one rule warns anchorites against becoming gossips, and another suggests that guests should not visit for longer than two days. So it is clear that those who withdrew from the secular world to a contemplative life within their anchorholds still maintained necessary connections to the world. As Christopher Cannon observes in his essay "Enclosure" in *The Cambridge Companion to Medieval Women's Writing,* a "well-lived anchoritic life always seemed to form communities around itself" (p. 114). This can be seen in the *Ancrene Wisse,* which addresses itself to three sisters (but a later version is addressed to twenty), and in *The Life of Christina of Markyate* (ca. 1156–1166), which implies the existence of a community of anchorites who lived miles apart but remained in communication with one another. Such texts suggest ways in which the life of Julian of Norwich may have expanded spiritually, emotionally, and imaginatively to include other people even as she remained enclosed physically.

Julian's cell and her profession as an anchoress give insight into the material realities of her life. Yet Julian herself was less concerned with material realities than with spiritual ones. This is evident in her major work, *A Revelation of Love.*

A REVELATION OF LOVE

In 1373, Julian of Norwich suffered a near fatal illness during which she experienced visions of the crucified Christ. She describes her "bodily sickness" vividly, giving enough detail to suggest that her physical symptoms included a fever, dehydration, exhaustion, weakness, numbness, paralysis, shortness of breath, and possibly choking. Various attempts have been made to correlate her symptoms to known illnesses, and scholars have suggested that she might have had diphtheria, Guillain-Barré syndrome, tick paralysis, botulism, or a severe chest or respiratory infection. Whatever the particular illness may have been, Julian believed she was going to die because of it, as did the priest who came to visit her at the time. Julian had a series of visionary experiences during this illness, and when she recovered, she recorded her revelations and her meditations on them. Before discussing the content of this work, it will be useful to review the forms in which it survives.

VERSIONS, MANUSCRIPTS, PRINTED EDITIONS

It is not known precisely how Julian of Norwich recorded, or caused to be recorded, her visions. Unlike *The Book of Margery Kempe,* Julian's work contains no outright statement that explains how her visions were transmitted from her memory to the page. Julian does plainly state in the second chapter of *A Revelation of Love* that "these revelations were shown to a simple creature who could no letter," but this statement can be interpreted variously. It might be an example of the humility topos and a deliberate understatement of Julian's abilities. It might indicate an inability to read or write Latin with no bearing whatsoever on her ability to read or write English—indeed, lack of skill in Latin might perfectly justify writing in the vernacular. It might mean Julian could not read or write Latin or English at the time of her visions, saying nothing about whether she later learned to read or write one or both languages at least passably well. The statement leaves room for the possibility that Julian had some ability to read and write and was aided by others. Such a circumstance might be comparable to the situation of Birgitta of Sweden who could write Old Swedish but dictated her visions to confessors who wrote them down in Latin; like Birgitta, Julian could have been partially literate but still have received help from others more literate than she. Finally Julian's statement could be simply a straightforward acknowledgment of illiteracy in both Latin and English, necessitating the help of another in order to produce her *Revelation of Love.*

This last possibility is the understanding of such scholars as Marion Glasscoe, who has argued that Julian's prose style imitates the rhythms of spoken discourse. Yet the breadth of knowledge of the Bible, the Church Fathers, and other authors that Julian reveals in her work seems to suggest that she had some sort of formal education beyond simply listening to sermons and cultivating an excellent memory. Edmund Colledge and James Walsh have argued that Julian must have been educated in her youth by one or more scholars and that she later read widely in Latin, scripture, and the liberal arts, particularly given her knowledge of Augustine, Gregory the Great, William of Saint-Thierry, and the terms and concepts of philosophers. Questions about the extent of Julian's literacy and her learning, and thus the nature of the transmission of her text, therefore, remain open.

However she did it, whether by writing or dictating her visions, two distinct versions of Julian's work came into being. They are called, in surviving manuscripts, *A Vision Showed . . . to a Devout Woman* (Short Text) and *A Revelation of Love* (Long Text). The versions resemble each other but differ in some interesting respects. Colledge and Walsh, whose two-volume *Book of Showings to the Anchoress Julian of Norwich* (1978) includes both versions along with extensive commentary, a glossary, bibliography, and index, have identified the major differences. These include additions, transpositions, and deletions or omissions. For example, the Long Text contains such additions as the prefatory chapter, which gives an overview of Julian's visions; a new sixth chapter on the preferability of direct prayer to God rather than to intermediaries; and the account of the Lord and his Servant in the fifty-first chapter. The Long Text transposes the meditation on the hazelnut with the story of Mary, and it omits Julian's reference to Saint Cecilia that appears in the first chapter of the Short Text. A thorough examination of the differences between *A Vision* and *A Revelation* can shed light on Julian's thoughts and revisionary process. For a complete account of the changes, see the Colledge and Walsh edition.

The differences between the two versions of Julian's visions have prompted scholars to argue about which came first, but the consensus now considers *A Vision* to be the original work, which Julian expanded with careful thought over twenty years into *A Revelation*. However, Nicolas Watson, after accepting this hypothesis for some years, later argued that *A Revelation* came first. So the matter is apparently still up for discussion.

The Short Text survives in a unique copy, British Library Additional MS 37790, sometimes known as the Amherst MS after Lord Amherst, the manuscript's last owner before the British Library obtained it in 1909. The manuscript was produced after 1435, and the *A Vision* it contains was copied from an exemplar dating to 1413, when Julian was still living. The manuscript makes a fascinating study in the anthologization of medieval texts. Written in one hand throughout and preserved by Carthusian monks, British Library Additional MS 37790 contains a wide selection of texts in Middle English on the contemplative life. A glance at the manuscript's contents reveals what at least one compiler

thought might be the appropriate literary context for Julian's *A Vision.*

As noted in the Colledge and Walsh edition, the contents of the Amherst manuscript include: Richard Misyn's translations of Richard Rolle's *De emendatione vitae* (On the Emendation of Life) and *Incendium amoris* (The Fire of Love); the Golden Epistle of Saint Bernard (an anonymous letter mistakenly attributed to Bernard); Julian of Norwich's *A Vision Showed . . . to a Devout Woman* (Short Text); a Middle English translation of Jan van Ruusbroec's *Van den Blickenden Steene,* from the Latin *De calculo sive de perfections filiorum dei,* entitled *The Treatise of Perfection of the Sons of God;* selections from Richard Rolle's *Forma vivendi (Form of Living);* selections from Richard Rolle's *Ego dormio* (I Sleep); selections from an English translation of Henry Suso's *Horologium sapientiae* (Clock of Wisdom); a Middle English translation of Marguerite Porete's *Le Mirouer des Simples Ames* (The Mirror of Simple Souls); selections from the spurious *Liber soliloquiorum animae ad deum* (The Book of Soliloquies of the Soul to God); tracts on contemplation and the contemplative life; and selections from Birgitta of Sweden's *Revelationes.* Each text explains or expounds upon some aspect of the contemplative life.

The earliest manuscript of the Long Text, Westminster Cathedral Treasury MS 4, dates to around 1500. However, it contains only fragments of Julian's *Revelation.* The Paris Manuscript, Bibliothèque Nationale de France Fonds anglais 40, dates to the seventeenth century and contains the Long Text alone. It is a Benedictine production and belonged to a Parisian monastery of nuns exiled from England during the Reformation. Two other manuscripts, British Library Sloane MS 2499 and British Library Sloane MS 3705, contain the entire *Revelation* as well, without any other texts to accompany it, and they date to the mid-seventeenth century and the eighteenth century respectively. BL Sloane MS 2499 may have been written out by Mother Clementina Cary, who founded the English Benedictine nunnery at Paris. The St. Joseph's College, Upholland MS contains selections from Julian's *Revelation* along with translations into English of spiritual classics by Augustine Baker for nuns at Cambrai; this manuscript dates circa 1640–1684. It was written out by Barbara Constable, who was a Benedictine nun of the abbey of Our Lady of Consolation at Cambrai by 1640.

The first printed edition of the Long Text appeared in 1670 under the title *XVI Revelations of Divine Love, Shewed to a Devout Servant of Our Lord, Called Mother Juliana, an Anchorete of Norwich: Who Lived in the Dayes of King Edward the Third. Published by R.F.S. Cressy.* As noted in the title, it was edited by Serenus de Cressy, an English Benedictine monk who was briefly a chaplain to the nuns at Paris. His edition was based on the Paris Manuscript and was most likely printed in England. As part of his endeavor, Cressy created marginal glosses for some words in his edition, modernized the spelling of others, and replaced still others that he must have deemed obsolete. Cressy's edition probably influenced the shape and appearance of the selections from *A Revelation of Love* that appear in the Upholland manuscript. As Alexandra Barratt notes, up until the nineteenth century the Long Text circulated only among English Catholics, usually Benedictine in persuasion, and the Short Text was virtually unknown (p. 29).

In 1843, George Hargreave Parker, an Anglican priest in Bethnal Green, London, reissued, with minor revisions, Cressy's edition. In 1877, Henry Collins, whom Barratt describes as "an Anglican convert to Roman Catholicism" (p. 31), issued the first printed edition based on BL Sloane MS 2499. In 1901, Grace Warrack produced *Revelations of Divine Love,* basing it on BL Sloane MS 2499 as well. Warrack's version went through numerous editions, the thirteenth appearing in 1958. In 1902, George Tyrrell, a Jesuit priest, reprinted Cressy's edition once again with some changes. Barratt notes that "Tyrrell's version was eventually reprinted but not until 1920, by which time Warrack's more successful version had reached its seventh edition" (p. 33). In 1911, Dundas Harford, an Anglican priest and vicar of St. Stephen's, Norwich, between 1901 and 1908, published his edited version of the Short Text from BL Additional MS 37790 under the title *Comfortable Words to Christ's Lovers.* The title was changed to *The Shewings of the Lady Julian* in later editions. Extracts from Warrack's edition appeared in the anonymous *All Shall Be Well* (1908) and in *The Shewing of a Vision* (1915), edited by George Congreve, S.S.J.E. In 1927, Dom Roger Hudleston, a Benedictine, published his edition based on BL Sloane MS 2499. (See Barratt, 29–34.)

Sister Anna Maria Reynolds worked on the Short Text and the Long Text for dissertations at the University of Liverpool, and in 1958 she produced what she called a "partially modernized" version of the Short Text. In 1961, James Walsh and Eric (later Edmund) Colledge published a modernized version of the extracts from the Westminster Manuscript titled *Of the Knowledge of Ourselves and of God.* Also in 1961, Walsh produced a version of the Long Text using transcripts of the Paris Manuscript and the BL Sloane MS 2499 that had been made by Sister Anna Maria Reynolds. In 1966, Clifton Wolters, an Anglican priest, edited and translated into modern English *Revelations of Divine Love* for Penguin Classics. His translation was based, like many others, on the Sloane Manuscript. (See Barratt, pp. 35–36.)

Marion Glasscoe produced a respectable scholarly edition of the Long Text, based on BL Sloane MS 2499, under the title *A Revelation of Love.* First published in 1976, Glasscoe's edition has been revised and reprinted several times. Frances Beer published the Short Text in 1978, and in the same year Colledge and Walsh produced their edition of the Short and Long Texts, basing the latter on the Paris Manuscript. The Colledge and Walsh edition is used by scholars, but the Glasscoe edition is better known and more widely available. Julian's *Revelation of Love* has now been translated into French, German, and Italian.

VISIONS, THEMES, CHARACTERS

In chapter 73 of her *Revelation,* Julian describes perceiving her visions in three ways: "by bodily sight, and by word formed in my understanding, and by ghostly sight." Her explanation indicates that she saw her visions with her eyes, that she heard her Lord speaking to her in her mind, and finally that she saw her visions inwardly with the eyes of her heart. Remarking on these three types of perception, Julian says:

> For the bodily sight, I have said as I saw as truly as I can; and for the words, I have said them right as our Lord showed them to me; and for the ghostly sight, I have said a certain amount, but I may never fully tell it, and therefore of this sight I am stirred to say more as God will give me grace.

The idea of "ghostly" or spiritual sight, of perceiving something inwardly that cannot be seen outwardly, clearly gave Julian pause for reflection and consideration.

Julian's three categories of visionary experience may be a way of putting in the vernacular what Augustine described in Latin when meditating on types of vision. In his *Literal Meaning of Genesis* (A.D. 401–415), Augustine identified three types of vision: corporeal, imaginary, and intellectual. He used an example to explain these types. If someone were meditating on Christ's perfect recapitulation of the Law in the phrase "Love your neighbor as yourself," he would see the letters of the verse with his physical eyes (corporeally), recall his neighbor in his memory (imaginatively), and behold love, as it were, in his very soul (intellectually). These three types of vision may correspond to Julian's three distinctions between "bodily sight," "word formed in my understanding," and "ghostly sight."

Certainly Julian's study of scripture would have lent support to her logical divisions of visionary experience. In the Acts of the Apostles she could have found an example of "bodily sight." Paul (then Saul) is on the road to Damascus when Christ appears to him and asks, "Why do you persecute me?" (Acts 9:4). Paul believed that he saw Jesus with his physical eyes, just as Julian saw him with hers, even though in neither case did their companions share in their vision. Julian could have found an example of "word formed in my understanding" in the account in Matthew's Gospel of Joseph's dreaming that an angel appears to him and speaks to him, telling him to flee with his wife Mary and the baby Jesus into Egypt. Julian records that she also heard a divine being, Jesus, speaking to her and saying that "All shall be well."

In the prophetic writings of the Old Testament and the New, Julian could have readily found instances of visionaries who had "ghostly sight" or perceptions of visions within their minds or souls. The Book of Daniel, for example, specifically states that Daniel "had a dream, and visions passed through his mind as he was lying on his bed" (7:1), when he saw "one like a son of man, coming with the clouds of heaven" (7:13). In this case "ghostly sight" rather than "bodily sight" seems to be the probable means by which Daniel perceived his vision, particularly since his physical eyes were closed, and he was asleep and dreaming. Yet the mystery of visionary experience in biblical writings, and the question of whether perception is physical ("bodily") or spiritual ("ghostly"), can be tricky to determine, as Paul's consideration of the matter in the twelfth chapter of his Second Letter to the Corinthians clearly indicates. Indeed Julian herself has a phrase or two which suggest some combination of "bodily" and "ghostly" perception: "ghostly in bodily likeness" and "more ghostly without bodily likeness."

The nature of Julian's visionary perception, though interesting, was perhaps not as important to the anchoress as the content of the visions themselves. Thus she does not address the nature of her perceptions until chapter 73 but from the first chapter of her *Revelation* she discusses the content of her visions. In her introductory prologue to the Long Text, Julian gives an overview of her sixteen visions, what she saw, and what they mean to her.

She begins by boldly stating: "This is a revelation of love that Jesus Christ, our endless bliss, made in sixteen showings or revelations in particular." The first revelation concerns Christ's crown of thorns; the second, the discoloring of his face during his Passion; and the third, that the all-powerful, all-wise God of love does everything that is done. The fourth depicts Christ's scourging, the fifth the overcoming of the fiend by the Passion of Christ, and the sixth the thanks and reward that God gives his servants in heaven. The seventh revelation shows that humanity, whether in joy or distress, is kept securely in love by the goodness of God. The eighth envisions Christ's suffering and death; the ninth, the satisfaction and joy that the whole Trinity has in the Passion of Christ and Christ's desire for everyone to be comforted with him in the fulfillment of heaven; and the tenth, Christ's heart cloven in two. The eleventh concerns Christ's mother and the twelfth Christ's worthiness. The thirteenth revelation involves several things: God's will for humanity to regard all the deeds he has done, including the excellence of the creation of humanity; God's redemption of humanity through Christ; and God's ability to turn all things that are evil to good ("I shall make well all that is not well and you shall see it"). The fourteenth asserts that the Lord is the ground or foundation of our beseeching as well as of our need for righteous prayer and sure trust in God. The fifteenth promises that pain shall end and heaven shall be the reward. The final vision emphasizes God's relationship with the individual human soul in ruling, giving, saving, and preserving that soul in and for love. "And," Julian concludes her introductory chapter, "we shall not be overcome by our enemy."

A quick analysis of Julian's overview reveals that several visions (the first, second, fourth, fifth, eighth, ninth, and perhaps tenth) meditate directly and primarily on the experience of the crucified Christ. Other visions meditate on Christian theological or spiritual truths. But all the visions, according to Julian, are in fact one revelation with one unifying theme: love. In chapter 86, the concluding chapter of her *Revelation,* Julian returns to this theme and emphasizes it powerfully. She remarks that from the time when she experienced her visions she wanted to understand "our Lord's meaning." So she explains:

> And fifteen years after and more I was answered in ghostly understanding, saying thus: "Would you know your Lord's meaning in this thing? Know it well: love was his meaning. Who showed it to you? Love. What did he show to you? Love. Why did he show it to you? For love. Hold yourself therein and you shall understand and know more in the same; but you shall never know nor understand therein another thing without end." Thus did I learn that

love was our Lord's meaning. And I saw very certainly in this and in all, that before God made us he loved us; and that his love never slackened, and never shall. And in this love he has done all his work; and in this love he has made all things profitable to us; and in this love our life is everlasting. In our making we had beginning; but the love wherein he made us was in him from without beginning; in which love we have our beginning. And all this shall be seen in God without end; which Jesus must grant us.

So, in concluding her work, Julian returns to a discussion of her work's beginning, though she does not locate that beginning on 13 May 1373 but within God even before the beginning of all created things.

Although Julian certainly identifies love as the main theme of her *Revelation,* the work treats several subsidiary themes as well. Clifton Wolters proposes four such themes in the introduction to his translation of Julian's work: God shows his love in the Cross; love triumphs over sin; love unites the soul to God; and love brings us to heaven. Certainly these ideas are consonant with Julian's visionary experience. Yet they leave out the centrality of suffering to Julian's revelatory understanding of love. Julian experienced her visions at a time when she was suffering intensely in her body and was meditating on the suffering Jesus endured on the Cross. Her visions are centered upon the Passion of the Christ, and all her understandings flow from and are integrated with that most vital event in Christian history. Thinking of Jesus, Julian remarks in the conclusion of her third chapter, "Therefore I desired to suffer with him." This desire is perhaps as old as Paul's Letter to the Philippians, in which he states, "I want to know Christ and the power of his resurrection and the fellowship of sharing in his sufferings, becoming like him in his death, and so, somehow, to attain to the resurrection from the dead" (3:10–11). Certainly many medieval Christians shared in this sentiment wholeheartedly. Julian's *Revelation* clearly indicates her desire to become one with Christ in his sufferings.

This theme points to the two central characters in *A Revelation of Love:* Julian and Christ, who is, for her, Love himself. Julian's work focuses on the central drama of their love relationship, a drama which unfolds inwardly in her own soul, and one which she caused to be recorded so that it might unfold in the souls of other Christians as well. She clearly identifies her audience as encompassing all Christians, regardless of gender, class, or place in the hierarchy of the Church. She might have written exclusively for women or for contemplatives or for those who had taken religious vows, but she did not. She wrote for everyone with faith in Jesus Christ. Thus in presenting two primary characters in her *Revelation,* herself and her Savior, Julian sought to affect the characters of her audience, her fellow Christians, with the power of love.

DIALECT, DICTION, LITERARY DEVICES

In conveying her experience of God's love in written form, Julian believed that she was at times relating the words of God. It comes as no surprise that she took special care with the choice and use of her own words. Thus an examination of the language of her work—her dialect, diction, and literary devices—can increase understanding of her purposes.

The dialect of Julian's *Revelation of Love* blends East Anglian and Northern dialects. In general Julian's language is comparable to the everyday speech of late-medieval Norwich. Often highly alliterative, it reflects the influence of biblical language and uses certain terms in special senses. For example, Julian's use of the binary opposition "sensuality and substance" suggests a contrast of the carnal nature of humanity and all that emerges from it (the flesh) with the divine nature of God and all that depends on him (the spirit). But as Ritamary Bradley explains in her essay "Julian of Norwich: Writer and Mystic," the two "can achieve unity again through Jesus Christ, who was fully human, and took sensuality, while remaining grounded in the Trinity" (p. 199). By "ground" Julian means, according to Bradley, the "unity of Christ in the Trinity," and by "ground of being" she means "that which knits the human soul to Christ" (ibid.). By "unmade kind" Julian means God. Julian's English vocabulary is wide, and it tends to use words of Latin

and French origin.

In the course of her work Julian uses a range of literary devices that would have been familiar, both generally and specifically, to her medieval audience: extended allegory, typological description, allusion, simile, metaphoric images, and a wide variety of rhetorical devices. In chapter 51 of *A Revelation of Love*, Julian creates an extended allegory, which she calls a "wonderful example," of a Lord and a Servant. The allegory answers her doubt and her desire to be comforted in two specific areas: her inability to discern between good and evil and her inability to love good and hate evil. In this part of her vision, Julian describes seeing two men, the first a Lord sitting peacefully and the second his Servant standing beside him ready to do his will. When the Lord bids his Servant do some errand, he runs forth in haste to do it, but falls along the way. In his fall, he experiences seven kinds of suffering: bruises, heaviness, feebleness, blindness in his reason and astonishment in his mind, the inability to rise, loneliness, and the hardness of the place where he fell. Julian looks to see if the Lord will blame the Servant for his fall, but the Lord does not do this because the cause of the Servant's fall was clearly only his good will and desire to serve his Lord. Instead of blame the Lord has tender regard for his fallen Servant and speaks courteously of his "beloved servant" and of his plans to reward him. From this, Julian says, "The Lord's meaning descended into my soul," and concludes that the Servant's fall will be turned into "worship and endless bliss."

Like other medieval allegories, Julian's allegory is an extended metaphor with several points of comparison between the figures she sees and the experiences they represent. It would seem that the relationship between Julian's allegorical Lord and Servant here parallels the relationship between Julian and God or between the individual human soul and the Savior. Yet Julian admits that full understanding of this part of her vision was not given to her at the time that she witnessed it. After twenty years of meditation, Julian says that she understood that the Lord was God and that the Servant was Adam—not only the particular Adam of the opening chapters of Genesis, but also the Adam who stands for all humanity and the second Adam as well, that is to say, Christ.

Julian's understanding of "Adam" is a typical medieval typological understanding. Typology, a Christian approach to reading the Bible, sees people, objects, and events in the Old Testament as prefigurations of people, objects, and events in the New Testament. Old Testament prefigurations are known as "types" and their New Testament fulfillments as "antitypes." The New Testament itself justifies and encourages such a mode of interpretation in several different instances.

For example, Matthew's Gospel depicts Jesus foretelling his death and resurrection by comparing his situation to that of Jonah: "For as Jonah was three days and three nights in the belly of a huge fish, so the Son of Man will be three days and three nights in the heart of the earth" (12:40). Here the typological comparison is between two events, Jonah's time in the whale's belly and Christ's time in the belly of the earth. In Luke's Gospel, Jesus focuses the typological comparison on two people, himself and Jonah: "For as Jonah was a sign to the Ninevites, so also will the Son of Man be to this generation" (11:30). In John's Gospel, Jesus makes a typological comparison between a person (himself) and an object (Moses's bronze snake) in order to foretell his crucifixion: "Just as Moses lifted up the snake in the desert, so the Son of Man must be lifted up, that everyone who believes in him may have eternal life" (3:14–15). Another prominent typological comparison in the Gospels is the identification of John the Baptist (antitype) with Elijah (type). In the Letter to the Galatians, the writer makes a typological comparison of Sarah and Hagar to the covenant of the law and the covenant of grace, respectively, a comparison that in fact develops into an extended allegory.

Patristic writers such as Augustine and Gregory the Great took a serious interest in typological interpretation of scripture, and they influenced a great many medieval people, lay and ecclesiastic alike, who began to see a plethora of typological correspondences between the Old and New Testaments. Medieval people took a particular interest in the typological comparison between the "old" Adam and the "new" Adam, in part because the comparison was rooted in the writings of the Apostle Paul, particularly the fifth chapter of the Letter to the Romans. There the writer emphasizes that just as death came through one man (Adam, the type), so grace came through one man (Jesus, the antitype). Paul's analogy is the ultimate source of Julian's typological understanding in chapter 51 of her *Revelation*.

In addition to allegory and typology, Julian alludes to saints and then identifies with them in some particular way. In the Short Text, for example, she makes an important reference to Saint Cecilia. The story of Saint Cecilia, perhaps familiar to some through Geoffrey Chaucer's Second Nun's Tale, concerns the chaste marriage of Cecilia and Valerian, the conversion of Valerian and his brother, and the martyrdom of both brothers and Cecilia. Cecilia's martyrdom was by partial beheading in a bath; she died after three days of bleeding, during which time she gave all she had to the poor. Julian took a particular interest in Cecilia's story and explains its relevance to her own desires in detail:

> I heard a man of holy church tell the story of Saint Cecilia, in which showing I understood that she had three wounds in the neck, by which she suffered unto death. By the stirring of this I conceived a mighty desire, praying to our Lord God that he would grant me three wounds in my lifetime, that is to say, the wound of contrition, the wound of compassion, and the wound of willful longing for God

Julian thus identifies herself with a martyred saint and turns the experience of the saint's martyrdom into a kind of allegory for her personal experience.

Julian's allusion to Mary Magdalene in the first chapter of the Short Text and the second chapter of the Long Text serves a similar function. There she writes: "I thought I would have been that time with Mary Magdalene and with others that were Christ's lovers. . . ." By making this assertion, Julian presents her love of Christ to her readers as similar to that of Mary Magdalene, a woman who, according to the New Testament, was freed by Christ from possession, and supported Christ during his ministry and who was the first to see Christ risen from the dead. Some medieval interpreters of the Gospels also identified her with the woman caught in adultery and with the woman who poured perfume on Christ in preparation for his burial. The saint's legend that grew up around Mary Magdalene depicted her as a prostitute who became a preacher. This legend never failed to emphasize the depth and intimacy, not only of Mary Magdalene's love for Christ, but also of Christ's love for Mary Magdalene. Julian's identification with the Magdalene thus proves to be an assertion of her love for Christ and Christ's love for her.

In chapter 38 of her *Revelation*, Julian alludes to several saints and biblical figures in a short catalog designed to demonstrate her understanding that sin can be turned to joy by God's mercy. She declares: "Then God brought merrily to my mind David and others in the old law without number, and in the new law he brought to my mind first Mary Magdalene, Peter and Paul, and those of India and Saint John of Beverley, and others also without number." In these cases, Julian points out, the people are known on earth and in the Church for their sins, but there is no shame in what they have done, only "worship."

In the Long Text, Julian then considers at greater length the particular example of Saint John of Beverley, noting that God allowed him to fall but mercifully kept him so that he lived and later rose in God's graces. She observes that, because of his contrite and meek living, God had given him greater joy in heaven than he would have had if he had not fallen at all, and she says God proves this is true by continuing to perform miracles around his body. By considering this aspect of the saint's life, an aspect with which Julian expects her readers to be familiar (even though it does not appear in Bede's *Ecclesiastical History of the English People* [ca. 731] or later versions of his legend), Julian emphasizes her theological point: God's ability to transform evil into good. As with Saint Cecilia and Mary Magdalene, Julian identifies with Saint John of Beverley and apparently encourages her readers to do the same.

Julian also makes use of powerful metaphors. She is best known for her discourses on Christ as Mother, a situation resulting from several factors:

anthologists often select the passages from Julian's *Revelation* that contain these discourses, with the result that students and general readers encounter these discourses first (and sometimes exclusively, if they never read the *Revelation* as a whole); scholars emphasize these discourses in their critical interpretations of Julian; and some modern readers have seen Julian's understanding of the maternal Christ as a reinterpretation of a masculine God and a re-empowerment of supposedly disempowered medieval women.

Actually Julian's ideas about God (and thus, in Christian Trinitarian thought, Christ) as a maternal figure derive from the Bible and traditional orthodox interpretations of it. Maternal imagery for God appears in such biblical books as Isaiah and the Psalms. Discussions of such imagery and free expansions thereupon appear in the writings of the Church Fathers, including Ambrose, Augustine, and Jerome, and in later writers, including, as cataloged by Ritamary Bradley, Cassiodorus, Remigius, Rabanus Maurus, Peter Lombard, Anselm, Bernard of Clairvaux, Albert the Great, Bonaventure, and Thomas Aquinas (p. 210). Thus it is not surprising that Julian would have thought about the maternal aspects of God and Christ in response to sermons, commentaries, and her own experience of God. The expression of her thought in her *Revelation* is beautiful.

Julian's most concentrated discussion of Christ's maternal nature appears in four chapters, 58–61, of her *Revelation*. It develops specifically in the context of Julian's understanding of the Trinitarian nature of God. For her, God is Father, Jesus is Mother, and the Holy Spirit is Lord, and because the Trinity is also a unity, all the Persons of the Trinity completely fulfill all the roles that Julian ascribes to each one individually. Thus she writes: "I beheld the working of all the blessed Trinity, in which beholding I saw and understood these three properties: the property of the fatherhood, the property of the motherhood and the property of the lordship *in one God*" (emphasis added). Julian is fascinated with Trinitarian patterns in this discourse, articulating a number of trinitarian constellations which all relate to one another: Father, Son, Holy Spirit; Father, Mother, Lord; and all-power, all-wisdom, all-love. When thinking of human nature, Julian also thinks in a trinitarian way, emphasizing the three stages of human life (being, growing, fulfilling) and the three things we receive from God (being, reforming, yielding).

Julian carefully distinguishes the ways in which Jesus is particularly "our Mother." The mercy, wisdom, and goodness of Jesus are important, but it is particularly his Incarnation that determines his maternal role. As Julian explains:

> Our *sensuality* is *only* in the second person, Christ Jesus, in whom is the Father and the Holy Ghost; and in him and by him we are mightily taken out of hell and out of the wretchedness in earth, and worshipfully brought up into heaven and blissfully united to our *substance* (emphasis added).

For Julian, Christ is the "ground of motherhood" the source and the origin of all true motherhood. Jesus is like a mother suckling her child in that he feeds his children with himself through the Sacrament of the Eucharist. A suckling mother proffers her breast to her child, but Jesus takes his children to his breast through his open side, thereby showing his children the joys of heaven. For Julian, Jesus is like a mother in that he is loving, wise, and knowing. His love for his children never changes, even if his manner with them changes as they grow and mature. Julian points out that though an earthly mother may suffer the death of her child, Jesus will never allow his children to perish. Julian's analogy has such force for her that she asserts that the word "mother"; is so sweet and kind in itself that it cannot be used truly to describe anyone except Jesus and Mary.

Julian uses other metaphors to explain her understanding of God and his relationship to his creation as well. As many have noted, in the fifth chapter of *A Revelation,* she describes seeing a "little thing" the size of a "hazel nut" in her palm. When she considers it, she realizes that it is all that has been made, and she marvels because its littleness suggests how easily it could fall to naught. Then she receives an answer in her understanding: God made it, he loves it, and he keeps and sustains it. Thus God is revealed as maker, lover, and keeper. In another place, Julian compares God to a point, the central point of all

life, and posits that human life is only a point in him. The metaphors of the "little thing" and the point emphasize the greatness and the glory of God and the ease with which it is possible for him to care for what he has made.

Julian also uses metaphors for other purposes. She compares the blood on Christ's face during her vision of his Passion to the scales of a red herring. She compares a vision of the fiend's face to newly fired brick. Both of these images emphasize the vivid redness of the faces, painful on the one hand and terrifying on the other. Elsewhere Julian compares life to a spiritual journey and describes spiritual lack of perception as blindness. She contrasts light and darkness and imagines the soul as a city. Though many of her metaphors are traditional, she uses them sparingly and with great effect. This is particularly true in chapter 51 of *A Revelation.*

In the allegory of the Lord and the Servant, Julian considers the symbolic significance of the colors, positions, and clothes of the figures in her vision. She writes of a "treasure in the earth"— perhaps comparable to that in the parable of the hidden treasure in the thirteenth chapter of Matthew's Gospel—which was a meat pleasant to the Lord, though Julian never saw the Lord served meat or drink. She further imagines the Servant as a gardener tending to the earth and its plants in a great labor of loving service. She describes the flesh Christ took on in the Incarnation as "Adam's kirtle," and she compares her own understanding of the marvelous example of the Lord and the Servant to a beginner's understanding of an ABC, a medieval text giving instruction in the alphabet. She likens Christ's work at the harrowing of hell to raising a "great root out of the deep depth," and Christ's crown to humanity, whom he saved. She also calls Christ the spouse who is at peace with "his beloved wife, which is the fair maiden of endless joy."

Julian's language is thus rich and varied. Through her use of allegory, typology, allusion, metaphor, and metaphoric imagery, Julian conveys her experience of divine revelation in precise yet evocative terms. She was able to use such language in part because she inherited it from her predecessors.

SOURCES

Many questions surround the sources of Julian's *Revelation of Love*. How, for instance, did the anchoress access her sources? The formative influence of the Bible is indisputable as is the importance of the sermons that she heard preached by the hundreds and thousands year in and year out through her window into the church. Particular ideas that she articulates, such as the perception of the maternal nature of God and Christ, certainly have a long history, but that does not mean she would have known the author of any particular idea. Like all thoughtful medieval persons, Julian inherited a body of knowledge from the medieval and ecclesiastical past that she then incorporated into her own thinking without always knowing where the ideas originated.

With that caveat, it is fair to consider the influences on Julian's work, beginning with the Bible. Julian makes hundreds of scriptural allusions and paraphrases in her *Revelation*, drawing from both testaments. From the New Testament, Julian especially draws on the four gospels, the letters of Paul and John, and the book of Hebrews. From the Old Testament, the Psalms; Wisdom literature such as Proverbs, Job, Ecclesiastes, and several apocryphal books; and the Book of Isaiah. Other influences on her thought and work include pseudo-Dionysius, Augustine, William of Ockham, Gregory the Great, William of Saint-Thierry, and possibly Walter Hilton, and Chaucer's translation of Boethius's *Consolation of Philosophy*. In addition to these sources Julian was steeped in one of the seven liberal arts: rhetoric.

Rhetoric, the art of persuasion, was widely taught and admired in the late medieval period. Its figures and modes of expression provided Julian with an orderly means of articulating her ideas. Colledge and Walsh have demonstrated in their edition of the Short and Long Texts that the anchoress made skillful use of numerous and diverse rhetorical figures in her work (see vol. 2, pp. 735–748, for a detailed enumeration and definition of the types of such figures that Julian employed). Julian's expansive use of diverse rhetorical figures strongly suggests that she wanted to use language to its best effect in order to influence her audience. It also suggests that her sources included skilled rhetoricians.

JULIAN'S LEGACY

Julian's life and *A Revelation of Love* left a legacy that influenced many communities. In her own time, Julian influenced Norwich through her presence, prayers, and counsel. She reached a larger community through the oral and written dissemination of her visionary experience, as evidenced by the testimony of wills and scribes and by Margery Kempe. During the Renaissance and Reformation, Julian's ideas exerted influence on English Benedictines living on the continent, particularly in France. Carthusians and Benedictines preserved and published her *Revelation*. As the textual fortunes of Julian's work show, Catholic and Protestant believers alike knew her work in later centuries. Beginning in the early twentieth century, Julian became a figure of particular interest for medieval, literary, and feminist scholars. At the same time, her importance to communities of faith continued to grow. Her legacy can perhaps best be understood in terms of her contributions to mysticism, theology, and literature.

MYSTICAL EXPERIENCE

The terms "mystic" and "mysticism" have been variously defined. They have been imagined to include a broad range of people and experiences, especially religious or ecstatic ones, in various eastern and western traditions. Modern scholarship identifies four or five late-medieval English mystics: Richard Rolle, Walter Hilton, the anonymous author of *The Cloud of Unknowing*, Julian of Norwich, and Margery Kempe. Yet what makes these authors "mystics" and their writings "mystical" has been the subject of debate. In his essay "The Middle English Mystics," Nicholas Watson has argued that "both the canon of 'Middle English mystics' and the term 'mysticism' have largely outlived their usefulness to scholars" (p. 539). He points to the ahistorical nature and use of the term, the tendency of devotional and historical exploration of mystics to be conflated, and the modern belief in the unifying nature of the "quality of experience" of the "Middle English mystics" as problematic factors in the study of mysticism which ought to lead to the abandonment of the term. Watson's argument notwithstanding, many people continue to understand Julian of Norwich as a mystic in a Christian mystical tradition.

The term "mystike" appears in Middle English writings and can mean "figurative" or "secret." Julian uses a related term at the beginning of her allegory of the Lord and Servant. There in chapter 51 she describes how God spoke to her in a showing or revelation "full mystely." Colledge and Walsh suggest that Julian's word choice combines the Old English "mist" with the Middle English "mystike" to mean "conveyed darkly and symbolically, after the manner of Scriptural parables" (p. 513). Julian's use of the term "mystely" thereby suggests on its own that her visionary experience, particularly of the Lord and his Servant, is a mystical experience. It involves an intimate interaction with her God. Her explanation makes clear that Julian sees her mystical experience as one that caused her difficulty in understanding, prompted her to meditate at length, and finally brought about new insight years later.

Julian's presentation of her mystical experience makes it possible to analyze the components of her mysticism. In a sense, Julian's mysticism begins with questions in her own heart that she then brings to God in prayer. Her *Revelation* depicts how she enjoys communion and fellowship of an intimate nature with God. In the context of that intimacy, God shows Julian a picture of relationship between himself and humanity, the picture of the Lord and his Servant. Julian then meditates on this revelation, spiritually and contemplatively, in order to reach the fullest possible understanding of its meaning. Over years of thoughtful consideration and devotion, Julian explores the myriad details of her vision and sees significance in all of them. She

also concludes that there is one overarching meaning to the vision: love.

Julian of Norwich's experience can profitably be compared to other so-called mystics of the fourteenth century. Several scholars have engaged in such comparisons, demonstrating therein that medieval mysticism does not have to be some murky, undefined, ahistorical field of inquiry. Instead Julian and other mystics can be explored on the terms and through the descriptions that they themselves set forth. Julian's use of the phrase "full mystely" is just one open door through which Julian invites those who are interested to come in and understand her experience. Her vision of the Lord and the Servant concretely suggests the outlines of a historically situated, readily defined Christian mysticism in late-medieval England, which is perhaps Julian's most significant contribution to the practice and understanding of mystical experience.

THEOLOGICAL INTERPRETATION

In general Julian's theology conforms to an orthodox, medieval Catholic worldview. She inherits a Trinitarian conception of God as three Persons in One—Father, Son, and Holy Spirit—from Augustine's interpretation of scripture. She, like most other medieval Christians, believes in the doctrines of the Church summarized in the Apostles' Creed, which include: the nature of God as Creator of heaven and earth; the events of Christ's conception, birth, crucifixion, resurrection, ascension, and role in the coming judgment; the importance of the Holy Spirit, the Church, and the saints; and the belief in the forgiveness of sins, the resurrection of the flesh, and eternal life.

Julian particularly emphasizes, as did the writer of the Gospel and letters of John, that God is love. She meditates intensely on the Incarnation of Christ, his fully divine and fully human nature, and she worships Jesus for his death on the cross, harrowing of hell, and resurrection to life again. She believes with the Apostle Paul that Christ's death was efficacious for the forgiveness of sins and the redemption of humanity, opening the way of restoration to relationship with God the Father.

She admires such saints as Cecilia, Mary Magdalene, and John of Beverley, as well as numerous figures from the Old and New Testaments of the Bible. While Julian is traditionally Catholic in her beliefs, her theology emphasizes particular aspects of her faith and makes meaningful contributions to the understanding of Christianity in the late Middle Ages as well.

The emphasis of Julian's theology is the love of God. She makes this fact plain in many places in her *Revelation,* including the beginning: "This is a revelation of love that Jesus Christ, our endless bliss, made." Famously she also claims in a later chapter that "love was his meaning." It is clear throughout Julian's *Revelation* that God's love is the center of her theology. Everything that exists does so in God's love, and it is this love that is the foundation of Julian's understanding of the relationship between God and humanity.

It is perhaps because of her overwhelming sense of God's love that she finds it impossible to perceive any wrath in God. For Julian, God is not angry or vengeful. He is worthy of worship and fear, but he is not angry with his children, servants, or lovers when they fall into the traps of sin. He is merciful, and he is able to turn everything to good. When Julian considers the problem of sin, it is with some perplexity. She is not at all certain why God would permit the existence of sin. Ultimately she does not resolve this question; instead she focuses on the work Christ accomplished through the cross and concludes that "all shall be well." Though through Adam sin entered the world, Jesus, the second Adam, made it possible through his atonement for humanity to receive forgiveness for sin and be reunited with God. Julian also believes, perhaps heterodoxically, that

in every soul that shall be saved is a godly will that never assented to sin nor never shall; just as there is a beastly will in the lower party that may will no good, just so there is a godly will in the higher party, which will is so good that it may never will ill but ever good.

(*Revelation*, ch. 37)

Such an assertion implies that human beings can escape sin in at least part of their will, but this

does not accord well with biblical or ecclesiastical teaching. Still it may only be Julian's attempt to agree with Paul's assertion in the seventh chapter of Romans that

I do not understand what I do. For what I want to do I do not do, but what I hate I do. . . . Now if I do what I do not want to do, it is no longer I who do it, but it is sin living in me that does it.

(Romans 7:15, 20)

Julian's theology also embraces the meaningfulness of such Christian disciplines as prayer, meditation, fasting, study, simplicity, solitude, submission, service, confession, worship, guidance, and celebration. She devotes three chapters of her *Revelation* to the discussion of prayer, and she records in the text multiple prayers that she herself prayed, for every question she asks of God is a prayer of petition. The importance of prayer in Julian's life cannot be understated because, as she says in chapter 43, "Prayer unifies the soul to God." Prayer is related to meditation, to the sustained and willful recalling to mind of divine things, and Julian carefully remembers in her *Revelation* how she meditated on the crucifix during her illness.

As part of her anchoritic life Julian certainly fasted during Lent and other seasons and applied herself to the study of scripture, whether she read it herself or had it read to her. She lived a life of simplicity within her enclosure, and her life was defined by solitude, even when it occasionally included other people. She submitted her life to the will of God and served God and "Christ's lovers" through prayer, counsel, and the sharing of her *Revelation* with the world. She participated in the sacrament of confession, she worshipped God, she guided others, and she celebrated the seasons of the liturgical year. Thus her theology is not explained simply in her *Revelation* but also exemplified in her life.

LITERARY INFLUENCE

The story of Julian's life, together with her *Revelation of Love,* influenced other writers and works of literature beginning as early as the fourteenth and fifteenth centuries. Julian certainly intended her audience to include her fellow Christians, and as Hugh Kempster argues in his "A Question of Audience: The Westminster Text and Fifteenth-Century Reception of Julian of Norwich," at least one manuscript of *A Revelation,* the abbreviated Westminster MS, probably reached an audience of pious lay people. Yet Julian might have been surprised that her legacy was not only mystical, theological, and practical, but also specifically literary. Sister Mary Arthur Knowlton shows that Julian probably influenced late-medieval devotional lyrics in Middle English. *The Book of Margery Kempe* explicitly testifies to the influence of Julian's life and visionary experience on Margery herself. Studies remain to be done on Julian's literary influence, exclusive of the textual tradition and transmission of her *Revelation,* during the sixteenth, seventeenth, eighteenth, and nineteenth centuries.

As Ritamary Bradley points out, Julian has influenced a number of modern authors and works of literature in the twentieth century. In the poem *Little Gidding,* T. S. Eliot makes repeated use of the phrase "All shall be well." Aldous Huxley ends a chapter of *Eyeless in Gaza* with what Bradley calls an "echo" of the same phrase from Julian's *Revelation.* In her prose poem *Holy the Firm,* Annie Dillard names a major character Julie Norwich and makes use of images, themes, and teachings from *A Revelation of Love.* Mary Gordon, in her novel *Final Payments,* depicts one character in a religious crisis discovering a prayer card with words from Julian printed on it. (pp. 214–215.)

Ralph Milton, a Canadian author, has written a work of historical fiction retelling Julian's life story. In *Julian's Cell: The Earthy Story of Julian of Norwich* (2002), Milton imagines Julian's life between the years 1358 and 1415. In his story Julian's given name is Katherine, which means "purity." She marries young and has two children, but her husband and children die of the plague. She experiences her amazing visions and then enters her anchorhold as Julian, a layperson (not a nun), and dies sometime later. While Milton's Julian is not quite the same as the Julian known to scholars and students of her *Revelation,* still the character that Milton imagines has great life

and determination. The very existence of Milton's Julian shows that the historical Julian of Norwich left a legacy for writers and readers to appreciate in works of literature for years to come.

Selected Bibliography

WORKS OF JULIAN OF NORWICH

MANUSCRIPTS

Bibliothèque Nationale de France Fonds anglais 40.

British Library Additional MS 37790.

British Library Sloane MS 2499.

British Library Sloane MS 3705.

Westminster Cathedral Treasury MS 4. (Extracts only.)

EDITIONS, TRANSLATIONS, MODERNIZATIONS, AND PARAPHRASES

Beer, Frances, trans. *Julian of Norwich: "Revelations of Divine Love,"* Translated from British Library Additional MS 37790; *"The Motherhood of God": An Excerpt, Translated from British Library MS Sloane 2477.* Woodbridge, Suffolk: D. S. Brewer, 1998.

Chambers, P. Franklin, ed. *Juliana of Norwich: An Introductory Appreciation and an Interpretive Anthology.* London: Victor Gollancz, 1955.

Colledge, Edmund, O.S.A., and James Walsh, S.J., eds. *A Book of Showings to the Anchoress Julian of Norwich.* 2 vols. Toronto: Pontifical Institute of Mediaeval Studies, 1978.

———, trans. *Julian of Norwich: Showings.* New York: Paulist Press, 1978.

Collins, Henry, ed. *Revelations of Divine Love Shewed to a Devout Anchoress.* London: T. Richardson, 1877.

Del Mastro, M. L., ed., *Revelations of Divine Love.* Garden City, N.Y.: Image Books, 1977.

Glasscoe, Marion, ed. *Julian of Norwich: A Revelation of Love.* Exeter, U.K.: University of Exeter Press, 1976. Rev. ed. 1986. Rev. again 1993.

Harford, Dundas, ed. *Comfortable Words for Christ's Lovers: Being the Visions and Voices Vouchsafed to Lady Julian Recluse at Norwich in 1373.* London: H. R. Allenson, 1911.

Hudleston, Dom Roger, O.S.B., ed. *Revelations of Divine Love Shewed to a Devout Ankress.* London: Burns, Oates, and Washbourne, 1927.

Reynolds, Sister Anna Maria, ed. *A Shewing of God's Love: The Shorter Version of Sixteen Revelations of Divine Love.* London: Longmans, Green, 1958.

Tyrrell, George, ed. *XVI Revelations of Divine Love Shewed to Mother Juliana of Norwich 1373.* London: Kegan Paul, Trench, Trübner, 1902.

Warrack, Grace, ed. *Revelations of Divine Love.* London: Methuen, 1901.

Wolters, Clifton, trans. *Revelations of Divine Love.* Harmondsworth, U.K.: Penguin, 1966. Reprint, 1974.

BIBLIOGRAPHY

Lagorio, Valerie Marie, and Ritamary Bradley. *The Fourteenth-Century English Mystics: A Comprehensive Annotated Bibliography.* New York: Garland, 1981.

CRITICAL AND BIOGRAPHICAL STUDIES

Abbott, Christopher. *Julian of Norwich: Autobiography and Theology.* Woodbridge, Suffolk: D. S. Brewer, 1999.

Baker, Denise Nowakowski. *Julian of Norwich's Showings: From Vision to Book.* Princeton, N.J.: Princeton University Press, 1994.

Barratt, Alexandra. "How Many Children Had Julian of Norwich?: Editions, Translations, and Versions of Her Revelations." In *Vox Mystica: Essays on Medieval Mysticism in Honor of Professor Valerie M. Lagorio.* Edited by Anne Clark Bartlett, et al. Woodbridge, Suffolk: D. S. Brewer, 1995. pp. 27–39.

Bauerschmidt, Frederick Christian. *Julian of Norwich and the Mystical Body Politic of Christ.* Notre Dame, Ind.: University of Notre Dame Press, 1999.

Bradley, Ritamary. "Julian of Norwich: Writer and Mystic." In *An Introduction to the Medieval Mystics of Europe.* Edited by Paul E. Szarmach. Albany: State University of New York Press, 1984. pp. 195–216.

Cannon, Christopher. "Enclosure." In *The Cambridge Companion to Medieval Women's Writing.* Edited by Carolyn Dinshaw and David Wallace. Cambridge, U.K.: Cambridge University Press, 2003. pp. 109–123.

Furlong, Monica. *Visions and Longings: Medieval Women Mystics.* Boston: Shambhala, 1996.

Glasscoe, Marion. *English Medieval Mystics: Games of Faith.* London: Longman, 1993.

Jantzen, Grace M. *Julian of Norwich: Mystic and Theologian.* London: SPCK, 1987. Reprint, Mahwah, N.J.: Paulist, 2000.

Kempster, Hugh. "A Question of Audience: The Westminster Text and Fifteenth-Century Reception of Julian of Norwich." In *Julian of Norwich: A Book of Essays.* Edited by Sandra J. McEntire. New York: Garland, 1998. pp. 257–289.

Knowlton, Sister Mary Arthur. *The Influence of Richard Rolle and of Julian of Norwich on the Middle English Lyrics.* The Hague, Netherlands: Mouton, 1973.

Krantz, M. Diane F. *The Life and Text of Julian of Norwich: The Poetics of Enclosure.* New York: Peter Lang, 1997.

Lawes, Richard. "Psychological Disorder and the Autobiographical Impulse in Julian of Norwich, Margery Kempe and Thomas Hoccleve." In *Writing Religious Women: Female Spiritual and Textual Practices in Late Medieval England.* Edited by Denis Renevey and Christiania Whitehead. Toronto: University of Toronto Press, 2000. pp. 217–243.

Madigan, Shawn, C.S.J., ed. *Mystics, Visionaries, and Prophets: A Historical Anthology of Women's Spiritual Writings.* Foreward by Benedicta Ward, S.L.G. Minneapolis: Fortress Press, 1998. pp. 191–208.

McAvoy, Liz Herbert, and Teresa Walters, eds. *Consuming Narratives: Gender and Monstrous Appetite in the Middle Ages and the Renaissance.* Cardiff: University of Wales, 2002.

McEntire, Sandra J., ed. *Julian of Norwich: A Book of Essays.* New York: Garland, 1998.

Meech, Sanford Brown, ed. *The Book of Margery Kempe: The Text from the Unique MS Owned by Colonel W. Butler-Bowdon.* Early English Text Society, Original Series, No. 212. London: Oxford University Press, 1940. Reprint, 1961.

Nuth, Joan M. *Wisdom's Daughter: The Theology of Julian of Norwich.* New York: Crossroad, 1991.

Warren, Ann K. *Anchorites and their Patrons in Medieval England.* Berkeley: University of California Press, 1985.

Watson, Nicholas. "The Composition of Julian of Norwich's Revelation of Love." *Speculum* 68, no. 3:637–683 (July 1993).

———. "The Middle English Mystics." In *The Cambridge History of Medieval English Literature.* Edited by David Wallace. Cambridge, U.K.: Cambridge University Press, 1999. pp. 539–565.

———. "Julian of Norwich." In *The Cambridge Companion to Medieval Women's Writing.* Edited by Carolyn Dinshaw and David Wallace. Cambridge, U.K.: Cambridge University Press, 2003. pp. 210–221.

HISTORICAL FICTION

Milton, Ralph. *Julian's Cell: The Earthy Story of Julian of Norwich.* Kelowna, British Columbia: Northstone, 2002.

Wangerin, Jr., Walter. *Saint Julian: A Novel.* San Francisco: HarperSanFrancisco, 2003.

MARGERY KEMPE

(c. 1373 – c. 1440)

Jane Beal

MARGERY KEMPE LIVED an extraordinary life. However, that life was little known until the twentieth-century rediscovery of her spiritual autobiography, *The Book of Margery Kempe*. In 1940, under the auspices of the Early English Texts Society (EETS), Sanford Meech and Hope Emily Allen published a critical edition of the book that made the story of Margery Kempe's life widely available. Since that edition, other editions, translations, and anthologizations have made Margery a figure of great interest and, at the same time, great dispute. A review of her life, book, and reception reveals why.

CHILDHOOD, MARRIAGE, AND BUSINESS ENDEAVORS

Margery Kempe was born in Bishop's Lynn (now King's Lynn), Norfolk, England, in the fourteenth century. Her father, John Burnham (or Brunham), was a financially and politically successful man. He served as town mayor five times, member of Parliament six times, alderman of the merchant guild, coroner, and justice of the peace. Margery had at least one sibling, a brother named Robert, who followed in his father's footsteps and served as a member of Parliament in 1402 and 1417. In her father's house Margery would have enjoyed a comfortable, middle-class lifestyle.

Neither Margery nor anyone else left a record of any formal education she might have been privileged to obtain as a young person. She did not read Latin, claimed she could not understand it when she heard it spoken, and certainly did not write it. When Margery became an adult, a priest read many works of religious devotion to her in English, which points up the fact that she could not read them in English herself. Yet Margery's lack of literacy did not prevent her from learning many things by memorization. Margery memorized scripture, at least partially because she heard it repeatedly in sermons, and she was very familiar with many Bible stories and saints' lives. Like most medieval Christians, Margery was taught the Paternoster, Ave Maria, Ten Commandments, virtues, vices, and articles of faith. She particularly mentions being tested in the latter by men of the Church and defending her knowledge and belief successfully.

Margery also learned by observation. She was conversant with the social expectations of her time and class, as her description of her fashionable style of dress, pride in her family accomplishments, and concern for her reputation all suggest. She would have gained an understanding of appropriate social decorum as the daughter of the mayor of Lynn, perhaps in part by listening to the conversations of politicians and businessmen in her father's house. At the same time, she would have understood much about her social and spiritual obligations as a Christian through regular church attendance. The influence of the Church on the course of her life would prove quite strong—even stronger, in fact, than that of her politically and financially savvy family.

At about age twenty Margery married John Kempe, a burgess of Lynn who may have been a brewer by trade. Records show that John Kempe served as a town chamberlain in 1394. Together Margery and John had fourteen children. At least one, the eldest, a son named John, lived to adulthood and married a Prussian. During her marriage Margery started two businesses, first brewing beer and then milling corn, but both businesses failed. In terms of her social standing, youthful marriage, prolific childbearing, and business ventures, Margery Kempe was an ordinary medieval Englishwoman. It was her spiritual experiences and expression of her Catholic faith, which she caused to be recorded in *The Book of Margery Kempe,* that distinguished her from the majority of her contemporaries and made her life extraordinary.

CONVERSIONARY EXPERIENCES

Although she was baptized a Catholic as an infant, Margery believed that she was called to greater intimacy with Christ through a series of experiences she had as an adult. The turning point in her spiritual life came after the birth of her first child. Her pregnancy and labor were so difficult that she "despaired of her life" (p. 21), and even after she delivered, she still did not trust that she would survive. This catalyzed her desire to confess something she had long concealed, which was on her conscience, and so she called for her confessor. She related to him a great many things, but she had not yet come to the point of saying the specific thing that was on her mind when her confessor began to sharply reprove her. Between her fear of her confessor and her fear of damnation for failing to confess, Margery testifies that she "went out of her mind" for more than half a year.

In her madness, Margery saw devils trying to attack her and telling her to forsake her faith, her family, and her friends. These temptations prompted Margery to slander everyone around her, pressured her to commit suicide, and caused her to do herself bodily harm. Margery's family kept her bound and guarded as a result. But she testifies that in this time of madness and suffering, on a day when she was alone, she had a vision of Jesus Christ, who came to her in the form of a man and asked her, "Daughter, why have you forsaken me, and I never forsook you?" (p. 23). Then she saw Jesus ascend slowly in the air. After this Margery's madness ceased, and her husband gave the keys to their food stores back to her. Margery resumed eating and interacting with her friends and family in her customary way.

Later, after she had recovered, Margery was lying in bed with her husband at night when she heard such a sweet melody that it was as if she were in paradise. This affected her greatly, first in that whenever she heard music on earth it would remind her of the music in heaven and cause her to weep, and second in that she completely lost her desire to have sexual relations with her husband. From the time that she heard this heavenly melody, she desired to live chastely. She often tried to live so and to convince her husband to live so as well, but when he would not, she consented to his will "with great weeping" (p. 26).

Since she could not, as a married person, give up sexual relations, Margery found other ways to express the intensity of her devotion to God. She prayed for a chaste marriage, went to confession two or three times a day, prayed early and often each day in church, wore a hair shirt, and willingly suffered whatever negative responses her community expressed in response to her extreme forms of devotion. Perhaps most of all, Margery wept. Her weeping was for Christ's mercy and the forgiveness of sin, for herself, and for the world, and it became the signature of her devotion throughout her life. Everywhere she went, but particularly in churches, during sermons, and in holy places, Margery would weep. Throughout her life, the fervor of her weeping and the number of her tears only increased. And she was always moved to tears on any occasion when she meditated on the Passion of Jesus Christ.

After being tempted to commit adultery, Margery went to the Church of Saint Margaret in her home town and begged God for forgiveness. She had a vision of Christ speaking to her and reassuring her that he had forgiven her sins "to the uttermost point" (p. 30). He then gave her several commands: to call him her love, to stop wearing the hair shirt, to give up eating meat, to take the Eucharist every Sunday, to pray the rosary only until six o'clock, to be still and speak to him in thought, and to make the anchorite at the Dominican Priory of Lynn her confessor. "And I shall flow so much in grace in you," she heard him say, "that all the world shall marvel thereof" (p. 31). Then, to his commands he added many promises: to give her victory over her enemies, to give her the ability to answer all clerks, to be with her and never forsake her, and to help her and never be parted from her.

From that point onward Margery Kempe lived a different life than her husband, her family, and her community might have expected she would live. She did her best to obey the commands she believed Christ had given her and the commands he continued to give her for the rest of her life. As a result, Margery became a weeper and a woman of prayer, living in the world for God.

SPIRITUAL PROGRESS

Significant milestones marked Margery's spiritual progress after her conversionary experiences. Specifically, Margery had visions, visited local holy places with her husband, and eventually convinced her husband to take a vow of chastity. She escaped more than one near-death experience, including the collapse of part of a church roof on her back and the threat of being burned to death by monks who accused her of heresy when she was visiting Canterbury. She grew in her ability to discern, and willingness to prophetically express, the sins and spiritual destinies of other people. At the same time, she continued to weep and to pray. She often sought out men in positions of ecclesiastical authority in order to obtain their affirmation that her life of devotion was godly, not misdirected, and that her feelings were true, not deceived. By the end of 1413, at approximately forty years of age, Margery undertook her first international pilgrimage.

Before heading across the English Channel, however, Margery made several local pilgrimages to holy places in Norwich, Canterbury, York, Bridlington, and Lincoln. In Norwich she met with Richard Caister, the vicar of the cathedral of Norwich, and visited and conversed with William Southfield, a Carmelite friar, who told her that her manner of living was the work of the Holy Spirit. She also sought out Julian of Norwich, an anchoress who experienced divine revelations of love from God, for similar reassurance, which Julian gave to her. Julian particularly reassured her about her weeping, telling her:

> When God visits a creature with tears of contrition, devotion, or compassion, he may and ought to believe that the Holy Ghost is in his soul. Saint Paul says that the Holy Ghost asks for us with mournings and weepings unspeakable, that is to say, he makes us to ask and pray with mournings and weepings so plentiful that the tears may not be numbered. No evil spirit can give these tokens, for Jerome says that tears torment the devil more than the pains of hell. God and the devil be evermore contrary to one another, and they shall never dwell together in one place, and the devil has no power in man's soul. Holy Writ says that the soul of a righteous man is the seat of God, and so I trust, sister, that you are. I pray that God grants you perseverance.

(p. 54)

Margery was despised for her weeping in Canterbury, however, by monks, priests, and secular men who accused her of heresy. She was rescued from burning by two young men who took her back to her hostel where she found her husband. Yet she was not too discouraged. For in Lincoln, Bishop Philip Repingdon greatly commended Margery's feelings and contemplations, saying they were inspired by the Holy Ghost, and it was he who accepted the profession of her vow of chastity and that of her husband. When Margery left him, the bishop gave her money and asked her to pray for him. Later, when Margery was once again in Canterbury, she met with the Archbishop Thomas Arundel, and he found no fault in her manner of living, her contemplations, or her tears. Indeed, he gave her a letter allowing her to choose her own confessor and directing priests, wherever she met them, to administer the sacrament of the Eucharist every week just as she had desired.

Although Margery's husband often joined her on her travels in England, he did not accompany her everywhere at all times, as the incident in Canterbury clearly indicates. Yet Margery grew in confidence that God would send friends to help her in need and that her Savior himself would accompany her everywhere. Indeed, even before she undertook visits to local shrines, she believed God was calling her to visit Rome, Jerusalem, and Santiago de Compostela in Spain, and that she had received a special promise from God: "I shall send enough friends of England in diverse countries to help you. And, daughter, I shall go with you in every country and provide for you. I shall lead you there and bring you back again in safety" (p. 45). Perhaps it was the combination of her experiences as a pilgrim in England and her promises from God that enabled her to undertake her much wider travels on the Continent, not with her husband but rather in the company, many times, of people she had never met before.

PILGRIMAGE TO JERUSALEM, ROME, AND SANTIAGO DE COMPOSTELA

Shortly after her father's death in 1413, Margery left Lynn in order to undertake a pilgrimage to the Holy Land. She spent the winter in Venice, Italy, staying there for thirteen weeks. Although Venice was then at the height of its medieval splendor, rich in commerce and holy relics, Margery makes very few observations about the city. Her focus is on her own experience: taking the Sacrament every Sunday in a great convent of nuns; crying plentiful tears during devotions; becoming deathly ill and then suddenly recovering. She vividly remembers her ongoing conflicts with her traveling companions, who resented her talk of the gospel at mealtimes and eventually excluded her from their fellowship, compelling her to eat alone in her rooms and using the services of her maidservant (i.e., cooking and washing) for themselves. While she was in Venice, Margery records hearing the Lord speak to her only once, warning her to sail in a galley rather than the sailing ship her traveling companions had chosen. Margery passed on the warning to her companions, and they quickly switched ships and ended up traveling with her.

As Anthony Goodman points out, the decision to take a galley was a wise one. The journey to Jerusalem was expensive, and a galley made it more so, but a galley had certain advantages a mere sailing ship did not: rowers. Such men could row the galley and its passengers out of trouble as well as position them off the coast so that passengers could disembark. All aboard could then take time to regain their land legs, stay the night on shore if desired, and purchase fresh food supplies. Margery's decision to take a galley may have been informed not only by God but also by her experience in Lynn, a town that was located on the North Sea coast on the east bank of the River Ouse and thus exposed her to the vicissitudes of the medieval shipping industry.

Margery's journey from Venice to Jerusalem takes up only a few sentences in her story, most of them devoted to the memory of a dispute with a fellow traveler, a priest, over the ownership of a sheet. But the company most likely landed in Jaffa, the usual port for arriving pilgrims, and headed inland from there. Before arriving in Jerusalem, Margery did her best to make up with her companions, asking their forgiveness and giving her forgiveness in turn, for it was appropriate to pilgrims to enter the Holy Land in a state of contrition. Margery records that she was riding on a donkey in the company of her fellow travelers when she saw Jerusalem for the first time, a realistic detail, and that she nearly fell off, so overcome was she by the vision before her and her sense of God's grace in her soul.

As part of her pilgrimage Margery visited many places that were holy to her and to other Catholics because of their association with Jesus and the gospel story. She stayed in Jerusalem for three weeks, so she had a fair amount of time to make her visits and contemplate the spiritual significance of the sites she saw. She went to Bethlehem where Christ was born. She recorded walking the way Christ did when he carried his Cross and visiting the mount of Calvary where he was crucified. She also visited Mount Sion, where she believed Jesus had washed his disciples' feet, and she received the Sacrament in the same place that Jesus and his disciples had shared the last supper. She saw the burial places of Jesus, his mother Mary, and the Cross itself, which had been unearthed by Constantine's mother. She spent some of her time in the place where the apostles received the Holy Ghost on the day of Pentecost and "our Lord gave her great devotion" (p. 79). She also came to the river Jordan and Mount Quarentyne (near Jericho), where it was believed Jesus had fasted forty days, and Bethany, where Mary, Martha, and Lazarus had lived. She also records that "she stood in the same place where Mary Magdalene stood when Christ said to her, 'Mary, why are you crying?' " (p. 81).

This identification with Mary Magdalene in the Holy Land proved to be quite important for Margery, who makes numerous references to the saint throughout her *Book*. Mary's tears gave Margery's tears a scriptural warrant and a spiritual justification. Indeed, Margery wept more and more in Jerusalem, and particularly at Calvary, where she experienced visions of Christ's Passion and a new kind of crying: a crying out loud, a "roaring," which was "the first cry that ever she cried in any contemplation" (p. 76). That kind of loud and heartbreaking cry would accompany Margery's weeping for most of the rest of her life.

Margery visited Jerusalem at a time when it was under the control of the sultan of Egypt, al Mu'ayyad Shaykh, and his Mamluk governors. Relatively tolerant Muslims permitted the presence of the Franciscans at Mount Sion, and Margery records how the friars led her and her company along their roads and routes to holy sites. She also records meeting "Saracens," who made much of her, and one who particularly befriended her and helped her up Mount Quarentyne when none of her own company would give her aid.

The picture of the relationship between Christianity and Islam in Margery's *Book* makes a fascinating addition to other medieval testaments. Notably, Margery makes no negative remarks about Islam, its followers, or its founder. Indeed, she says "Saracens . . . conveyed her and led her about in the country wherever she wanted to go, and she found all people good unto her and gentle—save her own countrymen" (p. 81). For Margery, the irony must have been inescapable: Muslims in the Holy Land were kinder to her than the hard-hearted Christians who voyaged with her from England.

Margery's experiences in Jerusalem and the surrounding areas made a lasting impression on her. There she was able to be intimately close to the places where Jesus had lived and died. She often remembered her time in the Holy Land in later years, and she used it to defend herself against accusations of heresy. Not everyone she met in England could believe that she had actually been to Jerusalem, but such a pilgrimage was considered quite meritorious.

From the Holy Land, Margery returned to Italy and stayed in Assisi before coming to Rome, the second great pilgrimage site of medieval Christendom. Margery stayed at the hospital of Saint Thomas of Canterbury in Rome, just as many other medieval English pilgrims did. She received the sacrament of the Eucharist there every Sunday, as she did customarily, until a priest came and spoke so badly of her that she was compelled to leave her lodgings at the hospital. She visited many churches, including San Giovanni in Laterano and Santa Maria Maggiore, which she mentions by name. She also visited Santi Apostoli, San Marcello, and St. Birgitta's Chapel. She stayed in Rome longer than in any other city on her pilgrimage, not leaving until Easter 1415.

Margery's visionary experiences in Rome were almost as intense as those she had experienced in Jerusalem. She confessed her life to St. John the Evangelist, whom Jesus sent to comfort her when she was excluded from the hospital of St. Thomas, and she heard God ask her to be wedded to himself in the Apostles' Church on Saint Lateran's Day (November 9). She saw "with her bodily eyes," as she says, "white things flying about her on every side as thick in manner as motes in the sun" (p. 92). She understood through a revelation that they signified angels. She had auditions as well of the Holy Ghost, who sounded at first like a pair of bellows, then a dove, and finally a little robin redbreast. She heard Jesus speaking to her many times, and, at his command, made a man named Winslowe her confessor. She also gave away all of her money and lived by begging for a time.

Margery's decision to choose poverty deliberately suggests both the tremendous impact of her pilgrimage on her devotion to Christ and her desire to express it as the Franciscans and Poor Clares did: by living without goods. Margery is remarkable for repudiating the comforts of her wealth and middle-class upbringing, however, because she did so without taking vows or regular orders as many of her contemporaries did. She had no specific monastic community to support her in her decision, and her traveling companions wanted nothing to do with her. As she records, her response to her reduced circumstances was to thank God for her poverty because she believed it increased her merit in God's eyes (p. 97). Her motivation does not lessen the fact that she was doing something incredibly brave for an English-woman in Rome in 1415. Homelessness, poverty, and daily begging for food risked not only her comfort but her physical safety, which she was generally terrified of endangering at other times, as her *Book* attests.

While in Rome, Margery made another dramatic decision. She began wearing white clothes, an event almost as important as her utterance of loud cries of devotion at Calvary. She had long believed that God wanted her to wear white, but Bishop Philip Repingdon had given her permission to do so only after she fulfilled her intention to visit Jerusalem. In order to understand the significance of Margery's white clothes, it is necessary to remember that there were strict sumptuary laws in place in late medieval England. Perhaps even more important than legal restrictions were social expectations. Clothes loudly declared a person's gender, social class, and religious vocation in Margery's day. White clothes in particular generally signified sexual purity and sexual chastity, states most often associated with virginity. Since Margery was in fact married, and the mother of fourteen children, her decision to wear white clothes was badly received in most of her circles. The reaction to her clothing could, in fact, be quite violent. Yet Margery persisted in her decision to wear white. For her, it was an outward sign of an inward transformation.

Before leaving Rome, Margery had other marvelous experiences, including an encounter with a woman who served St. Birgitta, an acquaintance with a German priest who could understand her English (but no one else's), and a vision of St. Jerome. Jerome told her that she was blessed for weeping for people's sins and that many people would be saved through her special gift, her "well of tears" (p. 103). Thus Margery left Rome with additional confirmation and surety of the life she believed God had called her to live.

Margery returned to Norwich, passing through Middelburg (in what is now the Netherlands) on the way, but in 1417 undertook a journey to Santiago de Compostela. "St. James," as Margery calls it, was the third great pilgrimage site of Western Christendom. Her *Book* is remarkably taciturn about what she did in Spain, focusing more on her prayer for a safe journey on calm seas and the length of time it took to go from Bristol to Santiago and then return (seven days there, five days back). Though she does not mention it, Margery doubtless visited the Cathedral of Compostela, viewed the relics of St. James, and worshipped God in her usual manner with "many great cries remembering our Lord's Passion" (p. 112). Upon her return she went to venerate the blood of Christ at the Abbey of Hailes in Gloucestershire.

CHALLENGES TO A LIFE OF DEVOTION

When Margery returned to England, she continued to worship with tears and cries just as she had while on international pilgrimage. However, not all the men of the Church in England responded as favorably to her weeping as the monks in Jerusalem had. The lack of understanding was due, in part, to the tension arising from the conflict between the Church in England and a reform movement known as Lollardy.

Lollardy had its origins in the teachings of John Wyclif, a priest and scholar at Oxford who died in 1384. Before his death Wyclif articulated critiques of several common Church teachings that became central to the beliefs of those in his expanding circle of influence who desired reform. Wyclif's followers denied, for example, that the bread and wine actually became the flesh and blood of Christ in the sacrament of the Eucharist, they denied that unbaptized infants were damned, and most importantly, they denied that the Church had a right to its goods and possessions. Wyclif actively promoted the "disendowment" of the Church by secular lords and kings. In Wyclif's view, Christ's poverty ought to have been shared by his followers, especially men of the Church. This view was popular among the nobility, partially because it enriched their coffers, and so it was widely disseminated among them. Wyclif's followers actively promoted a reform agenda among the clergy and the laity as well, composing not only in Latin but also in the vernacular and translating significant texts from Latin into English. The most important book to emerge from this program was the Wycliffite Bible, so called because its translation was inspired by Wyclif's influence, though the scholar himself probably had little to do with the actual work of translation. Even before the production of an English Bible, however, preaching in English, and translating scripture from Latin into English for sermons to the laity, had become popular among both orthodox and Lollard preachers.

The medieval English Catholic Church actively resisted the reformers within their ranks. Two pieces of legislation mitigated against the Lollards: *De Heretico Comburendo* (On the burning of the heretic), approved by Parliament in 1401, and the *Constitutions* of Arundel, Archbishop of Canterbury, issued in 1407–1409. Together these texts condemned Lollard positions and the means of promoting them (i.e., English preaching, English Bibles, and English translation). They also provided for punishments of heretical persons. The first man tried and condemned for Lollardy, and consequently burned, was William Sawtrey, the parish priest of Saint Margaret's Church in Margery's hometown of Lynn. There can be little doubt that Margery knew William, and knew him well, given her frequent presence in her local church. William's name is not mentioned in Margery's *Book* nor is her response to his death, perhaps a deliberate omission for a woman who wanted to present herself as an orthodox believer. Yet his death in 1401 must have been a shock to Margery and a scandal to her community. The trials and deaths of accused Lollards only continued thereafter.

It is fair to say that Margery lived her whole adult life in the shadow of the conflict between orthodox Catholicism and Lollardy. When she returned to England from her international pilgrimages, she was just five years removed in time from Cobham's Rebellion (1413). Lord Cobham, also known as Sir John Oldcastle, had been convicted of Lollardy in 1413, but his punishment was delayed to give him opportunity to recant, so in the intervening time he raised a rebellion attempting to unseat his former friend King Henry V. This rebellion was not successful. Oldcastle escaped, but he was brought to justice in 1417—the very same year that Margery returned from the Continent. Thus it is not surprising that the political and religious climate in her country was highly charged, and her particular forms of emotionally expressive devotion were badly received in 1417. She had been called a Lollard before, by monks who threatened to burn her for heresy when she was in Canterbury in 1413, but the mood of the country had worsened since then. In new conflicts, Margery was accused of being a Lollard and even called "Cobham's daughter." She faced quite serious municipal and ecclesiastical trials in Leicester, York, Cawood, and Beverley.

In Leicester, the mayor accused Margery of Lollardy and had her imprisoned. Her friends too were taken captive. While in custody, Margery faced the threat of sexual assault by the town steward but defended herself by saying she was a man's wife and the mother of fourteen children. Margery does not record being raped, and perhaps the attempted physical assault gave her the strength and courage to defend herself from the mayor's assault on her spiritual life. She was successful in answering questions and accusations and was set free. So were her friends, but Margery's *Book* records that they were none too pleased at being arrested because of her. Margery was later arrested at York, but she defended herself before the archbishop, who had met her before. She was also arrested by the duke of Bedford and accused of encouraging a wife to desert her husband, a charge she vehemently denied. When she finally managed to get away from Beverley, Margery apparently went back to Lynn.

Margery's experience testifies to the tension of her times but also to Margery's amazing resourcefulness. When other people were being arrested, tried for heresy, and sometimes burned at the stake, Margery managed to defend herself and her weeping. According to the self-presentation in her *Book,* Margery remained dedicated to Christ and the Church despite all challenges to her life of devotion.

RETURN TO LYNN AND A FINAL JOURNEY

Margery's life after she returned to Lynn was characterized by difficulty. She was sick for about eight years, suffering physical discomfort and pain. A Franciscan friar arrived in Lynn about 1420 who preached from the pulpit specifically against her and her emotional forms of worship, making her life in her community miserable. Her husband, from whom she had lived apart for many years, had a bad fall and required her help. Margery became his caretaker once more as he descended into senility. First her husband and then her son, who had come to visit from Germany with his Prussian wife, died about 1431. Margery's losses were painful.

Although her weeping and her cries were never cordially received in her hometown, Margery did gain favor with many of her fellow townspeople during a terrible fire that ravaged Lynn on January 23, 1431. The fire burned down the guildhall of the Trinity and part of Saint Margaret's Church. In fact, the whole town was in danger from the flames. Margery responded to the peril of the town with great cries and tears and prayers to God. Though in the past the citizens of Lynn had regarded this behavior with disdain, on the day of the fire their attitudes changed. They bid Margery continue and to, by all means, intercede with God to have mercy on them and their town. With Margery's permission, her confessor carried the Sacrament toward the church. Margery followed and prayed that God would "make it well" (p. 158) by sending rain or some weather to quench the fire. Shortly after, three men with snow on their clothes came into the church to tell Margery that God had shown grace to them and ended the fire with a snowfall.

After the fire and the deaths of her husband and son, Margery continued to host her son's wife in her home until the woman was ready to return to Germany, where her young daughter, Margery's granddaughter, was still living with caretakers. In 1433, at about sixty years of age, Margery accompanied her daughter-in-law to the port of Ipswich along with a monk sent along to help them. Then, though she had not intended to do so or obtained her confessor's permission, Margery took the journey by sea with her daughter-in-law toward the Continent. They were blown off course and spent Easter in Norway. Within a few days, they were able to sail with a fair wind into Germany.

In Gdansk (present-day Danzig in Poland), Margery stayed for five or six weeks. Her daughter-in-law, who had not wanted her mother-in-law (who had an injured foot) to come in the first place, was against her staying. On a day when she was praying in the local church, a man asked if she would like to go on a pilgrimage to the "Holy Blood" at Wilsnack. Margery had trouble leaving, for the Teutonic knights did not favor her, but she met up by chance with a merchant from Lynn who helped her get out of the country secretly. She sailed toward Stralsund and eventually came to Wilsnack, despite problems with her fellow traveler, and there she venerated Christ's blood. Her return journey took her by way of Aachen, where she saw more holy relics, including a cloak that had ostensibly belonged to Mary, the mother of Jesus. From Aachen she went to Calais, and from Calais, to Dover.

In England once more, Margery traveled through Canterbury and London, where people received her both positively and negatively. Some of the clergy slandered and reproved her, but many of the common people held her in high regard, believing that it was "the goodness of God which wrought that high grace in her soul" (p. 228). Margery then made her way to Syon Abbey, a Brigettine house at Isleworth, where she wept profoundly as she remembered the sufferings of Christ. There she met a monk named Reynald who was from Lynn, the very man who had accompanied her to Ipswich. He was not willing, initially, to accompany her back to Lynn; Margery's confessor had blamed him for Margery's sudden departure to the Continent. Yet Margery talked Reynald into accompanying her anyway, by offering to pay for his expenses, and so they both returned to Lynn.

COMPOSING HER BOOK

In 1436, Margery's then confessor, a priest, began to recopy the first part of her *Book* which had been written down at Margery's dictation sometime earlier by an Englishman living in Germany (possibly her son, some scholars have suggested). In 1438, the same priest copied down the second part of Margery's *Book*. An external record mentions that Margery was admitted to the Guild of the Trinity at Lynn on April 13, 1438. Another record mentions her on May 22, 1439. After that there are no further records of Margery's life.

THE BOOK OF MARGERY KEMPE: *CONFESSION, COMPOSITION, MANUSCRIPT*

The outline of Margery's life can be derived from her *Book,* placed in historical context, and considered in relation to medieval social expectations. However, Margery's *Book* itself is not at all a straightforward, chronological autobiography in the modern sense. In order to gain an understanding of the *Book of Margery Kempe,* it is useful to consider its generic qualities as a confession or spiritual autobiography. The process by which it was composed, which is foregrounded in prefaces to the work, must also be considered. The history of the unique manuscript of the *Book* and its partial survival in early modern printed editions gives insight into its use by later readers. These things can be evaluated before looking at other aspects of Margery's *Book.*

Margery Kempe's *Book* must be understood in relation to the medieval Catholic practice of confession. In confession, the penitent admitted sins to a man authorized by the Church to hear confession, such as a priest, and he in turn recommended the proper penance. The penitent went through three spiritual stages in this process: contrition (an inner conviction of wrongdoing combined with the desire and decision to repent), confession (the act of verbally admitting wrong-

doing to God and an authorized representative of the Church), and satisfaction (the acceptance and performance of penance). Admissions in the confessional were held in confidence and could not be betrayed even in legal proceedings, let alone in ordinary conversation or gossip. It was typical for a penitent to confess on a regular basis to the same person throughout his or her life. Given the intimacy and secrecy of the confessional, as well as the development and duration of the relationship between the penitent and the confessor, it is no surprise that the confessor had a privileged position of authority and respect in the lives of many medieval people. This is particularly true in the case of Margery Kempe.

The fact that Margery Kempe's *Book* exists at all is due in part to her confessors, to whom she dictated her life and through whom a written record of it was preserved. After introductory prefaces, her *Book* opens with a failed attempt at confession that leads to a period of severe psychological distress and ultimately provides the impetus for an intimate relationship with Christ. Margery's confessors play a central role in her life, listening to her confessions, validating her spiritual experiences, and defending her to other people, among other things. Indeed, Margery's *Book,* often considered the first autobiography in English, is in fact confessional in nature and genre. It is concerned with the problem of sin, the reception of grace, and the experience of God's love in a fallen world. Margery's *Book* is not an autobiography in the modern sense, with a focus on a historically situated self and a chronologically ordered set of events. Rather it is a spiritual autobiography, one that acknowledges God as the principal agent in a human life and which medieval people would have recognized as a confession, a testimony, or a witness of one person's journey of faith.

As set forth in the prefaces to her *Book,* Margery waited twenty years from the time of her first intense spiritual experiences (her "first feelings and revelations") before seeking to create a written record of them for others. When sufficient time for reflection had passed, she dictated her book to two men, one of whom was a priest authorized to hear confession. The first man, an

Englishman living in Germany with a wife and child, wrote down what she dictated but so poorly that the priest, to whom Margery later brought the manuscript, could not discern if he were reading English or German. The priest would not recopy the book and for four years or more claimed he could not read it, so Margery finally took it to another man who had known her first scribe and helper because he was supposed to be conversant with her scribe's ostensibly illegible script. That man copied very little of the text, perhaps a leaf, and then gave up because the handwriting was so poor and difficult to read. So once again Margery assayed the priest, and he tried to read the poor copy again, this time finding the task much more manageable. As he records, he began to write out Margery's *Book* shortly after St. Mary Magdalene's Day in 1436.

The process involved in the composition and transmission of Margery's *Book* complicates the question of its authorship. Although Margery dictated it, there is little way of knowing or discerning how complicit the priest or the original copyist may have been in adding, deleting, or changing material in Margery's narrative. Only one manuscript of the *Book* survives, British Library Additional 61823 (formerly belonging to Colonel William Erdeswick Ignatius Butler-Bowden), and it is a fifteenth-century copy by a scribe who calls himself Salthows on one of the pages. Neither the illegible copy made by the Englishman in Germany nor the new copy made by the priest survives, preventing interesting comparisons. Yet the fact that British Library Additional 61823 dates to as early as the fifteenth century suggests that it was fairly close to the original, as Sanford Meech and Hope Emily Allen suggest in their excellent edition of Margery's *Book.*

Although the manuscript of Margery's *Book* did not come to light until 1934, it did manage to influence a small audience in its time as annotations to the manuscript in four hands attest. The manuscript remained in the possession of the Carthusian monastery at Mount Grace initially, but what its fortunes were between the sixteenth and twentieth centuries is unknown. Colonel Butler-Bowden suggested that the monks of Mount Grace may have given the manuscript to his family, which was Catholic, for preservation during the upheaval of the Reformation.

Whatever the case may be, selections from the manuscript also survived in a seven-page quarto edition printed by Wynkyn de Worde, titled *A Shorte Treatyse of Contemplacyon . . . Taken Out of the Boke of Margerie Kempe of Lynn* (c. 1501). Henry Pepwell reprinted the treatise in 1521, mistakenly identifying Margery as an anchoress when he did so. The treatise appears as one part of Barry Windeatt's edition of *The Book of Margery Kempe* (2000). Such brief selections as those printed by Wynkyn de Worde, however, do not give the full sense of Margery Kempe's spiritual autobiography. The tale of her extraordinary life can only be fully appreciated in her *Book* itself.

AUDIENCE, PURPOSE, STRUCTURE

The preface that begins Margery's *Book* clearly reveals her anticipated audience and moral purposes in relating the story of her life. "Here begins a short and comfortable treatise for sinful wretches, wherein they may have great solace and comfort for themselves and understand the high and unspeakable mercy of our sovereign Savior Christ Jesus, whose name be worshipped and magnified without end, that now in our days, to us who are unworthy, he deigns to exercise his nobility and his goodness" (p. 17).

As this passage suggests, Margery is composing her *Book* for an audience of "sinful wretches." Her reasons for doing so include her desire to comfort sinners, to help them understand the mercy of their Savior, and to magnify the name, nobility, and goodness of that Savior, Jesus Christ. This is the clearly stated purpose of the book.

Margery might have had other reasons for causing her life story to be set down, and the confessors who helped her probably had their own motivations as well. Autobiography is often inspired by a desire to clarify events that took place in the past and relate them to an understanding of the self that has emerged over time. Sometimes autobiographers are seeking to justify or explain their actions to a perceived public.

Although these motivations might seem to be the preserve of modern writers, Margery's *Book* gives every suggestion that such purposes were part of Margery's reasons for composing. Her confessors had their own reasons. Like Margery, they doubtless shared the desire to see God glorified in Margery's life. Yet this motive was complicated by others. The priest responsible for the final copy of the first part of the *Book* and the original copy of the second part certainly had a complex relationship to Margery and Margery's spiritual autobiography.

As he admits, he was initially hesitant to copy Margery's life, though she pressed him. At various points in Margery's *Book,* he states that the criticism other people directed at Margery and her weeping caused him to doubt her sincerity and convinced him to abandon her. Obviously the priest does this, in part, to use himself as a model of someone whose doubt was converted to faith in Margery's sanctity and thus to set an example for readers who might have similar doubts that need assuaging. The priest was convinced of the holiness of Margery's tears by reading the lives of other holy women who were similarly tearful. As Janette Dillon has suggested, he might also have found in those lives examples of important confessors, priests, and amanuenses who, through affiliation with holy women, were able to promote their own importance in the Church. Yet this priest, if that was his hope, never gives his name in the *Book*—an omission that suggests the humility he might have possessed and which the Christian Middle Ages so often prized.

The stated purposes of the *Book*—to comfort, to promote understanding, and to glorify Christ Jesus—relate to the structure of the *Book.* The *Book* begins with two prefaces, the first long and the second short, both explaining the history of the composition of the "treatise." The first part, called Book I, has eighty-nine chapters. The second part, called Book II, has ten chapters. There follows a kind of appendix that describes Margery's habitual approach to prayer. In the first chapter of Book I, Margery begins by telling the story of an incomplete confession that led to madness from which she recovered through the intervention of Christ. In the last chapter of Book II, Margery ends by recording her prayers, her communication with Christ, and so concludes where she began: focusing on the central relationship in her life.

MARGERY AND JESUS

Margery's *Book* depicts stages in the development of her relationship to Jesus. In the opening chapter Jesus rescues her and restores her to sanity. Later Margery hears the heavenly melody that prompts her to want to live chastely. Both before and after her international pilgrimages, Margery also had visions of events from the life of Christ and his family in which she took an active part. These participatory visions gave Margery the chance to do for Jesus and his family what they had done for her: namely, help in times of need. Margery is not unique among medieval visionaries for having such desires and acting so dramatically in the gospel story.

While still in Lynn, Margery saw in contemplation the early life of Christ and envisioned herself participating in it: acting as the midwife to Saint Anne when Mary was born; carrying sweet, spiced wine for Mary and Joseph; visiting Elizabeth, the mother of John the Baptist, and receiving Elizabeth's commendation for her service to Mary; purchasing lodging for Mary and Joseph en route to Bethlehem; and begging for food, bedding, and swaddling clothes for Mary and the newborn Jesus. She also saw herself accompanying the holy family into Egypt and witnessing the adoration of the Magi.

Many times in her life, Margery had visions of the crucifixion of Jesus. His Passion was continually on her mind wherever she went. These visions intensified during her visits to holy places in Jerusalem and Rome. After her return from abroad, on a Thursday proceeding Easter, she saw "in her soul" a vision Mary, Mary Magdalene, the twelve apostles, and Jesus, bidding farewell to all of them before his ascension into heaven. She saw Mary at the time of Mary's death and wished to die in order to be reunited with Mary and Jesus. Mary responded by telling her that she could not come yet and reassuring her that her sins had been forgiven long before. Margery repeatedly had an intense and vividly detailed vision of the whole process of Christ's Passion in which she played a part: sympathizing with Mary before the Christ's arrest, witnessing the betrayal in the garden, and weeping at the scourging Jesus endured. She also saw the crucifixion and burial. At the foot of the Cross, she heard Jesus commend Mary to John and John to Mary. She spoke to Mary to comfort her and later made her something to drink in Mary's home. She heard Peter ask Mary's forgiveness for betraying her son, and she stood with Mary Magdalene in the garden where Jesus met her after his resurrection.

Margery's visions of Jesus and those closest to him, including his mother, his twelve disciples, and Saint Mary Magdalene, emphasize that Jesus was everything to Margery. Her visions also reveal the intensity of Marger's affective piety.

The focus of late medieval affective piety was the humanity of Jesus. By contemplating Christ's humanity, Margery and others sought to stir up within themselves great emotional responses indicative, to themselves and their community, of their love and total devotion to Christ. Indeed, Margery's devotion to the humanity of Jesus caused her to hesitate to accept the invitation to be married to God in the Apostles' Church in Rome: "for all her love and her affection was set in the manhood of Christ and . . . she would for nothing be parted therefrom" (p. 91). In her visions at that time, Margery heard Jesus ask the Father to excuse her for her inability to answer the invitation. Then Margery was spiritually married to God anyway despite her fear of being separated from her devotion to the humanity of Jesus.

Margery's devotion to the "manhood of Christ" caused her to be moved by the sight of babies, who recalled to her mind Jesus as an infant; by weddings, which reminded her of the marriage of Mary and Joseph and the "spiritual joining of man's soul to Jesus Christ" (p. 189); and by images and holy places and Corpus Christi plays, all of which returned her meditation to Christ's humanity. Margery perceived Jesus, the Second Person of the Trinity, in explicitly and consis-

tently human terms. Furthermore, she perceived her relationship to Jesus as absolutely vital, saying to him in contemplation: "You are my joy, Lord, my bliss, my comfort, and all the treasure that I have in this world." Elsewhere she heard him say of himself that he was the "true steward and true executor" (p. 183) of her good works. Margery had no doubts about the lordship and sovereignty of Jesus, and the final prayer that concludes her *Book* particularly acknowledges these aspects of her Savior when she repeatedly calls him "Lord," "Good Lord," "Lord God Almighty," "sovereign Lord Christ Jesus," and "Good Lord Christ Jesus" (p. 228–234). And always, Jesus was Margery's "love" (p. 156).

Margery understood Christ's love for her in incredibly intimate terms. Many times, as recorded in her *Book,* she heard Jesus call her daughter, mother, sister, wife, spouse, and dearworthy darling. Margery firmly believed that Jesus saw her as a part of his family. No other person was as meaningful to her. Margery's perception of Jesus, and her understanding of his perception of her, formed the core of Margery's identity.

This was important because not all perceptions of Margery were positive. Indeed, the perceptions Margery's contemporaries had of her were quite polarized. Other people's opinions affected Margery, as her *Book* makes plain, but they did not replace the central role of her savior in her life. Perhaps that is why Margery was able to tolerate negative responses to the woman she became even when she did not think she could.

MARGERY AND OTHER PEOPLE

The contrasting perceptions of Margery and her emotionally expressive worship are perhaps best exemplified by the anchorite at Lynn, her confessor, and the mayor of Leicester, her onetime accuser and jailor. The anchorite called Margery "a good woman, a lover of God, and highly inspired of the Holy Ghost." The mayor, in contrast, called her "a false strumpet, a false lollard, and a false deceiver of the people!" (p. 112–113). Margery's *Book,* perhaps not surprisingly, makes every effort to represent Margery as closer to the former than the latter description. Yet the *Book* does not omit references to other people's negative responses to Margery. This is because they were a part of Margery's life in the world, because they truly affected her, and because she saw Christ-like virtue in suffering other people's scorn.

Unlike many other medieval visionaries, Margery did not live as a nun or an anchoress under a rule. She carried out her life of devotion, prayer, and tears in public. She had a husband, fourteen children, and relationships with many citizens in the town of Lynn, churchmen in positions of ecclesiastical power, and pilgrims traveling throughout the world. These people were divided in their responses to her. Some saw her as wicked while others saw her as righteous. Some mocked her, and some aided her. By some she was called a heretic and a hypocrite; by others, mother and holy woman. Many individuals changed their view of Margery over time. The priest who copied her book is one example. Her husband is another. When they fought over the possibility of having a chaste marriage, John Kempe called her "no good wife" (p. 37), but later he agreed to chastity and to her way of devotion.

Margery's *Book* signals that she had complex attitudes about people's perceptions of her. She often desired approval and affirmation of her calling to her particular way of life. This can be seen in her tendency to seek out men of the Church as well as Julian of Norwich. In her conversations with such people, Margery sought to verify that her visions were true, not false, and that she was being led by the Holy Spirit, not some evil spirit. Conversely, Margery desired disapproval, at least insofar as she was disapproved for Christ's sake, because she believed that human scorn was sometimes a punishment for her sins, often efficacious for the exculpation of her sins, and consistently a means of meriting favor with God. According to the Gospel, Jesus himself had provoked mixed responses to his actions, and religious leaders of his day had accused him of being possessed by demons. Perhaps for that reason, Margery was willing to record an occasion when clerks accused her of having a devil within her after she affirmed that the gospel gave

her permission to talk about God whether the archbishop wanted her to do so or not (p. 126). For Margery, mockery and misunderstanding could be accepted in the light of Christ's example.

Certainly Margery could withstand other people's scorn, and did so on many occasions, as her *Book* attests. Yet she was clearly sensitive to other people's opinions. She retained a middle-class woman's awareness of the importance of her reputation, and that awareness was heightened by her understanding of how perfect a life a holy woman ought to lead. She would tolerate people maligning her tears, but outright falsehoods she refuted, as when churchmen impugned her orthodoxy or one man accused her of giving birth to a child while traveling overseas. To silence gossipers who said she was not living chastely after taking her vow, she lived apart from her husband until he fell ill.

If the self-presentations in her *Book* are any indication, Margery saw herself in a variety of ways. She knew her social roles included being a daughter, a wife, and a mother. She knew, spiritually, that she was a sinner and a captive wretch, but she believed that she had been transformed into God's servant. Metaphorically her *Book* compares her to a "pillar" and a "mirror," one who holds up the Church and one who reflects back truthfully what is shown to her. She also saw herself as a "creature," the term she consistently used to refer to herself in her *Book,* which means that she saw herself in relation to her Creator, the one who made her as she was and formed who she came to be. Perhaps most significantly, Margery saw herself as a woman who prayed and a woman who wept. Her spiritual autobiography might even be called a book of tears.

MARGERY'S "HOLY TEARS"

Margery's tears were the signs of her devotion. Her *Book* describes her "holy tears," her "crying, weeping, and sobbing," her "loud cries," "great weepings," and "boisterous sobbings," as well as her "roaring." The words alone evoke pitiful pictures and sounds, at times quiet and at other times loud. The *Book* suggests that Margery spent a lifetime expressing her devotion in tears while at the same time trying to understand why she was crying. But it is clear that she saw the value of her tears, even when others did not, and that she understood them as a gift of God, justified by scripture, and in imitation of Jesus, his mother Mary, and Saint Mary Magdalene.

For Margery tears could express compassion and contrition, devotion and compunction. Tears could be motivated by memories of sin, contemplation of forgiveness, and conversation with others, as when she met a man in Rome and told him "many good tales and and many good exhortations until God visited him with tears" (p. 97). In Margery's view, sometimes tears came from within her and sometimes they came to her from God. She prayed that God would give her a "well of tears" (p. 139) in order to prevent him from putting men's souls asunder from him. She also, on another occasion, prayed that Jesus would take away her tears. But he did not. Instead, he explained their value.

Margery records that when she first had her "wonderful cries" (p. 174), she asked her Lord to take them from her because people had told her that her crying was causing men to sin on account of her. Margery heard Jesus saying that he wanted Margery to be obedient to his will and cry when he willed it because of what her tears showed to others. He said that "small weepings and soft tears" show his love for her; "great cries and roarings" show his mother's sorrow over his sufferings. Her tears are a "token" to others that, if they will sorrow over Christ's Passion and cease their sins like Margery, they will have the bliss of heaven. Margery's tears show sinners, no matter how horrible they may be, that their past need not throw them into despair; they have the option of imitating Margery's example. Finally, Jesus tells Margery that her tears and her pain now are the reason why she will have no pain when she leaves the world and less pain when she is dying because her compassion for Christ's humanity motivates his compassion for her humanity in turn (pp. 175–176).

As this suggests, Margery saw her tears as expressive of divine love and imitative of Mary, the mother of Jesus. She saw them as appropriate to a mourner remembering Christ's death and efficacious for turning sinners toward repentance and, ultimately, heavenly bliss. She also saw them as, redemptive.

Margery knew, however, that tears could be motivated by secular rather than spiritual feelings. Margery's *Book* records that both men and women cry over lost property, over affections for their family and friends, and over inordinate loves and fleshly desires, especially for friends parted from them (p. 77). But Margery is clear, throughout her *Book,* that her tears are rarely of this kind. Her tears are holy. She gained this understanding from scripture, and in her advanced years, she even dared to use scripture to defend herself from the scorn to which she had become accustomed.

When she was about sixty years old, and traveling through Germany, she came to a house of Friars Minor, and there, with others, she saw the Eucharist on the Feast of Corpus Christi. She began weeping and sobbing at the sight, and a monk was furious at her and her company so that they all turned on her and rebuked her. But she answered them by quoting one of the Psalms, saying: "They that sow in tears shall reap in joy. He that goes forth and weeps, bearing precious seed, shall doubtless come again with rejoicing, bring his sheaves with him." (The part of this verse recorded in Margery's *Book* is preserved in Latin.) This only made them angrier, and they soon abandoned her. The episode is interesting, however, because it shows Margery using scripture in defense of her tears.

Margery also found in scripture and in extrabiblical literature precious models for her life of tears. She recalls a priest reading to her about the moment when Jesus saw Jerusalem and wept over it because of the sorrows that would befall it. When Margery heard this, she herself began weeping and crying aloud (p. 141). Christ's tears prompted Margery's imitative tears, and they also provided a justification for Margery's past and future weeping. Likewise, the tears that Mary, the mother of Jesus, cried over Christ's death were very much in Margery's heart, mind, and memory. At one point, Margery heard Jesus speaking to her about "the sorrows that my mother had here on earth" and "the tears that she wept" (p. 155). Margery's tears were often in imitation of Mary's tears over the death of her son. But it was Mary Magdalene who was Margery's foremost model of the weeping woman.

Margery's *Book* contains numerous references to Mary Magdalene, references that reveal Margery's personal sense of identification with the saint. Margery begins her book shortly after Mary Magdalene's day (preface to Book I), she makes special mention of the fact that she stood where Mary Magdalene stood in the Holy Land when Jesus spoke to her after his resurrection (p. 81), and she even hears Christ commend her for calling Mary Magdalene into her soul (p. 198). Margery also had a vivid vision of the scene described in John's gospel wherein Mary met Jesus in a garden, mistook him for the gardener, not realizing that he had come back to life again, and heard him ask her, "Woman, why are you weeping?" Margery was particularly pierced by Christ's command to Mary not to touch him *(noli me tangere),* and she experienced great sorrow whenever she heard that phrase repeated in a sermon "for love and desire that she had to be with our Lord" (p. 188).

Beyond scriptural warrants and models, Margery's *Book* also meditates on the examples of holy women from the Continent who wept holy tears. Margery herself was particularly interested in Birgitta of Sweden, whose maidservant she met with in Rome and whose book of *Revelations* she had read to her. Margery's priest and scribe was particularly attentive to the tradition of Continental piety among women, and it was that tradition that persuaded him to remain loyal to Margery even when she was attacked from the pulpit by the friar who came to Lynn (c. 1420). Women like Marie d'Oignies (c. 1177–1213) and Elizabeth of Hungary (1207–1231) persuaded him, as did the *Incendio Amoris* of Richard Hampole and the *Stimulis Amoris* of another writer (at that time supposed to be Saint Bonaventura). The priest's account of his renewed loyalty (pp. 148–151) provides one type of justification for Margery's life of devotion. Margery knew of these same people and their writings directly through a young priest who read to her for seven years, and

they served as examples to her, of lives of devotion expressed in tears.

RECEPTION OF MARGERY KEMPE

In her own day, as her *Book* attests, Margery faced a mixed reception. The split in public opinion in Margery's lifetime emerged again when her *Book* was rediscovered in the twentieth century. Critics were and are divided about Margery. Unlike many of her contemplative contemporaries, she has not been canonized by the Catholic Church, and her piety is frequently seen as imitative, egotistical, and hysterical. At times she has been unfavorably compared to Julian of Norwich, for example, and to the holy women of the Continental tradition. Yet she has attained literary canonicity, and portions of her story are included in most historical surveys of British literature and widely taught to college students. Her *Book* is often considered the first autobiography in English, and because it originates with a woman, it is important for feminist scholarship as well.

Interestingly, Margery's *Book,* like those of many famous authors, was strangely prophetic about its own reception. In one vision Margery hears Jesus say to her, "Daughter, I shall make all the world to wonder at you, and many men and many women shall speak of me for love of you and worship me in you" (p. 80). Certainly it is impossible to talk about *The Book of Margery Kempe* without considering the central relationship depicted in it, the relationship between Margery and Jesus, and in the early twenty-first century many people are discussing—and wondering—over Margery Kempe in college classrooms, medieval conferences, feminist symposia, and other venues.

How might Margery have responded to the divided reception of her *Book* so many years after its composition? Her wide range of emotional responses to public opinion in her lifetime suggest several possibilities. One is particularly inviting. After suffering at the hands of the men of the duke of Bedford, and being referred to the archbishop and then released by him, Margery encountered the steward who had badly harassed her before. She was laughing when she saw him, and he disapproved of her, and said, "Holy folk should not laugh." She answered him, "Sir, I have great cause to laugh, for the more shame and spite I suffer, the merrier I may be in our Lord Jesus Christ!" (p. 134). Margery, famous for her tears, could rejoice in her fifteenth-century sufferings. If she could see the criticism of her work in the twenty-first century, surely it would provoke her holy laughter.

Selected Bibliography

WORKS OF MARGERY KEMPE

MANUSCRIPT AND EDITIONS

The Book of Margery Kempe. British Library Additional MS 61823. (Manuscript.)

The Book of Margery Kempe. Edited by Sanford Brown Meech and Hope Emily Allen. EETS vol. 212. Oxford: Oxford University Press, 1940. Reprinted, 1961. (The standard edition. Indispensable.)

The Book of Margery Kempe. Edited by Lynn Staley. TEAMS Middle English Texts Series. Kalamazoo, Mich: Medieval Institute Publications, 1996. (Fine edition designed for student use. Includes introduction, select bibliography, footnotes, textual notes, and glossary.)

The Book of Margery Kempe. Edited by Barry Windeatt. New York: Longman, 2000. (Excellent textual apparatus: chronology of Margery's life, outline of the chapters of her book, explanation of editorial practice, clear introduction, edition of Wynkyn de Worde's "A Short Treatise of Contemplation," glossary of common words, and so forth.)

TRANSLATIONS AND PARAPHRASES

Collis, Louise. *Memoirs of a Medieval Woman: The Life and Times of Margery Kempe.* New York: Crowell, 1964. (Largely a paraphrase with some commentary, mostly condescending, about Margery's life and visions.)

McAvoy, Liz Herbert, trans. *The Book of Margery Kempe: An Abridged Translation.* Woodbridge, U.K.: Brewer, 2003. (Selects, translates, and organizes passages from the *Book* under three headings: narratives of motherhood; discourses of desire; and voice and authority. Includes a scholarly introduction, an interpretive essay on gendered performances, and Wynkyn de Worde's 1501 printed extracts in an appendix.)

Staley, Lynn, trans. and ed. *The Book of Margery Kempe: A New Translation, Contexts, Criticism.* New York: Norton, 2001. (Includes an introduction, lexicon, contexts from Thomas Arundel, *Meditations on the Life of Christ,* Julian of Norwich, Birgitta of Sweden, and the *Life of Marie d'Oignies* by Jacques de Vitry as well as brief criticism on female sanctity, authorship and authority, and so forth.)

CRITICAL AND BIOGRAPHICAL STUDIES

Atkinson, Clarissa W. *Mystic and Pilgrim: The Book and World of Margery Kempe.* Ithaca, N.Y.: Cornell University Press, 1983. (Treats Margery's book, mystical experience, family in King's Lynn, relationship to the Church, affective piety, and virginity discourses as well as various critical interpretations.)

Beckwith, Sarah. "A Very Material Mysticism: The Medieval Mysticism of Margery Kempe." In *Gender and the Text in the Later Middle Ages.* Edited by Jane Chance. Gainesville: University Press of Florida, 1996. pp. 195–215. (Applies literary theory, particularly of French feminist scholars, to identify the female mystic as the "Other," question her marginalization, and encourage questioning of patriarchal structures of power.)

Cholmeley, Katharine. *Margery Kempe: Genius and Mystic.* London: Longmans, Green, 1947. (Argues from a devout Catholic perspective that Margery was divinely inspired, even saintly, not hallucinatory.)

Dillon, Janette. "Holy Women and Their Confessors or Confessors and Their Holy Women? Margery Kempe and Continental Tradition." In *Prophets Abroad: The Reception of Continental Holy Women in Late-Medieval England.* Edited by Rosalynn Voaden. Woodbridge, U.K.: Brewer, 1996. pp. 115–140. (Analyzes the positions of power held by confessors in the lives of holy women with particular attention to Margery Kempe and her priestly scribe.)

Dinshaw, Carolyn. "Margery Kempe." In *The Cambridge Companion to Medieval Women's Writing.* Edited by Carolyn Dinshaw and David Wallace. Cambridge, U.K.: Cambridge University Press, 2003. pp. 222–238. (Considers influence of books on Margery's *Book,* Margery's emotional style of devotion, the sexuality of Margery's spirituality, and notions of time which may or may not be useful for understanding Margery.)

Fries, Maureen. "Margery Kempe." In *An Introduction to the Medieval Mystics of Europe.* Edited by Paul Szarmach. Albany: State University of New York Press, 1984. pp. 217–236. (Solid overview of the life and works of Margery Kempe.)

Gallyon, Margaret. *Margery Kempe of Lynn and Medieval England.* Norwich, U.K.: Canterbury Press, 1995. (Analyzes Margery's life particularly in relation to religious groups such as secular clergy, regular clergy, friars, and Lollards.)

Glenn, Cheryl. "Popular Literacy in the Middle Ages: *The Book of Margery Kempe*." In *Popular Literacy: Studies in Cultural Practices and Poetics*. Edited by John Trimbur. Pittsburgh: University of Pittsburgh Press, 2001. pp. 56–73. (Gives a fair introduction to the varieties of medieval literacy, in Latin and the vernacular, with special attention to Margery's book.)

Goodman, Anthony. *Margery Kempe and Her World*. London: Longman, 2002. (Takes a special interest in Margery's travels locally, in England, in Europe, and particularly in holy cities like Santiago de Compostela, Rome, and Jerusalem.)

Jones, Sarah Rees. "'A peler of Holy Cherch': Margery Kempe and the Bishops." In *Medieval Women: Texts and Contexts in Late Medieval Britain: Essays for Felicity Riddy*. Edited by Joycelyn Wogan-Browne, et al. Turnhout, Belgium: Brepols, 2000. pp. 377–392. (Focuses on the role of episcopal authority in structuring the *Book*.)

Lochrie, Karma. *Margery Kempe and Translations of the Flesh*. Philadelphia: University of Pennsylvania Press, 1991. (Argues for the interrelationship of bodies, speech, discourse, and books in mystical texts.)

McEntire, Sandra J. *Margery Kempe: A Book of Essays*. New York: Garland, 1992. (Essays on Margery's life, work, and world.)

Meale, Carol M. "'This Is a Deed Bok, the Tother a Quick': Theatre and the Drama of Salvation in the *Book* of Margery Kempe." In *Medieval Women: Texts and Contexts in Late Medieval Britain: Essays for Felicity Riddy*. Edited by Joycelyn Wogan-Browne, et al. Turnhout, Belgium: Brepols, 2000. pp. 49–68. (Analyzes popular drama as a context for and in relation to Margery's *Book*.)

Parsons, Kelly. "The Red Ink Annotator of *The Book of Margery Kempe* and His Lay Audience." In *The Medieval Professional Reader at Work: Evidence from Manuscripts of Chaucer, Langland, Kempe, and Gower*. Edited by Kathryn Kerby-Fulton and Maidie Hilmo. English Literary Studies vol. 85. Victoria, B.C.: University of Victoria, 2001. pp. 143–216. (Analyzes the annotations of a late-fifteenth- or early-sixteenth-century commentator on BL Additional 61823.)

Renevey, Denis, and Christiania Whitehead, eds. *Writing Religious Women: Female Spiritual and Textual Practices in Late Medieval England*. Cardiff: University of Wales Press, 2000. (Contains four essays on Margery Kempe investigating her journeys, her understanding of virgin martyrs, her body as performance, and her psychological disorder.)

Salih, Sarah. *Versions of Virginity in Late Medieval England*. Woodbridge, U.K.: Brewer, 2001. (Chapter on Margery in relation to the discourses, expectations, and martyrs of virginity.)

Stone, Robert Karl. *Middle English Prose Style: Margery Kempe and Julian of Norwich*. Paris: Mouton, 1970. (A comparative study of the prose styles of Margery Kempe and Julian of Norwich.)

Voaden, Rosalynn. *God's Words, Women's Voices: The Discernment of Spirits in the Writing of Late-Medieval Women Visionaries*. Suffolk, U.K.: York Medieval Press, 1999. (Discusses women's mysticism historically, Birgitta of Sweden, and Margery Kempe.)

PHILIP KERR

(1956—)

Patrick A. Smith

SCOTS BORN, THE novelist Philip Kerr found himself at home in London. That dual identity is perhaps the most apt starting point for an analysis of a career that, by any measure, has become increasingly difficult to categorize. Kerr's sensibility remains a capricious blend of Scottish attitudes and the more cosmopolitan trappings of success that attend his career as, first, an up-and-coming talent and, later, an A-list fixture. Kerr was born February 22, 1956 to Bill and Ann Kerr and spent much of his childhood in the Corstorphine section of Edinburgh. Growing up in a religious, middle-class family, Kerr led something of a sheltered life. The young Philip, "squeezed between the Baptist faith at home and the stiff-backed atmosphere of private school . . . remembers being shocked to spot his grandfather, a carpenter, ducking into a Haymarket boozer" (Gibb, p. 3). Apparently, such distress was short-lived. None of Kerr's novels would show the least bit of squeamishness in describing far more disturbing events. The question of identity surfaces repeatedly in Kerr's fiction, a theme that might be traced to the author's double life as Scot and Londoner, as well as an event that shaped his own father's life, when the man discovered after more than a quarter-century that the people he thought of as his biological parents were, in fact, his aunt and uncle. Kerr's father, a property developer, died at the age of forty-seven, when the aspiring writer was just twenty-two. Kerr did not receive any encouragement from his father to pursue a writing career, although his father did once begin a thriller. After moving with his family to England as a teenager, Kerr earned a law degree from the University of Birminghamin 1980 and spent seven years in the London-based advertising agency Saatchi & Saatchi, the same firm where Salman Rushdie had worked years before.

Despite the veneer of success in business that might have made his father proud, Kerr was determined to write:

> I spent my lunchtimes—throughout my entire 30s—living a double life. I was saying to someone yesterday that the Dr. Jekyll and Mr. Hyde duality is really about a writer: after the proper job in the day, at night you roam free in the world of your own making. I think the only thing that encouraged me was a sense—well, not even "a sense of my own worth" but that very Scottish thing, the "chippy" thing, the Scottish-Protestant work ethic. . . . I think it is the thing which matters most in life—the thing you have to prove to yourself.
>
> (Gibb, p. 3)

As with many aspects of Kerr's public life—including his often strained relationship with the media and fellow literati—those early experiences reveal a conflict between Kerr's childhood and his own attempt at reinventing himself. Mike Gillespie reminds readers of Kerr's offhand remarks about Edinburgh—"that it is one sexually repressed Glaswegian satellite" and concludes that the sentiment is "just plain daft" (p. C14). Gillespie also invokes Kerr's infamous slur toward his home country, when he says of his Scots accent that "I didn't lose that so much as wipe it off my shoe" (p. C14).

Regardless of how Kerr is reported in England's famously prying and opinionated periodicals, however, the author is more balanced in his own analysis of what it means to have made the transition between two different worlds. "When I came to England I would say I was offensively Scots. . . . I was utterly committed, from devolution to the defence of Scottish football," Kerr contends. "But you get to the stage where you get tired of it and I thought the world isn't going to change, so I basically just smoothed myself out. . . . I feel a sense of schizophrenia the Scottish boy has been the father of the more or less English man" (Gibb, p. 3).

Kerr and his wife, Jane Thynne, who has been a media correspondent for London's *Daily Telegraph,* live with their three children in the London suburb of Wimbledon.

EARLY PROMISE AND THE ANXIETY OF INFLUENCE

When Kerr was named one of *Granta*'s Best Young British Novelists in 1993, the recognition should have sent him along with the other honorees—Iain Banks, Esther Freud, Kazuo Ishiguro, Caryl Phillips, and Will Self chief among them—well on their way to careers as acclaimed writers. While some thrived, Kerr struggled for respect, his work both characterized as that of a gifted and driven writer—particularly the early detective novels—and denigrated as unambitious genre fiction. Kerr has found himself on the cusp of two distinct literary worlds: that of literary fiction, which admires the pastiche and gritty, ambitious prose of the early novels; and that of the thriller-science fiction world, which looks to Kerr for novels of ideas that, though certainly not lacking in expository ability, have pushed him solidly into the realm of mainstream "genre fiction." Kerr, attempting to explain his position on the matter, wrote in a 2002 article in the *New Statesman,*

> No single literary event in 1990s Great Britain caused as much sniping, backbiting, hissy-fitting, navel analysis and self-castigation as Granta's publication, in 1993, of those writers whom Bill Buford, Salman Rushdie, A. S. Byatt and John Mitchison judged to be worthy of inclusion on a list of the 20 best of British, aged under 40. Bliss was it in that dawn to be alive, but to be judged young was very heaven! For a couple of days, anyway. Because it wasn't very long before people started to piss on our parade.
>
> (p. 18)

Kerr goes on to name, in part, the formidable writers who were chosen for the first *Granta* list in 1983: Julian Barnes, Martin Amis, Salman Rushdie, Peter Ackroyd, Ian McEwan, Graham Swift—writers who have become the standard-bearers of British literature over the past twenty years. About being included in a group that has become Britain's literary elite, Kerr told the interviewer Michele Field, "Like a lot of people, I felt the Amis influence and wrote novels about randy young men in London and swiftly realized that there was only room for one person to do this—and that person was Martin Amis, who was doing it terribly well" (p. 43).

Criticism of Kerr's fiction is predicated primarily on the author's subject matter rather than any intellectual shortcomings. In an interview with Joyce Park, the British crime writer Maxim Jakubowski deemed Kerr's *Berlin Noir* trilogy (1989–1991) "a wonderful example [of noir fiction] which stands basically completely on its own." At the same time, says Jakubowski, "he's also a great disappointment" for the direction and tone of his later fiction. That ambivalence toward Kerr's work has followed him since his preference for novels of ideas over complex characters became apparent with the publication of *A Philosophical Investigation* (1992), a near-future techno-thriller that limns notions of privacy, genetic determination, and random violence years before such topics became fodder for cable-news pundits.

Kerr's characters most often inhabit worlds that are dystopian mirrors of the present. Whether as a researcher in Russia exploring that country's pervasive Mafia influence as a result of the collapse of Communism or the machinations of human evolution in the Himalayas or in outer space, Kerr transposes the world around him into a fresh, though still recognizable, context that allows him to examine the less palatable elements of society while maintaining audience interest; or, as Kerr told Michele Field, "One of my pet theories is that the modern thriller has replaced the didactic novel. . . .I am very pleased that I can allow myself stretches of 'thought-filled' prose—which are leavened by a plot which will still carry the reader (who is perhaps not interested in hearing my thoughts)" (p. 44).

In a review of Kerr's *Esau* (1996), a novel that explores the possibility of ape-like creatures inhabiting the Himalayas amid an apocalyptic confrontation between nations, Liam Callanan points out that the designation "genre fiction," as well as many other classifications of literature in general, has become nebulous, the synthesis of high and low forms suggestive of postmodern literature. "Better genre fiction is hard to categorize," Callanan writes. "Is it mystery or suspense? Fantasy or science fiction? Such books sit uncomfortably on one shelf and then another; the best of them manage to leap across the aisle into 'literary fiction'" (p. 25). Indeed, Kerr explores varied and timely themes, and he has garnered a reputation as a hardworking researcher who creates engaging scenes with accurate scientific and forensic details. The research stems from his willingness to explore worlds entirely unknown to him: "I begin as a layman and end up knowing just a little bit more than what I began with. . . . I include small points of detail rather than larger ones—points of color instead of broad brush strokes. Pointillism, in words. Only when you step back from the canvas do you see the whole effect. I hope" ("A Conversation").

Kerr's literary influences are as eclectic as his themes and genres. William Gibson and Isaac Asimov, among others, inform the science fiction and the techno-thrillers. Kerr looks to the American noir crime writers, including Dashiell Hammett, James M. Cain, and Raymond Chandler, for his noir novels. The works of the philosopher Ludwig Wittgenstein are the basis for *A Philosophical Investigation,* and the novel's criminal mastermind recalls details suggestive of Truman Capote's *In Cold Blood* (1965) as easily as he discusses motive in the novels of Albert Camus and Arthur Conan Doyle, images in the poems of John Keats, or Peter O'Toole's lines in the 1962 film *Lawrence of Arabia.* Such references are not the work of an author augmenting his fiction with erudition in order to pass it off as "literary" or "intelligent" writing. Rather, Kerr balances his passion for research, cultural allusion, and the necessary synthesis of information with the ideas that drive his plots.

While Kerr would make his name in thrillers, his reputation—and a spot on *Granta*'s list—was cemented with his first five novels, all of which explore the underbelly of society through the eyes of a jaded and cynical detective. Despite the generic differences, however, all of Kerr's novels are peopled with Orwellian characters who face the same existential dilemma of identity that prompted Kerr to write in the first place. On the surface, the novels are plot-driven stories about war, politics, and the downside of technology. More importantly, however, they are explorations of the human psyche, which, Kerr reminds his readers frequently, can be besieged and broken. It is only through dogged persistence that his characters discover hope. As the narrator of Kerr's 1998 science-fiction novel *The Second Angel* posits in a philosophy reminiscent of the American naturalists of the early twentieth century, "*All life-forms are merely vehicles for DNA survival; and genes are little bits of software that have but one goal—to make copies of themselves*" (p. 283). In order for Kerr's characters to overcome the limitations of their own evolution, they must find solace in the mundane details of everyday life.

NOIR NOVELS AND THE "NEW 'TECS"

Berlin Noir, the title of the collected trilogy comprising the novels *March Violets* (1989), *The Pale Criminal* (1990), and *A German Requiem* (1991), illustrates Kerr's early fascination with the American crime form and a thoroughgoing interest in history. The novels "both reinvigorate the scope of British crime writing and examine the key moments of twentieth-century European history from a distinctive and oblique perspective. In no way ponderous or pretentious, these novels may be read straightforwardly as thrillers, but that should not disguise their seriousness of purpose or their accomplishment" ("Philip Kerr"). Set in Berlin and Vienna immediately before World War II and in the aftermath of the war, during the first days of Russian occupation, the novels express themes that would also appear in the later "'tecs," or detective novels, set after the fall of the Berlin Wall (*Dead Meat*, 1993) and in a near-future dystopia (*A Philosophical Investigation*): greed, corruption, morality, and self-determination.

Bernhard Gunther, *Berlin Noir*'s protagonist, is a private detective cast in the mold of the American hard-boiled characters of Chandler, Cain, Hammett, and Ross MacDonald, noir writers who gained a reputation in the late 1920s and reached the peak of their popularity in the 1940s and 1950s with novels that examined the mores and attitudes of a society in transformation. Noir literature influenced a subsequent generation of writers, not the least Kerr, whose descriptions of society's rough edges are both parodic of the noir writers and act as homage, a touchstone that provides a familiar underpinning for the stories and neatly mirrors the darkness and depravity of Gunther's wartime Germany. Describing an informant for whom he has little but disdain, Gunther observes,

> If he was a member of the human race at all, Neumann was its least attractive specimen. His eyebrows, twitching and curling like two poisoned caterpillars, were joined together by an irregular scribble of poorly matched hair. Behind thick glasses that were almost opaque with greasy thumbprints, his grey eyes were shifty and nervous, searching the floor as if he expected that at any moment he would be lying flat on it. Cigarette smoke poured out from between teeth that were so badly stained with tobacco they looked like two wooden fences.
>
> (*Berlin Noir* p. 108)

Such descriptions pervade the trilogy, and based as they are on familiar types first expressed in noir literature and film, they draw the reader further into the work and allow Kerr to explore unfamiliar settings and events in a recognizable milieu. For instance, a Gestapo general who threatens Gunther warns, "'The ability to talk as toughly as your fictional counterpart is one thing. . . . Being it is quite another'" (p. 221). Earlier, Hitler's henchman Hermann Goering admits to Gunther, "'I've always wanted to meet a real private detective. . . . Tell me, have you ever read any of Dashiell Hammett's detective stories? He's an American, but I think he's wonderful'" (p. 132).

Setting, too, is important to the novels' overall effect. Gunther rarely reports weather more appealing than "grey and wet" (*March Violets,* p.

25), an atmosphere that matches the dreary tone of Gunther's career and relationships. Years later, after the war, as he considers Germany's fate amid the Russian occupation in *A German Requiem,* Gunther reports that "it snowed hard that night, and then the temperature fell into the sewers, freezing the whole of Vienna, to preserve it for a better day. I dreamed, not of a lasting city, but of the city which was to come" (p. 658). Even the buildings that should be imposing symbols of the power of the Third Reich now remind Gunther only of the oppression and squalor that are the regime's lasting legacy. When he passes the Reichstag, the Reich's most important and once its most imposing building, he observes a burned-out shell that was "the clearest piece of pyromancy that Germany could have been given as to what Adolf Hitler and his third nipple had in store for us" (p. 258).

Those elements are first explored in *March Violets,* the first installment of the well-reviewed trilogy and Kerr's keenest combination of research, ideas, and writing. Gunther, a former police "bull" who made a name for himself a decade before by apprehending an infamous serial killer, has opened his own detective agency. The novel is set in Germany during the nascence of the Third Reich, which has been in power since Hitler's coup in 1933, and opens in 1936 as Berlin readies itself for the Olympics. The March Violets, the ones who join Hitler, do so for their own gain. They are gathering strength, though posters that extol the hate journalism of Julius Streicher, the publisher of the rabidly anti-Semitic tabloid *Der Stürmer,* are being pulled down so as not to offend foreign visitors. Books banned by the Reich are placed in bookshops for the same reason, "'so that tourists won't think things are quite as repressive here as has been made out'" (p. 119). History is important to the reader's understanding of the novels from the outset— much of the first novel deals with relations between Jews and Germans—and Kerr uses a keen sense of the events and vivid descriptions to set the tone. The novel's underlying ideology is chillingly familiar: Jews are forbidden to practice law, and the number of missing-persons cases has skyrocketed in Hitler's Germany, as Jewish families searching for their loved ones are compelled to hire professional help.

Gunther's intimate knowledge of his society's history engenders his bitterness toward his country's imperialism, and he delivers his indictments of the government in scathing first-person narration. Arriving for a meeting on a street known for its museums, Gunther admits, "I'm not much interested in The Past and, if you ask me, it is this country's obsession with its history that has partly put us where we are now: in the shit" (p. 54). The most salient feature of past governments that has made its transition from regime to regime, Gunther points out, is the insatiable corruption of its bureaucrats. Gunther dispels the notion that to ignore history is to repeat it, instead believing that to give history too much credence and wishing to relive it is the least advised of all possible responses.

That attitude is borne out in the novel's first scenes, in which the Olympics are a metaphor for the divisiveness incited by Hilter's ascendancy to the head of German government. The racial issues that arise when the American Jesse Owens bests his German opponents on the track are expressed in terms similar to the Nazis' treatment of the Jews. Gunther admires Owens's prowess and concludes that Owens makes "a mockery of crackpot theories of Aryan superiority" and "to run like that was the meaning of the earth, and if ever there was a master-race it was certainly not going to exclude someone like Jesse Owens" (pp. 187–188). In fact, the Germans cheer Owens to the embarrassment of their "superior" athletes, and Gunther wonders if "Germany did not want to go to war after all" (p. 188). That bit of optimism—misguided as it turns out to be—is one of the few times Gunther finds hope in his and his country's situation.

Gunther pointedly notices the changes in both himself and society when he attends the wedding of his secretary, Dagmarr. At thirty-eight, he realizes that he is too old for her romantically, and his caustic cynicism—as a noir detective, the attitude is his stock-in-trade—is illustrated in a conversation with Dagmarr's new husband, a military pilot obsessed with winning glory for himself. Gunther expresses his disdain for war by

recalling that in World War I he won an Iron Cross, second class, simply "for staying out of trouble." "Most of the first-class medals," he explains to the idealistic, vain young man, "were awarded to men in cemeteries" (p. 7).

Gunther approaches Hitler's inner circle for the first time when he meets Hermann Six, one of the most powerful businessmen in Germany, a man who was present at Hilter's rise to power. Six professes loyalty to the Reich, despite the fact that he is more concerned with preserving his wealth than with carrying out Hitler's policies. He hires Gunther to discover his daughter's murderer. Gunther complicates matters by having an affair with Six's wife, a popular actress, who mistakenly believes that her husband has hired the detective to spy on her and sleeps with Gunther only to be able to blackmail him should he report her dalliances to Six.

After a search that leads back to Six and the convoluted passions and illicit relationships that prompted the murders, Gunther is forced to regain his freedom by going undercover in Dachau prison, where the horror of the place awes Gunther, and he muses that "there were many more articulate than me who were simply unable to find the words. It is a silence born of shame, for even the guiltless are guilty" (p. 229). The fragmentation that Gunther experiences in *March Violets* lingers as he searches for Inge Lorenz, a newfound love who has disappeared without a trace. Despite Gunther's inability to find her, he reconciles himself to the hard years that lay ahead. The relationship takes on an Orwellian tone and says much about Kerr's attitude throughout his fiction about experience and memory. Gunther continues long after such a search is feasible to visit her apartment, and "the memory of her grew more distant. Having no photograph, I forgot her face, and came to realize how little I had really known about her, beyond rudimentary pieces of information" (p. 244). The hopelessness that Gunther feels as the war nears is illustrated in his observation that, now that the Olympics were over, "The red *Der Stürmer* showcases were back on the street corners and, if anything, Streicher's paper seemed more rabid than ever" (p. 246).

Streicher and his legions of anti-Semites play a central role in Kerr's second Gunther novel, *The Pale Criminal* (1990), whose title was inspired by a quotation from the German philosopher Friedrich Nietzsche: "Much about your good people moves me to disgust, and it is not their evil I mean. How I wish they possessed a madness through which they could perish, like this pale criminal. Truly I wish their madness were called truth or loyalty or justice: but they possess their virtue in order to live long and in a miserable ease" (p. 249). The historical Streicher was an unsavory character—perhaps the most perverse of Hitler's acquaintances—despite having been an elementary school teacher until his conscription in the German Army before World War I. In 1923, he founded *Der Stürmer*, a periodical that fomented hatred of Jews by publishing articles and cartoons depicting Jews as pederasts and occult murderers intent upon undermining the purity of the Aryan race. At its height of popularity, *Der Stürmer*'s circulation was eight hundred thousand. Streicher was convicted of war crimes at Nuremburg in 1946, and his last reported words before his execution were "Heil Hitler." Kerr uses Streicher's character as both plot device and symbol of the Third Reich, the image of the balding, debauched soldier a metaphor for the dissolution of German society as Gunther knows it.

In a short prologue, Gunther describes his circumstances, referring to the disappearance of Inge two years before and bemoaning his own mortality and his struggle to establish a lasting relationship "in the long hot summer of 1938, [when] bestiality was callously enjoying something of an Aryan renaissance" (p. 253). Gunther's narrative is organized as a journal— the only novel of the three so arranged, although all are written from Gunther's point of view— and gives the effect of counting down the days until the onset of Hitler's spree of violence across Europe. Arthur Nebe, a police official who persuades Gunther to return to take a case involving the abduction and deaths of seven blonde teenage girls—"the Aryan stereotype that we know and love so well" (p. 317), Gunther quips— tersely defines the coming conflict: "There's no room for agnosticism in the Germany that Himmler and Heydrich have got planned for us. It'll be stand up and be counted or take the consequences" (p. 261). Blame falls squarely on the Jews, unnamed and unknown, but assumed to be guilty nonetheless, until Gunther discovers a connection between the disappearances and Julius Streicher.

An underlying irony is the groundswell of support for the occult in Hitler's inner circle and the occult's connection to Judaism. Gunther despises the hypocrisy of those who adhere to Freud's doctrines while at the same time denouncing the father of psychoanalysis in public; they are the same people, Gunther points out, who persecute German citizens as social outcasts for their sexual preferences and confiscate their pornographic materials for their own use. His disgust is piqued when he reads a headline in Streicher's magazine, "A flash across the top left-hand corner of the paper advertised it as 'A Special Ritual Murder Number.' Not that one needed reminding. The pen-and-ink illustration said it eloquently enough. Eight naked fair-haired German girls hanging upside-down, their throats slit, and their blood spilling into a great Communion plate that was held by an ugly caricature Jew" (p. 375). Streicher, who reminds Gunther of Al Capone, becomes a suspect in the killings.

An interesting sidebar to Gunther's inquiries into the murders is his introduction to the poetry of Charles-Pierre Baudelaire, which implies to Gunther the inevitability of a violent confrontation, or what Hannah Arendt would later term "the banality of evil": "In Baudelaire's interest in violence, in his nostalgia for the past and through his revelation of the world of death and corruption, I heard the echo of Satanic litany that was altogether more contemporary, and saw the pale reflection of a different kind of criminal, one whose spleen had the force of law" (p. 329). Gunther's ruminations on Baudelaire are juxtaposed to the earnest, passionate voice of Heinrich Stahlecker, the young son of Gunther's partner Bruno, who was recently killed while on assignment. The boy's words, a Nazi marching song imploring like-minded youth to "kill the

Jewish bastards, / Who poison all our lives" (p. 330), unnerve Gunther.

The Pale Criminal is as much social commentary as noir mystery. Although Streicher and his henchmen are never brought to justice for the murders, Gunther sees in their actions the moral degeneration and undoing of the Third Reich. The novel prefigures the silence that comes out of World War II—Kerr divulges little of Gunther's actions from 1938 to 1947—and the conflagration to come for the Jews, who will continue to be blamed for the ills of Hitler's corrupt society. As he walks through the Botanical Gardens with the trees' leaves burning in piles in the chill autumn air, Gunther interprets the image as a microcosm of society: "as I stood and watched the glowing embers of the fires, and breathed the hot gas of deciduous death, it seemed to me that I could taste the very end of everything" (p. 523).

The trilogy's final installment, *A German Requiem*, finds Gunther traveling to Vienna in 1947 to exonerate Emil Becker, a German accused of murdering an American soldier. The novel's backstory refers obliquely to Gunther's service in the German military during World War II ("the end of everything" to which Gunther presciently refers at the conclusion of *The Pale Criminal*) and stresses the importance of the silences, the conspicuous gap in the experiences that Gunther is willing to discuss. In the intervening decade since the events detailed in *The Pale Criminal*, Germany and her people have undergone extraordinary changes. Berlin is in a shambles, having been wracked and plundered just two years before, and Gunther observes that for Hitler's adherents, "it was not the defeat which gave the lie to that patriarchal view of society, but the rebuilding" (p. 560). The German society could not be any more despondent than in its failure to win the war and its inability to reconstruct society without outside help.

The Vienna in which Gunther finds himself is a synecdoche of Germany after that failure: the Russians and the Americans vie for control over the German state; former Nazis, many of whom faked their own deaths to avoid punishment for war crimes, work to repatriate themselves into

society; Gunther's wife, a schoolteacher-cum-cocktail waitress, determined to maintain some semblance of a life for her husband and herself, prostitutes herself to American soldiers for PX rations; even the most basic human functions are not immune to the machinations of society, as venereal disease is epidemic and penicillin a rare commodity. In attempting to prove Becker's innocence, Gunther uncovers a convoluted plot that points to the complicity of high-ranking Nazis who have gone into hiding. Kerr's approach to all three novels—the noir influence and his debt to the crime literature of the first half of the twentieth century is pervasive—emphasizes an important aspect of these novels, namely the serious philosophical issues just beneath the narratives' highly polished surface.

In a decade, Gunther evolves from a cynical former cop to a hard-bitten survivor whose memories of the war only reinforce his disillusionment with Germany society. The numbing contradictions that he faces in his daily life are a testament to his resilience. When Gunther recalls how he escaped killing innocent people during the war by refusing to further serve in the Nazi Secret Service, he realizes that, without the help of Arthur Nebe, a feared and ruthless Nazi, he probably would have been killed himself, and "it always gave me a strange kind of feeling to know that I very possibly owed my life to a mass-murderer" (p. 593).

In the end, Gunther, against his instinct, trusts the Russian, Belinsky, only to be betrayed. Even as he fights for his life in Vienna, the Russians close access to Berlin, prompting the Americans to implement the Marshall Plan as sides are drawn and Berlin divided into East and West. As he lies in a hospital bed during a debriefing by American investigators, the detritus of the past—hazy, distant memories of war—takes its place alongside the possibility of a new beginning.

A Philosophical Investigation, the novel that followed the *Berlin Noir* trilogy, takes a near-future dystopia for its setting and describes a society that classifies potential violent offenders according to their genetic makeup as a way of remedying "the increasingly apparent limitations of the criminal justice system [that] have eroded a foundational myth of modern society: the modern state can provide security, law, and order within its territory and can single-handedly cure the social problem of crime" (p. 380). Although the notion has become commonplace in both fiction and film, the narrative explores a theme central to *Berlin Noir,* namely society's reaction to governmental control. (Gerlach uses the term "biogovernance," which he defines as "the use of biotechnology to manage risky populations and populations at risk" [p. 372].) Although Kerr certainly would have known many of the uses for such a tool when he wrote the novel in the early 1990s, Gerlach notes that within a decade of the book's publication, biological boundaries were being crossed in reproduction technologies, cloning, the Human Genome Project, food production, gene therapy and—significant to the discussion at hand—DNA profiling and data banking.

The novel's title, a reference to Ludwig Wittgenstein's eponymous philosophical treatise, establishes a connection between the issue of genetic manipulation and Wittgenstein's philosophy. Wittgenstein, an intense man of contrary nature, once famously brandished a poker at his fellow philosopher Karl Popper at Cambridge in 1946 during a semantic dispute; the similarity between Wittgenstein and his philosophies and the killer known as Wittgenstein and his actions in the novel is worth noting. The connection has elicited various critical responses, both praising Kerr for his willingness to explore big ideas and condemning him for overreaching; still, the novel is at least as ambitious in its exploration of society's decisions as the trilogy that preceded it.

In the London of 2013, police investigators have at their disposal profound advances in determining genetic bases for crime. To aid in the apprehension of society's worst criminals, law enforcement has created the Lombroso database, which identifies and tracks men who are VMN (Ventro Medial Nucleus) negative; in short, they have little ability to control their own aggressive behavior. About three in ten thousand of British men are afflicted. The Lombroso program attempts to recruit men to its testing center through public service announcements that

imply such acquiescence is a sign of good citizenship. More stringent rules in hiring and insurance coverage ultimately make the question moot. Men who are unwilling to be tested are even more stigmatized by society than those who are tested and found to be at risk for violent behavior. As Jay Clayton writes, "The notion that the test is voluntary quickly becomes a sham, because a daunting array of social and economic pressures are brought to bear, making it difficult for citizens to exercise their right not to be tested. The novel's depiction of these pressures amounts to an incisive critique of similar forces today, which often effectively transform voluntary into mandatory screening programs" (pp. 11–12). Those identified as crime risks are given code names in the database to keep their identities secret. Isadora "Jake" Jakowicz, a detective and psychologist who specializes in tracking down serial killers, is put on the case of a killer who targets exclusively men, all of whom happen to be part of the Lombroso database.

The connection between Wittgenstein the philosopher and Wittgenstein the serial killer has another significant parallel: language. Wittgenstein the philosopher used his *Philosophical Investigations* (1963) to espouse the notion that language is the basis for meaning. Similarly, Wittgenstein the serial killer muses, "*A name means an object. The object is its meaning. I can only speak about names. I cannot put them into words. But to live your whole life with a meaning that is not of your own choosing would seem to me to be quite unbearable*" (p. 106). His notebooks, a dialectical examination of Ludwig Wittgenstein's work, alternate with the novel's plot chapters. In addition to echoing the sentiments of his philosophical namesake, the irony of the killer's statement refers to the near-absence of self-determination. A quirk of evolution and genetics has made him what he is. Compounding the problem on a societal level is, as Clayton points out, that "the world has become so accustomed to the statistical generalizations of genetic research about populations that characters feel free to engage in racial, ethnic, and sexual stereotyping too. The novel is full of racial epithets, sexual harassment, and homophobia" (p.

13). Kerr also makes clear that economic considerations have not been severed from the notion of social well-being when a bureaucrat reminds his audience, "I have a duty to my shareholders as well as to the patients" (p. 70). What is seen as a solution to a long-standing problem, in fact, only exacerbates the problem.

Dead Meat (1993), the last of the five noir and detective novels that begin Kerr's career, takes place in Russia after the collapse of Communism. The atmosphere is not unlike that of post-Third Reich Germany or twenty-first-century London, and Newgate Callender writes, "Perhaps the most interesting thing about the book is its grim depiction of a desperate Russia in the process of being taken over by crime, graft and corruption" (p. 39). The novel is timely—only four years removed from the disintegration of the Soviet Union—and the narrative benefits from Kerr's own experiences in Russia, where he spent a great deal of time interviewing and studying the people who would appear in the novel. The setting that Kerr creates is rich in historical detail as well as in an appreciation for Russian literature. *Dead Meat,* which was adapted in 1994 as a popular BBC miniseries titled *Grushko,* forms a sharp counterpoint to Kerr's exploration of the Third Reich in *Berlin Noir* and the dystopian near-future of *A Philosophical Investigation.* The novel opens with the narrator, a police detective from Moscow, arriving in St. Petersburg, ostensibly to observe the operations of his colleagues. His real mission, however, is to discover any complicity between police and the local Mafia. The narrator conjures images of Gunther—wise in many ways, relatively incompetent at other tasks, including interpersonal relationships—transposed onto a different culture where little, in reality, has changed.

The narrator and many other of the novel's characters are highly literate, and they view the world almost exclusively in terms of Russian literature and history, words and events as palpable as the land itself. The novel's opening line, "A Russian can never resist stories, even the ones he tells to himself" (p. 1), carries overtones of Leo Tolstoy's *Anna Karenina* (1877) and establishes context for the story that follows: the narrator begins his story on a train between Moscow and St. Petersburg to investigate the police there; at the same time, he tells a story that, in the manner of much Russian literature, must be told before it is lost to history. The narrator recalls how his journey began several weeks before, invoking Anton Chekhov, who "says that a storyteller should show life neither as it is nor as it ought to be, but as we see it in our dreams. Dozing in my warm berth that was indeed how it all seemed to me now, for in a sense, my story had started on this very train" (p. 2).

After the narrator's arrival in St. Petersburg, two men are executed by the Mafia near a memorial to World War II veterans. The narrator observes that the monument commemorates the high-water mark of the Nazi advance. Now, ironically, two bodies lie at its base. Kerr juxtaposes the extraordinary sacrifices that were made on behalf of Russia's soldiers in order to protect the country and the slaughter of two men for profit in the new democratic society. While the narrator investigates his peers, a famous Russian journalist, Mikhail Milyukin, is murdered. The prime suspects are soldiers of the Russian Mafia. Grushko and his men search in earnest for the killers, and the policeman's reaction to the murder is telling: "'Ever since the Openness,' he said, 'when Mikhail first started writing about the Mafia. That was when the government still denied such a thing as a Soviet Mafia ever existed. You could say that my own department owes its very existence to Mikhail Milyukin'" (pp. 21–22). The narrator is assigned to Grushko, the man who knows as much about the Mafia as anyone on the force, and the narrator's prime target in the corruption investigation. At first, the narrator flippantly likens Grushko to Elvis Presley; he soon realizes, however, that the man is not to be taken lightly. Perhaps, he thinks, he has discovered the only cadre of police in the country who are honest.

Milyukin is a symbol for the difficult struggle that resulted from the fall of the Berlin Wall. He understands the problems that plague the country—people who scrounge for dead lightbulbs so that they can swap them for live ones at work; prostitutes who hang used condoms on a clothesline to dry because they cannot afford new; young girls who aspire to become hard-currency prostitutes because the job is one of the most lucrative; the devaluation of the ruble—but succinctly delineates the lack of viable solutions: "'The urgent need for foreign capital seems obvious,' said Milyukin, 'but what is there that's actually worth investing in? Our factories are hopelessly antiquated. The rudiments of political stability are missing. Individually we lack something as 'ordinary as a work ethic': everyone knows the saying 'They pretend to pay us, and we pretend to work'" (p. 70). Indeed, the police uncover a garbage backhauling scheme in which meat—the denotation of the title, and a commodity worth more by weight than illegal narcotics—is tainted by radiation.

A counterpoint to the unsavory state of the country is the staid dignity of Russian literature. The novel is a litany of the great Russian novelists and poets—Fyodor Dostoyevsky, Anton Chekhov, Leo Tolstoy, Anna Akhmatova, Boris Pasternak, among others—and the narrator and Grushko often define their lives in terms of that literature: the room where Raskolnikov committed murder; the blood that Akhmatova said must be spilled in order to satisfy the Russian earth; Pasternak's notion that "poetry is murderous" (p. 30). The Russians believe in the literature that has come before and understand that they have a duty to live up to the reputation that has preceded them.

Significantly, the narrator repeatedly comments on the city's architecture, the buildings' size and grandeur, whose proportions dwarf the problems of society. Those comments often connect the individual to the machinations of society, especially when it comes to the country's prisons and police stations. The narrator comments, "Presumably there must have been an architect although, as with most of the modern buildings in this country, it is difficult to see how. . . . Something forbidden and inhuman anyway, and that I suppose was the whole of the architect's idea: to render the individual insignificant" (p. 9). Later, Grushko observes how much he enjoys the city's shabby beauty and longs for a time before the revolution. The narrator respects the notion, but

thinks to himself, in a parallel to Gunther's own observations in *Berlin Noir*,

I was no Communist, but you didn't have to be Lenin to see that a dynasty that could have built some palaces for themselves while peasants went hungry was headed for serious trouble. Yet I was glad that such places existed: without these magnificent reminders of our former glories it would have been hard to see ourselves as anything but a third-world banana republic. With an acute shortage of bananas.
(p. 132)

One of the most incongruous images to come out of any of Kerr's fiction is at the conclusion of *Dead Meat*, when the narrator watches an elk running through the city streets. The narrator muses, "There was precious little dignity to be found in any other variety of Russian life. It was true the beast seemed to have no idea where it was going any more than it knew why it was going there. But probably it would get there in the end and in that there might have been a message of hope for us all" (p. 214). The ambivalence appears repeatedly in Kerr's fiction as he abandons the hard-boiled mystery and begins to write thrillers that would draw on irony and pastiche as the delivery mechanism for his particular brand of social commentary.

THRILLERS AND TECHNO-THRILLERS

"Science is much more philosophical than it has ever been. Stephen Hawking treads on the toes of the Creationists. Mischievously so, in my opinion" ("A Conversation"), Kerr states, and the most successful novels of his post-crime period are the ones that deal with the ethics of science. The books that followed Kerr's successful appearance on the literary scene have met with ambivalence among critics, who are divided as to the relative merit of a handful of novels that may be classified as genre fiction, including *The Second Angel, The Shot* (1999), *The Gridiron* (1995; published in the United States in 1996 as *The Grid*), *A Five-Year Plan* (1997), and *Esau. The Shot* is a contemporary refashioning of the Kennedy assassination, and, as such, the novel stands in contradistinction to the known history and recalls the alternate histories of Harry Turtledove. *A Five-Year Plan* is a straight thriller that reads much like a screenplay: the actor Tom Cruise reportedly optioned the book, and a *Publishers Weekly* review deems the novel, "a slick, sometimes exciting, often rather slapdash comedy thriller, a caper really, of the kind Elmore Leonard pulls off with silky ease" (p. 74). Both passed relatively unnoticed by serious criticism.

The techno-thrillers were better received than the more traditional thrillers and among the champions of Kerr's later fiction has been Michele Field, who writes, "While contemporary novelists as diverse as Richard Powers and William Gibson have indeed experimented with the frightening implications of a society so besotted with technology, authors of thrillers rarely manage to convey as cogently ideas about science and society as Kerr does" (p. 44). Kerr posits that his success in the genre is a function of an increased interest in popular science, spawned by scientists whose work, previously relegated to the laboratory, has been brought to light. Now, he says, "People do have an appetite for science and that is clearly evidenced by the Stephen Hawking phenomenon, with interest in books that try to make science more intelligible to the layman. . . . The better thrillers have always provided insight and information about a secret world" (p. 3).

Much of what Kerr writes about the progress of technology is in a similar vein. *The Grid* and *Esau* in particular, novels that preceded *The Second Angel,* seem, in retrospect, to be rehearsals for the most polished and thought-provoking of the techno-thrillers. All three novels are as much explications of a philosophy—novels of ideas—as they are plot-driven narratives. According to Field, *The Grid,* which details the rebellion of a "smart building" against its creators, "has a strong cerebral undercurrent, punctuated by epigraphs about technology and building that float a philosophy along the surface of the story. On this level, *The Grid* reminds one of Ayn Rand's *The Fountainhead* (1943): buildings are the way people project their thoughts, and both Kerr and Rand spell out their correlations" (p. 43). Kerr recalls that the novel was born of the ennui and wanderlust that so often haunts his characters "I spent many years in a high-rise building somewhere, wishing I was somewhere else. I think *The Grid* is in part an exorcism of my fear of being back in a nine-to-five job, and being with people I didn't really know, and who didn't know each other" (Field, p. 43). Similarly, although the balance between philosophy and plot is not as finely wrought as in the other novels, *Esau* takes on issues of the preservation of isolated species and the possibility of widespread destruction through nuclear annihilation.

The most effective of the techno-thrillers, however, is *The Second Angel,* a work that explores the nexus of science fiction, evolution, and religion. The book has been compared to *A Philosophical Investigation* for its attention to the ethical issues attendant on science and the future of technology, about which Kerr says, "I sometimes see the novelist writing about science in the position of the priest in the chariot of some general accorded a great triumph, saying 'remember ye are but mortal.' Too often scientists ask only if something CAN be done, not if it SHOULD be done" ("A Conversation"). Charles Flowers finds in Kerr's fiction a philosophical thoroughness lacking in much genre fiction, and he praises a writer "more interested in the thematic underpinnings of his plot, projecting twentieth-century scientific theories into what turns out to be a surprisingly optimistic vision of human possibility" (p. 20). In *The Second Angel,* Kerr uses literary and scientific references ranging from Ovid to Alexander Pope; Leo Tolstoy, Oscar Wilde, William Blake, and Edgar Allan Poe to Richard Feynman, Albert Einstein, Frank Kermode, and Sir Kenneth Clark. All of these scientists, philosophers, and writers take on new significance when seen from the distance of a century, the novel's setting.

The plot-narrative is intertwined with the ruminations of an omniscient outside narrator, an entity that not only records the narrative's events but controls the text's action. The narrator interjects into the text, writing,

This would seem a suitable place for me to say something of myself. Perhaps you have wondered, perhaps you have not. Well, it is true, I have been careful not to be too free with the use of the personal pronoun, but this is as much to do with a wish not to slow down the story with irrelevant questions about whether your narrator might turn out to be unreliable in the great tradition of Joseph Conrad, Henry James, and Emily Brontë.

(pp. 98–99)

The purpose of the narrator is to manipulate the characters into colonizing the galaxy.

As the novel opens, most of the world's population is infected with the P2 virus, and pure blood is scarce. The presence of the virus, which can be eliminated from the body only through a complete transfusion, is a result of man's ability to manipulate natural processes. Scientists have created a universal blood substitute that, as an unintended consequence, facilitates the spread of the virus. Uninfected blood is worth half as much as gold (a parallel to a similar economic situation in the earlier novel *Dead Meat*) and violent crime that involves blood—"vamping"—is rampant. Blood has been given the status of a religion in a society divided by the disease along socioeconomic lines. "Blessed Are the Pure in Blood" is an invocation whose irony is neatly juxtaposed to the "traditional" religion that the worship of blood replaces, and the narrator posits that the science of hematology has superseded the importance of all other branches of science. Blood is not only essential for life but also acts as an information carrier. Scientists are determined to find a way to incorporate binary code and the tenets of quantum mechanics into a biological system that erases the boundary between man and machine.

In 2069, the one-hundredth anniversary of the first lunar landing, John Dallas is forced to make a difficult decision. His young daughter is stricken with thallassemia, a terminal condition if she is not given repeated transfusions of blood. Dallas, an architect for Terotechnology Corporation, the firm that designs security systems for blood banks, becomes a security risk because of his compromised position. His wife and daughter are murdered; Dallas survives. In an Orwellian flourish, Dallas's name is removed from the official company record and an attempt is made on his life. His own life having become meaning-less, Dallas decides to rob a blood bank—an institution more powerful than monetary systems—for which he has designed the security system.

The world that Kerr describes is dystopian in the manner of that in *A Philosophical Investigation* but still recognizable as a mirror of today's society. One of Kerr's strengths, even in his desire to create worlds that ask readers to suspend disbelief, is to provide a familiar context through which the reader is able to comprehend Kerr's motivation. Part of that motivation is to reconcile the role of history in both the present and the future and Dallas, as a reader among the nonliterate—an indication in Kerr's fiction of a character who will prevail—is well situated to provide a solution. (Dallas's holographic assistant describes Dallas as "a very old-fashioned person. Few people bothered to read anything these days, let alone books. It seemed such a pity when it took such an effort to write them" [p. 92].) Literature is connected to an understanding of history, and Kerr uses literary references to separate certain characters from others. When Dallas opines, "'All history is just a palimpsest'" (p. 93), he reiterates the reliance of subsequent generations on what has come before. The notion is one of the novel's key themes, and the exchange draws a sharp contrast between society as the keystone of civilization and the more abstract philosophy that holds memory as the repository for all of history, itself necessary for the perpetuation of civilization. Closely linked with history, and connected in some ways to Dallas's own statement that "history is just a palimpsest," is a narrative intrusion that comments on the sources of history: "If myth is a language, then theft is one of its most important nouns" (p. 173).

Kerr's commentary on anonymity and loneliness in cities that house millions of people is also an indictment of the inefficacy of language, communication, and imagination. Following analyses of the social theories of Aristotle, Kenneth Clark, and Henry Wotten, the narrator bemoans the fact that "there was no sense of permanence here, no perfect good, no self-sufficiency other than the exclusively selfish, no life desirable, no structure sound, no building suitable for the purpose for which it was being used, and no aesthetic pleasure that might have been derived from the contemplation of any man-made structure" (p. 128). Even Isaac Newton, in Kerr's next novel, *Dark Matter: The Private Life of Sir Isaac Newton* (2002), has much in common with the narrator of *The Second Angel,* who claims, *"There are no miracles except the science that is not already known. And man is the measure of all things"* (p. 254).

DARK MATTER

Kerr's eleventh novel was the culmination of his passion for research and a desire to articulate big ideas in accessible literary fiction. *Dark Matter* is a return to the author's early crime roots, with settings—including the Tower of London, Newgate Prison, Bedlam asylum, the busy streets of England's capital city, various taverns and whorehouses—richly drawn in an historical depth reminiscent of Umberto Eco's *The Name of the Rose* (1980) or, more recently, Iain Pears's *The Instance of the Fingerpost* (1998). Kerr pays homage to Arthur Conan Doyle in the novel, drawing implicit comparisons between his protagonist, Sir Isaac Newton, and Doyle's Sherlock Holmes. The characters who move through Newton's life are drawn from the fringes of history, familiar to readers in general, but, like Newton himself, little known in the details. Famous historical personages—Samuel Pepys, Daniel DeFoe, and John Hooke, among others—are involved in the story's action, often in distasteful ways. The critical response to *Dark Matter* was largely positive, although few critics acknowledge the work as both intriguing genre fiction and literary fiction. Scott Bernard Nelson writes, "There is one history lesson to be had, in any case: Nobody who reads *Dark Matter* will ever think of the real Isaac Newton quite the same way again" (p. C8). Jabari Asim commends that "Kerr successfully evokes a dangerous milieu, full of shadows, disease and nauseating smells. He's even better at describing people" (p. C2).

The two most prominent characters in *Dark Matter* are Isaac Newton and his mentee, Christopher Ellis. Ellis, the novel's narrator, recalls the events he is about to relate some thirty years after they have occurred, and only after Newton's death. Ellis's words offer a glimpse into his own life as well as that of Newton, and he begins by setting the tone and purpose for what follows: "There has been little poetry in my life. No fine words. Just guns and swords, bullets and bawds. . . . I had little thought that in recalling this story I might need to write it down. And yet how else might I improve upon the telling of it, except by writing it?" (p. 5) The subtitle of Kerr's novel suggests a focus on Isaac Newton, although the story's plot, at least superficially, deals with a scheme by London's Protestant population to exact revenge on the city's Roman Catholics for past wrongs against French Huguenots in Paris in 1572, more than a century before the narrative present. Newton, Ellis reports, is obsessed with discovering the workings of the universe, and Ellis points out that Newton "believed that a man who might decipher an earthly code might similarly fathom the heavenly one. He believed nothing unless he could prove it as a theorem or draw it as a diagram" (p. 2). In fact, Newton's young apprentice even chides his mentor for treating a series of murders in the Tower of London, where the Royal Mint operates, as an intellectual exercise rather than the serious matter it is.

Newton is cast as a free spirit, if a rigorous thinker, and the novel is not without a sly wit. Newton relates with great relish that in his various experiments, he has driven himself to the brink of madness with mercury poisoning and nearly blinded himself with a blunted bodkin in an attempt at discovering the nature of light. He confesses to Ellis that a fig, not an apple, was the creative impulse for his greatest discovery, and because of his scanty understanding of human nature, Newton uses his own Second Law of Motion to describe not physics, but the workings of the human mind and heart. Ellis learns much from Newton, whose job it is with the Royal Mint to discover forgers and to prosecute them. Despite his genius, though, the humor of Newton's story comes from his vast ignorance when it comes to women. Newton can offer little assistance in endearing Ellis to his niece, Miss Barton. The relationship ends badly when Ellis articulates his disdain for organized religion, siding with Newton and the rational.

The notion of religion is central to the story and links the novel's philosophical aspects. In a prologue, Ellis writes of his relationship with Miss Barton, "For one all too brief and brilliant moment my sky was quite lit up, as if by fireworks. The next, I lay overwhelmed and everything was consumed. My church maimed irreparably; my soul boiled away to nothing; my heart burned to a cold black cinder. In short, my life reduced to ashes" (p. 3). Later, in detailing Newton's own contrary religious beliefs, Ellis articulates his mentor's belief in the regulus and the crucible, his words the recognizable language of the alchemical arts. In fact, Newton's religion is so intermingled with alchemy as to make the two indistinguishable, and he is loath to forsake science by confirming any faith in religion. When Newton attempts to debunk the alchemical renderings of one of his competitors, he articulates his philosophy on the matter to Ellis. The irony of the statement, in the context of the murders, on the one hand, and the larger implications for religion, on the other, is not lost on the young man: "To my way of thinking, a man's trying to turn lead into gold is as absurd as expecting bread and wine to become the body and blood of Jesus Christ. It is what they represent that should inspire us. Nature is not merely chemical and physical, but also intellectual" (p. 70). In addition, Newton finds spiritual satisfaction in a discovered gnostic Christian text, whose "books that prove that Christ was only a man, that he did not rise from the dead, and that the established Christian dogma is a blasphemy of the truth and evil teaching" (p. 335).

On the whole, the novel is a commentary on late-seventeenth-century society, with some important analogues to current events (Kerr penned the author's note less than three months after the terrorist attacks in the United States on 11 September 2001). When Newton and Ellis visit the infamous Bedlam to discuss the details of the case with a madman, Ellis draws a connection between society inside the asylum and what he sees daily outside its walls, observing, "there was cruelty and callousness, drunkenness and despair, not to mention a great many whores who plied their trade in the hospital among the visiting public. In short, the picture was a facsimile of the world at large" (p. 157). Newton himself complains repeatedly that the metropolis of London was becoming unmanageable, "to the affright of those who lived there and were obliged to suffer its dirt and its general lawlessness" (p. 119). In a note at the novel's conclusion, Kerr draws a further connection between the present and Ellis's story, related more than three hundred years ago, noting that the "dark matter" to which he refers "does not give off or reflect much light" (p. 344). Kerr recognizes the double duty of science: as a rich source of wonder and truth, science provides the author with material through which he can examine his own philosophies; as a powerful metaphor, a primer on the nature of light and dark, fact and fiction, science comments in many ways on a current state of affairs that cannot help but come into focus, even when seen through the smudged lens of history.

CONCLUSION

Much has been made of the financial success Philip Kerr has achieved as his career has unfolded—at the expense, some reviewers and essayists insist, of his early literary promise. Kerr does not shy away from the criticism, though his response is perhaps not as brash as his detractors might expect. He told Eddie Gibb, "People ask me if I write for money and I can honestly say that I don't because I wrote for so long when I didn't have anything published. But I think what happened was that I made a conscious decision to write something that people actually want to read" (p. 3). The question of motivation is, perhaps, a valid one. In 2004, Kerr inked a seven-figure deal with Steven Spielberg for the film rights to a children's book—part of the planned series *Children of the Lamp*—titled *The Akhenaten Adventure*. The series' second installment, *The Blue Djinn of Babylon,* was published in 2006. The book details the lives of magical twelve-year-old twins, John and Phillipa Gaunt, who discover that they are descended from a tribe of dijnn. At the same time, six of his novels were under option for an average of better than $1.5

million. Despite his high profile, one of the few feature articles that attempts to penetrate the surface of the author's persona hints at the complexity of a man whose reputation as a contrarian has served him well:

> Dressed all in black with a crisp, cream raincoat over one arm and a light tan that suggests health rather than endless Caribbean holidays, no one would say this was a man on his uppers but neither is there any hint of the seven-digit bank balance. It would be easy to imagine he had prospered modestly as the lawyer his father wanted him to become.
> (Gibb, p. 3)

Marketplace success has not blunted Kerr's desire to remain opinionated and at times irascible. As of late 2004, he had published in the *New Statesman* more than one hundred installments of a regular, often volatile column on film, literature, and current events.

Indisputable is the fact that Kerr, after fulfilling the early promise as one of the most gifted British writers of his generation with the *Berlin Noir* trilogy, became, on his own terms, a writer better known for the novel of the big idea "in an era of fragmented knowledge and overspecialization, in an epoch of trial and error and of fluid results" (p. 13). The importance of Kerr's fiction in the rapidly evolving literary landscapes of Britain and the United States is its ability to meld setting, plot, and characters into readable and important novels that bridge the fissure between the literary and the mainstream. The eclecticism—and the controversy—that marks Kerr's career makes his consistent production of viable literature all the more remarkable. Kerr's fiction is a testament to his ability as a storyteller and stylist who appeals to a reading public hungry for intelligent writing and engaging storylines.

Selected Bibliography

WORKS OF PHILIP KERR

NOVELS

March Violets. London and New York: Viking, 1989.
The Pale Criminal. London and New York: Viking, 1990.

A German Requiem. London and New York: Viking, 1991.
A Philosophical Investigation. London: Chatto & Windus, 1992; New York: Farrar Straus and Giroux, 1993.
Berlin Noir. London and New York: Penguin, 1993.
Dead Meat. London: Chatto & Windus, 1993; New York: Mysterious Press, 1994.
The Gridiron. London: Chatto & Windus, 1995. Published as *The Grid*; New York: Warner Books, 1996.
Esau. London: Chatto & Windus, 1996; New York: Holt, 1997.
A Five-Year Plan. London: Hutchinson, 1997; New York: Holt, 1998.
The Second Angel. London: Orion, 1998; New York: Holt, 1999.
The Shot. London: Orion, 1999; New York: Pocket Books, 2001.
Dark Matter: The Private Life of Sir Isaac Newton. New York: Crown, 2002.
The Akhenaten Adventure. New York: Orchard, 2004.
Hitler's Peace: A Novel of the Second World War. New York: Putnams, 2005.
The Blue Djinn of Babylon. New York: Orchard, 2006.

EDITED ANTHOLOGIES

The Penguin Book of Fights, Feuds, and Heartfelt Hatreds: An Anthology of Antipathy. London: Viking, 1992.
The Penguin Book of Lies. London: Viking, 1990; New York: Penguin, 1990.

OTHER WORKS

"Remembering Dad" and "Manor Farm." *Granta* 43:143–151 (spring 1993). The two fictional vignettes are published in a section titled "Reference Points" in the issue that heralds Kerr as one of the "best young British Novelists."
Grushko. With Robin Mukherjee. Television series adapted from Kerr's novel *Dead Meat*. Directed by Tony Smith. British Broadcasting Corporation, 1994.
"The Writing's on the Wall." *New Statesman*, 22 July 2002, pp. 18–19. (Essay).

CRITICAL AND BIOGRAPHICAL STUDIES AND REVIEWS

Asim, Jabari. "Isaac Newton, Laying Down the Law." *Washington Post*, 15 October 2002, p. C2. (Review of *Dark Matter*.)
Callanan, Liam. Review of *Esau*. *New York Times Book Review*, 27 April 1997, p. 25.
Callendar, Newgate. Review of *Dead Meat*. *New York Times Book Review*, 22 May 1994, p. 39.
Clayton, Jay. "Crimes of the Genome: Philip Kerr's *A

Philosophical Investigation and the Propensity for Violence." (Unpublished manuscript.)

Publishers Weekly. Review of *A Five-Year Plan.* 23 March 1998, p. 74.

Flowers, Charles. "Blood on the Moon (Really!)." *New York Times Book Review,* 14 February 1999, p. 20. (Review of *The Second Angel.*)

Gerlach, Neil. "Criminal Biology: Genetic Crime Thrillers and the Future of Social Control." In Pastourmatzi, pp. 371–394.

Gillespie, Mike. Review of *The Shot. Ottawa Citizen,* 19 December 1999, p. C14.

Nelson, Scott Bernard. "Imagining Isaac Newton, Sleuth." *Boston Globe,* 23 October 2002, p. C8. (Review of *Dark Matter.*)

Pastourmatzi, Domna, ed. *Biotechnological and Medical Themes in Science Fiction.* Thessaloniki, Greece: University Studio Press, 2002.

INTERVIEWS AND PROFILES

Field, Michele. "Philip Kerr: Scottish Cynicism and Thriller Plots." *Publishers Weekly,* 8 April 1996, pp. 43–44.

"A Conversation with Philip Kerr, Author of *The Second Angel.*" Henry Holt and Company (http://216.247.214.252/releases/pr-secondangelconver.htm), 15 May 2004.

Gibb, Eddie. "A Plan to Thrill." *Sunday Times* (London), 16 June 1996, sec. Ecosse, p. 3.

Park, Joyce. "Maxim Jakubowski Interview." *MysteryGuide.com* (http://www.mysteryguide.com/jakubowski.html), 17 February 1998.

HUGH MacDIARMID

(1892– 1978)

Les Wilkinson

HUGH MACDIARMID WAS the most influential Scottish writer of the twentieth century. Not only was he the originator and focus of the Scottish Renaissance, an enormous upsurge in interest in the literature and the languages of Scotland that gave rise to a great range of poetry and prose from other writers, his writing and political activism were also central to the creation of a Scottish consciousness, without which, it could be argued, the Scottish Parliament would not have reconvened in May 1999 for the first time in almost three centuries.

Christopher Murray Grieve adopted the pseudonym "Hugh MacDiarmid" in 1922, the year T. S. Eliot's *The Waste Land* and James Joyce's *Ulysses* were published, and MacDiarmid stands comparison with both Eliot and Joyce in his breadth and genius. There are many reasons, however, why a reader might be intimidated upon approaching MacDiarmid's work for the first time. First, there is its sheer volume: aside from his prose works, his *Complete Poems,* published in 1978, the year of his death, runs to two volumes and 1,436 pages (Eliot's 1963 *Collected Poems,* by comparison, occupy a mere 234 pages). Clearly, such an output could not be consistent in its brilliance. When Norman MacCaig made the claim that MacDiarmid was Scotland's greatest poet in a radio program broadcast by the Scottish Home Service in May 1964, Alex Scott added, less than seriously, that he was "also the worst." MacDiarmid himself, with characteristic brio, admitted the unevenness of his work in a letter to George Bruce, dated 1 July 1964: "My job, as I see it, has never been to lay a tit's egg, but to erupt like a volcano, emitting not only flame, but a lot of rubbish" (MacDiarmid, p. 478). This essay will seek to concentrate on the flame of MacDiarmid's poetry—which is not to say that the poems not considered should be thought of as "rubbish"; there are nuggets of brilliance everywhere in his work, though they are less thick on the ground in some places than others.

Then there is MacDiarmid's language. Even his countrymen might be daunted by his "synthetic" Scots and find difficulty of making sense (at first reading, at least) of

I' the how-dumb-deid o' the cauld hairst nicht
The warl' like an eemis stane
Wags i' the lift
("The Eemis Stane")

(CP, p. 27)

To an Englishman or an American, it is almost a foreign language. Nor when he writes in English does MacDiarmid make any concessions to the layman, as the opening of his magnificent poem "On a Raised Beach" shows:

All is lithogenesis—or lochia,
Carpolite fruit of the forbidden tree,
Stones blacker than any in the Caaba;
Cream-coloured Caen-stone, chatoyant pieces,
Celadon and corbeau, bistre and beige,
Glaucous, hoar, enfouldered and cyathiform

(CP, p. 422)

"I never write with any thought of the potential reader," he wrote to Pittendrigh MacGillivary in 1926, although perhaps he wrote sometimes to impress, even intimidate; his notes on his long poem *To Circumjack Cencrastus; or, The Curly Snake* (1930) begin: "I do not consider any explication of my references to Valery, Husserl, Leontiev, Tyutchev and any others necessary here." It is to be hoped, however, that potential readers can be persuaded to persevere, and that this essay will encourage them to recognize MacDiarmid as one of the significant poetic voices of the twentieth century in any language (p. 293).

Christopher Murray Grieve was born on August 11, 1892 in Langholm, a Scottish border town twenty miles north of Carlisle. The main industry of the town was weaving and still is; it lies on a flat area of land where the river Esk meets the rivers Wauchope and Ewes; dominated by the hills of Eskdale, its landscape is a recurring motif in MacDiarmid's poetry. The house where Chris Grieve was born was itself high up a steep brae, or hillside, above the town. His father, John Grieve, was the local postman, devoutly religious and independent in his thought; he had married Elizabeth Graham, a domestic servant, in October 1891. Two years after their first child, a second son was born. The family moved to Henry Street and then, when Chris was seven, to a flat in the library buildings in the center of Langholm, where he began his lifelong passion for books, for he had free access to the library's contents. At school, he was no great scholar, although he was bookish and solitary compared to his brother. Nevertheless, one of his teachers, the composer Francis George Scott, who would later become a firm friend and collaborator, recognized his potential: "There's something in that big head of yours will come out some day" (*MacDiarmid*, p. 53). In 1908 he began training as a teacher at Broughton Higher Grade School in Edinburgh to please his father rather than himself, and indeed he left before completing the course in 1911. Grieve claimed that he left Broughton of his own accord upon his father's death, but in fact he was expelled six days before his father died, for stealing books—an offense that was also to cost him his first job. At Broughton, however, he did meet George Ogilvie, his English teacher, who remained an influence throughout his life. He had joined the Independent Labour Party in 1918, and his return to Langholm developed his radicalism and republicanism.

He began journalistic work in towns around Scotland, enlisting in the Royal Army Medical Corps in 1915. Between 1916 and 1918, he was posted to the 42nd General Hospital in Salonika, but he was sent back to England in 1918, suffering from malaria and holding the firm conviction that "never again must men be made to suffer these years of war" (*Annals of the Five Senses,* p. 89). In the same year he married Peggy Skinner, whom he had met in 1912, and in 1919 they moved to Montrose to begin work with the *Montrose Review*. The couple lived in Montrose, where their two children, Christine and Walter, were born, for the next ten years. While living there, Grieve edited *Northern Numbers* and the *Scottish Chapbook,* advocating a return to Scots as a literary language and becoming a political voice to be reckoned with. In 1922, he adopted the pseudonym Hugh MacDiarmid (not so much a nom de plume as a nom de guerre, as Kenneth Buthlay has remarked). More significantly, he published two collections of lyrics, *Sangschaw* in 1925 and *Penny Wheep* in 1926, in which he found a poetic voice, followed by the centrally important *A Drunk Man Looks at the Thistle* in 1926. He continued to be politically active, becoming a founding member of both the Scottish branch of the PEN literary and human rights organization and the National Party of Scotland. He was gaining a reputation as an iconoclast and a national figure.

In 1929, the family moved to London, where Grieve had been appointed the editor of *Vox*, a radio journal that soon collapsed. Here he fell from the top deck of an open-topped London bus onto the pavement below and suffered a concussion for three days. Doctors were convinced that only his extraordinarily thick head of hair had saved his life and prevented his skull from fracturing. The following year, he separated from Peggy and his children. He divorced in 1931, and shortly after met Valda Trevlyn in London, with whom he had a son, Michael, the following year. The couple married on September 12, 1934 at Islington Register Office.

In 1933, almost penniless, he moved to Whalsay, one of the Shetland Isles, where he was to live for nine years. It was to be a period of renewed political and literary activity with the publication of *Stony Limits and Other Poems* in 1934. MacDiarmid joined the Communist Party in 1934, but was expelled four years later for his Nationalist views. He felt himself viewed as "Scotland's public enemy number one," and in 1935 he suffered a nervous breakdown. In 1941, he was conscripted for National Service, and a year later he moved to Glasgow to work as a manual laborer in an engineering firm, where an industrial accident led to serious leg injuries in 1943, when a stack of copper cuttings fell on him. He transferred to the merchant navy and become a deckhand, later servicing vessels in the Clyde estuary.

In 1950, he was offered a house by the earl of Selkirk, but unfortunately the National Coal Board bought the whole estate in the same year. However, on MacDiarmid's return from Russia as a guest of the Scottish-USSR Friendship Society, the Grieves were offered the tenancy of Brownsbank Cottage in Biggar, where they moved in 1951 and where they were to live for the rest of their days. They had lived a hand-to-mouth existence for most of their married lives, but a civil list pension of 150 pounds per annum, which Grieve accepted "with great gratitude" in a letter to the Prime Minister, Clement Attlee, put their domestic finances on a solid basis from then on. He published *In Memoriam James Joyce* in 1955 and *The Kind of Poetry I Want* in 1961, but neither works consistently live up to the promise of his earlier poetry; more significantly, his *Collected Poems,* published in 1962, led to a real awareness of his achievement as a poet throughout Scotland and in the wider world. The later years of his life were also a time of of travel, of political activity, and of honors: he was awarded an honorary doctorate of laws by Edinburgh and Dublin Universities in 1957 and 1978 respectively. MacDiarmid controversially rejoined the Communist Party as many of its members left in the wake of the Russian invasion of Hungary in 1956; he also stood as a Communist candidate (and Scotsman) against the then prime minister, Sir Alec Douglas-Home, in the 1964 general election.

Hugh MacDiarmid died in Edinburgh on 9 September 1978 and was buried in Langholm Cemetery on 13 September.

AN OVERVIEW: WHAUR EXTREMES MEET

Fewer poets can have had a more apposite epitaph than MacDiarmid. Carved on the plain yellow-ocher headstone is this quatrain from *A Drunk Man:*

I'll ha'e nae hauf-way hoose, but aye be whaur
Extremes meet—it's the only way I ken
To dodge the curst conceit o' being richt
That damns the vast majority o' men.

(*CP,* p. 87)

Because MacDiarmid was so aware of the vastness of the physical universe and the vastness of human thought, he accepted as a fundamental tenet that truth can never be known with any certainty—"I dinna haud the world's end in my heid / As maist folk think they dae"; whatever knowledge we have is necessarily limited. We can never, therefore, presume to be right about anything, and so the honest thing to do is hold strong opinions—even when these contradict each other. In this way, it is wholly appropriate that MacDiarmid was expelled from the National Party of Scotland for his extreme socialist views in 1934 and from the Communist Party in 1938 for his Scottish nationalism. He could simultaneously be the fiery, polemic Hugh MacDiarmid, denouncing the Anglo-Scottish Establishment "together with the whole gang of high mucky-mucks, famous fatheads, old wives of both sexes, stuffed shirts . . . bird wits, lookers-under-beds, trained seals, creeping Jesuses, Scots Wha Hae'vers, Village idiots" (*Lucky Poet,* p. 149), and the courteous and gentle Chris Grieve, always ready to give friends a warm welcome and share glass of malt whisky with them. In poetry, he was elitist; in politics, egalitarian. He could be an atheist, and yet write in the poem "Lament for the Great Music" that "I believe . . ./ in the ineluctable certainty of the resurrection" (*CP,* p. 480); as Hugh MacDiarmid, he could advocate Scots as a literary language, while simultaneously, as C. M. Grieve, he could present himself as wholly opposed to Scots revivalism in an article published in the *Aberdeen Free Press* on January 30, 1922.

In *A Drunk Man,* MacDiarmid wrote that "A Scottish poet maun assume / The burden o' his people's doom." (lines 2638–2639) As a poet and thinker, he has assumed the "zigzag of convictions" that G. Gregory Smith identified as the

"Caledonian Antisyzygy" in *Scottish Literature: Character and Influence* (1919) and that MacDiarmid claimed was "one of the quintessential principles of the [Scottish Renaissance] Movement" in volume one of his quarterly journal *Voice of Scotland* (June–August 1938). His poetry is both fiercely nationalistic and political, yet only secondarily so; primarily, it is deeply philosophical, inquiring only in part into man's relationship with the body politic but more importantly into his place in the vastness of a universe without God.

EARLY POEMS IN ENGLISH

Before he became Hugh MacDiarmid, Christopher Grieve had written a number of poems in English, the most significant of which is a long poem in blank verse, "A Moment in Eternity," in which the poet sees himself as a tree shaken by the wind of immortality. By stages, he feels himself transformed into a tree in Paradise, then into "a flame of glorious and complex resolve / Within God's heart." The experience takes him deeper into God's heart, where he is aware of "A white light like a silence" before it restores him to his earthly existence with a sense of stillness and "new delight." The poem shows the influence of William Wordsworth in its subject matter and contains some verbal echoes of Wordsworth's *Ode on Immortality* (1807), as well some echoes of the verse of T. S. Cairncross, the minister of Langholm who was a considerable influence on the young poet.

Highly accomplished in itself, the poem is of particular interest in the way it anticipates some of the themes that were to predominate in MacDiarmid's later work, although its Christian overtones were not to recur. Typically, the poet is alone with his thoughts, which reach out into the infinity of the universe; poetic inspiration and spiritual truth are not differentiated and reach out to the silence that lies at the heart of all things— the Silence that all thought strives toward. The cosmic imagery of the poem was to recur in his first important collection of poems published as Hugh MacDiarmid, the 1925 volume titled *Sangschaw.*

EARLY LYRICS IN SCOTS

For some time, Grieve had argued that a Scottish poet would need to write in English. The London Burns Society had proposed that Scots could be used by modern poets, but Grieve was not convinced until Joyce's *Ulysses* showed him how Irish speech could be transformed into great art; however, he was to set about using the vernacular in a different way. He had always had a great delight in words, and he found inspiration in James Wilson's *Lowland Scotch as Spoken in the Lower Strathearn District of Perthshire* (1915). On two pages, he had found much of the vocabulary of "The Watergaw"; elsewhere he found the line "There is nae reek i' the laverock's hoose" in Wilson's "List of Proverbs and Sayings." "The Watergaw" (*CP,* p. 17) was the first poem published under the name of Hugh MacDiarmid, appearing in the *Scottish Chapbook,* a periodical edited by Christopher Grieve, in 1922. This was a significant moment in the poet's life and in the history of twentieth-century Scottish literature, and the poem deserves to be quoted in full:

Ae weet forenicht i' the yow trummle
I saw yon antrin thing,
A watergaw wi' its chitterin' licht
Ayont the on-ding;
An' I thocht o' the last wild look ye gied
Afore ye died!

(p. 25)

There was nae reek i' the laverock's hoose [smoke; skylark]
That nicht—an' nane i' mine;
But I hae thocht o' that foolish licht
Ever sin' syne; [then]
n' I think that mebbe at last I ken [know]
What your look meant then.

There is a density of dialect words in the first four lines—but translate them into English (One drizzling evening, during a cold spell in early summer that makes new-shorn sheep shiver, I saw an unusual thing: an indistinct rainbow with its shivering light just before the fall of heavy rain) and the poetry is lost. That is because the words came first for MacDiarmid: as he wrote in *Lucky Poet:* "The act of poetry [is] not an idea gradually shaping itself in words, but deriving entirely from words—and it was in fact . . . in this way that I wrote all the best of my Scots poems." (p. xxiii)

But it is not just in the choice of language that the success of this poem lies. He has also found a lyric form that breaks with the traditional verse forms used by Robert Burns (1759–1796) and his imitators: he is using old words in a new way. The variation of long and short lines may be reminiscent of the "standard Habbie" stanza used by Burns, but the rhyme scheme and arrangement are different. And then there is the idea itself behind the poem—the linking of an indistinct rainbow with the look of a dying man (probably the poet's father), suggesting that in his dying moments he has an intimation of immortality, just as the poet sees the rainbow as the precursor of the coming rain. Of course this is not defined, but only hinted, and therein lies the strength of the poem. It was a method MacDiarmid was to use again in his short lyrics: to begin his poem with a strong visual image in the first verse and to link it to a philosophical or metaphysical speculation in the second.

The poem was read by F. G. Scott, Grieve's former English teacher, who was more importantly a composer; he wished to set it to music, and he set out to trace the identity of "Hugh MacDiarmid." It was with considerable mutual surprise that he discovered the poet was none other than the boy he had taught in Langholm. The result was that Scott asked for more lyrics to be set as songs; MacDiarmid obliged, and he soon had enough Scots poems to make a collection, published as *Sangshaw* in 1925.

The linguistic inspiration for these lyrics was John Jamieson's two-volume *Etymological Dictionary of the Scottish Language* (1808–), in which MacDiarmid found words and phrases around which the poems accrued. These dialect words were combined with an orthographical representation of modern colloquial Scots pronunciation, resulting in a hybrid language called "synthetic Scots" by the poet. There is thus a poetic "otherness" in this language, together with the immediacy of the spoken word, that contributes to the poems' richness and effect. There is a distinctive poetic voice here, yet there is also

great range and variety, not only in the metrical forms and rhyming patterns, but also in the range of tone and subject matter. "Crowdieknowe" (*CP*, p. 26) takes an ironic look at the prospect of God wakening Scotsmen from the clay for the Last Judgment by anticipating the "feck [plenty] o' swearin" there will be because of their reluctance to be disturbed: MacDiarmid catches an aspect of the Scottish character here and presents it with immediacy and humor. Another poem in *Penny Wheep*, MacDiarmid's next collection, published in 1926, uses the ballad stanza to anticipate doomsday in a different way: In "Focherty" (*CP*, p. 53), the speaker looks forward with glee to the day when Duncan Gibb of Focherty, who "tramped me underfit [underfoot]" by stealing his lass, and against whom he had no chance, will have to account to God—and the poet—for himself and his behavior "like a bull in the sale-ring there." The linking of the cosmic and apocalyptic—the Day of Judgment—and the homely and earthy—a livestock sale ring—is characteristic of many of these poems.

MacDiarmid uses the ballad stanza to different effect in "The Innumerable Christ" (*CP*, p. 32). From the idea suggested by the epigraph (*"Other stars may have their Bethlehem, and their Calvary, too"*) he leaves the Earth behind and contemplates the vastness of the universe. If God lived and died on earth, surely he must do so on countless other planets "Yont [beyond] a' the stars oor een can see"; yet implicit in this view is a sense of infinite human sadness and suffering, too. That the human condition is predominantly one of sadness is also suggested in "The Bonny Broukit Bairn" (neglected child) (*CP*, p. 17), where the Earth is imagined almost as a Cinderella figure beside the finely dressed planets of the solar system. Once again, the poet ranges through the cosmos to come to rest in a homely image:

Mars is braw in crammasy, [crimson]
Venus in a green silk goun,
The auld mune shak's her gowden feathers,
Their starry talk's a wheen o' blethers, [pack of
  nonsense]
Nane for thee a thochtie sparin', [small thought]
Earth, thou bonnie broukit bairn!
—But greet, an' in your tears ye'll droun [weep]

The haill clanjamfrie! [rabble]

(p. 25)

The unusual, arcane vocabulary ("crammasy," "broukit," "clanjamfrie") combine in the last two lines with the colloquial idiom of a parent talking to a child in a way that enhances the poem considerably.

There are love songs, too, among these lyrics, but typically they do not address the beloved, reflecting rather the poet's mood after making love: in "Wheest, Wheest" (*CP,* p. 45), he contemplates his lover's stillness and refrains from starting up "auld ploys" (old games) again; "Scunner" ("disgust") (CP p. 64) is a more complex poem examining the speaker's feelings as he contemplates his lover, recognizing her beauty, which almost obliterates his sense of shame after sex, acknowledging this as an integral part of what is meant by "Love." Once again the imagery of the poem goes from the intimate and human to the "skinklan' [gleaming] stars," only for the poet to remind us that they are no more than "distant dirt"; MacDiarmid avoids the more usual romantic associations of the stars in love poetry to bring together the earthly and the heavenly in his postcoital mood.

It is difficult to generalize about the full effect of these early lyrics; the best way to convey their unique character is perhaps to end this consideration with a detailed commentary of two quite different examples. The first is "The Eemis Stane" (the unsteady stone) (*CP,* p. 27):

I' the how-dumb-deid o' the cauld hairst nicht [dead
  silent depth; cold harvest night]
The warl' like an eemis stane
Wags i' the lift; [sky]
An' my eerie memories fa'
Like a yowdendrift. [blizzard]

(p. 27)

Like a yowdendrift so's I couldna read
The words cut oot i' the stane
Had the fug o' fame [moss]
An' history's hazelraw [lichen]
No' yirdit thaim. [buried them]

Alan Bold finds this "perhaps the most haunting lyric in *Sangschaw*"; but pinpointing where this disconcerting quality comes from is no easy matter. The poet begins with his feet firmly on the ground, on a cold harvest night, contemplating the Earth, which seems like a huge, unsteady stone, balanced precariously—even dangerously—and yet he also seems to be seeing things *sub specie aeternitatis,* that is, under the aspect of eternity, from God's point of view. His memories (of what?) come between him and this vision of the Earth, which is now like a tombstone whose inscription is indecipherable beneath the moss and lichen of fame and history. Should we envisage him literally looking at a tombstone, illegible under the accretions of age, about to topple over? It seems more likely that the two images, the unsteady stone and the tombstone, are intended to modify one another, in the same way that the cold of the night is echoed by the wind-driven snow (the "yowdendrift"), and the word "deid" anticipates the tombstone image. The rhythm of the poem, particularly in its first line, echoes the spring rhythm of Gerard Manley Hopkins's verse, adding to the effect of the whole. In the end, the poem works by suggesting a response, rather than by defining one, in much the same way that music does: we are left facing a spiritual mystery in which man's history and achievements are no more than moss and lichen defacing the Earth.

The second lyric to consider closely is "Empty Vessel" (*CP,* pg. 66):

I met ayont the cairney [beyond a small cairn]
A lass wi' tousie hair [tousled]
Singin' till a bairnie [young child]
That was nae langer there.
Wunds wi' warlds to swing
Dinna sing sae sweet,
The licht that bends owre a' thing
Is less ta'en up wi'it.

(p. 66)

Here, MacDiarmid has taken his form from an anonymous folk song collected in David Herd's *Ancient and Modern Scots Songs* (1769):

I met ayont the cairney
Jenny Nettles, Jenny Nettles,
Singing til her bairny,
Robin Rattles bastard

206

The debt is obvious, but MacDiarmid takes the tale of a child conceived out of wedlock and transforms it into an image of human suffering almost universal in its application in the stark tradition of the ballad. Detail is sparse, and most is left to our imaginations; once again, something is suggested more than defined. The poem moves from a rural image to a cosmic viewpoint in the second verse, where the use of alliteration emphasizes the rhythm.

Taken as a whole, these lyrics are outstanding in their marriage of language, imagery, and thought. In *The Golden Lyric: An Essay on the Poetry of Hugh MacDiarmid* (1967), Iain Crichton Smith says that "in no other lyrics do I find their special combination of imaginative power, tenderness, wit, intelligence (but an intelligence which has not been divorced from feelings). . . . His lyrics are his greatest achievement." (*Hugh MacDiarmid,* p. 23)

A DRUNK MAN LOOKS AT THE THISTLE

MacDiarmid, however, was ready to move on to new challenges. He had announced in the *Glasgow Herald* on 17 December 1925 that he had completed a "long poem of over a thousand lines split into several sections," but when it was eventually published by Blackwood in 1926 it ran to 2,685 lines.

The poet makes considerable claims for its significance. He was aware that the publication of Eliot's *The Waste Land* in 1922 would be a landmark in the history of twentieth-century literature, but in *The Drunk Man* he asserts (perhaps with ironic modesty) that his work is greater.

A considerable claim—but then the poem looks out for someone not only to redeem Scotland through a rebirth of its literature but also to redeem all mankind in his search for "A greater Christ, a greater Burns" (line 116)—and who is to say that the awaited savior might not be the drunk man, or MacDiarmid himself, in his wide ranging, all–encompassing poem?

In the process of its composition, *A Drunk Man* was in some ways analogous to *The Waste Land;* just as Eliot had allowed Pound to give shape to the disparate elements that were to make up his great poem, so MacDiarmid turned to F. G. Scott to fulfill a similar role over a bottle of whisky one evening in Montrose. The extent of Scott's influence over the final shape of the poem is unclear, but the whisky bottle emptying over an evening gives a unity of time and place to MacDiarmid and Scott's collaboration that is missing from Eliot and Pound's.

A considerable claim—but then the poem looks out for someone not only to redeem Scotland through a rebirth of its literature but also to redeem all mankind in his search for "A greater Christ," and who is to say that the awaited savior might not be the drunk man, or McDiarmid himself, in his wide ranging, all-encompassing poem?

The plot of *A Drunk Man* can be easily stated: after a heavy night's drinking, a the poet stumbles into a ditch on his way home, where he is confronted by a giant thistle, and his thoughts range over Life, the Universe, and Everything (including Scotland and sex)—but that, however, is rather like saying that *Hamlet* is about a mixed-up young man who dies before his time.

MacDiarmid expressed his purpose in writing the poem in an article in the *Glasgow Herald* of February 13 1926: "The intention here has been to show that Braid Scots is adaptable to all kinds of poetry, and to a much greater variety of measures than might be supposed from the restricted practice of the last hundred years"(*MacDiarmid,* p. 213). There is certainly a variety in the Scots that MacDiarmid uses, from the colloquial "bar room" argot evident at the beginning of the poem, which frequently recurs (particularly when the poet bemoans the declining quality of whisky) to the complex "dictionary Scots" that is evident in some lyrics such as that beginning "Maun I tae perish in the keel o' Heaven" (lines 2335–2346). It is a language capable of developing philosophical discourse in several major sections of the poem, yet also hauntingly lyrical in others:

But I can gi'e ye kindness, lad,
And a pair o' willin' hands
And you sall ha'e my breists like stars,

My limbs like willow wands,

And on my lips ye'll heed nae mair,
And in my hair forget,
The seed o' a' the men that in
My virgin womb ha'e met

(p. 103)

The poem also encompasses a vast range of verse and meter. MacDiarmid recognized in *The Thistle Rises* that "largely, the engine that motivates the whole poem and keeps it going is the ballad measure" (p. 223); but there is a huge range of variation aside from this: there are sustained passages written in blank verse; passages sometimes in tetrameters and sometimes pentameters; there are quatrains of rhyming hexameters, and toward the end a sustained passage in rhyming triplets. The poem ends in heroic couplets: there is a tremendous dexterity in handling all these forms. Besides this, MacDiarmid shows that Scots is a medium for the translation of verse from other languages at several points in the poem, including work by Russian, Belgian, and German poets. These are not direct translations from the original languages, but versions derived from anthologies of verse in English translation, which MacDiarmid integrates into the fabric of his poem, suggesting not only the breadth of his reading, but also the universal, pan-European nature of the experiences he is describing.

In his preface to the first edition, MacDiarmid described the poem as a "Gallimaufry" (a lucky bag or odds and ends), and it is certainly wide-ranging in its references: besides Biblical allusions and those to which he draws our specific attention (Alexander Blok, George Ramaekers, Zinaida Hippius, Else Lakser-Schuler, Edmond Rocher, together with quotations in the original from Stephané Mallarmé and Dante Alighieri) there are the major influences of Fyodor Dostoyevsky and Herman Melville. Underlying the poem is the philosophy of both Friedrich Niezche and Lev Shestov, together with that of Romantic poets such as Percy Bysshe Shelley. And we must not forget Burns: the drunk man shares a number of characteristics with Tam o' Shanter, too! In all, the range of references and sources is certainly as broad as Eliot's in *The Waste Land,* but MacDiarmid has refused to provide us with the "handrails" of notes. Fortunately, Kenneth Buthlay's 1987 annotated edition of the poem does.

The most useful approach to answer the question "What is the poem about?" is to consider the elements of its title. The protagonist, the drunk man, shares many biographical details with the poet himself: he makes references to the Common Riding of Langholm (lines 457–460), he lives in Montrose, he has "sodgered 'neth the Grecian sky / And in Italy and Marseilles" (lines 2462–2463), he has a taste for good whisky. More importantly, he feels himself an intellectual outcast with little in common with "the feck o' men" yet as the one destined to save Scotland from itself. Kenneth Buthlay feels that "without quite bursting at the seams, [the poem] is able to hold all or almost all of MacDiarmid" (*1964*, p. 50); we too can safely infer that the speaker of the poem is the poet himself and not a persona. His drunkenness is also an important element of the poem: the whisky not only sheds a transforming light over things (as does the moonlight in the poem), so that reality seen from a drunk man's point of view is different from that of a man sober—more importantly, the drink frees his mind "owre continents unkent / And wine-dark oceans (to) waunder like Ulysses" (lines 399–400), allowing the poem to move forward thorough a free association of ideas and images, rather than by advancing a logical argument in measured stages. As Klaeber says in the preface to his edition of *Beowulf,* the poem "lacks steady advance," developing a circular, cumulative logic as themes and ideas recur—and interspersed with this there is much fun, as the poem includes passages of satire, flyting (that is, offering up disputation and personal abuse), parody, and quite a few good jokes. In his 1817 *Biographia Literaria,* Samuel Taylor Coleridge had described the imagination as revealing itself in "the balance or reconciliation of discordant qualities," and it is this kind of synthesis that MacDiarmid has set out to achieve not through argument (although that plays a part) but through a pattern of recurring themes and images:

And I in turn 'ud be an action
To pit in a concrete abstraction
My Country's contrair qualities
And mak' a unity of these

(p. 145)

The thistle, which is the focus of the drunk man's meditations, is the central image of the poem and has several symbolic applications. Initially, of course, it is the national flower and symbol for Scotland, and for the most part, MacDiarmid is scornful of his native country: it is "the barren fig" (line 707) whose only hope of redemption is "a miracle." (line 719) The poem begins with a sustained attack on Burns Clubs and the way they have replaced intellectual inquiry with unthinking sentiment, and toward the end the poet's fellow Scots are described as

—The only race in History who've

Bidden in the same category [remained]
Frae stert to present o' their story,
And deem their ignorance their glory.

And "Puir Auld Scotland" bleat wi' pride,
And wi' their minds made up to bide
A thorn in a' the wide world's side.

(p. 165)

Of course not all Scots are like this; Burns was not, and neither is MacDiarmid—but all but a dozen of the rest do not have souls worth the saving: "I widna gi'e five meenits wi' Dunbar [the Scottish poet William Dunbar, c. 1460–c. 1520] / For a' the millions o' ye as ye are" (lines 748–749).

This is a disconcerting sentiment from someone who loves his native country so passionately, yet MacDiarmid was to acknowledge in 1975 in a letter to David Daiches that "I have had to confess that on the whole I do not like people—and have no love of mankind en masse, but regard them as a failure and can only find interests in common with an individual or two" (*Letters,* p. 743). Hence the couplet: "Millions o' wimmen bring forth in pain / Millions o' bairns that are no' worth ha'en" (lines 636–637). This scorn for "the feck o' men" is illustrated by the drunk man's attitude to Cruivie and Gilsanquar, his drinking companions: if he were to speak of

his concerns to them, the former would merely "goam" (that is, stare vacuously) and the latter would "jalouse you're dottlin" (suspect you're going senile). (lines 785–786)

The symbolism of the thistle then expands from Scotland to represent everything that holds back not just the nation but all mankind from spiritual development: this is particularly apparent in a passage dealing in symbolic terms with the failure of the General Strike in 1926 (lines 1119–1218). The poet comes to realize that this sense of failure is a part of human life that all men, including himself, must suffer, although because he is more sensitive, he feels it more than others:

Aye—this is Calvary—to bear
Your cross wi'in you frae the seed,
And feel it grow by slow degrees
Until it rends your flesh apairt,
And turn, and see your fellow-men
In similar case but sufferin' less
Thro' bein' mair wudden frae the stert!

(p. 134)

The poet's inquiring mind does not take him any further forward than his fellow men: on the one hand, he is determined to follow the intellectual train of thought that he shares with Dostoyevsky, Melville, and the rest because it is what raises him above the mass; on the other, he acknowledges that "ye dinna need to pass ony exam. to dee" (lines 798–799)—the common fate of us all. Man's soul cannot be divorced from his body—yet therein lies a source of comfort, for through sex (the thistle also functions as a phallic symbol in the poem) and his relationship with his wife, the drunk man can find "A kind o' Christianity" (line 574)—although he is aware of the physical basis for this spiritual ecstasy: "Man's spreit is wi' his ingangs [innards] twined / In ways that he can ne'er unwind" (lines 584–585).

The poem comes to a conclusion by accepting the state of affairs that the drunk man has railed against so vehemently for two thousand lines or so. Alan Bold finds the later section of the poem known as "The Great Wheel" (lines 2395–2658) a less successful passage, yet in many ways it is the poem's climax. MacDiarmid's image of the Great Wheel is a synthesis of elements from William Butler Yeats's *A Vision* (1925), the notion of the Platonic year, and the model of the universe as discovered by Edwin Hubble in 1923 when he observed that it extended beyond its previously perceived limits. The drunk man comes to see Scotland's troubles—and his own—in the context of the vastness of the universe and of time:

Upon the huge circumference are
As neebor points the Heavenly War [neighbor]
That dung doun Lucifer sae far [cast]

And that upheaval in which I
Sodgered 'neth the Grecian sky
and in Italy and Marseilles

And there isna' room for men
Wha the haill o' history ken
To pit a pin twixt then and then.

(p. 159)

Since no one can comprehend the scale of the universe, or of history, we cannot hope to understand the objective world. The poem then turns round to direct the poet's gaze inward:

Oor universe is like an e'e
Turned in, man's benmaist hert to see [deepest]
And swamped in subjectivity.

(p. 163)

In time, the poet feels that mankind may evolve organs to be responsive to this "need divine;" until then

The function, as it seems to me
O' Poetry is to bring to be
At lang, lang last that unity . . .

(p. 163)

And this is what the poet will strive toward—although he cannot help but feel frustrated by the limitations of his fellow Scots, since, Christ-like, a Scottish poet has to "assume / The burden o' his people's doom / And dee to brak' their livin' tomb." (lines 2638–2640) There is no escape: his solution is to take the matter to "avizandum," a Scots legal term meaning to defer a decision.

The final irony is that this garrulous, loquacious poem ends in "Silence"—"the croon o'a" (the crown of all)—and a joke, as the drunk man anticipates his wife's reaction to his returning sober with the dawn:

O I ha'e Silence left
—"And well ye micht,"
Sae Jean'll say, "eftir sic a nicht!"

(p. 167)

The Silence he has found is a profound spiritual quality, similar to the stillness sought by Eliot in "Burnt Norton" (1935, from *Four Quartets*) at the still point of the turning world.

In *Hugh MacDiarmid,* Kenneth Buthlay despairs of giving a sense of the scope of *A Drunk Man.* No summary of this length can hope to give a sense of the richness the poem has to offer a responsive reader; one can only hope it will whet the appetite.

POEMS 1930–1933

In 1930, MacDiarmid published *To Circumjack Cencrastus,* a second long philosophical poem in the same mold as *A Drunk Man.* It had taken four years to write because of interruptions in his personal life and is less successful than the previous work—possibly because *A Drunk Man* had been such a tour de force that the form could not be developed further. The poem revisits many of the preoccupations MacDiarmid had dealt with four years earlier and casts some interesting light on the steadily growing discontent he was feeling as a provincial journalist who really wanted his poetic voice to be heard. As a whole, however, it lacks the consistency of tone so impressive in *A Drunk Man* and does not have the same focus. Nevertheless, it contains some fine passages, such as the wonderful lyric often anthologized as "Lourd on My Hert" (*CP,* pp. 204–205), in which MacDiarmid revisits his feelings on contemporary Scotland, using the country's weather as a metaphor for its regressive state: although he feels some optimism toward the end of the poem that Scotland's cultural winter may be drawing to a close because he can see the light of dawn heralding his country's renaissance, the poem ends in self-mocking anticlimax:

Nae wonder if I think I see
A lichter shadow that the neist [lighter, next]
I'm fain to cry: "The dawn, the dawn!
I see it brakin' in the East!"

But ah
—It's juist mair snaw!

(p. 205)

The language of this lyric is less densely Scots than much of *A Drunk Man;* although he does use some particularly Scottish expressions (for example, the word "fain" in the stanza above), much of the vocabulary is English spelled to suggest a Scots accent.

MacDiarmid was aware that his poetic ability was changing—or, as he felt at the time, deserting him. Mary MacDonald, a friend of the poet, recalled a conversation with him in 1935, saying "he would speak to me of his marriage to Peggy, his first wife, and the damage he feared the break-up and the loss of his children had done to his lyrical faculty. He seemed very depressed when he dwelt on this, and did so often." His art was to take off in a new direction: he was to write more directly political poems over the coming years, some in Scots and some in English, including the three "Hymns to Lenin" and perhaps his most successful political poem, "The Seamless Garment." He had already attacked the capitalist system through presenting his own personal frustrations as a regional journalist when reprimanded by his employer for daydreaming:

Curse the system that can gie
A coof like this control o' me [fool]
—No that he's in the least bit waur
Or better, than other bosses are . . .

. . . Curse his new house, his business, his cigar,
His wireless set, and motor car . . .
—A'thing included in his life . . .
And—if he has yin— his hereafter . . .

(CP, p. 235)

Whereas his nationalism had always been a constant and overt feature of his work, during this period he wrote poems that were more directly socialist in their tone. They are often stark and challenging, and the views put forward are uncompromising; for example in the "First Hymn to Lenin," where he condones institutional murder as a necessary means to a greater end:

As necessary, and insignificant, as death
Wi' a' its agonies in the cosmos still

The Cheka's horrors are in their degree; [State Secret Police]
And'll end suner! What maitters wha' we kill
To lessen that foulest murder that deprives
Maist men o' real lives?

(p. 298)

The poet turns to Lenin because he offers "the flower and iron of the truth"—an evocative and stirring phrase, but one that reflects an unyielding, hardline stance in encounters with his fellow man. This quality that he so much admires in Lenin is also recognizable in his short poem "The Skeleton of the Future (at Lenin's Tomb)" (*CP*, p. 386), where the geological language, combined with the coldness of the snow imagery and the violence of the lightning, suggest something of what the poet admired in the politician:

Red granite and black diorite, with the blue
Of the labradorite crystals gleaming like precious stones
In the light reflected from the snow; and behind them
The eternal lightning of Lenin's bones.

(p. 386)

"The Seamless Garment" (*CP*, pp. 311–314), however, is more accessible because, in Roderick Watson's words, it "attempts to persuade without arousing hate in us . . . fully combining polemic and poetry." (*Hugh MacDiarmid,* p. 43) The poem marries tone and style with apposite imagery to convey its message; the colloquial tone is expertly judged as the poet explains to his cousin, a worker in a cloth-weaving mill in Langholm, the importance of his political and poetic beliefs. As he stands in the woolen mill for the first time (despite being born in a weaving town), he finds the place "dumfoonderin," yet his cousin is perfectly at home here. He then uses weaving as a metaphor for Lenin's grasp of working class life and for the way Rainer Maria Rilke aimed to use his poetry to make "a single reality . . o' his love and pity and fear." His cousin is an expert weaver—but is the quality of his life equal to that of the cloth he produces? Should working men not contribute as much effort to their moral and political growth as they do to their marketable skills? MacDiarmid suggests that "many a loom [is] mair alive than the weaver"; he exhorts his cousin to seek for spiritual as well as material advancement. The poem then ends with an analogy between weaving and his own work as a poet: MacDiarmid himself must achieve in his poetry an integrity

> Indivisible, real,
> Woven owre close for the point of a pin
>   Onywhere to win in.

The poet and the weaver, then, are engaged in similar tasks. At one point in the poem, he suggests that his cousin's skill is greater than his own: the weaver's cloth is perfect, but the poet's work is not always so:

> Is't no' high time
> We were tryin' to come into line a' roon?
>   (I canna think o' a rhyme.)
>
>   (p. 313)

MacDiarmid's self-deprecating admission here suggests not so much the difficulty of his task but rather the greater workmanship of his cousin, a factor that rescues the poem from being patronizing in its tone.

MacDiarmid's lyric muse had not entirely deserted him, as a glance at the short poem "Milk-Wort and Bog-Cotton" (*CP*, p. 331) shows. A beautifully well-modulated love poem, it has the lyric intensity of his earlier work and also its haunting elusiveness: is the poet addressing the landscape or a woman—or is one cast as a metaphor for the other? Another poem worthy of note is "Water Music" (*CP*, pp. 333–337), an exuberant celebration both of MacDiarmid's ability to handle Scots and of the waters that flow around Langholm. His reference to Joyce in the first verse suggests that he was aiming to achieve something similar in this poem to the way language is used in *Finnegans Wake* (1939); certainly the onomatopoeia of the opening stanzas suggests the song of the Wauchope, Esk, and Ewes so strongly the reader can almost see the light playing on their surface, so that meaning almost becomes superfluous:

> Lively, louch, atweesh, atween
>   Auchimuty or aspate,
> Threidin' through the averins

> Or bightsome in the aftergait.

> Or barmybrained or barritchfu'
>   Or rinnin' like an attercap,
> Or shinin' like an Atchison
>   Wi' a blare or wi a blawp
>
>   (p. 333)

STONY LIMITS *AND* ON A RAISED BEACH

MacDiarmid had moved to the Shetland Island of Whalsay in 1933, and the first collection of poems he published after the move, *Stony Limits* (1934), confirmed a trend that had been apparent in his poetry for some time: more and more he had come to write in English rather than what Kenneth Buthlay describes as "a thin variety of Scots"; from now, the predominant language was to be English. This grew partly from MacDiarmid's growing interest in the importance of science and an awareness of the fact that Scots did not have an independent scientific vocabulary. Being MacDiarmid, however, he combined this interest in scientific terminology with an urge to find out recondite elements of the English vocabulary, resulting in a "synthetic English" that became the source of his new poetic voice, wholly distinctive from that of his earlier work.

This voice is particularly noticeable in the opening of "On a Raised Beach" (*CP*, pp. 422–433), the greatest of the poems in this collection and one of the greatest long poems of the twentieth century, comparable to Eliot's "Ash Wednesday" or *The Four Quartets* in its achievement. MacDiarmid had explored Whalsay in the company of a geologist, and he uses the scientific vocabulary he has learned extensively in the opening of the poem (already quoted in the introductory passages of this essay):

> All is lithogenesis—or lochia,
> Carpolite fruit of the forbidden tree,
> Stones blacker than any in the Caaba;
> Cream-coloured Caen-stone, chatoyant pieces,
> Celadon and corbeau, bistre and beige,
> Glaucous, hoar, enfouldered and cyathiform . . .
>
>   (p. 422)

This presents a challenge to any reader—and deliberately so, for MacDiarmid's intention in the poem is to make us face rigorous truths; we need to limber up intellectually for what is to follow. Roderick Watson provides a translation of these lines to save us from rushing between dictionary and poem in his title *MadDiarmid* and it is almost a surprise to find that they make sense, but in some ways it does not matter if we do not grasp the literal meaning of the words here: we are being prepared for what is to follow, which (thankfully) is in more accessible language, although the ideas that are presented in the long, blank verse lines may be difficult for us to grasp and require considerable concentration. We should come to realize, however, that many of them lead on naturally from the concerns explored in *A Drunk Man Looks at the Thistle*.

The poet is characteristically alone, on a raised beach: a geological feature of the Shetland Islands, which can often be some way inland from the sea, the remnant of a previous shoreline. He lies listening to the song of a solitary bird whose "inward gates are ever open," which leads (like Shelley's skylark) to the exuberance of its song. The stones on which he lies are open to the same influence, too, and are considerably more permanent than either the poet or the bird, examples of animal life, whose "purposive function is another question"; in other words, the stones' presence is fundamental to this or any other planet "No visitor comes from the stars / But is the same as they are," whereas the purpose of life is unclear—an optional planetary extra, rather than essential to its existence. If animal and vegetable life were to die out, the Earth would still continue to be.

Alan Bold draws our attention to a key word among the eclectic vocabulary in the opening stanza of the poem: "haecceity." The term is drawn from the work of a medieval Scots philosopher, Duns Scotus, who believed that what distinguishes one thing from another is form, not matter: "haecceity" is what distinguishes man from stones, or one stone from another—but essentially all things—man, bird, and stones and stars—are all part of the same universe: they are separate, but inseparable.

In comparison to the stones, all man's achievement is nothing—or, expressed in the poem's terms, "There are plenty of ruined buildings in the world but no ruined stones." It is therefore important that men see their place in the universe not as masters of creation, but subject to it:

What happens to us
Is irrelevant to the world's geology
But what happens to the world's geology
Is not irrelevant to us.
We must reconcile ourselves to the stones
Not the stones to us.

(p. 428)

Out of this austerity, the poet has already felt "all that can perish perishing in me"; realizing that "an emotion chilled is an emotion controlled", he comes to a state where "Death is a physical horror to me no more": he can face a godless universe (or at least a universe that does not contain a conventional Christian God, and promises no afterlife) without flinching or fear, since "in death—unlike in life—we lose nothing that is truly ours." There is a heroism in accepting that this life is all there is, and since that is the case, it is our moral duty to make the most we can out of it; if we do not do so, we are doomed:

men cannot hope
To survive the fall of mountains
Which we will no more see than we saw their rise
Unless they are more concentrated and determined,
Truer to themselves and with more to be true to . . .

(p. 427)

The message to mankind has changed little since *The Drunk Man:*

. . . manifest forevermair
Contempt o' ilka goal:

(pp. 136-137)

O' ilka goal—save ane alane:
To be yoursel' whatever that may be . . .

(lines 1713–1716)

In an allusion to Eliot, MacDiarmid tells us that "This is no heap of broken images"; rather he has found in these stones the symbol both of the unity and integrity, "indivisible, real" that he sought in "The Seamless Garment" and of the Silence sought by *The Drunk Man:*

But the kindred form I am conscious of here
Is the beginning and end of the world . . .
. . . the Omnific word.
These stones have the silence of supreme creative
  power
The direct and undisturbed way of working
Which alone leads to greatness.

(pp. 428–429)

Like William Blake, who can see the world in a grain of sand and hold infinity in the palm of his hand, MacDiarmid holds a stone and sees the universe; references above to "the beginning and end of the world" show he also sees eternity, as suggested in the final word of the poem, "epana-diplosis," a rhetorical term that describes a sentence beginning and ending with the same word—presumably the "Omnific word" above. Although the poem rejects orthodox religion in its closing stages in its reference to "the stone rolled away from the tomb of the Lord," MacDiarmid here acknowledges a spiritual (and creative) force that rolls through all things in the universe, and of which we are part.

The stones also function as a symbol of separateness, reminding him of his own isolation ("Great work cannot be combined with surrender to the crowd"), yet affirming the necessity of keeping himself separate and dedicated to his art,

as a stone remains
Essential to the world, inseparable from it
And rejects all other life yet.

Coupled with this is the image of the poet that the Romantics would have recognized:

I grasp one of them and I have in my grip
The beginning and the end of the world,
My own self, and as before I never saw
The empty hand of my brother man.
The humanity no other culture has reached, the mob.
Intelligentsia, our impossible and imperative job!

(p. 432)

Like Shelley in the final words of his essay *A Defence of Poetry* (1821), MacDiarmid believes that "Poets are the unacknowledged legislators of the world." The poem is a triumph over death. MacDiarmid has told us that "My disposition is towards spiritual issues / Made inhumanly clear"

and he presents us with the "barren but beautiful reality" of life and death in a universe were there is only life and death, and nothing beyond that.

LATER POEMS: THE "POETRY OF FACT"

In the 1940s and 1950s, MacDiarmid began to write long and seemingly shapeless poems that he often described as parts of longer work in progress: he was aiming for poetry that was all-inclusive in projected works such as "Mature Art" and "Cornish Heroic Song for Valda Trevlyn." He called this a "poetry of fact" or "a poetry of ideas"; in "The Caledonian Antisyzygy" (*CP,* p. 1052) he describes its style as "chopped up prose." "In Memoriam James Joyce" frequently seems to consist of lists of his recent reading:

Valery's *Poesie et Pensee Abstraite*
   Paulhan's *Les Fleurs des Tarbes,* And *Jacob Cow the Pirate* or *Whether Words are Signs*
   Parain's *Traite sur la Nature et les Fonctions de Langage,*
   Francis Ponge's *Le Parti-pris des Choses. . .*

(*CP,* p. 745)

MacDiarmid refers to this tendency with a vein of self-mockery at one point:

Shirokogofoff's *Psychomental Complex of the Tungus*
(If that line is not great poetry in itself
Then I don't know what poetry is!)

(*CP,* p. 793)

Sometimes there are just lists of names:

   . . . Chaim Bailik, Theodor Daubler,
   Domhnull Mac na Ceardiach, Yeats, AE, Dylan Thomas,
   Sturge Moore, T. S. Eliot, Austin Clarke, Fred Higgins,
   Mulk Raj Anad, Harindranath Chattopadhyaya...

(*CP,* p. 817)

Another habit is to take passages of prose verbatim from other writers, sometimes acknowledged and sometimes not, and present this as poetry by breaking it up into blank verse: the passage beginning "What was the inspiration of his best productivity?" (*CP,* p. 768) originated almost word for word as an article by Karl Kraus in the *Times Literary Supplement* of 8 May 1953. This literary borrowing was to lead to considerable controversy when Kenneth Buthlay printed the poem "Perfect" (*CP,* p. 573) in his 1964 study, *Hugh MacDiarmid,* praising it as "the poem which Ezra Pound and the other imagists talked about but did not write." The poem begins with an epigraph—"On the Western Seaboard of South Uist / (Los muertos abren los ojos a los que viven)"—and then reads:

I found a pigeon's skull on the machair,
All the bones pure white and dry, and chalky,
But perfect,
Without a crack or flaw anywhere.

At the back, rising out of the beak
Were twin domes like bubbles of thin bone,
Almost transparent, where the wings had been
That fixed the tilt of the wings.

Reading a review of Buthlay's book which reprinted the poem in its entirety in the *Times Literary Supplement,* the Welsh writer Glyn Jones pointed out that these words (with the exception of the epigraph and two substitutions—"machair" for "beach" and "pigeon" for "gull") came from his own short story "Porth-y-Rhyd," published in 1937. MacDiarmid apologized, claiming that "any plagiarism was certainly unconscious," (*Letters,* p. 829) but the occurrence suggests that he was in the habit of borrowing from other writers so regularly that he could at times, by writing passages in notebooks, not remembering their sources and later thinking they were his own, not realize he was doing it.

Edwin Morgan joined the debate in the *Times Literary Supplement,* asking whether prose could become poetry through typographical rearrangement. In a subsequent article, Kenneth Buthlay suggests it can: by arranging the lines as he does, MacDiarmid not only draws out attention to the word "perfect" (the key word of the poem), but also to the interplay of sound in second stanza: the alliteration on "back," "beak," "bubbles," "bone," "been"; the assonance and rhyme of "twin domes" and "thin bone"; and finally how the assonance of the final line—"that fixed the tilt of the wings"—underscores its regular rhythm. Perhaps the best of MacDiarmid's later poems is "Crystals Like Blood" (*CP,* p. 1054). Here, the poet brings two seemingly disparate images together to symbolize a third: first, there is the stone he remembers, "hard, greenish-grey, quartz-like" yet dappled with "veins and beads / Of bright magenta" —a disturbing image of animal and mineral existence in surreal conjunction; second, he remembers seeing the industrial process by which mercury is extracted from its ore by huge pile drivers, pounding and pulverizing repeatedly. These images are then related to his "living memory" of someone he had loved whose "dear body [is now] rotting here in the clay." It becomes apparent that the poem is in fact an elegy, celebrating the "bright torrents of felicity, naturalness and faith" (like the magenta beads) that are released by his "treadmill memory": like the pile drivers, his thoughts extract the essence of the person he remembers from memories of their past life.

CONCLUSION

This essay on MacDiarmid's poetry has taken no account of his prose works, beyond including short quotations to illustrate ideas underlying his poems. He wrote a vast amount of journalism and also a great deal of political literature—but it is principally as a poet that he has his greatest claim to fame. His greatest achievement was to have forged a new poetic language from archaic and dialect forms that he nevertheless made capable of expressing a twentieth-century consciousness in its entirety both in hauntingly evocative lyrics and in the sustained exploration of *A Drunk Man Looks at the Thistle.* Not only that, he was to find another, completely distinctive, poetic voice in the following decade to express truths in a different but no less brilliant and demanding way. There may have been some trailing off of his creative powers over the last decades of his life, but that cannot detract from his achievement, any more than Wordsworth's later years can take away from what he had achieved prior to 1807. Importantly, MacDiarmid never surrendered his integrity: in *To Circumjack Cencrastus* he proclaimed that "I'm no' the kind o' poet / That opens sales o'work" and he never became so. Although recognition of his achievement came to him in later years, he never lost his sense of who he was, his love of controversy, or the need to speak his mind, whatever the consequences.

Selected Bibliography

WORKS OF HUGH MACDIARMID

POETRY

Sangschaw. Edinburgh: Blackwood, 1925.

A Drunk Man Looks at the Thistle. Edinburgh: Blackwood, 1926.

A Drunk Man Looks at the Thistle: An Annotated Edition. Edited by Kenneth Buthlay. Edinburgh: Scottish Academic Press, 1987. (References to *A Drunk Man Looks at the Thistle* refer to line numbers in this edition.)

Penny Wheep. Edinburgh: Blackwood, 1926.

To Circumjack Cencrastus; or, The Curly Snake. Edinburgh: Blackwood, 1930.

First Hymn to Lenin and Other Poems. London: Unicorn, 1931.

Scots Unbound and Other Poems. Stirling, U.K.: Eneas Mackay, 1932.

Stony Limits and Other Poems. London: Gollancz, 1934.

Second Hymn to Lenin and Other Poems. London: Stanley Nott, 1935.

A Kist of Whistles. Glasgow: Maclellan, 1947.

In Memoriam James Joyce. Glasgow: Maclellan, 1955.

The Battle Continues. Edinburgh: Castle Wynd Printers, 1957.

The Kind of Poetry I Want. Edinburgh: Duval, 1961.

Direadh I, II, and III. Frenich, Foss, U.K.: Duval and Hamilton, 1974.

PROSE

Annals of the Five Senses. Montrose, U.K.: C. M. Grieve, 1923. 2nd ed. Edinburgh, Porpoise Press, 1930.

Contemporary Scottish Studies. London: Leonard Parsons, 1926.

The Lucky Bag. Edinburgh: Porpoise Press, 1927.

Scottish Scene; or, The Intelligent Man's Guide to Albyn. With Lewis Grassic Gibbon. London: Jarrolds, 1934.

Scottish Eccentrics. London: Routledge, 1936.

Lucky Poet: A Self-Study in Literature and Political Ideas. London: Methuen, 1943.

The Company I've Kept. London: Hutchinson, 1966.

Scotch Whisky. London: Macmillan, 1974.

Aesthetics in Scotland. Edited by Alan Bold. Edinburgh: Mainstream, 1984.

The Letters of Hugh MacDiarmid. Edited by Alan Bold. London: Hamilton, 1984.

COLLECTIONS

Collected Poems. New York: Macmillan, 1962; Edinburgh: Oliver and Boyd, 1962.

Selected Poems. Edited by David Craig and John Manson. Harmondsworth, U.K.: Penguin, 1970.

The Hugh MacDiarmid Anthology: Poems in Scots and English. Edited by Michael Grieve and Alexander Scott. London: Routledge and Kegan Paul, 1972.

The Complete Poems of Hugh MacDiarmid, 1920–1976. 2 vols. Edited by Michael Grieve and W. R. Aitken. London: Martin Brian and O'Keeffe, 1978; Harmondsworth, U.K.: Penguin, 1985.

The Socialist Poems of Hugh MacDiarmid. Edited by T. S. Law and Thurso Berwick. London: Routledge and Kegan Paul, 1978.

CRITICAL AND BIOGRAPHICAL STUDIES

Bold, Alan. *MacDiarmid: Christopher Murray Grieve: A Critical Biography.* London: Murray, 1988.

Buthlay, Kenneth. *Hugh MacDiarmid (C. M. Grieve).* Edinburgh: Oliver and Boyd, 1964. (Part of the Writers and Critics series.)

Crawford, Thomas, ed. *Scottish Literary Journal* 5, no. 2 (December 1978). (MacDiarmid memorial issue.)

Riach, Alan. *The Poetry of Hugh MacDiarmid.* Glasgow: Scottish Academic Press, 1999. (*Scotnotes* series, no. 15.)

Smith, Iain Crichton. *The Golden Lyric: An Essay on the Poetry of Hugh MacDiarmid.* Preston, U.K.: Akros, 1967.

Watson, Roderick. *Hugh MacDiarmid.* Milton Keynes, U.K.: Open University Press, 1976.

DAVID MALOUF

(1934—)

Brian Henry

BORN IN BRISBANE, Queensland, on March 20, 1934, David Malouf has emerged as one of Australia's most prominent literary figures. His own background reflects the multiculturalism of modern Australia. His father's family immigrated to Australia from Lebanon in the 1880s, and his mother's family moved to Australia from London in the 1910s. Because of his paternal grandfather's "temperament, or aristocratic pride, or lack of English, or contempt for the conventions of the place" (*12 Edmondstone Street,* p. 7), he refused to work or adapt to his new home, thus requiring his wife and children to support the family. Malouf's grandmother worked long days in a shop, learned English, and converted to Catholicism, thereby assimilating to Australian life. Malouf's father embodied this divide, speaking Arabic with his parents and English with his wife and children. Malouf's mother re-created in her family "her own life in Edwardian London," forbidding her children "to speak or act 'Australian'" (p. 33). Malouf grew up encouraged by his father to embrace an Australian identity while his mother urged him to retain her own Englishness. This tension becomes manifest throughout his writing.

Malouf attended Brisbane Grammar School and the University of Queensland, where he also taught for two years after graduation. He left Australia in 1959, at age twenty-four, to live in England, teaching in London and Birkenhead. In 1968, during the charged political climate of the Vietnam War, he returned to Australia to protest Australia's involvement in the war and to teach at the University of Sydney. Malouf quit teaching in 1977 to focus on his writing, living mainly in Italy (in the village of Campagnatico in Tuscany) until 1985, when he returned to Sydney in 1985, where he still resides.

Although known primarily for his fiction, Malouf began his career as a poet, publishing three books of poetry and a poetry anthology before his first novel appeared. His second book of poetry, *Neighbours in a Thicket* (1974), won the Grace Leven Prize for Poetry, a gold medal from the Australian Literature Society, and the James Cook Award for best Australian book of the year. Malouf achieved even wider recognition for his writing after shifting from poetry to fiction as his primary genre. The critic Philip Neilson has written that Malouf's early fiction demonstrates "the strengths of his verse—economy of expression, lyrical subtlety, descriptive detail and thematic reverberation—while demonstrating a sure sense of dramatic development, dialogue and narrative structure" (p. 7). Describing the differences between Malouf's poetry and fiction, the critic James Tulip writes, "Malouf's prose style in fiction has a clarity of surface, a pace and rhythmic fluidity to it" (p. xviii). Malouf also has developed a sweeping historical sense as a novelist; as the Australian poet and critic Andrew Taylor points out, Malouf's fiction covers two hundred years of Australian history, a feat "not found in any other Australian novelist" (p. 4).

Neilson and other critics have commented on the notable consistency of Malouf's writing, particularly his fiction, which has steadfastly pursued the themes of self-realization and self-transformation, the meaning and place of Australia, the importance of personal histories, the beauty of the natural world, and the power of language and imagination. This consistency has resulted in widespread acclaim for Malouf. His novels have received numerous awards internationally, including the 1978 New South Wales Premier's Literary Award (for *An Imaginary Life*); the 1982 *The Age* Book of the Year Award (for *Fly Away Peter*); the 1985 Vance Palmer Prize for fiction and the Victorian Premier's Literary Award (for *Antipodes*); the 1991 Miles Franklin Award and the 1991 Commonwealth Prize (for *The Great World*); the 1993 New South Wales Premier's Literary Award, the 1994 Commonwealth Prize, the 1994 *Los Angeles Times* Book Prize, and the 1996 International IMPAC Dublin Literary Award (for *Remembering Babylon*); and a 2000 Lannan Literary Award (for *Dream Stuff*).

One of the few criticisms frequently leveled at Malouf's fiction is its scarcity of fully realized female characters. These characters are often powerful and threatening to men, yet their roles remain largely subsidiary. Most of Malouf's novels center on pairs of men whose evolving relationships govern the books. The lack of a viable father figure haunts many of his novels, forcing young men to look beyond their families for men to emulate. And as the critic Ivor Indyk notes, "the activities of men at war provide Malouf with opportunities to explore the intricacies of the masculine relationship, the comradeship, the mutual dependencies, the soaring excitement from risks taken and survived, the sharing of confidences" (p. 42).

In addition to fiction and poetry, Malouf has written theater and opera criticism for newspapers and magazines as well as libretti for the operas *Voss,* which was first performed in 1986 at the Adelaide Festival, and *Mer de Glace,* which opened in 1991 at the Sydney Opera House. He also has written essays that provide some useful background on his life and artistic aims. In "A First Place: The Mapping of a World," Malouf writes that he is interested in "how the elements of a place and our inner lives cross and illuminate one another, how we interpret space, and in so doing make our first maps of reality" (p. 261). His essay "12 Edmondstone Street" meditates on houses, particularly first houses, which he considers "the grounds of our first experience" (p. 8). He claims that "each house has its own topography, its own lore: negotiable borders, spaces open or closed" (p. 9). In the essay, Malouf explores his childhood house "room by room" to find "what it was that I first learned there about how high, how wide the world is, how one space opens into another" as well as "what kind of real-

ity I had been born into, that body of myths, beliefs, loyalties, anxieties, affections that shapes a life" (p. 12). Malouf views his childhood as "a little world of its own, to be mapped, explored, re-mapped, interpreted and made the repository of its own powerful mythology" (p. 8). And in his essay "The Kyogle Line," Malouf writes about a scene in which he sees Australians verbally abusing three Japanese prisoners of war at a train station. The scene reminds him of his Lebanese grandfather's experience of alienation in Australia; because he was not an Australian citizen, he technically became an "enemy combatant" during World War II because of Lebanon's standing in the war. His grandfather's experience and that of the Japanese prisoners of war cause Malouf to question the arbitrariness of nationality. The ideas of belonging, and thus of home and exile, are major themes in all his work.

Malouf's experience in England and Italy has given his work a European background unique in Australian literature. Neither an expatriate nor a tourist, he has learned about European culture and customs without cutting his ties to Australia. The critic Amanda Nettelbeck has observed that Malouf's fiction also demonstrates "a long-standing preoccupation with the nature of white Australia's relationship to its European source culture" (p. 5). Thus his work exhibits as much an affinity for European literature and culture as it does for Australian literature and culture, and his primary influences include Shakespeare, Goethe, Thomas Mann, Marcel Proust, and E. M. Forster as well as the Australian Patrick White.

The concept of nationality and individual identity emerge as major themes for Malouf. As Taylor points out, "predominant in Malouf's fiction is the urge to explore and challenge difference and boundaries" (p. 5). Malouf is interested in the margins of life—the remote, largely coastal Australia; individuals who fail to flourish in society. Various critics have commented on Malouf's pairings of Australia and Europe, center and periphery, human and animal. As the critic Martin Leer has observed, writing from "the edge" provides a useful vantage point because it allows one to see both the "outside world" and the "interior" (p. 10). For Leer, "the edge" in

Malouf's fiction "is where things happen; where sudden discoveries illuminate hidden memories; where revelations and metamorphoses occur" (p. 11). The edge also "is where our consciousness is at now" and "where all the intellectual and creative functions of our consciousness are performed" (p. 11). In an interview, Malouf himself has remarked on his interest in "the question of what is at the edge and what is at the centre and what you make of the space between" (p. 251).

POETRY

Malouf's first individual volume of poetry, *Bicycle and Other Poems,* appeared in 1970. The Australian poet Thomas Shapcott has described the poems in *Bicycle* as "grave meditations that are inventive, even surprising in their development" (p. 8). Malouf's abiding concerns in the book's thirty-seven short poems include the passage of time—particularly aging and childhood—and Australian identity. In "The Comforters" he observes, "The time comes at last / to quit old comforters, / tin drum and tantrum, / the worn teddy-bear / we lug into exile with us" (p. 14).

In these poems "years unloosen / their bonds and let me go" (p. 27), demonstrating again and again an obsession with time and the effects of time.

Malouf's early poetic influences include the Australian poet Kenneth Slessor, the British poet W. H. Auden, and the American poet Wallace Stevens. Tulip has written that Malouf's early poems demonstrate "control, hard analytical edges, and teem with concreteness of image and emotion" (p. x), and according to Shapcott, the voice of Malouf's early poems is "almost distressingly in control, and very precise in defining its interests and territories" (p. 4). Malouf's predominant mode in his poems is first-person narrative. Shapcott has also noted that "celebrative meditation" and "anecdotal imagery" (p. 1) appear in many of Malouf's poems.

"The Year of the Foxes," which Malouf considers "a touchstone poem" (p. 271), takes place during World War II, when the poet's mother tried to sell fox fur to "Brisbane ladies, rather / the worse for war" (p. 1). The women would arrive at the poet's house, wearing "a G.I. on their arm" (p. 1), which links the soldiers to the "old foxes, rusty-red like dried-up wounds" (p. 2) and thus connects sexuality and death. According to Malouf the poem "introduces a whole set of oppositions that is right at the center of almost everything I do"; these oppositions occur "between suburbs and wilderness; between the settled life and a nomadic life; between a metropolitan center and an edge; between places made and places that are unmakeable or not yet made; between the perceiver . . . and all sorts of things which are 'other'" (p. 272). Many of Malouf's early poems benefit from naturalistic detail.

But nature often serves as a metaphor, as when "Sheer Edge" shifts focus from the "sheer edge" of a cliff to "the edge of darkness" from which "words slide off" (p. 60). Landscape remains central to Malouf's poetry, but the idea of country—and thus identity and belonging—can complicate his admiration of the natural world. In "This Day, Under My Hand" he narrates the sale of a house purchased for him by his father. As he relinquishes his "foothold / on a continent" (p. 41) and his last concrete connection to Australia, he recognizes the centrality of Australia—its landscape, people, and history—to his work.

According to Tulip, the poems in Malouf's second book, *Neighbours in a Thicket* (1974), offer "more of a reflexive subconsciousness, freer and discursive, drawing upon cultural and literary sources, yet always personal at the point of address and insight" (p. xii). As the book's three major awards suggest, this is Malouf's strongest book of poetry to date. Consisting of poignant lyric narratives, the book's primary concerns—childhood, family, mortality, history, and Australian identity—resemble those in *Bicycle* but are handled with more depth and sophistication. Some poems also introduce a new topic: what Shapcott calls "a Europe of the mind [and] . . . of close observation" (p. 9).

Childhood experience drives one of Malouf's strongest poems, "Asphodel." The wildness of a lily pond appeals to the young poet and his friends but also nearly kills him as he steps "from clear skies ankle deep / into aeons of mud" and "the clamourous bottom of the night" (*Selected Poems, 1959–1989*, p. 33). Having coughed up his "belly's mud," the poet "discovered / a lifelong taste for earth" (p. 33). Like the rest of the city of Malouf's youth, the pond later becomes tamed and is drained. Now, he notes, "Earth holds firm under my heel" (p. 34).

Familial concerns establish the center of "Confessions of an Only Child," which Malouf has dedicated to his sister, two years younger. Although he writes, "we were seldom on speaking terms," the realization that "my afternoons in fact / were yours" and "the poems are also yours, and empty / without you" (*Selected Poems, 1959–1989*, p. 35) allows Malouf to look at a childhood photograph of them and admit, "we grow like one another . . . [and] might be twins at last, with nothing / between us" (p. 36). This exploration of family forms a strong connection between his poetry and his fiction, for all of Malouf's writing examines family structures.

Stemming from his time in Europe, poems such as "The Little Aeneid," "Among the Ruins," and "Eternal City" look outside Australia for their genesis. In "The Little Aeneid," Malouf describes Italy as "a coast where every promontory / glitters with artifacts" (*Selected Poems, 1959–1989*, p. 53). The conjunction of past and present in Italy convinces Malouf to live there. Other poems in *Neighbours in a Thicket* take place in Germany, France, and Austria, where, he writes in "Bad Dreams in Vienna," "bad dreams have monuments" (*Selected Poems, 1959–1989*, p. 63). But it is Italy that emerges as the imaginative and emotional center of the book. These poems move beyond the surface level of artistic tourism to find deep significance in the landscape, history, and people of these European countries.

This fascination with Europe, however, does not stop Malouf from writing about landscape unattached to nation. In "Stooping to Drink," for example, the poet focuses on a specific landscape but does not identify it. The poem seems more concerned with exploring an image than with describing a specific place. Similarly "Off the Map" literally moves beyond nationhood and explores images of a city at night.

First Things Last (1980) demonstrates Malouf's attraction to longer forms, especially the poetic sequence ("Preludes," "Elegy: The Absences," "Deception Bay," "The Crab Feast," and "First Things Last") and the prose poem ("The Ladders," "The Switch," and "Carpenter's Shed"). The book also includes a seven-page prose piece, "A Poor Man's Guide to Southern Tuscany," which resembles an abbreviated travel essay. As in his earlier poems, a sense of place becomes a major theme. In "Preludes," for example, he claims to be "at home wherever I am" (p. 6). Time also remains an important subject for him; in "Wild Lemons" he writes, "The present is always / with us, always open" (p. 1). In "Deception Bay" memory and time become water—"the balance / of salt against salt" (p. 22).

In an elegy for his parents, "Elegy: The Absences," Malouf focuses on the presence of the dead in the lives of the living: "The dead are buried in us. We dream them / as they dreamed us and woke and found us / flesh" (p. 78). because having to "make room" for someone entails preparing a space for their arrival, and thus their presence, Malouf's decision to make room for his mother's death implies that her death, like his father's, will remain inside him.

Malouf's later poems become increasingly philosophical and didactic. With titles like "The Elements of Geometry," "A Commentary on Galatians," "Guide to the Perplexed," and "Gray's Anatomy," he clearly seeks to instruct and educate in these poems. Other poems, such as "The Fables" and "Metamorphoses," allude to or are based on earlier texts. Some of these poems (particularly most of the new poems in *Selected Poems, 1959–1989*) take place in Italy. The centerpiece, "A Place in Tuscany," is a suite of seven poems set in the Italian region and dependent upon the years the poet spent there for their imagery and details.

Some of Malouf's later poems take place in unspecified landscapes and use landscape as a link to the spiritual. In "The Blue Apron" a chance detail provides Malouf an opportunity for an otherworldly connection. "Pentecostal" recalls the good Fridays of the poet's youth, when he had to eat "mullet, whiting, bream" (p. 129), "their boneless ghosts lodged in my throat" (p. 129). Through the poet's imagination, the fish become spiritual conduits. In "Vocation" making bread emerges as "a minor form of praying" (p. 131) as hands "invoke domestic saints that gravely / watch over a task" (p. 131). Domestic work allows "a task" to become "a gift" when "the angels [are] willing" (p. 131). "Aerial views" aptly sums up Malouf's reverence for landscape, regardless of its location. Though integral to Malouf's poetry, those "familiar small fabulous lives" take their most enduring form in his fiction.

JOHNNO

Malouf's first novel, *Johnno* (1975), is a portrait of the writer as a young man. Indyk has called *Johnno* "the most deliberately autobiographical of Malouf's fictional works" (p. 3) even though the writer/narrator is not the ostensible subject of the portrait. Indyk points out that although Dante's friend Johnno is the focus of the novel, "the controlling perspective is Dante's, and he charts his hero's progressively more erratic and obsessive behaviour with what is at times chilling detachment" (p. 2). By telling the story through Dante, Malouf signals the beginning of his own career as a fiction writer. His first effort at fiction was favorably received. According to tulip, *Johnno* revealed "a sophistication to the mind of the writer, an appealing self-consciousness, and a subtle awareness of the boundaries of autobiography and fiction having to be mutually crossed" (p. ix).

Johnno begins with a prologue that takes place immediately after the narrator's father—"a great sportsman in his day" (p. 1)—has died unexpectedly of a heart attack. Returning from studying in London, the narrator becomes responsible for cleaning out his parents' house because his mother no longer wants to live there. In his former bedroom he finds a photograph of the still-water livesaving team, to which he belonged as a boy. He sees "a small boy at the very edge of the picture" (p. 9) and slowly realizes that the boy, Johnno, does not belong there; he was not a member of the team. His presence in the picture

is "a joke with a time fuse" (p. 11) and propels the narrator into the novel.

Johnno is described as "the class madcap" (p. 13). Frequently playing practical jokes, gambling, shoplifting, and exasperating his teachers, he shows "no sense of responsibility, no school spirit, no loyalty to his country or to his House, no respect for anything" (p. 16). Other boys fear and revere him because of this recklessness. Nearly expelled from school twice, he is given special consideration because he is "a war child" (p. 19): his father disappeared during World War II. Although *Johnno* focuses primarily on the narrator's childhood friend, the war sets the stage—psychologically, politically, culturally—and the novel can be read as a book about two boys growing up in Brisbane during and after the war. For Dante the war has "a private and more sinister dimension" (p. 25) not portrayed in the news. When American troops arrive in Brisbane, establishing it as the center of their Pacific campaign, the war emerges as "quite an exciting affair" (p. 26) because it is no longer distant or dreamlike. After the war Brisbane seems like "a huge shanty-town, set down in the middle of nowhere" (p. 83). The position of the city in Dante's mind becomes a prominent theme in the novel: "Brisbane was nothing: a city that blew neither hot nor cold, a place where nothing happened, and where nothing ever would happen, because it had no soul" (p. 84).

Despite the chaos of war, Dante's mother maintains a life of "utterly reasonable" (p. 37) rules and rituals; rather than rebel against them, Dante embraces discipline, which he considers "character-building" (p. 38). At the same time, however, he secretly develops doubts about the Catholic Church, a sense of humor, a fondness for masturbation, and a skepticism about the correlation between outward appearance and moral fiber. He considers becoming a "rebel" (p. 39) like Johnno and gradually becomes friendly with him. But Johnno himself changes, becoming "a reformed character" (p. 46) whose turnaround confuses his classmates because they no longer can use him as a point of comparison: "If Johnno was not Johnno where did any of us stand?" (p. 47). Now studious, well-mannered, and athletic,

Johnno outgrows others' conceptions of him, ceasing to serve as "a marker" (p. 48) against which others can measure themselves and forcing them to examine themselves to see if a "commensurate change" (p. 48) has occurred.

Dante claims to have received his nickname from Johnno "at the very moment when I was most in doubt about who I was, or where I stood" (p. 49). In *Johnno,* according to Nettelbeck, Malouf demonstrates that "a sense of identity is not something intrinsic but is something drawn from a relationship to others . . . [and] to place" (p. 27); and because people and places change, individual identity remains open to change. Nettelbeck has also noted that for Johnno and Dante, "the boundaries which define the self . . . flex, shift and are crossed . . . because for each of them, self-definition comes from the shifting perception of himself in the other's eyes" (p. 20). Later Johnno becomes a hard-drinking, disillusioned university student who seeks to enlist Dante in his many escapades, such as visiting brothels. Throughout the novel, Malouf positions Johnno and Dante as opposites: Johnno breaks rules while Dante upholds them, Johnno despises the Australia that Dante comes to embrace, Johnno seeks a transient life while Dante strives for permanence. Dante serves as both a foil for Johnno and his only source of stability.

Johnno moves to the Congo to work at a copper mine for three years, then goes to Europe, by which time nearly everyone Dante knows in Brisbane has left. He remains in Brisbane because he fears that, elsewhere, "some false glamour might dazzle me out of my recognition of what was common and ordinary" (p. 109). He prefers a static life, in which all of his "prospects . . . shrivelled into nothing" (p. 110). Four years after Johnno has left Australia, Dante visits him in Paris, then moves to northern England to teach. Despite this change, Dante leads in England "a life as suburban and ordinary in its way as anything I might have settled for at home" (p. 127). After three years away from Brisbane he finds that others consider him an expatriate. This puzzles him: "Expatriate? What did it mean? Nothing it seemed to me" (p. 129). He feels that expatriation involves a conscious choice and that his passive approach to life precludes willfully

becoming an expatriate. While Dante works in England, Johnno moves around Europe, from Switzerland to Austria to Greece.

After four years in England, Dante returns to Brisbane, where he unexpectedly encounters Johnno, who has returned to Australia to work in the oil industry. Dante wonders "what sort of defeat of his expectation, what moment of panic, had brought [Johnno] back full-circle" (pp. 148–149). Both discover that the Brisbane of their youth has changed rapidly: the brothels have been closed, buildings have been razed to make room for parking lots, a freeway has been built along the river. The city is in the process of becoming "a minor metropolis" (p. 148). The changes compel Dante to reflect on aging:

It is a sobering thing, at just thirty, to have outlived the landmarks of our youth. And to have them go, not in some violent cataclysm, an act of God, or under the fury of bombardment, but in the quiet way of our generation: by council ordinance and by-law; through shady land deals; in the name of order, and progress, and in contempt . . . of all that is untidy and shabbily individual.

(p. 148)

At the end of the novel Johnno drowns in the Condamine River, a "ghost of a river for two seasons of the year" (p. 151). Dante consider Johnno's death "a suicide with some of the shocking randomness of accident" (p. 164), observing that his death "would have to confound us . . . to be a mystery, and of his own making" (p. 164). Here and elsewhere in the book Dante emerges as a curious narrator because he has not been particularly perceptive. His insights into Johnno's and his own behavior and nature are often flawed, or belated, such that he recognizes too late Johnno's deep feelings for him. Only after Johnno's death, as he looks at the photograph with Johnno in disguise, does Dante understand that "maybe, in the end, even the lies we tell define us. And better, some of them, than our most earnest attempts at the truth" (p. 170).

AN IMAGINARY LIFE

Malouf's second novel, *An Imaginary Life* (1978), imagines the exile and final days of the "anarchic" and "fun" (p. 26) Roman poet Ovid. The book occurs in 8 A.D. after Ovid has been exiled by Emperor Augustus from Rome to Tomis, a "degenerate outpost of Rome" (p. 135) on the Black Sea where the "relatively savage" (p. 23) Getic tribe lives. Tomis serves as a conceptual corollary to Australia, which was once viewed in Europe as "the limits of the known world" (p. 26) and which served as a place of exile. Tomis also represents a place where life "has been stripped to the simplest terms" (p. 16). Many critics view *An Imaginary Life* as a masterpiece. Neilson claims that it "breaks important new ground for Malouf, and gives the agencies of imagination and language a central position" (p. 42). And Indyk describes the novel as "one of the finest achievements of recent Australian fiction" because of its "poetic reach and intensity" (p. 47).

Ovid does not know the language of the tribe, and his initial inability to make his language mesh with his surroundings parallels that of the original Australian settlers. Malouf has explained in an interview that Ovid interested him because of the "problem of the poet who's exiled not just to a wild place, but beyond the bounds of the language he can use" (p. 294). With no one to talk to, the great poet has been reduced to "a crazy, comic old man, grotesque, tearful, who understands nothing, can say nothing" (p. 17). As Nettelbeck points out, "Language is crucial to Ovid as a means of bringing the world (or his sense of it) into being. Access to or denial of language is what creates for Ovid a sense of belonging or of exile" (p. 32). Being "essentially a social creature" (p. 25), Ovid considers his exile a kind of torture, deprived as he is of society and language, and he feels "dead" in this "region of silence" (p. 27).

While on a hunting trip with men from the village, Ovid sees a wild boy, "the Child," whom he recognizes from a vision in his childhood. The Child lingers in Ovid's mind for two years, until he encounters him during another hunting trip. The Child seems increasingly curious about the men, and Ovid believes he will return with them the following year. In the meantime Ovid begins to learn the villagers' language, which he finds "oddly moving" (p. 65) because it is "closer to the first principle of creation" (p. 65). His despondency gives way to enthusiasm: "I belong to this place now. I have made it mine" (p. 95).

The next year the men bring the Child back to the village. Approximately eleven years old, he acts like an animal: he crawls, hisses, howls, and twitches in his sleep. Tall and thin, his limbs and back are "lightly haired" (pp. 74–75), and despite frequent washing he never seems clean. Ovid seeks to "free him into some clearer body" (p. 77) through kindness, which entails isolating the Child from the villagers, especially the women, who have shown only hostility toward him. Eventually the Child seems curious about Ovid and the objects around him, showing "the stirring . . . of renewed life" (p. 80). While Ovid teaches the Child human language and other skills like threading a needle, the Child teaches Ovid how to imitate birds and other animals. Ovid's "final metamorphosis" (p. 96) occurs when he embraces the natural world rather than just observing it. He realizes that "the true language . . . is that speech in silence in which we first communicated, the Child and I" (p. 97), and he believes this language will open "the secrets of the universe" (p. 98) to him.

During the Child's first winter with Ovid they must move back with the family responsible for Ovid. The Child contracts a fever that lasts five days, and the family is convinced the illness is the manifestation of the struggle between the animal and the human in the Child. They fear that the animal will enter the boy in their own family, and when the boy also contracts the fever, Ovid fears for his and the Child's lives. The boy recovers, but then the head of the family becomes seriously ill and dies. Concerned about revenge, Ovid takes the Child and they leave the village during the funeral ceremonies, heading north into the steppes.

As they move past the fringes of civilization, Ovid observes that his fate is "always to be pushing out like this, beyond what I know cannot be the limits" (p. 135). Here Ovid entrusts himself to the Child, and thus to the natural world, following him to the Ister River (now the Danube), the border of the Roman Empire and "the final boundary" (p. 136) of his life. Crossing the river means leaving the empire, and thus civilization as Ovid has known it, for an unknown world. Once he arrives in this world, the dying process begins: "I am growing bodiless. I am turning into the landscape" (p. 145). This comforts him as he dies, since he knows he will "settle deep into the earth," becoming a part of nature, "continuous with earth" (p. 147). Nettelbeck argues that "the ending of *An Imaginary Life* gestures toward an imaginary space where the boundaries between speech and silence, centre and edge, origin and destination can be crossed and overcome" (p. 41). When Ovid finally finds "the point on the earth's surface where I disappear" (p. 150), he dies "immeasurably, unbearably happy" (p. 152).

FLY AWAY PETER

Fly Away Peter (1982) explicitly juxtaposes Europe and Australia via World War I. Ashley Crowther, a twenty-three-year-old Australian landowner educated in England, hires the twenty-year-old Jim Saddler to watch and record the birds in the swamp on his property, which he has designated "an observing place, a sanctuary" (p. 17). Jim comes from a working-class family with an abusive father; Ashley, "in all ways cultivated" (p. 8) as well as "dreamy . . . and excitably inarticulate" (p. 9), is an aesthete at heart. With his wealth, devotion to European culture, and class consciousness, Ashley emerges as the prototypical English gentleman. Yet his respect for Jim and dependence upon Jim's knowledge allow him to treat his employee as an individual. Despite their different backgrounds, they both respect the natural world and take Jim's role as caretaker seriously.

Jim's job is to note each bird he sees in "The Book," and he believes that "making a place for them there was giving them existence in another form" (p. 44). In this way his occupation resembles that of their friend Imogen Harcourt, a fifty-year-old nature photographer from England, who also gives birds "existence in another form" through photographs. Both Imogen and Jim focus on details, a contrast to Ashley's broader view of the world. In a pivotal scene in the book, Jim begins to see how Ashley views the world when he rides in a biplane above Ashley's land, discovering that his mental map of the area, though made at ground level, is accurate.

Their peaceful existence is interrupted by World War I, in which both men volunteer to fight. (Ashley's social position allows him to enter as an officer, whereas Jim serves as a common soldier.) The book's structure dramatizes the tension between the Old World (Europe) and the New World (Australia) by giving half of its space to each. Australia emerges as a kind of paradise, in which bird-watching can occupy one's days; Europe, on the other hand, becomes the site of a terrible war. Thus the idyllic Australian landscape is replaced by the infernal landscape of war-torn France, which is "unlike anything [Jim] had ever known or imagined" (p. 58). According to Indyk, Jim and Ashley encounter "a world remade, renamed," operating through "a perverse economy . . . geared to death and destruction" (p. 40); furthermore, "in a grotesque remaking of the fruitful swamp . . . , this landscape gives birth to corpses, teems with unburied, swollen, ransacked bodies, has as its ruling deity rats instead of birds" (p. 40).

Nothing Jim has learned in Australia prepares him for the war in Europe. Yet his knowledge of birds provides an escape from his current situation to a realm—the sky—that he knows. He feels reassured whenever he sees birds overhead because they allow him "to make a map in his head of how the parts of his life were connected, there and here, and to find his way back at times to a natural cycle of things that the birds still followed undisturbed" (p. 61). Of course the sky, unlike nations, acknowledges no borders, nor do the birds, which are unconstrained by national boundaries and politics. But on the ground, he fights not only the German army but the "stinking water" (p. 80) in the trenches, which soaks his clothing and equipment, causes cave-ins, and exhumes corpses. The war makes him feel "immeasurably old" (p. 100), and he fears that "the war, or something like it with a different name, would go on growing out from here till the whole earth was involved" (p. 102). Ultimately the birds he sees allow him to move "out of himself . . .

floating" as if watching the war from a bird's perspective: "he moved in one place and saw things from another, and saw too, from up there, in a grand sweep, the whole landscape through which he was moving" (p. 116). Immediately after this epiphany, Jim is killed. Back in Australia, Imogen mourns him: "What had torn at her breast in the fact of Jim's death had been the waste of it, all those days that had been gathered towards nothing but his senseless and brutal extinction" (p. 131). With his unromantic depiction of the war, Malouf does not idealize it or the soldiers; rather, he seeks to humanize the event and its participants. He presents modern war as an unnatural act, dependent upon technology and working against the best interests of the natural world, which operates according to regeneration and flux—a view symbolized by the birds and by Jim's final vision.

HARLAND'S HALF ACRE

Harland's Half Acre (1984) depicts Frank Harland growing from a farm boy into a renowned and eccentric painter. His life begins in Killarney on a small plot of family land, which once was considerable but has dwindled to practically nothing: "Possession was easy. One brief bloody encounter established the white man's power and it was soon made official with white man's law" (p. 3). But within twenty years the Harlands "had squandered most of what they earned and were reduced to day-labouring for others" (p. 3). The novel depicts Frank's lifelong efforts to reacquire the Harland land.

Frank's father Clem is "dreamy" (p. 3), "full of notions, all cloudily unreal" (p. 4), and obsessed with "the mystery of *himself*" (p. 5). A widower at the age of twenty-three with two young sons, he takes care of the boys by himself, allowing no one to help him until he eventually remarries. When his new wife becomes pregnant, Clem sends Frank to live with his sister. After Clem's second wife dies eight years later he decides the entire family should live together, and Frank returns to Killarney to live with his older brother, Jim, and his three younger half-brothers, Clyde, Tam, and Pearsall. Frank finds

"permanency" (p. 20) in this new world consisting of six males, but Jim, now fifteen, grows hostile toward his father and the household becomes tense because of his rages. The family is "beginning to fall apart" (p. 28), and Clem cannot hold them together, making Frank realize his father is "all self-indulgence and wistfulness" (p. 28). Meanwhile Frank has discovered a talent for drawing, gradually attaining "a state in which mind was suspended and his hand did the thinking for him" (p. 29). His primary subject is the Harlands' former land, and his life plan is "to win all this back some day and restore it, acre by acre, to its true possessors" (p. 31) as a gift to his father and brothers. His drawings serve as "reminder and inventory" as well as "a first act of repossession" (p. 31).

Frank must leave his family, become a hermit, embrace the natural world, and endure physical and economic hardship to achieve the self-knowledge and the vision that lead to great art. Neilson points out the irony here when he writes, "The art that Frank has fashioned on the periphery, and out of his oneness with the natural, has firmly established him in the culture of Australia, adjudicated and collected in the urban centres" (p. 147). Another irony lies in the fact that Frank must live in "lifelong solitude" (p. 41) to regain the land for his family. His financial difficulties require that he work "with small means" (p. 45); he paints on boxes and newspapers, often using house paint, because he cannot afford proper supplies. Despite his difficulties, Frank flourishes as an artist. His brothers, however, do not adapt well to life outside the family: Jim disappears during the war, Clyde commits suicide, Pearsall becomes a derelict, and Tam becomes an overly sensitive radical.

Nearly half of the novel is narrated by Phil Vernon, who meets Frank while living with his grandparents and parents in Southport, the town where Frank has established his studio. Twelve years old at the time, Phil accompanies his father to Frank's studio—a condemned theater on a pier—and feels inextricably and mysteriously connected to Frank when he recognizes the woman in one of his paintings. Afterward Frank becomes a frequent dinner guest and awkward fixture in the household. After Phil's grandfather dies and he returns with his parents to Brisbane, he does not see Frank for ten years. During that time Frank experiences an artistic breakthrough when the deaths of two of his friends splatter blood on one of his paintings: Frank is "frighteningly dazzled by the possibilities, as if, without his knowing it, his own hand had broken through to something that was searingly alive, savage, triumphant, and stood witness at last to all terror and beauty" (p. 126).

A decade later Phil reencounters Frank. Now a law student, Phil becomes Frank's closest confidant, and Frank enlists him in helping with his business transactions, primarily land purchases. Their dealings always have an "aspect of conflict and drama" (p. 154); Phil is "variously puzzled, rewarded, exasperated, moved, amused, drawn deep into his world, then roughly pushed off again, dazzled by the largeness of his vision and brought up hard against some pettiness in him, some small-minded fear or superstition, that in no way fitted the boldness and scope of his thinking or the nobility of his dreams" (p. 155). Phil becomes "a sharer in his passion, an agent in the achieving of an ambition to which he had already devoted more than half his life" (p. 156).

Frank spends his final years on an island near Brisbane, where he lives in a tent in "almost complete isolation" (p. 186). He becomes "a household word" (p. 221), and Phil, as his lawyer, becomes Frank's "custodian and gatekeeper . . . to a storehouse of fragile, unpredictable, spasmodically brilliant occasions" (p. 189)—Frank's paintings. Frank remains on the island until his death, which happens after he falls and breaks his hip; by the time he is found, he has nearly died from exposure. He dies in the helicopter that arrives to take him to the hospital. At a posthumous retrospective, Phil claims that

> seeing the pictures unpacked from their cases and hung at last in the big white-walled rooms, I was astonished by their number, by how much space he had covered in the fifty years of his working life, how many square-yards of canvas, sheets of newsprint, sides of cartons and strips of board; and what sweeps of the imagination he had made that

had carried his intense encounters with a few square inches of the world into a dimension that could no longer be named or fixed at a particular latitude, . . . or in any decade.

(p. 222)

By the end of his life, Frank had painted enough canvases to cover half an acre and repurchase the Harland land.

THE GREAT WORLD

The Great World (1990) traces the lives of two Australian men—Digger Keen and Vic Curran—from their childhood in the 1930s to their experience as prisoners of war in World War II to the stock market crash of the 1980s. The novel progresses achronologically through a series of flashbacks that alternate between Digger's and Vic's perspectives. In the present, Digger and Vic are in their sixties; the scenes from the past occur during their childhood, adolescence, young adulthood, and middle age. According to Neilson, "The main characters spend much of their time in introspection and analysis of one another, while the narrative presents them as centres of consciousness in a complex network of speculation upon such abstractions as time, space, language, the animal, memory and fate" (p. 167). Indyk sees Malouf's "epic ambition" in the novel as a source of weakness, because the form "imposes considerable strain on Malouf's technique" (p. 91). But other critics, such as Vince Passaro, see the novel's accumulative use of vignettes as a source of power.

The Great World opens with "simple" Jenny Keen, an elderly store owner on a dead-end road near a river. Jenny is fiercely devoted to her older brother Digger, who is frequently visited by Vic. Because of Jenny's mental limitations, she feels threatened by Digger's introspective nature and by Vic's visits. Digger and Jenny live alone at Keen's Crossing, a defunct ferry crossing, because their mother, Marge, insisted on settling there in order to force their father, Billy, to accept stability and establish order in their lives. But Billy, a veteran of World War I, resents his wife and volunteers for World War II and, later, the Korean War, never returning home. Marge dies after World War II, leaving Keen's Crossing to Digger and Jenny. Digger remains attached to Keen's Crossing even after the ferry crossing is rendered obsolete by a nearby bridge; thus, as Neilson points out, Digger takes "imaginative possession of the land," which allows him to "mythologis[e] his own part of Australia" (p. 199). This fidelity mirrors that of his mother, who was fiercely committed to establishing a permanent home for her family.

Because Vic has grown up poor, and sometimes homeless, due to his father's alcoholism, he is determined to "make his own life, not just pick up what was passed on to him" (p. 74). Vic's mother dies when he is ten years old, then his father is killed in a drunken brawl the following year. Vic is adopted by Captain Warrender, who is listed as Vic's guardian in his father's will. Vic becomes extremely loyal to Mr. Warrender, his wife, and two daughters (Lucille, with whom he falls in love as a teenager, and the younger Ellie). Because the Warrenders own a soap factory, Vic lives comfortably for the first time in his life, until he enlists in the war. During the war Mrs. Warrender takes over managing the factory and makes it highly profitable.

Captured by the Japanese soon after the war begins, Digger and Vic are forced into manual labor in Malaya and Thailand, where they can no longer rely on "their unquestionable superiority as white men" (p. 152). Overworked and underfed, many soldiers become extremely ill—with cholera, malaria, dysentery, beriberi, or blood poisoning. Vic and Digger both fall ill, and each takes care of the other, giving rise to "a relationship that was so full of intimate and no longer shameful revelations that they lost all sense of difference" (p. 134). Digger and Vic are prisoners of war for three-and-a-half years, existing in a kind of limbo, as neither casualties nor heroes.

After the war Digger returns to Australia, living in the Kings Cross area of Sydney and working as a bouncer at a club. Having missed the social rituals of young adulthood, both Vic and Digger feel emotionally vulnerable in postwar Australia. But Digger finds peace in his love for Iris, the sister of a deceased soldier friend, while

Vic drifts until he eventually returns to the Warrenders. Shortly thereafter Vic marries Ellie and discovers in himself an uncanny business sense; working with his mother-in-law, he quickly becomes wealthy. But he remains unfulfilled, and like his own father, Vic fails to become a true father to his son Greg, thus figuratively orphaning his son with his emotional incapacity.

Because he returns to Keen's Crossing to live with Jenny and his mother, visiting Iris every week for twenty-six years, Digger is sure of his place in the world. But Vic needs confirmation from others, and his central question becomes "What does it mean to *be* except *to be known?*" (p. 287). As a result, he grows dependent on Digger, because being with Digger instills in him "a great calmness" (p 206). At times Vic internalizes the hardships of being a prisoner of war and feels resentful at having lost four years of his life. For him the war represents an unforgivable "injustice" that he considers "absolute" (p. 297) because an "especially precious," youthful "possibility had been killed in him then" (p. 298). Vic dies of a heart attack on his way to visit Digger, whom he saw increasingly in the final months of his life out of a need for Digger's equanimity. For Digger the war "had been one time of his life among others; a time, simply, that had laid hard responsibilities on him, but ones that were too deeply ingrained in his nature now for regret" (p. 297). Digger's peace of mind ultimately stems from his realization that "Every moment was dense with causes, possibilities, consequences; too many, even in the simplest case, to grasp. Every moment was dense too with lives, all crossing and interconnecting or exerting pressure on one another . . ." (p. 296). This outlook, Malouf implies, is essential if one is to grasp and live in "the great world."

REMEMBERING BABYLON

Remembering Babylon (1993) takes place in nineteenth-century Queensland, when settlements were being established and most of the land was mysterious to the settlers. The colonial setting allows Malouf to impose a contemporary postcolonial viewpoint onto an integral part of Australia's history. Part of the novel's postcolonialism emerges in its construction. According to Neilson, the plot of *Remembering Babylon* is "unpredictable" (p. 201), and the structure itself is "fragmented, combining lyrical sections with portions of historical saga" (p. 202). He argues that "such inconclusiveness and fragmentation support the post-colonial theme in the novel by failing to provide neat and reassuring verities about colonial settlement and the growth of the nation" (p. 202).

The novel opens with three children—the twelve-year-old Lachlan Beattie and his two female cousins—playing near the fence at the edge of their isolated settlement. A white man with "the mangy, half-starved look of a black" (p. 3) appears from the unknown territory beyond the settlement. Lachlan takes charge of the situation, pretending that the stick in his hand is a gun, and the man falls for the illusion, hopping onto the fence that separates the settlement from the area beyond and shouting, in English, "Do not shoot. . . . I am a B-b-british object!" (p. 3), confusing subject for object and inadvertently objectifying himself.

The settlement is bordered by a swamp, which is "forbidden" territory (p. 2), "the abode of everything savage and fearsome" (p. 3). The fence on the edge of the settlement is a borderline, much like the River Ister in *An Imaginary Life*. By balancing on the fence before falling into the settlement, the man, Gemmy, momentarily straddles the two worlds. The critic Claudia Egerer has observed that the novel "dramatizes Gemmy's position on the margins of two cultures" (p. 141) and that "on the one hand, Gemmy serves as a reminder that while the village may be their home, they are not *at home* in it; on the other, Gemmy raises the spectre of what the unknown country might do to them" (p. 146). Therefore he immediately becomes a controversial figure in the settlement.

Gemmy lives with the McIvors, the family of the children who found him. In exchange for food and shelter he helps the father, Jock, on the farm. The children, who feel "a proprietary right" (p. 34) to Gemmy, develop a special relationship with him: by giving in to their whims, he falls

under their protection. Because of the courage he showed when he first saw Gemmy, Lachlan becomes Gemmy's particular focus. Like others in the settlement, Jock feels anxious about Gemmy, partly because he does not want to lose his standing in the community; but he tries to be patient and accepting because of the feelings of his family. This contrasts with the "open hostility" (p. 37) Gemmy encounters off the McIvors' farm, where he is considered "a parody of a white man" (p. 39). The novel raises the question of what constitutes whiteness and thus racial identity. Originally from England, Gemmy had been thrown from a ship while sick sixteen years earlier and had been living in the north country with Aborigines. He had arrived as a similarly puzzling intruder in the Aborigines' lives when he washed up onto the shore and was found by a "mob of naked women and gleaming, big-eyed children" (p. 22). With his talent for mimicry, he quickly learned their language, losing his former language—English—in the process.

Gemmy therefore "started out white" (p. 40), but after living with Aborigines, his racial identity has become a mystery. He has lost the English language, his facial features seem non-European, he smells different, and he has "jerking and stammering fits" (p. 39). He also serves as a physical manifestation of the settlers' fear of Aborigines—"It was the monstrous strangeness and unwelcome likeness that made Gemmy Fairley so disturbing to them, since at any moment he could show either one face or the other" (p. 43)—as well as a reminder that the land the settlers have taken originally belonged to someone else. Their fear stems, in part, from guilt. Gemmy represents different things to different people in the settlement. To the McIvor family, he is at first a curiosity, then an object under their care. To the minister of the settlement, he represents a European who has learned to adapt to the Australian landscape rather than try to bend the land to his will. To the schoolmaster George Abbot, he demonstrates sheer endurance. To the rest of the settlement, Gemmy represents the threat of the uncivilized and the possibility of losing one's language and place in the world. Neilson sees Gemmy's "symbolic force" in his being "a subversive, postcolonial figure, a hybrid who combines both indigenous and European perspectives and knowledge" (p. 202).

When two Aborigines visit Gemmy at the McIvors' farm, the settlers' distrust increases, forcing Jock to choose his family over his neighbors. By trusting Gemmy, he draws closer to his family and farther apart from everyone else. A "wave of panic and suspicion" (p. 113) in the settlement leads to violence: three of the McIvors' geese are killed, a shed that Gemmy was repairing is smeared with human excrement, and Gemmy is attacked and nearly drowned. In order to protect Gemmy and themselves, the McIvors move him to a house outside the settlement. Although life in the settlement returns to normal, the McIvors feel shaken by their neighbors' acts of cruelty and remain distant from them. Gemmy eventually returns to the Aborigines, and colonial Australia continues to develop according to British laws. Nine years later Lachlan is working in northern Queensland as a road surveyor for the government when he hears that Gemmy might have been killed, with other Aborigines, by a group of cattle owners. Fifty years later Lachlan has become a minister of the Crown, and his cousin Janet has become a nun and beekeeper. In old age they realize that through Gemmy they are "inextricably joined and would always be" (p. 197). Thus their compassion and generosity allow a potentially divisive presence to unite them throughout their lives.

THE CONVERSATIONS AT CURLOW CREEK

The Conversations at Curlow Creek (1996) explores the idea of home and the forces of fate and coincidence by placing two Irishmen together in a hut in Australia in 1827 the night before one of them is to be executed. Michael Adair, a trooper who has arrived to supervise the execution, spends the night with Daniel Carney, a member of a gang of rebels, or "bushrangers," accused of inciting Aborigines to rebel against colonists. Carney's death is "announced" and "certain" (p. 4), and after receiving a beating from one of the troopers, he seems hardly hu-

man—"an agglomeration of rags with its knees drawn up" (p. 1)—when Adair arrives. During the course of the night Carney asks Adair questions about fate and forgiveness, which often startle Adair because "they went straight to the centre of his own thoughts, his own confusions, as if this illiterate fellow had somehow dipped into the dark of his head and drawn up the very questions he had chosen not to find words for" (p. 28).

While waiting with Carney, Adair thinks of his childhood. Orphaned by the death of his parents, both of whom were professional opera singers, he is adopted by a childhood friend of his mother, who is the matron of a large and decaying estate. His parents had lived "very much like gypsies, carefree and, except in the exercise of their art, entirely without discipline" (p. 36). "Torn between an obsessive fastidiousness and a fascination . . . with dirt" (p. 36), Adair constantly fights the lack of discipline within himself. Although others see "doggedness" and "sternness of manner" (p. 35) in him, he sees in himself "laxity, a tendency to dreamy confusion and a pleasure too in giving himself up to it, a dampness of soul for which he had a kind of hopeless scorn" (p. 35). Always aware that his place in the world depends on the goodwill of others, Adair feels "a need to be of service, to be necessary" (p. 40).

When Adair's foster mother gives birth to her own child, Fergus, she refuses to openly love the baby because she had lost all of her other children as infants. Being young, Adair has no such fear, and he becomes Fergus's closest companion, a combination of brother, father, mother, and nurse, "expert in the recognition of all his needs" (p. 49). Later, when Adair goes to a neighbor's house for tutoring, he meets Virgilia, a confident and intelligent girl with whom he grows up and falls in love. But the spirited Virgilia eventually falls in love with Fergus, whose own impetuousness, rebelliousness, and generosity contrast with Adair's caution and "horror of disorder" (p. 35). Yet Adair remains hopeful through the entire novel, believing that Virgilia's "vulnerability" will lead her to recognize in him "her only peace, her only safety" (p. 79) and hoping that "she would see at last that her passion for Fergus could have no outcome, and that it was he, who had always loved her and stayed patiently close . . . who was her natural partner" (p. 152). Fergus, however, directs his attentions outward, to the poor and unfortunate who live nearby. Receiving no guidance or discipline, he carouses with young men and women of all social classes, helping families whose fathers have been sent to prison in Australia.

At nineteen Adair leaves the family to become a soldier, eventually working in Australia at Virgilia's request to track down Fergus, who is rumored to have moved there. Here the novel alludes to a nineteenth-century ballad about the Wild Colonial Boy, the Irishman Jack Dolan, who moves to Australia to take from the rich and give to the poor and is eventually killed. Adair believes that the leader of Carney's gang, Dolan, is really Fergus. Although he never finds Fergus or Dolan, Adair feels Fergus's presence—"a shadow thrown on the heart" (p. 181)—between Carney and himself. But Fergus does not emerge as the focus or destination of the novel; instead, Adair assumes the central role, using Carney as a way to connect with Fergus, who in turn connects Adair to Virgilia. In Australia, Adair frequently writes to Virgilia, finding solace and "deepest privacy" (p. 160) in the act of writing; he also finds "a new means of wooing" as well as "a more eloquent, more perceptive, more passionate self" (p. 160) when he writes.

At the end of the novel Adair prepares to return to Ireland, where he will "appear before [Virgilia] untrammelled and without intermediaries, in his own form, as himself; the new self that something in this harsh land and the events of those last months have created; a self that has journeyed into the underworld and come back both more surely itself and changed" (pp. 211–212). He also will arrive in Ireland as a legend, for the final scene with Carney, in which he allows Carney to bathe in a stream before his execution, has been transformed into rumor: Adair, it has been told, allowed Carney to escape and went with him to join the rebels. Although false, the story reveals another facet of Adair, who would have preferred to set Carney free

rather than follow the rule of law. By simultaneously offering the "real" Adair and the legendary Adair, Malouf acknowledges the permeability of the membrane between reality and imagination—a membrane that all of his work has enriched through the powers of language and imagination.

Selected Bibliography

WORKS OF DAVID MALOUF

NOVELS AND NOVELLAS
Johnno. St. Lucia, Australia: University of Queensland Press, 1975.
An Imaginary Life. London: Chatto and Windus, 1978; New York: Braziller, 1978.
Child's Play, with Eustace and The Prowler. London: Chatto and Windus, 1982.
Fly Away Peter. London: Chatto and Windus, 1982.
Harland's Half Acre. London: Chatto and Windus, 1984; New York: Knopf, 1984.
The Great World. London: Chatto and Windus, 1990; New York: Pantheon, 1990.
Remembering Babylon. London: Chatto and Windus, 1993; New York: Pantheon, 1993.
The Conversations at Curlow Creek. London: Chatto and Windus, 1996; New York, Pantheon, 1996.

SHORT FICTION
Antipodes. London: Chatto and Windus, 1985.
Dream Stuff. New York: Pantheon, 2000.

POETRY
Bicycle and Other Poems. St. Lucia, Australia: University of Queensland Press, 1970.
Neighbours in a Thicket. St. Lucia, Australia: University of Queensland Press, 1974; 2nd ed., 1980.
Poems 1975–76. Sydney: Prism, 1976.
The Year of the Foxes and Other Poems. New York: Braziller, 1979.
First Things Last. St. Lucia, Australia, 1980; London: Chatto and Windus, 1981.
Selected Poems. Sydney: Angus and Robertson, 1981.
Selected Poems. Pymble, Australia: Angus and Robertson, 1991.

Selected Poems, 1959–1989. St. Lucia, Australia: University of Queensland Press, 1992; London: Chatto and Windus, 1994.

NONFICTION

12 Edmondstone Street. London: Chatto and Windus, 1985.

Untold Tales. Sydney: Paper Bark Press, 1999.

COLLECTED WORKS

Tulip, James, ed. *David Malouf: Johnno, Short Stories, Poems, Essays, and Interviews.* St. Lucia, Australia: University of Queensland Press, 1990.

DRAMA AND OPERA LIBRETTI

Blood Relations. Sydney: Currency Press, 1988.

Voss. With Richard Meale. Based on a novel by Patrick White. First performance 1986, Adelaide Festival.

Mer de Glace. With Richard Meale. First performance 1991, Sydney Opera House.

Baa Baa Black Sheep: A Jungle Tale. With Michael Berkeley. London: Chatto and Windus, 1993.

MISCELLANEOUS PROSE

"The Making of Literature." *Overland* 106:5–6 (March 1987).

"A Personal, Multi-cultural Biography." *Australian Studies* 5:73–80 (1990).

"Space, Writing and Historical Identity." With Paul Carter. *Thesis Eleven* 22 (1989).

"A Traveller's Tale." *Meanjin* 41 (1982).

AS EDITOR

Gesture of a Hand. Artarmon, Australia: Holt, Rinehart & Winston, 1975.

New Currents in Australian Writing. With Katharine Brisbane and R F. Brissenden. London and Sydney: Angus & Robertson, 1978.

CRITICAL AND BIOGRAPHICAL STUDIES

Ashcroft, Bill. "The Return of the Native: *An Imaginary Life* and *Remembering Babylon.*" *Commonwealth Essays and Studies* 16, no. 2:51–60 (1993).

Attar, Samar. "A Lost Dimension: The Immigrant's Experience in the Work of David Malouf." *Australian Literary Studies* 13, no. 3:308–321 (1988).

Buckridge, Patrick. "Colonial Strategies in the Writing of David Malouf." *Kunapipi* 8, no. 3:48–58 (1986).

Craven, Peter. "Crooked Versions of Art: The Novels of David Malouf." *Scripsi* 3, no. 1:99–126 (1985).

Egerer, Claudia. "Unhomely Lives and Homefulness in Malouf's *An Imaginary Life* and *Remembering Babylon.*" In her *Fictions of (In)Betweenness.* Göteborg, Sweden: Acta Universitatis Gothoburgensis, 1997.

Hansson, Karin. *Sheer Edge: Aspects of Identity in David Malouf's Writing.* Lund, Sweden: Lundus, 1991.

Hergenhan, Laurie. "Discoveries and Transformations: Aspects of David Malouf's Work." *Australian Literary Studies* 11, no. 3:328–341 (1984).

Indyk, Ivor. *David Malouf.* Melbourne and New York: Oxford University Press, 1993.

Knox-Shaw, Peter. "Malouf's Epic and the Unravelling of a National Stereotype." *Journal of Commonwealth Literature* 26, no. 1:79–100 (1991).

Laigle, Genevieve. "Approaching Prayer, Knowledge, One Another: David Malouf's *Remembering Babylon.*" *Commonwealth Essays and Studies* 18, no. 1:78–91 (1995).

Leer, Martin. "At the Edge: Geography and the Imagination in the Work of David Malouf." *Australian Literary Studies* 12, no. 1:3–21 (1985).

Lindsay, Ellen, and John Murray. "'Whether This Is Jerusalem or Babylon We Know Not': National Self-Discovery in *Remembering Babylon.*" *Southerly* 57, no. 4 (1997–1998).

Neilson, Philip. *Imagined Lives: A Study of David Malouf.* St. Lucia, Australia: University of Queensland Press, 1996.

Nettlebeck, Amanda. *Reading David Malouf.* Sydney: Sydney University Press, 1995.

Pierce, Peter. "David Malouf's Fiction." *Meanjin* 41, no. 4:225–233 (September 1982).

Spinks, Lee. "Allegory, Space, Colonialism: *Remembering Babylon* and the Production of Colonial History." *Australian Literary Studies* 17, no. 2:166–174 (1995).

Taylor, Andrew. "Origin, Identity, and the Body in David Malouf's Fiction." *Australian Literary Studies* 19, no. 1 (1999).

Whittick, Sheila. "Excavating Historical Guilt and Moral Failure in *Remembering Babylon:* An Exploration of the Faultlines in White Australian Identity." *Commonwealth Essays and Studies* 19, no. 2 (1997).

INTERVIEWS

Baker, Candida. In *Yacker: Australian Writers Talk About Their Work.* Sydney: Pan Books, 1986.

Copeland, Julie. *Australian Literary Studies* 10, no. 4 (1982).

Davidson, Jim. "Interview with David Malouf." *Meanjin* 39, no. 3:323–334 (1980).

Fabre, Michel. "Roots and Imaginations." *Commonwealth Essays and Studies* 4:59–67 (1979–1980).

Kavanagh, Paul. *Southerly* 46, no. 3:247–259 (1986).

Ondaatje, Michael. "A Conversation with David Malouf." *Brick* 47:50–58 (1993).

Tipping, Richard Kelly. "An Interview with David Malouf." *Southerly* 49, no. 3:492–502 (1989).

Turcotte, Gerry. In *Writers in Action.* Sydney: Currency Press, 1990.

Willbanks, Ray. *Antipodes* 4, no. 1:13–18 (spring 1990).

MARTIN McDONAGH

(1971—)

Kimberly Lewis

MARTIN MCDONAGH'S FIRST play, *The Beauty Queen of Leenane,* premiered at the Town Hall Theatre in Galway on February 1, 1996. The play went on to London's Royal Court Theatre and to the Walter Kerr Theater in New York, earning the new playwright numerous awards and the privileged recognition of instant success. Since then McDonagh has gone from rising star to permanent presence in British theater, adding five other plays of comparable acclaim to his name. These include the second two plays in *The Leenane Trilogy: A Skull in Connemara* (1997) and *The Lonesome West* (1997). They emerged shortly after his first success along with *The Cripple of Inishmaan* (1996), making McDonagh the first playwright since Shakespeare to have four plays on stage in London at the same time. The *Lieutenant of Inishmore* was produced in 2001 to critical and popular praise, and *The Pillowman* (2003) continued the trend. Still evolving, the resident playwright at the Royal National Theatre in London promises new surprises to come not only for the stage but also, if he has his way, for the cinema.

LIFE

The label of Anglo-Irish playwright takes on a slightly new meaning when applied to McDonagh, as reviewers including his perhaps most attentive reader, Fintan O'Toole, have often pointed out. McDonagh was born in London to working-class Irish parents in 1971, and he grew up in Elephant and Castle surrounded by other Irish expatriates. He returned every summer to his father's native Galway and his mother's native Sligo, but despite this McDonagh seems to consider himself something of an outsider to Ireland. When his parents moved back to Letter-mullan in Connemara, he and his brother opted to remain in London, though continuing to make frequent trips to the western Ireland that would become the setting for five of his six plays to date.

At a distance, then, from the modern everyday reality of Ireland, McDonagh found himself attracted to the storytelling potential offered by the land and its artistic heritage, but more importantly he was fascinated by the possibilities of a way of speaking that he found there. In a rarely granted interview with O'Toole, published on April 26, 1997, in the *Irish Times,* McDonagh explains that it was in an attempt to distinguish his voice from the American and English literature and cinema he so admired that he had rediscovered the theatrical possibilities of the structure and rhythm with which his Irish relatives spoke. Their way of speaking, the English of rural western Ireland, is the unvaried language of all the characters of his plays to date with the exception of *The Pillowman.* This unique voice, which brought McDonagh such instant praise, has also contributed to critical accusations of two-dimensionality in characters whose voices cannot be distinguished from one another. In addition, reaction to the plays indicates that they benefit greatly from a cast of all Irish actors, as the unique and rapid exchanges don't lend themselves well to less than adept pronunciation.

Nevertheless, it is McDonagh's talent for dialogue that most distinguishes his work, and his uniquely black and violent plots rest on verbal exchanges that are colorful, rapid, clever, and at times hilarious. If his harsher critics sometimes dwell on possible inauthenticities in McDonagh's reproduction of the speech of western Ireland's lower class, he seems unbothered. His overriding concern, as becomes clear in *The Pillowman,* is with what such a way of speaking might contribute to the art of storytelling. He is interested in the creation of a play that will entertain, not in the purely mimetic re-creation of either a political or linguistic reality. *The Pillowman,* which departs from both the language and the land of Ireland, seems to indicate that even without the accent of his ancestors, McDonagh's dialogues will continue to keep the attention of reader and spectator alike.

Artistic rather than sentimental motivations first led McDonagh to write about Ireland, but it was not admiration for the art and experience of theater that drew him to write plays. He claims to have spent the ten years between dropping out of high school at sixteen and fantastic success at twenty-six watching films and television, writing, and eating junk food. Living with his brother John, also an aspiring writer, McDonagh was finally forced for a short time to take a job as a civil servant. A self-declared slacker, virulently opposed to such regular employment, McDonagh resolved, with seemingly unflagging confidence, to make a career out of writing. He decided to try his hand at theater only after numerous rejections of his stories and of his radio plays, twenty or so of which were rejected by the BBC. Even now McDonagh says that he has relatively seldom attended plays that were not his own, finding the theater generally dull, and he is quite certain, it seems to most journalists who have spoken to him, that he is just the person to spice it up. It thus comes as no surprise that among his greatest influences he is most likely to cite such film directors as Quentin Tarantino, Martin Scorsese, John Woo, and David Lynch, and if he does speak of his theatrical influences it is usually of such cinematic playwrights as David Mamet and Sam Shepard.

It also comes as no surprise that McDonagh has acquired something of a cultured bad-boy image. The most notorious tale from his days as a newcomer to the world of British theater involves a verbally violent confrontation with Sean Connery at the 1996 *Evening Standard* Awards, where he was named the Most Promising New Playwright. Having arrived with his brother in an apparently inebriated state, the two began loudly to mock the queen, which initiated a rather unpleasant exchange with an unimpressed Connery. The fame of such petty incidents, however, is probably due as much to McDonagh's reluctance to play for too long in the spotlight as it is to any subversive or confrontational nature. Journalists have described him somewhere between confident and arrogant, nonchalant about his rapid rise toward the top of contemporary British theater; in an article in the December 1, 1996 *Observer,* Michael Coveney somewhat mockingly cites McDonagh's comparison of himself to young Orson Welles. This willingness to declare his own genius, however, is usually accompanied by a wink of irony. The playwright is in fact quite solitary and quite serious about the writing to which he has devoted most of his time, both before and after the success of *The Beauty Queen.*

Like his slacker confidence, McDonagh's lack of intimate knowledge of the theater might have been exaggerated. Despite his affinity for the cinema over the stage, McDonagh is clearly well acquainted—if only through his extensive reading—with modern British and American theater. Along with his admiration for Mamet and Shepard, critics cite the influence of the metaphysical absurdity of Samuel Beckett's theater and of Sean O'Casey's unromanticized portrayals of nationalistic violence. They also frequently note the echoes of the frantic confusion of Joe Orton's farcical comedies. Moving beyond general similarities, McDonagh's plays often seem to engage in quite specific dialogues with works from the past such as John Millington Synge's *The Playboy of the Western World,* Thomas Murphy's *Bailegangaire,* and Harold Pinter's *One for the Road.* The variations, developments, contradictions, and questions that such direct connections entail allow for a greater understanding not only of McDonagh's relationship to Ireland and his Irish past but also of the vision he advances of twenty-first-century theater. We must first, however, look at his plays.

THE LEENANE TRILOGY

The February 1996 debut of the first play of the yet unknown Martin McDonagh was directed by

Garry Hynes, who would take the production to London shortly after and to New York in late 1997. Collecting numerous awards in those three countries including four Tonys, *The Beauty Queen of Leenane* received nearly unanimously good reviews of both play and production. McDonagh wrote the play in just over a week, and at the time of its opening he had already completed the trilogy that also includes *A Skull in Connemara* and *The Lonesome West*. The plays are set in Leenane, a small town in Connemara, County Galway, that rather seems to have received little more from the twentieth century than a few appliances, some packaged snack foods, and Australian television programs. Although each play focuses on different main characters, the police officer, Tom Hanlon and the priest, Father Welsh, appear or are mentioned in all three plays, developing as characters more fully in the later two. The trilogy is held together not only by the plays' common setting and characters, however, but also by the quick, harsh dialogue and unwavering tone. In each, McDonagh's alternation between violence and silly Hollywood sentimentality, along with the absurd stupidity that he manages to lay over characters who are also devious and criminal, create a black comedy out of each tragic story.

The first play takes place in the home of the lonely, middle-aged Maureen, who cares for her nagging, infirm mother, Mag Folan. Maureen wants nothing more than to leave Leenane on the arm of a strong and handsome husband, and Pato Dooley, an Irish expatriate living in England who has returned to Leenane for a short trip before moving to America, is her best chance. Early on the characters fall into the easy categories of bitter spinster and senile mother, but as the play progresses the physical cruelty of Maureen and the psychological ruthlessness of Mag become increasingly shocking. When Mag burns a letter from Pato to Maureen in order to keep Maureen from leaving with him, Maureen burns her (onstage) with boiling oil. By the end of the next scene we understand that Maureen will not leave Mag in order to run to the station to meet Pato— she has killed her instead.

With the death of Mag, however, the seeming reality of the play wavers. The last scene takes place after Pato has left (without Maureen) and after Mag's funeral. Maureen is speaking with Ray Dooley—an ominous fireplace poker lurking always nearby—as they bicker over biscuits and a stolen tennis ball and as Ray tells her that Pato is getting married to an American girl. With one incidental detail, however, McDonagh throws Maureen's reality, which has been the reality of the play throughout, into question. Pato didn't leave from the station. He left in a taxi, and yet Maureen remembers seeing him at the station. Perhaps Mag lied to Maureen, and Pato never asked her to join him at all? Was Maureen unable to accept his rejection, or perhaps unable to resign herself to having missed the chance to depart with him because of Mag's delay? Either way, she has become, in Ray's words, a "fecking loon" and on top of it has become the spitting image of her mother. "The exact fecking image of your mother you are, sitting there pegging orders and forgetting me name!" (p. 83) Ray shouts as he leaves, and the play ends with Maureen rocking and listening to music. A song by the Chieftans is followed by Delia Murphy's appropriate "The Spinning Wheel," a song of a maiden who slips away from her work and her sleeping grandmother to meet her lover outside. Maureen seems willing to live in a dream, or at least incapable of fully understanding reality.

The reality of television, the "reality" of the stage, the vision of Maureen, the vision of the audience, ideas about places and the reality of places—all begin to blur in this play. Interestingly, Leenane is not far from the set of John Ford's 1952 film *The Quiet Man,* about an Irish American (played by John Wayne) who returns to the pastoral and slightly primitive bliss of a small town in western Ireland and a sassy, small-town Irish woman. Where, then, is the real Ireland? On the television or at the movies? Out the window or on the stage? Does the playwright have any responsibility to seek it out? What are the comical consequences of conceptions built by television, cinema, and by the spotty influence of that modern world on the still somewhat premodern towns of McDonagh's plays? It is a theme that will recur in his first four works.

In the next play in the trilogy, *A Skull in Connemara* (which takes its title from a line in Beckett's 1953 play *Waiting for Godot*,) McDonagh makes this exploration of truth and reality, and the question of morality, even more central to the witty exchanges of his characters. Here Mick Dowd must complete his yearly task of digging up bones to make room in the church graveyard, but this year he will have to dig up the remains of his own wife, Oona. Amid the humorous exchanges that occur between Mick, Mary, and Mairtin Hanlon around the destination of the bones is the suggestion that the death of Mick's wife in a car crash wasn't, in fact, an accident. Soon insinuations become accusations, and the usual task of space making in the graveyard has the secondary benefit of offering an opportunity for Mick, Mairtin, and the police guard Thomas Hanlon to exchange insults and dredge up the rumors of Mick's crime. The graveyard scene, a funny and macabre evocation of Shakespeare's gravediggers, is full of jokes, superstitions, and absurdities around the subject of skulls and dead bodies that veers as close to slapstick as it does to horror.

Scene 3 opens on Mairtin and Mick back in the kitchen surrounded by the bones that they have dug up, a few bottles of poteen, and a couple of mallets. McDonagh here raises the level of disrespect to the dead to such a level that even the most nonreligious member of the audience can do little but cringe and laugh. We learn that Mick's wife's body was missing from the grave, and bickering now about this mystery as well as over Mick's supposed guilt, the two men continue to smash skulls throughout the scene, eventually to the music of "All Kinds of Everything" by Dana (with the appropriate refrain "all kinds of everything remind me of you"). When Mairtin mentions a locket that was buried along with Mick's wife, however, Mick becomes serious. Thus it comes as no surprise in scene 4 when Mick returns to the house covered in blood, and when Thomas Hanlon shows up with his wife's cracked skull, Mick confesses not to her murder but to Mairtin's. For a moment the play teeters

on being serious, but soon the bloody and grinning Mairtin saunters in. As he has remained unaware of Mick's intentions, Mick is off the hook again.

In addition to playing with the story versus the reality of Oona's death, the play addresses the difference between representation, stereotypes, and reality. This time it is not only the cinematic image of Ireland that is overturned but Thomas Hanlon's television image of cops and criminals. So concerned with police dramas like *Hill Street Blues* and the less-esteemed *McMillan and Wife*, Hanlon not only doesn't see the crime in front of him (when Mick has supposedly killed Mairtin) but he has even dug up and cracked Oona's skull himself and then batters Mairtin later on for revealing this. Despite the efforts and insinuations of many, however, no murder seems to have occurred before or during this play, and thus McDonagh ends up able to mock not only Thomas Hanlon but the television shows that influence him, the detective story expectations of his audience, and the violent nature of this "innocent" Irish small town.

The curtain closes on the sentimental gesture of Mick rubbing the skull against his cheek and kissing it. The final dialogue is an almost touching discussion between the two old friends, Mick and Mary, in which Mick denies once again having killed his wife intentionally. This ending is one of the more pronounced examples of the almost banal but nevertheless welcome sentimentality with which McDonagh spatters these works that are otherwise so devoid of normal human emotion, especially between family members. McDonagh's characters so explode our notions of propriety, taboo, and familial interaction that we breathe a sigh of queasy relief when the suspected murderer shows even this macabre sign of affection for his dead wife.

We see other examples of this sentimentality in *The Lonesome West*, first in an exaggerated and farcical version between the feuding brothers, Coleman and Valene. The brothers fight over objects, over alcohol and money, but such disputes have begun as the result of a dark pact between them: Valene has agreed not to report his brother's killing of their father in return for

Coleman's portion of the inheritance. The latter has begun to resent the arrangement.

Father Welsh, who has been mentioned in the previous two plays but never seen, attempts to reconcile the brothers. Welsh (frequently called Father Walsh by the characters who, keep forgetting his name) is the softest and most morally grounded character of the trilogy. He is also, however, devastated by the state of things in Leenane and by his lack of influence over its violent and uncaring inhabitants.

An exchange with with Valene about the state of the town plagues Father Welsh, until Tom Hanlon's suicide and the truth about Coleman's murdered father send him over the edge. He drowns himself in the same lake as Tom, despite the touching and quite genuine efforts of Girleen, the beautiful and harsh catch of the town, to express her affection for him. Before committing suicide, he writes a comically sentimental last letter to Coleman and Valene pleading for their reconciliation.

Even as this play is the most farcical of the trilogy, Welsh's earnest and ingenuous letter along with Girleen's genuine despair at his death make it the most overtly sentimental as well. These gestures offer a glimpse into the sadness that awaits those who, like Father Welsh, "take things too much to heart." In spite of the trite and simple words in which Girleen and Father Welsh express their seriousness, the audience cannot help but sympathize with them even as all will soon be laughing at Coleman and Valene's continued bickering. Even the brothers, however, are touched, and though their peace is precarious at best, the play ends with Valene unable to burn Welsh's letter. If Mick's final kiss in *A Skull* left the audience with no certainty about the crimes of the past, then Valene's final gesture leaves no certainty about crimes to come. With both gestures, however, McDonagh offers us a sigh of relief, a final vision of peace and relative innocence in the present tense.

In the ruthless mix of violence and dripping sentimentality that characterize *The Leenane Trilogy,* McDonagh establishes a new voice not only in Anglo-Irish theater but in international theater as a whole. His plays do, however, interact in quite specific ways with those of his Irish predecessors, and the singularity of McDonagh's theater emerges more starkly in the comparison.

CONVERSATIONS THROUGH TIME

The playwright that is most often mentioned alongside McDonagh is John Millington Synge, and the play which the work of the former seems to most often recall is *The Playboy of the Western World.* Though born in Dublin, Synge left Ireland to study in Germany and France only to travel to the Aran Islands at the suggestion of W. B. Yeats, who felt that Synge, like McDonagh nearly a century later, might find expression in the life of the people of western Ireland. Thus Synge approached the land of his most famous play as an outsider, and like McDonagh he was fascinated with the linguistic creativity that his newfound setting offered. First performed in 1907 at the Abbey Theatre in Dublin, Synge's portrayal in *Playboy* of violent, hypocritical, superstitious, drunk, and lustful Irish people caused riots in a population that had just begun to relish the creation of a national theater. He was accused of harboring bitterness toward the Irish people, especially toward the rural poor who inhabited the ballads and the pastoral dramas of his contemporaries.

The play presents Christopher Mahon, a young man who has fled his homestead believing that he has killed his father and who arrives exhausted and filthy in a rural town of County Mayo. There he finds himself, to his apparent disbelief, the object of the attentions of all of the women in sight, including Pegeen, who immediately falls in love with the savage and poetic man she believes Christy to be. Soon, however, Old Mahon turns up still very much alive, expounding upon a quite different version of Christy as the weak and vain idiot whose cowardice led him to attempt to kill his own father and whose ineptitude caused him to fail even at that. In an attempt to prove that his newfound strength is not just an act, Christy attempts to kill Old Mahon once again. In the brief period during which all believe that he has finally succeeded, however, Christy discovers that the heroic reputation he had acquired in telling his early tale cannot be reclaimed through action. As Pegeen puts it, before taking her part in his condemnation to death, "I'll say, a strange man is a marvel, with his mighty talk; but what's a squabble in your back-yard, and the blow of a loy, have taught me that there's a great gap between a gallous story and a dirty deed." (p. 81). Luckily for Christy, Old Mahon has once again survived his death blow to the head, and he departs with bitter glee, leaving Pegeen to lament her lonely fate.

Playboy is a clear predecessor not only to Mc-Donagh's *The Lonesome West* (which takes its title from a line in the play) but to the entire *Leenane Trilogy.* In McDonagh's world, however, violence against a family member is neither heroic nor particularly reprehensible either in stories or in reality—the line between the truth and the tales is never drawn, and such violence is a possibility to which all have become accustomed. Both Maureen of *The Beauty Queen of Leenane* and Coleman of *The Lonesome West* are guilty of killing a parent, and while the question of their guilt arises often in banter and bickering, no one except Father Welsh seems particularly shocked, and only Tom Hanlon self-ishly and clumsily attempts to uncover the truth. They both commit suicide when thwarted. The characters in *A Skull in Connemara,* who suspect Mick of having killed his wife, are similarly complacent. In addition, when Mick finally does commit murder, he is saved from the hands of justice when the victim, Mairtin, saunters in with a crack down his head much like Synge's car-toonish Old Mahon. Very real violence thus remains a fiction, a legend, or a rumor in the minds of McDonagh's characters, who feel neither the desire nor the obligation to uncover the truth in order to draw a distinction between a dirty deed and a gallous story. It is not until *The Pillowman* that McDonagh's characters deal with this distinction as explicitly as Synge's Pegeen, and *The Leenane Trilogy* leaves even the audience vaguely unconcerned with the "real" psychological or moral position of the characters.

Like Synge's play, the plays of *The Leenane Trilogy* present the audience with an inseparable weaving of tragedy and comedy. McDonagh leaves his audience in a state of guilty amuse-ment, laughing at stories that, behind the comic dialogue, are tragic, and would be anything but funny should they cross over from gallous story to reality. The effect is not unlike that produced by the cartoonish violence of Tarantino's *Reservoir Dogs* (1992) or his script for Oliver Stone's *Natural Born Killers* (1994), the connection to which is even more apparent in the bloodbath of *The Lieutenant of Inishmore.* McDonagh's emphasis, unlike Synge's in *The Playboy,* is not on questioning the rather hypocritical manifesta-tions of religious morality in his characters but rather on presenting the absence of any moral system at all in both his creations and, perhaps, in his audience. Tragic tales of the underclass, like violence, have become a norm that barely disturbs the consciousness of the audience.

Many years after Synge's controversial por-trayal of the "real" Irish people, McDonagh has been occasionally accused of similarly harsh treatment of a class and disloyalty to people among whom he is a relative outsider, a summer tourist. Like his predecessor in antipastoral, non-romanticized Irish theater, he seeks, it seems, to overturn and to twist the pastoral vision of Ireland's most Irish west that persisted in theater and cinema even after Synge had succeeded in just such a reversal at the start of the twentieth century. McDonagh denies any desire to belittle the people upon whom his characters are based—he is concerned with the telling of a good story and little else. He also feels no militant connection to Ireland and no obligation to promote one vision or another of the country in his work. He does, however, despise all displays of nationalism, and this does lead to the only play so far in McDonagh's body of work that might be considered truly politically controversial with respect to Ireland, *The Lieutenant of Inishmore.* Nationalism and the violence commit-ted in its name are as nonsensical to McDonagh as its portrayal in that play, which enters political debate because of its very refusal to take Irish nationalism seriously.

McDonagh's first four plays, however, avoid such near-direct involvement in both current Irish politics and in social commentary. McDonagh refuses the sentimentality and hard realism of what was known in British theater of the 1960s as "kitchen-sink drama." These were plays that portrayed the reality of the everyday hardships and violence of the working class, their relationships and social difficulties. It is a type of theater that Thomas Murphy continued to develop. His 1984 play *Bailegangaire* is the main but not the only work of Murphy's that critics relate to McDonagh's first trilogy and, more specifically, to *The Beauty Queen of Leenane*. The comparison reveals the extent to which McDonagh overturns the social and political value of such "kitchen-sink" realism, even going so far as to do so metaphorically—the kitchen sink around which much of the drama unfolds smells like urine, and the violence of *The Lonesome West* takes place not only in but to the kitchen.

Murphy's play takes place in the kitchen of Mary and Mommo. Mary is a middle-aged spinster, educated and once quite independent, who has come back to her small town in order to take care of her babbling and sickly mother. Stifled, bored, frustrated, lonely, and all but unrecognized by her mother, Mary struggles with a desire to depart once again. Her sister Dolly, married, gallivanting, and all-too fertile, is Mary's polar opposite in all but unhappiness. The play is an often incommunicative dialogue between the sisters that occurs against the babble of Mommo's incessant retelling of a tale from the past that never reaches its end. This dialogue borders on the comical, but it mainly serves to deepen the spectator's or reader's understanding of the characters, of their complicated relationships to one another. While both Mommo's tale and the discussion of the sisters are laced with violent fantasies, half-memories and insinuations, none of this violence ever fully reaches the light of reality, and the obscured but very real love that exists between the characters remains at the center of the play. In the end their affection and need for one another seems to soothe the dissatisfaction and relieve the suffocation from which none of the three women seems capable of escaping.

This is quite the opposite of *The Beauty Queen*, in which McDonagh has adopted the confined setting and the general outline of the story of Mary and Mommo but with some important changes. The violence has become quite real, as Maureen burns her mother with hot oil onstage, proving that, as Mag has complained, she has been torturing the elderly woman for ages. Familial affection remains all but nonexistent in the play, and human need (both Mag's for Maureen and Maureen's for a man) is clutching, violent, selfish, and left perpetually unsatisfied. In typical McDonagh style, the escalation of Maureen's violence is accompanied by an even greater escalation of comedy, as Murphy's chaotic but revealing dialogue has been replaced by McDonagh's obscuring wit, which steers clear of the profoundly psychological. Perhaps we no longer need the author to explain character psychology in tales with which we are familiar, the tragedy of which has worn thin, the reality of which we no longer wish to consider entertaining. Most critics seem to appreciate the novelty of McDonagh's adaptation, but a few resent the emptiness that is the final result. This may account for the opinion of critics like Breandán Delap (in Bolger, ed.), who found that the translation of the play into Irish and the consequent elimination of much of the play's skittish and empty humor was a great improvement.

McDonagh's "kitchen sink" realism veers into the postmodern in more ways than one. Fintan O'Toole, in his introduction to the trilogy, describes the sinister undertones of everyday banality in the plays, in which the 1950s seem to have been laid over the 1990s with the disorienting effect of what he describes as a superimposed photograph. Actual news events from the 1990s (such as allusions to church abuse, Bosnia, and current Irish politics) appear in the dialogue alongside the timeless stories of small-town characters. In addition, the usual postmodern blend of kitsch and high art is present. Sitcom humor exists in Shakespeare's graveyard. Nods to Synge and Beckett are followed by winks at popular television shows, soap-opera dramas, and pop music. As John Waters points out in "The Irish Mummy: The Plays and Purpose of Martin McDonagh" (in Bolger, ed.), the playwright's stories themselves are comparable to traditional ballads gone punk in the music of the Pogues. Waters, however, objects to the use of the term "postmodern." Rather, he believes that McDonagh captures modern Irish reality, itself a mix of present and past tense, enthusiasm for the future and nostalgia for the past.

McDonagh's realism, however, is rather distorted. The objects of his plays, those background elements of realism-like Valene's stove and figurines, Mag's Complan (a brand of nutritional supplement), and the Taytos and various brands of biscuits—refuse to remain incidental details in a more important psychological drama. Instead characters spend more time discussing and debating them than they do addressing the murders and mayhem around them. Offering many occasions for laughter, this rather unsubtle commentary on the empty materialism of modern society allows not only the characters but also the audience to forgo analysis in favor of dwelling on the "real" details and disputes of everyday life.

Such exaggeration, however, according to some readers of McDonagh, creates a distance between the audience and these cartoon characters that allows the spectators to disassociate themselves from the materialism and violence that is in fact a very real part of our modern world. Vic Merriman (whose "Settling for More: Excess and Success in Contemporary Irish Theatre" is also included in Bolger's volume), compares the effect of McDonagh's caricatures to that created by shows like Jerry Springer's. We laugh at the white-trash antics of these characters, and we simultaneously revel in our own civilized and more ethical order. We turn to the theater for pure entertainment, not to question ourselves and the world around us. Merriman is not alone in his criticism of McDonagh's lack of genuine social commentary and of the false sense of relief from responsibility that his farcical portrayal of a poor, violent, rural world provides to his primarily wealthy, urban spectators. Despite the overall critical applause for McDonagh's trilogy and for the plays that followed, not everyone rejoices in seeing what they perceive as theater's renunciation of a serious political and social role, relegating itself to the realm of storytelling and entertainment. The first two plays of his still incomplete *Aran Trilogy* allow this debate to continue.

THE CRIPPLE OF INISHMAAN *AND* THE LIEUTENANT OF INISHMORE

With *The Cripple of Inishmaan* (1996), McDonagh begins to reveal his ability to tell a story that creates interest and laughter that are not necessarily accompanied by horror and guilt. Billy, or Cripple Billy as the other characters call him, is a rather broken version of a dreamer. Reading most of the time, or off watching the cows (though he later says that this isn't much fun), Billy has an intelligence that no other McDonagh character has possessed. The play centers around his trip to Inishmore to get involved in a film that some Americans are filming there (and that once again vaguely recalls Ford's *The Quiet Man,* though the play is set in 1934, well before the film was made). Billy departs, leaving his worried aunts Eileen and Kate, having managed to convince Babbybobby to take him along by telling him a rather clever lie—he claims to be dying of TB, the disease that killed Bobby's wife. Billy then continues on to America, leaving his fellow characters to imagine that he has died there, only to return to Inishmaan a few months later, happy to be back. Unsurprisingly, he discovers that he really does have TB, and this time his only desire is to spend time with Helen, who is almost the same character as the beautiful and sharp-tongued Girleen. The play ends on a sentimental but happy note when she agrees to be seen with him and even expresses a bit of affection. Overall, the jokes in the play involve a usual slew of drunk mammy references and relatively gentle mocking of each character by the others. It passes over into the realm of genuine cruelty or farcical insult that characterized *The Leenane Trilogy* only in a few of the cripple comments that Helen makes to Billy.

For the first time in a McDonagh play, each character is clearly defined and falls more or less within the realm of normal. Kate and Eileen are old, rather unintelligent but caring aunts. Johnnypateenmike is the town storyteller—a bit of a con man and certainly a gossip. Helen is hard on the edges but soft enough on the inside, and she eventually admits something that one might like to think is the guiding idea behind many of McDonagh's earlier characters: "I do have to be so violent, or if I'm not to be taken advantage of anyways I have to be so violent" (p. 105). Bobby is a similar mix, being kind and generous enough to fall for Billy's story but also violent enough to beat him badly for it later. Finally there is the tragic and yet heroic Billy. The other townspeople attempt incessantly to understand whether Inishmaan is a place to want to be or a place to escape, often reassuring themselves with the simple idea that if foreigners come, it can't be that bad. Billy is the only one who, despite his physical disabilities, is able to escape Inishmaan and return willingly, with at least a partial understanding both of what lies beyond and of what lies within.

McDonagh's consistently unique talent for dialogue works well in this rather conventional story with these rather traditional characters. In their exchanges they reveal an unconscious awareness of a theme that goes beyond the particular story of Billy. "We have only what you see," Eileen repeats over and over at the start of scene 2, as Bartley wistfully repeats his requests for new American candies. The truth, however, is that Eileen has the very candies that Bartley wants, but she and Kate have kept them for themselves. It seems perhaps to be an insignificant detail, but the entire play is filled with minor examples of the idea that what you see isn't exactly all that is there. Billy deceives Babbybobby about his disease, but he is in turn mistaken when he believes that Bobby will easily understand and forgive him. Helen puts forth a mean and violent front, but in fact she is sweet and generous to Billy and Bartley. The town can't imagine that Billy could be wanted by the American filmmaker, but even as they do in fact need a cripple, they decide they'd rather have a good actor playing a cripple than a real cripple who can't act.

Finally, the story of the death of Billy's parents, told repeatedly in various ways, always involves deceit of some kind. After passing through many versions, Billy is led to believe that his parents killed themselves in order to get him the insurance money that would pay for the medical treatment of his illness. Johnnypateenmike, who tells true stories for selfish reasons throughout the play, has invented this story for the unselfish reason of making Billy feel better. Not only is he so unexpectedly kind as to do this, but in the true telling of the same tale, Johnny also saved Billy from drowning when his reprehensible parents had tried to do away with him and stole from them the money for their son's hospital treatment.

Thus, in spite of Billy's imminent death, the play ends much less tragically than any of the early works of McDonagh, with the realization that all of the characters are essentially good, simple people. The cinematic violence of *The Leenane Trilogy* has given way to an almost realistic portrayal of life in a small town, tied to the 1930s only by the candy brand names and by a brief discussion of a famous German man with an indecisive mustache. The initial productions of the play were successful in Britain and elsewhere, opening at the Royal National Theatre in December 1996. Particularly in New York, however, where it played at the Joseph Papp Public Theater in March 1998, McDonagh's fourth play was much less critically acclaimed than *The Beauty Queen of Leenane,* which was onstage at the same time at the Walter Kerr. Performances and production were the main subjects of criticism, but reviewers saw the play itself as quaint and mediocre compared to the shocking novelty that the earlier play had offered. The work is nevertheless proof that McDonagh can move beyond violence and cartoon humor, as he does again in *The Pillowman.*

Before *The Pillowman,* however, comes *The Lieutenant of Inishmore.* McDonagh's goriest and most violent, farcical, and political play to date is set primarily in Inishmore in 1993. It was written in 1994, before splinter groups gained importance alongside the Irish Republican Army (IRA) but was first performed in London in April 2001 when peace talks were underway. The play was put on by the Royal Shakespeare Company at the Other Place Theatre, Stratford-upon-Avon, after being rejected for production by the National and the Royal Court Theatres. Like all of McDonagh's plays, *The Lieutenant* received fairly good reviews all around, but it did give rise to more debate about whether or not any of his work can be said to have any serious message or content that goes beyond pure entertainment.

The basic plot of the play is that the rabid patriot Padraic, founder of a splinter group of the Irish National Liberation Army (INLA, itself a split-off of the IRA) comes home to Inishmore to avenge the death of his cat, Wee Thomas. Believing that his cat has been run over by the bicycle of his father Donny's friend Davey, Padraic sets out to kill them both, only to discover that the cat was in fact killed by Christy and a group of INLA members who have tired of his antics. As they are about to kill Padraic, Mairead, an aspiring patriotic rebel, in love with Padraic since childhood, rescues him and helps him to kill the INLA crew. The two force Donny and Davey, who have been spared as Davey is now Padraic's brother-in-law-to-be, to begin chopping up the bodies of the victims (onstage). When Mairead finds her own cat dead in the midst of the rest of the gore (Donny and Davey had attempted to find a Wee Thomas look-alike, which had been killed by the perceptive Padraic), she too succumbs to her loyalty to cats by killing Padraic. Mairead exits singing "The Dying Rebel"—ironic, in that it is a song sung by a father at the death of his patriotic son—and Donny seems less than grief-stricken at the death of Padraic. The final entrance of the play is that of Wee Thomas—the dead cat was in fact just a look-alike. The events have been not only horrific but entirely gratuitous.

Critics have compared this play not only to the work of Tarantino and other obvious cinematic predecessors but also to the tradition of the Grand Guignol theater. This Parisian theater dominated the territory of onstage violence from the early twentieth century to the early 1960s, horrifying and entertaining audiences with grisly and macabre crime dramas and bawdy sex farces. The onstage effects that McDonagh's play require are comparable, including the torture of James by Padraic in scene 2, the exploding of a cat onstage, the chopping up of bodies throughout the last scene, and the death of Padraic at the end.

Such onstage events, along with the need to acquire a well-disciplined cat, make this play the most difficult of McDonagh's works to stage.

McDonagh seems to have left behind any real notion of development of character or story in favor of a farcical bloodbath that mocks either nothing at all or all violence in general. Most critics, such as Sean O'Hagan of the *Guardian* and Penelope Dening of the *Irish Times,* emphasize the antiviolence stand of McDonagh's play, speaking of both his nonviolent anarchy and his pacifist rage. The play does, however, continue a trend of violence that is as much highbrow entertainment as it is a political statement. Norma Jenckes advances this idea in an *Irish Times* article in which she describes the reemergence of onstage violence in serious theater, pointing out that violence had departed from the serious when the Grand Guignol took hold but that it has returned in recent years to the British and the international stage. It is unclear then, whether the playwright wished to shake up the theater world artistically or politically, but all seem to agree that he intended to cause a stir. McDonagh himself, however, focuses on the political. He expresses disgust with both nationalism and the crimes committed in its name, and he declares, in the same Dening article, that with *The Lieutenant* he aimed at being something of the Irish Salman Rushdie.

The play's connection to McDonagh's earlier plays is clear, but the parallels are more limited than between his first four works. Mairead is an exaggerated version of McDonagh's other female characters: violent, defensive, cruel, and strong, she also has a softer side that comes out when Padraic promises her his love. Like Billy, she has a fascination with the cows of Inishmore, but she prefers shooting out their eyes to looking at them. Padraic is ready to kill his father (like Coleman before him), but his nonsensical and self-righteous defense of the homeland and its people (he tortures James for selling marijuana to children) is without precedent. Compared to the first trilogy, the first two plays of *The Aran Trilogy* are not alike in tone, content, or characters. The quaint human drama of the first play, set almost sixty years earlier, has little in common with the modern plot and cartoon antics of the second. It remains to be seen what the third play, *The Banshees of Inisheer,* will add to the mix, perhaps clarifying whether or not the parts of the trilogy have anything in common besides geography.

THE PILLOWMAN

First performed on November 13, 2003, at the Cottesloe auditorium of the National Theatre in London, *The Pillowman* gathered mainly praise, starting with the 2004 Lawrence Olivier Award for best new play. McDonagh submitted a first version of the play to the Soho Theatre's Verity Bargate Award in 1995, thus classifying the play as one of many that the author has kept, waiting for the chance to revise it and see it onstage. In addition to acclaim for the play itself, the performances of actors Jim Broadbent and David Tennant in the roles of the two main characters, Tupolski and Katurian, were highly acclaimed. A few critics complained of the length of the play, and a few, including Charles Spenser of the *Daily Telegraph,* embarked upon the usual criticisms of McDonagh's empty and gratuitous violence. Most, however, found much to discuss and little to criticize.

The play is the story of Katurian Katurian, a rather unsuccessful writer who has been arrested by the police and is in the midst of an interrogation for reasons that remain unclear for the duration of the first scene. It is the first released McDonagh play not to be set in Ireland–Katurian is the helpless inhabitant of some seemingly totalitarian state, which will execute him for his crimes without trial or defense. The comparison to Franz Kafka is inevitable, though the dialogue is comical enough to border on creating a farce of an interrogation in a totalitarian state (or to recall the torture scene between James and Padraic in *The Lieutenant of Inishmore.*) "This feels like school, somehow," Katurian says. "Mm," Tupolski replies. "Except at school they didn't execute you at the end. Unless you went to a really fucking tough school" (p. 20).

The comparison to Harold Pinter's play *One for the Road* (1984) is also inevitable. In that very short play an intellectual named Nicholas is held for interrogation by the police of a totalitarian state. His wife is tortured and raped and his son is killed before the police release him. His crime is never quite known, though it has something to do with his intellectual opposition to the governing powers. The beginning of *The Pillowman* seems at first like a comical elaboration of Pinter's piece, as Katurian's mentally handicapped older brother is also being held and reportedly tortured in the next room. McDonagh quickly brings the play into his own territory, however, and the story behind Katurian's imprisonment gradually unravels. His interrogators, Topolski and Ariel, also eventually become too human, too personally revealed, to fall neatly into the category of servants of a nameless, faceless, and ruthless regime.

Katurian's offense is related to the short stories that he has been writing for years, which are horrific and often involve children in their violence. The tales that will be important to the rest of the play are read out loud: An abused girl tricks her father into swallowing carved apples filled with razor blades. A caged man remains unaware of his crime (which is written outside the cage), and a passing highwayman who has freed the other prisoners kills the confused criminal out of disgust for that unknown offense. A boy shares a sandwich with a sinister stranger, who cuts off the boy's toes before leaving, but as Katurian explains, the stranger is a version of the Pied Piper who has in fact saved the boy by crippling him. These gruesome tales, filled with images from the stories of classic folktales and the stories of the Brothers Grimm, reveal that McDonagh (and his character Katurian) has been influenced perhaps as much by a tradition of fairy tales and horror stories as he has by the cinematic and cartoon violence that are their contemporary manifestation. Katurian intermittently defends his right to write such stories, blaming first those who might misinterpret them and then those who might be sick enough to carry them out for any crimes that might result. Synge's theme of the difference between a gallous story and a dirty deed lurks behind Katurian's justifications. The stories have been carried out, however, and not by just anyone. His brother Michal has confessed to their enactment, which has resulted in the death of possibly three children.

The plot thickens in the second scene. In it, Katurian reenacts the story "The Writer and the Writer's Brother," which we are later assured is based on his own childhood. His parents made him the subject of an experiment, lavishing him with affection while abusing an invisible brother always within earshot, in order to see if such contradictions and imagined horrors would give birth to a great writer. Katurian snapped, killing his parents and freeing his brother, but their ploy in a sense succeeds. Katurian writes fantastic stories, so compelling that he becomes something of a Pied Piper himself, leading his brother into inhabiting his imaginings. The play takes on the narrative complications and mirror images of a Jorge Luis Borges story with this scene, as the story of "The Writer," Katurian, is being created as it is told, as it is enacted onstage. Likewise Katurian's stories are like confessions of acts committed by his confused brother. Michal, who, having lived through the horrifying reality of being the "Writer's Brother," sees little difference between reality and fiction.

The first scene of act 2 brings a conversation between the brothers, Michal's admission of guilt, and two more stories. First, and most important for obvious reasons, is Katurian's story of "The Pillowman," a creature made of pillows that convinces children who are destined to lead unhappy lives to kill themselves before they have a chance to grow up. His is the merciful persuasion behind the deaths of many children. As such, when one day a pillow boy mercifully sets him ablaze, his dying vision is not of all the children that he helped to kill but of all the ones he will no longer help to kill, who will go on to lead miserable lives and die miserable deaths as adults. The Pillowman is the hero of Michal, who, despite his faulty reasoning, makes a few pessimistic but serious points to his brother:

> Michal: I mean, you're my brother and I love you, but, y'know, you've just spent twenty minutes telling me a story about a bloke, his main thing in life's to get a bunch of little kids to, at minimum, set themselves on fire, so, y'know? And he's the

hero! And I'm not criticising. He's a very good character. He's a very very good character. He reminds me a lot of me.

> Katurian: How does he remind you of you?

> Michal: You know, getting little children to die. All that.

> Katurian: The Pillowman never killed anybody, Michal. And all the children that died were going to lead horrible lives anyway.

> Michal: You're right, all children are going to lead horrible lives. You might as well save them the hassle.

> Katurian: Not all children are going to lead horrible lives.

> Michal: Erm, hmm. Did *you* lead a horrible life since you was a child? Yes. Erm, did *I* lead a horrible life since I was a child? Yes. That's two out of two for a start.

(p. 52)

It is Katurian, however, who will fully embrace the symbolism and the title of "The Pillowman," stifling his brother with a pillow just as he had his parents, presumably to save him from the horror of execution.

The second story is that of "The Little Green Pig . . . ," made fun of for being green unlike all of the other pigs. The farmer finally paints him pink, and when a strange storm pours green paint over all the other pigs, his special pink paint sticks. "And as he looked at the strange sea of green pigs that lay around him, most of which were crying like babies, he smiled, and he thanked goodness, and he thanked God, because he knew that he was still, and he always would be, just a little bit peculiar" (pp. 66–67). A more conventional fairy tale for children, it is one of a very small number of nonviolent stories in Katurian's portfolio.

Before Katurian kills him, Michal confesses that yet a third story, "The Little Jesus," is the script for his final killing. The next scene is the enactment of that story, in which a little miracle-performing girl is crucified like Jesus and buried alive by her evil parents. The story ends up, however, proving Katurian's innocence of the murders. With the plan in mind of bargaining to save his stories, Katurian confesses to the child murders, to his brother's murder, and to the killing of his parents. When police discover that the last little girl had, in fact, been not buried alive but left with a bucket of green paint and three little pigs, they realize that Katurian, who doesn't know the real story, has taken the fall for his brother. He is executed nevertheless for his other crimes, but not before the investigator Tupolski elaborates on his own abuse at the hands of a father that he too murdered and reads his own allegorical story.

Despite warnings to the contrary, the brutish police detective, Ariel, does not destroy Katurian's stories, and the writer reappears onstage for a final encounter of Michal and the Pillowman. The ending is thus as bittersweet and slightly trite as the endings of many of McDonagh's plays, but after the violence and the death of the main character, such sweetness is similarly welcome.

Kafka, Borges, Pinter, the Brothers Grimm, and even a bit of Grand Guignol horror resonate in this play. It is McDonagh's most complicated work to date, perhaps because its black comedy is only a backdrop this time to an exploration of power, of narrative, and of the influence of story on reality and vice versa. Is Katurian a voice for McDonagh himself? As his character vehemently puts it:

> I say if you've got a political axe to grind, if you've got a political what-do-ya-call-it, go write a fucking essay, I will know where I stand. I say keep your left-wing this, keep your right-wing that and tell me a fucking story! You know? A great man once said, "The first duty of a storyteller is to tell a story," and I believe in that wholeheartedly, "The first duty of a storyteller is to tell a story." Or was it "The only duty of a storyteller is to tell a story?" Yeah, it might have been "The only duty of a storyteller is to tell a story." I can't remember, but anyway, that's what I do, I tell stories.

(p. 7)

McDonagh would be unlikely to disagree with Katurian's tirade—political and social commentary seem all but absent in this play and only a marginally serious aspect of the others. If we are to take both Katurian and Michal's concern for the preservation of K.'s gory creations as any indication, the writer seems absolved of all responsibility not only to take a political or moral stand but also to consider the negative effects that his art might have on his readers. The question of art's ability to corrupt and to mislead is nevertheless left open. Katurian's art did mislead, but as both he and his brother were honest products of the world in which they lived, the idea that he might avoid writing such stories never enters the realm of possibility.

Saved from tragedy by laughter, saved from callous emptiness by touching sentimentality, this play more than any other reveals McDonagh's talent for capturing an audience with his tales. As such it is a continuation and a development of all of his works, but especially of the two plays so far in *The Aran Trilogy*. *The Pillowman* comes close to reducing the protective disconnect between McDonagh's outlandish characters and his audience, who have been separated almost entirely from one another by the laughter and horror that dominate reactions to all but *The Cripple of Inishmaan*. Still comical and notably twisted, Katurian and Michal are quite unlike the characters in *A Skull in Connemara* and *The Lonesome West* and much closer to Billy. Compelling in their reasoning, and neither ignorant nor purposely immoral, they have unique reasons for turning out as they have and thus shed the cartoonish aura of characters like Coleman and Valene, Mick and Mairtin. Finally, like *The Lieutenant of Inishmore*, the play centers not around the banal and sinister interactions of average folk in their everyday lives but rather portrays extraordinary characters in an extraordinary situation. The elements of realism, the objects of daily existence so important to his first four plays have disappeared, and replacing them is a setting that balances between fairy tale, Orwellian nightmare, and television police drama.

With *The Pillowman*, McDonagh seems to have come into his own, and as it is a partially revised version of one among many rejections that the playwright ignored in the first half of the 1990s, it leaves one wondering what else is not far behind. Though McDonagh continues his success not only on the stages of Britain and America but on those of non-English-speaking theaters worldwide, critical work on him is still largely limited to the articles of theater critics and newspaper journalists. He seems reluctant to give comprehensive interviews, and extensive academic work on both his own work and his position with respect to his predecessors and his contemporaries has yet to emerge. If he has his way, however, he may pass to the columns of film criticism long before theater theory catches up with him.

Selected Bibliography

WORKS OF MARTIN McDONAGH

PLAYS

The Beauty Queen of Leenane. London: Methuen, 1996.

A Skull in Connemara. London: Methuen, 1997.

The Lonesome West. London: Methuen, 1997.

The Beauty Queen of Leenane and Other Plays. New York: Vintage, 1998. (Includes the title play; A Skull in Connemara; and The Lonesome West; which together make up *The Leenane Trilogy.* All text quotations from these plays refer to this edition.)

The Cripple of Inishmaan. London: Methuen, 1997; New York: Vintage, 1998.

The Lieutenant of Inishmore. London: Methuen, 2001.

The Pillowman. London: Faber, 2003.

RELATED DRAMATIC WORKS

Murphy, Tom. *Bailegangaire.* London: Methuen, 2001; First published in Dublin, 1986.

Pinter, Harold. *One for the Road.* London: Methuen, 1984.

Synge, John Millington Synge. *The Playboy of the Western World.* London: A & C Black, 1975. First published, 1907.

CRITICAL WORKS AND REVIEWS

Bolger, Dermot, ed. *Druids, Dudes and Beauty Queens: The Changing Face of Irish Theater.* Dublin: New Island, 2001. (Contains essays by John Waters, Merriman, and Breandán Delap that address McDonagh's work specifically.)

Dening, Penelope. "The Scribe of Kilburn." *Irish Times,* April 18, 2001.

Jenckes, Norma. "Skeletons Are Dancing Again." *Irish Times,* July 13, 2000.

Morash, Christopher. *A History of Irish Theatre, 1601–2000.* Cambridge, U.K.: Cambridge University Press, 2002.

Nightingale, Benedict. "What Does Realistic Mean on the Stage, Anyway?" *New York Times,* January 13, 2002.

"The Pillowman." *Times* (London), November 15, 2003.

O'Hagan, Sean. "The Wild West." *Guardian,* March 24, 2001. (Contains a brief discussion with McDonagh and general biography of the author.)

O'Toole, Fintan. "Nowhere Man." *Irish Times,* April 26, 1997. (Contains an interview with McDonagh.) Introduction to *Plays 1.* London: Methuen, 1998.

Segal, Victoria. "Are You Sitting Comfortably?" *Sunday Times* (London), November 11, 2003.

Spencer, Charles. "Devastating Masterpiece of Black Comedy." *Daily Telegraph,* June 28, 2002.

PATRICK O'BRIAN

(1914 – 2000)

John Lennard

NAPOLEONIC NAVAL FICTION is something of a puzzle. Ships have been an obvious narrative vehicle since Homer's *Odyssey,* but little before 1937 suggested the success of fictions of the Royal Navy during the Great Wars of 1792–1815. More than 250 have appeared, with assorted companion volumes, popular histories, and a sub-genre devoted to the Duke of Wellington's Peninsula Campaign of 1809–1814. Television and film have lagged (naval action is expensive to stage) but with computer-generated imagery are fast catching up. Runaway success for historically accurate novels laden with technical detail itself calls for explanation, but the literary problem is deeper: while most of the novelists are enjoyably competent, and some have real talent, the twenty volumes of Patrick O'Brian's Aubrey/Maturin series (1969–1999) form a roman-fleuve unmatched in twentieth-century literature in English. How did such apparently intractable material inform such an unlikely triumph?

A fictionalizing of facts begins soon after 1815. Captains William Glascock (*The Naval Sketch Book,* 1826), Frederick Marryat (*Frank Mildmay,* 1829; *Peter Simple,* 1834; *Mr. Midshipman Easy,* 1836), and Frederick Chamier (*The Life of a Sailor,* 1832; *Ben Brace,* 1836) all traded as novelists on experiences in the Great Wars but, like the seaman John Nicol, whose "edited" memoirs *The Life and Adventures of John Nicol, Mariner* were published in 1822, wrote with license. These captains, intervening in a protracted debate about reforming naval discipline, also had agendas beyond history or fiction. Memoirs, more or less embellished, continue well into the nineteenth century (Thomas Cochrane's *Autobiography of a Seaman* appeared in 1860, when he was eighty-five), but naval novels die away, despite a scattering of midcentury sea stories, including Herman Melville's *Moby-Dick* (1851) and several great Napoleonic novels, notably Leo Tolstoy's *War and Peace* (1865–1869). From 1878, Joseph Conrad was demonstrating for all to see the narrative value of a ship, at once closed and mobile, relaxed and disciplined, free of land and at the mercy of the sea. The consolidation of imperial adventure fiction as a mass genre by Rudyard Kipling in the 1890s whetted public appetite for far flung derring-do. Arthur Conan Doyle hit the nerve in 1896 and afterward with his tales of Brigadier Gerard, a French hussar at large in Napoleon's empire; but Gerard, though continuously in print, did not crystallize the genre as Sherlock Holmes had for the detective story a decade before.

The character who did finally achieve that was Captain Horatio Hornblower, created by C. S. Forester (1899–1966) in a trilogy that climbed best-seller lists: *The Happy Return* (1937; published in the U.S. as *Beat to Quarters*), *A Ship of the Line* (1938), and *Flying Colours* (1938), immediately issued in an omnibus, *Captain Hornblower, R.N.* (1939), that sold well throughout World War II. From 1945 to 1966 Forester extended Hornblower's career in seven further novels (plus an unfinished one published posthumously in 1967) and a *Hornblower Companion* (1964), establishing architectures for individual books and a series plan matching a successful career against the movement from the declaration of war in 1792 to Napoleon's final defeat in 1815 and death in 1821. A 1951 Hollywood film starring Gregory Peck, named for and adapted from the initial trilogy, if approximately faithful, tended to emphasize romantic and downplay naval detail—but Forester, Admiral Horatio Nelson's biographer in 1929, also produced a popular history, *The Age of Fighting Sail* (1956), offering sincere admiration of ordinary seamen in peace and war and thus establishing a powerful precedent linking fictions to naval history and honorable verisimilitude.

Patrick O'Brian was one of Forester's earliest successors, but in a distinct vein: his *The Golden Ocean* (1956) and *The Unknown Shore* (1959) are tales of Commodore George Anson's global circumnavigation in 1740–1744 and, though clear anticipations of the Aubrey/Maturin tales, were written as adventure stories for children, for money, and for pleasure. By the time O'Brian returned to sea stories in 1969, two writers of more modest talent had made themselves Forester's heirs. Dudley Pope, a World War II naval veteran established from the 1950s as a popular historian of Napoleonic oceangoing warfare, transformed himself with the creation of Captain Lord Nicholas Ramage in 1965, and between 1967 and 1989 wrote seventeen further Ramage novels, all best sellers. Even more prolific, another veteran established as a novelist of the modern navy, Douglas Reeman, writing under the pen name Alexander Kent, began in 1968 the Richard Bolitho novels, of which twenty-eight have appeared, with the author promising more. Before O'Brian completed his second Aubrey/Maturin novel in 1972, the historian Cyril Northcote Parkinson weighed in with a "biography" of Hornblower in 1970, and from 1973 to 1982 published six novels about a Guernseyman, Richard Delancey, whose fluent French enables perilous missions. By 1981, O'Brian had completed eight Aubrey/Maturin books and become a word-of-mouth recommendation, but Pope and Kent continued to dominate publicity; the seafaring Richard Woodman published the first of fourteen Nathaniel Drinkwater novels (1981–1998); and the television producer Bernard Cornwell added a dimension with the first of (to date) twenty-two novels about Richard Sharpe, whose military career tracks Wellington's from Seringapatam in 1799 to Waterloo in 1815.

O'Brian at last began to receive acclaim and find mass popularity in the 1990s, when his publishers cracked the U.S. market. As the scale of his achievement was recognized, his last five novels (1993–1999) enjoyed celebrity publication, hardback sales in great quantities, and lauda-tory reviews driving backlist sales. But by then he was in his eighties; he was widowed in 1998; and on 2 January 2000 died in a Dublin hotel room. The increased attention had also raised unwelcome questions about whether O'Brian was "really" R. P. Russ, a literary wunderkind in the 1930s and by 1939 a man with a family he abandoned. O'Brian wouldn't say, but it became clear the person he had been since 1945 was creation, not inheritance; that he wasn't, for example, Irish by birth or citizenship; and that there were mysteries in his life as well as the blazing enigma of Aubrey/Maturin, sustained afloat and ashore over thirty-one years, twenty volumes, and more than 6,300 printed pages.

R. P. RUSS, 1914–1945: FROM FABLES TO TRAUMATIZED PEACE

Richard Patrick Russ was born at Chalfont St. Peter in Buckinghamshire, England, on 12 December 1914, the fifth son and eighth child of Charles Russ (1876–1955) and Jessie Naylor Goddard (1878–1918). The Russes, of German extraction, were successful in the fur trade, but Charles chose medicine as a bacteriologist and would-be inventor. In 1908 he and Jessie bought a country house in Buckinghamshire, but extravagance steadily ate capital; in 1916 the eldest boys were withdrawn from school, and in 1917 the family had to move to a smaller house nearer London.

The slide accelerated terribly in 1918 when Jessie died, probably from abdominal cancer, and the grief-stricken Charles became deeply insensitive to his children. By 1921, after a further expedient move, the only children remaining at home were Patrick and his younger sister, Joan; both went years without formal schooling. There was, intermittently, heavy-handed paternal tuition with occasional beating, but dominantly a neglect that left Patrick introverted and insecure for life.

In 1922, Charles married Zoe Center, née Blakeway (1878–1964), the widow of a senior naval surgeon killed at the Dardanelles in 1916. The marriage was happy, and Zoe funded Charles's self-indulgence. She gave Patrick (but not Joan) sustained affection, and partly rescued him from his father's neglect; even so, he received only four years' schooling, at Lewes Grammar during 1925–1929, and didn't matriculate until 1934, after two years of evening classes at Birkbeck College in London. What he did all day as a child is intimated only by his autobiographical fiction, highly problematic as evidence; historically the record is largely blank, years passing without structure. Tellingly, he had no friends and besides Joan few playmates; only magazines and books, dustily piled in cellars, and an intense inner life both fueled and straitened by increasingly eclectic reading.

The major evidence of what he must have been doing is his first novel, *Caesar: The Life Story of a Panda Leopard,* written in 1927 when he was twelve and published in 1930—one arrangement his father did make on Patrick's behalf. Three more animal stories were published between 1931 and 1933, and twelve were collected in *Beasts Royal* in 1934; another four appeared in annuals published by the Oxford University Press from 1934 through 1937, from one of which grew *Hussein: An Entertainment* (1938), the first contemporary novel ever published by Oxford University Press. "An Entertainment" invokes Graham Greene, who so described his 1930s novels of action and intrigue, but the major influence on Patrick Russ was clearly Kipling's *Jungle Books.* Patrick O'Brian later disavowed Kipling, partly for his lifelong imperialism and political temper in bereaved old age, partly through an apparent fear that identification of Kipling as an influence would somehow impugn his own work, but the descriptive economy and narrative felicity of O'Brian's prose have honorable models in Kipling. Emotionally Patrick Russ's precocious animal tales are simpler, persistently featuring large predators that repeatedly enjoy violent triumph over human and animal adversaries before ending in noble death. The compensatory fantasies of an isolated and inward child are apparent, but in the human Hussein, patently an offspring of Kipling's *Kim,* greater maturity is equally clear. The writing throughout is of a quality consistent with prestigious publication and implies considerable revision, or superb absorption from reading of how extended prose narratives are structured and composed sentences dovetailed into sequent paragraphs.

Two additional stories appeared in annuals in 1938 and 1940, but events and World War II had by then overtaken Patrick Russ. In 1934 he briefly enlisted in the Royal Air Force but found he and service life were at odds. In 1935 he left his father's house and lived in London. Facts are very sparse, but in 1936 he married Elizabeth Jones (1912–1998); they had two children, Richard (born 1937) and Jane (1939–1942), born with spina bifida. He may have traveled to Ireland in 1937 and certainly did in 1938; he spent some weeks at Locarno in Switzerland as a travel-company representative and had at least one brief affair. More significantly in late 1938 he began a doubly adulterous affair with Countess Mary Tolstoy (née Wicksteed, 1915–1998). Her scandalized husband and family initially necessitated subterfuge, but during the early part of the war, with Elizabeth in East Anglia and Mary separated from her husband, she and Patrick Russ began cohabiting. He was named as co-respondent by Count Tolstoy in his 1942 petition for divorce, and Mary was denied contact with her children. Elizabeth seems to have remained ignorant of the affair until 1944, then petitioned for a divorce granted in 1945—following which Patrick and Mary immediately married.

After fire watching and ambulance driving in the Blitz of 1940–1941, Patrick (and later Mary) worked for the Political Warfare Executive, a shadow organization gathering intelligence and generating black propaganda. Despite speculation, it is unlikely either entered occupied France, but both spoke fluent French, gathered information on French affairs, and liaised with the resistance. The germ of Maturin's fictional activities as an intelligencer in the Great Wars is evident; equally seminal was O'Brian's discovery with Mary of the "long eighteenth century" (1688–1815) as a historical place of imaginative retreat, successor to the beast worlds of his youth.

They lived from 1942 until 1945 in Chelsea in a beautiful Queen Anne house that had been vacated early in the war; and acquiring early editions—like those he had read in childhood basements, redolent of their age as material objects as well as in content—became a mutual devotion. A theme in naval history emerged, unsurprising given Britain's long dependence on maritime competence, but never to the exclusion of domestic and country life, odd memoirs, manuals, periodicals, lexicons, and encyclopedias—all the detail and humdrum reality whose effortless realization in Aubrey/Maturin novels grounds their adventurous action in verisimilar history. The ebb and flow of reported and epistolary debates is also a primary record of the eighteenth-century mind, those beliefs and understandings of our ancestors we no longer inherit. This reading would prove crucial to Patrick O'Brian, but for Patrick Russ it was an indulgence unconnected with a career on hold since 1939.

War's end meant unemployment, poverty hedged only by a small trust of Mary's, and renewed responsibility for Richard, now nine. Patrick Russ was determined not to neglect his son as his father had neglected him, but options were limited. When chance brought an offer from the visionary architect Clough Williams-Ellis (1883–1978) of a tiny Welsh cottage at a bargain rent, he and Mary seized the opportunity and decamped, bag and baggage, from Chelsea to remote Cwm Croesor (*koom kroissor*) in Snowdonia. For income there was the trust and hopes of an anthology, hastily put together from wartime reading, which eventually appeared as *A Book of Voyages* in 1947; smallholding self-sufficiency and rigid budgeting would permit him, just, to meet Richard's school fees. And abruptly, between remarriage and departure, Patrick Russ legally changed his and Richard's surname to O'Brian, for reasons that must involve a formal break with his family past; not, as has been suggested, his first wife and surviving child, but his deeply unhappy history with his father (whose failings he now saw with painful clarity) and the symptomatically escapist writing it produced. Re-wed, beginning again elsewhere, he would quarry himself in a new manner but first needed distance from the child writer he had been; the change of name emphatically signaled a necessary break.

O'Brian persistently refused to remember Patrick Russ. His usual strategy was *suppressio veri* (suppressing truth), but he could indulge or be provoked into *suggestio falsi* (suggesting untruth). Mixed with vulgar Freudianism, this has fueled malicious postmortem commentary. It also undermined well-meaning efforts by Dean King, O'Brian's first biographer, leading him factually astray and to fill gaps with clichéd supposition. Matters have, however, been properly investigated by O'Brian's stepson, Nikolai Tolstoy, in a second biography. Writing to correct King and as both a professional historian and the son of a mother whose adultery with O'Brian led to her being forbidden all contact with him as a minor, Tolstoy manages a tactful and serious analysis. He identifies two methods by which elements of O'Brian's writing in the later 1940s and 1950s can be seined for probable facts, carefully indicating limits of certainty. But Tolstoy does not lend himself to summary; those interested in what exactly can and cannot be established should consult his work directly.

PATRICK O'BRIAN, 1945–1969: GROWING INTO TRANSLATION

The cottage, Fron Wen, proved for the most part an enjoyable adventure. Working largely from eighteenth-century manuals of husbandry and sport, the O'Brians survived three years, and stayed another when a larger house became available. For Richard, spending holidays there and eventually a long year of home tutoring, the scenery and outdoor life offered compensations, but it is painfully clear that Patrick O'Brian, alert and concerned as Charles Russ had never been, was nevertheless baffled and irritated by childishness. As an adult Richard broke contact with Patrick, as Patrick had with Charles, and while that breach did not come until the 1960s its roots reached back to Fron Wen.

There was local amusement at the improbable spectacle the O'Brians presented, but also growing admiration and liking, and always a warm welcome and generous hand. Acceptance was confirmed by steadfast attendance at the Ynysfor Hunt, led by a remarkable local patriarch, Captain Jack Jones. A Welsh fox hunt should not be confused with its lowland English counterpart: in Snowdonia huntsmen do not ride but scramble over miles of mountain badlands where wily foxes lair; the hunt is utterly to defend the lambs, the only available food for foxes and money-spinner for man. Those keeping up throughout with master and huntsman, turning out twice a week, were few, but both O'Brians were regularly among them—Patrick enchanted to sublime purpose by Jones's commanding vigor of tactics and language (he was a primary model for Jack Aubrey), and both passionately expending energy at a very high level.

The necessities of unplumbed, unelectrified life on a shoestring, growing one's own food, are exhausting and time-consuming; add tutoring, and spare moments are rare. Whether cause or symptom, the activities of living and following the Ynysfor Hunt left no energy for writing. Probably O'Brian was unready to begin fictionalizing the life he had abandoned. In any case, barring the odd short story and polishing older ones that had rested in draft, nothing literary was happening. The stories were collected as *The Last Pool and Other Stories* (1950), but that, after four years, was it; and with the valley lessened by Captain Jones's death in a rockfall O'Brian determined on another new start. Chance this time led him to the fishing port of Collioure on the Mediterranean coast of French Catalonia, and he and Mary, as abruptly as before, uprooted themselves and went in September 1949.

O'Brian had started procedures to clear Richard's removal to France, intending a lycée education, but in late autumn Elizabeth, now remarried, regained custody. Contact with Richard wasn't broken, but the degree of separation would never again diminish. In later years O'Brian was haunted by his incapacity as a father. His enforced habit of imaginative self-sufficiency had been breached once and for ever by Mary, but could not be overcome for or by his son. And time in delightful new surroundings was being put to use: first came two substantially autobiographical novels, *Three Bear Witness* (1952; published as *Testimonies* in the U.S.) and *The Catalans* (1953; published as *The Frozen Flame* in the U.K.); then a second adventure novel, *The Road to Samarcand* (1954), and an expanded collection of stories, *The Walker and Other Stories* (1955; *Lying in the Sun* in the U.K.); the novels

of Anson's circumnavigation, *The Golden Ocean* (1956) and *The Unknown Shore* (1959); and a third autobiographical novel, *Richard Temple* (1962). London editions were from Secker & Warburg, Hart-Davis, and Macmillan, New York ones from Harcourt, Brace—all respectable houses— and all secured respectable notices, but no more.

The autobiographical fiction is now most interesting for the light it casts on O'Brian's life, and if the second volume of Tolstoy's biography matches critically the scholarship of *The Making of the Novelist,* O'Brian may become a classic study in self-transformation. Even with fame, though, and eager republication of his early naval adventures, the slyly confessional and self-reconstructive fictions remain less available, curious and unsatisfying books their author needed to write but didn't really want readers to understand. They record and analyze much fantasy, exhibit considerable literary skill, sometimes venture deeper into the mirror than can have been tolerable, and contain disconnected moments that anticipate events or turns of phrase in the Aubrey/Maturin series—but not in ways that illuminate at large.

Better by far are the stories, initially forced in desperation from journal entries and observations of animals as prey; crabbed, spare vignettes humming with tension. With returning fluency of composition in Collioure, more refracted fictions of earlier life impinge: children in terror and boredom, marriages in vile, tightly wound tensions, fantasies of murder and revenge suasively accommodating sketched circumstance and evoked atmosphere. Many are as oddly framed in opening as closing, abrupt perspectives that recall Patrick Russ's self-projection as animals, but go far beyond him in alienating narrative vision. Violence flares from events in conjunction as much as people in action; obsessions tick as mechanically as clocks in an empty house. A highbrow flavor of mystery disdains explanations, but O'Brian did not, and probably could not, find the way of, say, Raymond Carver; though an admirer of Joyce, neither early modernist aesthetics of the fragment nor late modernist aesthetics of dissolute agency were ones he could develop.

It is telling that the Anson novels were written (and read) more easily than the choked *Richard Temple,* a protracted composition they gainfully interrupted. Midway in an eighteenth-century circumnavigation, contemporary accounts of which (in the *Gentleman's Magazine* for 1743–1745) he had long read for sheer pleasure, O'Brian was at home. Moreover, in Peter Palafox and Sean O'Mara of *The Golden Ocean* and Jack Byron and Tobias Barrow of *The Unknown Shore,* he created comedic duos, survivors who laugh because they are alive to do so, as a study in the attraction of opposites. *Richard Temple,* however, is talismanically isolated and tragically manqué, the product of an entrenched literary class conviction that serious writing must be sad and probably unpopular. O'Brian's talents were unleashed by comedic endurance, as they were strangled in pursuit of tragic distinction.

In class-raddled Britain, where literature is among many things divided and subdivided by supposedly generic merit, disaffected authors often find a comic note, ranging from reedy tenors like Anthony Powell (1905–2000) to baritones like Evelyn Waugh (1903–1966) and basso profundos like Lord Byron (1788–1824). Byron and his rare ilk lose no gravity in doing so (as Johann Wolfgang von Goethe acknowledged in calling *Don Juan* a comic epic), and O'Brian came tantalizingly close to that note: his Jack Byron is firmly based on the poet's grandfather, "Foulweather Jack" Byron (1723–1786), who did sail with Anson. But the work of Powell and Waugh gave O'Brian reason to think that a comedic stance forestalls greatness, and he seems to have internalized with cruel force a mess of misapprehensions in which writing genre novels was supposed a personal debasement. His downwardly mobile father and tense relations with his wife's socially elite first-marriage connections exacerbated the problem, and O'Brian had a stubborn pride in self-sufficiency that would have made ease of composition and increase of royalties equally suspicious. A foundation of taught snobbery must also be acknowledged: one that led him to mischannel his efforts for a decade after two clear indications of the ingredients his imagination truly needed.

In the meantime there were bills, even living simply on the Mediterranean coast. With fluent French, Catalan, and Latin, translation beckoned, and with *Richard Temple* complete, became a mainstay. Beginning in 1961 with Jacques Soustelle's *Daily Life of the Aztecs,* O'Brian translated thirty-one substantial books, most in the 1960s at two or three a year; notably seven books by Simone de Beauvoir and two best-selling memoirs by Henri Charrière, *Papillon* (1970) and *Banco: The Further Adventures of Papillon* (1973). The rest were mostly history. Many were praised; all seem as felicitous as one may hope; and with de Beauvoir a fully literary act. But energy was still being diverted from fiction.

Yet others' words are weak fare after the pleasures of composition. Long years had passed without inspiration, and epics will, like murder, out. Forester had died in 1966, Dudley Pope was one novel in, and Alexander Kent unestablished. A wily American editor at J. B. Lippincott, Robert White Hill (who published Pope), had read the Anson novels, thought O'Brian could exploit Forester's market, and in 1967 tracked him down to suggest it. Patrick Russ had read *Captain Hornblower, R.N.* during the war but only half-enjoyed *The Commodore* (1945), which he found historically slight; and Patrick O'Brian had no thought of Forester in his Anson novels, which marry detailed knowledge of primary sources with a grasp of adventure narrative evident since *Caesar.* Perhaps with Forester dead, a personal approach to the navy of the Great Wars seemed acceptable, as competitive publication with a living Forester had not. Whatever the reason, Hill's proposal was welcome, and reaching back to his comedic duos in the Anson novels, O'Brian produced, somewhat as Zeus from his ear, the redoubtable pair of Jack Aubrey and Stephen Maturin, alive to their mutually irritated fingertips at a recital in Port Mahon in 1800 and only a finale away from one of the most productive quarrels in postwar English literature.

AUBREY/MATURIN I: MUSIC AND MAINSTAYS

The music-room in the Governor's House at Port Mahon, a tall, handsome, pillared octagon, was filled with the triumphant first movement of Locatelli's C major quartet. The players, Italians pinned against the far wall by rows and rows of little round gilt chairs, were playing with passionate conviction as they mounted towards the penultimate crescendo, towards the tremendous pause and the deep, liberating final chord. And on the little gilt chairs at least some of the audience were following the rise with an equal intensity: there were two in the third row, on the left-hand side; and they happened to be sitting next to one another. The listener farther to the left was a man of between twenty and thirty whose big form overflowed his seat, leaving only a streak of gilt wood to be seen here and there. He was wearing his best uniform—the white-lapelled blue coat, white waistcoat, breeches and stockings of a lieutenant in the Royal Navy, with the silver medal of the Nile in his buttonhole—and the deep white cuff of his gold-buttoned sleeve beat the time, while his bright blue eyes, staring from what would have been a pink-and-white face if it had not been so deeply tanned, gazed fixedly at the bow of the first violin. The high note came, the pause, the resolution; and with the resolution the sailor's fist swept firmly down upon his knee. He leant back in his chair, extinguishing it entirely, sighed happily and turned towards his neighbour with a smile. The words "Very finely played, sir, I believe" were formed in his gullet if not quite in his mouth when he caught the cold and indeed inimical look and heard the whisper, "If you really must beat the measure, sir, let me entreat you to do so in time, and not half a beat ahead."

(pp. 7–8)

In this the splendid opening passage of *Master and Commander* (1969), the initial volume of Aubrey/Maturin, the English lieutenant, often half a beat ahead (a considerable maritime quality), is Jack Aubrey; his irritated neighbor, Stephen Maturin:

A covert glance showed that he was a small, dark, white-faced creature in a rusty black coat—a civilian. It was difficult to tell his age, for not only had he that kind of face that does not give anything away, but he was wearing a wig, a grizzled wig, apparently made of wire, and quite devoid of powder: he might have been anything between twenty and sixty. "About my own age, in fact, however,"

thought Jack. "The ill-looking son of a bitch, to give himself such airs."

(p. 8)

Jack's perceptions are typically as shrewd as they are blunt; he and Maturin are indeed of an age, and Maturin, the natural son of an Irish father and Catalan mother, has like all Irishmen and Catalans good reason to give nothing away. During the centuries of Anglo-French rivalry, Ireland was the underbelly of the English state and saw a hopelessly compromised uprising in 1798—so Irishmen were vulnerable to English suspicions, as Catalans to Spanish ones. Yet though an observant Catholic advocate of Irish and Catalan independence, Maturin had been sickened by the gutted vainglory of 1798 and harbored a profound conviction that Napoleonic tyranny would be far worse for Ireland than British, and for Catalonia than Castilian, colonialism.

Shortly after the concert Jack to his immense joy finds himself promoted master and commander of H.M.S. *Sophie,* a fourteen-gun brig, so when he sees Maturin next morning in the street he is more inclined to offer hospitality than to pursue the quarrel; Maturin, a scholar-naturalist, Royal Societarian, and skilled physician at a loose end, is moved to accept. As both men in differing manners had greatly admired the Locatelli and are themselves amateur players (Jack of the violin, Stephen of the cello), the *Sophie* soon sails under Aubrey's command with Maturin, his "particular friend," as ship's surgeon and partner in musical evenings; a balm in the new loneliness of command at sea and, as a hopeless landlubber (like most readers), a marvelous device to allow naturally within the narrative Jack's expert explanations of hull, masts, cordage, and maneuvers.

So O'Brian's epic, sometimes called the *Aubreiad,* was launched. Every theme of that first paragraph—attraction and friction of opposites, harmonies of music, honor of combat, twists of perception and social protocols, formality of eighteenth-century speech, period detail in uniform, furniture, manners, and wig—would be worked and reworked against a driven succession of wartime actions and lulls, snags and bureaucracies. Most historical novels (like period films) rely on incidental detail while cleaving to modern minds, generating a historicized surface yet profoundly careless of how "the past is another country" where "they do things differently" because they understood and thought differently. O'Brian, conversely, always perceives the early nineteenth century through the eyes and ears of men born in the 1770s, invoking the then popular, now forgotten Pietro Antonio Locatelli (rather than, say, George Frideric Handel), rhythmically generating the automatic medial "sir" of each speaker, and finessing a clear sense that the nature and condition of Maturin's wig surprises rather than his being bewigged at all. O'Brian's wide Georgian reading and experience of eighteenth-century manuals coalesced in profound imagination of a lost world intimately connected to our own; guided in naval detail and probability by ships' logs, officers' journals, admiralty papers, and news reports, he focused on a naval career that would sweep around the Napoleonic world, at once fiction, a mosaic of facts, and a fully historical enterprise.

Equally important are the dry humor of the wig's description and the coarser joke of the chair's eclipse by Aubrey's bulk, a wit and belly laugh that the eighteenth century distinctively combined. As in the Anson tales, O'Brian lets his comedic genius off its leash, and Aubrey and Maturin, however epic, are recognizably an odd couple akin to Laurel and Hardy and all jolly-fattypuff/morose-thinnifer pairs: Samuel Beckett's *Waiting for Godot* (1953) had shown what the twentieth century could make of such a pair, suitably adapted.

As Aubrey and Maturin began to live for themselves, O'Brian set himself to explore uses in the Great Wartime navy for an odd couple at large with a fourteen-gun sloop. To the facilitation of technical explanation were added explorations of character, establishing Maturin (with nice plausibility) as a Catalonian advisor to Naval Intelligence, and Aubrey as professionally superb at sea, yet as all at sea on land as Maturin is landlubberly at sea, and deeply anxious about his career; wider context and deeper politics cease to be explanations and become perceptions between friends, colored by emotion to reveal character with situation.

Locatelli and his ilk bring harmony; the burden of recurrent technical detail about sailing a wooden battleship registers the unremitting vigilance required at sea. The complex contrasts of Aubrey and Maturin constantly expand the narrative with new angles—Jack, despite his bulk, is more athletic and the finer musician, as well as a late-blooming mathematician-astronomer, while Stephen ("such a deep old file," as Jack often says), is the better swordsman and a deadly duelist-while providing a set of comedic topoi, from Stephen's botanizing and beetles to Jack's delight in old jokes and passions for particular sails, that can be recursively intensified and delicately varied.

Beginning with Jack's first command, his desperation to achieve the crucial step to full captain (after which advancement was rigidly governed by seniority) is understandable—a subordinate protagonist is a very different challenge, as Austen shows in *Mansfield Park*—but starting as late as 1801, on the eve of the brief Peace of Amiens (1802–1803), seeded a problem, for the sheer duration of sea voyages to the far sides of the world would make mapping the fictional sequence onto the true calendar of the Great Wars progressively harder. The interruption of Aubrey's naval prospects by the peace also forced a narrative hiatus, but by ending *Master and Commander* with Aubrey's blameless capture by superior French forces, O'Brian provided an introduction to the enemy, the then very gentlemanly codes of an officer's war, and the practice of prisoner exchange, with a grandstand view of Admiral James Saumarez's battles against de Moreno and Durand-Linois in the Gut of Gibraltar (Algeciras, 6–12 July 1801).

The peacefully land-bound opening of *Post Captain* (1972) then allowed him to establish the England Aubrey loves and fights to defend, with his landowning-class status and family roots, and to settle the romantic issue by involving Aubrey and Maturin with cousins, Sophie Williams (beautiful and proper, with a dreadful mother) and the widowed, wild, and graceful Diana Villiers. Jack in love and lust is an inarticulate bull, Stephen a wooden post libidinally suppressed by laudanum, and their joint relations with Diana bring them very near a duel; eventually Jack marries Sophie (remaining a cheerful adulterer overseas), while it takes Stephen several further novels to marry Diana, and their relationship remains explosively unstable, as fascinating as it is heartbreaking. Nowhere is O'Brian's love of Jane Austen more luminous than in the country scenes of *Post Captain,* and it is a measure of his historical understanding and the sly capacities of his prose that some passages and scenes are as close to her as anyone has ever come.

The short peace ends, the navy recommissions, and our heroes (nearly trapped in France by Napoleon's unprecedented order to intern all aliens) are again away to sea. *H.M.S. Surprise* (1973) is named for the last foundation of the epic, the eventual reward for Jack's successes in the *Sophie:* an old-fashioned, undersized, sweet-sailing twenty-eight-gun frigate which was again (after many vicissitudes) bearing him and Stephen when O'Brian's death ended the series in 2000. In tracking with Jack's career a particular warship's service O'Brian anticipated such "biographies" of ships as Anthony Deane's *Nelson's Favourite: H.M.S. Agamemnon at War* (1996) and David Cordingly's *Billy Ruffian: The Bellerophon and the Downfall of Napoleon* (2003), and opened another axis of historical awareness, reaching from the yards where H.M.S. *Surprise* was laid down in the 1760s to the reputation individual ships gained in the fleet, the evolving body of men who crewed her on one or another voyage, and the various dockyards that maintained her as, successively, warship, letter of marque, H.M. hired vessel, and private yacht.

In the nature of sea service and the absolute authority of wartime captains, the social and fighting unit of the ship's company must be happily established for maximal efficiency in storm and battle; the wooden machine to which all entrust their lives, from the depths of its hold to its quarterdeck and aerial ropeways, functions as a village within which "families" making up the messes and watches of the crew live, love, fight, and die. As the series progressed bit-part players in Aubrey's crew could be fleshed out, while a small band who accompany him in almost all things (including his coxswain, Barret Bonden, and personal servant, the gloriously morose Preserved Killick) become orchestrations of the melody Aubrey and Maturin play.

The achievements of the Royal Navy in effectively blockading continental Europe for twenty-two years while maintaining a worldwide presence and winning a dozen major fleet actions are astonishing; conditions for officers and men alike defy modern belief, and to endure such privation, risk, and oppression commands awe. O'Brian paid direct homage in a small explanatory guide aimed at young readers and requested by his publishers, *Men-of-War: Life in Nelson's Navy* (1974), but each Aubrey/Maturin novel is an act of praise. The exemplary *Surprise,* bearing all yet Aubrey's burden, is at once a resonating chamber for Jack and Stephen's emotions (as for their music) and the tool with which Aubrey's tactical brilliance, guided by Maturin's political and strategic understanding, can wreak its havoc, volume by volume, on a tyranny both loathe. With the personal, emotional, rational, official, naval, and historical so intimately fused within a fully responsive narrative vehicle, and the sweep of the Great Wars before him, all was set for O'Brian: who turned instead to an apparently quite different project.

INTERLUDE I: PICASSO AND MEDITERRANEAN CULTURE

Pablo Ruiz Picasso: A Biography (1976) appeared only three years after the artist's death and remains an important account embodying a powerful, coherent view of Picasso's life and work as distinctively Mediterranean. O'Brian had met Picasso at Collioure, and he creates a vivid sense of the man; they spoke Catalan, a language Picasso (born an Andalou) acquired early and always adored. Picasso's Catalan connections were known, but O'Brian first insisted that Catalan identity and experience as a specifically Mediterranean culture was necessary to understand his artistic development and maturity.

O'Brian wasn't a professional art historian, critic, or biographer, and there is refreshing directness (and masterful prose) in his approach to life and pictures. Art history rolls on, and O'Brian's is not the last word; feminist objections to his treatment of Picasso's many women, moreover, are well grounded; but neither consideration affects the literary interest of his book. Catalonia is an old land and as a seafaring Mediterranean culture has historical mercantile links ranging from Barbary to Byzantium and the once numerous fiefdoms and city-states of the Aegean and Adriatic.

In *Master and Commander* the *Sophie's* orders took her from Port Mahon (where Catalan is often heard) to the eastern Mediterranean, and the understanding of Catalonia's place in the maritime cultural jigsaw he had developed for Aubrey/Maturin informed O'Brian's reading of Picasso's early life and artistic coordinates. In return the gravitas he gave the Mediterranean within Picasso's artistic career reinforced his historical reading of its place in understanding the Great Wars—so that even when Aubrey and Maturin repeatedly stray to the far side of the world the whole European sphere glows behind and before them, not merely the longing of individuals for a particular English or Catalan spot they know as home. Actions in the Atlantic and Baltic, the northern European world in general, are never slighted, but in its eastern and African shores and rich classical history the Mediterranean is always honored, and there is overall a clear corrective emphasis (like that of Linda Colley's revisionist *Britons: Forging the Nation, 1707–1837,* 1992; and *Captives: Britain, Empire and the World, 1600–1850,* 2002) to the anglocentricism of British historiography.

It is striking that O'Brian, an introvert most at ease in an imaginary Georgian battleship, could so suasively enter the mind of as outgoing and cheerfully libidinous a man as Picasso, and penetrate the modernist rigors and creative formations and deformations of his art. It is tempting to see connections between the personalities of Aubrey and Maturin and the aspects of Picasso that O'Brian chose to limn, Jack's zest and childlike humor reflecting one reality, Stephen's codebook complexity and awareness of multiple meanings another. O'Brian knew Picasso before creating Jack Aubrey and Stephen Maturin, so the patterns of influence are potentially complex. After the biography was done, O'Brian's intense awareness of the interplay within Picasso of many identities enriched his imagination of the emotional life of a ship's company with Aubrey and Maturin as the unified expression of its consciousness.

AUBREY/MATURIN II: IN THE WAKE OF COCHRANE

H.M.S. *Surprise* had taken Aubrey and Maturin to India and the East Indies, in connection with the China trade, and when O'Brian returned to them he was ready to expand still further. *The Mauritius Command* (1977) follows the British campaign to capture those islands in 1810, while *Desolation Island* (1978), *The Fortune of War* (1979), and *The Surgeon's Mate* (1980) take Aubrey and Maturin in a great sweep to the far southern roaring forties, the Far East, North America (just in time for the War of 1812), the Baltic, and briefly, as prisoners, France. *The Ionian Mission* (1981) and *Treason's Harbour* (1983) return to the Mediterranean, but *The Far Side of the World* (1984) again sends Aubrey to the Pacific, this time to protect the whaling trade, whither he returns in *The Reverse of the Medal* (1986), only to become embroiled in the strangest episode of his career.

Maturin's intelligence and counterintelligence activities during the voyage beginning in *Desolation Island* provide a wide-angle view of Anglo-Franco-American spy networks and practices circa 1812, and the later Mediterranean mission brings him perilously close to a high-ranking British traitor, Andrew Wray. Aubrey, whose irresponsible father is causing the government political difficulties, becomes Wray's target, and is implicated in a scheme to defraud the stock market. Convicted in a rigged trial, he is automatically dismissed from the navy and sentenced to stand in the pillory—a vindictive punishment intended to achieve a political end but utterly backfiring when thousands of angry sailors surround and cheer Aubrey throughout his ordeal. The loss of professional standing is nevertheless a form of death, and Aubrey's abiding misery throughout *The Letter of Marque* (1988)—in which he captains the *Surprise,* sold out of service and purchased by Maturin, as a licensed privateer—is a fascinating narrative achievement. Higher-ranking sailors than those who protested the pillory are aware of Aubrey's victimization, and once Wray has been exposed as a traitor and fled the country, pardon and naval reinstatement are secured—which seems too melodramatic to be true, yet (setting aside the egregious Wray and some time compression) the episode is in its bones factual.

The remarkable officer dismissed from the navy on conviction for fraud in 1814, and eventually reinstated in 1832, was Thomas Cochrane, tenth earl of Dundonald (1775–1860). He made his name in May 1801, when with the fourteen-gun sloop *Speedy* (158 tons, 54 crew, 28-pound broadside) he took the Spanish xebec-frigate *Gamo* (600+ tons, 319 crew, 190-pound broadside); frequently distinguishing himself thereafter, and a Member of Parliament from 1806, he exposed dockyard and prize-court corruption and publicly criticized Admiral "Dismal Jimmy" Gambier for the missed opportunities of the Basque Roads (1809). After his politically motivated conviction in an 1814 stock-exchange scandal, denied Royal Naval service for eighteen years despite the payment of his legal fines by popular penny-subscription, he accepted in 1817–1822 command of the Chilean navy, securing Chilean and Peruvian independence from Spain; from 1823 to 1825 he did as much for Brazil, forcing independence from Portugal; and in 1825–1828, as admiral of the Greek navy, helped win independence from Ottoman Turkey. After reinstatement in the Royal Navy in 1832, he served until the Crimean War (1855), dying a full admiral in 1860. A pioneer of steam-powered warships, he urged adoption of screw propulsion, besides writing accounts of his South American service and an autobiography.

In constructing Aubrey's career, O'Brian drew on many real officers, including the outstanding frigate captains Edward Pellew (1757–1833) and William Hoste (1780–1828), but none more than Cochrane. The *Sophie* matches the *Speedy,* and

her great success in *Master and Commander* is to take the *Cacafuego,* a Spanish xebec-frigate replicating the *Gamo;* later incidents follow events from Cochrane's cruises in the frigates *Pallas and Imperieuse;* the fraud trial concludes *The Reverse of the Medal;* and a version of Cochrane's Chilean adventures fills the last novel, *Blue at the Mizzen* (1999). Cochrane was truly extraordinary, and using him as a model allows wild action to remain grounded in the historical record while narratively opening the politics of yet another continent. O'Brian also rendered Aubrey's exceptionally rapid pardon more plausible by having him become, after the death of his father, an MP for a pocket borough—with the benefit of adding to subsequent novels further aspects of British wartime and postwar domestic politics.

Maturin is in large part a projection of O'Brian himself, but if he is, as a scientist, based on anyone it is Joseph Banks (1743-1820). Banks who sailed with Captain James Cook in 1768–1771, was responsible for creating the penal colony at Botany Bay, played critical roles in establishing Merino sheep in Britain and in developing Kew Gardens, and served as President of the Royal Society for forty years. Like Maturin, who compulsively keeps a journal (allowing a first-person narrative variation), Banks was a great writer, whose thousands of surviving letters are a major source for later eighteenth-century thought and manners; Maturin's discoveries (including a giant Indian Ocean island tortoise he dubs *Testudo aubreii* in Jack's honor) resemble those of Banks and Cook. O'Brian had long raided Banks's papers for beetle details and the like, and in return Banks now occasioned the last interruption in the Aubrey/Maturin series.

INTERLUDE II: JOSEPH BANKS AND CIRCUMNAVIGATION

Joseph Banks: A Life (1987), the only available biography, is an absorbingly odd book. Outside the letters, surviving detail, especially of Banks's early life, is scarce; and quarrying all known letters for their detail would be a decade's work. The Banks biography is far slimmer than the Picasso, and, if everything is covered, nothing receives sustained attention except the voyages, especially the great circumnavigation. There O'Brian goes to the other extreme, quoting verbatim and unmodernized long passages detailing botanizing walks and specimens collected; this does indeed bring "one directly into touch with Banks" (p. 41), but the biography nevertheless leaves an impression of a core wrapped in necessary packaging.

The scientific world in which Banks moved was in flux, rapidly developing many cornerstones and systematic classifications of modern knowledge. Banks himself (like Maturin) was primarily concerned with the greatest of all, the Linnaean classification of all living things with a Latin tag. For this enterprise everything in an exotic location was potentially "nondescript," unknown to the system and so in need of killing and anatomizing, just as for admiralty hydrographers (including Cook) every newly mapped cape and shoal needed a name. In fiction the encyclopedic impulse is a source of comedy, as Stephen, quivering like a hound held in check despite a clear scent, is dragged helplessly away from island after exotic island by the urgencies of Jack's command. On Cook's peacetime voyage discovery was the purpose, and the number of things he and Banks named is staggering. Moreover, the circumnavigation was both broadly political, in imperial outreach and impositions of nomenclature, and immediately political—as in Banks's prompt recommendation of Botany Bay as a destination for those sentenced to transportation (an urgent issue since American independence had closed the New World). The unintended consequence, founding modern Australia, is an outstanding example of the curious debts the contemporary world owes to past exigencies, an idea that is a guiding principle of the *Aubreiad* as an act of historical illumination.

AUBREY/MATURIN III: THE GLOBAL PICTURE IN 1813B

The Mauritius Command is set in 1810 and *The Reverse of the Medal* in 1814, but there is insufficient time between them for the intervening six novels. The deepening time constrictions were noted by the critic John Bayley (a champion of O'Brian) in the mid-1980s, with the satisfying suggestion that some books must happen "in 1813b." Yet even supposing Aubrey's privateering voyage and reinstatement to take no time at all, O'Brian was running out of war. His solution was again to loop the world in a voyage filling *The Thirteen-Gun Salute* (1989), *The Nutmeg of Consolation* (1991), *Clarissa Oakes* (1992; published in the U.S. as *The Truelove*), and *The Wine-Dark Sea* (1993), set in 1813b and so distant from other theaters that incongruity causes no difficulty.

The continuing plot is served by having Maturin find (and dissect) the traitor Wray in the Malay state of Pulo Prabang, and by setting up the South American connections necessary for Aubrey's later emulation of Cochrane; this also allows O'Brian to reintroduce Jack's illegitimate mixed-race son Sam Panda, educated by Catholic missionaries, granted through Stephen's influence dispensation for a bastard to be ordained, and now an important priest in Spanish colonies racked by the fallout of the French Revolution. The suspended anxieties of Europe are hauntingly present through personal and financial concerns of Jack's and Stephen's, and there is an addition to the main cast, Clarissa Oakes, an escapee from Botany Bay who marries one of Jack's midshipmen and later as a widow becomes companion to Stephen's autistic daughter Bridie.

But the heart of the novels is the circumnavigation itself and the extended botanizing the diplomatic layover in Pulo Prabang allows Stephen. Episodes including a visit to an isolated Buddhist temple and an encounter with a submarine volcano dilate O'Brian's normally crisp action but hold their place for sheer curiosity and as narrative tours de force. These four novels of circumnavigation also all but complete O'Brian's picture of the early nineteenth-century world, adding to his European and international maritime theaters the state of mercantile-imperial penetration of Pacific archipelagos, while framing all in global dynamics of trade and scientific discovery; philosophically, they explore in non-European locations what all humans might then (as now) share despite differing cultural understandings of the world.

Marking time has limits, and eventually O'Brian returned to Europe with three precisely positioned novels: *The Commodore* (1994) fuses a campaign against the slave trade in the Bight of Benin (anytime after 1806) with a French expedition to Ireland (a perennial danger), placing both in (de facto, by this stage) 1813c; *The Yellow Admiral* (1997), often land bound, otherwise concerns the Brest blockade during the cruel winter of 1813–1814; and *The Hundred Days* (1998) explores the Mediterranean naval side of Napoleon's last flourish, the campaign of March and June 1815 that led to Waterloo.

While O'Brian was writing this novel, Mary died, and his grief found immediate expression in the deaths of Diana in a coaching accident and Barret Bonden in action. Writing briefly helped keep him going, and the long-planned novel based on Cochrane's South American service, *Blue at the Mizzen* (1999), took the *Aubreiad* to its twentieth volume and finally saw Jack promoted to rear admiral. The opening of another novel survives (*The Final Unfinished Voyage of Jack Aubrey,* 2004), but with Jack promoted, giving a kind of closure to the sequence, and his own grief unbearable, O'Brian died in his sleep on 2 January 2000.

CODA: FOR THE SHEER PLEASURE OF WORDS

All naval novel writers love terminology. Their exotically exact language of "mizzen topmast skysails," "kedges," "bunting," "transom," "ratlines," "by the mark ten," "waisters," "three-water grog" and so on constitute a litany even readers who never grasp the difference between a brace and a sheet nor why the weather gauge matters in battle and a lee shore is a terrible thing, may still enjoy. Via Stephen Maturin, O'Brian added fascinating words from eighteenth-century medicine and learned manners, as "marthambles" (a supposed disease) or "mammothrept" (a mother's boy); familiar words are also tweaked, as "nondescript" in its Linnaean sense of "undescribed by science" and "crass" as a noun. He

also caught superbly in dialogue a variety of national, regional, and personal locutions such as Stephen's terminal use of "joy," Preserved Killick's habit of beginning sentences with "Which it," and Diana's mannish way of using bare surnames—sustained acts of precise literary ventriloquy and a primary pleasure in reading.

The dynamics of language are suggested by the need for a dictionary, which (far from proving off-putting) led to Dean King's *A Sea of Words,* a handy lexicon, first published in 1995 and in its third edition by 2000, that has sold over a hundred thousand copies—substantially more than *Harbors and High Seas* (third edition, 2000), an illustrated guide to O'Brian's locations that one might think the more accessible companion. The recovered and technical words are also a principal means of generating both sensibility and individual character, as in this exchange between Aubrey and Maturin in *The Ionian Mission:*

"But tell me now, how can I best confound Professor Graham?" [asked Stephen.]

"Why, as to that," said Jack, blowing on his coffee-cup and staring out of the stern-window at the harbour, "as to that . . . if you do not choose to call him a pragmatical clinchpoop and kick his breech, which you might think ungenteel, perhaps you could tell him to judge the pudding by its fruit."

"You mean, prove the tree by its eating."

"No, no, Stephen, you are quite out: eating a tree would prove nothing. And then you might ask him, had he ever seen many poltroons in the Navy?"

"I am not quite sure what you mean by poltroons."

"You might describe them as something that cannot be attempted to be tolerated in the Navy—like wombats," he added, with a sudden recollection of the creatures Stephen had brought aboard an earlier command. "Mean-spirited worthless wretches: cowards, to put it in a word."

"You are unjust to wombats, Jack; and you were unjust to my three-toed sloth—such illiberal reflections. But leaving wombats to one side, and confining ourselves to your poltroons, Graham might reply that he had seen a good many bullies in the Navy; and for him, perhaps, the two are much the same."

"But they ain't, you know. They ain't the same thing at all. I thought they were once, when I was a youngster in the Queen, and I stood up to a tyrannical brute, quite sure he would prove a barnyard cock and turn shy. Lord, how he did bang me up and down,"—laughing heartily at the recollection—"and when I could no longer hear or see or keep my feet he stood over me with a cobbing-board."

(pp. 292–293)

Besides the rich humor of Jack's typical confusion with sayings, the pleasing cross-purpose about wombats, and the interests of "poltroon" or the conventional naval use of "shy" for "cowardly," there are subtler pleasures. "Cobbing-boards" were legal instruments of naval beating, bringing ironic legitimacy to the bully's final stance and chiming with Jack's laughter at his own suffering. "Clinchpoop," apparently Jack's invention, combines "clinch" in the sense of seizing a rope to itself with "poop" as a verb, to be mortally struck from behind by a wave—a parallel to "kicking his breech," or backside: an action Jack's class would have thought perfectly "gentlemanly" (inferiors might properly be so treated), but the rising middle classes would indeed have thought "ungenteel" (demeaning to one's own status). Also far-reaching is Jack's "pragmatical" as an insult, presumably in the sense (old-fashioned even then) of "officious, needlessly interfering," but as Stephen's dispute with Professor Graham is quasi-scientific, with a complex echo of the philosophical sense allied to "empiricism"—a form of argument to which Jack turns in suggesting Stephen should appeal to Graham's own experience of naval personnel.

This dense yet flowing conversation is a great part of O'Brian's world and corresponds to the importance the Georgian era placed on conversation in all its senses. Yet O'Brian could also, as in this passage from *The Reverse of the Medal,* create jeweled evocations:

"Why do I feel such an intense pleasure, such an intense satisfaction?" asked Stephen. For some time he searched for a convincing reply, but finding none he observed "The fact is that I do." He sat on as the sun's rays came slowly down through the trees, lower and lower, and when the lowest reached a branch not far above him it caught a dewdrop poised upon a leaf. The drop instantly blazed crimson, and a slight movement of his head made it show all the colours of the spectrum with extraordinary purity, from a red almost too deep to be seen through all the others to the ultimate violet and back again. Some minutes later a cock pheasant's explosive call broke the silence and the spell and he stood up.

(p. 178)

Science and nature at one; or again, in the same narrative mode (created as a third-person variant on Stephen's first-person diary entries), such as this from *The Commodore:*

Stephen had been put to sleep in his usual room, far from children and noise, away in that corner of the house which looked down to the orchard and the bowling-green, and in spite of his long absence it was so familiar to him that when he woke about three he made his way to the window almost as quickly as if dawn had already broken, opened it and walked out on to the balcony. The moon had set: there was barely a star to be seen. The still air was delightfully fresh with falling dew, and a late nightingale, in indifferent voice, was uttering a routine jug-jug far down in Jack's plantations; closer at hand, and more agreeable by far, nightjars churred in the orchard, two of them, or perhaps three, the sound rising and falling, intertwining so that the source could not be made out for sure. There were few birds he preferred to nightjars, but it was not they that had brought him out of bed: he stood leaning on the balcony rail and presently Jack Aubrey, in a summer-house by the bowling-green, began again, playing very gently in the darkness, improvising wholly for himself, dreaming away on his violin with a mastery that Stephen had never heard equalled, though they had played together for years and years.

(p. 72)

The skill with which description, evocation, and narrative are blended, report and opinion melding toward revelation, could but should not pass unnoticed; nor the habitual specificities of "bowling-green," "a late nightingale," "jug-jug," and "churred," spicing the diction with a countryman's knowledge and a wordsmith's art. Social and natural setting, living friendship, and the drive of suspense and revelation are as harmonious as the nightjars, as intertwined as Stephen's thoughts and Jack's violin, with O'Brian the half-heard third.

CONCLUSION: THE NAVAL ROMAN-FLEUVE

In almost every way the Great Wars sparked by the French Revolution and Terror, and sustained by Napoleonic imperialism, mark the beginnings of the modern age. Decades long, with action on all continents and in all oceans, they are our World War Zero, and their polarities are legion: in French land power and British sea power; in legal philosophy, where forced introduction throughout continental Europe of the Napoleonic Code laid the basis of much modern law; in imperial history, where utter defeat of the Franco-Spanish fleet at Trafalgar in 1805 sounded the death knell of the Spanish maritime empire and the coronation salute of its British successor, while the proxy war in India completed foundations for the British raj; in natural science, where London's Royal Society and the Paris *Académie des Sciences* continued to cooperate, and the grasp of Enlightened thought, empirical classification, and reason became critically dominant in the world; even in the murky history of secret services, where the need for accurate intelligence and the economic foundations of successful belligerence forced rapid systematic development. Technologies from semaphore to rockets, explosive shells, and the ultrarapid clipper ships of the Victorian tea trade originate in perceived wartime necessities, and the navy was at the heart of the British effort and, often enough, the forefront of the public mind.

N. A. M. Rodger, concluding *The Command of the Ocean* (2004), the second volume of his *Naval History of Britain,* comments on the long-term consequences of the Glorious Revolution of 1688, which wrested further powers for Parliament from the crown:

> The location [after 1688] of the main revenue-raising and revenue-spending departments on the efficient, Parliamentary side of British government is one of the most distinctive and important features of British constitutional development. Because

Parliament captured the Navy, it was able to realize the character of British sea power as the ideal expression of the nation in arms which was founded on the folk-memory of the Elizabethan age. It made the Navy an expression of the liberty of the people, where the army was an expression of the power of the crown.

(p. 579)

This is not a kind of awareness Aubrey or Maturin could themselves express, but it is a perception they embody, and O'Brian's primary achievement in their conception is marrying a comedic duo shaped for endurance with a set of circumstances that put the world on edge; the mutual resonance of private and public, love and duty, survival and slaughter are amplified throughout the secondary achievement of the series itself, sustained (with preface and coda) across the Napoleonic Wars of 1803–1815 and bookended by Aubrey's promotions into individual command, and out of it to flag rank. The global reach and frequent extremity of action convey in the end plain truths, and the recurrent technical detail, faithfully recording the consuming exertions demanded by wooden ships, conveys also O'Brian's warm admiration for the sung and unsung heroes of the age he loved, from which our own visibly descends. In consequence the Aubreiad is as warm (and often funny) as it is long-reaching and farseeing, and the whole, at its twin heart, is wise about men's minds, drawing deeply on interpretative skills of biography and the searching self-critique to which O'Brian subjected himself after 1945.

In literary terms O'Brian must also be granted a bold inspiration in increasingly allowing his plot and Aubrey's voyages to flow from novel to novel, as Forester's, Pope's, and Kent's do not. The generic norm of one voyage per novel is obvious and understandable, but in breaking it O'Brian was able to expand his scope enormously. He had one prompt in Anthony Powell's twelve-volume *Dance to the Music of Time* (1951–1975), almost the only valid comparison, but the *Aubreiad* is twice as long, far wilder, and yet more scholarly in every way; the two do, however, share a notable constancy of chapter length and hence a steadiness of increment that is probably a necessity for the long haul of a sequence. Powell and O'Brian were close contemporaries, despite sharply dissimilar lives; the comparison is a reminder that O'Brian, however historical a writer, lived through the great military convulsions of his own century, and after a very close encounter with its seamiest aspects rejected contemporary political life as dishonorably unworthy.

To that extent the *Aubreiad* might be thought, with all Napoleonic naval adventures, escapist—a nostalgic retreat by the readers of a nation whose empire was imploding to a time when greatness was being achieved; a yearning fantasy for an age when warfare was noble and civilized, before the grotesque barbarism of nuclear war and the Holocaust. There is some truth in that, but far less in O'Brian's case than most, his sense of Georgian England and its navy including quite as many warts and acerbic judgments as glories and hallelujahs. It should also be noted that O'Brian's unremitting attention to the late eighteenth-century mind and world, as to the distinct speech and manners of Jack and Stephen, represents a writerly and imposes a readerly burden that is anything but escapist. Additionally, if O'Brian's historical portrait is exceptionally broad, he nevertheless gives some things and themes more attention than others, and his selection of those things, whether Stephen and Diana's tormented relationship or the importance of the Pacific to world affairs, necessarily reflected his own twentieth-century life and concerns.

In some sense, then, O'Brian is an exception to prove the rule, reworking a genre so thoroughly that it became of a quite different order. At the same time great generic novels do not achieve greatness by rejecting or transcending genre; they amplify and purify it, and Rodger's insight about the genuine historical popularity of the Royal Navy as a parliamentarian institution, "the ideal expression of the nation in arms," goes far to explain an underlying warmth and cheerfulness in the genre that O'Brian most magnificently realizes. In the light of Jane Austen (and Dorothy L. Sayers's transformation of the detective novel), one might also think of O'Brian as fundamentally a novelist of manners and his battles as the continuation of manners by other

means—a view that would explain the central functions in the *Aubreiad* of spoken and musical conversation, and the moralization they commonly offer. It is also clear that Patrick O'Brian's extraordinary life was *in toto* a source for his fiction and that a set of personal traumas and compensations was combined to their mutual ease in a profoundly historical imagination that became his center of mental life. If the genre gave a great writer the space and structure he needed for his major work, that is a testimony to the genre as well as an X-ray of the writer.

Selected Bibliography

WORKS AS R. P. RUSS

NOVELS

Caesar: The Life Story of a Panda Leopard. London and New York: Putnam, 1930. Reprint under the name Patrick O'Brian with a foreword, Boston Spa: British Library, 1999; New York: Norton, 1999.

Hussein: An Entertainment. London: Oxford University Press, 1938. Reprint under the name Patrick O'Brian with a foreword, Boston Spa: British Library, 1999; New York: Norton, 1999.

SHORT STORIES

"Skogula—the Sperm Whale." *Chums,* 1931, pp. 314–315.

"Wang Khan of the Elephants." In *The Oxford Annual for Scouts.* Edited by Herbert Strang. London: Oxford University Press, 1933, pp. 107–112.

"A Tale about a Great Peregrine Falcon." *Great-Heart: The Church of Scotland Magazine—for Boys and Girls,* 1933, pp. 50–52.

Beasts Royal. London: Putnam, 1934.

"The White Cobra." *In The Oxford Annual for Scouts.* Edited by Herbert Strang. London: Oxford University Press, 1934, pp. 66–70.

"Cheetah." In *The Oxford Annual for Boys.* Edited by Herbert Strang. London: Oxford University Press, 1935 pp. 144–152.

"Noughts and Crosses." *In The Oxford Annual for Boys.* Edited by Herbert Strang. London: Oxford University Press, 1936.

"Two's Company." *In The Oxford Annual for Boys.* Edited by Herbert Strang. London: Oxford University Press, 1937 pp. 5–18.

"One Arctic Summer." *In The Oxford Annual for Boys.* Edited by Herbert Strang. London: Oxford University Press, 1938 pp. 88–96.

"No Pirates Nowadays." *In The Oxford Annual for Boys.* Edited by Herbert Strang. London: Oxford University Press, 1940 pp. 5–22.

WORKS AS PATRICK O'BRIAN

NOVELS OTHER THAN AUBREY/MATURIN

Three Bear Witness. London: Secker & Warburg, 1952. Reprint with the title *Testimonies,* New York: Harcourt, Brace, 1952. Rev. ed. with a preface by Delmore Schwartz, New York: Norton, 1993; London: HarperCollins, 1994.

The Catalans. New York: Harcourt, Brace, 1953. Reprint with the title *The Frozen Flame,* London: Hart-Davis, 1953.

The Road to Samarcand. London: Hart-Davis, 1954.

The Golden Ocean. London: Hart-Davis, 1956; New York: J. Day, 1957. Rev. ed., London: Macmillan, 1970; New York: Norton, 1994; London: HarperCollins, 1996.

The Unknown Shore. London: Hart-Davis, 1959; New York: Norton, 1995; London: HarperCollins, 1996.

Richard Temple. London: Macmillan, 1962; New York: Norton, 2006.

SHORT-STORY COLLECTIONS

The Last Pool and Other Stories. London: Secker & Warburg, 1950.

The Walker and Other Stories. New York: Harcourt, Brace, 1955. Reprint with the title *Lying in the Sun and Other Stories,* London: Hart-Davis, 1956.

The Chian Wine and Other Stories. London: Collins, 1974.

The Collected Short Stories. London: HarperCollins, 1994. Reprint with the title *The Rendezvous and Other Stories,* New York: Norton, 1994. (As many stories are omitted, this might better have been called Selected Stories.).

THE AUBREY/MATURIN NOVELS

Publication details of first U.K. and U.S. editions only are given, but all the novels in the series have often been reprinted. Music by Pietro Antonio Locatelli (1695–1764) and other composers mentioned in the novels is available on a compact disc by the Philharmonia Virtuosi, *Musical Evenings with the Captain* (1996). Peter Weir's Oscar-winning film *Master and Commander: The Far Side of the World* (2003), fusing the novels its title names, is available in a two-disc DVD edition including interviews and other documentary material.

Master and Commander. Philadelphia: Lippincott, 1969; London: Collins, 1970.

Post Captain. Philadelphia: Lippincott, 1972; London: Collins, 1972.

H.M.S. Surprise. Philadelphia: Lippincott, 1973; London: Collins, 1973.

The Mauritius Command. London: Collins, 1977; New York: Stein & Day, 1978.

Desolation Island. London: Collins, 1978; New York: Stein & Day, 1979.

The Fortune of War. London: Collins, 1979; New York: Norton, 1991.

The Surgeon's Mate. London: Collins, 1980; New York: Norton, 1992.

The Ionian Mission. London: Collins, 1981; New York: Norton, 1992.

Treason's Harbour. London: Collins, 1983; New York: Norton, 1992.

The Far Side of the World. London: Collins, 1984; New York: Norton, 1992.

The Reverse of the Medal. London: Collins, 1986; New York: Norton, 1992.

The Letter of Marque. London: Collins, 1988; New York: Norton, 1990.

The Thirteen-Gun Salute. London: Collins, 1989; New York: Norton, 1991.

The Nutmeg of Consolation. London: Collins, 1991; New York: Norton, 1991.

Clarissa Oakes. London: HarperCollins, 1992. Reprint with the title *The Truelove,* New York: Norton, 1992.

The Wine-Dark Sea. London: HarperCollins, 1993; New York: Norton, 1993.

The Commodore. London: HarperCollins, 1995; New York: Norton, 1995.

The Yellow Admiral. New York: Norton, 1996; London: HarperCollins, 1997.

The Hundred Days. London: HarperCollins, 1998; New York: Norton, 1998.

Blue at the Mizzen. London: HarperCollins, 1999; New York: Norton, 1999.

The Final Unfinished Voyage of Jack Aubrey. London: HarperCollins, 2004. Reprint with the title *21: The Final Unfinished Voyage of Jack Aubrey,* New York: Norton, 2004.

BIOGRAPHIES

Pablo Ruiz Picasso: A Biography. London: Collins, 1976; New York: Putnam, 1976.

Joseph Banks: A Life. London: Collins Harvill, 1987; Boston: David R. Godine, 1993.

OTHER NONFICTION

A Book of Voyages. London: Home & Van Thal, 1947.

Men-of-War: Life in Nelson's Navy. London: Collins, 1974; New York: Norton, 1995.

Foreword to *Nelson's Navy: The Ships, Men and Organisation, 1793–1815,* by Brian Lavery. London: Conway Maritime Press, 1989.

"The Great War." In *Brooks's: A Social History.* Edited by Philip Ziegler and Desmond Seward. London: Constable, 1991.

Introduction to *Mansfield Park. In The Complete Novels of Jane Austen.* Glasgow: HarperCollins, 1993.

"Black, Choleric & Married?" In *Patrick O'Brian: Critical Appreciations and a Bibliography.* Edited by A. E. Cunningham. Boston Spa: British Library, 1994.

SELECTED TRANSLATIONS

Soustelle, Jacques. *The Daily Life of the Aztecs on the Eve of the Spanish Conquest.* London: Weidenfeld & Nicolson, 1961.

de Beauvoir, Simone. *A Very Easy Death.* London: Deutsch, Weidenfeld & Nicolson, 1966; New York: Putnam, 1966.

———. *Les Belles Images.* New York: Putnam, 1968; Douglas, Isle of Man: Fontana/Collins, 1969.

———. *The Woman Destroyed.* London: Collins, 1969; New York: Putnam, 1969.

Charrière, Henri. *Papillon.* London: Hart-Davis, 1970; New York: Morrow, 1973.

de Beauvoir, Simone. *Old Age.* London: Deutsch, Weidenfeld & Nicolson, 1972; New York: Putnam, 1972.

Charrière, Henri. *Banco: The Further Adventures of Papillon.* London: Hart-Davis, MacGibbon, 1973; New York: Morrow, 1973.

de Beauvoir, Simone. *All Said and Done.* London: Deutsch, Weidenfeld & Nicolson, 1974; New York: Putnam, 1974.

———. *When Things of the Spirit Come First: Five Early Tales.* London: Deutsch, Weidenfeld & Nicolson, 1982; New York: Pantheon, 1982.

———. *Adieux: A Farewell to Sartre.* London: Deutsch, Weidenfeld & Nicolson, 1984; New York: Pantheon, 1984.

CRITICAL AND BIOGRAPHICAL STUDIES

Bayley, John. "The Matter of India." *London Review of Books,* 3 March 1987, pp. 19–21.

———. "In Which We Serve." *New York Review of Books,* 7 November 1991, pp. 7–8.

Cunningham, A. E., ed. *Patrick O'Brian: Critical Appreciations and a Bibliography.* Boston Spa: British Library, 1994. Reprint with the title *Patrick O'Brian: Critical Essays and a Bibliography,* New York: Norton, 1994. (The British Library's first bibliography of a living writer. Includes articles by O'Brian, John Bayley, Stuart Bennett, Charlton Heston, Brian Lavery, Richard Ollard, N. A. M. Rodger, and Louis Jolyon West.)

Flanagan, Thomas. "Elegantly, They Sail Against Bonaparte." *New York Times Book Review,* 4 August 1991, p. 9.

King, Dean. *Patrick O'Brian: A Life Revealed.* New York: Holt, 2000. Rev. ed. with the title *Patrick O'Brian: A Life,* 2001. (The first biography, honorably intended but factually mistaken and misleading; use only as an adjunct to Tolstoy's biography.)

King, Dean, and John B. Hattendorf. *Harbors and High Seas: An Atlas and Geographical Guide to the Aubrey-Maturin Novels of Patrick O'Brian.* New York: Holt, 1996. 3d ed. with the title *Harbors and High Seas: An Atlas and Geographical Guide to the Complete Aubrey-Maturin Novels of Patrick O'Brian,* 2000.

King, Dean, John B. Hattendorf, and J. Worth Estes. *A Sea of Words: A Lexicon and Companion for Patrick O'Brian's Seafaring Tales.* New York: Holt, 1995. 3d ed. with the title *A Sea of Words: A Lexicon and Companion to the Complete Seafaring Tales of Patrick O'Brian,* 2000.

Luckett, Richard. "Master at the Literary Helm." *Daily Telegraph,* 23 July 1993, p. 15.

O'Neill, Richard, ed. *Patrick O'Brian's Navy: The Illustrated Companion to Jack Aubrey's World.* Philadelphia: Running Press, 2003.

Ringle, Ken. "Is This the Best Writer You Never Heard Of?" *Washington Post,* 2 August 1992, §F, pp. 1, 4–5.

Simson, Maria. "Patrick O'Brian: Full Speed Ahead at Norton." *Publishers Weekly,* 26 October 1992, p. 28.

Snow, Richard. "An Author I'd Walk the Plank For." *New York Times Book Review,* 6 January 1991, pp. 1, 37–38.

Tolstoy, Nikolai. *Patrick O'Brian: The Making of the Novelist.* London: Century, 2004; New York: Norton, 2005. (This second biography, written by O'Brian's stepson, is seminal.)

ADDITIONAL SOURCES

Cochrane, Thomas, Earl of Dundonald. *The Autobiography of a Seaman.* London: R. Bentley, 1861. Facsimile ed., London: Constable, 1995.

Colley, Linda. *Britons: Forging the Nation, 1707–1837.* London: Jonathan Cape, 1992; New Haven, Conn.: Yale University Press, 1992.

———. *Captives: Britain, Empire and the World, 1600–1850.* London: Jonathan Cape, 2002; New York: Pantheon, 2002.

Cordingly, David. *Billy Ruffian: The Bellerophon and the Downfall of Napoleon: The Biography of a Ship of the Line, 1782–1836.* London: Bloomsbury, 2003.

Deane, Anthony. *Nelson's Favourite: H.M.S. Agamemnon at War, 1781–1809.* London: Chatham, 1996; Annapolis, Md.: Naval Institute Press, 1996.

Pope, Stephen. *Dictionary of the Napoleonic Wars.* London: Cassell, 1999; New York: Facts on File, 2000.

Rodger, N. A. M. *The Command of the Ocean: A Naval History of Britain, 1649–1815.* London: Allen Lane, 2004; New York: Norton, 2005.

Woodman, Richard. *The Victory of Seapower: Winning the Napoleonic War, 1806–1814.* London: Duckworth, 1998; London: Chatham/National Maritime Museum, 1998.

FLORA ANNIE STEEL

(1847–1929)

Phillip Mallett

IN THE ENTRY on Flora Annie Steel in his *Longman Companion to Victorian Fiction* (1988), John Sutherland notes her support for women's suffrage, and comments that "On this, as on every other matter, her views seem to have been eminently sensible" (p. 601). This is engaging but also a little dispiriting; it suggests a writer at once worthy and dull. The photograph that appears as the frontispiece to Flora Steel's autobiography, *The Garden of Fidelity* (1929), tells a more encouraging story. Taken late in her long life, it shows her wearing what seems to be a turban over frizzled gray hair and swathed in a heavy robe or gown; like all her clothes, these had been made by her own hand, to suit her own tastes, and with little regard to other people's ideas of fashion. She stands facing the camera, one hand raised as if to emphasize a point, her eyes bright, and with the hint of a smile: energetic, opinionated, uncompromising. In retrospect it is possible and even necessary to place her and her work in a number of contexts—as a type of the British memsahib and author of a manual entitled *The Complete Indian Housekeeper and Cook;* as a writer about India who became known, much to her annoyance, as "the female Rudyard Kipling" and as a woman novelist who like many New Women of the 1890s developed strong views on eugenics, suffrage, and female sexuality. She was, inevitably, a woman of her age, but more than most she found her own distinct voice: often sensible, certainly, but at times eccentric; liable to prejudice, even where she struggled to resist it, but capable too of the imaginative sympathy that enables the artist to reach out beyond the limits of her formal beliefs.

EARLY YEARS, AND LIFE IN INDIA

The Garden of Fidelity remains the fullest account of Flora Steel's life. It is at times oddly circumspect and even misleading—she frequently omits names, for example, even that of her husband—but for the most part it is typically forthright. So on the first page she conjectures that her birth, in Harrow, England, on April 2, 1847, was the result of a truce between her parents after a temporary "cessation of marital relations" during a dispute between an "autocratic mother-in-law, an equally autocratic husband, and an heiress wife who ought to have had control over her own money" (p. 1). These family tensions may have contributed to what Steel referred to as her "inborn dislike to the sensual side of life" (p. 1); they certainly have a bearing on her fiction, which frequently turns into what the Victorian press called "the woman question"—in fact a series of interrelated questions about women's sexuality, their moral nature, and their economic and legal status. One of the features that distinguishes Steel's fiction is that she recognized that these were issues for Indian women too, and not just for women like herself in the British middle class.

Her father, George Webster, was a Scottish parliamentary agent; her mother, born Isabella MacCallum, was heiress to property in Jamaica. Despite the difficulties between them, they produced eleven children; Flora was the sixth, the second of four daughters. In 1850 Webster found himself bankrupt and in 1856 moved his family to Forfarshire in Scotland, where they could live more cheaply. Financial pressures restricted Flora's formal education to six months at a school in Brussels; otherwise she helped with the running of a large house, roamed the surrounding countryside of the West Highlands, and educated herself by reading widely in her parents' library. Her brothers stayed on at school in Harrow, and it was through the Harrow connection that she came to know her future husband, Henry Steel (1840–1923), whose father was a housemaster there. In her autobiography she wonders frankly why they married; she had not loved him—she thought that she had never been in love—and he was so nervous of her that he proposed by letter. Nonetheless, on December 31, 1867, they entered on what was to prove a companionable if passionless marriage and the following day set off for India. Henry, a member of the Indian Civil Service, was soon appointed district officer of Kasur in the Punjab (now in Pakistan), and though he was regularly moved to other posts, usually at short notice, it was a region they came to know well over the next two decades before returning to Britain in 1889—in the same year, as chance would have it, that the young Rudyard Kipling also returned from India, to take literary London by storm.

Her husband was content to retire, but Flora had no wish to do so. In 1891, she published a short story, "Lal," the first of many she was to write for *Macmillan's Magazine,* where Kipling too was a regular contributor, and over the remaining thirty-eight years of her life she produced or had a hand in more than thirty volumes, mostly fiction and mostly novels but also six collections of short stories, four nonfiction works about India, four books for children, a book on animals, educational materials for use in Indian schools, and her autobiography. In nothing was she more Victorian than in her productivity.

Her twenty-two years in India were similarly energetic. It was, on the whole, a happy life. Her deepest grief was the loss of a child, stillborn, at a time when she herself was seriously ill; the loss haunted her through her life, but another child, Mabel, was born soon after, in December 1870, who "somehow completed and filled up my world" (*Garden,* p. 52). Her talent for theatricals, and for music, kept her in demand among her fellow Anglo-Indians, and she made friends easily. But she also liked to accompany her husband on his tours of inspection, to see Indian life at first hand, to ask questions, and to challenge official opinion. When he fell ill she took over from him an inquiry into some financial malpractice; the administrative chaos she found convinced her that "the best form of Government is a beneficent Autocracy" (*Garden,* p. 46), and

that her success in putting it right showed that she had the ability and temperament for autocratic rule. Back in Kasur in 1873, after Mabel had been taken "home" to be raised in the kinder British climate, and with few Europeans for company, she acted as doctor to the local women and children. She began with a case of puerperal fever, which she treated with such success that had she ordered a patient to be "painted . . . pea-green it would have been done" (*Garden,* p. 61). Most Victorian memsahibs had little knowledge of or interest in Indians other than their servants, or those they were obliged to meet at official functions, while British administrators, all of course male, had virtually no access to Indian domestic life. Here as so often the exception, Steel taught herself Punjabi and studied local customs and folklore. This interest brought her into print, with a collection of Indian tales called *Wide-Awake Stories,* published in Bombay in 1884 and in a revised form in London ten years later, now under the title *Tales of the Punjab,* with illustrations by Lockwood Kipling (Rudyard's father), whom Flora knew in his role as Curator of Native Arts and Crafts at the Museum in Lahore, and with the original notes, by the soldier and scholar R. C. Temple, greatly expanded. These were folktales in the strict sense of the word, all but three of them taken down as well as translated by Steel herself, as she sat among villagers who for the most part could neither read nor write. In its revised version this, her first book, was a popular as well as a critical success, though she herself preferred it in its earlier form, as a book intended for children (*Garden,* p. 187).

She continued to take every opportunity to meet Indians in all walks of life and became a discerning advocate for Indian handicrafts, which were under threat from attempts to satisfy European taste; she produced an illustrated monograph on phulkari embroidery (a Punjabi style, based mainly on flower motifs), and took a particular interest in opportunities for women's employment in the embroidery industry. More significantly, her involvement in doctoring soon took her into teaching, at first working with boys and then at a school for girls. The success of her methods led to a semiofficial position as the first female inspectress of schools, making her responsible for an area of some 141,000 square miles, with duties that ranged from determining the level of grant a school should receive to rewriting and illustrating (again with the help of Lockwood Kipling) the primers to be used in them. Over the years tens of thousands of Indian women received their education in schools under her management.

This was by any standard a significant achievement as well as the source of many friendships among Indian women; when her life was rumored to be in danger after she had exposed a case of corruption in high places, forty or fifty of them would come up from the city at night to ensure her safety. But despite her sympathy with many aspects of Indian life, there was much of which she disapproved, and which seemed to her, as it did to most of her contemporaries, to cry out for British guidance. Indians, she believed, welcomed rulers; she insisted on "the absolute necessity for high-handed dignity in dealing with those who for thousands of years have been accustomed to it" (*Garden*, p. 133). Quoting this comment in *Delusions and Discoveries* (1998), Benita Parry suggests that it exhibits "the insolence of the powerful" and calls into question Steel's confident assumption of her intimacy with the Indians whom she regarded as friends (p. 104). This is fair comment; in Steel's defense one can only note that she based her views on the current state of relations between the British and the Indians rather than on notions of racial superiority, and that elsewhere she was ready to admit how little she or other Westerners understood. Even so, she was always ready to use what she termed her "special knowledge" (*Garden*, p. 183), as when she drew the attention of police officials to cases where a newborn female infant was exposed outside the village, for the jackals to carry off. In her later years she was mistrustful of even the limited steps being taken toward Indian self-government, not least because of the restraints placed on Indian women by the zenana system (the requirement for high-caste women to remain secluded), which she condemned in and out of season as the "plague-spot of India," and in her less temperate moments she was inclined to lump all Indian nationalists together as extremists at best, terrorists at worst. An independent India would be a democratic nation, and she had little faith in a democracy that gave equal rights to both the well—and the poorly educated. But unlike some old India hands, including Rudyard Kipling, she did not take the view that Indians as a race were inherently unfit for self-rule. "In time," she wrote, "India will govern herself, but only in time" (*Garden*, p. 253); until then, she saw it as her role to support the British administration but also to challenge it wherever she felt she could make it more effective and more responsible.

She published only one other book before leaving India, which she coauthored with Grace Gardiner. This was *The Complete Indian Housekeeper and Cook* (1888), dedicated to those "English Girls to whom Fate may assign the task of being Housemothers in our Eastern Empire" and intended as a practical guide for setting up house in an unfamiliar land and clime, among a host of servants—cooks, ayahs, grooms, sweepers, gardeners, water carriers—who were unwilling to adopt English ways and standards. As more than one commentator has noticed, in Steel's view the same qualities of authority, efficiency, and watchfulness were needed to rule a household as to govern an empire. Servants should be treated like children, kindly but firmly, and with a system of rewards and punishments. Beyond this, the young memsahib had to equip herself with as much knowledge as possible: the duties of an ayah (including brushing the memsahib's hair); how to make snipe pudding, or broth for invalids (most memsahibs, sooner or later, had to nurse husbands or guests sick with fever); how to prepare mange ointment for dogs, get rid of white ants, or dose a cow with colic; how to grow English vegetables and to ensure that the kitchen was properly stocked and organized. This and much more, together with warnings against idleness or romantic intrigues, Steel set down with such success that the *Complete Indian Housekeeper* was soon in its tenth edition. One reader must have been her daughter, Mabel, who in 1900 followed her mother by taking a husband in the Indian Civil Service.

EARLY FICTION

EARLY FICTION

The work for which Steel remains best known, the novels and stories of Indian life, began after her return to Britain with the publication of her first story, "Lal" (*Macmillan's Magazine* LXIII) in April 1891. It opens with a recollection of the problems of mapping a land regularly disturbed by floods:

> For year after year, armed with the majesty of law and bucklered by foot-rules and maps, the Government of India in the person of one of its officers came gravely and altered the proportion of land and water on the surface of the globe, while the river [Indus] gurgled and dimpled as if it were laughing in its sleeve
>
> (p. 452)

Steel had watched her husband trying to resolve questions of land ownership in an area periodically altered by flooding, not with foot rules but by the traditional method of floating pots on the water to decide where the currents ran strongest. But the idea of an unmappable land works on two levels: both as a statement about the problems of governing India and as a metaphor for the human condition, with the implication that India stands for all that is unstable or intractable in life itself.

There are similar suggestions in Kipling's writings. The epigraph to "In the House of Suddhoo" (1886) reads:

A stone's throw out on either hand
From that well-ordered road we tread,
And all the world is wild and strange...

(p. 143)

The pattern in many of Kipling's Indian stories is to enter this "wild and strange" world for a few pages and then return to the "well-ordered road"—the world of the club and the mess, with their reassuring and familiar rituals. Structuring the stories in such a way allows the limits of Western systems of knowledge to be rewritten as the eternal incomprehensibility of India. This is the paradigm that Edward Said describes in *Orientalism* (1978) as "a Western style for dominating, restructuring and having authority over the

Orient" (p. 3). Steel frequently adopts a similar narrative position, as when she writes of "the strange old Indian tale of transience and permanence" ("At the Great Durbar," *Cornhill,* October 1896 (pp. 502–516)), as if the mysteries of Time, with uppercase "T," were somehow a product of the East. "Lal" itself is a teasing story in which the narrator's question "Who is Lal?" is never fully answered. It is unclear whether Lal has died and been buried, as the villagers seem to suggest, or even if he has ever existed; he is rather a spirit of the land than a real person, the embodiment of a peasant way of life that constantly evolves in answer to the changing configurations of landscape, climate, and administration. Victorian writers liked to make assumptions about the "timelessness" of Indian village life, and often, as here, the intention is sympathetic: this is a way of life that has outlasted a succession of ruling dynasties. But the effect can also be to suggest that India exists almost unconsciously, without history. History, it is implied, together with the sense of deliberate purpose, belongs to the West.

Like "Lal," "Heera Nund," published in *Macmillan's* a year later, resists easy explanation. It tells of a gardener driven half-mad by his wife's infidelity, who finally kills her and is hanged. His crazed state of mind is evident in his treatment of his daughter, Dhrapadi, whom he idolizes but cares for as if she were a plant; he keeps her beside him during the day in a cloche (a transparent cover to protect plants from the elements), amusing her as best he can, sometimes by dancing for her. The story ends with the narrator learning of his execution, and a remarkable final sentence: "But as I turned away I could think of nothing but that *can-can* among the *sootullians* [sweet williams], with little Dhrapadi beating time with a carrot" (*Macmillan's Magazine* LXIV, pp. 283–288). The story of murder and execution seems entirely natural to the villagers but leaves the narrator baffled; the "winking stars . . . knew more of life within [the village] than I did." But if it eludes Western understanding, and is to that extent typically Orientalist, it is also a compassionate account of a mind hurt by love, with its literary antecedents in poems such as

William Wordsworth's "The Thorn" in the *Lyrical Ballads* (1798).

The opposition between East and West provides the framework for many of the stories Steel published in *Macmillan's*. "The Footsteps of Death" (1892), another elliptical piece, includes a tale within a tale, told by a fakir, whose blindness signals the gap between his vision of things and that of the Western mind. In "The Bhut-Baby" (1893) a Brahman devotes himself to the service of the doctor who restored his sight. When the doctor falls ill the Brahman arranges the death of the "Bhut-Baby," an albino child cared for by the doctor but regarded by the villagers as a devil or succubus; soon after, the doctor recovers. The narrator refuses to insist that the villagers were wholly wrong; the Brahman believes that the doctor's return to health had to be paid for, and the narrator allows that the child's death may have been the payment required by the gods.

In all these tales, the irregularities in the physical world—infidelity and murder, blindness, the albino child—serve as an image of the moral and spiritual uncertainties which engage the sahib narrator. This is not unlike those early Kipling stories—"Beyond the Pale," "The Strange Ride of Morrowbie Jukes," "The Mark of the Beast"—in which a threat to the identity of the English protagonist is similarly figured by the scarred or wounded body of an Indian. In such stories India stands to the West as unreason does to reason, or night to day; it becomes the dangerous Other against which "we" define ourselves. This is balanced, in Steel's case, by tales that concern themselves directly with Indian domestic life. She rejected popular notions of the degradation or sensuality of Indian women and refused to condemn arranged marriages, arguing that they were often more successful than those based on Western notions of romantic love: a reflection, perhaps, of her own contented but emotionally low-key married life. Her stories focus instead on the dynamics of Indian households: the tensions between wives and mothers-in-law, or between first and later wives, or between mother and son, as in "Gunesh Chund" (in *From the Five Rivers*, 1893); the sorrow of the child widow prohibited from remarrying, or of the childless wife, as in "Uma Himavutee" (*In the Permanent Way*, 1903).

There is much here that is sympathetic. Steel takes some pains, for example, to understand Indian ideas of the sanctity of widowhood; contemporary reviewers sometimes worried that she was too tolerant of Indian beliefs and customs. Two aspects of these stories, however, may cause a modern reader some disquiet. First, they often include moments of violence, cruelty, or the grotesque—snakebites, poisonings, the deaths of children, and the like. This can partly be set down to the need in the short story for narrative excitement, but it also suggests that beneath the apparent inertia of Indian life (another version of its supposed timelessness) there lies the hateful and the malignant. India is, by implication, a treacherous land. Second, there is a suggestion that the ills of Indian society are irremediable, or at least that they are not open to Western ideas of reform. In "On the Second Story" (*In the Permanent Way*), Ramamund, a descendant of Brahman priests as well as a science teacher and reformer, argues that an outbreak of cholera should be met with filtered water and better hygiene rather than offerings at the shrine of the goddess Kali. The outcome, after a plot involving treacherous priests, human sacrifice, and delirium, is the death of the widow he had hoped to marry and his own loss of faith in reform. India, it appears, lacks the capacity to change, or to be changed; it is trapped in custom and tradition, where the West looks toward the future. Yet Steel is also ready to subject notions of the well-ordered Western mind to a degree of irony, as she does in her first novel, *Miss Stuart's Legacy* (1893). Here she contrasts "the parallelogram of white roads . . . bordered by red and blue houses" of the Europeans with the world of the Indians, "the tillers of the soil, the hewers of wood and drawers of water, who pay the bills for the great Empire" (*Macmillan's Magazine*, LXIII, p. 352): what is at issue is not the inherent opposition of Western rationality and Indian obscurity but the casual ignorance, on the part of those who rule the land, of the people on whose labor they depend. Steel's politics were imperialist and autocratic, but in her fiction, at its best, she shows herself more flexible.

Miss Stuart's Legacy, first published in serial form in *Macmillan's Magazine,* is in some ways a typical magazine story. Belle Stuart arrives in India to be united with her father, his Eurasian second wife, and her stepsisters, only to find that Colonel Stuart is irresponsible, selfish, and a gambler. She marries unwisely; her husband, the unscrupulous John Raby, chooses her for her legacy and not for herself. In the end she is released by his death, brought about by his own dishonesty, and marries Philip Marsden, whom—as is often the way in Victorian fiction— she meets, and dislikes, at the start of the novel. Partly buried under the errors, secrets, lost documents, and financial misdeeds that drive the plot is some more personal material. Like her creator, Belle never sees her stillborn child and longs for work as a means to alleviate her sadness, while the narrator's reflections, on the gulf between the realities of sexual life and the sentimental and spiritualized idea of love woman were expected to bring into marriage, owe as much to Steel's experience as to Belle's.

But *Miss Stuart's Legacy* is a thoughtful as well as an uneven book. Though it is hinted that intrigue is a racial characteristic of the Indians, both the native and European communities are given to financial double-dealing and sexual rivalry; that each group is baffled by the behavior of the other serves to confirm the narrator's insistence that both East and West, mankind is made much the same way. The most devious of the Europeans, and the most interesting, is John Raby. Crucially, he is a member of neither the army nor the administration; he dismisses notions of duty and probity as a mixture of sentimental illusion and a cover for self-esteem. There may be an element of anti-Semitism in this, since Raby's Jewish ancestry is mentioned more than once; if so it runs counter to Steel's usual moral decency. But the issue that concerns her is the broader one, that without attachment to an institution or the supra-personal ideas of duty and service, human weakness will range unchecked. This is the territory that Joseph Conrad was soon to take as his own, with the advantage that he

(like Raby) stood outside the British imperial dream and—unlike Steel, but again like Raby— was ready to admit that duty might indeed be a disguise for self-admiration. Conrad is by far the greater writer; the comparison marks Steel's limitations, but that it can be made at all points to the critical intelligence at work in her fiction.

This intelligence does not extend to questioning the British right to rule India. Yet the novel makes both implicit and explicit demands for racial tolerance. How the white races regard the nonwhite is one of its moral yardsticks: whether, for example, they are willing to learn or are merely indifferent; whether they aim to rule fairly or to seek personal gain. This is fair-minded but essentially Eurocentric; it makes India into a moral testing ground for the Europeans. More suggestive is the use Steel makes of a familiar Western narrative, in which a restless youth is given the opportunity to work and in the process discovers his own identity: the boy becomes a man. What is interesting here is that Dick, the young man, is of mixed European and Eurasian parentage. In Kipling's story "His Chance in Life" (1887), the Eurasian Michele D'Cruze, seven-eighths native, is able to draw on that one-eighth of his nature that is "white" to act briefly as a hero, but as soon as the crisis is past and the pure-blooded English arrive, he relapses into hysterical tears: "It was the White drop in Michele's veins dying out, though he did not know it." (*Plain Tales from the Hills,* ed. cit., p. 95) This is repellent; but in Steel's story Dick dies bravely, without tears, and without any condescension from the narrator. Significantly both stories deal with telegraph messages, evoking the first warning of the "Mutiny" of 1857 in the telegram sent to Delhi after the opening shots had been fired in Meerut; Dick's heroism in sending his message associates him with one of the iconic moments in British imperial history. Kipling would not have been so hospitable.

Miss Stuart's Legacy was moderately successful, and in *The Potter's Thumb* (1894) Steel returned to similar material. In this novel too there is a character recently arrived in India, this time a young official, George Keene, whose perceptions help to focus points of difference between the European and native populations. The plot follows the fortunes of two English-women, Gwen Boynton and Rose Tweedie, the one widowed and worldly, the other young and spirited, and a Eurasian woman named Azizan, as they face the issues of love and marriage; as Steel and her readers understood, while some women went to India in search of independence, many more went to find husbands. The story also deals with corruption, involving irrigation, which she had already brought into *Miss Stuart's Legacy,* and horse racing, which reappears in *On the Face of the Waters;* Steel liked to get her facts straight, and these were subjects about which her husband knew a good deal. Again there are scenes set wholly among Indians, with no Westerners present. Some of these take place in the court of the Hodinuggur Mughals, which is portrayed as a corrupt and fallen society, its older inhabitants caught in dreams of lost glories and its young heir, Dalal Beg, weak and immoral. Like many Victorians, Steel admired the Mughal rulers of an earlier time; in his poem "Akbar's Dream," published in 1892 in his final collection, Tennyson even sees Akbar (1542–1605) as a Mughal counterpart to King Arthur and his dream of a united people as a first statement of Britain's imperial mission in India. But Bahadur Shah, the last of the Mughal emperors, had been sent into exile after the 1857 Mutiny, and the only historical process of which India was thought capable was that of decline. Elsewhere in *The Potter's Thumb* the emphasis is again on timelessness: in the final chapter, Rose, now married, remarks that Hodinuggur looks just as it had when she first saw it, to which her husband replies that "these people do not change except under pressure from without, and then they disintegrate suddenly" (p. 313). Steel of course knew of the emerging middle class in India—the first meeting of the Indian National Congress took place in 1885, four years before she left—but for her, as for many others, the "real" India ("these people") was still a land of rajahs and peasants. India, in British eyes, would remain "timeless" until after World War I.

ON THE FACE OF THE WATERS

In 1894, Flora Steel made a return visit to Kasur, leaving her husband and daughter to follow later. The plot of the novel she was now planning, *On the Face of the Waters* (1896), required that an Englishwoman should live undetected in an Indian house during the siege of Delhi in 1857, and Steel wanted at least to experience the house; she was far too well known to live unnoticed and was soon doctoring Indian women. Her stay in Kasur, together with the time she spent among the Mutiny archives in Delhi, was less to acquire local color than to make sure, as she put it in the preface, that fiction should not "interfere with fact." This was to be a novel written out of a sense of historical responsibility—hence the occasional footnote—which can sensibly be read alongside a modern narrative history such as Saul David's *The Indian Mutiny, 1857* (2002).

It was also written in a spirit of reconciliation. This was no easy matter. The contemporary reaction to the horrors of 1857–1858 had been to demand promiscuous revenge. Charles Dickens wrote that given the chance he would "exterminate the Race upon whom the stain of the late cruelties rested" (*Letters,* ed. Walter Dexter. 3 vols. Bloomsbury: Nonesuch Press, 1937–1938. 2.889); John Nicholson, the hero of the siege of Delhi and an important presence in Steel's novel, advocated "flaying alive, impalement, or burning." The savagery of the punishments inflicted on the mutineers was widely reported, and applauded, in the press and from the pulpit. Small children, including Steel herself, made and tormented models of Nana Sahib, the villain of Cawnpore, and over the succeeding decades numerous plays, poems, and novels had continued to promulgate images of Indian treachery, cruelty, and sexual depravity. Benita Parry writes in *Delusions and Discoveries* that Steel too "is able to glory in the overpowering satisfaction at British retribution" (p. 119). This is too rash a judgment. In the final chapter of the novel, when Nicholson is reminded that he had once demanded something worse than hanging for the mutineers, he replies: "I was not so near death myself. It makes a difference (pp. 412–413)." If this is not quite a retraction, it comes as near to it as Steel could without interfering with the facts. The same chapter reports the arrest and summary execution of Bahadur Shah's sons by William Hodson. Hodson, writes Steel, "gloried in the deed," but her own revulsion is unmistakable; she describes him as "shooting down with his own hand, men who had surrendered without stipulations to his generosity and clemency" and pointedly rejects as a "strange perversion of the truth" the supposedly justifying claim that Englishwomen had been "outraged" in the place where the princes' bodies were left to rot (p. 416). *On the Face of the Waters* is, as Steel intended it to be, more nuanced than a simple account of the conflict of good and evil, each wholly embodied in a single race.

The novel opens strikingly at the auction of a menagerie formerly owned by the deposed King of Oudh, where Major Erlton buys a cockatoo for his mistress, Alice Gissing. Ominously, the bird has been taught the Islamic cry to arms; that, and the auctioneer's cry of "Going, going, gone" echo through the text. Impulsively Alice gives the bird to Erlton's wife, Kate, whose experiences, trapped in Delhi during the siege, form the center of the novel. Her survival there depends in part on the protection of another Englishman, Jim Douglas, a former soldier now working as an undercover agent, and of his servant Tara, a widow whom Douglas has prevented from self-immolation on her husband's funeral pyre. Alice is killed during the first wave of violence; sexually transgressive women conventionally come to a bad end in Victorian fiction, but Steel puts the emphasis on Alice's honesty and fearlessness, in life as in death, rather than on her status as a fallen woman. Erlton too is killed, in the battle for Delhi; in the chaos of the final assault, Tara achieves her ambition to become suttee, putting on her wedding-dress and throwing herself into a fire. Zora, Douglas's native mistress, dies early in the novel; at its close he and Kate return to Britain and are about to be married. Interwoven with the adventures of the fictional characters is a historically based account of the fall and recapture of Delhi and, less firmly grounded, of the political maneuverings and vacillations in the court of Bahadur Shah—

though even here Steel draws as far as she can on contemporary records.

This is an ambitious story. It tracks the lives of English and Indian characters, both inside and outside Delhi, at both the military-political and the personal level, and includes a host of minor players. It is necessarily episodic and at times pays the penalty for that; as in the similarly crowded novels of Charles Dickens, some characters appear trapped in a single mood or gesture, with little room for development. Even this limitation, however, can be turned to good effect. Hafzan, the crippled and embittered scribe to the Queen, is essentially a choric figure, a commentator rather than an actor, until the penultimate chapter, when she is seen as a terrified woman threatened by the bayonets of British troops. Saved from death, her last action is to tend the body of an Indian killed by the soldiers, turning him "gently" onto his back, straightening his limbs, and closing his eyes: a silent witness to a truth lost or ignored in the violence. The shift of perspective is eloquent and moving.

On the Face of the Waters is generally described as one of the more sympathetic accounts of the Mutiny, which was, and remains, a difficult topic for British writers. Even the nomenclature is disputed. "Mutiny," which implies disobedience to legitimate authority, is clearly a tendentious term, though still widely used. In her preface Steel uses both "Mutiny" and "Great Rebellion" the latter comes closer to some revisionist accounts, which see the events of 1857 as steps in the Indian struggle for independence. Benita Parry complains that Steel oscillates between acknowledging reasons for the uprising—in particular, British insensitivity to Indian religious beliefs and to the humiliations felt by the dispossessed Mughal rulers—and regarding it as an explosion of aimless and barbarous violence. This is only partly just. Most modern historians, like Steel, see the uprising as "aimless" in the sense that there was no coherent plan to unite Hindu and Muslim opponents of British rule, and there was in truth barbarity on both sides. Parry quotes one passage in which a young Englishman, Mainwaring, in love with Alice Gissing, is filled with an insane desire for revenge: "He gave a little faint sob of sheer satisfaction as he felt the first resistance, which meant that his sword had cut sheer into flesh and blood." (p. 233) But this is Mainwaring's response, not Steel's; frequently in the novel she protests against the way notions of the sanctity of English womanhood were used as an excuse for hatred and slaughter. It is true, as Parry also points out, that even the kindly Kate Erlton feels a momentary pleasure in the thought of English men exacting revenge on behalf of English women; but she is also "aghast" at the vision of horror this opens up. It is the British forces, not Steel, who see themselves as "Men" and the Indians as "Murderers," and the claim has no explanatory power in the novel: Hodson, still widely revered as a hero, is shown as a murderer, or little better; the British soldiers who rampage through Delhi, "seeking victims, seeking plunder," kill as indiscriminately as the Indian rioters. It would be absurd to claim that Steel was impartial, but the whole enterprise of creating individual Indian characters is an implicit assertion that they cannot simply be lumped together, whether as murderers or victims.

There are similar attempts to suggest a degree of moral equivalence between the two communities can be found elsewhere in the novel. Both Douglas and Kate Erlton are forced to disguise themselves as native Indians, and both find themselves drawn to the way of life the disguise opens up to them—though it should be admitted that neither Steel nor her readers would have felt comfortable with the idea of an Indian successfully disguised as a European. Douglas is secretly thankful that the child born him by his Indian mistress dies at birth and is puzzled by the sensuality of Indian women. Yet Steel knew what it was to be the mother of a stillborn child, and Douglas, we are reminded, bought his young mistress; however tender their relationship has since become, it began with his sensual needs, not hers. He himself has left the army under a cloud, seemingly because of an illicit relationship with an Englishwoman; Erlton, who dies a hero and is expected to receive a posthumous VC (Victoria Cross), was about to resign because of his liaison with Alice Gissing. It is true that neither Kate nor Alice can be accused of sensuality, yet it is also true that neither deeply loves Erlton, even though Kate has married him and Alice is expecting his child. Steel does not dispute the right and duty of the British to rule India, but they are not offered as unequivocal moral exemplars in the novel.

LATER LIFE AND WRITINGS

On the Face of the Waters was rejected by Macmillan—why, is unclear—and brought out instead by Heinemann, who now took over as Steel's publishers. It was an instant success, reprinted six times in twelve months. Steel and her husband were living in London, and in her new role as literary lioness she celebrated the Queen's Jubilee by organizing a celebration dinner for 120 women, each distinguished in her own right and each responsible for inviting a distinguished male partner. She continued to express her views on Indian affairs, even on such contentious topics as the moves to limit the spread of venereal disease among troops stationed in India. Toward the end of the year she made her last visit to the country, staying mainly in Lucknow, where she gathered material for her novel *Voices in the Night* (1900), but despite her usually robust health she fell ill with fever and afterward could remember little of her stay except that the hashish the doctors gave her reduced her to "smiling placidity, full of beautiful dreams" (*Garden,* p. 241).

Voices in the Night deals with the predicament of a young Brahmin, married to an English girl during a period of study in London. Back in his native city, however, he finds himself drawn to the goddess Kali, unable to resolve his dual identity as Chris Davenant and Krishn Davenund. The general theme, of the unwisdom of trying to fuse two distinct cultures, is echoed in a background story of the foundation ceremonies for an Anglo-Vernacular College. The novel also takes in the domestic conflict between the dissolute Jehan Aziz and his neglected wife, Noormahal, and an attempt by the young and seductive Sobrai Begum to rebel against a life of poverty and boredom, as well as religious disputes, theft, riot and arson, and the usual theme of love and courtship among the English characters. It was not, as Steel admitted, as successful a novel as *On the Face of the Waters,* but she was already at work on another, *The Hosts of the Lord,* also published in 1900. She took time off to move into a large unfurnished house in rural Wales, but the move coincided with her daughter's marriage to a cousin, Jack Webster, of whom both she and Henry Steel disapproved, and it was two years before she found the will to write again.

The Hosts of the Lord has a plot as complicated as any Steel was to devise. It makes use of her recollection of religious festivals she had seen in India, including one at Benares during an eclipse of the sun, as well as the favorite topic of irrigation. Among the British characters are the canal engineer, Eugene Smith, his elegant but fickle wife Muriel, the mission lady Erda, and her eventual husband Lancelot Carlyon; among the Indians are the Muslim soldier Roshan Khan, descendant of the Mughal Nawab, his cousin Laila Bonaventura, descended from an Indian princess and an Italian adventurer, and Roshan's grandmother, Mumtaza Mahal, who is determined to restore the family's fortunes and status. The action includes a jailbreak and religious riot, as well as a reckless liaison between Captain Dering and Laila, her death at the hands of the jealous Roshan, and a fatal duel between Roshan and the Roman Catholic priest Father Ninian, who has for many years been her guardian.

Both *Voices in the Night* and *The Hosts of the Lord* have their merits, but both are heavily overplotted and even in 1900 must have seemed oldfashioned. The three-volume novel favored by mid-Victorian writers had begun to give way in the 1890s to the shorter, more concentrated onevolume form. Steel's novels were published in single volumes, typically of around four hundred pages, but they retained much of the creaking machinery of the earlier "triple-decker." Combined with the Indian setting, the elaborate plots leave them stranded in a no-man's-land between the external, romance world of crisis and adventure and the inner, psychological world that writers like Thomas Hardy, Henry James, and Joseph Conrad had begun to claim as the true territory of the realist novel. Moreover, form here deter-

mines content in that the romance elements seem to have drawn Steel toward racial stereotypes at the expense of the tolerance and flexibility that marks her best work. Benita Parry quotes a passage in *The Hosts of the Lord* where Roshan runs amok after killing Laila, in "that curious phase of the Oriental mind when once it oversteps the hard and fast lines of custom in which it breathes and has its being." (p. 297) The generalizing tone does Steel no credit; there is nothing in the words to remind the reader that she had firsthand knowledge of Indian life, let alone respect and affection for it.

The birth of Mabel's first child, in 1903, helped reconcile her parents to her marriage, and Steel returned to writing. Not all of her new work was fiction. In 1905, she brought out *A Book of Mortals: Being a Record of the Good Deeds and Good Qualities of What Humanity Is Pleased to Call the Lower Animals*—among other things, a tribute to her dachshund, Angelo, whom she expected to meet again in the afterlife—but neither the public nor her publisher were enthusiastic. In the same year she had a hand in the less whimsically titled *India,* essentially a coffee-table book for which she supplied the text, a series of essays on such topics as "Women" and "Morals," and Mortimer Mempes the rather dull illustrations. Three years later, she wrote a more conventional history, *India Through the Ages: A Popular and Picturesque History of Hindustan.* As its subtitle suggests, this was a relatively relaxed account, even though it was written during a time of growing tension, with bombs hurled at British officials in Bengal and debate in London and Simla about steps to increase Indian autonomy.

Steel was also writing novels with a British background. The first of these, *A Sovereign Remedy* (1906), is set in Wales and Cornwall. There is the usual abundance of incident—a shipwreck on the Cornish coast, a hotel fire, an illegitimate child buried in unconsecrated ground, religious revivalism—as well as a concern with economic and social matters, ranging from free education to factory productivity, these last no doubt prompted by the same national mood that led to a landslide victory for the Liberals in the election of 1906. Later she would publish a collection of stories set in Scotland, *Tales of the Tides* (1923), but in 1908 Steel returned to Indian themes with the first of a quartet of novels based on the lives of the great Mughal emperors, *A Prince of Dreamers*. This takes Akbar the Great as hero, and Fatehpur Sikri, built to celebrate the birth of his first son, as its setting. It was to this great sandstone palace, still hauntingly beautiful, that Akbar summoned teachers from a whole range of religions—Hindu, Muslim, Sufi, Sikh, and Christian—to search for a core "Divine Faith" that could satisfy all believers. Like Elizabeth I of England, his near-contemporary, Akbar had personality and adventures enough to fill a dozen novels, though as usual Steel added numerous complications of plot, including a woman who takes up the traditionally male role of bard to the emperor, and a courtesan of unparalleled beauty.

With *King-Errant* (1912) Steel stepped back to the reign of Akbar's grandfather, Babar, descendant of both Tamerlane and Genghis Khan, a boy king who became the conqueror of Delhi and the founder of the Mughal dynasty. Like later historians, such as Abraham Eraly in his *The Mughal Throne* (1997), Steel made use of Babar's own poetry and memoirs and like them found herself drawn by his charm, wisdom, and generosity; no doubt it helped that he, like Steel, loved orchards and gardens. The story of Babar's struggle to unite the land and rule justly, despite intense heat and cholera as well as opponents on the battlefield, is made into an exemplum for the British, who in Steel's eyes had inherited the task the Mughals had begun. Babar is even described as a "gentleman," a key term in the moral lexicon of the Victorians; and as a gentleman he learns to deal fairly with others and to take on the responsibility of ruling justly over those whose territories he had annexed on the battlefield. His death, willingly accepted in exchange for the life of his son Humayun, is a "good end" in the tradition beloved of the nineteenth century.

The third novel of the quartet, *Mistress of Men*, appeared in 1917. As its title suggests, its real subject is not the emperor Jahangir, the successor to Akbar, but Nur Jahan, Jahangir's wife; the novel opens with her as a baby exposed in the desert by her parents and left to die (in fact her father became one of Jahangir's chief ministers). Both the novel and the historical evidence reveal Nur Jahan as a woman of exceptional beauty, courage, and intelligence. For much of Jahangir's reign she was the de facto ruler, helping him fight off several attempts at rebellion; that after his death she survived the transition from public to private life, despite the failure of one last bid to remain the power behind the throne, testifies to her skill in managing the intrigues of the Mughal court. Steel herself was now seventy, and like Nur Jahan had come into her own in the second half of her life; in her autobiography she insists that, for her, menopause brought "not any diminution of energy, any failure physical or mental; but the exact contrary" (*Garden*, p. 200). *Mistress of Men* allowed her to link the history of India to her recurring interest in women with ambitions beyond the domestic sphere, in the constraints placed upon them, and in the means they found to secure control of their own destinies.

The fourth novel in the quartet, *The Builder*, was not to appear until 1928. Like many of her contemporaries and many more recent historians, Steel dated the decline of the Mughal dynasty from the reign of Shah Jahan. He might, she thought, have been "the ablest monarch of them all" (*Garden*, p. 290), but despite his celebrity as the builder of the Taj Mahal, built in memory of his wife Mumtaz Mahal, and of the Jama Masjid, then the largest mosque in India, he had consoled himself after her death with numerous mistresses at the same time as he acquiesced in the religious intolerance that was to mark the reign of his successor, Aurangzeb. Here, for Steel, were signs of the strange mixture of religiosity and sensuality that caused India's fall from its golden age and, eventually, its need to be reinvigorated by British rule. The issue, as she put it in *The Law of the Threshold* (1924), was whether a backward, caste-ridden land would be better governed by itself or by a race admittedly alien but accustomed to accepting and to exercising authority.

Steeped as she was in the imperial tradition, to Steel such a question could admit of only one answer.

Sensuality, or what in *The Builder* Steel called "the smirch of sex," was an increasing preoccupation, and not only as a theme for fiction. At one level this was simply a reflex of her years, and her disquiet at the changes taking place around her; she wrote of the distress it caused her to see a young girl, "so ignorant of eternal values, so hopelessly deluded," put on a fur coat and silk stockings in order to "spend hours at a cinema with a boy's arm round her waist" (*Garden*, p. 285). The contrast between "eternal values" and the cinema suggests how little Steel could feel at home in the 1920s.

But she was also concerned at a more general level. On a train journey into London she found herself looking down into a warren of crowded dwellings: evidence, it seemed to her, that human reproduction had run out of control. Others were thinking along similar lines. The atrocities of Nazism have overshadowed the importance of ideas of rational reproduction, not least among feminist thinkers, in the two decades on either side of the end of the nineteenth century, but as scholars like Angelique Richardson have shown, in *Love and Eugenics in the Late Nineteenth Century* (2003), there was nothing strange or sinister in Steel's interest in eugenics and in the work of the Eugenics Education Society (later, more briefly, the Eugenics Society). True, for some writers rational reproduction resolved itself into an attempt to discourage the poor, the criminal, or the feebleminded from adding to their numbers, but for others, as for Steel, it offered a means for women to assert their autonomy and for the poor and disadvantaged to reclaim control of their lives.

This in turn suggested broader, more philosophical questions about the nature of human sexuality and the extent to which it was the site of women's disabilities. During the 1920s Steel spent many hours in the British Museum studying books on human sexuality. Her conclusion, mixed with some quasi-mystical thoughts about Oneness, was that women had become oversexed and female celibacy undervalued. This seems on the face of it an antifeminist position, but as Lucy Bland has demonstrated in *Banishing the Beast* (1995) and Sheila Jeffreys in *The Spinster and Her Enemies* (1985), similar arguments had long been advanced by "social purity" feminists. Steel's last novel, *The Curse of Eve* (1929), set in England in the years after World War I, turns partly on issues of overpopulation, illegitimacy, and stillborn children and partly on the troubled sexual relationships of the Graham siblings. Alan, a doctor, becomes obsessed with a dancer; Eve fascinates and is fascinated by the fiancé of her friend; George is believed to be in love with an aging society hostess but proposes instead to her daughter. Women, knowingly or otherwise, endlessly repeat the sin of Eve by leading men into temptation. In effect the novel provides reasoned support for that "inborn dislike to the sensual side of life" to which Steel admitted on the first page of her autobiography. Was it possible, she now asked, for sex to become once more a "seasonal racial instinct," to have a social dimension, rather than a matter of "individual pleasure"? "Can woman find her lost reserve, and man his lost sense of fatherhood?" (*Garden*, p. 291). Four years earlier, in a very different spirit, Dora Russell had argued that "the most important task of modern feminism is to accept and proclaim sex" (*Hypatia*, 1925, p. 23). Steel's feminism, whatever its merits, was not "modern" she was becoming, as she acknowledged ruefully, "a complete back-number" (*Garden*, p. 281).

Over the twenty years that separated *A Prince of Dreamers* from *The Builder* her life had indeed undergone a series of changes. In 1913 she and her husband had moved into a late-seventeenth-century house in Shropshire, then known as Court o' Hill, and it was from there that she had tried to be of service during the years of the Great War, only to find that her efforts were rebuffed. She did her bit by knitting socks for the troops, organizing the wives of local quarrymen into a Women's Institute, and giving war lectures around the countryside, but she needed a wider field of action and was frustrated not to find it. In the aftermath of the war, however, she seized on the evidence that women had successfully performed work previously reserved for men and took her energies into political campaigning, albeit as a speaker—on one occasion to an audience of fifteen hundred women—rather than as a parliamentary candidate. She and her husband made one final move, to Cheltenham, where their grandson Neil Webster was at school. Then, in 1923, Henry Steel died. Their marriage had been long and contented and it was a hard loss to bear; her daughter, Mabel, wrote that to her father "my mother was the one entirely right thing in this world, and the loss to her of this background to all her life and activity was immense" (*Garden,* p. 289). Yet life and activity remained. In 1928, after completing *The Curse of Eve,* she traveled to Jamaica to visit the family property, toured widely while there, and on her return wrote up her experiences with her usual gusto before beginning work on her memoir, *The Garden of Fidelity.* It was still unfinished when, as her daughter recorded, she turned to a tale planned much earlier, to be called *The Gates of Pearl,* "and while telling of those who sought them, suddenly and splendidly passed within them" (*Garden,* p. 293).

Selected Bibliography

WORKS OF FLORA ANNIE STEEL

NOVELS AND STORIES

Wide-Awake Stories: A Collection of Tales Told by Little Children between Sunset and Sunrise, in the Punjab and Kashmi. With Richard C. Temple. Bombay: Education Society, 1884. Republished as *Tales of the Punjab Told by the People.* London and New York: Macmillan, 1894.

From the Five Rivers. London: Heinemann, 1893.

Miss Stuart's Legacy. London and New York: Macmillan, 1893.

The Flower of Forgiveness and Other Stories. London: Macmillan, 1894.

The Potter's Thumb. New York: Harper, 1894; London: Heinemann, 1898.

Red Rowans. London and New York: Macmillan, 1895.

The Swimmers. London and New York: Macmillan, 1895.

On the Face of the Waters. London: Nelson, 1896; Rahway, N.J., 1896.

The Gift of the Gods. New York: J. Chartres, 1897.

In the Permanent Way. London and New York: Macmillan, 1897.

In the Tideway. London and New York: Macmillan, 1897.

The Hosts of the Lord. New York, London: Macmillan, 1899; Toronto: Copp, Clark, 1900.

Voices in the Night. London: Heinemann, 1900. Published as *Voices in the Night: A Chromatic Fantasia,* London and New York: Macmillan, 1900.

In the Guardianship of God. London: Heinemann; New York: Macmillan, 1903.

A Sovereign Remedy. London: Heinemann, 1906; New York: Trow, 1906.

A Prince of Dreamers. London: Heinemann, 1908; New York: Doubleday, 1909.

India through the Ages: A Popular and Picturesque History of Hindustan, 1908.

King-Errant. London: Heinemann, 1912; New York: Stokes, 1912.

The Adventures of Akbar. London: Heinemann, 1913.

The Mercy of the Lord. London: Heinemann, 1914; New York: Doran, 1914.

Marmaduke. London: Heinemann, 1917.

Mistress of Men. London: Lane, 1917; New York: Stokes, 1917.

English Fairy Tales. London: Macmillan, 1918.

Tales of the Tides, and Other Stories. London: Heinemann, 1923.

A Tale of Indian Heroes: Being the Stories of the Mâhâbhârata and the Râmâyana. London: Hutchinson, 1923.

The Law of the Threshold. London: Heinemann, 1924; New York: Macmillan, 1924.

The Builder. London: Lane, 1928.

The Curse of Eve. London: Lane, 1929.

Indian Scene: Collected Short Stories of Flora Annie Steel. London: Arnold, 1933.

NONFICTION AND MEMOIR

The Complete Indian Housekeeper & Cook: Giving the Duties of Mistress and Servants, the General Management of the House, and Practical Recipes for Cooking in All Its Branches. With Grace Gardiner. Edinburgh, 1888.

The Modern Marriage Market. With Marie Corelli, Lady Jeune, and Susan, Countess of Malmsbury. London: Hutchinson, 1898; Philadelphia: J. B. Lippincott, 1900.

A Book of Mortals: Being a Record of the Good Deeds and Good Qualities of What Humanity Is Pleased to Call the Lower Animals. London: Heinemann, 1905.

India. London: A. C. Black, 1905. Republished as *Socio-Religious History of India.* Delhi, 1984.

India Through the Ages: A Popular and Picturesque History of Hindustan. New York: Dutton, 1908; London: Routledge, 1909.

The Garden of Fidelity: Being the Autobiography of Flora Annie Steel, 1847–1929. London: Macmillan, 1929.

PAPERS AND CORRESPONDENCE

The largest collection of Steel's papers, including the manuscript of *In the Permanent Way,* is in the Harry Ransom Humanities Research Center, University of Texas at Austin; some of her correspondence to her first publishers, Macmillan, is included in the Macmillan Archive at the British Library in London.

CRITICAL AND BIOGRAPHICAL STUDIES

Attridge, Steve. *Nationalism, Imperialism, and Identity in Late Victorian Culture.* London and New York: Palgrave Macmillan, 2003.

Barr, Pat. *The Memsahibs: In Praise of The Women of Victorian India.* London: Secker and Warburg, 1976.

Brantlinger, Patrick. *Rule of Darkness: British Literature and Imperialism, 1830–1914.* Ithaca, N.Y., and London: Cornell University Press, 1988.

Diver, Maud. *The Englishwoman in India.* Edinburgh and London: Blackwood, 1909.

Gregg, Hilda. "The Indian Mutiny in Fiction." *Blackwood's Magazine* 161:218–231, 1897.

Oaten, Edwin Farley. *A Sketch of Anglo-Indian Literature.* London: K. Paul, Trench, Trübner, 1908.

Parry, Benita. *Delusions and Discoveries: Studies on India in the British Imagination, 1880–1930.* London: Allen Lane, 1972; republished 1998.

(Contains a chapter on Steel, emphatically not written from the standpoint of an admirer of British imperialism. Occasionally unjustly hostile but remains the account any admirer of Steel must address.)

Patwardhan, Daya. *A Star of India: Flora Annie Steel, Her Life, Works, and Times.* Bombay: 1963.

(An admiring account by an Indian scholar, published by herself.)

Paxton, Nancy. "Feminism Under the Raj: Complicity and Resistance in the Writings of Flora Annie Steel and Annie Besant." *Women's Studies International Forum* 13, no. 4:333–346, 1990.

Powell, Violet. *Flora Annie Steel: Novelist of India.* London: Heinemann, 1981.

(Includes some critical discussion but is essentially an old-fashioned study in the "life and letters" mode.)

Saunders, Rebecca. "Gender, Colonialism, and Exile: Flora Annie Steel and Sara Jeannette Duncan in India." In *Women's Writing in Exile.* Edited by Mary Lynn Broe and Angela Ingram. Chapel Hill: University of North Carolina Press, 1989.

Sharpe, Jenny. *Allegories of Empire: The Figure of Woman in the Colonial Text.* Minneapolis: University of Minnesota Press, 1993

Sutherland, John. "Flora Steel" and "*On the Face of the Waters.*" *Longman Companion to Victorian Fiction.* London: Longman, 1988.

(Succinct dictionary entries.)

Tuson, Penelope, ed. *The Queen's Daughters: An Anthology of Victorian Feminist Writings on India, 1857–1900.* Reading, U.K.: Ithaca Press, 1996.

(A useful way into the debate among Victorian women about the roles they might hope or expect to play in an imperial age; includes Steel's 1899 essay "East Indian Women.")

R. S. THOMAS

(1913–2000)

William V. Davis

IF EVERY WRITER's life might in some ways be described as a pilgrimage, the life and work of Ronald Stuart Thomas, a Welsh poet and Anglican priest was quite literally a pilgrimage toward a sacred place. Thomas, however, was a man of contradictions, and these are evident in his life and in his work. And despite Thomas's protests—especially with respect to his most controversial political and theological positions—the seeming contradictions between his professional life as a priest and his work as a poet (which he often vehemently denied) provide an intriguing sequence of developments through which his life and career can be described and evaluated. Indeed it was out of the conflicts and contradictions of his life, which Thomas never flinched from describing, that much of his best and most memorable poetry grew.

But, more than the conflicts and contradictions themselves, it is in the margins and boundaries of his life that the essence of Thomas's personal and poetic pilgrimages can best be seen and evaluated. These interstices provide the thematic focus for much of his most important poetry, which, like his life, was obsessively focused on theological themes and concerns. In a very real sense Thomas lived a crisscrossed (and indeed a Christ-crossed) existence, and the most memorable moments in his life, as well as his most memorable and important poems, often occur at those points where things or themes cross or intersect. Yet these crossings, these paradoxes, in his life and in his lines, were more apparent to others than they were to Thomas, and while his readers were often confused or disturbed by them, Thomas never seemed to be.

Although R. S. Thomas was born in Cardiff and raised in a series of sizable cities, in adulthood he chose to live in rural, out-of-the-way places, often on the geographical margins of Wales, places not even on most maps. Throughout his life Thomas remained a staunch supporter of Welsh nationalism, and he regularly railed against the English, "Scavenging among the remains / Of our culture," as he says in "Reservoirs" (*Collected Poems,* p. 194), and against the English language, contending that in large part the decay of the Welsh countryside and of Welsh culture and tradition resulted directly from English incursions and usurpations in Wales and led to the domination of the alien English over Welsh as the primary language of the people, a denigration that, ironically, Welsh apathy helped to advance or at least did not sufficiently resist. In spite of his strong opinions and fierce nationalism, Thomas did not endorse Plaid Cymru, the Welsh Nationalist Party, because it acknowledged the British role and rule in Wales.

Thomas lamented the fact that, as a Welshman, he had been taught English as his first language. The fact that he wrote his poetry exclusively in English, arguing that one could write poetry only in his "native" language, remains perhaps the most conspicuous irony in Thomas's life. He learned Welsh as an adult and finally came to speak it as his primary language; late in his life he spoke Welsh almost exclusively, and he wrote most of his major prose works in Welsh. Yet Thomas wrote his poems in English, published them with British publishers, married a British wife, and sent his only child, Gwydion, a son named after a character in the medieval collection of Welsh tales known as the Mabinogion, to an English boarding school.

A pacifist, Thomas frequently followed the lead of other outspoken Welsh activists, such as Saunders Lewis (1893–1985), the flamboyant supporter of Plaid Cymru. Thomas took an active role in various causes, including the controversial Campaign for Nuclear Disarmament, and he even

he would collect in his first books, and here too Gwydion was born in 1945.

After twelve years at Manafon, Thomas was appointed vicar of Eglwys-fach in Cardiganshire, near Aberystwyth, a predominantly Welsh—speaking area. He was disappointed to find, however, that many of the inhabitants were English transplants to the area and that they were crowding out the Welsh natives and supplanting the Welsh language. Even so Thomas gave one sermon in Welsh every Sunday during his twelve years at Eglwys-fach.

In 1967, Thomas took his final priestly post, as vicar of St. Hywyn's Church in Aberdaron. Aberdaron was a tiny, primarily Welsh-speaking village at the very tip of the Llŷn Peninsula in northwest Wales. And here, finally, Thomas felt fully at home, in what he considered "home" territory. Offshore lay Bardsey Island, famous as a place of pilgrimage since the Middle Ages, and on it was a bird observatory where Thomas could easily indulge his obsession with watching birds.

At Easter 1978, having reached his sixty-fifth birthday, Thomas retired from the priesthood and moved, not far from Aberdaron, to a small stone cottage, already more than four hundred years old, overlooking Porth Neigwl ("The Mouth of Hell") on the Plas-yn-Rhiw National Trust estate, made available to him and his wife by the Keating sisters, longtime residents in the area and well-known for their philanthropic activities. Thomas was to live in this cottage until 1994. He spent much of his time in retirement watching birds, speaking out on causes that he felt were important—many of which he had been constrained from speaking about while he was in the ministry—and nursing his wife, who had had serious health problems for many years and was also going blind.

Following Elsi's death in 1991, left alone again, Thomas moved in 1994 back to north Wales where he had been most happy as a boy, and took up residence in the remote village of Llanfairynghornwy in northwest Anglesey. In 1996, he married a Canadian widow, Elisabeth Vernon, who was known as Betty. They moved to Pentrefelin, near Criccieth, not far from where the Llŷn Peninsula joins the mainland of Wales

and not far from the area that Thomas had always regarded as the most beautiful in Wales. There on 25 September 2000 at the age of eighty-seven Thomas died.

Thomas's first book of poetry, *The Stones of the Field* (1946), was followed by more than twenty additional individual collections, through *No Truce with the Furies* (1995), the last book of poems he saw into print. In addition to these, Thomas published several volumes of selected poems (1955, 1973; a posthumous edition appeared in 2004), a collected volume, *Collected Poems: 1945–1990* (1993; the title is a misnomer since well over two hundred poems published in the volumes encompassed by this collection were excluded from it), and the posthumous *Collected Later Poems, 1988–2000* (2004), which includes *Residues* (2002), a selection of fifty-seven poems culled from the large number of poems in manuscript that Thomas left in the care of his literary executor and friend M. Wynn Thomas. Thomas also edited several books, including *The Penguin Book of Religious Verse* (1963) and selections of poems by Edward Thomas (1964), George Herbert (1967), and William Wordsworth (1971). He published numerous essays and reviews, many of them written and published initially or only in Welsh, and other occasional items. Since Thomas kept such poor records and often published in small short-lived journals of limited circulation, it seems certain that more poems (and possibly essays) will appear before his canon is finally complete—something that is desperately needed. Even so, more than a thousand poems are available in various places.

In the course of his long career Thomas received many awards and honors. Among the most notable are the Heinemann Award from the Royal Society of Literature (1955), the Queen's Gold Medal for Poetry (1964), four Welsh Arts Council Awards, the Cholmondeley Award (1978), the Cheltenham Prize (1993), the Horst Bienek Prize for Poetry from the Bavarian Academy of Fine Arts (1996), the Lannan Lifetime Achievement Award for Poetry (1996), and a nomination for the Nobel Prize for Literature (1996).

R. S. THOMAS

THE EARLY POETRY

"The young man was sent unprepared to expose his ignorance of life in a leafless pulpit."—*The Echoes Return Slow* (*Echoes*, p. 24).

Thomas's poetry, especially the poems in the first half of his career, can be conveniently considered in terms of several biographical and thematic sequences. In some ways such a consideration follows the outline of Thomas's life as summarized above. His first three books, *The Stones of the Field* (1946), *An Acre of Land* (1952), and *The Minister* (1953)—collected in *Song at the Year's Turning: Poems, 1942–1954* (1955)—contain poems focused on the Welsh landscape and the Welsh people, especially the farmers and laborers in the small rural villages and parishes where Thomas spent most of his life.

In some ways Manafon was the quintessential place for Thomas, and it became the paradigmatic setting for much of his major early work. The poems written in Manafon are both place—and people—oriented. They frequently concern nature (often dealt with in terms of Welsh history), and philosophical or theological trappings overlie many of them. These early poems, perhaps not surprisingly, are the most overtly formal poems Thomas wrote—although in spite of appearances, especially later on, he never abandoned his own kind of often subtle formality. Likewise, most of these early poems are short, a practice Thomas kept to throughout his life. In his large canon few poems exceed a single page.

Among the poems in his first books are several thematically important, indeed seminal, poems. These are the poems that put Thomas on the poetic map and, for some Welsh readers and others, these early poems, with their Welsh characters and settings, are what have kept Thomas on that map. Among them are poems, such as "Welsh History," "Welsh Landscape," "The Welsh Hill Country," and "A Welshman to Any Tourist," that focus specifically on Wales. In these Thomas seems to be greeting his readers—both those in Wales and those elsewhere—although, as is equally and immediately evident, his "invitation" to things and places Welsh is not without its warning. Although the sheep are "[a]rranged

romantically" on the hillsides "in the usual manner" (*Collected Poems,* p. 22) in a quintessential Welsh setting, as if posed for a travel brochure, and even though the inevitable "[w]ind-bitten towers" (*Collected Poems,* p. 37) of ruined castles fabled by history and the tourist trade scattered artistically around the Welsh hills, these are the relics of a past peopled with "sham ghosts" (*Collected Poems,* p. 37) and "bred on legends," (*Collected Poems,* p. 36) whereas the present truth is that Wales is home to "an impotent people" who, "[s]ick with inbreeding," continue to worry the "carcass of an old" and outmoded "song" (*Collected Poems,* p. 37). From lines like these it is easy enough to see how some of Thomas's early poems disturbed some Welsh readers and embarrassed others.

But other early poems, especially those that emphasize his pride of place, endeared Thomas to many readers and helped to establish his reputation at home and abroad. These poems are of several sorts. First, there are poems like the often anthologized "Cynddylan on a Tractor" (*Collected Poems,* p. 30). Cynddylan, on his tractor, with his "nerves of metal and his blood oil," is the paradigm of the new Welshman, here depicted as passing "proudly up the lane." But there are also more ominous hints both toward the future and from the past in the poem, since Thomas here introduces, in his mention of "the machine" and the way it has mechanized man, a theme he will return to repeatedly throughout his career. But, even more importantly, Cynddylan would remind history-conscious Welsh readers of the tragic seventh-century Cynddylan, Prince of Powys, long lamented in a tenth-century Welsh saga, which Justin Wintle has called in *Furious Interiors: Wales, R. S. Thomas and God* (1996) a "classic expression of *hiraeth*" (p. 156). (*Hiraeth* is an almost untranslatable Welsh word used to describe the nostalgia or longing for a time or a place long past.)

Two other paradigmatic kinds of poems appear in these early collections. The first can perhaps best be represented by "In a Country Church" (*Collected Poems,* p. 67), which John Powell Ward calls in *The Poetry of R. S. Thomas* (1987) "the nodal spiritual poem" (p. 34) in Thomas's early career. Here we find Thomas alone in an empty church, in his typical posture, "kneeling," waiting for God's word to come to him. All the traditional trappings are in place—indeed, the place itself seems to be likened to a huge trap into which God might be lured and finally contained and constrained—as in the later companion poem "The Empty Church" (*Collected Poems,* p. 349), in which Thomas makes this metaphor even more explicit by saying, "They laid this stone trap / for him," as if imagining that God would suddenly appear out of the darkness "like some huge moth" and be drawn to it. But in spite of such hopes, prayers, or expectations, "no word came," and "the God" (as Thomas often calls the deity) refuses to appear or to present himself, having once before "burned himself / . . . in the human flame." "In a Country Church," then, and other poems like it introduce early in his career what became one of Thomas's dominant and most consistently mined themes.

But perhaps the most conspicuous poem in *The Stones of the Field,* one that likewise introduces a dominant theme that runs a long course through Thomas's career and canon, is the signature poem "A Peasant" (*Collected Poems,* p. 4). One of the first poems Thomas published, "A Peasant" opens by introducing his most recognizable protagonist: "Iago Prytherch his name." In his essay "Abercuawg" (1976), Thomas describes how "When I began writing I devised a character called Iago Prytherch—an amalgam of some farmers I used to see at work on the Montgomeryshire hillsides." (*Selected Prose,* p. 126). Prytherch quickly became, as Thomas himself said, "my symbol of the hill farmers" ("Autobiographical Essay," in Davis, *Miraculous Simplicity,* p. 10). In "A Peasant" he describes Prytherch as "just an ordinary man of the bald Welsh hills, / Who pens a few sheep in a gap of cloud." His clothing "sour with years of sweat" from the hard labor of the fields, he sits "fixed" (just as Thomas "fixes" him here) before his fire at night or "leans to gob" into the fire. His "half-witted grin" and his rare "spittled mirth" define the "frightening . . . vacancy of his mind." Yet—Thomas tells us in no uncertain terms—he "is your prototype." Prytherch, no doubt lonely, stands solitary and alone, "season

by season" and year by year, against "siege of rain and the wind's attrition," as firm as an "impregnable fortress," not to be taken or "stormed even in death's confusion." This prototypical man, as Thomas suggests in "Abercuawg," developed for many of his readers "into a symbol of something greater." (*Selected Prose,* 3d. ed., p. 126). Even so, Thomas says, "I had to ask myself whether he was real at all." (*Selected Prose,* 3d ed., p. 126). Nonetheless, as Thomas insists, Prytherch needs to be remembered and perhaps even revered for the simple reason that he is, that he exists, and that he will endure. "A Peasant" ends: "Remember him, then, for he, too, is a winner of wars, / Enduring like a tree under the curious stars."

Thomas wrote more than twenty poems about Iago Prytherch, a character who can easily be seen simultaneously as his protagonist and antagonist, his personal persona, even as a kind of alter ego. Clearly Thomas and his early readers alike took to Prytherch and even identified Thomas's work largely in terms of this character. Many readers were disappointed when Thomas turned away from Prytherch and, with him, away from the other early poems in which rural folk and their interests and activities figure so prominently. Some of these folk elements are also evident in Thomas's radio play "The Minister" (1953), which was written for the BBC in Wales.

THE MIDDLE YEARS

"The Cross always is avant-garde."—*The Echoes Return Slow* (*Echoes,* p. 82)

Thomas was now ready to turn, if often with a rather personal focus, toward more politically sensitive and philosophical and theological themes. In his next five volumes, *Poetry for Supper* (1958), *Tares* (1961), *The Bread of Truth* (1963), *Pietà* (1966), and *Not That He Brought Flowers* (1968), Thomas's two most conspicuous concerns have to do with Welsh nationalism and his growing concern for, and emphasis on, theological issues. In terms of the first of these emphases, because Thomas was taking increasingly atypical, untraditional, and unconventional stances, his poems often confused, annoyed, and even angered his readers—especially many of his Welsh readers who had grown accustomed to, and were comfortable with, his more bucolic treatments of Wales and of Welsh characters such as Iago Prytherch.

The incipient emphasis on more overt theological themes is perhaps most conspicuous, and most important, here in the middle of Thomas's career because it represents what was to be the dominant focus of much of the major work yet to come. One of the earliest poems to emphasize this theological theme, "Souillac: Le Sacrifice d'Abraham," appears in *The Bread of Truth* and is based on the Old Testament story of Abraham and Isaac. In focusing on this biblical father-son story Thomas introduced the theme of family and family relationships, an important and, given Thomas's notorious obsession with privacy, somewhat surprising theme that appeared briefly during this period in his career. ("Gifts," another poem, in *Pietà*, is perhaps Thomas's most explicitly personal poem.) But what is most suggestive about "Souillac: Le Sacrifice d'Abraham," anticipating his later poems on paintings, is the way that Thomas associates theology with art and literature—beyond the fact that he is writing literature—by suggesting that art can interpret faith. And indeed many of Thomas's most important poems do precisely that—interpret, or reinterpret, faith or theological doctrine.

Several other poems in this period signal additional concurrent themes: "Pietà" introduces the symbol of the "untenanted" cross, an image that Thomas will return to in other important poems. "Kierkegaard" is the first of several crucial poems that concentrate on the Danish philosopher, a thinker whom Thomas read closely throughout his life, as he makes clear in his essay "The Creative Writer's Suicide" (1978) and in other poems on Kierkegaard, including "S. K." in *No Truce with the Furies* (1995), and who provided Thomas with several central metaphors, as William V. Davis has shown in his essay "At the Foot of the Precipice of Water," (1998). And "The Moor" mines the Wordsworthian theme of the relationship between God and nature, another important and ongoing issue for Thomas.

But in the context of Thomas's primary focus during this period perhaps the two major poems are "In Church" and "Llanrhaeadr ym Mochnant," both portraits of priests. Llanrhaeadr ym Mochnant is the small village in central Wales where Bishop William Morgan (ca. 1545–1604) lived and where he translated the Bible into Welsh by forcing, as Thomas says, the "unmanageable bone" of the Welsh language into "passages of serene prose," and thereby "expiating the sin / Of his namesake" (*Collected Poems*, p. 192)—by which Thomas meant the fourth-century monk and theologian Pelagius, who argued that people initiated their own paths toward salvation without the assistance of divine grace. Thomas himself has emphatically stated that he intended to conflate Morgan and Pelagius. His reason for doing so is based on wordplay, since the name Pelagius is a latinization of Morgan. Thomas was intrigued with Morgan and remained so, as his later poem "R. I. P." in *Mass for Hard Times* (1992) attests, because by translating the Bible into Welsh, Morgan was able to illustrate the importance of the Welsh language to, Welsh, to the English, and to the English government as well. Morgan's translation of the Bible was instrumental in cementing Welsh as the language (thereafter so recognized throughout the British Isles) for all official matters having to do with religion conducted in Wales—even if English was to remain the official language of politics and bureaucracy. Obviously Morgan is one of Thomas's heroes, and "Llanrhaeadr ym Mochnant" is a testament to the "heirloom" that Morgan left for all Welshmen.

If "Llanrhaeadr ym Mochnant" is a historical portrait of the priest in Wales, "In Church" (p. 180) is Thomas's contemporary portrait of the priest, essentially a self-portrait. The poem begins by focusing on the setting ("Often I try / To analyse the quality / Of its silences," p. 180) and by speculating as to how it might be that God would choose to hide from the priest ("Is this where God hides / From my searching?") in, of all places, the church—especially when the priest has waited, in hope and expectation, until "the few people have gone" for God to appear to him. But he finds that he waits in vain, and then he realizes that the church too, since it was built centuries before, has been waiting in vain for God to appear ("It has waited like this / Since the stones grouped themselves about it."). But neither the enticing building nor the expectant priest at his prayers has been able to "animate" the divine to make its presence known. The only sound in the resounding silence of the vacant church is the priest's breath, "testing his faith / On emptiness," and "nailing his questions / One by one to an untenanted cross." And so the priest, alone again and, as always, lonely, finds not the presence he seeks, but only the voluble, indeed almost visible, presence of God's absence, finds his questions unanswered and his faith tested by this ever absent (but hauntingly present) presence of God.

If "In a Country Church" introduces the posture of obeisance as "kneeling," in the poem "Kneeling" (p. 199), Thomas reintroduces this posture. "Kneeling" positions the poet-priest on his knees before an altar "waiting for the God / To speak." Remembering Saint Augustine's request "Save me, God; but not yet," Thomas says, "Prompt me, God; / But not yet." He wishes for God's word, not his own, even though he knows that God can and might well speak through him. He wishes and waits because he knows that the "meaning" of what he awaits "is in the waiting." "Kneeling" thus both anticipates and provides a convenient transition to Thomas's major period, which begins with his enigmatically titled book *H'm* (1972) and runs throughout most of the 1970s, encompassing two of Thomas's most important books, *Laboratories of the Spirit* (1975) and *Frequencies* (1978).

This is Thomas's apocalyptic period, the climax of his career. This period also represents and details Thomas's "dark night of the soul," to use St. John of the Cross's famous phrase. Certainly this is the time that Thomas most definitively felt the presence of God's absence, the *deus absconditus*, and it is the most important and productive decade in his career, a period filled with many powerful poems on his crucial theological theme. Indeed in his autobiographical essay "No-One" (1986), Thomas himself says that during this phase of his life "he turned increasingly to the question of the soul, the nature and existence of God, and the problem of time in the universe" and that "he had reached the destination of his own personal pilgrimage." (*Autobiographies,* pp. 76–77).

"Via Negativa" (*Collected Poems,* p. 220), a poem from *H'm* in which Thomas deals explicitly with this important apocalyptic theme, is therefore conspicuous and important. It begins: "Why no! I never thought other than / That God is the great absence / In our lives" (p. 220). God is here described as an "empty silence," a void— even though he "keeps" the gaps in our knowledge, even though we follow in his "footprints" and hear his disappearing "echoes" in our own voices, and even though we seek and fail to find him. In spite of all this, as Thomas was later to say in "Nuance" in *No Truce with the Furies* (p. 32), we "must not despair"; rather we must remember that even an "invisible" God can be "inferred." Perhaps only Thomas would not despair under such circumstances.

"Emerging" is a key word in Thomas's vocabulary during this period, and it is therefore perhaps not surprising that Thomas titles two different poems with this single word. The first "Emerging" (*Collected Poems,* p. 263), the opening poem in *Laboratories of the Spirit,* describes prayer as the "annihilation of difference" between God and mankind, the recognition of "myself in you, / of you in me." This "annihilation of difference" provides a way of "emerging / from the adolescence of nature / into the adult geometry / of the mind," and also a way of dealing with "the machine": "My life is not what it was. / Yours, too, accepts the presence of / the machine?" (p. 263). This attention to "the machine" resurfaced in Thomas's poetry at about this time as a symbol for the increasingly mechanized society that he saw impinging on the life of the spirit, and this emphasis on the machine would continue throughout much of the remainder of his career.

The companion "Emerging" (p. 355), in *Frequencies,* begins with the poet, now living on the Llŷn Peninsula, waiting for God on "some peninsula / of the spirit." But then there is the realization that God, beyond the anthropomorphic trappings he is so often clothed in, "must be put together / like a poem," that "what he conforms to / is art." This kind of description, if it isn't something new for Thomas, is here newly evident in his poetry, and it adds a complication to his theological musings and to his meanings. The poem itself goes on "emerging" as it suggests that "no God" will bend down out of thin air "to take the hand / extended to him." Rather "it is matter is the scaffolding / of spirit" and God is simultaneously revealed and concealed by the "mind's tooling."

"The Gap" (p. 324), the first poem in *Frequencies,* is also seminal. In it Thomas describes humanity's "verbal hunger" for God and God's fear of human approaches and entreaties. The poem opens with God, seemingly startled, as he suddenly awakens to the "nightmare" of man's "nearness," as "Word by word / the tower of speech grew" upward toward him. God wishes to maintain the "gap" between himself and his creation, and he is terrified that it seems to be diminishing as a result of repeated human appeals to him through incessant petitions, prayers, and entreaties: "One word more and / it would be on a level / with him" (p. 7). God is afraid of this potential personal contact between himself and his creation, and he is therefore relieved to discover, when he "looked in the dictionary / they used," that "There was the blank still / by his name." And then "the darkness" of God, which is as his blood, swells and is then "let" as a "sign in the space / on the page." This enigmatic image—and poem—seems to satisfy two almost contradictory positions simultaneously. On the one hand, this "sign" might be read as a symbol of God's potential bridging of the "gap" between himself and mankind in Jesus; on the other hand, it might be read as an ongoing symbol of the distance God created and maintains between himself and his creation, a distance that he insists on since he wishes to keep his "eternal / silence" and thus his "repose." As with so many of Thomas's poems, the reader here, as Thomas says in "Fishing" (p. 327), is left waiting for a "withheld answer to an insoluble / problem." If Thomas gives an answer to any of these insoluble problems, that answer throws the questions back to the speaker or seeker.

"Abercuawg" (pp. 340–341), another poem in *Frequencies,* is based on the mysterious and enigmatic place first mentioned in a ninth-century cycle of traditional Welsh poetry. Thomas used the title on several occasions in his poetry and in his prose to designate an important but mythic or imaginary place. In his 1976 National Eisteddfod lecture (the *eisteddfod,* a Welsh-language competition involving both poetry and music, is an annual assembly of poets begun in the twelfth century), also entitled "Abercuawg," Thomas asked, "Where is Abercuawg?" And even though he acknowledged that he "half fear[ed]" that it might not exist, he also said, "I see no meaning to my life if there is no such place as Abercuawg." (p. 122) And, he added, "For such a place I am ready to make sacrifices, maybe even to die."(p. 125) It is obvious that, for Thomas, Abercuawg is as important and necessary to believe in as God is—even if Abercuawg, like God, can never be fully or finally found, since both are "above time," and yet "ever on the verge of being." (p. 130) Therefore, as he says at the end of his poem, Thomas is "a seeker / in time for that which is / beyond time," for that which is "always / about to be" and "whose duration is / of the mind" alone (p. 340). In short, Thomas's quest, both in this poem and his essay, and in indeed in many of the poems of these books of his middle period, is ultimately more epistemological than it is ontological.

Frequencies includes other important poems. In "The Empty Church" (*Collected Poems,* p. 349), which is both a companion poem as well as a kind of complement to "In a Country Church" and "In Church," Thomas asks:

Why, then, do I kneel still
striking my prayers on a stone
heart? Is it in hope one
of them will ignite yet and throw
on its illumined walls the shadow
of someone greater than I can understand?

(p. 35)

Likewise, "Perhaps" begins and ends in questions, none of which are answered; "The Answer" provides no answer; "The Absence" (p. 361) describes a "great absence / that is like a presence," but "he is no more here / than before."

In "Pilgrimages" (p. 364), the last poem in *Frequencies*, Thomas describes the journey of his middle career as the pilgrimage it has been and asks, "Am I too late?" His final answer here is again only another question:

Was the pilgrimage
I made to come to my own
self, to learn that in times
like these and for one like me
God will never be plain and
out there, but dark rather and
inexplicable, as though he were in here

(p. 52)

In many ways, then, Thomas's poems during this time of self-questionings alternate between those that are bitter and biting (such as "The Island" and "H'm") and others (for example, "The Coming" and "Sea-watching") that are moving and often beautiful descriptions of the power of a personal relationship between God and humanity—and between God and the man R. S. Thomas.

A LATE INTERLUDE

"He was too insignificant for it to be a kind of dark night of the soul."—*The Echoes Return Slow* (*Echoes*, p. 116)

After this major decade filled with poems of self-questionings and self-questings, Thomas's career took a brief turn into ekphrastic poetry—that which describes and interprets works of art. This seems to have been something like a necessary deep breath before he set out again on his pilgrimage toward what he must have realized was the end of his long journey, both literally and poetically. *Between Here and Now* (1981) and *Ingrowing Thoughts* (1985) contain fifty-four poems based on paintings (thirty-three "impressions" in *Between Here and Now* based on Germain Bazin's *Impressionist Paintings in the Louvre* (1958), twenty-one poems in *Ingrowing Thoughts* focused on surrealist, cubist, and twentieth-century expressionist paintings). This turn toward graphic art as a source of inspiration would seem quite natural for Thomas since his wife was a painter and their house was filled with art and books on art.

But Thomas had always been a painterly poet, one who looked closely and carefully at things and rendered them precisely. Therefore, in looking at works of art—which are meant to be studied and interpreted—it was almost inevitable that (following Horace's dictum *ut pictura poesis*, "painting is like poetry") he should provide his own iconographical "impressions" of these "impressions." As John Powell Ward points out in *The Poetry of R. S. Thomas* (1987), French impressionism appeared at a time "when old certainties about essential and 'inner' reality were breaking" up. And it appeared almost in tandem with Edmund Husserl's philosophy known as phenomenology, which may be simplistically defined as a "philosophy of appearances." Ward argues that the reaction against the impressionist painters was the charge that by concentrating on the surface of reality they seemed to "omit" the "inside," whereas, somewhat ironically, Thomas, after "having sought . . . nothing less than the heart of reality itself (God)," turned, in his poems on paintings, to the "immediate world of . . . appearance[s]."(*Ward,* 1987, p. 111)

After this brief respite, or even in the midst of it, in the thirty poems in *Between Here and Now* not based on paintings and in the forty-plus new poems published in *Later Poems, 1972–1982* (1983), Thomas returned to his theological themes and to his obsessive pilgrimage. Indeed the first of the non-ekphrastic poems in *Between Here and Now* is "Directions," while the last is "Threshold"—as if Thomas were giving himself new directions and firming up a base from which to move onward. In short, Thomas was off again and looking forward, even if still balanced on "the edges of . . . an abyss," as he says in "Threshold" (*Later Poems*, p. 155), a poem that posits briefly a new point of departure for his continuing quest.

Among other important poems in *Between Here and Now,* "The Presence" is memorable for its treatment of the relationship between prayer, Thomas's constant search for God, and the resounding silence that he continues to encounter in that search. "The Presence" (*Collected Poems,*

p. 391) begins, "I pray and incur / silence." This is a silence similar to "my own / silence," but nonetheless pregnant with possibility, with a prescient presence of presence. As he writes in "Suddenly" (p. 426), "I have no need / to despair" since everything "round me: weeds, stones, instruments, / the machine itself," is "all / speaking to me in the vernacular / of the purposes of One who is."

Thomas's next two important books are *Experimenting with an Amen* (1986), in which he continues his theological quest, and *The Echoes Return Slow* (1988), perhaps his most unique book, in which he draws on his own life as source and summarizes—in parallel passages of prose or prose poems and lined poems printed on facing pages—his life and work to date. The obvious transition between these two books occurs in *The Echoes Return Slow*, where Thomas writes: "Concede / the Amens." (p. 45) Having done so, he makes "the traveling" itself "all." (p. 45) Or, as he says in another of the prose poems, "For some there is no future but the one that is safeguarded by a return to the past." (p. 66) Thomas is here attempting to commit "his silence to paper." (p. 48) In doing so, he lets silence itself speak.

The Echoes Return Slow begins abruptly and memorably with a description of Thomas's birth: "Pain's climate." This is reminiscent of the opening of his essay in the *Contemporary Authors Autobiography Series* (1986), where he writes: "Pain, and a woman bearing it; the child, too, but only half-aware" (p. 301). In the companion poem in *The Echoes Return Slow*, as in *Neb*, Thomas says, "I have no name." (p. 3) This book of "echoes," then, describes and details events and circumstances in Thomas's life, in antiphonal fashion, and in his usual guarded manner, more through metaphor than through literal detail. This guardedness is especially evident in Thomas's treatment of close family ties, which (except for the several masterly lyrical poems for his wife Elsi, as, for instance, the final poem in the collection, "I look out over the timeless sea"), like his own life, he never describes in any detailed way. *The Echoes Return Slow* is perhaps Thomas's most private book, as it is no doubt his most personal. Certainly it contains some of his strongest work—in prose and in poetry.

An excellent example is the brace of poems beginning with "Minerva's bird, Athene noctua" (the prose poem, p. 78) and "There are nights that are so still" (p. 457). The prose poem contains a sequence of doubles, literal or implied, which work well within the prose poem itself but which also implicate the companion poem in lines. "Minerva's bird" is the owl "Athene noctua," a small night owl (but active during the day as well, "unlike its tawnier cousin," the barn owl) that sounds or calls its "lyrical" "double note" "under the stars in counterpoint to the fall of the waves." "Counterpoint," a carefully chosen word, joins, as it contrasts, the two owls, their "double noted" songs during day and dark, and the stars and moon above the ocean waves. To all of these doubled details Thomas links "There are nights that are so still" on the facing page—a perfect "counterpoint" (and counterpart) that both complements and contrasts the birds with their human listeners. In this lined poem the poet describes himself as a kind of "night owl," awake and awakened to the sounds of nature: "I can hear the small owl calling / far off, and a fox barking / miles away," and

I lie
in the lean hours awake, listening
to the swell born somewhere in the Atlantic
rising and falling, rising and falling
wave on wave on the long shore. . . .

This vigilance stirs a "companionless" recognition in the poet's mind—one typical of Thomas's constant quest for a relationship with "that other being" who, he imagines, is also awake in the dark, and is also waiting for, even anticipating, "companionship."

"There are nights that are so still," surely one of Thomas's finest and best-known poems—it is inscribed on a stone marker outside Thomas's church in Aberdaron—ends with these memorable lines:

And the thought comes
of that other being who is awake, too,
letting our prayers break on him

not like this for a few hours,
but for days, years, for eternity.

THE FINAL DECADE

"From a parsonage to a cottage."—*The Echoes Return Slow* (*Echoes*, p. 104)

During the 1990s, Thomas's final decade, he published three significant books: *Counterpoint* (1990), *Mass for Hard Times* (1992), and *No Truce with the Furies* (1995). *Counterpoint*, like *The Echoes Return Slow*, is unique; it might loosely be regarded as a book-length poem in four parts. The parts are titled "*B.C.*,," "Incarnation," "Crucifixion," and "*A.D.*" Each part is "counterpointed" with another, the means played off against the extremes, and everything hung on a theological line—as Thomas's lifelong pilgrimage here takes its final turn toward home. The divisions and the arrangement of the individual parts of the book and of the poems, all of which, as in *The Echoes Return Slow*, are untitled, forces the issue of the figure of Jesus into the forefront of human history. In this sense this book is easily Thomas's most insistent theological text.

Counterpoint begins before history began, before humans were human. The opening line of the first poem reads, "This page should be left blank." The poem then attempts to "imagine a brow puckered / before thought," and "man rising / from on all fours." (p. 8) The last poem in "*B.C.*" describes God's staring "down into the empty /womb" (p. 22) of the world. The two central sections of the book conflate Christ's birth and his death on the cross as if there was nothing between these two events. Nonetheless, in "*A. D.*," although there is the recognition of the modern ("the Middle Ages / are over") and of the persuasive presence of modern science ("with radiation / for candle, we make sacrifices / to the god of quasars / and pulsars," p. 49), there are still all the old truths and the inevitable movement "from unfathomable / darkness into unfathomable light." (p. 40) The book ends characteristically, with Thomas still face to face with an "illimitable" absence as the only presence, and with his asking, as he has always asked, "How can I / find God?" (p. 58).

Mass for Hard Times is a difficult and diverse collection, but all of Thomas's central themes are represented in it as he re-girds himself "for the agon" ("The Reason," p. 27). Just Junas the universe (a pun implying "one turn" and "turned toward" and no doubt meant to be taken literally and personally as well as poetically and globally) stretches, so God himself "stretches" "to embrace" the universe, even though it is hurriedly "drawing / away . . . at the speed of light" ("Tell Us," p. 46). This world, in which the "electron's confinement gives / birth to excess of speed" ("Could Be," p. 54) is, for many, a world where God has become "an extinct concept" ("Eschatology," p. 48).

This eclectic collection is dedicated to Thomas's late wife, and it includes one of his most moving and best-known poems, one of several memorable poems that he wrote for Elsi. "A Marriage" (*Collected Poems*, p. 533) documents the couple's long marriage: "We met / under a shower / of bird-notes. / Fifty years passed." When death comes, saying "Come" to her,

> she,
>   who in life
> had done everything
>   with a bird's grace,
> opened her bill now
>   for the shedding
> of one sigh no
>   heavier than a feather.

(p. 533)

Of the other poems in *Mass for Hard Times* that revisit Thomas's recurring themes, perhaps most significant are ones in which he focuses again on his beloved Wales ("Plas-yn-Rhiw," "Pen Llŷn," and "Afon Rhiw") and those that have to do with poetry per se or with language in general ("Question" and "The Letter"). But the most intriguing poems in this collection deal with themes of nature ("Moth," "The Seasons," and "Newts"), literature ("Nativity," "The Letter," and "One Day"), philosophy ("Markers" and "I"), and science ("The Word," "Adam Tempted," "Winter," and the title poem), or with Thomas's quintessential theological themes ("Preference," "Aside," "Tell Us," "Bleak Liturgies," "What Then?" and "Migrants"). One poem, "Sonata in

X," employing an image of "the spirit's / adultery with the machine," (p. 84) interestingly combines science and theology. In a disconnected sequence of poems spaced intermittently throughout the book, Thomas also turns (or somewhat adjusts) his obsessive Christian symbolism. In this theological revisitation Thomas reconfigures the symbol of the cross, a symbol that has been important to him throughout his career, both literally and literarily.

While in the past Thomas had depicted the cross as an "untenanted" tree, which, though vacant, had a clear symbolic and historical presence, here in the title poem of this late book, he asks, "how contemporary / is the Cross?" He then defines it as a "long-bow drawn / against love." (p. 13) This typically elaborate image is punningly accurate in several ways: the cross is simultaneously an "old-fashioned / weapon" (as he describes it in "Sure," where the extended image—"its bow / is drawn unerringly / against the heart" (p. 53)—is almost identical to the image here in "Mass for Hard Times") and something to bow down before. Thomas then complicates his metaphor by calling Christ on the cross an "[i]mperishable // scarecrow" ("The Word," p. 71) and likening the hanging body to "lightning" ("Retired," p. 23). And then, in "What Then?" (p. 75) he asks,

What boughs,
. . . will need to be crossed
and what body crucified
upon them for salvation
to be won . . . ?

(p. 75)

In the poem somewhat ironically entitled "Bleak Liturgies," (*Mass for Hard Times,* p. 63) Thomas finally finds that, "as the day dawned," there will be those who will still find "his body hanging upon the crossed tree / of man, as though he were man, too." Clearly Thomas will be among those at the foot of that cross—among those who find, in the mystery of Christ's incarnation and crucifixion, their ultimate hope and identity.

In *Counterpoint* Thomas wrote, "On an evening like this / the furies have receded." (p. 57) In a poem called "Question," in *Mass for Hard Times,*

Thomas asked, "what after-life is there / for the furies?" (p. 42) *No Truce with the Furies,* Thomas's final book, published when he was in his eighties, addresses this question with a vengeance. Indeed the book addresses most of Thomas's familiar themes with a vengeance, as it takes head-on the reality of his situation in life. "Geriatric," (p. 9) the opening poem, begins with a question:

What god is proud
    of this garden
of dead flowers, this underwater
    grotto of humanity?

It ends:

       I come away
comforting myself, as I can,
    that there is another
garden, all dew and fragrance,
    and that these are the brambles
about it we are caught in,
    a sacrifice prepared
by a torn god to a love fiercer
    than we can understand.

(p. 9)

No Truce with the Furies ends with "Anybody's Alphabet," in which an anonymous speaker (someone like "No one" perhaps?), in a playful, alphabetically arranged sequence, catalogs the themes his mind and his poems have played over during the course of his long life and career. "Reflections" focuses unblinkingly on the world and on the poet himself at the end of his life. It begins: "The furies are at home / in the mirror . . . ." But then Thomas warns us that we can "Never think to surprise them"; that there can be "no truce // with the furies." Certainly Thomas never sought "truce" with any of his "furies," but he also never avoided confrontation with any of them.

The image of the raptor and of the owl figure prominently and powerfully in *No Truce with the Furies,* often in conjunction with each other. In "Raptor" Thomas describes the deity in terms of a bird of prey. To those who "have made God small" Thomas responds that he thinks "of him rather / as an enormous owl" who is "abroad in

291

the shadows" and who brushes him "sometimes / with his wing," a creature who can fasten his talons either "in his great / adversary, or in some lesser / denizen . . . like you or me." (p. 52) Again, there is a buried pun in Thomas's metaphor: if God is a raptor, humanity is his prey, wrapped in his claws and at the same time willingly enraptured by being so captured.

And so R. S. Thomas makes no truce with his furies. And here, at the end of his life, at the end of the long pilgrimage that that life has been, Thomas includes a poem, entitled, appropriately enough, "At the End" (*No Truce,* p. 42). It begins:

Few possessions: a chair,
a table, a bed
to say my prayers by,
and, gathered from the shore,
the bone-like, crossed sticks
proving that nature
acknowledges the Crucifixion.

"All night," Thomas says,

I am at
a window not too small
to be frame to the stars
that are no further off
than the city lights
I have rejected.

He knows that "the passers-by, who are not / pilgrims, stare" at him "through the rain's / bars, seeing [him] as prisoner / of the one view"— even though, he now knows, that he has

been made free
by the tide's pendulum truth
that the heart that is low now
will be at the full tomorrow.

(p. 42)

Years before, in "The Combat" (*Collected Poems,* p. 291), Thomas described his wrestling with God in a passage reminiscent of the description of Jacob's wrestling with God in the Book of Genesis. And now, he reports, as "night approaches," still "anonymous / you withdraw." There is, ever and always, "the failure of language" to express the inexpressible. There is not even any way of knowing "why / on the innocent marches / of vocabulary you should choose / to engage us," while all along "belaboring us / with your silence." At the end, then, all we know is that:

We die, we die
with the knowledge that your resistance
is endless at the frontier of the great poem.

(p. 291)

If God's "resistance / is endless," Thomas's quest, his pilgrimage, is also endless, and at the end of his long career, as he said in "Near and Far" (*No Truce,* p. 46), he finds God still "vibrating" within him "with the resonance" of a blessing, "of an Amen." In the course of his long life R. S. Thomas moved from pilgrim to prophet. His pilgrimage will long be retraced by faithful followers and by readers still to come.

Selected Bibliography

WORKS OF R. S. THOMAS

POETRY

The Stones of the Field. Carmarthen, Wales: Druid Press, 1946.

An Acre of Land. Newtown, Wales: Montgomeryshire Printing Co., 1952.

The Minister. Newtown, Wales: Montgomeryshire Printing Co., 1953.

Song at the Year's Turning: Poems 1942–1954. London: Rupert Hart-Davis, 1955.

Poetry for Supper. London: Rupert Hart-Davis, 1958.

Tares. London: Rupert Hart-Davis, 1961.

The Bread of Truth. London: Rupert Hart-Davis, 1963.

Pietà. London: Rupert Hart-Davis, 1966.

Not That He Brought Flowers. London: Rupert Hart-Davis, 1968.

H'm. London: Macmillan, 1972.

Young and Old. London: Chatto & Windus, 1972.

Selected Poems, 1946–1968. London: Rupert Hart-Davis, MacGibbon, 1973.

What Is a Welshman? Llandybie, Wales: Christopher Davies, 1974.

Laboratories of the Spirit. London: Macmillan, 1975.

The Way of It. Sunderland, U.K.: Ceolfrith Press, 1977.

Frequencies. London: Macmillan, 1978.

Between Here and Now. London: Macmillan, 1981.

Later Poems, 1972–1982. London: Macmillan, 1983.

Destinations. Shipston-on-Stour, England: Celandine Press, 1985.

Ingrowing Thoughts. Bridgend: Poetry Wales Press, 1985.

Experimenting with an Amen. London: Macmillan, 1986.

Welsh Airs. Bridgend: Poetry Wales Press, 1987.

The Echoes Return Slow. London: Macmillan, 1988.

Counterpoint. Newcastle-upon-Tyne, U.K.: Bloodaxe Books, 1990.

Frieze. Schondorf am Ammersee, Germany: Babel, 1992.

Mass for Hard Times. Newcastle-upon-Tyne, U.K.: Bloodaxe Books, 1992.

Collected Poems, 1945–1990. London: J. M. Dent, 1993.

No Truce with the Furies. Newcastle-upon-Tyne, U.K.: Bloodaxe Books, 1995.

Residues. Edited by M. Wynn Thomas. Tarset, U.K.: Bloodaxe Books, 2000.

Selected Poems. London: Penguin, 2004.

Collected Later Poems, 1988–2000. Tarset, U.K.: Bloodaxe Books, 2004.

PROSE

"A Frame for Poetry." *Times Literary Supplement,* 1966, 169. Reprinted in *R. S. Thomas: Selected Prose.* 3d ed. Edited by Sandra Anstey. Bridgend, Wales: Seren, 1995.

"Abercuawg." Llandysul, Wales: Gwasg Gomer, 1976.

Translated (Anstey is not the translator of "Abercuawg"!) by Sandra Anstey. In her *R. S. Thomas: Selected Prose.* 3d ed. Bridgend, Wales: Seren, 1995.

"The Creative Writer's Suicide." *Planet* 41:30–33 1978. Reprinted in *R. S. Thomas: Selected Prose.* 3d ed. Edited by Sandra Anstey. Bridgend, Wales: Seren, 1995.

Neb. Caernarfon, Wales: Gwasg Gwynedd, 1985. Translated as "No-One" by Jason Walford Davies. In his *Autobiographies.* London: J. M. Dent, 1997.

"R. S. Thomas." In *Contemporary Authors Autobiography Series,* vol. 4. Edited by Adele Sarkissian. Detroit: Gale, 1986. Reprinted in *Miraculous Simplicity: Essays on R. S. Thomas.* Edited by William V. Davis. Fayetteville: University of Arkansas Press, 1993.

R. S. Thomas: Selected Prose. 3d ed. Edited by Sandra Anstey. Bridgend, Wales: Seren, 1995.

ABC Neb. Edited by Jason Walford Davies. Caernarfon, Wales: Gwasg Gwynedd, 1995.

Autobiographies. Edited and translated by Jason Walford Davies. London: J. M. Dent, 1997.

BOOKS EDITED

The Batsford Book of Country Verse. London: Batsford, 1961.

The Penguin Book of Religious Verse. Harmondsworth: Penguin, 1963.

Selected Poems of Edward Thomas. London: Faber, 1964.

A Choice of George Herbert's Verse. London: Faber, 1967.

A Choice of Wordsworth's Verse. London: Faber, 1971.

CRITICAL AND BIOGRAPHICAL STUDIES

Anstey, Sandra, ed. *Critical Writings on R. S. Thomas.* Bridgend: Poetry Wales Press, 1982. Rev. and enl., Bridgend: Seren, 1992.

Davis, William V. "R. S. Thomas: Poet-Priest of the Apocalyptic Mode." *South Central Review* 4, no. 4: 92–106 (winter 1987). *Reprinted in his Miraculous Simplicity.*

———, ed. *Miraculous Simplicity: Essays on R. S. Thomas.* Fayetteville: University of Arkansas Press, 1993.

———. "'At the Foot of the Precipice of Water . . . Sea Shapes Coming to Celebration': R. S. Thomas and Kierkegaard." *Welsh Writing in English: A Yearbook of Critical Essays* 4:94–117 (1998).

Dyson, A. E. *Yeats, Eliot and R. S. Thomas: Riding the Echo.* London: Macmillan, 1981. Reprint, Atlantic Highlands, N.J.: Humanities Press, 1981.

Merchant, W. Moelwyn. *R. S. Thomas.* Cardiff: University of Wales Press, 1979. Reprint, Fayetteville: University of Arkansas Press, 1990.

Morgan, Christopher. *R. S. Thomas: Identity, Environment, and Deity.* Manchester, U.K.: Manchester University Press, 2003.

Ormond, John. "R. S. Thomas: Priest and Poet." BBC TV broadcast, 2 April 1972. Transcript, *Poetry Wales* 7, no. 4:47–57 (spring 1972).

Phillips, D. Z. *R. S. Thomas: Poet of the Hidden God: Meaning and Meditation in the Poetry of R. S. Thomas.* London: Macmillan, 1986.

Shepherd, Elaine. *R. S. Thomas: Conceding an Absence: Images of God Explored.* New York: St. Martin's, 1996.

Thomas, M. Wynn. *The Page's Drift: R. S. Thomas at Eighty.* Bridgend, Wales: Seren, 1993.

Van Buuren, Martinus Johannes Joseph. *Waiting: The Religious Poetry of Ronald Stuart Thomas, Welsh Priest and Poet.* Dordrecht, Netherlands: ICG Printing, 1993.

Volk, Sabine. *Grenzfähle der Wirklichkeit: Approaches to the Poetry of R. S. Thomas.* Frankfurt am Main, Germany: Peter Lang, 1985.

Ward, John Powell. *The Poetry of R. S. Thomas.* Bridgend: Poetry Wales Press, 1987. Rev. ed. Bridgend: Seren, 2001.

Wintle, Justin. *Furious Interiors: Wales, R. S. Thomas and God.* London: HarperCollins, 1996.

INTERVIEWS

Lethbridge, J. B. "R. S. Thomas Talks to J. B. Lethbridge." *Anglo–Welsh Review* 74:36–56 (1983).

Owen, Molly Price. "R. S. Thomas in Conversation with Molly Price Owen." *David Jones Journal* 3:93–102 (2001).

Thomas, Ned, and John Barnie. "Probings: An Interview with R. S. Thomas." *Planet* 80:28–52 (April/May 1990). Reprinted in *Miraculous Simplicity: Essays on R. S. Thomas.* Edited by William V. Davis. Fayetteville: University of Arkansas Press, 1993.

SPECIAL ISSUES OF JOURNALS ON THOMAS

Poetry Wales 7 (spring 1972).

Poetry Wales 14 (spring 1979).

New Welsh Review 20 (1993).

Poetry Wales 29 (spring 1993).

Agenda 36 (1998).

MASTER INDEX

The following index covers the entire British Writers series through Supplement XII. All references include volume numbers in boldface Roman numerals followed by page numbers within that volume. Subjects of articles are indicated by boldface type.

A.*Couleii Plantarum Libri Duo* (Cowley), **II:** 202
A. D. Hope (Hart), **Supp. XI:** 123
"A. G. A. V." (Blunden), **Supp. XI:** 45
A la recherche du temps perdu (Proust), **Supp. IV:** 126, 136
A Laodicean (Hardy), **Retro. Supp. I:** 112, 114
"A Propos of Lady Chatterley's Lover" (Lawrence), **IV:** 106; **VII:** 91
"Aaron" (Herbert), **Retro. Supp. II:** 179
Aaron's Rod (Lawrence), **VII:** 90, 94, 106–107; **Retro. Supp. II:** 230
Abaft the Funnel (Kipling), **VI:** 204
"Abasement of the Northmores, The" (James), **VI:** 69
"Abbé Delille and Walter Landor, The" (Landor), **IV:** 88*n*, 92–93
Abbess of Crewe, The (Spark), **Supp. I:** 200, 201, 210
"Abbey Mason, The" (Hardy), **Retro. Supp. I:** 119
Abbey Theatre, **VI:** 212, 218, 307, 309, 316; **VII:** 3, 6, 11
Abbey Walk, The (Henryson), **Supp. VII:** 146, 147
Abbot, The (Scott), **IV:** 39
Abbott, C. C., **V:** 379, 381
ABC Murders, The (Christie), **Supp. II:** 128, 130, 135
"ABC of a Naval Trainee" (Fuller), **Supp. VII:** 69
"Abomination, The" (Murray), **Supp. VII:** 273
Abyssophone (Redgrove), **Supp. VI:** 236
Abdelazer; or, The Moor's Revenge (Behn), **Supp. III:** 27, 36
Abercrombie, Lascelles, **II:** 247
"Abercuawg," **Supp. XII:** 284, 287
Aberdeen Free Press, **Supp. X:** 203
"Abernethy" (Dunn), **Supp. X:** 77
"Abiding Vision, The" (West), **Supp. III:** 442
Abinger Harvest (Forster), **VI:** 411, 412; **Supp. II:** 199, 223
"Abject Misery" (Kelman), **Supp. V:** 244
Ableman, Paul, **Supp. IV:** 354
Abolition of Man, The (Lewis), **Supp. III:** 248, 255, 257
Abortive (Churchill), **Supp. IV:** 181
About the House (Auden), **Retro. Supp. I:** 13
"About Two Colmars" (Berger), **Supp. IV:** 85
"Above the Dock" (Hulme), **Supp. VI:** 134, 136

"Abraham Men" (Powys), **VIII:** 250
Abridgement of the History of England, An (Goldsmith), **III:** 191
Abridgement of the Light of Nature Pursued, An (Hazlitt), **IV:** 139
Abroad; British Literary Traveling Between the Wars (Fussell), **Supp. IV:** 22
Absalom and Achitophel (Dryden), **II:** 292, 298–299, 304
"Absalom, My Son" (Warner), **Supp. VII:** 380
"Absence" (Jennings), **Supp. V:** 218
"Absence" (Thompson), **V:** 444
"Absence, The" (Thomas), **Supp. XII:** 287–288
"Absence, The" (Warner), **Supp. VII:** 373
Absence of War, The (Hare), **Supp. IV:** 282, 294, 297–298
"Absences" (Larkin), **Supp. I:** 277
Absent Friends (Ayckbourn), **Supp. V:** 2–3, 10, 13, 14
Absent in the Spring (Christie), **Supp. II:** 133
Absentee, The (Edgeworth), **Supp. III:** 154, **160–161,** 165
"Absent–Minded Beggar, The" (Kipling), **VI:** 203
"Absent–Mindedness in a Parish Choir" (Hardy), **VI:** 22
Abstract of a Book Lately Published, A: A Treatise of Human Nature . . . (Hume), **Supp. III:** 230–231
Absurd Person Singular (Ayckbourn), **Supp. V:** 2, 5–6, 9
"Abt Vogler" (Browning), **IV:** 365, 366, 370
Abuses of Conscience, The (Sterne), **III:** 135
Academy (periodical), **VI:** 249
"Academy, The" (Reid), **Supp. VII:** 331
Academy Notes (Ruskin), **V:** 178
Acceptable Sacrifice, The (Bunyan), **II:** 253
Acceptance World, The (Powell), **VII:** 347, 348, 350
"Access to the Children" (Trevor), **Supp. IV:** 504
Accident (Bennett), **VI:** 250
Accident (Pinter), **Supp. I:** 374, 375; **Retro. Supp. I:** 226
Accidental Man, An (Murdoch), **Supp. I:** 227
"Accidents" (Adcock), **Supp. XII:** 9
"Accompanist, The" (Desai), **Supp. V:** 65

"According to His Lights" (Galsworthy), **VI:** 276–277
"Account, The" (Cowley), **II:** 197
Account of Corsica, An (Boswell), **III:** 236, 239, 243, 247
Account of the European Settlements in America, An (Burke), **III:** 205
Account of the Growth of Popery and Arbitrary Government, An (Marvell), **I:** 207–208, 219; **Retro. Supp. II:** 266–268
Account of the Life of Dr. Samuel Johnson . . . by Himself, An (Johnson), **III:** 122
Account of the Life of Mr. Richard Savage, An (Johnson), **Retro. Supp. I:** 142
Account of the Settlement at Port Jackson, **Supp. IV:** 348
Account Rendered (Brittain), **Supp. X:** 45
Ace of Clubs (Coward), **Supp. II:** 155
Achilles (Gay), **III:** 55, 66, 67
Achilles in Scyros (Bridges), **VI:** 83
"Achronos" (Blunden), **Supp. XI:** 45
Ackroyd, Peter, **Supp. VI: 1–15**
"Acid" (Kelman), **Supp. V:** 245
Acis and Galatea (Gay), **III:** 55, 67
Acre of Land, The (Thomas), **Supp. XII:** 283
"Across the Estuary" (Nicholson), **Supp. VI:** 216
"Across the Moor" (Adcock), **Supp. XII:** 8
Across the Plains (Stevenson), **V:** 389, 396
"Act, The" (Harrison), **Supp. V:** 161–162
Act of Creation, The (Koestler), **Supp. I:** 37, 38
Act of Grace (Keneally), **Supp. IV:** 347
"Act of Reparation, An" (Warner), **Supp. VII:** 380
Act of Terror, An (Brink), **Supp. VI: 55– 56,** 57
Act Without Words I (Beckett), **Supp. I:** 46, 55, 57
Act Without Words II (Beckett), **Supp. I:** 46, 55, 57
Actaeon and Diana (Johnson), **I:** 286
Acte (Durrell), **Supp. I:** 126, 127
Actions and Reactions (Kipling), **VI:** 204
Acton, John, **IV:** 289, 290; **VI:** 385
"Acts of Restoration" (Fallon), **Supp. XII:** 107
"Ad Amicam"sonnets (Thompson), **V:** 441
Ad Patrem (Milton), **Retro. Supp. II:** 272

Adam and Eve and Pinch Me (Coppard), **VIII:** 85, 88, 89, 91–93

"Adam and Eve and Pinch Me" (Coppard), **VIII:** 90

Adam and Eve and Pinch Me (Rendell), **Supp. IX:** 189, 195

Adam and the Sacred Nine (Hughes), **Supp. I:** 357, 363

Adam Bede (Eliot), **V:** xxii, 2, 191–192, 194, 200; **Retro. Supp. II:** 104–106

"Adam Pos'd" (Finch), **Supp. IX:** 68

"Adam Tempted" (Thomas), **Supp. XII:** 290

Adams, Henry, **VI:** 65

Adam's Breed (Hall), **Supp. VI:** 120, 122, 128

"Adam's Curse" (Yeats), **III:** 184; **VI:** 213

"Adam's Dream" (Muir), **Supp. VI:** 207–208

"Adapting *Nice Work* for Television" (Lodge), **Supp. IV:** 373, 381

Adcock, Fleur, **Supp. XII:** 1–16

"Adders' Brood" (Powys), **VIII:** 248, 249

Addison, Joseph, **II:** 195, 200; **III:** 1, 18, 19, 38–53, 74, 198; **IV:** 278, 281, 282

"Additional Poems" (Housman), **VI:** 161

Address to the Deil (Burns), **III:** 315, 317

Address to the Irish People, An (Shelley), **IV:** 208; **Retro. Supp. I:** 245

"Address to the Unco Guid" (Burns), **III:** 319

"Addy" (Blackwood), **Supp. IX:** 12

Adéle: Jane Eyre's Hidden Story (Tennant), **Supp. IX:** 239

Adepts of Africa, The (Williams, C. W. S.), see *Black Bastard, The*

"Adina" (James), **VI:** 69

Administrator, The (MacNeice), **VII:** 401

Admirable Bashville, The (Barker), **VI:** 113

Admiral Crichton, The (Barrie), **Supp. III:** 6, 9, 14–15

Admiral Guinea (Stevenson), **V:** 396

"Admonition on a Rainy Afternoon" (Nye), **Supp. X:** 203

Adolphe (Constant), **Supp. IV:** 125, 126, 136

Adonais (Shelley), **I:** 160; **VI:** 73; **IV:** xviii, 179, 196, 205–206, 207, 208; **Retro. Supp. I:** 255

Adonis and the Alphabet (Huxley), **VII:** 206–207

Adonis, Attis, Osiris: Studies in the History of Oriental Religion (Frazer), **Supp. III:** 175, 180

Adored One, The (Barrie), **Supp. III:** 5, 9

Adorno, Theodor, **Supp. IV:** 29, 82

"Adrian and Bardus" (Gower), **I:** 54

"Advanced Lady, The" (Mansfield), **VII:** 172

Advancement of Learning, An (Hill, R.), **Supp. IX:** 122

Advancement of Learning, The (Bacon), **I:** 261–265; **II:** 149; **IV:** 279

Advantages Proposed by Repealing the Sacramental Test, The (Swift), **III:** 36

"Adventure of Charles Augustus Milverton, The" (Doyle), **Supp. II:** 173

"Adventure of Charles Wentworth" (Brontë), **V:** 118–119

"Adventure of the Abbey Grange, The" (Doyle), **Supp. II:** 168, 173, 176

"Adventure of the Blanched Soldier, The" (Doyle), **Supp. II:** 168

"Adventure of the Blue Carbuncle, The" (Doyle), **Supp. II:** 173

"Adventure of the Bruce–Partington Plans, The" (Doyle), **Supp. II:** 170, 175

"Adventure of the Copper Beeches, The" (Doyle), **Supp. II:** 168

"Adventure of the Creeping Man, The" (Doyle), **Supp. II:** 165

"Adventure of the Devil's Foot, The" (Doyle), **Supp. II:** 167, 176

"Adventure of the Empty House, The" (Doyle), **Supp. II:** 160

"Adventure of the Engineer's Thumb, The" (Doyle), **Supp. II:** 170

"Adventure of the Golden Pince–Nez, The" (Doyle), **Supp. II:** 175

"Adventure of the Illustrious Client, The" (Doyle), **Supp. II:** 169

"Adventure of the Lion's Mane, The" (Doyle), **Supp. II:** 168–169

"Adventure of the Missing Three–Quarter, The" (Doyle), **Supp. II:** 165, 171

"Adventure of the Norwood Builder, The" (Doyle), **Supp. II:** 169, 170, 173

"Adventure of the Retired Colourman, The" (Doyle), **Supp. II:** 172

"Adventure of the Second Stain, The" (Doyle), **Supp. II:** 175, 176

"Adventure of the Six Napoleons, The" (Doyle), **Supp. II:** 170–171, 174–175

"Adventure of the Speckled Band, The" (Doyle), **Supp. II:** 165–166

"Adventure of the Sussex Vampire, The" (Doyle), **Supp. II:** 169

"Adventure of the Three Garridebs, The" (Doyle), **Supp. II:** 165

"Adventure of Wisteria Lodge, The" (Doyle), **Supp. II:** 168

Adventure Story (Rattigan), **Supp. VII:** 316–317

Adventures Aboard the Maria Celeste (Carey), **Supp. XII:** 52

Adventures in the Skin Trade (Thomas), **Supp. I:** 182

Adventures of Caleb Williams, The (Godwin), **III:** 332, 345; **IV:** 173

Adventures of Covent Garden, The (Farquhar), **II:** 352, 354, 364

Adventures of Eovaai, Princess of Ijaveo, The (Haywood), **Supp. XII:** 135, 141–142, 146

Adventures of Ferdinand Count Fathom, The (Smollett), see *Ferdinand Count Fathom*

Adventures of Harry Richmond, The (Meredith), **V:** xxiii, 228, 234

Adventures of Johnny Walker, Tramp, The (Davies), **Supp. XI:** 93

Adventures of Peregrine Pickle, The (Smollett), see *Peregrine Pickle*

Adventures of Philip on His Way Through the World, The (Thackeray), **V:** 19, 29, 35, 38

Adventures of Robina, The (Tennant), **Supp. IX:** 239

Adventures of Roderick Random, The (Smollett), see *Roderick Random*

Adventures of Sir Launcelot Greaves, The (Smollett), see *Sir Launcelot Greaves*

Adventures of the Black Girl in Her Search for God, The (Shaw), **VI:** 124, 127, 129

Adventures of Ulysses, The (Lamb), **IV:** 85

"Adventurous Exploit of the Cave of Ali Baba, The" (Sayers), **Supp. III:** 340

Advice: A Satire (Smollett), **III:** 152n, 158

Advice to a Daughter (Halifax), **III:** 40

"Advice to a Discarded Lover" (Adcock), **Supp. XII:** 5

Advice to a Son (Osborne), **II:** 145

Advocateship of Jesus Christ, The (Bunyan), *II:* 253

A. E. Housman (Gow), **VI:** 164

A. E. Housman: A Divided Life (Watson), **VI:** 164

A. E. Housman: An Annotated Handlist (Sparrow), **VI:** 164

AE. See Russell, George William

Ælfric of Eynsham, Abbot, **Retro. Supp. II:** 297–298

Aeneid (tr. Douglas), **III:** 311

Aeneid (tr. Surrey), **I:** 116–119

Aeneid of Virgil, The (tr. Day Lewis), **Supp. III:** 118

Aeneids of Virgil, Done into English Verse, The (Morris), **V:** 306

Aeneis (Dryden), **II:** 290, 293, 297, 301

"Aerial Views" (Malouf), **Supp. XII:** 221

Aeschylus, **IV:** 199

"Aesculapian Notes" (Redgrove), **Supp. VI:** 234

Aesop (Vanbrugh), **II:** 324, 332, 336

"Aesop and Rhodopè" (Landor), **IV:** 94

Aesop's Fables (Behn), **Supp. III:** 37

"Aesthetic Apologia, An" (Betjeman), **VII:** 357–358

"Aesthetic Poetry" (Pater), **V:** 356, 357

Aethiopian History (Heliodorus), **I:** 164

Affair, The (Snow), **VII:** xxi, 324, 329–330

"Affliction" (Herbert), **II:** 125, 127; **Retro. Supp. II:** 179

"Affliction" (Vaughan), **II:** 187–188

Affliction (Weldon), **Supp. IV:** 531, 532–533

"Affliction of Childhood, The" (De Quincey), **IV:** 152–153, 154

"Afon Rhiw" (Thomas), **Supp. XII:** 290

African Elegy, An (Okri), **Supp. V:** 359

"African Socialism: Utopian or Scientific?" (Armah), **Supp. X:** 2

African Stories (Lessing), **Supp. I:** 240, 243

African Witch, The (Cary), **VII:** 186

"After a Childhood away from Ireland" (Boland), **Supp. V:** 36

"After a Death" (Stevenson), **Supp. VI:** 254

"After a Journey" (Hardy), **VI:** 18; **Retro. Supp. I:** 118

"After an Operation" (Jennings), **Supp. V:** 214

"After a Romantic Day" (Hardy), **Retro. Supp. I:** 118

After Bakhtin (The Art of Fiction: Illustrated from Classic and Modern Texts) (Lodge), **Supp. IV:** 366–367

"After Closing Time" (Dunn), **Supp. X:** 69

"After Dunkirk" (Lewis), **VII:** 445

"After Eden" (MacCaig), **Supp. VI:** 187

After Hannibal (Unsworth), **Supp. VII:** 357, 365–366

"After Her Death" (Stevenson), **Supp. VI:** 254

After Julius (Howard), **Supp. XI:** 138, 139, 142–144, 145, 147, 148

After Leaving Mr. Mackenzie (Rhys), **Supp. II:** 388, **392–394,** 400

"After Long Silence" (Yeats), **VI:** 212

After Magritte (Stoppard), **Supp. I:** 443, 444–445, 447, 451; **Retro. Supp. II:** 346–347

After Many a Summer (Huxley), **VII:** xviii, 205

"After Rain" (Thomas), **Supp. III:** 406

After Rain (Trevor), **Supp. IV:** 505

After Strange Gods (Eliot), **VI:** 207; **VII:** 153

After the Ark (Jennings), **Supp. V:** 217

After the Ball (Coward), **Supp. II:** 155

After the Dance (Rattigan), **Supp. VII:** 310–311, 312, 318

After the Death of Don Juan (Warner), **Supp. VII:** 376, 377

"After the funeral" (Thomas), **Supp. I:** 176, 177

"After the Irish of Aodghan O'Rathaille" (Boland), **Supp. V:** 36

"After the Swim" (Dutton), **Supp. XII:** 93

"After the Vision" (Warner), **Supp. XI:** 298

"After the War" (Dunn), **Supp. X:** 70–71

After–Dinner Joke, The (Churchill), **Supp. IV:** 181

"Afterflu Afterlife, The" (Ewart), **Supp. VII:** 42–43

Aftermath, The (Churchill), **VI:** 359

"Afternoon Dancing" (Trevor), **Supp. IV:** 503–504

"Afternoon in Florence" (Jennings), **Supp. V:** 210

Afternoon Men (Powell), **VII:** 343–345

Afternoon Off (Bennett), **VIII:** 27

"Afternoons" (Larkin), **Supp. I:** 281

"Afterthought, An" (Rossetti), **V:** 258

"Afterwards" (Hardy), **VI:** 13, 19; **Retro. Supp. I:** 119

Against a Dark Background (Banks), **Supp. XI:** 1, 12–13

"Against Absence" (Suckling), **II:** 227

"Against Coupling" (Adcock), **Supp. XII:** 5

"Against Dryness" (Murdoch), **Supp. I:** 216, 218, 219, 221

Against Entropy (Frayn), see *Towards the End of Morning*

"Against Fruition" (Cowley), **II:** 197

"Against Fruition" (Suckling), **II:** 227

Against Hasty Credence (Henryson), **Supp. VII:** 146, 147

Against Religion (Wilson), **Supp. VI:** 297, **305–306,** 309

"Against Romanticism" (Amis), **Supp. II:** 3

"Against the Sun" (Dutton), **Supp. XII:** 88, 94

Against Venomous Tongues (Skelton), **I:** 90

Agamemnon (Seneca), **II:** 71

Agamemnon (Thomson), **Supp. III:** 411, 424

Agamemnon, a Tragedy Taken from Aeschylus (FitzGerald), **IV:** 349, 353

Agamemnon of Aeschylus, The (tr. Browning), **IV:** 358–359, 374

Agamemnon of Aeschylus, The (tr. MacNeice), **VII:** 408–409

Agate, James, **Supp. II:** 143, 147

Age of Anxiety, The (Auden), **VII:** 379, 388, 389–390, **Supp. IV:** 100, **Retro. Supp. I:** 11

Age of Bronze, The (Byron), **IV:** xviii, 193

Age of Indiscretion, The (Davis), **V:** 394

Age of Iron (Coetzee), **Supp. VI:** 76, **85**

Age of Longing, The (Koestler), **Supp. I:** 25, 27, 28, 31–32, 35

Age of Reason, The (Hope), **Supp. VII:** 164

Age of Shakespeare, The (Swinburne), **V:** 333

Age of the Rainmakers, The (Harris), **Supp. V:** 132

Agents and Patients (Powell), **VII:** 345–346

Aglaura (Suckling), **II:** 226, 238

Agnes Grey (Brontë), **V:** xx, 129–130, 132, 134–135, 140–141, 153; **Supp. IV:** 239; **Retro. Supp. I:** 52, 54–55

"Agnes Lahens" (Moore), **VI:** 98

Agnostic's Apology, An (Stephen), **VI:** 289

"Agonies of Writing a Musical Comedy" (Wodehouse), **Supp. III:** 451

"Agnus Dei" (Nye), **Supp. X:** 202

Ah, But Your Land Is Beautiful (Paton), **Supp. II:** **353–355**

"Ah, what avails the sceptred race" (Landor), **IV:** 88

"Ahoy, Sailor Boy!" (Coppard), **VIII:** 97

Aids to Reflection (Coleridge), **IV:** 53, 56

Aiken, Conrad, **VII:** 149, 179; **Supp. III:** 270

Aimed at Nobody (Graham), **Supp. VII:** 106

Ainger, Alfred, **IV:** 254, 267

"Air and Angels" (MacCaig), **Supp. VI:** 185

Ainsworth, Harrison, **IV:** 311; **V:** 47

"Air" (Traherne), **Supp. XI:** 267

"Air Disaster, The" (Ballard), **Supp. V:** 33

"Aire and Angels" (Donne), **II:** 197

Airship, The (Caudwell), **Supp. IX:** 35

"Aisling" (Muldoon), **Supp. IV:** 418–419

"Aisling Hat, The" (McGuckian), **Supp. V:** 286, 288, 289

Aissa Saved (Cary), **VII:** 185

"Akbar's Bridge" (Kipling), **VI:** 201

Akerman, Rudolph, **V:** 111

Akhenaten Adventure, The (Kerr), **Supp. XII:** 198

Akhmatova, Anna, **Supp. IV:** 480, 494

"Al Som de l'Escalina" (Eliot), **VII:** 152

Alaham (Greville), **Supp. XI:** 110, 120

Alamanni, Luigi, **I:** 110–111

Alamein to Zem–Zem (Douglas), **VII:** xxii, 441

Alarcos (Disraeli), **IV:** 306, 308

Alaric at Rome (Arnold), **V:** 216

"Alas, Poor Bollington!" (Coppard), **VIII:** 94–95

"Alaska" (Armitage), **VIII:** 5

Alastair Reid Reader, An: Selected Poetry and Prose (Reid), **Supp. VII:** 333, 336

Alastor (Shelley), **III:** 330, 338; **IV:** xvii, 195, 198, 208, 217; **Retro. Supp. I:** 247

"Albergo Empedocle" (Forster), **VI:** 399, 412

Albert's Bridge (Stoppard), **Supp. I:** 439, 445

Albigenses, The (Maturin), **VIII:** 201, 207, 208

"Albinus and Rosemund" (Gower), **I:** 53–54

Albion! Albion! (Hill, R.), **Supp. IX:** 111

"Albion & Marina" (Brontë), **V:** 110

Albion and Albanius (Dryden), **II:** 305

Album Verses (Lamb), **IV:** 83, 85

Alcazar (Peele), see *Battle of Alcazar, The*

Alcestis (Euripides), **IV:** 358

Alchemist, The (Jonson), **I:** 304–341, 342; **II:** 4, 48; **Retro. Supp. I:** 163

"Alchemist in the City, The" (Hopkins), **V:** 362

"Alchemy of Happiness, The" (Kureishi), **Supp. XI:** 163

Alcott, Louisa May, **Supp. IV:** 255

Aldington, Richard, **VI:** 416; **VII:** xvi, 36, 121

Aldiss, Brian, **III:** 341, 345; **Supp. V:** 22

Aldous Huxley (Brander), **VII:** 208

Alexander, Peter, **I:** 300n, 326

Alexander, William (earl of Stirling), **I:** 218; **II:** 80

"Alexander and Zenobia" (Brontë), **V:** 115

Alexander Pope (Sitwell), **VII:** 138–139

Alexander Pope (Stephen), **V:** 289

Alexander Pope as Critic and Humanist (Warren), **II:** 332n

Alexander's Feast; or, The Power of Musique (Dryden), **II:** 200, 300, 304

Alexanders saga, **VIII:** 237, 242

Alexandria: A History and Guide (Forster), **VI:** 408, 412

Alexandria Quartet (Durrell), **Supp. I:** 94, 96, 97, 98, 100, 101, **104–110,** 113, 122

"Alfieri and Salomon the Florentine Jew" (Landor), **IV:** 91

"Alford" (Crawford), **Supp. XI:** 78–79

Alfred (Thomson and Mallet), **Supp. III:** 412, 424–425

Alfred Lord Tennyson: A Memoir (Tennyson), **IV:** 324, 338

Alfred the Great of Wessex, King, **Retro. Supp. II:** 293, 295–297

Algernon Charles Swinburne (Thomas), **VI:** 424

Ali the Lion: Ali of Tebeleni, Pasha of Jannina, 1741–1822 (Plomer), **Supp. XI:** 225

Alice (Potter, D.), **Supp. X:** 228, 230–233

Alice Fell (Tennant), **Supp. IX:** 235, 236

Alice in Wonderland (Carroll), *see Alice's Adventures in Wonderland*

Alice Sit–by–the–Fire (Barrie), **Supp. III:** 8, 9

Alice's Adventures in Wonderland (Carroll), **V:** xxiii, 261–265, **266–269,** 270–273

Alice's Adventures Under Ground (Carroll), **V:** 266, 273; *see Alice's Adventures in Wonderland*

"Alicia's Diary" (Hardy), **VI:** 22

Alien (Foster), **III:** 345

"Alien Corn, The" (Maugham), **VI:** 370, 374

Alien Sky, The (Scott), **Supp. I:** 261–263

"Alien Soil" (Kincaid), **Supp. VII:** 221, 229

All About Mr. Hatterr (Desani), **Supp. IV:** 445

"All blue and bright, in glorious light" (Brontë), **V:** 115

"All Day It Has Rained" (Lewis), **VII:** 445

All Day on the Sands (Bennett), **VIII:** 27

"All Flesh" (Thompson), **V:** 442

All Fools (Chapman), **I:** 235, 238, 244

All for Love (Dryden), **II:** 295–296, 305

All for Love (Southey), **IV:** 71

All Hallow's Eve (Williams, C. W. S.), **Supp. IX:** 281, 282, 284, 285

All My Eyes See: The Visual World of G. M. Hopkins (ed. Thornton), **V:** 377n, 379n, 382

All My Little Ones (Ewart), **Supp. VII:** 36

All Ovid's Elegies (Marlowe), **I:** 280, 291, 293

"All philosophers, who find" (Swift), **IV:** 160

All Quiet on the Western Front (Remarque), **VII:** xvi

All Religions Are One (Blake), **III:** 292, 307; **Retro. Supp. I:** 35

"All Saints: Martyrs" (Rossetti), **V:** 255

"All Souls Night" (Cornford), **VIII:** 112

All That Fall (Beckett), **Supp. I:** 58, 62; **Retro. Supp. I:** 25

All the Conspirators (Isherwood), **VII:** 310

"All the hills and vales along" (Sorley), **VI:** 421–422

All the Usual Hours of Sleeping (Redgrove), **Supp. VI:** 230

All the Year Round (periodical), **V:** 42

"All Things Ill Done" (Cameron), **Supp. IX:** 23–24

All Trivia (Connolly), **Supp. III:** 98

All What Jazz: A Record Diary, 1961–1968 (Larkin), **Supp. I:** 286, 287–288

Allan Quatermain (Haggard), **Supp. III:** 213, 218

"Allegiance, An" (Wallace–Crabbe), **VIII:** 315

Allegory of Love: A Study in Medieval Tradition (Lewis), **Supp. III:** 248, 249–250, 265

Allen, John, **IV:** 341, 349–350, 352

Allen, Walter Ernest, **V:** 219; **VI:** 257; **VII:** xvii, xxxvii, 71, 343

Allestree, Richard, **III:** 82

Allott, Kenneth, **IV:** 236; **VI:** xi, xxvii, 218

Allott, Miriam, **IV:** x, xxiv, 223n, 224, 234, 236; **V:** x, 218

All's Well That Ends Well (Shakespeare), **I:** 313, 318

All You Who Sleep Tonight (Seth), **Supp. X:** 283–284, 288

"Allusion to the Tenth Satire of the Second Book of Horace" (Rochester), **II:** 259

Almayer's Folly (Conrad), **VI:** 135–136, 148; **Retro. Supp. II:** 70–71

Almeria (Edgeworth), **Supp. III:** 158

Almond Tree, The (Stallworthy), **Supp. X:** 293–294

"Almond Tree, The" (Stallworthy), **Supp. X:** 293–294, 302

"Almswoman" (Blunden), **Supp. XI:** 42

"Aloe, The" (Mansfield), **VII:** 173–174

Alone (Douglas), **VI:** 293, 294, 297, 304, 305

Alpers, Antony, **VII:** 176

"Alphabetical Catalogue of Names . . . and Other Material Things Mentioned in These Pastorals, An" (Gay), **III:** 56

Alphabetical Order (Frayn), **Supp. VII:** 60

"Alphabets" (Heaney), **Retro. Supp. I:** 131

Alphonsus, King of Aragon (Greene), **VIII:** 139–140

Alps and Sanctuaries (Butler), **Supp. II:** 114

"Alps in Winter, The" (Stephen), **V:** 282

Alroy (Disraeli), **IV:** 296, 297, 308

"Altar, The" (Herbert), **II:** 128

"Altar of the Dead, The" (James), **VI:** 69

"Altarwise by owl–light" (Thomas), **Supp. I: 174–176**

Alteration, The (Amis), **Supp. II:** 12–13

"Alternative to Despair, An" (Koestler), **Supp. I:** 39

Althusser, Louis, **Supp. IV:** 90

Alton, R. E., **I:** 285

Alton Locke (Kingsley), **V:** vii, xxi, 2, 4; **VI:** 240

"Altruistic Tenderness of LenWing the Poet, The" (Cameron), **Supp. IX:** 19

Altus Prosator (tr. Morgan, E.), **Supp. IX:** 169

Alvarez, A., **II:** 125n

Alvíssmál, **VIII:** 231

Amadeus (Shaffer), **Supp. I:** 326–327

Amadis of Gaul (tr. Southey), **IV:** 71

Amado, Jorge, **Supp. IV:** 440

Amalgamemnon (Brooke–Rose), **Supp. IV:** 99, 110–111, 112

Amateur Emigrant, The (Stevenson), **V:** 389, 396

"Amateur Film–Making" (Fuller), **Supp. VII:** 73

Amazing Marriage, The (Meredith), **V:** 227, 232, 233, 234

Ambarvalia: Poems by T. Burbidge and A. H. Clough, **V:** 159–160, 161, 170

Ambassadors, The (James), **VI:** 55, 57–59; **Supp. IV:** 371

"Amber Bead, The" (Herrick), **II:** 106

Amberley, Lady, **V:** 129

"Ambiguities" (Fuller), **Supp. VII:** 73

Ambition and Other Poems (Davies), **Supp. XI:** 102

Ambler, Eric, **Supp. IV: 1–24**

Amboyna (Dryden), **II:** 305

Amelia (Fielding), **III:** 102–103, 105; **Retro. Supp. I:** 81, 89–90

"Amen" (Rossetti), **V:** 256

Amendments of Mr. Collier's False and Imperfect Citations (Congreve), **II:** 339, 340, 350

America. A Prophecy (Blake), **III:** 300, 302, 307; **Retro. Supp. I:** 40–41

America I Presume (Lewis), **VII:** 77

American, The (James), **VI:** 24, 28–29, 39, 67

"American Dreams" (Carey), **Supp. XII:** 54, 55, 56

American Ghosts and Other World Wonders (Carter), **Supp. III:** 91

American Notes (Dickens), **V:** 42, 54, 55, 71

American Scene, The (James), **VI: 54, 62–64,** 67

American Senator, The (Trollope), **V:** 100, 102

American Visitor, An (Cary), **VII:** 186

"Americans in My Mind, The" (Pritchett), **Supp. III:** 316

"Ametas and Thestylis Making Hay–Ropes" (Marvell), **II:** 211

Aminta (Tasso), **II:** 49

"Amir's Homily, The" (Kipling), **VI:** 201

Amis, Kingsley, **Supp. II: 1–19; Supp. IV:** 25, 26, 27, 29, 377; **Supp. V:** 206

Amis, Martin, **Supp. IV: 25–44,** 65, 75, 437, 445

"Among All Lovely Things My Love Had Been" (Wordsworth), **IV:** 21

"Among School Children" (Yeats), **VI:** 211, 217

Among the Believers: An Islamic Journey (Naipaul), **Supp. I:** 399, 400–401, 402

Among the Cities (Morris, J.), **Supp. X:** 183

"Among the Ruins" (Malouf), **Supp. XII:** 220

Among the Walls (Fallon), **Supp. XII:** 102

Amores (tr. Marlowe), **I:** 276, 290

Amoretti and Epithalamion (Spenser), **I:** 124, 128–131

Amorous Cannibal, The (Wallace–Crabbe), **VIII:** 319, 320–321

"Amorous Cannibal, The" (Wallace–Crabbe), **VIII:** 319

Amorous Prince, The; or, The Curious Husband (Behn), **Supp. III:** 26

"Amos Barton" (Eliot), **V:** 190

Amours de Voyage (Clough), **V:** xxii, 155, 156, 158, 159, 161–163, 165, 166–168, 170

Amphytrion; or, The Two Sosias (Dryden), **II:** 296, 305

"Ample Garden, The" (Graves), **VII:** 269

Amrita (Jhabvala), **Supp. V:** 224–226

"Amsterdam" (Murphy), **Supp. V:** 326

Amusements Serious and Comical (Brown), **III:** 41

"Amy Foster" (Conrad), **VI:** 134, 148

An Duanaire: An Irish Anthology, Poems of the Dispossessed, 1600–1900 (Kinsella), **Supp. V:** 266

An Giall (Behan), **Supp. II:** 71–73

Anacreontiques (Johnson), **II:** 198

"Anactoria" (Swinburne), **V:** 319–320, 321

"Anahorish" (Heaney), **Retro. Supp. I:** 125, 128

Anand, Mulk Raj, **Supp. IV:** 440

"Anarchist, An" (Conrad), **VI:** 148

Anathemata, The (Jones), **Supp. VII:** 167, 168, 169, 170, 175–178

Anatomy of Exchange–Alley, The (Defoe), **III:** 13

Anatomy of Frustration, The (Wells), **VI:** 228

Anatomy of Melancholy (Burton), **II:** 88, 106, 108; **IV:** 219

Anatomy of Oxford (eds. Day Lewis and Fenby), **Supp. III:** 118

Anatomy of Restlessness: Selected Writings, 1969–1989 (Chatwin), **Supp. IV:** 157, 160; **Supp. IX:** 52, 53, 61

"Ancestor" (Kinsella), **Supp. V:** 274

"Ancestor to Devotee" (Adcock), **Supp. XII:** 12–13

Ancestors (Brathwaite), **Supp. XII:** 33, 41–42, 45, 46

"Ancestors" (Cornford), **VIII:** 106

Ancestral Truths (Maitland), **Supp. XI:** 170–172

Anchises: Poems (Sisson), **Supp. XI:** 257

"Anchored Yachts on a Stormy Day" (Smith, I. C.), **Supp. IX:** 211

Ancient Allan, The (Haggard), **Supp. III:** 222

Ancient and English Versions of the Bible (Isaacs), **I:** 385

"Ancient Ballet, An" (Kinsella), **Supp. V:** 261

"Ancient Historian" (Wallace–Crabbe), **VIII:** 311

Ancient Lights (Ford), **VI:** 319, 320

"Ancient Mariner, The" (Coleridge), **III:** 330, 338; **IV:** viii, ix, 42, 44–48, 54, 55; **Retro. Supp. II:** 53–56

"Ancient Sage, The" (Tennyson), **IV:** 329

"Ancient to Ancients, An" (Hardy), **VI:** 13

"And country life I praise" (Bridges), **VI:** 75

"And death shall have no dominion" (Thomas), **Supp. I:** 174

And Our Faces, My Heart, Brief as Photos (Berger), **Supp. IV:** 94, 95

And Then There Were None (Christie), *see Ten Little Niggers*

And What if the Pretender Should Come? (Defoe), **III:** 13

Anderson, Lindsay, **Supp. IV:** 78

Anderson, Sherwood, **VII:** 75

Anderton, Basil, **II:** 154, 157

"Andrea del Sarto" (Browning), **IV:** 357, 361, 366; **Retro. Supp. II:** 27–28

Andrea of Hungary, and Giovanna of Naples (Landor), **IV:** 100

Andreas, **Retro. Supp. II:** 301

"Andrey Satchel and the Parson and Clerk" (Hardy), **VI:** 22

Androcles and the Lion (Shaw), **VI:** 116, 124, 129; **Retro. Supp. II:** 322

"Andromeda" (Hopkins), **V:** 370, 376

Andromeda Liberata (Chapman), **I:** 235, 254

Ane Prayer for the Pest (Henryson), **Supp. VII:** 146, 148

Anecdotes (Spence), **II:** 261

"Anecdotes, The" (Durrell), **Supp. I:** 124

Anecdotes of Johnson (Piozzi), **III:** 246

Anecdotes . . . of Mr. Pope . . . by the Rev. Joseph Spence (ed. Singer), **III:** 69, 78

Anecdotes of Sir W. Scott (Hogg), **Supp. X:** 111

Angel and Me: Short Stories for Holy Week (Maitland), **Supp. XI:** 177

"Angel and the Sweep, The" (Coppard), **VIII:** 92

Angel at the Gate, The (Harris), **Supp. V:** 137, 139

Angel Maker: The Short Stories of Sara Maitland (Maitland), **Supp. XI:** 165, 176

Angel Pavement (Priestley), **VII:** xviii, 211, 216–217

"Angelica" (Blackwood), **Supp. IX:** 12

Angels and Insects (Byatt), **Supp. IV:** 139, 151, 153–154

Angels and Insects (film), **Supp. IV:** 153

"Angels at the Ritz" (Trevor), **Supp. IV:** 503

Angels at the Ritz (Trevor), **Supp. IV:** 504

"Angle" (Dutton), **Supp. XII:** 90

"Angle–Land" (Jones), **Supp. VII:** 176

Anglican Essays (Sisson), **Supp. XI:** 255

Anglo–Italian Review (periodical) **VI:** 294

"Anglo–Saxon, The" (Golding), **Supp. I:** 78

Anglo–Saxon Attitudes (Wilson), **Supp. I:** 154, 155, 156, 159–160, 161, 162, 163

Anglo–Saxon Chronicle, **Retro. Supp. II:** 296, 297, 298, 307

Angrian chronicles (Brontë), **V:** 110–111, 120–121, 122, 124–125, 126, 135

"Anima and Animus" (Jung), **Supp. IV:** 10–11

Anima Poetae: From the Unpublished Notebooks (Coleridge), **IV:** 56

Animadversions upon the Remonstrants Defense Against Smectymnuus (Milton), **II:** 175

Animal Farm (Orwell), **VII:** xx, 273, 278, 283–284; **Supp. I:** 28*n*, 29; **Supp. IV:** 31

Animal Lover's Book of Beastly Murder, The (Highsmith), **Supp. V:** 179

Animal's Arrival, The (Jennings), **Supp. V:** 208

Animated Nature (Goldsmith), *see History of the Earth . . . .*

Ann Lee's (Bowen), **Supp. II:** 81

Ann Veronica: A Modern Love Story (Wells), **VI:** 227, 238

"Anna, Lady Braxby" (Hardy), **VI:** 22

Anna of the Five Towns (Bennett), **VI:** xiii, 248, 249, 252, 253, 266

Annals of a Publishing House (Oliphant), **Supp. X:** 221

Annals of Chile, The (Muldoon), **Supp. IV:** 428–432

Annals of the Five Senses (MacDiarmid), **Supp. XII:** 202

Annan, Gabriele, **Supp. IV:** 302

Annan, Noel, **V:** 284, 290

Anne Brontë (Gérin), **V:** 153

"Anne Killigrew" (Dryden), **II:** 303

Anne of Geierstein (Scott), **IV:** 39

Annie, Gwen, Lily, Pam, and Tulip (Kincaid), **Supp. VII:** 222

Annie John (Kincaid), **Supp. VII:** 217, 223 225, 229, 230

Anniversaries (Donne), **I:** 361–362, 364, 367; **Retro. Supp. II:** 88

"Anniversary" (Nye), **Supp. X:** 201

Annotations of Scottish Songs by Burns (Cook), **III:** 322

Annual Register (periodical), **III:** 194, 205

Annunciation, The (Henryson), **Supp. VII:** 146, 148

"Annunciation, The" (Jennings), **Supp. V:** 212

"Annunciation, The" (Muir), **Supp. VI:** 207

Annunciation in a Welsh Hill Setting (Jones), **Supp. VII:** 180

Annus Domini (Rossetti), **V:** 260

"Annus Mirabilis" (Larkin), **Supp. I:** 284

Annus Mirabilis: The Year of Wonder (Dryden), **II:** 292, 304

"Anorexic" (Boland), **Supp. V:** 49

Another Death in Venice (Hill, R.), **Supp. IX:** 111–112, 117

"Another Grace for a Child" (Herrick), **II:** 114

Another Mexico (Greene), *see Lawless Roads, The*

Another Part of the Wood (Bainbridge), **Supp. VI:** 17–19

"Another September" (Kinsella), **Supp. V:** 260

"Another September" (Kinsella), **Supp. V:** 260

"Ansell" (Forster), **VI:** 398

Anstey, Christopher, **III:** 155

"Answer, The" (Thomas), **Supp. XII:** 287

"Answer, The" (Wycherley), **II:** 322

Answer from Limbo, An (Moore, B.), **Supp. IX:** 141, 142, 148, 150

"Answer to a Paper Called 'A Memorial of true Poor Inhabitants'" (Swift), **III:** 35

Answer to a Poisoned Book (More), **Supp. VII:** 245

Answer to a Question That No Body Thinks of, An (Defoe), **III:** 13

"Answer to Davenant" (Hobbes), **II:** 256n

"Answers" (Jennings), **Supp. V:** 206

"Ant, The" (Lovelace), **II:** 231

Ant and the Nightingale or Father Hubburd's Tales, The (Middleton), **II:** 3

"Ant–Lion, The" (Pritchett), **Supp. III:** 105–106

Antal, Frederick, **Supp. IV:** 80

"Antecedents of History, The" (Russell), **VIII:** 277

Antechinus: Poems 1975–1980 (Hope), **Supp. VII:** 159

"Antheap, The" (Lessing), **Supp. I:** 242

"Anthem for Doomed Youth" (Owen), **VI:** 443, 447, 448, 452; **Supp. IV:** 58

"Anthem of Earth, An" (Thompson), **V:** 448

Anthology of War Poetry, An (ed. Nichols), **VI:** 419

Anthony Trollope: A Critical Study (Cockshut), **V:** 98, 103

Antic Hay (Huxley), **VII:** 198, 201–202

"Anti–Christ; or, The Reunion of Christendom" (Chesterton), **VI:** 340–341

Anticipations of the Reaction of Mechanical and Scientific Progress upon Human Life and Thought (Wells), **VI:** 227, 240

Anti–Coningsby (Disraeli), **IV:** 308

Anti–Death League, The (Amis), **Supp. II:** 14–15

Antidotes (Sisson), **Supp. XI:** 262

Antigua, Penny, Puce (Graves), **VII:** 259

"Antigua Crossings" (Kincaid), **Supp. VII:** 220, 221

"Anti–Marriage League, The" (Oliphant), **Supp. X:** 221–222

Anti–Pamela; or, Feign'd Innocence Detected (Haywood), **Supp. XII:** 136

Antipodes (Malouf), **Supp. XII:** 217–218

Antipodes, The (Brome), **Supp. X:** 49, 56, 58–61, 63

Antiquarian Prejudice (Betjeman), **VII:** 358, 359

Antiquary, The (Scott), **IV:** xvii 28, 32–33, 37, 39

Anti–Thelyphthora (Cowper), **III:** 220

Antonina; or, The Fall of Rome (Collins), **Supp. VI:** 92, 95

Antonio and Mellida (Marston), **II:** 27–28, 40

Antonioni, Michelangelo, **Supp. IV:** 434

Antonio's Revenge (Marston), **II:** 27–29, 36, 40

Antony and Cleopatra (Sedley), **II:** 263, 271

Antony and Cleopatra (Shakespeare), **I:** 318, 319–320; **II:** 70; **III:** 22; **Supp. IV:** 263

Antony and Octavus. Scenes for the Study (Landor), **IV:** 100

Ants, The (Churchill), **Supp. IV:** 180–181

"Antwerp" (Ford), **VI:** 323, 416

"Anxious in Dreamland" (Menand), **Supp. IV:** 305

"Any Other Enemy" (Nye), **Supp. X:** 204–205

"Any Saint" (Thompson), **V: 444**

"Anybody's Alphabet" (Thomas), **Supp. XII:** 291

Anything for a Quiet Life (Middleton and Webster), **II:** 21, 69, 83, 85

Anzac Sonata, The (Stallworthy), **Supp. X:** 294, 298, 302

Apartheid and the Archbishop: The Life and Times of Geoffrey Clayton, Archbishop of Cape Town (Paton), **Supp. II:** 343, 356, 357–358

"Apartheid in Its Death Throes" (Paton), **Supp. II:** 342

"Ape, The" (Pritchett), **Supp. III:** 325

Apes of God, The (Lewis), **VII:** xv, 35, 71, 73, 74, 77, 79

Aphorisms on Man (Lavater), **III:** 298

Aphrodite in Aulis (Moore), **VI:** 88, 95, 99

Apocalypse (Lawrence), **VII:** 91; **Retro. Supp. II:** 234

"Apollo and the Fates" (Browning), **IV:** 366

"Apollo in Picardy" (Pater), **V:** 355, 356

"Apollonius of Tyre" (Gower), **I:** 53

"Apologia pro Poemate Meo" (Owen), **VI:** 452

Apologia pro Vita Sua (Newman), **Supp. VII:** 289, 290, 291, 294, 295, 296, 298, 299–300

Apologie for Poetry (Sidney), *see Defence of Poesie, The Apologie for the Royal Party, An . . . By a Lover of Peace and of His Country* (Evelyn), **II:** 287

Apology Against a Pamphlet Call'd A Modest Confutation of the Animadversions upon the Remonstrant Against Smectymnuus, An (Milton), **II:** 175

"Apology for Plainspeaking, An" (Stephen), **V:** 284

Apology for Poetry, An (Sidney), **Retro. Supp. I:** 157

"Apology for Smectymnuus" (Milton), **Retro. Supp. II:** 269

Apology for the Bible (Watson), **III:** 301

Apology for the Life of Mrs. Shamela Andrews, An (Fielding), *see Shamela*

"Apology for the Revival of Christian Architecture in England, A" (Hill), **Supp. V:** 189, 191–192

Apology for the Voyage to Guiana (Ralegh), **I:** 153

Apophthegms (Bacon), **I:** 264, 273

"Apostasy, The" (Traherne), **II:** 191

Apostles, The (Moore), **VI:** 88, 96, 99

Apostes, The (Cambridge Society), **IV:** 331; **V:** 278; **VI:** 399

"Apotheosis of Tins, The" (Mahon), **Supp. VI:** 172

"Apparition of His Mistresse Calling Him to Elizium, The" (Herrick), **II:** 113

Appeal from the New to the Old Whigs, An (Burke), **III:** 205

Appeal to England, An (Swinburne), **V:** 332

Appeal to Honour and Justice, An (Defoe), **III:** 4, 13; **Retro. Supp. I:** 66, 67

Appeal to the Clergy of the Church of Scotland, An (Stevenson), **V:** 395

"Appius and Virginia" (Gower), **I:** 55

Appius and Virginia (R. B.), **I:** 216

Appius and Virginia (Webster), **II:** 68, 83, 85

Apple Broadcast, The (Redgrove), **Supp. VI:** 235

Apple Cart, The: A Political Extravaganza (Shaw), **VI:** 118, 120, 125–126, 127, 129

"Apple Picking" (Maitland), **Supp. XI:** 177

"Apple Tragedy" (Hughes), **Supp. I:** 351, 353

"Apple Tree, The" (du Maurier), **Supp. III:** 138

"Apple Tree, The" (Galsworthy), **VI:** 276

"Apple Tree, The" (Mansfield), **VII:** 173

Applebee, John, **III:** 7

Appley Dapply's Nursery Rhymes (Potter), **Supp. III:** 291

Apollonius of Tyre, **Retro. Supp. II:** 298

Apology for Poetry, An (Sidney), **Retro. Supp. II:** 332–334, 339

"Appraisal, An" (Compton–Burnett), **VII:** 59

Appreciations (Pater), **V:** 338, 339, 341, 351–352, 353–356

"Apprehension, The" (Traherne), **Supp. XI:** 270

"Apprentice" (Warner), **Supp. VII:** 380

"April" (Kavanagh), **Supp. VII:** 188

"April Epithalamium, An" (Stevenson), **Supp. VI:** 263

April Love (Hughes), **V:** 294

April Shroud, An (Hill, R.), **Supp. IX:** 113–114

"Apron of Flowers, The" (Herrick), **II:** 110

Apropos of Dolores (Wells), **VI:** 240

"Aquae Sulis" (Hardy), **Retro. Supp. I:** 121

"Aquarius" (Armitage), **VIII:** 12

"Arab Love Song" (Thompson), **V:** 442, 445, 449

"Arabella" (Thackeray), **V:** 24

"Arabesque—The Mouse" (Coppard), **VIII:** 88

Arabian Nights, The, **III:** 327, 335, 336; **Supp. IV:** 434

"Araby" (Joyce), **Retro. Supp. I:** 172

Aragon, Louis, **Supp. IV:** 466

"Aramantha" (Lovelace), **II:** 230, 231

Aran Islands, The (Synge), **VI:** 308–309; **Retro. Supp. I:** 291–294

Aran Trilogy (McDonagh), **Supp. XII:** 240, 242–243, 245

Ararat (Thomas), **Supp. IV:** 484

Aratra Pentelici (Ruskin), **V:** 184

Arbuthnot, John, **III:** 19, 34, 60

"Arcades" (Milton), **II:** 159

Arcadia (Sidney), **I:** 161, 163–169, 173, 317; **II:** 48, 53–54; **III:** 95; **Retro. Supp. II:** 330–332, 340

Arcadia (Stoppard), **Retro. Supp. II:** 355–356

Arcadian Rhetorike (Fraunce), **I**: 164

"Archdeacon Truggin" (Powys), **VIII:** 256

Archeology of Love, The (Murphy), **Supp. V:** 317

Archer, William, **II:** 79, 358, 363, 364; **V:** 103, 104, 113

Architectural Review (periodical), **VII:** 356, 358

Architecture in Britain: 1530–1830 (Reynolds), **II:** 336

Architecture, Industry and Wealth (Morris), **V:** 306

"Arctic Summer" (Forster), **VI:** 406

Arden of Feversham (Kyd), **I:** 212, 213, 218–219

Arden, John, **Supp. II: 21–42**

"Ardour and Memory" (Rossetti), **V:** 243

Ardours and Endurances (Nichols), **VI:** 423

"Are You Lonely in the Restaurant" (O'Nolan), **Supp. II:** 323

Area of Darkness, An (Naipaul), **Supp. I,** 383, 384, 387, 389, 390, 391–392, 394, 395, 399, 402

Arendt, Hannah, **Supp. IV:** 306

Areopagitica (Milton), **II:** 163, 164, 169, 174, 175; **IV:** 279; **Retro. Supp. II:** 277–279

Aretina (Mackenzie), **III:** 95

"Argonauts of the Air, The" (Wells), **VI:** 244

Argonauts of the Pacific (Malinowski), **Supp. III:** 186

Argufying (Empson), **Supp. II:** 180, 181

Argument . . . that the Abolishing of Christianity .. . . May . . . be Attended with some Inconveniences, An (Swift), **III:** 26, 35

"Argument of His Book, The" (Herrick), **II:** 110

Argument Shewing that a Standing Army . . . Is Not Inconsistent with a Free Government, An (Defoe), **III,** 12

Ariadne Florentina (Ruskin), **V:** 184

Ariel Poems (Eliot), **VII:** 152

Arians of the Fourth Century, The (Newman), **Supp. VII:** 291

Arion and the Dolphin (Seth), **Supp. X:** 288

Aristocrats (Friel), **Supp. V:** 122

Aristomenes: or, The Royal Shepherd (Finch), **Supp. IX:** 74–76

Aristophanes, **V:** 227

Aristophanes' Apology (Browning), **IV:** 358, 367, 370, 374; **Retro. Supp. II:** 30

Aristos, The: A Self–Portrait in Ideas (Fowles), **Supp. I:** 293–294, 295, 296

Arky Types (Maitland and Wandor), **Supp. XI:** 165, 170

"Armada, The" (Macaulay), **IV:** 283, 291

Armadale (Collins), **Supp. VI:** 91, 93–94, **98–100,** 101, 103

Armah, Ayi Kwei, **Supp. X: 1–16**

Armitage, Simon, **VIII: 1–17**

Arms and the Covenant (Churchill), **VI:** 356

Arms and the Man (Shaw), **VI:** 104, 110, 120; **Retro. Supp. II:** 313

Arms and the Women: An Elliad (Hill, R.), **Supp. IX:** 122

Armstrong, Isobel Mair, **V:** xi, xxvii, 339, 375

Armstrong, William, **V:** xviii, xxxvii

Armstrong's Last Goodnight (Arden), **Supp. II:** 29, 30

Arnold, Matthew, **IV:** 359; **V:** viii–xi, 14, 156–158, 160, **203–218,** 283, 285, 289, 342, 352–353; works, **III:** 23, 174, 277; **V:** 206–215; literary criticism, **I:** 423; **III:** 68, 277; **IV:** 220, 234, 323, 371; **V:** 160, 165–169, 352, 408; **Supp. II:** 44, 57; **Retro. Supp. I:** 59

Arnold, Thomas, **V:** 155–156, 157, 165, 207, 208, 277, 284, 349

Arnold Bennett (Lafourcade), **VI:** 268

Arnold Bennett (Pound), **VI:** 247, 268

Arnold Bennett (Swinnerton), **VI:** 268

Arnold Bennett: A Biography (Drabble), **VI:** 247, 253, 268; **Supp. IV:** 203

Arnold Bennett: A Last Word (Swinnerton), **VI:** 268

Arnold Bennett and H. G. Wells: A Record of a Personal and Literary Friendship (ed. Wilson), **VI:** 246, 267

Arnold Bennett in Love (ed. and tr. Beardmore and Beardmore), **VI:** 251, 268

Arnold Bennett: The AEvening Standard–"Years (ed. Mylett), **VI:** 265n, 266

Arouet, Françoise Marie, *see* Voltaire

Around Theatres (Beerbohm), **Supp. II:** 54, 55

"Aromatherapy" (Redgrove), **Supp. VI:** 236

Arragonian Queen, The (Haywood), **Supp. XII:** 135

Arraignment of London, The (Daborne and Tourneur), **II:** 37

Arraignment of Paris (Peele), **I:** 197–200

"Arrangements" (Dunn), **Supp. X:** 76

"Arrest of Oscar Wilde at the Cadogan Hotel, The" (Betjeman), **VII:** 356, 365–366

Arrival and Departure (Koestler), **Supp. I:** 27, 28, 30–31

Arrivants, The: A New World Trilogy (Brathwaite), **Supp. XII:** 33, 34, 36–40, 41, 42, 44, 45

Arrow in the Blue (Koestler), **Supp. I:** 22, 25, 31, 34, 36

Arrow of Gold, A (Conrad), **VI:** 134, 144, 147

Ars Longa, Vita Brevis (Arden and D'Arcy), **Supp. II:** 29

Ars Poetica (Horace), **Retro. Supp. I:** 166

"Arsonist" (Murphy), **Supp. V:** 326

Art and Action (Sisson), **Supp. XI:** 253

"Art and Criticism" (Harris), **Supp. V:** 140

"Art and Extinction" (Harrison), **Supp. V:** 156

Art & Lies: A Piece for Three Voices and a Bawd (Winterson), **Supp. IV:** 542, 547, 552–553, 554–555, 556, 557

"Art and Morality" (Stephen), **V:** 286

Art and Reality (Cary), **VII:** 186

Art and Revolution: Ernst Neizvestny and the Role of the Artist in the U.S.S.R. (Berger), **Supp. IV:** 79, 88

"Art and Science" (Richards), **Supp. II:** 408–409

Art History and Class Consciousness (Hadjinicolaou), **Supp. IV:** 90

"Art McCooey" (Kavanagh), **Supp. VII:** 190

Art Objects: Essays on Ecstasy and Effrontery (Winterson), **Supp. IV:** 541, 542, 544, 557

Art of Angling, The (Barker), **II:** 131

Art of Being Ruled, The (Lewis), **VII:** 72, 75, 76

"Art of Dying, The" (Caudwell), **Supp. IX:** 35–38

Art of English Poetry, The (Puttenham), **I:** 94, 146, 214

Art of Fiction, The (James), **VI:** 46, 67

Art of Fiction, The (Kipling), **VI:** 204

Art of Fiction, The (Lodge), **Supp. IV:** 381

"Art of Fiction, The" (Woolf), **VII:** 21, 22

Art of Love, The (Ovid), **I:** 237–238

"Art of Malingering, The" (Cameron), **Supp. IX:** 18

Art of Sinking in Poetry, The (Pope), **IV:** 187

Art of the Big Bass Drum, The (Kelman), **Supp. V:** 256

Art of the Novel, The (James), **VI:** 67

"Art Work" (Byatt), **Supp. IV:** 155

"Arthur Snatchfold" (Forster), **VI:** 411

Article of Charge Against Hastings (Burke), **III:** 205

"Articles of Inquiry Concerning Heavy and Light" (Bacon), **I:** 261

Articulate Energy (Davie), **Supp. VI:** 114

"Artifice of Versification, An" (Fuller), **Supp. VII:** 77

Artificial Princess, The (Firbank), **Supp. II:** 199, 205, 207–208

Artist Descending a Staircase (Stoppard), **Retro. Supp. II:** 349

Artist of the Floating World, An (Ishiguro), **Supp. IV:** 301, 304, 306, 309–311

"Artist to His Blind Love, The" (Redgrove), **Supp. VI:** 234

"Artistic Career of Corky, The" (Wodehouse), **Supp. III:** 459

"Artistic Temperament of Stephen Carey, The" (Maugham), **VI:** 373

"Artists, The" (Thackeray), **V:** 22, 37

"Artists and Value" (Kelman), **Supp. V:** 257

Arts and Crafts Movement, The (Naylor), **VI:** 168

"Arundel Tomb, An" (Larkin), **Supp. I:** 280

As I Saw the USA (Morris), *see* *Coast to Coast*

As If By Magic (Wilson), **Supp. I:** 163–**165,** 166

"As It Should Be" (Mahon), **Supp. VI:** 170

"As kingfishers catch fire" (Hopkins), **V:** 371

"As So Often in Scotland" (Dutton), **Supp. XII:** 97

"As the Team's Head–Brass" (Thomas), **VI:** 425; **Supp. III:** 405

As You Like It (Shakespeare), **I:** 278, 312; **III:** 117; **Supp. IV:** 179

"Ascent into Hell" (Hope), **Supp. VII:** 153

Ascent of F6, The (Auden and Isherwood), **VII:** 312, 380, 383, 385; **Retro. Supp. I:** 7

Ascent to Omai (Harris), **Supp. V:** 135, 136, 138

"Ash Grove, The" (Thomas), **Supp. III:** 402

Ashenden (Maugham), **VI:** 371; **Supp. IV:** 9–10

Ashford, Daisy, **V:** 111, 262

Ashley, Lord, *see* Shaftesbury, seventh earl of

Ash–Wednesday (Eliot), **VII:** 144, 150, 151–152

Ashworth, Elizabeth, **Supp. IV:** 480

Asiatic Romance, An (Sisson), **Supp. XI:** 251

"Aside" (Thomas), **Supp. XII:** 290

Asimov, Isaac, **III:** 341

"Ask Me No More" (Tennyson), **IV:** 334

"Askam Unvisited" (Nicholson), **Supp. VI:** 214

"Askam Visited" (Nicholson), **Supp. VI:** 214

Asking Around (Hare), **Supp. IV:** 282, 298

Asking for the Moon (Hill, R.), **Supp. IX:** 118

"Asleep" (Owen), **VI:** 455

Asolando (Browning), **IV:** 359, 365, 374; **Retro. Supp. II:** 31

"Aspects" (MacCaig), **Supp. VI:** 188

Aspects of E. M. Forster (Stallybrass), **VI:** 413

Aspects of Religion in the United States of America (Bird), **Supp. X:** 23

Aspects of the Novel (Forster), **V:** 229; **VI:** 397, 411, 412; **VII:** 21, 22; **Retro. Supp. II:** 149

"Aspens" (Thomas), **Supp. III:** 406

Aspern Papers, The (James), **VI:** 38, **46–48**

"Asphodel" (Malouf), **Supp. XII:** 219–220

Asquith, Herbert, **VI:** 417

Asquith, Raymond, **VI:** 417, 428

"Ass, The" (Vaughan), **II:** 186

"Assassination of John Fitzgerald Kennedy Considered as a Downhill Motor Race" (Ballard), **Supp. V:** 21

Assassins, The (Shelley), **Retro. Supp. I:** 247

Assignation, The; or, Love in a Nunnery (Dryden), **II:** 305

"Assisi" (MacCaig), **Supp. VI:** 189–190, 194–195

"Assunta 2" (Chatwin), **Supp. IV:** 173

"Astarte Syriaca" (Rossetti), **V:** 238, 240

Astonished Heart, The (Coward), **Supp. II:** 152

Astonishing the Gods (Okri), **Supp. V:** 347, 349, 353, 359, 360–361

"Assault, The" (Nichols), **VI:** 419

Assembling a Ghost (Redgrove), **Supp. VI:** 236

"Assumption" (Beckett), **Retro. Supp. I:** 17

Astraea Redux. A Poem on the Happy Restoration . . . of . . . Charles the Second (Dryden), **II:** 292, 304

Astride the Two Cultures (Koestler), **Supp. I:** 36

"Astronomy" (Housman), **VI:** 161

Astronomy of Love, The (Stallworthy), **Supp. X:** 292, 298, 302

Astrophel (collection), **I:** 160

Astrophel. A Pastoral Elegy (Spenser), **I:** 126; **IV:** 205

Astrophel and Other Poems (Swinburne), **V:** 333

Astrophel and Stella (Sidney), **I:** 161, 169–173; **Retro. Supp. II:** 334–339, 340–341

Astrophil and Stella (Greville), **Supp. XI:** 111

Asylum Piece and Other Stories (Kavan), **Supp. VII:** 210–211, 212, 214

"At a Calvary near the Ancre" (Owen), **VI:** 450, 451

"At a Potato Digging" (Heaney), **Supp. II:** 270

"At a Warwickshire Mansion" (Fuller), **Supp. VII:** 73

"At Bedtime" (Stallworthy), **Supp. X:** 294

"At Castle Boterel" (Hardy), **VI:** 18

"At Christ Church, Greyfriars" (Blunden), **Supp. XI:** 44

"At East Coker" (Day Lewis), **Supp. III:** 130

"At Falkland Place" (Dunn), **Supp. X:** 77

"At First Sight" (Reid), **Supp. VII:** 328

At Freddie's (Fitzgerald), **Supp. V:** 96, 98, 101, 103–104

"At Grass" (Larkin), **Supp. I:** 277

"At Great Hampden" (Adcock), **Supp. XII:** 13

At Home: Memoirs (Plomer), **Supp. XI:** 223, 226

"At Isella" (James), **VI:** 69

"At Laban's Well" (Coppard), **VIII:** 95

At Lady Molly's (Powell), **VII:** 348

"At Last" (Kincaid), **Supp. VII:** 220–221

"At Last" (Nye), **Supp. X:** 204

"At Lehmann's" (Mansfield), **VII:** 172, 173

"At Rugmer" (Blunden), **Supp. XI:** 44

"At Senlis Once" (Blunden), **VI:** 428

At Swim–Two–Birds (O'Nolan), **Supp. II:** **323–326,** 332, 336, 338

"At the Ball" (Fuller), **Supp. VII:** 80

"At the Bay" (Mansfield), **VII:** 175, 177, 179, 180

At the Bottom of the River (Kincaid), **Supp. VII:** 217, 221, 222, 223, 224, 225

"At the British War Cemetery, Bayeux" (Causley), **VII:** 448

"At the Centre" (Gunn), **Supp. IV:** 267

"At the Crossroads" (Kinsella), **Supp. V:** 267

"At the Edge of a Birchwood" (Dunn), **Supp. X:** 76–77

"At the Edge of the Wood" (Redgrove), **Supp. VI:** 228

"At the End" (Cornford), **VIII:** 106

"At the End" (Thomas), **Supp. XII:** 292

"At the End of the Passage" (Kipling), **VI:** 173–175, 183, 184, 193

"At the Funeral of Robert Garioch" (Smith, I. C.), **Supp. IX:** 218–219

"At the Grave of Henry James" (Auden), **VII:** 380; **Retro. Supp. I:** 2

"At the Great Durbar" (Steel), **Supp. XII:** 268

"At the Great Wall of China" (Blunden), **VI:** 429

"At the 'Mermaid'" (Browning), **IV:** 35

"At the Head Table" (Kinsella), **Supp. V:** 273

"At the Musical Festival" (Nicholson), **Supp. VI:** 219

"At the Sale" (Smith, I. C.), **Supp. IX:** 220

"At the White Monument" (Redgrove), **Supp. VI:** 228–229, 237

Atalanta in Calydon (Swinburne), **IV:** 90; **V:** xxiii, 309, 313, 318, **321–324,** 331, 332; **VII:** 134

"Atheism" (Bacon), **III:** 39

"Atheist, The" (Powys), **VIII:** 249

Atheist's Tragedy, The (Tourneur), **II:** 29, 33, 36, 37, **38–40,** 41, 70

Athenaeum (periodical), **IV:** 252, 254, 262, 310, 315; **V:** 32, 134; **VI:** 167, 234, 374; **VII:** 32

"Athene's Song" (Boland), **Supp. V:** 39

Athenian Mercury (newspaper), **III:** 41

"Atlantic" (Russell), **VIII:** 291

Atlantic Monthly (periodical), **VI:** 29, 33

"Atlantis" (Auden), **Retro. Supp. I:** 10

Atlas (periodical), **V:** 144

Atrocity Exhibition, The (Ballard), **Supp. V:** 19, 21, 25

"Attack" (Sassoon), **VI:** 431

Attempt to Describe Hafod, An (Cumberland), **IV:** 47

Attenborough, Richard, **Supp. IV:** 455

Atterbury, Francis, **III:** 23

"Attic, The" (Mahon), **Supp. VI:** 175

Attlee, Clement, **VI:** 358

"Attracta" (Trevor), **Supp. IV:** 502

"Atumpan" (Brathwaite), **Supp. XII:** 38, 39

Atwood, Margaret, **Supp. IV:** 233

"Aubade" (Empson), **Supp. II:** 191

"Aubade" (Larkin), **Supp. I:** 284

"Aubade" (Sitwell), **VII:** 131

Aubreiad (O'Brian), **Supp. XII:** 253, 258, 259, 261–262

Aubrey, John, **I:** 260; **II:** 45, 46, 205–206, 226, 233

"Auction" (Murphy), **Supp. V:** 317

"Auction of the Ruby Slippers, The" (Rushdie), **Supp. IV:** 443

Auden, W. H., **I:** 92, **IV:** 106, 208; **V:** 46; **VI:** 160, 208; **VII:** xii, xviii, xix–xx, 153, **379–399,** 403, **407; Supp. II:** 143–144, 190, 200, 213, 267, 481–

482, 485, 486, 493, 494; **Supp. III:** 60, 100, 117, 119, 123, 131; **Supp. IV:** 100, 256, 411, 422, 423; **Retro. Supp. I: 1–15**

"Audenesque for an Initiation" (Ewart), **Supp. VII:** 37

"Auditors In" (Kavanagh), **Supp. VII:** 195–196

"Audley Court" (Tennyson), **IV:** 326n

"Auguries of Innocence" (Blake), **III:** 300

"August for the People" (Auden), **Retro. Supp. I:** 7

August Is a Wicked Month (O'Brien), **Supp. V:** 339

"August Midnight, An" (Hardy), **Retro. Supp. I:** 119

"August 1914" (Rosenberg), **VI:** 434

Augusta Triumphans; or, The Way to Make London the Most Flourishing City . . . (Defoe), **III:** 14

Augustan Ages, The (Elton), **III:** 51n

Augustan Lyric (Davie), **Supp. VI:** 115

Augustans and Romantics (Butt and Dyson), **III:** 51n

Augustus Does His Bit (Shaw), **VI:** 120

"Auld Enemy, The" (Crawford), **Supp. XI:** 81

"Auld Lang Syne" (Burns), **III:** 321

Auld Licht Idylls, When a Man's Single (Barrie), **Supp. III:** 2, 3

Ault, Norman, **III:** 69, 78

"Aunt and the Sluggard, The" (Wodehouse), **Supp. III:** 447–448, 455, 457

Aunt Judy's (periodical), **V:** 271

Aunts Aren't Gentlemen (Wodehouse), **Supp. III:** 455

Aunt's Story, The (White), **Supp. I:** 131, **134–136,** 148

Aureng-Zebe (Dryden), **II:** 295, 305

Aurora Floyd (Braddon), **VIII:** 35, 38, 42–44, 48

Aurora Leigh (Browning), **IV:** xxi, 311, 312, 314–315, 316–318, 321

Aus dem Zweiten Reich [From the Second Reich] (Bunting), **Supp. VII:** 4

Ausonius, **II:** 108, 185

"Auspicious Occasion" (Mistry), **Supp. X:** 138

Austen, Alfred, **V:** 439

Austen, Cassandra, **Retro. Supp. II:** 13–14

Austen, Jane, **III:** 90, 283, 335–336, 345; **IV:** xi, xiv, xvii, 30, **101–124; V:** 51; **Supp. II:** 384; **Supp. IV:** 154, 230, 233, 236, 237, 319; **Retro. Supp. II: 1–16,** 135

Austen–Leigh, J. E., **III:** 90

Austerlitz (Sebald), **VIII:** 295, 305–307

Austin, J. L., **Supp. IV:** 115

"Australia" (Hope), **Supp. VII:** 153

Australia and New Zealand (Trollope), **V:** 102

Australian Nationalists, The: Modern Critical Essays (Wallace–Crabbe), **VIII:** 3 **VIII:** 21, 320

Austri's effort (Þórðarson), **VIII:** 235

"Auteur Theory" (Hill, R.), **Supp. IX:** 118

"Author of 'Beltraffio,' The," (James), **VI:** 69

"Author to the Critical Peruser, The" (Traherne), **Supp. XI:** 274

"Author Upon Himself, The" (Swift), **III:** 19, 32

Authoress of the Odyssey, The (Butler), **Supp. II:** 114–116

Authorized Version of the Bible, *see* King James Version

Author's Apology, The (Bunyan), **II:** 246n

Author's Farce, The (Fielding), **III:** 105

"Autobiographical Essay" (Thomas), **Supp. XII:** 284

"Autobiographical Reflections on Politics" (Sisson), **Supp. XI:** 247

Autobiographical Writings (Newman), **Supp. VII:** 289, 290

Autobiographies (Thomas), **Supp. XII:** 281, 286

Autobiographies (Yeats), **V:** 301, 304, 306, 404; **VI:** 317

"Autobiographies, The" (James), **VI:** 65

"Autobiography" (Gunn), **Supp. IV:** 270

"Autobiography" (MacNeice), **VII:** 401

"Autobiography" (Reid), **Supp. VII:** 325

Autobiography (Russell), **VII:** 90

"Autobiography" (Thomas), **Supp. XII:** 280–281

Autobiography, An (Muir), **Supp. VI:** 197, **198–200,** 201, 205

Autobiography, An (Trollope), **V:** 89, 90–93, 96, 101, 102

Autobiography and Letters of Mrs. M. O. W. Oliphant (Oliphant), **Supp. X:** 212–213, 223

Autobiography and Other Essays, An (Trevelyan), **VI:** 383, 386, 388

Autobiography of a Supertramp (Davies), **Supp. III:** 398; **Supp. XI:** 88, 90–91, 92

Autobiography of Alice B. Toklas, The (Stein), **Supp. IV:** 557

Autobiography of Edward Gibbon, The (ed. Smeaton), **III:** 229n

Autobiography of My Mother, The (Kincaid), **Supp. VII:** 217, 229–230

"Autumn" (Hulme), **Supp. VI:** 134, 136, 142

Autumn (Thomson), **Supp. III:** 414–415, 416, 417, 420

"Autumn Evening" (Cornford), **VIII:** 102, 103, 112

Autumn Journal (MacNeice), **VII:** 412

Autumn Midnight (Cornford), **VIII:** 104, 105, 109

"Autumn Morning at Cambridge" (Cornford), **VIII:** 102, 103, 107

"Autumn 1939" (Fuller), **Supp. VII:** 69

"Autumn 1942" (Fuller), **VII:** 430–431

"Autumn on Nan-Yueh" (Empson), **Supp. II:** 191–192

Autumn Sequel (MacNeice), **VII:** 407, 412, 415

"Autumn Sunshine" (Trevor), **Supp. IV:** 504

"Autumnall, The" (Donne), **II:** 118

Available for Dreams (Fuller), **Supp. VII:** 68, 79, 80, 81

Avatars, The (Russell), **VIII:** 277, 285, 290–291, 292

Ave (Moore), **VI:** 99

"Ave Atque Vale" (Swinburne), **V:** 314, 327

"Ave Imperatrix" (Kipling), **VI:** 201

Aveling, Edward, **VI:** 102

Avignon Quintet (Durrell), **Supp. I:** 100, 101, **118–121**

"Avising the bright beams of those fair eyes" (Wyatt), **I:** 110

Avoidance of Literature, The: Collected Essays (Sisson), **Supp. XI:** 247,

Avowals (Moore), **VI:** 97–98, 99

"Awake, my heart, to be loved" (Bridges), **VI:** 74, 77

Awakened Conscience, The (Dixon Hunt), **VI:** 167

"Awakening, The" (Brathwaite), **Supp. XII:** 39

Awakening Conscience, The (Holman Hunt), **V:** 45, 51, 240

"Away with the Birds" (Healy), **Supp. IX:** 107

Awesome God: Creation, Commitment and Joy (Maitland), **Supp. XI:** 164, 165

Awfully Big Adventure, An (Bainbridge), **Supp. VI:** 18, **23–24**

Awkward Age, The (James), **VI:** 45, 56, 67

"Axeing Darkness / Here Below" (Dutton), **Supp. XII:** 94

"Axel's Castle" (Mahon), **Supp. VI:** 177

Ayala's Angel (Trollope), **V:** 100, 102

Ayckbourn, Alan, **Supp. V: 1–17**

Ayesha: The Return of She (Haggard), **Supp. III:** 214, 222

Aylott & Jones (publishers), **V:** 131

"Baa, Baa Black Sheep" (Kipling), **VI:** 166

"Babby" (Crawford), **Supp. XI:** 76

Babees Book, The (Early English Poems and Treatises on Manners and Meals in Olden Time) (ed. Furnival), **I:** 22, 26

Babel Tower (Byatt), **Supp. IV:** 139, 141, 149–151

"Babes" (Fallon), **Supp. XII:** 102

Babes in the Darkling Wood (Wells), **VI:** 228

"Baby Nurse, The" (Blackwood), **Supp. IX:** 5, 9

"Baby's cradle with no baby in it, A" (Rossetti), **V:** 255

Babylon Hotel (Bennett), *see Grand Babylon Hotel, The*

"Babysitting" (Galloway), **Supp. XII:** 126

Bachelors, The (Spark), **Supp. I:** 203, 204

Back (Green), **Supp. II:** 254, 258–260

"Back of Affluence" (Davie), **Supp. VI:** 110

"Back to Cambo" (Hartley), **Supp. VII:** 124

Back to Methuselah (Shaw), **VI: 121– 122,** 124; **Retro. Supp. II:** 323

"Background Material" (Harrison), **Supp. V:** 155

Background to Danger (Ambler), **Supp. IV:** 7–8

Backward Place, A (Jhabvala), **Supp. V:** 229

Backward Son, The (Spender), **Supp. II:** 484, 489

Bacon, Francis, **I: 257–274; II:** 149, 196; **III:** 39; **IV:** 138, 278, 279; annotated list of works, **I:** 271–273; **Supp. III:** 361

Bad Boy (McEwan), **Supp. IV:** 400

"Bad Dreams in Vienna" (Malouf), **Supp. XII:** 220

"Bad Five Minutes in the Alps, A" (Stephen), **V:** 283

Bad Land: An American Romance (Raban), **Supp. XI:** 236, 239, 241

"Bad Night, A" (Auden), **Retro. Supp. I:** 14

Bad Sister, The (Tennant), **Supp. IX:** 229, 230, 231–234, 235–236, 238, 239, 240

Bagehot, Walter, **IV:** 289, 291; **V:** xxiii, 156, 165, 170, 205, 212

"Baggot Street Deserta" (Kinsella), **Supp. V:** 259–260

Bagman, The; or, The Impromptu of Muswell Hill (Arden), **Supp. II:** 31, 32, 35

"Bagpipe Music" (MacNeice), **VII:** 413

Bailey, Benjamin, **IV:** 224, 229, 230, 232–233

Bailey, Paul, **Supp. IV:** 304

Baillie, Alexander, **V:** 368, 374, 375, 379

Bainbridge, Beryl, **Supp. VI: 17–27**

Baines, Jocelyn, **VI:** 133–134

Baird, Julian, **V:** 316, 317, 318, 335

"Baite, The" (Donne), **IV:** 327

Bajazet (tr. Hollinghurst), **Supp. X:** 132–134

Bakerman, Jane S., **Supp. IV:** 336

"Baker's Dozen, The" (Saki), **Supp. VI:** 243

Bakhtin, Mikhail, **Supp. IV:** 114

"Balakhana" (McGuckian), **Supp. V:** 284

"Balance, The" (Waugh), **Supp. VI:** 271

Balance of Terror (Shaffer), **Supp. I:** 314

Balaustion's Adventure (Browning), **IV:** 358, 374; **Retro. Supp. II:** 30

"Balder Dead" (Arnold), **V:** 209, 216

Baldrs draumar, **VIII:** 231

Baldwin, Stanley, **VI:** 353, 355

Bale, John, **I:** 1, 3

Balfour, Arthur, **VI:** 226, 241, 353

Balfour, Graham, **V:** 393, 397

Balin; or, The Knight with Two Swords (Malory), **I:** 79

Ball and the Cross, The (Chesterton), **VI:** 338

Ballad at Dead Men's Bay, The (Swinburne), **V:** 332

"Ballad of Bouillabaisse" (Thackeray), **V:** 19

"Ballad of Death, A" (Swinburne), **V:** 316, 317–318

Ballad of Jan Van Hunks, The (Rossetti), **V:** 238, 244, 245

"Ballad of Kynd Kittok, The" (Dunbar), **VIII:** 126

"Ballad of Life, A" (Swinburne), **V:** 317, 318

Ballad of Peckham Rye, The (Spark), **Supp. I:** 201, 203–204

Ballad of Reading Gaol, The (Wilde), **V:** xxvi, 417–418, 419; **Retro. Supp. II:** 372–373

Ballad of Sylvia and Ted, The (Tennant), **Supp. IX:** 239, 240

"Ballad of the Investiture 1969, A" (Betjeman), **VII:** 372

"Ballad of the Long–legged Bait" (Thomas), **Supp. I:** 177

"Ballad of the Three Spectres" (Gurney), **VI:** 426

"Ballad of the Two Left Hands" (Dunn), **Supp. X:** 73

"Ballad of the White Horse, The" (Chesterton), **VI:** 338–339, 341

"Ballad of Villon and Fat Madge, The" (tr. Swinburne), **V:** 327

"Ballad upon a Wedding, A" (Suckling), **II:** 228–229

Ballade du temps jadis (Villon), **VI:** 254

"Ballade of Barnard Stewart, The" (Dunbar), **VIII:** 118

Ballade of Truthful Charles, The, and Other Poems (Swinburne), **V:** 333

Ballade on an Ale–Seller (Lydgate), **I:** 92

Ballads (Stevenson), **V:** 396

Ballads (Thackeray), **V:** 38

Ballads and Lyrical Pieces (Scott), **IV:** 38

Ballads and Other Poems (Tennyson), **IV:** 338

Ballads and Poems of Tragic Life (Meredith), **V:** 224, 234

Ballads and Sonnets (Rossetti), **V:** xxiv, 238, 244, 245

Ballads of the English Border (Swinburne), **V:** 333

Ballard, J. G., **III:** 341; **Supp. V: 19–34**

Ballast to the White Sea (Lowry), **Supp. III:** 273, 279

"Ane Ballat of Our Lady" (Dunbar). *See* "Hale, sterne superne"

Balliols, The (Waugh), **Supp. VI:** 273

Ballot (Smith), **Supp. VII:** 351

"Ballroom of Romance, The" (Trevor), **Supp. IV:** 503

"Bally *Power Play*" (Gunn), **Supp. IV:** 272

Ballygombeen Bequest, The (Arden and D'Arcy), **Supp. II:** 32, 35

Balthazar (Durrell), **Supp. I:** 104–105, 106, 107

Balzac, Honoré de, **III:** 334, 339, 345; **IV:** 153n; **V:** xvi, xviii, xix–xxi, 17, 429; **Supp. IV:** 123, 136, 238, 459

"Bamboo: A Ballad for Two Voices" (Plomer), **Supp. XI:** 226

Bamborough, J. B., **Retro. Supp. I:** 152

Bananas (ed. Tennant), **Supp. IX:** 228–229

Banco: The Further Adventures of Papillon (tr. O'Brian), **Supp. XII:** 252

Bancroft, John, **II:** 305

Bandamanna saga, **VIII:** 238, 241

"Bangor Requiem" (Mahon), **Supp. VI:** 177

"Banim Creek" (Harris), **Supp. V:** 132

Banished Misfortune (Healy), **Supp. IX:** 96, 103–106

Banks, Iain, **Supp. XI: 1–15**

Banks, John, **II:** 305

"Bann Valley Eclogue" (Heaney), **Retro. Supp. I:** 134

Banshees of Inisheer, The (McDonagh), **Supp. XII:** 243

"Barbara of the House of Grebe" (Hardy), **VI:** 22; **Retro. Supp. I:** 117

Barbara, pseud. of Arnold Bennett

"Barbarian Catechism, A" (Wallace–Crabbe), **VIII:** 324

"Barbarian Pastorals" (Dunn), **Supp. X:** 72

Barbarians (Dunn), **Supp. X: 71–73,** 77

"Barbarians" (Dutton), **Supp. XII:** 90

Barbauld, Anna Laetitia, **III:** 88, 93

"Barber Cox and the Cutting of His Comb" (Thackeray), **V:** 21, 37

Barcellona; or, The Spanish Expedition under . . . Charles, Earl of Peterborough (Farquhar), **II:** 353, 355, 364

Barchester Towers (Trollope), **V:** xxii, 93, 101

"Bard, The" (Gray), **III:** 140–141

Bardic Tales (O'Grady), **Supp. V:** 36

"Bards of Passion . . ." (Keats), **IV:** 221

"Bare Abundance, The" (Dutton), **Supp. XII:** 89

Bare Abundance, The: Selected Poems, 1975–2001 (Dutton), **Supp. XII:** 83, 86, 88, 89–99

Barker, Granville, *see* Granville Barker, Harley

Barker, Sir Ernest, **III:** 196

Barker, Pat, **Supp. IV: 45–63**

Barker, Thomas, **II:** 131

Barker's Delight (Barker), *see* Art of Angling, The

Barksted, William, **II:** 31

"Barley" (Hughes), **Supp. I:** 358–359

"Barn, The" (Welch), **Supp. IX:** 268

Barnaby Rudge (Dickens), **V:** 42, 54, 55, 66, 71

Barnes, William, **VI:** 2

Barnes, Julian, **Supp. IV: 65–76,** 445, 542

"Barney Game, The" (Friel), **Supp. V:** 113

"Barnfloor and Winepress" (Hopkins), **V:** 381

"Barnsley Cricket Club" (Davie), **Supp. VI:** 109

Barrack–Room Ballads (Kipling), **VI:** 203, 204

Barrel of a Pen: Resistance to Repression in Neo–Colonial Kenya (Ngũgĩ), **VIII:** 225

Barreca, Regina, **Supp. IV:** 531

Barren Fig Tree, The; or, The Doom . . . of the Fruitless Professor (Bunyan), **II:** 253

Barrett, Eaton Stannard, **III:** 335

Barrie, James M., **V:** 388, 392; **VI:** 265, 273, 280; **Supp. III: 1–17,** 138, 142

Barry Lyndon (Thackeray), **V:** 24, 28, 32, 38

Barrytown Trilogy, The (Doyle), **Supp. V:** 78, 80–87, 88, 89

Barsetshire novels (Trollope), V: 92–96, 98, 101

Bartas, Guillaume du, **II:** 138

Bartered Bride, The (Harrison), **Supp. V:** 150

Barth, John, **Supp. IV:** 116

Barthes, Roland, **Supp. IV:** 45, 115

Bartholomew Fair (Jonson), **I:** 228, 243, 324, 340, 342–343; **II:** 3; **Retro. Supp. I:** 164

Bartlett, Phyllis, **V:** x, xxvii

Barton, Bernard, **IV:** 341, 342, 343, 350

Barton, Eustace, **Supp. III:** 342

"Base Details" (Sassoon), **VI:** 430

Basement, The (Pinter), **Supp. I:** 371, 373, 374; **Retro. Supp. I:** 216

"Basement Room, The" (Greene), **Supp. I:** 2

Bashful Lover, The (Massinger), **Supp. XI:** 185

Basic Rules of Reason (Richards), **Supp. II:** 422

Basil: A Story of Modern Life (Collins), **Supp. VI:** 92, 95

Basil Seal Rides Again (Waugh), **VII:** 290

"Basking Shark" (MacCaig), **Supp. VI:** 192

Bate, Walter Jackson, **Retro. Supp. I:** 185

Bateman, Colin, **Supp. V:** 88

Bateson, F. W., **IV:** 217, 323*n*, 339

Bath (Sitwell), **VII:** 127

Bath Chronicle (periodical), **III:** 262

"Bath House, The" (Gunn), **Supp. IV:** 268–269

Bath–Intrigues: In Four Letters to a Friend in London (Haywood), **Supp. XII:** 135

Bathurst, Lord, **III:** 33

"Bats' Ultrasound" (Murray), **Supp. VII:** 281

Batsford Book of Light Verse for Children (Ewart), **Supp. VII:** 47

Batsford Book of Verse for Children (Ewart), **Supp. VII:** 47

"Battalion History, A" (Blunden), **Supp. XI:** 35

Battenhouse, Roy, **I:** 282

"Batter my heart, three person'd God" (Donne), **I:** 367–368; **II:** 122

"Batterer" (Adcock), **Supp. XII:** 4

Battiscombe, Georgina, **V:** xii, xxvii, 260

"Battle Hill Revisited" (Murphy), **Supp. V:** 323

Battle of Alcazar, The (Peele), **I:** 205, 206

Battle of Aughrim, The (Murphy), **Supp. V:** 321–324

"Battle of Aughrim, The" (Murphy), **Supp. V:** 317, 321–322

"Battle of Blenheim, The" (Southey), **IV:** 58, 67–68

Battle of Brunanburh, The, **Retro. Supp. II:** 307

Battle of Life, The (Dickens), **V:** 71

Battle of Maldon, The, **Retro. Supp. II:** 307

Battle of Marathon, The (Browning), **IV:** 310, 321

Battle of Shrivings, The (Shaffer), **Supp. I:** 323–324

Battle of the Books, The (Swift), **III:** 17, 23, 35; **Retro. Supp. I:** 276, 277

"Battle of the Goths and the Huns, The", *See Hlǫðskviða*

Baucis and Philemon (Swift), **III:** 35

Baudelaire, Charles **III:** 337, 338; **IV:** 153; **V:** xiii, xviii, xxii–xxiii, 310–318, 327, 329, 404, 405, 409, 411; **Supp. IV:** 163

Baum, L. Frank, **Supp. IV:** 450

Baumann, Paul, **Supp. IV:** 360

Baumgartner's Bombay (Desai), **Supp. V:** 53, 55, 66, 71–72

Bay (Lawrence), **VII:** 118

Bay at Nice, The (Hare), **Supp. IV:** 282, 293

Bayley, John, **Supp. I:** 222

Bayly, Lewis, **II:** 241

"Baymount" (Murphy), **Supp. V:** 328

"Be It Cosiness" (Beerbohm), **Supp. II:** 46

Be my Guest! (Ewart), **Supp. VII:** 41

"Be still, my soul" (Housman), **VI:** 162

Beach, J. W., **V:** 221*n*, 234

"Beach of Fales, The" (Stevenson), **V:** 396; **Retro. Supp. I:** 270

Beachcroft, T. O., **VII:** xxii

Beaconsfield, Lord, *see* Disraeli, Benjamin

"Bear in Mind" (Cameron), **Supp. IX:** 29

Beardsley, Aubrey, **V:** 318*n*, 412, 413

"Beast in the Jungle, The" (James), **VI:** 55, 64, 69

Beastly tales from Here and There (Seth), **Supp. X:** 287–288

Beasts and Super-Beasts (Saki), **Supp. VI:** 245, 251

Beasts' Confession to the Priest, The (Swift), **III:** 36

Beasts Royal (O'Brian), **Supp. XII:** 249

Beatrice (Haggard), **Supp. III:** 213

Beattie, James, **IV:** 198

Beatty, David, **VI:** 351

Beau Austin (Stevenson), **V:** 396

Beauchamp's Career (Meredith), **V:** xxiv, 225, 228–230, 231, 234

Beaumont, Francis, **II:** **42–67**, 79, 82, 87

Beaumont, Joseph, **II:** 180

Beaumont, Sir George, **IV:** 3, 12, 21, 22

Beauties and Furies, The (Stead), **Supp. IV:** 463–464

Beauties of English Poesy, The (ed. Goldsmith), **III:** 191

"Beautiful Lofty Things" (Yeats), **VI:** 216; **Retro. Supp. I:** 337

"Beautiful Sea, The" (Powys), **VIII:** 251

Beautiful Visit, The (Howard), **Supp. XI:** 137–138, 140–141, 148–149

"Beautiful Young Nymph Going to Bed, A" (Swift), **III:** 32, 36; **VI:** 256

"Beauty" (Thomas), **Supp. III:** 401–402

Beauty and the Beast (Hughes), **Supp. I:** 347

Beauty in a Trance, **II:** 100

Beauty Queen of Leenane, The (McDonagh), **Supp. XII:** 233, 234, 235–236, 238, 239, 241

Beautyful Ones Are Not Yet Born, The (Armah), **Supp. X:** 1–6, 12–13

Beauvoir, Simone de, **Supp. IV:** 232

Beaux' Stratagem, The (Farquhar), **II:** 334, 353, 359–360, 362, 364

"Beaver Ridge" (Fallon), **Supp. XII:** 113–114

"Because of the Dollars" (Conrad), **VI:** 148

"Because the pleasure-bird whistles" (Thomas), **Supp. I:** 176

Becket (Tennyson), **IV:** 328, 338

Beckett, Samuel, **Supp. I:** **43–64; Supp. IV:** 99, 106, 116, 180, 281, 284, 412, 429; **Retro. Supp. I:** 17–32

Beckford, William, **III:** 327–329, 345; **IV:** xv, 230

Bed Among the Lentils (Bennett), **VIII:** 27–28

"Bedbug, The" (Harrison), **Supp. V:** 151

Beddoes, Thomas, **V:** 330

Beddoes, Thomas Lovell, **Supp. XI:** **17–32**

Bedford–Row Conspiracy, The (Thackeray), **V:** 21, 37

"Bedroom Eyes of Mrs. Vansittart, The" (Trevor), **Supp. IV:** 500

Bedroom Farce (Ayckbourn), **Supp. V:** 3, 12, 13, 14

Beds in the East (Burgess), **Supp. I:** 187

Bedtime Story (O'Casey), **VII:** 12

"Bedtime Story for my Son" (Redgrove), **Supp. VI:** **227–228**, 236

Bee (periodical), **III:** 40, 179

Bee Hunter: Adventures of Beowulf (Nye), **Supp. X:** 193, 195

"Bee Orchd at Hodbarrow" (Nicholson), **Supp. VI:** 218

"Beechen Vigil" (Day Lewis), **Supp. III:** 121

Beechen Vigil and Other Poems (Day Lewis), **Supp. III:** 117, 120–121

"Beehive Cell" (Murphy), **Supp. V:** 329

Beekeepers, The (Redgrove), **Supp. VI:** 231

"Beeny Cliff" (Hardy), **Retro. Supp. I:** 118

Beerbohm, Max, **V:** 252, 390; **VI:** 365, 366; **Supp. II:** **43–59**, 156

"Before Action" (Hodgson), **VI:** 422

Before Dawn (Rattigan), **Supp. VII:** 315

"Before Her Portrait in Youth" (Thompson), **V:** 442

"Before I knocked" (Thomas), **Supp. I:** 175

Before She Met Me (Barnes), **Supp. IV:** 65, 67–68

"Before Sleep" (Kinsella), **Supp. V:** 263

Before the Knowledge of Evil (Braddon), **VIII:** 36

"Before the Mirror" (Swinburne), **V:** 320

"Before the Party" (Maugham), **VI:** 370

Beggars (Davies), **Supp. XI:** 87, 88

Beggars Banquet (Rankin), **Supp. X:** 245–246, 253, 257

Beggar's Bush (Beaumont, Fletcher, Massinger), **II:** 66

Beggar's Opera, The (Gay), **III:** 54, 55, **61–64**, 65–67; **Supp. III:** 195; **Retro. Supp. I:** 80

"Beggar's Soliloquy, The" (Meredith), **V:** 220

Begin Here: A War–Time Essay (Sayers), **Supp. III:** 336

"Beginning, The" (Brooke), **Supp. III:** 52

Beginning of Spring, The (Fitzgerald), **Supp. V:** 98, 106

Behan, Brendan, **Supp. II: 61–76**

Behind the Green Curtains (O'Casey), **VII:** 11

Behn, Aphra, **Supp. III: 19–33**

"Behold, Love, thy power how she despiseth" (Wyatt), **I:** 109

"Being Boring" (Cope), **VIII:** 80

"Being Stolen From" (Trevor), **Supp. IV:** 504

"Being Treated, to Ellinda" (Lovelace), **II:** 231–232

"Beldonald Holbein, The" (James), **VI:** 69

"Beleaguered City, A" (Oliphant), **Supp. X:** 220

"Belfast vs. Dublin" (Boland), **Supp. V:** 36

"Belief" (Dutton), **Supp. XII:** 96

Belief and Creativity (Golding), **Supp. I:** 88

Belief in Immortality and Worship of the Dead, The (Frazer), **Supp. III:** 176

Believe As You List (Massinger), **Supp. XI:** 185

Belin, Mrs., **II:** 305

Belinda (Edgeworth), **Supp. III: 157–158,** 162

Belinda, An April Folly (Milne), **Supp. V:** 298–299

Bell, Acton, pseud. of Anne Brontë

Bell, Clive, **V:** 345

Bell, Currer, pseud. of Charlotte Brontë

Bell, Ellis, pseud. of Emily Brontë

Bell, Julian, **Supp. III:** 120

Bell, Quentin, **VII:** 35; **Retro. Supp. I:** 305

Bell, Robert, **I:** 98

Bell, Vanessa, **VI:** 118

Bell, The (Murdoch), **Supp. I:** 222, 223–224, 226, 228–229

"Bell of Aragon, The" (Collins), **III:** 163

"Bell Ringer, The" (Jennings), **Supp. V:** 218

"Belladonna" (Nye), **Supp. X:** 198

Bellamira; or, The Mistress (Sedley), **II:** 263

Belle Assemblée, La (tr. Haywood), **Supp. XII:** 135

"Belle Heaulmière" (tr. Swinburne), **V:** 327

"Belle of the Ball–Room" (Praed), **V:** 14

Belloc, Hilaire, **VI:** 246, 320, 335, 337, 340, 447; **VII:** xiii; **Supp. IV:** 201

Belloc, Mrs. Lowndes, **Supp. II:** 135

Bellow, Saul, **Supp. IV:** 26, 27, 42, 234

Bells and Pomegranates (Browning), **IV:** 356, 373–374

Belmonte, Thomas, **Supp. IV:** 15

Below Loughrigg (Adcock), **Supp. XII:** 6

Belsey, Catherine, **Supp. IV:** 164

Belton Estate, The (Trollope), **V:** 100, 101

"Bench of Desolation, The" (James), **VI:** 69

Bend for Home, The (Healy), **Supp. IX:** 95, 96, 98–100, 101, 103, 106

Bend in the River, A (Naipaul), **Supp. I:** 393, **397–399,** 401

Bender, T. K., **V:** 364–365, 382

Bending of the Bough, The (Moore), **VI:** 87, 95–96, 98

Benedict, Ruth, **Supp. III:** 186

Benjamin, Walter, **Supp. IV:** 82, 87, 88, 91

Benlowes, Edward, **II:** 123

Benn, Gotfried, **Supp. IV:** 411

"Bennelong" (Wallace–Crabbe), **VIII:** 319–320

Bennett, Alan, **VIII: 19–34**

Bennett, Arnold, **VI:** xi, xii, xiii, 226, 233n, **247–268,** 275; **VII:** xiv, xxi; **Supp. III:** 324, 325; **Supp. IV:** 229, 230–231, 233, 239, 241, 249, 252; **Retro. Supp. I:** 318

Bennett, Joan, **II:** 181, 187, 201, 202; **V:** 199, 201

Benson, A. C., **V:** 133, 151; **Supp. II:** 406, 418

Benstock, Bernard, **Supp. IV:** 320

Bentham, Jeremy, **IV:** xii, xv, 50, 130–133, 278, 295; **V:** viii

Bentley, Clerihew, **IV:** 101

Bentley, E. C., **VI:** 335

Bentley, G. E., Jr., **III:** 289n, 307

Bentley, Richard, **III:** 23

Bentley's Miscellany (periodical), **V:** 42

Benveniste, Émile, **Supp. IV:** 115

"Benvolio" (James), **VI:** 69

Beowulf, **I:** 69; **Supp. VI:** **29–44**; **Retro. Supp. II:** 298, 299, 305–306, 307

Beowulf (tr. Morgan), **Supp. IX:** 160–162

"Beowulf: The Monsters and the Critics" (Tolkien), **Supp. II:** 521

Beppo (Byron), **IV:** xvii, 172, 177, **182–184,** 186, 188, 192

Bequest to the Nation, A (Rattigan), **Supp. VII:** 320

Berdoe, Edward, **IV:** 371

Bérénice (Racine), **II:** 98

Bergerac, Cyrano de, *see* Cyrano de Bergerac

Bergonzi, Bernard, **VII:** xxi, xxxvii; **Supp. IV:** 233, 364

"Berkeley and 'Philosophic Words'" (Davie), **Supp. VI:** 107

Berkeley, George, **III:** 50

Berlin Noir (Kerr), **Supp. XII:** 186, 187–191, 192, 193, 194, 199

Berlin stories (Isherwood), **VII:** 309, 311–312

"Bermudas" (Marvell), **II:** 208, 210, 211, 217

Bernard, Charles de, **V:** 21

Bernard, Richard, **II:** 246

Bernard Shaw and Mrs. Patrick Campbell: Their Correspondence (ed. Dent), **VI:** 130

Bernard Shaw's Letters to Granville Barker (ed. Purdom), **VI:** 115n, 129

Bernard Shaw's Rhyming Picture Guide . . . (Shaw), **VI:** 130

"Bertie Changes His Mind" (Wodehouse), **Supp. III:** 458

Bertram; or, The Castle of St. Aldobrand; A Tragedy in Five Acts (Maturin), **VIII:** 201, 205–207

Bertrams, The (Trollope), **V:** 101

Besant, Annie, **VI:** 103, 249

Beside the Ocean of Time (Brown), **Supp. VI:** 64, **67–68**

"Best Friend, The" (Davies), **Supp. XI:** 99

Best of Defoe's Review, The (ed. Payne), **III:** 41

Best of Enemies, The (Fry), **Supp. III:** 195

Best of Roald Dahl, The (Dahl), **Supp. IV:** 209

"Best of the Young British Novelists, The" (Granta special issue), **Supp. IV:** 304

Best Wine Last: An Autobiography through the Years 1932–1969, The (Waugh), **Supp. VI:** 268, **271–272,** 273, 275–276

"Bestre" (Lewis), **VII:** 77

Bethell, Augusta, **V:** 84

Betjeman, John, **VII:** xxi–xxii, **355–377**

Betrayal (Pinter), **Supp. I:** 377

Betrayal, The (Hartley), **Supp. VII:** 121, 131, 132

Betrayal of the Left, The (Orwell), **VII:** 284

"Betrayer, The" (Cornford), **VIII:** 112

Betrothed, The (Scott), **IV:** 39

Better Class of Person, A (Osborne), **Supp. I:** 329

Better Dead (Barrie), **Supp. III:** 2

"Better Resurrection, A" (Rossetti), **V:** 254

Between (Brooke–Rose), **Supp. IV:** 98, 99, 104, 105, 108–109, 112

Between Here and Now (Thomas), **Supp. XII:** 288–289

"Between Mouthfuls" (Ayckbourn), **Supp. V:** 11

Between the Acts (Woolf), **VII:** 18, 19, 22, 24, 26; **Retro. Supp. I:** 308, 321

"Between the Conceits" (Self), **Supp. V:** 402–403

Between the Iceberg and the Ship (Stevenson), **Supp. VI:** 257, 259, 264

Between the Lines: Yeats's Poetry in the Making (Stallworthy), **Supp. X:** 291

"Between the Lotus and the Robot" (Koestler), **Supp. I:** 34n

Between These Four Walls (Lodge and Bradbury), **Supp. IV:** 365

"Between Two Nowheres" (MacCaig), **Supp. VI:** 192

Between Us Girls (Orton), **Supp. V:** 363, 366–367, 372

"Bevel, The" (Kelman), **Supp. V:** 245

"Beware of Doubleness" (Lydgate), **I:** 64

"Beware of the Dog" (Dahl), **Supp. IV:** 209

Beyle, Marie Henri, *see* Stendhal

Beyond (Richards), **Supp. II:** 421, 426, **428–429**

Beyond Good and Evil (Nietzsche), **IV:** 121; **V:** xxv; **Supp. IV:** 50

"Beyond Howth Head" (Mahon), **Supp. VI:** 170, 175

Beyond Personality (Lewis), **Supp. III:** 248

Beyond Reductionism: New Perspectives in the Life Sciences (Koestler), **Supp. I:** 37, 38

Beyond the Bone (Hill), see *Urn Burial*

Beyond the Fringe (Bennett et al.), **VIII:** 19, 21, 22

Beyond the Mexique Bay (Huxley), **VII:** 201

"Beyond the Pale" (Kipling), **VI:** 178–180

"Beyond the Pale" (Trevor), **Supp. IV:** 502

"Beyond Words" (Okri), **Supp. V:** 360

BFG, The (Dahl), **Supp. IV:** 204, 207, 225

"Bhut–Baby, The" (Steel), **Supp. XII:** 269

Bhutto, Benazir, **Supp. IV:** 444, 455

Bhutto, Zulfikar Ali, **Supp. IV:** 444

Biala, Janice, **VI:** 324

"Bianca Among the Nightingales" (Browning), **IV:** 315

Biathanatos (Donne), **I:** 370; **Retro. Supp. II:** 96–97

Bible, *see* English Bible

Bible in Spain, The; or, The Journeys, Adventures, and Imprisonments of an Englishman in an Attempt to Circulate the Scriptures on the Peninsula (Borrow), **Supp. XII:** 17–18, 18–20, 31

Bibliography of Henry James, A (Edel and Laurence), **VI:** 66

Bickerstaff, Isaac, pseud. of Sir Richard Steele and Joseph Addison

Bicycle and Other Poems (Malouf), **Supp. XII:** 219

Big Bazoohley, The (Carey), **Supp. XII:** 54

Big Day, The (Unsworth), **Supp. VII:** 354, 357

"Big Deaths, Little Deaths" (Thomas), **Supp. IV:** 492

Big H, The (Harrison), **Supp. V:** 150, 164

Big House, The (Behan), **Supp. II:** 70–71

"Big House in Ireland, A" (Blackwood), **Supp. IX:** 6

Big Toys (White), **Supp. I:** 131, 151

Bill for the Better Promotion of Oppression on the Sabbath Day, A (Peacock), **IV:** 170

Bim, **Supp. XII:** 35, 43

Bingo (Bond), **Supp. I:** 423, 433–434

"Binsey Poplars" (Hopkins), **V:** 370, 371

Binyon, Laurence, **VI:** 416, 439

Biographia Literaria (Coleridge), **IV:** xvii, **4,** 6, 18, 25, 41, **44–45,** 50, 51, 52–53, 56; **Retro. Supp. II:** 62–64

"Biographical Notice of Ellis and Acton Bell" (Brontë), **V:** 131, 134, 152, 153

"Biography" (Thomas), **Supp. XII:** 279

"Bird and Beast" (Rossetti), **V:** 258

"Bird Auction, The" (McGuckian), **Supp. V:** 284

"Bird in the House" (Jennings), **Supp. V:** (Jennings), **Supp. V:** 218

Bird, Isabella, **Supp. X: 17–32**

Bird of Paradise, The (Davies), **Supp. XI:** 99

Bird of Paradise (Drabble), **Supp. IV:** 230

"Bird Poised to Fly, The" (Highsmith), **Supp. V:** 180

"Bird Study" (Jennings), **Supp. V:** 218

"Birds" (Davies), **Supp. XI:** 100

"Birds, The" (du Maurier), **Supp. III:** 143, 147, 148

Birds, The (film), **III:** 343; **Supp. III:** 143

"Birds at Winter Nightfall" (Hardy), **Retro. Supp. I:** 119

Birds, Beasts and Flowers (Lawrence), **VII:** 90, 118, 119; **Retro. Supp. II:** 233–234

Birds Fall Down, The (West), **Supp. III:** 440, 444

Birds in Tiny Cages (Comyns), **VIII:** 56, 59–60

Birds of Heaven (Okri), **Supp. V:** 359, 360

"Birds of Paradise" (Rossetti), **V:** 255

Birds of Paradise, The (Scott), **Supp. I:** 259, **263–266,** 268

Birds of Passage (Kureishi), **Supp. XI:** 156, 157

Birds of Prey (Braddon), **VIII:** 47

Birds Without Wings (De Bernières), **Supp. XII:** 65–66, 68, 69, 77–78

Birthday Letters (Hughes), **Retro. Supp. II:** 202, 216–218

Birkenhead, Lord (F. E. Smith), **VI:** 340–341

Birmingham Colony, **VI:** 167

Birney, Earle, **Supp. III:** 282

Birrell, A., **II:** 216

Birth by Drowning (Nicholson), **Supp. VI: 222–223**

Birth of Manly Virtue, The (Swift), **III:** 35

"Birth of the Squire, The" (Gay), **III:** 58

Birth of Tragedy, The (Nietsche), **Supp. IV:** 3, 9

"Birth Place" (Murphy), **Supp. V:** 328

"Birth–Bond, The" (Rossetti), **V:** 242

Birthday (Frayn), **Supp. VII:** 57

"Birthday, A" (Mansfield), **VII:** 172, 173

"Birthday, A" (Muir), **Supp. VI:** 207

"Birthday, A" (Rossetti), **V:** 252

Birthday Boys, The (Bainbridge), **Supp. VI: 24–25,** 26

Birthday Party (Milne), **Supp. V:** 309

Birthday Party, The (Pinter), **Supp. I:** 367, 369–370, 373, 380; **Retro. Supp. I:** 216–217, 224

"Birthdays" (MacCaig), **Supp. VI:** 192

"Birthplace, The" (James), **VI:** 69

"Birthright" (Nye), **Supp. X:** 205

Birthstone (Thomas), **Supp. IV:** 479, 480–481, 492

"Bishop Blougram's Apology" (Browning), **IV:** 357, 361, 363

"Bishop Burnet and Humphrey Hardcastle" (Landor), **IV:** 91

"Bishop Orders His Tomb at St. Praxed's Church, The" (Browning), **IV:** 356, 370, 372

Bishop's Bonfire, The (O'Casey), **VII:** xvii 10

"Bishop's Fool, The" (Lewis), **VII:** 80

Bishton, John, **Supp. IV:** 445

Bit o' Love, A (Galsworthy), **VI:** 280

"Bit of Honesty, A" (Nye), **Supp. X:** 202

"Bit of Young Life, A" (Gordimer), **Supp. II:** 232

Bit Off the Map, A (Wilson), **Supp. I:** 155

"Bit Off the Map, A" (Wilson), **Supp. I:** 155, 157, 161

"Bitch" (Dahl), **Supp. IV:** 220

Bitter Fame (Stevenson), **Supp. VI: 263**

Bitter Lemons (Durrell), **Supp. I:** 104, 111–113

"Bitter Salvage" (Warner), **Supp. XI:** 298

Bitter Sweet (Coward), **Supp. II:** 142, 146, 147

Bjarnar saga Hítdœlakappa, **VIII:** 239

Black Album, The (Kureishi), **Supp. XI:** 153–155, 158–159

Black and Blue (Rankin), **Supp. X:** 243–245, 253–254

Black and Silver (Frayn), **Supp. VII:** 57

"Black and Tans," **VII:** 2

Black and the Red, The (Smith, I. C.), **Supp. IX:** 210

Black and White (Collins), **Supp. VI:** 102

Black Arrow, The (Stevenson), **V:** 396

Black Bastard, The (Williams, C. W. S.), **Supp. IX:** 279

Black Book, The (Durrell), **Supp. I:** 93, 94, 96, **97–100,** 118, 122, 123

Black Book, The (Middleton), **II:** 3

Black Book, The (Rankin), **Supp. X:** 244, 251–252

Black Bryony (Powys), **VIII:** 250

Black Comedy (Shaffer), **Supp. I:** 317, 318, 321–322, 324

Black Daisies for the Bride (Harrison), **Supp. V:** 164

Black Dog, The (Coppard), **VIII:** 94–95, 97

"Black Dog, The" (Coppard), **VIII:** 90, 94

Black Dogs (McEwan), **Supp. IV:** 389, 390, 398, 404–406

Black Dwarf, The (Scott), **IV:** 39

"Black Goddess, The" (Graves), **VII:** 261, 270

"Black Guillemot, The" (Nicholson), **Supp. VI: 218**

Black Hermit, The (Ngũgĩ), **VIII:** 214, 222–223

Black Hill, On the (Chatwin, B.), **Supp. IX:** 56–57, 59

Black House, The (Highsmith), **Supp. V:** 180

Black Knight, The (Lydgate), *see Complaint of the Black Knight, The Black Lamb and Grey Falcon* (West), **Supp. III:** 434, 438–439, 445

"Black Lace Fan My Mother Gave Me, The" (Boland), **Supp. V:** 46–47

"Black Madonna, The" (Lessing), **Supp. I:** 242–243

"Black March" (Smith), **Supp. II:** 469

Black Marina (Tennant), **Supp. IX:** 239

Black Marsden (Harris), **Supp. V:** 138–139

Black Mass (Bond), **Supp. I:** 423, 429

"Black Mass, The" (Ewart), **Supp. VII:** 45

"Black Mate, The" (Conrad), **VI:** 135, 148

Black Mischief (Waugh), **VII:** 290, 294–295

"Black Mountain Poets: Charles Olson and Edward Dorn, The" (Davie), **Supp. VI:** 116

"Black Peril" (Plomer), **Supp. XI:** 218

Black Prince, The (Murdoch), **Supp. I:** 226, 228, 229–230

Black Robe (Moore, B.), **Supp. IX:** 144, 145, 151, 152–153

Black Robe, The (Collins), **Supp. VI:** 102–103

Black Goddess and the Sixth Sense, The (Redgrove), **Supp. VI:** 234–235

"Black Takes White" (Cameron), **VII:** 426

Black Tower, The (James), **Supp. IV:** 319, 320, 325, 327–328

"Black Virgin" (McGuckian), **Supp. V:** 288

"Blackberry–Picking" (Heaney), **Retro. Supp. I:** 123

"Blackbird in a Sunset Bush" (MacCaig), **Supp. VI:** 192

Blackeyes (Potter, D.), **Supp. X:** 229

Black–out in Gretley (Priestley), **VII:** 212, 217

"Blackness" (Kincaid), **Supp. VII:** 221, 223, 229

Blackstone, Bernard, **VII:** xiv, xxxvii

Blackstone, Sir William, **III:** 199

"Blackthorn Spray, The" (Stallworthy), **Supp. X:** 296–297

Blackwood, Caroline, **Supp. IX: 1–16**

Blackwood's (periodical), **IV:** xvii, 129, 145, 269–270, 274; **V:** 108–109, 111, 137, 142, 190, 191

Blair, Robert, **III:** 336

Blair, Tony, **Supp. IV:** 74

Blake (Ackroyd), **Supp. VI:** 10, **11**

Blake, Nicholas (pseud.), *see* Day Lewis, Cecil

Blake, Robert, **IV:** 296, 304, 306–308

Blake, William, **II:** 102, 115, 258; **III:** 174, **288–309**, 336; **IV:** 178; **V:** xiv–xvi, xviii, **244**, 316–317, 325, 329–330, 403; **V:** viii, 163; **VI:** viii; **VII:** 23–24; **Supp. II:** 523, 531; **Supp. IV:** 188, 410, 448; **Retro. Supp. I: 33–47**

Blake, William (neé Blech), **Supp. IV:** 459, 461

Blake's Chaucer: The Canterbury Pilgrims (Blake), **III:** 307

"Blake's Column" (Healy), **Supp. IX:** 105

"Blakesmoor in H—shire" (Lamb), **IV:** 76–77

Blandings Castle (Wodehouse), **Supp. III:** 453

"Blank, A" (Gunn), **Supp. IV:** 278

Blank Cheque, The (Carroll), **V:** 274

Blank Verse (Lloyd and Lamb), **IV:** 78, 85

Blasphemers' Banquet, The (Harrison), **Supp. V:** 164

Blast (periodical), **VII:** xiii, 72

Blasted (Kane), **VIII:** 147, 148, 149, 151–155, 156, 157, 158, 159

Blasting and Bombardiering (Lewis), **VII:** 72, 76, 77

Blather (periodical), **Supp. II:** 323, 338

Blatty, William Peter, **III:** 343, 345

Bleak House (Dickens), **IV:** 88; **V:** 4, 42, 47, 53, 54, 55, 59, 62–66, 68, 69, 70, 71; **Supp. IV:** 513

"Bleak Liturgies" (Thomas), **Supp. XII:** 290, 291

Bleeding Hearts (Rankin), **Supp. X:** 245

Blenheim (Trevelyan), **VI:** 392–393

"Blessed Among Women" (Swinburne), **V:** 325

"Blessed Are Ye That Sow Beside All Waters: A Lay Sermon" (Coleridge), **IV:** 56

Blessed Body (More), **Supp. VII:** 245

"Blessed Damozel, The" (Rossetti), **V:** 236, 239, 315

Blessing, The (Mitford), **Supp. X:** 151, 158, 161, 163–165

"Blighters" (Sassoon), **VI:** 430

Blind Beggar of Alexandria, The (Chapman), **I:** 234, 243

Blind Date (film; Ambler), **Supp. IV:** 3

Blind Fireworks (MacNeice), **VII:** 411

Blind Love (Collins), **Supp. VI:** 103

"Blind Love" (Pritchett), **Supp. III: 325–327**

Blind Love and Other Stories (Pritchett), **Supp. III:** 313, 325

Blind Mice, The (Friel), **Supp. V:** 115

"Blinded Bird, The" (Hardy), **Retro. Supp. I:** 119

Blindness (Green), **Supp. II: 249–251**

Bliss (Carey), **Supp. XII:** 52–53, 55–56, 57, 58, 62

"Bliss" (Mansfield), **VII:** 174

"Blisse" (Traherne), **Supp. XI:** 270

Blithe Spirit (Coward), **Supp. II:** 154–155, 156

"Blizzard Song" (Thomas), **Supp. IV:** 494

Bloch, Robert, **III:** 342

Blomberg, Sven, **Supp. IV:** 88

Blood (Galloway), **Supp. XII:** 117, 120–123, 124

"Blood" (Galloway), **Supp. XII:** 122

"Blood" (Murray), **Supp. VII:** 273, 281, 282

Blood and Family (Kinsella), **Supp. V:** 270, 271

Blood Doctor, The (Rendell), **Supp. IX:** 200–201, 203

"Blood–feud of Toad–Water, The" (Saki), **Supp. VI:** 246

Blood Hunt (Rankin), **Supp. X:** 245

"Blood Is the Water" (Wallace–Crabbe), **VIII:** 316–317

Blood of the Bambergs, The (Osborne), **Supp. I:** 335

Blood Red, Sister Rose (Keneally), **Supp. IV:** 346

Blood, Sweat and Tears (Churchill), **VI:** 349, 361

Blood Sympathy (Hill, R.), **Supp. IX:** 123

Blood Will Tell (Christie), *see Mrs. McGinty's Dead*

"Bloodlines" (Motion), **Supp. VII:** 263

"Bloody Chamber, The" (Carter), **Supp. III:** 88

Bloody Chamber and Other Stories, The (Carter), **Supp. III:** 79, 87, 88–89

"Bloody Cranesbill, The" (Nicholson), **Supp. VI:** 219

"Bloody Men" (Cope), **VIII:** 76

"Bloody Son, The" (Swinburne), **V:** 321

Bloom, Harold, **III:** 289n, 307; **V:** 309, 316, 329, 402

Bloomfield, Paul, **IV:** xii, xxiv, 306

Bloomsbury: A House of Lions (Edel), **VII:** 39

Bloomsbury Group, The (Johnstone), **VI:** 413

Blot in the Scutcheon, A (Browning), **IV:** 374

"Blow, The" (Hardy), **VI:** 17

Blow Your House Down (retitled *Liza's England;* Barker), **Supp. IV:** 45, 46, 50–53, 57

"Blucher and Sandt" (Landor), **IV:** 92

Bludy Serk, The (Henryson), **Supp. VII:** 146, 148

"Blue Apron, The" (Malouf), **Supp. XII:** 220

Blue at the Mizzen (O'Brian), **Supp. XII:** 257, 259

"Blue bell is the sweetest Flower, The" (Brontë), **V:** 134

"Blue Closet, The" (Morris), **IV:** 313

Blue Djinn of Babylon, The (Kerr), **Supp. XII:** 198

"Blue Dress, The" (Trevor), **Supp. IV:** 501

"Blue Eyes" (Warner), **Supp. VII:** 371

Blue Flower, The (Fitzgerald), **Supp. V:** 95, 96, 98, 99, 100, 107–108

"Blue Lenses, The" (du Maurier), **Supp. III:** 147

Blue Remembered Hills and Other Plays (Potter, D.), **Supp. X:** 229, 231–237

"Bluebeard's Ghost" (Thackeray), **V:** 24, 38

Blunden, Edmund, **IV:** xi, xxiv, 86, 210, 254, 267, 316; **VI:** 416, **427–429,** 439, 454; **VII:** xvi; **Supp. XI: 33–48**

Blunderer, The (Highsmith), **Supp. V:** 170

Blyton, Enid, **Supp. IV:** 434

Boarding House, The (Trevor), **Supp. IV:** 501, 506–507, 511

Boas, F. S., **I:** 218, 275

Boat, The (Hartley), **Supp. VII:** 123, 127, 128

"Boat House, Bank Ground, Coniston, The" (Nicholson), **Supp. VI:** 216

Boat of Fate, The (Roberts, K.), **Supp. X:** 272–273

Boat That Mooed, The (Fry), **Supp. III:** 195

Boating for Beginners (Winterson), **Supp. IV:** 541, 542, 545–547, 555

"Bob Hope Classic Show (ITV) and 'Shelley Among the Ruins,' Lecture by Professor Timothy Webb—both Saturday evening, 26.9.81" (Ewart), **Supp. VII:** 45

"Bob Robinson's First Love" (Thackeray), **V:** 24, 38

"Bob's Lane" (Thomas), **Supp. III:** 394, 405

Boccaccio, Giovanni, **II:** 292, 304; **Supp. IV:** 461

Body, The (Kureishi), **Supp. XI:** 163

Body Below (film; Ambler), **Supp. IV:** 3

Body in the Library (Christie), **Supp. II:** 131, 132

Body Language (Ayckbourn), **Supp. V:** 3, 10, 11

Body Snatcher, The (Stevenson), **V:** 396

"Body's Beauty" (Rossetti), **V:** 237

Boehme, Jacob, **IV:** 45

"Boeotian Count, The" (Murray), **Supp. VII:** 275

Boethius, **I:** 31, 32; **II:** 185

Bog of Allen, The (Hall), **Supp. II:** 322

Bog People, The (Glob), **Retro. Supp. I:** 128

"Bogland" (Heaney), **Supp. II:** 271–272

"Bogy Man, The" (Coppard), **VIII:** 96

"Bohemians, The" (Gurney), **VI:** 427

Boiardo, Matteo, **IV:** 231

Boileau, Nicolas, **IV:** 92, 93

Boke of Eneydos, The (Skelton), **I:** 82

Boklund, Gunnar, **II:** 73

Boland, Eavan, **Supp. V: 35–52**

Bold, Alan, **Supp. IV:** 256

Böll, Heinrich, **Supp. IV:** 440

"Bombers" (Day Lewis), **Supp. III:** 127

"Bombing Practice" (Nicholson), **Supp. VI:** 214

Bonadventure, The: A Random Journal of an Atlantic Holiday (Blunden), **Supp. XI:** 36

Bond, Edward, **Supp. I: 421–436; Supp. IV:** 182

"Bond" (Dutton), **Supp. XII:** 92

Bond Honoured, A (Osborne), **Supp. I:** 335–336, 337–338

Bondman, The: And Antient Storie (Massinger), **Supp. XI:** 184, 185

Bonduca (Fletcher), **II:** 45, 58, 60, 65

"Bone Elephant, The" (Motion), **Supp. VII:** 262

"Bonfire Under a Black Sun" (O'Casey), **VII:** 13

Bonnefon, Jean de, **II:** 108

"Bonny Broukit Bairn, The" (MacDiarmid), **Supp. XII:** 205–206

Boodle, Adelaide, **V:** 391, 393, 397

"Book, The" (Vaughan), **II:** 187

"Book Ends" (Harrison), **Supp. V:** 153–154

Book for Boys and Girls, A; or, Country Rhimes for Children (Bunyan), **II:** 253

Book of Ahania, The (Blake), **III:** 307; **Retro. Supp. I:** 44

Book of Answers, A (Hope), **Supp. VII:** 164

Book of Balaam's Ass, The (Jones), **Supp. VII:** 170

Book of Common Praise, The (Newman), **Supp. VII:** 291

Book of Los, The (Blake), **III:** 307

Book of Margery Kempe, The (Kempe), **Supp. XII:** 167–168, 169–171, 172, 173, 174, 175–181, 182

Book of Matches (Armitage), **VIII:** 1, 6–8

"Book of Matches" (Armitage), **VIII:** 8

Book of Mortals, A: Being a Record of the Good Deeds and Good Qualities of What Humanity Is Pleased to Call the Lower Animals (Steel), **Supp. XII:** 274

"Book of Nature" (Sisson), **Supp. XI:** 262

Book of Nonsense, A (Lear), **V:** xx, 76, 82–83, 87

Book of Prefaces, The (Gray, A.), **Supp. IX:** 92

"Book of Settlements, The", *See Landnámabók*

Book of Sir Lancelot and Queen Guinevere, The (Malory), **I:** 70–71, 77; **Retro. Supp. II:** 249–250

Book of Snobs, The (Thackeray), **V:** 24–25, 28, 38

Book of Spells, A (Maitland), **Supp. XI:** 170, 176, 177

Book of the Church, The (Southey), **IV:** 71

Book of the Duchess, The (Chaucer), **I:** 29, 31, 43, 54; **Retro. Supp. II:** 36–38

"Book of the Icelanders, The" (Ari), *See Íslendingabók*

Book of Thel, The (Blake), **III:** 302, 307; **Retro. Supp. I:** 35–36

Book of Tristram de Lyonesse (Malory), **Retro. Supp. II:** 248

Book of Urizen, The (Blake), *see First Book of Urizen, The*

Book of Victorian Narrative Verse, A (ed. Williams, C. W. S.), **Supp. IX:** 276

Book of Voyages, A (ed. O'Brian), **Supp. XII:** 249

Booke of Balettes, A (Wyatt), **I:** 97

Books and Persons: Being Comments on a Past Epoch (Bennett), **VI:** 265, 267

Books Do Furnish a Room (Powell), **VII:** 352

Books of Bale (Arden), **Supp. II:** 41

"Books of the Ocean's Love to Cynthia, The" (Ralegh), **I:** 147, 148, 149

Bookshop, The (Fitzgerald), **Supp. V:** 95, 97, 100, 101–102

Boon (Wells), **VI:** 227, 239–240, 333

Border Antiquities (Scott), **IV:** 38

Border Ballads (Swinburne), **V:** 333

"Border Campaign, The" (Heaney), **Retro. Supp. I:** 134

Borderers, The (Wordsworth), **III:** 338; **IV:** 3, 5–6, 25

Borderline (Kureishi), **Supp. XI:** 156–157

Borderline Ballads (Plomer), **Supp. XI:** 226

Borges, Jorge Luis, **Supp. IV:** 558

Borges: A Reader (tr. Reid), **Supp. VII:** 332

"Borgia, thou once wert almost too august" (Landor), **IV:** 98

"Boris Is Buying Horses" (Berger), **Supp. IV:** 93

Born Guilty (Hill, R.), **Supp. IX:** 123

Born in Exile (Gissing), **V:** 425, 428, 429–430, 437

"Born 1912" (Fuller), **Supp. VII:** 80

Born 1925: A Novel of Youth (Brittain), **Supp. X:** 46

"Born Yesterday" (Larkin), **Supp. I:** 278

Borough, The (Crabbe), **III:** 273–274, 275, 280, 281, 283–285, 286

Borrow, George, **Supp. XII: 17–32**

Borstal Boy (Behan), **Supp. II: 61–63,** 64, 69, 70, 72, 73

Bosch, Hieronymus, **Supp. IV:** 199, 249

"Boscombe Valley Mystery, The" (Doyle), **Supp. II:** 171

Bostock, Anya, **Supp. IV:** 87

Bostonians, The (James), **VI: 39–41,** 67

Boswell, James, **III:** 54, 107, 110–115, 117, 119–122, **234–251; IV:** xv, xvi, 27, 88n, 280; **Retro. Supp. I:** 145–149

"Boswell and Rousseau" (Leigh), **III:** 246n

Boswell for the Defence 1769–1774 (ed. Pottle and Wimsatt), **III:** 249

Boswell in Extremis 1776–1778 (ed. Pottle and Weis), **III:** 249

Boswell in Holland 1763–1764 (ed. Pottle), **III:** 249

Boswell in Search of a Wife 1766–1769 (ed. Brady and Pottle), **III:** 249

Boswell: Lord of Auchinleck 1778–1782 (ed. Pottle and Reed), **III:** 249

Boswell on the Grand Tour: Germany and Switzerland 1764 (ed. Pottle), **III:** 249

Boswell on the Grand Tour: Italy . . . 1765–1766 (ed. Brady and Pottle), **III:** 249

Boswell: The Ominous Years 1774–1776 (ed. Pottle and Ryskamp), **III:** 249

Boswelliana . . . Memoir and Annotations by the Rev. Charles Rogers (Rogers), **III:** 249

Boswell's Book of Bad Verse (ed. Werner), **III:** 249

Boswell's London Journal 1762–1763 (ed. Pottle), **III:** 249

Boswell's Notebook, 1776–1777 (Boswell), **III:** 244, 249

"Botany Bay Eclogues" (Southey), **IV:** 60

Bothie of Tober-na-Vuolich, The (Clough), **V:** 155, 156, 158, 159, 161–164, 166, 167, 169, 170

Bothie of Toper-na-Fuosich, The (Clough), **V:** 170

Bothwell (Swinburne), **V:** 314, 330, 331, 332

Botticelli, Sandro, **V:** 345

Bottle Factory Outing, The (Bainbridge), **Supp. VI:** 18–20, 24, 27

"Bottle Imp, The" (Stevenson), **V:** 396

Bottle in the Smoke, A (Wilson), **Supp. VI:** 304, 307

"Bottle of Ink, A" (Stallworthy), **Supp. X:** 296

Bottle's Path and Other Stories (Powys), **VIII:** 249, 255

Boucicault, Dion, **V:** 415; **VII:** 2

Bouge of Court, The (Skelton), **I:** 83, 84–85

Boughner, D. C., **I:** 186

"Bourgeois Psychology" (Caudwell), **Supp. IX:** 45

Boursault, Edme, **II:** 324, 332

Bow Down (Harrison), **Supp. V:** 164

"Bow in the Cloud, The" (Nicholson), **Supp. VI:** 215

Bowen, Elizabeth, **Supp. II: 77–95; Supp. IV:** 151, 500, 514

Bowen, Stella, **VI:** 324

Bowen's Court (Bowen), **Supp. II:** 78, 84, 91

Bowers, Fredson, **II:** 44

Bowles, Caroline, **IV:** 62, 63

"Bowling Alley and the Sun, or, How I Learned to Stop Worrying and Love America, The" (Lodge), **Supp. IV:** 373

Bowra, C. M., **VI:** 153

Bowra, Maurice, **V:** 252–256, 260

Boy and the Magic, The (tr. Fry), **Supp. III:** 195

Boy book see (Galloway), **Supp. XII:** 117

Boy Comes Home, The (Milne), **Supp. V:** 299

"Boy from Birnam, The" (Dunn), **Supp. X:** 68

Boy Hairdresser, The (Orton), **Supp. V:** 363, 364, 367

Boy in the Bush, The (Lawrence), **VII:** 114; **Retro. Supp. II:** 230–231

Boy: Tales of Childhood (Dahl), **Supp. IV:** 204, 205, 206, 208, 225

Boy Who Followed Ripley, The (Highsmith), **Supp. V:** 171

"Boy Who Talked with Animals, The" (Dahl), **Supp. IV:** 223, 224

Boy with a Cart, The; Cuthman, Saint of Sussex (Fry), **Supp. III:** 191, 194, 195, 196

Boyd, H. S., **IV:** 312

Boyer, Abel, **II:** 352

Boyfriends and Girlfriends (Dunn), **Supp. X:** 67–69

"Boyhood" (Nye), **Supp. X:** 204

Boyhood: Scenes from Provincial Life (Coetzee), **Supp. VI:** 77–78

Boyle, Robert, **III:** 23, 95

"Boys, The" (Nye), **Supp. X:** 201

"Boys' Weeklies" (Orwell), **Supp. III:** 107

Boys Who Stole the Funeral, The: A Novel Sequence (Murray), **Supp. VII:** 270, 284–286

"Boys with Coats" (Dunn), **Supp. X:** 71

Bradbrook, M. C., **I:** xi, 292, 329; **II:** 42, 78; **VII:** xiii–xiv, xxxvii, 234

Bradbury, Ray, **III:** 341

Bradbury, Malcolm, **Supp. IV:** 303, 365

Braddon, Mary Elizabeth, **V:** 327; **VIII:** 35–52

Bradley, A. C., **IV:** 106, 123, 216, 235, 236

Bradley, F. H., **V:** xxi, 212, 217

Bradley, Henry, **VI:** 76

Brady, F., **III:** 249

Braine, John, **Supp. IV:** 238

Brand (Hill), **Supp. V:** 199, 200–201

Brander, Laurence, **IV:** xxiv; **VII:** xxii

Brantley, Ben, **Supp. IV:** 197–198

Branwell Brontë (Gerin), **V:** 153

Branwell's Blackwood's (periodical), **V:** 109, 123

Branwell's Young Men's (periodical), *see Branwell's Blackwood's*

Brass Butterfly, The (Golding), **Supp. I:** 65, 75

"Brassneck" (Armitage), **VIII:** 5

Brassneck (Hare and Brenton), **Supp. IV:** 281, 282, 283, 284–285, 289

Brathwaite, Kamau (Edward), **Supp. XII: 33–48**

Brave and Cruel (Welch), **Supp. IX:** 267–269

"Brave and Cruel" (Welch), **Supp. IX:** 267, 269

Brave New World (Huxley), **III:** 341; **VII:** xviii, 200, 204

Brave New World Revisited (Huxley), **VII:** 207

"Bravest Boat, The" (Lowry), **Supp. III:** 281

Brawne, Fanny, **IV:** 211, 216–220, 222, 226, 234

Bray, Charles, **V:** 188

Bray, William, **II:** 275, 276, 286

Brazil (Gilliam), **Supp. IV:** 442, 455

"Breach, The" (Murray), **Supp. VII:** 276

Bread of Truth, The (Thomas), **Supp. XII:** 284, 285

"Bréagh San Réilg, La" (Behan), **Supp. II:** 73

"Break My Heart" (Golding), **Supp. I:** 79

"Break of Day in the Trenches" (Rosenberg), **VI:** 433, 434

"Breake of day" (Donne), **Retro. Supp. II:** 88

Breakfast on Pluto (McCabe), **Supp. IX:** 127, 135–136, 138

"Breaking Ground" (Gunn), **Supp. IV:** 271

"Breaking the Blue" (McGuckian), **Supp. V:** 287

Breath (Beckett), **Supp. I:** 60; **Retro. Supp. I:** 26

Brecht, Bertolt, **II:** 359; **IV:** 183; **VI:** 109, 123; **Supp. II:** 23, 25, 28; **Supp. IV:** 82, 87, 180, 194, 198, 281, 298

"Bredon Hill" (Housman), **VI:** 158

Brendan (O'Connor), **Supp. II:** 63, 76

Brendan Behan's Island (Behan), **Supp. II:** 64, 66, 71, 73, 75

Brendan Behan's New York (Behan), **Supp. II:** 75

Brennoralt (Suckling), *see Discontented Colonel, The*

Brenton, Howard, **Supp. IV:** 281, 283, 284, 285

Brethren, The (Haggard), **Supp. III:** 214

"Breton Walks" (Mahon), **Supp. VI:** 168, 172

Brett, Raymond Laurence, **IV:** x, xi, xxiv, 57

Brickfield, The (Hartley), **Supp. VII:** 131–132

Bricks to Babel (Koestler), **Supp. I:** 37

Bridal of Triermain, The (Scott), **IV:** 38

"Bride and Groom" (Hughes), **Supp. I:** 356

"Bride in the 30's, A" (Auden), **Retro. Supp. I:** 8

Bride of Abydos, The (Byron), **IV:** xvii, 172, 174–175, 192

Bride of Frankenstein (film), **III:** 342

Bride of Lammermoor, The (Scott), **IV:** xviii, 30, 36, 39

Brides of Reason (Davie), **Supp. VI:** 106–107

"Brides, The" (Hope), **Supp. VII:** 154

"Bride's Prelude, The" (Rossetti), **V:** 239, 240

Brides' Tragedy, The (Beddoes), **Supp. XI:** 17, 20–22, 29

Brideshead Revisited (Waugh), **VII:** xx–xxi, 290, 299–300; **Supp. IV:** 285

Bridge, The (Banks), **Supp. XI:** 6–7

"Bridge, The" (Galloway), **Supp. XII:** 126–127

"Bridge, The" (Thomas), **Supp. III:** 401

"Bridge for the Living" (Larkin), **Supp. I:** 284

"Bridge of Sighs, The" (Hood), **IV:** 252, 261, 264–265

Bridges, Robert, **II:** 160; **V:** xx, 205, 362–368, 370–372, 374, 376–381; **VI:** xv, 71–83, 203

Brief History of Moscovia . . . , A (Milton), **II:** 176

Brief Lives (Aubrey), **I:** 260

Brief Lives (Brookner), **Supp. IV:** 131–133

Brief Notes upon a Late Sermon . . . (Milton), **II:** 176

Briefing for a Descent into Hell (Lessing), **Supp. I:** 248–249

Briggflatts (Bunting), **Supp. VII:** 1, 2, 5, 7, 9–13

Bright, A. H., **I:** 3

"Bright Building, The" (Graham), **Supp. VII:** 109, 110–111

"Bright–Cut Irish Silver" (Boland), **Supp. V:** 49–50

Bright Day (Priestley), **VII:** 209, 218–219

"Bright Star!" (Keats), **IV:** 221

Brighton Rock (Greene), **Supp. I:** 2, 3, 7–9, 11, 19; **Retro. Supp. II:** 153–155

"Brigid's Girdle, A" (Heaney), **Retro. Supp. I:** 132

"Brilliance" (Davie), **Supp. VI:** 113

"Brilliant Career, A" (Joyce), **Retro. Supp. I:** 170

Brimstone and Treacle (Potter, D.), **Supp. X:** 232, 234

"Bring Back the Cat!" (Hill, R.), **Supp. IX:** 118

Bring Larks and Heroes (Keneally), **Supp. IV:** 345, 347, 348–350

"Bringing to Light" (Gunn), **Supp. IV:** 269–270

Brink, Andre, **Supp. VI: 45–59**

Brinkmanship of Galahad Threepwood, The (Wodehouse), *see Galahad at Blandings*

Brissenden, R. F., **III:** 86n

Bristow Merchant, The (Dekker and Ford), **II:** 89, 100

Britain and West Africa (Cary), **VII:** 186

Britannia (periodical), **V:** 144

Britannia (Thomson), **Supp. III:** 409, 411, 420

Britannia Rediviva: A Poem on the Birth of the Prince (Dryden), **II:** 304

"Britannia Victrix" (Bridges), **VI:** 81

"British Church, The" (Herbert), **I:** 189

British Dramatists (Greene), **Supp. I:** 6, 11

"British Guiana" (Ewart), **Supp. VII:** 38

British History in the Nineteenth Century (Trevelyan), **VI:** 390

British Magazine (periodical), **III:** 149, 179, 188

British Museum Is Falling Down, The (Lodge), **Supp. IV:** 363, 365, 367, 369–370, 371

British Women Go to War (Priestley), **VII:** 212

Briton (Smollett), **III:** 149

Brittain, Vera, **II:** 246; **Supp. X:** 33–48

Britten, Benjamin, **Supp. IV:** 424

Brittle Joys (Maitland), **Supp. XI:** 165, 174–175

"Broad Bean Sermon, The" (Murray), **Supp. VII:** 275

"Broad Church, The" (Stephen), **V:** 283

Broadbent, J. B., **II:** 102, 116

Broadcast Talks (Lewis), **Supp. III:** 248

"Broagh" (Heaney), **Retro. Supp. I:** 128

"Brodgar Poems" (Brown), **Supp. VI:** 71

Broken Chariot, The (Sillitoe), **Supp. V:** 411, 421

Broken Cistern, The (Dobrée), **V:** 221, 234

"Broken heart, The" (Donne), **Retro. Supp. II:** 90

Broken Heart, The (Ford), **II:** 89, 92, 93–98, 99, 100

"Broken Wings, The" (James), **VI:** 69

Brome, Richard, **II:** 87; **Supp. X:** 49–64

Brontë, Anne, **IV:** 30; **V:** xviii, xx, xxi, 105, 106, 108, 110, 112–119, 122, 126, **128–130**, 131, 132, **134–135, 140–141, 145, 150, 153; Supp. III:** 195; **Supp. IV:** 239; **Retro. Supp. I:** 55–56

Brontë, Branwell, **V:** xvii, 13, 105, 106, 108–112, 117–119, 121–124, 126, 130, 131, 135, 141, 145, 150, 153

Brontë, Charlotte, **III:** 338, 344, 345; **IV:** 30, 106, 120; **V:** xvii, xx–xxii, 3, 13–14, 20, 68, 105–107, **108–112**, 113–118, **119–126**, 127, 129, 130–140, 144, 145–150, 152, 286; **Supp. III:** 144, 146; **Supp. IV:** 146, 471; **Retro. Supp. I:** 58–61

Brontë, Emily, **III:** 333, 338, 344, 345; **IV:** ix, xvii, xx–xxi, 13, 14, 105, 106, 108, 110, **112–117**, 118, 122, 130, 131, **132–135, 141–145**, 147, 150, 152–153, 254; **Supp. III:** 144; **Supp. IV:** 462, 513; **Retro. Supp. I:** 56–58

Brontë, Patrick, **V:** 105–108, 109, 122, 146, 151

Brontë Poems (ed. Benson), **V:** 133, 151

Brontë Sisters, **Retro. Supp. I:** 49–62

Brontë Story, The: A Reconsideration of Mrs. Gaskell's "Life of Charlotte Brontë" (Lane), **V:** 13n, 16

Brontës, The, Their Lives, Friendships and Correspondence (ed. Wise and Symington), **V:** 117, 118, 151

Brontës of Haworth, The (Fry), **Supp. III:** 195

Brontës' Web of Childhood, The (Ratchford), **V:** 151

"Bronze Head, The" (Yeats), **VI:** 217

Bronze Horseman: Selected Poems of Alexander Pushkin (tr. Thomas), **Supp. IV:** 495

Brooke, Arthur, **I:** 305

Brooke, Jocelyn, **VII:** xviii, xxxvii; **Supp. II:** 202, 203

Brooke, Rupert, **VI:** xvi, 416, **419–420**, 439; **VII:** 35; **Supp. II:** 310; **Supp. III:** **45–61**

Brooke Kerith, The. A Syrian Story (Moore), **VI:** xii, 88, 89, **93–94**, 99

Brooke-Rose, Christine, **Supp. IV:** 97–118

Brookner, Anita, **Supp. IV:** 119–137

Brooks, C., **IV:** 323n, 339

"Brooksmith" (James), **VI:** 48, 69

Brophy, Brigid, **IV:** 101

"Brother Fire" (MacNeice), **VII:** 414

"Brothers" (Hopkins), **V:** 368–369

Brothers and Sisters (Compton–Burnett), **VII:** 61, 66, 67, 69

Brother's Keeper (Hill, R.), **Supp. IX:** 118

Brown, Charles, **IV:** 211, 221, 231–233

Brown, E. K., **V:** 211–212, 217

Brown, Ford Madox, **V:** 248

Brown, George Mackay, **Supp. VI:** 61–73

Brown, John, **V:** 245, 253, 254

Brown, Tom, **III:** 41

Brown Owl, The (Ford), **VI:** 320

Brownbread (Doyle), **Supp. V:** 77, 87–88

Browne, Moses, **II:** 142

Browne, Sir Thomas, **II:** **145–157**, 185, 345n; **III:** 40

"Brownie" (Gissing), **V:** 437

"Brownie of Black Haggs, The" (Hogg), **Supp. X:** 110

Brownie of Bodsbeck and Other Tales, The (Hogg), **Supp. X:** 111–113, 117

Browning, Elizabeth Barrett, **IV:** xvi, xix–xxii, **310–322**, 356, 357; **Retro. Supp. II:** 23–24

Browning, Robert, **IV:** viii, xii, xiii, xix–xxiii, 240, 248, 252, 254, 311–312, 314, 318–319, 352, **354–375**; **V:** xxv, 209, 287, 315, 330; **VI:** 336; **Supp. IV:** 139; **Retro. Supp. II:** 17–32

Browning Box, The; or, The Life and Works of Thomas Lovell Beddoes as Reflected in Letters by His Friends and Admirers (Beddoes)

Browning: "Men and Women" and Other Poems: A Casebook (ed. Watson), **IV:** 375

Browning Version, The (Rattigan), **Supp. VII:** 307, 315–316

Browning's Essay on Chatterton (ed. Smalley), **IV:** 374

Browning's Major Poetry (Jack), **IV:** 375

"Bruno" (Warner), **Supp. VII:** 381

"Bruno's Revenge" (Carroll), **V:** 270

"Brutal Sentimentalist, A" (Plomer), **Supp. XI:** 220

"Brute, The" (Conrad), **VI:** 148

Brutus (Pope), **III:** 71–72

Brutus's Orchard (Fuller), **Supp. VII:** 73–74

Bryan, Michael, *see* Moore, Brian

Bryce, James, **IV:** 289

Brydon, Diana, **Supp. IV:** 459, 462

Bryskett, Lodowick, **I:** 124

Bubble, The (Swift), **III:** 35

Bucer, Martin, **I:** 177

Buchan, John, **Supp. II:** 299, 306; **Supp. IV:** 7

Buchanan, Robert, **V:** 238, 245

"Bucket and the Rope, The" (Powys), **VIII:** 254–255

Buckhurst, Lord, *see* Dorset, earl of (Charles Sackville)

Buckingham, duke of (George Villiers), **II:** 206, 255, 294

Buckle, G. E., **IV:** 306–308

"Buckles of Superior Dosset, The" (Galsworthy), **VI:** 270

Bucolic Comedies (Sitwell), **VII:** 131, 132

"Bucolics" (Auden), **Retro. Supp. I:** 13

Buddha of Suburbia, The (Kureishi), **Supp. XI:** 157, 159

Budgell, Eustace, **III:** 48

Buffon, Georges–Louis, **Supp. II:** 106, 107, 108; **III:** 189

Buff (Fuller), **Supp. VII:** 74

"Bugle Call" (Thomas), **Supp. III:** 404

"Bugler's First Communion, The" (Hopkins), **V:** 368–369

Builder, The (Steel), **Supp. XII:** 275, 276

"Building, The" (Larkin), **Supp. I:** 280, 282, 283

"Build–Up" (Ballard), **Supp. V:** 21

"Bujak and the Strong Force" (Amis), **Supp. IV:** 40

"Buladelah–Taree Song Cycle, The" (Murray), **Supp. VII:** 276–277

Bulgakov, Mikhail, **Supp. IV:** 445

"Bull" (MacCaig), **Supp. VI:** 188

Bull: A Farce (Self), **Supp. V:** 405–406

Bull from the Sea, The (Renault), **Supp. IX:** 180–181

"Bull Ring, The" (Hill, R.), **Supp. IX:** 118

"Bull That Thought, The" (Kipling), **VI:** 189, 190

"Bulldog" Drummond series (Sapper), **Supp. IV:** 500

"Bulletin" (Dutton), **Supp. XII:** 98

Bullett, Gerald, **V:** 196, 199, 200

Bulwer–Lytton, Edward, **III:** 340, 345; **IV:** 256, 295, 311; **V:** 22, 47

Bundle, The (Bond), **Supp. I:** 423

Bundle of Letters, A (James), **VI:** 67, 69

"Bungalows, The" (Plomer), **Supp. XI:** 226

Bunting, Basil, **Supp. VII: 1–15**

Bunyan, John, **I:** 16; **II: 240–254; III:** 82; **V:** 27

Buoyant Billions: A Comedy of No Manners in Prose (Shaw), **VI:** 127, 129

Burbidge, Thomas, **IV:** 159

Burckhardt, Jakob, **V:** 342

"Burden of Itys, The" (Wilde), **V:** 401

"Burden of Ninevah, The" (Rossetti), **V:** 240, 241

Bürger, Gottfried August, **IV: 44, 48**

Burger's Daughter (Gordimer), **Supp. II:** 225, 228, 230, 231, 232, **234–237,** 241, 242, 243

Burgess, Anthony, **Supp. I: 185–198; Supp. IV:** 4, 13, 234, 449

"Burghers, The" (Hardy), **Retro. Supp. I:** 120

"Burial of the Dead, The" (Eliot), **Retro. Supp. II:** 126

"Burial of the Rats, The" (Stoker), **Supp. III:** 382

Buried Alive (Bennett), **VI:** 250, 252, 257, 266

Buried Day, The (Day Lewis), **Supp. III:** 116, 128

Buried Harbour, The: Selected Poems of Giuseppe Ungaretti (ed. Hart), **Supp. XI:** 130

"Buried Life, The" (Arnold), **V:** 210

Burke, Edmund, **III:** 185, **193–206,** 274; **IV:** xii–xvi, 54, 127, 130, 133, 136–138, 271, 275; **VI:** 356; **Supp. III:** 371, 467, 468, 470

Burke, Kenneth, **Supp. IV:** 114

Burke and Bristol, 1774–1780 (Barker), **III:** 196

"Burleigh" (Macaulay), **IV:** 279

Burlington Magazine, **Supp. IV:** 121

"Burma Casualty" (Lewis), **VII:** 447

Burmann, Peter, **III:** 96

Burmese Days (Orwell), **VII:** 276, 278

Burn, The (Kelman), **Supp. V:** 243, 249, 250–251

Burne–Jones, Edward, **IV:** 346; **V:** 236, 293–296, 302, 318n, 355; **VI:** 166; **Supp. V:** 98, 99

Burney, Charles, **Supp. III:** 65–67

Burney, Frances, **Supp. III: 63–78**

Burning Cactus, The (Spender), **Supp. II:** 488

Burning of the Brothel, The (Hughes), **Supp. I:** 348

"Burning Times, The" (Maitland), **Supp. XI:** 176

"Burning Want" (Murray), **Supp. VII:** 283–284

Burning World, The (Ballard), **Supp. V:** 24

"Burns Ayont Auld Reekie/Burns Beyond Edinburgh" (Crawford), **Supp. XI:** 69

Burnshaw, Stanley, **Supp. IV:** 460, 473

Burnt Diaries (Tennant), **Supp. IX:** 228, 229, 239

Burnt Ones, The (White), **Supp. I:** 131, 136, 143

Burnt–Out Case, A (Greene), **Supp. I:** 7, 13, 15, 16, 18; **Retro. Supp. II:** 162

"Burrington Combe" (Sisson), **Supp. XI:** 261

Burroughs, William S., **Supp. V:** 26

Busconductor Hines, The (Kelman), **Supp. V:** 242, 246–247

Business, The (Banks), **Supp. XI:** 13

Business of Good Government, The (Arden), **Supp. II:** 29

Busker, The (Kelman), **Supp. V:** 256

Busman's Honeymoon (Sayers), **Supp. III:** 335, 336, 347–348

"Busted Scotch" (Kelman), **Supp. V:** 249

"Busy" (Milne), **Supp. V:** 302

"But at the Stroke of Midnight" (Warner), **Supp. VII:** 381

...but the Clouds (Beckett), **Retro. Supp. I:** 29

Butcher Boy, The (McCabe), **Supp. IX:** 127, 128, 129–133, 135, 137, 138

Butcher's Dozen (Kinsella), **Supp. V:** 267

Butler, Samuel, **Supp. II: 97–119**

Butor, Michel, **Supp. IV:** 115

"Butterflies" (McEwan), **Supp. IV:** 391

"Buzzard and Alder" (Stevenson), **Supp. VI:** 261

"By Achmelrich Bridge" (MacCaig), **Supp. VI:** 182

By and Large (Wallace–Crabbe), **VIII:** 324

"By Ferry to the Island" (Smith, I. C.), **Supp. IX:** 212

"By the burn" (Kelman), **Supp. V:** 250–251

By Jeeves (Ayckbourn and Webber), **Supp. V:** 3

"By Leave of Luck" (Cameron), **Supp. IX:** 24

By Night Unstarred (Kavanagh), **Supp. VII:** 189

By Still Waters (Russell), **VIII:** 286

"By the Fire–Side" (Browning), **Retro. Supp. II:** 23–24

By the Line (Keneally), **Supp. IV:** 345

"By the Sea" (Smith, I. C.), **Supp. IX:** 216

By Way of Introduction (Milne), **Supp. V:** 300

Byatt, A. S.(neé Antonia Drabble), **Supp. IV: 139–156,** 229

Bye–Bye, Blackbird (Desai), **Supp. V:** 55, 60–62

"Bylot Island" (Armitage), **VIII:** 4

"Byre" (MacCaig), **Supp. VI:** 188, 190, 194

Byron, George Gordon, Lord, **III:** 329; **IV:** x, xi, 46, 61, 91, 129, 132, 168, **171–194,** 198–199, 202, 206, 215, 281, 299; **V:** 111–112, 247, 324; **Supp. III:** 356, 365; and Coleridge, **IV:** 46, 48; and Hazlitt, **IV:** 129; and Shelley, **IV:** 159, 172, 176–177, 179, 181, 182, 198–199, 202, 206; **Retro. Supp. I:** 250–251; and Southey, **IV:** 61, 184–187; literary style, **III:** 336, 337–338; **IV:** viii, ix, xi, 129, 281; **V:** 17, 116; **VII:** xix

"Byron" (Durrell), **Supp. I:** 126

"Byron" (Macaulay), **IV:** 281

Byron, Robert, **Supp. IV:** 157

Byron and the Ruins of Paradise (Gleckner), **IV:** 173, 194

Byron in Italy (Quennell), **IV:** 194

Byron: The Years of Fame (Quennell), **IV:** 194

Byronic Hero, The Types and Prototypes (Thorslev), **IV:** 173, 194

Byron's Conspiracy (Chapman), **I:** 249–251

Byron's Tragedy (Chapman), *see Tragedy of Byron, The*

"Byzantium" (Yeats), **VI:** 215; **Retro. Supp. I:** 336–337

C (Reading), **VIII:** 265, 266–268, 269, 271, 273

"C. G. Jung's First Years" (Kinsella), **Supp. V:** 269

C. H. Sisson (Sisson), **Supp. XI:** 252

Cab at the Door, A (Pritchett), Supp. III: 311, 312

Cabinet of Dr. Caligari, The (film), **III:** 342

Cadenus and Vanessa (Swift), **III:** 18, 31, 35; **Retro. Supp. I:** 283–284

"Caedmon" (Nicholson), **Supp. VI:** 216

Caesar and Cleopatra (Shaw), **VI:** 112; **Retro. Supp. II:** 316–317

Caesar and Pompey (Chapman), **I:** 252–253

Caesar Borgia (Lee), **II:** 305

Caesar: The Life Story of a Panda Leopard (O'Brian), **Supp. XII:** 249, 252

"Caesarean" (Fallon), **Supp. XII:** 109–110

Caesar's Fall (Drayton, Middleton, Munday, Webster, et al.), **II:** 68, 85

Caesar's Wife (Maugham), **VI:** 369

"Cage of Sand" (Ballard), **Supp. V:** 24

Cage Without Grievance (Graham), **Supp. VII:** 105, 107–109, 112

"Caged Skylark, The" (Hopkins), **Retro. Supp. II:** 190

Cagliostro, Alessandro di, **III:** 332

Cahier d'un retour au pays natal (Césaire), **Supp. IV:** 77

Cain (Byron), **IV:** xviii, 173, 177, **178–182,** 193

Caitaani mūtharaba–in? (Ngũgĩ), **VIII:** 212, 215, 216, 221–222, 224

Cakes and Ale (Maugham), **VI:** 367, 371, 374, 377

Calderón de la Barca, Pedro, **II:** 312n, 313n; **IV:** 206, 342, 349

Caleb Field: A Tale of the Puritans (Oliphant), **Supp. X:** 219

Caleb Williams (Godwin), *see Adventures of Caleb Williams, The*

Caledonia (Defoe), **III:** 13

"Caledonian Antisyzygy, The" (MacDiarmid), **Supp. XII:** 214

"Calendar–Flush, A" (Cameron), **Supp. IX:** 24

Calendar of Love, A (Brown), **Supp. VI:** 64

Calendar of Modern Letters (periodical), **VII:** 233

"Calenture" (Reid), **Supp. VII:** 328

"Caliban upon Setebos" (Browning), **IV:** 358, 364, 370, 372; **Retro. Supp. II:** 26

"Calidore" (Keats), **IV:** 214

Caliph's Design, The (Lewis), VII: 72, 75n

Call for the Dead (le Carré), **Supp. II:** 299, **305–307**, 308, 311

Called to Be Saints (Rossetti), V: 260

Call–Girls, The (Koestler), **Supp. I:** 28n, 32

"Calling of Arthur, The" (Williams, C. W. S.), **Supp. IX:** 282

Callista: A Tale of the Third Century (Newman), **Supp. VII:** 299

"Calm, The" (Donne), **Retro. Supp. II:** 86

"Calmative, The" (Beckett), **Supp. I:** 50, 59; **Retro. Supp. I:** 21

Calvin, John, **I:** 241

Calvino, Italo, **Supp. IV:** 558

"Calypso" (Brathwaite), **Supp. XII:** 41

"Camberwell Beauty, The" (Pritchett), **Supp. III:** 312, **327–328**, 329

Camberwell Beauty and Other Stories, The (Pritchett), **Supp. III:** 313, 327

Cambises (Preston), **I:** 122, 213–214

"Cambridge" (Ewart), **Supp. VII:** 36

Cambridge (Phillips), **Supp. V:** 380, 386, 388–390

"Cambridge Autumn" (Cornford), **VIII:** 107

Cambridge Bibliography of English Literature, **III:** 51, 52

"Cambridgeshire" (Cornford), **VIII:** 106

Cambyses (Preston), *see* Cambises

Camden, William, **Retro. Supp. I:** 152–153

Cameron, Norman, **VII:** 421, 422, 426; **Supp. IX: 17—32**

"Cameronian Preacher's Tale, The" (Hogg), **Supp. X:** 110

Camilla; or, A Picture of Youth (Burney), **Supp. III:** 64, 65, 68, 72, 73–75, 76

Cammaerts, Emile, **V:** 262, 274

"Camouflage" (Longley), **VIII:** 168

Camp, The (Sheridan), **III:** 253, 264

Camp One (Dutton), **Supp. XII:** 87–88, 95

Campaign, The (Addison), **III:** 46

Campaspe (Lyly), **I:** 198, 199–200

Campbell, Ian, **IV:** xii, xxiv, 250

Campbell, Joseph, **VII:** 53

Campbell, Roy, **IV:** 320; **VII:** 422, 428; **Supp. III:** 119

Campbell, Sue Ellen, **Supp. IV:** 336

Campbell's Kingdom (film, Ambler), **Supp. IV:** 3

Campensis, Joannes, **I:** 119

Camus, Albert, **Supp. IV:** 259

Can You Find Me: A Family History (Fry), **Supp. III:** 192, 193

Can You Forgive Her? (Trollope), **V:** 96, 101

"Can You Remember?" (Blunden), **Supp. XI:** 45

Canaan (Hill), **Supp. V:** 192–194

"Canacee" (Gower), **I:** 53–54, 55

"Canal Bank Walk" (Kavanagh), **Supp. VII:** 197

Canal Dreams (Banks), **Supp. XI:** 8, 9

Canavans, The (Gregory), **VI:** 315

"Canberra Remnant" (Murray), **Supp. VII:** 273

"Cancer Hospital, The" (Fuller), **Supp. VII:** 80

Candida (Shaw), **III:** 263; **VI:** 108, 110–111, 113; **Retro. Supp. II:** 313–314

Candidate, The (Crabbe), **III:** 286

"Candidate, The" (Gray), **III:** 142

Candide (tr. Cameron, N.), **Supp. IX:** 28

Candide (Voltaire), **IV:** 295; **Supp. IV:** 221

"Candle Indoors, The" (Hopkins), **V:** 370

Candle of Vision, The (Russell), **VIII:** 277, 278–280, 288, 292

Candy Floss Tree, The (Nicholson), **Supp. VI:** 218–219

"Canoes, The" (Dunn), **Supp. X:** 67

Canning, George, **IV:** 132, 164

Canon of Thomas Middleton's Plays, The (Lake), **II:** 1, 21

Canopus in Argos, Archives (Lessing), **Supp. I: 250–253**

"Canterbury Cathedral" (Murphy), **Supp. V:** 328

Canterbury Tales, The (Chaucer), **I:** 1, 2, **20–47**; **Retro. Supp. I:** 45; **Retro. Supp. II:** 45–49, 125

Canticle of the Rose, The (Sitwell), **VII:** xvii, 130, 137

"Canto 45" (Pound), **Supp. IV:** 114, 115

Cantos (Pound), **V:** 317n; **Supp. IV:** 100, 115

Cantos of Mutability (Spenser), **I:** 140

Cap, The, and, The Falcon (Tennyson), **IV:** 338

"Cap and Bells, The" (Keats), **IV:** 217

Cape of Storms: The First Life of Adamastor (Brink), **Supp. VI: 54–55**, 57

Capell, Edward, **I:** 326

Caprice (Firbank), **Supp. II:** 201, 204, 205, **211–213**

Captain, The (Beaumont and Fletcher), **II:** 65

Captain Brassbound's Conversion (Shaw), **VI:** 110; **Retro. Supp. II:** 317

Captain Corelli's Mandolin (De Bernières), **Supp. XII:** 65, 68–69, 74–76, 78

Captain Fantom (Hill, R.), **Supp. IX:** 117

"Captain Henry Hastings" (Brontë), **V:** 122, 123–124, 135, 138, 151

Captain Lavender (McGuckian), **Supp. V:** 280, 287–289

"Captain Lavender" (McGuckian), **Supp. V:** 289

"Captain Nemo" (Gunesekera), **Supp. X:** 86

"Captain Parry" (Hood), **IV:** 267

Captain Patch (Powys), **VIII:** 258

"Captain Rook and Mr. Pigeon" (Thackeray), **V:** 21, 37

Captain Singleton (Defoe), **III:** 8, 13; **Retro. Supp. I:** 72

Captains Courageous (Kipling), **VI:** 204

"Captain's Doll, The" (Lawrence), **VII:** 90

Captive Lion and Other Poems, The (Davies), **Supp. XI:** 98

Captives, The (Gay), **III:** 60–61, 67

Car, Thomas, **II:** 181

Caravaggio, Michelangelo Merisi da, **Supp. IV:** 95, 262

"Carboniferous" (Morgan, E.), **Supp. IX:** 167

Carceri d'invenzione (Piranesi), **III:** 325

Card, The (Bennett), **VI:** 250, 258–259, 266; **Supp. III:** 324, 325

Card, The (film, Ambler), **Supp. IV:** 3

Card Castle (Waugh), **Supp. VI:** 270

Cardenio (Fletcher and Shakespeare), **II:** 43, 66, 87

"Cards" (Fallon), **Supp. XII:** 105

Cards on the Table (Christie), **Supp. II:** 131, 135

"Care" (Murphy), **Supp. V:** 327

"Careless Lover, The" (Suckling), **II:** 227

"Careless Talk" (Bowen), **Supp. II:** 93

Careless Widow and Other Stories, A (Pritchett), **Supp. III:** 328, 329

Caretaker, The (Pinter), **Supp. I:** 367, 368, 369, **372–374**, 379, 380, 381; **Retro. Supp. I:** 224–225

Carew, Thomas, **I:** 354; **II:** **222–225,** 237

Carey, John, **V:** ix, xxvii, 39, 62, 73

Carey, Peter, **Supp. XII: 49–64**

Carlingford, Lord, *see* Fortescue, Chichester

"Carlow Village Schoolhouse" (Murphy), **Supp. V:** 328

Carlyle, A. J., **III:** 272n

Carlyle, Jane, **IV:** 239, 240

Carlyle, R. M., **III:** 272n

Carlyle, Thomas, **IV:** xii, 38, 41–42, 70, 231, **238–250,** 266n, 273, 289, 295, 301–302, 311, 324, 341–342; **V:** vii, ix, xii, 3, 5, 165, 182, 213n, 285, 319

"Carlyon Bay Hotel" (Murphy), **Supp. V:** 328

"Carmen Becceriense, Cum Prolegomenis et Commentario Critico, Edidit H. M. B."(Beerbohm), **Supp. II:** 44

Carmen Deo Nostro, Te Decet Hymnus, Sacred Poems, Collected (Crashaw), **II:** 180, 181, 184, 201

"Carmen Mortis" (Dutton), **Supp. XII:** 89

Carmen Triumphale, for the Commencement of the Year 1814 (Southey), **IV:** 71

"Carmilla" (Le Fanu), **III:** 340, 345; **Supp. III:** 385–836

Carmina V (Herrick), **II:** 108

Carn (McCabe), **Supp. IX:** 127, 128–129, 137, 138

Carnal Island, The (Fuller), **Supp. VII:** 77–78, 81

"Carnal Knowledge" (Gunn), **Supp. IV:** 258

Carnall, Geoffrey Douglas, **IV:** xxiv, 72, 156

Carnival Trilogy, The (Harris), **Supp. V:** 135, 136, 138, 140–141

"Carol" (Nicholson), **Supp. VI:** 214–215

"Carol on Corfu" (Durrell), **Supp. I:** 123–124, 126

Caroline (Maugham), **VI:** 369

"Caroline Vernon" (Brontë), **V:** 112, 122, 123, 124, 125, 138, 151

Carpenter, Edward, **VI:** 407, 408

"Carpenter, The" (Hart), **Supp. XI:** 130, 131

"Carpenter's Shed" (Malouf), **Supp. XII:** 220

Carr, John Dickson, **Supp. IV:** 285

"Carrickfergus" (MacNeice), **VI:** 401

Carrington, Charles, **VI:** 166

"Carrion Comfort" (Hopkins), **V:** 374

Carroll, Lewis, **V:** xi, xix, xxii, xxvi, 86, 87, **261–275; Supp. IV:** 199, 201

Carry On, Jeeves (Wodehouse), **Supp. III:** 455, 461, 462

Carter, Angela, **III:** 341, 345; **Supp. III:** **79–93; Supp. IV:** 46, 303, 459, 549, 558

Carter, Frederick, **VII:** 114

Cartoons: The Second Childhood of John Bull (Beerbohm), **Supp. II:** 51

Cartwright, John, **IV:** 103

Cartwright, William, **II:** 134, 185, 222, 237, 238

Cary, Joyce, **VII:** xvii, **185–196**

Caryl Churchill, A Casebook (King), **Supp. IV:** 194–195

"Casa d'Amunt" (Reid), **Supp. VII:** 329

Casa Guidi Windows (Browning), **IV:** 311, 314, 318, 321

"Casadh Súgáin Eile" (Behan), **Supp. II:** 68

Casanova's Chinese Restaurant (Powell), **VII:** 348–349

Cascando (play, Beckett), **Supp. I:** 60

"Cascando" (poem, Beckett), **Supp. I: 44**

Case, A. E., **III:** 25, 36

Case for African Freedom, The (Cary), **VII:** 186

"Case for Equality, The" (Drabble), **Supp. IV:** 31, 233

Case is Alter'd, The (Jonson), **Retro. Supp. I:** 156–157

Case is Altered, The (Plomer), **Supp. XI:** 217–219

"Case of Bill Williams, The" (Kavan), **Supp. VII:** 210

Case of Conscience Resolved, A (Bunyan), **II:** 253

Case of Elijah, The (Sterne), **III:** 135

Case of General Ople and Lady Camper, The (Meredith), **V:** 230–231, 234

"Case of Identity, A" (Doyle), **Supp. II:** 171

Case of Ireland . . . Stated, The (Molyneux), **III:** 27

Case of the Abominable Snowman, The (Day Lewis), **Supp. III:** 130

Case of the Midwife Toad, The (Koestler), **Supp. I:** 38

Case of Walter Bagehot, The (Sisson), **Supp. XI:** 250

Cashel Byron's Profession (Shaw), **VI:** 102, 103, 105–106, 109–110, 113, 129

"Cask of Amontillado, The" (Poe), **III:** 339

"Cassandra" (Maitland), **Supp. XI:** 174

Cassinus and Peter (Swift), **Retro. Supp. I:** 284

"Castalian Spring" (Heaney), **Retro. Supp. I:** 134

"Castaway, The" (Cowper), **III:** 218–219

Casting Off (Howard), **Supp. XI:** 145, 147, 148

Castle, The (Kafka), **III:** 340, 345; **Supp. IV:** 439

Castle Corner (Cary), **VII:** 186

Castle Dangerous (Scott), **IV:** 39

Castle of Indolence, The (Thomson), **III:** 162, 163, 171, 172; **Supp. III:** 412, **425–428**

Castle of Otranto, The (Walpole), **III:** 324, **325–327,** 336, 345; **IV:** 30; **Supp. III:** 383–384

Castle of the Demon, The (Hill, R.), **Supp. IX:** 116

Castle Rackrent (Edgeworth), **Supp. III:** 154–155; **Supp. IV:** 502

Castle Richmond (Trollope), **V:** 101

Castle–Croquet (Carroll), **V:** 274

Castles of Athlin and Dunbayne, The (Radcliffe), **IV:** 35

Casualties of Peace (O'Brien), **Supp. V:** 339

"Casualty" (Heaney), **Retro. Supp. I:** 130

Casuarina Tree, The (Maugham), **VI:** 370, 371

"Cat–Faith" (Reid), **Supp. VII:** 328

Cat Nappers, The (Wodehouse), *see Aunts Aren't Gentlemen*

Cat on a Houseboat (Desai), **Supp. V:** 55, 62

Catalans, The (O'Brian), **Supp. XII:** 251

"Catarina to Camoens" (Browning), **IV:** 314

Catcher in the Rye, The (Salinger), **Supp. IV:** 28

Catepillar Stew (Ewart), **Supp. VII:** 47

Catharine and Petruchio, **I:** 327; *see also Taming of the Shrew, The*

Cather, Willa, **Supp. IV:** 151

Catherine (Thackeray), **V:** 22, 24, 28, 37

Cathleen ni Houlihan (Yeats and Gregory), **VI:** 218, 222, 309; **VII:** 4

Catholic Church, The (Newman), **Supp. VII:** 292

"Catholic Church and Cultural Life, The" (Lodge), **Supp. IV:** 376

"Catholic Homilies" (Ælfric of Eynsham), **Retro. Supp. II:** 297–298

"Catholic Novel in England from the Oxford Movement to the Present Day, The" (Lodge), **Supp. IV:** 364

Catholics (Moore, B.), **Supp. IX:** 143, 151, 152

Cathures (Morgan, E.), **Supp. IX:** 160, 164, 170

Catiline (Jonson), **I:** 345–346; **Retro. Supp. I:** 161, 164

Cato (Addison), **III:** 46

Catriona (Stevenson), **V:** 387, 396; **Retro. Supp. I:** 267

Cat's Cradle Book, The (Warner), **Supp. VII:** 369, 381–382

Catullus, **II:** 108; **IV:** 327; **Supp. IV:** 491

Caudwell, Christopher, **Supp. III:** 120; **Supp. IX: 33–48**

Caught (Green), **Supp. II: 254–256**

Cause Célèbre (Rattigan), **Supp. VII:** 318, 321

Cause For Alarm (Ambler), **Supp. IV:** 8–9

Causeries du lundi (Sainte–Beuve), **III:** 226

Causley, Charles, **VII:** 422, 434–435

"Caught in a Hurry" (Redgrove), **Supp. VI:** 231

Causeway (Longley ed.), **VIII:** 165–166

Caution to Stir up to Watch Against Sin (Bunyan), **II:** 253

Cavafy, C. P., **VI:** 408

Cavalcade (Coward), **VI:** 264; **Supp. II:** 147, 149, 150–151

Cave, Edward, **III:** 107

Cave and the Spring, The: Essays in Poetry (Hope), **Supp. VII:** 155, 163

Cave Birds (Hughes), **Supp. I:** 351, 356–357, 363

Cavendish, George, **I:** 114

"Caverns of the Grave I've Seen, The" (Blake), **III:** 305

Cawelti, John, **Supp. IV:** 7

Caxton, William, **I:** 67, 82; **Retro. Supp. II:** 242–2

Cayley, Charles Bagot, **V:** 250–251, 253, 259

Ceausescu, Nicolae, **Supp. IV:** 195, 196

Cecil Rhodes (Plomer), **Supp. XI:** 221

Cecilia; or, Memoirs of an Heiress (Burney), **Supp. III:** 63, 64, 67, 70, 71, 72

Cefalû (Durrell), **Supp. I:** 100, 101

"Ceix and Alceone" (Gower), **I:** 53–54

Celan, Paul, **Supp. V:** 189–190, 199–200

Celebrations (Plomer), **Supp. XI:** 222

Celebrations and Elegies (Jennings), **Supp. V:** 217

"Celestial Omnibus" (Forster), **Supp. I:** 153

Celestial Omnibus, The (Forster), **VI:** 399

Celestials, **Supp. IV:** 344–345

Celibate Lives (Moore), **VI:** 95

Celibates (Moore), **VI:** 87, 91, 95

Cellular Pathologie (Virchow), **V:** 348

Celt and Saxon (Meredith), **V:** 234

"Celtic Twilight" (MacCaig), **Supp. VI:** 187

Celtic Twilight, The, Men and Women, Ghouls and Faeries (Yeats), **VI:** 221

Cement Garden, The (McEwan), **Supp. IV:** 390, 392–393, 400, 407

Cenci, The (Shelley), **III:** 338; **IV:** xviii, 202, 208; **Supp. IV:** 468; **Retro. Supp. I:** 254

"Censored, Banned, Gagged" (Gordimer), **Supp. II:** 237

"Censors and Unconfessed History" (Gordimer), **Supp. II:** 237

"Centaur Within, The" (Wallace–Crabbe), **VIII:** 315

"Centaurs, The" (Longley), **VIII:** 168, 169, 171

"Centenary of Charles Dickens, The" (Joyce), **V:** 41

Centlivres, Susanna, **Supp. III:** 70

Centuries of Meditations (Traherne), **II:** 189n, 190, 192–193, 202; **Supp. XI:** 263, 264, 265–266, 269–273

Century of Roundels, A (Swinburne), **V:** 332

Century Was Young, The (Aragon), **Supp. IV:** 466

Century's Daughter, The (retitled *Liza's England,* Barker), **Supp. IV:** 45, 46, 53–56

"Ceremony after a fire raid" (Thomas), **Supp. I:** 178

"Certain Mercies" (Graves), **VII:** 265

Certain Noble Plays of Japan (Yeats), **VI:** 218

Certain Satires (Marston), **II:** 25

Certaine Learned and Elegant Workes of the Right Honourable Fulke, Lord Brooke, Written in His Youth and Familiar Exercise with Sir Philip Sidney (Greville), **Supp. XI:** 106, 107–117

Cervantes, Miguel de, **IV:** 190

Césaire, Aimé, **Supp. IV:** 77

Cestus of Aglaia, The (Ruskin), **V:** 180–181, 184

Cetywayo and His White Neighbours (Haggard), **Supp. III:** 213, 214, 216–217

"Ceud Mile Failte" (Crawford), **Supp. XI:** 81

Chabot, Admiral of France (Chapman), **I:** 252–253

Chadourne, Marc, **III:** 329

"Chaffinch Map of Scotland, The" (Morgan, E.), **Supp. IX:** 166

"Chair that Will sat in, I sat in the best, The" (FitzGerald), **IV:** 341

Chain of Voices, A (Brink), **Supp. VI:** **51–52,** 57

"Chalet" (Murphy), **Supp. V:** 329

Chalk Giants, The (Roberts, K.), **Supp. X:** 272–273

Chalkhill, John, **II:** 133

Chamber Music (Joyce), **VII:** 41, 42; **Retro. Supp. I:** 171

Chamberlain, Neville, **VI:** 353, 355–356

"Chambermaid's Second Song, The" (Yeats), **VI:** 215

Chambers, E. K., **I:** 299; **II:** 187; **IV:** 41, 57

Chambers, R. W., **I:** 3; **Retro. Supp. I:** 143

"Chamois, The" (du Maurier), **Supp. III:** 143, 147

Champion (periodical), **III:** 97–98, 105

"Champion of the World, The" (Dahl), **Supp. IV:** 214, 223

Chance (Conrad), **VI:** 144, 146; **Supp. IV:** 250; **Retro. Supp. II:** 82

"Chance, The" (Carey), **Supp. XII:** 54, 55

Chance Encounters (Hope), **Supp. VII:** 152

Chancer, A (Kelman), **Supp. V:** 242, 247–249

Chances, The (Fletcher), **II:** 65

Chandler, Edmund, **V:** 354, 359

Chandler, Raymond, **Supp. II:** 130, 135

"Chanel" (Durrell), **Supp. I:** 125

"Change" (Donne), **Retro. Supp. II:** 89

"Change of Policy, A" (Pritchett), **Supp. III:** 329

Change the Name (Kavan), **Supp. VII:** 212

"Changed Man, A" (Hardy), **VI:** 22

Changed Man, A, The Waiting Supper, and Other Tales (Hardy), **VI:** 20, 22

"Changeling, The" (Byatt), **Supp. IV:** 140

Changeling, The (Middleton and Rowley), **II:** 1, 3, 8, **14–18,** 21, 93

"Changing Face of Fiction, The" (Weldon), **Supp. IV:** 522, 533

Changing Places: A Tale of Two Campuses (Lodge), **Supp. IV:** 363, 365, 371, 372–375, 376, 377, 385

Changing Room, The (Storey), **Supp. I:** 408, 416–417

"Channel Passage, A" (Brooke), **Supp. III:** 53

Channel Passage, A, and Other Poems (Swinburne), **V:** 333

Chant of Jimmie Blacksmith, The (Keneally), **Supp. IV:** 345, 347–348, 350–352, 360

Chant of the Celestial Sailors, The (Pater), **V:** 357

"Chant–Pagan" (Kipling), **VI:** 203

Chants for Socialists (Morris), **V:** 306

Chaos and Night (Montherlant), **II:** 99n

"Chapel Organist, The" (Hardy), **Retro. Supp. I:** 120

"Chaperon, The" (James), **VI:** 69

Chapman, George, **I:** **232–256,** 278, 288; **II:** 30, 37, 47, 55, 70, 71, 85; **IV:** 215, 255–256

Chapman, John, **V:** 189

Chapman, R. W., **III:** 249

Chappell, E., **II:** 288

"Chaps" (Crawford), **Supp. XI:** 74

Character and Opinions of Dr. Johnson, The (Swinburne), **V:** 333

Character of a Trimmer (Halifax), **III:** 40

"Character of a Virtuous Widow" (Webster), **II:** 77

Character of England, A, as It Was Lately Presented . . . (Evelyn), **II:** 287

"Character of Holland, The" (Marvell), **II:** 211, 219

"Character of Mr. Burke" (Hazlitt), **IV:** 136

Character of Robert Earl of Salisbury, The (Tourneur), **II:** 37, 41

Characterismes of Vertues and Vice (Hall), **II:** 81

Characteristicks (Shaftesbury), **III:** 44

"Characteristics" (Carlyle), **IV:** 241

Characteristics: In the Manner of Rochefoucault's Maxims (Hazlitt), **IV:** 132, 139

"Characters" (Dickens), **V:** 46

Characters (Theophrastus), **III:** 50

Characters (Webster), **II:** 68, 81

"Characters of Dramatic Writers Contemporary with Shakespeare" (Lamb), **IV:** 79, 80

Characters of Love, The: A Study in the Literature of Personality (Bayley), **Supp. I:** 222, 224

Characters of Shakespeare's Plays (Hazlitt), **I:** 329; **IV:** xvii, 129, 139

"Characters of the First Fifteen" (Ewart), **Supp. VII:** 36

Charge Delivered to the Grand Jury, A (Fielding), **III:** 105

"Charge of the Light Brigade, The" (Tennyson), **IV:** xxi, 325

Charioteer, The (Renault), **Supp. IX:** 172, 176–178, 187

"Charity" (Cowper), **III:** 212

Charles, Amy, **Retro. Supp. II:** 174

"Charles Augustus Milverton" (Ewart), **Supp. VII:** 42

Charles Darwin, 1809–1882: A Centennial Commemoration (ed. Chapman), **Supp. XI:** 195

Charles Dickens (Swinburne), **V:** 333

Charles Dickens: A Critical Study (Gissing), **V:** 424, 435, 437

Charles I (Shelley), **IV:** 206

"Charles Lamb" (De Quincey), **IV:** 148

Charles Lamb and His Contemporaries (Blunden), **IV:** 86

"Charles Lamb, to those who know thee justly dear" (Southey), **IV:** 85

"Charles Maurras and the Idea of the Patriot King" (Sisson), **Supp. XI:** 246

Charley Is My Darling (Cary), **VII:** 186, 188, 189, 190–191

Charlie and the Chocolate Factory (Dahl), **Supp. IV:** 202–203, 207, 222–223

Charlie and the Great Glass Elevator (Dahl), **Supp. IV:** 207

"Charlotte Brontë as a Critic of *Wuthering Heights*" (Drew), **V:** 153

Charlotte Brontë, 1816–1916: A Centenary Memorial (ed. Wood), **V:** 152

"Charlotte Brontë in Brussels" (Spielman), **V:** 137n

Charlotte Brontë: The Evolution of Genius (Gérin), **V:** 111, 152

Charlotte Mew and Her Friends (Fitzgerald), **Supp. V:** 98–99

"Charm Against Amnesia, A" (Nye), **Supp. X:** 202

Charmed Circle, A (Kavan), **Supp. VII:** 203, 205, 206–207

Chartism (Carlyle), **IV:** xix, 240, 244–245, 249, 250; **V:** viii

Chase, The, and William and Helen (Scott), **IV:** 29, 38

Chaste Maid in Cheapside, A (Middleton), **II:** 1, 3, **6–8,** 10, 21

Chaste Wanton, The (Williams, C. W. S.), **Supp. IX:** 276–277

Chastelard (Swinburne), **V:** 313, 330, 331, 332

Chatterton (Ackroyd), **Supp. VI:** **7–8**

Chatterton, Thomas, **IV:** iv, 228; **V:** 405; **Supp. IV:** 344

Chatwin, Bruce, **Supp. IV:** **157–177,** **Supp. IX:** **49–63**

Chaucer, Geoffrey, **I:** 2, 15, 16, **19–47,** 49, 60, 67, 126; **II:** 70, 292, 302, 304; **IV:** 189; **V:** 298, 303; **Supp. IV:** 190; **Retro. Supp. II:** **33–50,** 125

Châtiments, Les (Hugo), **V:** 324

"Cheap in August" (Greene), **Supp. I:** 16

"Chearfulness" (Vaughan), **II:** 186

"Cheek, The" (Hope), **Supp. VII:** 157–158

Cheery Soul, A (White), **Supp. I:** 131, 150

"Cheery Soul, A" (White), **Supp. I:** 143

Chekhov, Anton, **VI:** 372

"Chekhov and Zulu" (Rushdie), **Supp. IV:** 445

Cherry Orchard, The (tr. Frayn), **Supp. VII:** 61

"Cherry-ripe" (Herrick), **II:** 115

"Cherry Stones" (Milne), **Supp. V:** 302–303

"Cherry Tree, The" (Coppard), **VIII:** 94

"Cherry Tree, The" (Gunn), **Supp. IV:** 271

"Chest" (Self), **Supp. V:** 403

Chester Nimmo trilogy (Cary), **VII:** 186, 191, 194–195; *see also Prisoner of Grace, Except the Lord, Not Honour More*

Chester, Robert, **I:** 313

Chesterton, G. K., **IV:** 107; **V:** xxiv, 60, 262, 296, 383, 391, 393, 397; **VI:** 200, 241, 248, **335–345; VII:** xiii

Chettle, Henry, **I:** 276, 296; **II:** 47, 68

"Chevalier" (Crawford), **Supp. XI:** 73

Chief of Staff (Keneally), **Supp. IV:** 347

"Chief Petty Officer" (Causley), **VII:** 434

"Chiffonier, The" (Adcock), **Supp. XII:** 9

"Child, The" (Friel), **Supp. V:** 113

"Child and the Shadow, The" (Jennings), **Supp. V:** 210

Child Christopher and Goldilind the Fair (Morris), **V:** 306

"Child Dying, The" (Muir), **Supp. VI:** 207

"Child in the House, The" (Pater), **V:** 337, 357

Child in Time, The (McEwan), **Supp. IV:** 389, 390, 400–402, 404, 406, 407

"Child Lovers" (Davies), **Supp. XI:** 100

"Child of God" (Fallon), **Supp. XII:** 105

Child of Misfortune (Day Lewis), **Supp. III:** 118, 130–131

Child of Queen Victoria and Other Stories, The (Plomer), **Supp. XI:** 214–215

Child of Storm (Haggard), **Supp. III:** 214

Child of the Jago, The (Morrison), **VI:** 365–366

Childe Harold's Pilgrimage (Byron), **III:** 337, 338; **IV:** x, xvii, 172, **175–178,** 180, 181, 188, 192; **V:** 329

"Childe Roland to the Dark Tower Came" (Browning), **IV:** 357; **VI:** 16

"Childe-hood" (Vaughan), **II:** 188, 189, 190

Childermass (Lewis), **VII:** 71, 79, 80–81

"Childhood" (Clare), **Supp. XI:** 52–53

"Childhood" (Cornford), **VIII:** 112

"Childhood" (Muir), **Supp. VI:** 204–205

"Childhood Incident" (Nye), **Supp. X:** 203

Childhood of Edward Thomas, The (Thomas), **Supp. III:** 393

"Childish Prank, A" (Hughes), **Supp. I:** 353

"Children, Follow the Dwarfs" (Smith, I. C.), **Supp. IX:** 214

Children of Dynmouth, The (Trevor), **Supp. IV:** 501, 510–511

Children of Men, The (James), **Supp. IV:** 320, 338–339, 340

Children of the Chapel (Gordon), **V:** 313

"Children of the Zodiac, The" (Kipling), **VI:** 169, 189, 191–193

Children of Violence (Lessing), **Supp. I:** 238, **243–246**

Children's Encyclopedia (Mee), **Supp. IV:** 256

"Child's Christmas in Wales, A" (Thomas), **Supp. I:** 183

"Child's Calendar, A" (Brown), **Supp. VI:** 71

Child's Garden of Verses, A (Stevenson), **V:** 385, 387, 395; **Retro. Supp. I:** 264

Child's History of England, A (Dickens), **V:** 71

Child's Play: A Tragi-comedy in Three Acts of Violence With a Prologue and an Epilogue (Hill, R.), **Supp. IX:** 115–116

Chimeras, The (Mahon), **Supp. VI:** 173

Chimes, The (Dickens), **V:** 42, 64, 71

"Chimney Sweeper" (Blake), **III:** 297; **Retro. Supp. I:** 36, 42

China. A Revised Reprint of Articles from Titan . . . (DeQuincey), **IV:** 155

China Diary (Spender), **Supp. II:** 493

Chinamen (Frayn), **Supp. VII:** 57–58

"Chinese Button, The" (Brooke-Rose), **Supp. IV:** 103

"Chinese Letters" (Goldsmith), *see Citizen of the World, The*

"Chinese Lobster, The" (Byatt), **Supp. IV:** 155

Chinese Love Pavilion, The (Scott), **Supp. I:** 259, 263

Chinese Pictures (Bird), **Supp. X:** 31

"Chinoiserie" (Reading), **VIII:** 273

"Chip of Glass Ruby, A" (Gordimer), **Supp. II:** 232

"Chippenham" (Adcock), **Supp. XII:** 9

Chit-chat (periodical), **III:** 50

Chitty Chitty Bang Bang (film, Dahl), **Supp. IV:** 213

Chitty Chitty Bang Bang (Fleming), **Supp. IV:** 212–213

Chivers, Thomas Holley, **V:** 313

Chloe (Meredith), **V:** 231n, 234

Chloe Marr (Milne), **Supp. V:** 310

Choice of Ballads, A (Plomer), **Supp. XI:** 222

Choice of George Herbert's Verse, A (ed. Thomas), **Supp. XII:** 282

Choice of Kipling's Prose, A (Maugham), **VI:** 200, 204

Choice of Wordsworth's Verse, A (ed. Thomas), **Supp. XII:** 282

"Choir School" (Murphy), **Supp. V:** 328

Chomei at Toyama (Bunting), **Supp. VII:** 4, 6–7

Chomsky, Noam, **Supp. IV:** 113–114

"Chorale" (Hope), **Supp. VII:** 158

Chorus of Disapproval, A (Ayckbourn), **Supp. V:** 3, 9–10, 14

"Chorus Sacerdotum" (Greville), **Supp. XI:** 108, 117–118

"Chorus Tartaorum" (Greville), **Supp. XI:** 117–118

Christ a Compleat Saviour in His Intercession (Bunyan), **II:** 253

Christ and Satan, **Retro. Supp. II:** 301

Christ in the Cupboard (Powys), **VIII:** 255

Christ Stopped at Eboli (Levi), **VI:** 299

"Christ Surprised" (Jennings), **Supp. V:** 217

"Christ upon the Waters" (Newman), **Supp. VII:** 298

Christabel (Coleridge), **II:** 179; **III:** 338; **IV:** ix, xvii, 29, 44, 48–49, 56, 218, 313; **Retro. Supp. II:** 58–59

Christe's Bloody Sweat (Ford), **II:** 88, 100

"Christening" (Murphy), **Supp. V:** 322

Christian Behaviour (Lewis), **Supp. III:** 248

Christian Behaviour . . . (Bunyan), **II:** 253

Christian Captives, The (Bridges), **VI:** 83

Christian Dialogue, A (Bunyan), **II:** 253

Christian Ethicks (Traherne), **II:** 190, 191, 201; **Supp. XI:** 263, 264, 265, 267, 277–279

Christian Hero, The (Steele), **III: 43, 44,** 53

Christian Morals (Browne), **II:** 149, 153, 154, 156; **III:** 40

Christie, Agatha, **III:** 341; **Supp. II: 123–135; Supp. III:** 334; **Supp. IV:** 500

Christina Alberta's Father (Wells), **VI:** 227

Christina Rossetti (Packer), **V:** 251, 252–253, 260

Christina Rossetti: A Divided Life (Battiscombe), **V:** 260

Christina Stead (Brydon), **Supp. IV:** 463

Christina Stead: A Biography (Rowley), **Supp. IV:** 459

"Christine's Letter" (Coppard), **VIII:** 96

"Christmas" (Smith, I. C.), **Supp. IX:** 221

"Christmas Antiphones" (Swinburne), **V:** 325

"Christmas at Sea" (Stevenson), **V:** 396

Christmas at Thompson Hall (Trollope), **V:** 102

Christmas Books (Dickens), **V:** 71

Christmas Carol, A (Dickens), **V:** xx, 42, 56–57, 71

"Christmas Carol, A" (Swinburne), **V:** 315

"Christmas Childhood, A" (Kavanagh), **Supp. VII:** 194

Christmas Comes But Once a Year (Chettle, Dekker, Heywood, Webster), **II:** 68, 85

"Christmas Day At Home" (Hollinghurst), **Supp. X:** 121

"Christmas Day in the Workhouse" (Wilson), **Supp. I:** 153, 157

"Christmas Eve" (Nye), **Supp. X:** 202, 205

Christmas Eve and Easter Day (Browning), **Retro. Supp. II:** 25–26

"Christmas Garland Woven by Max Beerbohm, A" (Beerbohm), **Supp. II:** 45

Christmas Garland, A (Beerbohm), **Supp. II:** 45, 49

Christmas His Masque (Jonson), **Retro. Supp. I:** 165

Christmas Holiday (Maugham), **VI:** 377

"Christmas Life, The" (Cope), **VIII:** 80

"Christmas Oratorio, A" (Auden), **Retro. Supp. I:** 10–11

Christmas Pudding (Mitford), **Supp. X:** 154–155

"Christmas Storms and Sunshine" (Gaskell), **V:** 15

Christmas–Eve and Easter–Day (Browning), **IV:** 357, 363, 370, 372, 374

Christopher, John, **Supp. V:** 22

Christopher and His Kind (Isherwood), **VII:** 318

"Christopher At Birth" (Longley), **VIII:** 167

Christopher Columbus (MacNeice), **VII:** 406

"Christopher Columbus and Queen Isabella of Spain Consummate Their Relationship" (Rushdie), **Supp. IV:** 452

Christopher Homm (Sisson), **Supp. XI:** 247–248, 249

"Christopher Marlowe" (Swinburne), **V:** 332

Christopher Marlowe in Relation to Greene, Peele and Lodge (Swinburne), **V:** 333

Christ's Hospital, A Retrospect (Blunden), **IV:** 86

"Christ's Hospital Five–and–Thirty Years Ago" (Lamb), **IV:** 42, 76

"Chronicle, The" (Cowley), **II:** 198

Chronicle Historie of Perkin Warbeck, The (Ford), *see Perkin Warbeck*

chronicle history, **I:** 73

Chronicle of Carlingford series (ed. Fitzgerald), **Supp. V:** 98

Chronicle of Friendships, A, 1873–1900 (Low), **V:** 393, 397

Chronicle of Queen Fredegond, The (Swinburne), **V:** 333

Chronicle of the Cid (tr. Southey), **IV:** 71

"Chronicle of the Drum, The" (Thackeray), **V:** 17, 38

Chronicle of Youth: War Diary, 1913–1917 (Brittain), **Supp. X:** 47

Chronicles (Hall), **II:** 43

Chronicles of Barset (Trollope), **Supp. IV:** 231

Chronicles of Carlingford (Oliphant), **Supp. X:** 214, 219

Chronicles of Clovis, The (Saki), **Supp. VI:** 240–243, 245, 249

Chronicles of Narnia, The (Lewis), **Supp. III:** 247, 248, **259–261**

Chronicles of the Canongate (Scott), **IV:** 39

Chroniques (Froissart), **I:** 21

"Chronopolis" (Ballard), **Supp. V:** 22

"Chrysalides" (Kinsella), **Supp. V:** 262

Chrysaor (Landor), **IV:** 96

Church, Dean R. W., **I:** 186

Church and Queen. Five Speeches, 1860–1864 (Disraeli), **IV:** 308

"Church–floore, The" (Herbert), **Retro. Supp. II:** 178–179

"Church Going" (Larkin), **Supp. I:** 277, 279, 280, 285

"Church Service" (Vaughan), **II:** 187

"Church Windows, The" (Herbert), **II:** 127

"Churche–Floore, The" (Herbert), **II:** 126

Church in Crisis, The (Wilson), **Supp. VI:** 305

"Churches of Northern France, The" (Morris), **V:** 293, 306

"Church's Year Book" (Traherne), **Supp. XI:** 264, 274

Churchill, Caryl, **Supp. IV: 179–200**

Churchill, Lady Randolph, **VI:** 349

Churchill, Winston, **III:** 27; **VI:** xv, 261, 274, **347–362**, 369, 385, 392; **Supp. III:** 58–59; speeches, **VI:** 361

Churchill by His Contemporaries (ed. Eade), **VI:** 351*n*, 361

"Church–monuments" (Herbert), **II:** 127

"Church–warden and the Curate, The" (Tennyson), **IV:** 327

"Churl and the Bird, The" (Lydgate), **I:** 57

Chymist's Key, The (tr. Vaughan), **II:** 185, 201

Cibber, Colley, **I:** 327; **II:** 314, 324–326, 331, 334, 337

Cicadas, The (Huxley), **VII:** 199

"Cicero and His Brother" (Landor), **IV:** 90, 91

Ciceronianus (Harvey), **I:** 122

Ciceronis Amor: Tullies Love (Greene), **VIII:** 135, 143

"Cinders" (Hulme), **Supp. VI:** 133, 135–136, 140, **141,** 146

Cinkante balades (Gower), **I:** 56

Cinque Ports, The (Ford), **VI:** 238, 332

Cinthio, Giraldi, **I:** 316; **II:** 71

Circe (Davenant), **II:** 305

"Circe" (Longley), **VIII:** 167

"Circe Truggin" (Powys), **VIII:** 249

Circle, The (Maugham), **VI:** 369

"Circle of Deception" (Waugh), **Supp. VI:** 275

"Circled by Circe" (Gunesekera), **Supp. X:** 86

"Circuit of the World, The", *See Heimskringla*

Circular Billiards for Two Players (Carroll), **V:** 273

"Circulation, The" (Traherne), **Supp. XI:** 267

"Circus Animals' Desertion, The" (Yeats), **V:** 349; **VI:** 215; **Supp. III:** 102; **Retro. Supp. I:** 338

"Circus Wheel" (Redgrove), **Supp. VI:** 236

Citation and Examination of William Shakespeare . . . (Landor), **IV:** 100

Cities (Morris, J.), **Supp. X:** 172

"Cities, The" (Russell), **VIII:** 291

Cities, Plains and People (Durrell), **Supp. I:** 126

"Citizen" (Wallace–Crabbe), **VIII:** 311

Citizen of the World, The; or, Letters from a Chinese Philosopher . . . (Goldsmith), **III:** 177, 179, 185, 188–189, 191

City Madam, The (Massinger), **Supp. XI:** 183, 184, 185, 186, 190–192

"City of Brass, The" (Kipling), **VI:** 203

"City Sunset, A" (Hulme), **Supp. VI:** 136

"City Ways" (Amis), **Supp. II:** 2

City Witt: or, The Woman Wears the Breeches, The (Brome), **Supp. X:** 62

City Wives' Confederacy, The (Vanbrugh), *see Confederacy, The*

"Civilised, The," (Galsworthy), **VI:** 273, 274, 276

Civilization in the United States (Arnold), **V:** 216

Civilization of the Renaissance in Italy, The (Burckhardt), **V:** 342

Civitatis Amor (Middleton), **II:** 3

Cixous, Hélène, **Supp. IV:** 99, 117, 232, 547, 558

"Clachtoll" (MacCaig), **Supp. VI:** 186

Clancy, Laurie, **Supp. IV:** 348

Clapp, Susannah, **Supp. IV:** 164

Clara (Galloway), **Supp. XII:** 117, 127–130

Clara Florise (Moore), **VI:** 96

Clare, John, **IV:** 260; **Supp. XI: 49–65**

Clare Drummer (Pritchett), **Supp. III:** 313

Clarel (Melville), **V:** 211

"Clarence Mangan" (Kinsella), **Supp. V:** 260

"Clare's Ghost" (Blunden), **Supp. XI:** 44

"Clarice of the Autumn Concerts" (Bennett), **VI:** 266

Clarissa (Richardson), **III:** 80–81, **85–89,** 91, 92, 95; **VI:** 266; **Supp. III:** 30–31; **Supp. IV:** 150; **Retro. Supp. I:** 81

"Clarissa": Preface, Hints of Prefaces and Postscripts (ed. Brissenden), **III:** 86*n*

"Clarissa Harlowe Poem, The" (Ewart), **Supp. VII:** 41

Clarissa Oakes (O'Brian), **Supp. XII:** 258–259

Clark, Kenneth, **III:** 325, 346

Clark, Sir George, **IV:** 290

Clarke, Charles Cowden, **IV:** 214, 215

Clarke, Herbert E., **V:** 318*n*

Clarke, Samuel, **II:** 251

Clarkson, Catherine, **IV:** 49

Classic Irish Drama (Armstrong), **VII:** 14

Classical Tradition, The: Greek and Roman Influence on Western Literature (Highet), **II:** 199*n*

Classics and Commercials (Wilson), **Supp. II:** 57

Claude Lorrain's House on the Tiber (Lear), **V:** 77

Claudius novels (Graves), **VII:** xviii, 259

Claudius the God and His Wife Messalina (Graves), **VII:** 259

"Claud's Dog" (Dahl), **Supp. IV:** 214

Claverings, The (Trollope), **V:** 99–100, 101

Clayhanger (Bennett), **VI:** 248, 250, 251, 257–258

Clayhanger series(Bennett), **VI:** xiii, 247, 248, 250, 251, 257–258

Clea (Durrell), **Supp. I:** 103, 104, 106, 107

"Clean Bill, A" (Redgrove), **Supp. VI:** 234

"Cleaned Out" (Motion), **Supp. VII:** 263

"Cleaning Out the Workhouse" (McGuckian), **Supp. V:** 291

Cleanness (*Gawain*–Poet), **Supp. VII:** 83, 84, 98–99

Cleansed (Kane), **VIII:** 148, 151, 152, 156, 158–159, 160

Clear Light of Day (Desai), **Supp. V:** 53, 55, 62, 65–67, 68, 73

Clear State of the Case of Elizabeth Canning, A (Fielding), **III:** 105

"Clearances" (Heaney), **Supp. II:** 279–280; **Retro. Supp. I:** 131

"Cleator Moor" (Nicholson), **Supp. VI:** 214

"Cleggan Disaster, The" (Murphy), **Supp. V:** 313, 319–320

Cleomenes, The Spartan Hero (Dryden), **II:** 296, 305

"Cleon" (Browning), **IV:** 357, 360, 363

Cleopatra (Daniel), **I:** 162

Cleopatra (Haggard), **Supp. III:** 213, 222

"Cleopatra" (Swinburne), **V:** 332

"Clergy, The" (Wilson), **Supp. VI:** 305

Clergyman's Daughter, A (Orwell), **VII:** 274, 278

"Clergyman's Doubts, A" (Butler), **Supp. II:** 117

Clergymen of the Church of England (Trollope), **V:** 101

"Cleric, The" (Heaney), **Supp. II:** 279

Clerk, N. W., *see* Lewis, C. S.

Clerk's Prologue, The (Chaucer), **I:** 29

Clerk's Tale, The (Chaucer), **I:** 34; **Supp. IV:** 190

Cleveland, John, **II:** 123

"Clicking of Cuthbert, The" (Wodehouse), **Supp. III:** 462

Clifford, J. L., **III:** 244n

Clifford, W. K., **V:** 409n

"Clinical World of P. D. James, The" (Benstock), **Supp. IV:** 320

Clio: A Muse (Trevelyan), **VI:** 383–384

Clishbotham, Jedidiah, pseud. of Sir Walter Scott

"Clive" (Browning), **IV:** 367

"Clock (for Albert Ayler)" (Brathwaite), **Supp. XII:** 44

"Clock Ticks at Christmas, A" (Highsmith), **Supp. V:** 180

"Clocks, The" (Christie), **Supp. II:** 135

Clockwork Orange, A (Burgess), **Supp. I:** 190–191

Clockwork Testament, The; or, Enderby's End (Burgess), **Supp. I:** 189

Clodd, Edward, **V:** 429

Cloning of Joanna May, The (Weldon), **Supp. IV:** 535, 536

"Clopton Hall" (Gaskell), **V:** 3

"Clorinda and Damon" (Marvell), **II:** 210, 211

Clorinda Walks in Heaven (Coppard), **VIII:** 89, 93–94

"Clorinda Walks in Heaven" (Coppard), **VIII:** 88, 97

"Close of Play" (Dunn), **Supp. X:** 70

Close Quarters (Golding), **Retro. Supp. I:** 104

Closed Eye, A (Brookner), **Supp. IV:** 120, 133

Closing the Ring (Churchill), **VI:** 361

"Clothes Pit, The" (Dunn), **Supp. X:** 69

"Cloud, The" (Fowles), **Supp. I:** 304

"Cloud, The" (Shelley), **IV:** 196, 204

Cloud Nine (Churchill), **Supp. IV:** 179, 180, 188–189, 198

CloudCuckooLand (Armitage), **VIII:** 1, 11–14

"Clouds" (Brooke), **VI:** 420

Clouds (Frayn), **Supp. VII:** 61

"Cloud–Sculptors of Coral–D, The" (Ballard), **Supp. V:** 26

Clouds of Witness (Sayers), **Supp. III:** 338, 339

"Cloud's Swan Song, The" (Thompson), **V:** 443

Clough, Arthur Hugh, **IV:** 371; **V:** ix, xi, xviii, xxii, 7, **155–171,** 207, 208n, 209, 211, 212

"Club in an Uproar, A" (Thackeray), **V:** 25

Clubbable Woman, A (Hill, R.), **Supp. IX:** 110, 112–113

Clune, Frank, **Supp. IV:** 350

Cnut, King, **Retro. Supp. II:** 293

Co–operation and Nationality (Russell), **VIII:** 286, 287

Coakley, Thomas P., **Supp. IV:** 350

"Coal, The" (Caudwell), **Supp. IX:** 38

Coal Face (Auden), **Retro. Supp. I:** 7

"Coast, The" (Fuller), **VII:** 431

Coast to Coast: An Account of a Visit to the United States (Morris, J.), **Supp. X:** 175, 181–182, 184

Coasting (Raban), **Supp. XI:** 227, 228–232

"Coat, A" (Yeats), **Retro. Supp. I:** 330

"Coat of Many Colors, A" (Desai), **Supp. V:** 53

Cobbett, William, **VI:** 337

Cobra Verde (film), **Supp. IV:** 168

Coburn, Kathleen, **IV:** 52, 55–57

Cocaine Nights (Ballard), **Supp. V:** 31–32, 34

"Cock: A Novelette" (Self), **Supp. V:** 404–405

Cock and Bull (Self), **Supp. V:** 404–406

Cock and the Fox, The (Henryson), **Supp. VII:** 136, 137–138, 147

Cock and the Jasp, The (Henryson), **Supp. VII:** 136, 137

"Cock Crows" (Hughes), **Retro. Supp. II:** 211

"Cock o' the North" (Crawford), **Supp. XI:** 68

Cock–a–Doodle Dandy (O'Casey), **VII:** xviii, 9–10

Cockatoos, The (White), **Supp. I:** 132, 147

Cockburn, Alexander, **Supp. IV:** 449

"Cockcrow" (Herrick), **II:** 114

"Cock–crowing" (Vaughan), **II:** 185

Cockrill, Maurice, **Supp. IV:** 231

Cockshut, A. O. J., **V:** 98, 100–101, 103

Cocktail Party, The (Eliot), **VII:** 158, 159, 160–161; **Retro. Supp. II:** 132

"Coda" (Kinsella), **Supp. V:** 271

Code of the Woosters, The (Wodehouse), **Supp. III:** 459–460

"Codham, Cockridden, and Childerditch" (Thomas), **Supp. III:** 401

Coelum Britannicum . . . (Carew), **II:** 222

Coetzee, J(ohn) M(ichael), **Supp. VI:** **75–90**

Coffin for Dimitrios, A (Ambler), **Supp. IV:** 9–11, 12

"Coffin on the Hill, The" (Welch), **Supp. IX:** 267–268

Coggan, Donald, archbishop of Canterbury, **I:** vi

Cohen, Francis, **IV:** 190

Cohn, Ruby, **Retro. Supp. I:** 215

Co–Incidence of Flesh (Fallon), **Supp. XII:** 102

Colasterion: A Reply to a Nameless Answer Against the Doctrine and Discipline of Divorce (Milton), **II:** 175

Colburn, Henry, **IV:** 254, 293; **V:** 135

"Cold, The" (Warner), **Supp. VII:** 380

"Cold, clear, and blue, The morning heaven" (Brontë), **V:** 115

Cold Coming, A (Harrison), **Supp. V:** 150

"Cold Coming, A" (Harrison), **Supp. V:** 161–163

Cold Heaven (Moore, B.), **Supp. IX:** 143, 144, 151–152

"Cold in the earth" (Brontë), **V:** 114, 133, 134

Cold Lazarus (Potter, D.), **Supp. X:** 228, 240–241

Colenso, Bishop John William, **V:** 283

Coleridge, Derwent, **IV:** 48–49, 52

Coleridge, Hartley, **IV:** 44; **V:** 105, 125

Coleridge, Samuel Taylor, **III:** 338; **IV:** viii–xii, **41–57,** 59, 75–78, 82, 84, 115, 204, 253, 257, 281; **V:** 244; **Retro. Supp. II: 51–67;** and De Quincey, **IV:** 143, 144, 150; and Hazlitt, **IV:** 125–130, 133–134, 137, 138; and Peacock, **IV:** 161–162, 167; and Wordsworth, **IV:** 3–4, 6, 15, 128; at Christ's Hospital, **IV:** 75–78, 82; critical works, **II:** 42, 119n, 155, 179, 249–250, 298; **III:** 174, 281, 286; **IV:** 4, 6, 18, 96, 253, 257; **Retro. Supp. II:** 172; literary style, **II:** 154; **III:** 336, 338; **IV:** viii, xi, 18, 180; **V:** 62, 361, 447; Pater's essay in "*ppreciations*, **V:** 244, 340–341; **Supp. IV:** 425, 426–427

"Coleridge" (Mill), **IV:** 50, 56

"Coleridge" (Pater), **V:** 338, 340–341, 403

Coleridge on Imagination (Richards), **Supp. II:** 422–423, 429

Coleridge's Miscellaneous Criticism (ed. Raysor), **IV:** 46

Coleridge's Shakespearean Criticism (ed. Raysor), **IV:** 51, 52, 56

Colette, **Supp. III:** 86; **Supp. IV:** 136

"Coleum; or, The Origin of Things" (Bacon), **I:** 267

Colin Clout (Skelton), **I:** 84, 86, 87, 91–92

Colin Clout's Come Home Again (Spenser), **I:** 124, 127–128, 146–147

"Collaboration" (James), **VI:** 48, 69

Collaborators, The (Hill, R.), **Supp. IX:** 118

"Collar, The" (Herbert), **II:** 120–121, 216; **Retro. Supp. II:** 180

Collected Essays (Greene), **Supp. I:** 9

Collected Essays, Papers, etc. (Bridges), **VI:** 83

Collected Ewart 1933–1980, The (Ewart), **VII:** 423, **Supp. VII:** 35, 36, 37, 38, 41, 43

Collected Impressions (Bowen), **Supp. II:** 78, 82

Collected Later Poems, 1988–2000 (Thomas), **Supp. XII:** 282

Collected Letters (Cowen), **VI:** 448

Collected Papers on Analytical Psychology (Jung), **Supp. IV:** 3, 4

Collected Plays (Maugham), **VI:** 367

Collected Plays (Rattigan), **Supp. VII:** 311, 312, 318

Collected Poems (Amis), **Supp. II:** 15

Collected Poems (Brooke), **Supp. III:** 55–56

Collected Poems (Bunting), **Supp. VII:** 6, 13–14

Collected Poems (Cameron), **Supp. IX:** 18, 24, 31

Collected Poems (Caudwell), **Supp. IX:** 33, 37

Collected Poems (Cornford), **VIII:** 104, 112, 114

Collected Poems (Davies), **Supp. XI:** 89, 96

Collected Poems (Durrell), **Supp. I: 124–126**

Collected Poems (Empson), **Supp. II:** 179, 181, 192

Collected Poems (Ford), **VI:** 323, 332

Collected Poems (Jennings), **Supp. V:** 216

Collected Poems (MacCaig), **Supp. VI:** 185, 187, 192

Collected Poems (MacDiarmid), **Supp. XII:** 203

Collected Poems (Mahon), **Supp. VI:** 165–167, 169–170, 172–177

Collected Poems (Morgan **Supp. IX:** 157, 158, 160–161, 163

Collected Poems (Muir), **Supp. VI:** 201, 204–205, 208

Collected Poems (Murray), **Supp. VII:** 271, 273, 275, 277, 278, 279, 281, 283, 284

Collected Poems (Nicholson), **Supp. VI:** 213–214, 217–219

Collected Poems (Nye), **Supp. X:** 200, 202–205

Collected Poems (Plomer), **Supp. XI:** 213, 214, 216, 222

Collected Poems (Russell), **VIII:** 277, 2887

Collected Poems, The (Seth), **Supp. X:** 279, 281, 284

Collected Poems (Sillitoe), **Supp. V:** 424

Collected Poems (Sisson), **Supp. XI:** 243, 245, 246, 248, 250, 251, 252, 253, 254, 255, 256, 257, 258, 259

Collected Poems (Smith), **Supp. II:** 464

Collected Poems (Smith, I. C.), **Supp. IX:** 209, 211, 214, 217, 219, 221

Collected Poems (Thomas), **Supp. I:** 169, 170, 171, 175, 179, 184; **Supp. III:** 393

Collected Poems (Warner), **Supp. VII:** 371, 372, 373

Collected Poems (Yeats), **Retro. Supp. I:** 330

Collected Poems 1909–1962 (Muir), **Supp. VI:** 205

Collected Poems 1928–1985 (Spender), **Supp. II:** 486, 493

Collected Poems 1930–1965 (Hope), **Supp. VII:** 153, 155, 156, 157, 159, 162, 164, 165

Collected Poems, 1945–1990 (Thomas), **Supp. XII:** 279, 280, 282, 283, 284, 285, 286, 287, 288–289, 290, 292

Collected Poems 1950–1970 (Davie), **Supp. VI:** 105–106, 108, 110, 114

Collected Poems, 1953–1985 (Jennings), **Supp. V:** 211, 216, 218

Collected Poems 1955–1995 (Stevenson), **Supp. VI:** 254, 256–257, 260–262, 264–265

Collected Poems, 1956–1994 (Kinsella), **Supp. V:** 273, 274

Collected Poems 1980–1990 (Ewart), **Supp. VII:** 35, 43, 44, 46

Collected Poems of A. E. Coppard (Coppard), **VIII:** 91, 98

Collected Poems of Robert Louis Stevenson (ed. Smith), **V:** 393

Collected Poetry of Malcolm Lowry, The (ed. Scherf), **Supp. III:** 283

Collected Stories (Carey), **Supp. XII:** 54

Collected Stories (Maugham), **VI:** 370

Collected Stories (Thomas), **Supp. I:** 180, 181–182, 183

Collected Tales of A. E. Coppard, The (Coppard), **VIII:** 85, 89, 97

Collected Translations (Morgan, E.), **Supp. IX:** 169

Collected Translations (Sisson), **Supp. XI:** 252

Collected Verse, The (Carroll), **V:** 270, 273

Collected Works (Smith), **Supp. VII:** 340

Collected Works of Izaak Walton (Keynes), **II:** 134

Collected Writings of T. E. Hulme (Hulme), **Supp. VI:** 134–136, 139–146

Collection, The (Pinter), **Supp. I:** 373, 374, 375

"Collection, The" (Pritchett), **Supp. III:** 315

Collection of Meditations and Devotions in Three Parts, A (Traherne), **II:** 191, 201

Collection of Original Poems, A (Boswell), **III:** 247

Collection of Poems 1955–1988, A (Nye), **Supp. X:** 193–194, 197, 202–205

"Collective Invention, The" (Wallace–Crabbe), **VIII:** 317

Collector, The (Fowles), **Supp. I:** 291, 292, 293, 294–295, 297, 307, 310

Collector, The (Redgrove), **Supp. VI:** 227–228

"Collector Cleans His Picture, The" (Hardy), **Retro. Supp. I:** 120

"Collectors, The" (Mistry), **Supp. X:** 139

"College Garden, The" (Bridges), **VI:** 82

"College in the Reservoir, The" (Redgrove), **Supp. VI:** 235–236

"College Magazine, A" (Stevenson), **Retro. Supp. I:** 261

Collier, Jeremy, **II:** 303, 325, 331–332, 338, 340, 356; **III: 44**

Collier, John Payne, **I:** 285; **IV:** 52, 56

Collier's Friday Night, A (Lawrence), **VII:** 89, 121

Collingwood, R. G., **VI:** 203

Collingwood, S. D., **V:** 270, 273, 274

Collins, Michael, **VI:** 353

Collins, Phillip, **V:** 46, 73

Collins, Wilkie, **III:** 334, 338, 340, 345; **V:** xxii–xxiii, 42, 62; **Supp. III:** 341; **Supp. VI: 91–104**

Collins, William, **II:** 68, 323n; **III: 160–176**, 336; **IV:** 227

Collinson, James, **V:** 249

Colloquies on the Progress and Prospects of Society (Southey), *see* Sir Thomas More; or, Colloquies on the Progress . . .

Colman, George, **IV:** 271

Colombe's Birthday (Browning), **IV:** 374

"Colonel Fantock" (Sitwell), **VII:** 133

Colonel Jack (Defoe), **III:** 5, 6, 7, 8, 13

Colonel Quaritch, V. C. (Haggard), **Supp. III:** 213

Colonel Sun (Markham), **Supp. II:** 12

"Colonel's Lady, The" (Maugham), **VI:** 370

Color of Blood, The (Moore, B.), **Supp. IX:** 142, 144–145, 151, 152–153

"Color of Herring, The" (Reid), **Supp. VII:** 331

"Colour Machine, The" (Gunn), **Supp. IV:** 267

Colour of Rain, The (Tennant), **Supp. IX:** 228, 229, 239

Coloured Countries, The (Waugh), **Supp. VI:** 272

"Colours of Good and Evil" (Bacon), *see* "Examples of the Colours of Good and Evil"

"Colubriad, The" (Cowper), **III:** 217–218

"Columban" (Crawford), **Supp. XI:** 76

"Columba's Song" (Morgan, E.), **Supp. IX:** 170

"Columbus in Chains" (Kincaid), **Supp. VII:** 223, 224

Colvin, Sidney, **V:** 386, **389–396**

"Coma Berenices" (Thomas), **Supp. IV:** 491

"Comála" (Macpherson), **VIII:** 188

"Combat, The" (Muir), **Supp. VI:** 200, 207

"Combat, The" (Thomas), **Supp. XII:** 292

Come and Go (Beckett), **Supp. I:** 60

Come and Welcome, to Jesus Christ (Bunyan), **II:** 253

Come Dance with Kitty Stobling and Other Poems (Kavanagh), **Supp. VII:** 193

"Come, Fool" (Smith, I. C.), **Supp. IX:** 221

Comedians, The (Greene), **Supp. I:** 10, 13, 15–16; **Retro. Supp. II:** 162–164

"Comedy" (Fry), **Supp. III:** 201

Comedy of Dante Alighieri, The (tr. Sayers), **Supp. III:** 333, 336, 350

Comedy of Errors, The (Shakespeare), **I:** 302, 303, 312, 321

"Come–on, The" (Dunn), **Supp. X:** 72

Comfort of Strangers, The (McEwan), **Supp. IV:** 390, 396–398, 400, 402

Comfortable Words to Christ's Lovers (Julian of Norwich), **Supp. XII:** 155

"Comforters, The" (Malouf), **Supp. XII:** 219

Comforters, The (Spark), **Supp. I:** 199, 200, 201–202, 213

Comic Annual, The (Hood), **IV:** 251, 252, 253–254, 258, 259, 266

"Comic Cuts" (Kelman), **Supp. V:** 256

Comic Romance of Monsieur Scarron, The (tr. Goldsmith), **III:** 191

Comical Revenge, The (Etherege), **II:** 266, 267–268, 271

Comicall Satyre of Every Man Out of His Humour, The (Jonson), **Retro. Supp. I:** 158, 159–160

"Coming" (Larkin), **Supp. I:** 285

"Coming, The" (Thomas), **Supp. XII:** 288

"Coming Down Through Somerset" (Hughes), **Retro. Supp. II:** 211–212

"Coming Home" (Bowen), **Supp. II:** 81, 82

Coming of Gabrielle, The (Moore), **VI:** 96, 99

"Coming of the Anglo–Saxons, The" (Trevelyan), **VI:** 393

Coming of the Kings, The (Hughes), **Supp. I:** 347

"Coming to Visit" (Motion), **Supp. VII:** 256

Coming Up for Air (Orwell), **VII:** 281–282

"Commemoration of King Charles the I, martyr'd on that day (King), **Supp. VI:**162

Commendatory Verses Prefixed to Heywood's Apology for Actors (Webster), **II:** 85

Commendatory Verses Prefixed to . . . Munday's Translation of Palmerin . . . (Webster), **II:** 85

"Comment on Christmas, A" (Arnold), **V:** 216

Commentaries of Caesar, The (Trollope), **V:** 102

Commentarius solutus (Bacon), **I:** 263, 272

"Commentary" (Auden), **Retro. Supp. I:** 9

"Commentary on Galatians, A" (Malouf), **Supp. XII:** 220

Commentary on Macaulay's History of England, A (Firth), **IV:** 290, 291

Commentary on the "Memoirs of Mr. Fox" (Landor), **IV:** 100

Commentary on the Collected Plays of W. B. Yeats (Jeffares and Knowland), **VI:** 224; **VI:** 224

Commentary on the Complete Poems of Gerard Manley Hopkins, A (Mariani), **V:** 373n, 378n 382

Comming of Good Luck, The (Herrick), **II:** 107

Commitments, The (Doyle), **Supp. V:** 77, 80–82, 93

"Committee Man of 'The Terror,' The" (Hardy), **VI:** 22

Commodore, The (O'Brian), **Supp. XII:** 259, 260–261

Common Asphodel, The (Graves), **VII:** 261

"Common Breath, The" (Stallworthy), **Supp. X:** 292

Common Chorus, The (Harrison), **Supp. V:** 164

"Common Entry" (Warner), **Supp. VII:** 371

Common Grace, A (MacCaig), **Supp. VI:** **187,** 194

Common Pursuit (Leavis), **VII:** 234, 246

Common Reader, The (Woolf), **VII:** 22, 28, 32–33

Common Sense of War and Peace, The: World Revolution or War Unending (Wells), **VI:** 245

Commonplace and Other Short Stories (Rossetti), **V:** 260

Commonplace Book of Robert Herrick, **II:** 103

"Commonsense About the War" (Shaw), **VI:** 119, 129

Commonweal (periodical), **V:** 302

Commonweal, The: A Song for Unionists (Swinburne), **V:** 332

"Commonwealth Literature Does Not Exist" (Rushdie), **Supp. IV:** 454–455

Communication Cord, The (Friel), **Supp. V:** 124–125

Communicating Doors (Ayckbourn), **Supp. V:** 3, 9, 11, 12

Communication to My Friends, A (Moore), **VI:** 89, 99

"Communion" (Coppard), **VIII:** 88, 93

"Communist to Others, A" (Auden), **Retro. Supp. I:** 8

"Communitie" (Donne), **Retro. Supp. II:** 89

Companion to the Theatre, The (Haywood), **Supp. XII:** 135

Companions of the Day (Harris), **Supp. V:** 136, 138

Company (Beckett), **Supp. I:** 62; **Retro. Supp. I:** 29

"Company of Laughing Faces, A" (Gordimer), **Supp. II:** 232

"Company of Wolves, The" (Carter), **Supp. III:** 88

Compassion: An Ode (Hardy), **VI:** 20

"Compassionate Fool, The" (Cameron), **Supp. IX:** 24–25

Compendium of Authentic and Entertaining Voyages, A (Smollett), **IV:** 158

"Competition, The" (Dunn), **Supp. X:** 71

Complaint of Chaucer to His Purse (Chaucer), **I:** 31

Complaint of the Black Knight, The (Lydgate), **I:** 57, 60, 61, 65

Complaint of Venus, The (Chaucer), **I:** 31

Complaints (Spenser), **I:** 124

Compleat Angler, The (Walton), **II:** 131–136, **137–139,** 141–143

Compleat English Gentleman, The (Defoe), **III:** 5, 14

Compleat Gard'ner, The; or, Directions for . . . Fruit–Gardens and Kitchen–Gardens . . . (tr. Evelyn), **II:** 287

Compleat Tradesman, The (Defoe), **Retro. Supp. I:** 63

Compleat Vindication of the Licensers of the Stage, A (Johnson), **III:** 121; **Retro. Supp. I:** 141–142

"Complement, The" (Carew), **II:** 223–224

Complete Clerihews of Edward Clerihew Bentley (Ewart), **Supp. VII:** 43, 46

Complete Collected Essays (Pritchett), **Supp. III:** 313, 315

Complete Collected Stories (Pritchett), **Supp. III:** 312

Complete Collection of Genteel and Ingenious Conversation, A (Swift), **III:** 29, 36

Complete Doctor Stories, The (Dutton), **Supp. XII:** 82, 85

Complete English Tradesman, The (Defoe), **III:** 5, 14

Complete History of England . . . (Smollett), **III:** 148, 149, 158

Complete Indian Housekeeper & Cook, The: Giving the Duties of Mistress and Servants, the General Management of the House, and Practical Recipes for Cooking in All Its Branches (Steel), **Supp. XII:** 265, 267

Complete Little Ones (Ewart), **Supp. VII:** 45

Complete Plays, The (Behan), **Supp. II:** 67, 68, 69, 70, 73, 74

Complete Plays (Kane), **VIII:** 149

Complete Plays of Frances Burney, The (ed. Sabor), **Supp. III:** 64

Complete Poems (Muir), **Supp. VI:** 204

Complete Poems (Day Lewis), **Supp. III:** 130

Complete Poems and Fragments of Wilfred Owen, The (Stallworthy), **VI:** 458, 459; **Supp. X:** 292

Complete Poems of Emily Brontë, The (ed. Hatfield), **V:** 133, 152

Complete Poems of Hugh MacDiarmid, 1920–1976, The (MacDiarmid), **Supp. XII:** 201

Complete Poems of W. H. Davies, The (Davies), **Supp. XI:** 93, 95

"Complete Poetical Works of T.E. Hulme" (Hulme), **Supp. VI:** 136

Complete Saki, The (Saki), **Supp. VI:** 240

Complete Short Stories (Pritchett), **Supp. III:** 313

"Complete Stranger" (Dunn), **Supp. X:** 82

Complete Works of John Webster, The (ed. Lucas), **II:** 70n

"Complicated Nature, A" (Trevor), **Supp. IV:** 500

Complicity (Banks), **Supp. XI:** 3–4, 5, 7, 12

Compton–Burnett, Ivy, **VII:** xvii, **59–70; Supp. IV:** 506

Comte, Auguste, **V:** 428–429

Comus (Milton), **II:** 50, 159–160, 166, 175; **Retro. Supp. II:** 273–275

Comyns, Barbara, **VIII:** **53–66**

"Con Men, The" (Reading), **VIII:** 267

"Concealment, The" (Cowley), **II:** 196

"Conceit Begotten by the Eyes" (Ralegh), **I:** 148, 149

Concept of Nature in Nineteenth–Century Poetry, The (Beach), **V:** 221n

"Concentration City, The" (Ballard), **Supp. V:** 21

"Concerned Adolescent, The" (Cope), **VIII:** 77

"Concerning Geffray Teste Noir" (Morris), **V:** 293

Concerning Humour in Comedy (Congreve), **II:** 338, 341, 346, 350

"Concerning the Beautiful" (tr. Taylor), **III:** 291

Concerning the Eccentricities of Cardinal Pirelli (Firbank), **Supp. II:** 202, **220–222**

"Concerning the regal power" (King), **Supp. VI:** 158

Concerning the Relations of Great Britain, Spain, and Portugal . . . (Wordsworth), **IV:** 24

Concerning the Rule of Princes (tr. Trevisa), see *De Regimine Principum*

"Concert Party: Busseboom" (Blunden), **VI:** 428

Conciones ad Populum (Coleridge), **IV:** 56

Concluding (Green), **Supp. II:** **260–263**

Concordance to the Poems of Robert Browning, A (Broughton and Stelter), **IV:** 373

Concrete Garden, The (Dutton), **Supp. XII:** 83, 89, 97

Concrete Island (Ballard), **Supp. V:** 27, 28

Condemned Playground, The: Essays 1927–1944 (Connolly), **Supp. III:** **107–108**

"Condition of England, The" (Masterman), **VI:** viii, 273

Condition of the Working Class in England in 1844, The (Engels), **IV:** 249

"Condition of Women, The" (Oliphant), **Supp. X:** 222

"Condolence Visit" (Mistry), **Supp. X:** 140

Conduct of the Allies, The (Swift), **III:** 19, 26–27, 35; **Retro. Supp. I:** 274, 275

"Coney, The" (Muldoon), **Supp. IV:** 422

Confederacy, The (Vanbrugh), **II:** 325, 336

Confederates, The (Keneally), **Supp. IV:** 346, 348

Conference of Pleasure, A (Bacon), **I:** 265, 271

Confessio amantis (Gower), **I:** 48, 49, 50–56, 58, 321

Confession of My Faith, A, . . . (Bunyan), **II:** 253

"Confessional Poetry" (Harrison), **Supp. V:** 153

Confessions (St. Augustine), **Supp. III:** 433

Confessions of a Justified Sinner (Tennant), **Supp. IX:** 231–232

"Confessions of a Kept Ape" (McEwan), **Supp. IV:** 394

Confessions of a Young Man (Moore), **VI:** 85–86, 87, 89, 91, 96

Confessions of an English Opium–Eater (De Quincey), **III:** 338; **IV:** xviii, 141, 143, 148–149, 150–153, 154, 155

Confessions of an Inquiring Spirit (Coleridge), **IV:** 53, 56

Confessions of an Irish Rebel (Behan), **Supp. II:** 63, 64–65, 71, 75, 76

"Confessions of an Only Child" (Malouf), **Supp. XII:** 220

Confidence (James), **VI:** 67

Confidence Man, The (Melville), **Supp. IV:** 444

Confidential Agent, The (Greene), **Supp. I:** 3, 4, 7, 10; **Retro. Supp. II:** 155–156

Confidential Chats with Boys (Hollinghurst), **Supp. X:** 119, 121–122

Confidential Clerk, The (Eliot), **VII:** 161–162; **Retro. Supp. II:** 132

"Confined Love" (Donne), **Retro. Supp. II:** 89

Confines of Criticism, The (Housman), **VI:** 164

"Confirmation, The" (Muir), **Supp. VI:** 206

"Confirmation Suit, The" (Behan), **Supp. II:** 66–67

"Conflict, The" (Day Lewis), **Supp. III:** 120, 126

Confusion (Howard), **Supp. XI:** 145, 146, 147, 148

Confusions (Ayckbourn), **Supp. V:** 3, 11

Confutation of Tyndale's Answer (More), **Supp. VII:** 245

Congreve, William, **II:** 269, 289, 302, 304, 325, 336, **338–350**, 352; **III:** 45, 62

Coningsby (Disraeli), **IV:** xii, xx, 294, 300–303, 305, 307, 308; **V:** 4, 22

Conjugal Lewdness; or, Matrimonial Whoredom (Defoe), **III:** 14

"Conjugation" (Crawford), **Supp. XI:** 79–80

"Conjugial Angel, The" (Byatt), **Supp. IV:** 153

Connell, John, **VI:** xv, xxxiii

"Connoisseur" (MacCaig), **Supp. VI:** 192–193

Connolly, Cyril, **VI:** 363, 371; **VII:** xvi, 37, 138, 310; **Supp. II:** 156, 199, 489, 493; **Supp. III:** **95–113**

Connolly, T. L., **V:** 442n, 445, 447, 450, 451

"Connor Girls, The" (O'Brien), **Supp. V:** 339–340

Conny–Catching (Greene), **VIII:** 144

Conquest, Robert, **Supp. IV:** 256

Conquest of Granada by the Spaniards, The (Dryden), **II:** 294, 305

"Conquest of Syria, The: If Complete" (Lawrence), **Supp. II:** 287

Conrad, Joseph, **VI:** xi, **133–150**, 170, 193, 242, 270, 279–280, 321; **VII:** 122; **Retro. Supp. II:** **69–83**; list of short stories, **VI:** 149–150; **Supp. I:** 397–398; **Supp. II:** 290; **Supp. IV:** 5, 163, 233, 250, 251, 302, 403

Conrad in the Nineteenth Century (Watt), **VI:** 149

"Conrad's Darkness" (Naipaul), **Supp. I:** 397, 402, 403

Conrad's Prefaces to His Works (Garnett), **VI:** 149

"Conquistador" (Hope), **Supp. VII:** 158

Conscience of the Rich, The (Snow), **VII:** 324, 326–327

"Conscious" (Owen), **VI:** 451

Conscious and Verbal (Murray), **Supp. VII:** 271, 286–287

"Conscious Mind's Intelligible Structure, The: A Debate" (Hill), **Supp. V:** 183

"Conscript" (Larkin), **Supp. I:** 277

Conscription for Ireland: A Warning to England (Russell), **VIII:** 288

Consequently I Rejoice (Jennings), **Supp. V:** 217

Conservationist, The (Gordimer), **Supp. II:** 230–231, 232, 239

"Consider" (Auden), **Retro. Supp. I:** 5

Consider (Rossetti), **V:** 260

Consider Phlebas (Banks), **Supp. XI:** 1, 10, 11–12

Consider the Lilies (Smith, I. C.), **Supp. IX:** 209–210

Considerations Touching the Likeliest Means to Remove Hirelings out of the Church (Milton), **II:** 176

"Considering the Snail" (Gunn), **Supp. IV:** 262–263

"Consolation" (Stallworthy), **Supp. X:** 292

Consolation of Philosophy (Boethius), **I:** 31; **Retro. Supp. II:** 36, 296–297

Consolations (Fuller), **Supp. VII:** 79, 80, 81

Consolidator, The (Defoe), **III:** 4, 13

Constance (Durrell), **Supp. I:** 119, 120

"Constant" (Cornford), **VIII:** 107

Constant, Benjamin, **Supp. IV:** 125, 126, 136

Constant Couple, The; or, A Trip to the Jubilee (Farquhar), **II:** 352, 356–357, 364

Constant Wife, The (Maugham), **VI:** 369

"Constantine and Silvester" (Gower), **I:** 53–54

Constantine the Great (Lee), **II:** 305

"Constellation" (Kelman), **Supp. V:** 255

"Constellation, The" (Vaughan), **II:** 186, 189

Constitutional (periodical), **V:** 19

Constitutional History of England, The (Hallam), **IV:** 283

Constructing Postmodernism (McHale), **Supp. IV:** 112

"Construction for I. K. Brunel" (Morgan, E.), **Supp. IX:** 158

Constructions (Frayn), **Supp. VII:** 51, 53, 58, 64

Contacts (Carey), **Supp. XII:** 51

"Contemplation" (Thompson), **V:** 442, 443

"Contemporaries" (Cornford), **VIII:** 105

Contemporaries of Shakespeare (Swinburne), **V:** 333

Contemporary Authors Autobiography Series (ed. Sarkissian), **Supp. XI:** 243, 244, 245, 249, 250, 251, 252

"Contemporary Film of Lancasters in Action, A" (Ewart), **Supp. VII:** 44

"Contemporary Sagas", *See Samtíðarsögur*

Continual Dew (Betjeman), **VII:** 365

Continuation of the Complete History, A (Smollett), **III:** 148, 149, 158

Continuous: 50 Sonnets from "The School of Elegance" (Harrison), **Supp. V:** 150

Contractor, The (Storey), **Supp. I:** 408, 416–417, 418

Contrarini Fleming (Disraeli), **IV:** xix, 292–293, 294, 296–297, 299, 308

Contrary Experience, The (Read), **VI:** 416

"Contrasts" (Smith, I. C.), **Supp. IX:** 216

Contre–Machiavel (Gentillet), **I:** 283

"Controversial Tree of Time, The" (Brathwaite), **Supp. XII:** 43

Conundrum (Morris, J.), **Supp. X:** 171– 174, 179, 184

"Convenience" (Murphy), **Supp. V:** 328

"Convergence of the Twain, The" (Hardy), **II:** 69; **VI:** 16; **Retro. Supp. I:** 119–120

"Conversation of prayer, The" (Thomas), **Supp. I:** 178

"Conversation, The" (Gunn), **Supp. IV:** 272; **Supp. IV:** 273

"Conversation with a Cupboard Man" (McEwan), **Supp. IV:** 392

"Conversation with Calliope" (Hope), **Supp. VII:** 162–163

Conversation with My Younger Self (Plomer), **Supp. XI:** 223

Conversations at Curlow Creek, The (Malouf), **Supp. XII:** 229–230

Conversations in Ebury Street (Moore), **V:** 129, 153; **VI:** 89, 98, 99

Conversations of James Northcote, Esq., R. A. (Hazlitt), **IV:** 134, 140

"Conversations with Goethe" (Lowry), **Supp. III:** 286

ConVERSations with Nathaniel Mackey (Brathwaite), **Supp. XII:** 46 inline"Conversion" (Hulme), **Supp. VI:** 136

"Conversion" (Smith, I. C.), **Supp. IX:** 221

"Convert, The" (Hart), **Supp. XI:** 123, 124

"Convict and the Fiddler, The" (Hardy), **Retro. Supp. I:** 121

Convivio (Dante), **I:** 27

Cook, D., **III:** 322

Cook, Eliza, **IV:** 259, 320

Cook, J. D., **V:** 279

Cooke, W., **III:** 184n

"Cool Web, The" (Graves), **VII:** 266

"Coole Park" (Yeats), **VI:** 212; **Retro. Supp. I:** 336

"Coole Park and Ballylee" (Yeats), **VI:** 215; **Retro. Supp. I:** 336

Cooper, Lettice Ulpha, **V:** x, xxvii, 397, 398

Cooper, William, **VII:** xxi, xxxvii

"Co–ordination" (Forster), **VI:** 399

Coover, Robert, **Supp. IV:** 116

Cope, Wendy, **VIII:** **67–84**

Copeland, T. W., **III:** 245n, 250

Copenhagen (Frayn), **Supp. VII:** 63–64

Coppard, A. E., **VIII:** **85–99**

"Coppersmith" (Murphy), **Supp. V:** 325

Coppy of a Letter Written to . . . Parliament, A (Suckling), **II:** 238

Coral Island, The (Ballantyne), **Supp. I:** 68; **Retro. Supp. I:** 96

Corbett, Sir Julian, **I:** 146

Cordelia Gray novels (James) **Supp. IV:** 335–337

"Corinna's Going a–Maying" (Herrick), **II:** 109–110

"Coriolan" (Eliot), **VII:** 152–153, 158

Coriolanus (Shakespeare), **I:** 318; **II:** 70

Coriolanus (Thomson), **Supp. III:** 411, 423

Corke, Helen, **VII:** 93

Corker's Freedom (Berger), **Supp. IV:** 79, 84, 85

Corkery, Daniel, **Supp. V:** 37, 41

"Cornac and His Wife, The" (Lewis), **VII:** 77, 78

Corneille, Pierre, **II:** 261, 270, 271

Cornelia (Kyd), **I:** 162, 220

Cornélie (Garaier), **I:** 220

Cornelius: A Business Affair in Three Transactions (Priestley), **VII:** 224

Corner That Held Them, The (Warner), **Supp. VII:** 376, 377–378

"Corner of the Eye, The" (Longley), **VIII:** 169

"Cornet Love" (McGuckian), **Supp. V:** 291

Cornford, Frances, **VIII:** **101–115**

Cornhill (periodical), **V:** xxii, 1, 20, 279; **VI:** 31

"Cornish April" (Cornford), **VIII:** 106

"Cornish Heroic Song for Valda Trevlyn" (MacDiarmid), **Supp. XII:** 214

Corno di Bassetto, pseud. of George Bernard Shaw

Cornwall, Barry, **IV:** 311

Cornwall, David John Moore, *see* le Carré, John

Cornwallis, Sir William, **III:** 39–40

Coronation Everest (Morris, J.), **Supp. X:** 175, 179

"Coronet, The" (Marvell), **II:** 113, 211, 216

Coronet for His Mistress Philosophy, A (Chapman), **I:** 234

"Corposant" (Redgrove), **Supp. VI:** 228

"Corpse and the Flea, The" (Powys), **VIII:** 255

"Corregidor" (Nicholson), **Supp. VI:** 214

Correspondence (Flaubert), **V:** 353

Correspondence (Swift), **III:** 24

Correspondence of James Boswell and John Johnston . . . (ed. Walker), **III:** 249

Correspondence . . . of James Boswell Relating to the "Life of Johnson," The (ed. Waingrow), **III:** 249

Correspondence of James Boswell with . . . the Club, The (ed. Fifer), **III:** 249

Correspondences (Stevenson), **Supp. VI:** 254, 256, **257–260,** 261

Corrida at San Feliu, The (Scott), **Supp. I:** 259, 263, 266

"Corridor, The" (Sisson), **Supp. XI:** 258

Corridors of Power (Snow), **VII:** xxvi, 324, 330–331

Corrigan (Blackwood), **Supp. IX:** 7–8, 13–14, 16

"Corruption" (Vaughan), **II:** 185, 186, 189

Corsair, The (Byron), **IV:** xvii, 172, 173, 175, 192; *see also* Turkish tales

Corson, James C., **IV:** 27, 38–40

"Corymbus for Autumn" (Thompson), **V:** 442

"Cosmologist" (Dunn), **Supp. X:** 70

Cosmopolitans (Maugham), **VI:** 370

"Cost of Life" (Motion), **Supp. VII:** 265, 266

"Costa Pool Bums" (Warner), **Supp. XI:** 294

"Cottage at Chigasaki, The" (Blunden), **Supp. XI:** 47

"Cottage Hospital, The" (Betjeman), **VII:** 375

Cotter's England (Stead), **Supp. IV:** 473– 476

"Cotter's Saturday Night, The" (Burns), **III:** 311, 313, 315, 318

Cottle, Joseph, **IV:** 44, 45, 52, 56, 59

Cotton, Charles, **II:** 131 134, 137

Coué, Emile, **VI:** 264

"Could Be" (Thomas), **Supp. XII:** 290

"Council of the Seven Deadly Sins, The" (Nicholson), **Supp. VI:** 214–215

Count Belisarius (Graves), **VII:** xviii, 258

Count Julian (Landor), **IV:** 89, 96, 100

Count Robert of Paris (Scott), **IV:** 39

"Countdown" (Ayckbourn), **Supp. V:** 2, 4, 11

Counter–Attack (Sassoon), **VI:** 430, 431

"Counter Attack" (Stallworthy), **Supp. X:** 298

Counterblast (McLuhan), **VII:** 71n

Counterclock World (Dick), **Supp. IV:** 41

Counterparts (Fuller), **Supp. VII:** 72, 74

Counterpoint (Thomas), **Supp. XII:** 290, 291

"Counterpoint in Herbert" (Hayes), **Retro. Supp. II:** 181

Countess Cathleen, The (Yeats), **VI:** 87; **Retro. Supp. I:** 326

Countess Cathleen and Various Legends and Lyrics, The (Yeats), **VI:** 211, 309

Countess of Pembroke, **I:** 161, 163–169, 218

Countess of Pembroke's Arcadia, The (Sidney), *see Arcadia*
"Countess of Pembroke's Dream" (Hope), **Supp. VII:** 158
"Country Bedroom, The" (Cornford), **VIII:** 105
"Country Bedroom" (MacCaig), **Supp. VI:** 187
Country Comets (Day Lewis), **Supp. III:** 117, 120–121
"Country Dance" (MacCaig), **Supp. VI:** 192
"Country for Old Men, A" (Smith, I. C.), **Supp. IX:** 224
Country Girls, The (O'Brien), **Supp. V:** 333–336
Country Girls Trilogy and Epilogue, The (O'Brien), **Supp. V:** 338
"Country House" (MacCaig), **Supp. VI:** 185–186, 194
Country House, The (Galsworthy), **VI:** 271, 272, 273, 275, 278, 282
Country House, The (Vanbrugh), **II:** 325, 333, 336
"Country Kitchen" (Dunn), **Supp. X:** 78
Country Life, (Ackroyd), **Supp. VI:** 3
"Country Measures" (Warner), **Supp. VII:** 371
"Country Music" (Fallon), **Supp. XII:** 110
"Country of the Blind, The" (Wells), **VI:** 234
Country of the Blind, The, and Other Stories (Wells), **VI:** 228, 244
"Country Sunday" (Coppard), **VIII:** 88
"Country Walk, A" (Kinsella), **Supp. V:** 262
Country-Wife, The (Wycherley), **I:** 243; **II:** 307, 308, **314–318,** 321, 360
"Coup: A Story, A" (Chatwin), **Supp. IV:** 167
"Coup de Poing" (Crawford), **Supp. XI:** 68–69
"Courage Means Running" (Empson), **Supp. II:** 191
Courier (periodical), **IV:** 50
Course of Lectures on the English Law,A: Delivered at the University of Oxford 1767–1773 (Johnson), **Retro. Supp. I:** 143
Court and the Castle, The (West), **Supp. III:** 438
"Court of Cupid, The" (Spenser), **I:** 123
"Court Revolt, The" (Gunn), **Supp. IV:** 257
Courte of Venus, The (Wyatt), **I:** 97
"Courter, The" (Rushdie), **Supp. IV:** 438
"Courtesies of the Interregnum" (Gunn), **Supp. IV:** 277
"Courtship of Ossian, The" (Macpherson), **VIII:** 186
Courtyards in Delft (Mahon), **Supp. VI:** 173
"Courtyards in Delft" (Mahon), **Supp. VI:** 174
Cousin Henry (Trollope), **V:** 102
"Cousin Maria" (James), **VI:** 69
Cousin Phillis (Gaskell), **V:** 1, 2, 4, 8, 11, 15

Cousin Rosamund: A Saga of the Century (West), **Supp. III:** 443
Cousine Bette (Balzac), **V:** xx, 17
"Cousins, The" (Burne–Jones), **VI:** 167, 169
Covent Garden Drolery, The (Behn), **Supp. III:** 36
Covent Garden Journal, The (periodical), **III:** 103–104; **Retro. Supp. I:** 81
Covent Garden Tragedy, The (Fielding), **III:** 97, 105
Cover Her Face (James), **Supp. II:** 127; **Supp. IV:** 321–323
Coverdale, Myles, **I:** 377
"Covering End" (James), **VI:** 52, 69
Coward, Noël, **Supp. II:** **139–158**
Cowasjee, S., **VII:** 4
Cowell, Edward, **IV:** 342–346
Cowley, Abraham, **II:** 123, 179, **194–200, 202,** 236, 256, 259, 275, 347; **III:** 40, 118; **Retro. Supp. I:** 144
Cowper, William, **II:** 119n, 196, 240; **III:** 173, **207–220,** 282; **IV:** xiv–xvi, 93, 184, 281
"Cowper's Grave" (Browning), **IV:** 312, 313
"Cows on Killing Day, The" (Murray), **Supp. VII:** 282
"Cowyard Gates" (Murray), **Supp. VII:** 276
Cox, Charles Brian, **VI:** xi, xxxiii
"Cox's Diary" (Thackeray), *see* "Barber Cox and the Cutting of His Comb"
Coxcomb, The (Beaumont, Fletcher, Massinger), **II:** 66
Coxhead, Elizabeth, **VI:** xiv, xxxiii
"Coxon Fund, The" (James), **VI:** 69
Coyle, William, pseud. of Thomas Keneally
C. P. Snow (Karl), **VII:** 341
"Crab Feast, The" (Malouf), **Supp. XII:** 220
Crabbe, George, **III:** **272–287,** 338; **IV:** xv, xvii, 103, 326; **V:** 6; **VI:** 378
Crack, The (Tennant), *see Time of the Crack, The*
Cracking India (Sidhwa), **Supp. V:** 62
Craig, Hardin, **I:** 187, 326
Craig, W. J., **I:** 326
Craigie, Mrs., **VI:** 87
"Craigvara House" (Mahon), **Supp. VI:** 174
Crampton Hodnet (Pym), **Supp. II:** **364–366,** 370
Crane, Stephen, **VI:** 320; **Supp. IV:** 116
Cranford (Gaskell), **V:** xxi, 1–4, 8–10, 11, 14, 15
"Crankshaft" (Murray), **Supp. VII:** 283
"Crapy Cornelia" (James), **VI:** 69
Crash (Ballard), **Supp. V:** 19, 27, 28, 33–34
Crashaw, Richard, **II:** 90–91, 113, 122, 123, 126, **179–184, 200–201;** **V:** 325
Crave (Kane), **VIII:** 148, 150–151, 159–160
"Craven Arms" (Coppard), **VIII:** 90
"Craving for Spring" (Lawrence), **VII:** 118
Crawford, Robert, **Supp. XI:** **67–84**

"Crawford's Consistency" (James), **VI:** 69
Creative Element, The (Spender), **Supp. II:** 491
Creative Uses of Homosexuality in E. M. Forster, Ronald Firbank, and L. P. Hartley, The (Mistry), **Supp. X:** 120–121
"Creative Writer's Suicide, The" (Thomas), **Supp. XII:** 285
"Creative Writing: Can It/Should It Be Taught?" (Lodge), **Supp. IV:** 381
"Creator in Vienna" (Jennings), **Supp. V:** 218
Creators of Wonderland (Mespoulet), **V:** 266
Crediting Poetry (Heaney), **Retro. Supp. I:** 125
"Credits" (Stallworthy), **Supp. X:** 298
Creed or Chaos? and Other Essays in Popular Theology (Sayers), **Supp. III:** 336
Creighton, Joan, **Supp. IV:** 244
"Creosote" (Adcock), **Supp. XII:** 12
Cripple of Inishmaan, The (McDonagh), **Supp. XII:** 233, 240–241, 242–243, 245
Cricket Country (Blunden), **Supp. XI:** 37
Cricket on the Hearth, The (Dickens), **V:** 71
Crime in Kensington (Caudwell), **Supp. IX:** 35
Crime of the Century, The (Amis), **Supp. II:** 12
Crime Omnibus (Fuller), **Supp. VII:** 70
Crime Times Three (James), **Supp. IV:** 323, 324, 325
Crimes (Churchill), **Supp. IV:** 181
"Criminal Ballad"(Hughes), **Supp. I:** 354
Criminal Case, A (Swinburne), **V:** 333
Criminal Minded (Rankin), **Supp. X:** 257
Crimson in the Tricolour, The (O'Casey), **VII:** 12
"Crinoline" (Thackeray), **V:** 22
"Crippled Bloom" (Coppard), **VIII:** 90
Crisis, The, a Sermon (Fielding), **III:** 105
Crisis Examined, The (Disraeli), **IV:** 308
Crisis in Physics, The (Caudwell), **Supp. IX:** 33, 43, 45–46
Crist, **Retro. Supp. II:** 303
Criterion (periodical), **VI:** 248; **VII:** xv 143, 165
Critic (periodical), **V:** 134
Critic, The (Sheridan), **III:** 253, **263–266,** 270
"Critic, The" (Wilde), **Retro. Supp. II:** 367
"Critic as Artist, The" (Wilde), **V:** 407, 408, 409
Critical and Historical Essays (Macaulay), **IV:** xx, 272, 277, **278–282,** 291
Critical Bibliography of Katherine Mansfield, The (Mantz), **VII:** 182
Critical Essays (Orwell), **VII:** 282
Critical Essays of the Seventeenth Century (Spingarn), **II:** 256n
Critical Essays on George Eliot (Hardy), **V:** 201

Critical Essays on the Poetry of Tennyson (ed. Killham), **IV:** 323*n*, 338, 339

Critical Observations on the Sixth Book of the Aeneid (Gibbon), **III:** 233

Critical Review (periodical), **III:** 147–148, 149, 179, 188

Critical Strictures on the New Tragedy of Elvira . . . (Boswell, Dempster, Erskine), **III:** 246

Critical Studies of the Works of Charles Dickens (Gissing), **V:** 437

Criticism on Art: And Sketches of the Picture Galleries of England (Hazlitt), **IV:** 140

Crito (Plato), **Supp. IV:** 13

Croker, J. W., **IV:** 280

Crome Yellow (Huxley), **VII:** 197, 200

Cromwell (Carlyle), *see Oliver Cromwell's Letters and Speeches*

Cromwell (Storey), **Supp. I:** 418

Cromwell's Army (Firth), **II:** 241

Cronica tripertita (Gower), **I:** 50

Crook, Arthur, **Supp. IV:** 25

Crooked House (Christie), **Supp. II:** 125

Croquet Castles (Carroll), **V:** 274

Cross, John Walter, **V:** 13, 198, 200

Cross, Wilbur L, **III:** 125, 126, 135

Cross Channel (Barnes), **Supp. IV:** 65, 67, 75–76

"Crossing alone the nighted ferry" (Housman), **VI:** 161

Crossing the Border: Essays on Scottish Literature (Morgan, E.), **Supp. IX:** 162

Crossing the River (Phillips), **Supp. V:** 380, 386, 390–391

Crotchet Castle (Peacock), **IV:** xix, 165–166, 169, 170

Crow (Hughes), **Supp. I: 350–354,** 363; **Retro. Supp. II:** 206–208

"Crow Alights" (Hughes), **Supp. I:** 352

"Crow Blacker than Ever" (Hughes), **Supp. I:** 353

"Crow Hears Fate Knock on the Door" (Hughes), **Supp. I:** 350

"Crow on the Beach" (Hughes), **Supp. I:** 352; **Retro. Supp. II:** 207

Crow Road, The (Banks), **Supp. XI:** 5

"Crow Tyrannosaurus" (Hughes), **Supp. I:** 352

"Crowdieknowe" (MacDiarmid), **Supp. XII:** 205

"Crow's Account of the Battle" (Hughes), **Supp. I:** 353

"Crow's Last Stand" (Hughes), **Retro. Supp. II:** 207–208

"Crow's Song of Himself" (Hughes), **Supp. I:** 353

"Crowd of Birds and Children, The" (Graham), **Supp. VII:** 110

Crowley, Aleister, **VI:** 374; **Supp. II:** 204

Crowley, Robert, **I:** 1, 3

Crown of All Homer's Works, The (Chapman), **I:** 236

Crown of Life, The (Gissing), **V:** 437

Crown of the Year (Fry), **Supp. III:** 195

Crown of Wild Olive, The (Ruskin), **V:** 184

"Crowning of Offa, The" (Hill), **Supp. V:** 195

Crowning Privilege, The (Graves), **VII:** 260, 268

"Crowson" (Nye), **Supp. X:** 201

"Croy. Ee. Gaw. Lonker. Pit." (Crawford), **Supp. XI:** 81

Cruel Sea, The (film, Ambler), **Supp. IV:** 3

"Cruelty and Love" (Lawrence), **VII:** 118

Cruelty of a Stepmother, The, **I:** 218

"Cruiskeen Lawn" (O'Nolan), **Supp. II:** 323, **329–333,** 336

Crusader Castles (Lawrence), **Supp. II:** 283, 284

Crux Ansata: An Indictment of the Roman Catholic Church (Wells), **VI:** 242, 244

"Cry Hope, Cry Fury!" (Ballard), **Supp. V:** 26

"Cry of the Children, The" (Browning), **IV:** xx 313

"Cry of the Human, The" (Browning), **IV:** 313

Cry of the Owl, The (Highsmith), **Supp. V:** 173

Cry, The Beloved Country (Paton), **Supp. II:** 341, 342, 343, 344, **345–350,** 351, 354

Cry, the Peacock (Desai), **Supp. V:** 54, 58–59, 75

"Cryptics, The" (Ewart), **Supp. VII:** 39

Crystal and Fox (Friel), **Supp. V:** 118–119

Crystal World, The (Ballard), **Supp. V:** 24, 25–26, 34

"Crystals Like Blood" (MacDiarmid), **Supp. XII:** 215

C. S. Lewis (Wilson), **Supp. VI:** 304, **305**

Cuala Press, **VI:** 221

"Cub" (Reading), **VIII:** 268

Cub, at Newmarket, The (Boswell), **III:** 247

Cuckold in Conceit, The (Vanbrugh), **II:** 337

"Cuckoo, The" (Thomas), **Supp. III:** 399–400

Cuckoo in the Nest, The (Oliphant), **Supp. X:** 220

Cuirassiers of the Frontier, The (Graves), **VII:** 267

"Culture" (Dutton), **Supp. XII:** 94

Culture and Anarchy (Arnold), **III:** 23; **V:** 203, 206, 213, 215, 216

Culture and Society (Williams), **Supp. IV:** 380

Cumberland, George, **IV:** 47

Cumberland, Richard, **II:** 363; **III:** 257

Cumberland and Westmoreland (Nicholson), **Supp. VI:** 223

Cunningham, William, **VI:** 385

"Cup Too Low, A" (Ewart), **Supp. VII:** 39–40

"Cupid and Psyche" (tr. Pater), **V:** 351

"Cupid; or, The Atom" (Bacon), **I:** 267

Cupid's Revenge (Beaumont and Fletcher), **II:** 46, 65

Curate in Charge, The (Oliphant), **Supp. X:** 219–220

"Curate's Friend, The" (Forster), **VI:** 399

"Curate's Walk; The," (Thackeray), **V:** 25

Cure at Troy, The (Heaney), **Retro. Supp. I:** 131

Cure for a Cuckold, A (Rowley and Webster), **II:** 69, 83, 85

Curiosissima Curatoria (Carroll), **V:** 274

Curious Fragments (Lamb), **IV:** 79

"Curious if True" (Gaskell), **V:** 15

Curious Relations (ed. Plomer), **Supp. XI:** 221

"Curiosity" (Reid), **Supp. VII:** 330

Curlew River: A Parable for Church Performance (Plomer), **Supp. XI:** 222

"Curse, The" (Healy), **Supp. IX:** 103–104

Curse of Eve, The (Steel), **Supp. XII:** 276

Curse of Kehama, The (Southey), **IV:** 65, 66, 71, 217

Curse of Minerva, The (Byron), **IV:** 192

Curtain (Christie), **Supp. II:** 124, 125, 134

Curtis, Anthony, **VI:** xiii, xxxiii, 372

Curtis, L. P., **III:** 124*n*, 127*n*

Curtmantle (Fry), **Supp. III:** 195, **206–207,** 208

Custom of the Country, The (Fletcher [and Massinger]), **II:** 66, 340

"Custom–House, The" (Hawthorne), **Supp. IV:** 116

"Customs" (Crawford), **Supp. XI:** 74

Cut by the County (Braddon), **VIII:** 49

"Cut Grass" (Larkin), **Supp. I:** 285

Cut–Rate Kingdom, The (Keneally), **Supp. IV:** 346

"Cutting Trail" (Dutton), **Supp. XII:** 93–94

Cyclopean Mistress, The (Redgrove), **Supp. VI:** 231

"Cygnus A." (Thomas), **Supp. IV:** 490, 491

Cymbeline (Shakespeare), **I:** 322

Cymbeline Refinished (Shaw), **VI:** 129

"Cynddylan on a Tractor" (Thomas), **Supp. XII:** 283

"Cynic at Kilmainham Jail, A" (Boland), **Supp. V:** 36

Cynthia's Revels (Jonson), **I:** 346; **Retro. Supp. I:** 158, 160

"Cypress and Cedar" (Harrison), **Supp. V:** 161

Cyrano de Bergerac, **III:** 24

Cyrano de Bergerac (tr.. Fry), **Supp. III:** 195

Cyril Connolly: Journal and Memoirs (ed. Pryce–Jones), **Supp. III:** 96, 97, 112

"Cyril Tourneur" (Swinburne), **V:** 332

D. *G. Rossetti: A Critical Essay* (Ford), **VI:** 332

"D. G. Rossetti as a Translator" (Doughty), **V:** 246

D. H. Lawrence: A Calendar of His Works (Sugar), **VII:** 104, 115, 123

D. H. Lawrence: Novelist (Leavis), **VII:** 101, 234–235, 252–253

Da Silva da Silva's Cultivated Wilderness (Harris), **Supp. V:** 139, 140

Daborne, Robert, **II:** 37, 45

Dad's Tale (Ayckbourn), **Supp. V:** 2

"Daedalus" (Reid), **Supp. VII:** 331

"Daedalus; or, The Mechanic" (Bacon), **I:** 267

Daemon of the World, The (Shelley), **IV:** 209

Daffodil Murderer, The (Sassoon), **VI:** 429

"Daffodil Time" (Brown), **Supp. VI:** 72

Dahl, Roald, Supp. **IV: 201–227,** 449

Daiches, David, **V:** ix

Daily Graphic (periodical), **VI:** 350

Daily Life of the Aztecs (tr. O'Brian), **Supp. XII:** 252

Daily News (periodical), **VI:** 335

Daily Worker (periodical), **VI:** 242

Daisy Miller (James), **VI: 31–32,** 69

Dale, Colin (pseud., Lawrence), **Supp. II:** 295

Dali, Salvador, **Supp. IV:** 424

Dalinda; or, The Double Marriage (Haywood), **Supp. XII:** 144

Dalkey Archive, The (O'Nolan), **Supp. II:** 322, **337–338**

Dallas, Eneas Sweetland, **V:** 207

"Dalziel's Ghost" (Hill, R.), **Supp. IX:** 114

Damage (film, Hare), **Supp. IV:** 282, 292

Damage (play, Hare), **Supp. IV:** 282, 292

"Damnation of Byron, The" (Hope), **Supp. VII:** 159

Dampier, William, **III:** 7, 24

"Danac" (Galsworthy), *see Country House, The*

Danae (Rembrandt), **Supp. IV:** 89

Dan Leno and the Limehouse Golem (Ackroyd), **Supp. VI:** 10 13

Danby, J. F., **II:** 46, 53, 64

"Dance, The" (Kinsella), **Supp. V:** 271

Dance of Death, The, **I:** 15

Dance of Death, The (Strindberg), **Supp. I:** 57

"Dance the Putrefact" (Redgrove), **Supp. VI:** 234

Dance to the Music of Time, A (Powell), **VII:** xxi, 343, **347–353; Supp. II:** 4

Dancing Hippo, The" (Motion), **Supp. VII:** 257

Dancing Mad (Davies), **Supp. XI:** 92

Dancourt, Carton, **II:** 325, 336

"Dandies and Dandies" (Beerbohm), **Supp. II:** 46

Dangerous Corner (Priestley), **VII:** 223

Dangerous Love (Okri), **Supp. V:** 349, 359, 360

Dangerous Play: Poems 1974–1984 (Motion), **Supp. VII:** 251, 254, 255, 256–257, 264

Daniel, **Retro. Supp. II:** 301

Daniel, Samuel, **I:** 162

Daniel Deronda (Eliot), **V:** xxiv, 190, 197–198, 200; **Retro. Supp. II:** 115–116

Daniel Martin (Fowles), **Supp. I:** 291, 292, 293, **304–308,** 310

D'Annunzio, Gabriele, **V:** 310

"Danny Deever" (Kipling), **VI:** 203

Danny, the Champion of the World (Dahl), **Supp. IV:** 214, 223

"Dans un Omnibus de Londre" (Fuller), **Supp. VII:** 80

Dante Alighieri, **II:** 75, 148; **III:** 306; **IV:** 93, 187; **Supp. IV:** 439, 493; **Retro. Supp. I:** 123–124

Dante and His Circle (Rossetti), **V:** 245

"Dante and the Lobster" (Beckett), **Retro. Supp. I:** 19

"Dante at Verona" (Rossetti), **V:** 239, 240

"Dante ... Bruno. Vico ... Joyce" (Beckett), **Retro. Supp. I:** 17

Dante's Drum Kit (Dunn), **Supp. X:** 78–80

"Dantis Tenebrae" (Rossetti), **V:** 243

Danvers, Charles, **IV:** 60

Daphnaida (Spenser), **I:** 124

"Daphne" (Sitwell), **VII:** 133

"'Daphne with Her Thighs in Bark' [Ezra Pound]" (Boland), **Supp. V:** 39

"Daphnis, an Elegiac Eclogue" (Vaughan), **II:** 185

"Daphnis and Chloe" (Marvell), **II:** 209, 211, 212

"Daphnis and Chloe" (tr. Moore), **VI:** 89

D'Arcy, Margaretta, **Supp. II:** 21, 29, 30, 31, 32–38, 39, 40–41

Darcy's Utopia (Weldon), **Supp. IV:** 528–529, 531

Dark-Adapted Eye, A (Rendell), **Supp. IX:** 201–203

"Dark Angel, The," (Johnson), **VI:** 211

Dark As the Grave Wherein My Friend Is Laid (Lowry), **Supp. III:** 274–275, 279, 280, **283–284**

"Dark Crossroads, The" (Dunn), **Supp. X:** 77

"Dark Dialogues, The" (Graham), **Supp. VII:** 114

Dark Flower, The (Galsworthy), **VI:** 274

Dark Frontier, The (Ambler), **Supp. IV:** 1, 3, 5–7

Dark Is Light Enough, The (Fry), **Supp. III:** 195, 203–204, 207

Dark Labyrinth (Durrell), *see Cefalû*

"Dark Lady, The" (Russell), **VIII:** 290

Dark Lady of the Sonnets, The (Shaw), **VI:** 115, 129

Dark Matter (Kerr), **Supp. XII:** 197–198

Dark Night's Work, A (Gaskell), **V:** 15

Dark Places of the Heart (Stead), *see Cotter's England*

"Dark Rapture" (Russell), **VIII:** 290

Dark Side of the Moon, The (anon.), **Supp. IV:** 100

Dark Sisters, The (Kavan), **Supp. VII:** 205, 207

Dark Tide, The (Brittain), **Supp. X:** 37, 41

"Dark Times" (Harrison), **Supp. V:** 156–157

Dark Tower, The (MacNeice), **VII:** 407, 408

Darker Ends (Nye), **Supp. X:** 193, 200–202, 204

"Darkling Thrush, The" (Hardy), **VI:** 16; **Retro. Supp. I:** 119

Dark-Eyed Lady (Coppard), **VIII:** 89

Darkness at Noon (Koestler), **V:** 49; **Supp. I:** 22, 24, 27, 28, 29–30, 32, 33; **Supp IV:** 74

Darkness Visible (Golding), **Supp. I: 83–86; Retro. Supp. I:** 101–102

Darling, You Shouldn't Have Gone to So Much Trouble (Blackwood), **Supp. IX:** 15

Darwin, Charles, **Supp. II:** 98, 100, 105–107, 119; **Supp. IV:** 6, 11, 460; **Supp. VII: 17–31**

Darwin, Erasmus, **Supp. II:** 106, 107; **Supp. III:** 360

"Darwin Among the Machines" (Butler), **Supp. II:** 98, 99

Darwin and Butler: Two Versions of Evolution (Willey), **Supp. II:** 103

"Darwin and Divinity" (Stephen), **V:** 284

Das Leben Jesu (tr. Eliot), **V:** 189, 200

Daughter of Jerusalem (Maitland), **Supp. XI:** 163, 165–166

Daughter of the East (Bhutto), **Supp. IV:** 455

"Daughter of the House" (Dutton), **Supp. XII:** 87

Daughter-in-Law, The (Lawrence), **VII:** 119, 121

Daughters and Sons (Compton–Burnett), **VII:** 60, 63, 64–65

"Daughters of the Late Colonel, The" (Mansfield), **VII:** 175, 177, 178

"Daughters of the Vicar" (Lawrence), **VII.** 114

"Daughters of War" (Rosenberg), **VI:** 434

Davenant, Charles, **II:** 305

Davenant, Sir William, **I:** 327; **II:** 87, 185, 196, 259

Davenport, Arnold, **IV:** 227

David, Jacques–Louis, **Supp. IV:** 122

David and Bethsabe (Peele), **I:** 198, 206–207

"David Balfour" (Stevenson), *see Catriona*

David Copperfield (Dickens), **V:** xxi, 7, 41, 42, 44, 59–62, 63, 67, 71

David Lodge (Bergonzi), **Supp. IV:** 364

Davideis (Cowley), **II:** 195, 198, 202

Davidson, John, **V:** 318n

Davie, Donald, **VI:** 220; **Supp. IV:** 256; **Supp. VI: 105–118**

Davies, W. H., **Supp. III:** 398

Davies, William H., **Supp. XI: 85–103**

Davis, Clyde Brion, **V:** 394

Davis, H., **III:** 15n, 35

Davy, Sir Humphry, **IV:** 200; **Supp. III:** 359–360

Dawkins, R. M., **VI:** 295, 303–304

"Dawn" (Brooke), **Supp. III:** 53

"Dawn" (Cornford), **VIII:** 102, 103

Dawn (Haggard), **Supp. III:** 213, 222

"Dawn at St. Patrick" (Mahon), **Supp. VI:** 174

"Dawn on the Somme" (Nichols), **VI:** 419

"Dawnings of Genius" (Clare), **Supp. XI:** 49

Dawson, Christopher, **III:** 227

Dawson, W. J., **IV:** 289, 291

"Day Dream, A" (Brontë), **V:** 142

Day Lewis, Cecil, **V:** 220, 234; **VI:** x, xxxiii, 454, **VII:** 382, 410; **Supp. III: 115–132**

Day of Creation, The (Ballard), **Supp. V:** 29

"Day of Days, At" (James), **VI:** 69

"Day of Forever, The" (Ballard), **Supp. V:** 26

"Day of the Ox" (Brown), **Supp. VI:** 69

"Day of the Rabblement, The" (Joyce), **Retro. Supp. I:** 170

Day of the Scorpion, The (Scott), **Supp. I:** 260, 267

Day Out, A (Bennett), **VIII:** 26–27

"Day They Burned the Books, The" (Rhys), **Supp. II:** 401

"Day We Got Drunk on Cake, The" (Trevor), **Supp. IV:** 500

Day Will Come, The (Braddon), **VIII:** 49

Day Will Dawn, The (Rattigan), **Supp. VII:** 311

Daydreamer, The (McEwan), **Supp. IV:** 390, 406–407

Daylight Moon and Other Poems, The (Murray), **Supp. VII:** 270, 271, 279–280, 281

Daylight on Saturday (Priestley), **VII:** 212, 217–218

Day's Work, The (Kipling), **VI:** 204

De arte graphica (tr. Dryden), **II:** 305

De augmentis scientiarium (Bacon), **I:** 260–261, 264; *see also Advancement of Learning, The*

de Beer, E. S., **II:** 276*n*, 287

De Bello Germanico: A Fragment of Trench History (Blunden), **Supp. XI:** 35, 38–39

De Bernières, Louis, **Supp. XII: 65–80**

De casibus virorum illustrium (Boccaccio), **I:** 57, 214

De doctrina christiana (Milton), **II:** 176

De genealogia deorum (Boccaccio), **I:** 266

"De Grey: A Romance" (James), **VI:** 25–26, 69

De Guiana Carmen Epicum (Chapman), **I:** 234

"'De Gustibus—'" (Browning), **IV:** 356–357

De inventione (Cicero), **I:** 38–39

"De Jure Belli ac Pacis" (Hill), **Supp. V:** 192

de la Mare, Walter, **III:** 340, 345; **V:** 268, 274; **VII:** xiii; **Supp. III:** 398, 406

de Man, Paul, **Supp. IV:** 114, 115

De Profundis (Wilde), **V:** 416–417, 418, 419; **Retro. Supp. II:** 371–372

De Proprietatibus Rerum (tr. Trevisa), **Supp. IX:** 243, 247, 251–252

De Quincey, Thomas, **III:** 338; **IV:** ix, xi–xii, xv, xviii, xxii, 49, 51, 137, **141–156**, 260, 261, 278; **V:** 353

De Quincey Memorials (ed. Japp), **IV:** 144, 155

"De Quincey on 'The Knocking at the Gate'" (Carnall), **IV:** 156

De re publica (Cicero), **Retro. Supp. II:** 36

De Regimine Principum (tr. Trevisa), **Supp. IX** 252, 255

De rerum natura (tr. Evelyn), **II:** 275, 287

De sapientia veterum (Bacon), **I:** 235, 266–267, 272

de Selincourt, E., **IV:** 25

De tranquillitate animi (tr. Wyatt), **I:** 99

De tristitia Christi (More), **Supp. VII:** 245, 248

"De Wets Come to Kloof Grange, The" (Lessing), **Supp. I:** 240–241

Deacon Brodie (Stevenson), **V:** 396; **Retro. Supp. I:** 260

"Dead Cat, On a" (Caudwell), **Supp. IX:** 38

"Dead, The" (Brooke), **VI:** 420; **Supp. III:** 57–58, 59; **Retro. Supp. I:** 19, 172

"Dead, The" (Joyce), **VII:** xiv, 44–45; **Supp. II:** 88; **Supp. IV:** 395, 396

Dead Air (Banks), **Supp. XI:** 4–5, 13

"Dead and Alive" (Gissing), **V:** 437

Dead Babies (Amis), **Supp. IV:** 26, 29–31

"Dead Bride, The" (Hill), **Supp. V:** 189

"Dead Love" (Swinburne), **V:** 325, 331, 332

Dead Man Leading (Pritchett), **Supp. III:** 311, 312, 313, 314

"Dead Man's Dump" (Rosenberg), **VI:** 432, 434

Dead Meat (Kerr), **Supp. XII:** 187, 193–194, 196

"Dead on Arrival" (Kinsella), **Supp. V:** 261

"Dead One, The" (Cornford), **VIII:** 106

"Dead Painter, The" (Cornford), **VIII:** 106

Dead School, The (McCabe), **Supp. IX:** 133–135, 137, 138–139

Dead Sea Poems, The (Armitage), **VIII:** 1, 8–11, 15

Dead Secret, The (Collins), **Supp. VI:** 92, 95

Dead Souls (Rankin), **Supp. X:** 245, 255

"Dead–Beat, The" (Owen), **VI:** 451, 452

"Deadlock in Darwinism, The" (Butler), **Supp. II:** 108

Deadheads (Hill, R.), **Supp. IX:** 115

Dealings with the Firm of Dombey and Son . . . (Dickens), *see Dombey and Son*

Dean, L. F., **I:** 269

"Dean Swift Watches Some Cows" (Ewart), **Supp. VII:** 40

Deane, Seamus, **Supp. IV:** 424

Dear Brutus (Barrie), **Supp. III:** 5, 6, 8, 9, **11–14**, 138

"Dear Bryan Wynter" (Graham), **Supp. VII:** 115

Dear Deceit, The (Brooke–Rose), **Supp. IV:** 98, 99, 102–103

Dearest Emmie (Hardy), **VI:** 20

"Death" (Macpherson), **VIII:** 181

"Death and Doctor Hornbook" (Burns), **III:** 319

"Death and Dying Words of Poor Mailie, The" (Burns), **IV:** 314, 315

Death and the Princess (Cornford), **VIII:** 103–104

"Death and the Professor" (Kinsella), **Supp. V:** 260

"Death Bed" (Kinsella), **Supp. V:** 267

"Death by Water" (Eliot), **VII:** 144–145; **Retro. Supp. II:** 128

"Death Clock, The" (Gissing), **V:** 437

Death Comes as the End (Christie), **Supp. II:** 132–133

"Death in Bangor" (Mahon), **Supp. VI:** 177

"Death in Ilium" (Kinsella), **Supp. V:** 263

Death in the Clouds (Christie; U.S. title, *Death in the Air*), **Supp. II:** 131

"Death in the Desert, A" (Browning), **IV:** 358, 364, 367, 372; **Retro. Supp. II:** 26

Death in Venice (Mann), **Supp. IV:** 397

Death of a Dormouse (Hill, R.), **Supp. IX:** 119

Death of a Naturalist (Heaney), **Supp. II:** 268, **269–270**, 271; **Supp. IV:** 412; **Retro. Supp. I:** 123, 124, 126–127

Death of a Salesman (Miller), **VI:** 286

"Death of a Scientific Humanist, The" (Friel), **Supp. V:** 114

"Death of a Tsotsi" (Paton), **Supp. II:** 345

"Death of a Tyrant" (Kinsella), **Supp. V:** 261

Death of an Expert Witness (James), **Supp. IV:** 319, 328–330

"Death of an Old Lady" (MacNeice), **VII:** 401

"Death of an Old Old Man" (Dahl), **Supp. IV:** 210

"Death of Bernard Barton" (FitzGerald), **IV:** 353

Death of Christopher Marlowe, The (Hotson), **I:** 275

Death of Cuchulain, The (Yeats), **VI:** 215, 222

"Death of King George, The" (Betjeman), **VII:** 367

Death of Oenone, The, Akbar's Dream, and Other Poems (Tennyson), **IV:** 338

"Death of Oscur, The" (Macpherson), **VIII:** 183

"Death of Simon Fuge, The" (Bennett), **VI:** 254

Death of Sir John Franklin, The (Swinburne), **V:** 333

"Death of the Duchess, The" (Eliot), **VII:** 150

Death of the Heart, The (Bowen), **Supp. II:** 77, 78, 79, 82, 84, **90–91**

"Death of the Lion, The" (James), **VI:** 69

"Death of Marilyn Monroe, The" (Morgan, E.), **Supp. IX:** 164–165

"Death of the Rev. George Crabbe" (FitzGerald), **IV:** 353

Death of Wallenstein, The (Coleridge), **IV:** 56

Death of William Posters, The (Sillitoe), **Supp. V:** 409, 410, 414, 421–422, 423

"Death stands above me, whispering low" (Landor), **IV:** 98

Death Takes the Low Road (Hill, R.), **Supp. IX:** 116–117

"Death, the Cat" (Healy), **Supp. IX:** 106

"Death the Drummer" (Lewis), **VII:** 79

Death–Trap, The (Saki), **Supp. VI:** 250

Death Under Sail (Snow), **VII:** 323

"Deathbeds" (Ewart), **Supp. VII:** 45

"Death–Mask of John Clare, The" (Blunden), **Supp. XI:** 44

Deaths and Entrances (Thomas), **Supp. I:** 177–178

"Death's Chill Between" (Rossetti), **V:** 252

Death's Duel (Donne), **Retro. Supp. II:** 98

Death's Jest-Book (Hill, R.), **Supp. IX:** 122

Death's Jest-Book; or, The Fool's Tragedy (Beddoes), **Supp. XI:** 17, 18, 22, 24, 25–28, 29, 30–31

"Deathshead" (Hare), **Supp. IV:** 283

Debates in Parliament (Johnson), **III:** 108, 122

Debits and Credits (Kipling), **VI:** 173, 204

"Debt, The" (Kipling), **VI:** 201

Debut, The (Brookner; first published as *A Start in Life*), **Supp. IV:** 122, 123–124, 131

Decameron (Boccaccio), **I:** 313; **Supp. IV:** 461; **Retro. Supp. II:** 45–46

"Decapitation of Is" (Cameron), **Supp. IX:** 19

"Decay of Lying, The" (Wilde), **V:** 407–408; **Retro. Supp. II:** 366–367

"Deceased, The" (Douglas), **VII:** 440

"December" (Clare), **Supp. XI:** 59

"December's Door" (Dunn), **Supp. X:** 77

"Deception Bay" (Malouf), **Supp. XII:** 220

"Deceptions" (Larkin), **Supp. I:** 278

Deceptive Grin of the Gravel Porters, The (Ewart), **Supp. VII:** 39–40

Declaration (Maschler), **Supp. I:** 237, 238

Declaration of Rights (Shelley), **IV:** 208

Decline and Fall (Waugh), **VII:** 289–290, 291; **Supp. II:** 218

Decline and Fall of the Roman Empire, The (Gibbon), **III:** 109, 221, **225–233**

"Decline of the Novel, The" (Muir), **Supp. VI:** 202

Decline of the West, The (Spengler), **Supp. IV:** 12

Decolonizing the Mind: The Politics of Language in African Literature (Ngũgĩ), **Supp. V:** 56; **VIII:** 215, 223, 225

"Décor" (MacCaig), **Supp. VI:** 185

Decorative Art in America: A Lecture (Wilde), **V:** 419

"Dedicated Spirits, The" (Smith, I. C.), **Supp. IX:** 211

"Dedication" (Motion), **Supp. VII:** 260

"Dedicatory Letter" (Ford), **VI:** 331

Deep Blue Sea, The (Rattigan), **Supp. VII:**309, 315, 317–318

Deep Water (Highsmith), **Supp. V:** 171–172

"Deepe Groane, fetch'd at the Funerall of that incomparable and Glorious Monarch, Charles the First, King of Great Britaine, France, and Ireland, etc., A" (King), **Supp. VI: 159–161**

Deer on the High Hills (Smith, I. C.), **Supp. IX:** 212

Deerfield Series, The: Strength of Heart (Fallon), **Supp. XII:** 113–114

Defeat of Youth, The (Huxley), **VII:** 199

"Defence of an Essay of 'Dramatick Poesie'" (Dryden), **II:** 297, 305

Defence of English Commodities, A (Swift), **III:** 35

Defence of Guenevere, The (Morris), **V:** xxii, 293, 305–306, 312

Defence of Poesie, The (Sidney), **I:** 161–163, 169, 170, 173; **Retro. Supp. II:** 332–334, 339

"Defence of Poetry, A" (Shelley), **IV:** 168–169, 204, 208, 209; **Retro. Supp. I:** 250

Defence of the Doctrine of Justification, A, . . . (Bunyan), **II:** 253

"Defense of Cosmetics, A" (Beerbohm), **Supp. II:** 45, 53

Defense of Curates (tr. Trevisa), see *Defensio Curatorum*

Defensio Curatorum (tr. Trevisa), **Supp. IX:** 252, 253–254

"Definition of Love, The" (Marvell), **II:** 208, 211, 215

Defoe, Daniel, **II:** 325; **III: 1–14**, 24, 39, 41–42, 50–53, 62, 82; **V:** 288; **Supp. III:** 22, 31; **Retro. Supp. I: 63–77**

"Deformed Mistress, The" (Suckling), **II:** 227

Deformed Transformed, The (Byron), **IV:** 193

"Degas's Laundresses" (Boland), **Supp. V:** 39–40

Degeneration (Nordau), **VI:** 107

Degrees of Freedom: The Novels of Iris Murdoch (Byatt), **Supp. IV:** 145

Deighton, Len, **Supp. IV:** 5, 13

"Deincarnation" (Crawford), **Supp. XI:** 78

Deirdre (Russell), **VIII:** 284, 287

Deirdre (Yeats), **VI:** 218

Deirdre of the Sorrows (Synge), **Retro. Supp. I:** 301–302

"Dejection" (Coleridge), **IV:** 41, 49, 50; **Retro. Supp. II:** 61

Déjuner sur l'herbe (Manet), **Supp. IV:** 480

Dekker, Thomas, **I:** 68, 69; **II:** 3, 21, 47, 71, 89, 100; **Retro. Supp. I:** 160

"Delay" (Jennings), **Supp. V:** 208

"Delay Has Danger" (Crabbe), **III:** 285

Delight (Priestley), **VII:** 212

"Delight in Disorder" (Herrick), **II:** 104

Delillo, Don, **Supp. IV:** 487

"Deluding of Gylfi, The", See *Gylfaginning*

"Demephon and Phillis" (Gower), **I:** 53–54

Demeter, and Other Poems (Tennyson), **IV:** 338

"Demeter and Persephone" (Tennyson), **IV:** 328

"Demo" (Murray), **Supp. VII:** 284

"Democracy" (Lawrence), **VII:** 87–88

"Demolishers, The" (Morgan, E.), **Supp. IX:** 165

"Demon at the Walls of Time, The" (Morgan, E.), **Supp. IX:** 170

Demon in My View, A (Rendell), **Supp. IX:** 195

Demon Lover, The (Bowen; U.S. title, *Ivy Gripped the Steps*), **Supp. II:** 77, 92, 93

Demon of Progress in the Arts, The (Lewis), **VII:** 74

"Demonstration" (Adcock), **Supp. XII:** 9

"Demonstration, The" (Traherne), **Supp. XI:** 270

Demos (Gissing), **V:** 432–433, 437

Denham, Sir John, **II:** 236, 238

"Deniall" (Herbert), **II:** 127, 128; **Retro. Supp. II:** 180–181

Denis Duval (Thackeray), **V:** 27, 34, 36, 38

Dennis, John, **II:** 69, 310, 338, 340

Dennis, Nigel, **III:** 23, 37

"Dennis Haggarty's Wife" (Thackeray), **V:** 23–24

"Dennis Shand" (Rossetti), **V:** 239

Denry the Audacious (Bennett), *see Card, The*

Dent, Arthur, **II:** 241, 246

Denzil Quarrier (Gissing), **V:** 437

Deor, **Retro. Supp. II:** 304

"Departing Ship" (Hart), **Supp. XI:** 122–123

Departmental Ditties (Kipling), **VI:** 168, 204

Departure, The (Hart), **Supp. XI:** 122–124

"Depression, A" (Jennings), **Supp. V:** 214

Der Rosenkavalier (Strauss), **Supp. IV:** 556

Derham, William, **III:** 49

Derrida, Jacques, **Supp. IV:** 115

Derry Down Derry, pseud. of Edward Lear

Dervorgilla (Gregory), **VI:** 315

Des Imagistes: An Anthology (ed. Pound), **Supp. III:** 397

Desai, Anita, **Supp. IV:** 440; **Supp. V: 53–76**

Desani, G. V., **Supp. IV:** 443, 445

Descartes, René, **Supp. I:** 43–44

Descent into Hell (Williams, C. W. S.), **Supp. IX:** 281–282

"Descent into the Maelstrom, The" (Poe), **III:** 339

Descent of Man and Selection in Relation to Sex, On the (Darwin), **Supp. VII:** 17, 19, 25–28

"Descent of Odin, The" (Gray), **III:** 141

Descent of the Dove, The (Williams, C. W. S.), **Supp. IX:** 284

Descent of the Gods, The (Russell), **VIII:** 278–279, 288, 289

"Description of a City Shower, A" (Swift), **III:** 30

"Description of an Author's Bedchamber" (Goldsmith), **III:** 184

Description of Antichrist and His Ruin, A (Bunyan), **II:** 253

"Description of the Morning, A" (Swift), **III:** 30; **Retro. Supp. I:** 282–283

Description of the Scenery of the Lakes in the North of England, A (Wordsworth), **IV:** 25

Description of the Western Islands (Martin), **III:** 117

Descriptive Catalogue of Pictures . . . , A (Blake), **III:** 305, 307

Descriptive Sketches (Wordsworth), **IV:** xv, 1, 2, 4–5, 24

"Desecration" (Jhabvala), **Supp. V:** 236

"Desert, The" (Morgan, E.), **Supp. IX:** 167

Desert Highway (Priestley), **VII:** 227–228

"Deserted Garden, The" (Browning), **IV:** 312

Deserted Parks, The (Carroll), **V:** 274

Deserted Village, The (Goldsmith), **III:** 177, 180, 185, 186–187, 191, 277

Design for Living (Coward), **Supp. II:** 151–152, 156

"Desire" (Hart), **Supp. XI:** 125

Desolation Island (O'Brian), **Supp. XII:** 256–257

Desperate Remedies (Hardy), **VI:** 2, 19–20; **Retro. Supp. I:** 111–112

"Despite and Still" (Graves), **VII:** 268

"Despondency, an Ode" (Burns), **III:** 315

Destinations (Morris, J.), **Supp. X:** 172, 183

"Destinie" (Cowley), **II:** 194, 195, 198

"Destiny and a Blue Cloak" (Hardy), **VI:** 20

"Destroyers in the Arctic" (Ross), **VII:** 433

Destructive Element, The (Spender), **Supp. II:** 487–488, 489, 491

Detained: A Writer's Prison Diary (Ngũgĩ), **VIII:** 216, 221, 223, 224

"Developing Worlds" (Crawford), **Supp. XI:** 80

"Development" (Browning), **IV:** 365

Development of Christian Doctrine, The (Newman), **V:** 340

Development of Creole Society in Jamaica, 1770–1820, The (Brathwaite), **Supp. XII:** 35

"Development of Genius, The" (Browning), **IV:** 310

Devices and Desires (James), **Supp. IV:** 320, 331–333

"Devil, The" (Murray), **Supp. VII:** 284

"Devil and the Good Deed, The" (Powys), **VIII:** 251

Devil and the Lady, The (Tennyson), **IV:** 338

Devil Is an Ass, The: A Comedie (Jonson), **Retro. Supp. I:** 165

Devil of a State (Burgess), **Supp. I:** 187

Devil of Dowgate, The (Fletcher), **II:** 67

Devil on the Cross (Ngũgĩ). *See Caitaani mũtharaba-in?*

Devil, The World and the Flesh, The (Lodge), **Supp. IV:** 364

Devil to Pay, The (Sayers), **Supp. III:** 336, 349

"Devil–Dancers, The" (Plomer), **Supp. XI:** 214

"Devil's Advice to Story–tellers, The" (Graves), **VII:** 259, 263

Devil's Disciple, The (Shaw), **VI:** 104, 105, 110, 112; **Retro. Supp. II:** 316

"Devil's Due, The" (Swinburne), **V:** 332

Devil's Elixir, The (Hoffmann), **III:** 334, 345

"Devil's Jig, The" (Nye), **Supp. X:** 204–205

Devil's Law–Case, The (Webster), **II:** 68, 82–83, 85

Devils of Loudon, The (Huxley), **VII:** 205–206

Devil's Walk, The (Coleridge and Southey), **IV:** 56, 208

Devil's Walk, The (Shelley), **IV:** 208

Devlin, Christopher, **V:** 372, 373, 381

Devolving English Literature (Crawford), **Supp. XI:** 71, 82, 83

"Devoted Friend, The" (Wilde), **Retro. Supp. II:** 365

Devotions upon Emergent Occasions and severall steps in my Sicknes (Donne), **Retro. Supp. II:** 97–98

Devout Trental for Old John Clarke (Skelton), **I:** 86

Dhomhnaill, Nuala Ní, **Supp. V:** 40–41

Diabolical Principle and the Dithyrambic Spectator (Lewis), **VII:** 72, 76, 83

Dialectic of the Enlightenment (Adorno), **Supp. IV:** 29

Dialogue between a Lord and a Clerk on Translation (Trevisa), **Supp. IX:** 246, 248–249

Dialogue between a Soldier and a Clerk (tr. Trevisa), see *Dialogus inter Militem et Clericum*

Dialogue Between the Devil, The Pope, and the Pretender, The (Fielding), **III:** 105

"Dialogue Between the Resolved Soul and Created Pleasure, A" (Marvell), **II:** 208, 211, 216

"Dialogue Between the Soul and Body, A" (Marvell), **II:** 208, 211, 216

"Dialogue Between the Two Horses, The" (Marvell), **II:** 218

"Dialogue Between Thyrsis and Dorinda, A" (Marvell), **II:** 211

Dialogue Concerning Heresies, The (More), **Supp. VII:** 244

Dialogue of Comfort against Tribulation, A (More), **Supp. VII:** 245, 247–248

"Dialogue of Self and Soul" (Kavanagh), **Supp. VII:** 191

"Dialogue of Self and Soul, A" (Yeats), **Retro. Supp. I:** 336

"Dialogue on Dramatic Poetry" (Eliot), **VII:** 157; **Retro. Supp. II:** 131–132

Dialogue with Death (Koestler), **Supp. I:** 23–24

Dialogues Concerning Natural Religion (Hume), **Supp. III:** 240, 242–243

Dialogues of the Dead (Hill, R.), **Supp. IX:** 122

Dialogus inter Militem et Clericum (tr. Trevisa), **Supp. IX:** 252–253, 254

Diamond of Jannina, The (Plomer), **Supp. XI:** 221

Diana (Montemayor), **I:** 164, 302

Diana of the Crossways (Meredith), **V:** xxv, 227, 232–233, 234

Diana Trelawny (Oliphant), **Supp. X:** 217

"Diaphanéité" (Pater), **V:** 345, 348, 356

Diaries (Warner), **Supp. VII:** 382

Diaries of Jane Somers, The (Lessing), **Supp. I:** 253–255

Diaries of Lewis Carroll, The (ed. Green), **V:** 264, 274

Diaries, Prayers, and Annals (Johnson), **Retro. Supp. I:** 143

Diarmuid and Grania (Moore and Yeats), **VI:** 87, 96, 99

Diary (Evelyn), **II: 274–280, 286–287**

Diary (Pepys), **II: 274, 280–286, 288,** 310

Diary and Letters of Madame D'Arblay (ed. Barrett), **Supp. III:** 63

"Diary from the Trenches" (Hulme), **Supp. VI:** 139–141

Diary of a Dead Officer (West), **VI:** 423

Diary of a Good Neighbour, The (Lessing), **Supp. I:** 253

[am.2]Diary of a Journey into North Wales . . . , A (Johnson), **III:** 122

Diary of a Madman, The (Gogol), **III:** 345

Diary of a Man of Fifty, The (James), **VI:** 67, 69

Diary of Fanny Burney (Burney), **III:** 243

Diary, Reminiscences and Correspondence of H. Crabb Robinson, The, **IV:** 52, 56, 81

Dibb, Michael, **Supp. IV:** 88

Dick, Philip K., **Supp. IV:** 41

"Dick King" (Kinsella), **Supp. V:** 261

Dick Willoughby (Day Lewis), **Supp. III:** 117

Dickens, Charles, **II:** 42; **III:** 151, 157, 340; **IV:** 27, 34, 38, 88, 240, 241, 247, 251, 252, 259, 295, 306; **V:** viii, ix, 3, 5, 6, 9, 14, 20, 22, 41–74, 148, 182, 191, 424, 435; **VI:** viii; **Supp. I:** 166–167; **Supp. IV:** 120, 202–203, 229, 379, 460, 505, 513, 514

Dickens (Ackroyd), **Supp. VI: 8–9**

Dickens and Daughter (Storey), **V:** 72

Dickens and the Twentieth Century (ed. Cross and Pearson), **V:** 63, 73

Dickens from Pickwick to Dombey (Marcus), **V:** 46

"Dickens in Memory" (Gissing), **V:** 437

Dickens: Interviews and Recollections (ed. Collins), **V:** 46

Dickens the Novelist (Leavis), **VII:** 250–251

Dickens Theatre, The (Garis), **V:** 70, 73

Dickinson, Goldsworthy Lowes, **VI:** 398, 399

Dickinson, Emily, **Supp. IV:** 139, 480

Dickson, Lovat, **VI:** 239

Dictionary of Madame de Sévigné (FitzGerald and Kerrich), **IV:** 349, 353

Dictionary of National Biography (ed. Stephen and Lee), **V:** xxv, 280–281, 290

Dictionary of the English Language, A (Johnson), **III:** 113–114, 115, 121; **Retro. Supp. I:** 137, 141, 142

Dictionary of the Khazars: A Lexicon Novel in 100,000 Words (Pavic), **Supp. IV:** 116

"Did any Punishment attend" (Sedley), **II:** 265

Did He Steal It? (Trollope), **V:** 102

Diderot, Denis, **Supp. IV:** 122, 136

Didion, Joan, **Supp. IV:** 163

"Didn't He Ramble" (Brathwaite), **Supp. XII:** 37, 44

Dido, Queen of Carthage (Marlowe), **I:** 278–279, **280–281,** 292; **Retro. Supp. I:** 211

Die Ambassador (Brink), **Supp. VI: 46–47**

Die Eerste lewe van Adamastor (Brink), **Supp. VI:** 54

Die muur van die pes (Brink), **Supp. VI:** 52

Die Räuber (Schiller), **IV:** xiv, 173

Die Spanier in Peru (Kotzebue), **III:** 254, 268

Dierdre of the Sorrows (Synge), **VI:** 310, 313

"Dies Irae" (Morgan, E.), **Supp IX:** 160–162

"Dietary" (Lydgate), **I:** 58

Differences in Judgement about Water Baptism . . . (Bunyan), **II:** 253

Different Days (Cornford), **VIII:** 105–106

"Difficulties of a Bridegroom" (Hughes), **Supp. I:** 346

"Difficulties of a Statesman" (Eliot), **VII:** 152 153

Difficulties with Girls (Amis), **Supp. II:** 18

"Diffugere Nives" (Housman), **VI:** 155

"Digging" (Heaney), **Supp. II:** 270; **Retro. Supp. I:** 124, 126–127

"Digging for Pictures" (Golding), **Supp. I:** 65

"Digging Up Scotland" (Reid), **Supp. VII:** 336

Dilecta (Ruskin), **V:** 184

Dilke, Charles, **IV:** 254, 262, 306

"Dill Pickle, A" (Mansfield), **VII:** 174

"Dining" (Dunn), **Supp. X:** 76

"Dining Room Tea" (Brooke), **Supp. III:** 49, 52

Dinner at Noon (documentary, Bennett), **VIII:** 25

"Dinner at Poplar, A" (Dickens), **V:** 41, 47*n*

"Dinner in the City, A" (Thackeray), **V:** 25

"Dinosaur, The" (Fallon), **Supp. XII:** 102

Diodorus Siculus (tr. Skelton), **I:** 82

"Diogenes and Plato" (Landor), **IV:** 91

"Dip in the Pool" (Dahl), **Supp. IV:** 217

Diplopic (Reading), **VIII:** 265, 266, 267, 271

Dipsychus (Clough), **V:** 156, 159, 161, 163–165, 167, 211

"Diptych" (Reading), **VIII:** 264

"Dirce" (Landor), **IV:** 96–97

"Directions" (Thomas), **Supp. XII:** 288

Directions to Servants (Swift), **III:** 36

"Dirge" (Eliot), **VII:** 150

"Dirge for the New Sunrise" (Sitwell), **VII:** 137

"Dirge of Jephthah's Daughter, The: Sung by the Virgins" (Herrick), **II:** 113

Dirty Beasts (Dahl), **Supp. IV:** 226

Dirty Story (Ambler), **Supp. IV:** 16

"Dis aliter visum; or, Le Byron de nos jours" (Browning), **IV:** 366, 369

"Disabled" (Owen), **VI:** 447, 451, 452

"Disabused, The" (Day Lewis), **Supp. III:** 130

"Disappointmnt, The" (Behn), **Supp. III:** 39

Disappointment, The (Southern), **II:** 305

"Disc's Defects, A" (Fuller), **Supp. VII:** 80

Discarded Image, The: An Introduction to Medieval and Renaissance Literature (Lewis), **Supp. III:** 249, 264

Discarnation, The (Sisson), **Supp. XI:** 249, 256

"Discharge, The" (Herbert), **II:** 127

Discontented Colonel, The (Suckling), **II:** 238

Discourse, Introductory to a Course of Lectures on Chemistry, A (Davy), **Supp. III:** 359–360

"Discourse from the Deck" (Gunn), **Supp. IV:** 269

"Discourse of a Lady Standing a Dinner to a Down–and–Out Friend" (Rhys), **Supp. II:** 390

Discourse of Civil Life (Bryskett), **I:** 124

Discourse of the Building of the House of God, A (Bunyan), **II:** 253

Discourse of the Contests and Dissensions between the Nobles and the Commons in Athens and Rome (Swift), **III:** 17, 35

Discourse on Pastoral Poetry, A (Pope), **III:** 56

Discourse on Satire (Dryden), **II:** 297

Discourse on the Love of Our Country (Price), **IV:** 126

Discourse on the Pindarique Ode, A (Congreve), **II:** 346–347

Discourse on 2 Corinthians, i, 9 . . . , A (Crabbe), **III:** 286

Discourse upon Comedy, A (Farquhar), **II:** 332, 355

Discourse upon the Pharisee and the Publicane, A (Bunyan), **II:** 253

Discourses Addressed to Mixed Congregations (Newman), **Supp. VII:** 297

Discourses by Way of Essays (Cowley), **III:** 40

Discourses in America (Arnold), **V:** 216

Discoveries (Jonson), **I:** 270; **Retro. Supp. I:** 166

Discovery of Guiana, The (Ralegh), **I:** 145, 146, 149, 151–153

Discovery of the Future, The (Wells), **VI:** 244

"Discretioun in Taking" (Dunbar), **VIII:** 122

"Disdaine Returned" (Carew), **II:** 225

"Disease of the Mind" (Cameron), **Supp. IX:** 18

Disenchantment (Montague), **VII:** 421

"Disenchantments" (Dunn), **Supp. X:** 78–79

Disgrace (Coetzee), **Supp. VI:** 76, **86–88**

"Disguises" (McEwan), **Supp. IV:** 391–392

"Disinheritance" (Jhabvala), **Supp. V:** 223–224, 228, 230, 232

"Disinherited, The" (Bowen), **Supp. II:** 77, 87–88

Disney, Walt, **Supp. IV:** 202, 211

"Disobedience" (Milne), **Supp. V:** 301

"Disorderly, The" (Murray), **Supp. VII:** 287

"Displaced Person" (Murphy), **Supp. V:** 326

"Dispute at Sunrise" (Hart), **Supp. XI:** 129

Disraeli, Benjamin, **IV:** xii, xvi, xviii, xix, xx, xxiii, 271, 288, **292–309; V:** viii, x, xxiv, 2, 22; **VII:** xxi; **Supp. IV:** 379

Disraeli (Blake), **IV:** 307, 308

"Dissatisfaction" (Traherne), **II:** 192

"Dissolution, The" (Donne), **Retro. Supp. II:** 92

"Distant Fury of Battle, The" (Hill), **Supp. V:** 186

Disaffection, A (Kelman), **Supp. V:** 243, 249, 251–252

"Dissertation" (Macpherson), **VIII:** 188, 190

"Distant Past, The" (Trevor), **Supp. IV:** 504

"Distracted Preacher, The" (Hardy), **VI:** 22; **Retro. Supp. I:** 116

"Distraction" (Vaughan), **II:** 188

"Distress of Plenty" (Connolly), **Supp. III:** 108

Distress'd Wife, The (Gay), **III:** 67

"Disturber of the Traffic, The" (Kipling), **VI:** 169, **170–172**

"Disused Shed in County Wexford, A" (Mahon) **Supp. VI:** 169–170, 173

"Divali" (Seth), **Supp. X:** 279–280

"Dive" (Dutton), **Supp. XII:** 93

Diversions of Purley and Other Poems, The (Ackroyd), **Supp. VI:** 3Diversions of Purley and Other Poems, The (Ackroyd), Supp. VI: 3

"Diversity and Depth" (Wilson), **Supp. I:** 167

"Divided Life Re–Lived, The" (Fuller), **Supp. VII:** 72

Divine and Moral Songs for Children (Watts), **III:** 299

Divine Comedy, The (Dante), **II:** 148; **III:** 306; **IV:** 93, 187, 229; **Supp. I:** 76; Supp. IV: 439

"Divine Judgments" (Blake), **III:** 300

"Divine Meditations" (Donne), **Retro. Supp. II:** 98

Divine Poems (Waller), **II:** 238

Divine Vision and Other Poems, The (Russell), **VIII:** 284–285

"Divine Wrath and Mercy" (Blake), **III:** 300

Diviner, The (Friel), **Supp. V:** 113

"Diviner, The" (Friel), **Supp. V:** 115

"Diviner, The" (Heaney), **Supp. II:** 269–270

"Division, The" (Hardy), **VI:** 17

Division of the Spoils, A (Scott), **Supp. I:** 268, 271

Divisions on a Ground (Nye), **Supp. X:** 193, 200–202

Divorce (Williams, C. W. S.), **Supp. IX:** 272, 274

Dixon, Richard Watson, **V:** 362–365, 371, 372, 377, 379; **VI:** 76, 83, 167

Dixon Hunt, John, **VI:** 167

"Dizzy" (Strachey), **IV:** 292

"Do not go gentle into that good night" (Thomas), **Supp. I:** 178

"Do Take Muriel Out" (Smith), **Supp. II:** 471, 472

Do What You Will (Huxley), **VII:** 201

"Do You Love Me?" (Carey), **Supp. XII:** 54, 55, 56, 57

"Do you remember me? or are you proud?" (Landor), **IV:** 99

Dobell, Sydney, **IV:** 310; **V:** 144–145

Dobrée, Bonamy, **II:** 362, 364; **III:** 33, 51, 53; **V:** 221, 234; **VI:** xi, 200–203; **V:** xxii

"Dockery and Son" (Larkin), **Supp. I:** 281, 285

Doctor, The (Southey), **IV:** 67*n*, 71

Doctor Birch and His Young Friends (Thackeray), **V:** 38

Dr. Faust's Sea-Spiral Spirit (Redgrove), **Supp. VI:** 231, 233–234

Doctor Faustus (film), **III:** 344

Doctor Faustus (Marlowe), **I:** 212, 279–280, **287–290; Supp. IV:** 197

Doctor Fischer of Geneva; or, The Bomb Party (Greene), **Supp. I:** 1, 17–18

Doctor Is Sick, The (Burgess), **Supp. I:** 186, 189, 195

Doctor Therne (Haggard), **Supp. III:** 214

Doctor Thorne (Trollope), **V:** xxii, 93, 101

Doctors' Delusions, Crude Criminology, and Sham Education (Shaw), **VI:** 129

Doctor's Dilemma, The (Shaw), **VI:** xv 116, 129; **Retro. Supp. II:** 321–322

"Doctor's Family, The" (Oliphant), **Supp. X:** 214

"Doctor's Journal Entry for August 6, 1945, A" (Seth), **Supp. X:** 284

"Doctor's Legend, The" (Hardy), **VI:** 20

Doctors of Philosophy (Spark), **Supp. I:** 206

Doctor's Wife, The (Braddon), **VIII:** 44–46

Doctor's Wife, The (Moore, B.), **Supp. IX:** 144, 146, 147–148

Doctrine and Discipline of Divorce . . . , The (Milton), **II:** 175; **Retro. Supp. II:** 271

"Doctrine of Scattered Occasions, The" (Bacon), **I:** 261

Doctrine of the Law and Grace Unfolded, The (Bunyan), **II:** 253

Documents in the Case, The (Sayers and Eustace), **Supp. III:** 335, 342–343

Documents Relating to the Sentimental Agents in the Volyen Empire (Lessing), **Supp. I:** 252–253

Dodge, Mabel, **VII:** 109

Dodgson, Charles Lutwidge, *see* Carroll, Lewis

"Does It Matter?" (Sassoon), **VI:** 430

"Does That Hurt?" (Motion), **Supp. VII:** 263–264

"Dog and the Lantern, The" (Powys), **VIII:** 255

"Dog and the Waterlily, The" (Cowper), **III:** 220

Dog Beneath the Skin, The (Auden and Isherwood), **VII:** 312, 380, 385; **Retro. Supp. I:** 7

Dog Fox Field (Murray), **Supp. VII:** 280–281, 282

"Dogged" (Saki), **Supp. VI:** 239

Dog's Ransom, A (Highsmith), **Supp. V:** 176–177

"Dogs" (Hughes), **Supp. I:** 346

"Doing Research for Historical Novels" (Keneally), **Supp. IV:** 344

Doktor Faustus (Mann), **III:** 344

Dolben, Digby Mackworth, **VI:** 72, 75

"Doldrums, The" (Kinsella), **Supp. V:** 261

"Doll, The" (O'Brien), **Supp. V:** 340

Doll's House, A (Ibsen), **IV:** xxiii, 118–119; **V:** xxiv; **VI:** ix, 111

"Doll's House, The" (Mansfield), **VII:** 175

"Doll's House on the Dal Lake, A" (Naipaul), **Supp. I:** 399

"Dollfuss Day, 1935" (Ewart), **Supp. VII:** 36

Dolly (Brookner), **Supp. IV:** 134–135, 136–137

Dolores (Compton-Burnett), **VII:** 59, 68

"Dolores" (Swinburne), **V:** 313, 320–321

"Dolorida" (Swinburne), **V:** 332

Dolphin, The (Lowell), **Supp. IV:** 423

Dombey and Son (Dickens), **IV:** 34; **V:** xxi, 42, 44, 47, 53, 57–59, 70, 71

"Domestic Interior" (Boland), **Supp. V:** 50

"Domicilium" (Hardy), **VI:** 14

Don Fernando (Maugham), **VI:** 371

Don Juan (Byron), **I:** 291; **II:** 102*n*; **IV:** xvii, 171, 172, 173, 178, 183, 184, 185, **187–191,** 192

Don Quixote (Cervantes), **II:** 49; **IV:** 190; **V:** 46; **Retro. Supp. I:** 84

Don Quixote in England (Fielding), **III:** 105

Don Sebastian, King of Portugal (Dryden), **II:** 305

"Donald MacDonald" (Hogg), **Supp. X:** 106

"Dong with a Luminous Nose, The" (Lear), **V:** 85

"Donkey, The" (Smith), **Supp. II:** 468

"Donkey's Ears: Politovsky's Letters Home, The" (Dunn), **Supp. X:** 80–82

Donkeys' Years (Frayn), **Supp. VII:** 60–61

Donne, John, **I: 352–369; II:** 102, 113, 114, 118, 121–124, 126–128, 132, 134–138, 140–143, 147, 185, 196, 197, 209, 215, 221, 222, 226; **IV:** 327; **Supp. II:** 181, 182; **Supp. III:** 51, 57; **Retro. Supp. II: 85–99,** 173, 175, 259, 260

Donne, William Bodham, **IV:** 340, 344, 351

Donnelly, M. C., **V:** 427, 438

Donohue, J. W., **III:** 268

Don't Look Now (du Maurier), **Supp. III:** 148

Don't Tell Alfred (Mitford), **Supp. X:** 152, 158, 164–167

"Doodle Bugs" (Harrison), **Supp. V:** 151

Dog Beneath the Skin, The — continued

"Doom of the Griffiths, The" (Gaskell), **V:** 15

Doom of Youth, The (Lewis), **VII:** 72

"Door in the Wall, The" (Wells), **VI:** 235, 244

Door Into the Dark (Heaney), **Supp. II:** 268, **271–272; Retro. Supp. I:** 127

Dorando, A Spanish Tale (Boswell), **III:** 247

Dorian Gray (Wilde), *see Picture of Dorian Gray, The*

"Dorinda's sparkling Wit, and Eyes" (Dorset), **II:** 262

Dorking Thigh and Other Satires, The (Plomer), **Supp. XI:** 222

Dorothy Wordsworth (Selincourt), **IV:** 143

Dorset, earl of (Charles Sackville), **II:** 255, **261–263,** 266, 268, 270–271

Dorset Farm Laborer Past and Present, The, (Hardy), **VI:** 20

Dostoyevsky, Fyodor, **Supp. IV:** 1, 139

Dostoevsky: The Making of a Novelist (Simmons), **V:** 46

Doting (Green), **Supp. II:** 263, 264

Double Falsehood, The (Theobald), **II:** 66, 87

"Double Life" (MacCaig), **Supp. VI:** 186

Double Lives: An Autobiography (Plomer), **Supp. XI:** 210, 214, 215, 223

"Double Looking Glass, The" (Hope), **Supp. VII:** 159

Double Man, The (Auden), **Retro. Supp. I:** 10

Double Marriage, The (Fletcher and Massinger), **II:** 66

"Double Rock, The" (King), **Supp. VI:** 151

Double Tongue, The (Golding), **Retro. Supp. I:** 106–107

"Double Vision of Michael Robartes, The" (Yeats), **VI:** 217

Double-Dealer, The (Congreve), **II:** 338, 341–342, 350

Doublets: A Word-Puzzle (Carroll), **V:** 273

Doubtfire (Nye), **Supp. X:** 193–196, 203, 206

Doubtful Paradise (Friel), **Supp. V:** 115

Doughty, Charles, **Supp. II:** 294–295

Doughty, Oswald, **V:** xi, xxvii, 246, 297*n*, 307

Douglas, Gavin, **I:** 116–118; **III:** 311

Douglas, Keith, **VII:** xxii, 422, **440–444**

Douglas, Lord Alfred, **V:** 411, 416–417, 420

Douglas, Norman, **VI: 293–305**

Douglas Cause, The (Boswell), **III:** 247

Douglas Jerrold's Weekly (periodical), **V:** 144

"Dovecote" (McGuckian), **Supp. V:** 280

"Dover" (Auden), **VII:** 379

Dover Road, The (Milne), **Supp. V:** 299

"Down" (Graves), **VII:** 264

Down Among the Women (Weldon), **Supp. IV:** 524–525

Down and Out in Paris and London (Orwell), **VII:** xx, 275, 277; **Supp. IV:** 17

"Down at the Dump" (White), **Supp. I:** 143

Down by the River (O'Brien), **Supp. V:** 344–345

"Down by the Sally–Garden" (Yeats), **VII:** 368

"Down Darkening" (Nye), **Supp. X:** 205

Down from the Hill (Sillitoe), **Supp. V:** 411

"Down Kaunda Street" (Fuller), **Supp. VII:** 80

"Down on the Farm" (Plomer), **Supp. XI:** 214

Down There on a Visit (Isherwood), **VII:** 315–316

Downfall and Death of King Oedipus, The (FitzGerald), **IV:** 353

Downs, Brian, **III:** 84, 93

"Downs, The" (Bridges), **VI:** 78

Downstairs (Churchill), **Supp. IV:** 180

Downstream (Kinsella), **Supp. V:** 259, 260, 261–262

"Downstream" (Kinsella), **Supp. V:** 262

"Downward Pulse, The" (Cameron), **Supp. IX:** 27

Dowson, Ernest, **V:** 441; **VI:** 210

Doyle, Arthur Conan, **III:** 341, 345; **Supp. II:** 126, 127, **159–176**

Doyle, Roddy, **Supp. V:** **77–93**

Dr. Goldsmith's Roman History Abridged by Himself . . . (Goldsmith), **III:** 191

Dr. Jekyll and Mr. Hyde (Stevenson), *see Strange Case of Dr. Jekyll and Mr. Hyde, The*

"Dr. Woolacott" (Forster), **VI:** 406

Dr. Wortle's School (Trollope), **V:** 100, 102

Drabble, Antonia, *see* Byatt, A. S.

Drabble, Margaret, **VI:** 247, 253, 268; **Supp. IV:** 141, **229–254**

Dracula (Stoker), **III:** 334, 342, 345; **Supp. III:** **375–377,** 381, 382, 383, **386–390**

Dracula (films), **III:** 342; **Supp. III:** 375–377

"Dracula's Guest" (Stoker), **Supp. III:** 383, 385

"Draff" (Beckett), **Retro. Supp. I:** 19

Drafts and Fragments of Verse (Collins), **II:** 323n

"Dragon Class" (Dutton), **Supp. XII:** 88–89

"Dragon Dreams" (Maitland), **Supp. XI:** 170

Dragon of the Apocalypse (Carter), **VII:** 114

"Dragonfly" (Fallon), **Supp. XII:** 103

Drake, Nathan, **III:** 51

"Drama and Life" (Joyce), **Retro. Supp. I:** 170

Drama in Muslin, A (Moore), **VI:** 86, 89, **90–91,** 98

"Drama of Exile, A" (Browning), **IV:** 313

Dramatic Character in the English Romantic Age (Donohue), **III:** 268n

Dramatic Historiographer, The; or, The British Theatre Delineated (Haywood), **Supp. XII:** 135

Dramatic Idyls (Browning), **IV:** xxiii, 358, 374; **V:** xxiv

Dramatic Lyrics (Browning), **IV:** xx, 374

Dramatic Romances and Lyrics (Browning), **IV:** 374

Dramatic Works of Richard Brinsley Sheridan, The (ed. Price), **III:** 258

Dramatis Personae (Browning), **IV:** xxii, 358, 364, 374; **Retro. Supp. II:** 26–27

Dramatis Personae (Yeats), **VI:** 317

Drapier's Letters, The (Swift), **III:** 20n, 28, 31, 35; **Retro. Supp. I:** 274

"Drawing Room, Annerley, 1996" (Hart), **Supp. XI:** 131

"Drawing you, heavy with sleep" (Warner), **Supp. VII:** 373

Drayton, Michael, **I:** 196, 278; **II:** 68 134, 138

"Dread of Height, The" (Thompson), **V:** 444

Dreadful Pleasures (Twitchell), **Supp. III:** 383

"Dream" (Heaney), **Supp. II:** 271

"Dream" (Kinsella), **Supp. V:** 273

"Dream, A" (Healy), **Supp. IX:** 106

"Dream, The" (Galsworthy), **VI:** 280

"Dream, The" (MacCaig), **Supp. VI:** 185

"*Dream, The. A Song*" (Behn), **Supp. III:** 37–38

Dream and Thing (Muir), **Supp. VI:** 208

Dream Children (Wilson), **Supp. VI:** **308–309**

"Dream in Three Colours, A" (McGuckian), **Supp. V:** 285

Dream of Darkness (Hill, R.), **Supp. IX:** 119

Dream of Destiny, A (Bennett), **VI:** 262

"Dream of Eugene Aram, The Murderer, The" (Hood), **IV:** 256, 261–262, 264, 267; **Supp. III:** 378

Dream of Fair to Middling Women, A (Beckett), **Retro. Supp. I:** 17

"Dream of France, A" (Hart), **Supp. XI:** 123

Dream of Gerontius, The (Newman), **Supp. VII:** 293, 300, 301

"Dream of Heaven, A" (Fallon), **Supp. XII:** 105

Dream of John Ball, A (Morris), **V:** 301, 302–303, 305, 306

"Dream of Nourishment" (Smith), **Supp. II:** 466

"Dream of Private Clitus, The" (Jones), **Supp. VII:** 175

Dream of Scipio, The (Cicero), **IV:** 189

Dream of the Rood, The, **I:** 11; **Retro. Supp. II:** 302, 307

"Dream Play" (Mahon), **Supp. VI:** 178

Dream State: The New Scottish Poets (Crawford), **Supp. XI:** 67

Dream Stuff (Malouf), **Supp. XII:** 218

"Dream Work" (Hope), **Supp. VII:** 155

Dreamchild (Potter, D.), **Supp. X:** 236

"Dream–Fugue" (De Quincey), **IV:** 153–154

"Dream–Language of Fergus, The" (McGuckian), **Supp. V:** 285–286

"Dream–Pedlary" (Beddoes), **Supp. XI:** 30

Dreaming in Bronze (Thomas), **Supp. IV:** 490

"Dreaming Spires" (Campbell), **VII:** 430

"Dreams" (Spenser), **I:** 123

Dreams of Leaving (Hare), **Supp. IV:** 282, 289

"Dreams Old and Nascent" (Lawrence), **VII:** 118

"Dream–Tryst" (Thompson), **V:** 444

Drebbel, Cornelius, **I:** 268

Dressed as for a Tarot Pack (Redgrove), **Supp. VI:** 236

"Dressing" (Vaughan), **II:** 186

Dressing Up—Transvestism and Drag: The History of an Obsession (Ackroyd), **Supp. VI:** 3–4, 12

Dressmaker, The (Bainbridge), **Supp. VI:** 19–20, 24

"Dressmaker, The" (Hart), **Supp. XI:** 130–131

Drew, Philip, **IV:** xiii, xxiv, 375

"Drink to Me Only with Thine Eyes" (Jonson), **I:** 346; **VI:** 16

Drinkers of Infinity (Koestler), **Supp. I:** 34, 34n

"Drinking" (Cowley), **II:** 198

Driver's Seat, The (Spark), **Supp. I:** 200, 209–210, 218n

"Driving Through Sawmill Towns" (Murray), **Supp. VII:** 271

Droe wit seisoen, 'n (Brink), **Supp. VI:** **50–51**

"Droit de Seigneur: 1820" (Murphy), **Supp. V:** 321

Drought, The (Ballard), **Supp. V:** 24–25, 34

"Drowned Field, The" (Hollinghurst), **Supp. X:** 121

"Drowned Giant, The" (Ballard), **Supp. V:** 23

Drowned World, The (Ballard), **Supp. V:** 22–23, 24, 34

"Drowning" (Adcock), **Supp. XII:** 9

Drumlin (ed. Healy), **Supp. IX:** 95

"Drummer Hodge" (Housman), **VI:** 161; **Retro. Supp. I:** 120

Drummond of Hawthornden, William, **I:** 328, 349

Drums of Father Ned, The (O'Casey), **VII:** 10–11

Drums under the Windows (O'Casey), **VII:** 9, 12

Drunk Man Looks at the Thistle, A (MacDiarmid), **Supp. XII:** 202, 203, 207–210, 211, 213, 215

Drunken Sailor, The (Cary), **VII:** 186, 191

"Dry Point" (Larkin), **Supp. I:** 277

Dry Salvages, The (Eliot), **V:** 241; **VII:** 143, 144, 152, 154, 155

Dry, White Season, A (Brink), **Supp. VI:** **50–51**

Dryden, John, **I:** 176, 327, 328, 341, 349; **II:** 166–167, 195, 198, 200, **289–306,** 325, 338, 340, 348, 350, 352, 354–355; **III:** 40, 47, 68, 73–74, 118; **IV:** 93, 196, 287; **V:** 376; **Supp. III:** 19, 24, 27, 36, 37, 40; **Supp. V:** 201–202

Dryden, John, The younger, **II:** 305

"Dryden's Prize–Song" (Hill), **Supp. V:** 201–202

Du Bellay, Joachim, **I:** 126; **V:** 345

Du Bois, W. E. B., **Supp. IV:** 86

du Maurier, Daphne, **III:** 343; **Supp. III: 133–149**

du Maurier, George, **V:** 403; **Supp. III:** 133–137, 141

du Maurier, Guy, **Supp. III:** 147, 148

Du Mauriers, The (du Maurier), **Supp. III:** 135–136, 137, 139

Dual Tradition: An Essay on Poetry and Politics in Ireland (Kinsella), **Supp. V:** 272, 273–274

Dubliners (Joyce), **VII:** xiv, 41, 43–45, 47–52; critical studies, **VII:** 57; **Supp. I: 45; Supp. IV:** 395; **Retro. Supp. I:** 171–173

"Dubious" (Seth), **Supp. X:** 279

"Duchess of Hamptonshire, The" (Hardy), **VI:** 22

Duchess of Malfi, The (Webster), **II:** 68, 70–73, **76–78,** 79, 81, 82, 84, 85

Duchess of Padua, The (Wilde), **V:** 419; **Retro. Supp. II:** 362–363

"Duddon Estuary, The" (Nicholson), **Supp. VI:** 214

Due Preparations for the Plague (Defoe), **III:** 13

"Duel, The" (Conrad), **VI:** 148

Duel of Angels (Fry), **Supp. III:** 195

"Duel of the Crabs, The" (Dorset), **II:** 271

Duenna, The (Sheridan), **III:** 253, 257, 259–261, 270

"Duffy's Circus" (Muldoon), **Supp. IV:** 415

Dufy, Raoul, **Supp. IV:** 81

Dugdale, Florence Emily, **VI:** 17*n*

Dugdale, Sir William, **II:** 274

Dugmore, C. W., **I:** 177*n*

Dujardin, Edouard, **VI:** 87

Duke of Gandia, The (Swinburne), **V:** 333

Duke of Guise, The (Dryden), **II:** 305

Duke of Millaine, The (Massinger), **Supp. XI:** 183

Duke's Children, The (Trollope), **V:** 96, 99, 101, 102

"Duke's Reappearance, The" (Hardy), **VI:** 22

"Dulce et Decorum Est" (Owen), **VI:** 448, 451

"Dull London" (Lawrence), **VII:** 94, 116, 121

"Dulwich Gallery, The" (Hazlitt), **IV:** 135–136

Dumas père, Alexandre, **III:** 332, 334, 339

Dumb Instrument (Welch), **Supp. IX:** 269–270

Dumb Virgin, The; or, The Force of Imagination (Behn), **Supp. III:** 31

Dumb Waiter, The (Pinter), **Supp. I:** 369, 370–371, 381; **Retro. Supp. I:** 222

"Dumnesse" (Traherne), **II:** 189; **Supp. XI:** 270

Dun Cow, The (Landor), **IV:** 100

Dun Emer Press, **VI:** 221

"Dunbar and the Language of Poetry" (Morgan, E.), **Supp. IX:** 160

Dunbar, William, **I:** 23; **VIII: 117–130**

"Dunbar at Oxinfurde" (Dunbar), **VIII:** 122–123

Duncan, Robert, **Supp. IV:** 269

Dunciad, The (Pope), **II:** 259, 311; **III:** 73, 77, 95; **IV:** 187; **Supp. III:** 421–422; **Retro. Supp. I:** 76, 231, 235, 238–240

"Dunciad Minimus" (Hope), **Supp. VII:** 161

Dunciad Minor: A Heroick Poem (Hope), **Supp. VII:** 161–163

Dunciad of Today, The; and, The Modern Aesop (Disraeli), **IV:** 308

Dunciad Variorum, The (Pope), **Retro. Supp. I:** 238

Dunn, Douglas **Supp. X:** 65–84

Dunn, Nell, **VI:** 271

Dunne, John William, **VII:** 209, 210

Duns Scotus, John, **V:** 363, 370, 371; **Retro. Supp. II:** 187–188

"Duns Scotus's Oxford" (Hopkins), **V:** 363, 367, 370

Dunsany, Lord Edward, **III:** 340

Dunton, John, **III:** 41

Dupee, F. W., **VI:** 31, 45

"Dura Mater" (Kinsella), **Supp. V:** 272

Dürer, Albrecht, **Supp. IV:** 125

"Duriesdyke" (Swinburne), **V:** 333

"During Wind and Rain" (Cornford), **VIII:** 114

"During Wind and Rain" (Hardy), **VI:** 17

Durrell, Lawrence, **Supp. I: 93–128**

Dusklands (Coetzee), **Supp. VI: 78–80,** 81

"Dusky Ruth" (Coppard), **VIII:** 88, 90, 93

Dusky Ruth and Other Stories (Coppard), **VIII:** 90

"Dust" (Brooke), **Supp. III:** 52

"Dust, The" (Brathwaite), **Supp. XII:** 37–38, 40, 45

"Dust, The" (Redgrove), **Supp. VI:** 228

"Dust As We Are" (Hughes), **Retro. Supp. II:** 214

Dutch Courtesan, The (Marston), **II:** 30, 40

Dutch Love, The (Behn), **Supp. III:** 26–27, 40

Duties of Clerks of Petty Sessions in Ireland, The (Stoker), **Supp. III:** 379

Dutiful Daughter, A (Keneally), **Supp. IV:** 345

Dutton, G. F., **Supp. XII: 81–99**

"Duty—that's to say complying" (Clough), **V:** 160

Dwarfs, The (play, Pinter), **Supp. I:** 373

"Dwarfs, The" (unpublished novel, Pinter), **Supp. I:** 367

Dyer, John, **IV:** 199

Dyer, Sir Edward, **I:** 123

Dyer's Hand, The, and Other Essays (Auden), **V:** 46; **VII:** 394, 395

Dyet of Poland, The (Defoe), **III:** 13

Dying Gaul and Other Writings, The (Jones), **Supp. VII:** 171, 180

"Dying Is Not Setting Out" (Smith, I. C.), **Supp. IX:** 211

Dying Paralytic (Greuze), **Supp. IV:** 122

"Dying Race, A" (Motion), **Supp. VII:** 254

"Dying Swan, The" (Tennyson), **IV:** 329

"Dykes, The" (Kipling), **VI:** 203

Dymer (Lewis), **Supp. III:** 250

Dynamics of a Particle, The (Carroll), **V:** 274

Dynasts, The: A Drama of the Napoleonic Wars (Hardy), **VI:** 6–7, **10–12;** **Retro. Supp. I:** 121

Dyson, A. E., **III:** 51

"Dyvers thy death doo dyverslye bemone" (Surrey), **I:** 115

E. *M. Forster: A Study* (Trilling), **VI:** 413

E. M. Forster: A Tribute, with Selections from His Writings on India (Natwar–Singh), **VI:** 413

E. M. Forster: The Critical Heritage (ed. Gardner), **VI:** 413

"Eagle Pair" (Murray), **Supp. VII:** 283

Eagles' Nest (Kavan), **Supp. VII:** 213–214

Eagle's Nest, The (Ruskin), **V:** 184

Eagleton, Terry, **Supp. IV:** 164, 365, 380

Eames, Hugh, **Supp. IV:** 3

"Earl Robert" (Swinburne), **V:** 333

Earle, John, **IV:** 286

"Earlswood" (Adcock), **Supp. XII:** 9

Early Days (Storey), **Supp. I:** 419

Early Diary of Frances Burney, The (eds. Troide et al.), **Supp. III:** 64

Early Essays (Eliot), **V:** 200

Early Italian Poets, The (Rossetti), **V:** 245

Early Kings of Norway, The (Carlyle), **IV:** 250

Early Lessons (Edgeworth), **Supp. III:** 152

"Early Life of Ben Jonson, The" (Bamborough), **Retro. Supp. I:** 152

Early Morning (Bond), **Supp. I:** 422, 423, 426–428, 430

"Early One Morning" (Warner), **Supp. VII:** 379

Early Plays, The (Hare), **Supp. IV:** 283

Early Poems of John Clare, The (Clare), **Supp. XI:** 51

"Early Spring" (Smith, I. C.), **Supp. IX:** 221

"Early Stuff" (Reading), **VIII:** 263

Early Years of Alec Waugh, The (Waugh), **Supp. VI:** 267–270, 272, 274

Earnest Atheist, The (Muggeridge), **Supp. II:** 118, 119

"Ears in the turrets hear" (Thomas), **Supp. I:** 174

Earth Breath and Other Poems, The (Russell), **VIII:** 282

Earth Owl, The (Hughes), **Supp. I:** 348

Earthly Paradise, The (Morris), **V:** xxiii, **296–299,** 302, 304, 306

Earthly Paradise (Stallworthy), **Supp. X:** 291, 301–302

Earthly Powers (Burgess), **Supp. I:** 193

Earths in Our Solar System (Swedenborg), **III:** 297

Earthworks (Harrison), **Supp. V:** 149, 150

"East Anglian Church–yard" (Cornford), **VIII:** 113

"East Coker" (Eliot), **II:** 173; **VII:** 154, 155

East into Upper East: Plain Tales from New York and Delhi (Jhabvala), **Supp. V:** 235

"East London" (Arnold), **V:** 209

East of Suez (Maugham), **VI:** 369

"East Riding" (Dunn), **Supp. X:** 81–82

East, West: Stories (Rushdie), **Supp. IV:** 438, 443, 452

"East Window" (Dutton), **Supp. XII:** 90–91

Eastaway, Edward (pseud.), *see* Thomas, Edward

"Easter 1916" (Yeats), **VI:** 219, 220; **Retro. Supp. I:** 332

"Easter Day" (Crashaw), **II:** 183

"Easter Day, Naples, 1849" (Clough), **V:** 165

"Easter Day II" (Clough), **V:** 159

Easter Greeting for Every Child Who Loves AAlice,"An (Carroll), **V:** 273

"Easter Hymn" (Housman), **VI:** 161

"Easter 1916" (Yeats), **VI:** 219, 220

"Easter Prayer" (Fallon), **Supp. XII:** 114

Easter Rebellion of 1916, **VI:** 212; **VII:** 3

"Easter Wings" (Herbert), **II:** 128; **Retro. Supp. II:** 178

Eastern Front, The (Churchill), **VI:** 359

Eastern Tales (Voltaire), **III:** 327

Eastlake, Lady Elizabeth, **Retro. Supp. I:** 59

Eastward Ho! (Chapman, Jonson, Marston), **I:** 234, 254 **II:** 30, 40; **Retro. Supp. I:** 162

Easy Death (Churchill), **Supp. IV:** 180

Easy Virtue (Coward), **Supp. II:** 145, 146, 148

Eating Pavlova (Thomas), **Supp. IV:** 488–489

Eaton, H. A., **IV:** 142n, 155, 156

"Eaves, The" (Nye), **Supp. X:** 200

Ebb–Tide, The (Stevenson), **V:** 384, 387, 390, 396

Ebony Tower, The (Fowles), **Supp. I:** 303–304

"Ebony Tower, The" (Fowles), **Supp. I:** 303

Ecce Ancilla Domini! (Rossetti), **V:** 236, 248

"Ecchoing Green, The" (Blake), **Retro. Supp. I:** 37, 42

Ecclesiastical History of the English People (Bede), **Retro. Supp. II:** 296

Ecclesiastical Polity (Hooker), **II:** 147

Ecclesiastical Sonnets (Wordsworth), **IV:** 22, 25

"Echo from Willowwood, An" (Rossetti), **V:** 259

Echo Gate, The (Longley), **VIII:** 166, 172, 173–174

Echoes Return Slow, The (Thomas), **Supp. XII:** 280, 281, 283, 284, 288, 289, 290

Echo's Bones (Beckett), **Supp. I:** 44, 60–61

"Eclipse" (Armitage), **VIII:** 11, 12–14

"Eclogue for Christmas, An" (MacNeice), **VII:** 416

Eclogues (Vergil), **III:** 222n

Eclogues of Virgil, The (tr. Day Lewis), **Supp. III:** 118

Eco, Umberto, **Supp. IV:** 116

Economics of Ireland, and the Policy of the British Government, The (Russell), **VIII:** 289

"Economies or Dispensations of the Eternal" (Newman), **Supp. VII:** 291

Ecstasy, The (Donne), **I:** 238, 355, 358

Edel, Leon, **VI:** 49, 55

"Eden" (Traherne), **II:** 189; **Supp. XI:** 266

Eden End (Priestley), **VII:** 224

Edge of Being, The (Spender), **Supp. II:** 486, 491

Edge of the Unknown (Doyle), **Supp. II:** 163–164

Edgeworth, Maria, **Supp. III: 151–168; Supp. IV:** 502

Edgeworth, Richard Lovell, **Supp. III:** 151–153, 163

"Edinburgh Court" (MacCaig), **Supp. VI:** 194

Edinburgh: Picturesque Notes (Stevenson), **V:** 395; **Retro. Supp. I:** 261

Edinburgh Review (periodical), **III:** 276, 285; **IV:** xvi, 129, 145, 269–270, 272, 278; **Supp. XII:** 119

"Edinburgh Spring" (MacCaig), **Supp. VI:** 194

Edith Sitwell (Bowra), **VII:** 141

Edith's Diary (Highsmith), **Supp. V:** 177–178, 180

Editor's Tales, An (Trollope), **V:** 102

Edmonds, Helen, *see* Kavan, Anna

Edmund Blunden: Poems of Many Years (Blunden), **Supp. XI:** 33, 34, 35, 36, 37

Education and the University (Leavis), **VII:** 238, 241

"Education of Otis Yeere, The" (Kipling), **VI:** 183, 184

Edward I (Peele), **I:** 205–206, 208

Edward II (Marlowe), **I:** 278, **286–287;** **Retro. Supp. I:** 201–202, 209–211

Edward III (anon.), **V:** 328

Edward and Eleonora (Thomson), **Supp. III:** 411, 424

Edward Burne–Jones (Fitzgerald), **Supp. V:** 98

"Edward Dorn and the Treasures of Comedy" (Davie), **Supp. VI:** 116

Edward Lear in Greece (Lear), **V:** 87

Edward Lear's Indian Journal (ed. Murphy), **V:** 78, 79, 87

"Edward the Conqueror" (Dahl), **Supp. IV:** 215

Edwards, H. L. R., **I:** 87

"Edwin and Angelina: A Ballad" (Goldsmith), **III:** 185, 191

Edwin Drood (Dickens), **V:** xxiii, 42, 69, 72

"Edwin Morris" (Tennyson), **IV:** 326n

Edwy and Elgiva (Burney), **Supp. III:** 67, 71

"Eemis Stane, The" (MacDiarmid), **Supp. XII:** 206

"Eftir Geving I Speik of Taking" (Dunbar), **VIII:** 122

Egan, Pierce, **IV:** 260n

"Egg–Head" (Hughes), **Supp. I:** 348–349

Egils saga Skalla–Grímssonar, **VIII:** 238, 239

Egoist, The (Meredith), **V:** x, xxiv, 227, 230–232, 234

"Egremont" (Nicholson), **Supp. VI:** 214

"Egypt" (Fraser), **VII:** 425

"Egypt from My Inside" (Golding), **Supp. I:** 65, 83, 84, 89

"Egypt from My Outside" (Golding), **Supp. I:** 84, 89

Egyptian Journal, An (Golding), **Supp. I:** 89–90; **Retro. Supp. I:** 103

"Egyptian Nights" (Pushkin), **Supp. IV:** 484

Eh Joe (Beckett), **Supp. I:** 59–60

Eichmann in Jerusalem (Arendt), **Supp. IV:** 306

"Eight Arms to Hold You" (Kureishi), **Supp. XI:** 161

"Eight Arms to Hold You" (Kureishi), **Supp. XI:** 161

"Eight Awful Animals" (Ewart), **Supp. VII:** 39

Eight Dramas of Calderón (tr. FitzGerald), **IV:** 353

"Eight o'clock" (Housman), **VI:** 160

Eight or Nine Wise Words about Letter–Writing (Carroll), **V:** 273

Eight Short Stories (Waugh), **Supp. VI:** 273

"Eight Suits, The" (Ewart), **Supp. VII:** 39

Eighteen Poems (Thomas), **Supp. I:** 170, 171, 172

Eighteen–Eighties, The (ed. de la Mare), **V:** 268, 274

"Eighth Planet, The" (Maitland), **Supp. XI:** 174

85 Poems (Ewart), **Supp. VII:** 34–35, 46

ΕΙΚΟΝΟΚΛΑΣΤΗΣ: . . . (Milton), **II:** 175

Einstein's Monsters (Amis), **Supp. IV:** 40, 42

Eiríks saga rauða, **VIII:** 240

Ekblad, Inga Stina, **II:** 77, 86

"El Dorado" (Fallon), **Supp. XII:** 105

El maestro de danzar (Calderón), **II:** 313n

Elder Brother, The (Fletcher and Massinger), **II:** 66

Elder Statesman, The (Eliot), **VII:** 161, 162; **Retro. Supp. II:** 132

Elders and Betters (Compton–Burnett), **VII:** 63, 66

Eldest Son, The (Galsworthy), **VI:** 269, 287

"Eldorado" (Lessing), **Supp. I:** 240

Eleanor's Victory (Braddon), **VIII:** 36, 44

Election, An (Swinburne), **V:** 332

"Election in Ajmer, The" (Naipaul), **Supp. I:** 395

Elections to the Hebdomadal Council, The (Carroll), **V:** 274

Electric Light (Heaney), **Retro. Supp. I:** 133–135

"Electric Orchard, The" (Muldoon), **Supp. IV:** 413

"Elegiac Stanzas, Suggested by a Picture of Peele Castle . . . . A (Wordsworth), **IV:** 21–22

"Elegie. Princesse Katherine, An" (Lovelace), **II:** 230

"Elegie upon the Death of . . . Dr. John Donne" (Carew), **II:** 223

Elegies (Donne), **I:** 360–361; **Retro. Supp. II:** 89–90

Elegies (Dunn), **Supp. X:** 75–77

Elegies (Johannes Secundus), **II:** 108

Elegies for the Dead in Cyrenaica (Henderson), **VII:** 425

"Elegy" (Gunn), **Supp. IV:** 271–272, 274

"Elegy, An" (Wallace–Crabbe), **VIII:** 322

"Elegy: The Absences" (Malouf), **Supp. XII:** 220

Elegy and Other Poems, An (Blunden), **Supp. XI:** 45

"Elegy Before Death" (Day Lewis), **Supp. III:** 129

"Elegy for an Irish Speaker" (McGuckian), **Supp. V:** 285, 290

"Elegy for Margaret" (Spender), **Supp. II:** 490

"Elegy for W. H. Auden" (Jennings), **Supp. V:** 217

"Elegy in April and September" (Owen), **VI:** 453

"Elegy on Dead Fashion" (Sitwell), **VII:** 133

Elegy on Dicky and Dolly, An (Swift), **III:** 36

Elegy on Dr. Donne, An (Walton), **II:** 136

"Elegy on Marlowe's Untimely Death" (Nashe), **I:** 278

"Elegy on the Death of a Mad Dog" (Goldsmith), **III:** 184

Elegy on the Death of an Amiable Young Lady . . ., An (Boswell), **III:** 247

"Elegy on the Dust" (Gunn), **Supp. IV:** 264

Elegy on the Usurper O. C., An (Dryden), **II:** 304

"Elegy to the Memory of an Unfortunate Lady" (Pope), **III:** 70, 288

Elegy upon the Death of My Lord Francis Villiers, An (Marvell), **II:** 219

"Elegy upon the most Incomparable King Charls the First, An" (King), **Supp. VI:** 159

"Elegy Written in a Country Church–yard" (Gray), **III:** 119, 137, **138–139,** 144–145; **Retro. Supp. I:** 144

"Elementary Sketches of Moral Philosophy" (Smith), **Supp. VII:** 342

Elementary, The (Mulcaster), **I:** 122

Elements of Drawing, The (Ruskin), **V:** 184

"Elements of Geometry, The" (Malouf), **Supp. XII:** 220

Elements of Perspective, The (Ruskin), **V:** 184

Elene, **Retro. Supp. II:** 302–303

Eleonora: A Panegyrical Poem (Dryden), **II:** 304

"Elephant and Colosseum" (Lowry), **Supp. III:** 281

"Elephant and the Tragopan, The" (Seth), **Supp. X:** 287

Elephants Can Remember (Christie), **Supp. II:** 135

Eleutheria (Beckett), **Retro. Supp. I:** 23

"Elgin Marbles, The" (Crawford), **Supp. XI:** 75

Elia, pseud. of Charles Lamb

"Eliduc" (Fowles), **Supp. I:** 303

Elinor and Marianne: A Sequel to Jane Austen's Sense and Sensibility (Tennant), **Supp. IX:** 237–238, 239–240

"Elinor Barley" (Warner), **Supp. VII:** 379

"Elinor and Marianne" (Austen), *see Sense and Sensibility*

Eliot, George, **III:** 157; **IV:** 238, 323; **V:** ix–x, xviii, xxii–xxiv, 2, 6, 7, 14, 45, 52, 56, 57, 63, 66, 67, **187–201,** 212, **VI:** 23; **Supp. IV:** 146, 169, 230, 233, 239–240, 243, 379, 471, 513; **Retro. Supp. II:** **101–117**

Eliot T. S., **II:** 148; **IV:** 271; **V:** xxv, 241 309 402; **VII:** xii–xiii, xv, 34, **143–170;** **Retro. Supp. II:** **119–133;** and Matthew Arnold, **V:** 204, 205–206, 210, 215; and Yeats, **VI:** 207, 208; influence on modern literature, **I:** 98; **VII:** xii–xiii, xv, 34 143–144, 153–154, 165–166; **Retro. Supp. I:** 3; list of collected essays, **VII:** 169–170; literary criticism, **I:** 232, 275, 280; **II:** 16, 42, 83, 179, 196, 204, 208, 219; **III:** 51, 305; **IV:** 195, 234; **V:** 204–206, 210, 215, 310, 367; **VI:** 207, 226; **VII:** 162–165; **Retro. Supp. I:** 166; **Retro. Supp. II:** 173–174; style, **II:** 173; **IV:** 323, 329; in drama, **VII:** 157–162; in poetry, **VII:** 144–157; **Supp. I:** 122–123; **Supp. II:** 151, 181, 420, 428, 487; **Supp. III:** 122; **Supp. IV:** 58, 100, 139, 142, 180, 249, 260, 330, 377, 558

"Elixir" (Murphy), **Supp. V:** 326

"Ella Wheeler Wilcox Woo, The" (Ewart), **Supp. VII:** 41

"Elvers, The" (Nicholson), **Supp. VI:** 214

"Ely Place" (Kinsella), **Supp. V:** 267

Elizabeth Alone (Trevor), **Supp. IV:** 509–510

Elizabeth and Essex (Strachey), **Supp. II:** **514–517**

Elizabeth and Her German Garden (Forster), **VI:** 406

Elizabeth Cooper (Moore), **VI:** 96, 99

Elizabeth I, Queen of England, **Supp. IV:** 146

Elizabethan Drama and Shakespeare's Early Plays (Talbert), **I:** 224

"Elizas, The" (Gurney), **VI:** 425

"Ellen Orford" (Crabbe), **III:** 281

Ellen Terry and Bernard Shaw, a Correspondence (ed. St. John), **VI:** 130

Ellis, Annie Raine, **Supp. III:** 63, 65

Ellis, Havelock, **I:** 281

Ellis–Fermor, U. M., **I:** 284, 292

"Elm Tree, The" (Hood), **IV:** 261–262, 264

"Eloisa to Abelard" (Pope), **III:** 70, 75–76, 77; **V:** 319, 321

Elopement into Exile (Pritchett), *see Shirley Sanz*

Eloquence of the British Senate, The (Hazlitt), **IV:** 130, 139

Elton, Oliver, **III:** 51

Emancipated, The (Gissing), **V:** 437

"Embankment, The" (Hulme), **Supp. VI:** 134, 136

Embarrassments (James), **VI:** 49, 67

Embers (Beckett), **Supp. I:** 58

Emblem Hurlstone (Hall), **Supp. VI:** 129–130

"Emerald Dove, The" (Murray), **Supp. VII:** 281

Emerald Germs of Ireland (McCabe), **Supp. IX:** 135, 137–138

"Emerging" (Thomas), **Supp. XII:** 286–287

Emerson, Ralph Waldo, **IV:** xx, 54, 81, 240; **V:** xxv

Emigrant Ship, The (Stevenson), **Retro. Supp. I:** 262

Emigrant Train, The (Stevenson), **Retro. Supp. I:** 262

Emigrants, The (Lamming), **Supp. IV:** 445

Emigrants, The (Sebald), **VIII:** 295, 300–303, 308

Emilia in England (Meredith), *see Sandra Belloni*

Emilie de Coulanges (Edgeworth), **Supp. III:** 158

Emily Brontë: *A Biography* (Gérin), **V:** 153

"Emily Dickinson" (Cope), **VIII:** 73

"Emily Dickinson" (Longley), **VIII:** 167

Eminent Victorians (Wilson), **Supp. VI:** 305

Eminent Victorians (Strachey), **V:** 13, 157, 170; **Supp. II:** 498, 499, **503–511**

Emma (Austen), **IV:** xvii, 108, 109, 111, 112, 113, 114, 115, 117, 119, 120, 122; **VI:** 106; **Supp. IV:** 154, 236; **Retro. Supp. II:** 11–12

Emma in Love: Jane Austen's Emma Continued (Tennant), **Supp. IX:** 238, 239–240

Emotions Are Not Skilled Workers, The (Wallace–Crabbe), **VIII:** 318

Empedocles on Etna (Arnold), **IV:** 231; **V:** xxi, 206, 207, 209, 210, 211, 216

"Emperor Alexander and Capo d'Istria" (Landor), **IV:** 92

"Emperor and the Little Girl, The" (Shaw), **VI:** 120

Emperor Constantine, The (Sayers), **Supp. III:** 336, 350

"Emperor's Tomb Found in China" (Fuller), **Supp. VII:** 80

Emperor of Ice–Cream (Moore, B.), **Supp. IX:** 141, 142–143, 144, 146, 147

Emperour of the East, The (Massinger), **Supp. XI:** 184

Empire of the Sun (Ballard), **Supp. V:** 19, 29–30, 31, 35

Empire State (Bateman), **Supp. V:** 88

"Empires" (Dunn), **Supp. X:** 72–73

"Employment (I)" (Herbert), **Retro. Supp. II:** 180

Empson, William, **I:** 282; **II:** 124, 130; **V:** 367, 381; **Supp. II: 179–197**

"Empty Birdhouse, The" (Highsmith), **Supp. V:** 180

"Empty Church, The" (Thomas), **Supp. XII:** 284, 287

"Empty Heart, The" (Nye), **Supp. X:** 204

Empty Purse, The (Meredith), **V:** 223, 234

"Empty Vessel" (MacDiarmid), **Supp. XII:** 206–207

"Enallos and Cymodameia" (Landor), **IV:** 96

Enchafèd Flood, The (Auden), **VII:** 380, 394

Enchanted Isle, The (Dryden), **I:** 327

Enchantment and Other Poems (Russell), **VIII:** 290

"Enchantment of Islands" (Brown), **Supp. VI:** 61

Enchantress, The, and Other Poems (Browning), **IV:** 321

Encounter, **Supp. II:** 491

Encounters (Bowen), **Supp. II:** 79, 81

Encyclopaedia Britannica, **Supp. III:** 171

"End, An" (Nye), **Supp. X:** 204

"End, The" (Beckett), **Supp. I:** 50; **Retro. Supp. I:** 21

"End, The" (Cornford), **VIII:** 107

"End, The" (Milne), **Supp. V:** 303

"End, The" (Owen), **VI:** 449

"End of a Journey" (Hope), **Supp. VII:** 156–157

End of a War, The (Read), **VI:** 436, 437

End of the Affair, The (Greene), **Supp. I:** 2, 8, 12–13, 14; **Retro. Supp. II:** 159–160

End of the Beginning, The (O'Casey), **VII:** 12

End of the Chapter (Galsworthy), **VI:** 275, 282

"End of the City" (Fuller), **Supp. VII:** 69

"End of the Relationship, The" (Self), **Supp. V:** 403

"End of the Tether, The" (Conrad), **VI:** 148

Enderby Outside (Burgess), **Supp. I:** 189, 194–195

Enderby's Dark Lady; or, No End to Enderby (Burgess), **Supp. I:** 189

Endgame (Beckett), **Supp. I:** 49, 51, 52, 53, 56–57, 62; **Retro. Supp. I:** 24–25

"Ending, An" (Cope), **VIII:** 81

Ending in Earnest (West), **Supp. III:** 438

Ending Up (Amis), **Supp. II:** 18

Endiomion (Lyly), **I:** 202

Endless Night (Christie), **Supp. II:** 125, 130, 132, 135

Ends and Beginnings (Smith, I. C.), **Supp. IX:** 221–222

Ends and Means (Huxley), **VII:** xvii 205

Endymion (Disraeli), **IV:** xxiii, 294, 295, 296, 306, 307, 308; **V:** xxiv

"Endymion" (Keats), **III:** 174, 338; **IV:** x, xvii, 205, 211, 214, 216–217, 218, 222–224, 227, 229, 230, 233, 235; **Retro. Supp. I:** 184, 189–192

"Enemies, The" (Jennings), **Supp. V:** 211

Enemies of Promise (Connolly), **VI:** 363; **Supp. III:** 95, 96, 97, 98, **100–102**

"Enemy, The" (Naipaul), **Supp. I:** 386n

"Enemy Dead, The" (Gutteridge), **VII:** 433

Enemy in the Blanket, The (Burgess), **Supp. I:** 187–188

"Enemy Interlude" (Lewis), **VII:** 71

Enemy of the People, An (Ibsen), **VI:** ix

Enemy of the Stars, The (Lewis), **VII:** 72, 73, 74–75

Enemy Within, The (Friel), **Supp. V:** 115–116

Enemy's Country, The: Word, Contexture, and Other Circumstances of Language (Hill), **Supp. V:** 196, 201

"Engineer's Corner" (Cope), **VIII:** 71

England (Davie), **Supp. VI:** 111–112

"England" (Stevenson), **Supp. VI:** 255–256, 264

"England" (Thomas), **Supp. III:** 404

England and the Italian Question (Arnold), **V:** 216

England in the Age of Wycliffe (Trevelyan), **VI:** 385–386

England Made Me (Greene; U.S. title, *The Shipwrecked*), **Supp. I:** 6, 7

"England, My England" (Lawrence) **VII:** xv, 114; **Retro. Supp. II:** 153

England, My England, and Other Stories (Lawrence), **VII:** 114

England Under Queen Anne (Trevelyan), **VI: 391–393**

England Under the Stuarts (Trevelyan), **VI:** 386

England Your England (Orwell), **VII:** 282

"England's Answer" (Kipling), **VI:** 192

England's Helicon, **I:** 291

England's Hour (Brittain), **Supp. X:** 45

"England's Ireland" (Hare), **Supp. IV:** 281

England's Pleasant Land (Forster), **VI:** 411

"English and the Afrikaans Writer" (Brink), **Supp. VI:** 48–49

English, David, **Supp. IV:** 348

English Bards and Scotch Reviewers (Byron), **IV:** x, xvi, 129, 171, 192

English Bible, **I: 370–388**; list of versions, **I:** 387

"English Climate" (Warner), **Supp. VII:** 380

English Comic Characters, The (Priestley), **VII:** 211

English Eccentrics, The (Sitwell), **VII:** 127

English Folk–Songs (ed. Barrett), **V:** 263n

English Grammar (Jonson), **Retro. Supp. I:** 166

English Historical Review, **VI:** 387

English Hours (James), **VI:** 46, 67

English Humour (Priestley), **VII:** 213

English Humourists of the Eighteenth Century, The (Thackeray), **III:** 124, 146n; **V:** 20, 31, 38

English Journey (Bainbridge), **Supp. VI:** 22–23

English Journey (Priestley), **VII:** 212, 213–214

English Literature: A Survey for Students (Burgess), **Supp. I:** 189

English Literature and Society in the Eighteenth Century (Stephen), **III:** 41; **V:** 290

"English Literature and the Small Coterie" (Kelman), **Supp. V:** 257

English Literature, 1815–1832 (ed. Jack), **IV: 40, 140**

English Literature in Our Time and the University (Leavis), **VII:** 169, 235, 236–237, 253

English Literature in the Sixteenth Century, Excluding Drama (Lewis), **Supp. III:** 249, 264

"English Mail–Coach, The" (De Quincey), **IV:** 149, 153, 155

English Mirror, The (Whetstone), **I:** 282

English Moor, The (Brome), **Supp. X:** 62

English Music (Ackroyd), **Supp. VI: 9–10,** 11, 12

English Novel, The (Ford), **VI:** 322, 332

English Novel, The: A Short Critical History (Allen), **V:** 219

English Novelists (Bowen), **Supp. II:** 91–92

English Pastoral Poetry (Empson), *see Some Versions of Pastoral*

English People, The (Orwell), **VII:** 282

English Poems (Blunden), **VI:** 429

"English Poet, An" (Pater), **V:** 356, 357

English Poetry (Bateson), **IV:** 217, 323n, 339

English Poetry and the English Language (Leavis), **VII:** 234

English Poetry 1900 1950: An Assessment (Sisson), **Supp. XI:** 249–250, 257

English Poetry of the First World War (Owen), **VI:** 453

English Poets (Browning), **IV:** 321

English Prisons under Local Government (Webb), **VI:** 129

English Protestant's Plea, The (King), **Supp. VI:** 152

"English Renaissance of Art, The" (Wilde), **V:** 403–404

English Renaissance Poetry (ed. Williams), **Supp. XI:** 116, 117

English Review (periodical), **VI:** xi–xii, 294, 323–324; **VII:** 89

English Revolution, 1688–1689 (Trevelyan), **VI:** 391

"English School, An" (Kipling), **VI:** 201

English Seamen (Southey and Bell), **IV:** 71

English Sermon, 1750–1850, The (ed. Nye), **Supp. X:** 205

English Social History: A Survey of Six Centuries (Trevelyan), **VI:** xv, 393–394

English Songs of Italian Freedom (Trevelyan), **V:** 227

English South African's View of the Situation, An (Schreiner), **Supp. II:** 453

English Through Pictures (Richards), **Supp. II:** 425, 430

English Town in the Last Hundred Years (Betjeman), **VII:** 360

English Traits (Emerson), **IV:** 54

English Utilitarians, The (Stephen), **V:** 279, 288–289

"English Wife, The" (Ewart), **Supp. VII:** 36

English Without Tears (Rattigan), **Supp. VII:** 311

English Works of George Herbert (Palmer), **Retro. Supp. II:** 173

Englishman (periodical), **III:** 7, 50, 53

Englishman Abroad, An (Bennett), **VIII:** 30, 31

"Englishman in Italy, The" (Browning), **IV:** 368

Englishman in Patagonia, An (Pilkington), **Supp. IV:** 164

Englishman Looks at the World, An (Wells), **VI:** 244

Englishman's Home, An (du Maurier), **Supp. III:** 147, 148

"Englishmen and Italians" (Trevelyan), **V:** 227; **VI:** 388n

Englishness of English Literature, The (Ackroyd), **Supp. VI:** 12

Englishwoman in America, The (Bird) **Supp. X:** 19–22, 24, 29

"Enigma, The" (Fowles), **Supp. I:** 303–304

Enjoy (Bennett), **VIII:** 28–29

Ennui (Edgeworth), **Supp. III:** 154, 156, **158–160**

Enoch Arden (Tennyson), **IV:** xxii, 388; **V:** 6n

"Enoch Soames" (Beerbohm), **Supp. II:** 56

Enormous Crocodile, The (Dahl), **Supp. IV:** 207

"Enormous Space, The" (Ballard), **Supp. V:** 33

"Enough" (Nye), **Supp. X:** 205

Enough Is as Good as a Feast (Wager), **I:** 213

Enough of Green, (Stevenson), **Supp. VI:** 260

"Enquirie, The" (Traherne), **Supp. XI:** 268

Enquiry Concerning Human Understanding, An (Hume), **Supp. III:** 231, 238, 243–244

Enquiry Concerning Political Justice, An (Godwin), **IV:** xv, 181; **Supp. III:** 370; **Retro. Supp. I:** 245

Enquiry Concerning the Principles of Morals, An (Hume), **Supp. III:** 231, 238, 244

Enquiry into the Causes of the Late Increase of Robbers (Fielding), **III:** 104; **Retro. Supp. I:** 81

Enquiry into the Occasional Conformity of Dissenters . . . . An (Defoe), **III:** 12

Enquiry into the Present State of Polite Learning in Europe, An (Goldsmith), **III:** 179, 191

Enright, D. J., **Supp. IV:** 256, 354

"Enter a Cloud" (Graham), **Supp. VII:** 103

"Enter a Dragoon" (Hardy), **VI:** 22

Enter a Free Man (Stoppard), **Supp. I:** 437, 439–440, 445

"Enter One in Sumptuous Armour" (Lowry), **Supp. III:** 285

Entertainer, The (Osborne), **Supp. I:** 332–333, 336–337, 339

Entertaining Mr. Sloane (Orton), **Supp. V:** 364, 367, 370–371, 372, 373–374

Entertainment (Middleton), **II:** 3

"Entertainment for David Wright on His Being Sixty, An" (Graham), **Supp. VII:** 116

"Entertainment of the Queen and Prince at Althorpe (Jonson), **Retro. Supp. I:** 161

"Entire Fabric, The" (Kinsella), **Supp. V:** 268

"Entrance" (Kinsella), **Supp. V:** 271

"Entreating of Sorrow" (Ralegh), **I:** 147–148

"Envoi" (Stallworthy), **Supp. X:** 297

Envoy Extraordinary: A Study of Vijaya Lakshmi Pandit and Her Contribution to Modern India (Brittain), **Supp. X:** 47

"Envoy Extraordinary" (Golding), **Supp. I:** 75, 82, 83

"Eolian Harp, The" (Coleridge), **IV:** 46; **Retro. Supp. II:** 52

Epicoene (Johnson), **I:** 339, 341; **Retro. Supp. I:** 163

"Epicure, The" (Cowley), **II:** 198

"Epicurus, Leontion and Ternissa" (Landor), **IV:** 94, 96–97

Epigram CXX (Jonson), **I:** 347

"Epigram to My Muse, the Lady Digby, on Her Husband, Sir Kenelm Digby" (Jonson), **Retro. Supp. I:** 151

Epigrammata (More), **Supp. VII:** 234, 236–237

Epigrammatum sacrorum liber (Crashaw), **II:** 179, 201

Epigrams (Jonson), **Retro. Supp. I:** 164

Epilogue (Graves), **VII:** 261

"Epilogue: Seven Decades" (Morgan, E.), **Supp. IX:** 164

"Epilogue to an Empire" (Stallworthy), **Supp. X:** 295

Epilogue to the Satires (Pope), **III:** 74, 78

"Epipsychidion" (Shelley), **IV:** xviii, 204, 208; **VI:** 401; **Retro. Supp. I:** 254–255

Epistle (Trevisa), **Supp. IX:** 248, 249

"Epistle, An: Edward Sackville to Venetia Digby" (Hope), **Supp. VII:** 159

"Epistle from Holofernes, An" (Hope), **Supp. VII:** 157

Epistle to a Canary (Browning), **IV:** 321

Epistle to a Lady . . . , An (Swift), **III:** 36

Epistle to Augustus (Pope), **II:** 196

Epistle to Cobham, An (Pope), *see Moral Essays*

"Epistle to Davie" (Burns), **III:** 316

Epistle to Dr. Arbuthnot (Pope), **III:** 71, 74–75, 78; **Retro. Supp. I:** 229

"Epistle to Henry Reynolds" (Drayton), **I:** 196

Epistle to Her Grace Henrietta . . . , An (Gay), **III:** 67

"Epistle to John Hamilton Reynolds" (Keats), **IV:** 221

Epistle to . . . Lord Carteret, An (Swift), **III:** 35

"Epistle to Mr. Dryden, An, . . ." (Wycherley), **II:** 322

Epistle to the . . . Earl of Burlington, An (Pope), *see Moral Essays*

Epistle upon an Epistle, An (Swift), **III:** 35

Epistles to the King and Duke (Wycherley), **II:** 321

Epistola adversus Jovinianum (St. Jerome), **I:** 35

"Epitaph" (Sisson), **Supp. XI:** 243

"Epitaph for a Reviewer" (Cornford), **VIII:** 113

Epitaph For A Spy (Ambler), **Supp. IV:** 8

"Epitaph for Anton Schmidt" (Gunn), **Supp. IV:** 264

Epitaph for George Dillon (Osborne), **Supp. I:** 329–330, 333

"Epitaph on a Fir-Tree" (Murphy), **Supp. V:** 317–318

"Epitaph on a Jacobite" (Macaulay), **IV:** 283

"Epitaph on an Army of Mercenaries" (Housman), **VI:** 161, 415–416

Epitaph on George Moore (Morgan), **VI:** 86

"Epitaph on the Admirable Dramaticke Poet, W. Shakespeare, An" (Milton), **II:** 175

"Epitaph on the Lady Mary Villers" (Carew), **II:** 224

"Epitaphs" (Warner), **Supp. VII:** 371

Epitaphs and Occasions (Fuller), **Supp. VII:** 72

"Epitaphs for Soldiers" (Fuller), **Supp. VII:** 72

Epitaphium Damonis (Milton), **II:** 175

"Epithalamion" (Hopkins), **V:** 376, 377

Epithalamion (Spenser), **I:** 130–131; *see also Amoretti and Epithalamion*

"Epithalamion for Gloucester" (Lydgate), **I:** 58

"Epithalamion Thamesis" (Spenser), **I:** 123

"Epithalamium" (Motion), **Supp. VII:** 266

Epoch and Artist (Jones), **Supp. VII:** 168, 170, 171

Epping Hunt, The (Hood), **IV:** 256, 257, 267

Equal Music, An (Seth), **Supp. X:** 277, 288–290

Equal Skies, The (MacCaig), **Supp. VI:** 193

Equus (Shaffer), **Supp. I:** 318, 323, **324–326,** 327

Erdman, D. V., **III:** 289n, 307

Erechtheus (Swinburne), **V:** 314, 331, 332

Erewhon (Butler), **Supp. II:** 99–101

Erewhon Revisited (Butler), **Supp. II:** 99, 111, 116–117

Eric Ambler (Lewis), **Supp. IV:** 13

Eric Brighteyes (Haggard), **Supp. III:** 214

Eridanus (Lowry), **Supp. III:** 280

Ernie's Incredible Illucinations (Ayckbourn), **Supp. V:** 2

Eros and Psyche (Bridges), **VI:** 83

"Erotion" (Swinburne), **V:** 320

Erpingham Camp, The (Orton), **Supp. V:** 367, 371, 375–376

"Errata" (Rushdie), **Supp. IV:** 442

Erskine, Andrew, **III:** 247

"Erstwhile" (Wallace–Crabbe), **VIII:** 323

Esau (Kerr), **Supp. XII:** 186–187, 194, 195

Escape (Galsworthy), **VI:** 275, 287

"Escaped Cock, The" (Lawrence), **VII:** 91, 115

"Escapement" (Ballard), **Supp. V:** 21

"Escapist, The" (Day Lewis), **Supp. III:** 127–128

"Eschatology" (Thomas), **Supp. XII:** 290

"Escorial, The" (Hopkins), **V:** 361

Esio Trot (Dahl), **Supp. IV:** 225

Esmond in India (Jhabvala), **Supp. V:** 226–227

Espalier, The (Warner), **Supp. VII:** 370, 371

"Especially when the October Wind" (Thomas), **Supp. I:** 173

Espedair Street (Banks), **Supp. XI:** 5–6

Esprit de Corps (Durrell), **Supp. I:** 113

Essai sur l'étude de la littérature (Gibbon), **III:** 222, 223

Essais (Montaigne), **III:** 39

Essay Concerning Human Understanding (Locke), **III:** 22; **Supp. III:** 233

"Essay Concerning Humour in Comedy, An" (Congreve), *see Concerning Humour in Comedy*

Essay of Dramatick Poesy (Dryden), **I:** 328, 349; **II:** 301, 302, 305; **III:** 40

"Essay on Burmese Days" (Orwell), **VII:** 276

"Essay on Christianity, An" (Shelley), **IV:** 199, 209

Essay on Comedy and the Uses of the Comic Spirit, An (Meredith), **V:** 224–225, 234

Essay on Criticism, An (Pope), **II:** 197; **III:** 68, 72, 77; **Retro. Supp. I:** 230, 231, 233

Essay on Irish Bulls (Edgeworth), **Supp. III:** 155–156

Essay on Man, An (Pope), **III:** 72, 76, 77–78, 280; **Retro. Supp. I:** 229–231, 235

Essay on Mind, An (Browning), **IV:** 310, 316, 321

"Essay on Percy Bysshe Shelley, An" (Browning), **IV:** 357, 366, 374

Essay on the Development of Christian Doctrine, An (Newman), **Supp. VII:** 296–297, 301

Essay on the Dramatic Poetry of the Last Age (Dryden), **I:** 328

Essay on the External use of Water . . ., An (Smollett), **III:** 158

Essay on the First Book of T. Lucretius Carus de Rerum Natura, An (Evelyn), *see De rerum natura*

"Essay on Freewill" (Caudwell), **Supp. IX:** 38

Essay on the Genius and Writings of Pope (Warton), **III:** 170n

Essay on the Genius of George Cruikshank, An (Thackeray), **V:** 37

Essay on the History and Reality of Apparitions, An (Defoe), **III:** 14

Essay on the Idea of Comedy (Meredith), **I:** 201–202

Essay on the Lives and Works of Our Uneducated Poets (Southey), **IV:** 71

Essay on the Principle of Population (Malthus), **IV:** xvi, 127

Essay on the Principles of Human Action, An (Hazlitt), **IV:** 128, 139

Essay on the Theatre; Or, A Comparison Between the Laughing and Sentimental Comedy (Goldsmith), **III:** 187, 256

Essay on the Theory of the Earth (Cuvier), **IV:** 181

Essay to Revive the Antient Education of Gentlewomen, An (Makin), **Supp. III:** 21

Essay Towards an Abridgement of the English History, An (Burke), **III:** 205

Essay upon Projects, An (Defoe), **III:** 12; **Retro. Supp. I:** 64, 75

Essayes (Cornwallis), **III:** 39

Essays (Bacon), **I:** 258, 259, 260, 271; **III:** 39

Essays (Goldsmith), **III:** 180

Essays and Leaves from a Note–book (Eliot), **V:** 200

Essays and Reviews (Newman), **V:** 340

Essays and Studies (Swinburne), **V:** 298, 332

Essays and Treatises on Several Subjects (Hume), **Supp. III:** 238

Essays from "The Guardian" (Pater), **V:** 357

Essays Illustrative of the Tatler (Drake), **III:** 51

Essays in Criticism (Arnold), **III:** 277; **V:** xxiii, 203, 204–205, 212, 213, 214, 215, 216

Essays in Divinity (Donne), **I:** 353, 360, 363; **Retro. Supp. II:** 95

Essays in London and Elsewhere (James), **VI:** 49, 67

Essays in Verse and Prose (Cowley), **II:** 195

Essays, Moral and Political (Hume), **Supp. III:** 231, 237

Essays, Moral and Political (Southey), **IV:** 71

Essays of Elia (Lamb), **IV:** xviii, 73, 74, 75, 76, 82–83, 85

Essays of Five Decades (Priestley), **VII:** 212

Essays on Freethinking and Plainspeaking (Stephen), **V:** 283, 289

Essays on His Own Times (Coleridge), **IV:** 56

Essays on Literature and Society (Muir), **Supp. VI:** 202

Essays on Shakespeare (Empson), **Supp. II:** 180, 193

Essays, Theological and Literary (Hutton), **V:** 157, 170

Essence of Christianity, The (tr. Eliot), **V:** 200

Essence of the Douglas Cause, The (Boswell), **III:** 247

"Essential Beauty" (Larkin), **Supp. I:** 279

Essential Gesture (Gordimer), **Supp. II:** 226, 237, 239, 242, 243

"Essential Gesture, The" (Gordimer), **Supp. II:** 225

Essential Reading (Reading), **VIII:** 270–271

Essex Poems (Davie), **Supp. VI:** **109–111**

Esslin, Martin, **Supp. IV:** 181; **Retro. Supp. I:** 218–219

Estate of Poetry, The (Muir), **Supp. VI:** 197–198, 202, **203,** 209

Esther Waters (Moore), **VI:** ix, xii, 87, 89, 91–92, 96, 98

"Et Dona Ferentes" (Wilson), **Supp. I:** 157

Et Nobis Puer Natus Est (Dunbar), **VIII:** 128

"Et Tu, Healy" (Joyce), **Retro. Supp. I:** 169

"Eternal City" (Malouf), **Supp. XII:** 220

"Eternal Contemporaries" (Durrell), **Supp. I:** 124

Eternal Moment, The (Forster), **VI:** 399, 400

Eternity to Season: Poems of Separation and Reunion (Harris), **Supp. V:** 132, 136

Etherege, Sir George, **II:** 255, 256, **266–269, 271,** 305

Etherege and the Seventeenth–Century Comedy of Manners (Underwood), **II:** 256n

Ethical Characters (Theophrastus), **II:** 68

Ethics of the Dust, The (Ruskin), **V:** 180, 184

Ethnic Radio (Murray), **Supp. VII:** 270, 276–277

Etruscan Places (Lawrence), **VII:** 116, 117

Euclid and His Modern Rivals (Carroll), **V:** 264, 274

Eugene Aram (Bulwer–Lytton), **IV:** 256; **V:** 22, 46

"Eugene Aram" (Hood), *see* "Dream of Eugene Aram, The Murderer, The"

Eugene Onegin (Pushkin), **Supp. IV:** 485

"Eugene Pickering" (James), **VI:** 69

Eugenia (Chapman), **I:** 236, 240

Eugénie Grandet (Balzac), **Supp. IV:** 124

Eugenius Philalethes, pseud. of Thomas Vaughan

Euphranor: A Dialogue on Youth (FitzGerald), **IV:** 344, 353

Euphues and His England (Lyly), **I:** 194, 195–196

Euphues, The Anatomy of Wit (Lyly), **I:** 165, 193–196

Euripides, **IV:** 358; **V:** 321–324

Europa's Lover (Dunn), **Supp. X:** 75

"Europe" (James), **VI:** 69

Europe. A Prophecy (Blake), **III:** 302, 307; **Retro. Supp. I:** 39, 41–42

European Tribe, The (Phillips), **Supp. V:** 380, 384–385

European Witness (Spender), **Supp. II:** 489–490

Europeans, The (James), **VI:** 29–31

"Eurydice" (Sitwell), **VII:** 136–137

Eurydice, a Farce (Fielding), **III:** 105

"Eurydice to Orpheus" (Browning), **Retro. Supp. II:** 28

"Eurynome" (Nye), **Supp. X:** 203

Eustace and Hilda: A Trilogy (Hartley), **Supp. VII:** 119, 120, 122, 123–124, 127, 131, 132

Eustace Diamonds, The (Fuller), **Supp. VII:** 72

Eustace Diamonds, The (Trollope), **V:** xxiv, 96, 98, 101, 102

Eustace, Robert, *see* Barton, Eustace

Eva Trout (Bowen), **Supp. II:** 82, 94

"Evacuees, The" (Nicholson), **Supp. VI:** 214

Evagatory (Reading), **VIII:** 272–273

Evan Harrington (Meredith), **V:** xxii, 227, 234

Evangelium Nicodemi (tr. Trevisa), **Supp. IX:** 252, 254–255

Evans, Abel, **II:** 335

Evans, G. Blakemore, **I:** 326

Evans, Marian, *see* Eliot, George

"Eve"(Rossetti), **V:** 258

"Eve of St. Agnes, The" (Keats), **III:** 338; **IV:** viii, xviii, 212, **216–219,** 231, 235; **V:** 352; **Retro. Supp. I:** 193

Eve of Saint John, The (Scott), **IV:** 38

"Eve of St. Mark, The" (Hill), **Supp. V:** 191

"Eve of St. Mark, The" (Keats), **IV:** 212, 216, 218, 220, 226

"Eveline" (Joyce), **Retro. Supp. I:** 172

"Evening Alone at Bunyah" (Murray), **Supp. VII:** 272

Eve's Ransom (Gissing), **V:** 437

Evelina (Burney), **III:** 90, 91; **IV:** 279; **Supp. III:** 64, 67, 68, 69, 70, 71–72, 75–76

"Eveline" (Joyce), **VII: 44**

Evelyn, John, **II:** 194, 196, **273–280, 286–287**

Evelyn Innes (Moore), **VI:** 87, 92

Evelyn Waugh (Lodge), **Supp. IV:** 365

"Even So" (Rossetti), **V:** 242

"Even Such Is Time" (Ralegh), **I:** 148–149

Evening (Macaulay), **IV:** 290

Evening Colonnade, The (Connolly), **Supp. III:** 98, 110, 111

Evening Standard (periodical), **VI:** 247, 252, 265

Evening Walk, An (Wordsworth), **IV:** xv 2, 4–5, 24

Evening's Love, An; or, The Mock Astrologer (Dryden), **II:** 305

Events and Wisdom (Davie), **Supp. VI:** 109

"Events at Drimaghleen" (Trevor), **Supp. IV:** 505

"Events in your life" (Kelman), **Supp. V:** 251

Ever After (Swift), **Supp. V:** 438–440

"Ever drifting down the stream" (Carroll), **V:** 270

"Ever Fixed Mark, An" (Amis), **Supp. II:** 3

"Ever mine hap is slack and slow in coming" (Wyatt), **I:** 110

"Everlasting Gospel" (Blake), **III:** 304

Everlasting Man, The (Chesterton), **VI:** 341–342

Everlasting Spell, The: A Study of Keats and His Friends (Richardson), **IV:** 236

"Evermore" (Barnes), Supp. IV: 75–76

Every Changing Shape (Jennings), **Supp. V:** 207, 213, 215

Every Day of the Week (Sillitoe), **Supp. V:** 423

Every Good Boy Deserves Favour (Stoppard), **Supp. I:** 450, 451, 453; **Retro. Supp. II:** 351

Every Man for Himself (Bainbridge), **Supp. VI: 25–26,** 27

Every Man out of His Humor (Jonson), **I:** 336–337, 338–340; **II:** 24, 27

Every–Body's Business, Is No–Body's Business (Defoe), **III:** 13–14

Everybody's Political What's What? (Shaw), **VI:** 125, 129

Everyman, **II:** 70

Everyman in His Humor (Jonson), **I:** 336–337; **Retro. Supp. I:** 154, 157–159, 166

"Everything that is born must die" (Rossetti), **V:** 254

Evidence for the Resurrection of Jesus Christ as Given by the Four Evangelists, Critically Examined (Butler), **Supp. II:** 99, 102

Evidences of Christianity (Paley), **IV:** 144

Evil Genius: A Domestic Story, The (Collins), **Supp. VI:** 103

Evolution and Poetic Belief (Roppen), **V:** 221n

"Evolution of Tears, The" (Wallace–Crabbe), **VIII:** 322–323

Evolution Old and New (Butler), **Supp. II:** 106, 107

Ewart, Gavin, **VII:** 422, 423–424, **Supp. VII: 33–49**

Ewart Quarto, The (Ewart), **Supp. VII:** 44

"Ewes" (Fallon), **Supp. XII:** 108

"Ex Lab" (Reading), **VIII:** 265

Ex Voto (Butler), **Supp. II:** 114

"Exact Fare Please" (Dutton), **Supp. XII:** 91

Examen Poeticum (ed. Dryden), **II:** 290, 291, 301, 305

Examination, The (Pinter), **Supp. I:** 371

"Examination at the Womb Door" (Hughes), **Supp. I:** 352; **Retro. Supp. II:** 207

Examination of Certain Abuses, An (Swift), **III:** 36

Examiner (periodical), **III:** 19, 26, 35, 39; **IV:** 129

"Example of a Treatise on Universal Justice; or, The Fountains of Equity" (Bacon), **I:** 261

"Examples of Antitheses" (Bacon), **I:** 261

"Examples of the Colours of Good and Evil" (Bacon), **I:** 261, 264

Examples of the Interposition of Providence in . . . Murder (Fielding), **III:** 105

"Excellent New Ballad, An" (Montrose), **II:** 236–237

Excellent Women (Pym), **Supp. II: 367–370**

Except the Lord (Cary), **VII:** 186, 194–195

Excession (Banks), **Supp. XI:** 12

"Exchange of Letters" (Cope), **VIII:** 78–79

Excursion, The (Wordsworth), **IV:** xvii, 5, 22–24, 95, 129, 214, 230, 233

Excursions in the Real World (Trevor), **Supp. IV:** 499

"Excuse, The" (Davies), **Supp. XI:** 98

"Execration Upon Vulcan, An" (Jonson), **Retro. Supp. I:** 165

"Execution of Cornelius Vane, The" (Read), **VI:** 436

"Exequy To his Matchlesse never to be forgotten Friend, An" (King), **Supp. VI:** 153

"Exequy, The" (King), **Supp. VI: 153–155,** 159, 161

"Exercisers" (Mistry), **Supp. X:** 139–140

Exeter Book, The, **Retro. Supp. II:** 303–305

"Exeunt Omnes" (Cornford), **VIII:** 114

"Exhortation" (Shelley), **IV:** 196

Exiles (Joyce), **VII:** 42–43; **Supp. II:** 74; **Retro. Supp. I:** 175–176

Exiles, The (Smith, I. C.), **Supp. IX:** 218–219

"Existentialists and Mystics" (Murdoch), **Supp. I:** 216–217, 219, 220

"Exit" (Kinsella), **Supp. V:** 271

Exit Lines (Hill, R.), **Supp. IX:** 115

Exorcist, The (film), **III:** 343, 345

Exodus, **Retro. Supp. II:** 301

"Exotic Pleasures" (Carey), **Supp. XII:** 55

"Expanding Universe, The" (Nicholson), **Supp. VI:** 217

Expedition of Humphrey Clinker, The (Smollett), *see* Humphrey Clinker

Expedition of Orsua and the Crimes of Aquirre, The (Southey), **IV:** 71

"Expelled, The" (Beckett), **Supp. I:** 49–50; **Retro. Supp. I:** 21

Experience of India, An (Jhabvala), **Supp. V:** 235

"Experience with Images" (MacNeice), **VII:** 401, 414, 419

Experiment, The (Defoe), **III:** 13

Experiment in Autobiography (Wells), **V:** 426–427, 429, 438; **VI:** xi, 225, 320, 333

Experiment in Criticism, An (Lewis), **Supp. III:** 249, 264

Experimental Drama (Armstrong), **VII:** 14

Experimenting with an Amen (Thomas), **Supp. XII:** 289

Experiments (Douglas), **VI:** 296, 305

"Expiation" (Jhabvala), **Supp. V:** 236

"Explained" (Milne), **Supp. V:** 303

"Explaining France" (Motion), **Supp. VII:** 256

Exploded View, An (Longley), **VIII:** 166, 169–172

Explorations (Knights), **II:** 123

"Explorer, The" (Plomer), **Supp. XI:** 213
"Explorers, The" (Hope), **Supp. VII:** 154
"Explosion, The" (Larkin), **Supp. I:** 285–286
Exposition of the First Ten Chapters of Genesis, An (Bunyan), **II:** 253
Expostulation (Jonson), **I:** 243
"Expostulation and Inadequate Reply" (Fuller), **Supp. VII:** 73
"Expostulation and Reply" (Wordsworth), **IV:** 7
"Exposure" (Heaney), **Supp. II:** 275
"Exposure" (Owen), **VI:** 446, 450, 452, 455, 457
Exposure of Luxury, The: Radical Themes in Thackeray (Hardy), **V:** 39
Expression of the Emotions in Man and Animals, The (Darwin), **Supp. VII:** 26–28
"Expurgations" (Nye), **Supp. X:** 200
"Ex–Queen Among the Astronomers, The" (Adcock), **Supp. XII:** 7
"Exstasie, The" (Donne), **II:** 197; **Retro. Supp. II:** 88
"Extempore Effusion on the Death of the Ettrick Shepherd" (Wordsworth), **IV:** 73
Extending the Territory (Jennings), **Supp. V:** 216
Extravagant Strangers: A Literature of Belonging (ed. Phillips), **Supp. V:** 380
Extravagaria (tr. Reid), **Supp. VII:** 332
Exultations (Pound), **Supp. III:** 398
Eye for an Eye, An (Trollope), **V:** 102
Eye in the Door, The (Barker), **Supp. IV:** 45, 46, 57, 59–61
"Eye of Allah, The" (Kipling), **VI:** 169, 190–191
Eye of the Hurricane, The (Adcock), **Supp. XII:** 1, 4
Eye of the Scarecrow, The (Harris), **Supp. V:** 136–137, 139, 140
Eye of the Storm, The (White), **Supp. I:** 132, 146–147
Eye to Eye (Fallon), **Supp. XII:** 105, 110–112, 114
Eyeless in Gaza (Huxley), **II:** 173; **VII:** 204–205
"Eyes and Tears" (Marvell), **II:** 209, 211
Eyes of Asia, The (Kipling), **VI:** 204
"Eyewitness" (Armitage), **VIII:** 4
Eyrbyggja saga, **VIII:** 235, 239, 240
Ezra Pound and His Work (Ackroyd), **Supp. VI:** 4
"Ezra Pound in Pisa" (Davie), **Supp. VI:** 110, 113
Ezra Pound: Poet as Sculptor (Davie), **Supp. VI:** 115

Faber Book of Contemporary Irish Poetry, The (ed. Muldoon), **Supp. IV:** 409, 410–411, 422, 424
Faber Book of Pop, The (ed. Kureishi and Savage), **Supp. XI:** 159
Faber Book of Sonnets (ed. Nye), **Supp. X:** 193
Faber Book of Twentieth–Century Women's Poetry, The (ed. Adcock), **Supp. XII:** 2

"Faber Melancholy, A" (Dunn), **Supp. X:** 70
Fabian Essays in Socialism (Shaw), **VI:** 129
Fabian Freeway (Martin), **VI:** 242
Fabian Society, **Supp. IV:** 233
"Fable" (Golding), **Supp. I:** 67, 83
"Fable of the Widow and Her Cat, A" (Swift), **III:** 27, 31
Fables (Dryden), **II:** 293, 301, 304; **III:** 40; **IV:** 287
Fables (Gay), **III:** 59, 67
Fables (Powys). *See No Painted Plumage*
Fables (Stevenson), **V:** 396
"Fables, The" (Malouf), **Supp. XII:** 220
Façade (Sitwell and Walton), **VII:** xv, xvii, 128, 130, 131n, 132
"Face of an Old Highland Woman" (Smith, I. C.), **Supp. IX:** 213
Face of the Deep, The (Rossetti), **V:** 260
Face to Face: Short Stories (Gordimer), **Supp. II:** 226
"Faces, The" (James), **VI:** 69
Facial Justice (Hartley), **Supp. VII:** 131
Facilitators, The (Redgrove), **Supp. VI:** 231
"Facing the Pacific at Night" (Hart), **Supp. XI:** 129
"Factory–Owner, The" (Plomer), **Supp. XI:** 213
Fadiman, Clifton, **Supp. IV:** 460
Faerie Queene, The (Spenser), **I:** 121, 123, 124, **131–141,** 266; **II:** 50; **IV:** 59, 198, 213; **V:** 142
"Faery Song, A" (Yeats), **VI:** 211
"Faeth Fiadha: The Breastplate of Saint Patrick" (Kinsella), **Supp. V:** 264
"Fafaia" (Brooke), **Supp. III:** 55–56 ·
"Fag Hags" (Maitland), **Supp. XI:** 174
Fagrskinna, **VIII:** 242
"Failed Mystic" (MacCaig), **Supp. VI:** 188, 194
"Failure, A" (Thackeray), **V:** 18
Fair Haven, The (Butler), **Supp. II:** 99, **101–103,** 104, 117
"Fair Ines" (Hood), **IV:** 255
Fair Jilt, The; or, The Amours of Prince Tarquin and Miranda (Behn), **Supp. III:** 29, 31–32
Fair Maid of the Inn, The (Ford, Massinger, Webster), **II:** 66, 69, 83, 85
Fair Margaret (Haggard), **Supp. III:** 214
Fair Quarrel, A (Middleton and Rowley), **II:** 1, 3, 21
"Fair Singer, The" (Marvell), **II:** 211
Fairfield, Cicely, *see* West, Rebecca
Fairly Dangerous Thing, A (Hill, R.), **Supp. IX:** 111, 114
Fairly Honourable Defeat, A (Murdoch), **Supp. I:** 226, 227, 228, 232–233
Fairy and Folk Tales of the Irish Peasantry (ed. Yeats), **VI:** 222
Fairy Caravan, The (Potter), **Supp. III:** 291, 303–304, 305, 306, 307
Fairy Knight, The (Dekker and Ford), **II:** 89, 100
"Faith" (Herbert), **II:** 127
Faith Healer (Friel), **Supp. V:** 123

"Faith Healing" (Larkin), **Supp. I:** 280–281, 282, 285
"Faith on Trial, A" (Meredith), **V:** 222
Faithful Fictions: The Catholic Novel in British Literature (Woodman), **Supp. IV:** 364
Faithful Friends, The, **II:** 67
Faithful Narrative of . . . Habbakkuk Hilding, A (Smollett), **III:** 158
Faithful Shepherdess, The (Fletcher), **II:** 45, 46, 49–52, 53, 62, 65, 82
"Faithfulness of GOD in the Promises, The" (Blake), **III:** 300
"Faithless Nelly Gray" (Hood), **IV:** 257
"Faithless Sally Brown" (Hood), **IV:** 257
Faiz, Faiz Ahmad, **Supp. IV:** 434
"Falk" (Conrad), **VI:** 148
Falkner (Shelley), **Supp. III:** 371
"Fall in Ghosts" (Blunden), **Supp. XI:** 45
"Fall of a Sparrow" (Stallworthy), **Supp. X:** 294
Fall of Hyperion, The (Keats), **IV:** xi, 211–213, 220, **227–231,** 234, 235
Fall of Kelvin Walker, The (Gray, A.), **Supp. IX:** 80, 85, 89
Fall of Princes, The (Lydgate), **I:** 57, 58, 59, 64
Fall of Robespierre, The (Coleridge and Southey), **IV:** 55
"Fall of Rome, The" (Auden), **Retro. Supp. I:** 11
"Fall of the House of Usher, The" (Poe), **III:** 339
"Fall of the West, The" (Wallace–Crabbe), **VIII:** 321
Fallen Angels (Coward), **Supp. II:** 141, 145
Fallen Leaves, The (Collins), **Supp. VI:** 93, 102
"Fallen Majesty" (Yeats), **VI:** 216
"Fallen Yew, A" (Thompson), **V:** 442
Falling (Howard), **Supp. XI:** 142, 144–145
Falling into Language (Wallace–Crabbe), **VIII:** 323
Falling Out of Love and Other Poems, A (Sillitoe), **Supp. V:** 424
Fallon, Peter, **Supp. XII:** **101–116**
"Fallow Deer at the Lonely House, The" (Hardy), **Retro. Supp. I:** 119
Fallowell, Duncan, **Supp. IV:** 173
"Falls" (Ewart), **Supp. VII:** 39
Falls, The (Rankin), **Supp. X:** 245
False Alarm, The (Johnson), **III:** 121
False Friend, The (Vanbrugh), **II:** 325, 333, 336
"False Morality of the Lady Novelists, The" (Greg), **V:** 7
False One, The (Fletcher and Massinger), **II:** 43, 66
"False though she be to me and love" (Congreve), **II:** 269
Falstaff (Nye), **Supp. X:** 193, 195
Fame's Memoriall; or, The Earle of Devonshire Deceased (Ford), **II:** 100
Familiar and Courtly Letters Written by Monsieur Voiture (ed. Boyer), **II:** 352, 364

"Familiar Endeavours" (Wallace–Crabbe), **VIII:** 317

Familiar Letters (Richardson), **III:** 81, 83, 92

Familiar Letters (Rochester), **II:** 270

Familiar Studies of Men and Books (Stevenson), **V:** 395; **Retro. Supp. I:** 262–263

Familiar Tree, A (Stallworthy), **Supp. X:** 294, 297–298, 302

Family (Doyle), **Supp. V:** 78, 91

Family Album (Coward), **Supp. II:** 153

Family and a Fortune, A (Compton–Burnett), **VII:** 60, 61, 62, 63, 66

Family and Friends (Brookner), **Supp. IV:** 127–129

Family Instructor, The (Defoe), **III:** 13, 82; **Retro. Supp. I:** 68

Family Madness, A (Keneally), **Supp. IV:** 346

Family Matters (Mistry), **Supp. X:** 144, 147–148

Family Memories (West), **Supp. III:** 431, 432, 433, 434

Family of Love, The (Dekker and Middleton), **II:** 3, 21

Family of Swift, The (Swift), **Retro. Supp. I:** 274

Family Prayers (Butler), **Supp. II:** 103

Family Reunion, The (Eliot), **VII:** 146, 151, 154, 158, 160; **Retro. Supp. II:** 132

Family Romance, A (Brookner), *see Dolly*

"Family Sagas", *See Íslendinga sögur*

"Family Seat" (Murphy), **Supp. V:** 328

Family Sins (Trevor), **Supp. IV:** 505

"Family Supper, A" (Ishiguro), **Supp. IV:** 304

Family Tree, The (Plomer), **Supp. XI:** 216

Family Voices (Pinter), **Supp. I:** 378

Famished Road, The (Okri), **Supp. V:** 347, 348, 349, 350, 351, 352–353, 357–359

Famous for the Creatures (Motion), **Supp. VII:** 252

"Famous Ghost of St. Ives, The" (Redgrove), **Supp. VI:** 235–237

Famous History of Sir Thomas Wyat, The (Webster), **II:** 85

Famous Tragedy of the Queen of Cornwall . . . , The (Hardy), **VI:** 20

Famous Victoria of Henry V, The, **I:** 308–309

Fan, The: A Poem (Gay), **III:** 67

Fanatic Heart, A (O'Brien), **Supp. V:** 339

Fancies, Chaste and Noble, The (Ford), **II:** 89, 91–92, 99, 100

"Fancy" (Keats), **IV:** 221

"Fancy, A" (Greville), **Supp. XI:** 109

Fancy and Imagination (Brett), **IV:** 57

Fanfare for Elizabeth (Sitwell), **VII:** 127

"Fanny and Annie" (Lawrence), **VII:** 90, 114, 115

Fanny Brawne: A Biography (Richardson), **IV:** 236

Fanny's First Play (Shaw), **VI:** 115, 116, 117, 129

Fanon, Frantz, **Supp. IV:** 105

"Fanon the Awakener" (Armah), **Supp. X:** 2

Fanshawe, Sir Richard, **II:** 49, 222, 237

Fanshen (Hare), **Supp. IV:** 282, 284

Fanshen (Hinton), **Supp. IV:** 284

"Fantasia" (Redgrove), **Supp. VI:** 231

Fantasia of the Unconscious (Lawrence), **VII:** 122; **Retro. Supp. II:** 234

"Fantasia on 'Horbury'" (Hill), **Supp. V:** 187

Fantastic Mr. Fox (Dahl), **Supp. IV:** 203, 223

fantasy fiction, **VI:** 228–235, 338, 399

Fantasy and Fugue (Fuller), **Supp. VII:** 71–72

Fantomina (Haywood), **Supp. XII:** 135

Far Cry (MacCaig), **Supp. VI:** 184–185

"Far—Far—Away" (Tennyson), **IV:** 330

Far from the Madding Crowd (Hardy), **VI:** 1, 5–6; **Retro. Supp. I:** 113–114

Far Journey of Oudin, The (Harris), **Supp. V:** 132, 134, 135

Far Journeys (Chatwin), **Supp. IV:** 157

Far Side of the World, The (O'Brian), **Supp. XII:** 256

"Fare Thee Well" (Byron), **IV:** 192

Fares Please! An Omnibus (Coppard), **VIII:** 89

"Farewell, A" (Arnold), **V:** 216

Farewell the Trumpets: An Imperial Retreat (Morris, J.), **Supp. X:** 179, 181

"Farewell to Angria" (Brontë), **V:** 125

"Farewell to Essay–Writing, A" (Hazlitt), **IV:** 135

Farewell to Military Profession (Rich), **I:** 312

Farewell to Poesy (Davies), **Supp. XI:** 96

"Farewell to Tobacco" (Lamb), **IV:** 81

Farfetched Fables (Shaw), **VI:** 125, 126

Farina (Meredith), **V:** 225, 234

Farm, The (Storey), **Supp. I:** 408, 411, 412, 414

Farmer Giles of Ham (Tolkien), **Supp. II:** 521

"Farmer's Ingle, The" (Fergusson), **III:** 318

Farmer's Year, A (Haggard), **Supp. III:** 214

Farnham, William, **I:** 214

Farquhar, George, **II:** 334–335, 351–365

Farrell, Barry, **Supp. IV:** 223

Farther Adventures of Robinson Crusoe, The (Defoe), **III:** 13; **Retro. Supp. I:** 71

Farthing Hall (Walpole and Priestley), **VII:** 211

Fascinating Foundling, The (Shaw), **VI:** 129

"Fashionable Authoress, The" (Thackeray), **V:** 22, 37

Fashionable Lover, The (Cumberland), **III:** 257

"Fasternis Eve in Hell" (Dunbar), **VIII:** 126

Fasti (Ovid), **II:** 110n

"Fat Contributor Papers, The" (Thackeray), **V:** 25, 38

"Fat Man in History, The" (Carey), **Supp. XII:** 54

Fat Man in History, The: Short Stories (Carey), **Supp. XII:** 52, 54

Fat Man in History and Other Stories, The (Carey), **Supp. XII:** 52, 55

Fat Woman's Joke, The (Weldon), **Supp. IV:** 521, 522–524, 525

"Fatal Boots, The" (Thackeray), **V:** 21, 37

Fatal Dowry, The (Massinger and Field), **Supp. XI:** 182, 184

Fatal Gift, The (Waugh), **Supp. VI:** 276

Fatal Inversion, A (Rendell), **Supp. IX:** 201

Fatal Revenge, The; or, The Family of Montorio (Maturin), **VIII:** 200, 207

Fatal Secret, The (Haywood), **Supp. XII:** 135

"Fatal Sisters, The" (Gray), **III:** 141

Fatality in Fleet Street (Caudwell), **Supp. IX:** 35

Fate of Homo Sapiens, The (Wells), **VI:** 228

Fate of Mary Rose, The (Blackwood), **Supp. IX:** 11–12

"Fate Playing" (Hughes), **Retro. Supp. II:** 217

"Fates, The" (Owen), **VI:** 449

Fates of the Apostles, **Retro. Supp. II:** 301

Father and His Fate, A (Compton–Burnett), **VII:** 61, 63

"Father and Lover" (Rossetti), **V:** 260

"Father and Son" (Butler), **Supp. II:** 97

Father Brown stories (Chesterton), **VI:** 338

Father Damien (Stevenson), **V:** 383, 390, 396

"Father Mat" (Kavanagh), **Supp. VII:** 194

Fathers and Sons (tr. Friel), **Supp. V:** 124

Father's Comedy, The (Fuller), **Supp. VII:** 74, 75–76, 77, 81

"Fathers, Sons and Lovers" (Thomas), **Supp. IV:** 493

Fathers, The; or, The Good–Natur'd Man (Fielding), **III:** 98, 105

"Fatigue, The" (Jones), **Supp. VII:** 175

Faulkner, Charles, **VI:** 167

"Fault" (Dutton), **Supp. XII:** 95–96

"Faunal" (Reading), **VIII:** 273

Faust (Goethe), **III:** 344; **IV:** xvi, xix, 179

Faust (Nye), **Supp. X:** 195

"Faustine" (Swinburne), **V:** 320

Faustine (Tennant), **Supp. IX:** 231, 238

Faustus and the Censor (Empson), **Supp. II:** 180, **196–197**

Faustus Kelly (O'Nolan), **Supp. II:** 323, **335–337**

Fawkes, F., **III:** 170n

Fawn, The (Marston), **II:** 30, 40

Fay Weldon's Wicked Fictions (Weldon), **Supp. IV:** 522, 531

"Fear" (Collins), **III:** 166, 171, 336

"Fear, A" (Jennings), **Supp. V:** 214

Fear, The (Keneally), **Supp. IV:** 345

Fearful Pleasures (Coppard), **VIII:** 91, 97

"Fearless" (Galloway), **Supp. XII:** 121–122

Fears in Solitude . . . (Coleridge), **IV:** 55

Feast of Bacchus, The (Bridges), **VI:** 83

"Feast of Famine, The" (Stevenson), **V:** 396

Feast of Lupercal, The (Moore, B.), **Supp. IX:** 142, 143, 146–147

"Feastday of Peace, The" (McGuckian), **Supp. V:** 291

"February" (Hughes), **Supp. I:** 342

Feed My Swine (Powys), **VIII:** 249, 255

"Feeding Ducks" (MacCaig), **Supp. VI:** 187

Feeding the Mind (Carroll), **V:** 274

"Feeling into Words" (Heaney), **Supp. II:** 272, 273

Feersum Endjinn (Banks), **Supp. XI:** 12, 13

Felicia's Journey (Trevor), **Supp. IV:** 505, 517

"Félise" (Swinburne), **V:** 321

Felix Holt, The Radical (Eliot), **V:** xxiii, 195–196, 199, 200; **Retro. Supp. II:** 111–112

"Felix Randal" (Hopkins), **V:** 368–369, 371; **Retro. Supp. II:** 196

Fell of Dark (Hill, R.), **Supp. IX:** 110–111

"Fellow–Townsmen" (Hardy), **VI:** 22

Fellowship of the Ring (Tolkien), **Supp. II:** 519

Felony: The Private History of the Aspern Papers (Tennant), **Supp. IX:** 239

Female Friends (Weldon), **Supp. IV:** 534–535

Female God, The (Rosenberg), **VI:** 432

Female Spectator (Haywood), **Supp. XII:** 136, 142–144

"Female Vagrant, The" (Wordsworth), **IV:** 5

"Feminine Christs, The" (McGuckian), **Supp. V:** 290

Feminine Mystique, The (Freidan), **Supp. IV:** 232

"Feminist Writer's Progress, A" (Maitland), **Supp. XI:** 163, 164, 168

Fen (Churchill), **Supp. IV:** 179, 188, 191–192, 198

Fénelon, François, **III:** 95, 99

Fenton, James, **Supp. IV:** 450

Fenwick, Isabella, **IV:** 2

Ferdinand Count Fathom (Smollett), **III:** 153, 158

Fergus (Moore, B.), **Supp. IX:** 143, 148, 150, 154

Ferguson, Helen, *see* Kavan, Anna

Fergusson, Robert, **III:** 312–313, 316, 317, 318

Ferishtah's Fancies (Browning), **IV:** 359, 374

Fermor, Patrick Leigh, **Supp. IV:** 160

"Fern Hill" (Thomas), **Supp. I:** 177, 178, 179

Fernandez, Ramon, **V:** 225–226

Ferrex and Porrex (Norton and Sackville), *see* Gorboduc

Festival at Farbridge (Priestley), **VII:** 219–210

"Festubert: The Old German Line" (Blunden), **VI:** 428

"Fetching Cows" (MacCaig), **Supp. VI:** 188

"Fetish" (Harris), **Supp. V:** 138

Feuerbach, Ludwig, **IV:** 364

"Feuille d'Album" (Mansfield), **VII:** 364

"Few Crusted Characters, A" (Hardy), **VI:** 20, 22

Few Green Leaves, A (Pym), **Supp. II:** 370, **382–384**

Few Late Chrysanthemums, A (Betjeman), **VII:** 369–371

Few Sighs from Hell, A (Bunyan), **II:** 253

Fichte, Johann Gottlieb, **V:** 348

Ficino (philosopher), **I:** 237

"Ficino Notebook" (Traherne), **Supp. XI:** 264

Fiction (Reading), **VIII:** 264, 273

"Fiction" (Reading), **VIII:** 264

Fiction and the Reading Public (Leavis), **VII:** 233, 234

Fiction–Makers, The (Stevenson), **Supp. VI: 262–263**

"Fiction: The House Party" (Ewart), **Supp. VII:** 42

"Fictions" (Reid), **Supp. VII:** 334

"Fiddler of the Reels, The" (Hardy), **VI:** 22

Field, Isobel, **V:** 393, 397

Field, Nathaniel, **II:** 45, 66, 67

Field of Mustard, The (Coppard), **VIII:** 95–96

"Field of Mustard, The" (Coppard), **VIII:** 90, 96

"Field of Vision" (Heaney), **Retro. Supp. I:** 132

Field of Waterloo, The (Scott), **IV:** 38

Field Work (Heaney), **Supp. II:** 268, **275–277**; **Retro. Supp. I:** 124, 130

Fielding, Henry, **II:** 273; **III:** 62, 84, **94–106**, 148, 150; **IV:** 106, 189; **V:** 52, 287; **Supp. II:** 57, 194, 195; **Supp. IV:** 244; **Retro. Supp. I: 79–92**

Fielding, K. J., **V:** 43, 72

Fifer, C. N., **III:** 249

Fifine at the Fair (Browning), **IV:** 358, 367, 374; **Retro. Supp. II:**25

Fifteen Dead (Kinsella), **Supp. V:** 267

"Fifth Philosopher's Song" (Huxley), **VII:** 199

Fifth, Queen, The (Ford), **VI:** 324

Fifth Queen Crowned, The (Ford), **VI:** 325, 326

"Fifties, The" (Fuller), **Supp. VII:** 73

"Fifty Faggots" (Thomas), **Supp. III:** 403

"Fifty Pounds" (Coppard), **VIII:** 96

Fifty Years of English Literature, 1900–1950 (Scott–James), **VI:** 21

Fifty Years of Europe: An Album (Morris, J.), **Supp. X:** 185–186

"Fig Tree, The" (Ngũgĩ). *See* "Mugumo"

"Fight, The" (Thomas), **Supp. I:** 181

Fight for Barbara, The (Lawrence), **VII:** 120

"Fight to a Finish" (Sassoon), **VI:** 430

"Fight with a Water Spirit" (Cameron), **Supp. IX:** 19, 20, 22

Fighting Terms (Gunn), **Supp. IV:** 256, 257–259

"Figure in the Carpet, The" (James), **VI:** 69

Figure of Beatrice: A Study of Dante, The (Williams, C. W. S.), **Supp. IX:** 279, 284–285

"Figures on the Freize" (Reid), **Supp. VII:** 330

File on a Diplomat (Brink), **Supp. VI:** 46

Filibusters in Barbary (Lewis), **VII:** 83

Fille du Policeman (Swinburne), **V:** 325, 333

Film (Beckett), **Supp. I:** 51, 59, 60

Filostrato (Boccaccio), **I:** 30

Filthy Lucre (Bainbridge), **Supp. VI:** 23

Final Demands (Reading), **VIII:** 271, 273

Final Passage, The (Phillips), **Supp. V:** 380–383

"Final Problem, The" (Doyle), **Supp. II:** 160, 172–173

Final Unfinished Voyage of Jack Aubrey, The (O'Brian), **Supp. XII:** 259

"Finale" (Dutton), **Supp. XII:** 99

Finch, Anne, **Supp. IX: 65–78**

Finden's Byron Beauties (Finden), **V:** 111

Finding the Dead (Fallon), **Supp. XII:** 104

Findlater, Richard, **VII:** 8

Fine Balance, A (Mistry), **Supp. X:** 142, 145–149

Finer Grain, The (James), **VI:** 67

Fingal (Macpherson), **VIII:** 181–182, 186–189, 190, 191, 192, 193, 194

"Fingal's Visit to Norway" (Macpherson), **VIII:** 186

Finished (Haggard), **Supp. III:** 214

"Finistére" (Kinsella), **Supp. V:** 268

Finnegans Wake (Joyce), **VII:** 42, 46, 52–54; critical studies, **VII:** 58; **Supp. III:** 108; **Retro. Supp. I:** 169, 179–181

Firbank, Ronald, **VII:** 132, 200; **Supp. II: 199–223**

"Fire and Ice" (Kinsella), **Supp. V:** 261

Fire and the Sun, The: Why Plato Banished the Artists (Murdoch), **Supp. I:** 230, 232

"Fire and the Tide" (Stevenson), **Supp. VI:** 260

Fire Down Below (Golding), **Retro. Supp. I:** 104–105

"Fire, Famine and Slaughter" (Coleridge), **Retro. Supp. II:** 53

Fire from Heaven (Renault), **Supp. IX:** 184–185

"Fire in the Wood, The" (Welch), **Supp. IX:** 267

Fire of the Lord, The (Nicholson), **Supp. VI:** 219

Fire on the Mountain (Desai), **Supp. V:** 53, 55, 64–65, 73

"Fire Sermon, The" (Eliot), **Retro. Supp. II:** 127–128

"Fireworks Poems" (Cope), **VIII:** 81

"Firing Practice" (Motion), **Supp. VII:** 251, 254, 257, 260

"Firm of Happiness, Ltd., The" (Cameron), **Supp. IX:** 25–26

"Firm Views" (Hart), **Supp. XI:** 129

First Affair, The (Fallon), **Supp. XII:** 101, 102–103

First and Last Loves (Betjeman), **VII:** 357, 358, 359

First & Last Things (Wells), **VI:** 244

First Anniversary, The (Donne), **I:** 188, 356; **Retro. Supp. II:** 94

"First Anniversary of the Government under O. C., The" (Marvell), **II:** 210, 211; **Retro. Supp. II:** 262–263

First Book of Odes (Bunting), **Supp. VII:** 5, 13

First Book of Urizen, The (Blake), **III:** 299, 300, 306, 307; **Retro. Supp. I:** 43–44

"First Countess of Wessex, The" (Hardy), **VI:** 22

First Earthquake, The (Redgrove), **Supp. VI: 236**

First Eleven, The (Ewart), **Supp. VII:** 41

First Episode (Rattigan), **Supp. VII:** 308

First Flight, The (Heaney), **Supp. II:** 278

First Folio (Shakespeare), **I:** 299, 324, 325

First Grammatical Treatise, **VIII:** 236

First Hundred Years of Thomas Hardy, The (Weber), **VI:** 19

"First Hymn to Lenin" (MacDiarmid), **Supp. III:** 119; **Supp. XII:** 211

"'First Impression' (Tokyo), A" (Blunden), **Supp. XI:** 35

"First Impressions" (Austen), *see Pride and Prejudice*

"First Journey, The" (Graham), **Supp. VII:** 109

First Lady Chatterley, The (Lawrence), **VII:** 111–112

First Light (Ackroyd), **Supp. VI:** 1, 8

"First Light" (Kinsella), **Supp. V:** 263

First Life of Adamastor, The (Brink), **Supp. VI: 54–55,** 57

"First Love" (Beckett), **Retro. Supp. I:** 21

First Love, Last Rites (McEwan), **Supp. IV:** 390–392

"First Man, The" (Gunn), **Supp. IV:** 264–265

First Men in the Moon, The, (Wells), **VI:** 229, 234, 244

"First Men on Mercury, The" (Morgan, E.), **Supp. IX:** 169

First Ode of the Second Book of Horace Paraphras'd, The (Swift), **III:** 35

"*First Place, A: The Mapping of a World*" *(Malouf), Supp. XII:* 218

First Poems (Muir), **Supp. VI:** 198, **204–205**

First Satire (Wyatt), **I:** 111

First Satire of the Second Book of Horace, Imitated, The (Pope), **III:** 234

First Steps in Reading English (Richards), **Supp. II:** 425

First Things Last (Malouf), **Supp. XII:** 220

"First Things Last" (Malouf), **Supp. XII:** 220

"First Winter of War" (Fuller), **Supp. VII:** 69

First World War, see World War I

First Year in Canterbury Settlement, A (Butler), **Supp. II:** 98, 112

Firstborn, The (Fry), **Supp. III:** 195, 196, 198–199, 207

Firth, Sir Charles Harding, **II:** 241; **III:** 25, 36; **IV:** 289, 290, 291

Fischer, Ernst, **Supp. II:** 228

"Fish" (Lawrence), **VII:** 119

"Fish, The" (Brooke), **Supp. III:** 53, 56, 60

Fish Preferred (Wodehouse), **Supp. III:** 460

"Fisherman, The" (Yeats), **VI:** 214; **Retro. Supp. I:** 331

"*Fishermen with Ploughs: A Poem Cycle* (Brown), **Supp. VI:** 63

"Fishing" (Thomas), **Supp. XII:** 287

Fishmonger's Fiddle (Coppard), **VIII:** 89, 95

"Fishmonger's Fiddle" (Coppard), **VIII:** 95

"Fishy Waters" (Rhys), **Supp. II:** 401

Fit for the Future: The Guide for Women Who Want to Live Well (Winterson), **Supp. IV:** 542

"Fitz–Boodle Papers, The" (Thackeray), **V:** 38

FitzGerald, Edward, **IV:** xvii, xxii, xxiii, 310, **340–353; V:** xxv

Fitzgerald, Penelope, **Supp. V: 95–109**

Fitzgerald, Percy, **III:** 125, 135

Five (Lessing), **Supp. I:** 239, 240, 241, 242

Five Autumn Songs for Children's Voices (Hughes), **Supp. I:** 357

"Five Dreams" (Nye), **Supp. X:** 205

"Five Eleven Ninety Nine" (Armitage), **VIII:** 9–11, 15

Five Finger Exercise (Shaffer), **Supp. I:** 313, **314–317,** 319, 322, 323, 327

Five Looks at Elizabeth Bishop (Stevenson), **Supp. VI:** 264–265

"Five Minutes" (Nicholson), **Supp. VI:** 216

Five Metaphysical Poets (Bennett), **II:** 181, 202

Five Nations, The (Kipling), **VI:** 204

Five Novelettes by Charlotte Brontë (ed. Gérin), **V:** 151

"Five Orange Pips, The" (Doyle), **Supp. II:** 174

"Five Poems on Film Directors" (Morgan, E.), **Supp. IX:** 163

Five Red Herrings, The (Sayers), **Supp. III:** 334, 343–344

Five Rivers (Nicholson), **Supp. VI: 213–215,** 216

Five Sermons on the Errors of the Roman Catholic Church (Maturin), **VIII:** 197, 208

"Five Songs" (Auden), **Retro. Supp. I:** 11–12

"Five Students, The" (Hardy), **VI:** 17

Five Tales (Galsworthy), **VI:** 276

Five Uncollected Essays of Matthew Arnold (ed. Allott), **V:** 216

Fivefold Screen, The (Plomer), **Supp. XI:** 213

Five–Year Plan, A (Kerr), **Supp. XII:** 194, 195

Fixed Period, The (Trollope), **V:** 102

Flag on the Island, A (Naipaul), **Supp. I:** 394

Flame of Life, The (Sillitoe), **Supp. V:** 410, 421, 424

Flame Tree (Hart), **Supp. XI:** 126–127

"Flaming Heart Upon the Book and Picture of the Seraphicall Saint Teresa, The" (Crashaw), **II:** 182

"Flaming sighs that boil within my breast, The" (Wyatt), **I:** 109–110

Flare Path (Rattigan), **Supp. VII:** 311–312, 313, 314

Flatman, Thomas, **II:** 133

Flaubert, Gustave, **V:** xviii–xxiv, 340, 353, 429; **Supp. IV:** 68, 69, 136, 157, 163, 167

Flaubert's Parrot (Barnes), **Supp. IV:** 65, 67, 68–70, 72, 73

Flaws in the Glass: A Self–Portrait (White), **Supp. I:** 129, 130, 132, 149

Flea, The (Donne), **I:** 355; **Retro. Supp. II:** 88

"Fleckno, an English Priest at Rome" (Marvell), **II:** 211

"Fleet" (Coppard), **VIII:** 88

Fleming, Ian, **Supp. IV:** 212

Fleshly School of Poetry, The (Buchanan), **V:** 238, 245

Fletcher, Ian, **V:** xii, xiii, xxvii, 359

Fletcher, Ifan Kyrle, **Supp. II:** 201, 202, 203

Fletcher, John, **II: 42–67,** 79, 82, 87–88, 90, 91, 93, 185, 305, 340, 357, 359

Fletcher, Phineas, **II:** 138

Fletcher, Thomas, **II:** 21

Fleurs du Mal (Baudelaire), **V:** xxii, 316, 329, 411

Fleurs du Mal (Swinburne), **V:** 329, 331, 333

"Flickerbridge" (James), **VI:** 69

Flight from the Enchanter, The (Murdoch), **Supp. I: 220–222**

Flight into Camden (Storey), **Supp. I:** 408, 410–411, 414, 415, 419

"Flight of the Duchess, The" (Browning), **IV:** 356, 361, 368; **Retro. Supp. II:** 24

"Flight of the Earls, The" (Boland), **Supp. V:** 36

Flight of the Falcon, The (du Maurier), **Supp. III:** 139, 141

Flint Anchor, The (Warner), **Supp. VII:** 376, 378–379

"Flitting, The" (McGuckian), **Supp. V:** 281

Flood, A (Moore), **VI:** 99

Flood, The (Rankin), **Supp. X:** 244, 246–247, 250

"Flooded Meadows" (Gunn), **Supp. IV:** 267

Floor Games (Wells), **VI:** 227

"Flora" (Dutton), **Supp. XII:** 88

Flora Selbornesis (White), **Supp. VI:** 282–283

"Florent" (Gower), **I:** 55

Florentine Painting and Its Social Background (Antal), **Supp. IV:** 80

Flores Solitudinis (Vaughan), **II:** 185, 201

Floud, Peter, **V:** 296, 307

"Flower, The" (Herbert), **II:** 119n 125; **Retro. Supp. II:** 177–178

Flower Beneath the Foot, The (Firbank), **Supp. II:** 202, 205, **216–218**

Flower Master, The (McGuckian), **Supp. V:** 277, 278, 281–282

"Flower Master, The" (McGuckian), **Supp. V:** 281

Flower Master and Other Poems, The (McGuckian), **Supp. V:** 281

"Flower Poem" (Hope), **Supp. VII:** 154

Flowers and Shadows (Okri), **Supp. V:** 347–348, 350, 352, 354–355

Flower of Courtesy (Lydgate), **I:** 57, 60, 62

Flowering Death of a Salesman (Stoppard), **Supp. I:** 439

Flowers and Insects (Hughes), **Retro. Supp. II:** 214

"Flowers of Empire, The" (Kincaid), **Supp. VII:** 229

"Flowers of Evil" (Kincaid), **Supp. VII:** 219

Flowering Rifle (Campbell), **VII:** 428

Flowering Wilderness (Galsworthy), **VI:** 275, 282

Flowers of Passion (Moore), **VI:** 85, 98

Flurried Years, The (Hunt), **VI:** 333

Flush: A Biography (Woolf), **Retro. Supp. I:** 308, 320–321

Flute–Player, The (Thomas), **Supp. IV:** 479–480, 481

"Fly, The" (Blake), **III:** 295–296

"Fly, The" (Chatwin), **Supp. IV:** 158

"Fly, The" (Mansfield), **VII:** 176

Fly Away Peter (Malouf), **Supp. XII:** 217, 224–225

"Flying Above California" (Gunn), **Supp. IV:** 263

"Flying Ace, The" (Redgrove), **Supp. VI:** 236

"Flying Bum, The" (Plomer), **Supp. XI:** 222

Flying Hero Class (Keneally), **Supp. IV:** 347

Flying in to Love (Thomas), **Supp. IV:** 486–487

Flying Inn, The (Chesterton), **VI:** 340

"Flyting of Crawford and Herbert, The" (Crawford and Herbert), **Supp. XI:** 68

"Flyting of Dunbar and Kennedie, The" (Dunbar), **VIII:** 117, 118, 126–127

"Focherty" (MacDiarmid), **Supp. XII:** 205

Foe (Coetzee), **Supp. VI:** 75–76, **83–84**

Foe–Farrell (Quiller–Couch), **V:** 384

Folding Star, The (Hollinghurst), **Supp. X:** 120–122, 128–134

"Folk Wisdom" (Kinsella), **Supp. V:** 263

"Folklore" (Murray), **Supp. VII:** 276

Folk–Lore in the Old Testament (Frazer), **Supp. III:** 176

Follow My Leader (Rattigan), **Supp. VII:** 310

"Follower" (Heaney), **Supp. IV:** 410

"Followers, The" (Thomas), **Supp. I:** 183

Following a Lark (Brown), **Supp. VI:** 72

"Folly" (Murphy), **Supp. V:** 327

Folly of Industry, The (Wycherley), **II:** 322

"Fond Memory" (Boland), **Supp. V:** 35

Fontaine amoureuse, **I:** 33

"Food of the Dead" (Graves), **VII:** 269

Fool, The (Bond), **Supp. I:** 423, 434, 435

"Fool's Song" (Cornford), **VIII:** 107

Fools of Fortune (Trevor), **Supp. IV:** 502, 503, 512–514, 517

Foot of Clive, The (Berger), **Supp. IV:** 79, 84–85

"Football at Slack" (Hughes), **Retro. Supp. II:** 210–211

Foote, Samuel, **III:** 253; **V:** 261

Footfalls (Beckett), **Retro. Supp. I:** 28

Footnote to History, A: Eight Years of Trouble in Samoa (Stevenson), **V:** 396

"Footsteps of Death, The" (Steel), **Supp. XII:** 269

"For a Five–Year–Old" (Adcock), **Supp. XII:** 5

"For a Greeting" (MacCaig), **Supp. VI:** 185

"For a Young Matron" (McGuckian), **Supp. V:** 284–285

For All That I Found There (Blackwood), **Supp. IX:** 3–6, 8–9, 11

"For All We Have and Are" (Kipling), **VI:** 415

"For Andrew" (Adcock), **Supp. XII:** 5

"For Ann Scott–Moncrieff" (Muir), **Supp. VI:** 207

For Children: The Gates of Paradise (Blake), **III:** 307

"For Conscience' Sake" (Hardy), **VI:** 22

For Crying Out Loud (Wallace–Crabbe), **VIII:** 322–323

"For Heidi with Blue Hair" (Adcock), **Supp. XII:** 9

"For John Heath–Stubbs" (Graham), **Supp. VII:** 116

For Love Alone (Stead), **Supp. IV:** 470–473

For Love and Life (Oliphant), **Supp. X:** 220

For Love & Money: Writing, Reading, Traveling, 1967–1987 (Raban), **Supp. XI:** 228

"For M. S. Singing *Frühlingsglaube* in 1945" (Cornford), **VIII:** 111

For Queen and Country: Britain in the Victorian Age (ed. Drabble), **Supp. IV:** 230

"For Ring–Givers" (Reid), **Supp. VII:** 329

For Services Rendered (Maugham), **VI:** 368

"For St. James" (Nicholson), **Supp. VI:** 214

"For the Fallen" (Binyon), **VI:** 416; **VII:** 448

For the Islands I sing (Brown), **Supp. VI:** 61–66, 68–69

For the Municipality's Elderly (Reading), **VIII:** 262–263

"For the Previous Owner" (McGuckian), **Supp. V:** 283

For the Sexes: The Gates of Paradise (Blake), **III:** 307

For the Time Being (Auden), **VII:** 379; **Retro. Supp. I:** 10–11

For the Unfallen: Poems (Hill), **Supp. V:** 184–186

"For to Admire" (Kipling), **VI:** 203

"Forbidden Love of Noreen Tiernan, The" (McCabe), **Supp. IX:** 136–137

"Force, The" (Redgrove), **Supp. VI:** 231

Force, The (Redgrove), **Supp. VI:** 231

Force of Nature, The (Haywood), **Supp. XII:** 135

"Force that through the green fuse drives the flower, The" (Thomas), **II:** 156; **Supp. I: 171–173,** 177

Forc'd Marriage, The; or, The Jealous Bridegroom (Behn), **Supp. III:** 22, 24, 25–26

Ford, Charles, **III:** 33, 34

Ford, Ford Madox, **VI:** 145–146, 238, **319–333,** 416, 439; **VII:** xi, xv, xxi, 89

Ford, John, **II:** 57, 69, 83, 85, **87–101**

Ford Madox Ford (Rhys), **Supp. II:** 388, 390, 391

Ford Madox Ford: Letters (ed. Ludwig), **VI:** 332

"Fordham Castle" (James), **VI:** 69

"Forefathers" (Blunden), **Supp. XI:** 42–43, 45

Foreign Parts (Galloway), **Supp. XII:** 117, 123–126, 129, 130

Foreigners, The (Tutchin), **III:** 3

"Foregone Conclusion, The" (Warner), **Supp. VII:** 380

"Foreplay" (Maitland), **Supp. XI:** 175

"Forerunners, The" (Herbert), **Retro. Supp. II:** 180

Forest, The (Galsworthy), **VI:** 276, 287

Forest, The (Jonson), **Retro. Supp. I:** 164

Forest Minstrel, The (Hogg), **Supp. X:** 106

"Forest Path to the Spring, The" (Lowry), **Supp. III:** 270, 282

Forester, C. S., **Supp. IV:** 207, 208

"Foresterhill" (Brown), **Supp. VI:** 59

Foresters, The (Tennyson), **IV:** 328, 338

Forests of Lithuania, The (Davie), **Supp. VI:** 108, 115

Forewords and Afterwords (Auden), **VII:** 394; **Retro. Supp. I:** 1, 6

Forge, The (Hall), **Supp. VI:** 120–121, 124–125

"Forge, The" (Heaney), **Supp. II:** 271; **Retro. Supp. I:** 128

"Forge, The" (Russell), **VIII:** 291

"Forget about me" (tr. Reid), **Supp. VII:** 332

"Forget not yet" (Wyatt), **I:** 106

Forging of Fantom, The (Hill, R.), **Supp. IX:** 117

Forgive Me, Sire (Cameron), **Supp. IX:** 17, 29

"Forgive Me, Sire" (Cameron), **Supp. IX:** 25–27

"Forgiveness" (Jennings), **Supp. V:** 217–218

"Forgiveness, A" (Browning), **IV:** 360

Forgiveness of Sins, The (Williams, C. W. S.), **Supp. IX:** 284

"Forgotten" (Milne), **Supp. V:** 303

"Forgotten of the Foot" (Stevenson), **Supp. VI:** 262

"Form and Realism in the West Indian Artist" (Harris), **Supp. V:** 145

"Former House, A" (Nye), **Supp. X:** 205

"Former Paths" (Thomas), **Supp. XII:** 281

Fornaldarsögur, **VIII:** 236

Forrest, James F., **II:** 245n

Fors Clavigera (Ruskin), **V:** 174, 181, 184

"Forsaken Garden, A" (Swinburne), **V:** 314, 327

Forster, E. M., **IV:** 302, 306; **V:** xxiv, 208, 229, 230; **VI:** xii, 365, **397–413; VII:** xi, xv, 18, 21, 34, 35, 122, 144; **Supp. I:** 260; **Supp. II:** 199, 205, 210, 223, 227, 289, 293; **Supp. III:** 49; **Supp. IV:** 440, 489; **Retro. Supp. II: 135– 150**

Forster, John, **IV:** 87, 89, 95, 99, 100, 240; **V:** 47, 72

Forsyte Saga, The (Galsworthy), **VI:** xiii, 269, 272, 274; *see also Man of Property, The;* "Indian Summer of a Forsyte"; *In Chancery; To Let*

Fortescue, Chichester, **V:** 76–83, 85

Fortnightly Review (periodical), **V:** 279, 338

Fortunate Isles, and Their Union, The (Jonson), **Retro. Supp. I:** 165

Fortunate Mistress, The: or, A History of . . . Mademoiselle de Beleau . . . (Defoe), **III:** 13

"Fortune, A" (Fallon), **Supp. XII:** 112– 113

Fortune of War, The (O'Brian), **Supp. XII:** 256

Fortunes and Misfortunes of the Famous Moll Flanders, The (Defoe), *see Moll Flanders*

Fortunes of Falstaff, The (Wilson), **III:** 116n

Fortunes of Nigel, The (Scott), **IV:** 30, 35, 37, 39

Forty New Poems (Davies), **Supp. XI:** 97

Forty Years On (Bennett), **VIII:** 20–21, 22–23

"Forty–seventh Saturday, The" (Trevor), **Supp. IV:** 501

Forward from Liberalism (Spender), **Supp. II:** 488

Fóstbræðra saga, **VIII:** 239, 241

Foster, A. D., **III:** 345

"Fostering" (Fallon), **Supp. XII:** 107– 108, 109

Foucault, Michel, **Supp. IV:** 442

Foucault's Pendulum (Eco), **Supp. IV:** 116

"Found" (Rossetti), **V:** 240

Found in the Street (Highsmith), **Supp. V:** 171, 178–179

"Foundation of the Kingdom of Angria" (Brontë), **V:** 110–111

Foundations of Aesthetics, The (Richards and Ogden), **Supp. II:** 408, **409–410**

Foundations of Joy, The (Wallace–Crabbe), **VIII:** 318

"Fountain" (Jennings), **Supp. V:** 210, 212

Fountain of Self–love, The (Jonson), **Retro. Supp. I:** 158, 160

Fountain Overflows, The (West), **Supp. III:** 431–432, 443

Fountains in the Sand (Douglas), **VI:** 294, 297, 299, 300, 305

Four Ages of Poetry, The (Peacock), **IV:** 168–169, 170

Four and a Half Dancing Men (Stevenson), **Supp. VI: 264**

Four Banks of the River of Space, The (Harris), **Supp. V:** 137, 140, 142–144

Four Countries (Plomer), **Supp. XI:** 216, 222

Four Day's Wonder (Milne), **Supp. V:** 310

Four–Dimensional Nightmare, The (Ballard), **Supp. V:** 23

Four Dissertations (Hume), **Supp. III:** 231, 238

4.50 from Paddington (Christie; U.S. title, *What Mrs. McGillicuddy Saw*), **Supp. II:** 132

Four Georges, The (Thackeray), **V:** 20, 34–35, 38

Four Hymns (Spenser), **I:** 124

Four Last Things (More), **Supp. VII:** 234, 246–247

Four Lectures (Trollope), **V:** 102

"Four Letter Word, A" (Sisson), **Supp. XI:** 253

Four Loves, The (Lewis), **Supp. III:** 249, 264–265

"Four Meetings" (James), **VI:** 69

Four Plays (Stevenson and Henley), **V:** 396

Four Plays (White), **Supp. I:** 131

Four Plays for Dancers (Yeats), **VI:** 218

4.48 Psychosis (Kane), **VIII:** 148, 149, 150–151, 155, 159–160

Four Prentices of London with the Conquest of Jerusalem (Heywood), **II:** 48

Four Quartets (Eliot), **VII:** 143, 148, 153–157; **Retro. Supp. II:** 121, 130– 131; *see also* "The Dry Salvages," "East Coker," "Little Gidding"

"Four Walks in the Country near Saint Brieuc" (Mahon) **Supp. VI:** 168

Four Zoas, The (Blake), **III:** 300, 302– 303, 307; **Retro. Supp. I:** 44

Four–Gated City, The (Lessing), **Supp. I:** 245, 248, 250, 251, 255

Foure–footed Beastes (Topsel), **II:** 137

"14 November 1973" (Betjeman), **VII:** 372

Fourteenth Century Verse and Prose (Sisam), **I:** 20, 21

"Fourth of May, The" (Ewart), **Supp. VII:** 36

Fowler, Alastair, **I:** 237

Fowler, H. W., **VI:** 76

Fowles, John, **Supp. I: 291–311**

Foxe, The (Jonson), **Retro. Supp. I:** 163, 164

Fox and the Wolf, The (Henryson), **Supp. VII:** 136, 138, 140

Fox, Caroline, **IV:** 54

Fox, Chris, **Supp. IV:** 88

Fox, George, **IV:** 45

Fox, Ralph, **Supp. IV:** 464, 466

"Fox, The" (Lawrence), **VII:** 90, 91

Fox, the Wolf, and the Cadger, The (Henryson), **Supp. VII:** 136, 140

Fox, the Wolf, and the Husbandman, The (Henryson), **Supp. VII:** 136, 140

"Fox Trot" (Sitwell), **VII:** 131

Foxe, that begylit the Wolf, in the Schadow of the Mone, The (Henryson), see *Fox, the Wolf, and the Husbandman, The*

"Fra Lippo Lippi" (Browning), **IV:** 357, 361, 369; **Retro. Supp. II:** 27

Fra Rupert: The Last Part of a Trilogy (Landor), **IV:** 100

"Fracture" (Dutton), **Supp. XII:** 97–98

"Fragment" (Brooke), **VI:** 421

"Fragment of a Greek Tragedy" (Housman), **VI:** 156

Fragmenta Aurea (Suckling), **II:** 238

Fragments (Armah), **Supp. X:** 1–6, 12

"Fragments" (Hulme), **Supp. VI:** 137– 138

Fragments of Ancient Poetry (Macpherson), **VIII:** 183–185, 187, 189, 194

"Fragoletta" (Swinburne), **V:** 320

"Frail as thy love, The flowers were dead" (Peacock), **IV:** 157

"Frame for Poetry, A" (Thomas), **Supp. XII:** 279

Framley Parsonage (Trollope), **V:** xxii, 93, 101

"France" (Dunn), **Supp. X:** 76

"France, an Ode" (Coleridge), **IV:** 55

"France, December 1870" (Meredith), **V:** 223

"Frances" (Adcock), **Supp. XII:** 13

"Frances" (Brontë), **V:** 132

Francophile, The (Friel), **Supp. V:** 115

Francillon, R. E., **V:** 83

Francis, Dick, **Supp. IV:** 285

Francis, G. H., **IV:** 270

Francis, P., **III:** 249

"Francis Beaumont" (Swinburne), **V:** 332

Franck, Richard, **II:** 131–132

"Frank Fane: A Ballad" (Swinburne), **V:** 332

Frankenstein; or, The Modern Prometheus (Shelley), **III: 329–331,** 341, 342, 345; **Supp. III:** 355, **356– 363,** 369, 372, 385; **Retro. Supp. I:** 247

Frankenstein Un–bound (Aldiss), **III:** 341, 345

Franklin's Tale, The (Chaucer), **I:** 23

Fraser, Antonia, **Supp. V:** 20

Fraser, G. S., **VI:** xiv, xxxiii; **VII:** xviii, 422, 425, 443

Fraser's (periodical), **IV:** 259; **V:** 19, 22, 111, 142

"Frater Ave atque Vale" (Tennyson), **IV:** 327, 336

Fraternity (Galsworthy), **VI:** 274, 278, 279–280, 285

"Frau Brechenmacher Attends a Wedding" (Mansfield), **VII:** 172

"Frau Fischer" (Mansfield), **VII:** 172

Fraud (Brookner), **Supp. IV:** 134

Fraunce, Abraham, **I:** 122, 164

Frayn, Michael, **Supp. VII: 51–65**

Frazer, Sir James George, **V:** 204; **Supp. III: 169–190; Supp. IV:** 11, 19

Fred and Madge (Orton), **Supp. V:** 363, 366–367, 372

Frederick the Great (Mitford), **Supp. X:** 167

Fredy Neptune (Murray), **Supp. VII:** 271, 284–286

"Freddy" (Smith), Supp. **II:** 462

Fredolfo (Maturin), **VIII:** 207, 208, 209

Free and Offenceless Justification of a Lately Published and Most Maliciously Misinterpreted Poem Entitled "Andromeda Liberata, A" (Chapman), **I:** 254

Free Fall (Golding), **Supp. I: 75–78,** 81, 83, 85; **Retro. Supp. I:** 98

Free Inquiry into the Nature and Origin of Evil (Jenyns), **Retro. Supp. I:** 148

"Free Radio, The" (Rushdie), **Supp. IV:** 438

Free Thoughts on Public Affairs (Hazlitt), **IV:** 139

"Free Verse: A Post Mortem" (Hope), **Supp. VII:** 155

"Free Women" (Lessing), **Supp. I:** 246–247

Freedom of the City, The (Friel), **Supp. V:** 111, 112, 120–121

Free-Holder (periodical), **III:** 51, 53

Free-Holders Plea against . . . Elections of Parliament–Men, The (Defoe), **III:** 12

Freelands, The (Galsworthy), **VI:** 279

Freeman, Rosemary, **Retro. Supp. II:** 178

Freidan, Betty, **Supp. IV:** 232

French, Sean, **Supp. IV:** 173

French Eton, A (Arnold), **V:** 206, 216

"French Flu, The" (Koestler), **Supp. I:** 35

French Gardiner, The: Instructing How to Cultivate All Sorts of Fruit–Trees . . . (tr. Evelyn), **II:** 287

French Lieutenant's Woman, The (Fowles), **Supp. I:** 291, **300–303**

French Lyrics (Swinburne), **V:** 333

French Poets and Novelists (James), **VI:** 67

French Revolution, The (Blake), **III:** 307; **Retro. Supp. I:** 37

French Revolution, The (Carlyle), **IV:** xii, xix, 240, 243, 245, 249, 250

French Without Tears (Rattigan), **Supp. VII:** 308–310, 311

Frenchman's Creek (du Maurier), **Supp. III:** 144

Frequencies (Thomas), **Supp. XII:** 286, 287–288

Frere, John Hookham, **IV:** 182–183

"Fresh Water" (Motion), **Supp. VII:** 259, 262, 263, 264

Freud, Sigmund, **Supp. IV:** 6, 87, 331, 481, 482, 488, 489, 493

"Freya of the Seven Isles" (Conrad), **VI:** 148

Friar Bacon and Friar Bungay (Greene), **II:** 3; **VIII:** 139, 140–&142

Friar's Tale, The (Chaucer), **I:** 30

"Friary" (Murphy), **Supp. V:** 329

"Friday; or, The Dirge" (Gay), **III:** 56

Friedman, A., **III:** 178, 190

Friel, Brian, **Supp. V: 111–129**

Friend (periodical), **IV:** 50, 55, 56

"Friend, The" (Milne), **Supp. V:** 303

Friend from England, A (Brookner), **Supp. IV:** 129–130

"Friendly Epistle to Mrs. Fry, A" (Hood), **IV:** 257, 267

Friendly Tree, The (Day Lewis), **Supp. III:** 118, 130–131

Friendly Young Ladies, The (Renault), **Supp. IX:** 174–175

Friends and Relations (Bowen), **Supp. II:** 84, **86–87**

"Friends of the Friends, The" (James), **VI:** 69

Friendship's Garland (Arnold), **V:** 206, 213n, 215, 216

Fringe of Leaves, A (White), **Supp. I:** 132, 147–148

"Frog and the Nightingale, The" (Seth), **Supp. X:** 287

Frog He Would A–Fishing Go, A (Potter), **Supp. III:** 298

Frog Prince and Other Poems (Smith), **Supp. II:** 463

"Frogs, The" (Nye), **Supp. X:** 203

Froissart, Jean, **I:** 21

Frolic and the Gentle, The (Ward), **IV:** 86

"From a Brother's Standpoint" (Beerbohm), **Supp. II:** 53–54

From a View to a Death (Powell), **VII:** 345, 353

"From an Unfinished Poem" (Stevenson), **Supp. VI:** 262–263

From Bourgeois Land (Smith, I. C.), **Supp. IX:** 213–214, 216, 220–221

From Centre City (Kinsella), **Supp. V:** 272

From Doon with Death (Rendell), **Supp. IX:** 190–191, 197

From Every Chink of the Ark (Redgrove), **Supp. VI:** 234, 236

From Feathers to Iron (Day Lewis), **Supp. III:** 118, 122, 123–124

From Glasgow to Saturn (Morgan, E.), **Supp. IX:** 157–159, 162, 163, 167–170

From Heaven Lake: Travels Through Sinkiang and Tibet (Seth), **Supp. X:** 277, 280–281, 290

From Man to Man (Schreiner), **Supp. II:** 439, 440, 441, 442, **450–452**

"From My Diary. July 1914" (Owen), **VI:** 446

From My Guy to Sci-Fi: Genre and Women's Writing in the Postmodern World (ed. Carr), **Supp. XI:** 164

"From my sad Retirement" (King), **Supp. VI:** 159

"From My Study" (Stevenson), **Supp. VI:** 264

"From Sorrow Sorrow Yet Is Born" (Tennyson), **IV:** 329

"From the Answers to Job" (Redgrove), **Supp. VI:** 235

From the Five Rivers (Steel), **Supp. XII:** 269

From the Four Winds (Galsworthy), **VI:** 276

"From the Frontier of Writing" (Heaney), **Supp. II:** 280

"From the Greek" (Landor), **IV:** 98

From the Joke Shop (Fuller), **Supp. VII:** 79

"From the Life of a Dowser" (Redgrove), **Supp. VI:** 235, 237

"From the Middle Distance" (Armitage), **VIII:** 9

"From the New World" (Davie), **Supp. VI:** 110

"From the Night of Forebeing" (Thompson), **V:** 443, 448

"From the Painting *Back from Market* by Chardin" (Boland), **Supp. V:** 40

From "The School of Eloquence" (Harrison), **Supp. V:** 150

"From the Top" (Crawford), **Supp. XI:** 80

"From the Wave" (Gunn), **Supp. IV:** 267

"From Tuscan cam my ladies worthi race" (Surrey), **I:** 114

"Frontliners" (Gunesekera), **Supp. X:** 87

Frost, Robert, **VI:** 424; **Supp. III:** 394–395; **Supp. IV:** 413, 420, 423, 480, 487

"Frost at Midnight" (Coleridge), **IV:** 41, 44, 55; **Retro. Supp. II:** 60

Frost in the Flower, The (O'Casey), **VII:** 12

Froude, James Anthony, **IV:** 238, 240, 250, 324; **V:** 278, 287

Frozen Deep, The (Collins), **V:** 42; **Supp. VI:** 92, 95

Frozen Flame, The (O'Brian), **Supp. XII:** 251

"Fruit" (Betjeman), **VII:** 373

Fry, Christopher, **IV:** 318; **Supp. III:** **191**–210

Fry, Roger, **VII:** xii, 34

Fuel for the Flame (Waugh), **Supp. VI:** 276

Fuentes, Carlos, **Supp. IV:** 116, 440

Fugitive, The (Galsworthy), **VI:** 283

"Fugitive" (Russell), **VIII:** 291

Fugitive Pieces (Byron), **IV:** 192

Fulbecke, William, **I:** 218

"Fulbright Scholars" (Hughes), **Retro. Supp. II:** 217

Fulford, William, **VI:** 167

"Full Measures" (Redgrove), **Supp. VI:** 235

Full Moon (Wodehouse), **Supp. III:** 459

"Full Moon and Little Frieda" (Hughes), **Supp. I:** 349–350

Full Moon in March, A (Yeats), **VI:** 222

Fuller, Roy, **VII:** 422, 428–431, **Supp. VII: 67–82**

Fuller, Thomas, **I:** 178; **II:** 45; **Retro. Supp. I:** 152

Fully Empowered (tr. Reid), **Supp. VII:** 332

Fumed Oak (Coward), **Supp. II:** 153

Fumifugium; or, The Inconvenience of Aer and Smoak . . . (Evelyn), **II:** 287

"Function of Criticism at the Present Time, The" (Arnold), **V:** 204–205, 212, 213

"Funeral, The" (Redgrove), **Supp. VI:** 235

Funeral, The (Steele), **II:** 359
"Funeral Blues" (Auden), **Retro. Supp. I:** 6
Funeral Games (Orton), **Supp. V:** 367, 372, 376–377
Funeral Games (Renault), **Supp. IX:** 186–187
"Funeral Music" (Hill), **Supp. V:** 187–188
"Funeral of Youth, The: Threnody" (Brooke), **Supp. III:** 55
"Funeral Poem Upon the Death of . . . Sir Francis Vere, A,"**II:** 37, 41
"Funerall, The" (Donne), **Retro. Supp. II:** 89–90
"Fungi" (Stevenson), **Supp. VI:** 256
"Funnel, The" (Coppard), **VIII:** 96
Furbank, P. N., **VI:** 397; **Supp. II:** 109, 119
Furetière, Antoine, **II:** 354
"Furies, The" (Nye), **Supp. X:** 200
Furies, The (Roberts, K.), **Supp. X:** 261, 263–264
"Furnace, The" (Kinsella), **Supp. V:** 271
Furness, H. H., **I:** 326
Furnivall, F. J., **VI:** 102
Further Studies in a Dying Culture (Caudwell), **Supp. IX:** 33, 43–47
Fussell, Paul, **Supp. IV:** 22, 57
"Fust and His Friends" (Browning), **IV:** 366
"Futility" (Owen), **VI:** 453, 455
Futility Machine, The (Carey), **Supp. XII:** 51–52
"Future, The" (Arnold), **V:** 210
"Future, The" (Murray), **Supp. VII:** 277
Future in America, The: A Search After Reality (Wells), **VI:** 244
Future of Ireland and the Awakening of the Fires, The (Russell), **VIII:** 282
"Future Work" (Adcock), **Supp. XII:** 6
"Futures in Feminist Fiction" (Maitland), **Supp. XI:** 164
"Futurity" (Browning), **IV:** 313
Fyvel, T. R., **VII:** 284

G. (Berger), **Supp. IV:** 79, 85–88, 94
G. B. Shaw (Chesterton), **VI:** 130
G. M. Trevelyan (Moorman), **VI:** 396
"Gabor" (Swift), **Supp. V:** 432
"Gabriel–Ernest" (Saki), **Supp. VI:** 244
Gabriel's Gift (Kureishi), **Supp. XI:** 158–159
"Gabrielle de Bergerac" (James), **VI:** 67, 69
Gadfly, The (Voynich), **VI:** 107
"Gaelic Proverb, The" (Smith, I. C.), **Supp. IX:** 222
"Gaelic Songs" (Smith, I. C.), **Supp. IX:** 215–216
"Gaels in Glasgow/Bangladeshis in Bradford" (Crawford), **Supp. XI:** 73
Gager, William, **I:** 193
"Gala Programme: An Unrecorded Episode in Roman History, The" (Saki), **Supp. VI:** 242
Galahad at Blandings (Wodehouse), **Supp. III:** 460
Galile (Brecht), **IV:** 182
Galland, Antoine, **III:** 327

Gallathea (Lyly), **I:** 200–202
"Gallery, The" (Hart), **Supp. XI:** 123
"Gallery, The" (Marvell), **II:** 211
Galloway, Janice, **Supp. XII: 117–132**
Galsworthy, Ada, **VI:** 271, 272, 273, 274, 282
Galsworthy, John, **V:** xxii, 270n; **VI:** ix, xiii, 133, 260, **269–291; VII:** xii, xiv; **Supp. I:** 163; **Supp. IV:** 229
Galsworthy the Man (Sauter), **VI:** 284
Galt, John, **IV:** 35
"Game, The" (Boland), **Supp. V:** 35
Game, The (Byatt), **Supp. IV:** 139, 141, 143–145, 154
"Game, The" (Motion), **Supp. VII:** 265
Game at Chess, A (Middleton), **II:** 1, 2, 3, **18–21**
Game for the Living, A (Highsmith), **Supp. V:** 172
"Game of Chess, A" (Eliot), **Retro. Supp. II:** 127
Game of Cricket, A (Ayckbourn), **Supp. V:** 3
"Game of Glass, A" (Reid), **Supp. VII:** 327
Game of Logic, The (Carroll), **V:** 273
"Games at Twilight" (Desai), **Supp. V:** 65
Games at Twilight and Other Stories (Desai), **Supp. V:** 55, 65
Gandhi (film), **Supp. IV:** 455
Gandhi, Indira, **Supp. IV:** 165, 231
"Ganymede" (du Maurier), **Supp. III:** 135, 148
Gaol Gate, The (Gregory), **VI:** 315
"Gap, The" (Thomas), **Supp. XII:** 287
"Garbh mac Stairn" (Macpherson), **VIII:** 186
García Márquez, Gabriel, **Supp. IV:** 93, 116, 440, 441, 454, 558
Garden Kalendar (White), **Supp. VI:** 279, 282
"Garden, The" (Cowley), **II:** 194
"Garden, The" (Marvell), **II:** 208, 210, 211, 212, 213–214; **Supp. IV:** 271; **Retro. Supp. II:** 261, 263
"Garden in September, The" (Bridges), **VI:** 78
Garden of Cyrus, The (Browne), **II:** 148, **150–153,** 154, 155, 156
"Garden of Eros, The" (Wilde), **V:** 401, 402
Garden of Fidelity, The: Being the Autobiography of Flora Annie Steel, 1847–1929 (Steel), **Supp. XII:** 265, 266, 267, 273, 275, 276, 277
"Garden of Love, The" (Blake), **Retro. Supp. I:** 42
"Garden of Proserpine, The" (Swinburne), **V:** 320, 321
"Garden of Remembrance" (Kinsella), **Supp. V:** 261
"Garden of the Innocent" (Nicholson), **Supp. VI:** 215
"Garden of Time, The" (Ballard), **Supp. V:** 22
"Garden on the Point, A" (Kinsella), **Supp. V:** 261
Garden Party, A (Behan), **Supp. II:** 67, 68

"Garden Party, The" (Davie), **Supp. VI:** 106
Garden Party, The (Mansfield), **VII:** xv, 171, 177
"Gardener, The" (Kipling), **VI:** 197
"Gardeners" (Dunn), **Supp. X:** 72
Gardeners and Astronomers (Sitwell), **VII:** 138
"Gardener's Daughter, The" (Tennyson), **IV:** 326
Gardener's Year, A (Haggard), **Supp. III:** 214
"Gardens go on forever" (Kelman), **Supp. V:** 256
Gardiner, S. R., **I:** 146
Gardiner, Judith Kegan, **Supp. IV:** 459
Gardner, Helen, **II:** 121, 129
Gardner, Philip, **VI:** xii, xxxiii
Gareth and Lynette (Tennyson), **IV:** 338
Gargantua and Pantagruel (Rabelais), **Supp. IV:** 464
Garibaldi and the Making of Italy (Trevelyan), **VI:** 388–389
Garibaldi and the Thousand (Trevelyan), **VI:** 388–389
Garibaldi, Giuseppe, **Supp. IV:** 86
Garibaldi's Defence of the Roman Republic (Trevelyan), **VI:** xv, **387–389,** 394
Garis, Robert, **V:** 49–50, 70, 73
Garland of Laurel, The (Skelton), **I:** 81, 82, 90, 93–94
Garmont of Gud Ladeis, The (Henryson), **Supp. VII:** 146, 148
Garner, Ross, **II:** 186
Garnered Sheaves: Essays, Addresses, and Reviews (Frazer), **Supp. III:** 172
Garnett, Edward, **VI:** 135, 149, 273, 277, 278, 283, 366, 373; **VII:** xiv, 89
Garnier, Robert, **I:** 218
Garrett, John, **Supp. IV:** 256
Garrick, David, **I:** 327
Garrick Year, The (Drabble), **Supp. IV:** 230, 236–237
"Garrison, The" (Auden), **Retro. Supp. I:** 13
Garrod, H. W., **III:** 170n, 176
Gascoigne, George, **I:** 215–216, 298
Gaskell, Elizabeth, **IV:** 241, 248; **V:** viii, x, xvi, xxi–xxiii, **1–16,** 108, 116, 122, 137, 147–150; **VI:** viii; **Supp. IV;** 119, 379
Gaskill, William, **II:** 6
"Gaspar Ruiz" (Conrad), **VI:** 148
Gaston de Latour (Pater), **V:** 318n, 357
"Gate" (Fallon), **Supp. XII:** 114–115
Gate, The (Day Lewis), **Supp. III:** 118, 129–130
Gate of Angels, The (Fitzgerald), **Supp. V:** 96, 98, 106–107
Gates of Ivory, The (Drabble), **Supp. IV:** 231, 250–252
Gates of Paradise, The (Blake), *see For Children: The Gates of Paradise; For the Sexes: The Gates of Paradise*
Gates of Pearl, The (Steel), **Supp. XII:** 277
Gates of Wrath, The (Bennett), **VI:** 249
"Gathered Church, A" (Davie), **Supp. VI:** 107

Gathered Church, The (Davie), **Supp. VI:** 105, 115

"Gathering Mushrooms" (Muldoon), **Supp. IV:** 420

"Gathering Sticks on Sunday" (Nicholson), **Supp. VI:** 217

Gathering Storm, The (Churchill), **VI:** 361

Gathering Storm, The (Empson), **Supp. II:** 179, 184, 190

Gatty, Margaret, **V:** 270

Gaudete (Hughes), **Supp. I: 359–363;** **Retro. Supp. II:**209–210

Gaudy Night (Sayers), **Supp. III:** 334, 341, 343, 346–347

Gaunt, William, **VI:** 169

Gautier, Théophile, **IV:** 153*n*; **V:** 320*n*, 346, 404, 410–411; **Supp. IV:** 490

Gavin Ewart Show, The (Ewart), **Supp. VII:** 40

Gawain–Poet, The, **Supp. VII:** 83–101

Gay, John, **II:** 348; **III:** 19, 24, 44, **54–67,** 74

Gayton, Edward, **I:** 279

Gaze of the Gorgon, The (Harrison), **Supp. V:** 160, 164

Gebir (Landor), **IV:** xvi, 88, 95, 99, 100, 217

Gebirus, poema (Landor), **IV:** 99–100

"Geese, The" (Sisson), **Supp. XI:** 258

Gem (periodical), **IV:** 252

"Gemini" (Kipling), **VI:** 184

"General, The" (Sassoon), **VI:** 430

General, The (Sillitoe), **Supp. V:** 410, 415

"General Election, A" (Rushdie), **Supp. IV:** 456

General Grant: An Estimate (Arnold), **V:** 216

General History of Discoveries . . . in Useful Arts, A (Defoe), **III:** 14

General History of Music (Burney), **Supp. III:** 66

General History of the Robberies and Murders of . . . Pyrates, A (Defoe), **III:** 13

General History of the Turkes (Knolles), **III:** 108

General Inventorie of the History of France (Brimeston), **I:** 249

General Prologue, The (Chaucer), **I:** 23, 26, 27–28, 38–40

"General Satyre, A" (Dunbar), **VIII:** 122, 126

"Generations" (Stevenson), **Supp. VI:** 257

Generous Days, The (Spender), **Supp. II:** 493

Genesis, **Retro. Supp. II:** 301

"Genesis" (Hill), **Supp. V:** 184–185

"Genesis" (Swinburne), **V:** 325

"Genesis and Catastrophe" (Dahl), **Supp. IV:** 221

Genesis B, **Retro. Supp. II:** 301

Geneva (Shaw), **VI:** 125, 127–128, 129; **Retro. Supp. II:** 324

Genius of the Future: Studies in French Art Criticism, The (Brookner), **Supp. IV:** 122–123

Genius of the Thames, The (Peacock), **IV:** 169

Genius of Thomas Hardy, The (ed. Drabble), **Supp. IV:** 230

"Gentians" (McGuckian), **Supp. V:** 281

Gentle Island, The (Friel), **Supp. V:** 119–120

"Gentle Sex, The" (Ewart), **Supp. VII:** 42

Gentleman Dancing–Master, The (Wycherley), **II:** 308, 309, **313–314,** 321

Gentleman in the Parlour, The (Maugham), **VI:** 371

Gentleman Usher, The (Chapman), **I:** 244–245

Gentleman's Magazine (periodical), **III:** 107

Gentlemen in England (Wilson), **Supp. VI:** 302–303, 305

Gentler Birth, A (Fallon), **Supp. XII:** 104

Gentlewomen's Companion, The (Woolley), **Supp. III:** 21

Geoffrey de Vinsauf, **I:** 23 39–40, 59

Geography and History of England, The (Goldsmith), **III:** 191

George, Henry, **VI:** 102

"George and the Seraph" (Brooke–Rose), **Supp. IV:** 103

George Bernard Shaw (Chesterton), **VI:** 344

George Crabbe and His Times (Huchon), **III:** 273*n*

George Eliot (Stephen), **V:** 289

George Eliot: Her Life and Books (Bullet), **V:** 196, 200–201

George Eliot, Selected Essays, Poems and Other Writings (Byatt), **Supp. IV:** 151

George Eliot's Life as Related in Her Letters and Journals (ed. Cross), **V:** 13, 200

George Gissing: Grave Comedian (Donnelly), **V:** 427*n*, 438

"George Herbert: The Art of Plainness" (Stein), **Retro. Supp. II:** 181

George Moore: L'homme et l'oeuvre (Noel), **VI:** 98, 99

George Orwell (Fyvel), **VII:** 287

George Passant (Snow), **VII:** 324, 325–326

George Silverman's Explanation (Dickens), **V:** 72

George's Ghosts (Maddox), **Retro. Supp. I:** 327, 328

George's Marvellous Medicine (Dahl), **Supp. IV:** 204–205

"Georgian Boyhood, A" (Connolly), **Supp. III:** 1–2

Georgian Poetry 1911–1912 (ed. Marsh), **VI:** 416, 419, 420, 453; **VII:** xvi; **Supp. III:** 45, 53–54, 397

Georgics of Virgil, The (tr. Day Lewis), **Supp. III:** 118

"Georgina's Reasons" (James), **VI:** 69

Gerard; or, The World, the Flesh, and the Devil (Braddon), **VIII:** 49

Gerald: A Portrait (du Maurier), **Supp. III:** 134–135, 138–139

Gerard Manley Hopkins: A Critical Symposium (Kenyon Critics), **V:** 382

Gerard Manley Hopkins: The Classical Background . . . (Bender), **V:** 364–365, 382

"Geriatric" (Thomas), **Supp. XII:** 291

Géricault, Théodore, **Supp. IV:** 71–72, 73

Gérin, Winifred, **V:** x, xxvii, 111, 151, 152, 153

Germ (periodical), **V:** xxi, 235–236, 249

"German Chronicle" (Hulme), **Supp. VI:** 139

German Requiem, A (Kerr), **Supp. XII:** 187, 188, 191

"Germinal" (Russell), **VIII:** 290

"Gerontion" (Eliot), **VII:** 144, 146, 147, 152; **Retro. Supp. II:** 123–124

Gerugte van Reen (Brink), **Supp. VI:** 49

Gesta Romanorum, **I:** 52 53

"Gethsemane" (Nicholson), **Supp. VI:** 214

Get Ready for Battle (Jhabvala), **Supp. V:** 228–229

"Getting at Stars" (Armitage), **VIII:** 4

Getting It Right (Howard), **Supp. XI:** 135, 141, 143–144, 148

Getting Married (Shaw), **VI:** 115, 117–118

"Getting Off the Altitude" (Lessing), **Supp. I:** 240

Getting On (Bennett), **VIII:** 20, 21, 25–26

"Getting Poisoned" (Ishiguro), **Supp. IV:** 303

"Getting there" (Kelman), **Supp. V:** 249

Getting to Know the General (Greene), **Supp. I:** 1, 13, 14, 17

Geulincx, Arnold, **Supp. I: 44**

"Geve place ye lovers" (Surrey), **I:** 120

"Geysers, The" (Gunn), **Supp. IV:** 268, 269, 276

Ghastly Good Taste (Betjeman), **VII:** 357, 361

"Ghetto–Blastir" (Crawford), **Supp. XI:** 68

Ghost Child, The (Tennant), **Supp. IX:** 239

Ghost in the Machine, The (Koestler), **Supp. I:** 37, 38

"Ghost of Ferozsha Baag, The" (Mistry), **Supp. X:** 138–139

Ghost of Lucrece, The (Middleton), **II:** 3

Ghost Orchid, The (Longley), **VIII:** 175–177

"Ghost Orchid, The" (Longley), **VIII:** 175–176

Ghost Road, The (Barker), **Supp. IV:** 45, 46, 57, 61–63

Ghost Trio (Beckett), **Retro. Supp. I:** 29

"Ghost–Crabs" (Hughes), **Supp. I:** 349, 350; **Retro. Supp. II:** 206

"Ghostkeeper" (Lowry), **Supp. III:** 285

"Ghostly Father, The" (Redgrove), **Supp. VI:** 228

"Ghosts" (Redgrove), **Supp. VI:** 228, 236

"Ghosts" (Reid), **Supp. VII:** 327

"Ghost's Moonshine, The" (Beddoes), **Supp. XI:** 29

Giants' Bread (Christie), **Supp. II:** 133

Giaour, The (Byron), **III:** 338; **IV:** xvii, 172, 173–174, 180, 192

Gibbon, Edward, **III:** 109, **221–233; IV:** xiv, xvi, 93, 284; **V:** 425; **VI:** 347, 353, 383, 390n

Gibbons, Brian, **I:** 281

Gibson, W. W., **VI:** 416

Gide, André, **V:** xxiii, 402

Gidez, Richard B., **Supp. IV:** 326, 339–340

Gifford, William, **II:** 96; **IV:** 133

"Gift of Boxes, A" (Longley), **VIII:** 176

"Gifts" (Thomas), **Supp. XII:** 285

"Giggling" (Adcock), **Supp. XII:** 13

"Gigolo and Gigolette" (Maugham), **VI:** 370

Gil Blas (tr. Smollett), **III:** 150

Gil Perez, The Gallician (tr. FitzGerald), **IV:** 344

Gilbert, Elliott, **VI:** 194

"Gilbert" (Brontë), **V:** 131–132

Gilbert, Peter, **Supp. IV:** 354

Gilbert, Sandra, **Retro. Supp. I:** 59–60

"Gilbert's Mother" (Trevor), **Supp. IV:** 505

Gilchrist, Andrew, **Retro. Supp. I:** 46

Gilfillan, George, **I:** 98

"Gilles de Retz" (Keyes), **VII:** 437

Gilliam, Terry, **Supp. IV:** 455

Gillman, James, **IV:** 48–49, 50, 56

Gilman, Charlotte Perkins, **Supp. III:** 147

Gilpin, William, **IV:** 36, 37

Gilson, Étienne, **VI:** 341

"Gin and Goldenrod" (Lowry), **Supp. III:** 282

"Ginger Hero" (Friel), **Supp. V:** 113

Ginger, You're Barmy (Lodge), **Supp. IV:** 364–365, 368–369, 371

Giorgione da Castelfranco, **V:** 345, 348

"Giorgione" (Pater), **V:** 345, 348, 353

"Gipsy Vans" (Kipling), **VI:** 193, 196

"Giraffes, The" (Fuller), **VII:** 430, **Supp. VII:** 70

"Girl" (Kincaid), **Supp. VII:** 220, 221, 223

"Girl at the Seaside" (Murphy), **Supp. V:** 313, 318

"Girl From Zlot, The" (Stallworthy), **Supp. X:** 299–300

Girl in Winter, A (Larkin), **Supp. I:** 286, 287

Girl, 20 (Amis), **Supp. II:** 15–16; **Supp. IV:** 29

Girl Weeping for the Death of Her Canary (Greuze), **Supp. IV:** 122

"Girl Who Loved Graveyards, The" (James), **Supp. IV:** 340

Girlhood of Mary Virgin, The (Rossetti), **V:** 236, 248, 249

Girlitude: A Memoir of the 50s and 60s (Tennant), **Supp. IX:** 239

Girls in Their Married Bliss (O'Brien), **Supp. V:** 334, 337–338

"Girls in Their Season" (Mahon), **Supp. VI:** 167

Girls of Slender Means, The (Spark), **Supp. I:** 200, 204, 206

"Girls on a Bridge" (Mahon), **Supp. VI:** 174

Gisborne, John, **IV:** 206

Gísla saga Súrssonar, **VIII:** 241

Gismond of Salerne (Wilmot), **I:** 216

Gissing, George, **V:** xiii, xxii, xxv–xxvi, 69, **423–438; VI:** 365; **Supp. IV:** 7–8

Gittings, Robert, **Supp. III:** 194

"Give Her A Pattern" (Lawrence), **II:** 330n

Give Me Your Answer, Do! (Friel), **Supp. V:** 127–128

"Given Heart, The" (Cowley), **II:** 197

Giving Alms No Charity . . . (Defoe), **III:** 13

Gladiators, The (Koestler), **Supp. I:** 27, 28, 29n

"Glanmore Revisited" (Heaney), **Retro. Supp. I:** 132

"Glanmore Sonnets" (Heaney), **Supp. II:** 276

Glanvill, Joseph, **II:** 275

"Glasgow 5 March 1971" (Morgan, E.), **Supp. IX:** 162

"Glasgow Green" (Morgan, E.), **Supp. IX:** 158

Glasgow Herald, **Supp. XII:** 207

"Glasgow October 1971" (Morgan, E.), **Supp. IX:** 162

Glass–Blowers, The (du Maurier), **Supp. III:** 136, 138

Glass Cell, The (Highsmith), **Supp. V:** 174

Glass Cottage, A Nautical Romance, The (Redgrove), **Supp. VI:** 230–231

Glass of Blessings, A (Pym), **Supp. II:** **377–378**

Glass Town chronicles (Brontës), **V:** 110–111

Gleanings from the Menagerie and Aviary at Knowsley Hall (Lear), **V:** 76, 87

Gleckner, R. F., **IV:** 173, 194

Glen, Heather, **III:** 297

Glendinning, Victoria, **Supp. II:** 78, 80, 90, 95

"Glimpse, The" (Cornford), **VIII:** 106

Glimpse of America, A (Stoker), **Supp. III:** 380

Glimpse of Reality, The (Shaw), **VI:** 129

Gloag, Julian, **Supp. IV:** 390

"Globe in North Carolina, The" (Mahon), **Supp. VI:** 174

"Gloire de Dijon" (Lawrence), **Retro. Supp. II:** 233

Gloriana: Opera in Three Acts (Plomer), **Supp. XI:** 222

Glorious First of June, The, **III:** 266

"Glory, A" (Armitage), **VIII:** 11

"Glory of Women" (Sassoon), **VI:** 430

"Gnomes" (Ewart), **Supp. VII:** 39

gnomic moralizing poem, **I:** 57

"Go for" (Thomas), **Supp. III:** 399

"Go, Lovely Rose!" (Waller), **II:** 234

Go, Piteous Heart (Skelton), **I:** 83

Go When You See the Green Man Walking (Brooke–Rose), **Supp. IV:** 103–104

"Goal" (Dutton), **Supp. XII:** 96–97

"Goal of Valerius" (Bacon), **I:** 263

Go–Between, The (Hartley), **Supp. VII:** 119, 120, 121, 127–129, 131, 132; **Retro. Supp. I:** 227

Goat Green; or, The Better Gift (Powys), **VIII:** 255

Goat's Song, A (Healy), **Supp. IX:** 96–98, 101–103

"Goblin Market" (Rossetti), **V:** 250, 256–258

Goblin Market and Other Poems (Rossetti), **V:** xxii, 250, 260

Goblins, The (Suckling), **II:** 226

"God" (Powys), **VIII:** 248

God and His Gifts, A (Compton–Burnett), **VII:** 60, 64, 65

God and the Bible (Arnold), **V:** 216

"God and the Jolly Bored Bog–Mouse" (Cope), **VIII:** 74

God Bless Karl Marx! (Sisson), **Supp. XI:** 251

"God! How I Hate You, You Young Cheerful Men" (West), **VI:** 423

"God Moves in a Mysterious Way" (Cowper), **III:** 210

God of Glass, The (Redgrove), **Supp. VI:** 231

God of Small Things (Roy), **Supp. V:** 67, 75

God that Failed, The (Crossman), **Supp. I:** 25

"God the Eater" (Smith), **Supp. II:** 468

God the Invisible King (Wells), **VI:** 227

"God Who Eats Corn, The" (Murphy), **Supp. V:** 313, 323–324

"Godfather Dottery" (Powys), **VIII:** 258

"God's Eternity" (Blake), **III:** 300

"God's Funeral" (Hardy), **Retro. Supp. I:** 121

God's Funeral (Wilson), **Supp. VI:** 298, 306, 308, **309**

"God's Grandeur" (Hopkins), **V:** 366; **Retro. Supp. II:** 195

"God's Judgement on a Wicked Bishop" (Southey), **IV:** 67

"Gods of the Copybook Heading, The" (Ewart), **Supp. VII:** 41

Gods of War, with Other Poems (Russell), **VIII:** 287

God's Revenge Against Murder (Reynolds), **II:** 14

Godber, Joyce, **II:** 243, 254

"Goddess, The" (Gunn), **Supp. IV:** 266, 271

Godman, Stanley, **V:** 271, 274

Godolphin, Sidney, **II:** 237, 238, 271

Godwin, E. W., **V:** 404

Godwin, Mary Wollstonecraft, *see* Shelley, Mary Wollstonecraft

Godwin, William, **III:** 329, 330, 332, 340, 345; **IV:** xv, 3, 43, 127, 173, 181, 195–197; **Supp. III:** 355, 363, 370, 474, 476, 480

Goethe, Johann Wolfgang von, **III:** 344; **IV:** xiv–xix, 179, 240, 245, 249; **V:** 214, 343, 344, 402; **Supp. IV:** 28, 479

Goethe's Faust (MacNeice), **VII:** 408–410

Gogh, Vincent van, **Supp. IV:** 148, 154

Gogol, Nikolai, **III:** 340, 345; **Supp. III:** 17

"Going, The" (Hardy), **VI:** 18; **Retro. Supp. I:** 118

"Going Back" (Adcock), **Supp. XII:** 8

"Going Back" (Stevenson), **Supp. VI:** 265

"Going, Going" (Larkin), **Supp. I:** 283

Going Home (Lessing), **Supp. I:** 237

"Going Home" (Mahon), **Supp. VI:** 172

"Going Home (A Letter to Colombo)" (Gunesekera), **Supp. X:** 86

Going On (Reading), **VIII:** 207, 268, 269

Going Solo (Dahl), **Supp. IV:** 206, 208, 210, 211, 222, 225

Going Their Own Ways (Waugh), **Supp. VI:** 273

"Going to Italy" (Davie), **Supp. VI:** 107

"Going to See a Man Hanged" (Thackeray), **V:** 23, 37

Gold, Mike, **Supp. IV:** 464

Gold: A Poem (Brooke–Rose)), **Supp. IV:** 99, 100

Gold Coast Customs (Sitwell), **VII:** xvii, 132, 133–134

Gold in the Sea, The (Friel), **Supp. V:** 113

"Gold in the Sea, The" (Friel), **Supp. V:** 114

"Golden Age, The" (Behn), **Supp. III:** 39–40

Golden Ass (Apulius), **Supp. IV:** 414

Golden Bird, The (Brown), **Supp. VI:** 64

Golden Book of St. John Chrysostom, The, Concerning the Education of Children (tr. Evelyn), **II:** 275, 287

Golden Bough, The (Frazer), **V:** 204; **Supp. III:** 170, 172, 173, 174, 175, 176–182, 184, 185, 186, 187; **Supp. IV:** 12

Golden Bowl, The (James), **VI:** 53, 55, 60–62, 67; **Supp. IV:** 243

Golden Calf, The (Braddon), **VIII:** 49

"Golden Calf" (MacCaig), **Supp. VI:** 186

Golden Chersonese, The (Bird), **Supp. X:** 19, 30–31

Golden Child, The (Fitzgerald), **Supp. V:** 98, 100–101

Golden Echo, The (Garnett), **VI:** 333

Golden Gate: A Novel in Verse, The (Seth), **Supp. X:** 277–279, 281–283, 285–290

"Golden Hair" (Owen), **VI:** 449

Golden Labyrinth, The (Knight), **IV:** 328n, 339

Golden Lads: Sir Francis Bacon, Anthony Bacon, and Their Friends (du Maurier), **Supp. III:** 139

Golden Lion of Granpère, The (Trollope), **V:** 102

"Golden Lyric, The" (Smith, I. C.), **Supp. IX:** 222

Golden Mean, The (Ford), **II:** 88, 100

Golden Notebook, The (Lessing), **Supp. I:** 238, **246–248,** 254, 256; **Supp. IV:** 473

Golden Ocean, The (O'Brian), **Supp. XII:** 248, 251, 252

"Golden Stool, The" (Brathwaite), **Supp. XII:** 39

Golden Targe, The (Dunbar), **I:** 23

Golden Treasury, The (Palgrave), **II:** 208; **IV:** xxii, 196, 337

"Goldfish Nation" (Cope), **VIII:** 77

Golding, Arthur, **I:** 161

Golding, William, **Supp. I: 65–91; Supp. IV:** 392–393; **Retro. Supp. I: 93–107**

Goldring, Douglas, **VI:** 324, 419

Goldsmith, Oliver, **II:** 362, 363; **III:** 40, 110, 149, 165, 173, **177–192,** 256, 277, 278; **Retro. Supp. I:** 149

Goldsworthy Lowes Dickinson (Forster), **VI:** 411

Goldyn Targe, The (Dunbar), **VIII:** 120, 123–124

"Goldyn Targe, The" (Dunbar), **VIII:** 118

Gollancz, Victor, **VII:** xix, 279, 381

Gondal literature (Brontë), **V:** 113–117, 133, 142

Gondal Poems (Brontë), **V:** 152

Gondal's Queen (Ratchford), **V:** 133, 152

Gondibert (Davenant), **II:** 196, 259

Gonne, Maud, **VI:** 207, 210, 211, 212

Good and Faithful Servant, The (Orton), **Supp. V:** 364, 367, 370, 371, 372, 374–375

Good Apprentice, The (Murdoch), **Supp. I:** 231, 232, 233

"Good Aunt, The" (Edgeworth), **Supp. III:** 162

"Good Climate, Friendly Inhabitants" (Gordimer), **Supp. II:** 232

Good Companions, The (Priestley), **VII:** xviii, 209, 211, 215–216

"Good Counsel to a Young Maid" (Carew), **II:** 224

Good Fight, The (Kinsella), **Supp. V:** 267

Good Hanging and Other Stories, A (Rankin), **Supp. X:** 244, 246, 250

"Good Friday" (Herbert), **II:** 128

"Good Friday: Rex Tragicus; or, Christ Going to His Crosse" (Herrick), **II:** 114

"Good Friday, 1613" (Donne), **I:** 368

Good Kipling, The (Gilbert), **VI:** 194

"Good ladies ye that have" (Sumy), **I:** 120

Good Morning. Midnight (Rhys), **Supp. II:** 388, **396–398**

"Good Morrow, The" (MacCaig), **Supp. VI:** 185

Good Natur'd Man, The (Goldsmith), **III:** 111, 180, 187, 191

Good News for the Vilest of Men; or, A Help for Despairing Souls (Bunyan), **II:** 253

"Good Night" (Kinsella), **Supp. V:** 267

Good Night Sweet Ladies (Blackwood), **Supp. IX:** 8, 12–13

Good Soldier, The (Ford), **VI:** 49; **VI:** 319, 323, **327–328,** 329

Good Son, The (film), **Supp. IV:** 390, 400

Good Terrorist, The (Lessing), **Supp. I:** 255–256

Good Time Was Had by All, A (Smith), **Supp. II:** 462

Good Times, The (Kelman), **Supp. V:** 243, 254–256

"Good Town, The" (Muir), **Supp. VI:** 207

Goodbye (Adcock), **Supp. XII:** 14–15

Goodbye Earth and Other Poems (Richards), **Supp. II:** 427, 428

"Good-bye in fear, good-bye in sorrow" (Rossetti), **V:** 255

"Goodbye Marcus, Goodbye Rose" (Rhys), **Supp. II:** 401

Goodbye to All That (Graves), **VI:** xvi; **VII:** xviii, 257, 258

Goodbye to Berlin (Isherwood), **VII:** xx

Goodbye to Berlin (Wilson), **Supp. I:** 156

"Good–Bye to the Mezzogiorno" (Auden), **Retro. Supp. I:** 13

"Goodbye to the USA" (Davie), **Supp. VI:** 113

"Good–Morrow, The" (Donne), **II:** 197

"Goodness—the American Neurosis" (Rushdie), **Supp. IV:** 455–456

"Good–night" (Thomas), **Supp. III:** 400

Goopy Gyne Bagha Byne (film), **Supp. IV:** 450

"Goose, The" (Longley), **VIII:** 172–173

Goose Cross (Kavan), **Supp. VII:** 208

"Goose Fair" (Lawrence), **VII:** 114

"Goose to Donkey" (Murray), **Supp. VII:** 282

"Gooseberry Season" (Armitage), **VIII:** 5

Gorboduc (Norton and Sackville), **I:** 161–162, 214–216

Gordimer, Nadine, **Supp. II: 225–243**

Gordon, D. J., **I:** 237, 239

Gordon, Ian Alistair, **VII:** xvii, xxxvii

Gorgon's Head and Other Literary Pieces, The (Frazer), **Supp. III:** 176

Gorse Fires (Longley), **VIII:** 166, 169, 174–175

Gorton, Mary, **V:** 312, 313, 315–316, 330

Gospel of Nicodemus (tr. Trevisa), see *Evangelium Nicodemi*

Gosse, Edmund, **II:** 354, 361, 363, 364; **V:** 311, 313, 334, 392, 395

Gossip from the Forest (Keneally), **Supp. IV:** 346

Gosson, Stephen, **I:** 161

Gothic Architecture (Morris), **V:** 306

Gothic fiction, **III: 324–346; IV:** 110, 111; **V:** 142–143

Gothic Revival, The (Clark), **III:** 325, 346

"Gourmet, The" (Ishiguro), **Supp. IV:** 304, 306

Government of the Tongue: The 1986 T. S. Eliot Memorial Lectures and Other Critical Writings (Heaney), **Supp. II:** 268, 269; **Retro. Supp. I:** 131

Gower, John, **I:** 20, 41, **48–56,** 57, 321

Goya, Francisco de, **Supp. IV:** 125

Grace Abounding to the Chief of Sinners (Bunyan), **II:** 240, 241, 243–245, 250, 253; **Supp. IV:** 242

Grace Darling (Swinburne), **V:** 333

"Grace of the Way" (Thompson), **V:** 442

Graffigny, Mme de, **Supp. III:** 75

Graham Greene (Lodge), **Supp. IV:** 365

Graham, James, *see* Montrose, marquess of

Graham, W. S., **Supp. VII: 103–117**

Grain Kings, The (Roberts, K.), **Supp. X:** 270–271

"Grain Kings, The" (Roberts, K.), **Supp. X:** 271

Grain of Wheat, A (Ngũgĩ), **VIII:** 212, 219–220

"Gra´inne" (Roberts, K.), **Supp. X:** 273–274

Grammar of Assent, An Essay in Aid of a (Newman), **V:** 340, **Supp. VII:** 301–302

Grammar of Metaphor, A (Brooke–Rose)), **Supp. IV:** 98, 113

"Grammarian's Funeral, A" (Browning), **IV:** 357, 361, 366

Grand Alliance, The (Churchill), **VI:** 361

Grand Babylon Hotel, The (Bennett), **VI:** 249, 253, 262, 266

"Grand Ballet" (Cornford), **VIII:** 113

Grand Meaulnes, Le (Alain–Fournier), **Supp. I:** 299

"Grandmother's Story, The" (Murray), **Supp. VII:** 280

"Grandparent's" (Spender), **Supp. II:** 494

Grania (Gregory), **VI:** 316

Granny Scarecrow (Stevenson), **Supp. VI: 265**

Grant, Duncan, **VI:** 118

Granta (publication), **Supp. IV:** 304; **Supp. XII:** 66

"Grantchester" (Brooke), **Supp. III:** 52, 60

Granville Barker, Harley, **I:** 329; **VI:** ix, 104, 113, 273

Grass, Günter, **Supp. IV:** 440

Grass Is Singing, The (Lessing), **Supp. I:** 237, 239, 243, 248

"Grass Widows, The" (Trevor), **Supp. IV:** 503

Grasshopper (Rendell), **Supp. IX:** 189, 203

"Gratiana Dancing and Singing" (Lovelace), **II:** 230

Grave, The (Blair), **Retro. Supp. I:** 45

"Grave, The" (tr. Morgan), **Supp. IX:** 161

"Grave by the Handpost, The" (Hardy), **VI:** 22

"Gravel Walks, The" (Heaney), **Retro. Supp. I:** 133

Graves, Robert, **II:** 94; **VI:** xvi, 207, 211, 219, 419; **VII:** xvi, xviii–xx, **257–272;** **Supp. II:** 185; **Supp. III:** 60; **Supp. IV:** 558; **Retro. Supp. I:** 144

"Gravities: West" (Fallon), **Supp. XII:** 111

Gravity's Rainbow (Pynchon), **Supp. IV:** 116

Gray, Alasdair, **Supp. IX: 79–93**

Gray, Thomas, **II:** 200; **III:** 118, 119, **136–145,** 173, 294, 325

"Gray's Anatomy" (Malouf), **Supp. XII:** 220

Great Adventure, The (Bennett), **VI:** 250, 266; *see also Buried Alive*

Great Apes (Self), **Supp. V:** 398–400

"Great Automatic Grammatisator, The" (Dahl), **Supp. IV:** 216–217

Great Boer War, The (Doyle), **Supp. II:** 160

Great Broxopp, The (Milne), **Supp. V:** 299

Great Catherine (Shaw), **VI:** 119

Great Contemporaries (Churchill), **VI:** 354, 356

Great Depression, **VII:** xix

Great Divorce, The (Lewis), **Supp. III:** 56

Great Duke of Florence, The (Massinger), **Supp. XI:** 184

Great Exhibition, The (Hare), **Supp. IV:** 281

Great Expectations (Dickens), **V:** xxii, 42, 60, 63, 66–68, 72

Great Favourite, The; or, The Duke of Lerma (Howard), **II:** 100

Great Fire of London, The (Ackroyd), **Supp. VI:** 4–5, 10

"Great Good Place, The" (James), **VI:** 69

Great Granny Webster (Blackwood), **Supp. IX:** 2, 6, 10–11, 16

Great Hoggarty Diamond, The (Thackeray), **V:** 21, 38

Great Hunger, The (Kavanagh), **Supp. VII:** 187, 190–192, 193, 194, 199

Great Instauration, The (Bacon), **I:** 259, 272

Great Law of Subordination Consider'd, The (Defoe), **III:** 13

"Great Lover, The" (Brooke), **Supp. III:** 556

"Great Man, The" (Caudwell), **Supp. IX:** 35, 37

"Great Man, The" (Motion), **Supp. VII:** 256

"Great McEwen, Scottish Hypnotist, The" (Crawford), **Supp. XI:** 71

"Great men have been among us" (Wordsworth), **II:** 208

Great Moments in Aviation (film), **Supp. IV:** 542

Great Port: A Passage through New York, The (Morris, J.), **Supp. X:** 182

Great Short Stories of Detection, Mystery and Horror (ed. Sayers), **III:** 341; **Supp. III:** 340, 341

"Great Spirits Now on Earth Are Sojourning . . . A (Keats), **IV:** 214

Great Trade Route (Ford), **VI:** 324

Great Tradition, The (Leavis), **VI:** 68, 149; **VII:** 234, **248–251;** **Retro. Supp. I:** 90

"Great Unknown, The" (Hood), **IV:** 267

Great Victorian Collection, The (Moore, B.), **Supp. IX:** 143–144, 154

Great War and Modern Memory, The (Fussell), **Supp. IV:** 57

Great World, The (Malouf), **Supp. XII:** 218, 226–227

Greater Lakeland (Nicholson), **Supp. VI:** 223

"Greater Love" (Owen), **VI:** 450

Greater Trumps, The (Williams, C. W. S.), **Supp. IX:** 281

"Greatest TV Show on Earth, The" (Ballard), **Supp. V:** 28

Greatness of the Soul, A, . . . (Bunyan), **II:** 253

Greber, Giacomo, **II:** 325

Grecian History, The (Goldsmith), **III:** 181, 191

Greek Christian Poets, The, and the English Poets (Browning), **IV:** 321

"Greek Interpreter, The" (Doyle), **Supp. II:** l67

Greek Islands, The (Durrell), **Supp. I:** 102

Greek Studies (Pater), **V:** 355, 357

Greeks have a word for it, The (Unsworth), **Supp. VII:** 354, 355–356, 357, 359

Green Fool, The (Kavanagh), **Supp. VII:** 183, 186, 187, 188, 194, 199

Green, Henry, **Supp. II: 247–264**

"Green Hills of Africa, The" (Fuller), **Supp. VII:** 69

"Greenhouse Effect, The" (Adcock), **Supp. XII:** 12

Green, Joseph Henry, **IV:** 57

Green, Roger Lancelyn, **V:** 265n, 273, 274

Green Crow, The (O'Casey), **VII:** 13

"Green Geese" (Sitwell), **VII:** 131

"Green, Green Is Aghir" (Cameron), **VII:** 426; **Supp. IX:** 27

Green Helmet, The (Yeats), **VI:** 222

"Green Hills of Africa" (Fuller), **VII:** 429, 432

"Green Leaf, The" (Smith, I. C.), **Supp. IX:** 223

Green Man, The (Amis), **Supp. II:** 13–14

"Green Mountain, Black Mountain" (Stevenson), **Supp. VI:** 256–257, 261–262, 266

Green Shore, The (Nicholson), **Supp. VI: 219–220**

Green Song (Sitwell), **VII:** 132, 135, 136

"Green Tea" (Le Fanu), **III:** 340, 345

Greene, Graham, **VI:** 329, 370; **VII:** xii; **Supp. I: 1–20; Supp. II:** 311, 324; **Supp. IV:** 4, 10, 13, 17, 21, 157, 365, 369, 373–374, 505; **Supp. V:** 26; **Retro. Supp. II: 151–167**

Greene, Robert, **I:** 165, 220, 275, 286, 296, 322; **II:** 3; **VIII: 131–146**

Greene's Arcadia (Greene). *See Menaphon*

Greenlees, Ian Gordon, **VI:** xxxiii

"Greenshank" (MacCaig), **Supp. VI:** 192

Greenvoe (Brown), **Supp. VI:** 64, **65–66**

"Greenwich—Whitebait" (Thackeray), **V:** 38

Greenwood, Edward Baker, **VII:** xix, xxxvii

Greenwood, Frederick, **V:** 1

Greer, Germaine, **Supp. IV:** 436

Greg, W. R., **V:** 5, 7, 15

Greg, W. W., **I:** 279

Gregory, Lady Augusta, **VI:** 210, 218, **307–312, 314–316,** 317–318; **VII:** 1, 3, 42

Gregory, Sir Richard, **VI:** 233

Greiffenhagen, Maurice, **VI:** 91

Gremlins, The (Dahl), **Supp. IV:** 202, 211–212

"Grenadier" (Housman), **VI:** 160

Grenfell, Julian, **VI:** xvi, 417–418, 420

"Gretchen" (Gissing), **V:** 437

"Gretna Green" (Behan), **Supp. II:** 64

Grettis saga, **VIII:** 234–235, 238, 241

Greuze, Jean–Baptiste, **Supp. IV:** 122

Greuze: The Rise and Fall of an Eighteenth Century Phenomenon (Brookner), **Supp. IV:** 122

Greville, Fulke, **I:** 160, 164; **Supp. IV:** 256; **Supp. XI: 105–119**

Grey Area (Self), **Supp. V:** 402–404

Grey Eminence (Huxley), **VII:** 205

Grey of Fallodon (Trevelyan), **VI:** 383, 391
"Grey Woman, The" (Gaskell), **V:** 15
Greybeards at Play (Chesterton), **VI:** 336
Greyhound for Breakfast (Kelman), **Supp. V:** 242, 249–250
"Greyhound for Breakfast" (Kelman), **Supp. V:** 250
Grid, The (Kerr), **Supp. XII:** 194, 195
Gridiron, The (Kerr), **Supp. XII:** 194, 195
"Grief" (Browning), **IV:** 313, 318
Grief Observed, A (Lewis), **Supp. III:** 249
"Grief on the Death of Prince Henry, A" (Tourneur), **II:** 37, 41
Grierson, Herbert J. C., **II:** 121, 130, 196, 200, 202, 258; **Retro. Supp. II:** 173
Grigson, Geoffrey, **IV:** 47; **VII:** xvi
Grim Smile of the Five Towns, The (Bennett), **VI:** 250, 253–254
Grímnismál, **VIII:** 230
Grimus (Rushdie), **Supp. IV:** 435, 438–439, 443, 450
Gris, Juan, **Supp. IV:** 81
"Grisly Folk, The" (Wells), **Retro. Supp. I:** 96
Groatsworth of Wit, A (Greene), **I:** 275, 276; **VIII:** 131, 132
Grœnlendinga saga, **VIII:** 240
Grosskurth, Phyllis, **V:** xxvii
Grote, George, **IV:** 289
Group of Noble Dames, A (Hardy), **VI:** 20, 22
"Grove, The" (Muir), **Supp. VI:** 206
"Growing, Flying, Happening" (Reid), **Supp. VII:** 328
"Growing Old" (Arnold), **V:** 203
Growing Pains: The Shaping of a Writer (du Maurier), **Supp. III:** 135, 142, 144
Growing Points (Jennings), **Supp. V:** 217
Growing Rich (Weldon), **Supp. IV:** 531, 533
Growth of Love, The (Bridges), **VI:** 81, 83
Growth of Plato's Ideal Theory, The (Frazer), **Supp. III:** 170–171
"Grub First, Then Ethics" (Auden), **Retro. Supp. I:** 7, 13
Grünewald, Mathias, **Supp. IV:** 85
Gryffydh, Jane, **IV:** 159
Gryll Grange (Peacock), **IV:** xxii, 166–167, 170
Grylls, R. Glynn, **V:** 247, 260; **VII:** xvii, xxxviii
Guardian (periodical), **III:** 46, 49, 50
Guardian, The (Cowley), **II:** 194, 202
Guardian, The (Massinger), **Supp. XI:** 184
Guarini, Guarino, **II:** 49–50
Gubar, Susan, **Retro. Supp. I:** 59–60
"Gude Grey Katt, The" (Hogg), **Supp. X:** 110
"Guerrillas" (Dunn), **Supp. X:** 70–71
Guerrillas (Naipaul), **Supp. I:** 396–397
Guest from the Future, The (Stallworthy), **Supp. X:** 298–302
"Guest from the Future, The" (Stallworthy), **Supp. X:** 298

Guest of Honour, A (Gordimer), **Supp. II:** 229–230, 231
Guide Through the District of the Lakes in the North of England, A (Wordsworth), **IV:** 25
Guide to Kulchur (Pound), **VI:** 333
"Guide to the Perplexed" (Malouf), **Supp. XII:** 220
Guido della Colonna, **I:** 57
Guild of St. George, The, **V:** 182
Guillaume de Deguilleville, **I:** 57
Guillaume de Lorris, **I:** 71
"Guilt and Sorrow" (Wordsworth), **IV:** 5, 45
"Guinevere" (Tennyson), **IV:** 336–337, 338
Guise, The (Marlowe), *see Massacre at Paris, The*
Guise, The (Webster), **II:** 68, 85
"Guitarist Tunes Up, The" (Cornford), **VIII:** 114
Gulliver's Travels (Swift), **II:** 261; **III:** 11, 20, **23–26,** 28, 35; **VI:** 121–122; **Supp. IV:** 502; **Retro. Supp. I:** 274, 275, 276–277, 279–282
Gun for Sale, A (Greene; U.S. title, *This Gun for Hire*), **Supp. I:** 3, 6–7, 10; **Retro. Supp. II:** 153
Guncsckcra, Romcsh, **Supp. X:** 85–102
"Gunesh Chund" (Steel), **Supp. XII:** 269
Gunn, Ander, **Supp. IV:** 265
Gunn, Thom, **Supp. IV:** 255–279
Gunnlaugs saga ormstunga, **VIII:** 239
Guns of Navarone, The (film, Ambler), **Supp. IV:** 3
Gurdjieff, Georges I., **Supp. IV:** 1, 5
Gurney, Ivor, **VI:** 416, **425–427**
Gussow, Mel, **Retro. Supp. I:** 217–218
Gutch, J. M., **IV:** 78, 81
Guthlac, **Retro. Supp. II:** 303
Gutteridge, Bernard, **VII:** 422, 432–433
Guy Domville (James), **VI:** 39
Guy Mannering (Scott), **IV:** xvii, 31–32, 38
Guy of Warwick (Lydgate), **I:** 58
Guy Renton (Waugh), **Supp. VI:** 274–275
Guyana Quartet (Harris), **Supp. V:** 132, 133, 135
Guzman Go Home and Other Stories (Sillitoe), **Supp. V:** 410
Gyðinga saga, **VIII:** 237
Gylfaginning, **VIII:** 243
"Gym" (Murphy), **Supp. V:** 328
Gypsies Metamorphos'd (Jonson), **II:** 111*n*
"Gypsonhilia" (Hart), **Supp. XI:** 128–129
"Gyrtt in my giltetesse gowne" (Surrey), **I:** 115
"Healthy Landscape with Dormouse" (Warner), **Supp. VII:** 380
"Hee–Haw" (Warner), **Supp. VII:** 380
"House Grown Silent, The" (Warner), **Supp. VII:** 371

H. G. Wells and His Critics (Raknem), **VI:** 228, 245, 246
H. G. Wells: His Turbulent Life and Times (Dickson), **VI:** 246

H. G. Wells: The Critical Heritage (ed. Parrinder), **VI:** 246
Ha! Ha! Among the Trumpets (Lewis), **VII:** 447, 448
Habeas Corpus (Bennett), **VIII:** 25
Habermas, Jürgen, **Supp. IV:** 112
Habington, William, **II:** 222, 237, 238
Habit of Loving, The (Lessing), **Supp. I:** 244
"Habit of Perfection, The" (Hopkins), **V:** 362, 381
Hadjinicolaou, Nicos, **Supp. IV:** 90
"Hag, The" (Herrick), **II:** 111
Haggard, H. Rider, **Supp. III:** 211–228; **Supp. IV:** 201, 484
Haight, Gordon, **V:** 199, 200, 201
Hail and Farewell (Moore), **VI:** xii, 85, 88, 97, 99
"Hailstones" (Heaney), **Supp. II:** 280
"Hair, The" (Caudwell), **Supp. IX:** 37
Hakluyt, Richard, **I:** 150, 267; **III:** 7
Halcyon; or, The Future of Monogamy (Brittain), **Supp. X:** 39
Hale, Kathleen, **Supp. IV:** 231
"Hale, sterne superne" (Dunbar), **VIII:** 128–129
"Half–a–Crown's Worth of Cheap Knowledge" (Thackeray), **V:** 22, 37
Half–Mother, The (Tennant), *see Woman Beware Woman*
Halfway House (Blunden), **Supp. XI:** 46
Halidon Hill (Scott), **IV:** 39
Halifax, marquess of, **III:** 38, 39, 40, 46
Hall, Donald, **Supp. IV:** 256
Hall, Edward, **II:** 43
Hall, Joseph, **II:** 25–26, 81; **IV:** 286
Hall, Radclyffe, **VI:** 411; **Supp. VI:** 119–132
Hall, Samuel (pseud., O'Nolan), **Supp. II:** 322
"Hall, The" (Hart), **Supp. XI:** 124
Hall of Healing (O'Casey), **VII:** 11–12
Hall of the Saurians (Redgrove), **Supp. VI:** 236
Hallam, Arthur, **IV:** 234, 235, 328–336, 338
Hallam, Henry, **IV:** 283
Haller, Albrecht von, **III:** 88
Hallfreðar saga vandræðaskálds, **VIII:** 239
Halloran's Little Boat (Keneally), **Supp. IV:** 348
"Hallowe'en" (Burns), **III:** 315
Hallowe'en Party (Christie), **Supp. II:** 125, 134
"Hallway, The" (Healy), **Supp. IX:** 107
Ham Funeral, The (White), **Supp. I:** 131, 134, 149, 150
"Hamadryad, The" (Landor), **IV:** 96
Hamburger, Michael, **Supp. V:** 199
Hamilton, Sir George Rostrevor, **IV:** xxiv
Hamlet (early version), **I:** 212, 221, 315
Hamlet (Shakespeare), **I:** 188, 280, 313, 315–316; **II:** 29, 36, 71, 75, 84; **III:** 170, 234; **V:** 328; **Supp. IV:** 63, 149, 283, 295
Hamlet in Autumn (Smith, I. C.), **Supp. IX:** 215
"Hamlet, Princess of Denmark" (Beerbohm), **Supp. II:** 55

"Hammer, The" (Hart), **Supp. XI:** 127

Hammerton, Sir John, **V:** 393, 397

Hammett, Dashiell, **Supp. II:** 130, 132

Hampden, John, **V:** 393, 395

"Hampstead: the Horse Chestnut Trees" (Gunn), **Supp. IV:** 270–271

Hampton, Christopher, **Supp. IV:** 281

"Hand, The" (Highsmith), **Supp. V:** 179–180

"Hand and Soul" (Rossetti), **V:** 236, 320

Hand in Hand (Stallworthy), **Supp. X:** 294, 296

Hand of Ethelberta, The: A Comedy in Chapters (Hardy), **VI:** 4, 6, 20; **Retro. Supp. I:** 114

"Hand of Solo, A" (Kinsella), **Supp. V:** 267, 274

"Hand that signed the paper, The" (Thomas), **Supp. I:** 174

"Handful of Air, A" (Fallon), **Supp. XII:** 111

Handful of Dust, A (Waugh), **VII:** xx, 294, 295–297

"Handful of People, A" (Ewart), **Supp. VII:** 39

"Hands" (Ewart), **Supp. VII:** 39

"Hands" (Hughes), **Retro. Supp. II:** 212

Hands Across the Sea (Coward), **Supp. II:** 153

"Handsome Heart, The" (Hopkins), **V:** 368–369

Handsworth Songs (film), **Supp. IV:** 445

Hanged by the Neck (Koestler), **Supp. I:** 36

"Hanging, A" (Powell), **VII:** 276

Hanging Garden, The (Rankin), **Supp. X:**

Hanging Judge, The (Stevenson), **V:** 396

"Hangover Square" (Mahon), **Supp. VI:** 177

"Hangzhou Garden, A" (Seth), **Supp. X:** 281

Hapgood (Stoppard), **Retro. Supp. II:** 354–355

Happier Life, The (Dunn), **Supp. X:** 70–71

"Happily Ever After" (Huxley), **VII:** 199–200

"Happiness" (Owen), **VI:** 449, 458

"Happinesse to Hospitalitie; or, A Hearty Wish to Good House-keeping" (Herrick), **II:** 111

Happy Days (Beckett), **Supp. I:** 46, 52, 54, 56, 57, 60; **Retro. Supp. I:** 26–27

"Happy Family, A" (Trevor), **Supp. IV:** 503

Happy Haven, The (Arden), **Supp. II:** 29

Happy Hypocrite: A Fairy Tale for Tired Men, The (Beerbohm), **Supp. II:** 45, 46

"Happy Man, The" (Thomson), **Supp. III:** 417

"Happy old man, whose worth all mankind knows" (Flatman), **II:** 133

Happy Pair, The (Sedley), **II:** 266, 271

"Happy Prince, The" (Wilde), **V:** 406, 419; **Retro. Supp. II:** 365; **Retro. Supp. II:** 365

Happy Valley (White), **Supp. I:** 130, 132–133, 136

Haq, Zia ul–, **Supp. IV:** 444

Hárbarðsljóð, **VIII:** 230

Hard Life, The (O'Nolan), **Supp. II:** 336–337

Hard Times (Dickens), **IV:** 247; **V:** viii, xxi, 4, 42, 47, 59, 63–64, 68, 70, 71

Hardie and Baird: The Last Days (Kelman), **Supp. V:** 256–257

Hardie and Baird and Other Plays (Kelman), **Supp. V:** 256–257

"Hardness of Light, The" (Davie), **Supp. VI:** 109

Hardy, Barbara, **V:** ix, xxviii, 39, 73, 201

Hardy, G. H., **VII:** 239–240

Hardy, Thomas, **II:** 69; **III:** 278; **V:** xx–xxvi, 144, 279, 429; **VI:** x, **1–22,** 253, 377; **VII:** xvi; list of short stories, **VI:** 22; **Supp. IV:** 94, 116, 146, 471, 493; **Retro. Supp. I:** **109–122**

"Hardy and the Hag" (Fowles), **Supp. I:** 302, 305

Hardy of Wessex (Weber), **VI:** 21

Hare, J. C., **IV:** 54

Hare, David, **Supp. IV:** 182, **281–300**

"Harem Trousers" (McGuckian), **Supp. V:** 286

Harington, Sir John, **I:** 131

"Hark, My Soul! It Is the Lord" (Cowper), **III:** 210

"Hark! the Dog's Howl" (Tennyson), **IV:** 332

Harland's Half Acre (Malouf), **Supp. XII:** 225–226

Harlequinade (Rattigan), **Supp. VII:** 315–316

Harlot's House, The (Wilde), **V:** 410, 418, 419

Harm Done (Rendell), **Supp. IX:** 189, 196, 198, 199, 201

"Harmonies" (Kinsella), **Supp. V:** 271

"Harmony, The" (Redgrove), **Supp. VI:** 236

"Harmony of the Spheres, The" (Rushdie), **Supp. IV:** 445

Harness Room, The (Hartley), **Supp. VII:** 132

Harold (Tennyson), **IV:** 328, 338

Harold Muggins Is a Martyr (Arden and D'Arcy), **Supp. II:** 31

Harold the Dauntless (Scott), **IV:** 39

Harold's Leap (Smith), **Supp. II:** 462

Haroun and the Sea of Stories (Rushdie), **Supp. IV:** 433, 438, 450–451

Harriet Hume: A London Fantasy (West), **Supp. III:** 441–442

Harrington (Edgeworth), **Supp. III:** **161–163**

Harriet Said? (Bainbridge), **Supp. VI:** 17, **19**

Harriot, Thomas, **I:** 277, 278

Harris, Frank, **VI:** 102

Harris, Joseph, **II:** 305

Harris, Wilson, **Supp. V:** **131–147**

"Harris East End" (MacCaig), **Supp. VI:** 182

Harrison, Frederic, **V:** 428–429

Harrison, Tony, **Supp. V:** **149–165**

Harry Heathcote of Gangoil (Trollope), **V:** 102

"Harry Ploughman" (Hopkins), **V:** 376–377

Harsh Voice, The (West), **Supp. III:** 442

Hart, Kevin, **Supp. XI:** **121–133**

Hartley, David, **IV:** 43, 45, 50, 165

Hartley, L. P., **Supp. VII:** **119–133**

Hartmann, Edward von, **Supp. II:** 108

"Harvest Bow, The" (Heaney), **Supp. II:** 276–277

Harvest Festival, The (O'Casey), **VII:** 12

"Harvesting, The" (Hughes), **Supp. II:** 348

Harvesting the Edge: Some Personal Explorations from a Marginal Garden (Dutton), **Supp. XII:** 84–85

Harvey, Christopher, **II:** 138; **Retro. Supp. II:** 172

Harvey, Gabriel, **I:** 122–123, 125; **II:** 25

Harvey, T. W. J., **V:** 63, 199, 201

Harvey, William, **I:** 264

"Has Your Soul Slipped" (Owen), **VI:** 446

Hashemite Kings, The (Morris, J.), **Supp. X:** 175

"Hassock and the Psalter, The" (Powys), **VIII:** 255

Hastings, Warren, **IV:** xv–xvi, 271, 278

Hatfield, C. W., **V:** 133, 151, 152, 153

Háttatal, **VIII:** 243

Haunch of Venison, The (Goldsmith), **III:** 191

Haunted and the Haunters, The (Bulwer-Lytton), **III:** 340, 345

"Haunted House, The" (Graves), **VII:** 263

"Haunted House, The" (Hood), **IV:** 261, 262

Haunted Man and the Ghost's Bargain, The (Dickens), **V:** 71

"Haunter, The" (Hardy), **VI:** 18; **Retro. Supp. I:** 117

Haunter of the Dark, The . . . (Lovecraft), **III:** 345

Hávamál, **VIII:** 230, 232

Have His Carcase (Sayers), **Supp. III:** 345–346

Having a Wonderful Time (Churchill), **Supp. IV:** 180, 181

Haw Lantern, The (Heaney), **Supp. II:** 268, **279–281**; **Retro. Supp. I:** 131–132

Hawaiian Archipelago, The (Bird), **Supp. X:** 19, 24–26, 28

Hawes, Stephen, **I:** 49, 81

"Hawk, The" (Brown), **Supp. VI:** **71**

Hawk in the Rain, The (Hughes), **Supp. I:** 343, 345, 363

"Hawk in the Rain, The" (Hughes), **Supp. I:** 345; **Retro. Supp. II:** 200, 202–204

"Hawk Roosting" (Hughes), **Retro. Supp. II:** 204

Hawkfall (Brown), **Supp. VI:** 69

Hawkins, Lewis Weldon, **VI:** 85

Hawkins, Sir John, **II:** 143

Hawksmoor (Ackroyd), **Supp. VI:** 6–7, 10–11

Hawthorne, Nathaniel, **III:** 339, 345; **VI:** 27, 33–34; **Supp. IV:** 116

Hawthorne (James), **VI:** 33–34, 67

Haxton, Gerald, **VI:** 369

Hay Fever (Coward), **Supp. II:** 139, 141, **143–145,** 148, 156

Haydon, Benjamin, **IV:** 214, 227, 312

Hayes, Albert McHarg, **Retro. Supp. II:** 181

"Haymaking" (Thomas), **Supp. III:** 399, 405

"Haystack in the Floods, The" (Morris), **V:** 293

Hayter, Alethea, **III:** 338, 346; **IV:** xxiv–xxv, 57, 322

Haywood, Eliza, **Supp. XII: 133–148**

Hazard, Paul, **III:** 72

"Hazards of the House" (Dunn), **Supp. X:** 68

Hazlitt, William, **I:** 121, 164; **II:** 153, 332, 333, 337, 343, 346, 349, 354, 361, 363, 364; **III:** 68, 70, 76, 78, 165, 276–277; **IV:** ix, xi, xiv, xvii–xix, 38, 39, 41, 50, **125–140,** 217; **Retro. Supp. I:** 147; **Retro. Supp. II:** 51, 52

"He" (Lessing), **Supp. I:** 244

He Came Down from Heaven (Williams, C. W. S.), **Supp. IX:** 284

He Knew He Was Right (Trollope), **V:** 98, 99, 102

"He Revisits His First School" (Hardy), **VI:** 17

"He saw my heart's woe" (Brontë), **V:** 132

"He Says Goodbye in November" (Cornford), **VIII:** 114

He That Will Not When He May (Oliphant), **Supp. X:** 220

"He Thinks of His Past Greatness . . . When a Part of the Constellations of Heaven" (Yeats), **VI:** 211

"He thought he saw a Banker's Clerk" (Carroll), **V:** 270

"He Wonders Whether to Praise or to Blame Her" (Brooke), **Supp. III:** 55

Head to Toe (Orton), **Supp. V:** 363, 365–366

"Head Spider, The" (Murray), **Supp. VII:** 283, 284

Heading Home (Hare), **Supp. IV:** 288, 290–291

Headlong (Frayn), **Supp. VII:** 64, 65

Headlong Hall (Peacock), **IV:** xvii, **160–163,** 164, 165, 168, 169

Healers, The (Armah), **Supp. X:** 1–3, 6–11, 13

Healing Art, The (Wilson), **Supp. VI:** **299–300,** 301, 303, 308

Health and Holiness (Thompson), **V:** 450, 451

"Healthy Landscape with Dormouse" (Warner), **Supp. VII:** 380

Healy, Dermot, **Supp. IX: 95–108**

Heaney, Seamus, **Supp. II: 267–281; Supp. IV:** 410, 412, 416, 420–421, 427, 428; **Retro. Supp. I: 123–135**

Hear Us O Lord from Heaven Thy Dwelling Place (Lowry), **Supp. III: 281–282**

Hearing Secret Harmonies (Powell), **VII:** 352, 353

"Hears not my Phillis, how the Birds" (Sedley), **II:** 264

Heart and Science (Collins), **Supp. VI:** 102–103

"Heart, II, The" (Thompson), **V:** 443

Heart Clock (Hill, R.), **Supp. IX:** 111

"Heart Knoweth Its Own Bitterness, The" (Rossetti), **V:** 253–254

"Heart of a King, The" (Plomer), **Supp. XI:** 222

Heart of Darkness (Conrad), **VI:** 135, **136–139,** 172; **Supp. IV:** 189, 250, 403; **Retro. Supp. II:** 73–75

"Heart of John Middleton, The" (Gaskell), **V:** 15

Heart of Mid-Lothian, The (Scott), **IV:** xvii, 30, 31, 33–34, 35, 36, 39; **V:** 5

Heart of the Country, The (Weldon), **Supp. IV:** 526–528

Heart of the Matter, The (Greene), **Supp. I:** 2, 8, 11–12, 13; **Retro. Supp. II:** 157–159

Heart to Heart (Rattigan), **Supp. VII:** 320

Heartbreak (Maitland), **Supp. XI:** 163

"Heartbreak Hotel" (Brathwaite), **Supp. XII:** 42

Heartbreak House (Shaw), **V:** 423; **VI:** viii, xv, 118, **120–121,** 127, 129; **Retro. Supp. II:** 322–323

Heartland (Harris), **Supp. V:** 135, 136

"Heartland, The" (Fallon), **Supp. XII:** 109

Hearts and Lives of Men, The (Weldon), **Supp. IV:** 536

"Heart's Chill Between" (Rossetti), **V:** 249, 252

"Heat" (Hart), **Supp. XI:** 131

Heat and Dust (Jhabvala), **Supp. V:** 224, 230, 231–232, 238

Heat of the Day, The (Bowen), **Supp. II:** 77, 78, 79, 93, 95

"Heather Ale" (Stevenson), **V:** 396

Heather Field, The (Martyn), **IV:** 87, 95

"Heaven" (Brooke), **Supp. III:** 56, 60

Heaven and Earth (Byron), **IV:** 178, 193

Heaven and Its Wonders, and Hell (Swedenborg), **Retro. Supp. I:** 38

Heavenly Foot-man, The (Bunyan), **II:** 246, 253

Heaven's Command: An Imperial Progress (Morris, J.), **Supp. X:** 173, 179–180

Heaven's Edge (Gunesekera), **Supp. X:** 85–86, 96–100

"Heber" (Smith), **Supp. II:** 466

Hebert, Ann Marie, **Supp. IV:** 523

Hebrew Melodies, Ancient and Modern . . . (Byron), **IV:** 192

"Hebrides, The" (Longley), **VIII:** 168–169

Hecatommithi (Cinthio), **I:** 316

Hedda Gabler (Ibsen), **Supp. IV:** 163, 286

"Hedgehog" (Muldoon), **Supp. IV:** 414

"Hee-Haw" (Warner), **Supp. VII:** 380

Heel of Achilles, The (Koestler), **Supp. I:** 36

"Heepocondry" (Crawford), **Supp. XI:** 75

"Heera Nund" (Steel), **Supp. XII:** 268–269

Hegel, Georg Wilhelm Friedrich, **Supp. II:** 22

Heiðreks saga, **VIII:** 231

"Height-ho on a Winter Afternoon" (Davie), **Supp. VI:** 107–108

"Heil Baldwin" (Caudwell), **Supp. IX:** 38

Heilbrun, Carolyn G., **Supp. IV:** 336

Heimskringla, **VIII:** 235, 242

Heine, Heinrich, **IV:** xviii, 296

Heinemann, William, **VII:** 91

"Heiress, The" (McGuckian), **Supp. V:** 282

Heit, S. Mark, **Supp. IV:** 339

"Hélas" (Wilde), **V:** 401

Helen (Scott), **Supp. III:** 151, **165–166**

Helena (Waugh), **VII:** 292, 293–294, 301

Hélène Fourment in a Fur Coat (Rubens), **Supp. IV:** 89

Hellas (Shelley), **IV:** xviii, 206, 208; **Retro. Supp. I:** 255

Hellenics, The (Landor), **IV:** 96, 100

"Helmet, The" (Longley), **VIII:** 176

Héloïse and Abélard (Moore), **VI:** xii, 88, 89, **94–95,** 99

"Helplessly" (Smith, I. C.), **Supp. IX:** 217

Hemans, Felicia, **IV:** 311

Hemingway, Ernest, **Supp. III:** 105; **Supp. IV:** 163, 209, 500

Hemlock and After (Wilson), **Supp. I:** 155–156, 157, 158–159, 160, 161, 164

Hello, America (Ballard), **Supp. V:** 29

"Hen Woman" (Kinsella), **Supp. V:** 266–267

Henceforward (Ayckbourn), **Supp. V:** 3, 10, 11, 13

"Hendecasyllabics" (Swinburne), **V:** 321

"Hendecasyllabics" (Tennyson), **IV:** 327–328

Henderson, Hamish, **VII:** 422, 425–426

Henderson, Hubert, **VII:** 35

Henderson, Philip, **V:** xii, xviii, 335

Henderson, T. F., **IV:** 290n

Hengist, King of Kent; or, The Mayor of Quinborough (Middleton), **II:** 3, 21

Henley, William Ernest, **V:** 386, 389, 391–392; **VI:** 159; **Retro. Supp. I:** 260, 264

Henn, T. R., **VI:** 220

"Henrietta Marr" (Moore), **VI:** 87

Henrietta Temple (Disraeli), **IV:** xix, 293, 298–299, 307, 308

"Henrik Ibsen" (James), **VI:** 49

Henry Esmond (Thackeray), *see History of Henry Esmond, Esq. . . . , The*

Henry for Hugh (Ford), **VI:** 331

"Henry James" (Nye), **Supp. X:** 201

Henry James (ed. Tanner), **VI:** 68

Henry James (West), **Supp. III:** 437

"Henry James: The Religious Aspect" (Greene), **Supp. I:** 8

"Henry Petroski, The Pencil. A History. Faber and Faber, £14.95" (Dunn), **Supp. X:** 79

"Henry Purcell" (Hopkins), **V:** 370–371; **Retro. Supp. II:** 196

Henry Reed: Collected Poems (Stallworthy), **Supp. X:** 292

Henry II (Bancroft), **II:** 305

Henry IV (Shakespeare), **I:** 308–309, 320
Henry V (Shakespeare), **I:** 309; **V:** 383; **Supp. IV:** 258
Henry VI trilogy (Shakespeare), **I:** 286, 299–300, 309
Henry VI's Triumphal Entry into London (Lydgate), **I:** 58
Henry VIII (Shakespeare), **I:** 324; **II:** 43, 66, 87; **V:** 328
"Henry VIII and Ann Boleyn" (Landor), **IV:** 92
Henry Vaughan: Experience and the Tradition (Garner), **II:** 186n
Henry's Past (Churchill), **Supp. IV:** 181
Henryson, Robert, **Supp. VII: 135–149**
Henslowe, Philip, **I:** 228, 235, 284; **II:** 3 25, 68
Henty, G. A., **Supp. IV:** 201
"Her Second Husband Hears Her Story" (Hardy), **Retro. Supp. I:** 120
Her Triumph (Johnson), **I:** 347
Her Vertical Smile (Kinsella), **Supp. V:** 270–271
Her Victory (Sillitoe), **Supp. V:** 411, 415, 422, 425
Herakles (Euripides), **IV:** 358
Herbert, Edward, pseud. of John Hamilton Reynolds
Herbert, Edward, *see* Herbert of Cherbury, Lord
Herbert, George, **II:** 113, **117–130,** 133, 134, 137, 138, 140–142, 184, 187, 216, 221; **Retro. Supp. II: 169–184**
Herbert of Cherbury, Lord, **II:** 117–118, 222, 237, 238
Herbert's Remains (Oley), **Retro. Supp. II:** 170–171
Hercule Poirot's Last Case (Christie), **Supp. II:** 125
"Hercules" (Armitage), **VIII:** 12
"Hercules and Antaeus" (Heaney), **Supp. II:** 274–275
Hercules Oetaeus (Seneca), **I:** 248
"Here" (Larkin), **Supp. I:** 279, 285
"Here and There" (Dunn), **Supp. X:** 77–78
"Here Be Dragons" (Dunn), **Supp. X:** 72
Here Comes Everybody: An Introduction to James Joyce for the Ordinary Reader (Burgess), **Supp. I:** 194, 196–197
Here Lies: An Autobiography (Ambler), **Supp. IV:** 1, 2, 3, 4
"Heredity" (Harrison), **Supp. V:** 152
Heretics (Chesterton), **VI:** 204, 336–337
Hering, Carl Ewald, **Supp. II:** 107–108
Heritage and Its History, A (Compton-Burnett), **VII:** 60, 61, 65
Hermaphrodite Album, The (Redgrove), **Supp. VI:** 230
"Hermaphroditus" (Swinburne), **V:** 320
Hermetical Physick . . . Englished (tr. Vaughan), **II:** 185, 201
Hermit of Marlow, The, pseud. of Percy Bysshe Shelley
"Hero" (Rossetti), **V:** 260
"Hero and Leander" (Hood), **IV:** 255–256, 267

Hero and Leander (Marlowe), **I:** 234, 237–240, 276, 278, 280, 288, **290–291,** 292; **Retro. Supp. I:** 211
Hero and Leander, in Burlesque (Wycherley), **II:** 321
"Hero as King, The" (Carlyle), **IV:** 245, 246
Hero Rises Up, The (Arden and D'Arcy), **Supp. II:** 31
"Heroine, The" (Highsmith), **Supp. V:** 180
Herodotus, **Supp. IV:** 110
Heroes and Hero–Worship (Carlyle), **IV:** xx, 240, 244–246, 249, 250, 341
Heroes and Villains (Carter), **Supp. III:** 81, 84
Heroic Idylls, with Additional Poems (Landor), **IV:** 100
"Heroic Stanzas" (Dryden), **II:** 292
Heroine, The; or, The Adventures of Cherubina (Barrett), **III:** 335
"Heron, The" (Nye), **Supp. X:** 205
Heron Caught in Weeds, A (Roberts, K.), **Supp. X:** 273–275
Herrick, Robert, **II: 102–116,** 121
Herself Surprised (Cary), **VII:** 186, 188, 191–192
"Hertha" (Swinburne), **V:** 325
Hervarar saga, See Heiðreks saga
"Hervé Riel" (Browning), **IV:** 367
Herzog, Werner, **IV:** 180
"Hesperia" (Swinburne), **V:** 320, 321
Hesperides, The (Herrick), **II:** 102, 103, 104, 106, 110, 112, 115, 116
Hester (Oliphant), **Supp. X:** 217–218
"Hester Dominy" (Powys), **VIII:** 250
Hexameron; or, Meditations on the Six Days of Creation, and Meditations and Devotions on the Life of Christ (Traherne), **Supp. XI:** 264, 265, 273–274
Heyday of Sir Walter Scott, The (Davie), **Supp. VI:** 114–115
Heylyn, Peter, **I:** 169
Heywood, Jasper, **I:** 215
Heywood, Thomas, **II:** 19, 47, 48, 68, 83
"Hexagon" (Murphy), **Supp. V:** 328
Hibberd, Dominic, **VI:** xvi, xxxiii
Hide, The (Unsworth), **Supp. VII:** 354, 356
"Hide and Seek" (Gunn), **Supp. IV:** 272
Hide and Seek (Collins), **Supp. VI:** 92, 95
Hide and Seek (Rankin), **Supp. X:** 244, 246, 248–250
Hide and Seek (Swinburne), **V:** 334
"Hidden History, A" (Okri), **Supp. V:** 352
Hidden Ireland, The (Corkery), **Supp. V:** 41
"Hidden Law" (MacCaig), **Supp. VI:** 186
Higden, Ranulf, **I:** 22
Higgins, F. R., **Supp. IV:** 411, 413
"Higgler, The" (Coppard), **VIII:** 85, 90, 95
Higgler and Other Tales, The (Coppard), **VIII:** 90
"High Flats at Craigston, The" (Dutton), **Supp. XII:** 91

High Island: New and Selected Poems (Murphy), **Supp. V:** 313, 315, 316, 324–325
"High Life in Verdopolis" (Brontë), **V:** 135
High Tide in the Garden (Adcock), **Supp. XII:** 5
"High wavering heather . . . " (Brontë), **V:** 113
High Windows (Larkin), **Supp. I:** 277, 280, **281–284,** 285, 286
Higher Ground (Phillips), **Supp. V:** 380, 386–388
Higher Schools and Universities in Germany (Arnold), **V:** 216
"Higher Standards" (Wilson), **Supp. I:** 155
Highet, Gilbert, **II:** 199
Highland Fling (Mitford), **Supp. X:** 152–154
"Highland Funeral" (MacCaig), **Supp. VI:** 193
Highland Widow, The (Scott), **IV:** 39
Highlander, The (Macpherson), **VIII:** 181–182, 190
Highly Dangerous (Ambler), **Supp. IV:** 3
High–Rise (Ballard), **Supp. V:** 27
High Summer (Rattigan), **Supp. VII:** 315
Highsmith, Patricia, **Supp. IV:** 285; **Supp. V: 167–182**
"Highwayman and the Saint, The" (Friel), **Supp. V:** 118
Hilaire Belloc (Wilson), **Supp. VI:** 301–302
Hilda Lessways (Bennett), **VI:** 258; **Supp. IV:** 238
Hill, G. B., **III:** 233, 234n
Hill, Geoffrey, **Supp. V: 183–203**
"Hill, The" (Brooke), **Supp. III:** 51
Hill of Devi, The (Forster), **VI:** 397, 408, 411
"Hill of Venus, The" (Morris), **V:** 298
Hill, Reginald, **Supp. IX: 109–126**
Hilton, Walter, **Supp. I:** 74
Hind, The, and the Panther (Dryden), **II:** 291, 292, 299–300, 304
Hinge of Faith, The (Churchill), **VI:** 361
Hinman, Charlton, **I:** 326–327
Hinton, William, **Supp. IV:** 284
"Hints" (Reading), **VIII:** 265–266
Hints Towards the Formation of a More Comprehensive Theory of Life (Coleridge), **IV:** 56
Hippolytus (Euripides), **V:** 322, 324
Hips and Haws (Coppard), **VIII:** 89, 98
Hireling, The (Hartley), **Supp. VII:** 129–131
"His Age, Dedicated to his Peculiar Friend, M. John Wickes" (Herrick), **II:** 112
His Arraignment (Jonson), **Retro. Supp. I:** 158
"His Chosen Calling" (Naipaul), **Supp. I:** 385
"His Country" (Hardy), **Retro. Supp. I:** 120–121
His Darling Sin (Braddon), **VIII:** 49
"His Fare–well to Sack" (Herrick), **II:** 111

"His Father's Hands" (Kinsella), **Supp. V:** 268

"His Last Bow" (Doyle), **Supp. II:** 175

"His Letanie, to the Holy Spirit" (Herrick), **II:** 114

His Majesties Declaration Defended (Dryden), **II:** 305

His Majesty Preserved . . . Dictated to Samuel Pepys by the King . . . (ed. Rees–Mogg), **II:** 288

His Noble Numbers (Herrick), **II:** 102, 103, 112, 114, 115, 116

"His Returne to London" (Herrick), **II:** 103

His Second War (Waugh), **Supp. VI:** 274

Historia naturalis et experimentalis (Bacon), **I:** 259, 273

Historia regis Henrici Septimi (André), **I:** 270

Historiae adversum paganos (Orosius), **Retro. Supp. II:** 296

"Historian, The" (Fuller), **Supp. VII:** 74

"Historian of Silence, The" (Hart), **Supp. XI:** 130

Historical Account of the Theatre in Europe, An (Riccoboni), **II:** 348

Historical Register, The (Fielding), **III:** 97, 98, 105; **Retro. Supp. I:** 82

Historical Relation of the Island of Ceylon, An (Knox), **III:** 7

"Historical Sketches of the Reign of George Second" (Oliphant), **Supp. X:** 222

"Historical Society" (Murphy), **Supp. V:** 322

"History" (Macaulay), **IV:** 284

History and Adventures of an Atom, The (Smollett), **III:** 149–150, 158

History and Adventures of Joseph Andrews and of His Friend Mr. Abraham Adams (Fielding), **Retro. Supp. I:** 80, 83–86

History and Management of the East India Company (Macpherson), **VIII:** 193

History and Remarkable Life of . . . Col. Jack (Defoe), see *Colonel Jack*

History Maker, A (Gray, A.), **Supp. IX:** 80, 87–88

History of a Good Warm Watch–Coat, The (Sterne), see *Political Romance, A*

"History of a Piece of Paper" (Sisson), **Supp. XI:** 244

History of a Six Weeks' Tour Through a Part of France . . . (Shelley and Shelley), **IV:** 208; **Supp. III:** 355

"History of Angria" (Brontë), **V:** 110–111, 118

History of Antonio and Mellida, The (Marston), see *Antonio and Mellida*

History of Brazil (Southey), **IV:** 68, 71

History of Britain . . . , The (Milton), **II:** 176

History of British India, The, (Mill), **V:** 288

History of Dorastus and Fawnia, The (Greene). See *Pandosto: or, The Triumph of Time*

History of England (Hume), **II:** 148; **IV:** 273; **Supp. III:** 229, 238–239

History of England, An (Goldsmith), **III:** 180, 181, 189, 191

History of England, The (Trevelyan), **VI:** xv, 390–391, 393

History of England from the Accession of James II, The (Macaulay), **II:** 255; **IV:** xx, 272, 273, 280, 282, **283–290**, 291

History of England in the Eighteenth Century (Lecky), **Supp. V:** 41

History of English Thought in the Eighteenth Century (Stephen), **V:** 280, 288, 289

History of Frederick the Great, The (Carlyle), **IV:** xxi, 240, 246, 249, 250

History of Friar Francis, The, **I:** 218

History of Great Britain from the Restoration to the Accession of the House of Hanover (Macpherson), **VIII:** 192, 193

History of Henry Esmond, Esq. . . . , The (Thackeray), **V:** xxi, 20, **31–33**, 38

History of Jemmy and Jenny Jessamy, The (Haywood), **Supp. XII:** 144

History of King Richard III, The (More), **Supp. VII:** 234, 237–238, 246

History of Leonora Meadowson, The (Haywood), **Supp. XII:** 144

History of Madan, The (Beaumont), **II:** 67

History of Miss Betsy Thoughtless, The (Haywood), **Supp. XII:** 135, 136, 144–146

History of Mr. Polly, The (Wells), **VI:** xii, 225, 238–239

History of My Own Times (Burnet), **III:** 39

History of Orlando Furioso, The (Greene), **VIII:** 140

History of Pendennis, The (Thackeray), **V:** xxi, **28–31**, 33, 35, 38; **VI:** 354

History of Rasselas Prince of Abyssinia, The (Johnson), **III:** 112–113, 121; **IV:** 47; **Retro. Supp. I:** 139–140, 148

History of Samuel Titmarsh and the Great Hoggarty Diamond, The (Thackeray), see *Great Hoggarty Diamond, The*

History of Shikasta (Lessing), **Supp. I:** 251

History of Sir Charles Grandison, The (Richardson), see *Sir Charles Grandison*

History of the Adventures of Joseph Andrews . . . , The (Fielding), see *Joseph Andrews*

"History of the Boswell Papers" (Pottle), **III:** 240n

History of the Church of Scotland (Spottiswoode), **II:** 142

History of the Earth, and Animated Nature, An (Goldsmith), **III:** 180, 181, 189–190, 191

History of the English–Speaking Peoples, A (Churchill), **VI:** 356

History of the Four Last Years of Queen Anne, The (Swift), **III:** 27, 36

"History of the Hardcomes, The" (Hardy), **VI:** 22

History of the Italian Renaissance (Symonds), **V:** 83

History of the Kentish Petition, The (Defoe), **III:** 12

History of the League, The (tr. Dryden), **II:** 305

"History of the Next French Revolution, The" (Thackeray), **V:** 38

History of the Nun, The; or, The Fair Vow–Breaker (Behn), **Supp. III:** 32

History of the Peninsular War (Southey), **IV:** 58, 63, 71; **V:** 109

History of the Plague Year, A (Defoe), **Retro. Supp. I:** 68

History of the Pyrates, The (Defoe), **III:** 13

History of the Reign of Henry the Seventh, The (Bacon), **I:** 259, 269, 270, 272

History of the Royal Society of London (Sprat), **II:** 196; **III:** 29

History of the Union of Great Britain, The (Defoe), **III:** 4, 13; **Retro. Supp. I:** 65

"History of the Voice" (Brathwaite), **Supp. XII:** 44–45

History of the Wars of . . . Charles XII . . . , The (Defoe), **III:** 13

"History of the Winds" (Bacon), **I:** 263

History of the World in 10 Chapters, A (Barnes), **Supp. IV:** 65, 67, 71–72, 73

History of the World, The (Ralegh), **I:** 145, 146, 149, 153–157

History of Titus Andronicus, The, **I:** 305

History of Tom Jones, a Foundling, The (Fielding), see *Tom Jones*

History of Van's House, The, **II:** 335

History Plays, The (Hare), **Supp. IV:** 283

Histriomastix (Prynne), **II:** 339; **Supp. III:** 23

Histriomastix; or, The Player Whipt (Marston), **II:** 27, 28, 40

Hitchcock, Alfred, **III:** 342–343; **Supp. III:** 147, 148, 149

"Hitcher" (Armitage), **VIII:** 8

"Hitchhiker, The" (Dahl), **Supp. IV:** 201

Hitherto unpublished Poems and Stories . . . (Browning), **IV:** 321

Hjálmarr's Death–Song, **VIII:** 232

Hloðskviða, **VIII:** 231

H'm (Thomas), **Supp. XII:** 286

"H'm" (Thomas), **Supp. XII:** 288

H.M.S. Surprise (O'Brian), **Supp. XII:** 255, 256

Hoare, D.M., **V:** 299, 306

Hobbes, John Oliver, pseud. of Mrs. Craigie

Hobbes, Thomas, **II:** 190, 196, 256, 294; **III:** 22; **IV:** 121, 138

Hobbit, The (Tolkien), **Supp. II:** 520, 521, 525, 527–528, 529, 530, 531–532

Hobsbaum, Philip, **Retro. Supp. I:** 126; **Retro. Supp. II:** 200

Hoccleve, Thomas, **I:** 49

"Hock–Cart; or, Harvest Home, The" (Herrick), **II:** 110–111

Hockney's Alphabet (McEwan), **Supp. IV:** 389

Hodder, E., **IV:** 62n

Hodgkins, Howard, **Supp. IV:** 170

Hodgson, W. N., **VI:** 422, 423

Hoff, Benjamin, **Supp. V:** 311

Hoffman, Calvin, **I:** 277

Hoffman, Heinrich, **I:** 25; **Supp. III:** 296

Hoffmann, E. T. A., **III:** 333, 334, 345

"Hoffmeier's Antelope" (Swift), **Supp. V:** 432

Hofmeyr (Paton; U.S. title, *South African Tragedy: The Life and Times of Jan Hofmeyr*), **Supp. II: 356–357,** 358

Hogarth Press, **VII:** xv, 17, 34

Hogg, James, **IV:** xvii, 73; **Supp. X:** 103–118

Hogg, Thomas Jefferson, **IV:** 196, 198, 209

Hoggart, Richard, **VII:** xx, xxxviii; **Supp. IV:** 473

Hold Your Hour and Have Another (Behan), **Supp. II:** 65–66, 70

Holiday, The (Smith), **Supp. II:** 462, 474, **476–478**

Holiday Romance (Dickens), **V:** 72

Holiday Round, The (Milne), **Supp. V:** 298

"Holidays" (Kincaid), **Supp. VII:** 220

Hollinghurst, Alan, **Supp. X: 119–135**

Hollington, Michael, **Supp. IV:** 357

Hollis, Maurice Christopher, **VI:** xxxiii

Hollis, Richard, **Supp. IV:** 88

"Hollow Men, The" (Eliot), **VII:** 150–151, 158; **Retro. Supp. II:** 129–130

Hollow's Mill (Brontë), *see Shirley*

Holloway, John, **VII:** 82

Holroyd, Michael, **Supp. IV:** 231

"Holy Baptisme I" (Herbert), **II:** 128

Holy City, The; or, The New Jerusalem (Bunyan), **II:** 253

"Holy Fair, The" (Burns), **III:** 311, 315, 317

Holy Grail, The, and Other Poems (Tennyson), **IV:** 338

"Holy Experiment, The" (Nye), **Supp. X:** 203

Holy Life, The Beauty of Christianity, A (Bunyan), **II:** 253

"Holy Mountain, The" (Nicholson), **Supp. VI:** 215

"Holy Scriptures" (Vaughan), **II:** 187

"Holy Scriptures II, The" (Herbert), **Retro. Supp. II:** 174

Holy Sinner, The (Mann), **II:** 97n

Holy Sonnets (Donne), **I:** 362, 366, 367; **Retro. Supp. II:** 96

Holy War, The: Made by Shaddai . . . (Bunyan), **II:** 246, 250, 251–252, 253

"Holy Willie's Prayer" (Burns), **III:** 311, 313, 319

"Holy–Cross Day" (Browning), **IV:** 367

"Holyhead, September 25, 1717" (Swift), **III:** 32

"Homage to a Government" (Larkin), **Supp. I:** 284

Homage to Catalonia (Orwell), **VII:** 275, 280–281

Homage to Clio (Auden), **VII:** 392

"Homage to Burns" (Brown), **Supp. VI:** 72

"Homage to George Orwell" (Smith, I. C.), **Supp. IX:** 215

"Homage to the British Museum" (Empson), **Supp. II:** 182

"Homage to William Cowper" (Davie), **Supp. VI:** 106

"Homages" (Hart), **Supp. XI:** 123

Homans, Margaret, **Retro. Supp. I:** 189

"Home" (Ewart), **Supp. VII:** 37

"Home" (Fallon), **Supp. XII:** 106

Home (Storey), **Supp. I:** 408, 413, 417

Home and Beauty (Maugham), **VI:** 368–369

Home and Dry (Fuller), **Supp. VII:** 70, 81

"Home at Grasmere" (Wordsworth), **IV:** 3, 23–24

Home Chat (Coward), **Supp. II:** 146

"Home Conveyancing Kit, The" (Wallace–Crabbe), **VIII:** 320

"Home for a couple of days" (Kelman), **Supp. V:** 250

"Home for the Highland Cattle, A" (Lessing), **Supp. I:** 241–242

Home Front (Bishton and Reardon), **Supp. IV:** 445

Home Letters (Disraeli) **IV:** 296, 308

Home Letters of T. E. Lawrence and His Brothers, The (Lawrence), **Supp. II:** 286

"Home Thoughts from Abroad" (Browning), **IV:** 356

"Home Thoughts Abroad" (Newman), **Supp. VII:** 293

Home Truths (Maitland), **Supp. XI:** 163, 170–172, 175

"Home [2]" (Thomas), **Supp. III:** 405

"Home [3]" (Thomas), **Supp. III:** 404

Home University Library, **VI:** 337, 391

Homebush Boy (Keneally), **Supp. IV:** 344, 347

Homecoming, The (Pinter), **Supp. I:** 375, 380, 381; **Retro. Supp. I:** 225–226

Homecoming: Essays on African and Caribbean Literature, Culture, and Politics (Ngũgĩ), **VIII:** 214, 224

Homecomings (Snow), **VII:** xxi, 324, 329, 335

"Homemade" (McEwan), **Supp. IV:** 389, 391, 395

"Homemaking" (Kincaid), **Supp. VII:** 229

Homer, **I:** 236; **II:** 304, 347; **III:** 217, 220; **IV:** 204, 215

Homeric Hymns (tr. Chapman), **I:** 236

"Homesick in Old Age" (Kinsella), **Supp. V:** 263

"Homeward Prospect, The" (Day Lewis), **Supp. III:** 129

Homeward: Songs by the Way (Russell), **VIII:** 280, 282

Homiletic Fragment I, **Retro. Supp. II:** 301–302

Hone, Joseph, **VI:** 88

Hone, William, **IV:** 255

Honest Man's Fortune, The (Field, Fletcher, Massinger), **II:** 66

Honest Whore, The (Dekker and Middleton), **II:** 3, 21, 89

Honey for the Bears (Burgess), **Supp. I:** 191

Honeybuzzard (Carter), *see Shadow Dance*

Honeymoon Voyage, The (Thomas), **Supp. IV:** 490

Hong Kong House, A: Poems 1951–1961 (Blunden), **Supp. XI:** 34, 38

"Hong Kong Story" (Nye), **Supp. X:** 201–202

Honorary Consul, The (Greene), **Supp. I:** 7, 10, 13, 16; **Retro. Supp. II:** 164–165

Honour of the Garter, The (Peele), **I:** 205

Honour Triumphant; or, The Peeres Challenge (Ford), **II:** 88, 100

"Honourable Estate, An" (Gunesekera), **Supp. X:** 86

Honourable Estate: A Novel of Transition (Brittain), **Supp. X:** 41–43, 46–47

"Honourable Laura, The" (Hardy), **VI:** 22

Honourable Schoolboy, The (le Carré), **Supp. II:** 301, **313–314,** 315

Hood, Thomas, **IV:** xvi, xx, **251–267,** 311

Hood's (periodical), **IV:** 252, 261, 263, 264

"Hood's Literary Reminiscences" (Blunden), **IV:** 267

Hood's Own (Hood), **IV:** 251–252, 253, 254, 266

Hook, Theodore, **IV:** 254

Hooker, Richard, **I: 176–190,** 362; **II:** 133, 137, 140–142, 147

"Hope" (Cornford), **VIII:** 105, 112

"Hope" (Cowper), **III:** 212

Hope, A. D., **Supp. VII: 151–166**

"Hope Abandoned" (Davies), **Supp. XI:** 97

Hope for Poetry, A (Day Lewis), **Supp. III:** 117, 119

Hopes and Fears for Art (Morris), **V:** 301, 306

Hopkins, Gerard Manley, **II:** 123, 181; **IV:** xx; **V:** ix, xi, xxv, 53, 205, 210, 261, 309–310, 338, **361–382; VI:** 75, 83; **Supp. II:** 269; **Supp. IV:** 344, 345; **Retro. Supp. II:** 173, **185–198**

Hopkins (MacKenzie), **V:** 375n 382

Hopkinson, Sir Tom, **V:** xx, xxxviii

Horace, **II:** 108, 112, 199, 200, 265, 292, 300, 309, 347; **IV:** 327

"Horae Canonicae" (Auden), **Retro. Supp. I:** 12–13

Horae Solitariae (Thomas), **Supp. III:** 394

"Horatian Ode . . . , An" (Marvell), **II:** 204, 208, 209, 210, 211, 216–217; **Retro. Supp. II:** 263–264

"Horatius" (Macaulay), **IV:** 282

Horestes (Pickering), **I:** 213, 216–218

Horizon (periodical), **Supp. II:** 489; **Supp. III: 102–103,** 105, 106–107, 108–109

Horne, Richard Hengist, **IV:** 312, 321, 322

Hornet (periodical), **VI:** 102

Horniman, Annie, **VI:** 309; **VII:** 1

"Horns Away" (Lydgate), **I:** 64

Horse and His Boy, The (Lewis), **Supp. III:** 248, 260

"Horse Dealer's Daughter, The" (Lawrence), **VII:** 114

"Horse–Drawn Caravan" (Murphy), **Supp. V:** 329

"Horse, Goose and Sheep, The" (Lydgate), **I:** 57

Horseman's Word, The (Morgan, E.), **Supp. IX:** 166

"Horses" (Muir), **Supp. VI:** 204–205"Horses" (Muir), Supp. VI: 204–205

Horse's Mouth, The (Cary), **VII:** 186, 188, 191, 192, 193–194

Hoskins, John, **I:** 165–166, 167

"Hospital Barge" (Owen), **VI:** 454

Hostage, The (Behan), **Supp. II:** 70, **72–73,** 74

Hostages to Fortune (Braddon), **VIII:** 49

Hosts of the Lord, The (Steel), **Supp. XII:** 274

Hot Anger Soon Cold (Jonson), **Retro. Supp. I:** 157

Hot Countries, The (Waugh), **Supp. VI:** 272, 274

Hot Gates, The (Golding), **Supp. I:** 81; **Retro. Supp. I:** 93

Hotel, The (Bowen), **Supp. II: 82–83**

Hotel de Dream (Tennant), **Supp. IX:** 230

Hotel du Lac (Brookner), **Supp. IV:** 120, 121, 126–127, 136

Hotel in Amsterdam, The (Osborne), **Supp. I:** 338–339

"Hotel of the Idle Moon, The" (Trevor), **Supp. IV:** 501

"Hotel Room in Chartres" (Lowry), **Supp. III:** 272

Hothouse, The (Pinter), **Supp. I:** 377–378

Hothouse by the East River, The (Spark), **Supp. I:** 210

Hotson, Leslie, **I:** 275, 276

Hotspur: A Ballad for Music (Adcock and Whitehead), **Supp. XII:** 9

Houd–den–bek (Brink), **Supp. VI:** 51

Hough, Graham, **IV:** 323n, 339; **V:** 355, 359

Houghton, Lord, *see* Monckton Milnes, Richard

Hound of Death, The (Christie), **III:** 341

"Hound of Heaven, The" (Thompson), **V:** 445–447, 449, 450

Hound of the Baskervilles, The (Doyle), **III:** 341, 342, 345; **Supp. II:** 161, 163, 164, 170, 171, 172

"Hour and the Ghost, The" (Rossetti), **V:** 256

Hour of Magic and Other Poems, The (Davies), **Supp. XI:** 99

Hours in a Library (Stephen), **V:** 279, 285, 286, 287, 289

Hours of Idleness (Byron), **IV:** xvi 192

House, Humphry, **IV:** 167

"House" (Browning), **IV:** 359; **Retro. Supp. II:** 29

House and Its Head, A (Compton–Burnett), **VII:** 61

"House and Man" (Thomas), **Supp. III:** 403, 404

House at Pooh Corner, The (Milne), **Supp. V:** 295, 305, 306, 307, 308–309

"House Building" (Gunesekera), **Supp. X:** 86

House by the Churchyard, The (Le Fanu), **III:** 340, 345

House for Mr Biswas, A (Naipaul), **Supp. I:** 383, 386, **387–389**

"House Grown Silent, The" (Warner), **Supp. VII:** 371

House in Corfu: A Family's Sojourn in Greece, A (Tennant), **Supp. IX:** 239

House in Paris, The (Bowen), **Supp. II:** 77, 82, 84, 89–90

"House in the Acorn, The" (Redgrove), **Supp. VI:** 236

House of All Nations (Stead), **Supp. IV:** 464–467

"House of Aries, The" (Hughes), **Supp. I:** 346

"House of Beauty, The" (Christie), **Supp. II:** 124

House of Children, A (Cary), **VII:** 186, 187, 189

"House of Christmas, The" (Chesterton), **VI:** 344

House of Cobwebs, The (Gissing), **V:** 437

House of Doctor Dee (Ackroyd), **Supp. VI:** 4, 10

House of Dolls, The (Comyns), **VIII:** 53, 65

"House of Dreams, The" (Thomas), **Supp. IV:** 493

House of Fame, The (Chaucer), **I:** 23, 30; **Retro. Supp. II:** 38–39

House of Hospitalities, The (Tennant), **Supp. IX:** 239

House of Life, The (Rossetti), **V:** 237, 238, 241, 242, 243, 244, 245

House of Pomegranates, A (Wilde), **V:** 419; **Retro. Supp. II:** 365

House of Seven Gables, The (Hawthorne), **III:** 339, 345

House of Sleep, The (Kavan), **Supp. VII:** 212–213

House of Splendid Isolation (O'Brien), **Supp. V:** 341–344

House on the Beach, The (Meredith), **V:** 230–231, 234

House on the Strand, The (du Maurier), **Supp. III:** 138, 139, 140, 141, 147

House of Titans and Other Poems, The (Russell), **VIII:** 277, 290, 292

"House of Titans, The" (Russell), **VIII:** 290

"House We Lived In, The" (Smith, I. C.), **Supp. IX:** 214

House with the Echo, The (Powys), **VIII:** 248, 249, 254

"Household Spirits" (Kinsella), **Supp. V:** 272

Household Words (periodical), **V:** xxi, 3, 42

Householder, The (Jhabvala), **Supp. V:** 227–228, 237

Housman, A. E., **III:** 68, 70; **V:** xxii, xxvi, 311; **VI:** ix, xv–xvi, **151–164,** 415

Housman, Laurence, **V:** 402, 420

Housman: 1897–1936 (Richards), **VI:** 164

"House–martins" (Adcock), **Supp. XII:** 12

How About Europe? (Douglas), **VI:** 295, 305

"How Are the Children Robin" (Graham), **Supp. VII:** 115

How Brophy Made Good (Hare), **Supp. IV:** 281

How Can We Know? (Wilson), **Supp. VI:** 305

"How Distant" (Larkin), **Supp. I:** 284

"How Do You See"(Smith), **Supp. II:** 467

How Far Can You Go? (Lodge; U.S. title, *Souls and Bodies*), **Supp. IV:** 366, 368, 371, 372, 375–376, 381, 408

How He Lied to Her Husband (Shaw), **VI:** 129

How I Became a Holy Mother and Other Stories (Jhabvala), **Supp. V:** 235

"How I Became a Socialist" (Orwell), **VII:** 276–277

How It Is (Beckett), **Supp. I:** 43, 50, 52, 54–55, 58

"How It Strikes a Contemporary" (Browning), **IV:** 354, 367, 373

How Late It Was, How Late (Kelman), **Supp. V:** 243, 252–254

How Lisa Loved the King (Eliot), **V:** 200

"How Many Bards" (Keats), **IV:** 215

"How Pillingshot Scored" (Wodehouse), **Supp. III:** 449–450

How Right You Are, Jeeves (Wodehouse), **Supp. III:** 460, 461, 462

"How Sleep the Brave" (Collins), **III:** 166

"How soon the servant sun" (Thomas), **Supp. I:** 174

"How Sweet the Name of Jesus Sounds" (Newton), **III:** 210

How the "Mastiffs"Went to Iceland (Trollope), **V:** 102

How the Other Half Lives (Ayckbourn), **Supp. V:** 2, 4, 9, 11, 12

How the Whale Became (Hughes), **Supp. I:** 346

"How They Brought the Good News from Ghent to Aix (16—)" (Browning), **IV:** 356, 361

How this foirsaid Tod maid his Confession to Freir Wolf Waitskaith (Henryson), see *Fox and the Wolf, The*

"How to Accomplish It" (Newman), **Supp. VII:** 293

How to Become an Author (Bennett), **VI:** 264

"How to Kill" (Douglas), **VII: 443**

How to Live on 24 Hours a Day (Bennett), **VI:** 264

How to Read (Pound), **VII:** 235

How to Read a Page (Richards), **Supp. II:** 426

How to Settle the Irish Question (Shaw), **VI:** 119, 129

"How to Teach Reading" (Leavis), **VII:** 235, 248

"How would the ogling sparks despise" (Etherege), **II:** 268

"How You Love Our Lady" (Blackwood), **Supp. IX:** 9

Howard, Elizabeth Jane, **Supp. XI: 135–149**

Howard, Henry, earl of Surrey, *see* Surrey, Henry Howard, earl of

Howard, R., **V:** 418

Howard, Sir Robert, **II:** 100

Howards End (Forster), **VI:** viii, xii, 397, 398, 401, **404–406**, 407; **Supp. I:** 161; **Retro. Supp. II:** 143–145

Howarth, R. G., **II:** 69

Howe, Irving, **VI:** 41

Howells, William Dean, **VI:** 23, 29, 33

Howitt, William, **IV:** 212

Hrafnkels saga, **VIII:** 242

Hubert De Vere (Burney), **Supp. III:** 71

Huchon, René, **III:** 273n

Hudibras (Butler), **II:** 145

Hudson, Derek, **V:** xi, xxviii, 263, 274

Hudson, W. H., **V:** 429

Hudson Letter, The (Mahon), **Supp. VI:** 175–176

Hueffer, Ford Madox, *see* Ford, Ford Madox

"Hug, The" (Gunn), **Supp. IV:** 274–275, 276, 277

Huggan, Graham, **Supp. IV:** 170

Hugh Primas and the Archpoet (tr. Adcock), **Supp. XII:** 10

Hugh Selwyn Mauberley (Pound), **VI:** 417; **VII:** xvi

Hughes, Arthur, **V:** 294

Hughes, John, **I:** 121, 122; **III:** 40

Hughes, Ted, **Supp. I: 341–366; Supp. IV:** 257; **Supp. V:** xxx; **Retro. Supp. I:** 126; **Retro. Supp. II: 199–219**

Hughes, Thomas, **I:** 218; **V:** xxii, 170; **Supp. IV:** 506

Hughes, Willie, **V:** 405

Hugo, Victor, **III:** 334; **V:** xxii, xxv, 22, 320; **Supp. IV:** 86

Hugo (Bennett), **VI:** 249

Huis clos (Sartre), **Supp. IV:** 39

Hulme, T. E., **VI:** 416; **Supp. VI: 133–147**

Hulse, Michael, **Supp. IV:** 354

"Human Abstract, The" (Blake), **III:** 296

Human Age, The (Lewis), **VII:** 80

Human Face, The (Smith, I. C.), **Supp. IX:** 221–223

Human Factor, The (Greene), **Supp. I:** 2, 11, 16–17; **Retro. Supp. II:** 165–166

"Human Harvest, A" (Fallon), **Supp. XII:** 112–113

"Human Life, on the Denial of Immortality" (Coleridge), **Retro. Supp. II:** 65

Human Machine, The (Bennett), **VI:** 250

Human Odds and Ends (Gissing), **V:** 437

"Human Seasons, The" (Keats), **IV:** 232

Human Shows, Far Phantasies, Songs and Trifles (Hardy), **VI:** 20

Human Voices (Fitzgerald), **Supp. V:** 95, 100, 103

"Humanism and the Religious Attitude" (Hulme), **Supp. VI:** 135, 140

"Humanitad" (Wilde), **V:** 401–402

Humble Administrator's Garden, The (Seth), **Supp. X:** 281

"Humble Petition of Frances Harris" (Swift), **III:** 30–31

Humboldt's Gift (Bellow), **Supp. IV:** 27, 33, 42

Hume, David, **III:** 148; **IV:** xiv, 138, 145, 273, 288; **V:** 288, 343; **Supp. III: 220–245**

Humiliation with Honour (Brittain), **Supp. X:** 45

"Humility" (Brome), **Supp. X:** 55

Humorous Day's Mirth, A (Chapman), **I:** 243, 244

Humorous Lieutenant, The (Fletcher), **II:** 45, 60–61, 65, 359

Humours of the Court (Bridges), **VI:** 83

Humphrey Clinker (Smollett), **III:** 147, 150, **155–157,** 158

"Hunchback in the Park, The" (Thomas), **Supp. I:** 177, 178

Hundred Days, The (O'Brian), **Supp. XII:** 259

"Hundred Years, A" (Motion), **Supp. VII:** 266

Hundredth Story, The (Coppard), **VIII:** 89

Hungarian Lift-Jet, The (Banks), **Supp. XI:** 1

"Hunger" (Lessing), **Supp. I:** 240

"Hungry Eye, A" (Fallon), **Supp. XII:** 103

Hungry Hill (du Maurier), **Supp. III:** 144

Hunt, John, **IV:** 129, 132

Hunt, Leigh, **II:** 332, 355, 357, 359, 363; **IV:** ix, 80, 104, 129, 132, 163, 172, 198, 202, 205–206, 209, 212–217, 230, 306; **Retro. Supp. I:** 183, 248

Hunt, Violet, **VI:** 324

Hunt, William Holman, **V:** 45, 77–78, 235, 236, 240

Hunt by Night, The (Mahon), **Supp. VI:** 173–174, 177

"Hunt by Night, The" (Mahon), **Supp. VI:** 174

"Hunt of Eildon, The" (Hogg), **Supp. X:** 111

"Hunted Beast, The" (Powys), **VIII:** 247–248

Hunted Down (Dickens), **VI:** 66, 72

"Hunter, The" (Macpherson), **VIII:** 181

Hunter, G. K., **I:** 165; **II:** 29, 41

Hunting of Cupid, The (Peele), **I:** 205

Hunting of the Snark, The (Carroll), **V:** 270, 272, 273

Hunting Sketches (Trollope), **V:** 101

Huntley, F. L, **II:** 152, 157

"Huntsman, The" (Lowbury), **VII:** 431–432

"Huntsmen" (Nye), **Supp. X:** 198

Hurd, Michael, **VI:** 427

Hurd, Richard, **I:** 122

"Hurly Burly" (Coppard), **VIII:** 93–94

"Hurrahing in Harvest" (Hopkins), **V:** 366, 367, 368

"Husband and Wife" (Rossetti), **V:** 259

Husband His Own Cuckold, The (Dryden the younger), **II:** 305

Husband's Message, The, **Retro. Supp. II:** 305

Hussein: An Entertainment (O'Brian), **Supp. XII:** 249

Hussey, Maurice, **II:** 250, 254

Hutcheon, Linda, **Supp. IV:** 162

Hutchinson, F. E., **II:** 121, 123, 126, 129

Hutchinson, Sara, **IV:** 15, 49, 50, 54

Hutton, James, **IV:** 200

Hutton, R. H., **V:** 157–158, 168, 170

Huxley, Aldous, **II:** 105, 173; **III:** 341; **IV:** 303; **V:** xxii, 53; **VII:** xii, xvii–xviii, 79, **197–208; Retro. Supp. II:** 182

Huxley, Thomas, **V:** xxii, 182, 284

Hyacinth Halvey (Gregory), **VI:** 315, 316

Hyde, Douglas, **VI:** 307; **VII:** 1

Hyde–Lees, George, **VI:** 213

Hydriotaphia (Browne), **II: 150–153,** 154, 155, 156

Hygiasticon (Lessius), **II:** 181n

Hymenaei (Jonson), **I:** 239

Hymiskviða, **VIII:** 230

"Hymn before Sun–rise, in the Vale of Chamouni" (Coleridge), **Retro. Supp. II:** 59–60

"Hymn of Apollo" (Shelley), **II:** 200; **IV:** 203

Hymn of Nature, A (Bridges), **VI:** 81

"Hymn to Adversity" (Gray), **III:** 137

Hymn to Christ on the Cross (Chapman), **I:** 241–242

"Hymn to Colour" (Meredith), **V:** 222

Hymn to Diana (Jonson), **I:** 346; **Retro. Supp. I:** 162

"Hymn to God, my God, in my sickness" (Donne), **I:** 368; **II:** 114

Hymn to Harmony, A (Congreve), **II:** 350

"Hymn to Intellectual Beauty" (Shelley), **IV:** 198

"Hymn. To Light" (Cowley), **II:** 198, 200, 259

"Hymn to Mercury" (Shelley), **IV:** 196, 204

"Hymn to Pan" (Keats), **IV:** 216, 217, 222

"Hymn to Proust" (Ewart), **Supp. VII:** 38

"Hymn to the Name and Honor of the Admirable Sainte Teresa, A" (Crashaw), **II:** 179, 182

Hymn to the Pillory, A (Defoe), **III:** 13; **Retro. Supp. I:** 65, 67–68

"Hymn to the Sun" (Hood), **IV:** 255

"Hymn to the Winds" (du Bellay), **V:** 345

"Hymn to Venus" (Shelley), **IV:** 209

"Hymne of the Nativity, A" (Crashaw), **II:** 180, 183

"Hymne to God the Father, A" (Donne), **Retro. Supp. II:** 98

Hymns (Spenser), **I:** 131

Hymns Ancient and Modern (Betjeman), **VII:** 363–364

"Hymns to Lenin" (MacDiarmid), **Supp. XII:** 211

Hymnus in Cynthiam (Chapman), **I:** 240

Hyperion (Keats), **IV:** 95, 204, 211, 212, 213, **227–231,** 235; **VI:** 455; **Retro. Supp. I:** 194

Hypnerstomachia (Colonna), **I:** 134

Hypochondriack, The (Boswell), **III:** 237, 240, 243, 248

"Hypogram and Inscription" (de Man), **Supp. IV:** 115

Hysterical Disorders of Warfare (Yealland), **Supp. IV:** 58

"**I**" (Thomas), **Supp. XII:** 290
I abide and abide and better abide" (Wyatt), **I:** 108, 109
"I Am": The Selected Poetry of John Clare (Clare), **Supp. XI:** 51, 62
I Am a Camera (Isherwood), **VII:** 311
I Am Lazarus: Short Stories (Kavan), **Supp. VII:** 210–211
I Am Mary Dunne (Moore, B.), **Supp. IX:** 143, 148, 149–150, 153
"I am Raftery" (Mahon), **Supp. VI:** 170
"I Bring Her a Flower" (Warner), **Supp. VII:** 371
I Can Remember Robert Louis Stevenson (ed. Masson), **V:** 393, 397
"I care not if I live" (Bridges), **VI:** 81
I, Claudius (Graves), **VII:** 259
I Crossed the Minch (MacNeice), **VII:** 403, 411
"I dined with a Jew" (Macaulay), **IV:** 283
"I Do, You Do" (Motion), **Supp. VII:** 260
"I Dreamt Gallipoli Beach" (Hart), **Supp. XI:** 123
"I find no peace and all my war is done" (Wyatt), **I:** 110
"I go night–shopping like Frank O'Hara I go bopping" (Mahon), **Supp. VI:** 175
"I Have Been Taught" (Muir), **Supp. VI:** 208
"I have longed to move away" (Thomas), **Supp. I:** 174
"I have loved and so doth she" (Wyatt), **I:** 102
"I heard an Angel singing" (Blake), **III:** 296
"I, in my intricate image" (Thomas), **Supp. I:** 174
I Knock at the Door (O'Casey), **VII:** 12
"I know a Bank Whereon the Wild Thyme Grows" (Shakespeare), **IV:** 222
"I lead a life unpleasant"(Wyatt), **I:** 104
I Like It Here (Amis), **Supp. II: 8–10**, 12
I Live under a Black Sun (Sitwell), **VII:** 127, 135, 139
"I Look into My Glass" (Hardy), **VI:** 16
I Lost My Memory, The Case As the Patient Saw It (Anon.), **Supp. IV:** 5
"I love all beauteous things" (Bridges), **VI:** 72
"*I.M.* G.MacB." (Reading), **VIII:** 273
"I never shall love the snow again" (Bridges), **VI:** 77
"I Ordained the Devil" (McCabe), **Supp. IX:** 136
I promessi sposi (Manzoni), **III:** 334
"I Remember" (Hood), **IV:** 255
"I Remember, I Remember" (Larkin), **Supp. I:** 275, 277
"I Say I Say I Say" (Armitage), **VIII:** 9
"*I Say No*" (Collins), **Supp. VI:** 93, 103
"I see the boys of summer" (Thomas), **Supp. I:** 173
I Speak of Africa (Plomer), **Supp. XI:** 213, 214, 216
"I Stood Tip–toe" (Keats), **IV:** 214, 216
"I strove with none" (Landor), **IV:** 98

"I that in heill wes" (Dunbar), **VIII:** 121
"I took my heart in my hand" (Rossetti), **V:** 252
"I wake and feel the fell of dark" (Hopkins), **V:** 374n, 375
"I Wandered Lonely as a Cloud" (Wordsworth), **IV:** 22
I Want It Now (Amis), **Supp. II:** 15
"I Will Lend You Malcolm" (Graham), **Supp. VII:** 116
I Will Marry When I Want (Ngũgĩ). See *Ngaahika ndeenda*
"I will not let thee go" (Bridges), **VI:** 74, 77
I Will Pray with the Spirit (Bunyan), **II:** 253
"I will write" (Graves), **VII:** 269
"I would be a bird" (Bridges), **VI:** 81–82
Ian Hamilton's March (Churchill), **VI:** 351
"Ianthe"poems (Landor), **IV:** 88, 89, 92, 99
Ibrahim (Scudéry), **III:** 95
Ibsen, Henrik, **IV:** 118; **V:** xxiii–xxvi, 414; **VI:** viii–ix, 104, 110, 269; **Supp. III:** 4, 12; **Supp. IV:** 1, 286; **Retro. Supp. I:** 170; **Retro. Supp. II:** 309
Ibsen's Ghost; or, Toole Up to Date (Barrie), **Supp. III:** 4, 9
Ice (Kavan), **Supp. VII:** 201, 208, 214–215
Ice Age, The (Drabble), **Supp. IV:** 230, 245–246, 247
Ice in the Bedroom (Wodehouse), **Supp. III:** 460
Icelandic journals (Morris), **V:** 299, 300–301, 307
"Icy Road" (MacCaig), **Supp. VI:** 188–189
Idea of a University, The (Newman), **Supp. VII:** 294, 296, 298–299
Idea of Christian Society, The (Eliot), **VII:** 153
Idea of Comedy, The, and the Uses of the Comic Spirit (Meredith), *see Essay on Comedy and the Uses of the Comic Spirit*
"Idea of Entropy at Maenporth Beach, The" (Redgrove), **Supp. VI: 233–234**, 237
"Idea of Perfection, The" (Murdoch), **Supp. I:** 217, 220
Idea of the Perfection of Painting, An (tr. Evelyn), **II:** 287
Ideal Husband, An (Wilde), **V:** 414–415, 419
Ideals in Ireland (ed. Lady Gregory), **VI:** 98
Ideals in Ireland: Priest or Hero? (Russell), **VIII:** 282, 284
Ideas and Places (Connolly), **Supp. III:** 110
Ideas of Good and Evil (Yeats), **V:** 301, 306
"Idenborough" (Warner), **Supp. VII:** 380
Identical Twins (Churchill), **Supp. IV:** 181
Identifying Poets: Self and Territory in Twentieth–Century Poetry (Crawford), **Supp. XI:** 71

"Identities" (Muldoon), **Supp. IV:** 414, 424
"Ides of March, The" (Fuller), **Supp. VII:** 73
Idiocy of Idealism, The (Levy), **VI:** 303
"Idiot Boy, The" (Wordsworth), **IV:** 7, 11
"Idiots, The" (Conrad), **VI:** 148
"Idle Reverie, An" (Russell), **VIII:** 290
Idleness of Business, The, A Satyr . . . (Wycherley), *see Folly of Industry, The*
Idler (periodical), **III:** 111–112, 121; **Retro. Supp. I:** 145
Idol Hunter, The (Unsworth) see *Pascali's Island*
"Idyll" (Cope), **VIII:** 80
Idyllia heroica decem (Landor), **IV:** 100
"Idylls of the King" (Hill), **Supp. V:** 191
Idylls of the King (Tennyson), **IV:** xxii, 328, 336–337, 338
"If by Dull Rhymes Our English Must be Chained . . .." (Keats), **IV:** 221
"If I Could Tell You" (Auden), **Retro. Supp. I:** 10
If I Don't Know (Cope), **VIII:** 67, 70, 79–84
If I Were Four and Twenty: Swedenborg, Mediums and Desolate Places (Yeats), **VI:** 222
"If I were tickled by the rub of lover" (Thomas), **Supp. I:** 172
"If in the world there be more woes"(Wyatt), **I:** 104
"If, My Darling" (Larkin), **Supp. I:** 277, 285
"If my head hurt a hair's foot" (Thomas), **Supp. I:** 176–177
"If Only" (Dunn), **Supp. X:** 82
"If She's Your Lover Now" (Fallon), **Supp. XII:** 103
If the Old Could . . . (Lessing), **Supp. I:** 253, 254
"If This Were Faith" (Stevenson), **V:** 385
If You're Glad I'll Be Frank (Stoppard), **Supp. I:** 439, 445
Ignatius His Conclave (Donne), **Retro. Supp. I:** 95
"Ikey" (Brown), **Supp. VI:** 68
Ikons, The (Durrell), **Supp. I:** 121
"Il Conde" (Conrad), **VI: 148**
Il cortegiano (Castiglione), **I:** 265
Il Filostrato (Boccaccio), **Retro. Supp. II:** 40–42
Il pastor fido (Guarini), **II:** 49–50
Il pecorone (Fiorentino), **I:** 310
"Il Penseroso" (Milton), **II:** 158–159; **III:** 211n; **IV:** 14–15
Ilex Tree, The (Murray), **Supp. VII:** 270, 271–272
Iliad, The (tr. Cowper), **III:** 220
Iliad, The (tr. Macpherson), **VIII:** 192
Iliad, The (tr. Pope), **III:** 77
Ill Beginning Has a Good End, An, and a Bad Beginning May Have a Good End (Ford), **II:** 89, 100
"I'll come when thou art saddest" (Brontë), **V:** 127
I'll Leave It To You (Coward), **Supp. II:** 141
I'll Never Be Young Again (du Maurier), **Supp. III:** 139–140, 144

Ill Seen Ill Said (Beckett), **Retro. Supp. I:** 29

I'll Stand by You (Warner), **Supp. VII:** 370, 382

"Illiterations" (Brooke–Rose)), **Supp. IV:** 97

"Illuminated Man, The" (Ballard), **Supp. V:** 24

Illusion (Carey and Mullins), **Supp. XII:** 53

Illusion and Reality: A Study of the Sources of Poetry (Caudwell), **Supp. III:** 120, **Supp. IX:** 33–36, 40–44, 46

"Illusions" (Blunden), **Supp. XI:** 45

"Illusions of Anti–Realism" (Brooke–Rose)), **Supp. IV:** 116

Illustrated Excursions in Italy (Lear), **V:** 77, 79, 87

Illustrated London News (periodical), **VI:** 337

Illustrations of Latin Lyrical Metres (Clough), **V:** 170

Illustrations of the Family of Psittacidae, or Parrots (Lear), **V:** 76, 79, 87

Illywhacker (Carey), **Supp. XII:** 49, 50, 51, 53, 55, 56–57, 57–58, 62

I'm Deadly Serious (Wallace–Crabbe), **VIII:** 321–322

I'm Dying Laughing (Stead), **Supp. IV:** 473, 476

"I'm happiest when most away" (Brontë), **V:** 116

"Image, The" (Day Lewis), **Supp. III:** 115–116

"Image, The" (Fuller), **Supp. VII:** 73

"Image, The" (Warner), **Supp. VII:** 371

"Image from Beckett, An" (Mahon), **Supp. VI:** 169, 172

Image Men, The (Priestley), **VII:** 209, 210, 218, 221–223

Image of a Society (Fuller), **Supp. VII:** 68, 74–75

"Images" (Fuller), **Supp. VII:** 80

Imaginary Conversations (Landor), **IV:** xviii, 87, 88, 89, **90–94,** 96–97, 99, 100

Imaginary Conversations of Greeks and Romans (Landor), **IV:** 100

Imaginary Homelands: Essays and Criticism (Rushdie), **Supp. IV:** 171, 434

Imaginary Life, An (Malouf), **Supp. XII:** 217, 222–224, 228

Imaginary Love Affair, An (Ewart), **Supp. VII:** 41

Imaginary Portraits (Pater), **V:** 339, 340, 348–349, 355, 356

Imagination Dead Imagine (Beckett), **Supp. I:** 53, 61; **Retro. Supp. I:** 29

Imagination in the Modern World, The (Spender), **Supp. II:** 492

Imaginations and Reveries (Russell), **VIII:** 277, 281, 284, 287, 292

"Imaginative Woman, An" (Hardy), **VI:** 22

Imaginings of Sand (Brink), **Supp. VI:** **57**

Imitation Game, The (McEwan), **Supp. IV:** 390, 398–399

"Imitation of Spenser" (Keats), **IV:** 213; **Retro. Supp. I:** 187

Imitations of English Poets (Pope), **Retro. Supp. I:** 231–232

Imitation of the Sixth Satire of the Second Book of Horace, An (Swift), **III:** 36

Imitations of Horace (Pope), **II:** 298; **III:** 77; **Retro. Supp. I:** 230, 235–238

Immaturity (Shaw), **VI:** 105

"Immigrant" (Adcock), **Supp. XII:** 8

Immorality and Profaneness of the English Stage, A (Collier), *see Short View of the Immorality . . . , A*

Immorality, Debauchery and Prophaneness (Meriton), **II:** 340

Immortal Dickens, The (Gissing), **V:** 437

"Immortals, The" (Amis), **Supp. IV:** 40

"Immram" (Muldoon), **Supp. IV:** 415–418, 420, 421, 425

"Impercipient, The" (Hardy), **Retro. Supp. I:** 121

"Imperial Adam" (Hope), **Supp. VII:** 158

"Imperial Elegy, An" (Owen), **VI:** 448

Imperial Palace (Bennett), **VI:** xiii, 247, 250, 251, 262–263

Implements in Their Places (Graham), **Supp. VII:** 103, 115–116

Importance of Being Earnest, The (Wilde), **V:** xxvi, 415, 416, 419; **Supp. II:** 50, 143, 148; **Retro. Supp. II:** 350, 370, 314–315

"Importance of Glasgow in My Work, The" (Kelman), **Supp. V:** 257

Importance of the Guardian Considered, The (Swift), **III:** 35

"Impossibility" (Crawford), **Supp. XI:** 77

Impossible Thing, An: A Tale (Congreve), **II:** 350

Impressions and Opinions (Moore), **VI:** 87

Impressions of America (Wilde), **V:** 419

Impressions of Theophrastus Such (Eliot), **V:** 198, 200

Imprisonment (Shaw), **VI:** 129

"Improvement, The" (Traherne), **Supp. XI:** 267

"Improvisation" (Gunn), **Supp. IV:** 276

Improvisatore, in Three Fyttes, with Other Poems by Thomas Lovell Beddoes, The (Beddoes), **Supp. XI:** 17, 19–20, 21, 28

"In a Blue Time" (Kureishi), **Supp. XI:** 158

In a Bombed House, 1941: An Elegy in Memory of Anthony Butts (Plomer), **Supp. XI:** 222

"In a Country Church" (Thomas), **Supp. XII:** 283–284, 286, 287

"In a Dark Wood" (Sisson), **Supp. XI:** 248

In a Free State (Naipaul), **VII:** xx; **Supp. I:** 383, 390, 393, **394–396,** 397

"In a Free State"(Naipaul), **Supp. I:** 395, 396

In a German Pension (Mansfield), **VII:** 171, 172–173

In a Glass Darkly (Le Fanu), **III:** 345

"In a Shaken House" (Warner), **Supp. VII:** 380

"In a Strange City" (Russell), **VIII:** 291

In a Time of Violence (Boland), **Supp. V:** 43

"In an Artist's Studio" (Rossetti), **V:** 249

"In Another Country" (Ewart), **Supp. VII:** 45

In Between the Sheets (McEwan), **Supp. IV:** 390, 394–396

"In Broken Images"(Graves), **VII:** 267

"In California" (Davie), **Supp. VI:** 109

"In Carrowdore Churchyard" (Mahon), **Supp. VI:** 167–168

In Celebration (Storey), **Supp. I:** 408, 411, 412, 413–414

In Chancery (Galsworthy), **VI:** 274

"In Church" (Thomas), **Supp. XII:** 285–286, 287

In Custody (Desai), **Supp. V:** 53, 55, 65, 68, 69–71

"In Deep and Solemn Dreams" (Tennyson), **IV:** 329

"In Defence of Milton" (Leavis), **VII:** 246

"In Defense of Astigmatism" (Wodehouse), **Supp. III:** 454

"In Defense of the Novel, Yet Again" (Rushdie), **Supp. IV:** 455

"In dungeons dark I cannot sing"(Brontë), **V:** 115–116

In Excited Reverie: A Centenary Tribute to William Butler Yeats, 1865–1939 (ed. Jeffares and Cross), **VI:** 224

"In Flanders Fields" (McCrae), **VI:** 434

"In from Spain" (Powys), **VIII:** 251

"In God We Trust" (Rushdie), **Supp. IV:** 434, 456

"In Good Faith" (Rushdie), **Supp. IV:** 437, 450

In Good King Charles's Golden Days (Shaw), **VI:** 125, 127, 129

In Her Own Image (Boland), **Supp. V:** 48

"In Her Own Image" (Boland), **Supp. V:** 48, 49

"In His Own Image" (Boland), **Supp. V:** 48–49

"In Insula Avalonia" (Sisson), **Supp. XI:** 258

"In Lambeth Palace Road" (Fuller), **Supp. VII:** 76

In Light and Darkness (Wallace–Crabbe), **VIII:** 311

"In Love for Long" (Muir), **Supp. VI:** 206–207

"In Me Two Worlds" (Day Lewis), **Supp. III:** 126

"In Memoriam" (Longley), **VIII:** 169

In Memoriam (Tennyson), **IV:** xxi, 234, 248, 292, 310, 313, 323, 325–328, 330, 333–338, 371; **V:** 285, 455

"In Memoriam, Amada" (Reid), **Supp. VII:** 333

"In Memoriam (Easter, 1915)" (Thomas), **VI:** 424–425; **Supp. III:** 403, 404

"In Memoriam George Forrest" (Dutton), **Supp. XII:** 98–99

In Memoriam James Joyce (MacDiarmid), **Supp. XII:** 203

"In Memoriam James Joyce" (MacDiarmid), **Supp. XII:** 214

"In Memoriam W. H. Auden" (Hart), **Supp. XI:** 123

"In Memory of Ernst Toller" (Auden), **Retro. Supp. I:** 9

"In Memory of Eva Gore–Booth and Con Markiewicz" (Yeats), **VI:** 217

"In Memory of Major Robert Gregory" (Yeats), **Retro. Supp. I:** 331

"In Memory of my Cat, Domino" (Fuller), **Supp. VII:** 77

"In Memory of My Mother" (Kavanagh), **Supp. VII:** 198

"In Memory of Sigmund Freud" (Auden), **VII:** 379; **Retro. Supp. I:** 1

"In Memory of W. B. Yeats" (Auden), **VI:** 208; **Retro. Supp. I:** 1, 9

"In Memory of Zoe Yalland" (Motion), **Supp. VII:** 264

"In More's Hotel" (Nye), **Supp. X:** 202

"In my craft or sullen art"(Thomas), **Supp. I:** 178

"In My Dreams" (Smith), **Supp. II:** 466

In My Good Books (Pritchett), **Supp. III:** 313

"In My Own Album" (Lamb), **IV:** 83

In Our Infancy (Corke), **VII:** 93

In Our Time (Hemingway), **Supp. IV:** 163

In Parenthesis (Jones), **VI:** xvi, 437–438, **Supp. VII:** 167, 168, 169, 170, 171–175, 177

In Patagonia (Chatwin), **Supp. IV:** 157, 159, 161, 163–165, 173; **Supp. IX:** 53–55, 56, 59

"In Praise of Lessius His Rule of Health" (Crashaw), **II:** 181n

"In Praise of Limestone"(Auden), **VII:** 390, 391; **Retro. Supp. I:** 12

In Praise of Love (Rattigan), **Supp. VII:** 320–321

"In Procession" (Graves), **VII:** 264

In Pursuit of the English (Lessing), **Supp. I:** 237–238

"In Santa Maria del Popolo" (Gunn), **Supp. IV:** 262

In Search of Love and Beauty (Jhabvala), **Supp. V:** 223, 233

"In Sickness and in Health" (Auden), **Retro. Supp. I:** 10

In Single Strictness (Moore), **VI:** 87, 95, 99

"In Sobieski's Shield" (Morgan, E.), **Supp. IX:** 158, 164

"In Such a Poise Is Love" (Reid), **Supp. VII:** 328–329

"In Summer" (Wallace–Crabbe), **VIII:** 311

"In Tenebris II" (Hardy), **VI:** 14

In the Middle (Smith, I. C.), **Supp. IX:** 217–218

In the Middle of the Wood (Smith, I. C.), **Supp. IX:** 209

In the Beginning (Douglas), **VI:** 303, 304, 305

In the Cage (James), **VI:** 67, 69

"In the City of Red Dust" (Okri), **Supp. V:** 352

"In the Classics Room" (Smith, I. C.), **Supp. IX:** 214–215

In the Country of the Skin (Redgrove), **Supp. VI: 230**

In the Days of the Comet (Wells), **VI:** 227, 237, 244

"In the Garden at Swainston" (Tennyson), **IV:** 336

"In the Great Metropolis" (Clough), **V:** 164

In the Green Tree (Lewis), **VII:** 447

In the Heart of the Country (Coetzee), **Supp. VI:** 76, **80–81**

"In the House of Suddhoo" (Kipling), **VI:** 170

In the Labyrinth (Robbe–Grillet), **Supp. IV:** 116

In the Meantime (Jennings), **Supp. V:** 219

In the Night (Kelman), **Supp. V:** 256

"In the Night" (Jennings), **Supp. V:** 211–212

"In the Night" (Kincaid), **Supp. VII:** 220

"In the Nursery" (Stevenson), **Supp. VI:** 264

In the Permanent Way (Steel), **Supp. XII:** 269

In the Pink (Blackwood), **Supp. IX:** 14–15

"In the Ringwood" (Kinsella), **Supp. V:** 260

"In the rude age when science was not so rife" (Surrey), **I:** 115–116

"In the Same Boat" (Kipling), **VI:** 193

In the Scales of Fate (Pietrkiewicz), **Supp. IV:** 98

In the Seven Woods (Yeats), **VI:** 213, 222

In the Shadow of the Glen (Synge), **Retro. Supp. I:** 295–296

"In the Snack–bar" (Morgan, E.), **Supp. IX:** 158

In the South Seas (Stevenson), **V:** 396

In the Stopping Train (Davie), **Supp. VI:** 112

"In the Stopping Train" (Davie), **Supp. VI:** 112

In the Trojan Ditch: Collected Poems and Selected Translations (Sisson), **Supp. XI:** 243, 248, 250, 252, 253, 256–257

In the Twilight (Swinburne), **V:** 333

"In the Vermilion Cathedral" (Redgrove), **Supp. VI:** 234

In the Year of Jubilee (Gissing), **V:** 437

"In This Time" (Jennings), **Supp. V:** 214

"In Time of Absence" (Graves), **VII:** 270

"In Time of 'The Breaking of Nations'" (Hardy), **Retro. Supp. I:** 120

"In Time of War" (Auden), **Retro. Supp. I:** 9

"In to thir dirk and drublie days" (Dunbar), **VIII:** 121

In Touch with the Infinite (Betjeman), **VII:** 365

In Trouble Again: A Journey Between the Orinoco and the Amazon (O'Hanlon), **Supp. XI:** 196, 199–202, 207

In Which We Serve (Coward), **Supp. II:** 154

In Wicklow, West Kerry, and Connemara (Synge), **VI:** 309, 317

"In Youth" (Smith, I. C.), **Supp. IX:** 214

In Youth is Pleasure (Welch), **Supp. IX:** 261, 263, 264–266

Inadmissible Evidence (Osborne), **Supp. I:** 330, 333, 336–337

"Inarticulates" (MacCaig), **Supp. VI:** 191

Inca of Perusalem, The (Shaw), **VI:** 120

"Incarnate One, The" (Muir), **Supp. VI:** 208

"Incantata" (Muldoon), **Supp. IV:** 428–429, 430, 431–432

"Incendiary Method, The" (Murray), **Supp. VII:** 273

"Inchcape Rock, The" (Southey), **IV:** 58

"Incident" (Smith, I. C.), **Supp. IX:** 217

Incident Book, The (Adcock), **Supp. XII:** 3, 8–9

"Incident in Hyde Park, 1803" (Blunden), **Supp. XI:** 46

"Incident in the Life of Mr. George Crookhill" (Hardy), **VI:** 22

"Incident on a Journey" (Gunn), **Supp. IV:** 256, 258–259

Incidents at the Shrine (Okri), **Supp. V:** 347, 348, 352, 355–356

"Incidents at the Shrine" (Okri), **Supp. V:** 356–357

Incidents in the Rue Laugier (Brookner), **Supp. IV:** 135–136

Inclinations (Firbank), **Supp. II:** 201, 202, 209–211

Inclinations (Sackville–West), **VII:** 70

Incline Our Hearts (Wilson), **Supp. VI:** 307

Incognita; or, Love and Duty Reconcil'd (Congreve), **II:** 338, 346

Inconstant, The; or, The Way to Win Him (Farquhar), **II:** 352–353, 357, 362, 364

Incredulity of Father Brown, The (Chesterton), **VI:** 338

"Incubus, or the Impossibility of Self–Determination as to Desire (Self), **Supp. V:** 402

"Indaba Without Fear" (Paton), **Supp. II:** 360

"Indefinite Exposure" (Gunesekera), **Supp. X:** 86

"Independence" (Motion), **Supp. VII:** 255

Independent Labour Party, **VII:** 280

Independent Review (periodical), **VI:** 399

Independent Theatre Society, **VI:** 104

Index to A In Memoriam,"An (ed. Carroll), **V:** 274

Index to the Private Papers of James Boswell . . . (ed. Pottle et al.), **III:** 249

India (Steel), **Supp. XII:** 274

India: A Wounded Civilization (Naipaul), **Supp. I:** 385, 399, 401

India Through the Ages: A Popular and Picturesque History of Hindustan (Steel), **Supp. XII:** 274

Indian Education Minutes . . . , The (Macaulay), **IV:** 291

Indian Emperour, The; or, The Conquest of Mexico . . . , Being the Sequel to the Indian Queen (Dryden), **II:** 290, 294, 305

"Indian Fiction Today" (Desai), **Supp. V:** 67

Indian Ink (Stoppard), **Retro. Supp. II:** 356–357

Indian Journal (Lear), *see Edward Lear's Indian Journal*

Indian Queen, The (Dryden), **II:** 305

"Indian Serenade, The" (Shelley), **IV:** 195, 203

"Indian Summer of a Forsyte" (Galsworthy), **VI:** 274, 276, 283

"Indian Summer, Vermont" (Stevenson), **Supp. VI:** 255

"Indian Tree" (Gunesekera), **Supp. X:** 87

"Indifferent, The" (Donne), **Retro. Supp. II:** 89

Indiscretion in the Life of an Heiress, An (Hardy), **VI:** 20

"Induction" (Sackville), **I:** 169

Induction, The (Field), **II:** 66

Inebriety (Crabbe), **III:** 274, 278–279, 286

"Infancy" (Crabbe), **III:** 273, 281

"Infant–Ey, An" (Traherne), **Supp. XI:** 266, 267

"Inferior Religions" (Lewis), **VII:** 77

Infernal Desire Machine of Dr. Hoffman, The (Carter), **III:** 345; **Supp. III:** 84–85, 89

Infernal Marriage, The (Disraeli), **IV:** 297, 299, 308

Infernal World of Branwell Brontë, The (Carter), **Supp. III:** 139

Inferno (Dante), **Retro. Supp. II:** 36

Infidel, The (Braddon), **VIII:** 49

Infinite Rehearsal, The (Harris), **Supp. V:** 140, 141–142, 144

Information, The (Amis), **Supp. IV:** 26, 37–39, 42

"Informer, The" (Conrad), **VI:** 148

Infuence of the Roman Censorship on the Morals of the People, The (Swinburne), **V:** 333

Ingannati: The Deceived . . . and Aelia Laelia Crispis (Peacock), **IV:** 170

Inge, William Ralph, **VI:** 344

Ingelow, Jean, **Supp. IV:** 256

"Ingram Lake, or, Five Acts on the House" (Morgan, E.), **Supp. IX:** 161, 163

Ingrowing Thoughts (Thomas), **Supp. XII:** 288

"Inheritance" (Murphy), **Supp. V:** 322

Inheritors, The (Golding), **Supp. I:** 67, **70–72**, 75, 84; **Retro. Supp. I:** 96–97

Inheritors, The: An Extravagant Story (Conrad and Ford), **VI:** 146, 148, 321, 332

Inishfallen, Fare Thee Well (O'Casey), **VII:** 4, 12

Injur'd Husband, The; or, The Mistaken Resentment, **Supp. XII:** 140

Injur'd Husband, The; or, The Mistaken Resentment, and Lasselia; or, The Self-Abandoned (Haywood), **Supp. XII:** 137

Injury Time (Bainbridge), **Supp. VI:** 21

"Inland" (Motion), **Supp. VII:** 254, 255

Inland Voyage, An (Stevenson), **V:** 386, 395; **Retro. Supp. I:** 261

Inn Album, The (Browning), **IV:** 358, 367, 369–370, 374; **Retro. Supp. II:** 30

"Inn of the Two Witches, The" (Conrad), **VI:** 148

Inner and Outer Ireland, The (Russell), **VIII:** 289

Inner Harbour, The (Adcock), **Supp. XII:** 6–8

"Inniskeen Road: July Evening" (Kavanagh), **Supp. VII:** 188

Innocence (Fitzgerald), **Supp. V:** 100, 104–106

"Innocence" (Gunn), **Supp. IV:** 262

"Innocence" (Traherne), **Supp. XI:** 266

Innocence of Father Brown, The (Chesterton), **VI:** 338

Innocent, The (McEwan), **Supp. IV:** 390, 399, 402–404, 405, 406

Innocent and the Guilty, The (Warner), **Supp. VII:** 381

Innocent Birds (Powys), **VIII:** 251, 256, 258

Innocent Blood (James), **Supp. IV:** 337–338, 340

Innumerable Christ, The (MacDiarmid), **Supp. XII:** 205

Inquiry into the Nature & Causes of the Wealth of Nations (Smith), **IV:** xiv, 145

Insatiate Countess, The (Barsted and Marston), **II:** 31, 40

"Insect World, The" (Rhys), **Supp. II:** 402

"Insensibility" (Owen), **VI:** 453, 455

Inside a Pyramid (Golding), **Supp. I:** 82

Inside Mr Enderby (Burgess), **Supp. I:** 185, 186, 189, 194

Inside the Whale (Orwell), **VII:** 282

"Inside the Whale" (Orwell), **Supp. IV:** 110, 455

Insight and Outlook: An Enquiry into the Common Foundations of Science, Art and Social Ethics (Koestler), **Supp. I:** 37

"Insight at Flame Lake" (Amis), **Supp. IV:** 40

"Insomnia" (Hart), **Supp. XI:** 125

"Installation Ode" (Gray), **III:** 142

Instamatic Poems (Morgan, E.), **Supp. IX:** 162–163

"Instance, An" (Reid), **Supp. VII:** 328

"Instant, The" (Redgrove), **Supp. VI:** 231

Instant in the Wind, An (Brink), **Supp. VI:** 49

"Instead of an Interview" (Adcock), **Supp. XII:** 8

Instead of Trees (Priestley), **VII:** 209–210

"Instruction, The" (Traherne), **Supp. XI:** 268

Instructions Concerning Erecting of a Liberty (tr. Evelyn), **II:** 287

Instructions for the Ignorant (Bunyan), **II:** 253

"Instructions to a Painter . . . A (Waller), **II:** 233

"Instructions to an Actor" (Morgan, E.), **Supp. IX:** 164

Instrument of Thy Peace (Paton), **Supp. II: 358–359**

Inteendeel (Brink), **Supp. VI:** 56

"Intellectual Felicity" (Boswell), **III:** 237

Intelligence (journal), **III:** 35

Intelligent Woman's Guide to Socialism and Capitalism, The (Shaw), **VI:** 116, 125

"Intensive Care Unit, The" (Ballard), **Supp. V:** 28

Intentions (Wilde), **V:** 407, 419; **Retro. Supp. II:** 367–368

Intercom Conspiracy, The (Ambler), **Supp. IV:** 4, 16, 18, 20–21

"Intercom Quartet, The" (Brooke–Rose)), **Supp. IV:** 110–113

"Interference" (Barnes), **Supp. IV:** 75

"Interior Mountaineer" (Redgrove), **Supp. VI:** 236

"Interloper, The" (Hardy), **VI:** 17

"Interlopers at the Knapp" (Hardy), **VI:** 22

"Interlude, An" (Swinburne), **V:** 321

"Intermediate Sex, The" (Carpenter), **VI:** 407

"Intermezzo" (Kinsella), **Supp. V:** 271

"International Episode, An" (James), **VI:** 69

International Guerrillas (film), **Supp. IV:** 438

internationalism, **VI:** 241n; **VII:** 229

Interpretation in Teaching (Richards), **Supp. II:** 423, 430

Interpretation of Genesis, An (Powys), **VIII:** 246–247

Interpreters, The (Russell), **VIII:** 289, 290, 292

"Interrogator, The" (Jennings), **Supp. V:** 215

"Interruption" (Gunn), **Supp. IV:** 273, 274

"Interview" (Dutton), **Supp. XII:** 87, 95

"Interview, The" (Blackwood), **Supp. IX:** 9

"Interview" (Nye), **Supp. X:** 201

Interview, The (Sillitoe), **Supp. V:** 411

Intimacy (Kureishi), **Supp. XI:** 157, 158

Intimate Exchanges (Ayckbourn), **Supp. V:** 3, 6, 12, 14

"Intimate Supper" (Redgrove), **Supp. VI:** 234

"Intimate World of Ivy Compton–Burnett, The" (Karl), **VII:** 70

"Intimations of Immortality . . . A (Wordsworth), *see* AOde. Intimations of Immortality from Recollections of Early Childhood"

"Into Arcadia" (Heaney), **Retro. Supp. I:** 134

Into Battle (Churchill), **VI:** 356

"Into Battle" (Grenfell), **VI:** 418

"Into her Lying Down Head" (Thomas), **Supp. I:** 178

Into the Heart of Borneo: An Account of a Journey Made in 1983 to the Mountains of Batu Tiban with James Fenton (O'Hanlon), **Supp. XI:** 196–199, 202, 206, 207–208

Into Their Labours (Berger), **Supp. IV:** 80, 90–95

Intriguing Chambermaid, The (Fielding), **III:** 105

"Introduction" (Blake), **Retro. Supp. I:** 37

Introduction 7: Stories by New Writers (Faber & Faber), **Supp. IV:** 303

Introduction to the History of Great Britain and Ireland, An (Macpherson), **VIII:** 192

Introductory Lecture (Housman), **VI:** 164

"Introductory Rhymes" (Yeats), **Retro. Supp. I:** 330

Intruder, The (Hardy), **VI:** 20

"Invader, The" (Cameron), **Supp. IX:** 26, 27

Invaders, The (Plomer), **Supp. XI:** 219–221

Invasion of the Space Invaders (Amis), **Supp. IV:** 42

Invective against Jonson, The (Chapman), **I:** 243

Invention of Love, The (Stoppard), **Retro. Supp. II:** 357–358

"Inversion Layer: Oxfordshire" (Wallace–Crabbe), **VIII:** 323

Inversions (Banks), **Supp. XI:** 5, 10, 13

"Inversnaid" (Hopkins), **V:** 368, 372

Invisible Friends (Ayckbourn), **Supp. V:** 3, 12, 14–15

Invisible Man, The: A Grotesque Romance (Wells), **VI:** 226, 232–233, 244

Invisible Writing, The (Koestler), **Supp. I:** 22, 23, 24, 32, 37

"Invitation, The" (Shelley), **IV:** 196

"Invocation" (Hope), **Supp. VII:** 154

"Invocation" (Sitwell), **VII:** 136

"Inward Bound" (MacCaig), **Supp. VI:** 192

Inward Eye, The (MacCaig), **Supp. VI:** 184–185

"Iolaire" (Smith, I. C.), **Supp. IX:** 219

Ion (Plato), **IV:** 48

Ionian Mission, The (O'Brian), **Supp. XII:** 256, 259–260

"Iowa" (Davie), **Supp. VI:** 110

Iphigenia (Peele), **I:** 198

"Iphis and Araxarathen" (Gower), **I:** 53–54

Iqbal, Muhammad, **Supp. IV:** 448

"Ireland" (Swift), **III:** 31

Ireland and the Empire at the Court of Conscience (Russell), **VIII:** 289, 292

Ireland, Past and Future (Russell), **VIII:** 289

Ireland Since the Rising (Coogan), **VII:** 9

Ireland, Your Only Place (Morris, J.), **Supp. X:** 177

Ireland's Abbey Theatre (Robinson), **VI:** 317

Ireland's Literary Renaissance (Boyd), **VI:** 316

Irene: A Tragedy (Fielding), **III:** 109, 121

Irene: A Tragedy (Johnson), **Retro. Supp. I:** 138–139

Irigaray, Luce, **Supp. IV:** 232

"Irish Airman Foresees His Death, An" (Yeats), **Retro. Supp. I:** 331

"Irish Child in England" (Boland), **Supp. V:** 35

Irish Drama, The (Malone), **VI:** 316

Irish Dramatic Movement, The (Ellis–Fermor), **VI:** 317

Irish dramatic revival, **VI:** xiv, 207, 218, 307–310; **VII:** 3

Irish Essays and Others (Arnold), **V:** 216

Irish Faust, An (Durrell), **Supp. I:** 126, 127

Irish Impressions (Chesterton), **VI:** 345

"Irish Revel" (O'Brien), **Supp. V:** 340

Irish Sketch Book, The (Thackeray), **V:** 25, 38

Iron, Ralph (pseud., Schreiner), **Supp. II:** 448–449

Iron Man, The (Hughes), **Supp. I:** 346

Ironhand (Arden), **Supp. II:** 29

Irrational Knot, The (Shaw), **VI:** 102, 103, 105, 129

Irving, Washington, **III:** 54

Is He Popenjoy? (Trollope), **V:** 100, 102

"Is Nothing Sacred?" (Rushdie), **Supp. IV:** 437, 442–443

Is There a Church of England? (Sisson), **Supp. XI:** 251

Isabel Clarendon (Gissing), **V:** 437

"Isabella" (Keats), **IV:** xviii, 216, 217–218, 235; **Retro. Supp. I:** 193–194

"Isba Song" (McGuckian), **Supp. V:** 283

"Ischia" (Auden), **Retro. Supp. I:** 12

Isenheim Altar (Grünewald), **Supp. IV:** 85

Isherwood, Christopher, **VII:** xx, **309–320**; **Supp. II:** 408, 485, 486; **Retro. Supp. I:** 3, 7, 9

Ishiguro, Kazuo, **Supp. IV:** 75, **301–317**

Ishmael (Braddon), **VIII:** 49

Island (Huxley), **VII:** xviii, 206

Island, The (Byron), **IV:** xviii 173, 193

"Island, The" (Caudwell), **Supp. IX:** 37

"Island, The" (Jennings), **Supp. V:** 209

"Island, The" (Thomas), **Supp. XII:** 288

Island in the Moon, An (Blake), **III:** 290, 292; **Retro. Supp. I:** 34

Island in the Sun (Waugh), **Supp. VI:** 267, 274, **275**

Island Nights' Entertainments (Stevenson), **V:** 387, 396

Island of Dr. Moreau, The (Wells), **VI:** 230–231

Island of Statues, The (Yeats), **Retro. Supp. I:** 325

Island of Terrible Friends (Strutton), **Supp. IV:** 346

Island of the Mighty, The (Arden and D'Arcy), **Supp. II:** 30, **32–35**, 39

Island Pharisees, The (Galsworthy), **VI:** 271, 273, 274, 277, 281

Island Princess, The (Fletcher), **II:** 45, 60, 65

"Islanders, The" (Kipling), **VI:** 169, 203

Islands (Brathwaite), **Supp. XII:** 33, 38, 39–40, 45

Isle of Dogs, The (Jonson/Nashe), **Retro. Supp. I:** 156

Isle of Man, The (Bernard), **II:** 246

"Isle of Voices, The" (Stevenson), **V:** 396

Íslendinga sögur (Ari), **VIII:** 235, 236

"Isobel" (Golding), **Supp. I:** 66

"Isobel's Child" (Browning), **IV:** 313

"Isopes Fabules" (Lydgate), **I:** 57

Israel: Poems on a Hebrew Theme (Sillitoe), **Supp. V:** 411

Israel's Hope Encouraged (Bunyan), **II:** 253

"It Happened in 1936" (Waugh), **Supp. VI:** 273

"It is a beauteous evening, calm and free" (Wordsworth), **IV:** 22

"It May Never Happen" (Pritchett), **Supp. III:** 315

It May Never Happen and Other Stories (Pritchett), **Supp. III:** **318–319**

It Was a Lover and His Lass (Oliphant), **Supp. X:** 220

"It Was Upon a Lammas Night" (Burns), **III:** 315

It's a Battlefield (Greene), **Supp. I:** 2, 5–6; **Retro. Supp. II:** 152–153

"It's a Long, Long Way" (Thomas), **Supp. III:** 404

"It's a Woman's World" (Boland), **Supp. V:** 41

It's an Old Country (Priestley), **VII:** 211

"It's Hopeless" (MacCaig), **Supp. VI:** 191

It's Me O Lord! (Coppard), **VIII:** 85, 86, 88, 90

"It's No Pain" (Redgrove), **Supp. VI:** 234

Italian, The (Radcliffe), **III:** 331–332, 335, 337, 345; **IV:** 173; **Supp. III:** 384

Italian Hours (James), **VI:** 43, 67

Italian Mother, The, and Other Poems (Swinburne), **V:** 333

Italian Visit, An (Day Lewis), **Supp. III:** 118, 122, 129

"Italian Whirligig" (Coppard), **VIII:** 95

Italics of Walter Savage Landor, The (Landor), **IV:** 100

"Italio, Io Ti Saluto" (Rossetti), **V:** 250

"Italy and the World" (Browning), **IV:** 318

"It's Done This!" (Adcock), **Supp. XII:** 13

"Itylus" (Swinburne), **V:** 319

Ivanhoe (Scott), **IV:** xviii, 31, 34, 39

"I've Thirty Months" (Synge), **VI:** 314

Ivory Door, The (Milne), **Supp. V:** 300–301

Ivory Gate, The (Beddoes), **Supp. XI:** 29

Ivory Tower, The (James), **VI:** 64, 65

"Ivry: A Song of the Huguenots" (Macaulay), **IV:** 283, 291

Ivy Compton–Burnett (Iprigg), **VII:** 70

"Ivy Day in the Committee Room" (Joyce), **VII:** 44, 45

Ivy Gripped the Steps (Bowen), *see Demon Lover, The*

Ixion in Heaven (Disraeli), **IV:** 297, 299, 308

J. *B. Priestley, The Dramatist* (Lloyd–Evans), **VII:** 223, 231

J. M. Synge and the Irish Dramatic Movement (Bickley), **VI:** 317

"J. W. 51B A Convoy" (Ross), **VII:** 434

"Jabberwocky" (Carroll), **V:** 265

Jack, Ian Robert James, **II:** 298; **III:** 125n; **IV:** xi, xxv, 40, 140, 236, 373, 375

Jack Drum's Entertainment (Marston), **II:** 27, 40

Jack Flea's Birthday Celebration (McEwan), **Supp. IV:** 390, 398

Jack Maggs (Carey), **Supp. XII:** 49, 54, 60–61

Jack Straw (Maugham), **VI:** 368

Jack Straw's Castle (Gunn), **Supp. IV:** 257, 268–271

"Jack Straw's Castle" (Gunn), **Supp. IV:** 270

Jackdaw, The (Gregory), **VI:** 315

Jacko: The Great Intruder (Keneally), **Supp. IV:** 347

Jackson, T. A., **V:** 51

Jacob, Giles, **II:** 348

Jacob's Room (Woolf), **VII:** 18, 20, 26–27, 38; **Retro. Supp. I:** 307, 316

Jacobite's Journal, The (Fielding), **III:** 105; **Retro. Supp. I:** 81

Jacques–Louis David: A Personal Interpretation (Brookner), **Supp. IV:** 122

Jacta Alea Est (Wilde), **V:** 400

Jaggard, William, **I:** 307

"Jaguar, The" (Hughes), **Retro. Supp. II:** 203

Jaguar Smile: A Nicaraguan Journey, The (Rushdie), **Supp. IV:** 436, 454

Jake's Thing (Amis), **Supp. II:** 16–17; **Supp. IV:** 29

Jakobson, Roman, **Supp. IV:** 115

"Jam Tart" (Auden), **Retro. Supp. I:** 6

Jamaica Inn (du Maurier), **Supp. III:** 139, 144, 145, 147

James, Henry, **II:** 42; **III:** 334, 340, 345; **IV:** 35, 107, 319, 323, 369, 371, 372; **V:** x, xx, xiv–xxvi, 2, 48, 51, 70, 95, 97, 98, 102, 191, 199, 205, 210, 295, 384, 390–392; **VI:** x–xi, 5, 23–69, 227, 236, 239, 266, 320, 322; list of short stories and novellas, **VI:** 69; **Supp. II:** 80–81, 89, 487–488, 492; **Supp. III:** 47–48, 60, 217, 437; **Supp. IV:** 97, 116, 133, 153, 233, 243, 371, 503, 511

James, M. R., **III:** 340

James, P. D., **Supp. II:** 127; **Supp. IV:** **319–341**

James, Richard, **II:** 102

James, William, **V:** xxv, 272; **VI:** 24

James IV (Greene), **VIII:** 142

James and the Giant Peach (Dahl), **Supp. IV:** 202, 213, 222

James and the Giant Peach (film), **Supp. IV:** 203

James Hogg: Selected Poems (ed. Mack), **Supp. X:** 108–109

James Hogg: Selected Poems and Songs (ed. Groves), **Supp. X:** 110

James Hogg: Selected Stories and Sketches (ed. Mack), **Supp. X:** 110–111

"James Honeyman" (Auden), **Retro. Supp. I:** 8

James Joyce and the Making of AUlysses" (Budgen) **VII:** 56

"James Lee's Wife" (Browning), **IV:** 367, 369

James Rigg, Still Further Extract from The Recluse, A Poem (Hogg), **Supp. X:** 109–110

Jamie on a Flying Visit (Frayn), **Supp. VII:** 56–57

Jane and Prudence (Pym), **Supp. II:** **370–372**

Jane Austen: The Critical Heritage (ed. Southam), **IV:** 122, 124

Jane Austen's Literary Manuscripts (ed. Southam), **IV:** 124

Jane Eyre (Brontë), **III:** 338, 344, 345; **V:** xx, 106, 108, 112, 124, 135, **137–140,** 145, 147, 148, 152; **VII:** 101; **Supp. III:** 146; **Supp. IV:** 236, 452, 471; **Retro. Supp. I:** 50, 52, 53–55, 56, 58–60

"Janeites, The" (Kipling), **IV:** 106

"Jane's Marriage" (Kipling), **IV:** 106, 109

Janet (Oliphant), **Supp. X:** 219

"Janet's Repentance" (Eliot), **V:** 190–191; **Retro. Supp. II:** 104

Janowitz, Haas, **III:** 342

"January 12, 1996" (Longley), **VIII:** 177

Janus: A Summing Up (Koestler), **Supp. I:** 35, 37, 38–39

Japp, A. H., **IV:** 144*n*, 155

Jarrell, Randall, **VI:** 165, 194, 200; **Supp. IV:** 460

"Jars, The" (Brown), **Supp. VI:** 71–72

"Jasmine" (Naipaul), **Supp. I:** 383

"Jason and Medea" (Gower), **I:** 54, 56

"Jazz and the West Indian Novel" (Brathwaite), **Supp. XII:** 43–44

"Je est un autre" (Durrell), **Supp. I:** 126

"Je ne parle pas Français" (Mansfield), **VII:** 174, 177

"Je ne regretted rien" (Morgan, E.), **Supp. IX:** 165

"Je t'adore" (Kinsella), **Supp. V:** 263

"Jealousy" (Brooke), **Supp. III:** 52

Jeames's Diary; or, Sudden Wealth (Thackeray), **V:** 38

Jean de Meung, **I:** 49

Jeeves (Ayckbourn and Webber), **Supp. V:** 3

"Jeeves and the Hard–Boiled Egg" (Wodehouse), **Supp. III:** 455, 458

Jeeves and the Tie That Binds (Wodehouse), *see Much Obliged*

"Jeeves Takes Charge" (Wodehouse), **Supp. III:** 456, 457–458

Jeffares, Alexander Norman, **VI:** xxxiii–xxxiv, 98, 221

Jefferson, D. W., **III:** 182, 183

Jeffrey, Francis, **III:** 276, 285; **IV:** 31, 39, 60, 72, 129, 269

Jeffrey, Sara, **IV:** 225

Jenkin, Fleeming, **V:** 386

Jenkyn, D., **Supp. IV:** 346

Jennings, Elizabeth, **Supp. IV:** 256; **Supp. V:** **205–221**

"Jenny" (Rossetti), **V:** 240

Jenyns, Soame, **Retro. Supp. I:** 148

Jerrold, Douglas, **V:** 19

Jerrold, W. C., **IV:** 252, 254, 267

"Jersey Villas" (James), **III:** 69

Jerusalem (Blake), **III:** 303, 304–305, 307; **V:** xvi, 330; **Retro. Supp. I:** 45–46

Jerusalem: Its History and Hope (Oliphant), **Supp. X:** 222

Jerusalem Sinner Saved (Bunyan), *see Good News for the Vilest of Men*

Jerusalem the Golden (Drabble), **Supp. IV:** 230, 231, 238–239, 241, 243, 248, 251

Jesus (Wilson), **Supp. VI:** 306

Jess (Haggard), **Supp. III:** 213

Jesting Pilate (Huxley), **VII:** 201

Jew of Malta, The (Marlowe), **I:** 212, 280, **282–285, 310**; **Retro. Supp. I:** 208–209

Jew Süss (Feuchtwanger), **VI:** 265

Jewel in the Crown, The (Scott), **Supp. I:** 266–267, 269–270

Jeweller of Amsterdam, The (Field, Fletcher, Massinger), **II:** 67

Jewels of Song (Davies), **Supp. XI:** 93

"Jews, The" (Vaughan), **II:** 189

Jhabvala, Ruth Prawer, **Supp. V:** **223–239**

Jill (Larkin), **Supp. I:** 276, 286–287

Jill Somerset (Waugh), **Supp. VI:** 273

Jimmy Governor (Clune), **Supp. IV:** 350

Jitta's Atonement (Shaw), **VI:** 129

"Joachim du Bellay" (Pater), **V:** 344

Joan and Peter (Wells), **VI:** 240

Joan of Arc (Southey), **IV:** 59, 60, 63–64, 71

Joannis Miltonii Pro se defensio . . . (Milton), **II:** 176

Job (biblical book), **III:** 307

Jocasta (Gascoigne), **I:** 215–216

Jocelyn (Galsworthy), **VI:** 277

"Jochanan Hakkadosh" (Browning), **IV:** 365

Jocoseria (Browning), **IV:** 359, 374

"Joe Soap" (Motion), **Supp. VII:** 260–261, 262

Joe's Ark (Potter, D.), **Supp. X:** 229, 237–240

"Johann Joachim Quantz's Five Lessons" (Graham), **Supp. VII:** 116

"Johannes Agricola in Meditation" (Browning), **IV:** 360

Johannes Secundus, **II:** 108

"John Betjeman's Brighton" (Ewart), **Supp. VII:** 37

John Bull's Other Island (Shaw), **VI:** 112, **113–115**; **Retro. Supp. II:** 320–321

John Caldigate (Trollope), **V:** 102

"John Clare" (Cope), **VIII:** 82

John Clare: Poems, Chiefly from Manuscript (Clare), **Supp. XI:** 36, 63

John Clare by Himself (Clare), **Supp. XI:** 51

"John Fletcher" (Swinburne), **V:** 332

John Gabriel Borkman (Ibsen), **VI:** 110

"John Galsworthy" (Lawrence), **VI:** 275–276, 290

John Galsworthy (Mottram), **VI:** 271, 275, 290

"John Galsworthy, An Appreciation" (Conrad), **VI:** 290

"John Gilpin" (Cowper), **III:** 212, 220

John Keats: A Reassessment (ed. Muir), **IV:** 219, 227, 236

John Keats: His Like and Writings (Bush), **IV:** 224, 236

John Knox (Muir), **Supp. VI:** 198

"John Knox" (Smith, I. C.), **Supp. IX:** 211–212

"John Logie Baird" (Crawford), **Supp. XI:** 71

John M. Synge (Masefield), **VI:** 317

John Marchmont's Legacy (Braddon), **VIII:** 44, 46

"John Norton" (Moore), **VI:** 98

"John of the Cross" (Jennings), **Supp. V:** 207

"John Ruskin" (Proust), **V:** 183

John Ruskin: The Portrait of a Prophet (Quennell), **V:** 185

John Sherman and Dhoya (Yeats), **VI:** 221

John Thomas and Lady Jane (Lawrence), **VII:** 111–112

John Woodvil (Lamb), **IV:** 78–79, 85

Johnnie Sahib (Scott), **Supp. I:** 259, 261

Johnno (Malouf), **Supp. XII:** 221–222

Johnny I Hardly Knew You (O'Brien), **Supp. V:** 338, 339

Johnny in the Clouds (Rattigan), *see Way to the Stars, The*

Johnson, Edgar, **IV:** 27, 40; **V:** 60, 72

Johnson, James, **III:** 320, 322

Johnson, Joseph, **Retro. Supp. I:** 37

Johnson, Lionel, **VI:** 3, 210, 211

Johnson, Samuel, **III:** 54, 96, **107–123,** 127, 151, 275; **IV:** xiv, xv, 27, 31, 34, 88n, 101, 138, 268, 299; **V:** 9, 281, 287; **VI:** 363; **Retro. Supp. I: 137–150;** and Boswell, **III:** 234, 235, 238, 239, 243–249; and Collins, **III:** 160, 163, 164, 171, 173; and Crabbe, **III:** 280–282; and Goldsmith, **III:** 177, 180, 181, 189; dictionary, **III:** 113–116; **V:** 281, 434; literary criticism, **I:** 326; **II:** 123, 173, 197, 200, 259, 263, 293, 301, 347; **III:** 11, 88, 94, 139, 257, 275; **IV:** 101; on Addison and Steele, **III:** 39, 42, 44, 49, 51; **Supp. IV:** 271

Johnson, W. E., **Supp. II:** 406

Johnson over Jordan (Priestley), **VII:** 226–227

"Joker, The" (Wallace–Crabbe), **VIII:** 315–316

"Joker as Told" (Murray), **Supp. VII:** 279

Joking Apart (Ayckbourn), **Supp. V:** 3, 9, 13, 14

Jolly Beggars, The (Burns), **III:** 319–320

"Jolly Corner, The" (James), **Retro. Supp. I:** 2

Jonah Who Will Be 25 in the Year 2000 (film), **Supp. IV:** 79

Jonathan Swift (Stephen), **V:** 289

Jonathan Wild (Fielding), **III:** 99, 103, 105, 150; **Retro. Supp. I:** 80–81, 90

Jones, David, **VI:** xvi, 436, 437–439, **Supp. VII: 167–182**

Jones, Henry Arthur, **VI:** 367, 376

Jones, Henry Festing, **Supp. II:** 103–104, 112, 114, 117, 118

Jonestown (Harris), **Supp. V:** 144–145

Jonson, Ben, **I:** 228, 234–235, 270, **335–351; II:** 3, 4, 24, 25, 27, 28, 30, 45, 47, 48, 55, 65, 79, 87, 104, 108, 110, 111n, 115, 118, 141, 199, 221–223; **IV:** 35, 327; **V:** 46, 56; **Supp. IV:** 256; **Retro. Supp. I: 151–167**

Jonsonus Virbius (Digby), **Retro. Supp. I:** 166

Jonsonus Virbius (King), **Supp. VI:** 157

Joseph Andrews (Fielding), **III:** 94, 95, 96, 99–100, 101, 105; **Retro. Supp. I:** 80, 83–86

Joseph Banks: A Life (O'Brian), **Supp. XII:** 257–258

Joseph Conrad (Baines), **VI:** 133–134

Joseph Conrad (Ford), **VI:** 321, 322

Joseph Conrad (Walpole), **VI:** 149

Joseph Conrad: A Personal Reminiscence (Ford), **VI:** 149

Joseph Conrad: The Modern Imagination (Cox), **VI:** 149

Joseph Conrad and Charles Darwin: The Influence of Scientific Thought on Conrad's Fiction (O'Hanlon), **Supp. XI:** 195

"Joseph Grimaldi" (Hood), **IV:** 267

"Joseph Yates' Temptation" (Gissing), **V:** 437

Journal (Mansfield), **VII:** 181, 182

Journal, 1825–32 (Scott), **IV:** 39

Journal and Letters of Fanny Burney, The (eds. Hemlow et al.), **Supp. III:** 63

Journal of Bridget Hitler, The (Bainbridge), **Supp. VI:** 22

Journal of a Dublin Lady, The (Swift), **III:** 35

Journal of a Landscape Painter in Corsica (Lear), **V:** 87

Journal of a Tour in Scotland in 1819 (Southey), **IV:** 71

Journal of a Tour in the Netherlands in the Autumn of 1815 (Southey), **IV:** 71

Journal of a Tour to the Hebrides, The (Boswell), **III:** 117, 234n, 235, 243, 245, 248, 249

Journal of a Voyage to Lisbon, The (Fielding), **III:** 104, 105

Journal of Beatrix Potter from 1881 to 1897, The (ed. Linder), **Supp. III: 292–295**

"Journal of My Jaunt, Harvest 1762" (Boswell), **III:** 241–242

Journal of Researches into the Geology and Natural History of the various countries visited by HMS Beagle (Darwin), **Supp. VII:** 18–19

Journal of the Plague Year, A (Defoe), **III:** 5–6, 8, 13; **Retro. Supp. I:** 63, 73–74

Journal to Eliza, The (Sterne), **III:** 125, 126, 132, 135

Journal to Stella (Swift), **II:** 335; **III:** 32–33, 34; **Retro. Supp. I:** 274

Journalism (Mahon), **Supp. VI:** 166

Journalism for Women: A Practical Guide (Bennett), **VI:** 264, 266

Journals and Papers of Gerard Manley Hopkins, The (ed. House and Storey), **V:** 362, 363, 371, 378–379, 381

Journals 1939–1983 (Spender), **Supp. II:** 481, 487, 490, 493

Journals of a Landscape Painter in Albania etc. (Lear), **V:** 77, 79–80, 87

Journals of a Landscape Painter in Southern Calabria . . . (Lear), **V:** 77, 79, 87

Journals of a Residence in Portugal, 1800–1801, and a Visit to France, 1838 (Southey), **IV:** 71

Journals of Arnold Bennett (Bennett), **VI:** 265, 267

"Journals of Progress" (Durrell), **Supp. I:** 124

"Journey, The" (Boland), **Supp. V:** 41

"Journey Back, The" (Muir), **Supp. VI:** 207

Journey Continued (Paton), **Supp. II:** 356, 359

Journey from Cornhill to Grand Cairo, A (Thackeray), *see Notes of a Journey from Cornhill to Grand Cairo*

Journey from This World to the Next (Fielding), **Retro. Supp. I:** 80

Journey into Fear (Ambler), **Supp. IV:** 11–12

"Journey of John Gilpin, The" (Cowper), *see A John Gilpin*"

"Journey of the Magi, The" (Eliot), **VII:** 152

Journey Through France (Piozzi), **III:** 134

Journey to a War (Auden and Isherwood), **VII:** 312; **Retro. Supp. I:** 9

Journey to Armenia (Mandelstam), **Supp. IV:** 163, 170

"Journey to Bruges, The" (Mansfield), **VII:** 172

Journey to Ithaca (Desai), **Supp. V:** 56, 66, 73–74

Journey to London, A (Vanbrugh), **II:** 326, 333–334, 336

Journey to Oxiana (Byron), **Supp. IV:** 157, 170

Journey to the Hebrides (Johnson), **IV:** 281

Journey to the Western Islands of Scotland, A (Johnson), **III:** 117, 121; **Retro. Supp. I:** 143

Journey Without Maps (Greene), **Supp. I:** 9, **Retro. Supp. II:** 153

Journeys (Morris, J.), **Supp. X:** 172, 183

Journeys and Places (Muir), **Supp. VI:** 204, **205–206**

Journeys in Persia and Kurdistan (Bird), **Supp. X:** 31

Jovial Crew, A (Brome **Supp. X:** 49, 55–59, 62–63

Jowett, Benjamin, **V:** 278, 284, 285, 312, 338, 400

"Joy" (Dutton), **Supp. XII:** 94

Joy (Galsworthy), **VI:** 269, 285

"Joy Gordon" (Redgrove), **Supp. VI:** 236

Joyce (Oliphant), **Supp. X:** 218

Joyce, James, **IV:** 189; **V:** xxv, 41; **VII:** xii, xiv, 18, **41–58; VII:** 54–58; **Supp. I:** 43, 196–197; **Supp. II:** 74, 88, 327, 332, 338, 420, 525; **Supp. III:** 108; **Supp. IV:** 27, 233, 234, 363, 364, 365, 371, 390, 395, 396, 407, 411, 424, 426, 427, 500, 514; **Retro. Supp. I:** 18, 19, **169–182**

Joyce, Jeremiah, **V:** 174n

"Jubilate Matteo" (Ewart), **Supp. VII:** 44

"Judas Tree, The" (Welch), **Supp. IX:** 269

Jude the Obscure (Hardy), **VI:** 4, 5, 7, 8, 9; **Supp. IV:** 116; **Retro. Supp. I:** 110, 116

"Judge, The" (Crawford), **Supp. XI:** 75–76

Judge, The (West), **Supp. III:** 441, 442

"Judge's House, The" (Stoker), **Supp. III:** 382

"Judge Chutney's Final Summary" (Armitage), **VIII:** 6

Judgement of Martin Bucer . . . , The (Milton), **II:** 175

Judgement of Paris, The (Congreve), **II:** 347, 350

Judgement in Stone, A (Rendell), **Supp. IX:** 192, 194–195

Judge's Wife, The (Churchill), **Supp. IV:** 181

"Judging Distances" (Reed), **VII:** 422

Judgment on Deltchev (Ambler), **Supp. IV:** 4, 12–13, 21

Judith, **Supp. VI:** 29; **Retro. Supp. II:** 305, 306

Judith (Bennett), **VI:** 267

"Judith" (Coppard), **VIII:** 96

Judith (Giraudoux), **Supp. III:** 195

"Judkin of the Parcels" (Saki), **Supp. VI:** 245

Jugement du roi de Behaingne, **I:** 32

"Juggling Jerry" (Meredith), **V:** 220

"Julia" (Brontë), **V:** 122, 151

Julia and the Bazooka and Other Stories (Kavan), **Supp. VII:** 202, 205, 214

"Julia Bride" (James), **VI:** 67, 69

"Julia's Churching; or, Purification" (Herrick), **II:** 112

"Julian and Maddalo" (Shelley), **IV:** 182, 201–202; **Retro. Supp. I:** 251

"Julian M. & A. G. Rochelle" (Brontë), **V:** 133

Julian of Norwich, **I:** 20; **Retro. Supp. II:** 303; **Supp. XII:** 149–166

Julius Caesar (Shakespeare), **I:** 313, 314–315

"July Evening" (MacCaig), **Supp. VI:** 187, 194

"July Storm" (Healy), **Supp. IX:** 106

July's People (Gordimer), **Supp. II:** 231, 238–239, 241

Jumpers (Stoppard), **Supp. I:** 438, 444, 445–447, 451; **Retro. Supp. II:** 347–349

Jump-to-Glory Jane (Meredith), **V:** 234

"June Bracken and Heather" (Tennyson), **IV:** 336

"June the 30th, 1934" (Lowry), **Supp. III:** 285

"June to December" (Cope), **VIII:** 72

Jung, Carl, **Supp. IV:** 1, 4–5, 6, 10–11, 12, 19, 493

"Jungle, The" (Lewis), **VII:** 447

Jungle Books, The (Kipling), **VI:** 188, 199

Juniper Tree, The (Comyns), **VIII:** 53, 63–64, 65

Junius Manuscript, **Retro. Supp. II:** 298–299, 301

Junk Mail (Self), **Supp. V:** 406–407

"Junkie" (Morgan, E.), **Supp. IX:** 164

Juno and the Paycock (O'Casey), **VII:** xviii, 4–5, 6, 11

Juno in Arcadia (Brome), **Supp. X:** 52

Jure Divino (Defoe), **III:** 4, 13

"Jury, The" (Hart), **Supp. XI:** 125

Jusserand, Jean, **I:** 98

Just Between Ourselves (Ayckbourn), **Supp. V:** 3, 13

Just So Stories for Little Children (Kipling), **VI:** 188, 204

Just Vengeance, The (Sayers), **Supp. III:** 336, 350

Justice (Galsworthy), **VI:** xiii, 269, 273–274, 286–287

Justine (Durrell), **Supp. I:** 104, 105, 106

Juvenal, **II:** 30, 292, 347, 348; **III:** 42; **IV:** 188

Juvenilia 1 (Nye), **Supp. X:** 192, 194, 196–200, 202–203, 205

Juvenilia 2 (Nye), **Supp. X:** 192–194, 197–200, 204–205

"Kabla–Khun" (Dunn), **Supp. X:** 79

Kaeti and Company (Roberts, K.), **Supp. X:** 273

Kaeti on Tour (Roberts, K.), **Supp. X:** 273

Kafka, Franz, **III:** 340, 345; **Supp. IV:** 1, 199, 407, 439

Kafka's Dick (Bennett), **VIII:** 29–30

Kain, Saul, pseud. of Siegfried Sassoon

Kaisers of Carnuntum, The (Harrison), **Supp. V:** 164

Kakutani, Michiko, **Supp. IV:** 304

Kalendarium Hortense (Evelyn), **II:** 287

Kallman, Chester, **Supp. IV:** 422, 424; **Retro. Supp. I:** 9–10, 13

Kama Sutra, **Supp. IV:** 493

Kane, Sarah, **VIII:** 147–161

Kangaroo (Lawrence), **VII:** 90, 107–109, 119

Kant, Immanuel, **IV:** xiv, 50, 52, 145

Kanthapura (Rao), **Supp. V:** 56

"Karain: A Memory" (Conrad), **VI:** 148

Karaoke (Potter, D.), **Supp. X:** 228, 240–241

Karl, Frederick R., **VI:** 135, 149

Karl–Ludwig's Window, (Saki), **Supp. VI:** 250

"Karshish" (Browning), **IV:** 357, 360, 363

Katchen's Caprices (Trollope), **V:** 101

"Kathe Kollwitz" (Rukeyser), **Supp. V:** 261

Katherine Mansfield (Alpers), **VII:** 183

Kathleen and Frank (Isherwood), **VII:** 316–317

Kathleen Listens In (O'Casey), **VII:** 12

"Katina" (Dahl), **Supp. IV:** 210

Kavan, Anna, **Supp. VII:** 201–215

Kavanagh, Julia, **IV:** 108, 122

Kavanagh, Dan, pseud. of Julian Barnes

Kavanagh, Patrick, **Supp. IV:** 409, 410, 412, 428, 542; **Supp. VII:** 183–199; **Retro. Supp. I:** 126

Kazin, Alfred, **Supp. IV:** 460

Keats, John, **II:** 102, 122, 192, 200; **III:** 174, 337, 338; **IV:** viii–xii, 81, 95, 129, 178, 196, 198, 204–205, 211–237, 255, 284, 316, 323, 332, 349, 355; **V:** 173, 361, 401, 403; **Supp. I:** 218; **Supp. V:** 38; **Retro. Supp. I:** 183–197

Keats and the Mirror of Art (Jack), **IV:** 236

Keats Circle, The: Letters and Papers . . . (Rollins), **IV:** 231, 232, 235

Keats: The Critical Heritage (ed. Matthews), **IV:** 237

Keats's Publisher: A Memoir of John Taylor (Blunden), **IV:** 236; **Supp. XI:** 37

Keble, John, **V:** xix, 252

"Keel, Ram, Stauros" (Jones), **Supp. VII:** 177

"Keen, Fitful Gusts" (Keats), **IV:** 215

Keep the Aspidistra Flying (Orwell), **VII:** 275, 278–279

"Keep the Home Fires Burning" (Novello), **VI:** 435

"Keepsake, The" (Adcock), **Supp. XII:** 9

Keeton, G. W., **IV:** 286

Kell, Joseph, *see* Burgess, Anthony

Kellys and the O'Kellys, The (Trollope), **V:** 101

Kelman, James, **Supp. V:** 241–258

Kelmscott Press, publishers, **V:** xxv, 302

Kelsall, Malcolm Miles, **IV:** x, xxv

Kelvin, Norman, **V:** 221, 234

Kemble, Fanny, **IV:** 340, 350–351

Kemp, Harry, **Supp. III:** 120

Kempe, Margery, **Supp. XII:** 167–183

Keneally, Thomas, **Supp. IV:** 343–362

Kenilworth (Scott), **IV:** xviii, 39

Kennedy, John F., **Supp. IV:** 486

Kenner, Hugh, **VI:** 323

Kennis van die aand (Brink), **Supp. VI:** 47–48, 49

"Kensington Gardens" (Adcock), **Supp. XII:** 13, 14–15

Kenyon, Frederic, **IV:** 312, 321

Kenyon, John, **IV:** 311, 356

Kept (Waugh), **Supp. VI:** 270

Kept in the Dark (Trollope), **V:** 102

Kermode, Frank, **I:** 237; **V:** 344, 355, 359, 412, 420; **VI:** 147, 208

Kerr, Philip, **Supp. XII:** 185–200

Kettle, Thomas, **VI:** 336

Key of the Field, The (Powys), **VIII:** 255

Key to Modern Poetry, A (Durrell), **Supp. I:** 100, 121–123, 125, 126, 127

Key to My Heart, The (Pritchett), **Supp. III:** 324–325

"Key to My Heart, The" (Pritchett), **Supp. III:** 324

Key to the Door (Sillitoe), **Supp. V:** 410, 415

Keyes, Sidney, **VII:** xxii, 422, 433–440

Keynes, G. L., **II:** 134; **III:** 289n, 307, 308, 309

Kickleburys on the Rhine, The (Thackeray), **V:** 38

Kid (Armitage), **VIII:** 1, 4–6

"Kid" (Armitage), **VIII:** 5

Kidnapped (Stevenson), **V:** 383, 384, 387, 395; **Retro. Supp. I:** 266–267

Kierkegaard, Sören, **Supp. I:** 79

"Kierkegaard" (Thomas), **Supp. XII:** 285

"Kill, A" (Hughes), **Supp. I:** 352

"Killary Hostel" (Murphy), **Supp. V:** 328

Killham, John, **IV:** 323*n*, 338, 339; **VII:** **248–249**

Killing Bottle, The (Hartley), **Supp. VII:** 123

Killing Kindness, A (Hill, R.), **Supp. IX:** 114–115, 117, 122

Killing the Lawyers (Hill, R.), **Supp. IX:** 123

Killing Time (Armitage), **VIII:** 1, 15–16

"Killing Time" (Harrison), **Supp. V:** 156

"Kilmeny" (Hogg), **Supp. X:** 107–110

Kiltartan History Book, The (Gregory), **VI:** 318

Kiltartan Molière, The (Gregory), **VI:** 316, 318

Kiltartan Poetry Book, The (Gregory), **VI:** 318

Kilvert, Francis, **V:** 269; **Supp. IV:** 169

Kim (Kipling), **VI:** 166, 168, 169, **185– 189; Supp. IV:** 443

Kincaid, Jamaica, **Supp. VII: 217–232**

Kind Are Her Answers (Renault), **Supp. IX:** 173–174

"Kind Ghosts, The" (Owen), **VI:** 447, 455, 457

Kind Keeper, The; or, Mr Limberham (Dryden), **II:** 294305

Kind of Alaska, A (Pinter), **Supp. I:** 378

Kind of Anger, A (Ambler), **Supp. IV:** 16, 18–20

"Kind of Business: The Academic Critic in America, A" (Lodge), **Supp. IV:** 374

Kind of Poetry I Want, The (MacDiarmid), **Supp. XII:** 203

Kind of Scar, A (Boland), **Supp. V:** 35

"Kindertotenlieder" (Longley), **VIII:** 169–170

Kindness in a Corner (Powys), **VIII:** 248, 249, 256

Kindness of Women, The (Ballard), **Supp. V:** 24, 28, 31, 33

Kindly Light (Wilson), **Supp. VI:** 299, 308

Kindly Ones, The (Powell), **VII:** 344, 347, 348, 349, 350

King, Francis Henry, **VII:** xx, xxxviii; **Supp. IV:** 302

King, Bishop Henry, **II:** 121, 221; **Supp. VI: 149–163**

King, Kimball, **Supp. IV:** 194–195

King, S., **III:** 345

King, T., **III:** 336

King and Me, The (Kureishi), **Supp. XI:** 153–154

King and No King, A (Beaumont and Fletcher), **II:** 43, 45, 52, 54, 57–58, 65

King Arthur; or, The British Worthy (Dryden), **II:** 294, 296, 305

"King Arthur's Tomb" (Morris), **V:** 293

"King Billy" (Morgan, E.), **Supp. IX:** 158

"King Duffus" (Warner), **Supp. VII:** 373

"King James I and Isaac Casaubon" (Landor), **IV:** 92

King James Version of the Bible, **I:** 370, 377–380

King John (Shakespeare), **I:** 286, 301

"King John's Castle" (Kinsella), **Supp. V:** 260

King Lear (Shakespeare), **I:** 316–317; **II:** 69; **III:** 116, 295; **IV:** 232; **Supp. II:** 194; **Supp. IV:** 149, 171, 282, 283, 294, 335; **Retro. Supp. I:** 34–35

King Log (Hill), **Supp. V:** 186–189

King Must Die, The (Renault), **Supp. IX:** 178–180, 187

"King of Beasts" (MacCaig), **Supp. VI:** 189

King of Hearts, The (Golding), **Supp. I:** 82

King of Pirates, The . . . (Defoe), **III:** 13

King of the Golden River, The; or, The Black Brothers (Ruskin), **V:** 184

"King of the World, The" (Coppard), **VIII:** 92

"King Pim" (Powys), **VIII:** 248, 249

King Solomon's Mines (Haggard), **Supp. III:** 211, 213, **215–217, 218–219,** 227; **Supp. IV:** 484

King Stephen (Keats), **IV:** 231

King Victor and King Charles (Browning), **IV:** 373

"Kingdom of God, The" (Thompson), **V:** 449–450

"Kingdom of Heaven, The" (Powys), **VIII:** 256

Kingdom of the Wicked, The (Burgess), **Supp. I:** 186, 193

Kingdoms of Elfin (Warner), **Supp. VII:** 369, 371, 381

King-Errant (Steel), **Supp. XII:** 275

"Kingfisher" (Nye), **Supp. X:** 192, 205

"Kingfisher, The" (Davies), **Supp. XI:** 96–97

"Kingfisher, The" (Powys), **VIII:** 251

King's General, The (du Maurier), **Supp. III:** 146

"King's Tragedy, The" (Rossetti), **V:** 238, 244

"Kings" (Jennings), **Supp. V:** 211, 218

"Kings' Sagas", *See Konunga sögur*

Kingsland, W. G., **IV:** 371

Kingsley, Charles, **IV:** 195; **V:** viii, xxi, 2, 4, 283; **VI:** 266; **Supp. IV:** 256

Kinsayder, W., pseud. of John Marston

Kinsella, Thomas, **VI:** 220; **Supp. V:** **259–275**

Kinsley, James, **III:** 310n 322

Kipling, Rudyard, **IV:** 106, 109; **V:** xxiii– xxvi, **I:** xi, xi, xv, **165–206,** 415; **VII:** 33; poetry, **VI:** 200–203; list of short stories, **VI:** 205–206; **Supp. I:** 167, 261; **Supp. IV:** 17, 201, 394, 440, 506

Kipling and the Critics (Gilbert), **VI:** 195n

Kipling: Realist and Fabulist (Dobrée), **VI:** xi, 200–203, 205

Kipps: The Story of a Simple Soul (Wells), **VI:** xii, 225, 236–237

Kirk, Russell, **IV:** 276

Kirkpatrick, T. P. C. **III:** 180*n*

Kirsteen: The Story of a Scotch Family Seventy Years Ago (Oliphant), **Supp. X:** 217–219

"Kiss, The" (Sassoon), **VI:** 429

Kiss for Cinderalla, A (Barrie), **Supp. III:** 8, 9

Kiss Kiss (Dahl), **Supp. IV:** 214, 215, 218

"Kiss Me Again, Stranger" (du Maurier), **Supp. III:** 134

Kissing the Gunner's Daughter (Rendell), **Supp. IX:** 195, 196, 198

Kitaj, R. B., **Supp. IV:** 119

Kitay, Mike, **Supp. IV:** 256, 257

"Kitchen Sonnets" (Fuller), **Supp. VII:** 80

"Kitchen Window" (Nye), **Supp. X:** 198

Kitchener, Field Marshall Lord, **VI:** 351

Kiteworld (Roberts, K.), **Supp. X:** 261, 264, 271–273

Kittredge, G. L., **I:** 326

Klee, Paul, **Supp. IV:** 80

Klosterheim (De Quincey), **IV:** 149, 155

KMT: In the House of Life (Armah), **Supp. X:** 14

"Kneeling" (Thomas), **Supp. XII:** 286

"Kneeshaw Goes to War" (Read), **VI:** 437

Knife, The (Hare), **Supp. IV:** 282

"Knife-Play" (Adcock), **Supp. XII:** 4–5

Knight, G. W., **IV:** 328*n*, 339

"Knight, The" (Hughes), **Supp. I:** 356

Knight of the Burning Pestle, The (Beaumont), **II:** 45, 46, 48–49, 62, 65

"Knight of the Cart, The" (Malory), **I:** 70

Knight with the Two Swords, The (Malory), **I:** 73

Knights, L. C., **II:** 123, 126, 130

Knights of Malta, The (Field, Fletcher, Massinger), **II:** 66

Knight's Tale, The (Chaucer), **I:** 21, 23, 30, 31, 40

Knoblock, Edward, **VI:** 263, 267; **VII:** 223

"Knockbrack" (Murphy), **Supp. V:** 327

"Knole" (Fuller), **Supp. VII:** 72

Knolles, Richard, **III:** 108

Knots and Crosses (Rankin), **Supp. X:** 244–249

"Knowledge" (Crawford), **Supp. XI:** 76

Knowles, Sheridan, **IV:** 311

Knox, Robert, **III:** 7

Knox, Ronald, **Supp. II:** 124, 126

Knox Brothers, The (Fitzgerald), **Supp. V:** 95, 96, 98

Knuckle (Hare), **Supp. IV:** 282, 285–286

Koestler, Arthur, **V:** 49; **Supp. I: 21–41; Supp. III:** 107; **Supp. IV:** 68

Kokoschka, Oskar, **Supp. IV:** 81

Kontakian for You Departed (Paton), **Supp. II:** 343, 359

Konunga sögur, **VIII:** 236

Korea and Her Neighbors (Bird), **Supp. X:** 31

Kormaks saga

"Kosciusko and Poniatowski" (Landor), **IV:** 92

Kostakis, George, **Supp. IV:** 174

Kotzebue, August von, **III:** 254, 268

"Kraken, The" (Tennyson), **IV:** 329; **VI:** 16

Krapp's Last Tape (Beckett), **Supp. I:** 46, 55, 58, 61; **Retro. Supp. I:** 25–26

Krause, Ernest, **Supp. II:** 107

"Kristbjorg's Story: In the Black Hills" (Lowry), **Supp. III:** 285
Kristeva, Julia, **Supp. IV:** 115, 232
Krutch, J. W., **III:** 246
"Kubla Khan" (Coleridge), **IV:** ix, xvii, 44, 46–48, 56; **V:** 272, 447; **Supp. IV:** 425; **Retro. Supp. II:** 56–58
Kullus (Pinter), **Supp. I:** 368, 371
Kumar, Gobind, **Supp. IV:** 449
"Kumquat for John Keats, A" (Harrison), **Supp. V:** 160
Kundera, Milan, **Supp. IV:** 440
Kureishi, Hanif, **Supp. XI: 151–162**
Kurosawa, Akira, **Supp. IV:** 434
Kyd, Thomas, **I:** 162, **212–231,** 277, 278, 291; **II:** 25, 28, 74
"Kyogle Line, The" (Malouf), **Supp. XII:** 218

"La Belle Dame Sans Merci" (Keats), **IV:** 216, 219, 235, 313
La Bete Humaine (Zola), **Supp. IV:** 249
La Chapelle, Jean de, **II:** 358
La Die de Fénelon (Ramsay), **III:** 99
La Fayette, Madame de, **Supp. IV:** 136
"La Fontaine and La Rochefoucault" (Landor), **IV:** 91
"La Grosse Fifi" (Rhys), **Supp. II:** 390
La maison de campagne (Dancourt), **II:** 325
La Mordida (Lowry), **Supp. III:** 280
"La Nuit Blanche" (Kipling), **VI:** 193
La parisienne (Becque), **VI:** 369
La Princesse de Clèves (La Fayette), **Supp. IV:** 136
"La Rochefoucauld" (Durrell), **Supp. I:** 126
La Saisiaz (Browning), **IV:** 359, 364–365, 374
La Soeur de la Reine (Swinburne), **V:** 325, 333
La strage degli innocenti (Marino), **II:** 183
La traicion busca el castigo (Roias Zorilla), **II:** 325
La Vendée: An Historical Romance (Trollope), **V:** 101
La vida de la Santa Madre Teresa de Jesus, **II:** 182
La vida es sueño (Calderón), **IV:** 349
La vie de Fénelon (Ramsay), **III:** 99
Labels (De Bernières), **Supp. XII:** 66
Labels (Waugh), **VII:** 292–293
Laboratories of the Spirit (Thomas), **Supp. XII:** 286
Laborators, The (Redgrove), **Supp. VI:** 236
Labours of Hercules, The (Christie), **Supp. II:** 135
Laburnum Grove (Priestley), **VII:** 224
Labyrinth, The (Muir), **Supp. VI:** 204, **207**
Labyrinthine Ways, The (Greene), *see Power and the Glory, The*
Lacan, Jacques, **Supp. IV:** 99, 115
"Lachrimae, or Seven Tears Figured in Seven Passionate Pavanas" (Hill), **Supp. V:** 189, 190
"Lachrimae Amantis" (Hill), **Supp. V:** 191

"Lachrimae Verae" (Hill), **Supp. V:** 190
"Laconics: The Forty Acres" (Murray), **Supp. VII:** 276
"Ladder and the Tree, The" (Golding), **Supp. I:** 65
"Ladders, The" (Malouf), **Supp. XII:** 220
Ladies of Alderley, The (ed. Mitford), **Supp. X:** 156
Ladder of Perfection (Hilton), **Supp. I:** 74
Ladies from the Sea (Hope), **Supp. VII:** 160
Ladies Triall, The (Ford), *see Lady's Trial, The*
Ladies Whose Bright Eyes (Ford), **VI:** 327
"Ladle" (Berger), **Supp. IV:** 93
Lady Anna (Trollope), **V:** 102
"Lady Appledore's Mesalliance" (Firbank), **Supp. II:** 207
"Lady Artemis, The" (Maitland), **Supp. XI:** 175
Lady Athlyne (Stoker), **Supp. III:** 381
Lady Audley's Secret (Braddon), **VIII:** 35, 41–42, 43, 48, 50
"Lady Barbarina" (James), **VI:** 69
Lady Chatterley's Lover (Lawrence), **VII:** 87, 88, 91, **110–113; Supp. IV:** 149, 234, 369; **Retro. Supp. II:** 226, 231–232
"Lady Delavoy" (James), **VI:** 69
Lady Frederick (Maugham), **VI:** 367–368
"Lady Geraldine's Courtship" (Browning), **IV:** 311
Lady Gregory, **VI:** xiv
Lady Gregory: A Literary Portrait (Coxhead), **VI:** 318
"Lady Icenway, The" (Hardy), **VI:** 22
Lady in the Van, The (Bennett), **VIII:** 33
Lady into Woman: A History of Women from Victoria to Elizabeth II (Brittain), **Supp. X:** 46
Lady Jane (Chettle, Dekker, Heywood, Webster), **II:** 68
Lady Lisa Lyon (Mapplethorpe photography collection), **Supp. IV:** 170
"Lady Louisa and the Wallflowers" (Powys), **VIII:** 249
Lady Maisie's Bairn and Other Poems (Swinburne), **V:** 333
"Lady Mottisfont" (Hardy), **VI:** 22
Lady of Launay, The (Trollope), **V:** 102
Lady of May, The (Sidney), **I:** 161; **Retro. Supp. II:** 330
"Lady of Quality, A" (Kinsella), **Supp. V:** 260
"Lady of Shalott, The" (Tennyson), **IV:** xix, 231, 313, 329, 331–332
Lady of the Lake, The (Scott), **IV:** xvii, 29, 38
"Lady of the Pool, The" (Jones), **Supp. VII:** 176, 177, 178
Lady of the Shroud, The (Stoker), **Supp. III:** 381
"Lady Penelope, The" (Hardy), **VI:** 22
"Lady Rogue Singleton" (Smith), **Supp. II:** 466–467, 470
Lady Susan (Austen), **IV:** 108, 109, 122; **Supp. IV:** 230

Lady Windermere's Fan (Wilde), **V:** xxvi, 412, 413–414, 419; **Retro. Supp. II:** 369
Lady with a Laptop (Thomas), **Supp. IV:** 489–490
"Lady with the Dog, The" (Chekhov), **V:** 241
"Lady with Unicorn" (Maitland), **Supp. XI:** 170
"Ladybird, The" (Lawrence), **VII:** 115
"Lady's Dream, The" (Hood), **IV:** 261, 264
"Lady's Dressing Room, The" (Swift), **III:** 32
Lady's Life in the Rocky Mountains, A (Bird), **Supp. X:** 17, 19, 22, 24, 26–28, 30
Lady's Magazine (periodical), **III:** 179
"Lady's Maid, The" (Mansfield), **VII:** 174–175
Lady's Not for Burning (Fry), **Supp. III:** 195, 202
Lady's Pictorial (periodical), **VI:** 87, 91
Lady's Trial, The (Ford), **II:** 89, 91, 99, 100
Lady's World, The (periodical), **Retro. Supp. II:** 364
Lafourcade, Georges, **VI:** 247, 256, 259, 260, 262, 263, 268
"Lagoon, The" (Conrad), **VI:** 136, 148
Lair of the White Worm, The (Stoker), **Supp. III:** 381–382
Laird of Abbotsford: A View of Sirt Walter Scott, The (Wilson), **Supp. VI:** 301
Lake, David J., **II:** 1, 2, 21
Lake, The (Moore), **VI:** xii, 88, 89, 92–93, 98
"Lake Isle of Innisfree, The" (Yeats), **VI:** 207, 211; **Retro. Supp. I:** 329
Lake of Darkness, The (Rendell), **Supp. IX:** 196
"Lake of Tuonela, The" (Roberts, K.), **Supp. X:** 270–271
Lakers, The (Nicholson), **Supp. VI:** 223
"Lal" (Steel), **Supp. XII:** 266, 268
"L'Allegro" (Milton), **II:** 158–159; **IV:** 199
Lamarck, Jean–Baptiste, **Supp. II:** 105–106, 107, 118, 119
Lamb, Charles, **II:** 80, 86, 119n, 143, 153, 256, 340, 361, 363, 364; **IV:** xi, xiv, xvi xviii, xix, 41, **42, 73–86,** 128, 135, 137, 148, 252–253, 255, 257, 259, 260, 320, 341, 349; **V:** 328
Lamb, John, **IV:** 74, 77, 84
Lamb, Mary, **IV:** xvi, 77–78, 80, 83–84, 128, 135
"Lamb to the Slaughter" (Dahl), **Supp. IV:** 215, 219
Lambert, Gavin, **Supp. IV:** 3, 8
"Lament" (Gunn), **Supp. IV:** 277–278
Lament for a Lover (Highsmith), **Supp. V:** 170
"Lament for the Great Music" (MacDiarmid), **Supp. XII:** 203
"Lament for the Makaris, The" (Dunbar), **VIII:** 118, 121, 127–128
Lament of Tasso, The (Byron), **IV:** 192
"Lament of the Images" (Okri), **Supp. V:** 359

Lamia (Keats), **III:** 338; **IV:** xviii, 216, 217, 219–220, 231, 235; **Retro. Supp. I:** 192–193

Lamia, Isabella, The Eve of St. Agnes, and Other Poems (Keats), **IV:** xviii, 211, 235; **Retro. Supp. I:** 184, 192–196

Lamming, George, **Supp. IV:** 445

"Lamp and the Jar, The" (Hope), **Supp. VII:** 158

Lamp and the Lute, The (Dobrée), **VI:** 204

Lampitt Papers, The (Wilson), **Supp. VI:** 297, 304, **306–307**

Lanark: A Life in Four Books (Gray, A.), **Supp. IX:** 79–83, 84–86, 88–89

Lancelot and Guinevere (Malory), **I:** 70–71, 77

Lancelot du Laik, **I:** 73

Lancelot, The Death of Rudel, and Other Poems (Swinburne), **V:** 333

"Lancer" (Housman), **VI:** 160

"Land of Counterpane, The" (Stevenson), **Retro. Supp. I:** 260

Land of Heart's Desire, The (Yeats), **VI:** 221; **Retro. Supp. I:** 326

"Land of Loss, The" (Kinsella), **Supp. V:** 271

Land of Promise, The (Maugham), **VI:** 369

"Land under the Ice, The" (Nicholson), **Supp. VI:** 216

Landfall, **Supp. XII:** 3

Landing on the Sun, A (Frayn), **Supp. VII:** 62–63

"Landlady, The" (Behan), **Supp. II:** 63–64

"Landlady, The" (Dahl), **Supp. IV:** 215–216, 217

Landleaguers, The (Trollope), **V:** 102

Landlocked (Lessing), **Supp. I:** 245, 248

Landmarks in French Literature (Strachey), **Supp. II:** **502–503**

Landnámabók, **VIII:** 235, 238

Landon, Letitia, **IV:** 311

Landor, Walter Savage, **II:** 293; **III:** 139; **IV:** xiv, xvi, xviii, xix, xxii, **87–100**, 252, 254, 356; **V:** 320

Landscape (Pinter), **Supp. I:** 375–376

"Landscape Painter, A" (James), **VI:** 69

"Landscape with One Figure" (Dunn), **Supp. X:** 70

Landscapes Within, The (Okri), **Supp. V:** 347, 348, 350, 352, 353–354, 360

Landseer, Edwin, **V:** 175

Lane, Margaret, **V:** 13*n*, 16

Lang, Andrew, **V:** 392–393, 395; **VI:** 158; **Supp. II:** 115

Lang, C. Y., **V:** 334, 335

Langland, William, **I:** vii, **1–18**

"Language Ah Now You Have Me" (Graham), **Supp. VII:** 115

Language Made Plain (Burgess), **Supp. I:** 197

Language of Fiction: Essays in Criticism and Verbal Analysis of the English Novel (Lodge), **Supp. II:** 9; **Supp. IV:** 365, 366

Language, Truth and Logic (Ayer), **VII:** 240

Languages of Love, The (Brooke–Rose)), **Supp. IV:** 99, 100–101

Lannering, Jan, **III:** 52

"Lantern Bearers, The" (Stevenson), **V:** 385

"Lantern out of Doors, The," (Hopkins), **V:** 380

Lantern Slides (O'Brien), **Supp. V:** 341

Laodicean, A; or, The Castle of the De Stancys (Hardy), **VI:** 4–5, 20

Laon and Cynthia (Shelley), **IV:** 195, 196, 198, 208; **Retro. Supp. I:** 249–250; *see also* Revolt of Islam, The

"Lapis Lazuli" (Yeats), **Retro. Supp. I:** 337

Lara (Byron), **IV:** xvii, 172, 173, 175, 192; *see also* Turkish tales

"Large Cool Store, The" (Larkin), **Supp. I:** 279

Lark, The (Fry), **Supp. III:** 195

"Lark Ascending, The" (Meredith), **V:** 221, 223

"Larkin Automatic Car Wash, The" (Ewart), **Supp. VII:** 41

Larkin, Philip, **Supp. I:** 275–290; **Supp. II:** 2, 3, 375; **Supp. IV:** 256, 431

"Lars Porsena of Clusium" (Macaulay), **IV:** 282

Lars Porsena; or, The Future of Swearing and Improper Language (Graves), **VII:** 259–260

Lasselia; or, The Self–Abandoned (Haywood), **Supp. XII:** 137, 140

"Last Address, The" (Lowry), **Supp. III:** 272

Last and the First, The (Compton-Burnett), **VII:** 59, 61, 67

"Last Ark, The" (Tolkien), **Supp. II:** 522

Last Battle, The (Lewis), **Supp. III:** 248, 261

Last Chronicle of Barset, The (Trollope), **II:** 173; **V:** xxiii, 93–95, 101

"Last Confession, A" (Rossetti), **V:** 240–241

"Last Day of Summer, The" (McEwan), **Supp. IV:** 390

Last Days of Lord Byron, The (Parry), **IV:** 191, 193

Last Days of Sodom, The (Orton), **Supp. V:** 364

"Last Duchess" (Hardy), **Retro. Supp. I:** 120

Last Essay (Conrad), **VI:** 148

Last Essays of Elia, The (Lamb), **IV:** xix, 76–77, 82–83, 85

Last Essays on Church and Religion (Arnold), **V:** 212, 216

Last Fight of the Revenge at Sea, The (Ralegh), **I:** 145, 149–150

Last Fruit off the Old Tree, The (Landor), **IV:** 100

"Last Galway Hooker, The" (Murphy), **Supp. V:** 313, 316, 319

"Last Hellos, The" (Murray), **Supp. VII:** 283

"Last Instructions to a Painter, The" (Marvell), **II:** 217–218

Last Letters from Hav (Morris, J.), **Supp. X:** 171, 185–186

Last Loves (Sillitoe), **Supp. V:** 411, 414, 415–416, 425

"Last Man, The" (Gunn), **Supp. IV:** 264

Last Man, The (Shelley), **Supp. III:** **364–371**

"Last Moa, The" (Adcock), **Supp. XII:** 12

"Last of March (Written at Lolham Brigs), The" (Clare), **Supp. XI:** 57

Last of the Country House Murders, The (Tennant), **Supp. IX:** 230

Last of the Duchess, The (Blackwood), **Supp. IX:** 8, 13–14

"Last of the Fire Kings" (Mahon), **Supp. VI:** 172

Last of the Wine, The (Renault), **Supp. IX:** 182–183, 187

Last Orders (Swift), **Supp. V:** 440–441

Last Poems (Browning), **IV:** 312, 315, 357

Last Poems (Fuller), **Supp. VII:** 79

Last Poems (Housman), **VI:** 157, 158, 160, 161, 162, 164

Last Poems (Meredith), **V:** 234

Last Poems (Reading), **VIII:** 273

Last Poems (Yeats), **VI:** 214

Last Poems and Two Plays (Yeats), **VI:** 213

Last Pool and Other Stories, The (O'Brian), **Supp. XII:** 251

Last Post (Ford), **VI:** 319, 330–331

Last Pre–Raphaelite, The: A Record of the Life and Writings of Ford Madox Ford (Goldring), **VI:** 333

"Last Requests" (Longley), **VIII:** 173

Last September, The (Bowen), **Supp. II:** 77, 78, 79, 83–86, 89

Last Sheaf, A (Welch), **Supp. IX:** 267

Last Summer, The (Smith, I. C.), **Supp. IX:** 209

Last Testament of Oscar Wilde, The (Ackroyd), **Supp. VI:** 5

Last Thing (Snow), **VII:** xxi, 324, 332–333

"Last Things, The" (Ewart), **Supp. VII:** 40

"Last to Go" (Pinter), **Retro. Supp. I:** 217

"Last Tournament, The" (Tennyson), **V:** 327

"Last Will and Testament" (Auden), **Retro. Supp. I:** 7

Last Words of Thomas Carlyle, The (Carlyle), **IV:** 250

Late Augustans, The (Davie), **Supp. VI:** 115

Late Bourgeois World, The (Gordimer), **Supp. II:** 228, 229, 231, 233, 234, 236, 238

Late Call (Wilson), **Supp. I:** 156, 161–162, 163

Late Harvest (Douglas), **VI:** 300, 302–303, 305, 333

Late Mr. Shakespeare, The (Nye), **Supp. X:** 194, 196, 200, 202–203, 206

Late Murder in Whitechapel, The; or, Keep the Widow Waking, see Late Murder of the Son . . .

Late Murder of the Son Upon the Mother, A; or, Keep the Widow Waking (Dekker, Ford, Rowley, Webster), **II:** 85–86, 89, 100

"Late Period" (Fuller), **Supp. VII:** 78

Late Picking, A: Poems 1965–1974 (Hope), **Supp. VII:** 157, 158

Late Pickings (Ewart), **Supp. VII:** 45

Latecomers (Brookner), **Supp. IV:** 130–131, 136

Later and Italian Poems of Milton (tr. Cowper), **III:** 220

Later Days (Davies), **Supp. XI:** 91, 92

"Later Decalogue, The," (Clough), **V:** 155

"Later Poems" (Bridges), **VI:** 78, 83

Later Poems, 1972–1982 (Thomas), **Supp. XII:** 288

Latter–Day Pamphlets (Carlyle), **IV:** xxi, 240, 247–248, 249, 250

"Laud and Praise made for our Sovereign Lord The King" (Skelton), **I:** 88–89

Laugh and Lie Down (Swinburne), **V:** 312, 332

Laugh and Lie Down; or, The World's Folly (Tourneur), **II:** 37

Laughable Lyrics (Lear), **V:** 78, 85, 87

Laughing Anne (Conrad), **VI:** 148

"Laughter" (Beerbohm), **Supp. II:** 47–48

"Laughter Beneath the Bridge" (Okri), **Supp. V:** 355

Laughter in the Next Room (Sitwell), **VII:** 130, 135

Launch–Site for English Studies: Three Centuries of Literary Studies at the University of St. Andrews (ed. Crawford), **Supp. XI:** 76, 82

"Laundon, City of the Moon" (Redgrove), **Supp. VI:** 234

"Laundress, The" (Kinsella), **Supp. V:** 261

"Laus Veneris" (Swinburne), **IV:** 346; **V:** 316, 318, 320, 327, 346

L'Autre monde ou les états et empires de la lune (Cyrano de Bergerac), **III:** 24

Lavater, J. C., **III:** 298

"Lavatory Attendant, The" (Cope), **VIII:** 74

Lavengro: The Scholar, the Gipsy, the Priest (Borrow), **Supp. XII:** 17, 20–27, 31

Law, William, **IV:** 45

Law and the Grace, The (Smith, I. C.), **Supp. IX:** 212–213

Law and the Lady, The (Collins), **Supp. VI:** 102

Law Against Lovers, The (Davenant), **I:** 327

Law Hill poems (Brontë), **V:** 126–128

Law of the Threshold, The (Steel), **Supp. XII:** 275–276

Lawless Roads, The (Greene; U.S. title, *"nother Mexico*), **Supp. I:** 9, 10

Lawrence, D. H., **II:** 330; **IV:** 106, 119, 120, 195; **V:** xxv, 6, 47; **VI:** 235, 243, 248, 259, 275–276, 283, 363, 409, 416; **VI:** xii, xiv–xvi, 18, 75, **87–126,** 201, 203–204, 215; **Supp. II:** 492; **Supp. III:** 86, 91, 397–398; **Supp. IV:** 5, 94, 139, 233, 241, 369; **Retro. Supp. II: 221–235**

Lawrence, Frieda, **VII:** 90, 111

Lawrence, T. E., **VI:** 207, 408; **Supp. II:** 147, **283–297; Supp. IV:** 160

"Lawrence, of virtuous father virtuous son" (Milton), **II:** 163

Laws of Candy, The, **II:** 67

Lawson, Henry, **Supp. IV:** 460

Laxdæla saga, **VIII:** 238, 239, 240

"Lay By" (Hare), **Supp. IV:** 281, 283

Lay Down Your Arms (Potter, D.), **Supp. X:** 231

"Lay for New Lovers" (Reid), **Supp. VII:** 325

Lay Morals and Other Papers (Stevenson), **V:** 396

Lay of Lilies, A, and Other Poems (Swinburne), **V:** 333

"Lay of the Brown Rosary, The" (Browning), **IV:** 313

"Lay of the Labourer, The" (Hood), **IV:** 252, 261, 265–266

Lay of The Last Minstrel, The (Scott), **IV:** xvi, 29, 38, 48, 218

"Lay of the Laureate" (Southey), **IV:** 61, 71

Layamon, **I:** 72

Laying on of Hands, The: Stories (Bennett), **VIII:** 20

Lays of Ancient Rome (Macaulay), **IV:** xx, 272, 282–283, 290–291

"Lazarus and the Sea" (Redgrove), **Supp. VI: 225–227,** 231

"Lazarus Not Raised" (Gunn), **Supp. IV:** 259

Lazy Tour of Two Idle Apprentices, The (Collins), **Supp. VI:** 92

Lazy Tour of Two Idle Apprentices, The (Dickens), **V:** 72

Le Carré, John, **Supp. II: 299–319; Supp. IV:** 4, 5, 9, 13, 14, 15, 17, 22, 445, 449

"Le christianisme" (Owen), **VI:** 445, 450

Le dépit amoureux (Molière), **II:** 325, 336

Le Fanu, Sheridan, **III:** 333, 340, 342, 343, 345; **Supp. II:** 78–79, 81; **Supp. III:** 385–386

Le Gallienne, Richard, **V:** 412, 413

Le Jugement du Roy de Behaingne (Machaut), **Retro. Supp. II:** 37

Le misanthrope (Molière), **II:** 318

Le roman bourgeois (Furetière), **II:** 354

Le Roman de la Rose (Guillaurne), **Retro. Supp. II:** 36

Le Sage, Alain René, **II:** 325; **III:** 150

"Lead" (Kinsella), **Supp. V:** 260

"Lead, Kindly Light" (Newman), **Supp. VII:** 291

"Leaden Echo and the Golden Echo, The" (Hopkins), **V:** 371

Leader (periodical), **V:** 189

Leaf and the Marble, The (Smith, I. C.), **Supp. IX:** 209, 223

"Leaf Blown Upstream, A" (Nye), **Supp. X:** 201

"Leaf by Niggle" (Tolkien), **Supp. II:** 521

"Leaf Used as a Bookmark, A" (Nye), **Supp. X:** 203

Leak in the Universe, A (Richards), **Supp. II:** 426–427

Lean Tales (Kelman, Owens, and Gray), **Supp. V:** 249; **Supp. IX:** 80, 82, 90

"Leaning Tower, The" (Woolf), **VII:** 26; **Retro. Supp. I:** 310

Lear (Bond), **Supp. I:** 423, 427, **430–432,** 433, 435

Lear, Edward, **V:** xi, xvii, xv, xxv, **75–87,** 262; **Supp. IV:** 201

Lear Coloured Bird Book for Children, The (Lear), **V:** 86, 87

Lear in Sicily (ed. Proby), **V:** 87

Lear in the Original (ed. Liebert), **V:** 87

Learned Comment upon Dr. Hare's Excellent Sermon, A (Swift), **III,** 35

Learned Hippopotamus, The (Ewart), **Supp. VII:** 47

Learning Human: Selected Prose (Murray), **Supp. VII:** 271

Learning Laughter (Spender), **Supp. II:** 491

"Learning to Swim" (Swift), **Supp. V:** 431–432

Learning to Swim and Other Stories (Swift), **Supp. V:** 431–434

"Learning's Little Tribute" (Wilson), **Supp. I:** 157

Lease of Life (film, Ambler), **Supp. IV:** 3

"Leather Goods" (Redgrove), **Supp. VI:** 236

"Leaves from a Young Person's Notebook" (Welch), **Supp. IX:** 267, 268

"Leave–Taking, A" (Swinburne), **V:** 319

"Leaving Barra" (MacNeice), **VI:** 411–412

"Leaving Belfast" (Motion), **Supp. VII:** 254, 262

"Leaving Dundee" (Dunn), **Supp. X:** 77

Leavis, F. R., **II:** 254, 258, 271; **III:** 68, 78; **IV:** 227, 323, 338, 339; **V:** 195, 199, 201, 237, 309, 355, 375, 381, 382; **VI:** 13; **V:** xvi, xix, 72–73, 88, 101, 102, **233–256; Supp. II:** 2, 179, 429; **Supp. III:** 60; **Supp. IV:** 142, 229–230, 233, 256; **Retro. Supp. I:** 90

Leavis, Q. D., **II:** 250; **V:** 286, 290; **VI:** 377; **VII:** 233, 238, 250

Leben des Galilei (Brecht), **Supp. IV:** 298

"Lecknavarna" (Murphy), **Supp. V:** 328

Lecky, William, **IV:** 289

Lecky, William E. H., **Supp. V:** 41

L'école des femmes (Molière), **II:** 314

L'école des maris (Molière), **II:** 314

"Lecture on Modern Poetry, A" (Hulme), **Supp. VI:** 135–136, 138, 142–144

Lectures Chiefly on the Dramatic Literature of the Age of Elizabeth (Hazlitt), **IV:** xviii, 125, 129–130, 139

Lectures on Architecture and Paintings (Ruskin), **V:** 184

Lectures on Art (Ruskin), **V:** 184

Lectures on Certain Difficulties Felt by Anglicans in Submitting to the Catholic Church (Newman), **Supp. VII:** 297–298

Lectures on Justification (Newman), **II:** 243n; **Supp. VII:** 294, 301

Lectures on Shakespeare (Coleridge), **IV:** xvii, 52, 56

Lectures on the Early History of the Kingship (Frazer), **Supp. III:** 175

Lectures on the English Comic Writers (Hazlitt), **IV:** xviii, 129–130, 131, 136, 139

Lectures on the English Poets (Hazlitt), **IV:** xvii, 41, 129–130, 139; **Retro. Supp. II:** 51

Lectures on the Present Position of Catholics in England (Newman), **Supp. VII:** 298

Lectures on the Prophetical Office of the Church Viewed Relatively to Romanism and Popular Protestantism (Newman), **Supp. VII:** 293–294, 301, 302

"Leda and the Swan" (Yeats), **V:** 345

Lee, George John Vandeleur, **VI:** 101

Lee, Gypsy Rose, **Supp. IV:** 422, 423, 424

Lee, Hermione, **Retro. Supp. I:** 305

Lee, J., **II:** 336

Lee, Nathaniel, **II:** 305

Lee, Sidney, **V:** 280

Leech, Clifford, **II:** 44, 49, 52, 60, 62, 64, 70, 86, 90*n*, 100

Leech, John, **IV:** 258

Leenane Trilogy, The (McDonagh), **Supp. XII:** 233, 234–237, 238, 239, 240, 241

Left Bank and Other Stories, The (Rhys), **Supp. II:** 388, **389–390**

Left–Handed Liberty (Arden), **Supp. II:** 29, 30

Left Heresy in Literature and Art, The (Kemp and Riding), **Supp. III:** 120

Left Leg, The (Powys), **VIII:** 249, 250

"Left, Right, Left, Right: The Arrival of Tony Blair" (Barnes), **Supp. IV:** 74

"Legacie, The" (Donne), **Retro. Supp. II:** 88, 91–92

"Legacy, The" (King), **Supp. VI:** 152–153

"Legacy, The" (Motion), **Supp. VII:** 261

Legacy of Cain, The(Collins), **Supp. VI:** 103

"Legend" (Fallon), **Supp. XII:** 103

Legend of Good Women, The (Chaucer), **I:** 24–31, 38; **Retro. Supp. II:**40

Legend of Juba;, The, and Other Poems (Eliot), **V:** 200

Legend of Montrose, A (Scott), **IV:** xviii, 35, 39

Legend of the Rhine, A (Thackeray), **V:** 38

"Legacy on My Fiftieth Birthday, A" (Stevenson), **Supp. VI:** 262

Legendre's Elements of Geometry (Carlyle), **IV:** 250

"Legends of Ancient Eire, The" (Russell), **VIII:** 282

Legends of Angria (ed. Ratchford), **V:** 112

Léger, Fernand, **Supp. IV:** 81

"Legion Club, The" (Swift), **III:** 21, 31

Legion Hall Bombing, The (Churchill), **Supp. IV:** 181

Legion's Memorial to the House of Commons (Defoe), **III:** 12; **Retro. Supp. I:** 67

Legislation (Ruskin), **V:** 178

Legouis, Pierre, **II:** 207, 209, 218, 219, 220

Lehmann, John Frederick, **VII:** xvii, xxxviii

Leigh, R. A., **III:** 246*n*

Leigh Hunt's Examiner Examined (Blunden), **IV:** 236

Leila, A Tale (Browning), **IV:** 321

"Leisure" (Blunden), **Supp. XI:** 42

"Leisure" (Lamb), **IV:** 83

"Leith Races" (Fergusson), **III:** 317

Leland, John, **I:** 113

Lemady (Roberts, K.), **Supp. X:** 261

Lemon, Mark, **IV:** 263

"Lend Me Your Light" (Mistry), **Supp. X:** 141–142

"Lenin" (Smith, I. C.), **Supp. IX:** 212–213, 216

"Lenten Offering, The" (Warner), **Supp. VII:** 371

Leonard's War: A Love Story (Sillitoe), **Supp. V:** 411

"Leonardo Da Vinci" (Pater), **V:** 345–347, 348

Leonora (Edgeworth), **Supp. III:** 158

"'Leopard' George" (Lessing), **Supp. I:** 242

"Lepanto" (Chesterton), **VI:** 340

"Leper, The" (Swinburne), **V:** 315

LeQueux, William, **Supp. II:** 299

"Lerici" (Gunn), **Supp. IV:** 259

Les aventures de Télémaque (Fénelon), **III:** 95, 99

Les bourgeoises à la mode (Dancourt), **II:** 325, 336

Les carrosses d'Orleans (La Chapelle), **II:** 358

"Les Chats" (Baudelaire), **Supp. IV:** 115

Les Damnés de la terre (Fanon), **Supp. IV:** 105

Les fables d'Ésope (Boursault), **II:** 324

Les Misérables (Hugo), **Supp. IV:** 86

"Les Noyades" (Swinburne), **V:** 319, 320

"Les Vaches" (Clough), **V:** 168

Lesbia Brandon (Swinburne), **V:** 313, 325, 326–327, 332

Leslie Stephen (MacCarthy), **V:** 284, 290

Leslie Stephen and Matthew Arnold as Critics of Wordsworth (Wilson), **V:** 287, 290

Leslie Stephen: Cambridge Critic (Leavis), **VII:** 238

Leslie Stephen: His Thought and Character in Relation to His Time (Annan), **V:** 284–285, 290

Less Deceived, The (Larkin), **Supp. I:** 275, 277, 278, 279, 285

Less Than Angels (Pym), **Supp. II:** 372–374

"Lesser Arts, The" (Morris), **V:** 291, 301

Lessing, Doris, **Supp. I:** 237–257; **Supp. IV:** 78, 233, 234, 473

Lessing, Gotthold Ephraim, **IV:** 53

Lessius, **II:** 181*n*

Lessness (Beckett), **Supp. I:** 52, 61

"Lesson in Music, A" (Reid), **Supp. VII:** 324–325

"Lesson of the Master, The" (James), **VI:** 48, 67, 69

"Lessons of the Summer" (Fuller), **Supp. VII:** 80

Lessons of the War (Reed), **VII:** 422

L'Estrange, Sir Robert, **III:** 41

"Let Him Loose" (Cameron), **Supp. IX:** 24

Let It Bleed (Rankin), **Supp. X:** 244, 251, 253

"Let It Go" (Empson), **Supp. II:** 180, 194

Let Me Alone (Kavan), **Supp. VII:** 202–204, 205, 206, 207, 214

"Let that be a Lesson" (Kelman), **Supp. V:** 249

"Let the Brothels of Paris be opened" (Blake), **III:** 299

Let the People Sing (Priestley), **VII:** 217

"Let Them Call It Jazz" (Rhys), **Supp. II:** 402

"Let Us Now Praise Unknown Women and Our Mothers Who Begat Us" (Maitland), **Supp. XI:** 175

Let's Have Some Poetry! (Jennings), **Supp. V:** 206, 214

Lethaby, W. R., **V:** 291, 296, 306

"Letter, The" (Brontë), **V:** 132

"Letter, The" (Hart), **Supp. XI:** 130

Letter, The (Maugham), **VI:** 369

"Letter, The" (Smith, I. C.), **Supp. IX:** 215

"Letter, The" (Thomas), **Supp. XII:** 290

Letter Addressed to His Grace the Duke of Norfolk (Newman), **Supp. VII:** 302

Letter and Spirit: Notes on the Commandments (Rossetti), **V:** 260

Letter . . . concerning the Sacramental Test, A (Swift), **III:** 35

Letter from a Member . . . in Ireland to a Member in England, A (Defoe), **III:** 18

Letter from Amsterdam to a Friend in England, A, **II:** 206

"Letter from Armenia, A" (Hill), **Supp. V:** 189

"Letter from Artemiza . . . to Chloë, A" (Rochester), **II;** 260, 270; **Supp. III:** 70

"Letter from Hamnovoe" (Brown), **Supp. VI:** 64

"Letter from Home, The" (Kincaid), **Supp. VII:** 221

Letter . . . in Vindication of His Conduct with Regard to the Affairs of Ireland, A (Burke), **III:** 205

Letter of Advice to a Young Poet, A (Swift), **III:** 35

Letter of Marque (O'Brian), **Supp. XII:** 257

Letter of Thanks . . . to the . . . Bishop of S. Asaph, A (Swift), **III:** 35

Letter of Travell, A (Greville), **Supp. XI:** 108

Letter . . . on the Conduct of the Minority in Parliament, A (Burke), **III:** 205

"Letter to —, April 4, 1802, A" (Coleridge), **Retro. Supp. II:** 61

"Letter to a Brother of the Pen in Tribulation, A" (Behn), **Supp. III:** 40

Letter . . . to a Country Gentleman . . . , A (Swift), **III:** 35

Letter to a Friend, A (Browne), **II:** 153, 156

"Letter to a Friend" (Stallworthy), **Supp. X:** 295

Letter . . . to a Gentleman Designing for Holy Orders, A (Swift), **III:** 35

Letter to a Member of the National Assembly, A (Burke), **III:** 205

Letter to a Monk (More), **Supp. VII:** 240, 241–242

Letter to a Noble Lord (Burke), **IV:** 127

Letter to a Peer of Ireland on the Penal Laws (Burke), **III:** 205

"Letter to an Exile" (Motion), **Supp. VII:** 254, 257

Letter to an Honourable Lady, A (Greville), **Supp. XI:** 108

Letter to Brixius (More), **Supp. VII:** 241

"Letter to Curtis Bradford, A" (Davie), **Supp. VI:** 109

Letter to Dorp (More), **Supp. VII:** 240–241

Letter to Edward Lee (More), **Supp. VII:** 240

"Letter to John Donne, A" (Sisson), **Supp. XI:** 256

Letter to John Murray, Esq., "Touching"Lord Nugent (Southey), **IV:** 71

"Letter to Lord Byron" (Auden), **IV:** 106; **Supp. II:** 200; **Retro. Supp. I:** 7

Letter to Lord Ellenborough, A (Shelley), **IV:** 208

"Letter to Maria Gisborne" (Shelley), **IV:** 204

"Letter to Mr. Creech at Oxford, A" (Behn), **Supp. III:** 41

Letter to Mr. Harding the Printer, A (Swift), **III:** 35

Letter to Oxford (More), **Supp. VII:** 240–241

Letter to Peace–Lovers (Brittain), **Supp. X:** 45

Letter to Robert MacQueen Lord Braxfield . . . , A (Boswell), **III:** 248

Letter to Samuel Whitbread (Malthus), **IV:** 127

"Letter to Sara Hutchinson" (Coleridge), **IV:** 15

Letter to Sir Hercules Langrishe on . . . the Roman Catholics .. . . , A (Burke), **III:** 205

"Letter to Sylvia Plath" (Stevenson), **Supp. VI:** 263–264

"Letter to the Bishop of Llandaff" (Wordsworth), **IV:** 2

Letter to the Noble Lord on the Attacks Made upon Him . . . in the House of Lords, A (Burke), **III:** 205

Letter to the People of Scotland, on . . . the Articles of the Union, A (Boswell), **III:** 248

Letter to the People of Scotland, on the Present State of the Nation, A (Boswell), **III:** 248

Letter to the Shop–Keepers . . . of Ireland, A (Swift), **III:** 28, 35

Letter to the Whole People of Ireland, A (Swift), **III:** 35

Letter to Viscount Cobham, A (Congreve), **II:** 350

Letter to . . . Viscount Molesworth, A (Swift), **III:** 35

"Letter to William Coldstream" (Auden), **Retro. Supp. I:** 7

Letter to William Gifford, Esq., A (Hazlitt), **IV:** 139

Letter to William Smith, Esq., MP, A (Southey), **IV:** 71

Letter Writers, The (Fielding), **III:** 97, 105

Letter Written to a Gentleman in the Country, A . . . (Milton), **II:** 176

Letterbook of Sir George Etherege, The (ed. Rosenfeld), **II:** 271

"Letterfrack Industrial School" (Murphy), **Supp. V:** 316

Letters (Coleridge), **II:** 119n

Letters (Warner), **Supp. VII:** 377, 382

Letters Addressed to Lord Liverpool, and the Parliament . . . (Landor), **IV:** 100

Letters and Diaries (Newman), **Supp. VII:** 293, 297

Letters and Journals (Byron), **IV:** 185, 193

Letters and Journals of Lord Byron, with Notices of His Life, by T. Moore (Moore), **IV:** 193, 281; **V:** 116

Letters and Passages from . . . Clarissa (Richardson), **III:** 92

Letters and Private Papers of W. M. Thackeray (ed. Ray), **V:** 37, 140

Letters and Works of Lady Mary Wortley Montagu, **II:** 326n

Letters for Literary Ladies (Edgeworth), **Supp. III:** 153

Letters from a Citizen of the World (Goldsmith), *see Citizen of the World, The*

Letters from a Lost Generation: The First World War Letters of Vera Brittain and Four Friends, Roland Leighton, Edward Brittain, Victor Richardson, Geoffrey Thurlow (Brittain), **Supp. X:** 47

Letters from America (Brooke), **Supp. III:** 47, 50, 54–55, 59–60

Letters from Darkness (tr. Adcock), **Supp. XII:** 11

Letters from England: By Don Manuel Alvarez Espriella (Southey), **IV:** 60, 68–69, 71

Letters from Iceland (Auden and MacNeice), **VII:** 403; **Retro. Supp. I:** 7

Letters from John Galsworthy (ed. Garnett), **VI:** 290

Letters from London (Barnes), **Supp. IV:** 65, 74–75

Letters from the Lake Poets to D. Stuart (ed. Coleridge), **IV:** 144

"Letters from the Rocky Mountains" (Bird), **Supp. X:** 28

Letters from W. S. Landor to R. W. Emerson (Landor), **IV:** 100

Letters of a Conservative, The (Landor), **IV:** 100

"Letters of an Englishman" (Brontë), **V:** 111

Letters of an Old Playgoer (Arnold), **V:** 216

Letters of Charles Lamb . . . , The (ed. Lucas), **II:** 119n, **IV:** 84, 86

Letters of Elizabeth Barrett Browning (ed. Kenyon), **IV:** 312, 321

Letters of G. M. Hopkins to Robert Bridges (ed. Abbott), **VI:** 83

Letters of Hugh MacDiarmid, The (MacDiarmid), **Supp. XII:** 209

Letters of James Boswell . . . (ed. Francis), **III:** 249

Letters of James Boswell (ed. Tinker), **III:** 234n, 249

Letters of John Clare, The (Clare), **Supp. XI:** 55, 56, 57, 62

Letters of John Keats to Fanny Browne, **Retro. Supp. I:** 185

Letters of Laurence Sterne (ed. Curtis), **III:** 124n

Letters of Matthew Arnold, 1848–1888 (ed. Russell), **V:** 205, 206, 208, 211, 216

Letters of Mrs. Gaskell, The (ed. Chapell and Pollard), **V:** 108, 137, 151

Letters of Robert Browning and Elizabeth Barrett, 1845–46, **IV:** 318–319, 320, 321

Letters of Runnymede (Disraeli), **IV:** 298, 308

Letters of State, Written by Mr. John Milton . . . (Milton), **II:** 176

Letters of T. E. Lawrence, The (Lawrence), **Supp. II:** 287, 290

Letters of W. B. Yeats (ed. Wade), **VII:** 134

Letters of Walter Savage Landor, Private and Public (ed. Wheeler), **IV:** 89, 98, 100

Letters of William and Dorothy Wordsworth (ed. Selincourt), **IV:** 11, 25

Letters of Wit, Politicks and Morality, **II:** 352, 364

Letters on Several Occasions (Dennis), **II:** 338

Letters on the Subject of the Catholics, to my brother Abraham, who lives in the Country (Smith), **Supp. VII:** 343

Letters to a Young Gentleman . . . (Swift), **III:** 29

"Letters to a Young Man" (De Quincey), **IV:** 146

Letters to Alice on First Reading Jane Austen (Weldon), **Supp. IV:** 521–522, 536

Letters to Archdeacon Singleton (Smith), **Supp. VII:** 349–350

Letters to Henrietta (Bird), **Supp. X:** 23–27,

Letters to Malcolm: Chiefly on Prayer (Lewis), **Supp. III:** 249, 264, 265

Letters to T. E. Lawrence (Lawrence), **Supp. II:** 293

Letters to the Sheriffs of Bristol . . . (Burke), **III:** 205

"Letters to the Winner" (Murray), **Supp. VII:** 279

Letters with a Chapter of Biography, The (Sorley), **VI:** 421

Letters Written During a Short Residence in Spain and Portugal (Southey), **IV:** 71

Letters Written During a Short Residence in Sweden, Norway, and Denmark (Wollstonecraft), **Supp. III:** 473–475, 479

Letters Written to and for Particular Friends (Richardson), *see Familiar Letters*

Lettres d'une péruvienne (Graffigny), **Supp. III:** 75

Letty Fox: Her Luck (Stead), **Supp. IV:** 473

Levanter, The (Ambler), **Supp. IV:** 16

"Level–Crossing, The" (Warner), **Supp. VII:** 380

Levi, Peter, **Supp. IV:** 159

Leviathan (Hobbes), **II:** 190; **III:** 22; **IV:** 138

Levin, Harry, **I:** 288, 292

Levin, Ira, **III:** 343

Levin, Richard, **II:** 4, 23

Lévi–Strauss, Claude, **Supp. IV:** 115

Levitt, Morton, **Supp. IV:** 233

Levy, Paul, **Supp. IV:** 145

Lewes, George Henry, **IV:** 101, 122; **V:** 137, 189–190, 192, 198; **Retro. Supp. II:** 102–103

Lewis, Alun, **VII:** xxii, 422, **444–448**

Lewis, C. Day, *see Day Lewis, Cecil*

Lewis, C. S., **I:** 81, 95, 117; **III:** 51; **V:** 301, 306; **VII:** 356; **Supp. I:** 71, 72; **Supp. III: 247–268**

Lewis, Matthew, **III:** 331, 332–333, 336, 340, 343, 345; **Supp. III:** 384

Lewis, Peter, **Supp. IV:** 13

Lewis, Wyndham, **VI:** 118, 216, 247, 322; **VII:** xii, xv, 35, 41, 45, 49, 50, **71–85; Supp. IV:** 5

"Lewis Carroll" (de la Mare), **V:** 268, 274

Lewis Carroll (Hudson), **V:** 262–263, 274

Lewis Eliot stories (Snow), **VII:** 322; *see Strangers and Brothers* cycle

Lewis Seymour and Some Women (Moore), **VI:** 86, 89–90, 98, 99

"Lexicography" (Ewart), **Supp. VII:** 45

"Liar, The" (James), **VI:** 69

"Libbie Marsh's Three Eras" (Gaskell), **V:** 15

Libel on D[octor] Delany, A (Swift), **III:** 35

Liber Amoris (Hazlitt), **IV:** 128, 131–132, 133, 139

Liber niger (Edward IV), **I:** 25, 44

Liberal (periodical), **IV:** 132, 172

"Liberty" (Collins), **III:** 166, 172

Liberty (Thomson), **Supp. III:** 411–412, **419–422**

Libra (Delillo), **Supp. IV:** 487

"Libraries. A Celebration" (Dunn), **Supp. X:** 79

Library, The (Crabbe), **III:** 274, 280, 286

"Library Window, The" (Oliphant), **Supp. X:** 220

Licking Hitler (Hare), **Supp. IV:** 282, 287–288

"Licorice Fields at Pontefract, The" (Betjeman), **VII:** 368

Lidoff, Joan, **Supp. IV:** 459

"Lie, The" (Ralegh), **I:** 148

Lies of Silence (Moore, B.), **Supp. IX:** 146, 148–149

"Lieutenant Bligh and Two Midshipmen" (Brown), **Supp. VI:** 70

Lieutenant of Inishmore, The (McDonagh), **Supp. XII:** 233, 238, 241–243, 245

Life, A (Smith, I. C.), **Supp. IX:** 219–220

"Life, A" (Thomas), **Supp. XII:** 280

"Life, The" (Ewart), **Supp. VII:** 39

Life, Adventures, and Pyracies of . . . Captain Singleton, The (Defoe), *see Captain Singleton*

Life After Death (Toynbee), **Supp. I:** 40

Life and Adventures of Martin Chuzzlewit, The (Dickens), *see Martin Chuzzlewit*

Life and Adventures of Nicholas Nickleby, The (Dickens), *see Nicholas Nickleby*

Life and Art (Hardy), **VI:** 20

"Life and Character of Dean Swift, The" (Swift), **III:** 23, 32, 36

Life and Correspondence of Robert Southey, The (Southey), **IV:** 62, 72

Life and Correspondence of Thomas Arnold, The (Stanley), **V:** 13

"Life and Death of God, The" (Ballard), **Supp. V:** 28

Life and Death of Jason, The (Morris), **V:** 296, 297, 298, 304, 306

Life and Death of Mr. Badman, The (Bunyan), **II:** 242, 248, 250–251, 253

Life and Death of My Lord Gilles de Rais, The (Nyc), **Supp. X:** 195, 199

Life and Death of Robert Greene (Greene), **VIII:** 133

Life and Death of Tom Thumb, the Great, The (Fielding), **Retro. Supp. I:** 82

"Life and Fame" (Cowley), **II:** 196

Life and Habit (Butler), **Supp. II,** 102, 104–105, 106, 107, 111

Life and Labours of Blessed John Baptist De La Salle, The (Thompson), **V:** 450, 451

Life and Letters of John Galsworthy, The (Marrot), **V:** 270; **VI:** 287

Life and Letters of Leslie Stephen, The (Maitland), **V:** 277, 290

Life and Letters, The (Macaulay), **IV:** 270–271, 284, 291

Life and Loves of a She–Devil, The (Weldon), **Supp. IV:** 537–538

Life and Opinions of Tristram Shandy, Gentleman, The (Sterne), *see Tristram Shandy*

"Life and Poetry of Keats, The" (Masson), **IV:** 212, 235

Life and Strange Surprizing Adventures of Robinson Crusoe . . . . , The (Defoe), *see Robinson Crusoe*

Life and the Poet (Spender), **Supp. II:** 489

Life and Times of Laurence Sterne, The (Cross), **III:** 125

Life and Times of Michael K (Coetzee), **Supp. VI:** 76, **82–83**

Life and Work of Harold Pinter, The (Billington), **Retro. Supp. I:** 216

Life as We Have Known It (Woolf), **Retro. Supp. I:** 314

"Life and Writings of Addison" (Macaulay), **IV:** 282

Life Goes On (Sillitoe), **Supp. V:** 411

"Life in a Love" (Browning), **IV:** 365

Life in Greece from Homer to Menander (Mahafty), **V:** 400

"Life in London" (Egan), **IV:** 260

Life in Manchester (Gaskell), **V:** 15

Life, Letters, and Literary Remains of John Keats (Milnes), **IV:** 211, 235, 351; **Retro. Supp. I:** 185–186

Life of Addison (Johnson), **III:** 42

Life of Alexander Pope (Ruffhead), **III:** 69n, 71

Life of Algernon Charles Swinburne, The (Gosse), **V:** 311, 334

Life of Benjamin Disraeli, Earl of Beaconsfield, The (Monypenny and Buckle), **IV:** 292, 295, 300, 307, 308

Life of . . . Bolingbroke, The (Goldsmith), **III:** 189, 191

Life of Charlotte Brontë, The (Gaskell), **V:** xii, 1–2, 3, 13–14, 15, 108, 122

Life of Christina Rossetti, The (Sanders), **V:** 250, 260

Life of Cicero, The (Trollope), **V:** 102

Life of Collins (Johnson), **III:** 164, 171

Life of Crabbe (Crabbe), **III:** 272

Life of Dr. Donne, The (Walton), **II:** 132, 136, 140, 141, 142

Life of Dr. Robert Sanderson, The (Walton), **II:** 133, 135, 136–137, 140, 142

Life of Dryden, The (Scott), **IV:** 38

Life of George Moore, The (Horne), **VI:** 87, 96, 99

Life of Henry Fawcett, The (Stephen), **V:** 289

Life of John Bright, The (Trevelyan), **VI:** 389

Life of John Hales, The (Walton), **II:** 136

Life of John Milton, The (Wilson), **Supp. VI:** 301–302

Life of John Sterling (Carlyle), **IV:** 41–42, 240, 249, 250

Life of Johnson, The (Boswell), **I:** 30; **III:** 58, 114n, 115, 120, 234, 238, 239, 243–248; **IV:** xv, 280; **Retro. Supp. I:** 145–148

Life of Katherine Mansfield, The (Mantz and Murry), **VII:** 183

"Life of Ma Parker" (Mansfield), **VII:** 175, 177

Life of Man, The (Arden), **Supp. II:** 28

Life of Mr. George Herbert, The (Walton), **II:** 119–120, 133, 140, 142, 143; **Retro. Supp. II:** 171–172

Life of Mr. Jonathan Wild the Great, The (Fielding), *see Jonathan Wild*

Life of Mr. Richard Hooker, The (Walton), **II:** 133, 134, 135, 140–143

Life of Mr. Richard Savage (Johnson), **III:** 108, 121

Life of Mrs. Godolphin, The (Evelyn), **II:** 275, 287

"Life of Mrs. Radcliffe" (Scott), **IV:** 35

Life of Mrs. Robert Louis Stevenson, The (Sanchez), **V:** 393, 397

Life of Napoleon, The (Scott), **IV:** 38

Life of Napoleon Bonaparte, The (Hazlitt), **IV:** 135, 140

Life of Nelson, The (Southey), **IV:** xvii, 58, 69, 71, 280

Life of Our Lady, The (Lydgate), **I:** 22, 57, 65–66

Life of Pico (More), **Supp. VII:** 233, 234, 238

Life of Pope (Johnson), **Retro. Supp. I:** 144–145

Life of Richard Nash, The (Goldsmith), **III:** 189, 191

Life of Robert Louis Stevenson, The (Balfour), **V:** 393, 397

Life of Robert Louis Stevenson, The (Masson), **V:** 393, 397

Life of Rudyard Kipling, The (Carrington), **VI:** 166

Life of Saint Albion, The (Lydgate), **I:** 57

Life of Saint Cecilia, The (Chaucer), **I:** 31

Life of Saint Edmund, The (Lydgate), **I:** 57

Life of Saint Francis Xavier, The (tr. Dryden), **II:** 305

Life of Samuel Johnson, The (Boswell), *see Life of Johnson, The*

Life of Schiller (Carlyle), **IV:** 241, 249, 250

Life of Sir Henry Wotton, The (Walton), **II:** 133, 141, 142, 143

Life of Sir James Fitzjames Stephen, The (Stephen), **V:** 289

Life of Sterling (Carlyle), *see Life of John Sterling*

"Life of the Emperor Julius" (Brontë), **V:** 113

"Life of the Imagination, The" (Gordimer), **Supp. II:** 233–234

Life of the Renowned Sir Philip Sidney, The (Greville), **Supp. XI:** 106, 107–108, 117, 118

Life of the Rev. Andrew Bell, The (Southey and Southey), **IV:** 71

Life of the Seventh Earl of Shaftesbury (Hodder), **IV:** 62

Life of Thomas Hardy (Hardy), **VI:** 14–15

Life of Thomas More, The (Ackroyd), **Supp. VI: 12**, 13

"Life of Thomas Parnell" (Goldsmith), **III:** 189

Life of Wesley, The (Southey), **IV:** 68, 71

Life of William Blake (Gilchrist), **Retro. Supp. I:** 46

Life of William Morris, The (Mackail), **V:** 294, 297, 306

"Life Sentence" (West), **Supp. III:** 442

"Life to Come, The" (Forster), **VI:** 411

"Life with a Hole in It, The" (Larkin), **Supp. I:** 284

"Life-Exam, A" (Crawford), **Supp. XI:** 76

Life's Handicap (Kipling), **VI:** 204

Life's Little Ironies (Hardy), **VI:** 20, 22

Life's Morning, A (Gissing), **V:** 437

"Liffey Hill, The" (Kinsella), **Supp. V:** 267

"Lifted Veil, The" (Eliot), **V:** 198

Light and the Dark, The (Snow), **VII:** 324, 327

"Light breaks where no sun shines" (Thomas), **Supp. I:** 172

Light for Them That Sit in Darkness . . . (Bunyan), **II:** 253

Light Garden of the Angel King: Journeys in Afghanistan, The (Levi), **Supp. IV:** 159

Light Heart, The (Jonson), **Retro. Supp. I:** 165

"Light Man, A" (James), **VI:** 25, 69

Light Music, (Mahon), **Supp. VI:** 173

Light of Day, The (Ambler), **Supp. IV:** 4, 16–17

Light Shining in Buckinghamshire (Churchill), **Supp. IV:** 180, 186–188

"Light Shining Out of Darkness" (Cowper), **III:** 211

Light That Failed, The (Kipling), **VI:** 166, 169, 189–190, 204

"Light Woman, A" (Browning), **IV:** 369

Light Years, The (Howard), **Supp. XI:** 135, 145, 147, 148, 149

"Lightening Hours, The" (Fallon), **Supp. XII:** 103

Lighthouse, The (Collins), **Supp. VI:** 95

"Lighthouse Invites the Storm, The" (Lowry), **Supp. III:** 282

Lighthouse Invites the Storm, The (Lowry), **Supp. III:** 282

"Lights Among Redwood" (Gunn), **Supp. IV:** 263

"Lights Out" (Thomas), **Supp. III:** 401

"Liglag" (Crawford), **Supp. XI:** 78

"Like a Vocation" (Auden), **Retro. Supp. I:** 9

Like Birds, Like Fishes and Other Stories (Jhabvala), **Supp. V:** 235

Like It Or Not (Ewart), **Supp. VII:** 47

Lilac and Flag: An Old Wives' Tale of a City (Berger), **Supp. IV:** 93–95

Lilian (Bennett), **VI:** 250, 259–260

Lilliesleaf (Oliphant), **Supp. X:** 214

"Lilly in a Cristal, The" (Herrick), **II:** 104

"Lily Adair" (Chivers), **V:** 313

Limbo (Huxley), **VII:** 199, 200

Lincoln: A Foreigner's Quest (Morris, J.), **Supp. X:** 173, 182–183

Lincolnshire poems (Tennyson), **IV:** 327, 336

Linda Tressel (Trollope), **V:** 102

Linden Tree, The (Priestley), **VII:** 209, 228–229

Line of Life, A (Ford), **II:** 88, 100

"Lines: I Am" (Clare), **Supp. XI:** 49, 62

"Lines Composed a Few Miles Above Tintern Abbey" (Wordsworth), **IV:** ix, 3, 7, 8, 9–10, 11, 44, 198, 215, 233

"Lines Composed in a Wood on a Windy Day" (Brontë), **V:** 132

"Lines Composed While Climbing the Left Ascent of Brockley Combe" (Coleridge), **IV: 43–44**

"Lines for a Book" (Gunn), **Supp. IV:** 260, 261

"Lines for Cuscuscaraway . . . " (Elliot), **VII:** 163

"Lines for Thanksgiving" (McGuckian), **Supp. V:** 289

"Lines of Desire" (Motion), **Supp. VII:** 254, 260–261

Lines of the Hand, The (Hart), **Supp. XI:** 122, 123–125

"Lines on a Young Lady's Photograph Album" (Larkin), **Supp. I:** 285

"Lines on the Loss of the *Titanic*" (Hardy), **VI:** 16

"Lines Written Among the Euganean Hills" (Shelley), **IV:** 199; **Retro. Supp. I:** 250–251

"Lines Written in the Bay of Lerici" (Shelley), **IV:** 206

"Lines Written on a Seat" (Kavanagh), **Supp. VII:** 198

"Lingam and the Yoni, The" (Hope), **Supp. VII:** 154

"Linnet in the rocky dells, The" (Brontë), **V:** 115

Lion and the Fox, The (Lewis), **VII:** 72, 74, 82

Lion and the Mouse, The (Henryson), **Supp. VII:** 136, 139

Lion and the Ostrich, The (Koestler), **Supp. I:** 35

Lion and the Unicorn, The (Orwell), **VII:** 282

Lion, The Witch, and the Wardrobe, The (Lewis), **Supp. III:** 248, 260

Lions and Shadows (Isherwood), **VII:** 310, 312

Lipstick on Your Collar (Potter, D.), **Supp. X:** 231

Lipton Story: A Centennial Biography, A (Waugh), **Supp. VI:** 275

Listen to the Voice: Selected Stories (Smith, I. C.), **Supp. IX:** 210

"Listeners, The" (Nye), **Supp. X:** 192, 198, 202

"Litanie, The" (Donne), **Retro. Supp. II:** 96

Litanies de Satan (Baudelaire), **V:** 310

"Litany, A" (Swinburne), **V:** 320

"Literary Criticism and Philosophy: A Reply" (Leavis), **VII:** 241–242

Literary Criticisms by Francis Thompson (ed. Connolly), **V:** 450, 451

Literary History of England in the End of the Eighteenth and Beginning of the Nineteenth Century (Oliphant), **Supp. X:** 222

Literary Reminiscences (Hood), **IV:** 252, 253, 254, 259–260, 266

Literary Studies (Bagehot), **V:** 156, 170

Literary Taste: How to Form It (Bennett), **VI:** 266

Literature and Dogma (Arnold), **V:** xxiv, 203, 212, 216

"Literature and Offence" (Brink), **Supp. VI:** 47

"Literature and the Irish Language" (Moore), **VI:** 98

Literature and Western Man (Priestley), **VII:** 209, 214–215

Literature at Nurse; or, Circulating Morals (Moore), **VI:** 90, 98

Lithuania (Brooke), **Supp. III:** 47, 54

"Little Aeneid, The" (Malouf), **Supp. XII:** 220

"Little and a lone green lane" (Brontë), **V:** 112–113

"Little Black Boy, The" (Blake), **Supp. IV:** 188; **Retro. Supp. I:** 36

"Little Boy Lost, The" (Blake), **III:** 292

Little Dinner at Timmins's, A (Thackeray), **V:** 24, 38

Little Dorrit (Dickens), **V:** xxii, 41, 42, 47, 55, 63, 64–66, 68, 69, 70, 72

Little Dream, The (Galsworthy), **VI:** 274

Little Drummer Girl, The (le Carré), **Supp. II:** 305, 306, 307, 311, 313, **315–318**

Little French Lawyer, The (Fletcher and Massinger), **II:** 66

"Little Ghost Who Died for Love, The" (Sitwell), **VII:** 133

"Little Gidding" (Eliot), **VII:** 154, 155, 156

Little Girl, The (Mansfield), **VII:** 171

Little Girls, The (Bowen), **Supp. II:** 77, 82, 84, 94

Little Gray Home in the West (Arden and D'Arcy), **Supp. II:** 32, 35

Little Green Man (Armitage), **VIII:** 1

Little Hotel, The (Stead), **Supp. IV:** 473, 476

Little Learning, A (Waugh), **Supp. VI:** 271

Little Men (Alcott), **Supp. IV:** 255

Little Minister, The (Barrie), **Supp. III:** 1, 3, 8

"Little Paul and the Sea" (Stevenson), **Supp. VI:** 264

"Little Photographer, The" (du Maurier), **Supp. III:** 135

"Little Puppy That Could, The" (Amis), **Supp. IV:** 40

"Little Red Twin" (Hughes), **Supp. I:** 359

Little Tales of Misogyny (Highsmith), **Supp. V:** 177, 180

Little Tea, a Little Chat, A (Stead), **Supp. IV:** 462, 473

"Little Tembi" (Lessing), **Supp. I:** 241

Little Tour in France, A (James), **VI:** 45–46, 67

"Little Travels and Roadside Sketches" (Thackeray), **V:** 38

Little Wars: A Game for Boys (Wells), **VI:** 227, 244

"Little While, A" (Rossetti), **V:** 242

"Little while, a little while, A," (Brontë), **V:** 127–128

Littlewood, Joan, **Supp. II:** 68, 70, 73, 74

Live Like Pigs (Arden), **Supp. II:** 24–25, 29

Lively, Penelope, **Supp. IV:** 304

"Lively sparks that issue from those eyes, The" (Wyatt), **I:** 109

"Liverpool Address, A" (Arnold), **V:** 213, 216

Lives, (Mahon), **Supp. VI: 168–171,** 172

"Lives" (Mahon), **Supp. VI:** 169

Lives, The (Walton), **II:** 131, 134–137, 139, **140–143;** *see also* individual works: *Life of Dr. Donne; Life of Dr. Robert Sanderson; Life of Mr. George Herbert; Life of Mr. Richard Hooker; Life of Sir Henry Wotton*

Lives of the British Admirals (Southey and Bell), **IV:** 71

Lives of the English Poets, The (Johnson), **II:** 259; **III:** 118–119, 122, 160, 173, 189; **Retro. Supp. I:** 143–145, 274

Lives of the Hunted (Seton), **Supp. IV:** 158

Lives of the 'Lustrious: A Dictionary of Irrational Biography (Stephen and Lee), **V:** 290

Lives of the Novelists (Scott), **III:** 146n; **IV:** 38, 39

Lives of the Poets, The (Johnson), *see Lives of the English Poets, The*

Lives of the English Saints (Newman), **Supp. VII:** 296

Livia (Durrell), **Supp. I:** 118, 119

Living (Green), **Supp. II:** 251–253

Living and the Dead, The (White), **Supp. I:** 129, 130, 134

Living in America (Stevenson), **Supp. VI: 254–256**

"Living in Time" (Reid), **Supp. VII:** 329

Living Novel, The (Pritchett), **IV:** 306

Living Principle, The (Leaves), **VII:** 237

Living Quarters (Friel), **Supp. V:** 122

Living Room, The (Greene), **Supp. I:** 13; **Retro. Supp. II:** 161–162

Living Together (Ayckbourn), **Supp. V:** 2, 5

Living Torch, The (Russell), **VIII:** 277, 286, 290, 292

"Livings" (Larkin), **Supp. I:** 277, 282

Livingstone's Companions (Gordimer), **Supp. II:** 229, 233

Liza of Lambeth (Maugham), **VI:** 364–365

Liza's England (Barker), *see Century's Daughter, The*

"Lizbie Brown" (Hardy), **Retro. Supp. I:** 110

"Lizzie Leigh" (Gaskell), **V:** 3, 15

Ljósvetninga saga, **VIII:** 242

"Llanrhaeadr ym Mochnant" (Thomas), **Supp. XII:** 285

Lloyd, Charles, **IV:** 78

Lloyd George, David, **VI:** 264, 340, 352, 353; **VII:** 2

Loaves and Fishes (Brown), **Supp. VI:** 65, 71

"Lob" (Thomas), **Supp. III:** 394, 405

Lobo, Jeronimo, **III:** 107, 112

Local Habitation (Nicholson), **Supp. VI:** 213, **217–218**

Locations (Morris, J.), **Supp. X:** 172, 183

"Loch Ness Monster's Song, The" (Morgan, E.), **Supp. IX:** 162–163, 169

"Loch Roe" (MacCaig), **Supp. VI:** 182

"Loch Sionascaig" (MacCaig), **Supp. VI:** 195

"Lock, The" (Coppard), **VIII:** 88

"Lock the Door, Lariston" (Hogg), **Supp. X:** 110

"Lock up, fair lids, The treasure of my heart" (Sidney), **I:** 169

Locke, John, **III:** 22; **IV:** 169; **Supp. III:** 33, 233

Lockhart, J. G., **IV:** 27, 30, 34, 36, 38, 39, 294; **V:** 140

"Locksley Hall" (Tennyson), **IV:** 325, 333, 334–335

"Locksley Hall Sixty Years After" (Tennyson), **IV:** 328, 338

"Locust Songs" (Hill), **Supp. V:** 187

Lodge, David, **Supp. II:** 9, 10; **Supp. IV:** 102, 139, **363–387,** 546; **Retro. Supp. I:** 217

Lodge, Thomas, **I:** 306, 312

"Lodging for the Night, A" (Stevenson), **V:** 384, 395

"Lodging House Fire, The" (Davies), **Supp. XI:** 94–95

"Lodgings for the Night" (Caudwell), **Supp. IX:** 35, 37

Lodore (Shelley), **Supp. III:** 371, 372

Loftis, John, **III:** 255, 271

"Lofty in the Palais de Danse" (Gunn), **Supp. IV:** 258

"Lofty Sky, The" (Thomas), **Supp. III:** 401

Logan, Annie R. M., **VI:** 23

Logan Stone (Thomas), **Supp. IV:** 490

"Logan Stone" (Thomas), **Supp. IV:** 491, 492

"Loganair" (Crawford), **Supp. XI:** 75

"Logic of Dreams" (Fuller), **Supp. VII:** 74

Logic of Political Economy, The (De Quincey), **IV:** 155

"Logical Ballad of Home Rule, A" (Swinburne), **V:** 332

"Logos" (Hughes), **Supp. I:** 350

Loiners, The (Harrison), **Supp. V:** 149, 150–151

"Lois the Witch" (Gaskell), **V:** 15

Loitering with Intent (Spark), **Supp. I:** 204, 212, 213

Lokasenna, **VIII:** 230, 241

Lolita (Nabokov), **Supp. IV:** 26, 30

Lolly Willowes (Warner), **Supp. VII:** 370, 373–374, 375, 381

Lombroso, Cesare, **V:** 272

Londinium Redivivum (Evelyn), **II:** 287

"London" (Blake), **III:** 294, 295

"London" (Johnson), **III:** 57, 108, 114, 121; **Retro. Supp. I:** 137

London (Russell), **Supp. IV:** 126

London Assurance (Boucicault), **V:** 415

"London by Lamplight" (Meredith), **V:** 219

London Fields (Amis), **Supp. IV:** 26, 27, 35–37

"London hast thou accusèd me" (Surrey), **I:** 113, 116

London Journal 1762–1763 (Boswell), **III:** 239, 240, 242

London Kills Me: Three Screenplays and Four Essays (Kureishi), **Supp. XI:** 156–157, 159, 161

London Lickpenny (Ackroyd), **Supp. VI:** 3

London Life, A (James), **VI:** 67, 69

London Magazine (periodical), **III:** 263; **IV:** xviii, 252, 253, 257, 260; **V:** 386

London Mercury (periodical), **VII:** 211

London Pride (Braddon), **VIII:** 49

London Review of Books, **Supp. IV:** 121

"London Revisited" (Beerbohm), **Supp. II:** 52

Luck of Ginger Coffey, The (Moore, B.), **Supp. IX:** 142, 148–149, 153

Luck, or Cunning (Butler), **Supp. II:** 106, 107, 108, 113

"Lucky Break—How I Became a Writer" (Dahl), **Supp. IV:** 209, 211

Lucky Chance, The; or, An Alderman's Bargain (Behn), **Supp. III:** 26, 29

Lucky Jim (Amis), **Supp. II:** 2, 3, 4, 5–6, 7; **Supp. IV:** 25, 27, 28, 377

"Lucky Jim's Politics" (Amis), **Supp. II:** 11–12

Lucky Poet: A Self-Study in Literature and Political Ideas (MacDiarmid), **Supp. XII:** 203, 204–205

"Lucrece" (Gower), **I:** 54

Lucretia Borgia: The Chronicle of Tebaldeo Tebaldei (Swinburne), **V:** 325, 333

Lucretius, **II:** 275, 292, 300, 301; **IV:** 316

"Lucubratio Ebria" (Butler), **Supp. II:** 98, 99

Lucubrationes (More), **Supp. VII:** 240

Lucy (Kincaid), **Supp. VII:** 217, 219, 227–229

"Lucy Grange" (Lessing), **Supp. I:** 240

Lucy In Her Pink Jacket (Coppard), **VIII:** 90, 97

"Lucy"poems (Wordsworth), **IV:** 3, 18; **V:** 11

"Lui et Elles" (Moore), **VI:** 87

Lukács, György, **Supp. IV:** 81, 82, 87

"Lullaby" (Auden), **VII:** 383, 398; **Retro. Supp. I:** 6

"Lullaby" (Nye), **Supp. X:** 205

"Lullaby" (Sitwell), **VII:** 135

"Lullaby for Jumbo" (Sitwell), **VII:** 132

"Lumber Room, The" (Saki), **Supp. VI:** 245

Lunar Caustic (Lowry), **Supp. III:** 269, 270, **271–273,** 280, 283

Lunch and Counter Lunch (Murray), **Supp. VII:** 270, 275–276

"Lunch with Pancho Villa" (Muldoon), **Supp. IV:** 414–415

Lupercal (Hughes), **Supp. I:** 343, 345, 363; **Retro. Supp. I:** 126; **Retro. Supp. II:** 204–205

Luria: and a Soul's Tragedy (Browning), **IV:** 374

"Lust" (Brooke), **Supp. III:** 53

Luther (Osborne), **Supp. I:** 334–335, 338

"Lux Perpetua" (Brown), **Supp. VI:** 72

"Luxury" (Coppard), **VIII:** 94

"Lycidas" (Milton), **II:** 160–161, 164, 165, 168, 169, 175; **III:** 118–119, 120; **IV:** 205; **VI:** 73; **Retro. Supp. II:** 275–277

Lycidus; or, The Lover in Fashion (Behn), **Supp. III:** 37

"Lycus, The Centaur" (Hood), **IV:** 256, 267

Lydgate, John, **I:** 22, 49, **57–66**

Lydia Livingstone (Chatwin, B.), **Supp. IX:** 61

Lyell, Sir Charles, **IV:** 325

Lyfe of Johan Picus Erle of Myrandula (More), **Supp. VII:** 246

Lying Days, The (Gordimer), **Supp. II:** 226–227

Lying in the Sun (O'Brian), **Supp. XII:** 251

Lying Together (Thomas), **Supp. IV:** 485–486

Lyly, John, **I:** 191–211, 303

Lynch & Boyle (Seth), **Supp. X:** 283, 290

Lyric Impulse, The (Day Lewis), **Supp. III:** 118, 131

"Lyrical Ballad, A" (Motion), **Supp. VII:** 256–257

Lyrical Ballads (Wordsworth and Coleridge), **III:** 174, 336; **IV:** ix, viii, x, xvi, 3, 4, 5, **6–11,** 18, 24, **44–45,** 55, 77, 111, 138–139, 142; **Retro. Supp. II:** 53–54

Lyttelton, George, **III:** 118

Lyttleton, Dame Edith, **VII:** 32

Mabinogion, **I:** 73

"Mabinog's Liturgy" (Jones), **Supp. VII:** 177

Mac (Pinter), **Supp. I:** 367

Mac Flecknoe; or, A Satyre Upon the . . . Poet, T. S. (Dryden), **II:** 299, 304

"McAndrew's Hymn" (Kipling), **VI:** 202

Macaulay, Rose, **VII:** 37

Macaulay, Thomas Babington, **II:** 240, 241, 254, 255, 307; **III:** 51, 53, 72; **IV:** xii, xvi, xx, xxii, 101, 122, **268–291,** 295; **V:** viii; **VI:** 347, 353, 383, 392

Macbeth (Shakespeare), **I:** 317–318, 327; **II:** 97, 281; **IV:** 79–80, 188; **V:** 375; **Supp. IV:** 283

MacCaig, Norman, **Supp. VI: 181–195**

MacCarthy, Desmond, **V:** 284, 286, 290; **VI:** 363, 385; **VII:** 32; **Supp. III:** 98

McCabe, Patrick, **Supp. IX: 127–139**

McCarthy, Mary, **Supp. IV:** 234

McCartney, Colum, **Retro. Supp. I:** 131

McClintock, Anne, **Supp. IV:** 167

McClure, John, **Supp. IV:** 163

McCullers, Carson, **Supp. IV:** 422, 424

McCullough, Colleen, **Supp. IV:** 343

MacDermots of Ballycloran, The (Trollope), **V:** 101

MacDiarmid, Hugh, **III:** 310; **Supp. III:** 119; **Supp. XII: 201–216**

McDonagh, Martin, **Supp. XII: 233–246**

Macdonald, George, **V:** 266; **Supp. IV:** 201

Macdonald, Mary, **V:** 266, 272

McElroy, Joseph, **Supp. IV:** 116

McEwan, Ian, **Supp. IV:** 65, 75, **389–408; Supp. V:** xxx

McGann, Jerome J., **V:** 314, 335

McGrotty and Ludmilla (Gray, A.), **Supp. IX:** 80, 89

McGuckian, Medbh, **Supp. V: 277–293**

McHale, Brian, **Supp. IV:** 112

Machiavelli, Niccolò, **II:** 71, 72; **IV:** 279; **Retro. Supp. I:** 204

"Machine Stops, The" (Forster), **VI:** 399

Machynlleth Triad, A (Morris, J.), **Supp. X:** 185–186

McInherny, Frances, **Supp. IV:** 347, 353

Mack, Maynard, **Retro. Supp. I:** 229

Mackail, J. W., **V:** 294, 296, 297, 306

McKane, Richard, **Supp. IV:** 494–495

Mackay, M. E., **V:** 223, 234

Mackenzie, Compton, **VII:** 278

Mackenzie, Henry, **III:** 87; **IV:** 79

MacKenzie, Jean, **VI:** 227, 243

MacKenzie, Norman, **V:** 374*n*, 375*n*, 381, 382; **VI:** 227, 243

McKenney, Ruth, **Supp. IV:** 476

Mackenzie, Sir George, **III:** 95

"Mackery End, in Hertfordshire" (Lamb), **IV:** 83

MacLaren, Moray, **V:** 393, 398

McLeehan, Marshall, **IV:** 323*n*, 338, 339

Maclure, Millar, **I:** 291

Macmillan's (periodical), **VI:** 351; **Supp. XII:** 266, 268, 269, 270

MacNeice, Louis, **VII:** 153, 382, 385, **401–418; Supp. III:** 119; **Supp. IV:** 423, 424

Macpherson, James, **III:** 336; **VIII: 179–195; Supp. II:** 523

Macready, William Charles, **I:** 327

McTaggart, J. M. E., **Supp. II:** 406

Mad British Pervert Has a Sexual Fantasy About the 10th Street Bridge in Calgary, A (De Bernières), **Supp. XII:** 66

Mad Forest: A Play from Romania (Churchill), **Supp. IV:** 179, 188, 195–196, 198, 199

Mad Islands, The (MacNeice), **VII:** 405, 407

Mad Lover, The (Fletcher), **II:** 45, 55, 65

"Mad Maids Song, The" (Herrick), **II:** 112

"Mad Mullinix and Timothy" (Swift), **III:** 31

Mad Soldier's Song (Hardy), **VI:** 11

Mad World, My Masters, A (Middleton), **II:** 3, 4, 21

Madagascar; or, Robert Drury's Journal (Defoe), **III:** 14

Madame Bovary (Flaubert), **V:** xxii, 429; **Supp. IV:** 68, 69

"Madame de Mauves" (James), **VI:** 69; **Supp. IV:** 133

Madame de Pompadour (Mitford), **Supp. X:** 163

"Madame Rosette" (Dahl), **Supp. IV:** 209–210

Madan, Falconer, **V:** 264, 274

Maddox, Brenda, **Retro. Supp. I:** 327, 328

"Mademoiselle" (Stevenson), **Supp. VI:** 255

Mademoiselle de Maupin (Gautier), **V:** 320*n*

Madge, Charles, **VII:** xix

"Madman and the Child, The" (Cornford), **VIII:** 107

Madness of George III, The (Bennett), **VIII:** 31–33

Madoc (Muldoon), **Supp. IV:** 420, 424–427, 428

"Madoc" (Muldoon), **Supp. IV:** 422, 425–427, 430

Madoc (Southey), **IV:** 63, 64–65, 71

"Madoc" (Southey), **Supp. IV:** 425

"Madonna" (Kinsella), **Supp. V:** 273

Madonna and Other Poems (Kinsella), **Supp. V:** 272–273

Madonna of the Future and Other Tales, The (James), **VI:** 67, 69

"Madonna of the Trenches, A" (Kipling), **VI:** 193, **194–196**

Madras House, The (Shaw), **VI:** 118

Madwoman in the Attic, The (Gilbert/Gubar), **Retro. Supp. I:** 59–60

Maggot, A (Fowles), **Supp. I:** 309–310

"Magi" (Brown), **Supp. VI:** 71

Magic (Chesterton), **VI:** 340

Magic Box, The (Ambler), **Supp. IV:** 3

Magic Drum, The (Tennant), **Supp. IX:** 239

Magic Finger, The (Dahl), **Supp. IV:** 201

"Magic Finger, The" (Dahl), **Supp. IV:** 223–224

Magic Toyshop, The (Carter), **III:** 345; **Supp. III:** 80, 81, 82

Magic Wheel, The (eds. Swift and Profumo), **Supp. V:** 427

Magician, The (Maugham), **VI:** 374

Magician's Nephew, The (Lewis), **Supp. III:** 248

Magician's Wife, The (Moore, B.), **Supp. IX:** 141, 145–146

Maginn, William, **V:** 19

"Magna Est Veritas" (Smith), **Supp. II:** 471, 472

"Magnanimity" (Kinsella), **Supp. V:** 263

Magnetic Mountain, The (Day Lewis), **Supp. III:** 117, 122, 124–126

Magnetick Lady, The (Jonson), **Retro. Supp. I:** 165

Magnificence (Skelton), **I:** 90

"Magnolia" (Fuller), **Supp. VII:** 78

Magnus (Brown), **Supp. VI: 66–67**

"Magnus" (Macpherson), **VIII:** 186

Magnusson, Erika, **V:** 299, 300, 306

Magus, The (Fowles), **Supp. I:** 291, 292, 293, **295–299,** 310

Mahafty, John Pentland, **V:** 400, 401

Mahon, Derek, **Supp. IV:** 412; **Supp. VI: 165–180**

"Mahratta Ghats, The" (Lewis), **VII:** 446–447

Maid in the Mill, The (Fletcher and Rowley), **II:** 66

Maid in Waiting (Galsworthy), **VI:** 275

Maid Marian (Peacock), **IV:** xviii, 167–168, 170

Maid of Bath, The (Foote), **III:** 253

"Maid of Craca, The" (Macpherson), **VIII:** 186, 187

Maid of Honour, The (Massinger), **Supp. XI:** 184

"Maiden Name" (Larkin), **Supp. I:** 277

Maiden Voyage (Welch), **Supp. IX:** 261, 263–264

Maiden's Dream, A (Greene), **VIII:** 142

Maid's Tragedy, The (Beaumont and Fletcher), **II:** 44, 45, **54–57,** 58, 60, 65

Maid's Tragedy, Alter'd, The (Waller), **II:** 238

Mailer, Norman, **Supp. IV:** 17–18

"Maim'd Debauchee, The" (Rochester), **II:** 259–260

"Main Road" (Pritchett), **Supp. III:** 316–317

Mainly on the Air (Beerbohm), **Supp. II:** 52

Maitland, F. W., **V:** 277, 290; **VI:** 385

Maitland, Sara, **Supp. XI: 163–178**

Maitland, Thomas, pseud. of Algernon Charles Swinburne

Maitū njugīra (Ngũgĩ wa Thiong'o/Ngũgĩ wa Mĩriĩ), **VIII:** 216, 224, 225

Maiwa's Revenge (Haggard), **Supp. III:** 213

Majeske, Penelope, **Supp. IV:** 330

Major, John, **Supp. IV:** 437–438

Major Barbara (Shaw), **VII:** xv, 102, 108, **113–115,** 124; **Retro. Supp. II:** 321

Major Political Essays (Shaw), **VI:** 129

Major Victorian Poets, The: Reconsiderations (Armstrong), **IV:** 339

Make Death Love Me (Rendell), **Supp. IX:** 192–194

Make Thyself Many (Powys), **VIII:** 255

"Maker on High, The" (tr. Morgan, E.), see *Altus Prosator*

Makers of Florence, The (Oliphant), **Supp. X:** 222

Makers of Modern Rome, The (Oliphant), **Supp. X:** 222

Makers of Venice, The (Oliphant), **Supp. X:** 222

Makin, Bathsua, **Supp. III:** 21

"Making a Rat" (Hart), **Supp. XI:** 130

Making Cocoa for Kingsley Amis (Cope), **VIII:** 67, 69, 70–74, 81

Making History (Friel), **Supp. V:** 125

Making of a Poem, The (Spender), **Supp. II:** 481, 492

Making of an Immortal, The (Moore), **VI:** 96, 99

"Making of an Irish Goddess, The" (Boland), **Supp. V:** 44–45

"Making of the Drum" (Brathwaite), **Supp. XII:** 38

Making of the English Working Class, The (Thompson), **Supp. IV:** 473

Making of the Representative for Planet 8, The (Lessing), **Supp. I:** 252, 254

"Making Poetry" (Stevenson), **Supp. VI:** 262

Mal vu, mal dit (Beckett), **Supp. I:** 62

Malayan trilogy (Burgess), **Supp. I:** 187

Malcolm Lowry: Psalms and Songs (Lowry), **Supp. III:** 285

Malcolm Mooney's Land (Graham), **Supp. VII:** 104, 106, 109, 113–115, 116

Malcontent, The (Marston), **II:** 27, 30, **31–33,** 36, 40, 68

Malcontents, The (Snow), **VII:** 336–337

Male Child, A (Scott), **Supp. I:** 263

Malign Fiesta (Lewis), **VII:** 72, 80

Malinowski, Bronislaw, **Supp. III:** 186

Mallet, David, **Supp. III:** 412, 424–425

Malone, Edmond, **I:** 326

Malone Dies (Beckett), **Supp. I:** 50, 51, 52–53, 63; **Supp. IV:** 106; **Retro. Supp. I:** 18, 22–23

Malory, Sir Thomas, **I: 67–80;** **IV:** 336, 337; **Retro. Supp. II: 237–252**

Malouf, David, **Supp. XII: 217–232**

Malraux, André, **VI:** 240

"Maltese Cat, The" (Kipling), **VI:** 200

Malthus, Thomas, **IV:** xvi, 127, 133

Mamillia: A Mirror, or Looking–Glasse for the Ladies of England (Greene), **VIII:** 135, 140

"Man"(Herbert), **Retro. Supp. II:** 176–177

"Man"(Vaughan), **II:** 186, 188

Man, The (Stoker), **Supp. III:** 381

Man Above Men (Hare), **Supp. IV:** 282, 289

"Man and Bird" (Mahon), **Supp. VI:** 168

"Man and Boy" (Heaney), **Retro. Supp. I:** 132

Man and Boy (Rattigan), **Supp. VII:** 318, 320

"Man and Dog" (Thomas), **Supp. III:** 394, 403, 405

Man and Literature (Nicholson), **Supp. VI:** 213, 223

Man and Superman: A Comedy and a Philosophy (Shaw), **IV:** 161; **VI: 112–113,** 114, 127, 129; **Retro. Supp. II:** 309, 317–320

Man and Time (Priestley), **VII:** 213

Man and Two Women, A (Lessing), **Supp. I:** 244, 248

Man and Wife (Collins), **Supp. VI:** 102

Man Born to Be King, The (Sayers), **Supp. III:** 336, 349–350

"Man Called East, The" (Redgrove), **Supp. VI:** 236

Man Could Stand Up, A (Ford), **VI:** 319, 329

Man Does, Woman Is (Graves), **VII:** 268

"Man Friday" (Hope), **Supp. VII:** 164–165

"Man From the Caravan, The" (Coppard), **VIII:** 96

Man from the North, A (Bennett), **VI:** 248, 253

"Man from the South" (Dahl), **Supp. IV:** 215, 217–218

"Man I Killed, The" (Hardy), **Retro. Supp. I:** 120

"Man in Assynt, A" (MacCaig), **Supp. VI:** 191

Man in My Position, A (MacCaig), **Supp. VI: 191–192**

Man Lying On A Wall (Longley), **VIII:** 166, 172–173

"Man Lying On A Wall" (Longley), **VIII:** 172

Man Named East, The (Redgrove), **Supp. VI:** 235–236

Man of Destiny, The (Shaw), **VI:** 112

Man of Devon, A (Galsworthy), **VI:** 277

Man of Honour, A (Maugham), **VI:** 367, 368

Man of Law's Tale, The (Chaucer), **I:** 24, 34, 43, 51, 57

Man of Mode, The; or, Sir Fopling Flutter (Etherege), **II:** 256, 266, 271, 305

Man of Nazareth, The (Burgess), **Supp. I:** 193

Man of Property, A (Galsworthy), **VI:** 271, 272, 273, 274, 275, 276, 278, 282–283

Man of Quality, A (Lee), **II:** 336

Man of the Moment (Ayckbourn), **Supp. V:** 3, 7–8, 10

"Man of Vision" (Crawford), **Supp. XI:** 71

"Man Was Made to Mourn, a Dirge" (Burns), **III:** 315

"Man Who Changes His Mind, The" (Ambler), **Supp. IV:** 5

"Man Who Could Work Miracles, The" (Wells), **VI:** 235

"Man Who Died, The" (Lawrence), **VII:** 115; **Retro. Supp. II:** 233

Man Who Loved Children, The (Stead), **Supp. IV:** 460, 467–470, 473

"Man Who Loved Islands, The" (Lawrence), **VII:** 115

"Man Who Walked on the Moon, The" (Ballard), **Supp. V:** 33

Man Who Walks, The (Warner), **Supp. XI:** 282, 287, 290–293

Man Who Was Thursday, The (Chesterton), **VI:** 338

Man Who Wasn't There, The (Barker), **Supp. IV:** 45, 46, 56–57

"Man with a Past, The" (Hardy), **VI:** 17

"Man with Night Sweats, The" (Gunn), **Supp. IV:** 276–277

Man with Night Sweats, The (Gunn), **Supp. IV:** 255, 257, 274–278

"Man with the Dog, The" (Jhabvala), **Supp. V:** 236

"Man with the Twisted Lip, The" (Doyle), **Supp. II:** 171

Man Within, The (Greene), **Supp. I:** 2; **Retro. Supp. II:** 152

"Man Without a Temperament, The" (Mansfield), **VII:** 174, 177

"Mana Aboda" (Hulme), **Supp. VI:** 136

Manalive (Chesterton), **VI:** 340

Mañanas de abril y mayo (Calderón), **II:** 312*n*

Manchester Enthusiasts, The (Arden and D'Arcy), **Supp. II:** 39

"Manchester Marriage, The" (Gaskell), **V:** 6*n*, 14, 15

Manciple's Prologue, The (Chaucer), **I:** 24

Manciple's Tale, The (Chaucer), **I:** 55

"Mandela" (Motion), **Supp. VII:** 266

Mandelbaum Gate, The (Spark), **Supp. I:** 206–208, 213

Mandelstam, Osip, **Supp. IV:** 163, 493

Manet, Edouard, **Supp. IV:** 480

Manfred (Byron), **III:** 338; **IV:** xvii, 172, 173, 177, 178–182, 192

Mangan Inheritance, The (Moore), **Supp. IX** 144, 148, 150–151, 153

Manhatten '45 (Morris, J.), **Supp. X:** 182

"Manhole 69" (Ballard), **Supp. V:** 21

"Manifesto" (Morgan, E.), **Supp. IX:** 163

Manifold, John, **VII:** 422, 426–427

Manin and the Venetian Revolution of 1848 (Trevelyan), **VI:** 389

Mankind in the Making (Wells), **VI:** 227, 236

Manly, J. M., **I:** 1

"Man–Man" (Naipaul), **Supp. I:** 385

Mann, Thomas, **II:** 97; **III:** 344; **Supp. IV:** 397

Manner of the World Nowadays, The (Skelton), **I:** 89

Mannerly Margery Milk and Ale (Skelton), **I:** 83

Manners, Mrs. Horace, pseud. of Algernon Charles Swinburne

"Manners, The" (Collins), **III:** 161, 162, 166, 171

Manning, Cardinal, **V:** 181

Manoeuvring (Edgeworth), **Supp. III:** 158

"Manor Farm, The" (Thomas), **Supp. III:** 399, 405

"Mans medley" (Herbert), **Retro. Supp. II:** 181–182

Manservant and Maidservant (Compton–Burnett), **VII:** 62, 63, 67

Mansfield, Katherine, **IV:** 106; **VI:** 375; **VII:** xv, xvii, 171–184, 314; list of short stories, **VII:** 183–184

Mansfield Park (Austen), **IV:** xvii, 102–103, 108, 109, 111, 112, 115–119, 122; **Retro. Supp. II:** 9–11

Mantissa (Fowles), **Supp. I:** 308–309, 310

Manto, Saadat Hasan, **Supp. IV:** 440

Mantz, Ruth, **VII:** 176

Manuel (Maturin), **VIII:** 207, 208

"Manus Animam Pinxit" (Thompson), **V:** 442

Many Dimensions (Williams, C. W. S.), **Supp. IX:** 281

Manzoni, Alessandro, **III:** 334

"Map, The" (Hart), **Supp. XI:** 130

Map, Walter, **I:** 35

Map of Love, The (Thomas), **Supp. I:** 176–177, 180

"Map of the City, A" (Gunn), **Supp. IV:** 262, 274

Map of the World, A (Hare), **Supp. IV:** 282, 288–289, 293

Map of Verona, A (Reed), **VII:** 423

Mapp Showing . . . Salvation and Damnation, A (Bunyan), **II:** 253

Mappings (Seth), **Supp. X:** 279–280

Mapplethorpe, Robert, **Supp. IV:** 170, 273

Mara, Bernard, *see* Moore, Brian

Marble Faun, The (Hawthorne), **VI:** 27

March of Literature, The (Ford), **VI:** 321, 322, 324

March Violets (Kerr), **Supp. XII:** 187, 188–189

"Marchese Pallavicini and Walter Landor" (Landor), **IV:** 90

Marching Soldier (Cary), **VII:** 186

"Marching to Zion" (Coppard), **VIII:** 91–92

"Marchioness of Stonehenge, The" (Hardy), **VI:** 22

Marconi's Cottage (McGuckian), **Supp. V:** 284, 286–287

Marcus, Jane, **Retro. Supp. I:** 306

Marcus, S., **V:** 46, 73

Marfan (Reading), **VIII:** 262, 274–275

Margaret Drabble: Puritanism and Permissiveness (Myer), **Supp. IV:** 233

Margaret Ogilvy (Barrie), **Supp. III:** 3

Margin Released (Priestley), **VII:** 209, 210, 211

Margoliouth, H. M., **II:** 214*n*, 219

Mari Magno (Clough), **V:** 159, 168

Maria; or, The Wrongs of Woman (Wollstonecraft), **Supp. III:** 466, 476–480

"Mariana" (Tennyson), **IV:** 329, 331

"Mariana in the South" (Tennyson), **IV:** 329, 331

Mariani, Paul L., **V:** 373*n*, 378, 382

Marianne Thornton (Forster), **VI:** 397, 411

Marie (Haggard), **Supp. III:** 214

Marinetti, Filippo T., **Supp. III:** 396

"Marina" (Eliot), **Retro. Supp. II:** 130

"Marine Lament" (Cameron), **Supp. IX:** 19

"Mariner's Compass, The" (Armitage), **VIII:** 11

Marino, Giambattista, **II:** 180, 183

Marino Faliero (Swinburne), **V:** 332

Marino Faliero, Doge of Venice (Byron), **IV:** xviii, 178–179, 193

Marion Fay (Trollope), **V:** 102

Marionette, The (Muir), **Supp. VI:** 198, 203–204

Marius the Epicurean (Pater), **V:** xxv, 339, 348, 349–351, 354, 355, 356, 411

Marjorie, **VI:** 249; pseud. of Arnold Bennett

"Mark of the Beast, The" (Kipling), **VI:** 183, 193

Mark of the Warrior, The (Scott), **Supp. I:** 263

Mark Only (Powys), **VIII:** 250–251

Markandaya, Kamala, **Supp. IV:** 440

"Markers" (Thomas), **Supp. XII:** 290

"Market at Turk" (Gunn), **Supp. IV:** 260–261

Market Bell, The (Powys), **VIII:** 251, 258

Market of Seleukia, The (Morris, J.), **Supp. X:** 175

"Market Square" (Milne), **Supp. V:** 302

Markey, Constance, **Supp. IV:** 347, 360

Markham, Robert, **Supp. II:** 12; pseud. of Kingsley Amis

"Markheim" (Stevenson), **V:** 395; **Retro. Supp. I:** 267

Marking Time (Howard), **Supp. XI:** 145, 146, 147, 148

"Mark–2 Wife, The" (Trevor), **Supp. IV:** 503

Marlborough: His Life and Times (Churchill), **VI:** 354–355

Marlowe, Christopher, **I:** 212, 228–229, 275–294, 336; **II:** 69, 138; **III:** 344; **IV:** 255, 327; **Supp. IV:** 197; **Retro. Supp. I:** 199–213

Marlowe and His Circle (Boas), **I:** 275, 293

Marlowe and the Early Shakespeare (Wilson), **I:** 286

Marmion (Scott), **IV:** xvi, 29, 30, 38, 129

Marmor Norfolciense (Johnson), **III:** 121; **Retro. Supp. I:** 141

Marquise, The (Coward), **Supp. II:** 146

"Marriage, A" (Thomas), **Supp. XII:** 290

Marriage A–la–Mode (Dryden), **II:** 293, 296, 305

Marriage of Heaven and Hell, The (Blake), **III:** 289, 297–298, 304, 307; **V:** xv, 329–330, 331; **Supp. IV:** 448; **Retro. Supp. I:** 38–39

Marriage of Mona Lisa, The (Swinburne), **V:** 333

"Marriage of Tirzah and Ahirad, The" (Macaulay), **IV:** 283

Marriages Between Zones Three, Four and Five, The (Lessing), **Supp. I:** 251

Married Life (Bennett), *see Plain Man and His Wife, The*

Married Man, The (Lawrence), **VII:** 120

"Married Man's Story, A" (Mansfield), **VII:** 174

Married to a Spy (Waugh), **Supp. VI:** 276

Marryat, Captain Frederick, **Supp. IV:** 201

Marsh, Charles, **Supp. IV:** 214, 218

Marsh, Edward, **VI:** 416, 419, 420, 425, 430, 432, 452; **VII:** xvi; **Supp. III:** 47, 48, 53, 54, 60, 397

"Marsh of Ages, The" (Cameron), **Supp. IX:** 19

Marshall, William, **II:** 141

Marston, John, **I:** 234, 238, 340; **II:** 4, 24–33, 34–37, 40–41, 47, 68, 72; **Retro. Supp. I:** 160

Marston, Philip, **V:** 245

Marston, R. B., **II:** 131

Martha Quest (Lessing), **Supp. I:** 237, 239, 243–244; **Supp. IV:** 238

Martial, **II:** 104, 265

Martian, The (du Maurier), **Supp. III:** 134, 151

"Martian Sends a Postcard Home, A" (Cope), **VIII:** 74

Martin, John, **V:** 110

Martin, L. C., **II:** 183, 184n, 200

Martin, Martin, **III:** 117

Martin Chuzzlewit (Dickens), **V:** xx, 42, 47, 54–56, 58, 59, 68, 71; **Supp. IV:** 366, 381

Martin Chuzzlewit (teleplay, Lodge), **Supp. IV:** 366, 381

Martin Luther (Lopez and Moore), **VI:** 85, 95, 98

Martineau, Harriet, **IV:** 311; **V:** 125–126, 146

Martyn, Edward, **VI:** 309

Martyrdom of Man (Reade), **Supp. IV:** 2

"Martyrs' Song" (Rossetti), **V:** 256

Martz, Louis, **V:** 366, 382

Marvell, Andrew, **II:** 113, 121, 123, 166, 195–199, **204–220,** 255, 261; **Supp. III:** 51, 56; **Supp. IV:** 271; **Retro. Supp. II:** 253–268

Marvell and the Civic Crown (Patterson), **Retro. Supp. II:** 265

Marwick, A., **IV:** 290, 291

Marwood, Arthur, **VI:** 323, 331

Marxism, **Supp. I:** 24–25, 26, 30, 31, 238

Mary, A Fiction (Wollstonecraft), **Supp. III:** 466, 476

"Mary and Gabriel" (Brooke), **Supp. III:** 55

Mary Anne (du Maurier), **Supp. III:** 137

Mary Barton (Gaskell), **V:** viii, x, xxi, 1, 2, 4–5, 6, 15

"Mary Burnet" (Hogg), **Supp. X:** 110

"'Mary Gloster', The," (Kipling), **VI:** 202

Mary Gresley (Trollope), **V:** 101

"Mary Postgate" (Kipling), **VI:** 197, 206

"Mary Queen of Scots" (Swinburne), **V:** 332

Mary Rose (Barrie), **Supp. III:** 8, 9

"Mary Shelley on Broughty Ferry Beach" (Crawford), **Supp. XI:** 74

Mary Stuart (Swinburne), **V:** 330, 332

"Mary the Cook–Maid's Letter . . . " (Swift), **III:** 31

"Mary's Magnificat" (Jennings), **Supp. V:** 217

mas v. Mastermind (Ayckbourn), **Supp. V:** 2

"Masculine Birth of Time, The" (Bacon), **I:** 263

Masculinity (Crawford), **Supp. XI:** 67, 74–76

Masefield, John, **VI:** 429; **VII:** xii, xiii

Mask of Apollo (Renault), **Supp. IX:** 183–184, 187

Mask of Apollo and Other Stories, The (Russell), **VIII:** 285

Mask of Dimitrios, The (Ambler), **Supp. IV:** 21

"Mask of Love" (Kinsella), **Supp. V:** 262

Masks (Brathwaite), **Supp. XII:** 33, 38–39

Mason, William, **III:** 141, 142, 145

"Masque, The" (Auden), **Retro. Supp. I:** 11

"Masque of Anarchy, The" (Shelley), **IV:** xviii, 202–203, 206, 208; **Retro. Supp. I:** 253–254

Masque of Blackness, The (Jonson), **Retro. Supp. I:** 161–162

Masque of Queenes (Jonson), **II:** 111n; **Retro. Supp. I:** 162

Masque of the Manuscript, The (Williams, C. W. S.), **Supp. IX:** 276

Masqueraders, The (Haywood), **Supp. XII:** 135

Mass and the English Reformers, The (Dugmore), **I:** 177n

Mass for Hard Times (Thomas), **Supp. XII:** 285, 290–291

"Mass for Hard Times" (Thomas), **Supp. XII:** 290, 291

Massacre at Paris, The (Marlowe), **I:** 249, 276, 279–280, **285–286; Retro. Supp. I:** 211

Massinger, Philip, **II:** 44, 45, 50, 66–67, 69, 83, 87; **Supp. XI:** 179–194

Masson, David, **IV:** 212, 235

Masson, Rosaline, **V:** 393, 397

"Mastectomy" (Boland), **Supp. V:** (Boland), **Supp. V:** 49

Master, The (Brontë), *see Professor, The*

"Master, The" (Wilde), **Retro. Supp. II:** 371

Master and Commander (O'Brian), **Supp. XII:** 252–254, 256, 257

Master and Margarita, The (Bulgakov), **Supp. IV:** 448

Master Georgie (Bainbridge), **Supp. VI:** 26–27

Master Humphrey's Clock (Dickens), **V:** 42, 53–54, 71

"Master John Horseleigh, Knight" (Hardy), **VI:** 22

Master of Ballantrae, The (Stevenson), **V:** 383–384, 387, 396; **Retro. Supp. I:** 268–269

Master of Petersburg, The (Coetzee), **Supp. VI:** 75–76, **85–86,** 88

Master of the House, The (Hall), **Supp. VI:** 120, 122, 128

Masterman, C. F. G., **VI:** viii, 320

Masters, John, **Supp. IV:** 440

Masters, The (Snow), **VII:** xxi, 327–328, 330

"Match, The" (Marvell), **II:** 211

Match for the Devil, A (Nicholson), **Supp. VI:** **222**

"Match–Maker, The" (Saki), **Supp. VI:** 240

"Mater Dolorosa" (Swinburne), **V:** 325

"Mater Triumphalis" (Swinburne), **V:** 325

Materials for a Description of Capri (Douglas), **VI:** 305

Mathilda (Shelley), **Supp. III:** **363–364**

"Mathilda's England" (Trevor), **Supp. IV:** 504

Matigari (Ngũgĩ), **VIII:** 215, 216, 221–222

Matilda (Dahl), **Supp. IV:** 203, 207, 226

Matilda (film), **Supp. IV:** 203

Matisse, Henri, **Supp. IV:** 81, 154

Matisse Stories, The (Byatt), **Supp. IV:** 151, 154–155

Matlock's System (Hill), *see Heart Clock*

"Matres Dolorosae" (Bridges), **VI:** 81

"Matron" (Blackwood), **Supp. IX:** 12

"Mattens" (Herbert), **II:** 127; **Retro. Supp. II:** 179

"Matter of Fact, A" (Kipling), **VI:** 193

Matter of Wales: Epic Views of a Small Country, The (Morris), *see Wales: Epic Views of a Small Country*

Matthew Arnold: A Study in Conflict (Brown), **V:** 211–212, 217

Matthew Arnold: A Symposium (ed. Allott), **V:** 218

Matthews, Geoffrey Maurice, **IV:** x, xxv, 207, 208, 209, 237

Matthews, William, **I:** 68

Matthiessen, F. O., **V:** 204

Matthieu de Vendôme, **I:** 23, 39–40

"Mature Art" (MacDiarmid), **Supp. XII:** 214

Maturin, Charles, **III:** 327, 331, 333–334, 336, 345; **VIII:** 197–210; **Supp. III:** 384

Maud (Tennyson), **IV:** xxi, 325, 328, 330–331, 333–336, 337, 338; **VI:** 420

Maude: A Story for Girls (Rossetti), **V:** 260

"Maud-Evelyn" (James), **VI:** 69

Maugham, Syrie, **VI:** 369

Maugham, W. Somerset, **VI:** xi, xiii, 200, **363–381; VII:** 318–319; list of short stories and sketches, **VI:** 379–381; **Supp. II:** 7, 141, 156–157; **Supp. IV:** 9–10, 21, 500

Maumbury Ring (Hardy), **VI:** 20

Maupassant, Guy de, **III:** 340, **Supp. IV:** 500

Maurice (Forster), **VI:** xii, 397, **407–408,** 412; **Retro. Supp. II:** 145–146

Maurice, Frederick D., **IV:** 54; **V:** xxi, 284, 285

Mauritius Command, The (O'Brian), **Supp. XII:** 256, 258

Mavis Belfrage (Gray, A.), **Supp. IX:** 80, 91

Max in Verse (Beerbohm), **Supp. II:** 44

Maxfield, James F., **Supp. IV:** 336

May Day (Chapman), **I:** 244

"May Day, 1937" (Nicholson), **Supp. VI:** 214

"May Day Song for North Oxford" (Betjeman), **VII:** 356

"May 23" (Thomas), **Supp. III:** 405

Maybe Day in Kazakhstan, A (Harrison), **Supp. V:** 164

"Mayday in Holderness" (Hughes), **Supp. I:** 344

Mayer, Carl, **III:** 342

"Mayfly" (MacNeice), **VII:** 411

Mayo, Robert, **IV:** ix

"Mayo Monologues" (Longley), **VIII:** 174

Mayor of Casterbridge: The Life and Death of a Man of Character, The (Hardy), **VI:** 3, 5, 7, 8, 9–10, 20

Maze Plays (Ayckbourn), **Supp. V:** 12

Mazeppa (Byron), **IV:** xvii, 173, 192

Mazzini, Giuseppi, **V:** 313, 314, 324, 325

Me, I'm Afraid of Virginia Woolf (Bennett), **VIII:** 27

Me, Myself, and I (Ayckbourn), **Supp. V:** 13

Meaning of Meaning, The (Richards and Ogden), **Supp. II:** 405, 408, **410–411,** 414

"Meaning of the Wild Body, The" (Lewis), **VII:** 77

Meaning of Treason, The (West), **Supp. III:** 440, 445

Measure for Measure (Shakespeare), **I:** 313–314, 327; **II:** 30, 70, 168; **V:** 341, 351

Measures, (MacCaig), **Supp. VI: 188–189,** 194

"Meat, The" (Galloway), **Supp. XII:** 121

"Mechanical Genius, The" (Naipaul), **Supp. I:** 385

Mechanical Womb, The (Orton), **Supp. V:** 364

Medal: A Satyre Against Sedition, The (Dryden), **II:** 299, 304

Medea (Seneca), **II:** 71

Medea: A Sex–War Opera (Harrison), **Supp. V:** 164

"Medico's Song" (Wallace–Crabbe), **VIII:** 324

Medieval Heritage of Elizabethan Tragedy (Farnham), **I:** 214

"Meditation of Mordred, The" (Williams, C. W. S.), **Supp. IX:** 283

Meditation upon a Broom–Stick, A (Swift), **III:** 35

"Meditation with Mountains" (Wallace–Crabbe), **VIII:** 317–318

Meditations Collected from the Sacred Books . . . (Richardson), **III:** 92

"Meditations in Time of Civil War" (Yeats), **V:** 317; **VII:** 24; **Retro. Supp. I:** 334–335

Meditations of Daniel Defoe, The (Defoe), **III:** 12

"Meditations with Memories" (Wallace–Crabbe), **VIII:** 317

"Mediterranean" (Redgrove), **Supp. VI:** 231

Mediterranean Scenes (Bennett), **VI:** 264, 267

"Medussa's Ankles" (Byatt), **Supp. IV:** 154–155

Medwin, Thomas, **IV:** 196, 209

Mee, Arthur, **Supp. IV:** 256

Meet My Father (Ayckbourn), **Supp. V:** 2

"Meet Nurse!" (Hope), **Supp. VII:** 151

Meeting by the River, A (Isherwood), **VII:** 317

"Meeting My Former Self" (Cameron), **Supp. IX:** 24

Meeting the British (Muldoon), **Supp. IV:** 421–424

Meeting the Comet (Adcock), **Supp. XII:** 8

"Melancholia" (Bridges), **VI:** 80

"Melancholy" (Bridges), **VI:** 80

"Melancholy Hussar of the German Legion, The" (Hardy), **VI:** 20, 22; **Retro. Supp. I:** 116

"Melbourne" (Wallace–Crabbe), **VIII:** 313

"Melbourne in 1963" (Wallace–Crabbe), **VIII:** 313–314

Melbourne or the Bush (Wallace–Crabbe), **VIII:** 313–314, 319, 320

Melchiori, Giorgio, **VI:** 208

Meleager (Euripides), **V:** 322, 323

Melincourt (Peacock), **IV:** xvii, 162, 163–164, 165, 168, 170

Melly, Diana, **Supp. IV:** 168

Melmoth Reconciled (Balzac), **III:** 334, 339

Melmoth the Wanderer (Maturin), **III:** 327, 333–334, 335, 345; **VIII:** 197–200, 201–205, 208–209; **Supp. III:** 384–385

Melnikov, Konstantin, **Supp. IV:** 174

"Melon" (Barnes), **Supp. IV:** 75

Melville, Herman, **IV:** 97; **V:** xvii, xx–xxi, xxv, 211; **VI:** 363; **Supp. IV:** 160

Memento Mori (Spark), **Supp. I:** 203

"Memoir" (Scott), **IV:** 28, 30, 35–36, 39

"Memoir of Bernard Barton" (FitzGerald), **IV:** 353

"Memoir of Cowper: An Autobiography" (ed. Quinlan), **III:** 220

"Memoir"of Fleeming Jenkin (Stevenson), **V:** 386, 395

Memoir of Jane Austen (Austen–Leigh), **III:** 90

"Memoir of My Father, A" (Amis), **Supp. II:** 1

Memoir of the Author's Life and Familiar Anecdotes of Sir Walter Scott (Hogg), **Supp. X:** 105

Memoir of the Bobotes (Cary), **VII:** 185

Mémoire justificatif etc. (Gibbon), **III:** 233

Mémoires littéraires de la Grande Bretagne (periodical), **III:** 233

Memoirs (Amis), **Supp. IV:** 27

Memoirs (Temple), **III:** 19

Memoirs of a Cavalier, The (Defoe), **III:** 6, 13; **VI:** 353, 359; **Retro. Supp. I:** 66, 68, 71–72

Memoirs of a Certain Island Adjacent to the Kingdom of Utopia (Haywood), **Supp. XII:** 135, 141

Memoirs of a Midget (de la Mare), **III:** 340, 345

Memoirs of a Physician, The (Dumas père), **III:** 332

Memoirs of a Protestant, The (tr. Goldsmith), **III:** 191

Memoirs of a Survivor, The (Lessing), **Supp. I:** 249–250, 254

Memoirs of Barry Lyndon, Esq., The (Thackeray), *see Barry Lyndon*

Memoirs of Doctor Burney (Burney), **Supp. III:** 68

Memoirs of Himself (Stevenson), **V:** 396

"Memoirs of James Boswell, Esq." (Boswell), **III:** 248

Memoirs of Jonathan Swift (Scott), **IV:** 38

Memoirs of Lord Byron, The (Nye), **Supp. X:** 195–196

Memoirs of Martin Scriblerus, (Pope), **III:** 24, 77; **Retro. Supp. I:** 234

"Memoirs of M. de Voltaire" (Goldsmith), **III:** 189

Memoirs of My Dead Life (Moore), **VI:** 87, 88, 95, 96, 97, 98–99

"Memoirs of Percy Bysshe Shelley" (Peacock), **IV:** 158, 169, 170

Memoirs of the Author of A Vindication of the Rights of Woman (Godwin), **Supp. III:** 465

Memoirs of the Baron de Brosse (Haywood), **Supp. XII:** 135

Memoirs of the Late Thomas Holcroft . . . (Hazlitt), **IV:** 128, 139

Memoirs of the Life of Edward Gibbon, The (ed. Hill), **III:** 221n, 233

Memoirs of the Life of Sir Walter Scott, Bart. (Lockhart), **IV:** 27, 30, 34, 35–36, 39

Memoirs of the Life of William Collins, Esp., R.A. (1848) (Collins), **Supp. VI:** 92, 95

Memoirs of the Navy (Pepys), **II:** 281, 288

"Memoirs of the World" (Gunn), **Supp. IV:** 264

Memoirs Relating to . . . Queen Anne's Ministry (Swift), **III:** 27

"Memorabilia" (Browning), **IV:** 354–355

Memorable Masque of the Middle Temple and Lincoln's Inn, The (Chapman), **I:** 235

Memorial, The (Isherwood), **VII:** 205, 310–311

"Memorial for the City" (Auden), **VII:** 388, 393; **Retro. Supp. I:** 8

Memorials of a Tour on the Continent (Wordsworth), **IV:** 24–25

Memorials of Edward Burne–Jones (Burne–Jones), **V:** 295–296, 306

"Memorials of Gormandising"
(Thackeray), **V:** 23, 24, 38

Memorials of Thomas Hood (Hood and
Broderip), **IV:** 251, 261, 267

*Memorials of Two Sisters, Susanna and
Catherine Winkworth* (ed. Shaen), **V:**
149

Memories and Adventures (Doyle), **Supp.
II:** 159

Memories and Hallucinations (Thomas),
Supp. IV: 479, 480, 482, 483, 484,
486

Memories and Portraits (Stevenson), **V:**
390, 395

"Memories of a Catholic Childhood"
(Lodge), **Supp. IV:** 363–364

"Memories of a Working Women's Guild"
(Woolf), **Retro. Supp. I:** 311

Memories of the Space Age (Ballard),
Supp. V: 24

"Memories of the Space Age" (Ballard),
Supp. V: 33

Memories of Vailiona (Osborne and
Strong), **V:** 393, 397

"Memories of Youghal" (Trevor), **Supp.
IV:** 501

"Memory, A" (Brooke), **Supp. III:** 55

"Memory and Imagination" (Dunn),
Supp. X: 77

"Memory Man" (Ewart), **Supp. VII:** 41

*Memory of Ben Jonson Revived by the
Friends of the Muses, The* (Digby),
Retro. Supp. I: 166

"Memory Unsettled" (Gunn), **Supp. IV:**
277

"Men and Their Boring Arguments"
(Cope), **VIII:** 78

Men and Wives (Compton–Burnett), **VII:**
64, 65, 66–67

Men and Women (Browning), **IV:** xiii,
xxi, 357, 363, 374; **Retro. Supp. II:**
26, 27–28

Men at Arms (Waugh), **VII:** 304; *see also
Sword of Honour* trilogy

Men Like Gods (Wells), **VI:** 226 240 244;
VII: 204

Men on Women on Men (Ayckbourn),
Supp. V: 3

"Men Sign the Sea" (Graham), **Supp.
VII:** 110

"Men Who March Away" (Hardy), **VI:**
415, 421; **Retro. Supp. I:** 120

"Men With Coats Thrashing" (Lowry),
Supp. III: 283

Men Without Art (Lewis), **VII:** 72, 76

"Menace, The" (du Maurier), **Supp. III:**
139

"Menace, The" (Gunn), **Supp. IV:** 261

Menand, Louis, **Supp. IV:** 305

Mendelson, Edward, **Retro. Supp. I:** 12

"Menelaus and Helen" (Brooke), **Supp.
III:** 52

Menaphon (Greene), **I:** 165; **VIII:** 135,
138–139, 143

Mencius on the Mind (Richards), **Supp.
II:** 421

Men-of-War: Life in Nelson's Navy
(O'Brian), **Supp. XII:** 255

Men's Wives (Thackeray), **V:** 23, 35, 38

"Mental Cases" (Owen), **VI:** 456, 457

Mental Efficiency (Bennett), **VI:** 250, 266

Merchant of Venice, The (Shakespeare),
I: 310

Merchant's Tale, The (Chaucer), **I:** 36,
41–42

Mercian Hymns (Hill), **Supp. V:** 187,
189, 194–196

Mercier and Camier (Beckett), **Supp. I:**
50–51; **Retro. Supp. I:** 21

"Mercury and the Elephant" (Finch),
Supp. IX: 71–72

"Mercy" (Collins), **III:** 166

Mer de Glace (Meale and Malouf), **Supp.
XII:** 218

Mere Accident, A (Moore), **VI:** 86, 91

Mere Christianity (Lewis), **Supp. III:**
248

"Mere Interlude, A" (Hardy), **VI:** 22

Meredith (Sassoon), **V:** 219, 234

Meredith, George, **II:** 104, 342, 345; **IV:**
160; **V:** x, xviii, xxii–xxvi, **219–234,**
244, 432; **VI:** 2

Meredith, H. O., **VI:** 399

Meredith et la France (Mackay), **V:** 223,
234

"Meredithian Sonnets" (Fuller), **Supp.
VII:** 74

Meres, Francis, **I:** 212, 234, 296, 307

Merie Tales, The, **I:** 83, 93

Meriton, George, **II:** 340

Merkin, Daphne, **Supp. IV:** 145–146

Merleau–Ponty, Maurice, **Supp. IV:** 79,
88

Merlin (Nye), **Supp. X:** 195

"Merlin and the Gleam" (Tennyson), **IV:**
329

Mermaid, Dragon, Fiend (Graves), **VII:**
264

Merope (Arnold), **V:** 209, 216

"Merry Beggars, The" (Brome), **Supp.
X:** 55

Merry England (periodical), **V:** 440

Merry Jests of George Peele, The, **I:** 194

*Merry Men, and Other Tales and Fables,
The* (Stevenson), **V:** 395; **Retro. Supp.
I:** 267

Merry Wives of Windsor, The
(Shakespeare), **I:** 295, 311; **III:** 117

Merry–Go–Round, The (Lawrence), **VII:**
120

Merry–Go–Round, The (Maugham), **VI:**
372

Mescellanies (Fielding), **Retro. Supp. I:**
80

Meschonnic, Henri, **Supp. IV:** 115

Mespoulet, M., **V:** 266

"Message, The" (Donne), **Retro. Supp.
II:** 90

"Message, The" (Russell), **VIII:** 280–281

"Message Clear" (Morgan, E.), **Supp. IX:**
165

"Message from Mars, The" (Ballard),
Supp. V: 33

Messages (Fernandez), **V:** 225–226

"Messdick" (Ross), **VII:** 433

Messenger, The (Kinsella), **Supp. V:** 269–
270

"M. E. T." (Thomas), **Supp. III:** 401

"Metamorphoses" (Malouf), **Supp. XII:**
220

Metamorphoses (Ovid), **III:** 54; **V:** 321;
Retro. Supp. II: 36, 215

Metamorphoses (Sisson), **Supp. XI:** 249

Metamorphosis (Kafka), **III:** 340, 345

Metamorphosis of Pygmalion's Image
(Marston), **I:** 238; **II:** 25, 40

"Metaphor Now Standing at Platform 8,
The" (Armitage), **VIII:** 5–6

"Metaphorical Gymnasia" (Dutton),
Supp. XII: 97

*Metaphysical Lyrics and Poems of the
Seventeenth Century* (Grierson),
Retro. Supp. II: 173

Metempsycosis: Poêma Satyricon
(Donne), **Retro. Supp. II:** 94

"Methinks the poor Town has been
troubled too long" (Dorset), **II:** 262

"Method. For Rongald Gaskell" (Davie),
Supp. VI: 106

Metrical Tales and Other Poems
(Southey), **IV:** 71

Metroland (Barnes), **Supp. IV:** 65, 66–
67, 71, 76

Mew, Charlotte, **Supp. V:** 97, 98–99

Meynell, Wilfred, **V:** 440, 451

MF (Burgess), **Supp. I:** 197

"Mianserin Sonnets" (Fuller), **Supp. VII:**
79

Micah Clark (Doyle), **Supp. II:** 159, 163

"Michael" (Wordsworth), **IV:** 8, 18–19

Michael and Mary (Milne), **Supp. V:** 299

Michael Robartes and the Dancer (Yeats),
VI: 217; **Retro. Supp. I:** 331–333

"Michael X and the Black Power Killings in Trinidad" (Naipaul), **Supp. I:**
396

Michaelmas Term (Middleton), **II:** 3, 4,
21

Michelet, Jules, **V:** 346

Microcosmography (Earle), **IV:** 286

Micro–Cynicon, Six Snarling Satires
(Middleton), **II:** 2–3

Midas (Lyly), **I:** 198, 202, 203

"Middle Age" (Dunn), **Supp. X:** 80

Middle Age of Mrs Eliot, The (Wilson),
Supp. I: 160–161

Middle Ground, The (Drabble), **Supp. IV:**
230, 231, 234, 246–247, 248

Middle Mist, The (Renault), see *Friendly
Young Ladies, The*

"Middle of a War" (Fuller), **VII:** 429;
Supp. VII: 69

Middle Passage, The (Naipaul), **Supp. I:**
386, 390–391, 393, 403

"Middle–Sea and Lear–Sea" (Jones),
Supp. VII: 176

Middle Years, The (James), **VI:** 65, 69

"Middle Years, The" (Ewart), **Supp. VII:**
39

"Middle Years, The" (James), **VI:** 69

Middlemarch (Eliot), **III:** 157; **V:** ix–x,
xxiv, 196–197, 200; **Supp. IV:** 243;
Retro. Supp. II: 113–114

Middlemen: A Satire, The (Brooke–
Rose), **Supp. IV:** 99, 103

Middleton, D., **V:** 253

Middleton, Thomas, **II:** **1–23,** 30, 33, 68–
70, 72, 83, 85, 93, 100; **IV:** 79

Midnight All Day (Kureishi), **Supp. XI:**
158

"Midnight Hour, The" (Powys), **VIII:** 256

Midnight Oil (Pritchett), **Supp. III:** 312, 313

Midnight on the Desert (Priestley), **VII:** 209, 212

"Midnight Skaters, The" (Blunden), **VI:** 429; **Supp. XI:** 45

Midnight's Children (Rushdie), **Supp. IV:** 162, 433, 435, 436, 438, 439–444, 445, 448, 449, 456; **Supp. V:** 67, 68

"Midsummer Cushion, The" (Clare), **Supp. XI:** 60

"Midsummer Holiday, A, and Other Poems" (Swinburne), **V:** 332

"Midsummer Ice" (Murray), **Supp. VII:** 278

Midsummer Night's Dream, A (Shakespeare), **I:** 304–305, 311–312; **II:** 51, 281; **Supp. IV:** 198

"Mid–Term Break" (Heaney), **Retro. Supp. I:** 125

Mid–Victorian Memories (Francillon), **V:** 83

Mightier Than the Sword (Ford), **VI:** 320–321

Mighty and Their Full, The (Compton–Burnett), **VII:** 61, 62

Mighty Magician, The (FitzGerald), **IV:** 353

"Migrants" (Thomas), **Supp. XII:** 290

Miguel Street (Naipaul), **Supp. I:** 383, 385–386

"Mike: A Public School Story" (Wodehouse), **Supp. III:** 449

Mike Fletcher (Moore), **VI:** 87, 91

"Mildred Lawson" (Moore), **VI:** 98

Milesian Chief, The (Maturin), **VIII:** 201, 207

Milestones (Bennett), **VI:** 250, 263, 264

Milford, H., **III:** 208n

"Milford: East Wing" (Murphy), **Supp. V:** 328

Military Memoirs of Capt. George Carleton, The (Defoe), **III:** 14

Military Philosophers, The (Powell), **VII:** 349

"Milk–cart, The" (Morgan, E.), **Supp. IX:** 168

"Milk–Wort and Bog–Cotton" (MacDiarmid), **Supp. XII:** 212

Mill, James, **IV:** 159; **V:** 288

Mill, John Stuart, **IV:** 50, 56, 246, 355; **V:** xxi–xxii, xxiv, 182, 279, 288, 343

Mill on the Floss, The (Eliot), **V:** xxii, 14, 192–194, 200; **Supp. IV:** 240, 471; **Retro. Supp. II:** 106–108

Millais, John Everett, **V:** 235, 236, 379

Miller, Arthur, **VI:** 286

Miller, Henry, **Supp. IV:** 110–111

Miller, J. Hillis, **VI:** 147

Miller, Karl, **Supp. IV:** 169

"Miller's Daughter, The" (Tennyson), **IV:** 326

Miller's Tale, The (Chaucer), **I:** 37

Millet, Jean François, **Supp. IV:** 90

Millett, Kate, **Supp. IV:** 188

Millionairess, The (Shaw), **VI:** 102, 127

"Millom Cricket Field" (Nicholson), **Supp. VI:** 216

"Millom Old Quarry" (Nicholson), **Supp. VI:** 216

Mills, C. M., pseud. of Elizabeth Gaskell

Millstone, The (Drabble), **Supp. IV:** 230, 237–238

Milne, A. A., **Supp. V: 295–312**

"Milnes, Richard Monckton" (Lord Houghton), *see* Monckton Milnes, Richard

Milton (Blake), **III:** 303–304, 307; **V:** xvi 330; **Retro. Supp. I:** 45

Milton (Meredith), **V:** 234

"Milton" (Macaulay), **IV:** 278, 279

Milton, Edith, **Supp. IV:** 305–306

Milton in America (Ackroyd), **Supp. VI: 11–12,** 13

Milton, John, **II:** 50–52, 113, **158–178,** 195, 196, 198, 199, 205, 206, 236, 302; **III:** 43, 118–119, 167n, 211n, 220, 302; **IV:** 9, 11–12, 14, 22, 23, 93, 95, 185, 186, 200, 205, 229, 269, 278, 279, 352; **V:** 365–366; **Supp. III:** 169; **Retro. Supp. II: 269–289**

Milton's God (Empson), **Supp. II:** 180, **195–196**

Milton's Prosody (Bridges), **VI:** 83

Mimic Men, The (Naipaul), **Supp. I:** 383, 386, 390, 392, 393–394, 395, 399

"Mina Laury" (Brontë), **V:** 122, 123, 149, 151

Mind at the End of Its Tether (Wells), **VI:** xiii; **VI:** 228, 242

Mind Has Mountains, The (Jennings), **Supp. V:** 213, 215–216

Mind in Chains, The (ed. Day Lewis), **Supp. III:** 118

"Mind Is Its Own Place, The" (Wallace–Crabbe), **VIII:** 316

Mind of the Maker, The (Sayers), **Supp. III:** 345, 347

Mind to Murder, A (James), **Supp. IV:** 319, 321, 323–324

Mind's Eye, The (Blunden), **Supp. XI:** 35

"Mine old dear enemy, my froward master" (Wyatt), **I:** 105

"Miner's Hut" (Murphy), **Supp. V:** 328

"Miners" (Owen), **VI:** 452, 454

"Minerva's Bird, Athene Noctua" (Thomas), **Supp. XII:** 289

"Minimal" (Dutton), **Supp. XII:** 90, 91

Minister, The (Thomas), **Supp. XII:** 283, 284

Ministry of Fear, The (Greene), **Supp. I:** 10–11, 12; **Retro. Supp. II:** 157

Minor Poems of Robert Southey, The (Southey), **IV:** 71

Minpins, The (Dahl), **Supp. IV:** 204, 224

Minstrel, The (Beattie), **IV:** 198

Minstrelsy of the Scottish Border (ed. Scott), **IV:** 29, 39

"Mint" (Heaney), **Retro. Supp. I:** 133

Mint, The (Lawrence), **Supp. II:** 283, **291–294**

Minute by Glass Minute (Stevenson), **Supp. VI:** 261

Minute for Murder (Day Lewis), **Supp. III:** 130

"Minutes of Glory" (Ngũgĩ), **VIII:** 220

Minutes of the Negotiations of Monsr. Mesnager, . . . (Defoe), **III:** 13

"Mirabeau" (Macaulay), **IV:** 278

"Miracle Cure" (Lowbury), **VII:** 432

Miracles (Lewis), **Supp. III:** 248, 255, 258–259

"Miraculous Issue, The" (Dutton), **Supp. XII:** 89

Mirèio (Mistral), **V:** 219

Mirour de l'omme (Gower), **I:** 48, 49

Mirror for Magistrates, The, **I:** 162, 214

"Mirror in February" (Kinsella), **Supp. V:** 262

Mirror of the Sea: Memories and Impressions, The (Conrad), **VI:** 138, 148

Mirror Wall, The (Murphy), **Supp. V:** 313, 329–330

Mirrour; or, Looking–Glasse Both for Saints and Sinners, A (Clarke), **II:** 251

Misadventures of John Nicholson, The (Stevenson), **V:** 396

Misalliance (Shaw), **VI:** xv, 115, 117, 118, 120, 129; **Retro. Supp. II:** 321

Misalliance, The (Brookner), **Supp. IV:** 129

Misanthrope, The (tr. Harrison), **Supp. V:** 149–150, 163

"Misanthropos" (Gunn), **Supp. IV:** 264–265, 268, 270

"Misapprehension" (Traherne), **Supp. XI:** 266

Miscellanea (Temple), **III:** 40

Miscellaneous Essays (St. Évremond), **III:** 47

Miscellaneous Observations on the Tragedy of Macbeth (Johnson), **III:** 108, 116, 121

Miscellaneous Poems (Marvell), **II:** 207

Miscellaneous Studies (Pater), **V:** 348, 357

Miscellaneous Works of the Duke of Buckingham, **II:** 268

Miscellaneous Works . . . with Memoirs of His Life (Gibbon), **III:** 233

Miscellanies (Cowley), **II:** 198

Miscellanies (Pope and Swift), **II:** 335

Miscellanies (Swinburne), **V:** 332

Miscellanies; A Serious Address to the People of Great Britain (Fielding), **III:** 105

Miscellanies, Aesthetic and Literary . . . (Coleridge), **IV:** 56

Miscellany (Tonson), **III:** 69

Miscellany of New Poems, A (Behn), **Supp. III:** 36

Miscellany Poems (Wycherley), **II:** 321

Miscellany Poems, on Several Occasions (Finch), **Supp. IX:** 65, 67, 74, 77

Miscellany Tracts (Browne), **II:** 156

Mischmasch (Carroll), **V:** 274

"Mise Eire" (Boland), **Supp. V:** 45–46

Miser, The (Fielding), **III:** 105

"Miser and the Poet, The" (Finch), **Supp. IX:** 72–74

"Miserie" (Herbert), **II:** 128–129

Miseries of War, The (Ralegh), **I:** 158

Misfortunes of Arthur, The (Hughes), **I:** 218

Misfortunes of Elphin, The (Peacock), **IV:** xviii, 163, 167–168, 170

Mishan, E. J., **VI:** 240

"Misplaced Attachment of Mr. John Dounce, The" (Dickens), **V:** 46

"Miss Brill" (Mansfield), **VII:** 175

Miss Gomez and the Brethren (Trevor), **Supp. IV:** 507, 508–509

"Miss Gunton of Poughkeepsie" (James), **VI:** 69

Miss Herbert (The Suburban Wife) (Stead), **Supp. IV:** 473, 476

"Miss Kilmansegg and Her Precious Leg" (Hood), **IV:** 258–259

Miss Lucy in Town (Fielding), **III:** 105

Miss Mackenzie (Trollope), **V:** 101

Miss Marjoribanks (Oliphant), **Supp. X:** 214, 216–217, 219–220

Miss Marple's Last Case (Christie), **Supp. II:** 125

Miss Ogilvy Finds Herself (Hall), **Supp. VI:** 120–121, 128

"Miss Ogilvy Finds Herself" (Hall), **Supp. VI:** 121

"Miss Pulkinhorn" (Golding), **Supp. I:** 78–79, 80

"Miss Smith" (Trevor), **Supp. IV:** 502, 510

Miss Stuart's Legacy (Steel), **Supp. XII:** 269–270, 271

"Miss Tickletoby's Lectures on English History" (Thackeray), **V:** 38

"Miss Twye" (Ewart), **Supp. VII:** 36

"Missing" (Cornford), **VIII:** 1141

"Missing, The" (Gunn), **Supp. IV:** 276

"Missing Dates" (Empson), **Supp. II:** 184, 190

Mistake, The (Vanbrugh), **II:** 325, 333, 336

Mistakes, The (Harris), **II:** 305

Mistakes of a Night, The (Hogg), **Supp. X:** 105–106

Mr. A's Amazing Mr. Pim Passes By (Milne), **Supp. V:** 299

"Mr. and Mrs. Dove" (Mansfield), **VII:** 180

"Mr. and Mrs. Frank Berry" (Thackeray), **V:** 23

"Mr. Apollinax" (Eliot), **VII:** 144

Mr. Beluncle (Pritchett), **Supp. III:** 311, 313, 314–315

Mr. Bennett and Mrs. Brown (Woolf), **VI:** 247, 267, 275, 290; **VII:** xiv, xv

"Mr. Bennett and Mrs. Brown" (Woolf), **Supp. II:** 341; **Retro. Supp. I:** 309

"Mr. Bleaney" (Larkin), **Supp. I:** 281

"Mr. Bodkin" (Hood), **IV:** 267

Mr. Britling Sees It Through (Wells), **VI:** 227, 240

"Mr. Brown's Letters to a Young Man About Town" (Thackeray), **V:** 38

Mr. Bunyan's Last Sermon (Bunyan), **II:** 253

Mr. C[olli]n's Discourse of Free-Thinking (Swift), **III:** 35

"Mr. Crabbe—Mr. Campbell" (Hazlitt), **III:** 276

"Mr. Dottery's Trousers" (Powys), **VIII:** 248, 249

"Mr. Eliot's Sunday Morning Service" (Eliot), **VII:** 145

"Mr. Feasey" (Dahl), **Supp. IV:** 214

Mr. Foot (Frayn), **Supp. VII:** 57

Mr. Fortune's Maggot (Warner), **Supp. VII:** 370, 374–375, 379

Mr Fox (Comyns), **VIII:** 53, 56, 64–65

"Mr. Gilfil's Love Story" (Eliot), **V:** 190; **Retro. Supp. II:** 103–104

"Mr. Gladstone Goes to Heaven" (Beerbohm), **Supp. II:** 51

"Mr. Graham" (Hood), **IV:** 267

Mr. H (Lamb), **IV:** 80–81, 85

"Mr. Harrison's Confessions" (Gaskell), **V:** 14, 15

Mister Heracles (Armitage), **VIII:** 1

Mr. John Milton's Character of the Long Parliament and Assembly of Divines . . . (Milton), **II:** 176

Mister Johnson (Cary), **VII:** 186, 187, 189, 190–191

"Mr. Know-All" (Maugham), **VI:** 370

Mr. Macaulay's Character of the Clergy in the Latter Part of the Seventeenth Century Considered (Babington), **IV:** 291

"Mr. McNamara" (Trevor), **Supp. IV:** 501

Mr. Meeson's Will (Haggard), **Supp. III:** 213

Mr Noon (Lawrence), **Retro. Supp. II:** 229–230

"Mr. Norris and I" (Isherwood), **VII:** 311–312

Mr. Norris Changes Trains (Isherwood), **VII:** xx, 311–312

"Mr. Pim and the Holy Crumb" (Powys), **VIII:** 255, 257

Mr. Polly (Wells), *see History of Mr. Polly, The*

Mr. Pope's Welcome from Greece (Gay), **II:** 348

Mr. Prohack (Bennett), **VI:** 260, 267

"Mr. Reginald Peacock's Day" (Mansfield), **VII:** 174

"Mr. Robert Herricke His Farewell unto Poetrie" (Herrick), **II:** 112

"Mr. Robert Montgomery's Poems" (Macaulay), **IV:** 280

Mr Sampath (Naipaul), **Supp. I:** 400

Mr. Scarborough's Family (Trollope), **V:** 98, 102

"Mr. Sludge 'the Medium' " (Browning), **IV:** 358, 368; **Retro. Supp. II:** 26–27

Mr. Smirke; or, The Divine in Mode (Marvell), **II:** 219

Mr. Stone and the Knights Companion (Naipaul), **Supp. I:** 383, 389

"Mr. Strugnell" (Cope), **VIII:** 73

Mr. Tasker's Gods (Powys), **VIII:** 2 **VIII:** 51, 249–250

"Mr. Tennyson" (Trevor), **Supp. IV:** 502

Mr. Waller's Speech in the Painted Chamber (Waller), **II:** 238

"Mr. Waterman" (Redgrove), **Supp. VI:** 228–229, 231, 235, 237

Mr. Weston's Good Wine (Powys), **VII:** 21; **VIII:** 245, 248, 252–254, 255, 256

"Mr. Whatnot" (Ayckbourn), **Supp. V:** 2, 13

"Mr. Whistler's Ten O'Clock" (Wilde), **V:** 407

Mr. Wrong (Howard), **Supp. XI:** 141, 142

"Mrs. Acland's Ghosts" (Trevor), **Supp. IV:** 503

"Mrs. Bathurst" (Kipling), **VI:** 193–194

Mrs. Browning: A Poet's Work and Its Setting (Hayter), **IV:** 322

"Mrs. Cibber" (Roberts, K.), **Supp. X:** 273

Mrs. Craddock (Maugham), **VI:** 367

Mrs. Dalloway (Woolf), **VI:** 275, 279; **VII:** xv, 18, 21, 24, 28–29; **Supp. IV:** 234, 246; **Retro. Supp. I:** 316–317

Mrs. Dot (Maugham), **VI:** 368

Mrs. Eckdorf in O'Neill's Hotel (Trevor), **Supp. IV:** 501, 508

Mrs. Fisher; or, The Future of Humour (Graves), **VII:** 259–260

Mrs. Harris's Petition (Swift), **Retro. Supp. I:** 283

"Mrs. Jaypher found a wafer" (Lear), **V:** 86

Mrs. Leicester's School (Lamb and Lamb), **IV:** 80, 85

Mrs. McGinty's Dead (Christie; U.S. title, *Blood Will Tell*), **Supp. II:** 135

"Mrs. Medwin" (James), **VI:** 69

"Mrs. Nelly's Complaint," **II:** 268

"Mrs. Packletide's Tiger" (Saki), **Supp. VI:** 242

Mrs. Perkins's Ball (Thackeray), **V:** 24, 38

Mrs. Shakespeare: The Complete Works (Nye), **Supp. X:** 196

"Mrs. Silly" (Trevor), **Supp. IV:** 502

"Mrs. Simpkins" (Smith), **Supp. II:** 470

"Mrs. Temperley" (James), **VI:** 69

Mrs. Warren's Profession (Shaw), **V:** 413; **VI:** 108, 109; **Retro. Supp. II:** 312–313

Mistral, Frederic, **V:** 219

Mistras, The (Cowley), **II:** 194, 198, 202, 236

Mistress of Men (Steel), **Supp. XII:** 275

"Mistress of Vision, The" (Thompson), **V:** 447–448

Mistry, Rohinton, **Supp. X: 137–149**

"Mists" (Redgrove), **Supp. VI:** 228

Mist's Weekly Journal (newspaper), **III:** 4

Mitford, Mary Russell, **IV:** 311, 312

Mitford, Nancy, **VII:** 290; **Supp. X: 151–163**

Mithridates (Lee), **II:** 305

Mixed Essays (Arnold), **V:** 213n, 216

"Mixed Marriage" (Muldoon), **Supp. IV:** 415

Mo, Timothy, **Supp. IV:** 390

"Moa Point" (Adcock), **Supp. XII:** 6

Mob, The (Galsworthy), **VI:** 280, 288

Moby-Dick (Melville), **VI:** 363

Mock Doctor, The (Fielding), **III** 105

Mock Speech from the Throne (Marvell), **II:** 207

Mock-Mourners, The: . . . Elegy on King William (Defoe), **III:** 12

Mockery Gap (Powys), **VIII:** 251, 256

"Model Prisons" (Carlyle), **IV:** 247

Mock's Curse: Nineteen Stories (Powys), **VIII:** 251, 252, 256

Modern Comedy, A (Galsworthy), **VI:** 270, 275

Modern Fiction (Woolf), **VII:** xiv; **Retro. Supp. I:** 308–309

Modern Husband, The (Fielding), **III:** 105

"Modern Love" (Meredith), **V:** 220, 234, 244

Modern Love, and Poems of the English Roadside . . . (Meredith), **V:** xxii, 220, 234

Modern Lover, A (Moore), **VI:** 86, 89, 98

Modern Movement: 100 Key Books from England, France, and America, 1880–1950, The (Connolly), **VI:** 371

Modern Painters (Ruskin), **V:** xx, 175–176, 180, 184, 282

Modern Painting (Moore), **VI:** 87

Modern Poet, The: Poetry, Academia, and Knowledge Since the 1750s (Crawford), **Supp. XI:** 82–83

Modern Poetry: A Personal Essay (MacNeice), **VII:** 403, 404, 410

"Modern Times" (Wallace–Crabbe), **VIII:** 324

Modern Utopia, A (Wells), **VI:** 227, 234, 241, 244

"Modern Warning, The" (James), **VI:** 48, 69

Modernism and Romance (Scott–James), **VI:** 21

Modes of Modern Writing: Metaphor, Metonymy, and the Typology of Modern Literature, The (Lodge), **Supp. IV:** 365, 377

"Modest Proposal" (Ewart), **Supp. VII:** 46

Modest Proposal, A (Swift), **III:** 21, 28, 29, 35; **Supp. IV:** 482

"Moestitiae Encomium" (Thompson), **V:** 450

Moffatt, James, **I:** 382–383

Mohocks, The (Gay), **III:** 60, 67

Mohr, Jean, **Supp. IV:** 79

Moi, Toril, **Retro. Supp. I:** 312

"Moisture–Number, The" (Redgrove), **Supp. VI:** 235

Molière (Jean Baptiste Poquelin), **II:** 314, 318, 325, 336, 337, 350; **V:** 224

Moll Flanders (Defoe), **III:** 5, 6, 7, 8, 9, 13, 95; **Retro. Supp. I:** 72–73

Molloy (Beckett), **Supp. I:** 51–52; **Supp. IV:** 106; **Retro. Supp. I:** 18, 21–22

Molly Sweeney (Friel), **Supp. V:** 127

"Molly Gone" (Hardy), **Retro. Supp. I:** 118

Moly (Gunn), **Supp. IV:** 257, 266–268

"Moly" (Gunn), **Supp. IV:** 267

Molyneux, William, **III:** 27

"Moment, The: Summer's Night" (Woolf), **Retro. Supp. I:** 309

"Moment in Eternity, A" (MacDiarmid), **Supp. XII:** 204

"Moment of Cubism, The" (Berger), **Supp. IV:** 79

Moment of Love, A (Moore), see *Feast of Lupercal, The*

Moments of Being (Woolf), **VII:** 33; **Retro. Supp. I:** 305, 315

Moments of Grace (Jennings), **Supp. V:** 217–218

Moments of Vision, and Miscellaneous Verses (Hardy), **VI:** 20

Monastery, The (Scott), **IV:** xviii, 39

Monckton Milnes, Richard (Lord Houghton), **IV:** 211, 234, 235, 251, 252, 254, 302, 351; **V:** 312, 313, 334; **Retro. Supp. I:** 185–186

"Monday; or, The Squabble" (Gay), **III:** 56

Monday or Tuesday (Woolf), **VII:** 20, 21, 38; **Retro. Supp. I:** 307

Mondo Desperado (McCabe), **Supp. IX:** 127, 136–137

Money: A Suicide Note (Amis), **Supp. IV:** 26, 32–35, 37, 40

Money in the Bank (Wodehouse), **Supp. III:** 459

"Money–Man Only" (Smith, I. C.), **Supp. IX:** 213–214

"Money Singing" (Motion), **Supp. VII:** 261

Monk, The (Lewis), **III:** 332–333, 335, 345; **Supp. III:** 384

Monkfish Moon (Gunesekera), **Supp. X:** 85–88, 95, 100

Monks and the Giants, The (Frere), *see Whistlecraft*

Monks of St. Mark, The (Peacock), **IV:** 158, 169

Monk's Prologue, The (Chaucer), **II:** 70

Monk's Tale, The (Chaucer), **I:** 31

Monk's Tale, The (Lydgate), **I:** 57

"Monna Innominata" (Rossetti), **V:** 251

"Mono–Cellular" (Self), **Supp. V:** 402

Monody on the Death of the Right Hon. R. B. Sheridan . . . (Byron), **IV:** 192

Monro, Harold, **VI:** 448

"Mons Meg" (Crawford), **Supp. XI:** 81–82

Monsieur (Durrell), **Supp. I:** 118, 119

Monsieur de Pourceaugnac (Molière), **II:** 325, 337, 339, 347, 350

Monsieur d'Olive (Chapman), **I:** 244–245

"M. Prudhomme at the International Exhibition" (Swinburne), **V:** 333

Monsieur Thomas (Fletcher), **II:** 45, 61, 65

Monsignor Quixote (Greene), **Supp. I:** 18–19; **Retro. Supp. II:** 166

Monster (Beamish and Galloway), **Supp. XII:** 117

Monstre Gai (Lewis), **VII:** 72, 80

"Mont Blanc" (Shelley), **IV:** 198; **Retro. Supp. I:** 248

Montagu, Lady Mary Wortley, **II:** 326

Montague, John, **VI:** 220

Montaigne, Michel Eyquem de, **II:** 25, 30, 80, 104, 108, 146; **III:** 39

Monte Verité (du Maurier), **Supp. III:** 143–144, 147, 148

Montemayor, Jorge de, **I:** 164, 302

Montezuma's Daughter (Haggard), **Supp. III:** 214

Montgomery, Robert, **IV:** 280

Month (periodical), **V:** 365, 379

Month in the Country, A (tr. Friel), **Supp. V:** 124

Montherlant, Henry de, **II:** 99n

Monthly Review (periodical), **III:** 147, 188

Montrose, marquess of, **II:** 222, 236–237, 238

"Monument Maker, The" (Hardy), **Retro. Supp. I:** 117

Monumental Column, A. Erected to . . . Prince of Wales (Webster), **II:** 68, 85

"Monuments of Honour" (Webster), **II:** 68, 85

Monye, A. A., **Supp. II:** 350

Monypenny, W. F., **IV:** 292, 295, 300, 307, 308

"Moon and a Cloud, The" (Davies), **Supp. XI:** 91

Moon and Sixpence, The (Maugham), **VI:** xiii, 365, 374, **375–376**

Moon Country: Further Reports from Iceland (Armitage), **VIII:** 2

"Moon Fever" (Nye), **Supp. X:** 205

Mooncranker's Gift (Unsworth), **Supp. VII:** 354, 356–357

Moonlight (Pinter), **Retro. Supp. I:** 226

"Moonlight Night on the Port" (Keyes), **VII:** 439

Moonlight on the Highway (Potter, D.), **Supp. X:** 231

"Moonshine" (Murphy), **Supp. V:** 326

Moonstone, The (Collins), **Supp. VI:** 91, 93, **100–102**

"Moor, The" (Thomas), **Supp. XII:** 285

Moorcock, Michael, **Supp. V:** 24, 25, 32

Moonstone, The (Collins), **III:** 340, 345

Moore, Brian, **Supp. IX:** **141–155**

Moore, G. E., **Supp. I:** 217; **Supp. II:** 406–407; **Supp. III:** 46, 49

Moore, George, **IV:** 102; **V:** xxi, xxvi, 129, 153; **VI:** xii **85–99,** 207, 239, 270, 365

Moore, John Robert, **III:** 1, 12

Moore, Marianne, **IV:** 6; **Supp. IV:** 262–263

Moore, Thomas, **IV:** xvi, 193, 205; **V:** 116

"Moore's Life of Lord Byron" (Macaulay), **IV:** 281–282

"Moorings" (MacCaig), **Supp. VI:** 187

Moorland Cottage, The (Gaskell), **V:** 14, 15

Moorman, Mary, **IV:** 4, 25

Moor's Last Sigh, The (Rushdie), **Supp. IV:** 433, 438, 444, 446, 448, 451–454, 456

Moortown (Hughes), **Supp. I:** 354, 357; **Retro. Supp. II:** 211–212

"Mora Montravers" (James), **VI:** 69

Moral and Political Lecture, A (Coleridge), **IV:** 56

Moral Epistle, Respectfully Dedicated to Earl Stanhope (Landor), **IV:** 99

Moral Ending and Other Stories, A (Warner), **Supp. VII:** 379

Moral Essays (Pope), **III:** 74–75, 77, 78; **Retro. Supp. I:** 145; **Retro. Supp. I:** 235

Moralities (Kinsella), **Supp. V:** 260, 261

"Morality and the Novel" (Lawrence), **VII:** 87

Morality Play (Unsworth), **Supp. VII:** 362, 364–365

Morall Fabillis of Esope the Phrygian, The (Henryson), **Supp. VII:** 136–142, 145

Morando, the Tritameron of Love (Greene), **VIII:** 142–143

"Mordecai and Cocking" (Coppard), **VIII:** 95

More, Hannah, **IV:** 269

More, Paul Elmer, **II:** 152

More, Sir Thomas, **I:** 325; **II:** 24; **IV:** 69, **Supp. VII: 233–250**

"More a Man Has the More a Man Wants, The" (Muldoon), **Supp. IV:** 420–421, 425

More Dissemblers Besides Women (Middleton), **II:** 3, 21

"More Essex Poems" (Davie), **Supp. VI:** 110–111

More New Arabian Nights: The Dynamiter (Stevenson), **V:** 395

More Nonsense, Pictures, Rhymes, Botany (Lear), **V:** 78, 87

More Poems (Housman), **VI:** 152, 157, 161–162

More Pricks than Kicks (Beckett), **Supp. I: 45–46**; **Retro. Supp. I:** 19

More Reformation: A Satyr upon Himself . . . (Defoe), **III:** 13

More Short-Ways with the Dissenters (Defoe), **III:** 13

More Tales I Tell My Mother (ed. Fairbairns et al.), **Supp. XI:** 163

More Trivia (Connolly), **Supp. III:** 98

More Women than Men (Compton–Burnett), **VII:** 61–62

Morgan, Edwin, **Supp. IX: 157–170**

Morgan, Margery M., **VI:** xiii, xiv–xv, xxxiv

Morgann, Maurice, **IV:** xiv, 168

Morgante Maggiore (Pulci), **IV:** 182

Morison, James Augustus Cotter, **IV:** 289, 291

Morkinskinna, **VIII:** 242

Morland, Dick *see* Hill, Reginald

Morley, Frank, **IV:** 79, 86

Morley, John, **VI:** 2, 157, 336

Morley, Lord John, **III:** 201, 205; **IV:** 289, 291; **V:** 279, 280, 284, 290, 313, 334

"Morning" (Davie), **Supp. VI:** 112

"Morning Call" (Murphy), **Supp. V:** 326

Morning Chronicle, The (periodical), **IV:** 43, 128, 129; **V:** 41

"Morning Coffee" (Kinsella), **Supp. V:** 273

"Morning, Midday, and Evening Sacrifice" (Hopkins), **V:** 370

Morning Post (periodical), **III:** 269; **VI:** 351

Morning Star (Haggard), **Supp. III:** 214

"Morning Sun" (MacNeice), **III:** 411

Mornings in Mexico (Lawrence), **VII:** 116, 117

"Morning-watch, The" (Vaughan), **II:** 187

Moronic Inferno, The (AAnd Other Visits to America") (Amis), **Supp. IV:** 42, 43

"Morpho Eugenia" (Byatt), **Supp. IV:** 140, 153–154

Morrell, Ottoline, **VII:** 103

Morrell, Sir Charles, **V:** 111

Morris, Jan, **Supp. X: 171–189**

Morris, Margaret, **VI:** 274

Morris, May, **V:** 298, 301, 305

Morris, William, **IV:** 218; **V:** ix, xi, xii, xix, xxii–xxvi, 236–238, **291–307**, 312, 365, 401, 409; **VI:** 103, 167–168, 283

Morris & Co., **V:** 295, 296, 302

"Morris's Life and Death of Jason" (Swinburne), **V:** 298

Morrison, Arthur, **VI:** 365–366

Mortal Causes (Rankin), **Supp. X:** 244, 251–252

Mortal Coils (Huxley), **VII:** 200

Mortal Consequences (Symons), **Supp. IV:** 3

Morte Arthur, Le, **I:** 72, 73

Morte Darthur, Le (Malory), **I:** 67, 68–79; **V:** 294; **Retro. Supp. II:** 237–239, 240–251

"Morte d'Arthur" (Tennyson), **IV:** xx, 332–334, 336

"Mortier Water-Organ Called Oscar, The" (Redgrove), **Supp. VI:** 236

"Mortification" (Herbert), **II:** 127

Mortimer His Fall (Jonson), **Retro. Supp. I:** 166

Morvern Callar (Warner), **Supp. XI:** 281, 282–286, 287, 288, 289, 290, 293

Mosada, a Dramatic Poem (Yeats), **VI:** 221

Moseley, Humphrey, **II:** 89

Moses (Rosenberg), **VI:** 433

Moses the Lawgiver (Keneally), **Supp. IV:** 346

"Mosquito" (Lawrence), **VII:** 119

"Most Extraordinary Case, A" (James), **VI:** 69

Most Piteous Tale of the Morte Arthur Saunz Guerdon, The (Malory), **I:** 72, 77

"Moth" (Thomas), **Supp. XII:** 290

"Mother, The" (Stevenson), **Supp. VI:** 256

Mother and Son (Compton–Burnett), **VII:** 64, 65, 68–69

"Mother and Son" (Stallworthy), **Supp. X:** 297

Mother Bombie (Lyly), **I:** 203–204

"Mother Country" (Rossetti), **V:** 255

Mother Country, The (Kureishi), **Supp. XI:** 154

Mother Courage (Brecht), **VI:** 123

Mother Hubberd's Tale (Spenser), **I:** 124, 131

Mother Ireland (O'Brien), **Supp. V:** 338

"Mother Kamchatka; or, Mr. Mainchance in Search of the Truth" (Plomer), **Supp. XI:** 216

"Mother of the Muses, The" (Harrison), **Supp. V:** 161

"Mother of the World, The" (Powys), **VIII:** 251, 252

Mother Poem (Brathwaite), **Supp. XII:** 33, 41, 42, 46

Mother, Sing for Me (Ngũgĩ). *See Maitū njugĩra*

"Mother Speaks, The" (Day Lewis), **Supp. III:** 125

"Mother to Child Asleep" (Cornford), **VIII:** 107

"Mother Tongue" (Stallworthy), **Supp. X:** 298

Mother, What Is Man? (Smith), **Supp. II:** 462

Mother's Day (Storey), **Supp. I:** 420

"Mother's Sense of Fun" (Wilson), **Supp. I:** 153, 157–158

Motion, Andrew, **Supp. VII: 251–267**

"Motions of the Earth, The" (Nicholson), **Supp. VI:** 217

Motteux, Pierre, **II:** 352, 353

"Mount Badon" (Williams, C. W. S.), **Supp. IX:** 282–283

Mount of Olives, The; or, Solitary Devotions . . . (Vaughan), **II:** 185, 201

Mount Zion (Betjeman), **VII:** 364

"Mount Zion" (Hughes), **Supp. I:** 341

Mountain Bard, The (Hogg), **Supp. X:** 106

"Mountain Path" (Cornford), **VIII:** 107

"Mountain Shadow" (Gunesekera), **Supp. X:** 87

Mountain Town in France, A (Stevenson), **V:** 396

"Mountaineering Poetry: The Metaphorical Imperative" (Dutton), **Supp. XII:** 86

Mountains and Molehills (Cornford), **VIII:** 106, 107–108, 109

Mountolive (Durrell), **Supp. I:** 104, 106, 108, 109

"Mourning" (Marvell), **II:** 209, 212

Mourning Bride, The (Congreve), **II:** 338, 347, 350

Mourning Muse of Alexis, The: A Pastoral (Congreve), **II:** 350

Mousetrap, The (Christie), **Supp. II:** 125, 134

"Move, The" (Crawford), **Supp. XI:** 74–75

Movevent, The, **Supp. IV:** 256

Moving Finger, The (Christie), **Supp. II:** 132

Moving Out (Behan), **Supp. II:** 67, 68, 70

Moving Target, A (Golding), **Supp. I:** 88

Moving the Center: The Struggle for Cultural Freedoms (Ngũgĩ), **VIII:** 217, 225

"Mower to the Glo-Worms, The" (Marvell), **II:** 209

"Mowgli's Brothers" (Kipling), **VI:** 199

Moxon, Edward, **IV:** 83, 86, 252

Much Ado About Nothing (Shakespeare), **I:** 310–311, 327

Much Obliged (Wodehouse), **Supp. III:** 460

"Muchelney Abbey" (Sisson), **Supp. XI:** 258

"Mud Vision, The" (Heaney), **Supp. II:** 281

Mudlark Poems & Grand Buveur, The (Redgrove), **Supp. VI:** 236

"Mudtower, The" (Stevenson), **Supp. VI:** 253

Muggeridge, Malcolm, **VI:** 356; **VII:** 276; **Supp. II:** 118, 119
"Mugumo" (Ngũgĩ), **VIII:** 220
Muiopotmos (Spenser), **I:** 124
Muir, Edwin, **I:** 247; **IV:** 27, 40; **Supp. V:** 208; **Supp. VI: 197–209**
Muir, K., **IV:** 219, 236
Mulberry Bush, The (Wilson), **Supp. I:** 154–155
Mulberry Garden, The (Sedley), **II:** 263–264, 271
"Mulberry Tree, The" (Bowen), **Supp. II:** 78, 92
Mulberry Tree, The (Bowen), **Supp. II:** 80
Mulcaster, Richard, **I:** 122
Muldoon, Paul, **Supp. IV: 409–432**
Mule on the Minaret, The (Waugh), **Supp. VI:** 274
Mules (Muldoon), **Supp. IV:** 414–415
Mullan, John, **Retro. Supp. I:** 69–70
Müller, Max, **V:** 203
"Mulwhevin" (Dunn), **Supp. X:** 68
"Mum" (Crawford), **Supp. XI:** 70–71
Mum and Mr. Armitage (Bainbridge), **Supp. VI:** 23
Mummer's Wife, A (Moore), **VI:** xii, 86, 90, 98
"Mummia" (Brooke), **Supp. III:** 52, 60
"Mummy, The" (Morgan, E.), **Supp. IX:** 163
"Mummy to the Rescue" (Wilson), **Supp. I:** 153
"Mundus and Paulina" (Gower), **I:** 53–54
Mundus Muliebris; or, The Ladies–Dressing Room Unlock'd (Evelyn), **II:** 287
Mundy Scheme, The (Friel), **Supp. V:** 119
Munera Pulveris (Ruskin), **V:** 184
"Municipal Gallery Revisited, The" (Yeats), **VI:** 216; **Retro. Supp. I:** 337–338
Munnings, Sir Alfred, **VI:** 210
"Murad the Unlucky" (Brooke), **Supp. III:** 55
"Murder" (Nye), **Supp. X:** 198
Murder at the Vicarage (Christie), **Supp. II:** 130, 131
"Murder Considered as One of the Fine Arts" (De Quincey), **IV:** 149–150
Murder in the Calais Coach (Christie), *see Murder on the Orient Express*
Murder in the Cathedral (Eliot), **VII:** 153, 157, 159; **Retro. Supp. II:** 132
Murder in Triplicate (James), **Supp. IV:** 320, 327
"Murder, 1986" (James), **Supp. IV:** 340
Murder of John Brewer, The (Kyd), **I:** 218
Murder of Quality, A (le Carré), **Supp. II:** 300, **302–303**
Murder of Roger Ackroyd, The (Christie), **Supp. II:** 124, 128, 135
"Murder of Santa Claus, The" (James), **Supp. IV:** 340
Murder of the Man Who Was Shakespeare, The (Hoffman), **I:** 277
Murder on the Orient Express (Christie; U.S. title, *Murder in the Calais Coach*), **Supp. II:** 128, 130, 134, 135
Murderous Michael, **I:** 218

"Murdered Drinker, The" (Graham), **Supp. VII:** 115
"Murders in the Rue Morgue, The" (Poe), **III:** 339
Murdoch, Iris, **III:** 341, 345; **VI:** 372; **Supp. I: 215–235; Supp. IV:** 100, 139, 145, 234
Murmuring Judges (Hare), **Supp. IV:** 282, 294, 296–297, 298
Murnau, F. W., **III:** 342
Murphy (Beckett), **Supp. I:** 46–47, 48, 51, 62, 220; **Retro. Supp. I:** 19–20
Murphy, Richard, **VI:** 220; **Supp. V: 313–331**
Murray, Gilbert, **VI:** 153, 273, 274
Murray, John, **IV:** 182, 188, 190, 193, 294
Murray, Les, **Supp. VII: 269–288**
Murray, Nicholas, **Supp. IV:** 171
Murray, Sir James, **III:** 113
Murry, John Middleton, **III:** 68; **VI:** 207, 375, 446; **VII:** 37, 106, 173–174, 181–182
"Muse, The" (Cowley), **II:** 195, 200
"Muse Among the Motors, A" (Kipling), **VI:** 202
"Musée des Beaux Arts" (Auden), **VII:** 379, 385–386; **Retro. Supp. I:** 8
"Muses Dirge, The" (James), **II:** 102
"Museum" (MacNeice), **VII:** 412
Museum of Cheats, The (Warner), **Supp. VII:** 380
Museum Pieces (Plomer), **Supp. XI:** 221
"Music" (Owen), **VI:** 449
Music: An Ode (Swinburne), **V:** 333
Music at Night (Priestley), **VII:** 225–226
Music Cure, The (Shaw), **VI:** 129
"Music for Octopi" (Redgrove), **Supp. VI:** 234
Music of Division, The (Wallace–Crabbe), **VIII:** 311
Music of Time novel cycle (Powell), *see Dance to the Music of Time, A*
Music on Clinton Street (McCabe), **Supp. IX:** 127
"Music on the Hill, The" (Saki), **Supp. VI:** 243–244
"Musical Instrument, A" (Browning), **IV:** 315
"Musician, The" (Dunn), **Supp. X:** 73
Musicks Duell (Crashaw), **II:** 90–91
Musil, Robert, **Supp. IV:** 70
Muslin (Moore), **VI:** 98; *see Drama in Muslin, A*
Mustapha (Greville), **Supp. XI:** 108, 117
"Mute Phenomena, The" (Mahon), **Supp. VI:** 173
"Mutual Life" (MacCaig), **Supp. VI:** 188
"My Aged Uncle Arly" (Lear), **V:** 85–86
My Beautiful Laundrette (Kureishi), **Supp. XI:** 155–156
My Birds (Davies), **Supp. XI:** 92
My Brother (Kincaid), **Supp. VII:** 217, 230–231
My Brother Evelyn and Other Profiles (Waugh), **Supp. VI:** 269, 276
"My Canadian Uncle" (Smith, I. C.), **Supp. IX:** 224
"My Care" (Fallon), **Supp. XII:** 108, 109

My Child, My Sister (Fuller), **Supp. VII:** 74, 76, 77, 81
"My Christ Is No Statue" (Fallon), **Supp. XII:** 102
"My Company" (Read), **VI:** 437
My Cousin Rachel (du Maurier), **Supp. III:** 134, 139, 140, 141, 147
My Darling Dear, My Daisy Flower (Skelton), **I:** 83
My Dear Dorothea: A Practical System of Moral Education for Females (Shaw), **VI:** 109, 130
"My Death" (Hart), **Supp. XI:** 125
"My delight and thy delight" (Bridges), **VI:** 77
"My Diary": The Early Years of My Daughter Marianne (Gaskell), **V:** 15
"My Doves" (Browning), **IV:** 313
"My Dream" (Rossetti), **V:** 256
"My Dyet" (Cowley), **II:** 197, 198
My Early Life (Churchill), **VI:** 354
"My Father" (Adcock), **Supp. XII:** 12
My Father's Trapdoors (Redgrove), **Supp. VI:** 236
"My First Acquaintance with Poets" (Hazlitt), **IV:** 126, 132
"My First Book" (Stevenson), **Retro. Supp. I:** 260
"My First Marriage" (Jhabvala), **Supp. V:** 236
"My Friend Bingham" (James), **VI:** 69
My Fellow Devils (Hartley), **Supp. VII:** 127–128, 132
"My Friend Bruce Lee" (McCabe), **Supp. IX:** 136
"My galley charged with forgetfulness" (Wyatt), **I:** 110
My Garden (Davies), **Supp. XI:** 92
My Garden Book (Kincaid), **Supp. VII:** 217, 229, 230, 231
"My Ghost" (Wallace–Crabbe), **VIII:** 324
My Guru and His Disciple (Isherwood), **VII:** 318
My House in Umbria (Trevor), **Supp. IV:** 516–517
"My House Is Tiny" (Healy), **Supp. IX:** 106–107
"My Hundredth Tale" (Coppard), **VIII:** 97
My Idea of Fun: A Cautionary Tale (Self), **Supp. V:** 396–398
"My Joyce" (Lodge), **Supp. IV:** 364
"My Lady Love, My Dove" (Dahl), **Supp. IV:** 217
My Lady Ludlow (Gaskell), **V:** 15
"My Last Duchess" (Browning), **IV:** 356, 360, 372; **Retro. Supp. II:** 22–23
"My Last Mistress" (Stallworthy), **Supp. X:** 300–301
My Life as a Fake (Carey), **Supp. XII:** 54, 60, 61, 62
"My Life up to Now" (Gunn), **Supp. IV:** 255, 265, 266, 268, 269, 273
"My love whose heart is tender said to me" (Rossetti), **V:** 251
"My Lover" (Cope), **VIII:** 72–73
"My Luncheon Hour" (Coppard), **VIII:** 87
"My lute awake!" (Wyatt), **I:** 105–106

My Man Jeeves (Wodehouse), **Supp. III:** 455

"My Man of Flesh and Straw" (Stallworthy), **Supp. X:** 292

"My Mother" (Kincaid), **Supp. VII:** 221

"My own heart let me more have pity on" (Hopkins), **V:** 375–376

"My Own Life" (Hume), **Supp. III:** 229

"My pen take pain a little space" (Wyatt), **I:** 106

"My Picture Left in Scotland" (Jonson), **Retro. Supp. I:** 152

My Sad Captains (Gunn), **Supp. IV:** 257, 262–264

"My Sad Captains" (Gunn), **Supp. IV:** 263–264

"My Sailor Father" (Smith, I. C.), **Supp. IX:** 216

My Sister Eileen (McKenney), **Supp. IV:** 476

"My Sister's Sleep" (Rossetti), **V:** 239, 240, 242

"My Sister's War" (Thomas), **Supp. IV:** 492

"My Son the Fanatic" (Kureishi), **Supp. XI:** 157–158

My Son's Story (Gordimer), **Supp. II:** 233, 240 242

"My Spectre" (Blake), **V:** 244

"My spirit kisseth thine" (Bridges), **VI:** 77

"My true love hath my heart, and I have his" (Sidney), **I:** 169

"My Uncle" (Nye), **Supp. X:** 202

My Uncle Oswald (Dahl), **Supp. IV:** 213, 219, 220

My Very Own Story (Ayckbourn), **Supp. V:** 3, 11, 13

My World as in My Time (Newbolt), **VI:** 75

My Year (Dahl), **Supp. IV:** 225

Myer, Valerie Grosvenor, **Supp. IV:** 230

Myers, William Francis, **VII:** xx, xxxviii

Myles Before Myles, A Selection of the Earlier Writings of Brian O'Nolan (O'Nolan), **Supp. II:** 322, 323, 324

Myrick, K. O., **I:** 160, 167

"Myself in India" (Jhabvala), **Supp. V:** 227, 229–230

Myself When Young: Confessions (Waugh), **Supp. VI:** 270

Mysteries, The (Harrison), **Supp. V:** 150, 163

Mysteries of Udolpho, The (Radcliffe), **III:** 331–332, 335, 345; **IV:** xvi, 111; **Supp. III:** 384

Mysterious Affair at Styles, The (Christie), **Supp. II:** 124, 129–130

"Mysterious Kôr" (Bowen), **Supp. II:** 77, 82, 93

Mystery of Charles Dickens, The (Ackroyd), **Supp. VI:** 13

Mystery of Edwin Drood, The (Dickens), see *Edwin Drood*

"Mystery of Sasaesa Valley" (Doyle), **Supp. II:** 159

Mystery of the Blue Train (Christie), **Supp. II:** 125

Mystery of the Charity of Charles Péguy, The (Hill), **Supp. V:** 189, 196–198

Mystery of the Fall (Clough), **V:** 159, 161

Mystery of the Sea, The (Stoker), **Supp. III:** 381

Mystery Revealed: . . . Containing . . . Testimonials Respecting the . . . Cock Lane Ghost, The (Goldsmith), **III:** 191

Mystic Masseur, The (Naipaul), **Supp. I:** 383, 386, 387, 393

"Mystique of Ingmar Bergman, The" (Blackwood), **Supp. IX:** 6

"Mysticism and Democracy" (Hill), **Supp. V:** 192–193

Myth of Modernism (Bergonzi), **Supp. IV:** 364

Myth of Shakespeare, A (Williams, C. W. S.), **Supp. IX:** 276

"Mythical Journey, The" (Muir), **Supp. VI:** 206

Mythologiae sive explicationis fabularum (Conti), **I:** 266

"Mythological Sonnets" (Fuller), **Supp. VII:** 73

"Mythology" (Motion), **Supp. VII:** 266

N.

'n Droë wit seisoen (Brink), **Supp. VI:** 50

'n Oomblik in die wind (Brink), **Supp. VI:** 49

"Naaman" (Nicholson), **Supp. VI:** 216

"Nabara, The" (Day Lewis), **Supp. III:** 127

Nabokov, Vladimir, **Supp. IV:** 26–27, 43, 153, 302

Nacht and Traüme (Beckett), **Retro. Supp. I:** 29

Nada the Lily (Haggard), **Supp. III:** 214

Nadel, G. H., **I:** 269

Naipaul, V. S., **VII:** xx; **Supp. I: 383–405; Supp. IV:** 302

Naive and Sentimental Lover, The (le Carré), **Supp. II:** 300, **310–311**, 317

"Nakamura" (Plomer), **Supp. XI:** 216

Naked Warriors (Read), **VI:** 436

"Namaqualand After Rain" (Plomer), **Supp. XI:** 213

Name and Nature of Poetry, The (Housman), **VI:** 157, 162–164

Name of Action, The (Greene), **Supp. I:** 3

Name of the Rose, The (Eco), **Supp. IV:** 116

"Names" (Cope), **VIII:** 79

"Naming of Offa, The" (Hill), **Supp. V:** 195

"Naming of Parts" (Reed), **VII:** 422

Nannie's Night Out (O'Casey), **VII:** 11–12

Napier, Macvey, **IV:** 272

"Napier's Bones" (Crawford), **Supp. XI:** 74

Napoleon of Notting Hill, The (Chesterton), **VI:** 335, 338, 343–344

Napoleon III in Italy and Other Poems (Browning), see *Poems Before Congress*

Narayan, R. K., **Supp. IV:** 440

"Narcissus" (Gower), **I:** 53–54

"Narcissus Bay" (Welch), **Supp. IX:** 267, 268

Nares, Edward, **IV:** 280

Narrative of All the Robberies, . . . of John Sheppard, A (Defoe), **III:** 13

"Narrative of Jacobus Coetzee, The" (Coetzee), **Supp. VI:** 76, **79–80**

Narrow Corner, The (Maugham), **VI:** 375

Narrow Place, The (Muir), **Supp. VI:** 204, **206**

"Narrow Place, The" (Muir), **Supp. VI:** 206

Narrow Road to the Deep North (Bond), **Supp. I:** 423, 427, 428–429, 430, 435

"Narrow Sea, The" (Graves), **VII:** 270

"Narrow Vessel, A" (Thompson), **V:** 441

Nashe, Thomas, **I:** 114, 123, 171, 199, 221, 278, 279, 281, 288; **II:** 25; **Supp. II:** 188; **Retro. Supp. I:** 156

Nation (periodical), **VI:** 455

Nation Review (publication), **Supp. IV:** 346

National Being, The: Some Thoughts on Irish Polity (Russell), **VIII:** 277, 287, 288, 292

National Observer (periodical), **VI:** 350

National Standard (periodical), **V:** 19

National Tales (Hood), **IV:** 255, 259, 267

"National Trust" (Harrison), **Supp. V:** 153

Native Companions: Essays and Comments on Australian Literature 1936–1966 (Hope), **Supp. VII:** 151, 153, 159, 164

"Native Health" (Dunn), **Supp. X:** 68

"Nativity" (Thomas), **Supp. XII:** 290

"Natura Naturans" (Clough), **V:** 159–160

Natural Causes (Motion), **Supp. VII:** 254, 257–258, 263

Natural Curiosity, A (Drabble), **Supp. IV:** 231, 249–250

"Natural History" (Sisson), **Supp. XI:** 243

Natural History and Antiquities of Selborne, The, (White), **Supp. VI:** 279–284, **285–293**

Natural History of Religion, The (Hume), **Supp. III:** 240–241

"natural man," **VII:** 94

"Natural Son" (Murphy), **Supp. V:** 327, 329

Naturalist's Calendar, with Observations in Various Branches of Natural History, A (White), **Supp. VI:** 283

Naturalist's Journal (White), **Supp. VI:** 283, 292

"Naturally the Foundation Will Bear Your Expenses" (Larkin), **Supp. I:** 285

Nature (Davies), **Supp. XI:** 91

Nature in English Literature (Blunden), **Supp. XI:** 42, 43

"Nature, Language, the Sea: An Essay" (Wallace–Crabbe), **VIII:** 315

Nature of a Crime, The (Conrad), **VI:** 148

Nature of Blood, The (Phillips), **Supp. V:** 380, 391–394

Nature of Cold Weather, The (Redgrove), **Supp. VI: 227–229,** 236

"Nature of Cold Weather, The" (Redgrove), **Supp. VI:** 228,237

"Nature of Gothic, The" (Ruskin), **V:** 176

Nature of History, The (Marwick), **IV:** 290, 291

"Nature of Man, The" (Sisson), **Supp. XI:** 251

Nature of Passion, The (Jhabvala), **Supp. V:** 226

"Nature of the Scholar, The" (Fichte), **V:** 348

Nature Poems (Davies), **Supp. III:** 398

"Nature That Washt Her Hands in Milk" (Ralegh), **I:** 149

Natwar–Singh, K., **VI:** 408

Naufragium Joculare (Cowley), **II:** 194, 202

Naulahka (Kipling and Balestier), **VI:** 204

"Naval History" (Kelman), **Supp. V:** 250

"Naval Treaty, The" (Doyle), **Supp. II:** 169, 175

Navigation and Commerce (Evelyn), **II:** 287

"Navy's Here, The" (Redgrove), **Supp. VI:** 234

Naylor, Gillian, **VI:** 168

Nazarene Gospel Restored, The (Graves and Podro), **VII:** 262

Nazism, **VI:** 242

"NB" (Reading), **VIII:** 266

Neal, Patricia, **Supp. IV:** 214, 218, 223

Near and Far (Blunden), **VI:** 428

"Near Lanivet" (Hardy), **VI:** 17

"Near Perigord" (Pound), **V:** 304

Neb (Thomas), **Supp. XII:** 280, 289

"Necessary Blindness, A" (Nye), **Supp. X:** 204

Necessity of Art, The (Fischer), **Supp. II:** 228

Necessity of Atheism, The (Shelley and Hogg), **IV:** xvii, 196, 208; **Retro. Supp. I:** 244

"Necessity of Not Believing, The" (Smith), **Supp. II:** 467

Necessity of Poetry, The (Bridges), **VI:** 75–76, 82, 83

"Necessity's Child" (Wilson), **Supp. I:** 153–154

"Neck" (Dahl), **Supp. IV:** 217

"Ned Bratts" (Browning), **IV:** 370; **Retro. Supp. II:** 29–30

Ned Kelly and the City of the Bees (Keneally), **Supp. IV:** 346

"Ned Skinner" (Muldoon), **Supp. IV:** 415

"Need to Be Versed in Country Things, The" (Frost), **Supp. IV:** 423

Needham, Gwendolyn, **VI:** 60

Needle's Eye, The (Drabble), **Supp. IV:** 230, 234, 241, 242–243, 245, 251

"Needlework" (Dunn), **Supp. X:** 68

"Negative Love" (Donne), **Retro. Supp. II:** 93

"Neglected Graveyard, Luskentyre" (MacCaig), **Supp. VI:** 182, 189, 194

"Negus" (Brathwaite), **Supp. XII:** 44

"Neighbours" (Cornford), **VIII:** 107

Neighbours in a Thicket (Malouf), **Supp. XII:** 217, 219–220

Neizvestny, Ernst, **Supp. IV:** 88

"Nell Barnes" (Davies), **Supp. XI:** 97–98

"Nelly Trim" (Warner), **Supp. VII:** 371

Nelson, W., **I:** 86

"Neolithic" (Dutton), **Supp. XII:** 90

Nerinda (Douglas), **VI:** 300, 305

Nero Part I (Bridges), **VI:** 83

Nero Part II (Bridges), **VI:** 83

Nesbit, E., **Supp. II:** 140, 144, 149

"Nest in a Wall, A" (Murphy), **Supp. V:** 326

Nest of Tigers, A: Edith, Osbert and Sacheverell in Their Times (Lehmann), **VII:** 141

Nether World, The (Gissing), **V:** 424, 437

Netherwood (White), **Supp. I:** 131, 151

"Netting, The" (Murphy), **Supp. V:** 318

Nettles (Lawrence), **VII:** 118

"Netty Sargent's Copyhold" (Hardy), **VI:** 22

"Neurotic, The" (Day Lewis), **Supp. III:** 129

Neutral Ground (Corke), **VII:** 93

"Neutral Tones" (Hardy), **Retro. Supp. I:** 110, 117

New Age (periodical), **VI:** 247, 265; **VII:** 172

New and Collected Poems 1934–84 (Fuller), **Supp. VII:** 68, 72, 73, 74, 79

New and Collected Poems, 1952–1992 (Hill), **Supp. V:** 184

New and Improved Grammar of the English Tongue, A (Hazlitt), **IV:** 139

New and Selected Poems (Davie), **Supp. VI:** 108

New and Selected Poems (Hart), **Supp. XI:** 122

New and Useful Concordance, A (Bunyan), **II:** 253

New Apocalypse, The (MacCaig), **Supp. VI:** 184

New Arabian Nights (Stevenson), **V:** 384n, 386, 395; **Retro. Supp. I:** 263

New Arcadia (Sidney), **Retro. Supp. II:** 332

New Atlantis (Bacon), **I:** 259, 265, 267–269, 273

"New Ballad of Tannhäuser, A" (Davidson), **V:** 318n

New Bath Guide (Anstey), **III:** 155

New Bats in Old Belfries (Betjeman), **VII:** 368–369

New Bearings in English Poetry (Leavis), **V:** 375, 381; **VI:** 21; **VII:** 234, 244–246

"New Beginning, A" (Kinsella), **Supp. V:** 270

New Belfry of Christ Church, The (Carroll), **V:** 274

"New Cemetery, The" (Nicholson), **Supp. VI:** 219

New Characters . . . of Severall Persons . . . (Webster), **II:** 85

New Chatto Poets 2 (ed. Ehrhardt et al.), **Supp. XI:** 71

New Cratylus, The: Notes on the Craft of Poetry (Hope), **Supp. VII:** 151, 155

New Country (ed. Roberts), **VII:** xix, 411

"New Delhi Romance, A" (Jhabvala), **Supp. V:** 236–237

New Discovery of an Old Intreague, An (Defoe), **III:** 12; **Retro. Supp. I:** 67

New Divan, The (Morgan, E.), **Supp. IX:** 159, 161, 163

New Dominion, A (Jhabvala), **Supp. V:** 230–231

"New Drama" (Joyce), **Retro. Supp. I:** 170

New Dunciad, The (Pope), **III:** 73, 78; **Retro. Supp. I:** 238

"New Empire Within Britain, The" (Rushdie), **Supp. IV:** 436, 445

"New England Winter, A" (James), **VI:** 69

New Essays by De Quincey (ed. Tave); **IV:** 155

New Ewart, The: Poems 1980–82 (Ewart), **Supp. VII:** 34, 44, 45

New Family Instructor, A (Defoe), **III:** 14

"New Forge" (Murphy), **Supp. V:** 328

New Form of Intermittent Light for Lighthouses, A (Stevenson), **V:** 395

New Grub Street (Gissing), **V:** xxv, 426, 427, 429, 430, 434–435, 437; **VI:** 377; **Supp. IV:** 7

"New Hampshire" (Reid), **Supp. VII:** 326

New Inn; The Noble Gentlemen (Jonson), **II:** 65; **Retro. Supp. I:** 165

New Journey to Paris, A (Swift), **III:** 35

"New King for the Congo: Mobutu and the Nihilism of Africa" (Naipaul), **Supp. I:** 398

New Light on Piers Plowman (Bright), **I:** 3

New Lines (Conquest), **Supp. IV:** 256

New Lives for Old (Snow), **VII:** 323

New Love–Poems (Scott), **IV:** 39

New Machiavelli, The (Wells), **VI:** 226, 239, 244

New Magdalen, The (Collins), **Supp. VI:** 102

New Meaning of Treason, The (West), **Supp. III:** 440, 444

New Men, The (Snow), **VII:** xxi, 324, 328–329, 330

New Method of Evaluation as Applied to ð, The (Carroll), **V:** 274

New Monthly (periodical), **IV:** 252, 254, 258

"New Novel, The" (James), **VI:** xii

New Numbers (periodical), **VI:** 420; **Supp. III:** 47

New Oxford Book of Irish Verse, The (Kinsella), **Supp. V:** 274

New Oxford Book of Sixteenth Century Verse, The (ed. Jones), **Supp. XI:** 116

New Poems (Adcock), **Supp. XII:** 11, 13

New Poems (Arnold), **V:** xxiii, 204, 209, 216

"New Poems" (Bridges), **VI:** 77

New Poems (Davies), **Supp. III:** 398

New Poems (Davies), **Supp. XI:** 85, 88, 96, 97

New Poems (Fuller), **Supp. VII:** 76–77

New Poems (Kinsella), **Supp. V:** 266, 274

New Poems (Thompson), **V:** 444, 446, 451

New Poems by Robert Browning and Elizabeth Barrett Browning (ed. Kenyon), **IV:** 321

New Poems Hitherto Unpublished or Uncollected . . . (Rossetti), **V:** 260

New Quixote, The (Frayn), **Supp. VII:** 57

New Review (periodical), **VI:** 136

New Rhythm and Other Pieces, The (Firbank), **Supp. II:** 202, 205, 207, 222

New Satyr on the Parliament, A (Defoe), **Retro. Supp. I:** 67

New Selected Poems 1964–2000 (Dunn), **Supp. X:** 67, 70–71, 76, 81

New Selected Poems (Heaney), **Retro. Supp. I:** 131

New Signatures (Day Lewis), **Supp. III:** 125

New Signatures (ed. Roberts), **VII:** 411; **Supp. II:** 486

"New Song, A" (Heaney), **Supp. II:** 273

New Statesman (periodical), **VI:** 119, 250, 371; **VII:** 32; **Supp. IV:** 26, 66, 78, 80, 81; **Supp. XII:** 2, 186, 199

New Stories I (ed. Drabble), **Supp. IV:** 230

New Territory (Boland), **Supp. V:** 35, 36

New Testament in Modern English (Phillips), **I:** 383

New Testament in Modern Speech (Weymouth), **I:** 382

New Voyage Round the World, A (Dampier), **III:** 7, 24

New Voyage Round the World, A (Defoe), **III:** 3, 13

New Way to Pay Old Debts, A (Massinger), **Supp. XI:** 180, 184, 185, 186–190, 191

New Weather (Muldoon), **Supp. IV:** 412–414, 416

"New Weather" (Muldoon), **Supp. IV:** 413

New Witness (periodical), **VI:** 340, 341

"New World A'Comin'" (Brathwaite), **Supp. XII:** 36–37

New Worlds for Old (Wells), **VI:** 242

New Writings of William Hazlitt (ed. Howe), **IV:** 140

New Year Letter (Auden), **VII:** 379, 382, 388, 390, 393; **Retro. Supp. I:** 10

"New Year Wishes for the English" (Davie), **Supp. VI:** 110

"New Year's Burden, A" (Rossetti), **V:** 242

"New Year's Gift to the King" (Dunbar), **VIII:** 118

"New York" (Russell), **VIII:** 291

Newbolt, Henry, **VI:** 75, 417

Newby, T. C., **V:** 140

Newcomes, The (Thackeray), **V:** xxii, 18, 19, **28–31,** 35, 38, 69

Newell, K. B., **VI:** 235, 237

"Newgate"novels, **V:** 22, 47

Newman, F. W., **V:** 208n

Newman, John Henry, **II:** 243; **III:** 46; **IV:** 63, 64; **V:** xi, xxv, 156, 214, 283, 340; **Supp. VII: 289–305**

"News" (Traherne), **II:** 191, 194

News and Weather, The (Fallon), **Supp. XII:** 108–110, 114

"News from Ireland, The" (Trevor), **Supp. IV:** 504–505

News from Nowhere (Morris), **V:** xxv, 291, 301–304, 306, 409

"News from the Sun" (Ballard), **Supp. V:** 22

"News of the World" (Fallon), **Supp. XII:** 114

News of the World: Selected and New Poems (Fallon), **Supp. XII:** 114–115

News of the World: Selected Poems (Fallon), **Supp. XII:** 105–106, 112

Newspaper, The (Crabbe), **III:** 275, 286

Newspoems (Morgan, E.), **Supp. IX:** 163

"Newsreel" (Day Lewis), **Supp. III:** 127

"Newstead Abbey" (Fuller), **Supp. VII:** 73

Newton, Isaac, **Supp. III:** 418–419

Newton, J. F., **IV:** 158

Newton, John, **III:** 210

"Newts" (Thomas), **Supp. XII:** 290

"Next Time, The" (James), **VI:** 69

"Next, Please" (Larkin), **Supp. I:** 278

Ngaahika ndeenda (Ngũgĩ wa Thiong'o/ Ngũgĩ wa Mĩriĩ), **VIII:** 215–216, 223–224

Ngũgĩ wa Thiong'o, **Supp. V:** 56; **VIII: 211–226**

Nibelungenlied, **VIII:** 231

Nice and the Good, The (Murdoch), **Supp. I:** 226, 227

"Nice Day at School" (Trevor), **Supp. IV:** 504

"Nice to Be Nice" (Kelman), **Supp. V:** 245–246

Nice Valour, The (Fetcher and Middleton), **II:** 21, 66

Nice Work (Lodge), **Supp. IV:** 363, 366, 372, 378–380, 383, 385

Nice Work (television adaptation), **Supp. IV:** 381

Nicholas Nickleby (Dickens), **IV:** 69; **V:** xix, 42, 50–53, 54, 71

Nicholls, Bowyer, **V:** 98

Nichols, Robert, **VI:** 419

Nicholson, Norman, **Supp. VI: 211–224**

Nichomachean Ethics (Johnson), **Retro. Supp. I:** 149

"Nicht Flittin" (Crawford), **Supp. XI:** 70–71

Nicoll, Allardyce, **II:** 363

Nietzsche, Friedrich Wilhelm, **IV:** 121, 179; **Supp. IV:** 3, 6, 9, 10, 12, 17, 50, 108

Nigger of the "Narcissus,"The (Conrad), **VI:** 136, 137, 148; **Retro. Supp. II:** 71–73

Nigger Question, The (Carlyle), **IV:** 247, 250

Night (Pinter), **Supp. I:** 376

Night (Harris), **Supp. V:** 138, 139

Night (O'Brien), **Supp. V:** 338

"Night Before the War, The" (Plomer), **Supp. XI:** 222

"Nightclub" (MacNeice), **VII:** 414

Night–Comers, The (Ambler), *see State of Siege*

Night–Comers, The (film), **Supp. IV:** 3

Night Fears and Other Stories (Hartley), **Supp. VII:** 121–122

Night Feed (Boland), **Supp. V:** 50

"Night Feed" (Boland), **Supp. V:** 50

"Night Sister" (Jennings), **Supp. V:** 215

"Night Songs" (Kinsella), **Supp. V:** 261

"Nightwalker" (Kinsella), **Supp. V:** 263

Nightwalker and Other Poems (Kinsella), **Supp. V:** 262, 263–264

"Night, The" (Vaughan), **II:** 186, 188

Night and Day (Rosenberg), **VI:** 432

Night and Day (Stoppard), **Supp. I:** 451; **Retro. Supp. II:** 352–353

Night and Day (Woolf), **VII:** 20, 27; **Retro. Supp. I:** 307, 316

"Night and the Merry Man" (Browning), **IV:** 313

Night–Crossing (Mahon), **Supp. VI: 167–168,** 169

Night Feed (Boland), **Supp. V:** 50

"Night Mail" (Auden), **Retro. Supp. I:** 7

"Night of Frost in May" (Meredith), **V:** 223

Night on Bald Mountain (White), **Supp. I:** 131, 136, **149–151**

"Night Out" (Rhys), **Supp. II:** 402

Night Out, A (Pinter), **Supp. I:** 371–372, 375; **Retro. Supp. I:** 223

"Night Patrol" (West), **VI:** 423

Night School (Pinter), **Supp. I:** 373, 375

"Night Sister" (Jennings), **Supp. V:** 215

"Night Songs" (Kinsella), **Supp. V:** 261

"Night Taxi" (Gunn), **Supp. IV:** 272–273, 274

Night the Prowler, The (White), **Supp. I:** 131, 132

Night Thoughts (Young), **III:** 302, 307; **Retro. Supp. I:** 43

Night to Remember, A (Ambler), **Supp. IV:** 3

Night to Remember, A (film), **Supp. IV:** 2

Night Walker, The (Fletcher and Shirley), **II:** 66

"Night Wind, The" (Brontë), **V:** 133, 142

"Nightfall (For an Athlete Dying Young)" (Hollinghurst), **Supp. X:** 121

"Nightingale and the Rose, The" (Wilde), **Retro. Supp. II:** 365

"Nightingale's Nest, The" (Clare), **Supp. XI:** 50, 60

"Nightmare, A" (Rossetti), **V:** 256

Nightmare Abbey (Peacock), **III:** 336, 345; **IV:** xvii, 158, 162, 164–165, 170, 177

"Nightpiece to Julia, The" (Herrick), **II:** lll

Nightrunners of Bengal (film, Ambler), **Supp. IV:** 3

Nights at the Alexandra (Trevor), **Supp. IV:** 514–515

Nights at the Circus (Carter), **Supp. III:** 79, 87, 89–90, 91–92

"Night's Fall Unlocks the Dirge of the Sea" (Graham), **Supp. VII:** 110

Nightfishing, The (Graham), **Supp. VII:** 105, 106, 111–113, 114, 116

"Nightwalker" (Kinsella), **Supp. V:** 263

Nightwalker and Other Poems (Kinsella), **Supp. V:** 262, 263–264

Nin, Anaïs, **Supp. IV:** 110, 111

Nina Balatka (Trollope), **V:** 101

Nine Essays (Housman), **VI:** 164

Nine Experiments (Spender), **Supp. II:** 481, 486

Nine Tailors, The (Sayers), **Supp. III:** 343, 344–345

"Ninemaidens" (Thomas), **Supp. IV:** 494

"1938" (Kinsella), **Supp. V:** 271

1985 (Burgess), **Supp. I:** 193

Nineteen Eighty–four (Orwell), **III:** 341; **VII:** xx, 204, 274, 279–280, 284–285

1982 Janine (Gray, A.), **Supp. IX:** 80, 83–85, 86

1914 (Brooke), **Supp. III:** 48, 52, 56–58

"1914" (Owen), **VI:** 444

1914 and Other Poems (Brooke), **VI:** 420; **Supp. III:** 48, 55

1914. Five Sonnets (Brooke), **VI:** 420

1900 (West), **Supp. III:** 432, 445

"Nineteen Hundred and Nineteen" (Yeats), **VI:** 217; **Retro. Supp. I:** 335

"1916 Seen from 1922" (Blunden), **Supp. XI:** 45

"Nineteen Songs" (Hart), **Supp. XI:** 132

"1938" (Kinsella), **Supp. V:** 271

"Nineteenth Century, The" (Thompson), **V:** 442

Nineteenth Century: A Dialogue in Utopia, The (Ellis), **VI:** 241n

Nip in the Air, A (Betjeman), **VII:** 357

Niven, Alastair, **VII:** xiv, xxxviii

Njáls saga, **VIII:** 238, 240

"Njamba Nene" stories (Ngũgĩ), **VIII:** 222

No (Ackroyd), **Supp. VI:** 2

No Abolition of Slavery . . . (Boswell), **III:** 248

No Continuing City (Longley), **VIII:** 163, 165, 167–169, 170, 171, 175

"No Easy Thing" (Hart), **Supp. XI:** 132

No Enemy (Ford), **VI:** 324

No Exit (Sartre), **III:** 329, 345

"No Flowers by Request" (Ewart), **Supp. VII:** 36

No Fond Return of Love (Pym), **Supp. II: 374–375,** 381

No Fool Like an Old Fool (Ewart), **Supp. VII:** 41

"No Ghosts" (Plomer), **Supp. XI:** 222

"No Immortality?" (Cornford), **VIII:** 105, 109

No Laughing Matter (Wilson), **Supp. I:** 162–163

No Man's Land (Hill, R.), **Supp. IX:** 117–118, 121

No Man's Land (Pinter), **Supp. I:** 377

No Mercy: A Journey to the Heart of the Congo (O'Hanlon), **Supp. XI:** 196, 202–206, 207, 208

No More Parades (Ford), **VI:** 319, 329

No Name (Collins), **Supp. VI:** 91, 93–94, **97–98,** 102

No Other Life (Moore, B.), **Supp. IX:** 151, 152–153

No Painted Plumage (Powys), **VIII:** 245, 254–255, 256, 257, 258

No Quarter (Waugh), **Supp. VI:** 275

"No Rest for the Wicked" (Mahon), **Supp. VI:** 167

"No Return" (Smith, I. C.), **Supp. IX:** 218

"No Road" (Larkin), **Supp. I:** 285

"No Room" (Powys), **VIII:** 249, 254, 258

"No Smoking" (Ewart), **Supp. VII:** 47

No Star on the Way Back (Nicholson), **Supp. VI:** 217

"No, Thank You John" (Rossetti), **V:** 256

No Truce with the Furies (Thomas), **Supp. XII:** 282, 285, 286, 290, 291–292

No Truce with Time (Waugh), **Supp. VI:** 274

No Wit, No Help Like a Woman's (Middleton), **II:** 3, 21

"No Muses" (Smith, I. C.), **Supp. IX:** 222

"No Witchcraft for Sale" (Lessing), **Supp. I:** 241, 242

"No worst, There is none" (Hopkins), **V:** 374

Noah and the Waters (Day Lewis), **Supp. III:** 118, 126, 127

"Noble Child is Born, The" (Dunbar). *See Et Nobis Puer Natus Est*

Noble Jilt, The (Trollope), **V:** 102

Noble Numbers (Herrick), *see His Noble Numbers*

Nobleman, The (Tourneur), **II:** 37

Noblesse Oblige (Mitford), **Supp. X:** 163

"Nocturnal Reverie" (Finch), **Supp. IX:** 76

Nocturnal upon S. Lucy's Day, A (Donne), **I:** 358, 359–360; **II:** 128; **Retro. Supp. II:** 91

"Nocturne" (Coppard), **VIII:** 88

"Nocturne" (Murphy), **Supp. V:** 325

Noh theater, **VI:** 218

Noises Off (Frayn), **Supp. VII:** 61

"Noisy Flushes the Birds" (Pritchett), **Supp. III:** 324–325

"Noisy in the Doghouse" (Pritchett), **Supp. III:** 324, 325

"Noli emulari" (Wyatt), **I:** 102

Nollius, **II:** 185, 201

Nomadic Alternative, The (Chatwin, B.), **Supp. IX:** 52, 58

"Nona Vincent" (James), **VI:** 69

"Nones" (Auden), **Retro. Supp. I:** 2

Nonsense Songs, Stories, Botany and Alphabets (Lear), **V:** 78, 84, 87

Non–Stop Connolly Show, The (Arden and D'Arcy), **Supp. II:** 28, 30, **35–38,** 39

Nooks and Byways of Italy, The (Ramage), **VI:** 298

"Noon at St. Michael's" (Mahon), **Supp. VI:** 174

"Noonday Axeman" (Murray), **Supp. VII:** 272

"No–One" (Thomas), **Supp. XII:** 281, 286

Norman Douglas (Dawkins), **VI:** 303–304

Norman Conquests, The (Ayckbourn), **Supp. V:** 2, 5, 9, 10, 11, 14

Normyx, pseud. of Norman Douglas

North, Thomas, **I:** 314

North (Heaney), **Supp. II:** 268, **273–275; Supp. IV:** 412, 420–421, 427; **Retro. Supp. I:** 124, 125, 129–130

"North Africa" (Morgan, E.), **Supp. IX:** 167

North America (Trollope), **V:** 101

North and South (Gaskell), **V:** xxii, **1–6,** 8, 15

"North and South, The" (Browning), **IV:** 315

North Face (Renault), **Supp. IX:** 175–176

"North London Book of the Dead, The" (Self), **Supp. V:** 400

"North Sea" (Keyes), **VII:** 437

"North Sea off Carnoustie" (Stevenson), **Supp. VI:** 260

North Ship, The (Larkin), **Supp. I:** 276–277

"North Wind, The" (Bridges), **VI:** 80

Northanger Abbey (Austen), **III:** 335–336, 345; **IV:** xvii, 103, 104, 107–110, 112–114, 122; **Retro. Supp. II:** 4–6

Northanger Novels, The (Sadleir), **III:** 335, 346

"Northern Farmer, New Style" (Tennyson), **IV:** 327

"Northern Farmer, Old Style" (Tennyson), **IV:** 327

Northern Lasse, The (Brome), **Supp. X:** 52, 55, 61

Northern Lights: A Poet's Sources (Brown), **Supp. VI:** 61, 64

Northern Memoirs (Franck), **II:** 131

Northward Ho! (Dekker, Marston, Webster), **I:** 234–235, 236, 244; **II:** 68, 85

Norton, Charles Eliot, **IV:** 346; **V:** 3, 9, 299; **VI:** 41

Norton, Thomas, **I:** 214

"Nose, The" (Gogol), **III:** 340, 345

Nosferatu (film), **III:** 342; **IV:** 180

"Nostalgia in the Afternoon" (Heaney), **Retro. Supp. I:** 126

Nostromo (Conrad), **VI:** 140–143; **Retro. Supp. II:** 77–80

Not . . . not . . . not . . . not . . . not enough oxygen (Churchill), **Supp. IV:** 181

"Not Abstract" (Jennings), **Supp. V:** 217

"Not After Midnight" (du Maurier), **Supp. III:** 135

"Not Celia, that I juster am" (Sedley), **II:** 265

Not for Publication (Gordimer), **Supp. II:** 232

Not Honour More (Cary), **VII:** 186, 194–195

Not I (Beckett), **Supp. I:** 61; **Retro. Supp. I:** 27–28

"Not Ideas, But Obsessions" (Naipaul), **Supp. I:** 399

"Not Looking" (Nye), **Supp. X:** 201

"Not Not While the Giro" (Kelman), **Supp. V:** 246

Not Not While the Giro and Other Stories (Kelman), **Supp. V:** 242, 244–246

"Not Now for My Sins' Sake" (Reid), **Supp. VII:** 325–326

"Not on Sad Stygian Shore" (Butler), **Supp. II:** 111

"Not Palaces" (Spender), **Supp. II:** 494

"Not Proven" (Day Lewis), **Supp. III:** 130

Not–So–Stories (Saki), **Supp. VI:** 240

Not That He Brought Flowers (Thomas), **Supp. XII:** 284

Not to Disturb (Spark), **Supp. I:** 200, 201, 210

Not Waving But Drowning (Smith), **Supp. II:** 463

"Not Waving But Drowning" (Smith), **Supp. II:** 467

Not Without Glory (Scannell), **VII:** 424, 426

Not Without Honor (Brittain), **Supp. X:** 33, 38

"Not yet Afterwards" (MacCaig), **Supp. VI:** 185

"Notable Discovery of Cosenage, A" (Greene), **VIII:** 144

"Note for American Readers" (Byatt), **Supp. IV:** 149

"Notes from a Spanish Village" (Reid), **Supp. VII:** 334,335–336

Note on Charlotte Brontë, A (Swinburne), **V:** 332

"Note on F. W. Bussell" (Pater), **V:** 356–357

"Note on 'To Autumn,' A" (Davenport), **IV:** 227

"Note on Zulfikar Ghose's 'Nature Strategies'" (Harris), **Supp. V:** 145

"Note to the Difficult One, A" (Graham), **Supp. VII:** 115

Notebook (Maugham), **VI:** 370

"Notebook, A" (Hulme), **Supp. VI:** 135, 140, 145

Note–Book of Edmund Burke (ed. Somerset), **III:** 205

Notebook on William Shakespeare, A (Sitwell), **VII:** 127, 139, 140

Note–Books (Butler), **Supp. II:** 100, 102, 105, **108–111,** 115, 117, 118, 119

Notebooks (Thomas), **Supp. I:** 170

Notebooks of Henry James, The (ed. Matthiessen and Murdock), **VI:** 38

Notebooks of Robinson Crusoe, and Other Poems, The (Smith, I. C.), **Supp. IX:** 216, 217

Notebooks of Samuel Taylor Coleridge, The (ed. Coburn), **IV:** 48, 53, 56

Notes and Index to . . . the Letters of Sir Walter Scott (Corson), **IV:** 27, 39

Notes and Observations on the Empress of Morocco (Dryden), **II:** 297, 305

Notes and Reviews (James), **V:** 199

Notes by an Oxford Chiel (Carroll), **V:** 274

Notes for a New Culture: An Essay on Modernism (Ackroyd), **Supp. VI:** 2, 12–13

Notes for Poems (Plomer), **Supp. XI:** 213

"Notes from a Book of Hours" (Jennings), **Supp. V:** 211

Notes from the Land of the Dead and Other Poems (Kinsella), **Supp. V:** 266, 274

Notes of a Journey from Cornhill to Grand Cairo (Thackeray), **V:** 25, 37, 38

Notes of a Journey Through France and Italy (Hazlitt), **IV:** 134, 140

Notes of a Son and Brother (James), **VI:** 59, 65–66

Notes of an English Republican on the Muscovite Crusade (Swinburne), **V:** 332

"Notes on Being a Foreigner" (Reid), **Supp. VII:** 323

"Notes on Designs of the Old Masters at Florence" (Swinburne), **V:** 329

Notes on English Divines (Coleridge), **IV:** 56

Notes on Joseph Conrad (Symons), **VI:** 149

"Notes on Language and Style" (Hulme), **Supp. VI:** 135–136, 141–143, 146

Notes on Life and Letters (Conrad), **VI:** 67, 148

Notes on Novelists (James), **V:** 384, 392; **VI:** 149

Notes on Old Edinburgh (Bird), **Supp. X:** 23

Notes on . . . Pictures Exhibited in the Rooms of the Royal Academy (Ruskin), **V:** 184

Notes on Poems and Reviews (Swinburne), **V:** 316, 329, 332

Notes on Sculptures in Rome and Florence . . . (Shelley), **IV:** 209

"Notes on Technical Matters" (Sitwell), **VII:** 139

Notes on the Construction of Sheep–Folds (Ruskin), **V:** 184

Notes on the Royal Academy Exhibition, 1868 (Swinburne), **V:** 329, 332

Notes on "The Testament of Beauty" (Smith), **VI:** 83

Notes on the Turner Gallery at Marlborough House (Ruskin), **V:** 184

"Notes on Writing a Novel" (Bowen), **Supp. II:** 90

Notes Theological, Political, and Miscellaneous (Coleridge), **IV:** 56

Nothing (Green), **Supp. II: 263–264**

Nothing for Anyone (Reading), **VIII:** 264, 267, 274

Nothing Like Leather (Pritchett), **Supp. III:** 313–314

Nothing Like the Sun (Burgess), **Supp. I:** 194, 196

Nothing Sacred (Carter), **Supp. III:** 80, 86–87

Nothing So Simple as Climbing (Dutton), **Supp. XII:** 85

"Notice in Heaven" (Morgan, E.), **Supp. IX:** 163

"Notice in Hell" (Morgan, E.), **Supp. IX:** 163

Nott, John, **II:** 102

"Nottingham and the Mining Country" (Lawrence), **VII:** 88, 89, 91, 121; **Retro. Supp. II:** 221

Nouvelles (Beckett), **Supp. I:** 49–50

Novak, Maximillian, **Retro. Supp. I:** 66–67, 68–69

Novel and the People, The (Fox), **Supp. IV:** 466

Novel Now, The (Burgess), **Supp. I:** 194

Novel on Yellow Paper (Smith), **Supp. II:** 460, 462, 469, 473, **474–476**

Novelist, The (portrait; Kitaj), **Supp. IV:** 119

Novelist at the Crossroads, and Other Essays on Fiction, The (Lodge), **Supp. IV:** 365

"Novelist at Work, The" (Cary), **VII:** 187

"Novelist Today: Still at the Crossroads?, The" (Lodge), **Supp. IV:** 367

"Novelist's Poison, The" (Keneally), **Supp. IV:** 343

Novels of E. M. Forster, The (Woolf), **VI:** 413

Novels of George Eliot: A Study in Form, The (Hardy), **V:** 201

Novels of George Meredith, and Some Notes on the English Novel, The (Sitwell), **V:** 230, 234

Novels Up to Now (radio series), **VI:** 372

"November" (Armitage), **VIII:** 3–4

"November" (Bridges), **VI:** 79–80

"November 1, 1931" (Blunden), **Supp. XI:** 33

Novum organum (Bacon), **I:** 259, 260, 263–264, 272; **IV:** 279

"Now"(Thomas), **Supp. I:** 174

Now and in Time to Be (Keneally), **Supp. IV:** 347

"Now I know what love may be" (Cameron), see "Nunc Scio Quid Sit Amor"

"Now in the Time of This Mortal Living" (Nicholson), **Supp. VI:** 214

"Now Sleeps the Crimson Petal" (Tennyson), **IV:** 334

Now We Are Six (Milne), **Supp. V:** 295, 302–303

"Now Let Me Roll" (Cameron), **Supp. IX:** 27

"Now, Zero" (Ballard), **Supp. V:** 21

"Nuance" (Thomas), **Supp. XII:** 286

Nude with Violin (Coward), **Supp. II:** 155

Numbers (Sisson), **Supp. XI:** 249

"Numina at the Street Parties, The" (Redgrove), **Supp. VI:** 235

Numismata: A Discourse of Medals . . . (Evelyn), **II:** 287

"Nunc Dimittis" (Dahl), **Supp. IV:** 215, 217

"Nunc Scio Quid Sit Amor" (Cameron, N.), **Supp. IX:** 19–20, 22

Nunquam (Durrell), **Supp. I: 94,** 103, **113–118,** 120

Nuns and Soldiers (Murdoch), **Supp. I:** 231, 233

Nun's Priest's Tale, The (Chaucer), **I:** 21

"Nuptiall Song, A; or, Epithalamie, on Sir Clipseby Crew and his Lady" (Herrick), **II:** 105, 106

"Nuptials of Attilla, The" (Meredith), **V:** 221

"Nurse" (Cornford), **VIII:** 107

Nursery Alice, The (Carroll), **V:** 273

Nursery Rhymes (Sitwell), **VII:** 138

"Nursery Songs" (Reid), **Supp. VII:** 326

"Nurse's Song" (Blake), **III:** 292; **Retro. Supp. I:** 42

Nussey, Ellen, **V:** 108, 109, 113, 117, 118, 126, 152

Nutmeg of Consolation, The (O'Brian), **Supp. XII:** 258–259

Nuts of Knowledge, The (Russell), **VIII:** 284

Nye, Robert, **Supp. X:** 191–207

"Nymph Complaining for the Death of Her Faun, The" (Marvell), **II:** 211, 215–216

"Nympholept, A" (Swinburne), **V:** 328

"**O** Dreams, O Destinations" (Day Lewis), **Supp. III:** 122

"O! for a Closer Walk with God" (Cowper), **III:** 210

"O happy dames, that may embrace" (Surrey), **I:** 115, 120

"O land of Empire, art and love!" (Clough), **V:** 158

O Mistress Mine (Rattigan), see *Love in Idleness*

O Rathaille, Aogan, **Supp. IV:** 418–419

"O Tell Me the Truth About Love" (Auden), **Retro. Supp. I:** 6

Ó Tuama, Seán, **Supp. V:** 266

"O World of many Worlds" (Owen), **VI:** 445

"O Youth whose hope is high" (Bridges), **VI:** 159

Oak Leaves and Lavender (O'Casey), **VII:** 7, 8

Oases (Reid), **Supp. VII:** 333–337

Ob. (Reading), **VIII:** 273

"Oban" (Smith, I. C.), **Supp. IX:** 220

"Obedience" (Herbert), **II:** 126

"Obelisk, The" (Forster), **VI:** 411

"Obermann Once More" (Arnold), **V:** 210

Oberon (Jonson), **I:** 344–345

"Object Lessons" (Boland), **Supp. V:** 38–39

Object Lessons: The Life of the Woman and the Poet in Our Time (Boland), **Supp. V:** 35, 36, 37, 42, 43, 46

"Object of the Attack, The" (Ballard), **Supp. V:** 33

Objections to Sex and Violence (Churchill), **Supp. IV:** 182–183, 184, 198

"Objects, Odours" (Wallace–Crabbe), **VIII:** 321

O'Brian, Patrick, **Supp. XII: 247–264**

O'Brien, Conor Cruise, **Supp. IV:** 449

O'Brien, E. J., **VII:** 176

O'Brien, Edna, **Supp. V: 333–346**

O'Brien, Flann, *see* O'Nolan, Brian

Obsequies to the Memory of Mr. Edward King (Milton), **II:** 175

"Observation Car" (Hope), **Supp. VII:** 154

Observations on a Late State of the Nation (Burke), **III:** 205

Observations on Macbeth (Johnson), *see* Miscellaneous Observations on the Tragedy of Macbeth

Observations . . . on Squire Foote's Dramatic Entertainment . .. . (Boswell), **III:** 247

Observations Relative . . . to Picturesque Beauty . . . [in] the High–Lands of Scotland (Gilpin), **IV:** 36

Observations upon the Articles of Peace with the Irish Rebels .. . . (Milton), **II:** 176

Observator (periodical), **III:** 41; **Supp. IV:** 121

O'Casey, Sean, **VI:** xiv, 214, 218, 314–315; **VII:** xviii, **1–15**; list of articles, **VII:** 14–15; **Supp. II:** 335–336

Occasion for Loving (Gordimer), **Supp. II:** 227, 228, 231, 232, 233

Occasional Verses (FitzGerald), **IV:** 353

Occasions of Poetry, The (ed. Wilmer), **Supp. IV:** 255, 263

Ocean of Story (Stead), **Supp. IV:** 476

O'Connor, Frank, **Supp. IV:** 514

O'Connor, Monsignor John, **VI:** 338

O'Connor, Ulick, **Supp. II:** 63, 70, 76

October and Other Poems (Bridges), **VI:** 81, 83

"October Dawn" (Hughes), **Supp. I: 344**

October Ferry to Gabriola (Lowry), **Supp. III: 284–285**

October Man, The (film, Ambler), **Supp. IV:** 3

"October Dawn" (Hughes), **Retro. Supp. II:** 203

"October Salmon" (Hughes), **Supp. I:** 363; **Retro. Supp. II:** 213–214

Odd Girl Out, The (Howard), **Supp. XI:** 141, 142–143, 145

Odd Women, The (Gissing), **V:** 428, 433–434, 437

Oddments Inklings Omens Moments (Reid), **Supp. VII:** 327–329

Ode ad Gustavem regem. Ode ad Gustavem exulem (Landor), **IV:** 100

"Ode: Autumn" (Hood), **IV:** 255

"Ode for Music" (Gray), *see* "Installation Ode"

"Ode. Intimations of Immortality from Recollections of Early Childhood" (Wordsworth), **II:** 189, 200; **IV:** xvi, 21, 22

"Ode on a Distant Prospect of Eton College" (Gray), **III:** 137, 144

"Ode on a Grecian Urn" (Keats), **III:** 174, 337; **IV:** 222–223, 225, 226; **Supp. V:** 38; **Retro. Supp. I:** 195–196

"Ode on Indolence" (Keats), **IV:** 221, 225–226

"Ode on Melancholy" (Keats), **III:** 337; **IV:** 224–225

"Ode on Mrs. Arabella Hunt Singing" (Congreve), **II:** 348

Ode, on the Death of Mr. Henry Purcell, An (Dryden), **II:** 304

"Ode on the Death of Mr. Thomson" (Collins), **III:** 163, 175

"Ode on the Death of Sir H. Morison" (Jonson), **II:** 199

Ode on the Death of the Duke of Wellington (Tennyson), **II:** 200; **IV:** 338

Ode on the Departing Year (Coleridge), **IV:** 55

Ode on the Installation of . . . Prince Albert as Chancellor of . . . Cambridge (Wordsworth), **IV:** 25

"Ode on the Insurrection at Candia" (Swinburne), **V:** 313

"Ode on the Morning of Christ's Nativity" (Milton), **Retro. Supp. II:** 272

"Ode on the Pleasure Arising from Vicissitude" (Gray), **III:** 141, 145

"Ode on the Popular Superstitions of the Highlands of Scotland" (Collins), **III:** 163, 171–173, 175

Ode on the Proclamation of the French Republic (Swinburne), **V:** 332

"Ode on the Spring" (Gray), **III:** 137, 295

"Ode Performed in the Senate House at Cambridge" (Gray), **III:** 145

Ode Prefixed to S. Harrison's Arches of Triumph . . . (Webster), **II:** 85

"Ode to a Lady on the Death of Colonel Ross" (Collins), **III:** 162

"Ode to a Nightingale" (Keats), **II:** 122; **IV:** 212, 221, 222–223, 224, 226; **Retro. Supp. I:** 195–196

"Ode to Apollo" (Keats), **IV:** 221, 227

"Ode to Duty" (Wordsworth), **II:** 303

"Ode to Evening" (Blunden), **Supp. XI:** 43

"Ode to Evening" (Collins), **III:** 166, 173; **IV:** 227

"Ode to Fear" (Collins), *see* "Fear"

Ode to Himself (Jonson), **I:** 336

Ode to Independence (Smollett), **III:** 158

"Ode to John Warner" (Auden), **Retro. Supp. I:** 8

"Ode to Liberty" (Shelley), **IV:** 203

"Ode to Master Endymion Porter, Upon his Brothers Death, An" (Herrick), **II:** 112

"Ode to May" (Keats), **IV:** 221, 222

Ode to Mazzini (Swinburne), **V:** 333

"Ode to Memory" (Tennyson), **IV:** 329

"Ode to Mr. Congreve" (Swift), **III:** 30

"Ode to Naples" (Shelley), **II:** 200; **IV:** 195

Ode to Napoleon Buonaparte (Byron), **IV:** 192

"Ode to Pity" (Collins), **III:** 164

"Ode to Psyche" (Keats), **IV:** 221–222

"Ode to Rae Wilson" (Hood), **IV:** 261, 262–263

"Ode to Sir William Temple" (Swift), **III:** 30

"Ode to Sorrow" (Keats), **IV:** 216, 224

"Ode to the Moon" (Hood), **IV:** 255

"Ode to the Setting Sun" (Thompson), **V:** 448, 449

"Ode to the West Wind" (Shelley), **II:** 200; **IV:** xviii, 198, 203

Ode to Tragedy, An (Boswell), **III:** 247

"Ode upon Dr. Harvey" (Cowley), **II:** 196, 198

"Ode: Written at the Beginning of the Year 1746" (Collins), **III:** 169

Odes (Gray), **III:** 145

Odes and Addresses to Great People (Hood and Reynolds), **IV:** 253, 257, 267

Odes in Contribution to the Song of French History (Meredith), **V:** 223, 234

Odes on Several Descriptive and Allegorical Subjects (Collins), **III:** 162, 163, 165–166, 175

Odes on the Comic Spirit (Meredith), **V:** 234

Odes to . . . the Emperor of Russia, and . . . the King of Prussia (Southey), **IV:** 71

Odette d'Antrevernes (Firbank), **Supp. II:** 199, 201, 205–206

"Odour, The" (Traherne), **Supp. XI:** 269
"Odour of Chrysanthemums" (Lawrence), **VII:** 114; **Retro. Supp. II:** 232–233
"Odysseus of Hermes" (Gunn), **Supp. IV:** 275
Odyssey (Homer), **Supp. IV:** 234, 267, 428
Odyssey (tr. Cowper), **III:** 220
"Odyssey" (Longley), **VIII:** 167
Odyssey (tr. Pope), **III:** 70, 77
Odyssey, The (Butler translation), **Supp. II:** 114, 115
Odyssey of Homer, The (Lawrence translation), **Supp. II:** 283, 294
Odyssey of Homer, done into English Verse, The (Morris), **V:** 306
Oedipus Tyrannus; or, Swellfoot the Tyrant (Shelley), **IV:** 208
Of Ancient and Modern Learning (Temple), **III:** 23
"Of Commerce and Society: The Death of Shelley" (Hill), **Supp. V:** 186
"Of Democritus and Heraclitus" (Montaigne), **III:** 39
"Of Discourse" (Cornwallis), **III:** 39–40
"Of Divine Love" (Waller), **II:** 235
Of Dramatick Poesie, An Essay (Dryden), *see Essay of Dramatick Poesy*
Of Education (Milton), **II:** 162–163, 175
"Of Eloquence" (Goldsmith), **III:** 186
"Of English Verse" (Waller), **II:** 233–234
"Of Essay Writing" (Hume), **Supp. III:** 231–232
"Of Greatness" (Cowley), **III:** 40
Of Human Bondage (Maugham), **VI:** xiii, 365, 373–374
Of Justification by Imputed Righteousness (Bunyan), **II:** 253
"Of Liberty" (Cowley), **II:** 198
Of Liberty and Loyalty (Swinburne), **V:** 333
Of Liberty and Servitude (tr. Evelyn), **II:** 287
Of Magnanimity and Chastity (Traherne), **II:** 202
"Of Masques" (Bacon), **I:** 268
"Of My Self" (Cowley), **II:** 195
"Of Nature: Laud and Plaint" (Thompson), **V:** 443
"Of Only a Single Poem" (Dutton), **Supp. XII:** 95, 96
"Of Pacchiarotto" (Browning), **IV:** 366
"Of Plants" (Cowley), **Supp. III:** 36
"Of Pleasing" (Congreve), **II:** 349
"Of Poetry" (Temple), **III:** 23, 190
Of Prelatical Episcopacy . . . (Milton), **II:** 175
Of Reformation Touching Church Discipline in England (Milton), **II:** 162, 175
Of Style (Hughes), **III:** 40
Of the Characters of Women (Pope), *see Moral Essays*
Of the Friendship of Amis and Amile, Done into English (Morris), **V:** 306
Of the House of the Forest of Lebanon (Bunyan), **II:** 253
Of the Knowledge of Ourselves and of God (Julian of Norwich), **Supp. XII:** 155

Of the Lady Mary (Waller), **II:** 238
Of the Law and a Christian (Bunyan), **II:** 253
Of the Laws of Ecclesiastical Polity (Hooker), **I:** 176, 179–190
Of the Trinity and a Christian (Bunyan), **II:** 253
"Of the Uncomplicated Dairy Girl" (Smith, I. C.), **Supp. IX:** 216
Of the Use of Riches, an Epistle to . . . Bathurst (Pope), *see Moral Essays*
Of True Greatness (Fielding), **III:** 105
Of True Religion, Haeresie, Schism, Toleration, . . . (Milton), **II:** 176
"Of White Hairs and Cricket" (Mistry), **Supp. X:** 140–141
"Off the Map" (Malouf), **Supp. XII:** 220
"Offa's Leechdom" (Hill), **Supp. V:** 194
"Offa's Second Defence of the English People" (Hill), **Supp. V:** 195
Offer of the Clarendon Trustees, The (Carroll), **V:** 274
"Office for the Dead" (Kinsella), **Supp. V:** 263
"Office Friendships" (Ewart), **Supp. VII:** 39
"Office Girl" (Hart), **Supp. XI:** 123
Office Suite (Bennett), **VIII:** 27
Officers and Gentlemen (Waugh), **VII:** 302, 304; *see also Sword of Honour* trilogy
"Officers Mess" (Ewarts), **VII:** 423; **Supp. VII:** 37
Offshore (Fitzgerald), **Supp. V:** 96, 97, 98, 102
"Oflag Night Piece: Colditz" (Riviere), **VII:** 424
Ogden, C. K., **Supp. II:** 405, 406, 407–408, 409, 410, 411, 422, 424
Ogg, David, **II:** 243
O'Grady, Standish James, **Supp. V:** 36
"Oh, dreadful is the check—intense the agony" (Brontë), **V:** 116
"Oh, Madam" (Bowen), **Supp. II:** 92–93
"Oh! That 'Twere Possible" (Tennyson), **IV:** 330, 332
Oh What a Lovely War (musical), **VI:** 436
O'Hanlon, Redmond, **Supp. XI:** 195–208
Ohio Impromptu (Beckett), **Supp. I:** 61
Okri, Ben, **Supp. V:** 347–362
Óláfs saga helga, **VIII:** 242
"Olalla" (Stevenson), **V:** 395
"Old, The" (Hart), **Supp. XI:** 123
Old Adam, The (Bennett), *see Regent, The*
"Old Andrey's Experience as a Musician" (Hardy), **VI:** 22
"Old Atheist Pauses by the Sea, An" (Kinsella), **Supp. V:** 261
Old Batchelour, The (Congreve), **II:** 338, 340–341, 349
"Old Benchers of the Inner Temple, The" (Lamb), **IV:** 74
Old Boys, The (Trevor), **Supp. IV:** 505–506, 507, 517
Old Calabria (Douglas), **VI:** 294, 295–296, 297, 298, 299, 305
"Old Chartist, The" (Meredith), **V:** 220
"Old Chief Mshlanga, The" (Lessing), **Supp. I:** 242
"Old China" (Lamb), **IV:** 82

"Old Church Tower and the Garden Wall, The" (Brontë), **V:** 134
"Old Crofter" (MacCaig), **Supp. VI:** 192
Old Country, The (Bennett), **VIII:** 30
Old Curiosity Shop, The (Dickens), **V:** xx, 42, 53, 71
Old Debauchees, The (Fielding), **III:** 105
Old Devils, The (Amis), **Supp. II:** 3, 18–19; **Supp. IV:** 37
"Old Dispensary" (Murphy), **Supp. V:** 329
Old English (Galsworthy), **VI:** 275, 284
Old English Baron, The (Reeve), **III:** 345
"Old Familiar Faces, The" (Lamb), **IV:** 78
"Old Folks at Home" (Highsmith), **Supp. V:** 180
"Old Fools, The" (Larkin), **Supp. I:** 282–283, 285
Old Fortunatus (Dekker), **II:** 71, 89
"Old Francis" (Kelman), **Supp. V:** 249
Old French Romances, Done into English (Morris), **V:** 306
"Old Friend, The" (Cornford), **VIII:** 106
Old Gang and the New Gang, The (Lewis), **VII:** 83
"Old Garbo" (Thomas), **Supp. I:** 181
Old Glory: An American Voyage (Raban), **Supp. XI:** 227, 232–235
"Old Harry" (Kinsella), **Supp. V:** 261
"Old Holborn" (Kelman), **Supp. V:** 256
"Old Homes" (Blunden), **Supp. XI:** 34, 44
"Old House" (Redgrove), **Supp. VI:** 228
Old Huntsman, The (Sassoon), **VI:** 423, 430, 453
"Old John's Place" (Lessing), **Supp. I:** 240
Old Joiner of Aldgate, The (Chapman), **I:** 234, 244
"Old Lady" (Smith, I. C.), **Supp. IX:** 221
Old Lady Shows Her Medals, The (Barrie), **Supp. III:** 6, 9, 16
Old Law, The (Massigner, Middleton, Rowley), **II:** 21; **Supp. XI:** 182
Old Lights for New Chancels (Betjeman), **VII:** 361, 367, 368
"Old Main Street, Holborn Hill, Millom" (Nicholson), **Supp. VI:** 216–217
"Old Man" (Jennings), **Supp. V:** 210
"Old Man" (Thomas), **Supp. III:** 402
"Old Man, The" (du Maurier), **Supp. III:** 142–143
"Old Man and the Sea, The" (Morgan, E.), **Supp. IX:** 164
Old Man of the Mountains, The (Nicholson), **Supp. VI:** 220–221, 222
Old Man Taught Wisdom, An (Fielding), **III:** 105
"Old Man's Love, An* (Trollope), **V:** 102
"Old Meg" (Gunn), **Supp. IV:** 276
Old Men at the Zoo, The (Wilson), **Supp. I:** 154, 161
Old Mrs. Chundle (Hardy), **VI:** 20
Old Mortality (Scott), **IV:** 33, 39
Old Negatives (Gray, A.), **Supp. IX:** 91–92
Old Norse Literature, **VIII:** 227–244
"Old Nurse's Story, The" (Gaskell), **V:** 14, 15

Old Possum's Book of Practical Cats (Eliot), **VII:** 167

Old Pub Near the Angel, An (Kelman), **Supp. V:** 242, 244, 245

"Old Pub Near the Angel, An" (Kelman), **Supp. V:** 245

Old Reliable, The (Wodehouse), **Supp. III:** 451

Old Times (Pinter), **Supp. I:** 376–377

"Old Toy, The" (Fuller), **Supp. VII:** 79

"Old Vicarage, Grantchester, The" (Brooke), **Supp. III:** 47, 50, 54

Old Whig (periodical), **III:** 51, 53

Old Wife's Tale, The (Peele), **I:** 206–208

Old Wives' Tale, The (Bennett), **VI:** xiii, 247, 249, 250, 251, **254–257**

"Old Woman" (Smith, I. C.), **Supp. IX:** 211, 213

"Old Woman, An" (Sitwell), **VII:** 135–136

"Old Woman and Her Cat, An" (Lessing), **Supp. I:** 253–254

"Old Woman in Spring, The" (Cornford), **VIII:** 112

"Old Woman of Berkeley, The" (Southey), **IV:** 67

"Old Women, The" (Brown), **Supp. VI:** 71

"Old Women without Gardens" (Dunn), **Supp. X:** 67

"Oldest Place, The" (Kinsella), **Supp. V:** 268

Oldham, John, **II:** 259

Oley, Barnabas, **II:** 141; **Retro. Supp. II:** 170–171

"Olga" (Blackwood), **Supp. IX:** 12

Oliphant, Margaret, **Supp. X: 209–225**

"Olive and Camilla" (Coppard), **VIII:** 96

Oliver, H. J., **I:** 281

"Oliver Cromwell and Walter Noble" (Landor), **IV:** 92

Oliver Cromwell's Letters and Speeches (Carlyle), **IV:** 240, 244, 246, 249, 250, 342

Oliver Newman (Southey), **IV:** 71

"Oliver Plunkett" (Longley), **VIII:** 173

Oliver Twist (Dickens), **V:** xix, 42, 47–50, 51, 55, 56, 66, 71

Olney Hymns (Cowper), **III:** 210, 211, 220

Olor Iscanus . . . (Vaughan), **II:** 185, 201

Olympia (Manet), **Supp. IV:** 480

O'Malley, Mary, **Supp. IV:** 181

Oman, Sir Charles, **VI:** 387

Omega Workshop, **VI:** 118

Omen, The (film), **III:** 343, 345

Omniana; or, Horae otiosiores (Southey and Coleridge), **IV:** 71

"On a Brede of Divers Colours Woven by Four Ladies" (Waller), **II:** 233

On a Calm Shore (Cornford), **VIII:** 113–114

"On a Chalk Mark on the Door" (Thackeray), **V:** 34

On a Chinese Screen (Maugham), **VI:** 371

"On a Croft by the Kirkaig" (MacCaig), **Supp. VI:** 194

"On a Dead Child" (Bridges), **VI:** 77–78

"On a Drop of Dew" (Marvell), **II:** 211

"On a Girdle" (Waller), **II:** 235

"On a Joke I Once Heard from the Late Thomas Hood" (Thackeray), **IV:** 251–252

"On a Midsummer Eve" (Hardy), **Retro. Supp. I:** 119

"On a Mourner" (Tennyson), **IV:** 332

"On a Prayer Booke Sent to Mrs. M. R."(Crashaw), **II:** 181

"On a Raised Beach" (MacDiarmid), **Supp. XII:** 201, 212–214

"On a Return from Egypt" (Douglas), **VII:** 444

"On a Train" (Cope), **VIII:** 80

"On a Troopship" (Sisson), **Supp. XI:** 247, 248, 254

"On Actors and Acting" (Hazlitt), **IV:** 137

"On Adventure" (Rushdie), **Supp. IV:** 455

On Alterations in the Liturgy (Newman), **Supp. VII:** 292

"On an Insignificant" (Coleridge), **Retro. Supp. II:** 65

On Baile's Strand (Yeats), **VI:** 218, 309

On Ballycastle Beach (McGuckian), **Supp. V:** 282, 284–286

"On Ballycastle Beach" (McGuckian), **Supp. V:** 285

On Becoming a Fairy Godmother (Maitland), **Supp. XI:** 174–175

On Becoming a Writer (Brittain), **Supp. X:** 45

"On Being English but Not British" (Fowles), **Supp. I:** 292

On Beulah Height (Hill, R.), **Supp. IX:** 121–122, 123

"On Board the *West Hardaway*" (Lowry), **Supp. III:** 285

"On Byron and Byronism" (Williams, C. W. S.), **Supp. IX:** 278

On Christian Doctrine (Milton), **Retro. Supp. II:** 271

"On Dryden and Pope" (Hazlitt), **IV:** 217

On English Poetry (Graves), **VII:** 260

"On Fairy-Stories" (Tolkien), **Supp. II:** 521, 535

"On Familiar Style" (Hazlitt), **IV:** 138

"On Finding an Old Photograph" (Cope), **VIII:** 73

"On First Looking into Chapman's Homer" (Keats), **IV:** 214, 215–216; **Retro. Supp. I:** 188

"On First Looking into Loeb's Horace" (Durrell), **Supp. I:** 126

On Forsyte 'Change (Galsworthy), **VI:** 270, 275

On Gender and Writing (ed. Wandor), **Supp. XI:** 163, 174, 176

"On 'God' and 'Good' " (Murdoch), **Supp. I:** 217–218, 224–225

"On Greenhow Hill" (Kipling), **VI:** 191

"On Hearing Bartok's Concerto for Orchestra" (Fuller), **Supp. VII:** 72

"On Heaven" (Ford), **VI:** 323

"On Her Leaving Town After the Coronation" (Pope), **III:** 76

"On Her Loving Two Equally" (Behn), **Supp. III:** 38

"On Himself" (Herrick), **II:** 113

On His Grace the Duke of Marlborough (Wycherley), **II:** 322

"On His Heid-Ake" (Dunbar), **VIII:** 123

"On Home Beaches" (Murray), **Supp. VII:** 283

"On Installing an American Kitchen in Lower Austria" (Auden), **Retro. Supp. I:** 13

"On Jupiter" (Morgan, E.), **Supp. IX:** 167

"On Leaving the Cottage of My Birth" (Clare), **Supp. XI:** 59–60

"On Living for Others" (Warner), **Supp. VII:** 380

"On Living to One's-Self" (Hazlitt), **IV:** 137

"On Marriage" (Crashaw), **II:** 180

"On Men and Pictures" (Thackeray), **V:** 37

"On Milton" (De Quincey), **IV:** 146

"On Mr. Milton's 'Paradise Lost'" (Marvell), **II:** 206

"On My First Daughter" (Jonson), **Retro. Supp. I:** 155

"On My First Son" (Jonson), **Retro. Supp. I:** 155

"On My Thirty-fifth Birthday" (Nicholson), **Supp. VI:** 217

"On Not Being Milton" (Harrison), **Supp. V:** 152–153

"On Not Knowing Greek" (Woolf), **VII:** 35

"On Not Saying Anything" (Day Lewis), **Supp. III:** 130

"On Palestinian Identity: A Conversation with Edward Said" (Rushdie), **Supp. IV:** 456

"On Passing" (Dutton), **Supp. XII:** 95

"On Personal Character" (Hazlitt), **IV:** 136

"On Poetry: A Rhapsody" (Swift), **III:** 30, 36

"On Poetry in General" (Hazlitt), **IV:** 130, 138

"On Preaching the Gospel" (Newman), **Supp. VII:** 294

"On Preparing to Read Kipling" (Hardy), **VI:** 195

"On Reading That the Rebuilding of Ypres Approached Completion" (Blunden), **Supp. XI:** 40

"On Receiving News of the War" (Rosenberg), **VI:** 432

"On Renoir's *The Grape-Pickers*" (Boland), **Supp. V:** 40

"On Ribbons" (Thackeray), **V:** 34

"On Seeing England for the First Time" (Kincaid), **Supp. VII:** 218, 225, 228

"On Seeing the Elgin Marbles" (Keats), **IV:** 212–213, 214

On Seeming to Presume (Durrell), **Supp. I:** 124

"On Sentimental Comedy" (Goldsmith), *see Essay on the Theatre . . .*

"On Silence" (Pope), **Retro. Supp. I:** 233

"On Sitting Back and Thinking of Porter's Boeotia" (Murray), **Supp. VII:** 274

"On Some Characteristics of Modern Poetry" (Hallam), **IV:** 234, 235

"On Some Obscure Poetry" (Lander), **IV:** 98

"On Spies" (Jonson), **Retro. Supp. I:** 156

"On Stella's Birthday, . . . A.D. 1718–" (Swift), **III:** 31

"On Style" (De Quincey), **IV:** 148

"On the Application of Thought to Textual Criticism" (Housman), **VI:** 154, 164

On the Black Hill (Chatwin), **Supp. IV:** 158, 168–170, 173

On the Boiler (Yeats), **Retro. Supp. I:** 337

On the Choice of a Profession (Stevenson), **V:** 396

On the Choice of Books (Carlyle), **IV:** 250

"On the City Wall" (Kipling), **VI:** 184

"On the Cliffs" (Swinburne), **V:** 327

"On the Closing of Millom Iron Works" (Nicholson), **Supp. VI:** 218

"On the Conduct of the Understanding" (Smith), **Supp. VII:** 342

On the Constitution of the Church and State (Coleridge), **IV:** 54, 55, 56; **Retro. Supp. II:** 64

On the Contrary (Brink), **Supp. VI:** 56–57

"On the Death of Dr. Robert Levet" (Johnson), **III:** 120

"On the Death of General Schomberg . . . " (Farquhar), **II:** 351

"On the Death of Marshal Keith" (Macpherson), **VIII:** 181

"On the Death of Mr. Crashaw" (Cowley), **II:** 198

"On the Death of Mr. William Hervey" (Cowley), **II:** 198

"On the Death of Sir Henry Wootton" (Cowley), **II:** 198

"On the Departure" (Sisson), **Supp. XI:** 258

On the Dignity of Man (Mirandola), **I:** 253

"On the Discovery of a Lady's Painting" (Waller), **II:** 233

"On the Dismantling of Millom Ironworks" (Nicholson), **Supp. VI:** 218–219

"On the Dunes" (Cornford), **VIII:** 105

On the Edge of the Cliff and Other Stories (Pritchett), **Supp. III:** 328

"On the English Novelists" (Hazlitt), **IV:** 136–137

On the Face of the Waters (Steel), **Supp. XII:** 271–273, 274

"On the Feeling of Immortality in Youth" (Hazlitt), **IV:** 126

On the Frontier (Auden and Isherwood), **VII:** 312; **Retro. Supp. I:** 7

"On the Genius and Character of Hogarth" (Lamb), **IV:** 80

"On the Head of a Stag" (Waller), **II:** 233

On the Herpetology of the Grand Duchy of Baden (Douglas), **VI:** 300, 305

"On the Influence of the Audience" (Bridges), **VI:** 83

"On the Knocking at the Gate in 'Macbeth'" (De Quincey), **IV:** 146, 149

"On the Lancashire Coast" (Nicholson), **Supp. VI:** 216

"On the Living Poets" (Hazlitt), **IV:** 130

On the Look–out: A Partial Autobiography (Sisson), **Supp. XI:** 243, 244, 245, 246, 247, 248, 254

On the Margin (Bennett), **VIII:** 19, 22

On the Margin (Huxley), **VII:** 201

"On the means of improving people" (Southey), **IV:** 102

"On the Medusa of Leonardo da Vinci in the Florentine Gallery" (Shelley), **III:** 337

"On the Morning of Christ's Nativity" (Milton), **II:** 199; **IV:** 222

"On the Move" (Gunn), **Supp. IV:** 259–260, 261

"On the Origin of Beauty: A Platonic Dialogue" (Hopkins), **V:** 362; **Retro. Supp. II:** 187

On the Origin of Species by Means of Natural Selection (Darwin), **V:** xxii, 279, 287; **Supp. II:** 98

"On the Periodical Essayists" (Hazlitt), **IV:** 136

On the Place of Gilbert Chesterton in English Letters (Belloc), **VI:** 345

"On the Pleasure of Painting" (Hazlitt), **IV:** 137–138

"On the Profession of a Player" (Boswell), **III:** 248

"On the Receipt of My Mother's Picture" (Cowper), **III:** 208, 220

"On the Road with Mrs. G." (Chatwin), **Supp. IV:** 165

On the Rocks (Shaw), **VI:** 125, 126, 127; **Retro. Supp. II:** 324

"On Roofs of Terry Street" (Dunn), **Supp. X:** 69

"On the School Bus" (Adcock), **Supp. XII:** 9

"On the Scotch Character" (Hazlitt), **IV:** 132

"On the Sea" (Keats), **IV:** 216

"On the Second Story" (Steel), **Supp. XII:** 269

"On the Spirit of Monarchy" (Hazlitt), **IV:** 132

On the Study of Celtic Literature (Arnold), **V:** 203, 212, 216

On the Sublime and Beautiful (Burke), **III:** 195, 198, 205

"On the Table " (Motion), **Supp. VII:** 262–263, 264

On the Thermal Influence of Forests (Stevenson), **V:** 395

"On the Toilet Table of Queen Marie-Antoinette" (Nicholls), **IV:** 98

"On the Tragedies of Shakespeare . . . with Reference to . .. . Stage Representation" (Lamb), **IV:** 80

"On the Victory Obtained by Blake" (Marvell), **II:** 211

"On the Way to the Castle" (Adcock), **Supp. XII:** 10–11

"On the Western Circuit" (Hardy), **VI:** 22

"On the Wounds of Our Crucified Lord" (Crashaw), **II:** 182

"On the Zattere" (Trevor), **Supp. IV:** 502

"On This Island" (Auden), **Retro. Supp. I:** 7

"On Toleration" (Smith), **Supp. VII:** 347

On Translating Homer (Arnold), **V:** xxii, 212, 215, 216

On Translating Homer: Last Words (Arnold), **V:** 214, 215, 216

"On Whether Loneliness Ever Has a Beginning" (Dunn), **Supp. X: 82**

"On Wit and Humour" (Hazlitt), **II:** 332

"On Wordsworth's Poetry" (De Quincey), **IV:** 146, 148

"On Writing a Novel" (Fowles), **Supp. I:** 293

"On Yeti Tracks" (Chatwin), **Supp. IV:** 157

Once a Week (Milne), **Supp. V:** 298

"Once as me thought Fortune me kissed" (Wyatt), **I:** 102

"Once at Piertarvit" (Reid), **Supp. VII:** 327–328

"Once I Did Think" (Caudwell), **Supp. IX:** 35

"Once in a Lifetime, Snow" (Murray), **Supp. VII:** 273

Once in Europa (Berger), **Supp. IV:** 93, 94

Once on a Time (Milne), **Supp. V:** 298

"Once Upon a Time" (Gordimer), **Supp. II:** 233

"One" (Fallon), **Supp. XII:** 104

"One, The" (Kavanagh), **Supp. VII:** 198

One and Other Poems (Kinsella), **Supp. V:** 267–268

"One Before the Last, The" (Brooke), **Supp. III:** 51

"One by One" (Davies), **Supp. XI:** 101

One Day (Douglas), **VI:** 299, 300, 305

"One Day" (Stallworthy), **Supp. X:** 298

"One Day" (Thomas), **Supp. XII:** 290

"One Eye on India" (Sisson), **Supp. XI:** 247

One Fat Englishman (Amis), **Supp. II:** 10, 11, 15

One Fond Embrace (Kinsella), **Supp. V:** 272

One Foot in Eden (Muir), **Supp. VI:** 204, 206, **207–208**

One for the Grave (MacNeice), **VII:** 405, 406, 408

One for the Road (Pinter), **Supp. I:** 378, 381

One Hand Clapping (Burgess), **Supp. I:** 186

One Hundred Years of Solitude (García Márquez), **Supp. IV:** 116

One of Our Conquerors (Meredith), **V:** 232, 233, 234

"One Off the Short List" (Lessing), **Supp. I:** 244

"One Out of Many" (Naipaul), **Supp. I:** 395

"One Sea-side Grave" (Rossetti), **V:** 255

One Small Step (Hill, R.), **Supp. IX:** 123

"One Sunday" (Mistry), **Supp. X:** 138, 140

"One Thing and Another" (Dunn), **Supp. X:** 80

One Thing Is Needful (Bunyan), **II:** 253

One Thing More; or, Caedmon Construed (Fry), **Supp. III:** 191, 196–197

"One Thousand Days in a Balloon" (Rushdie), **Supp. IV:** 437

"One Token" (Davies), **Supp. XI:** 94

"One Viceroy Resigns" (Kipling), **VI:** 202

"One We Knew" (Hardy), **Retro. Supp. I:** 118

"One Who Disappeared" (Motion), **Supp. VII:** 258

One Who Set Out to Study Fear, The (Redgrove), **Supp. VI:** 231

"One Word More" (Browning), **IV:** 357

"One Writer's Education" (Armah), **Supp. X:** 1

One–Way Song (Lewis), **VII:** 72, 76

O'Neill, Eugene, **Supp. III:** 12 *Only Game, The* (Hill, R.), **Supp. IX:** 119–120

"Only our love hath no decay" (Donne), **II:** 221

Only Penitent, The (Powys), **VIII:** 255–256

Only Problem, The (Spark), **Supp. I:** 212–213

"Only the Devil" (Powys), **VIII:** 248–249

"Only This" (Dahl), **Supp. IV:** 211

O'Nolan, Brian, **Supp. II: 321–338; Supp. IV:** 412

Open Conspiracy, The, Blueprints for a World Revolution (Wells), **VI:** 240, 242

Open Court (Kinsella), **Supp. V:** 272, 273

"Open Court" (Kinsella), **Supp. V:** 273

Open Door (Fry), **Supp. III:** 194

"Open Door, The" (Oliphant), **Supp. X:** 220

Open Door, The (Sillitoe), **Supp. V:** 411, 415

Open Letter to the Revd. Dr. Hyde in Defence of Father Damien, An (Stevenson), *see Father Damien*

"Open Secrets" (Motion), **Supp. VII:** 255–256

Opened Ground (Heaney), **Retro. Supp. I:** 124

"Opening, The" (Crawford), **Supp. XI:** 80

"Opening a Place of Social Prayer" (Cowper), **III:** 211

Opera of Operas, The (Haywood and Hatchett), **Supp. XII:** 141

Operette (Coward), **Supp. II:** 152

"Opinions of the Press" (Reading), **VIII:** 264

Opium and the Romantic Imagination (Hayter), **III:** 338, 346; **IV:** 57

Oppenheim, E. Phillips, **VI:** 249

Opus 7 (Warner), **Supp. VII:** 372

Or Shall We Die? (McEwan), **Supp. IV:** 390

"Or, Solitude" (Davie), **Supp. VI:** 110

Or Where a Young Penguin Lies Screaming (Ewart), **Supp. VII:** 41

"Oracle, The" (Coppard), **VIII:** 88

"Oracles, The" (Housman), **VI:** 161

Orage, A. R., **VI:** 247, 265, **VII:** 172

"Oral" (Crawford), **Supp. XI:** 79

"Orange March" (Murphy), **Supp. V:** 322

Oranges Are Not the Only Fruit (Winterson), **Supp. IV:** 541, 542, 543–545, 546, 547–548, 552, 553, 555, 557

Orators, The (Auden), **VII:** 345, 380, 382; **Retro. Supp. I:** 5

Orchard End (Redgrove), **Supp. VI:** 236

"Orchards half the way, The" (Housman), **VI:** 159

Ordeal by Innocence (Christie), **Supp. II:** 125

Ordeal of George Meredith, The, A Biography (Stevenson), **V:** 230, 234

Ordeal of Gilbert Pinfold, The (Waugh), **VII:** 291, 293, 302–303

Ordeal of Richard Feverel, The (Meredith), **V:** xxii, 225, 226–227, 234

Ordeal of Sigbjorn Wilderness, The (Lowry), **Supp. III:** 280

"Ordered South" (Stevenson), **Retro. Supp. I:** 261

"Ordination, The" (Burns), **III:** 311, 319

Oresteia, The (tr. Harrison), **Supp. V:** 163

Orestes (Caudwell), **Supp. IX:** 37–39

"Orf"(Hughes), **Supp. I:** 359

"Orford" (Davie), **Supp. VI:** 110

Orford, fourth earl of, *see* Walpole, Horace

Orgel, Stephen, **I:** 237, 239

Orghast (Hughes), **Supp. I:** 354

Orient Express (Greene), **Supp. I:** *see* Stamboul Train

Orient Express (tr. Adcock), **Supp. XII:** 11

"Orient Ode" (Thompson), **V:** 448

"Oriental Eclogues" (Collins), *see* "Persian Eclogues"

Orientations (Maugham), **VI:** 367

Origin, Nature, and Object of the New System of Education, The (Southey), **IV:** 71

Origin of Species by Means of Natural Selection, or the Preservation of Favoured Races in the Struggle for Life (Darwin), **Supp. VII:** 17, 19, 23–25

Origin of the Family, Private Property, and the State, The (Engels), **Supp. II:** 454

Original and Progress of Satire, The (Dryden), **II:** 301

Original Letters &c of Sir John Falstaff (White and Lamb), **IV:** 79, 85

Original Michael Frayn, The (Frayn), **Supp. VII:** 51

Original Papers, containing the Secret of Great Britain from the Restoration to the Accession of the House of Hanover (Macpherson), **VIII:** 192, 193

"Original Place, The" (Muir), **Supp. VI:** 206

Original Poetry by Victor and Cazire (Shelley and Shelley), **IV:** 208

Original Power of the Collective Body of the People of England, Examined and Asserted, The (Defoe), **Retro. Supp. I:** 68

"Original Simplicitie" (Traherne), **Supp. XI:** 266

Original Sin (James), **Supp. IV:** 333–335

"Original Sins of Edward Tripp, The" (Trevor), **Supp. IV:** 503

Origine of Sciences, The (Pope), **Retro. Supp. I:** 234

Origins of the English Imagination, The (Ackroyd), **Supp. VI:** 13

Orkney Tapestry, An (Brown), **Supp. VI:** 64–65

"Orkney: The Whale Islands" (Brown), **Supp. VI:** 72

Orkneyinga saga, **VIII:** 236

Orlando (Woolf), **VII:** 21, 28, 35, 38; **Supp. IV:** 557; **Retro. Supp. I:** 314, 318–319

Orlando furioso (Ariosto), **I:** 131, 138

Orley Farm (Trollope), **V:** xxii, 100, 101

Ormond (Edgeworth), **Supp. III:** 154, 156, **163–165**

"Ornithological Section, The" (Longley), **VIII:** 168, 172

Oroonoko: A Tragedy (Southerne), **Supp. III:** 34–35

Oroonoko; or, The Royal Slave (Behn), **Supp. III:** 21, 22–23, 32–36, 39

Orpheus (Hope), **Supp. VII:** 165

Orpheus (Hughes), **Supp. I:** 347

Orpheus and Eurydice (Henryson), **Supp. VII:** 136, 145–146

"Orpheus in Hell" (Thomas), **Supp. IV:** 493

"Orpheus; or, Philosophy" (Bacon), **I:** 267

"Orr Mount" (Dunn), **Supp. X:** 68

Ortelius, Abraham, **I:** 282

Orthodoxy (Chesterton), **VI:** 336

Orton, Joe, **Supp. V: 363–378**

Orton Diaries, The (Orton), **Supp. V:** 363, 367–369

Orwell, George, **III:** 341; **V:** 24, 31; **VI:** 240, 242; **VII:** xii, xx, **273–287; Supp. I:** 28*n*; **Supp. III:** 96, 107; **Supp. IV:** 17, 81, 110–111, 440, 445

Osborne, John, **VI:** 101; **Supp. I: 329–340; Supp. II: 4,** 70, 139, 155; **Supp. III:** 191; **Supp. IV:** 180, 281, 283

Osbourne, Lloyd, **V:** 384, 387, 393, 395, 396, 397

Oscar and Lucinda (Carey), **Supp. XII:** 49, 50, 53, 57, 58–59

Oscar Wilde. Art and Egoism (Shewan), **V:** 409, 421

O'Shaughnessy, Arthur, **VI:** 158

Osiris Rising (Armah), **Supp. X:** 1–2, 11–12, 14

Othello (Shakespeare), **I:** 316; **II:** 71, 79; **III:** 116; **Supp. IV:** 285

"Other, The" (Thomas), **Supp. III:** 403

"Other Boat, The" (Forster), **VI:** 406, 411–412

Other House, The (James), **VI:** 48, 49, 67

Other House, The (Stevenson), **Supp. VI:** 263–265

"Other Kingdom" (Forster), **VI:** 399, 402

Other People: A Mystery Story (Amis), **Supp. IV:** 26, 39–40

Other People's Clerihews (Ewart), **Supp. VII:** 46

"Other People's Houses" (Reid), **Supp. VII:** 336

Other People's Worlds (Trevor), **Supp. IV:** 501, 506, 511–512, 517

Other Places (Pinter), **Supp. I:** 378

"Other Tiger, The" (tr. Reid), **Supp. VII:** 332–333

"Other Times" (Nye), **Supp. X:** 198–199

Other Tongues: Young Scottish Poets in English, Scots, and Gaelic (ed. Crawford), **Supp. XI:** 67

Other Voices (Maitland), **Supp. XI:** 163

"Others, The" (Ewart), **Supp. VII:** 39, 40

Otho the Great (Keats and Brown), **IV:** 231, 235

Otranto (Walpole), *see Castle of Otranto, The*

"Otter, An" (Hughes), **Retro. Supp. II:** 204–205

"Otters" (Longley), **VIII:** 174

Ouch (Ackroyd), **Supp. VI:** 3–4

Ounce, Dice, Trice (Reid), **Supp. VII:** 326

Our Betters (Maugham), **VI:** 368, 369

"Our Bias" (Auden), **VII:** 387

Our Corner (periodical), **VI:** 103

Our Country's Good (Keneally), **Supp. IV:** 346

Our Exagmination Round His Factification for Incamination of Work in Progress (Beckett et al.), **Supp. I:** 43*n*

Our Exploits at West Poley (Hardy), **VI:** 20

"Our Father" (Davie), **Supp. VI:** 113

"Our Father's Works" (Blunden), **Supp. XI:** 42

Our Family (Hood), **IV:** 254, 259

Our First Leader (Morris, J.), **Supp. X:** 186

Our Friend the Charlatan (Gissing), **V:** 437

"Our Hunting Fathers" (Auden), **VII:** 108

"Our Lives Now" (Fallon), **Supp. XII:** 114

Our Man in Havana (Greene), **Supp. I:** 7, 11, 13, 14–15; **Retro. Supp. II:** 161

"Our Mother" (Kinsella), **Supp. V:** 263

Our Mother's House (Gloag), **Supp. IV:** 390

Our Mutual Friend (Dickens), **V:** xxiii, 42, 44, 55, 68–69, 72; **Supp. IV:** 247

Our Old Home (Hawthorne), **VI:** 34

"Our Parish" (Dickens), **V:** 43, 46

Our Republic (Keneally), **Supp. IV:** 347

"Our Parish" (Dickens), **V:** 43, 46

Our Spoons Came From Woolworths (Comyns), **VIII:** 56–58

"Our Thrones Decay" (Russell), **VIII:** 285

"Our Village—by a Villager" (Hood), **IV:** 257

Our Women: Chapters on the Sex–Discord (Bennett), **VI:** 267

Out (Brooke–Rose)), **Supp. IV:** 99, 104, 105–106

"Out and Away" (Kavan), **Supp. VII:** 202

Out of Bounds (Stallworthy), **Supp. X:** 292–293

Out of India (Jhabvala), **Supp. V:** 235–236

Out of India (Kipling), **VI:** 204

Out of Ireland (Kinsella), **Supp. V:** 271

"Out of Ireland" (Kinsella), **Supp. V:** 271

Out of the Picture (MacNeice), **VII:** 405

Out of the Red, into the Blue (Comyns), **VIII:** 63

Out of the Shelter (Lodge), **Supp. IV:** 364, 365, 370–371, 372

"Out of the signs" (Thomas), **Supp. I:** 174

Out of the Silent Planet (Lewis), **Supp. III:** 249, 252–253

Out of the Whirlpool (Sillitoe), **Supp. V:** 411

Out of This World (Swift), **Supp. V:** 437–438

Outback (Keneally), **Supp. IV:** 346

"Outcast, The" (Tennyson), **IV:** 329

Outcast of the Islands, An (Conrad), **VI:** 136, 137, 148; **Retro. Supp. II:** 71

Outcasts, The (Sitwell), **VII:** 138

Outcry, The (Julia), **VI:** 67

"Outdoor Concert, The" (Gunn), **Supp. IV:** 269

"Outer Planet, The" (Nicholson), **Supp. VI:** 217

Outidana, or Effusions, Amorous, Pathetic and Fantastical (Beddoes), **Supp. XI:** 28–29

Outline of History: Being a Plain History of Life and Mankind, The (Wells), **VI:** 245

Outlines of Romantic Theology (Williams, C. W. S.), **Supp. IX:** 275, 284

"Outlook, Uncertain" (Reid), **Supp. VII:** 330

Outlying Stations, The (Warner), **Supp. XI:** 294

"Outpost of Progress, An" (Conrad), **VI:** 136, 148

Outriders: A Liberal View of Britain, The (Morris, J.), **Supp. X:** 175

"Outside the Whale" (Rushdie), **Supp. IV:** 455

Outskirts (Kureishi), **Supp. XI:** 154

"Outstation, The" (Maugham), **VI:** 370, 371, 380

"Outward Bound" (Morgan, E.), **Supp. IX:** 167

"Ovando" (Kincaid), **Supp. VII:** 225

"Over Mother, The" (McGuckian), **Supp. V:** 288

"Over Sir John's Hill" (Thomas), **Supp. I:** 179

Over the Frontier (Smith), **Supp. II:** 462, 474

"Over the Hill" (Warner), **Supp. VII:** 380

"Over the Hills" (Thomas), **Supp. III:** 400

"Over the Rainbow" (Rushdie), **Supp. IV:** 434

Over the River (Galsworthy), **VI:** 272, 275

Over the River (Gregory), **VI:** 318

Over to You: Ten Stories of Flyers and Flying (Dahl), **Supp. IV:** 208–211, 213

Overbury, Sir Thomas, **IV:** 286

"Overcoat, The" (Gogol), **III:** 340, 345

Overcrowded Barracoon, The (Naipaul), **Supp. I:** 384

"Overcrowded Barracoon, The" (Naipaul), **Supp. I:** 402

"Overloaded Man, The" (Ballard), **Supp. V:** 33

Overruled (Shaw), **VI:** 129

"Overture" (Kinsella), **Supp. V:** 270–271

"Overtures to Death" (Day Lewis), **Supp. III:** 122

Overtures to Death (Day Lewis), **Supp. III:** 118, 127–128

Ovid, **II:** 110*n*, 185, 292, 304, 347; **III:** 54; **V:** 319, 321

"Ovid on West 4th" (Mahon), **Supp. VI:** 176

"Ovid in the Third Reich" (Hill), **Supp. V:** 187

Ovid's Art of Love Paraphrased (Fielding), **III:** 105

Ovid's Banquet of Sense (Chapman), **I:** 237–238

Ovid's Epistles, Translated by Several Hands (Dryden), **Supp. III:** 36

Ovid's Fasti (tr. Frazer), **Supp. III:** 176

Owen, Wilfred, **VI:** xvi, 329, 416, 417, 419, 423, **443–460**; **VII:** xvi, 421; list of poems, **VI:** 458–459; **Supp. IV:** 57, 58

"Owen Wingrave," (James), **VI:** 69

"Owl, The" (Thomas), **VI:** 424; **Supp. III:** 403–404

"Owl and Mouse" (Smith, I. C.), **Supp. IX:** 218

"Owl and the Pussy–cat, The" (Lear), **V:** 83–84, 87

Owls and Artificers (Fuller), **Supp. VII:** 77

Owners (Churchill), **Supp. IV:** 179, 180, 181–182, 198

"Oxen, The" (Hardy), **VI:** 16

Oxford (Morris, J.), **Supp. X:** 176, 178

Oxford Book of English Verse, The (ed. Quiller–Couch), **II:** 102, 121

Oxford Book of Oxford, The (ed. Morris), **Supp. X:** 178

Oxford Book of Modern Verse, The, **VI:** 219

Oxford Book of Regency Verse, The (ed. Williams, C. W. S.), **Supp. IX:** 276

Oxford Book of Mystical Verse, The (ed. Williams, C. W. S.), **Supp. IX:** 274

Oxford Book of Twentieth–Century English Verse, The (Larkin), **Supp. I:** 286

Oxford Book of War Poetry, The (ed. Stallworthy), **Supp. X:** 292

Oxford Companion to English Literature, **Supp. IV:** 229, 231, 247, 252; **Supp. IX:** 276

Oxford Dictionary of Quotations, The (ed. Williams, C. W. S.), **Supp. IX:** 276

Oxford Lectures on Poetry (Bradley), **IV:** 216, 236

"Oxford Leave" (Ewart), **Supp. VII:** 37

"Oxford"papers (De Quincey), **IV:** 148

Oxford Poetry (eds. Day Lewis and Auden), **Supp. III:** 117; **Retro. Supp. I:** 3; **Supp. IX:** 17

"Oxford Staircase" (Murphy), **Supp. V:** 315

Oxford University and the Co–operative Movement (Russell), **VIII:** 287

Oxford University Chest (Betjeman), **VII:** 356

"P. & O.," (Maugham), **VI:** 370–371

"P. D. James' Dark Interiors" (Majeske), **Supp. IV:** 330

P. R. B.: An Essay on the Pre'Raphaelite Brotherhood, 1847–1854 (Waugh), **VII:** 291

"P.S." (Reading), **VIII:** 265–266

Pablo Ruiz Picasso: A Biography (O'Brian), **Supp. XII:** 255–256

Pacchiarotto and How He Worked in Distemper (Browning), **IV:** 359, 374; *see also* "Of Pacchiarotton"

Pacific 1860 (Coward), **Supp. II:** 155

Pacificator, The (Defoe), **III:** 12; **Retro. Supp. I:** 67

"Pack Horse and the Carrier, The" (Gay), **III:** 59–60

Pack My Bag: A Self Portrait (Green), **Supp. II: 247–248,** 251, 255

Packer, Lona Mosk, **V:** 251, 252–253, 260

"Pad, Pad" (Smith), **Supp. II:** 470

"Paddiad, The" (Kavanagh), **Supp. VII:** 193–194

Paddock and the Mouse, The (Henryson), **Supp. VII:** 136, 141–142, 147

Paddy Clarke Ha Ha Ha (Doyle), **Supp. V:** 78, 89–91, 92

Pagan Mysteries in the Renaissance (Wind), **V:** 317n

Pagan Place, A (O'Brien), **Supp. V:** 338–339

Pagan Poems (Moore), **VI:** 98

Page of Plymouth, The (Jonson/Dekker), **Retro. Supp. I:** 157

Pageant and Other Poems, A (Rossetti), **V:** 251, 260

"Pageant of Knowledge" (Lydgate), **I:** 58

"Pageants" (Spenser), **I:** 123

Paid on Both Sides (Auden), **Retro. Supp. I:** 4–5

Painful Adventures of Pericles, Prince of Tyre (Wilkins), **I:** 321

"Painful Case, A" (Joyce), **Retro. Supp. I:** 172

"Painful Pleasure of Suspense, The" (Dahl), **Supp. IV:** 222

"Pains of Sleep, The" (Coleridge), **IV:** xvii, 48, 56

Painter, William, **I:** 297; **II:** 76

Painter of His Own Dishonour, The (tr. FitzGerald), **IV: 344–345**

Painter of Our Time (Berger), **Supp. IV:** 79, 81–84, 88

Painter's Eye, The (James), **VI:** 67

Painting and the Fine Arts (Haydon and Hazlitt), **IV:** 140

"Painting It In" (Stevenson), **Supp. VI:** 264

Pair of Blue Eyes, A: A Novel (Hardy), **VI:** 3, 4, 20; **Retro. Supp. I:** 110, 111–112

"Palace of Art, The" (Tennyson), **IV:** 331

"Palace of Pan, The" (Swinburne), **V:** 328

Palace of Pleasure (Painter), **I:** 297, 313; **II:** 76

Palace of the Peacock (Harris), **Supp. V:** 132–136

"Pale Butterwort" (Longley), **VIII:** 177

Pale Companion, The (Motion), **Supp. VII:** 252

Pale Criminal, The (Kerr), **Supp. XII:** 187, 190–191

Pale Fire (Nabokov), **Supp. IV:** 26, 27

Pale Horse, The (Christie), **Supp. II:** 125, 135

Pale View of the Hills, A (Ishiguro), **Supp. IV:** 301, 303, 304, 305–306, 307–309, 310

Paleface (Lewis), **VII:** 72, 75

Paley, William, **IV:** 144

Paley, Grace, **Supp. IV:** 151

Palgrave, Francis Turner, **II:** 208; **IV:** xxii, 196

Palicio (Bridges), **VI:** 83

Palladas: Poems (Harrison), **Supp. V:** 163

Palladis Tamia (Meres), **I:** 296

"Palladium" (Arnold), **V:** 209

Palmer, George Herbert, **Retro. Supp. II:** 173

Palmer, John, **II:** 267, 271

Palmerin of England, **II:** 49; tr. Southey, **IV:** 71

"Palmer's 'Heroides' of Ovid" (Housman), **VI:** 156

Palmyra (Peacock), **IV:** 158, 169

Pamela (Richardson), **III:** 80, **82–85,** 92, 94, 95, 98; **Retro. Supp. I:** 80, 83, 85–86

Pamphlet Against Anthologies, A (Graves), **VI:** 207; **VII:** 260–261

"Pan and Pitys" (Landor), **IV:** 96

"Pan and Thalassius" (Swinburne), **V:** 328

"Pan; or, Nature" (Bacon), **I:** 267

"Pandora" (James), **VI:** 69

Pandosto (Greene), **I:** 165, 322; **VIII:** 131, 135–138, 139

"Panegerick to Sir Lewis Pemberton, A" (Herrick), **II:** 110

Panegyric to Charles the Second, Presented . . . the Day of His Coronation . . . (Evelyn), **II:** 287

Panegyrick to My Lord Protector, A (Waller), **II:** 238

Panic Spring (Durrell), **Supp. I:** 95, 96

Panofsky, Erwin, **I:** 237

"Panoptics" (Wallace–Crabbe), **VIII:** 321

"Panthea" (Wilde), **V:** 401

"Paperback Writer: Dream of the Perfect Novel" (Warner), **Supp. XI:** 281

Paoli, Pasquale di, **III:** 235, 236, 243

"Paolo to Francesca" (Wallace–Crabbe), **VIII:** 311

Paper Houses (Plomer), **Supp. XI:** 216

Paper Men, The (Golding), **Supp. I:** 88–89; **Retro. Supp. I:** 102–103

Paper Money Lyrics, and Other Poems (Peacock), **IV:** 170

Paperbark Tree, The: Selected Prose (Murray), **Supp. VII:** 270, 271, 273, 274, 277

"Papered Parlour, A" (Powys), **VIII:** 251

"Papers, The" (James), **VI:** 69

Papers by Mr. Yellowplush (Thackeray), *see Yellowplush Correspondence, The*

Papillon (tr. O'Brian), **Supp. XII:** 252

"Parable Island" (Heaney), **Supp. II:** 280

Paracelsus (Browning), **IV:** xix, 355, 365, 368, 373; **Retro. Supp. II:** 20

Parade's End (Ford), **VI:** 321, 324, 328, 329–330; **VII:** xv

Paradise Lost (Milton), **I:** 188–189; **II:** 158, 161, **165–171,** 174, 176, 198, 294, 302; **III:** 118, 302; **IV:** 11–12, 15, 47, 88, 93, 95, 186, 200, 204, 229; ed. Bentley, **VI:** 153; **Retro. Supp. I:** 184; **Retro. Supp. II:** 279–284

Paradise News (Lodge), **Supp. IV:** 366, 374, 381–383, 384, 385

Paradise Regained (Milton), **II:** 171–172, 174, 176; **Retro. Supp. II:** 284–285

"Paradox, The" (Donne), **Retro. Supp. II:** 91

Paradoxes and Problems (Donne), **Retro. Supp. II:** 97

"Paraffin Lamp, The" (Brown), **Supp. VI:** 69–70

Parallel of the Antient Architecture with the Modern, A (tr. Evelyn), **II:** 287

"Paraphrase on Oenone to Paris" (Behn), **Supp. III:** 36

Parasitaster (Marston), *see Fawn, The*

Parasites, The (du Maurier), **Supp. III:** 139, 143

Pardoner's Tale, The (Chaucer), **I:** 21, 42

"Parents" (Spender), **Supp. II:** 483

Parents and Children (Compton'Burnett), **VII:** 62, 65, 66, 67

Parent's Assistant, The (Edgeworth), **Supp. III:** 152

Pargiters, The (Woolf), **Retro. Supp. I:** 308, 320

Paridiso (Dante), **Supp. IV:** 439

Paris by Night (film), **Supp. IV:** 282, 292

Paris Nights (Bennett), **VI:** 259, 264

Paris Sketch Book, The (Thackeray), **V:** 22, 37

Parish Register, The (Crabbe), **III:** 275, 279, 283

Parisian Sketches (James), **VI:** 67

Parisina (Byron), **IV:** 173, 192

Parker, Brian, **II:** 6

Parker, W. R., **II:** 165n

Parkinson, T., **VI:** 220

Parlement of Foules (Chaucer), *see Parliament of Fowls, The*

Parleyings with Certain People of Importance in Their Day . . .. (Browning), **IV:** 359, 374

"Parliament, The" (Dunn), **Supp. X:** 73–74

Parliament of Birds (tr. FitzGerald), **IV:** 348–349, 353

Parliament of Fowls, The (Chaucer), **I:** 31, 38, 60; **Retro. Supp. II:** 39–40

Parliament of Love, The (Massinger), **Supp. XI:** 182, 183

Parliamentary Speeches of Lord Byron, The (Byron), **IV:** 193

Parnell, Thomas, **III:** 19

Parnell and His Island (Moore), **VI:** 86

Parochial and Plain Sermons (Newman), **Supp. VII:** 292

Parr, Samuel, **IV:** 88

Parrot (Haywood), **Supp. XII:** 142

Parry, William, **IV:** 191, 193

Parson's Daughter, The (Trollope), **V:** 101

"Parson's Pleasure" (Dahl), **Supp. IV:** 217

Parson's Tale, The (Chaucer), **I:** 34–35

"Part of Ourselves, A" (Fallon), **Supp. XII:** 111–112, 112–113

Part of the Seventh Epistle of the First Book of Horace Imitated (Swift), **III:** 35

"Parthenogenesis" (Dhomhnaill), **Supp. V:** 40–41

Partial Portraits (James), **V:** 95, 97, 102; **VI:** x, 46

"Particles of a Wave" (Maitland), **Supp. XI:** 168

"Partie Fine, The" (Thackeray), **V:** 24, 38

"Parting" (Thomas), **Supp. III:** 305

"Parting in War–Time" (Cornford), **VIII:** 112

"Partition" (Auden), **Retro. Supp. I:** 14

"Partner, The" (Conrad), **VI:** 148

Partnership, The (Unsworth), **Supp. VII:** 354–355, 356

"Party" (Smith, I. C.), **Supp. IX:** 215

Party Going (Green), **Supp. II:** 253–254

Pascal, Blaise, **II:** 146, 244; **V:** 339; **Supp. IV:** 160

Pascali's Island (Unsworth), **Supp. VII:** 355, 356, 357–359, 360

Pascoe's Ghost (Hill, R.), **Supp. IX:** 114, 118

Pasiphaë: A Poem (Swinburne), **V:** 333

Pasmore (Storey), **Supp. I:** 408, 410, 411–412, 413, 414–415

Pasquin (Fielding), **III:** 97, 98, 104, 105; **Retro. Supp. I:** 82

Passage of Arms (Ambler), **Supp. IV:** 16

"Passage to Africa, A" (Plomer), **Supp. XI:** 213

Passage to India, A (Forster), **VI:** 183, 397, 401, 401, **408–410; VII:** xv; **Retro. Supp. II:** 146–149

Passage to Juneau: A Sea and Its Meanings (Raban), **Supp. XI:** 228, 232, 237–238

Pastoral Care (Pope Gregory), **Retro. Supp. II:** 295

"Passage" (Dutton), **Supp. XII:** 97

Passages in the Life of an Individual (Brontë), *see Agnes Grey*

Passages in the Life of Mrs. Margaret Maitland of Sunnyside (Oliphant), **Supp. X:** 210–211, 214

Passages of Joy, The (Gunn), **Supp. IV:** 257, 271–274

Passenger (Keneally), **Supp. IV:** 346

Passenger to Frankfurt (Christie), **Supp. II:** 123, 125, 130, 132

"Passer'by, A" (Bridges), **VI:** 78

"Passing Events" (Brontë), **V:** 122, 123, 151

"Passing of the Dragons, The" (Roberts, K.), **Supp. X:** 270–271

Passing of the Essenes, The (Moore), **VI:** 96, 99

"Passing of the Shee, The" (Synge), **VI:** 314

Passion (Bond), **Supp. I:** 423, 429–430

"Passion, The" (Collins), **III:** 166, 168, 174

"Passion, The" (Vaughan), **II:** 187

Passion, The (Winterson), **Supp. IV:** 542, 548, 553–554, 555–556

Passion Fruit: Romantic Fiction with a Twist (Winterson), **Supp. IV:** 542

Passion of New Eve, The (Carter), **Supp. III:** 84, 85–86, 91

Passion Play, A (Shaw), **VI:** 107

Passion, Poison, and Petrification; or, The Fatal Gazogene (Shaw), **VI:** 129

Passionate Century of Love (Watson), **I:** 193

Passionate Friends, The (Ambler), **Supp. IV:** 3

"Passionate Man's Pilgrimage, The" (Ralegh), **I:** 148, 149

"Passionate Pilgrim, A" (James), **VI:** 69

Passionate Pilgrim, The, **I:** 291, 307

Passionate Pilgrim and Other Tales, A (James), **VI:** 67

Passionate Shepherd to His Love, The (Marlowe), **I:** 149, 284, 291; **IV:** 327; **Retro. Supp. I:** 203–204

"Passionate Woman, A" (Ewart), **Supp. VII:** 42

"Passions: An Ode. Set to Music, The" (Collins), **III:** 163, 175

Passions of the Mind (Byatt), **Supp. IV:** 139, 140, 141, 146, 151

"Passport to Eternity" (Ballard), **Supp. V:** 20

Passwords: Places, Poems, Preoccupations (Reid), **Supp. VII:** 324, 330, 336

Past and Present (Carlyle), **IV:** xx, 240, 244, 249, 250, 266n, 301

"Past ruin'd Ilion Helen lives" (Landor), **IV:** 99

"Past Ever Present, The" (Murray), **Supp. VII:** 280–281

"Paste" (James), **VI:** 69

Pastoral Lives of Daphnis and Chloë. Done into English (Moore), **VI:** 99

Pastorals (Blunden), **VI:** 427

Pastorals (Pope), **III:** 69

Pastorals of Virgil (tr. Thornton), **III:** 307

Pastors and Masters (Compton-Burnett), **VII:** 59, 65, 68

Pat and Roald (Farrell), **Supp. IV:** 223

"Pat Cloherty's Version of *The Maisie*" (Murphy), **Supp. V:** 325

"Patagonia, The," (James), **VI:** 49

Pater, Walter Horatio, **V:** xiii, xix, xxiv–xxvi, 286–287, 314, 323, 324, 329, **337–360,** 362, 400–401, 403, 408, 410, 411; **VI:** ix, 4 365

"Pater on Style" (Chandler), **V:** 359

Paterson, Banjo, **Supp. IV:** 460

"Path of Duty, The" (James), **VI:** 69

Patience (Gawain–Poet), **Supp. VII:** 83, 84, 96–98

"Patience, hard thing!" (Hopkins), **V:** 375

Patmore, Coventry, **V:** 372, 379, 441

"Patmos" (Durrell), **Supp. I:** 125

Paton, Alan, **Supp. II:** 341–359

"Patricia, Edith, and Arnold," (Thomas), **Supp. I:** 181

Patrician, The (Galsworthy), **VI:** 273, 278

"Patricians" (Dunn), **Supp. X:** 69

"Patrick Sarsfield's Portrait" (Murphy), **Supp. V:** 323

Patriot (Johnson), **III:** 121

Patriot for Me, A (Osborne), **Supp. I:** 335, 337

"Patrol: Buonomary" (Gutteridge), **VII:** 432–433

Patronage (Edgeworth), **Supp. III:** 151, 158

Pattern of Maugham, The (Curtis), **VI:** 379

Pattern of Painful Adventures, The (Twine), **I:** 321

Patterns of Culture (Benedict), **Supp. III:** 186

Paul (Wilson), **Supp. VI:** 306

Pauli, Charles Paine, **Supp. II:** 98, 116

Pauline: A Fragment of a Confession (Browning), **IV:** xix, 354, 355, 373; **Retro. Supp. II:** 19

Paul's Departure and Crown (Bunyan), **II:** 253

Paul's Letters to His Kinsfolk (Scott), **IV:** 38

Pausanias' Description of Greece (Frazer), **Supp. III:** 172, 173

"Pause en Route" (Kinsella), **Supp. V:** 261

"Pavana Dolorosa" (Hill), **Supp. V:** 190–191

Pavane (Roberts, K.), **Supp. X:** 261, 264–270, 275

Pavic, Milorad, **Supp. IV:** 116

"Pavilion on the Links, The" (Stevenson), **V:** 395; **Retro. Supp. I:** 263

"Pawnbroker's Shop, The" (Dickens), **V:** 45, 47, 48

Pax Britannica: The Climax of an Empire (Morris, J.), **Supp. X:** 179–181, 183

Paying Guest, The (Gissing), **V:** 437

Payne, W. L., **III:** 41n

"Peace" (Brooke), **VI:** 420; **Supp. III:** 56, 57

"Peace" (Collins), **III:** 166, 168

"Peace" (Hopkins), **V:** 370

"Peace" (Vaughan), **II:** 186, 187

Peace and the Protestant Succession, The (Trevelyan), **VI:** 392–393

Peace Conference Hints (Shaw), **VI:** 119, 129

"Peace from Ghosts" (Cameron), **Supp. IX:** 19

Peace in Our Time (Coward), **Supp. II:** 151, 154

Peace of the World, The (Wells), **VI:** 244

Peaceable Principles and True (Bunyan), **II:** 253

"Peaches, The" (Thomas), **Supp. I:** 181

Peacock, Thomas Love, **III:** 336, 345; **IV:** xv, xvii–xix, xxii, **157–170,** 177, 198, 204, 306; **V:** 220; **VII:** 200, 211

Peacock Garden, The (Desai), **Supp. V:** 55, 62–63

Pearl (Arden), **Supp. II:** 39–40

Pearl (*Gawain*–Poet), **Supp. VII:** 83, 84, 91–96, 98

"Pearl, Matth.13. 45., The" (Herbert), **Retro. Supp. II:** 175

"Pearl Necklace, A" (Hall), **Supp. VI:** 119

Pearl'Maiden (Haggard), **Supp. III:** 214

Pearsall Smith, Logan, **VI:** 76

"Peasant, A" (Thomas), **Supp. XII:** 284

Peasant Mandarin, The: Prose Pieces (Murray), **Supp. VII:** 270, 271

"Peasants, The" (Lewis), **VII:** 447

Pecket, Thomas, **Supp. III:** 385

Peckham, Morse, **V:** 316, 335

Pedlar, The (Wordsworth), **IV:** 24

"Peele Castle" (Wordsworth), *see* AElegiac Stanzas, Suggested by a Picture of Peele Castle . . . A

"Peep into a Picture Book, A" (Brontë), **V:** 109

Peer Gynt (Ibsen), **Supp. III:** 195

Pegasus (Day Lewis), **Supp. III:** 118, 129–130

"Pegasus" (Kavanagh), **Supp. VII:** 193

Pelagea and Other Poems (Coppard), **VIII:** 89, 98

Pelican History of English Literature, The, **I:** 102

Pell, J. P., **V:** 161

Pelles, George, **VI:** 23

Pemberly; or, Pride and Prejudice Continued (Tennant), *see Pemberly: The Sequel to Pride and Prejudice*

Pemberly: The Sequel to Pride and Prejudice (Tennant), **Supp. IX:** 237–238, 239–240

"Pen Llŷn" (Thomas), **Supp. XII:** 290

"Pen, Pencil and Poison" (Wilde), **V:** 405, 407; **Retro. Supp. II:** 367–368

Pen Portraits and Reviews (Shaw), **VI:** 129

Pen Shop, The (Kinsella), **Supp. V:** 272, 273, 274

Pendennis (Tackeray), *see History of Pendennis, The*

"Penelope" (Maitland), **Supp. XI:** 175

Penelope (Maugham), **VI:** 369

Penfriends from Portlock (Wilson), **Sup. VI:** 298, 304

Penguin Book of Contemporary British Poetry, The (ed. Motion), **Supp. VII:** 252, 254, 255, 257

Penguin Book of Contemporary Irish Poetry, The (ed. Fallon and Mahon), **Supp. XII:** 101

Penguin Book of Lesbian Short Stories, The (ed. Winterson), **Supp. IV:** 542

Penguin Book of Light Verse (ed. Ewart), **Supp. VII:** 43, 47

Penguin Book of Love Poetry, The (ed. Stallworthy), **Supp. X:** 292

Penguin Book of Modern British Short Stories (ed. Bradbury), **Supp. IV:** 304

Penguin Book of Religious Verse, The (ed. Thomas), **Supp. XII:** 282

Penguin Modern Poets II (Thomas), **Supp. IV:** 490

Penguin Modern Poets 9 (ed. Burnside, Crawford and Jamie), **Supp. XI:** 67

Peniel (Hart), **Supp. XI:** 122, 128–130, 132

Penitential Psalms (Wyatt), **I:** 101–102, 108, 111

Pennies from Heaven (Potter, D.), **Supp. X:** 229, 231

"Pennines in April" (Hughes), **Supp. I:** 344

"Penny Plain and Twopence Coloured, A" (Stevenson), **V:** 385

Penny Wheep (MacDiarmid), **Supp. XII:** 202, 205

Penny Whistles (Stevenson), *see Child's Garden of Verses, A*

Penpoints, Gunpoints, and Dreams: Towards a Critical Theory of the Arts and the State in Africa (Ngũgĩ), **VIII:** 216, 225

Pensées (Pascal), **Supp. IV:** 160

"Penshurst, To" (Jonson), **II:** 223

"Pension Beaurepas, The" (James), **VI:** 69

Pentameron and Pentalogia, The (Landor), **IV:** 89, 90–91, 93, 100

"Pentecost Castle, The" (Hill), **Supp. V:** 189, 190, 199

"Pentecostal" (Malouf), **Supp. XII:** 220–221

"Penthouse Apartment, The" (Trevor), **Supp. IV:** 502

Pentland Rising, The (Stevenson), **V:** 395; **Retro. Supp. I:** 260

Penultimate Poems (Ewart), **Supp. VII:** 45–46

"Penwith" (Thomas), **Supp. IV:** 492

People Who Knock on the Door (Highsmith), **Supp. V:** 178

People with the Dogs, The (Stead), **Supp. IV:** 473

People's Otherworld, The (Murray), **Supp. VII:** 270, 277–279

"People's Park and the Battle of Berkeley, The" (Lodge), **Supp. IV:** 374

Pepys, Samuel, **II:** 145, 195, 273, 274, 275, 278, **280–288,** 310

Per Amica Silentia Lunae (Yeats), **VI:** 209

"Perchance a Jealous Foe" (Ewart), **Supp. VII:** 42

Percy, Thomas, **III:** 336; **IV:** 28–29

Percy Bysshe Shelley (Swinburne), **V:** 333

"Perdita" (Warner), **Supp. VII:** 379

Perduta Gente (Reading), **VIII:** 265, 271–272, 273

Père Goriot (Balzac), **Supp. IV:** 238

Peregrine Pickle (Smollett), **III:** 149, 150, 152–153, 158

Perelandra (Lewis), **Supp. I:** 74; **Supp. III:** 249, 252, 253–254

Perennial Philosophy, The (Huxley), **VII:** xviii, 206

"Perfect" (MacDiarmid), **Supp. XII:** 215

Perfect Alibi, The (Milne), **Supp. V:** 310

"Perfect Critic, The" (Eliot), **VII:** 163

Perfect Fool, The (Fuller), **Supp. VII:** 74, 75

Perfect Happiness (Churchill), **Supp. IV:** 181

Perfect Spy, A (le Carré), **Supp. II: 300–302,** 304, 305

Perfect Wagnerite, The (Shaw), **VI:** 129

"Perfect World, A" (Motion), **Supp. VII:** 265, 266

Performing Flea (Wodehouse), **Supp. III:** 460

"Perhaps" (Thomas), **Supp. XII:** 287

Pericles (Shakespeare), **I:** 321–322; **II:** 48

Pericles and Aspasia (Landor), **IV:** xix, 89, 92, 94–95, 100

Pericles and Other Studies (Swinburne), **V:** 333

Perimeter: Caroline Blackwood at Greenham Common, On the (Blackwood), **Supp. IX:** 14–15

Peripatetic, The (Thelwall), **IV:** 103

Perkin Warbeck (Ford), **II:** 89, 92, 96, 97, 100

Perkin Warbeck (Shelley), **Supp. III:** 371

Perkins, Richard, **II:** 68

Permanent Red: Essays in Seeing (Berger), **Supp. IV:** 79, 81

Permanent Way, The (Warner), **Supp. XI:** 294

Pernicious Consequences of the New Heresie of the Jesuites . . . ., The (tr. Evelyn), **II:** 287

Peronnik the Fool (Moore), **VI:** 99

Perpetual Curate, The (Oliphant), **Supp. X:** 213–216

Perry, Thomas Sergeant, **VI:** 24

Persian Boy, The (Renault), **Supp. IX:** 185–186

"Persian Eclogues" (Collins), **III:** 160, 164–165, 175

"Persian Passion Play, A" (Arnold), **V:** 216

"Person, The" (Traherne), **Supp. XI:** 268, 270

Personae (Pound), **Supp. III:** 398

Personal and Possessive (Thomas), **Supp. IV:** 490

Personal Heresy, The: A Controversy (Lewis), **Supp. III:** 249

Personal History, Adventures, Experience, and Observation of David Copperfield, The (Dickens), *see David Copperfield*

Personal Landscape (periodical), **VII:** 425, 443

Personal Places (Kinsella), **Supp. V:** 272

"Personal Problem" (Kavanagh), **Supp. VII:** 198

Personal Record, A (Conrad), **VI:** 134, 148; **Retro. Supp. II:** 69

Personal Reminiscences of Henry Irving (Stoker), **Supp. III:** 381

Persons from Porlock (MacNeice), **VII:** 408

Persse, Jocelyn, **VI:** 55

Persuasion (Austen), **IV:** xvii, 106–109, 111, 113, 115–120, 122; **Retro. Supp. II:** 12–13

"Perturbations of Uranus, The" (Fuller), **Supp. VII:** 73

"Pervasion of Rouge, The" (Beerbohm), **Supp. II:** 45

"Peshawar Vale Hunt, The" (Stallworthy), **Supp. X:** 295–296

"Pessimism in Literature" (Forster), **VI:** 410

Petals of Blood (Ngũgĩ), **VIII:** 212, 215, 220–221

Peter Bell (Wordsworth), **IV:** xviii 2

Peter Bell the Third (Shelley), **IV:** 203, 207

"Peter Grimes" (Crabbe), **III:** 283, 284–285

Peter Ibbetson (du Maurier), **Supp. III:** 134, 135, 136, 137, 138, 139

Peter Pan; or, The Boy Who Would Not Grow Up (Barrie), **Supp. III:** 2, **6–8**

"Peter Wentworth in Heaven" (Adcock), **Supp. XII:** 13

Petrarch's Seven Penitential Psalms (Chapman), **I:** 241–242

Peveril of the Peak (Scott), **IV:** xviii, 36, 37, 39

Pfeil, Fred, **Supp. IV:** 94

Phaedra (tr. Morgan), **Supp. IX:** 157

Phaedra (Seneca), **II:** 97

Phaedra's Love (Kane), **VIII:** 148, 149, 156

"Phaèthôn" (Meredith), **V:** 224

"Phallus in Wonderland" (Ewart), **Supp. VII:** 36

Phantasmagoria (Carroll), **V:** 270, 273

"Phantom–Wooer, The" (Beddoes), **Supp. XI:** 30

Pharos, pseud. of E. M. Forster

Pharos and Pharillon (Forster), **VI:** 408

Pharsalia (tr. Marlowe), **I:** 276, 291

Phases of Faith (Newman), **V:** 208*n*

"Pheasant in a Cemetery" (Smith, I. C.), **Supp. IX:** 224

"Phebus and Cornide" (Gower), **I:** 55

Philadelphia, Here I Come! (Friel), **Supp. V:** 111, 116–118

Philanderer, The (Shaw), **VI:** 107, 109; **Retro. Supp. II:** 312

Philaster (Beaumont and Fletcher), **II:** 45, 46, **52–54,** 55, 65

Philby Conspiracy, The (Page, Leitch, and Knightley), **Supp. II:** 302, 303, 311–312

Philip (Thackeray), *see Adventures of Philip on His Way Through the World, The*

Philip Larkin (Motion), **Supp. VII:** 253

Philip Sparrow (Skelton), **I:** 84, 86–88

Philip Webb and His Work (Lethaby), **V:** 291, 292, 296, 306

Philips, Ambrose, **III:** 56

Philips, Katherine, **II:** 185

Phillips, Caryl, **Supp. V:** **379–394**

Phillipps, Sir Thomas, **II:** 103

Phillips, Edward, **II:** 347

"Phillis is my only Joy" (Sedley), **II:** 265

"Phillis, let's shun the common Fate" (Sedley), **II:** 263

Phillpotts, Eden, **VI:** 266

"Philosopher, The" (Brontë), **V:** 134

"Philosopher and the Birds, The" (Murphy), **Supp. V:** 318

Philosopher's Pupil, The (Murdoch), **Supp. I:** 231, 232–233

Philosophical Discourse of Earth, An, Relating to . . . . Plants, etc. (Evelyn), **II:** 287

Philosophical Enquiry into the Origin of Our Ideas of the Sublime and Beautiful, A (Burke), *see On the Sublime and Beautiful*

Philosophical Essays Concerning Human Understanding (Hume), **Supp. III:** 238

Philosophical Investigation, A (Kerr), **Supp. XII:** 186, 187, 191–193, 195, 196

Philosophical Lectures of S. T. Coleridge, The (ed. Coburn), **IV:** 52, 56

"Philosophical View of Reform, A" (Shelley), **IV:** 199, 209; **Retro. Supp. I:** 254

"Philosophy of Furniture, The" (Hart), **Supp. XI:** 130

"Philosophy of Herodotus" (De Quincey), **IV:** 147–148

Philosophy of Melancholy, The (Peacock), **IV:** 158, 169

Philosophy of Nesessity, The (Bray), **V:** 188

Philosophy of Rhetoric (Richards), **Supp. II:** 416, 423

Philosophy of the Unconscious (Hartmann), **Supp. II:** 108

Phineas Finn (Trollope), **V:** 96, 98, 101, 102

Phineas Redux (Trollope), **V:** 96, 98, 101, 102

Phoebe Junior (Oliphant), **Supp. X:** 214, 217, 219

Phoenix (Storey), **Supp. I:** 408, 420

Phoenix, The, **Retro. Supp. II:** 303

Phoenix, The (Middleton), **II:** 21, 30

Phoenix and the Turtle, The (Shakespeare), **I:** 34, 313

"Phoenix Park" (Kinsella), **Supp. V:** 264

"Phoenix Rose Again, The" (Golding), **Supp. I:** 66

Phoenix Too Frequent, A (Fry), **Supp. III:** 194–195, 201–202

Photographs and Notebooks (Chatwin, B.), **Supp. IX:** 61–62

"Photograph of Emigrants" (Smith, I. C.), **Supp. IX:** 221

Physicists, The (Snow), **VII:** 339–340

Physico'Theology (Derham), **III:** 49

"Pibroch" (Hughes), **Supp. I:** 350

Picasso, Pablo, **Supp. IV:** 81, 87, 88

Piccolomini; or, The First Part of Wallenstein, The (Coleridge), **IV:** 55–56

Pickering, John, **I:** 213, 216–218

Pickwick Papers (Dickens), **V:** xix, 9, 42, 46–47, 48, 52, 59, 62, 71

Pico della Mirandola, **II:** 146; **V:** 344

"Pictor Ignotus, Florence 15" A (Browning), **IV:** 356, 361; **Retro. Supp. II:** 27

"Pictorial Rhapsody, A" (Thackeray), **V:** 37

Picture, The (Massinger), **Supp. XI:** 184

Picture and Text (James), **VI:** 46, 67

"Picture of a Nativity" (Hill), **Supp. V:** 186

Picture of Dorian Gray, The (Wilde), **III:** 334, 345; **V:** xxv, 339, 399, 410–411, 417, 419; **Retro. Supp. II:** 368

"Picture of Little T. C. in a Prospect of Flowers, The" (Marvell), **II:** 211, 215

"Picture This" (Motion), **Supp. VII:** 266

Picturegoers, The (Lodge), **Supp. IV:** 364, 367–368, 369, 371, 372, 381, 382

"Pictures" (Kelman), **Supp. V:** 250

Pictures at an Exhibition (Thomas), **Supp. IV:** 487–488

"Pictures from a Japanese Printmaker" (Redgrove), **Supp. VI:** 234

"Pictures from an Ecclesiastical Furnisher's" (Redgrove), **Supp. VI:** 234

Pictures from Italy (Dickens), **V:** 71

Pictures in the Hallway (O'Casey), **VII:** 9, 12

Pictures of Perfection (Hill, R.), **Supp. IX:** 121, 122–123

Picturesque Landscape and English Romantic Poetry (Watson), **IV:** 26

"Piece of Cake, A" (Dahl), **Supp. IV:** 208, 209

"Pied Beauty" (Hopkins), **V:** 367; **Retro. Supp. II:** 196

"Pied Piper of Hamelin, The" (Browning), **IV:** 356, 367

Pied Piper of Lovers (Durrell), **Supp. I:** 95

"Pier Bar" (Murphy), **Supp. V:** 328

Pier'Glass, The (Graves), **VII:** 263–264

Pierrot mon ami (Queneau), **Supp. I:** 220

Piers Plowman (Langland), **I:** **1–18**

Pietà (Thomas), **Supp. XII:** 284, 285

"Pietà" (Thomas), **Supp. XII:** 285

Pietrkiewicz, Jerzy, **Supp. IV:** 98

"Piffingcap" (Coppard), **VIII:** 88, 92

"Pig"(Dahl), **Supp. IV:** 221

"Pig, The" (Lessing), **Supp. I:** 240

Pig Earth (Berger), **Supp. IV:** 90, 92, 93

Pigeon, The (Galsworthy), **VI:** 271, 274, 287–288

Pigeon Pie (Mitford), **Supp. X:** 156–157

"Pigeons" (Reid), **Supp. VII:** 329

"Pigs" (Gunesekera), **Supp. X:** 87

"Pigs" (Murray), **Supp. VII:** 282

Pigs Have Wings (Wodehouse), **Supp. III:** 453–454, 458–459, 462

"Pike, The" (Blunden), **Supp. XI:** 42, 43

Pilgrim, The (Fletcher), **II:** 65

Pilgrim, The (Vanbrugh), **II:** 289, 305, 325, 336

"Pilgrim Fathers" (Adcock), **Supp. XII:** 13

Pilgrim to Compostella, The (Southey), **IV:** 71

"Pilgrimage of Pleasure, The" (Swinburne), **V:** 332

Pilgrimage of the Life of Man (Lydgate), **I:** 57

"Pilgrimages" (Thomas), **Supp. XII:** 288

Pilgrims of Hope (Morris), **V:** 301, 306

Pilgrim's Progress, The (Bunyan), **I:** 16, 57; **II:** 240, 241, 243, 244, **245–250,** 253; **III:** 82; **V:** 27; **Supp. IV:** 242

Pilgrim's Progress (Hill, R.), **Supp. IX:** 121–122

Pilgrim's Regress, The (Lewis), **Supp. III:** 249, **250–252,** 264

Pilkington, John, **Supp. IV:** 164

"Pillar of the Cloud" (Newman), see "Lead, Kindly Light"

"Pillar of the Community, A" (Kinsella), **Supp. V:** 261

Pillars of Society, The (Ibsen), **V:** xxiv, 414

"Pillow hot . . . , The" (tr. McKane), **Supp. IV:** 494

"Pillow hot . . . , The" (tr. Thomas), **Supp. IV:** 494

Pillowman, The (McDonagh), **Supp. XII:** 233–234, 238, 241, 243–246

Pinch of Snuff, A (Hill, R.), **Supp. IX:** 114

Pincher Martin (Golding), **Supp. I:** 67, 72–75, 76, 77, 83, 218n; **Retro. Supp. I:** 97

Pindar, **II:** 198–199; **IV:** 95, 316

Pindaric Ode, Humbly Offer'd to the King . . . , A (Congreve), **II:** 350

"Pindaric Poem to the Reverend Doctor Burnet, A" (Behn), **Supp. III:** 41

Pindarique Ode on the victorious Progress of Her Majesties Arms, A (Congreve), **II:** 350

Pindarique Odes (Cowley), **II:** 197, 199, 202

Pinero, Arthur Wing, **V:** 413; **VI:** 269, 368

Pink Furniture (Coppard), **VIII:** 91, 97

Pinter, Harold, **Supp. I: 367–382; Supp. IV:** 180, 290, 390, 437, 456; **Retro. Supp. I: 215–228**

Pinter Problem, The (Quigley), **Retro. Supp. I:** 227

"Pioneers, The" (Plomer), **Supp. XI:** 213

Piozzi, Hester Lynch, **III:** 134, 246

Pipelines (Bevan and Galloway), **Supp. XII:** 117

Pippa Passes (Browning), **IV:** 356, 362–363, 370, 373; **Retro. Supp. II:** 20–21

Piranesi Giovanni Battista, **III:** 325, 338

Pirate, The (Scott), **IV:** 36, 39

"Pirate and the Apothecary, The" (Stevenson), **V:** 391

"Pisgah" (Nicholson), **Supp. VI: 219**

"Pit and the Pendulum, The" (Poe), **III:** 339

Pit Strike (Sillitoe), **Supp. V:** 411

Pithy, Pleasant, and Profitable Works of John Skelton, The (ed. Stow), **I:** 94

"Pity" (Collins), **III:** 166

"Pity of It, The" (Hardy), **Retro. Supp. I:** 120

"Pixie" (Brathwaite), **Supp. XII:** 42

Pizarro (Sheridan), **III: 267–270**

Place at Whitton, A (Keneally), **Supp. IV:** 345

"Place in Tuscany, A" (Malouf), **Supp. XII:** 220

Place of the Lion, The (Williams, C. W. S.), **Supp. IX:** 281, 284

Place Where Souls Are Born: A Journey to the Southwest, The (Keneally), **Supp. IV:** 343, 347, 357–358

"Placeless Heaven, The" (Heaney), **Supp. II:** 280; **Retro. Supp. I:** 131

Places (Morris, J.), **Supp. X:** 172, 183

"Places, Loved Ones" (Larkin), **Supp. I:** 278

Plain Man and His Plain Wife, The (Bennett), **VI:** 264, 267

Plain Speaker, The (Hazlitt), **IV:** 131, 134, 136, 140

Plain Tales from the Hills (Kipling), **VI:** 168, 204

Plain'Dealer, The (Wycherley), **II:** 308, **318–320,** 321, 322, 343

Plaine Mans Path'Way to Heaven, The (Dent), **II:** 241, 246

"Plains, The" (Fuller), **VII:** 430; **Supp. VII:** 69

"Plan, The" (O'Brien), **Supp. V:** 340

Plan of a Dictionary of the English Language, The (Johnson), **III:** 113, 121; *see also Dictionary of the English Language, A*

Plan of a Novel . . . With Opinions on AMansfield Park"and AEmma" . . . (Austen), **IV:** 112, 122

Plan of the English Commerce, A (Defoe), **III:** 14

Planes of Bedford Square, The (Plomer), **Supp. XI:** 222

"Planetist" (Crawford), **Supp. XI:** 79

"Planter of Malata, The" (Conrad), **VI:** 148

"Plas–yn–Rhiw" (Thomas), **Supp. XII:** 290

Plath, Sylvia, **Supp. I:** 346, 350; **Supp. IV:** 252, 430; **Retro. Supp. II:** 199, 200–201, 216–218

Plato, **IV:** 47–48, 54; **V:** 339; **Supp. III:** 125; **Supp. IV:** 13

Plato and Platonism (Pater), **V:** 339, 355, 356

Plato Papers: A Novel, The (Ackroyd), **Supp. VI:** 4, 11, 13

Plato Papers: A Prophesy, The (Ackroyd), **Supp. VI:** 13

"Platonic Blow, by Miss Oral" (Auden), **Retro. Supp. I:** 12

"Platonic Love" (Cowley), **II:** 197

Play (Beckett), **Supp. I:** 46, 58; **Retro. Supp. I:** 27

Play from Romania, A, see Mad Forest

Playboy of the Western World, The (Synge), **VI:** xiv, 308, 309–310, 312–313, 316; **Retro. Supp. I:** 291, 298–300

Player of Games, The (Banks), **Supp. XI:** 1, 9, 10

"Players, The" (Davies), **Supp. XI:** 100–101

Playground of Europe, The (Stephen), **V:** 282, 289

Playing Away (Phillips), **Supp. V:** 380

"Playing with Terror" (Ricks), **Supp. IV:** 398

Playmaker, The (Keneally), **Supp. IV:** 346

"Plays" (Landor), **IV:** 98

Plays and Poems of Thomas Lovell Beddoes (Beddoes), **Supp. XI:** 18, 21, 22, 23, 24, 26, 28–29, 30

Plays for England (Osborne), **Supp. I:** 335

Plays for Puritans (Shaw), **VI:** 109

Plays of William Shakespeare, The (ed. Johnson), **III:** 115–117, 121; **Retro. Supp. I:** 138, 144

Plays: One (Arden), **Supp. II:** 30

Plays: Pleasant and Unpleasant (Shaw), **VI:** ix, 104, **107–112; Retro. Supp. II:** 313–315

Plaza de Toros, The (Scott), **Supp. I:** 266

Plea for Justice, A (Russell), **VIII:** 289

"Poem" (Armitage), **VIII:** 5

Plea of the Midsummer Fairies, The (Hood), **IV:** 253, 255, 261, 267

Pleasant Notes upon Don Quixote (Gayton), **I:** 279

"Pleasaunce" (Dutton), **Supp. XII:** 95

"Please Baby Don't Cry" (Blackwood), **Supp. IX:** 9

"Please Identify Yourself" (Adcock), **Supp. XII:** 6

Pleasure (Waugh), **Supp. VI:** 270

Pleasure Dome, The (Greene), **Supp. I:** 3, 9

"Pleasure Island" (Auden), **Retro. Supp. I:** 12

Pleasure of Poetry, The (Sitwell), **VII:** 129–130

Pleasure of Reading, The (Fraser), **Supp. V:** 20

Pleasure Steamers, The (Motion), **Supp. VII:** 253–255, 257

Pleasures of a Tangled Life (Morris, J.), **Supp. X:** 183

"Pleasures of a Technological University, The" (Morgan, E.), **Supp. IX:** 158–159

Pleasures of the Flesh (Ewart), **Supp. VII:** 38–39

Pleasures of War, The (Maitland), **Supp. XI:** 163

Plebeian (periodical), **III:** 51, 53

Pléiade, **I:** 170

Plenty (Hare), **Supp. IV:** 282, 286–287, 293

Plomer, William, **Supp. XI: 209–225**

Plot Discovered, The (Coleridge), **IV:** 56

Plotinus, **III:** 291

Plotting and Writing Suspense Fiction (Highsmith), **Supp. V:** 167, 171, 174, 177

Plough, The (Walker), **V:** 377

Plough and the Stars, The (O'Casey), **VI:** 214; **VII:** xviii, 5–6

Ploughman and Other Poems (Kavanagh), **Supp. VII:** 187–188

Ploughman, and Other Poems, A (White), **Supp. I:** 130

Ploughman's Lunch, The (McEwan), **Supp. IV:** 389, 390, 399–400

Plumb, Sir John Harold, **IV:** 290; **VI:** xv, xxxiv, 391n

Plumed Serpent, The (Lawrence), **VII:** 87–88, 91, **109–110,** 123; **Retro. Supp. II:** 231

Plutarch, **II:** 185

Plutarch's Lives (tr. Goldsmith), **III:** 191

Plutarch's Lives. The translation called Dryden's . . . (ed. Clough), **V:** 157, 170

Plutus, The God of Riches (tr. Fielding), **III:** 105

Plymley, Peter, *see* Smith, Sydney
PN Review (publication), **Supp. IV:** 256
Podro, Joshua, **VII:** 262
Poe, Edgar Allan, **III:** 329, 333, 334, 338–339, 340, 343, 345; **IV:** 311, 319; **V:** xvi, xx–xxi; **VI:** 371
"Poem" (Welch), **Supp. IX:** 269–270
"Poem About a Ball in the Nineteenth Century" (Empson), **Supp. II:** 180–181, 183
"Poem about Poems About Vietnam, A" (Stallworthy), **Supp. X:** 294–295, 302
"Poem as Abstract" (Davie), **Supp. VI:** 106
"Poem by the Boy Outside the Fire Station" (Armitage), **VIII:** 4
"Poem Composed in Santa Barbara" (Cope), **VIII:** 78
"Poem from the North," (Keyes), **VII:** 439
"Poem for My Father" (Reid), **Supp. VII:** 325
"Poem in October" (Thomas), **Supp. I:** 177, 178–179
Poem in St. James's Park, A (Waller), **II:** 238
"Poem in Seven Books, A" (Blake), **Retro. Supp. I:** 37
"Poem in Winter" (Jennings), **Supp. V:** 213–214
"Poem of Lewis" (Smith, I. C.), **Supp. IX:** 211
"Poem of the Midway" (Thomas), **Supp. IV:** 493
"Poem on His Birthday" (Thomas), **Supp. I:** 179
Poem on the Late Civil War, A (Cowley), **II:** 202
"Poem on the Theme of Humour, A" (Cope), **VIII:** 81
Poem Sacred to the Memory of Sir Isaac Newton, A (Thomson), **Supp. III:** 411, 418–419
"Poem Upon the Death of O. C., A" (Marvell), **II:** 205, 211
"Poem with the Answer, A" (Suckling), **II:** 228
Poemata et Epigrammata, . . . (Crashaw), **II:** 201
Poemata et inscriptiones (Landor), **IV:** 100
Poems [1853] (Arnold), **V:** xxi, 165, 209, 216
Poems [1854] (Arnold), **V:** 216
Poems [1855] (Arnold), **V:** 216
Poems [1857] (Arnold), **V:** 216
Poems (Bridges), **VI:** 83
Poems (Brooke), **Supp. III:** 51–53
Poems [1844] (Browning), **IV:** xx, 311, 313–314, 321, 356
Poems [1850] (Browning), **IV:** 311, 321
Poems (Byron), **IV:** 192
Poems (Carew), **II:** 238
Poems (Caudwell), **Supp. IX:** 33, 35
Poems (Clough), **V:** 170
Poems (Cornford), **VIII:** 102, 103
Poems (Cowley), **II:** 194, 198, 199, 202
Poems (Crabbe), **III:** 286
Poems (Eliot), **VII:** 146, 150
Poems (Empson), **Supp. II:** 180

Poems (Gay), **III:** 55
Poems (Golding), **Supp. I:** 66
"Poems, 1912–13" (Hardy), **Retro. Supp. I:** 117
Poems (Hood), **IV:** 252, 261, 266
Poems (Jennings), **Supp. V:** 208
Poems (Keats), **IV:** xvii, 211, 213–214, 216, 235; **Retro. Supp. I:** 183, 187–188
Poems (Kinsella), **Supp. V:** 260
Poems (Lovell and Southey), **IV:** 71
Poems (Meredith), **V:** xxi, 219, 234
Poems (C. Rossetti), **V:** 260
Poems [1870] (D. G. Rossetti), **V:** xxiii, 237, 238, 245
Poems [1873] (D. G. Rossetti), **V:** 245
Poems [1881] (D. G. Rossetti), **V:** 238, 245
Poems (Ruskin), **V:** 184
Poems (Sassoon), **VI:** 429
Poems (Southey), **IV:** 71
Poems (Spender), **Supp. II:** 483, 486–487
Poems [1833] (Tennyson), **IV:** 326, 329, 338
Poems [1842] (Tennyson), **IV:** xx, 326, 333–334, 335, 338
Poems (Thompson), **V:** 439, 451
Poems (Waller), **II:** 238
Poems (Wilde), **V:** 401–402, 419; **Retro. Supp. II:** 361–362
Poems, The (Landor), **IV:** xvi, 99
Poems, The (Swift), **III:** 15n, 35
Poems, The (Thomas), **Supp. I:** 170
Poems Against Economics (Murray), **Supp. VII:** 270, 273–275
Poems and Ballads (Swinburne), **V:** xxiii, 309, 310, 313, **314–321**, 327, 330, 332
"Poems and Ballads of Goethe" (Clough), **V:** 170
Poems and Ballads: Second Series (Swinburne), **V:** xxiv, 314, 327, 332
Poems and Ballads: Third Series (Swinburne), **V:** 332
Poems and Letters of Bernard Barton (ed. FitzGerald), **IV:** 343–344, 353
Poems and Lyrics of the Joy of Earth (Meredith), **V:** 221, 224, 234
Poems and Melodramas (Davie), **Supp. VI:** 113
Poems and Metrical Tales (Southey), **IV:** 71
Poems and Prose Remains of A. H. Clough, The (ed. Clough and Symonds), **V:** 159, 170
Poems and Songs, The (Burns), **III:** 310n, 322
Poems and Songs (Ewart), **Supp. VII:** 34, 36–37
Poems and Translations (Kinsella), **Supp. V:** 264
Poems Before Congress (Browning), **IV:** 312, 315, 321
Poems by Alfred, Lord Tennyson (Lear), **V:** 78, 87
Poems by Currer, Ellis and Acton Bell (Brontës), **V:** xx, 131–134, 151
Poems by John Clare (Clare), **Supp. XI:** 63

Poems by the Author of the Growth of Love (Bridges), **VI:** 83
Poems by the Way (Morris), **V:** 306
Poems by Two Brothers (Tennyson and Tennyson), **IV:** 337–338
Poems, Centuries, and Three Thanksgivings (Traherne), **Supp. XI:** 263–264, 265, 266, 267, 268, 269, 270, 271, 272, 273, 274, 275, 276, 278
Poems Chiefly in the Scottish Dialect (Burns), **III:** 315
Poems, Chiefly Lyrical (Tennyson), **IV:** xix, 326, 329, 331, 338
Poems Chiefly of Early and Late Years (Wordsworth), **IV:** xx, 25
Poems, Descriptive of Rural Life and Scenery (Clare), **Supp. XI:** 49, 54–55
Poems, Elegies, Paradoxes, and Sonnets (King), **Supp. VI:** 162
"Poems for Angus" (MacCaig), **Supp. VI:** 193
Poems for Donalda (Smith, I. C.), **Supp. IX:** 217
Poems for Young Ladies (Goldsmith), **III:** 191
Poems from Centre City (Kinsella), **Supp. V:** 272
Poems from the Arabic and Persian (Landor), **IV:** 99
Poems from the Russian (Cornford), **VIII:** 110–111
Poems from Villon, and Other Fragments (Swinburne), **V:** 333
Poems in Prose (Wilde), **Retro. Supp. II:** 371
Poems, in Two Volumes (Wordsworth), **IV:** 22, 24
Poems, 1930 (Auden), **VII:** xix
Poems 1938–1945 (Graves), **VII:** 267–268
Poems, 1943–1947 (Day Lewis), **Supp. III:** 118, 128
Poems 1950 (Bunting), **Supp. VII:** 5, 13
Poems 1960–2000 (Adcock), **Supp. XII:** 2, 11, 13, 14–15
Poems 1962–1978 (Mahon), **Supp. VI:** 173–174
Poems of Conformity (Williams, C. W. S.), **Supp. IX:** 274
Poems of Dedication (Spender), **Supp. II:** 489, 490
Poems of Edmund Blunden, The (Blunden), **Supp. XI:** 36, 37, 44
Poems of Felicity (Traherne), **II:** 191, 202; **Supp. XI:** 266
Poems of Henry Vaughan, Silurist, The (ed. Chambers), **II:** 187
Poems of John Keats, The (ed. Allott), **IV:** 223n 224, 234–235
"Poems of 1912–13" (Hardy), **VI:** 14
Poems of Ossian, The (Macpherson), **III:** 336; **VIII:** 180, 181, 182, 183, 184, 185, 187, 188, 190, 191, 192, 193, 194
Poems of the War and After (Brittain), **Supp. X:** 41
Poems of William Dunbar, The (Dunbar), **VIII:** 118–119
Poems of Wit and Humour (Hood), **IV:** 257, 266

Poems on His Domestic Circumstances (Byron), **IV:** 192

Poems on Several Occasions (Haywood), **Supp. XII:** 135

Poems on the Death of Priscilla Farmer (Lloyd and Lamb), **IV:** 78, 85

Poems on the Theatre (Brecht), **Supp. IV:** 87

Poems on Various Occasions (Byron), **IV:** 192

Poems on Various Subjects (Coleridge), **IV:** 43, 55, 78, 85

Poems Original and Translated (Byron), **IV:** 192

Poems Translated from the French of Madame de la Mothe Guion (tr. Cowper), **III:** 220

Poems upon Several Occasions: With a Voyage to the Island of Love (Behn), **Supp. III:** 36

Poems, with the Tenth Satyre of Juvenal Englished (Vaughan), **II:** 184–185, 201

"Poet, The" (Hulme), **Supp. VI:** 135

"Poet, The" (Sillitoe), **Supp. V:** 425

Poet and Dancer (Jhabvala), **Supp. V:** 223, 234, 235

"Poet Hood, The" (Blunden), **IV:** 267

Poet in the Imaginary Museum, The (Davie), **Supp. VI:** 115, 117

"Poet in the Imaginary Museum, The" (Davie), **Supp. VI:** 115

poet laureateship, **IV:** 61, 310, 311, 324

"Poet on the Island, The" (Murphy), **Supp. V:** 318

"Poet O'Rahilly, The" (Kinsella), **Supp. V:** 263

"Poet with Sea Horse" (Reid), **Supp. VII:** 328

Poetaster (Jonson), **I:** 339, 340; **Retro. Supp. I:** 158

"Poetic Diction in English" (Bridges), **VI:** 73

Poetic Image, The (Day Lewis), **Supp. III:** 118

"Poetic Imagination, The" (Muir), **Supp. VI:** 202–203

Poetic Mirror, The (Hogg), **Supp. X:** 109–110

Poetic Unreason (Graves), **VII:** 257, 260

Poetical Blossomes (Cowley), **II:** 194, 202

Poetical Calendar (Fawkes and Woty), **III:** 170*n*

"Poetical Character, The" (Collins), **III:** 166, 168

Poetical Fragments (Swinburne), **V:** 333

Poetical Pieces (Lamb), **IV:** 74

Poetical Register (Jacob), **II:** 348

Poetical Sketches (Blake), **III:** 289, 290; **Retro. Supp. I:** 33–34

Poetical Works, The, . . . (Traherne), **II:** 201–202

Poetical Works, The (Southey), **IV:** 71

Poetical Works (Bridges), **VI:** 83

Poetical Works of George Crabbe, The (ed. Carlyle and Carlyle), **III:** 272*n*

Poetical Works of George Meredith, The (ed. Trevelyan), **V:** 223, 234

Poetical Works of Gray and Collins, The (ed. Poole and Stone), **III:** 161*n*

Poetical Works of John Gay, The (ed. Faber), **III:** 66, 67

"Poetics of Sex, The" (Winterson), **Supp. IV:** 547, 551–552, 553

Poetria nova (Geoffrey of Vinsauf), **I:** 59

"Poetry"[broadcast] (Bridges), **VI:** 83

"Poetry" (Moore), **IV:** 6

Poetry and Belief (Wallace–Crabbe), **VIII:** 316, 319

"Poetry and the Other Modern Arts" (Davie), **Supp. VI:** 115–116

Poetry and Philosophy of George Meredith, The (Trevelyan), **VI:** 383

Poetry and Prose (ed. Sparrow), **VI:** 83

"Poetry and Striptease" (Thomas), **Supp. IV:** 491

Poetry at Present (Williams, C. W. S.), **Supp. IX:** 277

Poetry by the Author of Gebir (Landor), **IV:** 99

Poetry for Children (Lamb and Lamb), **IV:** 85

Poetry for Supper (Thomas), **Supp. XII:** 284

"Poetry in Public" (Motion), **Supp. VII:** 265

Poetry in the Making (Hughes), **Supp. I:** 347

Poetry of Browning, The (Drew), **IV:** 375

"Poetry of Departures" (Larkin), **Supp. I:** 277, 278–279

Poetry of Edward Thomas, The (Motion), **Supp. VII:** 252, 253, 258, 263

Poetry of Ezra Pound, The (Kenner), **VI:** 333

Poetry of Meditation, The (Martz), **V:** 366, 382

Poetry of Nonsense, The (Cammaerts), **V:** 262, 274

"Poetry of Pope, The" (De Quincey), **IV:** 146

"Poetry of Protest, A" (Davie), **Supp. VI:** 116

Poetry of the First World War (Hibberd), **VI:** 460

Poetry of Thomas Hardy, The (Day Lewis), **VI:** 21

"Poetry of W. B. Yeats, The" (Eliot), **VI:** 207*n*, 223

Poetry of W. B. Yeats, The (MacNeice), **VII:** 404

"Poetry of Wordsworth, The" (De Quincey), **IV:** 146, 148

"Poetry Perpetuates the Poet" (Herrick), **II:** 115

Poet's Calendar, A (Davies), **Supp. XI:** 101

"Poet's Epitaph, A" (Davies), **Supp. XI:** 95–96

"Poet'Scholar, The" (Davie), **Supp. VI:** 105

"Poets Lie where they Fell, The" (Mahon), **Supp. VI:** 167

Poet's Notebook, A (Sitwell), **VII:** 127, 139

Poets of the First World War (Stallworthy), **VI:** 441

Poet's Pilgrimage, A (Davies), **Supp. XI:** 89–91

"Poet's Pilgrimage to Waterloo, The" (Southey), **IV:** 66, 71

Poet's Tongue, The (Auden and Garrett), **Supp. IV:** 256; **Retro. Supp. I:** 6–7

"Poet's Vow, The" (Browning), **IV:** 313

"Poggio" (Durrell), **Supp. I:** 126

Point Counter Point (Huxley), **VII:** xviii, 201, 202–204

"Point of It, The" (Forster), **V:** 208

Point Valaine (Coward), **Supp. II:** 152

Points of View (Maugham), **VI:** 374, 377

Pointz Hall (Woolf), **Retro. Supp. I:** 308

"Poison" (Dahl), **Supp. IV:** 206, 215

Pol Pot, **Supp. IV:** 247

Polanski, Roman, **III:** 343

Polaris (Weldon), **Supp. IV:** 521

"Police, The: Seven Voices" (Murray), **Supp. VII:** 276

Polidori, John, **III:** 329, 334, 338; **Supp. III:** 385

Polite Conversations (Swift), **III:** 36

Political Economy of Art, The (Ruskin), **V:** 184

Political Essays (Hazlitt), **IV:** 129, 139

Political History of the Devil, The (Defoe), **III:** 5, 14

Political Justice (Godwin), **IV:** 43

"Political Kiss, A" (Adcock), **Supp. XII:** 13

"Political Poem" (Ewart), **Supp. VII:** 36

Political Romance, A (Sterne), **III:** 127, 135

Political Situation, The (Schreiner), **Supp. I:** 453

Political Thought in England, 1848–1914 (Walker), **IV:** 304

Politicks of Laurence Sterne, The (Curtis), **III:** 127*n*

"Politics" (Durrell), **Supp. I:** 124

"Politics and the English Language" (Orwell), **Supp. III:** 107; **Supp. IV:** 455

"Politics of King Lear, The" (Muir), **Supp. VI:** 202

"Politics of Mecca, The" (Lawrence), **Supp. II:** 286–287

"Politics vs. Literature" (Orwell), **VII:** 273, 282

Poliziano, Angelo, **I:** 240

Poll Degree from a Third Point of View, The (Stephen), **V:** 289

Pollock, Jackson, **Supp. IV:** 80

Polly (Gay), **III:** 55, 65–67

"Polonius" (FitzGerald), **IV:** 353

Polonius: A Collection of Wise Saws and Modern Instances (FitzGerald), **IV:** 344, 353

Polychronicon (Higden), **I:** 22

Polychronicon (tr. Trevisa), **Supp. IX:** 243–252, 256–259

"Pomegranates of Patmos, The" (Harrison), **Supp. V:** 160

Pomes Penyeach (Joyce), **VII:** 42

Pomona (Evelyn), **II:** 287

Pompeii (Macaulay), **IV:** 290

Pompey the Great (tr. Dorset et al.), **II:** 270, 271

Pooh Perplex: A Freshman Casebook (Crews), **Supp. V:** 311

Poole, A. L., **III:** 161*n*

Poole, Thomas, **IV:** 42, 43, 51

Poor Clare (Hartley), **Supp. VII:** 132

"Poor Koko" (Fowles), **Supp. I:** 303

"Poor Man, The" (Coppard), **VIII:** 94

"Poor Man and the Lady, The" (Hardy), **VI:** 2, 20; **Retro. Supp. I:** 112

"Poor Man's Guide to Southern Tuscany, A" (Malouf), **Supp. XII:** 220

Poor Man's Plea, The (Defoe), **III:** 2, 12; **Retro. Supp. I:** 74–75

"Poor Mary" (Warner), **Supp. VII:** 380

"Poor Mathias" (Arnold), **V:** 207

Poor Miss Finch (Collins), **Supp. VI:** 102–103

Poor Mouth, The (O'Nolan), **Supp. II:** **333–335**

"Poor Richard" (James), **VI:** 69

Poor Things (Gray, A.), **Supp. IX:** 80, 85–87

Poor Tom (Muir), **Supp. VI:** 198

Pope, Alexander, **I:** 326, 328; **II:** **195–197**, 236, 259, 261, 263, 298, 308–309, 311, 321, 332, 335, 344; **III:** 1, 19, 20, 33, 46, 50, 54, 56, 60, 62, **68–79**, 95, 118, 167*n*, 234, 278, 280–282, 288; **IV:** 104, 182, 187, 189–190, 280; **V:** 319; **Supp. III:** 421–422; **Retro. Supp. I:** 76, **229–242**

Pope's Wedding, The (Bond), **Supp. I:** 422, **423–425**, 426, 427, 435

Popery: British and Foreign (Landor), **IV:** 100

"Poplar Field, The" (Cowper), **III:** 218

Popper, Karl, **Supp. IV:** 115

"Poppies" (Nye), **Supp. X:** 204–205

"Poppy grows upon the shore, A" (Bridges), **VI:** 78

Popular Education of France with Notices of that of Holland and Switzerland, The (Arnold), **V:** 216

"Popular Fallacies" (Lamb), **IV:** 82

Porcupine, The (Barnes), **Supp. IV:** 65, 67, 68, 73, 74

"Pornography and Obscenity" (Lawrence), **VII:** 91, 101, 122

"Pornography" (McEwan), **Supp. IV:** 394–395

"Porphyria's Lover" (Browning), **IV:** 360; **V:** 315; **Retro. Supp. II:** 22

Porson, Richard, **IV:** 63

"Portico" (Murphy), **Supp. V:** 327

"Portobello Road, The" (Spark), **Supp. I:** 200

"Portrait, The" (Gogol), **III:** 340, 345

"Portrait, The" (Oliphant), **Supp. X:** 220

"Portrait, The" (Rossetti), **V:** 239

Portrait, The (Swinburne), **V:** 333

Portrait of a Gentleman in Slippers (Milne), **Supp. V:** 300

"Portrait of a Grandfather, The" (Bridges), **VI:** 78

"Portrait of a Lady" (Eliot), **VII:** 144

Portrait of a Lady, The (James), **V:** xxiv, 51; **VI:** 25, 26, **35–38**; **Supp. IV:** 243

"Portrait of an Emperor, The" (Plomer), **Supp. XI:** 216

"Portrait of Mr. W. H., The" (Wilde), **V:** 405–406, 419; **Retro. Supp. II:** 365–366

Portrait of Rossetti (Grylls), **V:** 247, 249, 260

"Portrait of the Artist, A" (Kinsella), **Supp. V:** 272

"Portrait of the Artist, A" (Mahon), **Supp. VI:** 168

Portrait of the Artist as a Young Dog (Thomas), **Supp. I:** 176, 180, 181, 182

Portrait of the Artist as a Young Man, A (Joyce), **VII:** xiv, **45–47**; critical studies, **VII:** 57; **Supp. IV:** 364, 371; **Retro. Supp. I:** 169, 170, 173–175

"Portrait of the Artist as Émigré" (Berger), *see Painter of Our Time, A*

"Portrait of the Beatnik: Letter from California" (Blackwood), **Supp. IX:** 5–6, 9

"Portrait of the Engineer, A" (Kinsella), **Supp. V:** 261

Portrait of the Lakes (Nicholson), **Supp. VI:** 223

Portrait of Orkney (Brown), **Supp. VI:** 65

"Portraits" (Thomas), **Supp. IV:** 494

Portraits Contemporains (Sainte'Beuve), **V:** 212

Portraits from Memory (Russell), **VI:** 170

"Portraits in the Nude" (Plomer), **Supp. XI:** 214

Portraits of Places (James), **VI:** 67

Portugal History, The; or, A Relation of the Troubles . . . in the Court of Portugal . . . (Pepys), **II:** 288

"Pose (After the Painting *Mrs. Badham* by Ingres)" (Boland), **Supp. V:** 40

Positions (Mulcaster), **I:** 122

"Positive Season, The" (Fallon), **Supp. XII:** 104–105

Positives (Gunn), **Supp. IV:** 257, 264, 265, 266

Possession: A Romance (Byatt), **Supp. IV:** 139, 149, 151–153

Post Captain (O'Brian), **Supp. XII:** 254–255

"Post Office" (Adcock), **Supp. XII:** 9

Postal Problem, A (Carroll), **V:** 274

"Posterity" (Larkin), **Supp. I:** 282

Posthumous Fragments of Margaret Nicholson . . . (ed. Shelley), **IV:** 208

Posthumous Papers of the Pickwick Club, The (Dickens), *see Pickwick Papers*

Posthumous Poems (Day Lewis), **Supp. III:** 130

Posthumous Poems (Shelley), **IV:** 208

Posthumous Poems, The (Swinburne), **V:** 333

Posthumous Tales (Crabbe), **III:** 278, 286

"Postmodern Blues" (Wallace–Crabbe), **VIII:** 324

Post'Mortem (Coward), **Supp. II:** 149–150, 151

"Postponing the Bungalow" (Dunn), **Supp. X:** 68

"Postscript" (Fuller), **Supp. VII:** 81

"Postscript: for Gweno" (Lewis), **VII:** 444, 446

"Postscripts" (radio broadcasts), **VII:** 212

Poet Geranium, The (Nicholson), **Supp. VI:** 213, 216–217

Pot of Broth, The (Yeats), **VI:** 218

"Potato Gatherers, The" (Friel), **Supp. V:** 114

Potter, Beatrix, **Supp. III:** **287–309**

Potter, Cherry, **Supp. IV:** 181

Potter, Dennis, **Supp. X:** **227–242**

Potter's Thumb, The (Steel), **Supp. XII:** 270–271

Potting Shed, The (Greene), **Supp. I:** 13; **Retro. Supp. II:** 162

Pottle, F. A., **III:** 234*n*, 239, 240, 247, 249

Pound, Ezra, **I:** 98; **IV:** 323, 327, 329, 372; **V:** xxv, 304, 317*n*; **VI:** 207, 216, 247, 323, 417; **VII:** xiii, xvi, 89, 148, 149; **Supp. III:** 53–54, 397, 398; **Supp. IV:** 99, 100, 114–115, 116, 411, 559

Pound on Demand, A (O'Casey), **VII:** 12

"Pour Commencer" (Stallworthy), **Supp. X:** 297

"Poussin" (MacNeice), **VII:** 411

Powell, Anthony, **VI:** 235; **VII:** xxi, **343–359**; **Supp. II:** 4; **Supp. IV:** 505

Powell, Edgar, **VI:** 385

Powell, L F., **III:** 234*n*

Power and the Glory, The (Greene; U.S. title, *The Labyrinthine Ways*), **Supp. I:** 5, 8, 9–10, 13, 14, 18; **Retro. Supp. II:** 156–157

Power in Men (Cary), **VII:** 186, 187

Power of Grace Illustrated (tr. Cowper), **III:** 220

Powers, Mary, **Supp. IV:** 423, 428

Powys, T. F., **VII:** 21, 234; **VIII:** **245–259**

Practical Criticism (Richards), **Supp. II:** 185, 405, **418–421**, 423, 430

Practical Education (Edgeworth), **Supp. III:** 152

Practice of Piety, The (Bayly), **II:** 241

Practice of Writing, The (Lodge), **Supp. IV:** 366, 381

Praed, Winthrop Mackworth, **IV:** 269, 283; **V:** 14

Praeterita (Ruskin), **V:** 174, 175, 182, 184

"Prague Milk Bottle, The" (Motion), **Supp. VII:** 262

"Praise for Mercies, Spiritual and Temporal" (Blake), **III:** 294

"Praise for the Fountain Opened" (Cowper), **III:** 211

Praise of Age, The (Henryson), **Supp. VII:** 146, 148

"Praise of My Lady" (Morris), **V:** 295

"Praise of Pindar, The" (Cowley), **II:** 200

Praise Singer, The (Renault), **Supp. IX:** 181–182, 187

"Praise II" (Herbert), **II:** 129; **Retro. Supp. II:** 177

Praises (Jennings), **Supp. V:** 219

Prancing Nigger (Firbank; British title, *Sorrow in Sunlight*), **Supp. II:** 200, 202, 204, 205, 211, 213, **218–220**, **222, 223**

Prater Violet (Isherwood), **VII:** 313–314

Pravda (Hare and Brenton), **Supp. IV:** 282, 283, 284, 285, 286, 293

Praxis (Weldon), **Supp. IV:** 522, 525–526, 528, 533

"Prayer, A" (Joyce), **Retro. Supp. I:** 179

"Prayer Before Birth" (MacNeice), **VII:** 415

"Prayer for My Daughter, A" (Yeats), **VI:** 217, 220; **Supp. V:** 39; **Retro. Supp. I:** 333

"Prayer 1" (Herbert), **II:** 122; **Retro. Supp. II:** 179

"Prayers of the Pope, The" (Williams, C. W. S.), **Supp. IX:** 283

Prayers Written at Vailima (Stevenson), **V:** 396

Praz, Mario, **I:** 146, 292, 354; **II:** 123; **III:** 329, 337, 344–345, 346; **V:** 412, 420; **VII:** 60, 62, 70

"Preamble" (Nye), **Supp. X:** 198

"Precautions in Free Thought" (Butler), **Supp. II:** 99

Predictions for the Year 1708 (Swift), **III:** 35

Pre'eminent Victorian: A Study of Tennyson, The (Richardson), **IV:** 339

"Preface" (Arnold), **Supp. II:** 57

"Preface: Mainly About Myself" (Shaw), **VI:** 129

Preface to Paradise Lost, " (Lewis), **Supp. III:** 240, 265

Preface to the Dramatic Works of Dryden (ed. Congreve), **II:** 348, 350

Prefaces (Dryden), **IV:** 349

"Prefaces" (Housman), **VI:** 156

"Prefatory Letter on Reading the Bible for the First Time" (Moore), **VI:** 96

"Prefatory Poem to My Brother's Sonnets" (Tennyson), **IV:** 327, 336

"Preference" (Thomas), **Supp. XII:** 290

Preiching of the Swallow, The (Henryson), **Supp. VII:** 136, 139–140

"Prelude" (Brathwaite), **Supp. XII:** 36

"Prelude" (Mansfield), **VII:** 177, 179, 180

"Prelude, A" (Lawrence), **VII:** 114

Prelude, The (Wordsworth) **IV:** ix–x, xxi, 1, 2, 3, **11–17,** 24, 25, 43, 151, 315; **V:** 310

"Prelude and History" (Redgrove), **Supp. VI:** 236

"Preludes" (Eliot), **Retro. Supp. II:** 121

"Preludes" (Malouf), **Supp. XII:** 220

"Premature Rejoicing" (Blunden), **Supp. XI:** 43

Premonition to Princes, A (Ralegh), **I:** 154

Preoccupations: Selected Prose 1968–1978 (Heaney), **Supp. II:** 268–269, 272, 273

Pre'Raphaelite Imagination, The (Dixon Hunt), **VI:** 167

Pre'Raphaelitism (Ruskin), **V:** 184

Prerogative of Parliaments, The (Ralegh), **I:** 157–158

"Presage of the Ruin of the Turkish Empire, A" (Waller), **II:** 233

Presbyterians' Plea of Merit, The (Swift), **III:** 36

Prescott, William H., **VI:** 394

"Presence, The" (Thomas), **Supp. XII:** 288–289

Presence of Spain, The (Morris), see *Spain*

"Present" (Cope), **VIII:** 80–81

Present and the Past, The (Compton'Burnett), **VII:** 61, 62

"Present and the Past: Eliot's Demonstration, The" (Leavis), **VII:** 237

"Present Estate of Pompeii" (Lowry), **Supp. III:** 281–282

"Present King of France Is Bald, The" (Hart), **Supp. XI:** 130

Present Laughter (Coward), **Supp. II:** 153–154, 156

Present Position of History, The (Trevelyan), **VI:** 383

Present State of All Nations, The (Smollet), **III:** 158

Present State of the Parties in Great Britain, The (Defoe), **III:** 13

Present State of Wit, The (Gay), **III:** 44, 67

"Present Time, The" (Carlyle), **IV:** 247–248

Present Times (Storey), **Supp. I:** 408, 419–420

"Preserve and Renovate" (Dunn), **Supp. X:** 80

"Preserved" (Ewart), **Supp. VII:** 44

President's Child, The (Weldon), **Supp. IV:** 530–531

Press Cuttings: A Topical Sketch (Shaw), **VI:** 115, 117, 118–119, 129

Press, John, **VI:** xvi, xxxiv; **VII:** xxii, xxxviii

"Presser, The" (Coppard), **VIII:** 86, 96–97

Preston, Thomas, **I:** 122, 213

Pretty Lady, The (Bennett), **VI:** 250, 251, 259

"Pretty Maids All in a Row" (Cameron), **Supp. IX:** 19

Previous Convictions (Connolly), **Supp. III:** 110

Prévost, Antoine, **III:** 333

Price, Alan, **VI:** 314

Price, Cecil, **III:** 258n, 261, 264, 268, 271

Price, Cormell, **VI:** 166, 167

Price, Richard, **IV:** 126

"Price, The" (Stevenson), **Supp. VI:** 260

Price of Everything, The (Motion), **Supp. VII:** 253, 254, 260–262

Price of Salt, The (Highsmith), **Supp. V:** 167, 169–170

"Price of Sixpense, The" (Nicholson), **Supp. VI:** 219

Price of Stone, The (Murphy), **Supp. V:** 313, 315, 316, 326–329

"Price of Stone, The" (Murphy), **Supp. V:** 327

"Price of Things, The" (Ewart), **Supp. VII:** 42

Pride and Prejudice (Austen), **III:** 91, 336; **IV:** xvii, 103–104, 108–120, 122; **Supp. IV:** 235, 521; **Retro. Supp. II:** 7–9

Pride and Prejudice (television adaptation, Weldon), **Supp. IV:** 521

"Pride of the Village" (Blunden), **Supp. XI:** 44

Pride's Cure (Lamb), *see* John Woodvie

Priest to the Temple, A; or, The Country Parson His Character etc. (Herbert), **II:** 120, 141; **Retro. Supp. II:** 176

Priestley, J. B., **IV:** 160, 170; **V:** xxvi, 96; **VII:** xii, xviii, 60, **209–231**

Priestley, Joseph, **III:** 290

"Prima Belladonna" (Ballard), **Supp. V:** 21

"Prime Minister" (Churchill), **VI:** 349

Prime Minister, The (Trollope), **V:** xxiv, 96, 97, 98–99, 101, 102

Prime of Miss Jean Brodie, The (Spark), **Supp. I:** 200, 201, 204–206

Primer, The; or, Office of the B. Virgin Mary (Dryden), **II:** 304

Prince, F. T., **VII:** xxii 422, 427

Prince Caspian (Lewis), **Supp. III:** 248, 260

Prince Hohenstiel'Schwangau, Saviour of Society (Browning), **IV:** 358, 369, 374

Prince of Dreamers, A (Steel), **Supp. XII:** 275

Prince Otto (Stevenson), **V:** 386, 395

Prince Prolétaire (Swinburne), **V:** 333

"Prince Roman" (Conrad), **VI:** 148

"Prince's Progress, The" (Rossetti), **V:** 250, 258, 259

Prince's Progress and Other Poems, The (Rossetti), **V:** 250, 260

Princess, The (Tennyson), **IV:** xx, 323, 325, 328, 333–334, 336, 338

Princess Casamassima, The (James), **VI:** 27, 39, **41–43,** 67

Princess Cinderella and Her Wicked Sisters (Tennant), **Supp. IX:** 239

"Princess of Kingdom Gone, The" (Coppard), **VIII:** 92

Princess Zoubaroff, The (Firbank), **Supp. II:** 202, 204, 205, **215–216**

Principia Ethica (Moore), **Supp. III:** 49

Principles and Persuasions (West), **VI:** 241

Principles of Literary Criticism (Richards), **Supp. II:** 405, **411–417**

Pringle, David, **Supp. V:** 32

Prior, Matthew, **II:** 265

Prioress's Prologue, The (Chaucer), **I:** 37

Prioress's Tale, The (Chaucer), **I:** 22, 34

"Prison" (Murphy), **Supp. V:** 329

Prison Cell and Barrel Mystery, The (Reading), **VIII:** 263

"Prisoner, The" (Brontë), **V:** 142, 143, 254

"Prisoner, The" (Browning), **IV:** 313–314

Prisoner of Chillon, The (Byron), **IV:** 180, 192

Prisoner of Grace (Cary), **VII:** 186, 194–195

Prisoners (Stevenson), **Supp. VI:** 265

Prisoners of Mainz, The (Waugh), **Supp. VI:** 269

"Prisoner's Progress" (MacNeice), **VII:** 406

Prisons We Choose to Live Inside (Lessing), **Supp. I:** 239, 254–255

Pritchett, V. S., **IV:** 120, 298, 306; **Supp. III:** 99, 102, 211, **311–331**

(Pushkin), **III:**

t), **Supp. IX:**

-skin), **V:** 174,

rd), **Supp. III:**

ggard), **Supp.**

y), **Supp. II:**

The (Coward),

V: 333

: 31

Brooke' Rose),

urne), **V:** 312,

winburnc), **V:**

g), **Supp. X:**

ar), **V:** 87

iii, 192, 193,

: 107

IV: xviii, 37,

VI: 249

II: 380–381;

p. XII: 290,

314

V: 203

ngley), **VIII:**

The" (Reid),

4 (Bennett),

n), **Supp. X:**

Content, A"

-97–298

rger), **Supp.**

ewis), **Supp.**

owell), **VII:**

Seventh' Day
3

aves), **VII:**

V: 160

Retro. Supp.

e), **Supp. I:**
-69; **Retro.**

pp. VI:** 17,

nter), **Supp.**

Supp. VII:

Supp. VII:**

Profitable Meditations . . . (Bunyan), **II:** 253

"Programme Note" (Fuller), **Supp. VII:** 80

Progress and Poverty (George), **VI:** viii

Progress of Julius, The (du Maurier), **Supp. III:** 139, 140, 144

"Progress of Poesy" (Gray), **II:** 200; **III:** 140

"Progress of Poesy, The" (Arnold), **V:** 209

"Progress of the Soul, The" (Donne), **II:** 209

Progymnasmata (More), **Supp. VII:** 236

"Project for a New Novel" (Ballard), **Supp. V:** 21

Project for the Advancement of Religion . . . , A (Swift), **III:** 26, 35, 46

"Proletariat and Poetry, The" (Day Lewis), **Supp. III:** 120

Prolific and the Devourer, The (Auden), **Retro. Supp. I:** 10

Prologue (Henryson), **Supp. VII:** 136

"Prologue to an Autobiography" (Naipaul), **Supp. I:** 385

Prometheus Bound (Aeschylus), **IV:** 199

Prometheus Bound, Translated from the Greek of Aeschylus (Browning), **IV:** 310, 321

Prometheus on His Crag (Hughes), **Supp. I:** 354–355, 363

Prometheus the Firegiver (Bridges), **VI:** 83

Prometheus Unbound (Shelley), **III:** 331; **IV:** xviii, 176, 179, 196, 198, **199–201**, 202, 207, 208; **VI:** 449–450; **Supp. III:** 370; **Retro. Supp. I:** 250, 251–253

"Promise, The" (James), **VI:** 49

Promise and Fulfillment (Koestler), **Supp. I:** 33

Promise of Love (Renault), see *Purposes of Love*

Promos and Cassandra (Whetstone), **I:** 313

Promus of Formularies and Elegancies, A (Bacon), **I:** 264, 271

"Propagation of Knowledge" (Kipling), **VI:** 200

Proper Marriage, A (Lessing), **Supp. I:** 238, 244

Proper Studies (Huxley), **VII:** 198, 201

Properties of Things, On the (tr. Trevisa), see *De Proprietatibus Rerum*

"Property of Colette Nervi, The" (Trevor), **Supp. IV:** 500

Prophecy (Seltzer), **III:** 345

Prophecy of Dante, The (Byron), **IV:** 193

Prophesy to the Wind (Nicholson), **Supp. VI: 221–222**

Prophetess, The (Fletcher and Massinger), **II:** 55, 66

"Prophets, The" (Auden), **Retro. Supp. I:** 9

"Prophet's Hair, The" (Rushdie), **Supp. IV:** 438

Proposal for Correcting . . . the English Tongue, A (Swift), **III:** 29, 35

Proposal for Giving Badges to the Beggars . . . of Dublin, A (Swift), **III:** 36

Proposal for Making an Effectual Provision for the Poor, A (Fielding), **III:** 105; **Retro. Supp. I:** 81

Proposal for Putting Reform to the Vote, A (Shelley), **IV:** 208

Proposals for an Association of . . . Philanthropists . . . (Shelley), **IV:** 208

Proposals for Publishing Monthly . . . (Smollett), **III:** 148

Proposals for the Universal Use of Irish Manufacture . . . (Swift), **III:** 27–28, 35

Propositions for the Advancement of Experimental Philosophy, A (Cowley), **II:** 196, 202

Prose of John Clare, The (Clare), **Supp. XI:** 53, 58

Prose Works, The (Swift), **III:** 15n 35

Proserpine, The (Rossetti), **V:** 295

Prosody of A Paradise Lost" and A Samson Agonistes," The (Bridges), **VI:** 83

Prospero's Cell (Durrell), **Supp. I:** 96, 100, 110–111

Protestant Monastery, The; or, A Complaint against the Brutality of the Present Age (Defoe), **III:** 14

"Proteus; or, Matter" (Bacon), **I:** 267

Prothalamion (Spenser), **I:** 124, 131

"Proud word you never spoke, but you will speak" (Landor), **IV:** 99

Proust, Marcel, **V:** xxiv, 45, 174, 183; **Supp. I:** 44–45; **Supp. IV:** 126, 136, 139

Proust Screenplay, The (Pinter), **Supp. I:** 378

Provence (Ford), **VI:** 324

"Proverbs of Hell" (Blake), **III:** 298; **Retro. Supp. I:** 38

Providence (Brookner), **Supp. IV:** 124–125, 131

"Providence" (Herbert), **Retro. Supp. II:** 177

"Providence and the Guitar" (Stevenson), **V:** 395

Provincial Pleasures (Nicholson), **Supp. VI:** 223

Provok'd Husband, The (Cibber), **II:** 326, 337

Provok'd Wife, The (Vanbrugh), **II:** 325, **329–332,** 334, 336, 360

Provost, The (Galt), **IV:** 35

Prussian Officer, The, and Other Stories (Lawrence), **VII:** 114

Pryce' Jones, Alan, **VII:** 70

Prynne, William, **II:** 339; **Supp. III:** 23

"Psalm of Montreal, A" (Butler), **Supp. II:** 105

"Psalms of Assize" (Hill), **Supp. V:** 193

Pseudodoxia Epidemica (Browne), **II:** 149–150, 151, 155, 156, 345n

Pseudo–Martyr (Donne), **I:** 352–353, 362; **Retro. Supp. II:** 97

Psmith Journalist (Wodehouse), **Supp. III:** 450

Psyche's Task (Frazer), **Supp. III:** 185

Psycho (film), **III:** 342–343

Psycho Apocalypté, a Lyrical Drama (Browning and Horne), **IV:** 321

Psychoanalysis and the Unconscious (Lawrence), **VII:** 122; **Retro. Supp. II:** 234

"Psychology of Advertising, The" (Sayers), **Supp. III:** 345

Psychology of the Unconscious (Jung), **Supp. IV:** 3

"Psychopolis" (McEwan), **Supp. IV:** 395–396

Puberty Tree, The (Thomas), **Supp. IV:** 490

"Puberty Tree, The" (Thomas), **Supp. IV:** 492–493

Public Address (Blake), **III:** 305

Public Burning, The (Coover), **Supp. IV:** 116

Public Eye, The (Shaffer), **Supp. I:** 317, 318–319, 327

"Public–House Confidence" (Cameron), **Supp. IX:** 22–23

Public Image, The (Spark), **Supp. I:** 200, 208–209, 218n

Public Ledger (periodical), **III:** 179, 188

Public School Life: Boys, Parents, Masters (Waugh), **Supp. VI:** 267, 270

Public School Verse (Cameron), **Supp. IX:** 17

"Public Son of a Public Man, The" (Spender), **Supp. II:** 483

Publick Employment and an Active Life Prefer'd to Solitude (Evelyn), **II:** 287

Publick Spirit of the Whigs, The (Swift), **III:** 35

"Puck and Saturn" (Wallace–Crabbe), **VIII:** 323

"Puck Is Not Sure About Apollo" (Wallace–Crabbe), **VIII:** 321

Puck of Pook's Hill (Kipling), **VI:** viii, 169, 204

Puffball (Weldon), **Supp. IV:** 531, 533–534

Pulci, Luigi, **IV:** 182, 188

Pumpkin Eater, The (Pinter), **Supp. I:** 374

Punch (periodical), **IV:** 263; **V:** xx, 19, 23, 24–25; **VI:** 367, 368; **Supp. II:** 47, 49

Punch's Prize Novelists (Thackeray), **V:** 22, 38

"Punishment Enough" (Cameron), **Supp. IX:** 29

"Pupil, The" (James), **VI:** 49, 69

Purcell, Henry, **Retro. Supp. II:** 196

Purcell Commemoration Ode (Bridges), **VI:** 81

Purchas's Pilgrimage, **IV:** 46

Pure Poetry. An Anthology (Moore), **VI:** 99

Purgatorio (Dante), **Supp. IV:** 439

Purgatorio (Heaney), **Retro. Supp. I:** 124

Purgatorio II (Eliot), **VII:** 151

Purgatory (Yeats), **VI:** 219

Puritan, The (anonymous), **I:** 194; **II:** 21

Puritain and the Papist, The (Cowley), **II:** 202

Purity of Diction in English Verse (Davie), **Supp. VI:** 107, **114**

"Purl and Plain" (Coppard), **VIII:** 96

"Purple" (Owen), **VI:** 449

Purple Dust (O'Casey), **VII:** 7, 8

"Purple Jar, The" (Edgeworth), **Supp. III:** 153

Purple Plain, The (Ambler), **Supp. IV:** 3

Purposes of Love (Renault), **Supp. IX:** 172–173

Pursuit of Love, The (Mitford), **Supp. X:** 151–152, 156, 158–161, 163

Pushkin, Aleksander, **III:** 339, 345; **Supp. IV:** 484, 495

Put Out More Flags (Waugh), **VII:** 290, 297–298, 300, 313

Puttenham, George, **I:** 94, 114, 119, 146, 214

Puzzleheaded Girl, The (Stead), **Supp. IV:** 476

"Puzzling Nature of Blue, The" (Carey), **Supp. XII:** 55

"Pygmalion" (Beddoes), **Supp. XI:** 28–29

"Pygmalion" (Gower), **I:** 53–54

Pygmalion (Shaw), **VI:** xv, 108, 115, 116–117, 120; **Retro. Supp. II:** 322

"Pylons, The" (Spender), **Supp. II:** 48

Pym, Barbara, **Supp. II: 363–384**

Pynchon, Thomas, **Supp. IV:** 116, 163

Pynson, Richard, **I:** 99

Pyramid, The (Golding), **Supp. I:** 81–82; **Retro. Supp. I:** 100–101

"Pyramis or The House of Ascent" (Hope), **Supp. VII:** 154

"Pyramus and Thisbe" (Gower), **I:** 53–54, 55

"Qua cursum ventus" (Clough), **V:** 160

Quadrille (Coward), **Supp. II:** 155

"Quaint Mazes" (Hill), **Supp. V:** 191

"Quality of Sprawl, The" (Murray), **Supp. VII:** 278–279

Quality Street (Barrie), **Supp. III:** 6, 8

"Quantity Theory of Insanity, The" (Self), **Supp. V:** 402

Quantity Theory of Insanity, The: Together with Five Supporting Propositions (Self), **Supp. V:** 395, 400–402

Quare Fellow, The (Behan), **Supp. II:** 65, **68–70,** 73

Quaritch, Bernard, **IV:** 343, 346, 348, 349

Quarles, Francis, **II:** 139, 246

"Quarrel, The" (Cornford), **VIII:** 113

Quarterly Review (periodical), **IV:** xvi, 60–61, 69, 133, 204–205, 269–270; **V:** 140

Quartermaine, Peter, **Supp. IV:** 348

Quartet (Rhys), **Supp. II:** 388, **390–392,** 403

Quartet in Autumn (Pym), **Supp. II: 380–382**

Queen, The; or, The Excellency of Her Sex (Ford), **II:** 88, 89, 91, 96, 100

"Queen Annelida and False Arcite" (Browning), **IV:** 321

Queen Is Crowned, A (Fry), **Supp. III:** 195

Queen Mab (Shelley), **IV:** xvii, 197, 201, 207, 208; **Retro. Supp. I:** 245–246

Queen Mary (Tennyson), **IV:** 328, 338

Queen of Corinth, The (Field, Fletcher, Massinger), **II:** 66

Queen of Hearts, The (Collins), **Supp. VI:** 95

"Queen of Spades, The" 339–340, 345

Queen of Stones (Tenna 231, 233–235

Queen of the Air, The (F 180, 181, 184

Queen of the Dawn (Hagg 222

Queen Sheba's Ring (H **III:** 214

Queen Victoria (Strach **512–514**

Queen Was in the Parlor, **Supp. II:** 141, 146

Queen Yseult (Swinburne

Queenhoo'Hall (Strutt),

"Queenie Fat and Thin" **Supp. IV:** 103

Queen'Mother, The (Swin 313, 314, 330, 331, 33

Queen's Tragedy, The (S 333

Queen's Wake, The (Ho 106–107, 110

Queery Leary Nonsense (L

Quennell, Peter, **V:** xii, x 194; **VI:** 237; **Supp. II**

Quentin Durward (Scott), 39

"Quest, The" (Saki), **Supp**

Quest sonnets (Auden), **Retro. Supp. I:** 2, 10

"Question" (Thomas), **Su** 291

"Question, A" (Synge), **VI**

"Question, The" (Shelley),

"Question for Walter, A" (L 163–164

"Question in the Cobweb, **Supp. VII:** 326

Question of Attribution, **VIII:** 30, 31

Question of Blood, A (Rank 245, 257

"Question of Form and (Stallworthy), **Supp. X:**

"Question of Place, A" (B **IV:** 92

Question of Proof, A (Day **III:** 117, 131

Question of Upbringing, A 343, 347, 350, 351

Questions about the . . . *Sabbath* (Bunyan), **II:** 2

"Questions in a Wood" (C 268

"Qui laborat orat" (Clough)

"Quidditie, The" (Herbert), **II:** 179

Quiet American, The (Gree 7, 13, 14; **Supp. IV:** **Supp. II:** 160–161

Quiet Life, A (Bainbridge), ! 21–22, 26–27

Quiet Memorandum, The (F **I:** 374

"Quiet Neighbours" (Warner 371

Quiet Wedding (Rattigan), 311

"Quiet Woman, The" (Coppard), **VIII:** 93

"Quiet Woman of Chancery Lane, The" (Redgrove), **Supp. VI:** 235, 237

Quigley, Austin E., **Retro. Supp. I:** 227

Quiller'Couch, Sir Arthur, **II:** 121, 191; **V:** 384

Quillinan, Edward, **IV:** 143*n*

Quinlan, M. J., **III:** 220

Quinn Manuscript, **VII:** 148

Quintessence of Ibsenism, The (Shaw), **VI:** 104, 106, 129

"Quintets for Robert Morley" (Murray), **Supp. VII:** 278, 283

Quinx (Durrell), **Supp. I:** 119, 120

"Quip, The" (Herbert), **II:** 126

"Quis Optimus Reipvb. Status (What Is The Best Form of the Commonwealth?)" (More), **Supp. VII:** 238

"Quite Early One Morning" (Thomas), **Supp. I:** 183

"Quitting Bulleen" (Wallace–Crabbe), **VIII:** 316

Quoof (Muldoon), **Supp. IV:** 418–421, 422, 423, 425

"R. I. P." (Gissing), **V:** 43

"R. I. P." (Thomas), **Supp. XII:** 285

R.L.S. and His Sine Qua Non (Boodle), **V:** 391, 393, 397

R. S. Thomas: Selected Prose (Thomas), **Supp. XII:** 279, 282

Raban, Jonathan, **Supp. XI: 227–241**

"Rabbit Catcher, The" (Hughes), **Retro. Supp. II:** 217–218

Rabelais, François, **III:** 24; **Supp. IV:** 464

Rachel Papers, The (Amis), **Supp. IV:** 26, 27, 28–29, 30

Rachel Ray (Trollope), **V:** 101

Racine, Jean Baptiste, **II:** 98; **V:** 22

Racing Demon (Hare), **Supp. IV:** 282, 294–296, 298

Radcliffe (Storey), **Supp. I:** 408, 410, 414, 415–416, 418–419

Radcliffe, Ann, **III:** 327, 331–332, 333, 335–338, 345; **IV:** xvi, 30, 35, 36, 111, 173, 218; **Supp. III:** 384

Radcliffe Hall: A Case of Obscenity? (Brittain), **Supp. X:** 47

Radiant Way, The (Drabble), **Supp. IV:** 231, 234, 247–249, 250

Radical Imagination, The (Harris), **Supp. V:** 140, 145

Rafferty, Terrence, **Supp. IV:** 357, 360

Raffety, F. W., **III:** 199*n*

Raft of the Medusa, The (Géricault), **Supp. IV:** 71–72

"Rage for Order" (Mahon), **Supp. VI:** 170

Rage of the Vulture, The (Unsworth), **Supp. VII:** 356, 357, 359–360

Raiders' Dawn (Lewis), **VII:** 445, 448

"Railway Library, The" (Crawford), **Supp. XI:** 71

Railway Man and His Children, The (Oliphant), **Supp. X:** 219

Rain (Maugham), **VI:** 369

"Rain" (Thomas), **VI:** 424; **Supp. III:** 400, 401

Rain and the Glass: New and Selected Poems, The (Nye), **Supp. X:** 199

"Rain Charm for the Duchy" (Hughes), **Supp. I:** 365; **Retro. Supp. II:** 214

"Rain Horse, The" (Hughes), **Supp. I:** 348

"Rain in Spain, The" (Reid), **Supp. VII:** 328

"Rain in the Eaves, The" (Nye), **Supp. X:** 200

"Rain Stick, The" (Heaney), **Retro. Supp. I:** 132–133

Rain upon Godshill (Priestley), **VII:** 209, 210

"Rain Upon the Roof, The" (Nye), **Supp. X:** 202

Rainbow, The (Lawrence), **VI:** 232, 276, 283; **VII:** 88, 90, 93, **98–101**; **Retro. Supp. II:** 227–228

"Rainbow Sign, The" (Kureishi), **Supp. XI:** 159–161

Raine, Kathleen, **III:** 297, 308

"Rainy Night, A" (Lowry), **Supp. III:** 270

Raj Quartet (Scott), **Supp. I:** 259, 260, 261–262, **266–272**

"Rajah's Diamond, The" (Stevenson), **V:** 395

Rajan, B., **VI:** 219

Rake's Progress, The (Auden/Kallman), **Retro. Supp. I:** 10

Raknem, Ingwald, **VI:** 228

Ralegh, Sir Walter, **I: 145–159**, 277, 278, 291; **II:** 138; **III:** 120, 122, 245; **VI:** 76, 157; **Retro. Supp. I:** 203–204

Raleigh, Sir Walter, *see* Ralegh, Sir Walter

Ralph the Heir (Trollope), **V:** 100, 102

"Ram, The" (Armitage), **VIII:** 12

Rambler (Newman), **Supp. VII:** 299

Rambler (periodical), **II:** 142; **III:** 94, 110–111, 112, 119, 121; **Retro. Supp. I:** 137, 140–141, 149

Rambles Among the Oases of Tunisia (Douglas), **VI:** 305

Ramillies and the Union with Scotland (Trevelyan), **VI:** 392–393

Ramsay, Allan, **III:** 312, 313; **IV:** 28

Ramsay, Andrew, **III:** 99, 100

Randall, H. S., **IV:** 275

Randolph, Thomas, **II:** 222, 237, 238

Rank and Riches (Collins), **Supp. VI:** 93

Ranke, Leopold von, **IV:** 288

Rankin, Ian, **Supp. X:** 243–260

Rao, Raja, **Supp. IV:** 440; **Supp. V:** 56

Rape of Lucrece, The (Shakespeare), **I:** 306–307, 325; **II:** 3

Rape of the Lock, The (Pope), **III:** 70–71, 75, 77; **Retro. Supp. I:** 231, 233

"Rape of the Sherlock, The" (Milne), **Supp. V:** 297

Rape upon Rape (Fielding), **III:** 105

"Rapparees" (Murphy), **Supp. V:** 323

"Raptor" (Thomas), **Supp. XII:** 291–292

"Rapture, A" (Carew), **II:** 223

"Rapture, The" (Traherne), **Supp. XI:** 266

"Rapunzel Revisited" (Maitland), **Supp. XI:** 170

Rash Act, The (Ford), **VI:** 319, 331

Rash Resolve, The; or, The Untimely Discovery (Haywood), **Supp. XII:** 140

"Raspberry Jam" (Wilson), **Supp. I:** 154, 157

"Raspberrying" (Reading), **VIII:** 263

Rat Trap, The (Coward), **Supp. II:** 146

"Ratatouille" (Dunn), **Supp. X:** 74

"Ratcatcher, The" (Dahl), **Supp. IV:** 214

Ratchford, Fannie, **V:** 133, 151, 152

"Rats, The" (Sillitoe), **Supp. V:** 424

Rats and Other Poems, The (Sillitoe), **Supp. V:** 409, 424

Rattigan, Terence, **Supp. VII: 307–322**

Raven, The (Poe), **V:** xx, 409

"Ravenna" (Wilde), **V:** 401, 409

"Ravenswing, The" (Thackeray), **V:** 23, 35, 36

Raw Material (Sillitoe), **Supp. V:** 411, 414–415, 422, 423

Raw Spirit: In Search of the Perfect Dram (Banks), **Supp. XI:** 1, 13, 14

"Rawdon's Roof" (Lawrence), **VII:** 91

Rawley, William, **I:** 257

Ray, G. N., **V:** 37, 39

Ray, Satyajit, **Supp. IV:** 434, 450

Raymond Asquith: Life and Letters (Jolliffe), **VI:** 428

Raysor, T. M., **IV:** 46, 51, 52, 56, 57

Razor's Edge, The (Maugham), **VI:** 374, 377–378

Read, Herbert, **III:** 134; **VI:** 416, 436–437; **VII:** 437

Reade, Winwood, **Supp. IV:** 2

Reader (periodical), **III:** 50, 53

Reader's Guide to G. M. Hopkins, A (MacKenzie), **V:** 374, 382

Reader's Guide to Joseph Conrad, A (Karl), **VI:** 135

Readie & Easie Way to Establish a Free Commonwealth . . . (Milton), **II:** 176; **Retro. Supp. II:** 271

Reading, Peter, **VIII: 261–275**

"Reading, A" (Cope), **VIII:** 81–82

"Reading and Writhing in a Double Bind" (Lodge), **Supp. IV:** 385

"Reading Berryman's Dream Songs at the Writer's Retreat" (Cope), **VIII:** 79

"Reading Lesson, The" (Murphy), **Supp. V:** 316, 325

Reading of Earth, A (Meredith), **V:** 221, 234

Reading of George Herbert, A (Tuve), **II:** 124, 130; **Retro. Supp. II:** 174

Reading of Life, A, and Other Poems (Meredith), **V:** 234

"Reading Robert Southey to My Daughter" (Nye), **Supp. X:** 201

"Reading Scheme" (Cope), **VIII:** 71

"Reading the Banns" (Armitage), **VIII:** 8

"Reading the Elephant" (Motion), **Supp. VII:** 260, 263

Reading Turgenev (Trevor), **Supp. IV:** 516

Readings in Crabbe's ATales of the Hall" (Fitzgerald), **IV:** 349, 353

Reagan, Ronald, **Supp. IV:** 485

"Real and Made–Up People" (Amis), **Supp. II:** 10

"Real Estate" (Wallace–Crabbe), **VIII:** 318

Real Inspector Hound, The (Stoppard), **Supp. I:** 443–444; **Retro. Supp. II:** 345–346

Real Robert Louis Stevenson, The, and Other Critical Essays (Thompson), **V:** 450, 451

"Real Thing, The" (James), **VI:** 48, 69

Real Thing, The (Stoppard), **Supp. I:** 451–452; **Retro. Supp. II:** 353–354

"Real World, The" (Hart), **Supp. XI:** 127

Realists, The (Snow), **VII:** 338–339

Realms of Gold, The (Drabble), **Supp. IV:** 230, 232, 243–245, 246, 248, 251

"Realpolitik" (Wilson), **Supp. I:** 154, 157

Reardon, Derek, **Supp. IV:** 445

"Rear–Guard, The" (Sassoon), **VI:** 431; **Supp. III:** 59

"Reason, The" (Thomas), **Supp. XII:** 290

Reason and Sensuality (Lydgate), **I:** 57, 64

Reason of Church Government Urg'd Against Prelaty, The (Milton), **II:** 162, 175; **Retro. Supp. II:** 269, 276

"Reason our Foe, let us destroy" (Wycherley), **II:** 321

Reason Why, The (Rendell), **Supp. IX:** 196

Reasonable Life, The: Being Hints for Men and Women (Bennett), *see Mental Efficiency*

Reasons Against the Succession of the House of Hanover (Defoe), **III:** 13

Rebecca (du Maurier), **Supp. III:** 134, 135, 137–138, 139, 141, 142, 143, 144, 145–146, 147

Rebecca and Rowena: A Romance upon Romance (Thackeray), **V:** 38

Rebel General, The (Wallace–Crabbe), **VIII:** 314, 318

"Rebel General, The" (Wallace–Crabbe), **VIII:** 315

Rebels, The (Ngũgĩ), **VIII:** 222

Rebus: The St. Leonard's Years (Rankin), **Supp. X:** 251, 253

"Recall" (Crawford), **Supp. XI:** 75

Recalled to Life (Hill, R.), **Supp. IX:** 120–121

"Recantation, A" (Kipling), **VI:** 192–193

"Receipt to Restore Stella's Youth . . . , A" (Swift), **III:** 32

"Recessional" (Kipling), **VI:** 203

Recklings (Hughes), **Supp. I:** 346, 348

"Reckoning of Meter", *See Háttatal*

"Recollection, A" (Cornford), **VIII:** 103, 112

"Recollections" (Pearsall Smith), **VI:** 76

Recollections of Christ's Hospital (Lamb), **IV:** 85

"Recollections of Journey from Essex" (Clare), **Supp. XI:** 62

"Recollections of Solitude" (Bridges), **VI:** 74

Recollections of the Lake Poets (De Quincey), **IV:** 146n, 155

"Reconcilement between Jacob Tonson and Mr. Congreve, The" (Rowe), **II:** 324

"Record, The" (Warner), **Supp. VII:** 371

"Record of Badalia Herodsfoot, The" (Kipling), **VI:** 167, 168

Record of Friendship, A (Swinburne), **V:** 333

Record of Friendship and Criticism, A (Smith), **V:** 391, 396, 398

Records of a Family of Engineers (Stevenson), **V:** 387, 396

Recoveries (Jennings), **Supp. V:** 211

"Recovery, The" (Vaughan), **II:** 185

Recruiting Officer, The (Farquhar), **II:** 353, 358–359, 360, 361, 362, 364

"Rector, The" (Oliphant), **Supp. X:** 214

Rector and the Doctor's Family, The (Oliphant), **Supp. X:** 214–215

Rectory Umbrella and Mischmasch, The (Carroll), **V:** 264, 273

"Recycling" (Dutton), **Supp. XII:** 89

"Red"(Hughes), **Retro. Supp. II:** 218

Red Badge of Courage, The (Crane), **Supp. IV:** 116

Red Christmas (Hill, R.), **Supp. IX:** 116–117

Red Cotton Night–Cap Country (Browning), **IV:** 358, 369, 371, 374

Red Days and White Nights (Koestler), **Supp. I:** 23

Red Dog (De Bernières), **Supp. XII:** 65, 69, 77

"Red Front" (Warner), **Supp. VII:** 372

Red Harvest (Hammett), **Supp. II:** 130

Red House Mystery, The (Milne), **Supp. V:** 310

Red Peppers (Coward), **Supp. II:** 153

"Red, Red Rose, A" (Burns), **III:** 321

Red Roses for Me (O'Casey), **VII:** 9

"Red Rubber Gloves" (Brooke–Rose)), **Supp. IV:** 104

"Redeeming the Time" (Hill), **Supp. V:** 186

"Redemption" (Herbert), **II:** 126–127

Redgauntlet (Scott), **IV:** xviii, 31, 35, 39

Redgrove, Peter, **Supp. VI: 225–238**

"Red–Headed League, The" (Doyle), **Supp. II:** 170

Redimiculum Matellarum [A Necklace of Chamberpots] (Bunting), **Supp. VII:** 4

"Redriff" (Jones), **Supp. VII:** 176

"Reed, A" (Browning), **IV:** 313

Reed Bed, The (Healy), **Supp. IX:** 96, 106, 107

Reed, Henry, **VII:** 422–423, 449

Reed, J. W., **III:** 249

Reef (Gunesekera), **Supp. X:** 85–100

Rees–Mogg, W., **II:** 288

Reeve, C., **III:** 345

Reeve, Clara, **III:** 80

Reeve's Tale, The (Chaucer), **I:** 37, 41

"Reflection from Anita Loos" (Empson), **Supp. II:** 183–184

Reflections (Greene), **Retro. Supp. II:** 166–167

"Reflections" (Thomas), **Supp. XII:** 291

"Reflections of a Kept Ape" (McEwan), **Supp. IV:** 394

"Reflections on a Peninsula" (Koestler), **Supp. I:** 34

Reflections on Hanging (Koestler), **Supp. I:** 36

"Reflections on Leaving a Place of Retirement" (Coleridge), **IV:** 44

"Reflections on the Death of a Porcupine" (Lawrence), **VII:** 103–104, 110, 119

Reflections on the French Revolution (Burke), **III:** 195, 197, 201–205; **IV:** xv, 127; **Supp. III:** 371, 467, 468, 470

Reflections on the Late Alarming Bankruptcies in Scotland (Boswell), **III:** 248

Reflections on the Psalms (Lewis), **Supp. III:** 249, 264

Reflections on Violence (Hulme), **Supp. VI:** 145

Reflections upon Ancient and Modern Learning (Wotton), **III:** 23

Reflections upon the Late Great Revolution (Defoe), **Retro. Supp. I:** 64

Reflector (periodical), **IV:** 80

Reformation of Manners (Defoe), **III:** 12

"Refusal to mourn, A" (Thomas), **Supp. I:** 178

Refutation of Deism, in a Dialogue, A (Shelley), **IV:** 208

"Refutation of Philosophies" (Bacon), **I:** 263

"Regency Houses" (Day Lewis), **Supp. III:** 127–128

Regeneration (Barker), **Supp. IV:** 45, 46, 57–59

Regeneration (Haggard), **Supp. III:** 214

"Regeneration" (Vaughan), **II:** 185, 187

Regent, The (Bennett), **VI:** 259, 267

Regicide, The (Smollett), **III:** 158

"Regina Cara" (Bridges), **VI:** 81

Reginald (Saki), **Supp. VI:** 240–242

"Reginald at the Theatre" (Saki), **Supp. VI:** 241–242

Reginald in Russia and Other Sketches (Saki), **Supp. VI:** 243–246

"Reginald on the Academy" (Saki), **Supp. VI:** 240

"Reginald's Choir Treat" (Saki), **Supp. VI:** 241, 249

Region of the Summer Stars, The (Williams, C. W. S.), **Supp. IX:** 283

"Regret" (Swinburne), **V:** 332

Rehabilitations (Lewis), **Supp. III:** 249

Rehearsal, The (Buckingham), **II:** 206, 294

Rehearsal Transpros'd, The (Marvell), **II:** 205, 206–207, 209, 218, 219; **Retro. Supp. II:** 257–258, 264–266

Reid, Alastair, **Supp. VII: 323–337**

Reid, J. C., **IV:** 254, 267

Reign of Sparrows, The (Fuller), **Supp. VII:** 79

"Reiterative" (Reading), **VIII:** 274

Rejected Address (Smith), **IV:** 253

"Relapse, The" (Vaughan), **II:** 187

Relapse, The; or, Virtue in Danger (Vanbrugh), **II:** 324, 326–329, 332, 334, 335, 336; **III:** 253, 261

Relation Between Michael Angelo and Tintoret, The (Ruskin), **V:** 184

Relationship of the Imprisonment of Mr. John Bunyan, A (Bunyan), **II:** 253

Relative Values (Coward), **Supp. II:** 155

Relatively Speaking (Ayckbourn), **Supp. V:** 2, 4, 13

"Relativity" (Empson), **Supp. II:** 182

"Release from Fever" (Cameron), **Supp. IX:** 23

Religio Laici; or, A Layman's Faith (Dryden), **I:** 176, 189; **II:** 291, 299, 304

Religio Medici (Browne), **II:** 146–148, 150, 152, 156, 185; **III:** 40; **VII:** 29

"Religion" (Vaughan), **II:** 189

Religious Courtship: . . . Historical Discourses on . . . Marrying . . . (Defoe), **III:** 13

"Religious Musings" (Coleridge), **IV:** 43; **Retro. Supp. II:** 52

Reliques of Ancient English Poetry (Percy), **III:** 336; **IV:** 28–29

Reliquiae Wottonianae, **II:** 142

"Remain, ah not in youth alone" (Landor), **IV:** 99

Remains (Newman), **Supp. VII:** 295

Remains of Elmet (Hughes), **Supp. I:** 342; **Retro. Supp. II:** 210–211

Remains of Sir Fulke Grevill, Lord Brooke, The: Being Poems of Monarchy and Religion (Greville), **Supp. XI:** 108

Remains of Sir Walter Ralegh, The, **I:** 146, 157

Remains of the Day, The (Ishiguro), **Supp. IV:** 301–302, 304, 305, 306, 307, 311–314

Remake (Brooke–Rose)), **Supp. IV:** 98, 99, 102

"Remarkable Rocket, The" (Wilde), **Retro. Supp. II:** 365

Remarks on Certain Passages of the 39 Articles (Newman), **Supp. VII:** 295–296

Remarks Upon a Late Disingenuous Discourse (Marvell), **II:** 219; **Retro. Supp. II:** 266

"Rembrandt's Late Self–Portraits" (Jennings), **Supp. V:** 211

Remede de Fortune (Machaut), **Retro. Supp. II:** 37

"Remember" (Rossetti), **VII:** 64

Remember Me (Weldon), **Supp. IV:** 535–536

"Remember Me When I Am Gone Away" (Rossetti), **V:** 249

"Remember Young Cecil" (Kelman), **Supp. V:** 245

Remembering Babylon (Malouf), **Supp. XII:** 218, 227–229

"Remembering Carrigskeewaun" (Longley), **VIII:** 174

"Remembering Lunch" (Dunn), **Supp. X:** 74

"Remembering Old Wars" (Kinsella), **Supp. V:** 263

Remembering Sion (Ryan), **VII:** 2

"Remembering the 90s" (Mahon), **Supp. VI:** 177

"Remembering the Thirties" (Davie), **Supp. VI:** 106

"Remembrances" (Clare), **Supp. XI:** 52

Remembrances of Words and Matter Against Richard Cholmeley, **I:** 277

Reminiscences (Carlyle), **IV:** 70n, 239, 240, 245, 250

"Reminiscences of Charlotte Brontë" (Nussey), **V:** 108, 109, 152

Reminiscences of the Impressionistic Painters (Moore), **VI:** 99

Remorse (Coleridge), **IV:** 56

Remorse: A Study in Saffron (Wilde), **V:** 419

"Removal from Terry Street, A" (Dunn), **Supp. X** 69–70

Renaissance: Studies in Art and Poetry, The (Pater), *see Studies in the History of the Renaissance*

Renan, Joseph Ernest, **II:** 244

Renault, Mary, **Supp. IX: 171–188**

Rendell, Ruth, **Supp. IX: 189–206**

Renegade Poet, And Other Essays, A (Thompson), **V:** 451

Renegado, The (Massinger), **Supp. XI:** 182, 184, 193

"Renounce thy God" (Dunbar), **VIII:** 122

"Repeated Rediscovery of America, The" (Wallace–Crabbe), **VIII:** 319

"Repentance" (Herbert), **II:** 128

Repentance of Robert Greene, The (Greene), **VIII:** 132, 134

"Rephan" (Browning), **IV:** 365

Replication (Skelton), **I:** 93

Reply to the Essay on Population, by the Rev. T. R. Malthus, A (Hazlitt), **IV:** 127, 139

"Report from Below, A" (Hood), **IV:** 258

"Report on a Threatened City" (Lessing), **Supp. I:** 250n

"Report on an Unidentified Space Station" (Ballard), **Supp. V:** 33

"Report on Experience" (Blunden), **VI:** 428; **Supp. XI:** 39

Report on the Salvation Army Colonies (Haggard), **Supp. III:** 214

"Report to the Trustees of the Bellahouston Travelling Scholarship, A" (Gray, A.), **Supp. IX:** 79–80, 82, 90

"Reported Missing" (Scannell), **VII:** 424

Reports on Elementary Schools, 1852–1882 (Arnold), **V:** 216

Reprinted Pieces (Dickens), **V:** 72

Reprisal, The (Smollett), **III:** 149, 158

Reproof: A Satire (Smollett), **III:** 158

"Requiem" (Maitland), **Supp. XI:** 175

"Requiem" (Stevenson), **V:** 383; **Retro. Supp. I:** 268

"Requiem" (tr. Thomas), **Supp. IV:** 494–495

"Requiem for the Croppies" (Heaney), **Retro. Supp. I:** 127–128

"Requiescat" (Arnold), **V:** 211

"Requiescat" (Wilde), **V:** 400

Required Writing (Larkin), **Supp. I:** 286, 288

"Re–Reading Jane" (Stevenson), **Supp. VI:** 262

Rescue, The (Conrad), **VI:** 136, 147

Resentment (Waugh), **Supp. VI:** 270

"Reservoirs" (Thomas), **Supp. XII:** 279

Residues (Thomas), **Supp. XII:** 282

"Resignation" (Arnold), **V:** 210

"Resolution and Independence" (Wordsworth), **IV:** 19–20, 22; **V:** 352

"Resound my voice, ye woods that hear me plain" (Wyatt), **I:** 110

Responsibilities (Yeats), **VI:** 213; **Retro. Supp. I:** 330

"Responsibility" (MacCaig), **Supp. VI:** 189

Responsio ad Lutherum (More), **Supp. VII:** 242–243

Ressoning betuix Aige and Yowth, The (Henryson), **Supp. VII:** 146, 147

Ressoning betuix Deth and Man, The (Henryson), **Supp. VII:** 146, 147

Restoration (Bond), **Supp. I:** 423, 434, 435

Restoration of Arnold Middleton, The (Storey), **Supp. I:** 408, 411, 412–413, 414, 415, 417

"Resurrection, The" (Cowley), **II:** 200

Resurrection, The (Yeats), **VI:** xiv, 222

"Resurrection and Immortality" (Vaughan), **II:** 185, 186

Resurrection at Sorrow Hill (Harris), **Supp. V:** 144

Resurrection Men (Rankin), **Supp. X:** 245, 256–257

Resurrection of the Dead, The, . . . (Bunyan), **II:** 253

"Retaliation" (Goldsmith), **III:** 181, 185, 191

"Reticence of Lady Anne, The" (Saki), **Supp. VI:** 245

"Retired" (Thomas), **Supp. XII:** 291

"Retired Cat, The" (Cowper), **III:** 217

"Retirement" (Vaughan), **II:** 187, 188, 189

"Retreat, The" (King), **Supp. VI:** 153

"Retreate, The" (Vaughan), **II:** 186, 188–189

"Retrospect" (Brooke), **Supp. III:** 56

"Retrospect: From a Street in Chelsea" (Day Lewis), **Supp. III:** 121

"Retrospective Review" (Hood), **IV:** 255

"Return, The" (Conrad), **VI:** 148

"Return, The" (Muir), **Supp. VI:** 207

"Return, A" (Russell), **VIII:** 284

"Return, The" (Stallworthy), **Supp. X:** 298

Return from Parnassus, The, part 2, **II:** 27

"Return from the Freudian Islands, The" (Hope), **Supp. VII:** 155–156, 157

"Return from the Islands" (Redgrove), **Supp. VI:** 235

Return of Eva Peron, The (Naipaul), **Supp. I:** 396, 397, 398, 399

Return of the Druses, The (Browning), **IV:** 374

"Return of the Iron Man, The" (Hughes), **Supp. I:** 346

Return of the King, The (Tolkien), **Supp. II:** 519

Return of the Native, The (Hardy), **V:** xxiv, 279; **VI:** 1–2, 5, 6, 7, 8; **Retro. Supp. I:** 114

Return of the Soldier, The (West), **Supp. III:** 440, 441

Return of Ulysses, The (Bridges), **VI:** 83

Return to Abyssinia (White), **Supp. I:** 131

Return to My Native Land (tr. Berger), **Supp. IV:** 77

Return to Night (Renault), **Supp. IX:** 175

Return to Oasis (Durrell), **VII:** 425

"Return to the Council House" (Smith, I. C.), **Supp. IX:** 214

Return to Yesterday (Ford), **VI:** 149

Returning (O'Brien), **Supp. V:** 339

"Returning, We Hear the Larks" (Rosenberg), **VI:** 434–435

Revaluation (Leavis), **III:** 68; **VII:** 234, 236, 244–245

"Reveille" (Hughes), **Supp. I:** 350

Revelation of Love, A (Julian of Norwich), **Supp. XII:** 149, 150, 153–162, 163–165

Revelations of Divine Love (Julian of Norwich), **I:** 20–21; **Supp. XII:** 155

Revenge for Love, The (Lewis), **VII:** 72, 74, 81

Revenge Is Sweet: Two Short Stories (Hardy), **VI:** 20

Revenge of Bussy D'Ambois, The (Chapman), **I:** 251–252, 253; **II:** 37

Revenger's Tragedy, The, **II:** 1–2, 21, 29, **33–36,** 37, 39, 40, 41, 70, 97

Revengers' Comedies, The (Ayckbourn), **Supp. V:** 3, 10

Reverberator, The (James), **VI:** 67

"Reverie" (Browning), **IV:** 365

Reveries over Childhood and Youth (Yeats), **VI:** 222

Reversals (Stevenson), **Supp. VI:** 255–256

"Reversals" (Stevenson), **Supp. VI:** 256

Reverse of the Medal, The (O'Brian), **Supp. XII:** 256, 257, 258, 260

Review (periodical), **II:** 325; **III:** 4, 13, 39, 41, 42, 51, 53

"Review, The" (Traherne), **Supp. XI:** 269

Review of some poems by Alexander Smith and Matthew Arnold (Clough), **V:** 158

Review of the Affairs of France, A . . . (Defoe), **III:** 13; **Retro. Supp. I:** 65

Review of the State of the British Nation, A (Defoe), **Retro. Supp. I:** 65

"Reviewer's ABC, A" (Aiken), **VII:** 149

Revised Version of the Bible, **I:** 381–382

"Revision" (Adcock), **Supp. XII:** 8

Revolt in the Desert (Lawrence), **Supp. II:** 288, 289–290, 293

Revolt of Aphrodite, The (Durrell), *see Tunc; Nunquam*

Revolt of Islam, The (Shelley), **IV:** xvii, 198, 203, 208; **VI:** 455; **Retro. Supp. I:** 249–250

"Revolt of the Tartars" (De Quincey), **IV:** 149

"Revolution" (Housman), **VI:** 160

Revolution in Tanner's Lane, The (Rutherford), **VI:** 240

Revolution Script, The (Moore, B.), **Supp. IX:** 141, 143

Revolutionary Epick, The (Disraeli), **IV:** 306, 308

Revolving Lights (Richardson), **Retro. Supp. I:** 313–314

Revue des Deux Mondes (Montégut), **V:** 102

"Revulsion" (Davie), **Supp. VI:** 110, 112

"Rex Imperator" (Wilson), **Supp. I:** 155, 156

"Reynard the Fox" (Masefield), **VI:** 338

Reynolds, G. W. M., **III:** 335

Reynolds, Henry, **Supp. IV:** 350

Reynolds, John, **II:** 14

Reynolds, John Hamilton, **IV:** 215, 221, 226, 228, 229, 232, 233, 253, 257, 259, 281

Reynolds, Sir Joshua, **II:** 336; **III:** 305

"Rhapsody of Life's Progress, A" (Browning), **IV:** 313

"Rhapsody on a Windy Night" (Eliot), **Retro. Supp. II:** 121–122

Rhetor (Harvey), **I:** 122

"Rhetoric" (De Quincey), **IV:** 147

"Rhetoric" (Jennings), **Supp. V:** 218

"Rhetoric and Poetic Drama" (Eliot), **VII:** 157

"Rhetoric of a Journey" (Fuller), **Supp. VII:** 72

Rhetoric of the Unreal: Studies in Narrative and Structure, Especially of the Fantastic, A (Brooke–Rose)), **Supp. IV:** 97, 99, 115, 116

"Rhineland Journal" (Spender), **Supp. II:** 489

Rhoda Fleming (Meredith), **V:** xxiii, 227n, 234

"Rhodian Captain" (Durrell), **Supp. I:** 124

Rhododaphne (Peacock), **IV:** 158, 170

Rhyme? and Reason? (Carroll), **V:** 270, 273

Rhyme Stew (Dahl), **Supp. IV:** 226

Rhys, Jean, **Supp. II: 387–403; Supp. V:** 40; **Retro. Supp. I:** 60

"Rhythm and Imagery in British Poetry" (Empson), **Supp. II:** 195

"Ribblesdale" (Hopkins), **V:** 367, 372; **Retro. Supp. II:** 191

Ribner, Irving, **I:** 287

Riccoboni, Luigi, **II:** 348

Riceyman Steps (Bennett), **VI:** 250, 252, 260–261

Rich, Barnaby, **I:** 312

Rich Get Rich (Kavan), **Supp. VII:** 208–209

Richard II (Shakespeare), **I:** 286, 308

Richard III (Shakespeare), **I:** 285, 299–301

"Richard Martin" (Hood), **IV:** 267

Richard Rolle of Hampole, **I:** 20

Richard Temple (O'Brian), **Supp. XII:** 251, 252

Richards, I. A., **III:** 324; **V:** 367, 381; **VI:** 207, 208; **VII:** xiii, 233, 239; **Supp. II:** 185, 193, **405–431**

Richard's Cork Leg (Behan), **Supp. II:** 65, 74

Richards, Grant, **VI:** 158

Richardson, Betty, **Supp. IV:** 330

Richardson, Dorothy, **VI:** 372; **VII:** 20; **Supp. IV:** 233; **Retro. Supp. I:** 313–314

Richardson, Elaine Cynthia Potter, *see* Kincaid, Jamaica

Richardson, Joanna, **IV:** xxv, 236; **V:** xi, xviii

Richardson, Samuel, **III: 80–93,** 94, 98, 333; **VI:** 266 **Supp. II:** 10; **Supp. III:** 26, 30–31; **Supp. IV:** 150; **Retro. Supp. I:** 80

"Richey" (Adcock), **Supp. XII:** 6

"Richt Respeck for Cuddies, A" (tr. Morgan, E.), **Supp. IX:** 168

Ricks, Christopher, **Supp. IV:** 394, 398

Riddarasögur, **VIII:** 236

"Riddle of Houdini, The" (Doyle), **Supp. II:** 163–164

Riddle of Midnight, The (film, Rushdie), **Supp. IV:** 436, 441

"Ride from Milan, The" (Swinburne), **V:** 325, 333

Riders in the Chariot (White), **Supp. I:** 131, 132, 133, 136, **141–143,** 152

Riders to the Sea (Synge), **VI:** xvi, 308, 309, 310–311; **Retro. Supp. I:** 296

Ridiculous Mountains, The (Dutton), **Supp. XII:** 85

Riding, Laura, **VI:** 207; **VII:** 258, 260, 261, 263, 269; **Supp. II:** 185; **Supp. III:** 120

Riding Lights (MacCaig), **Supp. VI:** 181, **185–186,** 190, 194

Riffaterre, Michael, **Supp. IV:** 115

Rigby, Elizabeth, **V:** 138

"Right Apprehension" (Traherne), **Supp. XI:** 266

Right at Last and Other Tales (Gaskell), **V:** 15

Right Ho, Jeeves (Wodehouse), **Supp. III:** 458, 461

Right to an Answer, The (Burgess), **Supp. I:** 187, 188–189, 190, 195, 196

Righter, Anne, **I:** 224, 269, 329

Rights of Great Britain asserted against the Claims of America (Macpherson), **VIII:** 193

Rights of Passage (Brathwaite), **Supp. XII:** 33, 34, 36–38, 39, 40, 41, 45

Rígsþula, **VIII:** 231

Rilke, Rainer Maria, **VI:** 215; **Supp. IV:** 480

Rimbaud, Jean Nicolas, **Supp. IV:** 163

"Rime of the Ancient Mariner, The" (Coleridge), *see* "Ancient Mariner, The"

Riming Poem, The, **Retro. Supp. II:** 304

Ring, The (Wagner), **V:** 300

Ring and the Book, The (Browning), **IV:** xxiii, 358, 362, 369, 373, 374; **Retro. Supp. II:** 28–29

Ring Round the Moon (Fry), **Supp. III:** 195, 207

"Ringed Plover by a Water's Edge" (MacCaig), **Supp. VI:** 192

Rings of Saturn, The (Sebald), **VIII:** 295, 303–305, 308

Rings on a Tree (MacCaig), **Supp. VI:** 190

Ripley Under Ground (Highsmith), **Supp. V:** 171

Ripley Under Water (Highsmith), **Supp. V:** 171

Ripley's Game (Highsmith), **Supp. V:** 171

Ripple from the Storm, A (Lessing), **Supp. I:** 244–245

Rise and Fall of the House of Windsor, The (Wilson), **Sup. VI:** 308

"Rise of Historical Criticism, The" (Wilde), **V:** 401, 419

Rise of Iskander, The (Disraeli), **IV:** 308

"Rising Five" (Nicholson), **Supp. VI: 216**

Rising of the Moon, The (Gregory), **VI:** 315, 316

Rise of the Russian Empire, The (Saki), **Supp. VI:** 239

Ritchie, Lady Anne, **V:** 10

"Rite and Fore–Time" (Jones), **Supp. VII:** 176

Rite of the Passion, The (Williams, C. W. S.), **Supp. IX:** 276–277

"Rites" (Brathwaite), **Supp. XII:** 40, 45

Rites of Passage (Golding), **Supp. I:** 86–87; **Retro. Supp. I:** 103–104

"Rites of Passage" (Gunn), **Supp. IV:** 266

"Ritual of Departure" (Kinsella), **Supp. V:** 264

"Rival, The" (Warner), **Supp. VII:** 371

Rival Ladies, The (Dryden), **II:** 293, 297, 305

Rivals, The (Sheridan), **III:** 253, **257–259**, 270

Rive, Richard, **Supp. II:** 342–343, 350

River (Hughes), **Supp. I:** 363; **Retro. Supp. II:** 212–214

"River, The" (Muir), **Supp. VI:** 206

"River" (Wallace–Crabbe), **VIII:** 320

River Between, The (Ngũgĩ), **VIII:** 218–219

River Dudden, The, a Series of Sonnets (Wordsworth), **IV:** 24

River Girl, The (Cope), **VIII:** 69, 74–75

"River God, The" (Smith), **Supp. II:** 472

River Town, A (Keneally), **Supp. IV:** 347, 348

River War, The (Churchill), **VI:** 351

Rivers, W. H. R., **Supp. IV:** 46, 57, 58

Riverside Chaucer, The (ed. Benson), **Retro. Supp. II:** 49

Riverside Villas Murder, The (Amis), **Supp. II:** 12

Riviere, Michael, **VII:** 422, 424

"Road from Colonus, The" (Forster), **VI:** 399

Road Rage (Rendell), **Supp. IX:** 196, 198

"Road These Times Must Take, The" (Day Lewis), **Supp. III:** 126–127

"Road to Emmaus, The" (Brown), **Supp. VI:** 70

Road to Huddersfield: A Journey to Five Continents, The (Morris), see *World Bank: A Prospect, The*

Road to Samarcand, The (O'Brian), **Supp. XII:** 251

"Road to the Big City, A" (Lessing), **Supp. I:** 240

Road to Volgograd (Sillitoe), **Supp. V:** 409

Road to Wigan Pier, The (Orwell), **VII:** 274, 279–280

Road to Xanadu, The (Lowes), **IV:** 47, 57

"Road Uphill, The," (Maugham), **VI:** 377

"Roads" (Stevenson), **V:** 386

"Roads" (Thomas), **Supp. III:** 404, 406

Roald Dahl's Revolting Rhymes (Dahl), **Supp. IV:** 226

Roaring Girl, The (Dekker and Middleton), **II:** 3, 21

Roaring Queen, The (Lewis), **VII:** 82

Rob Roy (Scott), **IV:** xvii, 33, 34, 39

Robbe–Grillet, Alain, **Supp. IV:** 99, 104, 115, 116

Robbery Under Law (Waugh), **VII:** 292, 294

Robbins, Bruce, **Supp. IV:** 95

Robe of Rosheen, The (O'Casey), **VII:** 12

Robene and Makyne (Henryson), **Supp. VII:** 146, 147

Robert Bridges and Gerard Manley Hopkins (Ritz), **VI:** 83

Robert Bridges 1844–1930 (Thompson), **VI:** 83

"Robert Bridges: His Work on the English Language" (Daryush), **VI:** 76

Robert Browning (ed. Armstrong), **IV:** 375

Robert Browning (Chesterton), **VI:** 344

Robert Browning (Jack), **IV:** 375

Robert Browning: A Collection of Critical Essays (Drew), **IV:** 375

Robert Burns (Swinburne), **V:** 333

Robert Graves: His Life and Work (Seymour–Smith), **VII:** 272

Robert Louis Stevenson (Chesterton), **V:** 391, 393, 397; **VI:** 345

Robert Louis Stevenson (Cooper), **V:** 397, 398

Robert Louis Stevenson. An Essay (Stephen), **V:** 290

Robert Louis Stevenson: Man and Writer (Stewart), **V:** 393, 397

Robert Macaire (Stevenson), **V:** 396

Robert of Sicily: Opera for Children (Fry and Tippett), **Supp. III:** 194

Robert Southey and His Age (Carnall), **IV:** 72

Robert the Second, King of Scots (Jonson/Chettle/Dekker), **Retro. Supp. I:** 157

Roberts, Keith, **Supp. X:** 261–276

Roberts, Michael, **VII:** xix, 411

Roberts, Morley, **V:** 425, 427, 428, 438

Robertson, Thomas, **V:** 330; **VI:** 269

Robin Hood: A Fragment, by the Late Robert Southey, and Caroline Southey, **IV:** 71

Robinson, Henry Crabb, **IV:** 11, 52, 56, 81

Robinson, Henry Morton, **VII:** 53

Robinson, Lennox, **VI:** 96

Robinson (Spark), **Supp. I:** 201, 202–203

Robinson Crusoe (Defoe), **III:** 1, 5, 6, 7, 8, 10–12, 13, 24, 42, 50, 95; **Supp. I:** 73; **Retro. Supp. I:** 65–66, 68, 70–71

"Robinson Tradition, The" (Milne), **Supp. V:** 304

"Robinson's Life Sentence" (Armitage), **VIII:** 6

"Robinson's Resignation" (Armitage), **VIII:** 6

Roche, Denis, **Supp. IV:** 115

Roche, Maurice, **Supp. IV:** 116

Rochester, earl of, **II:** 208n, 255, 256, **257–261, 269–270; Supp. III:** 39, 40, 70

Rock, The (Eliot), **VII:** 153

"Rock, The" (Hughes), **Supp. I:** 341, 342; **Retro. Supp. II:** 199

Rock Face (Nicholson), **Supp. VI:** 213, **216–217**

Rock Pool, The (Connolly), **Supp. III: 98–100**

Rockaby (Beckett), **Supp. I:** 61; **Retro. Supp. I:** 28–29

"Rocking–Horse Winner, The" (Lawrence), **Supp. IV:** 511

Roderick Hudson (James), **VI:** 24, **26–28**, 42, 67

Roderick Random (Smollett), **III: 150–152**, 158

Roderick, The Last of the Goths (Southey), **IV:** 65–66, 68, 71

Rodker, John, **VI:** 327

Roe Head journals (Brontë), **V:** 119–122

"Roger Ascham and Lady Jane Grey" (Landor), **IV:** 92

"Roger Bear's Philosophical Pantoum" (Cope), **VIII:** 76–77

Roger Fry (Woolf), **Retro. Supp. I:** 308

Rogers, Charles, **III:** 249

Rogers, Woodes, **III:** 7

"Rois Fainéants" (Auden), **Retro. Supp. I:** 14

Rojas Zorilla, Francisco de, **II:** 325

Rokeby (Scott), **IV:** 38

Roland Whately (Waugh), **Supp. VI:** 270

"Roll for Joe, A" (Kelman), **Supp. V:** 244–245

"Rolling English Road, The" (Chesterton), **I:** 16

Rollins, Hyder, **IV:** 231, 232, 235

Rollo, Duke of Normandy (Chapman, Fletcher, Jonson, Massinger), **II:** 45, 66

Roman Actor, The (Massinger), **Supp. XI:** 180–181, 183

Roman de la rose, **I:** 28, 49; tr. Chaucer, **I:** 28, 31

Roman de Troie (Benoît de Sainte–Maure), **I:** 53

Roman expérimental (Zola), **V:** 286

Roman Forgeries; or, A True Account of False Records Discovering the Impostures and Counterfeit Antiquities of the Church of Rome (Traherne), **II:** 190, 191, 201; **Supp. XI:** 264, 265, 276–277

Roman History, The (Goldsmith), **III:** 180, 181, 191

Roman Poems (Sisson), **Supp. XI:** 249

Roman Quarry and Other Sequences, The (Jones), **Supp. VII:** 167, 171

"Roman Thoughts in Autumn" (Wallace–Crabbe), **VIII:** 317

Romance (Conrad and Ford), **VI:** 146, 148, 321

"Romance" (Sitwell), **VII:** 132–133

Romance and Realism (Caudwell), **Supp. IX:** 33, 43, 45–46

"Romance in Ireland" (Yeats), **Retro. Supp. I:** 330

"Romance of Certain Old Clothes, The" (James), **VI:** 69

"Romance of the Lily, The" (Beddoes), **Supp. XI:** 28

"Romania" (Adcock), **Supp. XII:** 11

Romantic Adventures of A Milkmaid, The (Hardy), **VI:** 20, 22

Romantic Agony, The (Praz), **III:** 337, 346; **V:** 412, 420

Romantic Image (Kermode), **V:** 344, 359, 412

Romantic Poetry and the Fine Arts (Blunden), **IV:** 236

"Romanticism and Classicism" (Hulme), **Supp. VI:** 135, 138, 142–145

Romany Rye, The; A Sequel to "Lavengro" (Borrow), **Supp. XII:** 17, 27–28

"Romaunt of Margaret, The" (Browning), **IV:** 313

Romeo and Juliet (Shakespeare), **I:** 229, 305–306, 320; **II:** 281; **IV:** 218

Romola (Eliot), **V:** xxii, 66, 194–195, 200; **Retro. Supp. II:** 110–111

Romulus and Hersilia; or, The Sabine War (Behn), **Supp. III:** 29

"Rondeau Redoublé" (Cope), **VIII:** 71

Rondeaux Parisiens (Swinburne), **V:** 333

"Roof–Tree" (Murphy), **Supp. V:** 329

Rookwood (Ainsworth), **V:** 47

Room, The (Day Lewis), **Supp. III:** 118, 129–130

"Room, The" (Day Lewis), **Supp. III:** 130

Room, The (Pinter), **Supp. I:** 367, 369; **Retro. Supp. I:** 216, 218, 221–222

"Room Above the Square" (Spender), **Supp. II:** 494

Room at the Top (Braine), **Supp. IV:** 238

Room of One's Own, A (Woolf), **VII:** 22–23, 25–26, 27, 38; **Supp. III:** 19, 41–42; **Supp. V:** 36; **Retro. Supp. I:** 310–314

Room with a View, A (Forster), **VI:** 398, 399, **403–404**; **Retro. Supp. II:** 141–143

"Rooms, The" (Stallworthy), **Supp. X:** 298

"Rooms of Other Women Poets, The" (Boland), **Supp. V:** 37

Root and Branch (Stallworthy), **Supp. X:** 293–296

Rootham, Helen, **VII:** 129

Roots (Brathwaite), **Supp. XII:** 43, 44, 45

"Roots" (Brathwaite), **Supp. XII:** 43

Roots of Coincidence (Koestler), **Supp. I:** 39

"Roots of Honour, The" (Ruskin), **V:** 179–180

Roots of the Mountains, The (Morris), **V:** 302, 306

Roppen, G., **V:** 221n

Rosalind and Helen (Shelley), **IV:** 208

Rosalynde (Lodge), **I:** 312

Rosamond, Queen of the Lombards (Swinburne), **V:** 312–314, 330, 331, 332, 333

Rose, Ellen Cronan, **Supp. IV:** 232

"Rose, The" (Southey), **IV:** 64

Rose, The (Yeats), **Retro. Supp. I:** 330

Rose and Crown (O'Casey), **VII:** 13

Rose and the Ring, The (Thackeray), **V:** 38, 261

Rose Blanche (McEwan), **Supp. IV:** 390

Rose in the Heart, A (O'Brien), **Supp. V:** 339

"Rose in the Heart of New York, A" (O'Brien), **Supp. V:** 340–341

"Rose Mary" (Rossetti), **V:** 238, 244

Rose of Life, The (Braddon), **VIII:** 49

Rosemary's Baby (film), **III:** 343

Rosenberg, Bruce, **Supp. IV:** 7

Rosenberg, Eleanor, **I:** 233

Rosenberg, Isaac, **VI:** xvi, 417, 420, **432–435**; **VII:** xvi; **Supp. III:** 59

Rosenberg, John, **V:** 316, 334

Rosencrantz and Guildenstern Are Dead (Stoppard), **Supp. I:** **440–443**, 444, 451; **Retro. Supp. II:** 343–345

Rosenfeld, S., **II:** 271

Rosengarten (Bevan and Galloway), **Supp. XII:** 117

"Roses on the Terrace, The" (Tennyson), **IV:** 329, 336

"Rosie Plum" (Powys), **VIII:** 251

Rosie Plum and Other Stories (Powys), **VIII:** 251, 252

"Rosiphelee" (Gower), **I:** 53–54

Ross (Rattigan), **Supp. VII:** 320, 321

Ross, Alan, **VII:** xxii, 422, 433–434

Ross, John Hume (pseud., Lawrence), **Supp. II:** 286, 295

Rossetti, Christina, **V:** xi–xii, xix, xxii, xxvi, **247–260**; **Supp. IV:** 139

Rossetti, Dante Gabriel, **IV:** 346; **V:** ix, xi, xii, xviii, xxiii–xxv, **235–246**, 247–253, 259, 293–296, 298, 299, 312–315, 320, 329, 355, 401; **VI:** 167

Rossetti, Maria **V:** 251, 253

Rossetti, William, **V:** 235, 236, 245, 246, 248–249, 251–253, 260

Rossetti (Waugh), **VII:** 291

Rossetti and His Circle (Beerbohm), **Supp. II:** 51

"Rossetti's Conception of the 'Poetic' " (Doughty), **V:** 246

Røstvig, Maren–Sofie, **I:** 237

"Rosyfingered, The" (MacCaig), **Supp. VI:** 186

"Rot, The" (Lewis), **VII:** 73

"Rotter, The" (Nye), **Supp. X:** 204

Rotting Hill (Lewis), **VII:** 72

Rough Justice (Braddon), **VIII:** 37, 49

Rough Shoot (film, Ambler), **Supp. IV:** 3

Round and Round the Garden (Ayckbourn), **Supp. V:** 2, 5

Round of Applause, A (MacCaig), **Supp. VI: 187–188**, 190, 194–195

Round Table, The (Hazlitt), **IV:** xvii, 129, 137, 139

Round Table, The; or, King Arthur's Feast (Peacock), **IV:** 170

"Round Table Manners" (Nye), **Supp. X:** 202–203

Round the Sofa (Gaskell), **V:** 3, 15

Roundabout Papers (Thackeray), **V:** 34, 35, 38

Roundheads, The; or, The Good Old Cause (Behn), **Supp. III:** 25

Rounding the Horn: Collected Poems (Stallworthy), **Supp. X:** 292–294, 298, 302

Rousseau, Jean Jacques, **III:** 235, 236; **IV:** xiv, 207; **Supp. III:** 239–240

Rover, The (Conrad), **VI:** 144, 147, 148

Rover, The; or, The Banish'd Cavaliers (Behn), **Supp. III:** 26, 27–29, 31

Royal Edinburgh (Oliphant), **Supp. X:** 222

Rowe, Nicholas, **I:** 326

Rowley, Hazel, **Supp. IV:** 459, 460

Rowley, William, **II:** 1, 3, 14, 15, 18, 21, 66, 69, 83, 89, 100

Roxana (Defoe), **III:** 8–9, 14; **Retro. Supp. I:** 69, 74

Roy, Arundhati, **Supp. V:** xxx, 67, 75

Royal Academy, The (Moore), **VI:** 98

Royal Beasts, The (Empson), **Supp. II:** 180, 184

Royal Combat, The (Ford), **II:** 100

Royal Court Theatre, **VI:** 101

Royal Hunt of the Sun, The (Shaffer), **Supp. I:** 314, **319–322**, 323, 324, 327

"Royal Jelly" (Dahl), **Supp. IV:** 221

"Royal Man" (Muir), **I:** 247

"Royal Naval Air Station" (Fuller), **Supp. VII:** 69

Royal Pardon, The (Arden and D'Arcy), **Supp. II:** 30

Rubáiyát of Omar Khayyám, The (FitzGerald), **IV:** xxii, 342–343, **345–348**, 349, 352, 353; **V:** 318

Rubin, Merle, **Supp. IV:** 360

Rudd, Margaret, **VI:** 209

Rudd, Steele, **Supp. IV:** 460

Rude Assignment (Lewis), **VI:** 333; **VII:** xv, 72, 74, 76

Rudolf II, Emperor of Holy Roman Empire, **Supp. IV:** 174

Rudyard Kipling, Realist and Fabulist (Dobrée), **VI:** 200–203

Rudyard Kipling to Rider Haggard (ed. Cohen), **VI:** 204

Ruell, Patrick, *see* Hill, Reginald

Ruffhead, O., **III:** 69n, 71

Ruffian on the Stair, The (Orton), **Supp. V:** 367, 370, 372, 373

"Rugby Chapel" (Arnold), **V:** 203

"Ruin, The" (tr. Morgan), **Supp. IX:** 160

Ruin, The, **Retro. Supp. II:** 305

Ruined Boys, The (Fuller), **Supp. VII:** 74, 75

"Ruined Cottage, The," (Wordsworth), **IV:** 23, 24

"Ruined Farm, The" (Plomer), **Supp. XI:** 213

"Ruined Maid, The" (Hardy), **Retro. Supp. I:** 120

Ruins and Visions (Spender), **Supp. II:** 486, 489

Ruins of Time, The (Spenser), **I:** 124

Rukeyser, Muriel, **Supp. V:** 261

Rule a Wife and Have a Wife (Fletcher), **II:** 45, 65

Rule Britannia (du Maurier), **Supp. III:** 133, 147

"Rule, Britannia" (Thomson), **Supp. III:** 412, 425

"Rules and Lessons" (Vaughan), **II:** 187

Rules for Court Circular (Carroll), **V:** 274
"Rummy Affair of Old Biffy, The" (Wodehouse), **Supp. III:** 455, 457
Ruling Passion (Hill, R.), **Supp. IX:** 113–114
Rumors of Rain (Brink), **Supp. VI:** **49–50**
Rumour at Nightfall (Greene), **Supp. I:** 3
"Run"(Motion), **Supp. VII:** 259
Rungs of Time (Wallace–Crabbe), **VIII:** 323–324, 325
"Running Stream, The" (Blunden), **Supp. XI:** 43–44
Running Wild (Ballard), **Supp. V:** 30–31
Rural Denmark (Haggard), **Supp. III:** 214
Rural England (Haggard), **Supp. III:** 214
Rural Minstrel, The (Brontë), **V:** 107, 151
Rural Muse, The: Poems (Clare), **Supp. XI:** 59, 60, 63
Rural Sports: A Poem (Gay), **III:** 67
Rushdie, Salman, **Supp. IV:** 65, 75, 116, 157, 160, 161, 162, 170–171, 174, 302, **433–456; Supp. V:** 67, 68, 74
Rushing to Paradise (Ballard), **Supp. V:** 31
Ruskin, John, **IV:** 320, 346; **V:** xii, xviii, xx–xxii, xxvi, 3, 9, 17, 20, 85–86, **173–185,** 235, 236, 291–292, 345, 362, 400; **VI:** 167
Ruskin's Politics (Shaw), **VI:** 129
Russ, R. P. *see* O'Brian, Patrick
Russell, Bertrand, **VI:** xi, 170, 385; **VII:** 90
Russell, G. W. E., **IV:** 292, 304
Russell, George William, **VIII: 277–293**
Russell, John, **Supp. IV:** 126
Russia House, The (le Carré), **Supp. II:** 300, 310, 311, 313, **318–319**
Russian Interpreter, The (Frayn), **Supp. VII:** 52–53, 54
Russian Nights (Thomas), **Supp. IV:** 483–486
Rusticus (Poliziano), **I:** 240
"Ruth" (Crabbe), **V:** 6
Ruth (Gaskell), **V:** xxi, 1, 6 7, 15
"Ruth" (Hood), **IV:** 255
Ryan, Desmond, **VII:** 2
Rymer, James Malcolm, **Supp. III:** 385
Rymer, Thomas, **I:** 328
Ryskamp, C., **III:** 249

"**S.** K." (Thomas), **Supp. XII:** 285
S. T. Coleridge (ed. Brett), **IV:** 57
"Sabbath" (Fallon), **Supp. XII:** 108
"Sabbath Morning at Sea, A" (Browning), **IV:** 313
"Sabbath Park" (McGuckian), **Supp. V:** 283–284
Sackville, Charles, *see* Dorset, earl of
Sackville, Thomas, **I:** 169, 214
Sackville–West, Edward, **VII:** 35, 59
Sacred and Profane Love Machine, The (Murdoch), **Supp. I:** 224
Sacred Flame, The (Maugham), **VI:** 369
Sacred Fount, The (James), **VI:** 56–57, 67
Sacred Hunger (Unsworth), **Supp. VII:** 353, 357, 361, 363–364
"Sacred Ridges above Diamond Creek" (Wallace–Crabbe), **VIII:** 320

Sacred Wood, The (Eliot), **I:** 293; **V:** 310, 334; **VII:** 149, 164; **Retro. Supp. I:** 166
"Sacrifice" (Kinsella), **Supp. V:** 267
"Sacrifice, The" (Herbert), **II:** 124, 128
"Sad Fortunes of the Reverend Amos Barton, The" (Eliot), **Retro. Supp. II:** 103
Sad One, The (Suckling), **II:** 226
Sad Shepherd, The (Jonson), **Retro. Supp. I:** 166
"Sad Steps" (Larkin), **Supp. I:** 284
"Sadak the Wanderer" (Shelley), **IV:** 20
Sade, marquis de, **V:** 316–317
Sadeian Woman, The: An Exercise in Cultural History (Carter), **Supp. III:** 87–88
Sadleir, Michael, **III:** 335, 346; **V:** 100, 101, 102
"Sadness of Cricket, The" (Ewart), **Supp. VII:** 45–46
Sado (Plomer), **Supp. XI:** 215 216
"Safe as Houses" (Drabble), **Supp. IV:** 231
"Safety" (Brooke), **Supp. III:** 57
"Saga of Bjǫrn Champion of the Folk of Hít–Dale, The", *See Bjarnar saga Hít-dœlakappa*
"Saga of Egill Skalla–Grimr's Son, The", *See Egils saga Skalla–Grímssonar*
"Saga of Eiríkr the Red, The", *See Eiríks saga rauða*
"Saga of Gísli Súrr's Son, The", *See Gísla saga Súrssonar*
"Saga of Glúmr of the Slayings, The", *See Víga–Glúms saga*
"Saga of Gunnlaugr Serpent–Tongue, The", *See Gunnlaugs saga ormstunga*
"Saga of Hallfreðr the Awkward Poet, The", *See Hallfreðar saga vandrœðaskálds*, 239
"Saga of Ljótr from Vellir, The", *See Val-la–Ljóts saga*
"Saga of Njáll of the Burning, The", *See Njáls saga*
"Saga of St Óláfr, The", *See Óláfs saga helga*
"Saga of the Confederates, The", *See Bandamanna saga*
"Saga of the Descendants of Sturla, The", *See Sturlunga saga*
"Saga of the Folk of Bright–Water, The", *See Ljósvetninga saga*
"Saga of the Folk of Laxdale, The", *Laxdœla saga*
"Saga of the Foster Brothers, The", *See Fóstbrœðra saga*
"Saga of the Greenlanders, The", *See Grœnlendinga saga*
"Saga of the Shingle–Dwellers, The", *See Eyrbyggja saga*
Saga Library, The (Morris, Magnusson), **V:** 306
Sagar, Keith, **VII:** 104
"Sagas of Ancient Times", *See Fornal-darsögur*
"Sagas of Icelanders", *See Íslendinga sögur*
"Sagas of Knights", *See Riddarasögur*
Sage, Lorna, **Supp. IV:** 346

"Sage to the Young Man, The" (Housman), **VI:** 159
Said, Edward, **Supp. IV:** 164, 449
Saigon: Year of the Cat (Hare), **Supp. IV:** 282, 289
Sail Away (Coward), **Supp. II:** 155
Sailing Alone Around the World (Slocum), **Supp. IV:** 158
"Sailing the High Seas" (Maitland), **Supp. XI:** 175–176
Sailing to an Island (Murphy), **Supp. V:** 317–320
"Sailing to an Island" (Murphy), **Supp. V:** 319
"Sailing to Byzantium" (Yeats), **Retro. Supp. I:** 333–334
"Sailor, What of the Isles?" (Sitwell), **VII:** 138
"Sailor's Mother, The" (Wordsworth), **IV:** 21
"Saint, The" (Maugham), **VI:** 377
"Saint, The" (Pritchett), **Supp. III:** 315, 318–319
"St. Alphonsus Rodriquez" (Hopkins), **V:** 376, 378
"St. Anthony's Shirt" (Day Lewis), **Supp. III:** 115
St. Augustine (West), **Supp. III:** 433
St Bartholomew's Eve: A Tale of the Sixteenth Century in Two Cantos (Newman), **Supp. VII:** 289
Sainte–Beuve, Charles, **III:** 226, 230; **V:** 212
"St. Botolph's" (Hughes), **Retro. Supp. II:** 217
St. Catherine's Clock (Kinsella), **Supp. V:** 271
St. Évremond, Charles de, **III:** 47
St. Francis of Assisi (Chesterton), **VI:** 341
Saint Ignatius Loyola (Thompson), **V:** 450, 451
St. Irvine (Shelley), **III:** 338
St. Irvyne; or, The Rosicrucian (Shelley), **IV:** 208
St. Ives (Stevenson and Quiller–Couch), **V:** 384, 387, 396
"St James" (Reading), **VIII:** 263
Saint Joan (Shaw), **VI:** xv, 120, **123–125; Retro. Supp. II:** 323–324
St. Joan of the Stockyards (Brecht), **VI:** 123
St. Kilda's Parliament (Dunn), **Supp. X:** 66, 73–75, 77
St. Leon (Godwin), **III:** 332
"St. Martin's Summer" (Browning), **IV:** 369
"Sainte Mary Magdalene; or, The Weeper" (Crashaw), *see* AWeeper, The"
"St. Mawr" (Lawrence), **VII:** 115; **Retro. Supp. II:** 232
"St. Patrick's Day" (Mahon), **Supp. VI:** 178
St. Patrick's Day (Sheridan), **III:** 253, 259, 270
St. Paul and Protestantism (Arnold), **V:** 216
St. Paul's boys' theater, **I:** 197
St. Ronan's Well (Scott), **IV:** 36, 37, 39

"St. Simeon Stylites" (Tennyson), **IV:** xx, 332

St. Thomas Aquinas (Chesterton), **VI:** 341

St. Valentine's Day (Scott), **IV:** 39

"St. Winefred's Well" (Hopkins), **V:** 371

"Saints and Lodgers" (Davies), **Supp. XI:** 94

Saint's Knowledge of Christ's Love, The (Bunyan), **II:** 253

Saint's Privilege and Profit, The (Bunyan), **II:** 253

Saint's Progress (Galsworthy), **VI:** 272, 279, 280–281

Saintsbury, George, **II:** 211; **IV:** 271, 282, 306; **V:** 31, 38; **VI:** 266

Saki (H. H. Munro), **Supp. II:** 140–141, 144, 149; **Supp. VI: 239–252**

Salem Chapel (Oliphant), **Supp. X:** 214–215, 221

Salámón and Absál . . . Translated from .. . . Jámí (FitzGerald), **IV:** 342, 345, 353

Salih, Tayeb, **Supp. IV:** 449

Salinger, J. D., **Supp. IV:** 28

"Salisbury Plain" poems (Wordsworth), **IV:** 2, 3, 4, 5–6, 23, 24

Sally Bowles (Isherwood), **VII:** 311

"Salmon Eggs" (Hughes), **Supp. I:** 363, 364; **Retro. Supp. II:** 213

Salomé (Wilde), **V:** xxvi, 412–413, 419; **Retro. Supp. II:** 370–371

Salsette and Elephanta (Ruskin), **V:** 184

Salt Lands, The (Shaffer), **Supp. I:** 314

"Salt of the Earth, The" (West), **Supp. III:** 442

Salt Stream, The (Redgrove), **Supp. VI:** 231–232

Salt Water (Motion), **Supp. VII:** 259, 262–264

Salter, F. M., **I:** 82

Salutation (Russell), **VIII:** 288

"Salutation, The" (Traherne), **II:** 191; **Supp. XI:** 268

Salutation, The (Warner), **Supp. VII:** 379–380

"Salvation of Swithin Forsyte, The" (Galsworthy), **VI:** 274, 277

"Salvatore" (Maugham), **VI:** 370

Salve (Moore), **VI:** 99

Salzburg Tales, The (Stead), **Supp. IV:** 461

"Same Day" (MacCaig), **Supp. VI:** 186

Sammy and Rosie Get Laid (Kureishi), **Supp. XI:** 156, 161

Samson Agonistes (Milton), **II:** 165, 172–174, 176; **Retro. Supp. II:** 285–288

Samtíðarsögur, **VIII:** 236

Samuel Johnson (Krutch), **III:** 246

Samuel Johnson (Stephen), **V:** 281, 289

"Samuel Johnson and John Horne (Tooke)" (Landor), **IV:** 92

Samuel Pepys's Naval Minutes (ed. Tanner), **II:** 288

Samuel Pepys's A Penny Merriments". . . Together with Comments . . . (ed. Thompson), **II:** 288

Samuel Taylor Coleridge: A Biographical Study (Chambers), **IV:** 41, 57

Samuel Titmarsh and the Great Hoggarty Diamond (Thackeray), *see Great Hoggarty Diamond, The*

Sanchez, Nellie, **V:** 393, 397

Sand, George, **V:** 22, 141, 207

"Sand–Between–the–Toes" (Milne), **Supp. V:** 302

"Sand Coast Sonnets, The" (Murray), **Supp. VII:** 283

Sandboy, The (Frayn), **Supp. VII:** 58

Sandcastle, The (Murdoch), **VII:** 66; **Supp. I:** 222–223, 225

Sanders, M. F., **V:** 250, 260

Sanderson, Robert, **II:** 136–137, 140, 142

Sandglass, The (Gunesekera), **Supp. X:** 85–86, 92–96, 98–100

Sandison, Alan G., **VI:** xi, xxxiv

Sanditon (Austen), **IV:** 108, 110, 122

Sandkastele (Brink), **Supp. VI: 57**

Sandra Belloni (Meredith), **V:** 226, 227, 234

"Sandro Botticelli" (Pater), **V:** 345, 348

"Sandstone Keepsake" (Heaney), **Supp. II:** 277

Sangschaw (MacDiarmid), **Supp. XII:** 202, 204, 205, 206

Sanity of Art, The (Shaw), **VI:** 106–107, 129

Sans (Beckett), **Supp. I:** *see Lessness*

Santal (Firbank), **Supp. II:** 202, 204, **214–215,** 223

Sapho and Phao (Lyly), **I:** 198, 201–202

"Sapho to Philænis" (Donne), **Retro. Supp. II:** 92–93

Sapper, **Supp. IV:** 500

"Sapphics" (Swinburne), **V:** 321

Sappho (Durrell), **Supp. I:** 126–127

"Sappho to Phaon" (Ovid), **V:** 319

Saramago, Jose, **Supp. V:** xxx

Sardanapalus (Byron), **IV:** xviii, 178–179, 193

Sarraute, Nathalie, **Supp. IV:** 99

Sarton, May, **Supp. II:** 82

Sartor Resartus (Carlyle), **IV:** xii, xix, 231, 239–240, 242–243, 249, 250

Sartre, Jean–Paul, **III:** 329, 345; **Supp. I:** 216, 217, 221, 222, 452–453; **Supp. III:** 109; **Supp. IV:** 39, 79, 105, 259

Sartre: Romantic Rationalist (Murdoch), **Supp. I:** 219–220, 222

Sassoon, Siegfried, **V:** 219, 234; **VI:** xvi, 416, **429–431,** 451, 454, 456–457; **VII:** xvi; **Supp. III:** 59; **Supp. IV:** 57–58

"Satan in a Barrel" (Lowry), **Supp. III:** 270

Satan in Search of a Wife (Lamb), **IV:** 84, 85

Satanic Verses, The (Rushdie), **Supp. IV:** 116, 433, 434, 436, 437, 438, 445–450, 451, 452, 456

Satire and Fiction (Lewis), **VII:** 72, 77

Satire on Satirists, A, and Admonition to Detractors (Landor), **IV:** 100

Satires (Donne), **I:** 361; **Retro. Supp. II:** 86

Satires (Wyatt), **I:** 100, 101–102, 111

Satires of Circumstance (Hardy), **VI:** 14, 20; **Retro. Supp. I:** 117

Satires of Circumstance (Sorley), **VI:** 421

"Satiric Muse, The " (Hope), **Supp. VII:** 163

"Satisfactory, The" (Pritchett), **Supp. III: 319–320**

Saturday Life, A (Hall), **Supp. VI:** 120–122

"Saturday Night" (Gunn), **Supp. IV:** 269

Saturday Night and Sunday Morning (Sillitoe), **Supp. V:** 409, 410, 413, 416–419

Saturday Review (periodical), **V:** 279; **VI:** 103, 106, 366; **Supp. II:** 45, 48, 53, 54, 55

"Saturday; or, The Flights" (Gay), **III:** 56

"Saturnalia" (Gunn), **Supp. IV:** 269

"Saturnalia" (Wilson), **Supp. I:** 158

"Satyr Against Mankind, A" (Rochester), **II:** 208n, 256, 260–261, 270

"Satyrical Elegy on the Death of a Late Famous General, A" (Swift), **III:** 31

Saucer of Larks, The (Friel), **Supp. V:** 113

"Saul" (Browning), **IV:** 363

Saunders, Charles, **II:** 305

Sauter, Rudolf, **VI:** 284

Sauve Qui Peut (Durrell), **Supp. I:** 113

Savage, Eliza Mary Ann, **Supp. II:** 99, 104, 111

Savage, Richard, **III:** 108

Savage and the City in the Work of T. S. Eliot, The (Crawford), **Supp. XI:** 67, 71, 82

Savage Gold (Fuller), **Supp. VII:** 70

Savage Pilgrimage, The (Carswell), **VII:** 123

Save It for the Minister (Churchill, Potter, O'Malley), **Supp. IV:** 181

Save the Beloved Country (Paton), **Supp. II:** 359, 360

Saved (Bond), **Supp. I:** 421, 422–423, 425–426, 427, 435

Saved By Grace (Bunyan), **II:** 253

Savile, George, *see* Halifax, marquess of

Saville (Storey), **Supp. I:** 419

Saviour of Society, The (Swinburne), **V:** 333

"Savonarola Brown" (Beerbohm), **Supp. II:** 5l, 56

Savonarola e il priore di San Marco (Landor), **IV:** 100

Savrola (Churchill), **VI:** 351

"Say not of me that weakly I declined" (Stevenson), **V:** 390

"Say not the struggle nought availeth" (Clough), **V:** 158–159, 165, 166, 167

Sayers, Dorothy L., **III:** 341; **VI:** 345; **Supp. II:** 124, 126, 127, 135; **Supp. III: 333–353; Supp. IV:** 2, 3, 500

"Scale" (Self), **Supp. V:** 403–404

"Scales, The" (Longley), **VIII:** 176

Scandal (Wilson), **Supp. VI:** 302–303, 308

"Scandal in Bohemia, A" (Doyle), **Supp. I:** 173

Scandal of Father Brown, The (Chesterton), **VI:** 338

Scandalous Woman, A (O'Brien), **Supp. V:** 339

Scannell, Vernon, **VII:** 422, 423–424

Scapegoat, The (du Maurier), **Supp. III:** 136, 139, 140–141

"Scapegoat, The" (Pritchett), **Supp. III:** 312, 317–318

Scapegoats and Rabies (Hughes), **Supp. I:** 348

Scarcity of Love, A (Kavan), **Supp. VII:** 213, 214

"Scarecrow in the Schoolmaster's Oats, The" (Brown), **Supp. VI:** 71

Scarlet Tree, The (Sitwell), **VII:** 128–129

Scarperer, The (Behan), **Supp. II:** 67

Scarron, Paul, **II:** 354

"Scenes" (Dickens), **V:** 44–46

Scenes and Actions (Caudwell), **Supp. IX:** 33, 37

Scenes from Italy's War (Trevelyan), **VI:** 389

"Scenes from the Fall of Troy" (Morris), **V:** 297

Scenes of Clerical Life (Eliot), **V:** xxii, 2, 190–191, 200; **Retro. Supp. II:** 103–104

Scenic Route, The (Adcock), **Supp. XII:** 6

Sceptick (Ralegh), **I:** 157

Schelling, Friedrich Wilhelm, **V:** 347

Scheme and Estimates for a National Theatre, A (Archer and Barker), **VI:** 104, 113

Schepisi, Fred, **Supp. IV:** 345

Schiller, Friedrich von, **IV:** xiv, xvi 173, 241

Schindler's Ark (Keneally), *see Schindler's List*

Schindler's List (Keneally), **Supp. IV:** 343, 346, 348, 354–357, 358

"Schir, I complayne off iniuris" (Dunbar), **VIII:** 119, 121

"Schir, Ye have mony Servitouris" (Dunbar), **VIII:** 122

Schirmer Inheritance, The (Ambler), **Supp. IV:** 4, 13–16, 21

Schlegel, A. W., **I:** 329; **IV:** vii, xvii; **V:** 62

Schneider, Elizabeth, **V:** 366, 382

"Scholar, The" (Cornford), **VIII:** 113

"Scholar and Gypsy" (Desai), **Supp. V:** 65

"Scholar Gipsy, The" (Arnold), **V:** xxi, 209, 210, 211, 216

School for Husbands (Mahon), **Supp. VI:** 175

School for Wives (Mahon), **Supp. VI:** 175

School for Scandal, The (Sheridan), **III:** 97, 100, 253, **261–264,** 270

School of Abuse (Gosson), **I:** 161

School of Athens, The (Renault), **Supp. IX:** 185

School of Donne, The (Alvarez), **II:** 125n

"School of Eloquence, The" (Harrison), **Supp. V:** 150, 151–157

"School Stories" (Wodehouse), **Supp. III:** 449

"School Story, A" (Trevor), **Supp. IV:** 502

"School Teacher" (Smith, I. C.), **Supp. IX:** 211

Schoolboy Verses (Kipling), **VI:** 200

"Schoolboys" (McEwan), **Supp. IV:** 393

Schools and Universities on the Continent (Arnold), **V:** 216

Schopenhauer, Arthur, **Supp. IV:** 6

Schreber's Nervous Illness (Churchill), **Supp. IV:** 181

Schreiner, Olive, **Supp. II: 435–457**

Schwindel. Gefühle (Sebald). *See Vertigo*

Science and Poetry (Richards), **VI:** 207, 208; **Supp. II:** 405, 412, 413, 414, **417–418,** 419

Science of Ethics, The (Stephen), **V:** 284–285, 289

"Science of History, The" (Froude), **IV:** 324

Science of Life, The (Wells), **VI:** 225

Scilla's Metamorphosis (Lodge), **I:** 306

"Scipio, Polybius, and Panaetius" (Landor), **IV:** 94

Scoop (Waugh), **VII:** 297

Scornful Lady, The (Beaumont and Fletcher), **II:** 65

"Scorpion, The" (Plomer), **Supp. XI:** 213–214

Scorpion and Other Poems (Smith), **Supp. II:** 463

Scorpion God, The (Golding), **Supp. I:** 82–83

Scot, William, **Supp. III:** 20, 22, 23

"Scotch Drink" (Burns), **III:** 315

"Scotland" (Crawford), **Supp. XI:** 72

"Scotland" (Reid), **Supp. VII:** 331

"Scotland in the 1890s" (Crawford), **Supp. XI:** 71

Scotland, the Place of Visions (Morris, J.), **Supp. X:** 177

"Scots and Off-Scots Words" (Crawford), **Supp. XI:** 80–81

"Scots Gamelan" (Crawford), **Supp. XI:** 69–70

Scots Musical Museum (Johnson), **III:** 320, 322

Scott, Geoffrey, **III:** 234n, 238, 249

Scott, John, **IV:** 252, 253

Scott, Paul, **Supp. I: 259–274; Supp. IV:** 440

Scott, Robert Falcon, **II:** 273

Scott, Sir Walter **II:** 276; **III:** 146, 157, 326, 335, 336, 338; **IV:** viii, xi, xiv, **27–40,** 45, 48, 102, 111, 122, 129, 133–136, 167, 168, 173, 254, 270, 281; **V:** 392; **VI:** 412; **Supp. III:** 151, 154, 167

Scott Moncrieff, Charles, **VI:** 454, 455

Scottish Assembly, A (Crawford), **Supp. XI:** 67, 70, 71–72, 73, 75, 78

Scottish Chapbook, **Supp. XII:** 204

Scottish Invention of English Literature, The (ed. Crawford), **Supp. XI:** 76, 82, 83

Scottish Journey (Muir), **Supp. VI:** 198, 201

Scott–James, Rolfe Arnold, **VI:** x, xxxiv, 1

Scott–Kilvert, Ian Stanley, **VI:** xvi, xxxiv; **VII:** xxii

Scott–King's Modern Europe (Waugh), **VII:** 301

"Scott's Arks" (Dunn), **Supp. X:** 82

Scotus, Duns, *see* Duns Scotus, John

Scourge of Villainy, The (Marston), **II:** 25, 26, 40

Scrapbook (Mansfield), **VII:** 181

Screams and Other Poems, The (Richards), **Supp. II:** 407, 427

Screwtape Letters, The (Lewis), **Supp. III:** 248, 255, 256–257

"Script for an Unchanging Voice" (McGuckian), **Supp. V:** 292

Scriptorum illustrium maioris Britanniae catalogus (Bale), **I:** 1

Scrutiny (periodical), **VII:** 233, 238, 243, 251–252, 256; **Supp. III:** 107

Scudéry, Georges de, **III:** 95

Sculptura; or, The History . . . of Chalcography and Engraving in Copper (Evelyn), **II:** 287

Scum of the Earth (Koestler), **Supp. I:** 26

"Scylla and Charybdis" (Kinsella), **Supp. V:** 261

Sea, The (Bond), **Supp. I:** 423, 427, 432–433, 435

Sea, The Sea, The (Murdoch), **Supp. I:** 231, 232

Sea and Sardinia (Lawrence), **VII:** 116–117

Sea and the Mirror, The (Auden), **VII:** 379, 380, 388, 389; **Retro. Supp. I:** 11

"Sea and the Skylark, The" (Hopkins), **V:** 367

Sea Change, The (Howard), **Supp. XI:** 135, 137, 139–140, 146

"Sea in Winter, The" (Mahon), **Supp. VI:** 173, 175

"Sea Limits" (Rossetti), **V:** 241

Sea Gull, The (tr. Frayn), **Supp. VII:** 61

"Sea–Sand" (Healy), **Supp. IX:** 106

Sea to the West (Nicholson), **Supp. VI:** 213, **218–219**

"Sea to the West" (Nicholson), **Supp. VI:** 219

Sea Voyage, The (Fletcher and Massinger), **II:** 43, 66

"Sea Voyage, The" (Hart), **Supp. XI:** 123

Seafarer, The, **Retro. Supp. II:** 303–304

"Seafarer, The" (tr. Morgan), **Supp. IX:** 160

"Seafarer, The" (Pound), **Supp. IV:** 100, 115

Sea–King's Daughter and *Eureka!, The* (Brown), **Supp. VI:** 71–73

"Seals at High Island" (Murphy), **Supp. V:** 324

"Sea–Mists of the Winter, The" (Lewis), **VII:** 84

"Seamless Garment, The" (MacDiarmid), **Supp. XII:** 211–212, 213

Sean O'Casey: The Man Behind the Plays (Cowasjee), **VII:** 4

Search, The (Snow), **VII:** 321–322, 323–324

"Search, The" (Vaughan), **VII:** 187

"Search After Happiness, The" (Brontë), **V:** 110

Search After Sunrise: A Traveller's Story (Brittain), **Supp. X:** 46

"Seaside Walk, A" (Browning), **IV:** 313

Season at Sarsaparilla, The (White), **Supp. I:** 131, 149

Season in Purgatory (Keneally), **Supp. IV:** 346

Season Songs (Hughes), **Supp. I:** 357–359; **Retro. Supp. II:** 208–209

Seasonable Counsel; or, Advice to Sufferers (Bunyan), **II:** 253

Season's Greetings (Ayckbourn), **Supp. V:** 3, 10, 13, 14

"Seasons, The" (Thomas), **Supp. XII:** 290

Seasons, The (Thomson), **Supp. III:** 409, 410, 411, **412–419,** 420, 428; **Retro. Supp. I:** 241

"Seated Woman" (Hart), **Supp. XI:** 123

"Sea–watching" (Thomas), **Supp. XII:** 288

Sebald, W. G., **VIII: 295–309**

Sebastian (Durrell), **Supp. I:** 120

Seccombe, Thomas, **V:** 425, 437

Second Angel, The (Kerr), **Supp. XII:** 187, 194, 195–197

"Second Best, The" (Arnold), **V:** 209

"Second Best" (Brooke), **Supp. III:** 49

Second Book of Odes (Bunting), **Supp. VII:** 13–14

Second Brother, The (Beddoes), **Supp. XI:** 22, 23

"Second Coming, The" (Yeats), **VI:** xiv; **Retro. Supp. I:** 332–333

Second Curtain, The (Fuller), **Supp. VII:** 71, 72, 81

Second Defence of the People of England, The (Milton), **II:** 164; **Retro. Supp. II:** 270

Second Epistle of the Second Book (Pope), **Retro. Supp. I:** 230

Second Funeral of Napoleon, The (Thackeray), **V:** 22, 38

"Second Hand Clothes" (Dunn), **Supp. X:** 74

"Second Hut, The" (Lessing), **Supp. I:** 240–241

Second Journal to Eliza, The, **III:** 135

Second Jungle Book, The (Kipling), **VI:** 204

Second Life, The (Morgan, E.), **Supp. IX:** 158, 159, 163–168

"Second Life, The" (Morgan, E.), **Supp. IX:** 165

Second Maiden's Tragedy, The (Middleton), **II:** 2, 3, **8–10,** 21

Second Mrs. Tanqueray, The (Pinero), **V:** 413

Second Nun's Tale, The (Chaucer), **I:** 31, 34, 43

"Second Opinion" (Dunn), **Supp. X:** 76

Second Part of Conny–Catching, The (Greene), **VIII:** 144–145

Second Part of Mr. Waller's Poems, The (Waller), **II:** 238

Second Part of Pilgrim's Progress, The (T. S.), **II:** 248

Second Part of the Bloody Conquests of Mighty Tamburlaine, The (Marlowe), *see Tamburlaine, Part 2*

Second Part of The Rover, The (Behn), **Supp. III:** 27

2nd Poems (Graham), **Supp. VII:** 109–110

Second Satire (Wyatt), **I:** 111

Second Sex, The (Beauvoir), **Supp. IV:** 232

"Second Sight" (Longley), **VIII:** 173

Second Treatise on Government (Locke), **Supp. III:** 33

"Second Visit, A" (Warner), **Supp. VII:** 380

Second World War (Churchill), **VI:** 359–360

Secord, Arthur Wellesley, **III:** 41

"Secret Agent, The" (Auden), **Retro. Supp. I:** 3

Secret Agent (Conrad), **Supp. IV:** 1

Secret Agent, The (Conrad), **VI: 143–144,** 148; **Retro. Supp. II:** 80–81

Secret Brother, The (Jennings), **Supp. V:** 216

Secret Dispatches from Arabia (Lawrence), **Supp. II:** 295

"Secret Garden, The" (Kinsella), **Supp. V:** 263

Secret Glass, The (Bainbridge), **Supp. VI:** 20

Secret History of the Present Intrigues of the Court of Caramania, The (Haywood), **Supp. XII:** 141

Secret History of the White Staff, The, . . . (Defoe), **III:** 13

"Secret History of World War 3, The" (Ballard), **Supp. V:** 33

Secret Ladder, The (Harris), **Supp. V:** 132, 135, 139

Secret Lives (Ngũgĩ), **VIII:** 220

Secret Love; or, The Maiden Queen (Dryden), **II:** 305

Secret Narratives (Motion), **Supp. VII:** 255–256, 257, 263

Secret of Father Brown, The (Chesterton), **VI:** 338

Secret Pilgrim, The (le Carré), **Supp. II:** 319

Secret Rapture, The (Hare), **Supp. IV:** 282, 292, 293–294, 296

Secret Rose (Yeats), **VI:** 222

"Secret Sharer, The" (Conrad), **VI: 145–147**

"Secret Sharer, The" (Gunn), **Supp. IV:** 256, 259

Secret Villages (Dunn), **Supp. X:** 67–68

Secret Water (Ransome), **Supp. I:** 68

Secrets (Davies), **Supp. XI:** 100

"Section 28" (Morgan, E.), **Supp. IX:** 160

"Secular, The" (Wallace–Crabbe), **VIII:** 315

Secular Lyrics of the XIVth and XVth Centuries (Robbins), **I:** 40

"Secular Masque, The" (Dryden), **II:** 289, 290, 305, 325

"Sedge–Warblers" (Thomas), **Supp. III:** 406

Sedley, Sir Charles, **II:** 255, 261, **263–266,** 271

"Seductio ad Absurdam" (Lowry), **Supp. III:** 285

"Seed Growing Secretly, The" (Vaughan), **II:** 189

Seed of Chaos: What Mass Bombing Really Means (Brittain), **Supp. X:** 45

"Seed Picture, The" (McGuckian), **Supp. V:** 281, 285

Seeing Things (Heaney), **Retro. Supp. I:** 124, 131–132

Seek and Find (Rossetti), **V:** 260

"Seers" (Blunden), **Supp. XI:** 34

"Seesaw" (Gunn), **Supp. IV:** 275–276

Seicentismo e Marinismo in Inghilterra (Praz), **II:** 123

Sejanus (Jonson), **I:** 235, 242, 249, 345–346; **Retro. Supp. I:** 161, 164

Select British Poets; or, New Elegant Extracts from Chaucer to the Present Time (Hazlitt), **IV:** 139

Select Collection of Original Scottish Airs (Thomson), **III:** 322

"Select Meditations" (Traherne), **Supp. XI:** 264, 265, 266

Select Poets of Great Britain (Hazlitt), **IV:** 139

Selected Essays of Cyril Connolly, The (ed. Quennell), **Supp. III:** 107

Selected Letters of Edwin Muir (Muir), **Supp. VI:** 203

Selected Life, A (Kinsella), **Supp. V:** 267

Selected Plays [of Lady Gregory] (ed. Coxhead), **VI:** 317

Selected Poems (Adcock), **Supp. XII:** 8

Selected Poems (Armitage), **VIII:** 1–2

Selected Poems (Gunn and Hughes), **Supp. IV:** 257

Selected Poems (Harrison), **Supp. V:** 150, 157, 160

Selected Poems (Hope), **Supp. VII:** 156, 159

Selected Poems (Hughes), **Supp. I: 364–365**

Selected Poems (Mahon), **Supp. VI:** 166–167, 169–174Selected Poems (Mahon), Supp. VI: 166–167, 169–174

Selected Poems (Muldoon), **Supp. IV:** 413

Selected Poems (Murray), **Supp. VII:** 270

Selected Poems (Plomer), **Supp. XI:** 223

Selected Poems (Smith), **Supp. II:** 463

Selected Poems (Russell), **VIII:** 292

Selected Poems (Spender), **Supp. II:** 486, 489

Selected Poems (Stevenson), **Supp. VI:** 256, 261–263

Selected Poems (D.M. Thomas), **Supp. IV:** 490, 494

Selected Poems (R.S. Thomas), **Supp. XII:** 282

Selected Poems of Boris Pasternak (tr. Stallworthy), **Supp. X:** 292

Selected Poems of Edward Thomas (ed. Thomas), **Supp. XII:** 282

Selected Poems of Fulke Greville (Greville), **Supp. XI:** 105, 109, 114, 116

Selected Poems of Malcolm Lowry (tr. Birney), **Supp. III:** 282

Selected Poems 1954–1992 (Brown), **Supp. VI:** 70–72

Selected Poems 1956–1994 (Wallace–Crabbe), **VIII:** 311, 312, 313, 314, 315, 317, 318, 319, 320

Selected Poems, 1959–1989 (Malouf), **Supp. XII:** 220

Selected Poems 1964–1983 (Dunn), **Supp. X:** 69

Selected Poems 1976–1997 (Motion), **Supp. VII:** 252, 257

Selected Prose (Housman), **VI:** 154

Selected Speeches (Disraeli), **IV:** 308

Selected Stories (Friel), **Supp. V:** 113

Selected Stories (Gordimer), **Supp. II:** 231, 232, 234, 242

Selected Stories (Plomer), **Supp. XI:** 223

"Selected Translations" (Sisson), **Supp. XI:** 248

Selected Writings of Fulke Greville (Greville), **Supp. XI:** 105, 117

Selection of Kipling's Verse (Eliot), **VI:** 202

Self, Will, **Supp. IV:** 26; **Supp. V: 395–408**

Self and Self–Management (Bennett), **VI:** 264

Self Condemned (Lewis), **VII:** 74, 81–82

"Self Justification" (Harrison), **Supp. V:** 155–156

Self Portrait (Kavanagh), **Supp. VII:** 197–198

"Self Portrait: Nearing Sixty" (Waugh), **Supp. VI:** 276

"Selfish Giant, The" (Wilde), **Retro. Supp. II:** 365

"Self–Release" (Kinsella), **Supp. V:** 270

"Self–Renewal" (Kinsella), **Supp. V:** 270

"Self–Scrutiny" (Kinsella), **Supp. V:** 270

"Self–Unseeing, The" (Hardy), **VI:** 13; **Retro. Supp. I:** 118

"Self's the Man" (Larkin), **Supp. I:** 281

Selimus, **I:** 220

Seltzer, David, **III:** 343, 345

"Selves" (Gunn), **Supp. IV:** 272

Selvon, Samuel, **Supp. IV:** 445

"Semi–Monde," (Coward), **Supp. II:** 146

"Semiology and Rhetoric" (de Man), **Supp. IV:** 114

Señor Vivo and the Coca Lord (De Bernières), **Supp. XII:** 65, 70, 72–73

"Send–Off, The" (Owen), **VI:** 447, 452

Seneca, **I:** 214–215; **II:** 25, 28, 71, 97

"Sensation Novels" (Oliphant), **Supp. X:** 221

Sense and Sensibility (Austen), **III:** 91, 336; **IV:** xvii, 108, 109, 111, 112, **114–122**; **Retro. Supp. II:** 6–7

Sense of Detachment, A (Osborne), **Supp. I:** 339

Sense of Movement, The (Gunn), **Supp. IV:** 257, 259–262

Sense of the Past, The (James), **VI:** 64–65

Sense of the World, A (Jennings), **Supp. V:** 210, 212, 214

"Sensitive Plant, The" (Shelley), **IV:** 203

"Sentence, The" (tr. McKane), **Supp. IV:** 494–495

"Sentence, The" (tr. Thomas), **Supp. IV:** 494–495

"Sentimental Blues" (Ewart), **Supp. VII:** 36

"Sentimental Education, The" (Ewart), **Supp. VII:** 40

Sentimental Journey, A (Sterne), **III:** 124, 127, 132–134, 135

Sentimental Tommy (Barrie), **Supp. III:** 3

Sentiments of a Church–of–England Man, The (Swift), **III:** 26

"Sentry, The" (Owen), **VI:** 448, 451

Separate Saga of St Óláfr, The, **VIII:** 235

Separate Tables: Table by the Window and Table Number Seven (Rattigan), **Supp. VII:** 313, 318–319

"Sephestia's Song to Her Child" (Greene), **VIII:** 143

"September 1, 1939" (Auden), **Retro. Supp. I:** 10, **Retro. Supp. I:** 14

"September Soliloquy" (Cornford), **VIII:** 114

"September Song" (Hill), **Supp. V:** 187

September Tide (du Maurier), **Supp. III:** 143

"Sepulchre" (Herbert), **II:** 128

Sequence for Francis Parkman, A (Davie), **Supp. VI:** 108–109, 115

"Sequence in Hospital" (Jennings), **Supp. V:** 214

Sequence of Sonnets on the Death of Robert Browning, A (Swinburne), **V:** 333

Serafino Aquilano, **I:** 103, 105, 110

"Seraph and the Zambesi, The," (Spark), **Supp. I:** 199

"Seraphim, The" (Browning), **IV:** 312, 313

Seraphim, The, and Other Poems (Browning), **IV:** xix, 311, 312–313, 321

"Serenade" (Sitwell), **VII:** 135

Sergeant Lamb (Graves), **VII:** 258

Serious and Pathetical Contemplation of the Mercies of God, in Several Most Devout and Sublime Thanksgivings for the Same, A (Traherne), **II:** 201; **Supp. XI:** 274–276

Serious Concerns (Cope), **VIII:** 67, 69, 75–79

Serious Money (Churchill), **Supp. IV:** 179, 180, 184, 192–195, 198

Serious Reflections During . . . A Robinson Crusoe" (Defoe), **III:** 12, 13; **Retro. Supp. I:** 71

Serjeant Musgrave's Dance (Arden), **Supp. II: 25–28,** 29, 30, 35, 38

"Sermon, The" (Redgrove), **Supp. VI:** 228–229, 232, 235, 237

Sermon Preached at Pauls Crosse, the 25. Of November. 1621, A (King), **Supp. VI:** 152

"Sermon to Our Later Prodigal Son" (Meredith), **V:** 223

Sermons (Donne), **I:** 364–366; **II:** 142; **Retro. Supp. II:** 96

Sermons: An Exposition upon the Lord's Prayer (King), **Supp. VI:** 152, 155, 158, 161

Sermons and Devotional Writings of Gerard Manley Hopkins, The (ed. Devlin), **V:** 372, 381

Sermons, Chiefly on the Theory of Religious Belief, Preached Before the University of Oxford (Newman), **Supp. VII:** 296

"Serpent–Charm, The" (Gissing), **V:** 437

Servant, The (Pinter), **Supp. I:** 374; **Retro. Supp. I:** 226

"Servant Boy" (Heaney), **Retro. Supp. I:** 128

"Servant Girl Speaks, A" (Lawrence), **VII:** 118

"Servants' Quarters, The" (Hardy), **Retro. Supp. I:** 121

"Serving Maid, The" (Kinsella), **Supp. V:** 263

Sesame and Lilies (Ruskin), **V:** 180, 184

"Session of the Poets, A" (Suckling), **II:** 229

"Sestina of the Tramp Royal" (Kipling), **VI:** 202, 203

Set in Darkness (Rankin), **Supp. X:** 245, 255–256

Set of Six, A (Conrad), **VI:** 148

Seth, Vikram, **Supp. X: 277–290**

Seton, Ernest Thempson, **Supp. IV:** 158

"Setteragic On" (Warner), **Supp. VII:** 380

Setting the World on Fire (Wilson), **Supp. I:** 165–166

"Settlers" (Adcock), **Supp. XII:** 8

"Seven Ages, The" (Auden), **Retro. Supp. I:** 11

Seven at a Stroke (Fry), **Supp. III:** 194

Seven Cardinal Virtues, The (ed. Fell), **Supp. XI:** 163

"Seven Conjectural Readings" (Warner), **Supp. VII:** 373

Seven Days in the New Crete (Graves), **VII:** 259

Seven Deadly Sins, The (ed. Fell), **Supp. XI:** 163

"Seven Deadly Sins: A Mask, The" (Nye), **Supp. X:** 202

"Seven Good Germans" (Henderson), **VII:** 426

Seven Journeys, The (Graham), **Supp. VII:** 111

Seven Lamps of Architecture, The (Ruskin), **V:** xxi, 176, 184

Seven Lectures on Shakespeare and Milton (Coleridge), **IV:** 56

"Seven Letters" (Graham), **Supp. VII:** 111

Seven Men (Beerbohm), **Supp. II:** 55–56

Seven Men and Two Others (Beerbohm), **Supp. II:** 55

Seven Men of Vision: An Appreciation (Jennings), **Supp. V:** 217

"7, Middagh Street" (Muldoon), **Supp. IV:** 411, 422, 424

Seven Pillars of Wisdom (Lawrence), **VI:** 408; **Supp. II:** 283, 284, 285, 286, **287–291**

"Seven Poets, The" (Brown), **Supp. VI:** 69

Seven Poor Men of Sydney (Stead), **Supp. IV:** 461–464

"Seven Rocks, The" (Nicholson), **Supp. VI: 216–217**

"Seven Sages, The" (Yeats), **Supp. II:** 84–85

Seven Seas, The (Kipling), **VI:** 204

Seven Short Plays (Gregory), **VI:** 315

Seven Types of Ambiguity (Empson), **I:** 282; **II:** 124, 130; **VII:** 260; **Supp.** 179, 180, 183, **185–189,** 190, 197

Seven Winters (Bowen), **Supp. II:** 77–78, 91

Seven Women (Barrie), **Supp. III:** 5

Sevenoaks Essays (Sisson), **Supp. XI:** 249, 256

"1740" (Kinsella), **Supp. V:** 271

"1738" (Stallworthy), **Supp. X:** 297

Seventh Man: Migrant Workers in Europe, A (Berger), **Supp. IV:** 79

Several Perceptions (Carter), **Supp. III:** 80, 81, 82–83

"Several Questions Answered" (Blake), **III:** 293

Severed Head, A (Murdoch), **Supp. I:** 215, 224, 225, 228

Severn and Somme (Gurney), **VI:** 425

"Sewage Pipe Pool, The" (Nye), **Supp. X:** 203

"Sex That Doesn't Shop, The" (Saki), **Supp. VI:** 246

Sexing the Cherry (Winterson), **Supp. IV:** 541, 542, 545, 547, 549, 552, 554, 556, 557

"Sexton's Hero, The" (Gaskell), **V:** 15

Sexual Politics (Millett), **Supp. IV:** 188

Seymour–Smith, Martin, **VII:** xviii, xxxviii

Shabby Genteel Story, A (Thackeray), **V:** 21, 35, 37

"Shack, The" (Cameron), **Supp. IX:** 27

Shade Those Laurels (Connolly), **Supp. III:** 111–112

Shadow Dance (Carter), **III:** 345; **Supp. III:** 79, 80, 81, 89

Shadow of a Gunman, The (O'Casey), **VI:** 316; **VII:** xviii, 3–4, 6, 12

"Shadow of Black Combe, The" (Nicholson), **Supp. VI:** 218

Shadow of Cain, The (Sitwell), **VII:** xvii, 137

Shadow of Dante, A (Rossetti), **V:** 253n

Shadow of Hiroshima, The (Harrison), **Supp. V:** 164

Shadow of Night (Chapman), **I:** 234, 237

Shadow of the Glen, The (Synge), **VI:** 308, 309, 310, 316

Shadow of the Sun, The (Byatt), **Supp. IV:** 140, 141, 142–143, 147, 148, 149, 155

Shadow Play (Coward), **Supp. II:** 152–153

"Shadow Suite" (Brathwaite), **Supp. XII:** 35

Shadow–Line, The: A Confession (Conrad), **VI:** 135, 146–147, 148

"Shadows" (Lawrence), **VII:** 119

"Shadows in the Water" (Traherne), **II:** 192; **Supp. XI:** 269

Shadows of Ecstasy (Williams, C. W. S.), **Supp. IX:** 279–280

Shadows of the Evening (Coward), **Supp. II:** 156

Shadowy Waters, The (Yeats), **VI:** 218, 222

Shadwell, Thomas, **I:** 327; **II:** 305, 359

"Shadwell Stair" (Owen), **VI:** 451

Shaffer, Anthony, **Supp. I:** 313

Shaffer, Peter, **Supp. I: 313–328**

Shaftesbury, earl of, **Supp. III:** 424

Shaftesbury, seventh earl of, **IV:** 62

Shaftesbury, third earl of, **III:** 44, 46, 198

Shahnameh (Persian epic), **Supp. IV:** 439

Shakes Versus Shav (Shaw), **VI:** 130

Shakespear, Olivia, **VI:** 210, 212, 214

Shakespeare, William, **I:** 188, **295–334; II:** 87, 221, 281, 302; **III:** 115–117; **IV:** 149, 232, 352; **V:** 41, 328; and Collins, **IV:** 165, 165n, 170; and Jonson, **I:** 335–337, **II:** 281; **Retro. Supp. I:** 158, 165; and Kyd, **I:** 228–229; and Marlowe, **I:** 275–279, 286; and Middleton, **IV:** 79–80; and Webster, **II:** 71–72, 74–75, 79; influence on English literature, **II:** 29, 42–43, 47, 48, 54–55, 79, 82, 84; **III:** 115–116, 167n; **IV:** 35, 51–52; **V:** 405; **Supp. I:** 196, 227; **Supp. II:** 193, 194; **Supp. IV:** 158, 171, 283, 558

Shakespeare (Swinburne), **V:** 333

"Shakespeare and Stage Costume" (Wilde), **V:** 407

Shakespeare and the Allegory of Evil (Spivack), **I:** 214

Shakespeare and the Goddess of Complete Being (Hughes), **Retro. Supp. II:** 202

Shakespeare and the Idea of the Play (Righter), **I:** 224

"Shakespeare and the Stoicism of Seneca" (Eliot), **I:** 275

"Shakespeare as a Man" (Stephen), **V:** 287

Shakespeare Wallah (Jhabvala), **Supp. V:** 237–238

Shakespeare's Sonnets Reconsidered (Butler), **Supp. II:** 116

Shall I Call Thee Bard: A Portrait of Jason Strugnell (Cope), **VIII:** 69

Shall We Join the Ladies? (Barrie), **Supp. III:** 6, 9, 16–17

"Shamdev; The Wolf–Boy" (Chatwin), **Supp. IV:** 157

Shame (Rushdie), **Supp. IV:** 116, 433, 436, 440, 443, 444–445, 448, 449

Shamela (Fielding), **III:** 84, 98, 105; **Retro. Supp. I:** 80; **Retro. Supp. I:** 82–83

Shape of Things to Come, The (Wells), **VI:** 228, 241

"Shape–Changer, The" (Wallace–Crabbe), **VIII:** 318–319

"Shapes and Shadows" (Mahon), **Supp. VI:** 178

SHAR: Hurricane Poem (Brathwaite), **Supp. XII:** 35–36

Sharawaggi: Poems in Scots (Crawford and Herbert), **Supp. XI:** 67–71, 72

Shards of Memory (Jhabvala), **Supp. V:** 233, 234–235

"Sharp Trajectories" (Davie), **Supp. VI:** 116

Sharp, William, **IV:** 370

Sharpeville Sequence (Bond), **Supp. I:** 429

Sharrock, Roger, **II:** 246, 254

Shaving of Shagpat, The (Meredith), **V:** 225, 234

Shaw, George Bernard, **III:** 263; **V:** xxii, xxv, xxvi, 284, 301, 305–306, 423, 433; **VI:** viii, ix, xiv–xv, **101–132,** 147, 343; **Supp. II:** 24, 45, 51, 54, 55, 117–118, 288, 296–297; **Supp. III:** 6; **Supp. IV:** 233, 288, 292; **Retro. Supp. II: 309–325**

Shaw Gives Himself Away: An Autobiographical Miscellany (Shaw), **VI:** 129

Shaw–Stewart, Patrick, **VI:** 418–419, 420

She (Haggard), **Supp. III:** 211, 212, 213, 219–222, 223–227

She Stoops to Conquer (Goldsmith), **II:** 362; **III:** 177, 181, 183, 188, 191, 256

She Wou'd if She Cou'd (Etherege), **II:** 266, 268, 271

Sheaf of Verses, A (Hall), **Supp. VI:** 119

"Sheep" (Hughes), **Retro. Supp. II:** 209

Sheep and the Dog, The (Henryson), **Supp. VII:** 136, 138–139, 141

"Sheepdog Trials in Hyde Park" (Day Lewis), **Supp. III:** 130

"Sheer Edge" (Malouf), **Supp. XII:** 219

"She's all my fancy painted him" (Carroll), **V:** 264

Shelf Life (Powell), **Supp. IV:** 258

Shelley, Mary Wollstonecraft, **III: 329–331,** 336, 341, 342, 345; **IV:** xvi, xvii, 118, 197, 201, 202, 203; **Supp. III: 355–373,** 385; **Supp. IV:** 546; **Retro. Supp. I:** 246

Shelley, Percy Bysshe, **II:** 102, 200; **III:** 329, 330, 333, 336–338; **IV:** vii–xii, 63, 132 158–159, 161, 163, 164, 168–169, l72, 176–179, 182, **195–210,** 217, 234, 281, 299, 349, 354, 357, 366, 372; **V:** 214, 330, 401, 403; **VI:** 453; **Supp. III:** 355, 357–358, 364–365, 370; **Supp. IV:** 468; **Retro. Supp. I: 243–257**

Shelley (Swinburne), **V:** 333

Shelley (Thompson), **V:** 450, 451

Shelley: A Life Story (Blunden), **IV:** 210

Shelley and Keats as They Struck Their Contemporaries (Blunden), **IV:** 210

Shelley's Idols of the Cave (Butler), **IV:** 210

"Shelley's Skylark" (Hardy), **Retro. Supp. I:** 119

Shells by a Stream (Blunden), **Supp. XI:** 37

Shelmalier (McGuckian), **Supp. V:** 280, 290–292

"Shelmalier" (McGuckian), **Supp. V:** 291

Shelter, The (Phillips), **Supp. V:** 380

Shepheardes Calendar (Spenser), *see Shepherd's Calendar, The*

Shepheard's Oracles, The (Quarles), **II:** 139

Shepherd, Ettrick, *see* Hogg, James

Shepherd, and Other Poems of Peace and War, The (Blunden), **Supp. XI:** 36, 42

"Shepherd and the Nymph, The" (Landor), **IV:** 96

Shepherd of the Giant Mountains, The (tr. Smedley), **V**: 265

"Shepherd's Brow, The" (Hopkins), **V**: 376, 378n

Shepherd's Calendar, The (Spenser), **I**: 97, 121, 123, 124–128, 162

Shepherd's Calendar, The; with Village Stories, and Other Poems (Clare), **Supp. XI**: 59

"Shepherd's Carol" (Nicholson), **Supp. VI**: 214–215

Shepherd's Life, A (Hudson), **V**: 429

Shepherd's Week, The (Gay), **III**: 55, 56, 67

Sheppey (Maugham), **VI**: 377

Sherburn, George, **III**: 73, 78

Sheridan, Richard Brinsley, **II**: 334, 336; **III**: 32, 97, 101, **252–271**

Sheridan, Susan, **Supp. IV**: 459

"Sherthursdaye and Venus Day" (Jones), **Supp. VII**: 177

Shewan, R., **V**: 409n, 421

Shewing of a Vision, The (Julian of Norwich), **Supp. XII**: 155

Shewings of the Lady Julian, The (Julian of Norwich), **Supp. XII**: 155

Shewing-Up of Blanco Posnet, The: A Sermon in Crude Melodrama (Shaw), **VI**: 115, 117, 124, 129

"Shian Bay" (Graham), **Supp. VII**: 110–111

"Shield of Achilles, The" (Auden), **VII**: 388, 390–391, 397–398; **Retro. Supp. I**: 10

Shikasta (Lessing), **Supp. I**: 250, 251, 252, 253

Shining, The (King), **III**: 345

"Shining Gift, The" (Wallace–Crabbe), **VIII**: 323

"Ship of The Wind, The" (Longley), **VIII**: 175

"Ship That Found Herself, The" (Kipling), **VI**: 170

Shipman's Tale, The (Chaucer), **I**: 36

"Ships" (Dunn), **Supp. X**: 70

Shipwreck (Fowles), **Supp. I**: 292

Shipwrecked, The (Greene), *see England Made Me*

Shires, The (Davie), **Supp. VI**: 111–112

Shirley, James, **II**: 44, 66, 87

Shirley (Brontë), **V**: xxi, 12, 106, 112, **145–147**, 152; **Retro. Supp. I**: 53, 54, 60

Shirley Sanz (Pritchett), **Supp. III**: 313

Shrimp and the Anemone, The (Hartley), **Supp. VII**: 119, 124–125

"Shoals Returning, The" (Kinsella), **Supp. V**: 263

Shoemaker of Merano, The (Hall), **Supp. VI**: 130

Shoemaker's Holiday, The (Dekker), **II**: 89

"Shooting an Elephant" (Orwell), **VII**: 273, 276, 282

Shooting Niagara—'nd After? (Carlyle), **IV**: xxii, 240, 247, 250

"Shore Road, The" (MacCaig), **Supp. VI**: 187, 195

Short Account of a Late Short Administration, A (Burke), **III**: 205

Short Character of . . . [the Earl of Wharton], A (Swift), **III**: 35

Short Historical Essay . . . , A (Marvell), **II**: 219

"Short History of British India, A" (Hill), **Supp. V**: 191

"Short History of the English Novel, A" (Self), **Supp. V**: 403

Short History of the English People (Green), **VI**: 390

Short Stories, Scraps, and Shavings (Shaw), **VI**: 129

short story, **VI**: 369–370; **VII**: xvii, 178–181

"Short Story, The" (Bowen), **Supp. II**: 86

Short View of the Immorality and Profaneness of the English Stage, A (Collier), **II**: 303, 325, 338, 340, 356; **III**: 44

Short View of the State of Ireland, A (Swift), **III**: 28, 35; **Retro. Supp. I**: 276

*Short Vindication of A*The Relapse"and A*The Provok'd Wife,"A, . . . by the Author* (Vanbrugh), **II**: 332, 336

Shortened History of England, A (Trevelyan), **VI**: 395

Shorter, Clement, **V**: 150, 151–153

Shorter Finnegans Wake, A (Burgess), **Supp. I**: 197

Shorter Poems (Bridges), **VI**: 72, 73, 81

Shortest Way to Peace and Union, The (Defoe), **III**: 13

Shortest Way with the Dissenters, The (Defoe), **III**: 2, 3, 12–13; **Retro. Supp. I**: 64–65, 67

"Shot, The" (Jennings), **Supp. V**: 210

Shot, The (Kerr), **Supp. XII**: 194–195

"Shot Down over Libya" (Dahl), **Supp. IV**: 202, 207–208, 209

Shot in the Park, A (Plomer), **Supp. XI**: 222

"Should lanterns shine" (Thomas), **Supp. I**: 174

Shoulder of Shasta, The (Stoker), **Supp. III**: 381

Shout, The (Graves), **VII**: 259

"Show me, dear Christ, thy spouse" (Donne), **I**: 367, 368

"Show Saturday" (Larkin), **Supp. I**: 283, 285

Shrapnel Academy, The (Weldon), **Supp. IV**: 529–530, 531

Shropshire Lad, A (Housman), **VI**: ix, xv, 157, 158–160, 164

Shroud for a Nightingale (James), **Supp. IV**: 319, 320, 323, 326–327

"Shrove Tuesday in Paris" (Thackeray), **V**: 22, 38

Shuttlecock (Swift), **Supp. V**: 429–431

"Sibylla Palmifera" (Rossetti), **V**: 237

Sibylline Leaves (Coleridge), **IV**: 56

"Sibyl's Prophecy, The", *See Voluspá*

"Sic Tydingis Hard I at the Sessioun" (Dunbar), **VIII**: 122

"Sic Vita" (King), **Supp. VI**: 162

Sicilian Carousel (Durrell), **Supp. I**: 102

Sicilian Romance, A (Radcliffe), **III**: 338

"Sick King in Bokhara, The" (Arnold), **V**: 210

Sidgwick, Henry, **V**: 284, 285

Sidhwa, Bapsi, **Supp. V**: 62

Sidley, Sir Charles, *see* Sedley, Sir Charles

Sidney, Sir Philip, **I**: 123, **160–175**; **II**: 46, 48, 53, 80, 158, 221, 339; **III**: 95; **Retro. Supp. I**: 157; **Retro. Supp. II**: **327–342**

Siege (Fry), **Supp. III**: 194

Siege of Corinth, The (Byron), **IV**: 172, 192; *see also* Turkish tales

Siege of London, The (James), **VI**: 67

Siege of Pevensey, The (Burney), **Supp. III**: 71

Siege of Thebes, The (Lydgate), **I**: 57, 61, 65

"Siena" (Swinburne), **V**: 325, 332

"Sierra Nevada" (Stevenson), **Supp. VI**: 254–255

"Siesta of a Hungarian Snake" (Morgan, E.), **Supp. IX**: 166

"Sigh, A" (Finch), **Supp. IX**: 67–68

"Sighs and Grones" (Herbert), **II**: 128

Sight for Sore Eyes, A (Rendell), **Supp. IX**: 195, 200–201

Sign of Four, The (Doyle), **Supp. II**: 160, 162–163, 164–165, 167, 171, 173, 176

Sign of the Cross, The (Barrett), **VI**: 124

Signal Driver (White), **Supp. I**: 131, 151

"Signpost, The" (Thomas), **Supp. III**: 403, 404

"Signs" (Stevenson), **Supp. VI**: 263

Signs of Change (Morris), **V**: 306

"Signs of the Times" (Carlyle), **IV**: 241–242, 243, 249, 324; **V**: viii

Sigurd the Volsung (Morris), *see Story of Sigurd the Volsung and the Fall of the Niblungs, The*

Silas Marner (Eliot), **V**: xxii, 194, 200; **Retro. Supp. II**: 108–110

"Silecroft Shore" (Nicholson), **Supp. VI**: 216

Silence (Pinter), **Supp. I**: 376

"Silence" (Traherne), **Supp. XI**: 270

Silence Among the Weapons (Arden), **Supp. II**: 41

Silence in the Garden, The (Trevor), **Supp. IV**: 505, 506, 515–516, 517

"Silent One, The" (Gurney), **VI**: 427

Silent Passenger, The (Sayers), **Supp. III**: 335

"Silent Voices, The" (Tennyson), **IV**: 329

Silent Voices: An Anthology of Romanian Women Poets (tr. Deletant and Walker), **Supp. XII**: 11

Silent Woman, The (Jonson), **Retro. Supp. I**: 163

Silex Scintillans: . . . (Vaughan), **II**: 184, 185, 186, 201

Sillitoe, Alan, **Supp. V**: **409–426**

Silmarillion, The (Tolkien), **Supp. II**: 519, 520, 521, 525, 527

Silver, Brenda, **Retro. Supp. I**: 305

"Silver Blaze" (Doyle), **Supp. II**: 167

Silver Box, The (Galsworthy), **VI**: 273, 284–285

Silver Bucket, The (Orton), **Supp. V**: 364

Silver Chair, The (Lewis), **Supp. III**: 248

Silver Circus (Coppard), **VIII:** 96–97

"Silver Crucifix on My Desk, A" (Hart), **Supp. XI:** 127–128

Silver Spoon, The (Galsworthy), **VI:** 275

Silver Stair, The (Williams, C. W. S.), **Supp. IX:** 273, 274

Silver Tassie, The (O'Casey), **VII:** 6–7

Silverado Squatters, The (Stevenson), **V:** 386, 395; **Retro. Supp. I:** 262

"Silvia" (Etherege), **II:** 267

Simenon, Georges, **III:** 341

Simisola (Rendell), **Supp. IX:** 196, 198–199

Simmons, Ernest, **V:** 46

Simmons, James, **Supp. IV:** 412

"Simon Lee" (Wordsworth), **IV:** 7, 8–9, 10

Simonetta Perkins (Hartley), **Supp. VII:** 122–123, 126

Simonidea (Landor), **IV:** 100

Simple and Religious Consultation (Bucer), **I:** 177

"Simple Simon" (Coppard), **VIII:** 97

"Simple Susan" (Edgeworth), **Supp. III:** 153

Simpleton of the Unexpected Isles, The (Shaw), **VI:** 125, 126, 127, 129

"Simplicities" (Wallace–Crabbe), **VIII:** 324–325

Simplicity (Collins), **III:** 166

"Simplify Me When I'm Dead" (Douglas), **VII:** 440

Simpson, Alan, **Supp. II:** 68, 70, 74

Simpson, Percy, **I:** 279

Simpson, Richard, **IV:** 107, 122

"Simultaneous Translation" (Crawford), **Supp. XI:** 73

Sinai Sort, The (MacCaig), **Supp. VI:** **186–187**

"Since thou, O fondest and truest" (Bridges), **VI:** 74, 77

"Sincerest Critick of My Prose, or Rhime" (Congreve), **II:** 349

"Sindhi Woman" (Stallworthy), **Supp. X:** 293

Singer, S. W., **III:** 69

"Singing, 1977" (Fuller), **Supp. VII:** 79

Singing Detective, The (Potter, D.), **Supp. X:** 229

Singing School: The Making of a Poet (Stallworthy), **Supp. X:** 291–292, 301–303

Singing the Sadness (Hill, R.), **Supp. IX:** 123

Single Man, A (Isherwood), **VII:** 309, 316–317

Singleton's Law (Hill), see *Albion! Albion!*

Sing–Song (Rossetti), **V:** 251, 255, 260

Singular Preference, The (Quennell), **VI:** 237, 245

Sinjohn, John, pseud. of John Galsworthy

Sins of the Fathers and Other Tales (Gissing), **V:** 437

Sir Charles Grandison (Richardson), **III:** 80, 90–91, 92; **IV:** 124

"Sir David Brewster Invents the Kaleidoscope" (Crawford), **Supp. XI:** 71

"Sir Dominick Ferrand" (James), **VI:** 69

"Sir Edmund Orme" (James), **VI:** 69

"Sir Eustace Grey" (Crabbe), **III:** 282

"Sir Galahad and the Islands" (Brathwaite), **Supp. XII:** 43

Sir Gawain and the Carl of Carlisle, **I:** 71

Sir Gawain and the Green Knight, (Gawain–Poet), **I:** 2, 28, 69, 71; **Supp. VII:** 83, 84–91, 94, 98

Sir George Otto Trevelyan: A Memoir (Trevelyan), **VI:** 383, 391

Sir Harry Hotspur of Humblethwaite (Trollope), **V:** 100, 102

Sir Harry Wildair, Being the Sequel of AThe Trip to the Jubilee" (Farquhar), **II:** 352, 357, 364

Sir Hornbook; or, Childe Launcelot's Expedition (Peacock), **IV:** 169

Sir John Vanbrugh's Justificahon of . . . the Duke of Marlborough's Late Tryal (Vanbrugh), **II:** 336

Sir Launcelot Greaves (Smollett), **III:** 149, 153, 158

Sir Martin Mar–All; or, The Feign'd Innocence (Dryden), **II:** 305

Sir Nigel (Doyle), **Supp. II:** 159

Sir Proteus, a Satirical Ballad (Peacock), **IV:** 169

Sir Thomas More; or, Colloquies on the Progress and Prospects of Society (Southey), **IV:** 69, 70, 71, 280

Sir Thomas Wyatt (Dekker and Webster), **II:** 68

Sir Tom (Oliphant), **Supp. X:** 219

Sir Tristrem (Thomas the Rhymer), **IV:** 29

"Sir Walter Scott" (Carlyle), **IV:** 38

Sir Walter Scott: The Great Unknown (Johnson), **IV:** 40

"Sir William Herschel's Long Year" (Hope), **Supp. VII:** 164–165

"Sire de Maletroit's Door, The" (Stevenson), **V:** 395

Siren Land (Douglas), **VI:** 293, 294, 295, 297, 305

"Sirens, The" (Manifold), **VII:** 426

Sirian Experiments, The: The Report by Ambien II, of the Five (Lessing), **Supp. I:** 250, 252

Sirocco (Coward), **Supp. II:** 141, 146, 148

"Siskin" (Stevenson), **Supp. VI:** 256

Sisson, C. H., **Supp. XI:** **243–262**

Sisson, C. J., **I:** 178*n*, 326

Sister Anne (Potter), **Supp. III:** 304

"Sister Helen" (Rossetti), **IV:** 313; **V:** 239, 245

"Sister Imelda" (O'Brien), **Supp. V:** 340

"Sister Maude" (Rossetti), **V:** 259

Sister Songs (Thompson), **V:** 443, 449, 450, 451

Sister Teresa (Moore), **VI:** 87, 92, 98

Sisterly Feelings (Ayckbourn), **Supp. V:** 3, 6, 10, 11–12, 13, 14

"Sisters" (Kinsella), **Supp. V:** 261

Sisters, The (Conrad), **VI:** 148

"Sisters, The" (Joyce), **Retro. Supp. I:** 171–172

Sisters, The (Swinburne), **V:** 330, 333

Sisters and Strangers: A Moral Tale (Tennant), **Supp. IX:** 235, 236

Sisters by a River (Comyns), **VIII:** 54, 55, 56

"Sitting, The" (Day Lewis), **Supp. III:** 128–129

Situation of the Novel, The (Bergonzi), **Supp. IV:** 233

Sitwell, Edith, **I:** 83; **III:** 73, 78; **VI:** 454; **VII:** xv–xvii, **127–141**

Sitwell, Osbert, **V:** 230, 234; **VII:** xvi, 128, 130, 135; **Supp. II:** 199, 201–202, 203

Sitwell, Sacheverell, **VII:** xvi, 128

Six Distinguishing Characters of a Parliament–Man, The (Defoe), **III:** 12

Six Dramas of Calderón. Freely Translated (FitzGerald), **IV:** 342, 344–345, 353

Six Epistles to Eva Hesse (Davie), **Supp. VI:** 111

"Six o'clock in Princes Street" (Owen), **VI:** 451

Six of Calais, The (Shaw), **VI:** 129

Six Poems (Thomas), **Supp. III:** 399

Six Queer Things, The (Caudwell), **Supp. IX:** 35

Six Stories Written in the First Person Singular (Maugham), **VI:** 374

Six Voices: Contemporary Australian Poets (Wallace–Crabb)e ed.), **VIII:** 314–315

"Six Weeks at Heppenheim" (Gaskell), **V:** 14, 15

"Six Years After" (Mansfield), **VII:** 176

"Six Young Men" (Hughes), **Supp. I:** 344; **Retro. Supp. II:** 203–204

"Sixpence" (Mansfield), **VII:** 175, 177

Sixteen Occasional Poems 1990–2000 (Gray, A.), **Supp. IX:** 88, 91–92

Sixteen Self Sketches (Shaw), **VI:** 102, 129

Sixth Beatitude, The (Hall), **Supp. VI:** 120, 122, **130**

Sixth Heaven, The (Hartley), **Supp. VII:** 124, 125, 127

"Sixth Journey, The" (Graham), **Supp. VII:** 109

Sizemore, Christine Wick, **Supp. IV:** 336

"Skating" (Motion), **Supp. VII:** 251, 256

Skeat, W. W., **I:** 17

"Skeleton, The" (Pritchett), **Supp. III:** 325

"Skeleton of the Future (at Lenin's Tomb), The" (MacDiarmid), **Supp. XII:** 211

Skelton, John, **I:** **81–96**

"Sketch, A" (Rossetti), **V:** 250

Sketch Book (Irving), **III:** 54

"Sketch from Private Life, A" (Byron), **IV:** 192

"Sketch of the Great Dejection, A" (Gunn), **Supp. IV:** 274

"Sketch of the Past, A" (Woolf), **Retro. Supp. I:** 314–315

Sketches and Essays (Hazlitt), **IV:** 140

Sketches and Reviews (Pater), **V:** 357

Sketches and Travels in London (Thackeray), **V:** 38

Sketches by Boz (Dickens), **V:** xix, 42, 43–46, 47, 52, 71

"Sketches for a Self–Portrait" (Day Lewis), **Supp. III:** 128

Sketches from Cambridge, by a Don (Stephen), **V:** 289

Sketches in the Life of John Clare, Written by Himself (Clare), **Supp. XI:** 50, 53

Sketches of the Principal Picture–Galleries in England (Hazlitt), **IV:** 132, 139

"Skin" (Dahl), **Supp. IV:** 216

Skin (Kane), **VIII:** 148, 149, 157–158

Skin Chairs, The (Comyns), **VIII:** 53, 55, 62–63

Skin Game, The (Galsworthy), **VI:** 275, 280, 288

Skírnismál, VIII: 230

Skotlands rímur, VIII: 243

Skriker, The (Churchill), **Supp. IV:** 179, 180, 197–198

Skull Beneath the Skin, The (James), **Supp. II:** 127; **Supp. IV:** 335–336, 337

Skull in Connemara, A (McDonagh), **Supp. XII:** 233, 235, 236, 237, 238, 245

"Sky Burning Up Above the Man, The" (Keneally), **Supp. IV:** 345

Skyhorse (Stallworthy), **Supp. X:** 301

"Skylarks" (Hughes), **Retro. Supp. II:** 206

Skylight (Hare), **Supp. IV:** 282, 298–299

"Skylight, The" (Heaney), **Retro. Supp. I:** 132

Slag (Hare), **Supp. IV:** 281, 283

"Slate" (Morgan, E.), **Supp. IX:** 167

"Sleep" (Cowley), **II:** 196

"Sleep, The" (Browning), **IV:** 312

"Sleep and Poetry" (Keats), **IV:** 214–215, 217, 228, 231; **Retro. Supp. I:** 184, 188

Sleep Has His House (Kavan), see *House of Sleep, The*

Sleep It Off, Lady (Rhys), **Supp. II:** 389, 401, 402

Sleep of Prisoners, A (Fry), **Supp. III:** 194, 195, 199–200

Sleep of Reason, The (Snow), **VII:** 324, 331–332

Sleep with Me (Kureishi), **Supp. XI:** 155

Sleepers of Roraima (Harris), **Supp. V:** 132

Sleep of the Great Hypnotist, The (Redgrove), **Supp. VI:** 231

"Sleeping at Last" (Rossetti), **V:** 251–252, 259

Sleeping Beauty, The (Sitwell), **VII:** 132

Sleeping Fires (Gissing), **V:** 437

Sleeping Lord and Other Fragments, The (Jones), **Supp. VII:** 167, 170, 178–180

Sleeping Murder (Christie), **Supp. II:** 125, 134

Sleeping Prince, The (Rattigan), **Supp. VII:** 318–319

Sleepwalkers, The: A History of Man's Changing Vision of the Universe (Koestler), **Supp. I:** 37–38

Sleuths, Inc. (Eames), **Supp. IV:** 3

Slight Ache, A (Pinter), **Supp. I:** 369, 371; **Retro. Supp. I:** 222–223

"Slips" (McGuckian), **Supp. V:** 281–282

Slipstream: A Memoir (Howard), **Supp. XI:** 135, 136, 141, 143, 144, 145–146

Slocum, Joshua, **Supp. IV:** 158

Slot Machine, The (Sillitoe), **Supp. V:** 411

"Slough" (Betjeman), **VII:** 366

"Slumber Did My Spirit Seal, A" (Wordsworth), **IV:** 18

"Small Boy" (MacCaig), **Supp. VI:** 194

Small Boy and Others, A (James), **VI:** 65

Small Family Business, A (Ayckbourn), **Supp. V:** 3, 12, 14

Small g: A Summer Idyll (Highsmith), **Supp. V:** 179

Small House at Allington, The (Trollope), **V:** xxiii, 101

"Small Personal Voice, The" (Lessing), **Supp. I:** 238

Small Place, A (Kincaid), **Supp. VII:** 217, 225–226, 230, 231

Small Town in Germany, A (le Carré), **Supp. II:** 300, **303–305,** 307

Small World: An Academic Romance (Lodge), **Supp. IV:** 363, 366, 371, 372, 374, 376–378, 384, 385

"*Small World:* An Introduction" (Lodge), **Supp. IV:** 377

Smeaton, O., **III:** 229*n*

"Smile" (Thomas), **Supp. IV:** 491–492

"Smile of Fortune, A" (Conrad), **VI:** 148

Smile Please (Rhys), **Supp. II:** 387, 388, 389, 394, 395, 396

Smiles, Samuel, **VI:** 264

Smiley's People (le Carré), **Supp. II:** 305, 311, **314–315**

Smith, Adam, **IV:** xiv, 144–145; **V:** viii

Smith, Alexander, **IV:** 320; **V:** 158

Smith, Edmund, **III:** 118

Smith, George, **V:** 13, 131, 132, 147, 149, 150, 279–280

Smith, Henry Nash, **VI:** 24

Smith, Iain Chrichton, **Supp. IX: 207–225**

Smith, James, **IV:** 253

Smith, Janet Adam, **V:** 391, 393, 395–398

Smith, Logan Pearsall, **Supp. III:** 98, 111

Smith, Nichol, **III:** 21

Smith, Stevie, **Supp. II: 459–478**

Smith, Sydney, **IV:** 268, 272; **Supp. VII: 339–352**

Smith, William Robertson, **Supp. III:** 171

Smith (Maugham), **VI:** 368

Smith and the Pharaohs and Other Tales (Haggard), **Supp. III:** 214, 222

Smith, Elder & Co. (publishers), **V:** 131, 140, 145, 150; *see also* Smith, George

Smith of Wootton Major (Tolkien), **Supp. II:** 521

Smithers, Peter, **III:** 42, 53

"Smoke" (Mahon), **Supp. VI:** 177

"Smokers for Celibacy" (Adcock), **Supp. XII:** 12

Smollett, Tobias, **III: 146–159; V:** xiv 52

Smyer, Richard I., **Supp. IV:** 338

"Snail Watcher, The" (Highsmith), **Supp. V:** 180

Snail Watcher and Other Stories, The (Highsmith), **Supp. V:** 180

"Snake" (Lawrence), **VII:** 119; **Retro. Supp. II:** 233–234

Snake's Pass, The (Stoker), **Supp. III:** 381

"Snap–dragon" (Lawrence), **VII:** 118

Snapper, The (Doyle), **Supp. V:** 77, 82–85, 88

"Snayl, The" (Lovelace), **II:** 231

"Sneaker's A (Mahon), **Supp. VI:** 175–176

"Sniff, The" (Pritchett), **Supp. III:** 319, **320–321**

"Sniper, The" (Sillitoe), **Supp. V:** 414

Snobs of England, The (Thackeray), *see Book of Snobs, The*

Snodgrass, Chris, **V:** 314

Snooty Baronet (Lewis), **VII:** 77

Snorra Edda, VIII: 243

Snow, C. P., **VI:** 235; **VII:** xii, xxi, 235, **321–341**

"Snow" (Hughes), **Supp. I:** 348

"Snow" (MacNeice), **VII:** 412

"Snow Joke" (Armitage), **VIII:** 3

Snow on the North Side of Lucifer (Sillitoe), **Supp. V:** 424, 425

Snow Party, The (Mahon), **Supp. VI:** 169, **172–173**

"Snow Party, The" (Mahon), **Supp. VI:** 172

"Snow White's Journey to the City" (Fallon), **Supp. XII:** 102

"Snowmanshit" (Redgrove), **Supp. VI:** 234

Snowstop (Sillitoe), **Supp. V:** 411

"Snow–White and the Seven Dwarfs" (Dahl), **Supp. IV:** 226

"So crewell prison howe could betyde, alas" (Surrey), **I:** 113

So Lovers Dream (Waugh), **Supp. VI:** 272

"So Much Depends" (Cope), **VIII:** 78

"So On He Fares" (Moore), **VI:** 93

"So sweet love seemed that April morn" (Bridges), **VI:** 77

"So to Fatness Come" (Smith), **Supp. II:** 472

Soaking The Heat (Kureishi), **Supp. XI:** 153

"Soap–Pig, The" (Muldoon), **Supp. IV:** 423

"Social Life in Roman Britain" (Trevelyan), **VI:** 393

Social Rights and Duties (Stephen), **V:** 289

Socialism and the Family (Wells), **VI:** 244

Socialism: Its Growth and Outcome (Morris and Box), **V:** 306

"Socialism: Principles and Outlook" (Shaw), **VI:** 129

Society for Pure English Tracts, **VI:** 83

"Sociological Cure for Shellshock, A" (Hibberd), **VI:** 460

"Sofa in the Forties, A" (Heaney), **Retro. Supp. I:** 133

Soft Side, The (James), **VI:** 67

Soft Voice of the Serpent and Other Stories, The (Gordimer), **Supp. II:** 226

"Soho Hospital for Women, The" (Adcock), **Supp. XII:** 7

"Sohrab and Rustum" (Arnold), **V:** xxi, 208, 209, 210, 216

"Soil Map, The" (McGuckian), **Supp. V:** 282

"Soldier, The" (Brooke), **VI:** 420, 421; **Supp. III:** 57, 58

"Soldier, The" (Hopkins), **V:** 372

Soldier and a Scholar, A (Swift), **III:** 36

Soldier of Humour (ed. Rosenthal), **VII:** 73

Soldier, Soldier (Arden), **Supp. II:** 28

Soldier's Art, The (Powell), **VII:** 349

"Soldiers Bathing" (Prince), **VII:** xxii 427

"Soldier's Declaration, A" (Sassoon), **Supp. IV:** 57

Soldier's Embrace, A (Gordimer), **Supp. II:** 232

"Soldiers of the Queen" (Kipling), **VI:** 417

"Soldiers on the Platform" (Cornford), **VIII:** 111

Soldiers Three (Kipling), **VI:** 204

"Sole of a Foot, The" (Hughes), **Supp. I:** 357

Solid Geometry (McEwan), **Supp. IV:** 390, 398

"Solid House, A" (Rhys), **Supp. II:** 402

Solid Mandala, The (White), **Supp. I:** 131, **143–145,** 148, 152

"Solid Objects" (Woolf), **VII:** 31

"Soliloquies" (Hill), **Supp. V:** 187

Soliloquies (St. Augustine), **Retro. Supp. II:** 297

Soliloquies of a Hermit (Powys), **VIII:** 246, 247, 249

"Soliloquy by the Well" (Redgrove), **Supp. VI:** 230

"Soliloquy of the Spanish Cloister" (Browning), **IV:** 356, 360, 367

Soliman and Perseda, **I:** 220

"Solitary Confinement" (Koestler), **Supp. I:** 36

"Solitary Reaper, The" (Wordsworth), **IV:** 22

"Solitary Shapers, The" (Wallace–Crabbe), **VIII:** 320

"Solitude" (Carroll), **V:** 263

"Solitude" (Milne), **Supp. V:** 303

"Solitude" (Traherne), **II:** 192

Sollers, Philippe, **Supp. IV:** 115, 116

Solomon, Simeon, **V:** 312, 314, 320

Solomon's Temple Spiritualized (Bunyan), **II:** 253

Solon, **II:** 70

Solstices (MacNeice), **VII:** 416

"Solution, The" (James), **VI:** 69

Some Advice . . . to the Members of the October Club (Swift), **III:** 35

Some Arguments Against Enlarging the Power of the Bishop (Swift), **III:** 35

Some Branch Against the Sky (Dutton), **Supp. XII:** 83

Some Branch Against the Sky: Gardening in the Wild (Dutton), **Supp. XII:** 84

"Some Days Were Running Legs" (Smith, I. C.), **Supp. IX:** 211

Some Do Not (Ford), **VI:** 319

Some Early Impressions (Stephen), **V:** 278, 281, 290

Some Free Thoughts upon the Present State of Affairs (Swift), **III:** 27, 36

Some Gospel–Truths Opened According to the Scriptures (Bunyan), **II:** 253

Some Imagist Poets (ed. Lowell), **Supp. III:** 397

Some Irish Essays (Russell), **VIII:** 286

"Some More Light Verse" (Cope), **VIII:** 77

Some Lie and Some Die (Rendell), **Supp. IX:** 191–192, 197–198

Some Observations upon a Paper (Swift), **III:** 35

Some Papers Proper to Be Read Before the Royal Society (Fielding), **III:** 105

Some Passages in the Life of Major Gahagan (Thackeray), *see Tremendous Adventures of Major Gahagan, The*

Some Popular Fallacies About Vivisection (Carroll), **V:** 273

Some Reasons Against the . . . Tyth of Hemp . . . (Swift), **III:** 36

Some Reasons to Prove That No Person Is Obliged . . . as a Whig, etc. (Swift), **III:** 35

Some Recent Attacks: Essays Cultural and Political (Kelman), **Supp. V:** 257

Some Remarks on the Barrier Treaty (Swift), **III:** 35

Some Remarks upon a Pamphlet (Swift), **III:** 35

Some Reminiscences (Conrad), **VI:** 148

Some Tame Gazelle (Pym), **Supp. II:** **366–367,** 380

Some Time Never: A Fable for Supermen (Dahl), **Supp. IV:** 211, 213, 214

"Some Time with Stephen: A Diary" (Kureishi), **Supp. XI:** 161

Some Versions of Pastoral (Empson; US. title, *English Pastoral Poetry*), **Supp. II:** 179, 184, 188, **189–190,** 197

"Someone Had To" (Galloway), **Supp. XII:** 126

Someone Like You (Dahl), **Supp. IV:** 206, 214, 215

Somers, Jane, *see Diaries of Jane Somers, The*

Somerset Maugham (Brander), **VI:** 379

Somerset Maugham (Curtis), **VI:** 379

Somervell, Robert, **VI:** 385

Something Childish, and Other Stories (Mansfield), **VII:** 171

"Something Else" (Priestley), **VII:** 212–213

Something Fresh (Wodehouse), *see Something New*

Something in Disguise (Howard), **Supp. XI:** 135, 141, 142

Something Leather (Gray, A.), **Supp. IX:** 80, 82, 83–86, 91

Something New (Wodehouse), **Supp. III:** 452, 453

"Something the Cat Dragged In" (Highsmith), **Supp. V:** 180

"Sometime I fled the fire that me brent" (Wyatt), **I:** 103–104

Somewhere Is Such a Kingdom: Poems, 1952–1971 (Hill), **Supp. V:** 184

Somnium Scipionis (Cicero), **IV:** 189

"Son, The" (Swift), **Supp. V:** 432–433

Son of Man (Potter, D.), **Supp. X:** 229, 236–237, 239

Son of the Soil, A (Oliphant), **Supp. X:** 219

Son of Frankenstein (film), **III:** 342

"Sonata Form" (Galloway), **Supp. XII:** 127

"Sonata in X" (Thomas), **Supp. XII:** 290–291

"Sonatas in Silence" (Owen), **VI:** 449, 451, 454

Sone and Air of the Foirsaid Foxe, called Father wer, The: Alswa the Parliament of fourfuttit Beistis, halden be the Lyoun (Henryson), see *Trial of the Fox, The*

"Song" (Blake), **III:** 290

"Song" (Collins), **III:** 170

"Song" (Congreve, two poems), **II:** 347–348

"Song" (Ewart), **Supp. VII:** 36

"Song" (Goldsmith), **III:** 184–185

"Song" (Lewis), **VII:** 446

"Song" (Nicholson), **Supp. VI:** 216

"Song" (Tennyson), **IV:** 329

"Song, A" (Rochester), **II:** 258

"Song [3]" (Thomas), **Supp. III:** 401

"Song, The" (Muir), **Supp. VI:** 208

Song and Its Fountains (Russell), **VIII:** 290, 292

"Song at the Beginning of Autumn" (Jennings), **Supp. V:** 214

Song at the Year's Turning: Poems, 1942–1954 (Thomas), **Supp. XII:** 283

Song at Twilight, A (Coward), **Supp. II:** 156–157

Song for a Birth or a Death (Jennings), **Supp. V:** 213, 215

"Song for a Birth or a Death" (Jennings), **Supp. V:** 215

"Song for a Corncrake" (Murphy), **Supp. V:** 324

"Song for a Phallus" (Hughes), **Supp. I:** 351

"Song for the Four Seasons" (Reid), **Supp. VII:** 326

"Song for the Swifts" (Jennings), **Supp. V:** 218

Song for St. Cecilia's Day, A (Dryden), **II:** 304

"Song for Simeon, A" (Eliot), **VII:** 152

"Song from Armenia, A" (Hill), **Supp. V:** 189

"Song from Cymbeline, A" (Collins), **III:** 163, 169–170

"Song from the Waters" (Beddoes), **Supp. XI:** 30

"Song in Storm, A" (Kipling), **VI:** 201

"Song in the Songless" (Meredith), **V:** 223

"Song of a Camera" (Gunn), **Supp. IV:** 273

Song of Hylas (Morris), **VII:** 164

Song of Italy, A (Swinburne), **V:** 313, 332

Song of Liberty, A (Blake), **III:** 307

"Song of Life, The" (Davies), **Supp. XI:** 98

Song of Life and Other Poems, The (Davies), **Supp. XI:** 98

Song of Los, The (Blake), **III:** 307; **Retro. Supp. I:** 44

"Song of Poplars" (Huxley), **VII:** 199

"Song of Rahero, The" (Stevenson), **V:** 396

Song of Roland, **I:** 69

Song of Songs (Redgrove), **Supp. VI:** 233

Song of Stone, A (Banks), **Supp. XI:** 8–9

"Song of the Amateur Psychologist" (Empson), **Supp. II:** 181

"Song of the Bower" (Rossetti), **V:** 243

Song of the Cold, The (Sitwell), **VII:** 132, 136, 137

"Song of the Fourth Magus" (Nye), **Supp. X:** 202

"Song of the Militant Romance, The" (Lewis), **VII:** 79

"Song of the Night" (Kinsella), **Supp. V:** 269

Song of the Night and Other Poems (Kinsella), **Supp. V:** 269

"Song of the Petrel, A" (Morgan, E.), **Supp. IX:** 161

"Song of the Rat" (Hughes), **Supp. I:** 348

"Song of the Shirt, The" (Hood), **IV:** 252, 261, 263–264

"Song Talk" (Nye), **Supp. X:** 206

"Song. To Celia" (Jonson), **Retro. Supp. I:** 164

"Song Written at Sea . . ." (Dorset), **II:** 261–262, 270

"Songbook of Sebastian Arrurruz, The" (Hill), **Supp. V:** 187, 188–189

Songlines, The (Chatwin), **Supp. IV:** 157, 158, 160, 161, 162, 163, 170–173, 174; **Supp. IX:** 49, 52, 57–59, 60, 61

Songs, The (Burns), **III:** 322

Songs and Sonnets (Donne), **I:** 357, 358, 360, 368

Songs Before Sunrise (Swinburne), **V:** xxiii, 313, 314, 324–325, 331, 332

"Songs for Strangers and Pilgrims" (Rossetti), **V:** 251, 254n, 260

"Songs in a Cornfield" (Rossetti), **V:** 258

Songs of Chaos (Read), **VI:** 436

Songs of Enchantment (Okri), **Supp. V:** 348–349, 350, 353, 358–359

Songes and Sonnettes . . . (pub. Tottel), *see Tottel's Miscellany*

Songs of Experience (Blake), **III:** 292, 293, 294, 297; **Retro. Supp. I:** 34, 36–37

Songs of Innocence (Blake), **III:** 292, 297, 307

Songs of Innocence and of Experience (Blake), **III:** 290, 299, 307; **V:** xv, 330; **Retro. Supp. I:** 36, 42–43

Songs of the Psyche (Kinsella), **Supp. V:** 270

"Songs of the PWD Man, The" (Harrison), **Supp. V:** 151

Songs of the Springtides (Swinburne), **V:** 332

Songs of Travel (Stevenson), **V:** 385, 396

Songs of Two Nations (Swinburne), **V:** 332

Songs Wing to Wing (Thompson), *see Sister Songs*

"Songster, The" (Smith), **Supp. II:** 465

"Sonnet" (Beddoes), **Supp. XI:** 29

"Sonnet, A" (Jennings), **Supp. V:** 207

"Sonnet, 1940" (Ewart), **VII:** 423

"Sonnet on the Death of Richard West" (Gray), **III:** 137

"Sonnet to Henry Lawes" (Milton), **II:** 175

"Sonnet to Liberty" (Wilde), **V:** 401

"Sonnet to Mr. Cyriack Skinner Upon His Blindness" (Milton), **II:** 164

"Sonnet to my Friend with an identity disc" (Owen), **VI:** 449

sonnets (Bridges), **VI:** 81

sonnets (Shakespeare), **I:** 307–308

"Sonnets for August 1945" (Harrison), **Supp. V:** 161–162

"Sonnets for August 1945" (Harrison), **Supp. V:** 161–162

"Sonnets for Five Seasons" (Stevenson), **Supp. VI:** 262

"Sonnets from Hellas" (Heaney), **Retro. Supp. I:** 133–134

Sonnets from Scotland (Morgan, E.), **Supp. IX:** 167

"Sonnets from the Portuguese" (Drowning), **IV:** xxi, 311, 314, 320, 321

Sonnets of William Wordsworth, The, **IV:** 25

Sonnets to Fanny Kelly (Lamb), **IV:** 81, 83

"Sonnets to the Left" (Wallace–Crabbe), **VIII:** 322

Sons and Lovers (Lawrence), **VII:** 88, 89, 91, 92, **95–98**; **Retro. Supp. II:** 227

"Sons of the Brave" (Kinsella), **Supp. V:** 261

Sons of Thunder, The (Chatwin, B.), **Supp. IX:** 61

Sorceress (Oliphant), **Supp. X:** 219

"Sorescu's Circles" (Longley), **VIII:** 176–177

"Sorrow" (Muir), **Supp. VI:** 207

Sort of Freedom, A (Friel), **Supp. V:** 113

"Son's Veto, The" (Hardy), **VI:** 22

Sophonisba (Marston), *see Wonder of Women, The*

Sopranos, The (Warner), **Supp. XI:** 282, 283, 287, 289–290, 294

Sordello (Browning), **IV:** xix, 355, 371, 373

Sorel, Georges, **VI:** 170

Sorley, Charles Hamilton, **VI:** xvi, 415, 417, 420, **421–422**

Sorrow in Sunlight (Firbank), *see Prancing Nigger*

"Sorrow of Socks, The" (Cope), **VIII:** 82

"Sorrow of true love is a great sorrow, The" (Thomas), **Supp. III:** 396

Sorrows of Young Werther, The (Goethe), **IV:** xiv, 59; **Supp. IV:** 28

"Sort of" (Fuller), **Supp. VII:** 80

"Sort of Exile in Lyme Regis, A" (Fowles), **Supp. I:** 292

"Sospetto d'Herode" (Crashaw), **II:** 180, 183–184

Sotheby, William, **IV:** 50

Sot–Weed Factor, The (Barth), **Supp. IV:** 116

"Souillac: Le Sacrifice d'Abraham" (Thomas), **Supp. XII:** 285

Soul and Body I, **Retro. Supp. II:** 301

Soul for Sale, A: Poems (Kavanagh), **Supp. VII:** 193, 199

"Soûl–Jeûn Parterre" (Morgan, E.), **Supp. IX:** 161

Soul of Man Under Socialism, The (Wilde), **V:** 409, 413, 415, 419

"Soul of Man Under Socialism, The" (Wilde), **Supp. IV:** 288; **Retro. Supp. II:** 367

"Soul Says" (Hart), **Supp. XI:** 131

Souls and Bodies (Lodge), *see How Far Can You Go?*

"Soul's Beauty," (Rossetti), **V:** 237

Soul's Destroyer and Other Poems, The (Davies), **Supp. XI:** 86, 93–96, 100

"Soul's Expression, The" (Browning), **IV:** 313

Souls of Black Folk, The (Du Bois), **Supp. IV:** 86

"Soul's Travelling, The" (Browning), **IV:** 313

Sound Barrier, The (Rattigan), **Supp. VII:** 318

"Sound Machine, The" (Dahl), **Supp. IV:** 214–215

"Sound of the River, The" (Rhys), **Supp. II:** 402

"Sounds of a Devon Village" (Davie), **Supp. VI:** 113

"Sounds of the Day" (MacCaig), **Supp. VI:** 189

Soursweet (film), **Supp. IV:** 390, 399

Soursweet (Mo), **Supp. IV:** 390, 400

South Africa (Trollope), **V:** 102

South African Autobiography, The (Plomer), **Supp. XI:** 223

South African Winter (Morris, J.), **Supp. X:** 175

"South African Writers and English Readers" (Plomer), **Supp. XI:** 209

South Sea Bubble (Coward), **Supp. II:** 155

South Seas, The (Stevenson), **V:** 396

South Wind (Douglas), **VI:** 293, 294, 300–302, 304, 305; **VII:** 200

Southam, Brian Charles, **IV:** xi, xiii, xxv, 122, 124, 337

Southern, Thomas, **II:** 305

"Southern Night, A" (Arnold), **V:** 210

Southerne, Thomas, **Supp. III:** 34–35

Southey, Cuthbert, **IV:** 62, 72

Southey, Robert, **III:** 276, 335; **IV:** viii–ix, xiv, xvii, 43, 45, 52, **58–72**, 85, 88, 89, 92, 102, 128, 129, 162, 168, 184–187, 270, 276, 280; **V:** xx, 105, 121; **Supp. IV:** 425, 426–427

"Southey and Landor" (Landor), **IV:** 93

"Southey and Porson" (Landor), **IV:** 93, 97

"Southey's *Colloquies*" (Macaulay), **IV:** 280

Southey's Common–place Book (ed. Warter), **IV:** 71

"South–Sea House, The" (Lamb), **IV:** 81–82

"South–Wester The" (Meredith), **V:** 223

Souvenirs (Fuller), **Supp. VII:** 67, 81

Sovereign Remedy, A (Steel), **Supp. XII:** 274–275

Sovereignty of Good, The (Murdoch), **Supp. I:** 217–218, 225

"Soviet Myth and Reality" (Koestler), **Supp. I:** 27

"Sow's Ear, The**"** (Sisson), **Supp. XI:** 258

Space Vampires (Wilson), **III:** 341

"Space–ship, The" (Smith, I. C.), **Supp. IX:** 216

Spain (Morris, J.), **Supp. X:** 176, 178–179

"Spain 1937" (Auden), **VII:** 384; **Retro. Supp. I:** 8

Spanbroekmolen (Roberts, K.), **Supp. X:** 274–275

Spanish Curate, The (Fletcher and Massinger), **II:** 66

Spanish Fryar, The; or, The Double Discovery (Dryden), **II:** 305

Spanish Gipsy, The (Middleton and Rowley), **II:** 100

Spanish Gypsy, The (Eliot), **V:** 198, 200

"Spanish Maids in England, The" (Cornford), **VIII:** 112–113

"Spanish Military Nun, The" (De Quincey), **IV:** 149

"Spanish Oranges" (Dunn), **Supp. X:** 80

Spanish Tragedy, The (Kyd), **I:** 212, 213, 218, 220, **221–229; II:** 25, 28–29, 69

Spanish Virgin and Other Stories, The (Pritchett), **Supp. III:** 316, 317

Spanner and Pen (Fuller), **Supp. VII:** 67, 68, 74, 81

Sparagus Garden, The (Brome), **Supp. X:** 52, 61–62

"Spared" (Cope), **VIII:** 84

Spark, Muriel, **Supp. I:** 199–214; **Supp. IV:** 100, 234

"Sparrow" (MacCaig), **Supp. VI:** 192

Sparrow, John, **VI:** xv, xxxiv; **VII:** 355, 363

Sparrow, The (Ayckbourn), **Supp. V:** 2

"Spate in Winter Midnight" (MacCaig), **Supp. VI:** 187

"Spätlese, The" (Hope), **Supp. VII:** 157

Speak, Parrot (Skelton), **I:** 83, 90–91

Speak for England, Arthur (Bennett), **VIII:** 22–25

"Speak to Me" (Tennyson), **IV:** 332

Speaker (periodical), **VI:** 87, 335

Speaker of Mandarin (Rendell), **Supp. IX:** 192, 198

"Speaking a Foreign Language" (Reid), **Supp. VII:** 330

Speaking Likenesess (Rossetti), **V:** 260

Speaking Stones, The (Fallon), **Supp. XII:** 104–105, 114

"Speaking Stones, The" (Fallon), **Supp. XII:** 104

"Special Type, The" (James), **VI:** 69

"Specimen of an Induction to a Poem" (Keats), **IV:** 214

Specimens of English Dramatic Poets (Lamb), **IV:** xvi 79, 85

Specimens of German Romance (Carlyle), **IV:** 250

Specimens of Modern Poets: The Heptalogia . . . (Swinburne), **V:** 332

Speckled Bird, The (Yeats), **VI:** 222; **Retro. Supp. I:** 326

Spectator (periodical), **III:** 39, 41, 44, **46–50,** 52, 53; **V:** 86, 238; **VI:** 87; **Supp. IV:** 121

Spectatorial Essays (Strachey), **Supp. II:** 497, 502

"Spectre of the Real, The" (Hardy), **VI:** 20

Speculations (Hulme), **Supp. VI:** 134, 140

Speculative Instruments (Richards), **Supp. I:** 426

Speculum hominis (Gower), **I:** 48

Speculum meditantis (Gower), **I:** 48

Speculum Principis (Skelton), **I:** 84

Spedding, James, **I:** 257n, 259, 264, 324

Speech Against Prelates Innovations (Waller), **II:** 238

Speech . . . Against Warren Hastings (Sheridan), **III:** 270

Speech . . . for the Better Security of the Independence of Parliament (Burke), **III:** 205

Speech, 4 July 1643 (Waller), **II:** 238

Speech . . . in Bristol upon . . . His Parliamentary Conduct, A (Burke), **III:** 205

Speech on American Taxation (Burke), **III:** 205

Speech . . . on Mr. Fox's East India Bill (Burke), **III:** 205

Speech on Moving His Resolutions for Conciliation with the Colonies (Burke), **III:** 205

Speech on Parliamentary Reform (Macaulay), **IV:** 274

Speech on the Anatomy Bill (Macaulay), **IV:** 277

Speech on the Army Estimates (Burke), **III:** 205

Speech on the Edinburgh Election (Macaulay), **IV:** 274

Speech on the People's Charter (Macaulay), **IV:** 274

Speech on the Ten Hours Bill (Macaulay), **IV:** 276–277

Speech Relative to the Nabob of Arcot's Debts (Burke), **III:** 205

Speech to the Electors of Bristol (Burke), **III:** 205

Speeches on Parliamentary Reform (Disraeli), **IV:** 308

Speeches on the Conservative Policy of the Last Thirty Years (Disraeli), **IV:** 308

Speeches, Parliamentary and Miscellaneous (Macaulay), **IV:** 291

Speedy Post, A (Webster), **II:** 69, 85

Spell, The (Hollinghurst), **Supp. X:** 120, 132–134

Spell, The: An Extravaganza (Brontë), **V:** 151

Spell for Green Corn, A (Brown), **Supp. VI: 72–73**

Spell of Words, A (Jennings), **Supp. V:** 219

"Spelt from Sybil's Leaves" (Hopkins), **V:** 372–373

Spence, Joseph, **II:** 261; **III:** 69, 86n

Spencer, Baldwin, **Supp. III:** 187–188

Spencer, Herbert, **V:** 182, 189, 284

Spender, Stephen, **VII:** 153, 382, 410; **Supp. II: 481–495; Supp. III:** 103, 117, 119; **Supp. IV:** 95

Spengler, Osvald, **Supp. IV:** 1, 3, 10, 11, 12, 17

Spenser, Edmund, **I: 121–144,** 146; **II:** 50, 302; **III:** 167n; **IV:** 59, 61, 93, 205; **V:** 318

Sphinx (Thomas), **Supp. IV:** 485

"Sphinx, The" (Rossetti), **V:** 241

Sphinx, The (Wilde), **V:** 409–410, 415, 419; **Retro. Supp. II:** 371

"Sphinx; or, Science" (Bacon), **I:** 267

"Spider, The" (Nye), **Supp. X:** 205

Spider (Weldon), **Supp. IV:** 521

Spielmann, M. H., **V:** 137, 152

Spiess, Johann, **III:** 344

Spingarn, J. E., **II:** 256n

"Spinoza" (Hart), **Supp. XI:** 123

"Spinster Sweet–Arts, The" (Tennyson), **IV:** 327

"Spiral, The" (Reid), **Supp. VII:** 330

Spire, The (Golding), **Supp. I:** 67, **79–81,** 83; **Retro. Supp. I:** 99–100

"Spirit, The" (Traherne), **Supp. XI:** 267

"Spirit Dolls, The" (McGuckian), **Supp. V:** 292

"Spirit is Too Blunt an Instrument, The" (Stevenson), **Supp. VI:** 256

Spirit Level, The (Heaney), **Retro. Supp. I:** 132–133

Spirit Machines (Crawford), **Supp. XI:** 67, 76–79

Spirit of British Administration and Some European Comparisons, The (Sisson), **Supp. XI:** 249, 258

Spirit of Man, The (ed. Bridges), **II:** 160; **VI:** 76, 83

Spirit of the Age, The (Hazlitt), **III:** 276; **IV:** xi, 39, 129, 131, 132–134, 137, 139

Spirit of Whiggism, The (Disraeli), **IV:** 308

Spirit Rise, A (Warner), **Supp. VII:** 380

Spirits in Bondage (Lewis), **Supp. III:** 250

Spiritual Exercises (Loyola), **V:** 362, 367, 371, 373n; **Retro. Supp. II:** 188

Spiritual Exercises (Spender), **Supp. II:** 489

"Spiritual Explorations" (Spender), **Supp. II:** 489, 490

"Spite of thy hap hap hath well happed" (Wyatt), **I:** 103

Spitzer, L., **IV:** 323n, 339

Spivack, Bernard, **I:** 214

Spivak, Gayatri, **Retro. Supp. I:** 60

"Spleen, The" (Finch), **Supp. IX:** 69–70, 76

Splitting (Weldon), **Supp. IV:** 535

Spoils, The (Bunting), **Supp. VII:** 5, 7–9

Spoils of Poynton, The (James), **VI: 49–50**

"Spoilt Child, The" (Motion), **Supp. VII:** 251

Sport of Nature, A (Gordimer), **Supp. II:** 232, 239–240, 241, 242

"Spot of Night Fishing (for Kenny Crichton), A" (Warner), **Supp. XI:** 294

Spottiswoode, John, **II:** 142

Sprat, Thomas, **II:** 195, 196, 198, 200, 202, 294; **III:** 29

"Spraying the Potatoes" (Kavanagh), **Supp. VII:** 190

Spreading the News (Gregory), **VI:** 309, 315, 316

Sprigg, Christopher St. John, *see* Caudwell, Christopher

"Sprig of Lime, The" (Nichols), **VI:** 419

"Spring, The" (Carew), **II:** 225

"Spring, The" (Cowley), **II:** 197

"Spring" (Crawford), **Supp. XI:** 70–71

"Spring" (Hopkins), **V:** 368

Spring (Thomson), **Supp. III:** 413–414, 415, 416,

"Spring and Fall" (Hopkins), **V:** 371–372, 381; **Retro. Supp. II:** 196–197

Spring Days (Moore), **VI:** 87, 91

Spring Fever (Wodehouse), **Supp. III:** 451

"Spring Hail" (Murray), **Supp. VII:** 272, 279, 281

Spring Morning (Cornford), **VIII:** 102, 103, 104, 112

"Spring Morning" (Milne), **Supp. V:** 302

"Spring Nature Notes" (Hughes), **Supp. I:** 358

"Spring 1942" (Fuller), **VII:** 429

"Spring Offensive" (Owen), **VI:** 455, 456, 458

"Spring Song" (Fallon), **Supp. XII:** 110

"Spring Song" (Milne), **Supp. V:** 309–310

Spring, Summer, Autumn, Winter (Hughes), **Supp. I:** 357

sprung rhythm, **V:** 363, 365, 367, 374, 376, 379, 380

Spy in the Family, A (Waugh), **Supp. VI:** 276

Spy on the Conjurer, A (Haywood), **Supp. XII:** 135

Spy Story, The (Cawelti and Rosenberg), **Supp. IV:** 7

Spy Who Came In from the Cold, The (le Carré), **Supp. II:** 299, 301, 305, **307–309**, 313, 315, 316, 317

Spy's Wife, The (Hill, R.), **Supp. IX:** 117, 119

Square Cat, The (Ayckbourn), **Supp. V:** 2

Square Egg and Other Sketches, The (Saki), **Supp. VI:** 242, 250–251

Square Rounds (Harrison), **Supp. V:** 164

Squaring the Circle (Stoppard), **Supp. I:** 449–450, 451

Squaring the Waves (Dutton), **Supp. XII:** 88–89

"Squarings" (Heaney), **Retro. Supp. I:** 132

"Squatter" (Mistry), **Supp. X:** 140–142

"Squaw, The" (Stoker), **Supp. III:** 382–383

Squire Arden (Oliphant), **Supp. X:** 220

"Squire Hooper" (Hardy), **Retro. Supp. I:** 121, 418, 420

Squire, J. C., **VII:** xvi

"Squire Petrick's Lady" (Hardy), **VI:** 22

Squire Trelooby (Congreve, Vanbrugh, Walsh), **II:** 325, 336, 339, 347, 350

Squire's Tale, The (Chaucer), **I:** 23, 24

"Squirrel and the Crow, The" (Cope), **VIII:** 81

"Sredni Vashtar" (Saki), **Supp. VI: 245–246**

"Stabilities" (Stevenson), **Supp. VI:** 256

Stade, George, **Supp. IV:** 402

"Staff and Scrip, The" (Rossetti), **V:** 240

Staffordshire Sentinel (periodical), **VI:** 248

"Stag in a Neglected Hayfield" (MacCraig), **Supp. VI:** 192

Stage Coach, The, **II:** 353, 358, 364

Stalin, Joseph, **Supp. IV:** 82

Stalky & Co. (Kipling), **VI:** 204; **Supp. IV:** 506

Stallworthy, Jon, **VI:** 220, 438; **Supp. X: 291–304**

Stallybrass, Oliver, **VI:** 397

Stamboul Train (Greene; US. title, *Orient Express*), **Supp. I:** 3, 4–5; **Retro. Supp. II:** 152

Stand Up, Nigel Barton (Potter, D.), **Supp. X:** 228, 230–233

Standard of Behavior, A (Trevor), **Supp. IV:** 505

Standing Room Only (Ayckbourn), **Supp. V:** 2, 11

Stanley, Arthur, **V:** 13, 349

Stanley and Iris (film), **Supp. IV:** 45

Stanley and The Women (Amis), **Supp. II:** 17–18

Stanleys of Alderley, The (ed. Mitford), **Supp. X:** 156

Stans puer ad mensam (Lydgate), **I:** 58

"Stanzas" (Hood), **IV:** 263

"Stanzas from the Grande Chartreuse" (Arnold), **V:** 210

"Stanzas in Memory of the Author of 'Obermann' " (Arnold), **V:** 206

"Stanzas Written in Dejection" (Shelley), **IV:** 201

Staple of News, The (Jonson), **Retro. Supp. I:** 165

Star (periodical), **VI:** 103

Star over Bethlehem (Fry), **Supp. III:** 195

Star Turns Red, The (O'Casey), **VII:** 7–8

Stares (Fuller), **Supp. VII:** 81

"Stare's Nest by My Window, The" (Yeats), **VI:** 212

Staring at the Sun (Barnes), **Supp. IV:** 65, 67, 70–71

"Starlight Night, The" (Hopkins), **V:** 366, 367; **Retro. Supp. II:** 190

"Stars" (Brontë), **V:** 133, 142

Stars of the New Curfew (Okri), **Supp. V:** 347, 348, 352, 355, 356–357

Start in Life, A (Brookner), *see Debut, The*

Start in Life, A (Sillitoe), **Supp. V:** 410, 413

Starting Point (Day Lewis), **Supp. III:** 118, 130–131

State of France, . . . in the IXth Year of . . . , Lewis XIII, The (Evelyn), **II:** 287

State of Independence, A (Phillips), **Supp. V:** 380, 383–384

State of Innocence, The (Dryden), **II:** 290, 294, 305

"State of Poetry, The" (Jennings), **Supp. V:** 215

"State of Religious Parties, The" (Newman), **Supp. VII:** 294

State of Siege (Ambler; formerly *The Night–Comers*), **Supp. IV:** 4, 16

State of the Art, The (Banks), **Supp. XI:** 10–11

"State of the Nation, The" (Fallon), **Supp. XII:** 111

States of Emergency (Brink), **Supp. VI: 53–54**

Statesman's Manual, The (Coleridge), **IV:** 56; **Retro. Supp. II:** 64

Statement, The (Moore, B.), **Supp. IX:** 152

"Statements, The" (Ewart), **Supp. VII:** 39

Station Island (Heaney), **Supp. II:** 268, **277–279**

"Station Island" (Heaney), **Supp. II:** 277 278; **Retro. Supp. I:** 124, 130–131

Stations (Heaney), **Retro. Supp. I:** 129

"Statue and the Bust, The" (Browning), **IV:** 366

"Statue in Stocks–Market, The" (Marvell), **II:** 218

"Statues, The" (Yeats), **VI:** 215

Staying On (Scott), **Supp. I:** 259, 272–274

Stead, Christina, **Supp. IV: 459–477**

"Steam Washing Co., The" (Hood), **IV:** 267

Steel, Flora Annie, **Supp. XII: 265–278**

"Steel, The" (Murray), **Supp. VII:** 278

Steel Glass, The (Gascoigne), **I:** 149

Steele, Richard, **II:** 359; **III:** 7, 18, 19, **38–53**

"Steep and her own world" (Thomas), **Supp. III:** 401

Steep Holm (Fowles), **Supp. I:** 292

"Steep Stone Steps" (Cameron), **Supp. IX:** 27

Steevens, G. W., **VI:** 351

Steevens, George, **I:** 326

Steffan, Truman Guy, **IV:** 179, 193

Stein, Arnold, **Retro. Supp. II:** 181

Stein, Gertrude, **VI:** 252; **VII:** 83; **Supp. IV:** 416, 542, 556, 557–558

Steiner, George, **Supp. IV:** 455

"Stella at Wood–Park" (Swift), **III:** 32

"Stella's Birth Day, 1725" (Swift), **III:** 32

"Stella's Birthday . . . A.D. 1720–21" (Swift), **III:** 32

"Stella's Birthday, March 13, 1727" (Swift), **III:** 32

Stella's Birth–Days: A Poem (Swift), **III:** 36

Stendhal, **Supp. IV:** 136, 459

Step by Step (Churchill), **VI:** 356

Stepdaughter, The (Blackwood), **Supp. IX:** 3, 10, 16

Stephen, Janus K., **IV:** 10–11, 268
Stephen, Leslie, **II:** 156, 157; **III:** 42;
　　IV: 301, 304–306; **V:** xix, xxv, xxvi,
　　277–290, 386; **VII:** xxii, 17, 238
Stephen Hero (Joyce), **VII:** 45–46, 48
Stephens, Frederick, **V:** 235, 236
Stephens, James, **VI:** 88
*Steps to the Temple. Sacred Poems, with
　　Other Delights of the Muses*
　　(Crashaw), **II:** 179, 180, 184, 201
Sterling, John, **IV:** 54
Stern, Gladys Bronwen, **IV:** 123; **V:** xiii,
　　xxviii, 395
Stern, J. B., **I:** 291
Stern, Laurence, **III: 124–135,** 150, 153,
　　155, 157; **IV:** 79, 183; **VII:** 20; **Supp.
　　II:** 204; **Supp. III:** 108
Sterts and Stobies (Crawford), **Supp. XI:**
　　67
Stet (Reading), **VIII:** 261, 269–271, 273
Steuart, J. A., **V:** 392, 397
Stevens, Wallace, **V:** 412; **Supp. IV:** 257,
　　414; **Supp. V:** 183
Stevenson, Anne, **Supp. VI: 253–268**
Stevenson, L., **V:** 230, 234
Stevenson, Robert Louis, **I:** 1; **II:** 153;
　　III: 330, 334, 345; **V:** xiii, xxi, xxv,
　　vxvi, 219, 233, **383–398; Supp. IV:**
　　61; **Retro. Supp. I: 259–272**
*Stevenson and Edinburgh: A Centenary
　　Study* (MacLaren), **V:** 393, 398
Stevenson Companion, The (ed.
　　Hampden), **V:** 393, 395
Stevensoniana (ed. Hammerton), **V:** 393,
　　397
Stewart, J. I. M., **I:** 329; **IV:** xxv; **VII:**
　　xiv, xxxviii
Stiff Upper Lip (Durrell), **Supp. I:** 113
Still Centre, The (Spender), **Supp. II:**
　　488, 489
"Still Falls the Rain" (Sitwell), **VII:** xvii,
　　135, 137
Still Life (Byatt), **Supp. IV:** 139, 145,
　　147–149, 151, 154
Still Life (Coward), **Supp. II:** 153
Stirling, William Alexander, earl of, *see*
　　Alexander, William
"Stoic, A" (Galsworthy), **VI:** 275, 284
Stoker, Bram, **III:** 334, 342, 343, 344,
　　345; **Supp. III: 375–391**
Stokes, John, **V:** xiii, xxviii
Stolen Bacillus, The, and Other Incidents
　　(Wells), **VI:** 226, 243
"Stolen Child, The" (Yeats), **Retro.
　　Supp. I:** 329
Stone, C., **III:** 161n
"Stone" (Dutton), **Supp. XII:** 92
"Stone Age Decadent, A" (Wallace–
　　Crabbe), **VIII:** 321
"Stone and Mr. Thomas, The" (Powys),
　　VIII: 258
"Stone Mania" (Murphy), **Supp. V:** 326
Stone Virgin (Unsworth), **Supp. VII:** 355,
　　356, 357, 360–361, 362, 365
"Stone–In–Oxney" (Longley), **VIII:** 169,
　　175
Stones of the Field, The (Thomas), **Supp.
　　XII:** 282, 283, 284
Stones of Venice, The (Ruskin), **V:** xxi,
　　173, 176–177, 180, 184, 292

"Stony Grey Soil "(Kavanagh), **Supp.
　　VII:** 189–190
Stony Limits and Other Poems
　　(MacDiarmid), **Supp. XII:** 202, 212–
　　216
"Stooping to Drink" (Malouf), **Supp.
　　XII:** 220
Stoppard, Tom, **Supp. I: 437–454; Retro.
　　Supp. II: 343–358**
Storey, David, **Supp. I: 407–420**
Storey, Graham, **V:** xi, xxviii, 381
Stories, Dreams, and Allegories
　　(Schreiner), **Supp. II:** 450
Stories from ABlack and White" (Hardy),
　　VI: 20
Stories of Red Hanrahan (Yeats), **VI:** 222
Stories of the Seen and Unseen
　　(Oliphant), **Supp. X:** 220
Stories, Theories and Things (Brooke–
　　Rose)), **Supp. IV:** 99, 110
"Stories, Theories and Things" (Brooke–
　　Rose)), **Supp. IV:** 116
"Storm" (Nye), **Supp. X:** 204-205
"Storm" (Owen), **VI:** 449
"Storm, The" (Brown), **Supp. VI:** 70–71
"Storm, The" (Donne), **Retro. Supp. II:**
　　86
"Storm, The" (Hart), **Supp. XI:** 126–127
*Storm, The; or, A Collection of . . .
　　Casualties and Disasters . . .* (Defoe),
　　III: 13; **Retro. Supp. I:** 68
Storm and Other Poems (Sillitoe), **Supp.
　　V:** 424
"Storm Bird, Storm Dreamer" (Ballard),
　　Supp. V: 26
"Storm is over, The land hushes to rest,
　　The" (Bridges), **VI:** 79
"Stormpetrel" (Murphy), **Supp. V:** 315
"Stormscape" (Davies), **Supp. XI:** 87
"Storm–Wind" (Ballard), **Supp. V:** 22
"Story, A" (Smitch, I. C.), **Supp. IX:** 222
"Story, A" (Thomas), **Supp. I:** 183
Story and the Fable, The (Muir), **Supp.
　　VI:** 198
"Story in It, The" (James), **VI:** 69
"Story of a Masterpiece, The" (James),
　　VI: 69
Story of a Non–Marrying Man, The
　　(Lessing), **Supp. I:** 253–254
"Story of a Panic, The" (Forster), **VI:** 399
"Story of a Year, The" (James), **VI:** 69
Story of an African Farm, The
　　(Schreiner), **Supp. II:** 435, 438, 439,
　　440, 441, **445–447,** 449, 451, 453, 456
Story of Fabian Socialism, The (Cole),
　　VI: 131
Story of Grettir the strong, The (Morris
　　and Magnusson), **V:** 306
Story of Rimini, The (Hunt), **IV:** 214
Story of San Michele, The (Munthe), **VI:**
　　265
*Story of Sigurd the Volsung and the Fall
　　of the Niblungs, The* (Morris), **V:** xxiv,
　　299–300, 304, 306
Story of the Glittering Plain, The
　　(Morris), **V:** 306
Story of the Injured Lady, The (Swift),
　　III: 27
Story of the Malakand Field Force
　　(Churchill), **VI:** 351

Story of the Sundering Flood, The
　　(Morris), **V:** 306
"Story of the Three Bears, The"
　　(Southey), **IV:** 58, 67
"Story of the Unknown Church, The"
　　(Morris), **V:** 293, 303
*Story of the Volsungs and . . . Songs from
　　the Elder Edda, The* (Morris and
　　Magnusson), **V:** 299, 306
Story So Far, The (Ayckbourn), **Supp. V:**
　　2
"Storyteller, The" (Berger), **Supp. IV:**
　　90, 91
Story–Teller, The (Highsmith), **Supp. V:**
　　174–175
Storyteller, The (Sillitoe), **Supp. V:** 410
Story–Teller's Holiday, A (Moore), **VI:**
　　88, 95, 99
Stout, Mira, **Supp. IV:** 75
Stovel, Nora Foster, **Supp. IV:** 245, 249
Stowe, Harriet Beecher, **V:** xxi, 3
Strachey, J. St. Loe, **V:** 75, 86, 87
Strachey, Lytton, **III:** 21, 28; **IV:** 292; **V:**
　　13, 157, 170, 277; **VI:** 155, 247, 372,
　　407; **VII:** 34, 35; **Supp. II: 497–517**
Strado, Famiano, **II:** 90
Strafford: An Historical Tragedy
　　(Browning), **IV:** 373
Strait Gate, The . . . (Bunyan), **II:** 253
"Strand at Lough Beg, The" (Heaney),
　　Supp. II: 278
Strange and the Good, The (Fuller),
　　Supp. VII: 81
"Strange and Sometimes Sadness, A"
　　(Ishiguro), **Supp. IV:** 303, 304
*Strange Case of Dr. Jekyll and Mr. Hyde,
　　The* (Stevenson), **III:** 330, 342, 345;
　　V: xxv, 383, 387, 388, 395; **VI:** 106;
　　Supp. IV: 61; **Retro. Supp. I:** 263,
　　264–266
"Strange Comfort Afforded by the Profes-
　　sion" (Lowry), **Supp. III:** 281
Strange Fruit (Phillips), **Supp. V:** 380
"Strange Meeting" (Owen), **VI:** 444, 445,
　　449, 454, 457–458
Strange Necessity, The (West), **Supp. III:**
　　438
"Strange Ride of Morrowbie Jukes, The"
　　(Kipling), **VI: 175–178**
Strange Ride of Rudyard Kipling, The
　　(Wilson), **VI:** 165; **Supp. I:** 167
Strange World, A (Braddon), **VIII:** 37
Stranger, The (Kotzebue), **III:** 268
Stranger Still, A (Kavan), **Supp. VII:**
　　207–208, 209
Stranger With a Bag, A (Warner), **Supp.
　　VII:** 380
Strangers: A Family Romance (Tennant),
　　Supp. IX: 239
Strangers and Brothers cycle (Snow),
　　VII: xxi, 322, **324–336**
Strangers on a Train (Highsmith), **Supp.
　　V:** 167, 168–169
Strapless (film), **Supp. IV:** 282, 291–292
"Strategist, The" (Saki), **Supp. VI:** 243
"Stratton Water" (Rossetti), **V:** 239
Strauss, Richard, **Supp. IV:** 556
"Strawberry Hill" (Hughes), **Supp. I:** 342
Strayed Reveller, The (Arnold), **V:** xxi,
　　209, 216

"Street in Cumberland, A" (Nicholson), **Supp. VI:** 216
Street Songs (Sitwell), **VII:** 135
"Streets of the Spirits" (Redgrove), **Supp. VI:** 235
"Strength of Heart" (Fallon), **Supp. XII:** 114
"Strephon and Chloe" (Swift), **III:** 32; **Retro. Supp. I:** 284, 285
Strickland, Agnes, **I:** 84
Strictures on AConingsby" (Disraeli), **IV:** 308
"Strictures on Pictures" (Thackeray), **V:** 37
Striding Folly (Sayers), **Supp. III:** 335
Strife (Galsworthy), **VI:** xiii, 269, 285–286
Strike at Arlingford, The (Moore), **VI:** 95
Strindberg, August, **Supp. III:** 12
Stringham, Charles, **IV:** 372
Strings Are False, The (MacNeice), **VII:** 406
Strip Jack (Rankin), **Supp. X:** 244, 250–251, 253
Strode, Ralph, **I:** 49
Strong, Roy, **I:** 237
Strong Poison (Sayers), **Supp. III:** 339, 342, 343, 345
Stronger Climate, A: Nine Stories (Jhabvala), **Supp. V:** 235
Structure and Distribution of Coral Reefs, On the (Darwin), **Supp. VII:** 19
Structural Analysis of Pound's Usura Canto: Jakobsonand Applied to Free Verse, A (Brooke–Rose)), **Supp. IV:** 99, 114
Structural Transformation of the Public Sphere, The (Habermas), **Supp. IV:** 112
Structure in Four Novels by H. G. Wells (Newell), **VI:** 245, 246
Structure of Complex Words, The (Empson), **Supp. II:** 180, **192–195,** 197
"Studies in a Dying Culture" (Caudwell), **Supp. IX:** 36
Struggle of the Modern, The (Spender), **Supp. II:** 492
Struggles of Brown, Jones and Robinson, The (Trollope), **V:** 102
"Strugnell's Christian Songs" (Cope), **VIII:** 78
"Strugnell's Sonnets" (Cope), **VIII:** 73–74
Strutt, Joseph, **IV:** 31
Strutton, Bill, **Supp. IV:** 346
Struwwelpeter (Hoffman), **I:** 25; **Supp. III:** 296
Stuart, D. M., **V:** 247, 256, 260
"Stubb's Calendar" (Thackeray), *see AFatal Boots, The"*
Studies in a Dying Culture (Caudwell), **Supp. IX:** 33, 43–47
Studies in Classic American Literature (Lawrence), **VII:** 90; **Retro. Supp. II:** 234
Studies in Ezra Pound (Davie), **Supp. VI:** 115
Studies in Prose and Poetry (Swinburne), **II:** 102; **V:** 333

Studies in Song (Swinburne), **V:** 332
Studies in the History of the Renaissance (Pater), **V:** xxiv, 286–287, 323, 338–339, **341–348,** 351, 355–356, 400, 411
Studies in the Prose Style of Joseph Addison (Lannering), **III:** 52
Studies in Words (Lewis), **Supp. III:** 249, 264
Studies of a Biographer (Stephen), **V:** 280, 285, 287, 289
"Studio 5, the Stars" (Ballard), **Supp. V:** 26
Study in Scarlet, A (Doyle), **Supp. II:** 159, 160, 162, 163, 164, 167, 169, 170, 171, 172, 173, 174, 176
Study in Temperament, A (Firbank), **Supp. II:** 201, 206–207
Study of Ben Jonson, A (Swinburne), **V:** 332
Study of Shakespeare, A (Swinburne), **V:** 328, 332
"Study of Thomas Hardy" (Lawrence), **VI:** 20; **Retro. Supp. II:** 234
Study of Victor Hugo, A (Swinburne), **V:** 332
"Stuff Your Classical Heritage" (Wallace–Crabbe), **VIII:** 321–322
Sturlunga saga, **VIII:** 242
"Style" (Pater), **V:** 339, 347, 353–355
Stylistic Development of Keats, The (Bate), **Retro. Supp. I:** 185
Subhuman Redneck Poems (Murray), **Supp. VII:** 271, 283–284
Subject of Scandal and Concern, A (Osborne), **Supp. I:** 334
"Sublime and the Beautiful Revisited, The" (Murdoch), **Supp. I:** 216–217, 223
"Sublime and the Good, The" (Murdoch), **Supp. I:** 216–217, 218, 220
Subsequent to Summer (Fuller), **Supp. VII:** 79
Substance of the Speech . . . in Answer to . . . the Report of the Committee of Managers (Burke), **III:** 205
Substance of the Speeches for the Retrenchment of Public Expenses (Burke), **III:** 205
"Suburban Dream" (Muir), **Supp. VI:** 207
Success (Amis), **Supp. IV:** 26, 27, 31–32, 37
"Success" (Empson), **Supp. II:** 180, 189
Success and Failure of Picasso, The (Berger), **Supp. IV:** 79, 88
"Successor, The" (Cameron), **Supp. IX:** 23, 27
Such (Brooke–Rose)), **Supp. IV:** 99, 104, 105, 106–108
Such a Long Journey (Mistry), **Supp. X:** 142–146
"Such Darling Dodos" (Wilson), **Supp. I:** 154
"Such nights as these in England . . . A" (Swinburne), **V:** 310
Such Stuff as Dreams Are Made On (tr. FitzGerald), **IV:** 349, 353
Such, Such Were the Joys (Orwell), **VII:** 275, 282
Such Was My Singing (Nichols), **VI:** 419

Suckling, Sir John, **I:** 337; **II:** 222, 223, **226–229**
"Sudden Light" (Rossetti), **V:** 241, 242
Sudden Times (Healy), **Supp. IX:** 96, 100–103
"Suddenly" (Thomas), **Supp. XII:** 289
Sue, Eugène, **VI:** 228
"Suet Pudding, A" (Powys), **VIII:** 255
Suffrage of Elvira, The (Naipaul), **Supp. I:** 386–387, 388
"Sufism" (Jennings), **Supp. V:** 217
Sugar and Other Stories (Byatt), **Supp. IV:** 140, 151
Sugar and Rum (Unsworth), **Supp. VII:** 357, 361–363, 366
"Suicide" (Blackwood), **Supp. IX:** 7
"Suicide Club, The" (Stevenson), **V:** 395; **Retro. Supp. I:** 263
Suitable Boy, A (Seth), **Supp. X:** 277, 279, 281–288, 290
Suite in Three Keys (Coward), **Supp. II:** 156–157
"Sullens Sisters, The" (Coppard), **VIII:** 90
Sultan in Oman (Morris, J.), **Supp. X:** 175
Sultry Month, A: Scenes of London Literary Life in 1846 (Hayter), **IV:** 322
Sum Practysis of Medecyn (Henryson), **Supp. VII:** 146, 147
Summer (Bond), **Supp. I:** 423, 434–435
Summer (Thomson), **Supp. III:** 411, 414, 416, 417, 418, 419
Summer Before the Dark, The (Lessing), **Supp. I:** 249, 253
Summer Bird–Cage, A (Drabble), **Supp. IV:** 230, 234–236, 241
Summer Day's Dream (Priestley), **VII:** 229
Summer Islands (Douglas), **VI:** 295, 305
"Summer Lightning" (Davie), **Supp. VI:** 112–113
Summer Lightning (Wodehouse), *see Fish Preferred*
"Summer Night, A" (Auden), **Retro. Supp. I:** 6
Summer Rites (Rankin), **Supp. X:** 246
"Summer Waterfall, Glendale" (MacCaig), **Supp. VI:** 182
Summer Will Show (Warner), **Supp. VII:** 376
"Summerhouse on the Mound, The" (Bridges), **VI:** 74
Summers, M., **III:** 345
"Summer's Breath" (Wallace–Crabbe), **VIII:** 324
"Summer's Day, On a" (Smith, I. C.), **Supp. IX:** 215
Summing Up, The (Maugham), **VI:** 364, 374
Summit (Thomas), **Supp. IV:** 485, 489
Summoned by Bells (Betjeman), **VII:** 355, 356, 361, 373–374
Sumner, Rosemary, **Retro. Supp. I:** 115
"Sun & Moon" (Longley), **VIII:** 176
"Sun and the Fish, The" (Woolf), **Retro. Supp. I:** 308
Sun Before Departure (Sillitoe), **Supp. V:** 424, 425
Sun King, The (Mitford), **Supp. X:** 167

Sun Poem (Brathwaite), **Supp. XII:** 33, 41, 46

"Sun used to shine, The" (Thomas), **Supp. III:** 395

"Sun Valley" (Thomas), **Supp. IV:** 493

"Sunburst" (Davie), **Supp. VI:** 110

"Sunday" (Hughes), **Supp. I:** 341–342, 348

"Sunday Afternoon" (Bowen), **Supp. II:** 77

Sunday Morning at the Centre of the World (De Bernières), **Supp. XII:** 66

"Sundew, The" (Swinburne), **V:** 315, 332

"Sunlight" (Gunn), **Supp. IV:** 268

"Sunlight in a Room" (Hart), **Supp. XI:** 127

"Sunlight on the Garden" (MacNeice), **VII:** 413

"Sunne Rising, The" (Donne), **II:** 127; **Retro. Supp. II:** 88–89, 90–91

"Sunny Prestatyn" (Larkin), **Supp. I:** 285

Sunny Side, The (Milne), **Supp. V:** 298

"Sunrise, A" (Owen), **VI:** 449

Sun's Darling, The (Dekker and Ford), **II:** 89, 100

Sun's Net, The (Brown), **Supp. VI:** 69

Sunset Across the Bay (Bennett), **VIII:** 27

Sunset and Evening Star (O'Casey), **VII:** 13

Sunset at Blandings (Wodehouse), **Supp. III:** 452–453

"Sunset on Mount Blanc" (Stephen), **V:** 282

"Sunsets" (Aldington), **VI:** 416

"Sunsum" (Brathwaite), **Supp. XII:** 39

"Suntrap" (Murphy), **Supp. V:** 328

"Sunup" (Murphy), **Supp. V:** 325

"Super Flumina Babylonis" (Swinburne), **V:** 325

"Superannuated Man, The" (Lamb), **IV:** 83

Supernatural Horror in Literature (Lovecraft), **III:** 340

Supernatural Omnibus, The (Summers), **III:** 345

"Superstition" (Bacon), **III:** 39

"Superstition" (Hogg), **Supp. X:** 104, 110

"Superstitious Man's Story, The" (Hardy), **VI:** 22

Supper at Emmaus (Caravaggio), **Supp. IV:** 95

Supplication of Souls (More), **Supp. VII:** 244–245

"Supports, The" (Kipling), **VI:** 189

"Supposed Confessions of a Second–rate Sensitive Mind in Dejection" (Owen), **VI:** 445

Supposes (Gascoigne), **I:** 298, 303

"Sure" (Thomas), **Supp. XII:** 291

"Sure Proof" (MacCaig), **Supp. VI:** 191

"Surface Textures" (Desai), **Supp. V:** 65

Surgeon's Daughter, The (Scott), **IV:** 34–35, 39

Surgeon's Mate, The (O'Brian), **Supp. XII:** 256

Surprise, The (Haywood), **Supp. XII:** 135

Surprised by Joy: The Shape of My Early Life (Lewis), **Supp. III:** 247, 248

"Surrender, The" (King), **Supp. VI:** 151, 153

Surrey, Henry Howard, earl of, **I:** 97, 98, 113

Surroundings (MacCaig), **Supp. VI: 189–190,** 195

Survey of Experimental Philosophy, A (Goldsmith), **III:** 189, 191

Survey of Modernist Poetry, A (Riding and Graves), **VII:** 260; **Supp. II:** 185

"Surview" (Hardy), **VI:** 13

"Survivor" (Kinsella), **Supp. V:** 267

Survivor, The (Keneally), **Supp. IV:** 345

"Survivors" (Ross), **VII:** 433

Suspense (Conrad), **VI:** 147

Suspension of Mercy, A (Highsmith), **Supp. V:** 174–175

"Suspiria de Profundis" (De Quincey), **IV:** 148, 153, 154

Sverris saga, **VIII:** 242

"Swallow, The" (Cowley), **II:** 198

Swallow (Thomas), **Supp. IV:** 483, 484–485

"Swan, The" (Dahl), **Supp. IV:** 207, 223, 224

"Swan, A Man, A" (Blunden), **Supp. XI:** 47

Swan Song (Galsworthy), **VI:** 275

"Swans Mating" (Longley), **VIII:** 171–172, 173

"Swans on an Autumn River" (Warner), **Supp. VII:** 380

Swearer's Bank, The (Swift), **III:** 35

Swedenborg, Emanuel, **III:** 292, 297; **Retro. Supp. I:** 39

Sweeney Agonistes (Eliot), **VII:** 157–158

"Sweeney Among the Nightingales" (Eliot), **VII:** xiii, 145

Sweeney Astray (Heaney), **Supp. II:** 268, 277, 278; **Retro. Supp. I:** 129

"Sweeney Erect" (Eliot), **VII:** 145

Sweeney poems (Eliot), **VII:** 145–146; *see also* ASweeney Among the Nightingales; ASweeney Erect"

"Sweeney Redivivus" (Heaney), **Supp. II:** 277, 278

Sweet Dove Died, The (Pym), **Supp. II: 378–380**

Sweet Dreams (Frayn), **Supp. VII:** 56, 58–60, 61, 65

Sweet Smell of Psychosis (Self), **Supp. V:** 406

Sweet–Shop Owner, The (Swift), **Supp. V:** 427–429

"Sweet Things" (Gunn), **Supp. IV:** 272

Sweet William (Bainbridge), **Supp. VI:** 18, 20–22, 24

"Sweet William's Farewell to Black–ey'd Susan" (Gay), **III:** 58

"Sweetheart of M. Brisieux, The" (James), **VI:** 69

Sweets of Pimlico, The (Wilson), **Supp. VI:** 297, **298–299,** 301

Swift, Graham, **Supp. IV:** 65; **Supp. V: 427–442**

Swift, Jonathan, **II:** 240, 259, 261, 269, 273, 335; **III: 15–37,** 39, 44, 53, 55, 76; **IV:** 160, 257, 258; **VII:** 127; **Retro. Supp. I: 273–287**

"Swift has sailed into his rest" (Yeats), **III:** 21

"Swifts" (Hughes), **Retro. Supp. II:** 208–209

"Swifts" (Stevenson), **Supp. VI:** 265

"Swigs" (Dunn), **Supp. X:** 79

Swimming Free: On and Below the Surface of Lake, River, and Sea (Dutton), **Supp. XII:** 83, 84, 92

"Swimming Lessons" (Mistry), **Supp. X:** 141–142

Swimming Lessons and Other Stories from Ferozsha Baag (Mistry), **Supp. X:** 138–142

Swimming Pool Library, The (Hollinghurst), **Supp. X:** 119–120, 122–129, 132, 134

"Swim in Co. Wicklow, A" (Mahon), **Supp. VI:** 178

Swinburne, Algernon Charles, **II:** 102; **III:** 174; **IV:** 90, 337, 346, 370; **V:** xi, xii, 236, 284, 286, 298–299, **309–335,** 346, 355, 365, 401

Swinburne: The Portrait of a Poet (Henderson), **V:** 335

"Swing, The" (Heaney), **Retro. Supp. I:** 133

"Swing, The" (Wallace–Crabbe), **VIII:** 311

"Swing of the Pendulum, The" (Mansfield), **VII:** 172

Swinging the Maelstrom (Lowry), **Supp. III:** 272

Swinnerton, Frank, **VI:** 247, 268; **VII:** 223

Switch, The (Malouf), **Supp. XII:** 220

Switch Bitch (Dahl), **Supp. IV:** 219

Sword of Honour trilogy (Waugh), **VII:** xx–xxi, 303–306; *see also Men at Arms; Officers and Gentlemen; Unconditional Surrender*

"Sword Music" (Stallworthy), **Supp. X:** 296

Sybil (Disraeli), **IV:** xii, xx, 296, 300, 301–302, 305, 307, 308; **V:** viii, x, 2, 4

Sycamore Tree, The (Brooke–Rose)), **Supp. IV:** 99, 101–102

"Sydney and the Bush" (Murray), **Supp. VII:** 276

Sykes Davies, Hugh, **IV:** xii, xxv; **V:** x, xxviii, 103

Sylva (Cowley), **II:** 202

Sylva; or, A Discourse of Forest–Trees (Evelyn), **II:** 275, 287

Sylva sylvarum (Bacon), **I:** 259, 263, 273

Sylvae (ed. Dryden), **II:** 301, 304

Sylvia and Ted: A Novel (Tennant), see *Ballad of Sylvia and Ted, The*

Sylvia's Lovers (Gaskell), **V:** 1, 4, 6, 7–8, 12, 15

Sylvie and Bruno (Carroll), **V:** 270–271, 273

Sylvie and Bruno Concluded (Carroll), **V:** 271, 273

Symbolic Logic (Carroll), **V:** 271, 274

Symbolist Movement in Literature, The (Symons), **VI:** ix

Symonds, John Addington, **V:** 83

Symons, Arthur, **VI:** ix

Symons, Julian, **Supp. IV:** 3, 339
"Sympathy in White Major" (Larkin), **Supp. I:** 282
Synge, John Millington, **II:** 258; **VI:** xiv, **307–314,** 317; **VII:** 3, 42; **Retro. Supp. I: 289–303**
Synge and Anglo–Irish Drama (Price), **VI:** 317
Synge and the Ireland of His Time (Yeats), **VI:** 222, 317
Syntactic Structures (Chomsky), **Supp. IV:** 113–114
"Syntax of Seasons, The" (Reid), **Supp. VII:** 330
"Synth" (Roberts, K.), **Supp. X:** 262–263
Syrie Maugham (Fisher), **VI:** 379
System of Logic (Mill), **V:** 279
System of Magick, A; or, A History of the Black Art (Defoe), **III:** 14
Systema medicinae hermeticae generale (Nollius), **II:** 201
Syzygies and Lanrick (Carroll), **V:** 273–274

T. E. Hulme: The Selected Writings (Hulme), **Supp. VI:** 135–136, 138, 140, 142, 143
T. E. Lawrence: The Selected Letters (Lawrence), **Supp. II:** 283, 286, 289, 290, 293, 295, 296, 297
T. Fisher Unwin (publisher), **VI:** 373
T. S. Eliot (Ackroyd), **Supp. VI:** 5–6, 8
T. S. Eliot (Bergonzi), **VII:** 169
"T. S. Eliot" (Forster), **VII:** 144
"T. S. Eliot and Ezra Pound" (Ewart), **Supp. VII:** 45
"T. S. Eliot as Critic" (Leavis), **VII:** 233
"Tabill of Confessioun, The" (Dunbar), **VIII:** 119
"Table, The" (Trevor), **Supp. IV:** 500
Table Book (Hone), **IV:** 255
Table Manners (Ayckbourn), **Supp. V:** 2, 5
Table Near the Band, A (Milne), **Supp. V:** 309
Table Talk (Hazlitt), **IV:** xviii, 131, 137, 139
Table Talk, and Other Poems (Cowper), **III:** 220
Table Talk 1941–1944 (Cameron), **Supp. IX:** 28
Tables Turned, The (Morris), **V:** 306
"Tables Turned, The" (Wordsworth), **IV:** 7, 225
Taburlaine the Great, Part I (Marlowe), **Retro. Supp. I:** 204–206
Taburlaine the Great, Part II (Marlowe), **Retro. Supp. I:** 206–207
"Tadnol" (Powys), **VIII:** 248
"Taft's Wife" (Blackwood), **Supp. IX:** 12
Tagore, Rabindranath, **Supp. IV:** 440, 454
Tailor of Gloucester, The (Potter), **Supp. III:** 290, 301–302
Taill of Schir Chantecleir and the Foxe, The (Henryson), see *Cock and the Fox, The*
Taill of the Uponlondis Mous and the Burges Mous, The (Henryson), see *Two Mice, The*

Táin, The (Kinsella), **Supp. V:** 264–266
Take a Girl Like You (Amis), Supp. II: 10–11, 18
Taken Care of (Sitwell), **VII:** 128, 132
Takeover, The (Spark), **Supp. I:** 211–212
"Taking Down the Christmas Tree" (Stevenson), **Supp. VI:** 262
Taking Steps (Ayckbourn), **Supp. V:** 3, 12, 13
Talbert, E. W., **I:** 224
"Talbot Road" (Gunn), **Supp. IV:** 272, 273–274
"Tale, The" (Conrad), **VI:** 148
Tale of a Town, The (Martyn), **VI:** 95
"Tale of a Trumpet, A" (Hood), **IV:** 258
Tale of a Tub, A (Swift), **II:** 259, 269; **III:** 17, 19, **21–23,** 35; **Retro. Supp. I:** 273, 276, 277–278
Tale of Balen, The (Swinburne), **V:** 333
Tale of Benjamin Bunny, The (Potter), **Supp. III:** 290, 299
Tale of Beowulf, Done out of the Old English Tongue, The (Morris, Wyatt), **V:** 306
Tale of Ginger and Pickles, The (Potter), **Supp. III:** 290, 299
Tale of Jemima Puddle–Duck, The (Potter), **Supp. III:** 290, 303
Tale of Johnny Town–Mouse, The (Potter), **Supp. III:** 297, 304, 307
Tale of King Arthur, The (Malory), **I:** 68
Tale of Little Pig Robinson, The (Potter), **Supp. III:** 288, 289, 297, 304–305
Tale of Mr. Jeremy Fisher, The (Potter), **Supp. III:** 298, 303
Tale of Mr. Tod, The (Potter), **Supp. III:** 290, 299
Tale of Mrs. Tiggy–Winkle, The (Potter), **Supp. III:** 290, 301–302
Tale of Mrs. Tittlemouse, The (Potter), **Supp. III:** 298, 301
Tale of Paraguay, A (Southey), **IV:** 66–67, 68, 71
Tale of Peter Rabbit, The (Potter), **Supp. III:** 287, 288, 290, 293, **295–296,** 299
Tale of Pigling Bland, The (Potter), **Supp. III.** 288–289, 290, 291, 304
Tale of Rosamund Gray and Old Blind Margaret, A (Lamb), **IV:** 79, 85
Tale of Samuel Whiskers, The (Potter), **Supp. III:** 290, 297, 301, 305
Tale of Sir Gareth of Orkeney that was called Bewmaynes, The (Malory), **I:** 72, 73; **Retro. Supp. II:** 243, 247
Tale of Sir Lancelot and Queen Guinevere (Malory), **Retro. Supp. II:** 243, 244
Tale of Sir Thopas, The (Chaucer), **I:** 67, 71
"Tale of Society As It Is, A" (Shelley), **Retro. Supp. I:** 245
Tale of Squirrel Nutkin, The (Potter), **Supp. III:** 288, 290, 301
Tale of the House of the Wolflings, A (Morris), **V:** 302, 306
Tale of the Noble King Arthur that was Emperor himself through Dignity of his Hands (Malory), **I:** 69, 72, 77–79
Tale of the Pie and the Patty–Pan, The (Potter), **Supp. III:** 290, 299

Tale of the Sankgreal, The (Malory), **I:** 69; **Retro. Supp. II:** 248–249
Tale of the Sea, A (Conrad), **VI:** 148
Tale of Timmy Tiptoes, The (Potter), **Supp. III:** 290
"Tale of Tod Lapraik, The" (Stevenson), **Retro. Supp. I:** 267
Tale of Tom Kitten, The (Potter), **Supp. III:** 290, 299, 300, 302, 303
Tale of Two Bad Mice, The (Potter), **Supp. III:** 290, 300–301
Tale of Two Cities, A (Dickens), **V:** xxii, 41, 42, 57, 63, 66, 72
"Talent and Friendship" (Kinsella), **Supp. V:** 270
Talent to Annoy, A (Mitford), **Supp. X:** 163
Talented Mr. Ripley, The (Highsmith), **Supp. V:** 170
Tales (Crabbe), **III:** 278, 285, 286; *see also Tales in Verse; Tales of the Hall; Posthumous Tales*
"Tales" (Dickens), **V:** 46
Tales and Sketches (Disraeli), **IV:** 308
Tales from a Troubled Land (Paton), **Supp. II: 344–345,** 348, 354
Tales from Angria (Brontë), **V:** 151
Tales from Ovid (Hughes), **Retro. Supp. II:** 202, 214–216
Tales from Shakespeare (Lamb and Lamb), **IV:** xvi, 80, 85
Tales I Tell My Mother (ed. Fairbairns et al.), **Supp. XI:** 163, 164, 175
Tales I Told My Mother (Nye), **Supp. X:** 195
Tales in Verse (Crabbe), **III:** 275, 278, 279, 281, 286
Tales of a Grandfather (Scott), **IV:** 38
Tales of All Countries (Trollope), **V:** 101
Tales of Good and Evil (Gogol), **III:** 345
Tales of Hearsay (Conrad), **VI:** 148
Tales of Hoffmann (Hoffmann), **III:** 334, 345
Tales of Mean Streets (Morrison), **VI:** 365
Tales of My Landlord (Scott), **IV:** 39
Tales of Natural and Unnatural Catastrophes (Highsmith), **Supp. V:** 179
Tales of St. Austin's (Wodehouse), **Supp. III:** 449–450
Tales of Sir Gareth (Malory), **I:** 68
Tales of the Crusaders (Scott), **IV:** 39
Tales of the Five Towns (Bennett), **VI:** 253
Tales of the Hall (Crabbe), **III:** 278, 285, 286; **V:** xvii, 6
"Tales of the Islanders" (Brontë), **V:** 107, 114, 135
Tales of the Punjab (Steel), **Supp. XII:** 266
Tales of the Tides, and Other Stories (Steel), **Supp. XII:** 275
Tales of Three Cities (James), **VI:** 67
Tales of Unrest (Conrad), **VI:** 148
Talfourd, Field, **IV:** 311
Taliesin (Nye), **Supp. X:** 193
"Taliessin on the Death of Virgil" (Williams, C. W. S.), 283
"Taliessin Returns to Logres" (Williams, C. W. S.), **Supp. IX:** 282

"There was never nothing more me pained" (Wyatt), **I:** 103

"There Will Be No Peace" (Auden), **Retro. Supp. I:** 13

"There's Nothing Here" (Muir), **Supp. VI:** 208

"Thermal Stair, The" (Graham), **Supp. VII:** 114

These Demented Lands (Warner), **Supp. XI:** 282, 285, 286–289, 294

"These Summer–Birds did with thy Master stay" (Herrick), **II:** 103

These the Companions (Davie), **Supp. VI:** 105, 109, 111, 113, 117

These Twain (Bennett), **VI:** 258

"Theses on the Philosophy of History" (Benjamin), **Supp. IV:** 87

Thespian Magazine (periodical), **III:** 263

"Thespians at Thermopylae, The" (Cameron), **Supp. IX:** 19

"They" (Kipling), **VI:** 199

"They" (Sassoon), **VI:** 430

"They" (Wallace–Crabbe), **VIII:** 322

"They All Go to the Mountains Now" (Brooke–Rose)), **Supp. IV:** 103

"They Are All Gone into the World of Light!" (Vaughan), **II:** 188

They Came to a City (Priestley), **VII:** 210, 227

"They flee from me" (Wyatt), **I:** 102

"They Shall Not Grow Old" (Dahl), **Supp. IV:** 210, 224

They Walk in the City (Priestley), **VII:** 217

They Went (Douglas), **VI:** 303, 304, 305

"Thief" (Graves), **VII:** 267

Thierry and Theodoret (Beaumont, Fletcher, Massinger), **II:** 66

Thieves in the Night (Koestler), **Supp. I:** 27–28, 32–33

"Thin Air" (Armitage), **VIII:** 11

"Thing Itself, The" (Wallace–Crabbe), **VIII:** 321

"Things" (Adcock), **Supp. XII:** 6

Things That Have Interested Me (Bennett), **VI:** 267

Things That Interested Me (Bennett), **VI:** 267

Things We Do for Love (Ayckbourn), **Supp. V:** 3–4, 12–13

Things Which Have Interested Me (Bennett), **VI:** 267

"Thinking as a Hobby" (Golding), **Supp. I:** 75

"Thinking of Mr. D." (Kinsella), **Supp. V:** 260

Thinking Reed, The (West), **Supp. III:** 442

"Thir Lady is Fair" (Dunbar), **VIII:** 122

"Third Journey, The" (Graham), **Supp. VII:** 109

Third Man, The (Greene), **Supp. I:** 11; **Retro. Supp. II:** 159

"Third Person, The" (James), **VI:** 69

Third Policeman, The (O'Nolan), **Supp. II:** 322, 326–329, 337, 338

"Third Prize, The" (Coppard), **VIII:** 96

Third Satire (Wyatt), **I:** 111

"Third Ypres" (Blunden), **Supp. XI:** 46

"Thirteen Steps and the Thirteenth of March" (Dunn), **Supp. X:** 76

Thirteen Such Years (Waugh), **Supp. VI:** 272–273

Thirteen–Gun Salute, The (O'Brian), **Supp. XII:** 258–259

Thirteenth Tribe, The (Koestler), **Supp. I:** 33

30 Days in Sydney: A Wildly Distorted Account (Carey), **Supp. XII:** 50, 52, 54, 60, 62

"30 December" (Cope), **VIII:** 80

"38 Phoenix Street" (Kinsella), **Supp. V:** 268

Thirty–Nine Steps, The (Buchan), **Supp. II:** 299, 306; **Supp. IV:** 7

31 Poems (Dutton), **Supp. XII:** 87

36 Hours (film), **Supp. IV:** 209

"Thirty–Three Triads" (Kinsella), **Supp. V:** 264

"This Be the Verse" (Larkin), **Supp. I:** 284

"This bread I break" (Thomas), **Supp. I:** 174

"This Day, Under My Hand" (Malouf), **Supp. XII:** 219

"This England" (Thomas), **Supp. III:** 404

This England: An Anthology from Her Writers (ed. Thomas), **Supp. III:** 404–405

This Gun for Hire (Greene), *see Gun for Sale, A*

This Happy Breed (Coward), **Supp. II:** 151, 154

"This Hinder Nicht in Dunfermeling" (Dunbar), **VIII:** 122

"This Is No Case of Petty Right or Wrong" (Thomas), **VI:** 424; **Supp. III:** 395

"This Is Thyself" (Powys), **VIII:** 247

This Is Where I Came In (Ayckbourn), **Supp. V:** 3, 11, 13

"This Is Your Subject Speaking" (Motion), **Supp. VII:** 257

"This Last Pain" (Empson), **Supp. II:** 184–185

This Life I've Loved (Field), **V:** 393, 397

"This Lime Tree Bower My Prison" (Coleridge), **IV:** 41, 44; **Retro. Supp. II:** 52

This Misery of Boots (Wells), **VI:** 244

This My Hand (Caudwell), **Supp. IX:** 33, 35, 37, 39–40, 46

This Real Night (West), **Supp. III:** 443

This Sporting Life (Storey), **Supp. I:** 407, **408–410,** 414, 415, 416

"This Stone Is Thinking of Vienna" (Hart), **Supp. XI:** 130

This Sweet Sickness (Highsmith), **Supp. V:** 172–173

This Time Tomorrow (Ngũgĩ), **VIII:** 213, 222

This Was a Man (Coward), **Supp. II:** 146

"This was for youth, Strength, Mirth and wit that Time" (Walton), **II:** 141

This Was the Old Chief's Country (Lessing), **Supp. I:** 239

This Year of Grace! (Coward), **Supp. II:** 146

Thistle Rises, The (MacDiarmid), **Supp. XII:** 208

"Thistles" (Hughes), **Retro. Supp. II:** 205–206

Thistles and Roses (Smith, I. C.), **Supp. IX:** 211–212

Thom Gunn and Ted Hughes (Bold), **Supp. IV:** 256, 257

"Thom Gunn at 60" (Hall), **Supp. IV:** 256

Thomas, D. M., **Supp. IV: 479–497**

Thomas, Dylan, **II:** 156; **Supp. I: 169–184; Supp. III:** 107; **Supp. IV:** 252, 263

Thomas, Edward, **IV:** 218; **V:** 313, 334, 355, 358; **VI:** 420–421, **423–425; VII:** xvi, 382; **Supp. III: 393–408**

Thomas, R. S., **Supp. XII: 279–294**

"Thomas Bewick" (Gunn), **Supp. IV:** 269

"Thomas Campey and the Copernican System" (Harrison), **Supp. V:** 151

Thomas Carlyle (Campbell), **IV:** 250

Thomas Carlyle (Froude), **IV:** 238–239, 250

Thomas Cranmer of Canterbury (Williams, C. W. S.), **Supp. IX:** 284

Thomas De Quincey: A Biography (Eaton), **IV:** 142, 156

Thomas De Quincey: His Life and Writings (Page), **IV:** 152, 155

"Thomas Gray" (Arnold), **III:** 277

Thomas Hardy (Blunden), **Supp. XI:** 37

Thomas Hardy: A Bibliographical Study (Purdy), **VI:** 19

Thomas Hardy and British Poetry (Davie), **Supp. VI:** 115

Thomas Hobbes (Stephen), **V:** 289

Thomas Hood (Reid), **IV:** 267

Thomas Hood and Charles Lamb (ed. Jerrold), **IV:** 252, 253, 267

Thomas Hood: His Life and Times (Jerrold), **IV:** 267

Thomas Love Peacock (Priestley), **IV:** 159–160, 170

Thomas Nabbes (Swinburne), **V:** 333

Thomas Stevenson, Civil Engineer (Stevenson), **V:** 395

Thomas the Rhymer, **IV:** 29, 219

Thomas Traherne: Centuries, Poems, and Thanksgivings (Traherne), **Supp. XI:** 266

Thompson, E. P., **Supp. IV:** 95, 473

Thompson, Francis, **III:** 338; **V:** xxii, xxvi, 439–452

Thompson, R., **II:** 288

Thomson, George, **III:** 322

Thomson, James, **III:** 162, 171, 312; **Supp. III:** 409–429; **Retro. Supp. I:** 241

Thor, with Angels (Fry), **Supp. III:** 195, 197–198

"Thorn, The" (Wordsworth), **IV:** 6, 7

Thornton, R. K. R., **V:** 377, 382

Thornton, Robert, **III:** 307

Thorsler, Jr., P. L., **IV:** 173, 194

Those Barren Leaves (Huxley), **VII:** 79, 199, 202

Those Were the Days (Milne), **Supp. V:** 298

Those Were the Days: The Holocaust through the Eyes of the Perpetrators and Bystanders, **Supp. IV:** 488

"Those White, Ancient Birds" (Hart), **Supp. XI:** 131–132

Those Who Walk Away (Highsmith), **Supp. V:** 175

"Thou art an Atheist, *Quintus,* and a Wit" (Sedley), **II:** 265–266

"Thou art fair and few are fairer" (Shelley), **IV:** 203

"Thou art indeed just, Lord" (Hopkins), **V:** 376, 378

"Thou damn'd Antipodes to Common sense" (Dorset), **II:** 263

"Thou that know'st for whom I mourne" (Vaughan), **II:** 187

"Though this the port and I thy servant true" (Wyatt), **I:** 106

"Though, Phillis, your prevailing charms," **II:** 257

"Thought" (Lawrence), **VII:** 119

Thought Power (Besant), **VI:** 249

"Thought–Fox, The" (Hughes), **Supp. I:** 347

Thoughts (Beddoes), **Supp. XI:** 20

"Thoughts" (Traherne), **Supp. XI:** 269

Thoughts and Details on Scarcity . . . (Burke), **III:** 205

Thoughts for a Convention (Russell), **VIII:** 288

Thoughts in the Wilderness (Priestley), **VII:** 212

"Thoughts of a Suicide" (Tennyson), *see* "Two Voices, The"

Thoughts of Murdo (Smith, I. C.), **Supp. IX:** 210–211

"Thoughts on Criticism, by a Critic" (Stephen), **V:** 286

Thoughts on the Ministerial Commission (Newman), **Supp. VII:** 291

Thoughts on South Africa (Schreiner), **Supp. II:** 453, 454, 457

Thoughts on the Cause of the Present Discontents (Burke), **III:** 197

Thoughts on the Education of Daughters; . . . (Wollstonecraft), **Supp. III:** 466

Thoughts on the . . . Falkland's Islands (Johnson), **III:** 121; **Retro. Supp. I:** 142

"Thoughts on the Shape of the Human Body" (Brooke), **Supp. III:** 52–53

"Thoughts on Unpacking" (Gunn), **Supp. IV:** 262

Thrale, Hester, *see* Piozzi, Hester Lynch

"Thrawn Janet" (Stevenson), **V:** 395; **Retro. Supp. I:** 267

Thre Deid Pollis, The (Henryson), **Supp. VII:** 146, 148

"Three Aquarium Portraits" (Redgrove), **Supp. VI:** 234, 236

"Three Baroque Meditations" (Hill), **Supp. V:** 187, 188

Three Bear Witness (O'Brian), **Supp. XII:** 251

"Three Blind Mice" (Christie), **Supp. II:** 134

Three Brothers, The (Muir), **Supp. VI:** 198

Three Brothers, The (Oliphant), **Supp. X:** 217

Three Cheers for the Paraclete (Keneally), **Supp. IV:** 345

Three Chinese Poets: Translations of Poems by Wang Wei, Li Bai and Du Fu (tr. Seth), **Supp. X:** 277, 284

Three Clerks, The (Trollope), **V:** 101

Three Continents (Jhabvala), **Supp. V:** 233–234, 235

Three Dialogues (Beckett), **Retro. Supp. I:** 18–19, 22

Three Essays, Moral and Political (Hume), **Supp. III:** 239

"Three Folk Poems" (Plomer), **Supp. XI:** 210

Three Friends (Bridges), **VI:** 72, 83

Three Glasgow Writers (Kelman), **Supp. V:** 241

Three Guineas (Woolf), **VII:** 22, 25, 27, 29, 38; **Supp. IV:** 399; **Retro. Supp. I:** 308, 311

Three Hours After Marriage (Gay), **III:** 60, 67

3 in 1 (Reading), **VIII:** 271

Three Letters, Written in Spain, to D. Francisco Riguelme (Landor), **IV:** 100

"Three Little Pigs, The" (Dahl), **Supp. IV:** 226

"Three Lives of Lucie Cabrol, The" (Berger), **Supp. IV:** 92–93, 94

Three Memorials on French Affairs . . . (Burke), **III:** 205

Three Men in New Suits (Priestley), **VII:** 218

Three Northern Love Stories (Morris and Magnusson), **V:** 306

Three of Them (Douglas), **VI:** 300, 305

Three Perils of Man, The (Hogg), **Supp. X:** 113–114

Three Perils of Woman, The (Hogg), **Supp. X:** 113–114

Three Plays (Williams, C. W. S.), **Supp. IX:** 276–277

Three Plays for Puritans (Shaw), **VI:** 104, 112, 129; **Retro. Supp. II:** 315–317

"Three Poems in Memory of My Mother, Miriam Murray neé Arnall" (Murray), **Supp. VII:** 278

"Three Poems of Drowning" (Graham), **Supp. VII:** 110

"Three Poets" (Dunn), **Supp. X:** 82–83

Three proper, and witty, familiar Letters (Spenser), **I:** 123

Three Regional Voices: Iain Crichton Smith, Barry Tebb, Michael Longley (Smith, I. C.), **Supp. IX:** 213

Three Sermons (Swift), **III:** 36

Three Short Stories (Powys), **VIII:** 249, 256

Three Sisters, The (tr. Frayn), **Supp. VII:** 61

Three Sisters, The (tr. Friel), **Supp. V:** 124

"Three Songs for Monaro Pubs" (Hope), **Supp. VII:** 158

"Three Strangers, The" (Hardy), **VI:** 20, 22

Three Sunsets and Other Poems (Carroll), **V:** 274

Three Times Table (Maitland), **Supp. XI:** 163, 168–170, 174

Three Voices of Poetry, The (Eliot), **VII:** 161, 162

Three Wayfarers, The: A Pastoral Play in One Act (Hardy), **VI:** 20

"Three Weeks to Argentina" (Ewart), **Supp. VII:** 45

"Three Women's Texts and a Critique of Imperialism" (Spivak), **Retro. Supp. I:** 60

Three Years in a Curatorship (Carroll), **V:** 274

Threnodia Augustalis (Goldsmith), **III:** 191

Threnodia Augustalis: A Funeral . . . Poem to . . . King Charles II (Dryden), **II:** 304

"Threshold" (Thomas), **Supp. XII:** 288

Thrice a Stranger (Brittain), **Supp. X:** 44

"Thrissil and the Rois, The" (Dunbar), **VIII:** 118

Thrissill and the Rois, The (Dunbar), **VIII:** 121

"Through the Looking Glass" (Auden), **VII:** 381

Through the Looking–Glass and What Alice Found There (Carroll), **V:** xxiii, 261, 262, 264, 265, 267–269, 270–273

Through the Panama (Lowry), **Supp. III:** 269, 280, 282, 283

"Through These Pale Gold Days" (Rosenberg), **VI:** 435

Thru (Brooke–Rose)), **Supp. IV:** 98, 99, 105, 109–110, 112

"Thrush in February, The" (Meredith), **V:** 222

"Thrushes" (Hughes), **Supp. I:** 345

"Thunder and a Boy" (Jennings), **Supp. V:** 218

Thurley, Geoffrey, **Supp. II:** 494

"Thursday; or, The Spell" (Gay), **III:** 56

Thursday's Child: A Pageant (Fry), **Supp. III:** 194

Thus to Revisit (Ford), **VI:** 321, 323

"Thy Beautiful Flock" (Powys), **VIII:** 254

Thyestes (Seneca), **I:** 215; **II:** 71

"Thyrsis" (Arnold), **V:** 157–158, 159, 165, 209, 210, 211; **VI:** 73

Thyrza (Gissing), **V:** 437

"Tiare Tahiti" (Brooke), **Supp. III:** 56

"Tibby Hyslop's Dream" (Hogg), **Supp. X:** 110

"Tich Miller" (Cope), **VIII:** 73

Tickell, Thomas, **III:** 50

Ticonderoga (Stevenson), **V:** 395

Tide and Stone Walls (Sillitoe), **Supp. V:** 424

"Tidings from the Sissioun" (Dunbar), **VIII:** 126

"Tierra del Fuego" (Caudwell), **Supp. IX:** 38

Tietjens tetralogy (Ford), **VI:** xii, 319, **328–331; VII:** xxi; *see also Last Post; Man Could Stand Up, A; No More Parades; Some Do Not*

"Tiger, The" (Coppard), **VIII:** 94, 97

Tiger at the Gates (Fry), **Supp. III:** 195
"Tiger! Tiger!" (Kipling), **VI:** 199
Tigers (Adcock), **Supp. XII:** 4–5
Tigers Are Better–Looking (Rhys), **Supp. II:** 389, 390, 401, 402
Tiger's Bones, The (Hughes), **Supp. I:** 346–347
"Till September Petronella" (Rhys), **Supp. II:** 401–402
Till We Have Faces (Lewis), **Supp. III:** 248, **262–264**, 265
Tillotson, Kathleen, **IV:** 34; **V:** 73
Timber (Jonson), **Retro. Supp. I:** 166
Timbuctoo (Tennyson), **IV:** 338
"Time" (Dutton), **Supp. XII:** 97
Time and the Conways (Priestley), **VII:** 212, 224–225
Time and Tide (O'Brien), **Supp. V:** 341
Time and Tide by Weare and Tyne (Ruskin), **V:** 184
Time and Time Again (Ayckbourn), **Supp. V:** 2, 4–5, 9, 10, 13–14
Time and Western Man (Lewis), **VII:** 72, 74, 75, 83, 262
"Time Disease, The" (Amis), **Supp. IV:** 40
Time Flies: A Reading Diary (Rossetti), **V:** 260
Time for a Tiger (Burgess), **Supp. I:** 187
Time Importuned (Warner), **Supp. VII:** 370, 371–372
Time in a Red Coat (Brown), **Supp. VI:** 66, 69–70
Time in Rome, A (Bowen), **Supp. II:** 80, 94
Time Machine, The: An Invention (Wells), **VI:** ix, xii, 226, 229–230
Time Must Have a Stop (Huxley), **VII:** 205
Time of Hope (Snow), **VII:** xxi, 321, 324–325
Time of the Crack, The (Tennant), **Supp. IX:** 229–230
Time of My Life (Ayckbourn), **Supp. V:** 3, 8, 10, 11, 13, 14
"Time of Plague, The" (Gunn), **Supp. IV:** 277
Time of the Angels, The (Murdoch), **III:** 341, 345; **Supp. I:** 225–226, 227, 228
"Time of Waiting, A" (Graves), **VII:** 269
Time Present (Osborne), **Supp. I:** 338
"Time the Tiger" (Lewis), **VII:** 74
Time to Dance, A (Day Lewis), **Supp. III:** 118, 126
Time to Go, A (O'Casey), **VII:** 12
Time to Keep, A (Brown), **Supp. VI:** 64, 70
Time Traveller, The: The Life of H. G. Wells (MacKenzie and MacKenzie), **VI:** 228, 246
"Timehri" (Brathwaite), **Supp. XII:** 34, 46
"Timekeeping" (Cope), **VIII:** 81
"Timer" (Harrison), **Supp. V:** 150
Time's Arrow; or The Nature of the Offence (Amis), **Supp. IV:** 40–42
Time's Laughingstocks and other Verses (Hardy), **VI:** 20
Times (periodical), **IV:** xv, 272, 278; **V:** 93, 279; **Supp. XII:** 2

Times Literary Supplement, **Supp. IV:** 25, 66, 121
"Time–Tombs, The" (Ballard), **Supp. V:** 21
Time–Zones (Adcock), **Supp. XII:** 10–11, 11–12
Timon of Athens (Shakespeare), **I:** 318–319, 321; **II:** 70
Tin Drum, The (Grass), **Supp. IV:** 440
Tin Men, The (Frayn), **Supp. VII:** 51–52, 64
Tinker, C. B., **III:** 234n, 249, 250
"Tinker, The" (Wordsworth), **IV:** 21
Tinker, Tailor, Soldier, Spy (le Carré), **Supp. II:** 306, **311–313,** 314
Tinker's Wedding, The (Synge), **VI:** 311, 313–314; **Retro. Supp. I:** 296–297
"Tintern Abbey" (Wordsworth), *see* "Lines Composed a Few Miles Above Tintern Abbey"
Tiny Tears (Fuller), **Supp. VII:** 78
Tip of my Tongue, The (Crawford), **Supp. XI:** 67, 79–82
"Tipperary" (Thomas), **Supp. III:** 404
"Tirade for the Mimic Muse" (Boland), **Supp. V:** 49
Tireless Traveller, The (Trollope), **V:** 102
"Tiresias" (Tennyson), **IV:** 328, 332–334, 338
"Tiriel" (Blake), **III:** 298, 302; **Retro. Supp. I:** 34–35
"Tirocinium; or, A Review of Schools" (Cowper), **III:** 208
'Tis Pity She's a Whore (Ford), **II:** 57, 88, 89, 90, 92–93, 99, 100
Tit–Bits (periodical), **VI:** 135, 248
"Tithe Barn, The" (Powys), **VIII:** 248, 249
Tithe Barn, The and The Dove and the Eage (Powys), **VIII:** 248
"Tithon" (Tennyson), **IV:** 332–334; *see also* "Tithonus"
"Tithonus" (Tennyson), **IV:** 328, 333
Title, The (Bennett), **VI:** 250, 264
Title and Pedigree of Henry VI (Lydgate), **I:** 58
Titmarsh, Michael Angelo, pseud. of William Makepeace Thackeray
Titus Andronicus (Shakespeare), **I:** 279, 305; **II:** 69
"Titus Hoyt, I A" (Naipaul), **Supp. I:** 385
"To a Black Greyhound" (Grenfell), **VI:** 418
"To a Brother in the Mystery" (Davie), **Supp. VI:** 113–114
"To a Butterfly" (Wordsworth), **IV:** 21
"To a Cretan Monk in Thanks for a Flask of Wine" (Murphy), **Supp. V:** 318
"To a Cold Beauty" (Hood), **IV:** 255
"To a Comrade in Flanders" (Owen), **VI:** 452
"To a Devout Young Gentlewoman" (Sedley), **II:** 264
"To a Dictionary Maker" (Nye), **Supp. X:** 201
"To a Fat Lady Seen from the Train" (Cornford), **VIII:** 102
"To a *Fine Singer,* who had gotten a *Cold;* . . . " (Wycherley), **II:** 320

"To a Fine Young *Woman* . . . " (Wycherley), **II:** 320
"To a Friend in Time of Trouble" (Gunn), **Supp. IV:** 274, 275
"To a Friend mourning the Death of Miss—" (Macpherson), **VIII:** 181
"To A. L." (Carew), **II:** 224–225
"To a Lady in a Letter" (Rochester), **II:** 258
To a Lady More Cruel Than Fair (Vanbrugh), **II:** 336
"To a Lady on Her Passion for Old China" (Gay), **III:** 58, 67
"To a Lady on the Death of Colonel Ross . . . " (Collins), **III:** 166, 169
"To a Louse" (Burns), **III:** 315, 317–318
"To a Mountain Daisy" (Burns), **III:** 313, 315, 317, 318
"To a Mouse" (Burns), **III:** 315, 317, 318
"To a Nightingale" (Coleridge), **IV:** 222
"To a Skylark" (Shelley), **III:** 337
"To a Snail" (Moore), **Supp. IV:** 262–263
"To a Very Young Lady" (Etherege), **II:** 267
"To Alastair Campbell" (Adcock), **Supp. XII:** 4
"To Althea from Prison" (Lovelace), **II:** 231, 232
"To Amarantha, That She Would Dishevell Her Haire" (Lovelace), **II:** 230
"To Amoret Gone from Him" (Vaughan), **II:** 185
"To Amoret, of the Difference 'twixt Him, . . . " (Vaughan), **II:** 185
"To an English Friend in Africa" (Okri), **Supp. V:** 359
"To an Infant Daughter" (Clare), **Supp. XI:** 55
"To an Old Lady" (Empson), **Supp. II:** 182–183
"To an Unborn Pauper Child" (Hardy), **Retro. Supp. I:** 121
"To an Unknown Reader" (Fuller), **Supp. VII:** 78
"To and Fro" (McEwan), **Supp. IV:** 395
"To Anthea" (Herrick), **II:** 105–106, 108
"To Any Dead Officer" (Sassoon), **VI:** 431
To Asmara (Keneally), **Supp. IV:** 346
"To Augustus" (Pope), **Retro. Supp. I:** 230–231
"To Autumn" (Keats), **IV:** 221, 226–227, 228, 232
To Be a Pilgrim (Cary), **VII:** 186, 187, 191, 192–194
"To Be a Poet" (Stevenson), **Supp. VI:** 260
"To Be Less Philosophical" (Graves), **VII:** 266
"To Blossoms" (Herrick), **II:** 112
"To Call Paula Paul" (McGuckian), **Supp. V:** 286
To Catch a Spy (Ambler), **Supp. IV:** 4, 17
"To cause accord or to agree" (Wyatt), **I:** 109
"To Celia" (Johnson), **IV:** 327
"To Charles Cowden Clarke" (Keats), **IV:** 214, 215

"To Certain English Poets" (Davie), **Supp. VI:** 110

"To Charles Cowden Clarke" (Keats), **Retro. Supp. I:** 188

To Circumjack Cencrastus; or, The Curly Snake (MacDiarmid), **Supp. XII:** 201, 210–211, 216

"To Constantia Singing" (Shelley), **IV:** 209

"To Daffodills" (Herrick), **II:** 112

"To Deanbourn" (Herrick), **II:** 103

"To Dianeme" (Herrick), **II:** 107, 112

"To E. Fitzgerald" (Tennyson), **IV:** 336

"To Edward Thomas" (Lewis), **VII:** 445

"To E. L., on his Travels in Greece" (Tennyson), **V:** 79

"To Electra" (Herrick), **II:** 105

"To Everlasting Oblivion" (Marston), **II:** 25

"To Fanny" (Keats), **IV:** 220–221

"To George Felton Mathew" (Keats), **IV:** 214

"To Germany" (Sorley), **VI:** 421

"To God" (Gurney), **VI:** 426

"To Helen" (Thomas), **Supp. III:** 401

"To His Coy Mistress" (Marvell), **II:** 197, 198, 208–209, 211, 214–215; **Retro. Supp. II:** 259, 261

"To his inconstant Friend" (King), **Supp. VI:** 151

"To His Lost Lover" (Armitage), **VIII:** 8

"To His Love" (Gurney), **VI:** 426

"To His Lovely Mistresses" (Herrick), **II:** 113

To His Sacred Majesty, a Panegyrick on His Coronation (Dryden), **II:** 304

"To His Sweet Savior" (Herrick), **II:** 114

"To His Wife" (Hill), **Supp. V:** 189

"To Hope" (Keats), **Retro. Supp. I:** 188

"To Ireland in the Coming Times" (Yeats), **Retro. Supp. I:** 330

"To J. F. H. (1897–1934)" (Muir), **Supp. VI:** 206

"To Joan Eardley" (Morgan, E.), **Supp. IX:** 165

"To Julia, The Flaminica Dialis, or Queen–

To Keep the Ball Rolling (Powell), **VII:** 351

"To King Henry IV, in Praise of Peace" (Gower), **I:** 56

"To Leonard Clark" (Graham), **Supp. VII:** 116

To Let (Galsworthy), **VI:** 272, 274, 275, 282

To Lighten My House (Reid), **Supp. VII:** 325–327

"To Live Merrily, and to Trust to Good Verses" (Herrick), **II:** 115

To Live with Little (Chapman), **I:** 254

"To Lizbie Browne" (Hardy), **VI:** 16

"To Lord Stanhope" (Coleridge), **IV:** 43

"To Louisa in the Lane" (Thomas), **Supp. IV:** 493

"To Lucasta, Going to the Warres" (Lovelace), **II:** 229

"To Marguerite—Continued" (Arnold), **V:** 211

"To Mary Boyle" (Tennyson), **IV:** 329, 336

"To Mr. Dryden" (Congreve), **II:** 338

To Mr. Harriot (Chapman), **I:** 241

"To Mr. Hobs" (Cowley), **II:** 196, 198

To Mistress Anne (Skelton), **I:** 83

"To My Brother George" (Keats), **IV:** 214

"To My Brothers" (Keats), **IV:** 215

"To My Daughter in a Red Coat" (Stevenson), **Supp. VI: 254**

"To my dead friend Ben: Johnson" (King), **Supp. VI:** 157

"To My Desk" (Dunn), **Supp. X:** 80

To My Fellow Countrymen (Osborne), **Supp. I:** 330

"To My Friend, Mr. Pope, . . . " (Wycherley), **II:** 322

"To My Inconstant Mistris" (Carew), **II:** 225

To My Lady Morton (Waller), **II:** 238

To My Lord Chancellor . . . (Dryden), **II:** 304

"To My Lord Northumberland Upon the Death of His Lady" (Waller), **II:** 233

To My Mother on the Anniversary of Her Birth, April 27, 1842 (Rossetti), **V:** 260

"To My Sister" (Wordsworth), **IV:** 8

"To Night" (Lovelace), **II:** 231

"To Nobodaddy" (Blake), **III:** 299

"To Olga Masson" (tr. Thomas), **Supp. IV:** 495

"To One Who Wanted a Philosophy from Me" (Russell), **VIII:** 290

"To One Who Was with Me in the War" (Sassoon), **VI:** 431

"To Penshurst" (Jonson), **Retro. Supp. I:** 164

"To Perilla" (Herrick), **II:** 113

"To P. H. T" (Thomas), **Supp. III:** 401

"To Please His Wife" (Hardy), **VI:** 20, 22

"To Poet Bavius" (Behn), **Supp. III:** 40

To Present the Pretense (Arden), **Supp. II:** 30

"To R. B." (Hopkins), **V:** 376, 378

"To Rilke" (Lewis), **VII:** 446

"To Room Nineteen" (Lessing), **Supp. I:** 248

"To Saxham" (Carew), **III:** 223

To Scorch or Freeze (Davie), **Supp. VI:** 113–115

"To seek each where, where man doth live" (Wyatt), **I:** 110

"To seem the stranger lies my lot" (Hopkins), **V:** 374–375

"To Sir Henry Cary" (Jonson), **Retro. Supp. I:** 154

To Sir With Love (Braithwaite), **Supp. IV:** 445

"To Sleep" (Graves), **VII:** 267

"To Sleep" (Keats), **IV:** 221

"To Solitude" (Keats), **IV:** 213–214

"To Stella, Visiting Me in My Sickness" (Swift), **III:** 31

"To Stella, Who Collected and Transcribed His Poems" (Swift), **III:** 31

"To Stella . . . Written on the Day of Her Birth . . . " (Swift), **III:** 32

To the Air, **Supp. IV:** 269

"To the Athenian Society" (Defoe), **Retro. Supp. I:** 67

"To the Author of a Poem, intitled, Successio" (Pope), **Retro. Supp. I:** 233

"To the Coffee Shop" (Kinsella), **Supp. V:** 274

"To the Evening Star" (Blake), **Retro. Supp. I:** 34

"To the fair Clarinda, who made Love to Me, imagin'd more than Woman" (Behn), **Supp. III:** 8

"To the High Court of Parliament" (Hill), **Supp. V:** 192, 193

"To the King" (Waller), **II:** 233

"To the King: Complane I Wald" (Dunbar), **VIII:** 117

To the King, upon His . . . Happy Return (Waller), **II:** 238

To the Lighthouse (Woolf), **V:** 281; **VI:** 275, 278; **VII:** xv, 18, 21, 26, 27, 28–29, 36, 38; **Supp. IV:** 231, 246, 321; **Supp. V:** 63; **Retro. Supp. I:** 308, 317–318

"To the Master of Balliol" (Tennyson), **IV:** 336

To the Memory of Charles Lamb (Wordsworth), **IV:** 86

"To the Memory of My Beloved, the Author Mr William Shakespeare" (Jonson), **Retro. Supp. I:** 165

"To the Memorie of My Ever Desired Friend Dr. Donne" (King), **Supp. VI:** 156

"To the Merchants of Edinburgh" (Dunbar), **VIII:** 126

"To the Muses" (Blake), **III:** 289; **Retro. Supp. I:** 34

"To the Name of Jesus" (Crashaw), **II:** 180

"To the Nightingal" (Finch), **Supp. IX:** 68–69

"To the Nightingale" (McGuckian), **Supp. V:** 283

To the North (Bowen), **Supp. II:** 85, 88–89

"To the Pen Shop" (Kinsella), **Supp. V:** 274

"To the Queen" (Tennyson), **IV:** 337

To the Queen, upon Her . . . Birthday (Waller), **II:** 238

"To the Reader" (Jonson), **Retro. Supp. I:** 165

"To the Reader" (Webster), **I:** 246

"To the Reverend Shade of His Religious Father" (Herrick), **II:** 113

"To the Rev. W. H. Brookfield" (Tennyson), **IV:** 329

"To the Royal Society" (Cowley), **II:** 196, 198

"To the Sea" (Larkin), **Supp. I:** 283, 285

"To the Shade of Elliston" (Lamb), **IV:** 82–83

"To the Slow Drum" (Ewart), **Supp. VII:** 42

"To the Small Celandine" (Wordsworth), **IV:** 21

"To the Spirit" (Hart), **Supp. XI:** 127

"To the (Supposed) Patron" (Hill), **Supp. V:** 184

"To the Virgins, to Make Much of Time" (Herrick), **II:** 108–109

To the Wedding (Berger), **Supp. IV:** 80

To This Hard House (Friel), **Supp. V:** 115
"To Thom Gunn in Los Altos, California" (Davie), **Supp. VI:** 112
"To Three Irish Poets" (Longley), **VIII:** 167–168
"To True Soldiers" (Jonson), **Retro. Supp. I:** 154
"To Vandyk" (Waller), **II:** 233
"To Virgil" (Tennyson), **IV:** 327
"To wet your eye withouten tear" (Wyatt), **I:** 105–106
"To what serves Mortal Beauty?" (Hopkins), **V:** 372, 373
"To Whom It May Concern" (Motion), **Supp. VII:** 264
To Whom She Will (Jhabvala), **Supp. V:** 224–226
"To William Camden" (Jonson), **Retro. Supp. I:** 152
"To William Godwin" (Coleridge), **IV:** 43
"To X" (Fuller), **Supp. VII:** 74
"To Yvor Winters, 1955" (Gunn), **Supp. IV:** 261
"Toads" (Larkin), **Supp. I:** 277, 278, 281
"Toads Revisited" (Larkin), **Supp. I:** 281
"Toccata of Galuppi's, A" (Browning), **IV:** 357
To–Day (periodical), **VI:** 103
Todhunter, John, **V:** 325
Todorov, Tzvetan, **Supp. IV:** 115–116
Together (Douglas), **VI:** 299–300, 304, 305
Toil & Spin: Two Directions in Modern Poetry (Wallace–Crabbe), **VIII:** 319, 325
Tolkien, J. R. R., **Supp. II: 519–535; Supp. IV:** 116
"Tollund Man, The" (Heaney), **Supp. II:** 273, 274; **Retro. Supp. I:** 128
Tolstoy (Wilson), **Supp. VI:** 304
Tolstoy, Leo, **Supp. IV:** 94, 139
"Tom Brown Question, The" (Wodehouse), **Supp. III:** 449
Tom Brown's Schooldays (Hughes), **V:** xxii, 157, 170; **Supp. IV:** 506
Tom Jones (Fielding), **III:** 95, 96–97, 100–102, 105; **Supp. II:** 194, 195; **Retro. Supp. I:** 81, 86–89, 90–91; **Retro. Supp. I:** 81, 86–89, 90–91
Tom O'Bedlam's Beauties (Reading), **VIII:** 264–265
Tom Thumb (Fielding), **III:** 96, 105
"Tom–Dobbin" (Gunn), **Supp. IV:** 267
Tomlin, Eric Walter Frederick, **VII:** xv, xxxviii
"Tomlinson" (Kipling), **VI:** 202
"Tomorrow" (Conrad), **VI:** 148
"Tomorrow" (Harris), **Supp. V:** 131
"Tomorrow Is a Million Years" (Ballard), **Supp. V:** 26
Tomorrow Morning, Faustus! (Richards), **Supp. II:** 427–428
"Tom's Garland" (Hopkins), **V:** 376
"Tone of Time, The" (James), **VI:** 69
"Tongue in My Ear: On Writing and Not Writing *Foreign Parts*" (Galloway), **Supp. XII:** 123–124
"Tongues of Fire" (Wallace–Crabbe), **VIII:** 325

Tonight at 8:30 (Coward), **Supp. II:** 152–153
Tono–Bungay (Wells), **VI:** xii, 237–238, 244
Tonson, Jacob, **II:** 323; **III:** 69
"Tony Kytes, The Arch–Deceiver" (Hardy), **VI:** 22
"Tony White's Cottage" (Murphy), **Supp. V:** 328
"Too Dearly Bought" (Gissing), **V:** 437
Too Good to Be True (Shaw), **VI:** 125, 127, 129
"Too Late" (Browning), **V:** 366, 369
Too Late the Phalarope (Paton), **Supp. II:** 341, **351–353**
Too Many Husbands (Maugham), **VI:** 368–369
"Too Much" (Muir), **Supp. VI:** 207
"Toot Baldon" (Motion), **Supp. VII:** 253
Tooth and Nail (Rankin), see *Wolfman*
Top Girls (Churchill), **Supp. IV:** 179, 183, 189–191, 198
Topkapi (film), **Supp. IV:** 4
"Torridge" (Trevor), **Supp. IV:** 501
"Tortoise and the Hare, The" (Dahl), **Supp. IV:** 226
Tortoises (Lawrence), **VII:** 118
Tortoises, Terrapins and Turtles (Sowerby and Lear), **V:** 76, 87
"Torturer's Apprenticeship, The" (Murray), **Supp. VII:** 280
"Tory Prime Minister, Maggie May . . . , A" (Rushdie), **Supp. IV:** 456
Totemism (Frazer), **Supp. III:** 171
"Totentanz" (Wilson), **Supp. I:** 155, 156, 157
Tottel's Miscellany, **I:** 97–98, 114
Touch (Gunn), **Supp. IV:** 257, 264, 265–266
"Touch" (Gunn), **Supp. IV:** 265–266
Touch and Go (Lawrence), **VII:** 120, 121
Touch of Love, A (screenplay, Drabble), **Supp. IV:** 230
Touch of Mistletoe, A (Comyns), **VIII:** 54–55, 56, 58–59, 65
Tour Thro' the Whole Island of Great Britain (Defoe), **III:** 5, 13; **Retro. Supp. I:** 75–76
Tour to the Hebrides, A (Boswell), see *Journal of a Tour to the Hebrides*
Tourneur, Cyril, **II:** 24, 33, **36–41,** 70, 72, 85, 97
Toward Reality (Berger), see *Permanent Red: Essays in Seeing*
"Toward the Imminent Days" (Murray), **Supp. VII:** 274
"Towards an Artless Society" (Lewis), **VII:** 76
Towards the End of Morning (Frayn), **Supp. VII:** 53–54, 65
Towards the Human (Smith, I. C.), **Supp. IX:** 209
Towards the Mountain (Paton), **Supp. II:** 346, 347, 351, 359
Towards Zero (Christie), **Supp. II:** 132, 134
Tower, The (Fry), **Supp. III:** 194, 195
Tower, The (Yeats), **VI:** 207, 216, 220; **Retro. Supp. I:** 333–335

Towers of Silence, The (Scott), **Supp. I:** 267–268
Town (periodical), **V:** 22
"Town and Country" (Brooke), **VI:** 420
"Town Betrayed, The" (Muir), **Supp. VI:** 206
Townley plays, **I:** 20
Townsend, Aurelian, **II:** 222, 237
Townsend Warner, George, **VI:** 485
Town–Talk (periodical), **III:** 50, 53
"Trace Elements" (Wallace–Crabbe), **VIII:** 323
"Track 12" (Ballard), **Supp. V:** 21
Trackers of Oxyrhyncus, The (Harrison), **Supp. V:** 163, 164
Tract 90 (Newman), see *Remarks on Certain Passages of the 39 Articles*
"Tractor" (Hughes), **Retro. Supp. II:** 211
Tracts for the Times (Newman), **Supp. VII:** 291, 293
"Traction–Engine, The" (Auden), **Retro. Supp. I:** 3
"Tradition and the Individual Talent" (Eliot), **VII:** 155, 156, 163, 164
"Tradition of Eighteen Hundred and Four, A" (Hardy), **VI:** 22
Tradition of Women's Fiction, The (Drabble), **Supp. IV:** 231
Tradition, the Writer and Society (Harris), **Supp. V:** 145, 146
"Traditional Prize Country Pigs" (Cope), **VIII:** 82–83
"Traditions, Voyages" (Wallace–Crabbe), **VIII:** 318
Traffics and Discoveries (Kipling), **VI:** 204
"Tragedy and the Essay, The" (Brontë), **V:** 135
Tragedy of Brennoralt, The (Suckling), **II:** 226
Tragedy of Byron, The (Chapman), **I:** 233, 234, 241n, 251
Tragedy of Count Alarcos, The (Disraeli), **IV:** 306, 308
Tragedy of Doctor Faustus, The (Marlowe), **Retro. Supp. I:** 200, 207–208
"Tragedy of Error, A" (James), **VI:** 25
Tragedy of Sir John Van Olden Barnavelt, The (Fletcher and Massinger), **II:** 66
Tragedy of Sophonisba, The (Thomson), **Supp. III:** 411, 422, 423, 424
Tragedy of the Duchess of Malfi, The (Webster), see *Duchess of Malfi, The*
Tragedy of Tragedies; or, The Life . . . of Tom Thumb, The (Fielding), see *Tom Thumb*
"Tragedy of Two Ambitions, A" (Hardy), **VI:** 22
Tragic Comedians, The (Meredith), **V:** 228, 234
Tragic History of Romeus and Juliet, The (Brooke), **I:** 305–306
Tragic Muse, The (James), **VI:** 39, **43–55,** 67
"Tragic Theatre, The" (Yeats), **VI:** 218
Tragical History of Doctor Faustus, The (Hope), **Supp. VII:** 160–161

Tragical History of Dr. Faustus, The (Marlowe), **III:** 344

Traherne, Thomas, **II:** 123, **189–194, 201–203; Supp. XI: 263–280**

Trail of the Dinosaur, The (Koestler), **Supp. I:** 32, 33, 36, 37

Traill, H. D., **III:** 80

Train of Powder, A (West), **Supp. III:** 439–440

Trained for Genius (Goldring), **VI:** 333

Traité du poeme épique (Le Bossu), **III:** 103

Traitor's Blood (Hill, R.), **Supp. IX:** 117

"Trampwoman's Tragedy, The" (Hardy), **VI:** 15; **Retro. Supp. I:** 120

transatlantic review (periodical), **VI:** 324

Transatlantic Sketches (James), **VI:** 67

"Transfiguration, The" (Muir), **Supp. VI:** 207

Transformed Metamorphosis, The (Tourneur), **II:** 37, 41

"Transients and Residents" (Gunn), **Supp. IV:** 271, 273

transition (quarterly periodical), **Supp. I:** 43*n*

Transitional Poem (Day Lewis), **Supp. III:** 117, 121–123

"Translation of Poetry, The" (Morgan, E.), **Supp. IX:** 168–169

Translations (Friel), **Supp. V:** 123–124

Translations and Tomfooleries (Shaw), **VI:** 129

"Translations from the Early Irish" (Kinsella), **Supp. V:** 264

Translations of the Natural World (Murray), **Supp. VII:** 281–282

"Transparencies" (Stevenson), **Supp. VI:** 262

"Transvaal Morning, A" (Plomer), **Supp. XI:** 214

Traps (Churchill), **Supp. IV:** 179, 180, 183–184, 188, 198

Traulus (Swift), **III:** 36

Travelers (Jhabvala), **Supp. V:** 230

"Traveling to My Second Marriage on the Day of the First Moonshot" (Nye), **Supp. X:** 202

"Traveller" (Kinsella), **Supp. V:** 263

Traveller, The (Goldsmith), **III:** 177, 179, 180, 185–186, 191; **Retro. Supp. I:** 149

"Traveller, The" (Stevenson), **Supp. VI:** 254, 265

"Travelling" (Healy), **Supp. IX:** 106

Travelling Behind Glass (Stevenson), **Supp. VI:** 256–257

"Travelling Behind Glass" (Stevenson), **Supp. VI:** 257, 261

"Travelling Companion, The" (Kinsella), **Supp. V:** 261

"Travelling Companions" (James), **VI:** 25, 69

Travelling Grave, The (Hartley), see *Killing Bottle, The*

Travelling Home (Cornford), **VIII:** 109, 111, 112

"Travelling Letters" (Dickens), **V:** 71

Travelling Sketches (Trollope), **V:** 101

Travels (Morris, J.), **Supp. X:** 172, 183

Travels in Arabia Deserta (Doughty), **Supp. II:** 294–295

Travels in Italy (Addison), **III:** 18

Travels in Nihilon (Sillitoe), **Supp. V:** 410

Travels Through France and Italy (Smollett), **III:** 147, **153–155,** 158

Travels with a Donkey in the Cevennes (Stevenson), **V:** 389, 395; **Retro. Supp. I:** 262

Travels with My Aunt (Greene), **Supp. I:** 2, 13, 16; **Retro. Supp. II:** 161

Travesties (Stoppard), **Supp. I:** 438, 445, 446, **447–449,** 451; **Retro. Supp. II:** 349–351

Trawler: A Journey Through the North Atlantic (O'Hanlon), **Supp. XI:** 196, 206–207

"A Treading of Grapes" (Brown), **Supp. VI:** 70

Treason's Harbour (O'Brian), **Supp. XII:** 256

Treasure Island (Stevenson), **V:** xxv, 383, 385, 386, 394, 395; **Retro. Supp. I:** 263

"Treasure of Franchard, The" (Stevenson), **V:** 395

"Treasure, The" (Brooke), **Supp. III:** 57, 58

"Treatise for Laundresses" (Lydgate), **I:** 58

Treatise of Civil Power in Ecclesiastical Causes . . . , The (Milton), **II:** 176

Treatise of Human Nature, A (Hume), **IV:** 138; **Supp. III:** 229, 230–231, **232–237,** 238

Treatise of the Fear of God, A (Bunyan), **II:** 253

Treatise of the Soul, A (Ralegh), **I:** 157

Treatise on Method (Coleridge), **IV:** 56

Treatise on the Astrolabe, A (Chaucer), **I:** 31

Treatise on the Passion (More), **Supp. VII:** 245

Trebitsch, Siegfried, **VI:** 115

Tree, Herbert Beerbohm, **Supp. II:** 44, 46, 53–54, 55

"Tree, The" (Thomas), **Supp. I:** 180

"Tree, The" (Wallace–Crabbe), **VIII:** 317

"Tree of Knowledge, The" (James), **VI:** 69

Tree of Man, The (White), **Supp. I:** 129, 131, 134, 136, 137–138, 143

Tree of Strings (MacCaig), **Supp. VI:** 192–193

Tree of the Sun, The (Harris), **Supp. V:** 139–140

Tree on Fire, A (Sillitoe), **Supp. V:** 409, 410, 414, 421, 422–423

"Tree Unleaved, The" (Warner), **Supp. VII:** 371

"Trees, The" (Larkin), **Supp. I:** 284, 285

Trelawny, Edward, **IV:** xiv, 203, 207, 209

Tremaine (Ward), **IV:** 293

Trembling of the Veil, The (Yeats), **VI:** 210

Tremendous Adventures of Major Gahagan, The (Thackeray), **V:** 22, 37

Tremor of Forgery, The (Highsmith), **Supp. V:** 175–176

Tremor of Intent (Burgess), **Supp. I:** 185, 191–192

Trench Town Rock (Brathwaite), **Supp. XII:** 36

"Trenches St. Eloi" (Hulme), **Supp. VI:** 140

Trespass of the Sign, The: Deconstruction, Theology, and Philosophy (Hart), **Supp. XI:** 122, 128

Trespasser, The (Lawrence), **VII:** 89, 91, 93–95; **Retro. Supp. II:** 227

Tretis of the Tua Mariit Wemen and the Wedo, The (Dunbar), **VIII:** 120, 123, 124–126

Trevelyan, G. M., **I:** 375; **V:** xxiv, 223, 227, 234; **VI:** xv, 347, **383–396;** list of works, **VI:** 394–396

Trevenen (Davie), **Supp. VI:** 111

Trevisa, John, **Supp. IX: 243–260**

Trevor, William, **Supp. IV: 499–519**

Trevor–Roper, Hugh, **Supp. IV:** 436

Trial, The (Kafka), **III:** 340

Trial of a Judge (Spender), **Supp. II:** 488

Trial of Dedan Kimathi, The (Ngũgĩ/ Mūgo), **VIII:** 223

Trial of Elizabeth Cree: A Novel of the Limehouse Murders, The (Ackroyd), **Supp. VI:** 10

Trial of the Fox, The (Henryson), **Supp. VII:** 136, 138, 139, 140

Trial of the Honourable Augustus Keppel, The (Burke), **III:** 205

"Tribune's Visitation, The" (Jones), **Supp. VII:** 175, 179–180

"Tribute of a Legs Lover" (Dunn), **Supp. X:** 70

Tributes (Jennings), **Supp. V:** 216

Trick is to Keep Breathing, The (Galloway), **Supp. XII:** 117, 119–120, 124, 129

Trick of It, The (Frayn), **Supp. VII:** 61–62

Trick to Catch the Old One, A (Middleton), **II:** 3, 4–5, 21

"Trickster and the Sacred Clown, Revealing the Logic of the Unspeakable, The" (Belmonte), **Supp. IV:** 15–16

Trieste and the Meaning of Nowhere (Morris, J.), **Supp. X:** 171, 173, 176, 178, 186–187

Trilby (du Maurier), **Supp. III:** 134, 135, 136

Trilogy (Beckett), **Retro. Supp. I:** 18, 20–23

Trilogy of Death (James), **Supp. IV:** 328, 329, 335, 337

"Trim" (Dutton), **Supp. XII:** 88

"Trinity at Low Tide" (Stevenson), **Supp. VI:** 264

Trinity College (Trevelyan), **VI:** 383, 393

Trip to Scarborough, A (Sheridan), **II:** 334, 336; **III:** 253, 261, 270

Triple Thinkers, The (Wilson), **VI:** 164

"Triple Time" (Larkin), **Supp. I:** 279

"Tristia" (Sisson), **Supp. XI:** 259 inline e"Tristram and Iseult" (Arnold), **V:** 210

"Tristram and Iseult: Prelude of an Unfinished Poem" (Swinburne), **V:** 332

Tristram Shandy (Sterne), **III:** 124, 126, **127–132,** 135, 150, 153; **IV:** 183; **Supp. II:** 204, 205

Triumph and Tragedy (Churchill), **VI:** 361

Triumph of Death (Fletcher), **II:** 66

Triumph of Gloriana, The (Swinburne), **V:** 333

Triumph of Honour (Field), **II:** 66

"Triumph of Life, The" (Shelley), **IV:** xi, 197, 206–207, 209; **Retro. Supp. I:** 256

Triumph of Love (Field), **II:** 66

Triumph of Love, The (Hill), **Supp. V:** 183, 189, 198–199, 202

Triumph of the Four Foster Children of Desire (Sidney), **Retro. Supp. II:** 329–330

Triumph of Time (Fletcher), **II:** 66

"Triumph of Time, The" (Swinburne), **V:** 311, 313, 318–319, 331

"Triumphal March" (Eliot), **VII:** 152–153

Triumphs of Love and Innocence, The (Finch), **Supp. IX:** 74–76

"Triumphs of Odin, The" (Gray), **III:** 142

"Triumphs of Sensibility" (Warner), **Supp. VII:** 371

Triumphs of Truth, The (Middleton), **II:** 3

Triumphs of Wealth and Prosperity, The (Middleton), **II:** 3

Trivia (Connolly), **Supp. III:** 98

Trivia; or, The Art of Walking the streets of London (Gay), **III:** 55, 57, 67

"Troglodyte, The" (Brooke–Rose)), **Supp. IV:** 103

Troilus and Cressida (Dryden), **II:** 293, 305

Troilus and Cressida (Shakespeare), **I:** 313, 314; **II:** 47, 70; **IV:** 225; **V:** 328

Troilus and Criseyde (Chaucer), **I:** 24, 30, 31, 32–34, 41, 43, 44; **IV:** 189; **Retro. Supp. II:** 40–45

Trójumanna saga, **VIII:** 237

Trollope, Anthony, **II:** 172–173; **IV:** 306; **V:** x, xvii, xxii–xxv, 11, **89–103; VII:** xxi; **Supp. IV:** 229, 230

Trollope, Frances, **V:** 89

Trollope: A Commentary (Sadleir), **V:** 100, 102

"Trollope and His Style" (Sykes Davies), **V:** 103

Trooper Peter Halket of Mashonaland (Schreiner), **Supp. II:** 454

"Troopship" (Fuller), **Supp. VII:** 69

"Troopship in the Tropics, A" (Lewis), **VII:** 446

Tropic Seed (Waugh), **Supp. VI:** 275

Troubled Eden, A, Nature and Society in the Works of George Meredith (Kelvin), **V:** 221, 234

Troublesome Offspring of Cardinal Guzman, The (De Bernières), **Supp. XII:** 65, 69, 73–74

Troublesome Reign of John, King of England, The, **I:** 301

"Trout, A" (Nye), **Supp. X:** 201

"Trout Stream, The" (Welch), **Supp. IX:** 267

"Troy" (Muir), **Supp. VI:** 206

Troy Park (Sitwell), **VII:** 138

Troy-book (Lydgate), **I:** 57, 58, 59–65, 280

"Truant Hart, The" (Coppard), **VIII:** 96

"Truce of the Bear, The" (Kipling), **VI:** 203

True Born Irishman, The (Friel), **Supp. V:** 126

"True Function and Value of Criticism, The" (Wilde), **Retro. Supp. II:** 367

True Heart, The (Warner), **Supp. VII:** 370, 375

True History (Lucian), **III:** 24

True History of Squire Jonathan and His Unfortunate Treasure, The (Arden), **Supp. II:** 31

True History of the Kelly Gang (Carey), **Supp. XII:** 49, 51, 54, 57, 60, 61–62

"True Love" (Nye), **Supp. X:** 199–200, 202

True Patriot, The (Fielding), **III:** 105; **Retro. Supp. I:**

True Relation of the Apparition of . . . Mrs. Veal . . . to . . . Mrs. Bargrave . . . (Defoe), **III:** 13

True State of the Case of Bosavern Penlez, A (Fielding), **III:** 105

True Traveller, The (Davies), **Supp. XI:** 86, 91

True Travellers: A Tramps Opera in Three Acts (Davies), **Supp. XI:** 93

True Widow, The (Shadwell), **II:** 115305

True–Born Englishman, The (Defoe), **III:** 3, 12; **Retro. Supp. I:** 64, 67

Truelove, The (O'Brian), **Supp. XII:** 258–259

"Truly Great" (Davies), **Supp. XI:** 85

Trumpet–Major, The: A Tale (Hardy), **VI:** 5, 6–7, 20; **Retro. Supp. I:** 114

"Trustie Tree, The" (Roberts, K.), **Supp. X:** 270

"Truth" (Bacon), **III:** 39

"Truth" (Cowper), **III:** 212

Truth About an Author (Bennett), **VI:** 264–265

Truth About Blayds, The (Milne), **Supp. V:** 299

"Truth in the Cup" (Warner), **Supp. VII:** 381

"Truth of Masks, The" (Wilde), **Retro. Supp. II:** 368

"Truthful Adventure, A" (Mansfield), **VII:** 172

Trying to Explain (Davie), **Supp. VI:** 115

"Tryst at an Ancient Earthwork, A" (Hardy), **VI:** 22

Trystram of Lyonesse (Swinburne), **V:** 299, 300, 314, 327–328, 332

Tsvetayeva, Marina, **Supp. IV:** 493

Tucker, Abraham, pseud. of William Hazlitt

Tudor trilogy (Ford), **VI:** 319, 323, 325–327; *see also Fifth Queen, The; Fifth Queen Crowned, The; Privy Seal*

"Tuesday; or, The Ditty" (Gay), **III:** 56

"Tulips" (McGuckian), **Supp. V:** 281

Tumatumari (Harris), **Supp. V:** 136, 137

Tumble–down Dick (Fielding), **III:** 105

"Tumps" (Cope), **VIII:** 78

Tunc (Durrell), **Supp. I:** 113–118, 120

"Tunnel" (Barnes), **Supp. IV:** 75, 76

Tunning of Elinour Rumming, The (Skelton), **I:** 82, 86–87, 92

"Tunstall Forest" (Davie), **Supp. VI:** 110

Tuppenny Stung (Longley), **VIII:** 164, 165

Turbott Wolfe (Plomer), **Supp. XI:** 209, 210–212, 213, 214, 219, 222, 223

"Turf, The" (Sisson), **Supp. XI:** 258

Turkish Delight (Churchill), **Supp. IV:** 181

Turkish Mahomet and Hiren the Fair Greek (Peele), **I:** 205

Turkish tales (Byron), **IV:** x, 172, 173–175

"Turn for the Better, A" (Nicholson), **Supp. VI:** 217

Turn of the Screw, The (James), **III:** 334, 340, 345; **V:** xxvi, 14; **VI:** 39, **52–53,** 69; **Supp. IV:** 97, 116, 503, 511

Turn of the Years, The (Pritchett), **Supp. III:** 311

Turner, J. M. W., **V:** xix, xx, 174–175, 178

"Turns" (Harrison), **Supp. V:** 154–155

Turning of the Tide, The (Hill), *see Castle of the Demon, The*

"Tursac" (Dunn), **Supp. X:** 76

Tutchin, John, **III:** 3

"Tutelar of the Place, The" (Jones), **Supp. VII:** 179–180

Tuve, Rosamund, **II:** 124, 130; **Retro. Supp. II:** 174

"TV" (Smith, I. C.), **Supp. IX:** 221

"Twa Dogs, The" (Burns), **III:** 315, 316

"Twa Herds, The" (Burns), **III:** 311, 319

Twain, Mark, **IV:** 106; **V:** xix, xxiv–xxv

Twelfth Night (Shakespeare), **I:** 312, 320

Twelve Adventurers and Other Stories (Brontë), **V:** 151

Twelve, and Other Poems by Aleksandr Blok, The (tr. Stallworthy), **Supp. X:** 292

Twelve Apostles (Ewart), **Supp. VII:** 40

12 Edmondstone Street (Malouf), **Supp. XII:** 217

"12 Edmondstone Street" (Malouf), **Supp. XII:** 218

Twelve Months in a Curatorship (Carroll), **V:** 274

Twelve Pound Look, The (Barrie), **Supp. III:** 6, 8, 9, 15–16

"Twelve Songs" (Auden), **VII:** 383, 386

"Twentieth Century Blues" (Coward), **Supp. II:** 147

"Twenty Pounds" (Gissing), **V:** 437

Twenty five (Gregory), **VI:** 309

Twenty–five Poems (Thomas), **Supp. I:** 174, 176, 180

"Twenty–four years" (Thomas), **Supp. I:** 177

"24th March 1986" (Ewart), **Supp. VII:** 46

"29 February, 1704" (Fallon), **Supp. XII:** 114

Twenty–One Poems (Sisson), **Supp. XI:** 249

"Twenty–Seven Articles, The" (Lawrence), **Supp. II:** 287

Twilight Bar (Koestler), **Supp. I:** 25

Twilight in Italy (Lawrence), **VII:** 116

Twin Rivals, The (Farquhar), **II:** 353, 357–358, 364

"Twin Sets and Pickle Forks" (Dunn), **Supp. X:** 67–68

Twine, Laurence, **I:** 321

Twits, The (Dahl), **Supp. IV:** 205, 207, 223

'Twixt Land and Sea: Tales (Conrad), **VI:** 148

"Two Analogies for Poetry" (Davie), **Supp. VI:** 115

Two Autobiographical Plays (Arden), **Supp. II:** 31

Two Biographical Plays (Arden), **Supp. II:** 31

"Two Blond Flautists" (Fuller), **Supp. VII:** 79

"Two Chairs" (Powys), **VIII:** 251, 252

Two Cheers for Democracy (Forster), **VI:** 397, 411

"Two Chorale–Preludes" (Hill), **Supp. V:** 199

"Two Countries" (James), **VI:** 69

Two Destinies, The (Collins), **Supp. VI:** 102

Two Drovers, The (Scott), **IV:** 39

"Two Early French Stories" (Pater), **V:** 344

"Two Faces, The" (James), **VI:** 69

Two Faces of January, The (Highsmith), **Supp. V:** 173–174

Two Foscari, The (Byron), **IV:** xviii, 178, 193

"Two Fragments: March 199–" (McEwan), **Supp. IV:** 395

"Two Frenchmen" (Strachey), **Supp. II:** 500, 502

"Two Fusiliers" (Graves), **VI:** 452

"Two Gallants" (Joyce), **VII:** 44

Two Generals, The (FitzGerald), **IV:** 353

Two Gentlemen of Verona (Shakespeare), **I:** 302, 311–312

"Two Girls Singing" (Smith, I. C.), **Supp. IX:** 213

Two Great Questions Consider'd, The (Defoe), **III:** 12

Two Guardians, The (Yonge), **V:** 253

Two Heroines of Plumplington, The (Trollope), **V:** 102

"Two Houses" (Thomas), **Supp. III:** 399

"Two Impromptus" (Amis), **Supp. II:** 15

"Two in the Campagna" (Browning), **IV:** 357, 369

"Two Kinds of Motion" (Stevenson), **Supp. VI:** 255

"Two Kitchen Songs" (Sitwell), **VII:** 130–131

"Two Knights, The" (Swinburne), **V:** 315, 333

Two Letters on the Conduct of Our Domestic Parties (Burke), **III:** 205

Two Letters on the French Revolution (Burke), **III:** 205

Two Letters . . . on the Proposals for Peace (Burke), **III:** 205

Two Letters . . . to Gentlemen in the City of Bristol . . . (Burke), **III:** 205

Two Lives (Seth), **Supp. X:** 290

Two Lives (Trevor), **Supp. IV:** 516

Two Magics, The (James), **VI:** 52, 69

Two Mice, The (Henryson), **Supp. VII:** 136, 137, 140

Two Noble Kinsmen, The (Shakespeare), **I:** 324, 325; **II:** 43, 66, 87

Two of Us, The (Frayn), **Supp. VII:** 57

"Two Old Men Outside an Inn" (Cornford), **VIII:** 113

Two on a Tower: A Romance (Hardy), **VI:** 4, 5, 20; **Retro. Supp. I:** 114

Two or Three Graces (Huxley), **VII:** 201

Two Paths, The (Ruskin), **V:** 180, 184

"Two Peacocks of Bedfont, The" (Hood), **IV:** 256, 267

Two People (Milne), **Supp. V:** 310

"Two Races of Men, The" (Lamb), **IV:** 82

"Two Spirits, The" (Shelley), **IV:** 196

Two Stories: "Come and Dine" and "Tadnol" (Powys), **VIII:** 248

"2000: Zero Gravity" (Motion), **Supp. VII:** 266

"2001: The Tennyson/Hardy Poem" (Ewart), **Supp. VII:** 40

Two Thieves, The (Powys), **VIII:** 248, 255

Two Thousand Seasons (Armah), **Supp. X:** 1–3, 6–11, 13

Two Towers, The (Tolkien), **Supp. II:** 519

Two Voices (Thomas), **Supp. IV:** 490

"Two Voices, The" (Tennyson), **IV:** 329

"Two Ways of It" (MacCaig), **Supp. VI:** 187

Two Women of London: The Strange Case of Ms. Jekyll and Mrs. Hyde (Tennant), **Supp. IX:** 238–239, 240

Two Worlds and Their Ways (Compton–Burnett), **VII:** 65, 66, 67, 69

"Two Year Old" (MacCaig), **Supp. VI:** 192

"Two Years Old" (Cornford), **VIII:** 113

"Two–Headed Beast, The" (Fallon), **Supp. XII:** 102

Two–Part Inventions (Howard), **V:** 418

"Two–Party System in English Political History, The" (Trevelyan), **VI:** 392

"Two–Sided Man, The" (Kipling), **VI:** 201

Twyborn Affair, The (White), **Supp. I:** 132, 148–149

"Tyes, The" (Thomas), **Supp. III:** 401

"Tyger, The" (Blake), **III:** 296; **Retro. Supp. I:** 42–43

Tyler, F. W., **I:** 275n

Tylney Hall (Hood), **IV:** 254, 256, 259, 267

Tynan, Katherine, **V:** 441

Tynan, Kenneth, **Supp. II:** 70, 140, 147, 152, 155; **Supp. IV:** 78

Tyndale, William, **I:** 375–377

"Typhoon" (Conrad), **VI:** 136, 148

Tyrannicida (tr. More), **Supp. VII:** 235–236

Tyrannick Love; or, The Royal Martyr (Dryden), **II:** 290, 294, 305

"Tyre, The" (Armitage), **VIII:** 11

"Tyronic Dialogues" (Lewis), **VII:** 82

*U*dolpho (Radcliffe), *see* Mysteries of Udolpho, The

Ugly Anna and Other Tales (Coppard), **VIII:** 89

"Uist" (Crawford), **Supp. XI:** 81

Ukulele Music (Reading), **VIII:** 265, 268–269, 270, 271

"Ula Masondo" (Plomer), **Supp. XI:** 214

Ulick and Soracha (Moore), **VI:** 89, 95, 99

"Ultima" (Thompson), **V:** 441

"Ultima Ratio Regum" (Spender), **Supp. II:** 488

Ultramarine (Lowry), **Supp. III:** 269, 270, **271–272**, 280, 283, 285

Ulysses (Butler), **Supp. II:** 114

Ulysses (Joyce), **V:** 189; **VII:** xv, 42, 46–47, 48–52; **Retro. Supp. I:** 169, 176–179; critical studies, **VII:** 57–58; **Supp. IV:** 87, 370, 390, 426

"Ulysses" (Tennyson), **IV:** xx, 324, 328, 332–334

"Uma Himavutee" (Steel), **Supp. XII:** 269

"Umbrella Man, The" (Dahl), **Supp. IV:** 221

"Un Coeur Simple" (Flaubert), **Supp. IV:** 69

Un Début dans la vie (Balzac), **Supp. IV:** 123

"Unarmed Combat" (Reed), **VII:** 422–423

"Unattained Place, The" (Muir), **Supp. VI:** 206

Unbearable Bassington, The (Saki), **Supp. VI: 245–248**

Unbeaten Tracks in Japan (Bird), **Supp. X:** 19, 29–30

"Unbidden Guest, The" (Powys), **VIII:** 251

"Unbuilders, The" (Crawford), **Supp. XI:** 70

Uncensored (Rattigan), **Supp. VII:** 311

"Unchangeable, The" (Blunden), **Supp. XI:** 43

Unclassed, The (Gissing), **V:** 437

Unclay (Powys), **VIII:** 256

Uncle Bernac (Doyle), **Supp. II:** 159

Uncle Dottery: A Christmas Story (Powys), **VIII:** 248

"Uncle Ernest" (Sillitoe), **Supp. V:** 414

Uncle Fred in the Springtime (Wodehouse), **Supp. III:** 460–461

Uncle Silas (Le Fanu), **III:** 345; **Supp. II:** 78–79, 81

Uncle Vanya (tr. Frayn), **Supp. VII:** 61

Unclouded Summer (Waugh), **Supp. VI:** 274

Uncollected Essays (Pater), **V:** 357

Uncollected Verse (Thompson), **V:** 451

Uncommercial Traveller, The (Dickens), **V:** 72

Unconditional Surrender (Waugh), **VII:** 303, 304; *see also* Sword of Honour trilogy

Unconscious Memory (Butler), **Supp. II:** 107–108

Unconsoled, The (Ishiguro), **Supp. IV:** 301, 302, 304, 305, 306–307, 314–316

"Uncovenanted Mercies" (Kipling), **VI:** 175

"Under a Lady's Picture" (Waller), **II:** 234–235

"Under Ben Bulben" (Yeats), **VI:** 215, 219–220; **Retro. Supp. I:** 338

"Under Brinkie's Brae" (Brown), **Supp. VI:** 64

"Under Carn Brea" (Thomas), **Supp. IV:** 492

Under Milk Wood (Thomas), **Supp. I:** 183–184

Under Plain Cover (Osborne), **Supp. I:** 335–336

Under the Greenwood Tree: A Rural Painting of the Dutch School (Hardy), **VI:** 1, 2–3, 5, 20; **Retro. Supp. I:** 112–113

Under the Hill (Beardsley), **VII:** 292

Under the Hill (Firbank), **Supp. II:** 202

Under the Microscope (Swinburne), **IV:** 337; **V:** 329, 332, 333

Under the Net (Murdoch), **Supp. I:** 220, 222, 228, 229–230

Under the Sunset (Stoker), **Supp. III:** 381

Under the Volcano (Lowry), **Supp. III:** 269, 270, 273, **274–280,** 283, 285

Under the Reservoir (Redgrove), **Supp. VI:** 236

Under Twenty–five: An Anthology (ed. O'Donovan, Sanderson, and Porteous), **Supp. XII:** 51

Under Western Eyes (Conrad), **VI:** 134, 144–145, 148; **Retro. Supp. II:** 81–82

"'Under Which King, Bezonian?'" (Leavis), **VII:** 242

Under World (Hill, R.), **Supp. IX:** 120, 121

Undergraduate Sonnets (Swinburne), **V:** 333

Underhill, Charles, *see* Hill, Reginald

"Understanding the Ur–Bororo" (Self), **Supp. V:** 401–402

Undertones of War (Blunden), **VI:** 428, 429; **Supp. XI:** 33, 36, 38, 39–41, 47

Underwood (Jonson), **Retro. Supp. I:** 166

Underwood, Dale, **II:** 256n

Underwoods (Stevenson), **V:** 390n, 395; **Retro. Supp. I:** 267–268

Undine (Schreiner), **Supp. II: 444–445**

"Undiscovered Planet, The" (Nicholson), **Supp. VI:** 217

"Undressing" (Nye), **Supp. X:** 198, 200

Undying Fire, The (Wells), **VI:** 242

Unequal Marriage; or, Pride and Prejudice Twenty Years Later, An (Tennant), see *Unequal Marriage: Pride and Prejudice Continued, An*

Unequal Marriage: Pride and Prejudice Continued, An (Tennant), **Supp. IX:** 237–238, 239–240

"Unfinished Draft, An" (Beddoes), **Supp. XI:** 30

Unfinished Portrait (Christie), **Supp. II:** 133

"Unfortunate" (Brooke), **Supp. III:** 55

"Unfortunate Lover, The" (Marvell), **II:** 211

Unfortunate Traveller, The (Nashe), **I:** 114, 281

"Ungratefulnesse" (Herbert), **II:** 127

Unguarded Hours (Wilson), **Supp. VI:** 299, 308

"Unhappy Families" (Carter), **Supp. IV:** 459

Unhappy Favorite, The (Banks), **II:** 305

Unholy Trade, The (Findlater), **VII:** 8–9, 14

Unicorn, The (Murdoch), **III:** 341, 345; **Supp. I:** 215, 225, 226, 228

Unicorn, The (Rosenberg), **VI:** 433

Unicorn from the Stars, The (Yeats and Gregory), **VI:** 318

"Unimportant Fire, An" (Rushdie), **Supp. IV:** 445

Union of the Two Noble and Illustre Families of Lancaster and York, The (Hall), **I:** 299

"Union Reunion" (Wilson), **Supp. I:** 153, 155, 157

Union Street (Barker), **Supp. IV:** 45, 46–50, 57

Universal Chronicle (periodical), **III:** 111

Universal Gallant, The (Fielding), **III:** 105

"University of Mainz, The" (Waugh), **Supp. VI:** 269

"University Feud, The: A Row at the Oxford Arms" (Hood), **IV:** 258

Unjust War: An Address to the Working–men of England (Morris), **V:** 305

Unkindness of Ravens, An (Rendell), **Supp. IX:** 199

Unknown, The (Maugham), **VI:** 369

"Unknown Bird, The" (Thomas), **Supp. III:** 402

Unknown Shore, The (O'Brian), **Supp. XII:** 248, 251, 252

"Unknown Shores" (Thomas), **Supp. IV:** 490

Unlikely Stories, Mostly (Gray, A.), **Supp. IX:** 80, 90

Unlimited Dream Company, The (Ballard), **Supp. V:** 28–29

Unlit Lamp, The (Hall), **Supp. VI:** 120–122, **123–125**

"Unluckily for a Death" (Thomas), **Supp. I:** 178

Unnamable, The (Beckett), **Supp. I:** 45, 51, 52, 53–54, 55, 56, 60; **Supp. IV:** 106; **Retro. Supp. I:** 22–23

Unnatural Causes (James), **Supp. IV:** 320, 321, 324–326

Unnatural Death (Sayers), **Supp. II:** 135; **Supp. III:** 338–339, 340, 343

Unnaturall Combat, The (Massinger), **Supp. XI:** 183

Unofficial Rose, An (Murdoch), **Supp. I:** 222, 223–224, 229, 232

Unpleasantness at the Bellona Club, The (Sayers), **Supp. III:** 330, 340

Unprofessional Tales (Douglas), **VI:** 293, 305

Unpublished Early Poems (Tennyson), **IV:** 338

Unquiet Grave, The: A Word Cycle by Palinurus (Connolly), **Supp. III: 103–105**

Unrelenting Struggle, The (Churchill), **VI:** 356

"Unremarkable Year, The" (Fuller), **Supp. VII:** 78

Unruly Times: Wordsworth and Coleridge in Their Time (Byatt), **Supp. IV:** 145

"Unseen Centre, The" (Nicholson), **Supp. VI:** 217

"Unsettled Motorcyclist's Vision of His Death, The" (Gunn), **Supp. IV:** 260

Unsocial Socialist, An (Shaw), **VI:** 103, 104, 105, 106, 129

"Unstable dream" (Wyatt), **I:** 103, 109

Unsuitable Attachment, An (Pym), **Supp. II: 375–377**

Unsuitable Job for a Woman, An (James), **Supp. IV:** 320, 335, 336

Unsworth, Barry, **Supp. VII: 353–367**

"Until Eternal Music Ends" (Fallon), **Supp. XII:** 102

"Until My Blood Is Pure" (Chatwin), **Supp. IV:** 173

Until the End of the World (Wenders and Carey), **Supp. XII:** 53

Untilled Field, The (Moore), **VI:** 88, 93, 98

Untitled Sea Novel (Lowry), **Supp. III:** 280

Unto This Last (Ruskin), **V:** xii, xxii, 20, 179–180

Unusual Life of Tristan Smith, The (Carey), **Supp. XII:** 52, 53, 54, 60, 62

"Unusual Young Man, An" (Brooke), **Supp. III:** 50–51

Up Against It (Orton), **Supp. V:** 363, 366, 369–370

"Up and Awake" (Kinsella), **Supp. V:** 268

"Up and Down" (Smith), **Supp. II:** 470

"Up at a Villa—Down in the City" (Browning), **IV:** 360

Up the Rhine (Hood), **IV:** 254, 259, 267

Up to Midnight (Meredith), **V:** 234

Updike, John, **Supp. IV:** 27, 136, 480, 483

"Upon a Child That Dyed" (Herrick), **II:** 115

"Upon a Cloke Lent Him by Mr. J. Ridsley" (Vaughan), **II:** 184

Upon a Dead Man's Head (Skelton), **I:** 84

"Upon Ancient and Modern Learning" (Temple), **III:** 40

"Upon Appleton House" (Marvell), **II:** 208, 209–210, 211, 212–213; **Retro. Supp. II:** 261–262

Upon Cromwell's Return from Ireland (Marvell), **II:** 199

Upon Her Majesty's New Buildings (Waller), **II:** 238

"Upon Heroick Virtue" (Temple), **III:** 40

"Upon Julia's Clothes" (Herrick), **II:** 107

"Upon Julia's Fall" (Herrick), **II:** 107

"Upon Julia's Unlacing Herself" (Herrick), **II:** 106

"Upon Julia's Voice" (Herrick), **II:** 107

"Upon Nothing" (Rochester), **II:** 259, 270

"Upon Our Late Loss of the Duke of Cambridge" (Waller), **II:** 233

"Upon Poetry" (Temple), **III:** 40

"Upon the Death of a Gentleman" (Crashaw), **II:** 183

"Upon the Death of Mr. R. W . . . ." (Vaughan), **II:** 184
"Upon the Earl of Roscommon's Translation of Horace" (Waller), **II:** 234
"Upon the Gardens of Epicurus" (Temple), **III:** 40
"Upon the Hurricane" (Finch), **Supp. IX:** 68–71
Upon the Late Storme, and of the Death of His Highnesse (Waller), **II:** 238
"Upon the Lonely Moor" (Carroll), **V:** 265, 267
Upstairs Downstairs (teleplay, Weldon), **Supp. IV:** 521
Upton, John, **I:** 121
Ure, Peter, **VI:** 220
Urgent Copy (Burgess), **Supp. I:** 186, 190, 194, 197
Uriah on the Hill (Powys), **VIII:** 255, 256
Urn Burial (Hill, R.), **Supp. IX:** 117
"Us" (Crawford), **Supp. XI:** 74
Use of Poetry and the Use of Criticism, The (Eliot), **VII:** 153, 158, 164; **Retro. Supp. II:** 65–66
Use of Weapons (Banks), **Supp. XI:** 10, 12
Useful and Instructive Poetry (Carroll), **V:** 263, 264, 273
Uses of Literacy, The (Hoggart), **Supp. IV:** 473
"Uses of the Many–Charactered Novel" (Stead), **Supp. IV:** 466
Using Biography (Empson), **Supp. II:** 180
Usk, Thomas, **I:** 2
"Usk, The" (Sisson), **Supp. XI:** 257–258
U.S. Martial (Harrison), **Supp. V:** 163
"Usquebaugh" (Cope), **VIII:** 74
"Usura Canto,"see "Canto 45"
Utility Player, The (Keneally), **Supp. IV:** 347
Utopia (More), **III:** 24; **Supp. VII:** 233, 235, 236, 238–240, 243, 248
"Utter Rim, The" (Graves), **VII:** 270
Utz (Chatwin), **Supp. IV:** 159, 163, 173, 174–175; **Supp. IX:** 59–60, 61

"V." (Harrison), **Supp. V: 153, 157–160**
V. (Pynchon), **Supp. IV:** 116
V. and Other Poems (Harrison), **Supp. V:** 160
V. C. O'Flaherty (Shaw), **VI:** 119–120, 129
Vafþrúðnismál, **VIII:** 230
Vagrant Mood, The (Maugham), **VI:** 374
Vailima Letters (Stevenson), **V:** 391, 396
Vain Fortune (Moore), **VI:** 87, 91
Vainglory (Firbank), **Supp. II:** 201, 203–204, 205, 208–209
Val D'Arno (Ruskin), **V:** 184
Vala; or, The Four Zoas (Blake), *see Four Zoas, The*
Vale (Moore), **VI:** 99
Vale and Other Poems (Russell), **VIII:** 290, 291, 292
"Valediction, A: Forbidding Mourning" (Donne), **II:** 185, 197; **Retro. Supp. II:** 87–88

"Valediction, A: Of Weeping" (Donne), **II:** 196
"Valediction of my name, in the window, A" (Donne), **Retro. Supp. II:** 92
"Valentine" (Cope), **VIII:** 76
Valentinian (Fletcher), **II:** 45, 58–60, 65
Valentinian: A Tragedy . . . (Rochester), **II:** 270
Valiant Pilgrim (Brittain), **Supp. X:** 46
Valiant Scot, The (Webster), **II:** 69, 85
Valla–Ljóts saga, **VIII:** 241
Valley of Bones, The (Powell), **VII:** 349
"Valley of Couteretz" (Tennyson), **IV:** 330
Valley of Fear, The (Doyle), **Supp. II:** 162, 163, 171, 172, 173, 174
Valmouth: A Romantic Novel (Firbank), **Supp. II:** 199, 201, 202, 205, **213–214**
"Value of Money, The" (Berger), **Supp. IV:** 92
"Values" (Blunden), **Supp. XI:** 46
Vamp Till Ready (Fuller), **Supp. VII:** 81
Vampirella (Carter), **III:** 341
Vampyre, The (Polidori), **III:** 329, 334; **Supp. III:** 385
"Van Gogh among the Miners" (Mahon), **Supp. VI:** 168
Van, The (Doyle), **Supp. V:** 78, 85–87
Van Vechten, Carl, **Supp. II:** 200, 203, 218
Vanbrugh, Sir John, **II:** 289, **323–337,** 339, 347, 360; **III:** 253, 261
Vandaleur's Folly (Arden and D'Arcy), **Supp. II:** 35, 39
"Vanitie" (Herbert), **II:** 127
Vanity Fair (Thackeray), **IV:** 301; **V:** xxi, 17, 19, 20, 23, **25–28,** 30, 31, 35, 38; **Supp. IV:** 238
"Vanity of Human Wishes, The" (Johnson), **III:** 109–110, 121, 280, 281; **IV:** 188; **Supp. IV:** 271; **Retro. Supp. I:** 139, 148
"Vanity of Spirit" (Vaughan), **II:** 185
"Vaquero" (Muldoon), **Supp. IV:** 415
Vargas Llosa, Mario, **Supp. IV:** 440
Variation of Public Opinion and Feelings, The (Crabbe), **III:** 286
"Variations of Ten Summer Minutes" (MacCaig), **Supp. VI:** 193
Variation on a Theme (Rattigan), **Supp. VII:** 315, 319–320
"Variations and Excerpts" (Ewart), **Supp. VII:** 43
Variations on a Time Theme (Muir), **Supp. VI:** 204
"Variations on a Time Theme" (Muir), **Supp. VI:** 205
Varieties of Parable (MacNeice), **VII:** 405
Varma, D. P., **III:** 338, 346
Varney the Vampire (Pecket and Rymer), **Supp. III:** 385
Vasari, Georgio, **V:** 346
"Vastness" (Tennyson), **IV:** 329, 330
Vathek (Beckford), **III:** **327–329,** 345; **IV:** xv, 230
Vaughan, Henry, **II:** 123, 126, **184–189,** 190, **201–203,** 221; **Retro. Supp. II:** 172

Vaughan, Thomas, **II:** 184, 185
"Vauxhall Gardens by Day" (Dickens), **V:** 47n
"Velvet Glove, The" (James), **VI:** 69
Venables, Robert, **II:** 131, 137
Vendor of Sweets, The (Naipaul), **Supp. I:** 400
Venerable Bede, The, **I:** 374–375
Venetia (Disraeli), **IV:** xix, 298, 299, 307, 308
Veni, Creator Spiritus (Dryden), **II:** 300
Venice (Morris, J.), **Supp. X:** 175–177
Venus and Adonis (Shakespeare), **I:** 291, 306, 325; **IV:** 256
Venus and Tannhäuser (Beardsley), **V:** 318n
Venus and the Rain (McGuckian), **Supp. V:** 277, 282–284, 287
"Venus and the Rain" (McGuckian), **Supp. V:** 277–278
"Venus and the Sun" (McGuckian), **Supp. V:** 283
"Venus Fly–trap" (MacCaig), **Supp. VI:** 192
Venus Observed (Fry), **Supp. III:** 195, 202–203, 207, 208
"Venus Smiles" (Ballard), **Supp. V:** 26
Venusberg (Powell), **VII:** 344, 345
Vera; or, The Nihilists (Wilde), **V:** 401, 419; **Retro. Supp. II:** 362
Veranilda (Gissing), **V:** 435, 437
Verbivore (Brooke–Rose), **Supp. IV:** 100, 111–112
Vercelli Book, **Retro. Supp. II:** 301–303
"Verdict, The" (Cameron), **Supp. IX:** 27
Vergil, **II:** 292, 300, 304; **III:** 222, 311, 312; **IV:** 327; **Supp. III:** 415–416, 417
Vergil's Gnat (Spenser), **I:** 123
Vérité de la réligion Chrétienne (tr. Sidney), **I:** 161
Verlaine, Paul, **V:** 404, 405
Vermeer, Jan, **Supp. IV:** 136
Vernacular Republic, The (Murray), **Supp. VII:** 270
Verne, Jules, **III:** 341; **VI:** 229
Veronese, Paolo, **V:** 179
"Vers de Société" (Larkin), **Supp. I:** 282, 285
Vers d'Occasion (Day Lewis), **Supp. III:** 130
Verse (Murray), **Supp. VII:** 270
Verse (Wallace–Crabbe), **VIII:** 316
"Verse and Mathematics: A Study of the Sources of Poetry" (Caudwell), *see* "Illusion and Reality: A Study of the Sources of Poetry"
"Verse from an Opera—The Village Dragon" (Ewart), **Supp. VII:** 37
Verses (Rossetti), **V:** 260
Verses of V. A. D. (Brittain), **Supp. X:** 35
"Verses for a Christmas Card" (Morgan, E.), **Supp. IX:** 161, 162
Verses, in the Character of a Corsican (Boswell), **III:** 248
Verses Lately Written upon Several Occasions (Cowley), **II:** 202
Verses on the Death of Dr. Swift (Swift), **III:** 21, 32; **Retro. Supp. I:** 274
"Verses . . . to Sir Thomas Hanmer" (Collins), **III:** 160, 175

Versions and Perversions of Heine (Sisson), **Supp. XI:** 247

Vertical Man: Sequel to A Selected Life (Kinsella), **Supp. V:** 267

Vertigo (Sebald), **VIII:** 295, 296, 297, 298–300

"Verulam" (Roberts, K.), **Supp. X:** 275

Very Fine Clock, The (Spark), **Supp. I:** 213

Very Good Hater, A (Hill, R.), **Supp. IX:** 111

Very Private Eye, A: An Autobiography in Diaries and Letters (Pym), **Supp. II:** 363, 374

Very Private Life, A (Frayn), **Supp. VII:** 54–56

"Very Simply Topping Up the Brake Fluid" (Armitage), **VIII:** 4

Very Woman, A (Fletcher and Massinger), **II:** 66; **Supp. XI:** 184

"Vespers" (Auden), **Retro. Supp. I:** 13

"Vespers" (Milne), **Supp. V:** 301–302

Vet's Daughter, The (Comyns), **VIII:** 53, 60, 61–62

Vexilla Regis (Jones), **Supp. VII:** 180

Vexilla Regis (Skelton), **I:** 84

Via Media, The (Newman), **Supp. VII:** 295, 302

"Via Maestranza" (Cameron), **Supp. IX:** 27

"Via Negativa" (Thomas), **Supp. XII:** 286

"Via Portello" (Davie), **Supp. VI:** 107

"Vicar, The" (Praed), **V:** 14

Vicar of Bullhampton, The (Trollope), **V:** 102

Vicar of Sorrows, The (Wilson), **Supp. VI:** 308

Vicar of Wakefield, The (Goldsmith), **III:** 177, 178, 179, 180, **181–184,** 185, 188, 191

Viceroy of Ouidah, The (Chatwin), **Supp. IV:** 158, 165–168, 173; **Supp. IX:** 55–56

"Victim" (Fallon), **Supp. XII:** 104

Victim of Circumstances, A, and Other Stories (Gissing), **V:** 437

Victim of the Aurora, A (Keneally), **Supp. IV:** 346, 352–354

Victims (Fallon), **Supp. XII:** 104

"Victor Hugo" (Swinburne), **V:** 333

Victoria, queen of England, **IV:** 303–304, 305; **V:** xvii, xix, xxv–xxvi, 77, 114, 117

Victoria Station (Pinter), **Supp. I:** 378

Victorian Age in Literature (Chesterton), **VI:** 337

Victorian Age of English Literature, The (Oliphant), **Supp. X:** 222

Victorian and Edwardian London from Old Photographs (Betjeman), **VII:** 358

"Victorian Guitar" (Cornford), **VIII:** 114

Victorian Lady Travellers (Middleton), **V:** 253

Victorian Ode for Jubilee Day, 1897 (Thompson), **V:** 451

Victorian Romantic, A: D. G. Rossetti (Doughty), **V:** 246, 297*n*, 307

Victory (Conrad), **VI:** 144, 146, 148; **Supp. IV:** 250; **Retro. Supp. II:** 82

"Victory, The" (Stevenson), **Supp. VI:** 256, 264

Vidal, Gore, **Supp. IV:** 546

"Video, The" (Adcock), **Supp. XII:** 13

Vienna (Spender), **Supp. II:** 486, 487

"Vienna. Zürich. Constance" (Thomas), **Supp. IV:** 493

"Vienne" (Rhys), **Supp. II:** 388, 389–390

Viet Rock (play), **Supp. IV:** 435

"Vietnam Project, The" (Coetzee), **Supp. VI:** 76, **78–79,** 80

"View of Exmoor, A" (Warner), **Supp. VII:** 380

"View of Poetry, A" (Muir), **Supp. VI:** 202–203

View of the Edinburgh Theatre . . . , A (Boswell), **III:** 247

View of the English Stage, A (Hazlitt), **IV:** 129, 139

View of the Present State of Ireland (Spenser), **I:** 139

Views and Reviews (James), **VI:** 67

Views in Rome and Its Environs (Lear), **V:** 76, 87

Views in the Seven Ionian Islands (Lear), **V:** 87

Víga–Glúms saga, **VIII:** 241

"Vigil and Ode for St. George's Day" (Sisson), **Supp. XI:** 251–252

"Vigil of Corpus Christi, The" (Gunn), **Supp. IV:** 266

Vigny, Alfred de, **IV:** 176

Vile Bodies (Waugh), **VII:** 289, 290–291

Villa Rubein (Galsworthy), **VI:** 277

Village, The (Crabbe), **III:** 273, 274, 275, 277–278, 283, 286

"Village, The" (Reid), **Supp. VII:** 325

"Village, The" (Smith, I. C.), **Supp. IX:** 220–221

Village and Other Poems, The (Smith, I. C.), **Supp. IX:** 220–221

Village Betrothal (Greuze), **Supp. IV:** 122

Village by the Sea (Desai), **Supp. V:** 55, 63, 68–69

Village Minstrel, and Other Poems, The (Clare), **Supp. XI:** 56–57

"Village Priest, The" (Ngũgĩ), **VIII:** 220

Village Wooing (Shaw), **VI:** 127, 129

"Villain, The" (Davies), **Supp. XI:** 98–99

Villainy of Stock–Jobbers Detected, The (Defoe), **III:** 12

"Villanelle" (Empson), **Supp. II:** 183

Villette (Brontë), **V:** xxi, 112, 125–126, 130, 132, 136, 145, **147–150,** 152; **Retro. Supp. I:** 53, 54, 60–61

Villiers, George, *see* Buckingham, duke of

Villon (Bunting), **Supp. VII:** 3, 6

Villon, François, **V:** 327, 384

Vinaver, Eugéne, **Retro. Supp. II:** 242, 246

Vindication etc., The (Dryden), **II:** 305

Vindication of a Natural Diet . . . , A (Shelley), **IV:** 208

Vindication of . . . Lord Carteret, A (Swift), **III:** 35–36

Vindication of Natural Society, A (Burke), **III:** 195, 198, 205

Vindication of . . . Some Gospel–Truths, A (Bunyan), **II:** 253

Vindication of Some Passages in . . . the Decline and Fall . . . , A (Gibbon), **III:** 233

Vindication of the English Constitution (Disraeli), **IV:** 298, 308

Vindication of the Rights of Men, A (Wollstonecraft), **Supp. III:** **467–470,** 474, 476

Vindication of the Rights of Women, A (Wollstonecraft), **IV:** xv, 118; **Supp. III:** 465, **470–473,** 476

Vindiciae Ecclesiae Anglicanae: Letters to Charles Butler . . . . (Southey), **IV:** 71

Vine, Barbara, *see* Rendell, Ruth

Vinegar Tom (Churchill), **Supp. IV:** 181, 184–186, 198

Vinland (Brown), **Supp. VI:** 67

Vintage London (Betjeman), **VII:** 358–359

"Vintage to the Dungeon, The" (Lovelace), **II:** 231

Violent Effigy, The: A Study of Dickens's Imagination (Carey), **V:** 73

"Violent Noon, The" (Ballard), **Supp. V:** 20

Viper and Her Brood, The (Middleton), **II:** 3, 33

Virchow, Rudolf, **V:** 348

Virgidemiarum (Hall), **II:** 25

Virgil, *see* Vergil

Virgin and the Gipsy, The (Lawrence), **VII:** 91, 115

Virgin and the Nightingale, The: Medieval Latin Lyrics (tr. Adcock), **Supp. XII:** 10

Virgin in the Garden, The (Byatt), **Supp. IV:** 139, 145–147, 149

Virgin Martyr, The (Massinger and Dekker), **Supp. XI:** 182, 183, 192–193

"Virgin Mary to the Child Jesus, The" (Browning), **IV:** 313

"Virgin Russia" (Cameron), **Supp. IX:** 19

Virgin Territory (Maitland), **Supp. XI:** 163, 166–168, 170, 171, 172

"Virgini Senescens" (Sisson), **Supp. XI:** 255–256

Virginia (O'Brien), **Supp. V:** 334

Virginia Woolf: A Biography (Bell), **VII:** 38; **Retro. Supp. I:** 305

Virginia Woolf Icon (Silver), **Retro. Supp. I:** 305

Virginians, The (Thackeray), **V:** 29, **31–33,** 38

Virginibus Puerisque and Other Papers (Stevenson), **V:** 395; **Retro. Supp. I:** 262

Virtuous Villager, The (Haywood), **Supp. XII:** 136

Vision, A (Yeats), **VI:** 209, 213, 214, 222

"Vision, The" (Burns), **III:** 315

"Vision, The" (Traherne), **Supp. XI:** 266, 267

"Vision and Prayer" (Thomas), **Supp. I:** 178

Vision of Bags, A (Swinburne), **V:** 333

Vision of Battlements, A (Burgess), **Supp. I:** 185, 187, 195–196

Vision of Cathkin Braes, The (Morgan, E.), **Supp. IX:** 160–163

"Vision of Cathkin Braes, The" (Morgan, E.), **Supp. IX:** 163

Vision of Delight, The (Jonson), **Retro. Supp. I:** 165

Vision of Don Roderick, The (Scott), **IV:** 38

Vision of Gombold Proval, The (Orton), **Supp. V:** 365–366, 370

Vision of Judgement, A (Southey), **IV:** 61, 71, 184–187

Vision of Judgment, The (Byron), **IV:** xviii, 58, 61–62, 132, 172, 178, **184–187,** 193

"Vision of Poets, A" (Browning), **IV:** 316

"Vision of the Empire, The" (Williams, C. W. S.), **Supp. IX:** 282

"Vision of the Last Judgment, A" (Blake), **III:** 299

"Vision of the Mermaids, A" (Hopkins), **V:** 361, 381

Vision of the Three T's, The (Carroll), **V:** 274

"Vision of that Ancient Man, The" (Motion), **Supp. VII:** 260, 261

Vision of William Concerning Piers the Plowman . . . , The (ed. Skeat), **I:** 17

Vision Showed ... to a Devout Woman, A (Julian of Norwich), **Supp. XII:** 153–154, 159

Visions of the Daughters of Albion (Blake), **III:** 307; **Retro. Supp. I:** 39–40

"Visit in Bad Taste, A" (Wilson), **Supp. I:** 157

"Visit to Grandpa's, A" (Thomas), **Supp. I:** 181

"Visit to Morin, A" (Greene), **Supp. I:** 15, 18

"Visit to the Dead, A" (Cameron), **Supp. IX:** 27

"Visitation, The" (Jennings), **Supp. V:** 212

Visitations (MacNeice), **VII:** 416

"Visiting Hour" (Kinsella), **Supp. V:** 273

"Visiting Hour" (Murphy), **Supp. V:** 326

"Visiting Julia" (Hart), **Supp. XI:** 123

Visiting Mrs. Nabokov and Other Excursions (Amis), **Supp. IV:** 42, 43

"Visiting Rainer Maria" (McGuckian), **Supp. V:** 286

Visiting the Caves (Plomer), **Supp. XI:** 213, 214

"Visitor, The" (Bowen), **Supp. II:** 81

"Visitor, The" (Blunden), **Supp. XI:** 36

"Visitor, The" (Dahl), **Supp. IV:** 219–220

Visitor, The (Orton), **Supp. V:** 363, 367

"Visitors, The" (Fuller), **Supp. VII:** 77

"Visits, The" (James), **VI:** 49, 69

"Visits to the Cemetery of the Long Alive" (Stevenson), **Supp. VI:** 264

Vita Nuova (tr. Rossetti), **V:** 238

"Vitai Lampada" (Newbolt), **VI:** 417

Vittoria (Meredith), **V:** 227–228, 234

Vivian (Edgeworth), **Supp. III:** 158

Vivian Grey (Disraeli), **IV:** xvii, 293–294, 297, 299, 308

Vivisector, The (White), **Supp. I:** 132, 145–146

Vizetelly (publisher), **VI:** 86

"Vocation" (Malouf), **Supp. XII:** 221

"Voice, The" (Brooke), **Supp. III:** 52

"Voice, The" (Hardy), **VI:** 18

"Voice from the Dead, A" (Connolly), **Supp. III:** 111

"Voice of Brisbane, The" (Hart), **Supp. XI:** 131

"Voice of Nature, The" (Bridges), **VI:** 79

Voice of Scotland, **Supp. XII:** 204

"Voice of the Ancient Bard, The" (Blake), **Retro. Supp. I:** 37

"Voice of Things, The" (Hardy), **Retro. Supp. I:** 121

Voice Over (MacCaig), **Supp. VI:** 194

Voice Through a Cloud, A (Welch), **Supp. IX:** 262–263; 266–267, 268

Voices in the City (Desai), **Supp. V:** 54, 59–60, 72

Voices in the Night (Steel), **Supp. XII:** 273 274

Voices of the Stones (Russell), **VIII:** 290

"Voices of Time, The" (Ballard), **Supp. V:** 22, 24, 29, 34

Volpone (Jonson), **I:** 339, 343–344, 348; **II:** 4, 45, 70, 79; **V:** 56; **Retro. Supp. I:** 163, 164

Vǫlsunga saga, **VIII:** 231

Voltaire, **II:** 261, 348; **III:** 149, 235, 236, 327; **IV:** xiv, 290, 295, 346; **Supp. IV:** 136, 221

"Voltaire at Ferney" (Auden), **Retro. Supp. I:** 8

Voltaire in Love (Mitford), **Supp. X:** 163

Vǫlundarkviða, **VIII:** 230

"Volunteer, The" (Asquith), **VI:** 417

Volunteers (Friel), **Supp. V:** 111, 112, 121–122

Vǫluspá, **VIII:** 230, 231, 235, 243

Vonnegut, Kurt, Jr., **III:** 341; **Supp. IV:** 116

Vortex, The (Coward), **Supp. II:** 139, 141–143, 144, 149

Voss (Meale and Malouf), **Supp. XII:** 218

Voss (White), **VII:** 31; **Supp. I:** 130, 131, **138–141,** 142

Vote, Vote, Vote for Nigel Barton (Potter, D.), **Supp. X:** 228, 231–232

Votive Tablets (Blunden), **IV:** 86; **Supp. XI:** 36

Vox clamantis (Gower), **I:** 48, 49–50

"Vox Humana" (Gunn), **Supp. IV:** 261–262

Voyage, The (Muir), **Supp. VI:** 204, **206–207**

Voyage In the Dark (Rhys), **Supp. II:** **394–396**

Voyage of Captain Popanilla, The (Disraeli), **IV:** 294–295, 308

"Voyage of Mael Duin," **Supp. IV:** 415–416

Voyage of the Dawn Treader, The (Lewis), **Supp. III:** 248, 260

Voyage of the Destiny, The (Nye), **Supp. X:** 195–196

"Voyage Out, The" (Adcock), **Supp. XII:** 6

Voyage Out, The (Woolf), **VII:** 20, 27, 37; **Retro. Supp. I:** 307, 315–316

Voyage That Never Ends, The (Lowry), **Supp. III:** 276, 280

Voyage to Abyssinia, A (tr. Johnson), **III:** 107, 112, 121; **Retro. Supp. I:** 139

Voyage to New Holland, A (Dampier), **III:** 24

Voyage to the Island of Love, A (Behn), **Supp. III:** 37

Voyage to Venus (Lewis), **Supp. III:** 249

Voyages (Hakluyt), **I:** 150, 267; **III:** 7

"Voyages of Alfred Wallis, The" (Graham), **Supp. VII:** 110

Vulgar Errors (Browne), *see Pseudodoxia Epidemica*

Vulgar Streak, The (Lewis), **VII:** 72, 77

"Vulgarity in Literature" (Huxley), **V:** 53; **VII:** 198

"Vulture, The" (Beckett), **Supp. I:** 44

W. B. Yeats, Man and Poet (Jeffares), **VI:** 223

W. B. Yeats. The Critical Heritage (Jeffares), **VI:** 224

"W. Kitchener" (Hood), **IV:** 267

W. Somerset Maugham and the Quest for Freedom (Calder), **VI:** 376n

Waagen, Gustav Friedrich, **III:** 328

Wager, William, **I:** 213

Waggoner, The (Blunden), **Supp. XI:** 36, 42

Waggoner, The (Wordsworth), **IV:** 24, 73

"Wagner" (Brooke), **Supp. III:** 53

Wagner the Werewolf (Reynolds), **III:** 335

Wagstaff, Simon, pseud. of Jonathan Swift

Waif Woman, The (Stevenson), **V:** 396

Wain, John, **VI:** 209

Wainewright, Thomas, **V:** 405

Waingrow, W., **III:** 249

Waith, Eugene, **II:** 51, 64

"Waiting" (Self), **Supp. V:** 402

"Waiting at the Station" (Thackeray), **V:** 25

"Waiting for Breakfast" (Larkin), **Supp. I:** 277

"Waiting for Columbus" (Reid), **Supp. VII:** 334

Waiting for Godot (Beckett), **I:** 16–17; **Supp. I:** 51, 55–56, 57, 59; **Supp. IV:** 281, 429; **Retro. Supp. I:** 17–18, 20–21, 23–24; **Retro. Supp. II:** 344

"Waiting for J." (Ishiguro), **Supp. IV:** 303

Waiting for the Barbarians (Coetzee), **Supp. VI:** 75–76, **81–82**

Waiting for the Telegram (Bennett), **VIII:** 28

"Waiting Grounds, The" (Ballard), **Supp. V:** 21, 22

"Waiting in Hospital" (Cornford), **VIII:** 113

Waiting in the Wings (Coward), **Supp. II:** 155

Waiting Room, The (Harris), **Supp. V:** 136, 137–138, 140

"Waiting Supper, The" (Hardy), **VI:** 22

"Waking Father, The" (Muldoon), **Supp. IV:** 416–417

"Waking in a Newly Built House" (Gunn), **Supp. IV:** 263

Waking of Angantýr, The, **VIII:** 232

Waldegrave, Frances, **V:** 77, 80, 81

Waldere, **Retro. Supp. II:** 306–307

Wales: Epic Views of a Small Country (Morris, J.), **Supp. X:** 185

Wales, the First Place (Morris, J.), **Supp. X:** 177, 185

Walk in Chamounix, A, and Other Poems (Ruskin), **V:** 184

Walk on the Water, A (Stoppard), **Supp. I:** 437, 439

Walker, Ernest, **IV:** 304

Walker, London (Barrie), **Supp. III:** 4

Walker, R. S., **III:** 249

Walker, Shirley, **Supp. IV:** 347

Walker and Other Stories, The (O'Brian), **Supp. XII:** 251

Walking on Glass (Banks), **Supp. XI:** 7–8

"Walking to the Cattle Place" (Murray), **Supp. VII:** 274–275, 280, 281

"Walking with God" (Cowper), **III:** 212

"Walking Wounded" (Scannell), **VII:** 423

"Wall, The" (Jones), **Supp. VII:** 175

"Wall I Built, The" (Healy), **Supp. IX:** 107

Wall of the Plague, The (Brink), **Supp. VI: 52–53**

Wallace–Crabbe, Christopher, **VIII: 311–325**

Waller, Edmund, **II:** 138, 222, **232–236,** 256, 271

Walpole, Horace, **III:** 324, **325–327,** 336, 345; **Supp. III:** 383–384

Walpole, Hugh, **VI:** 55, 247, 377; **VII:** 211

Walpole, Robert, **Retro. Supp. I:** 235–236

"Walrus and the Carpenter, The" (Carroll), **V:** 268

Walsh, William, **II:** 325, 337, 339, 347; **Retro. Supp. I:** 232

Walter Pater: A Critical Study (Thomas), **V:** 355, 358; **VI:** 424

Walter Pater: The Idea in Nature (Ward), **V:** 347, 359

Walter Savage Landor: A Biography (Forster), **IV:** 87, 100

Walton, Izaak, **I:** 178; **II:** 118, 119, 130, **131–144; Retro. Supp. II:** 171–172

Walton, William, **VII:** xv

Walts, Janet, **Supp. IV:** 399

Waltz: An Apostrophic Hymn by Horace Hornem, Esq. (Byron), **IV:** 192

Wanderer, The, **Retro. Supp. II:** 304

Wanderer, The (Auden), **VII:** 380

"Wanderer, The" (tr. Morgan), **Supp. IX:** 160–161

"Wanderer, The" (Smith), **Supp. II:** 465

Wanderer, The; or, Female Difficulties (Burney), **Supp. III:** 64, 67, 74, 75, 76–77

"Wandering Angus, The" (Yeats), **Supp. IV:** 424

Wandering Islands, The (Hope), **Supp. VII:** 153–156, 157, 159

Wandering Jew, The (Shelley), **IV:** 209

"Wanderings of Brendan,"**Supp. IV:** 415

Wanderings of Oisin, The (Yeats), **IV:** 216; **VI:** 220, 221; **Supp. V:** 36; **Retro. Supp. I:** 325

Want of Wyse Men, The (Henryson), **Supp. VII:** 146–147

Wanting Seed, The (Burgess), **Supp. I:** 186, 190, 192–193

War (Doyle), **Supp. V:** 77, 87, 88–89

War and Common Sense (Wells), **VI:** 244

"War Cemetery" (Blunden), **Supp. XI:** 35

War Crimes (Carey), **Supp. XII:** 52, 54

"War Crimes" (Carey), **Supp. XII:** 54–55

"War Death in a Low Key" (Ewart), **Supp. VII:** 44

War Fever (Ballard), **Supp. V:** 33

"War Fever" (Ballard), **Supp. V:** 33

War in Heaven (Williams, C. W. S.), **Supp. IX:** 279, 280–281

War in Samoa (Stevenson), **V:** 396

War in South Africa, The: Its Cause and Conduct (Doyle), **Supp. II:** 161

War in the Air . . . , The (Wells), **VI:** 234, 244

War Issues for Irishmen (Shaw), **VI:** 119

War of Don Emmanuel's Nether Parts, The (De Bernières), **Supp. XII:** 65, 68, 69, 70–72

War of the Worlds, The (Wells), **VI:** 226, 233–234

War Plays, The (Bond), **Supp. I:** 423, 434

"War Poets, The" (Longley), **VIII:** 173

War Speeches (Churchill), **VI:** 361

"War That Will End War, The" (Wells), **VI:** 227, 244

"War–time" (Ewart), **Supp. VII:** 38

Ward, A. C., **V:** xiii, xxviii, 85, 86, 347, 348, 349

Ward, Edward, **III:** 41

Ward, Mrs. Humphry, **VI:** 387

Ward, R. P., **IV:** 293

"Ward 1G" (Fuller), **Supp. VII:** 80

"Ward 9" (Self), **Supp. V:** 401

Warden, The (Trollope), **V:** xxii, 92, 93, 101

"Warden's Daughter, The" (Gissing), **V:** 437

Ware the Hawk (Skelton), **I:** 88

"Waring" (Browning), **IV:** 356

Warner, Alan, **Supp. XI: 281–296**

Warner, Sylvia Townsend, **Supp. VII:** 369–383

"Warning to Children" (Graves), **VII:** 265

Warren, Austin, **II:** 155, 332*n*

"Warriors of the North, The" (Hughes), **Supp. I:** 342, 350

"Warriors Soul, The" (Conrad), **VI:** 148

War's Embers (Gurney), **VI:** 425

Warton, Joseph, **III:** 162, 170*n*

"Was He Married?" (Smith), **Supp. II:** 468

"Was, Is, Will Be" (Reid), **Supp. VII:** 327

Washington Square (James), **VI: 32–33**

Wasp Factory, The (Banks), **Supp. XI:** 1–3, 6

Wasp in a Wig, The (Carroll), **V:** 274

"Waste Land, The" (Eliot), **VI:** 137, 158; **VII:** xv, 143, **147–150; Supp. III:** 122; **Supp. IV:** 58, 249, 377; **Retro. Supp. I:** 3; **Retro. Supp. II:** 120, 121, 124–129

"Waste Land, The" (Paton), **Supp. II:** 345

"Wasted Day, A" (Cornford), **VIII:** 103

Wasted Years, The (Phillips), **Supp. V:** 380

"Wat o' the Cleugh" (Hogg), **Supp. X:** 110

Wat Tyler (Southey), **IV:** 59, 62, 66, 71, 185

"Watch, The" (Cornford), **VIII:** 102–103, 107

"Watch, The" (Swift), **Supp. V:** 433–434

Watch and Ward (James), **VI:** 24, 26, 67

Watch in the Night, A (Wilson), **Supp. VI:** 307

Watched Pot, The (Saki), **Supp. VI:** 250

"Watching Post" (Day Lewis), **Supp. III:** 128

Watchman, The (periodical), **IV:** 43, 55, 56

Watchman, The (Rankin), **Supp. X:** 244

Water and Waste (Reading), **VIII:** 261, 262

Water Beetle, The (Mitford), **Supp. X:** 151, 167

"Water Cinema" (Redgrove), **Supp. VI:** 236

"Water Lady, The" (Hood), **IV:** 255

"Water Music" (MacDiarmid), **Supp. XII:** 212

Water of Life, The (Bunyan), **II:** 253

Water of the Wondrous Isles, The (Morris), **V:** 306

"Watercress Girl, The" (Coppard), **VIII:** 90, 95

"Waterfall" (Fallon), **Supp. XII:** 103

Waterfall, The (Drabble), **Supp. IV:** 230, 239–241

"Waterfall, The" (Longley), **VIII:** 177–178

"Waterfall of Winter" (Redgrove), **Supp. VI:** 234

"Watergaw, The" (MacDiarmid), **Supp. XII:** 204–205

"Waterglass, The" (Reid), **Supp. VII:** 326

"Waterkeeper's Bothy" (Murphy), **Supp. V:** 328

"Water–Lady" (Redgrove), **Supp. VI:** 230

Waterland (Swift), **Supp. V:** 427, 434–437

"Watermark" (Gunesekera), **Supp. X:** 87

Waters of Babylon, The (Arden), **Supp. II:** 21, 22, 23–24, 25, 29

"Watershed, The" (Auden), **Retro. Supp. I:** 3

"Water–Witch, Wood–Witch, Wine–Witch" (Redgrove), **Supp. VI:** 234

Watson, George L., **VI:** 152

Watson, John B., **Supp. II:** 451

Watson, John Richard, **IV:** ix, xxv, 26, 375

Watson, Peter, **Supp. III:** 102–103, 105, 109

Watson, Richard, **III:** 301

Watson, Sir William, **VI:** 415

Watson, Thomas, **I:** 193, 276

Watsons, The (Austen), **IV:** 108, 122

Watson's Apology (Bainbridge), **Supp. VI:** 23

Watt, Ian, **VI:** 144; **Retro. Supp. I:** 70

Watt (Beckett), **Supp. I:** 46, **47–49,** 50, 51; **Retro. Supp. I:** 17, 20

Watteau (Brookner), **Supp. IV:** 122

Watteau, Jean–Antoine, **Supp. IV:** 122

Watter's Mou', The (Stoker), **Supp. III:** 381

"Wattle Tent" (Murphy), **Supp. V:** 329

Watts, Isaac, **III:** 118, 211, 288, 294, 299, 300

Watts–Dunton, Theodore, **V:** 314, 334

Waugh, Alec, **Supp. VI:** **267–277**

Waugh, Evelyn, **V:** 33; **VII:** xviii, xx–xxi, **289–308; Supp. II:** 4, 74, 199, 213, 218; **Supp. III:** 105; **Supp. IV:** 27, 281, 287, 365, 505

Waverly novels (Scott), **IV:** 28, 30–34, 38

Waverly; or, 'Tis Sixty Years Since (Scott), **III:** 335; **IV:** xvii, 28, 30–31, 37, 38; **Supp. III:** 151, 154

Waves, The (Woolf), **VI:** 262; **VII:** xv, 18, 22, 27, 38; **Supp. III:** 45; **Supp. IV:** 461, 557; **Retro. Supp. I:** 308, 314, 319–320

"Waves Have Gone Back, The" (Dutton), **Supp. XII:** 93

"Waxwing Winter" (McGuckian), **Supp. V:** 289

Waxwings (Raban), **Supp. XI:** 227, 228, 238–241

"Way of Literature: An Apologia, The" (Brown), **Supp. VI:** 70

"Way It Came, The" (James), **VI:** 69

Way of All Flesh, The (Butler), **VI:** ix; **Supp. II:** 97, 98, 99, 104, **111–114,** 117, 119

Way of Being Free, A (Okri), **Supp. V:** 353, 359, 360

"Way of Imperfection, The" (Thompson), **V:** 451

Way of Looking, A (Jennings), **Supp. V:** , 210, 211, 214

"Way of the Cross, The" (du Maurier), **Supp. III:** 147

Way of the Spirit (Haggard), **Supp. III:** 214, 222

Way of the World, The (Congreve), **II:** 339, **343–346,** 347, 350

"Way the Wind Blows, The" (Caudwell), **Supp. IX:** 36

Way to the Stars, The (Rattigan), **Supp. VII:** 313, 319

"Way up to Heaven, The" (Dahl), **Supp. IV:** 218–219

Way Upstream (Ayckbourn), **Supp. V:** 3, 10, 14

Way We Live Now, The (Trollope), **IV:** 307; **V:** xxiv, 98–99, 100, 102

Ways and Means (Coward), **Supp. II:** 153

Ways of Escape (Greene), **Supp. I:** 3, 7, 11, 18

Ways of Seeing (Berger), **Supp. IV:** 79, 82, 88–90

Ways of Telling: The World of John Berger (Dyer), **Supp. IV:** 81

"Wayside Station, The" (Muir), **Supp. VI:** 206

"We All Try" (Caudwell), **Supp. IX:** 36, 37

"We Are Seven" (Wordsworth), **IV:** 8, 10

"We have a pritty witty king" (Rochester), **II:** 259

"We lying by seasand" (Thomas), **Supp. I:** 176

"We Must Act Quickly" (Paton), **Supp. II:** 359

We Were Dancing (Coward), **Supp. II:** 153

Weak Woman (Davies), **Supp. XI:** 92

"Wealth, The" (Dunn), **Supp. X:** 66

Wealth of Mr. Waddy, The (Wells), *see Kipps*

Wealth of Nations, The (Smith), *see Inquiry into the Nature & Causes of the Wealth of Nations*

Wearieswa': A Ballad (Swinburne), **V:** 333

Weather in Japan, The (Longley), **VIII:** 166, 177–178

"Weather in Japan, The" (Longley), **VIII:** 177

Weatherboard Cathedral, The (Murray), **Supp. VII:** 270, 272–273, 282

Weathering (Reid), **Supp. VII:** 323, 330–331

Webb, Beatrice, **VI:** 227, 241; **Supp. IV:** 233

Webb, Mary, **Supp. IV:** 169

Webb, Philip, **V:** 291, 296

Webb, Sidney, **VI:** 102; **Supp. IV:** 233

Webber, Andrew Lloyd, **Supp. V:** 3

Webster, John, **II:** 21, 31,, 33, **68–86,** 82359, 97, 100; **Supp. IV:** 234

Webster: "The Dutchess of Malfi" (Leech), **II:** 90*n*

Wedd, Nathaniel, **VI:** 398, 399

"Wedding, The" (Smith, I. C.), **Supp. IX:** 224

"Wedding Gown, The" (Moore), **VI:** 93

"Wedding Guest, A" (Plomer), **Supp. XI:** 222

Wedding of Cousins, A (Tennant), **Supp. IX:** 239

"Wedding Morning" (Kinsella), **Supp. V:** 261

"Wedding Wind" (Larkin), Supp. I: 277, 285

Wedding–Day, The (Fielding), **III:** 105

"Weddings" (Thomas), **Supp. IV:** 491

Weddings at Nether Powers, The (Redgrove), **Supp. VI:** 235

Wedgwood, Tom, **IV:** 127–128

Wednesday Early Closing (Nicholson), **Supp. VI:** 212, 214

"Wednesday; or, The Dumps" (Gay), **III:** 56

Wee Willie Winkie (Kipling), **VI:** 204

"Weed Species" (Dutton), **Supp. XII:** 94–95

"Weeds" (Nicholson), **Supp. VI:** 219

"Week with Uncle Felix, A" (Galloway), **Supp. XII:** 122–123

Weekend with Claude, A (Bainbridge), **Supp. VI:** 17–19, 24

Weekly Journal (newspaper), **III:** 7

Weep Not, Child (Ngũgĩ), **VIII:** 212, 213, 214, 218–219

"Weep Not My Wanton" (Coppard), **VIII:** 88, 93

"Weeper, The" (Crashaw), **II:** 180, 181, 183

"Weighing" (Heaney), **Retro. Supp. I:** 133

"Weights" (Murray), **Supp. VII:** 278

"Weignachtsabend" (Roberts, K.), **Supp. X:** 270

Weil, Simone, **Supp. I:** 217

Weinraub, Judith, **Supp. IV:** 345

Weir of Hermiston, The (Stevenson), **V:** 383, 384, 387, 390, 392, 396; **Retro. Supp. I:** 270

Weis, C. McC., **III:** 249

Weismann, August, **Supp. II:** 108

Welch, Denton, **Supp. III:** 107, **Supp. IX:** **261–270**

"Welcome, The" (Cowley), **II:** 196

"Welcome to Sack, The" (Herrick), **II:** lll

Weldon, Fay, **Supp. IV:** **521–539**

Well at the World's End, The (Morris), **V:** 306

Well of Loneliness, The (Hall), **VI:** 411; **Supp. VI:** 119–120, 122, **125–128,** 129, 131

Well of Lycopolis, The (Bunting), **Supp. VII:** 4

"Well of Pen–Morta, The" (Gaskell), **V:** 15

Well of the Saints, The (Synge), **VI:** 308, 311, 312–313; **Retro. Supp. I:** 297–298

"Well–Spring, The" (Nye), **Supp. X:** 195, 205

Well–Beloved, The: A Sketch of a Temperament (Hardy), **VI:** 14, 20; **Retro. Supp. I:** 114–115

"Wellington College" (Murphy), **Supp. V:** 328

Wells, H. G., **III:** 341; **V:** xxiii, xxvi, 388, 426–427, 429, 438; **VI:** x–xiii, 102, **225–246,** 287; **VII:** xiv, 197; list of works and letters, **VI:** 243–246; **Supp. II:** 295; **Supp. III:** 434; **Supp. IV:** 256

"Wells, Hitler, and the World State" (Orwell), **VII:** 274

"Wells, The" (Redgrove), **Supp. VI:** 234, 237

Well–Wrought Urn, The (Brooks), **IV:** 323*n*, 339

Welsh Ambassador, The, **II:** 100

"Welsh Hill Country, The" (Thomas), **Supp. XII:** 283

"Welsh History" (Thomas), **Supp. XII:** 283

Welsh, Irvine, **Supp. IV:** 26

"Welsh Landscape" (Thomas), **Supp. XII:** 283

Welsh Opera, The (Fielding), **III:** 105

"Welshman to Any Tourist, A" (Thomas), **Supp. XII:** 283

"Welshness in Wales" (Morris, J.), **Supp. X:** 184–185

We're Not Going to Do Anything (Day Lewis), **Supp. III:** 118

"Werewolf, The" (Carter), **Supp. III:** 88

Werner, J., **III:** 249

Werner: A Tragedy (Byron), **IV:** 193

Werther (Goethe), *see Sorrows of Young Werther, The*

Wesker, Arnold, **VI:** 101

Wesley, Charles, **III:** 211

Wesley, John, **II:** 273

Wessex Poems (Hardy), **VI:** 14; **Retro. Supp. I:** 110

Wessex Tales: Strange, Lively and Commonplace (Hardy), **VI:** 20

West, Anthony, **VI:** 241, 242

West, Arthur Graeme, **VI:** 423

"West End, The" (Healy), **Supp. IX:** 107

West, Moris, **Supp. IV:** 343

West, Rebecca, **VI:** 226, 227, 252, 371; **Supp. II:** 146–147; **Supp. III:** 431–445

"West Indies, The" (Macaulay), **IV:** 278

West Indies and the Spanish Main, The (Trollope), **V:** 101

West of Suez (Osborne), **Supp. I:** 339

West Window, The (Hartley), see *Shrimp and the Anemone, The*

"Westland Row" (Kinsella), **Supp. V:** 263

"Westland Well" (Swinburne), **V:** 333

Westmacott, Mary (pseud., Christie), **Supp. II:** 123, 133

"Westminster Abbey" (Arnold), **V:** 208–209

Westminster Alice, The (Saki), **Supp. VI:** 239

Westminster Review, The (periodical), **V:** xviii, 189

Westward Ho! (Dekker and Webster), **II:** 68, 85

Westwind (Rankin), **Supp. X:** 244

Wet Fish (Arden), **Supp. II:** 28

"Wet Night, A" (Beckett), **Supp. I:** 45; **Retro. Supp. I:** 19

"Wet Snow" (MacCaig), **Supp. VI:** 186

Wetherby (Hare), **Supp. IV:** 282, 289–290

"What a Misfortune" (Beckett), **Supp. I:** 45

What Am I Doing Here (Chatwin), **Supp. IV:** 157, 163, 173; **Supp. IX:** 52, 53, 60–61

What Became of Jane Austen? (Amis), **Supp. II:** 1, 2, 11

What D'Ye Call It, The (Gay), **III:** 58, 60, 67

"What Do Hippos Eat?" (Wilson), **Supp. I:** 156–157

"What Does It Matter?" (Forster), **VI:** 411

What Every Woman Knows (Barrie), **Supp. III:** 6, 9, **10–11**

"What Gets Lost *Lo Que Se Pierde*" (Reid), **Supp. VII:** 331

"What Happened to Blake?" (Hare), **Supp. IV:** 281, 283

What Happened to Burger's Daughter: or How South African Censorship Works (Gordimer), **Supp. II:** 237

"What I Believe" (Spender), **Supp. II:** 494

"What I Have Been Doing Lately" (Kincaid), **Supp. VII:** 221

What I Really Wrote About the War (Shaw), **VI:** 129

What Is He? (Disraeli), **IV:** 308

"What Is the Language Using Us For?" (Graham), **Supp. VII:** 115

"What Is There to Discuss?" (Ramsey), **VII:** 240

What Lack I Yet? (Powys), **VIII:** 255

What Maisie Knew (James), **VI: 50–52,** 67

"What meaneth this?" (Wyatt), **I:** 104

What Mrs. McGillicuddy Saw (Christie), *see 4.50 from Paddington*

"What rage is this" (Wyatt), **I:** 104

What the Black Mirror Saw (Redgrove), **Supp. VI:** 236

What the Butler Saw (Orton), **Supp. V:** 367, 371, 377–378

What the Hammer (Healy), **Supp. IX:** 96, 106–107

What the Public Wants (Bennett), **VI:** 263–264

"What the Shepherd Saw" (Hardy), **VI:** 22

"What the Thrush Said" (Keats), **IV:** 225

"What the Thunder Said" (Eliot), **Retro. Supp. II:** 128–129

"What Then?" (Thomas), **Supp. XII:** 290, 291

"What Then?" (Yeats), **Retro. Supp. I:** 337

What Where (Beckett), **Supp. IV:** 284

"What will they do?" (Thomas), **Supp. III:** 400, 401

What You Will (Marston), **II:** 29–30, 40

Whately, Richard, **IV:** 102, 122

"Whatever Sea" (Dutton), **Supp. XII:** 92–93

What's Become of Waring? (Powell), **VII:** 346, 353

"What's Your Success?" (Smith, I. C.), **Supp. IX:** 214

Wheatcroft, Geoffrey, **Supp. IV:** 173

"Wheel of Time, The" (James), **VI:** 69

Wheels of Chance, The: A Holiday Adventure (Wells), **VI:** 231–232, 244

"Wheest, Wheest" (MacDiarmid), **Supp. XII:** 206

"When a Beau Goes In" (Ewart), **VII:** 423; **Supp. VII:** 37

"When all my five and country senses see" (Thomas), **Supp. I:** 176

"When Earth's Last Picture Is Painted" (Kipling), **VI:** 169

"When I Am Dead, My Dearest" (Rossetti), **V:** 249

"When I Have Fears" (Keats), **IV:** 221

"When I Was Thirteen" (Welch), **Supp. IX:** 268–269

When Is a Door Not a Door? (Arden), **Supp. II:** 29

"When Israel came out of Egypt" (Clough), **V:** 160

"When My Girl Comes Home" (Pritchett), **Supp. III:** 312, **321–324**

When My Girl Comes Home (Pritchett), **Supp. III:** 313, 321

"When the Camel Is Dust it Goes Through the Needle's Eye" (Stevenson), **Supp. VI:** 264

"When the Kye Comes Hame" (Hogg), **Supp. X:** 110

When the Moon Has Set (Synge), **VI:** 310n; **Retro. Supp. I:** 294

"When the Sardines Came" (Plomer), **Supp. XI:** 215

When the Sleeper Wakes (Wells), **VI:** 234

When the Wicked Man (Ford), **VI:** 319, 332

"When They Want to Know What We Were Like" (Healy), **Supp. IX:** 107

When We Dead Awaken (Ibsen), **VI:** 269; **Retro. Supp. I:** 170, 175

"When we that were dear . . . A (Henley), **V:** 392

When We Were Very Young (Milne), **Supp. V:** 295, 301–302

When William Came (Saki), **Supp. VI: 248–250**

"When Windsor walles sustained my wearied arm" (Surrey), **I:** 113

"When You Are Old" (Yeats), **Retro. Supp. I:** 329

"When You Go" (Morgan, E.), **Supp. IX:** 168

"When you see millions of the mouthless dead" (Sorley), **VI:** 422

Where Adam Stood (Potter, D.), **Supp. X:** 232–234

Where Angels Fear to Tread (Forster), **VI:** 400–401; **Retro. Supp. II:** 136–139

"Where once the waters of your face" (Thomas), **Supp. I:** 173–174

Where Shall We Go This Summer (Desai), **Supp. V:** 53, 55, 63–64, 66, 73

"Where Tawe Flows" (Thomas), **Supp. I:** 180

Where the Wind Came (Wallace–Crabbe), **VIII:** 315–317, 318

Where There Is Darkness (Phillips), **Supp. V:** 380

"Where They Are Wrong" (Paton), **Supp. II:** 360

Where You Find It (Galloway), **Supp. XII:** 117, 126–127

"Where You Find It" (Galloway), **Supp. XII:** 126

Whereabouts: Notes on Being a Foreigner (Reid), **Supp. VII:** 323, 335–336

"Whereto Art Thou Come" (Thompson), **V:** 444

Whether a Dove or Seagull (Warner), **Supp. VII:** 370, 371, 372–373, 376

Whetstone, George, **I:** 282, 313

Whibley, Charles, **II:** 259

"Which New Era Would Be?" (Gordimer), **Supp. II:** 242

Whig Examiner (periodical), **III:** 51, 53

Whig Interpretations of History, The (Butterfield), **IV:** 291

While the Sun Shines (Rattigan), **Supp. VII:** 313

Whims and Oddities (Hood), **IV:** 253, 255, 257, 267

Whimsicalities (Hood), **IV:** 254, 267

Whirling (Wallace–Crabbe), **VIII:** 323–324, 325

Whirlpool, The (Gissing), **V:** 437

"Whisht" (Crawford), **Supp. XI:** 75

"Whisperer, The" (Nicholson), **Supp. VI:** 218

Whispering Roots, The (Day Lewis), **Supp. III:** 116, 118, 129–130

"Whispers" (Tennyson), **IV:** 332

"Whispers of Immortality" (Eliot), **VII:** 145

Whistlecraft (Frere), **IV:** 182–183

Whistler, James McNeill, **V:** 238, 245, 320, 407

Whit; or, Isis Amongst the Unsaved (Banks), **Supp. XI:** 14

White, Gilbert, **Supp. VI:** **279–295**

White, James, **IV:** 79

White, Norman, **V:** 379*n*

White, Patrick, **Supp. I:** **129–152; Supp. IV:** 343

White, Tony, **Supp. IV:** 256, 272, 273–274

"White Air of March, The" (Smith, I. C.), **Supp. IX:** 216–217

White Bird, The (Berger), **Supp. IV:** 89

White Bird, The (MacCaig), **Supp. VI:** 192

White Cockade, The (Gregory), **VI:** 315

White Company, The (Doyle), **Supp. II:** 159, 163

White Devil, The (Webster), **I:** 246; **II:** 68, 70, 72, 73–75, 76, 79, 80–85, 97; **Supp. IV:** 234–235

White Doe of Rylstone, The (Wordsworth), **IV:** xvii, 24

White Goddess, The (Graves), **VII:** xviii, 257, 259, 261–262

White Horseman, The (MacCaig), **Supp. VI:** 184

White Hotel, The (Thomas), **Supp. IV:** 479, 481–483, 486, 490, 493

"White Island, The; or, Place of the Blest" (Herrick), **II:** 113

White Liars (Shaffer), **Supp. I:** 322–323

White Lies (Shaffer), **Supp. I:** 322

White Monkey, The (Galsworthy), **VI:** 274

"White Negro, The" (Mailer), **Supp. IV:** 17–18

"White Noon, The" (Smith, I. C.), **Supp. IX:** 211

White Paternoster and Other Stories, The (Powys), **VIII:** 248, 256

White Peacock, The (Lawrence), **VII:** 88, 89, **91–93; Retro. Supp. II:** 222–223, 226

"White Poet, The" (Dunn), **Supp. X:** 71

"White Queen, The" (Harrison), **Supp. V:** 151

"White Ship, The" (Rossetti), **V:** 238, 244

"White Stocking, The" (Lawrence), **VII:** 114

White Threshold, The (Graham), **Supp. VII:** 110–111

"White Windsor Soap" (McGuckian), **Supp. V:** 288

White Writing: On the Culture of Letters in South Africa (Coetzee), **Supp. VI:** **84–85**

White–Eagles over Serbia (Durrell), **Supp. I:** 100

Whitehall, Harold, **V:** 365, 382

Whitelock, Derek, **Supp. IV:** 348

"Whitewashed Wall, The" (Hardy), **Retro. Supp. I:** 120

Whitman, Walt, **IV:** 332; **V:** 418; **VI:** 55, 63; **Supp. IV:** 163, 487

Whitsun Weddings, The (Larkin), **Supp. I:** 276, **279–281,** 285

"Whitsun Weddings, The" (Larkin), **Supp. I:** 285

"Whitsunday" (Herbert), **II:** 125

"Whitsunday in Kirchstetten" (Auden), **VII:** 396, 397

"Who Are These Coming to the Sacrifice?" (Hill), **Supp. V:** 191

Who Are You? (Kavan), **Supp. VII:** 214

"Who Goes Home?" (Day Lewis), **Supp. III:** 130

Who Guards a Prince? (Hill, R.), **Supp. IX:** 117

Who Is Sylvia? (Rattigan), **Supp. VII:** 317

"Who Needs It?" (Blackwood), **Supp. IX:** 9

Who was Changed and Who was Dead (Comyns), **VIII:** 53, 60–61

Who Was Oswald Fish? (Wilson), **Supp. VI:** **300–301**

Whole Armour, The (Harris), **Supp. V:** 132, 134, 135

Whole Duty of Man, The (Allestree), **III:** 82

"Whole of the Sky, The" (Armitage), **VIII:** 11

"Whole Truth, The" (Motion), **Supp. VII:** 256

Whole Works of Homer, The (Chapman), **I:** 235

Whoroscope (Beckett), **Supp. I:** 43; **Retro. Supp. I:** 19

"Who's Who" (Auden), **Retro. Supp. I:** 2

Whose Body? (Sayers), **Supp. III:** 334, 336–338, 340, 350

"Whose Endless Jar" (Richards), **Supp. II:** 426, 429

Whose Is the Kingdom? (Arden and D'Arcy), **Supp. II:** 39, 40–41

"Whoso list to hunt" (Wyatt), **I:** 101, 109

Why Are We So Blest? (Armah), **Supp. X:** 1–2, 5–9, 13–14

"Why Brownlee Left" (Muldoon), **Supp. IV:** 409, 410, 415, 418, 426

Why Come Ye Not to Court? (Skelton), **I:** 92–93

Why Do I Write? (Bowen), **Supp. II:** 80, 81, 91

Why Frau Frohmann Raised Her Prices and Other stories (Trollope), **V:** 102

"Why Has Narrative Poetry Failed" (Murphy), **Supp. V:** 320–321

"Why I Became a Plumber" (Maitland), **Supp. XI:** 175

"Why I Have Embraced Islam" (Rushdie), **Supp. IV:** 437

"Why I Ought Not to Have Become a Dramatic Critic" (Beerbohm), **Supp. II:** 54

"Why Not Take Pater Seriously?" (Fletcher), **V:** 359

Why Scots Should Rule Scotland (Gray, A.), **Supp. IX:** 80, 85

"Why She Would Not" (Shaw), **VI:** 130

"Why Should Not Old Men Be Mad?" (Yeats), **Retro. Supp. I:** 337

Why So, Socrates? (Richards), **Supp. II:** 425

"Why the Novel Matters" (Lawrence), **VII:** 122

"Why We Are in Favour of This War" (Hulme), **Supp. VI:** 140

"Why Write of the Sun" (Armitage), **VIII:** 3

Wi the Haill Voice (tr. Morgan, E.), **Supp. IX:** 168

Wicked Heat (Hart), **Supp. XI:** 121, 130–133

"Wicked Stepmother's Lament, The" (Maitland), **Supp. XI:** 175

"Wicked Tunge Wille Sey Amys, A" (Lydgate), **I:** 57

Wide Sargasso Sea (Rhys), **Supp. II:** 387, 389, **398–401,** 441; **Retro. Supp. I:** 60

Wide–Awake Stories: A Collection of Tales Told by Little Children between Sunset and Sunrise, in the Punjab and Kashmi (Steel), **Supp. XII:** 266

Widow, The (Middleton), **II:** 3, 21

"Widow, The" (Smith, I. C.), **Supp. IX:** 211

Widow Ranter, The (Behn), **Supp. III:** 34

Widow Ranter, The (Belin), **II:** 305

"Widower in the Country, The" (Murray), **Supp. VII:** 271

Widower's Son, The (Sillitoe), **Supp. V:** 410, 414, 415, 425

Widowers' Houses (Shaw), **VI:** 104, 107, 108, 129; **Retro. Supp. II:** 310–312

"Widowhood System, The" (Friel), **Supp. V:** 113

Widowing of Mrs. Holroyd, The (Lawrence), **VII:** 120, 121

Widow's Tears, The (Chapman), **I:** 243–244, 245–246

Widsith, **Retro. Supp. II:** 304

Wiene, Robert, **III:** 342

Wife for a Month (Fletcher), **II:** 65

Wife of Bath, The (Gay), **III:** 60, 67

Wife of Bath's Prologue, The (Chaucer), **I:** 24, 34, 39, 40

Wife of Bath's Tale, The (Chaucer), **I:** 27, 35–36

"Wife of Ted Wickham, The" (Coppard), **VIII:** 95

"Wife Speaks, The" (Day Lewis), **Supp. III:** 125

Wife's Lament, The, **Retro. Supp. II:** 305

Wigs on the Green (Mitford), **Supp. X:** 155–156

Wilberforce, William, **IV:** 133, 268; **V:** 277

Wild Ass's Skin, The (Balzac), **III:** 339, 345

"Wild Boar and the Ram, The" (Gay), **III**: 59

Wild Body, The (Lewis), **VII**: 72, 77, 78, 79

"Wild Colonial Puzzler, The" (Wallace–Crabbe), **VIII**: 318

Wild Duck, The (Ibsen), **VI**: ix

"Wild Flowers" (Howard), **V**: 48

Wild Gallant, The (Dryden), **II**: 305

Wild Garden, The; or, Speaking of Writing (Wilson), **Supp. I**: 153, 154–155, 156, 158, 160

Wild Goose Chase, The (Fletcher), **II**: 45, 61–62, 65, 352, 357

Wild Honey (Frayn), **Supp. VII**: 61

Wild Irish Boy, The (Maturin), **VIII**: 207, 209

Wild Knight, The (Chesterton), **VI**: 336

"Wild Lemons" (Malouf), **Supp. XII**: 220

Wild Nights (Tennant), **Supp. IX**: 230, 233–234

Wild Swans at Coole, The (Yeats), **VI**: 207, 213, 214, 217; **Retro. Supp. I**: 331

Wild Wales: Its People, Language, and Scenery (Borrow), **Supp. XII**: 17, 28–31

"Wild with All Regrets" (Owen), **VI**: 446, 452, 453

Wilde, Oscar, **III**: 334, 345; **V**: xiii, xxi, xxv, xxvi, 53, 339, **399–422**; **VI**: ix, 365; **VII**: 83; **Supp. II**: 43, 45–46, 48, 50, 51, 53, 54, 141, 143, 148, 155; **Supp. IV**: 288; **Retro. Supp. II**: 314–315, **359–374**

Wilder Hope, The: Essays on Future Punishment . . . (De Quincey), **IV**: 155

"Wilderness, The" (Keyes), **VII**: 439

Wilderness of Zin (Woolley and Lawrence), **Supp. II**: 284

Wildest Dreams (Ayckbourn), **Supp. V**: 3, 10, 12, 14

"Wildgoose Chase, A" (Coppard), **VIII**: 95

"Wildlife" (Adcock), **Supp. XII**: 12

"Wilfred Owen and the Georgians" (Hibberd), **VI**: 460

Wilfred Owen: Complete Poems and Fragments (Stallworthy), see *Complete Poems and Fragments of Wilfred Owen, The*

Wilfred Owen: War Poems and Others (Hibberd), **VI**: 446, 459

"Wilfred Owen's Letters" (Hibberd), **VI**: 460

Wilhelm Meister (Goethe), **IV**: 241; **V**: 214

Wilhelm Meister's Apprenticeship (tr. Carlyle), **IV**: 241, 250

Wilkes, John, **IV**: 61, 185

Wilkes, Thomas, **II**: 351, 363

Wilkie, David, **IV**: 37

Wilkins, George, **I**: 321

Wilkinson, Martin, **Supp. IV**: 168

"Will, The" (Donne), **Retro. Supp. II**: 91

Will Drew and Phil Crewe and Frank Fane . . . (Swinburne), **V**: 333

"Will o' the Mill" (Stevenson), **V**: 395

Will Warburton (Gissing), **V**: 435, 437

"Will Ye No' Come Back Again?" (Wallace–Crabbe), **VIII**: 323

Willey, Basil, **II**: 145, 157; **Supp. II**: 103, 107, 108

"William and Mary" (Dahl), **Supp. IV**: 218, 219

William B. Yeats: The Poet in Contemporary Ireland (Hone), **VI**: 223

William Blake (Chesterton), **VI**: 344

William Blake (Swinburne), **V**: 313, 314, 317, 329–330, 332

William Cobbett (Chesterton), **VI**: 341, 345

"William Cobbett: In Absentia" (Hill), **Supp. V**: 183

"William Congreve" (Swinburne), **V**: 332

William Dunbar, Selected Poems (Dunbar), **VIII**: 119

William Morris (Bloomfield), **V**: 306

William Morris, Artist, Writer, Socialist (Morris), **V**: 301, 305

"William Morris as I Knew Him" (Shaw), **VI**: 129

William Pitt . . . an Excellent New Ballad . . . (Boswell), **III**: 248

William Posters trilogy (Sillitoe), **Supp. V**: 410, 413, 421–424

"William Tennissippi" (Morgan, E.), **Supp. IX**: 161

William Wetmore Story and His Friends (James), **VI**: 67

"William Wordsworth" (De Quincey), **IV**: 146

William Wordsworth: A Biography (Moorman), **IV**: 4, 25

Williams, Basil, **VI**: 234

Williams, Charles Walter Stansby, **Supp. IX: 271–286**

Williams, H., **III**: 15n, 35

Williams, Hugo, **Supp. IV**: 168

Williams, Iolo, **VII**: 37

Williams, Raymond, **Supp. IV**: 95, 380

Williams, William Carlos, **Supp. IV**: 257, 263

Williams Manuscript and the Temple, The (Charles), **Retro. Supp. II**: 174

Willis, W., **III**: 199n

"Willowwood" sonnets (Rossetti), **V**: 243, 259

Willy Wonka and the Chocolate Factory (film), **Supp. IV**: 203

Wilmot, John, *see* Rochester, earl of

Wilson, A. N., *see* Wilson, Angus

Wilson, Angus, **V**: 43, 72; **VI**: 165; **Supp. I: 153–168**; **Supp. II**: 92; **Supp. IV**: 229, 231, 234, 346; **Supp. VI: 297–310**

Wilson, Colin, **III**: 341

Wilson, Dover, *see* Wilson, J. Dover

Wilson, Edmund, **III**: 27; **V**: 66, 69, 72; **VI**: 56, 62, 363; **VII**: 53; **Supp. II**: 57, 118, 124, 200, 204, 223; **Supp. III**: 95, 101, 105

Wilson, F. A. C., **VI**: 208, 220

Wilson, F. P., **I**: 286

Wilson, J. Dover, **I**: 326; **III**: 116n; **V**: 287, 290

Wilson, J. H., **II**: 257, 271

Wilson, John, **IV**: 11

Wilson, Rae, **IV**: 262

Wimsatt, M. K., Jr., **III**: 249

Winckelman, Johann, **V**: 341, 343, 344

"Winckelmann" (Pater), **V**: 341, 343, 344

Wind, Edgar, **I**: 237; **V**: 317n

"Wind" (Hughes), **Supp. I**: 343–344

Wind Among the Reeds, The (Yeats), **VI**: 211, 222

Wind from Nowhere, The (Ballard), **Supp. V**: 22

"Windfalls" (Fallon), **Supp. XII**: 110–111

"Windfarming" (Crawford), **Supp. XI**: 81

"Windhover, The" (Hopkins), **V**: 366, 367; **Retro. Supp. II**: 190, 191, 195–196

Winding Paths: Photographs by Bruce Chatwin (Chatwin, B.), **Supp. IX**: 62

Winding Stair, The (Yeats), **Supp. II**: 84–85; **Retro. Supp. I**: 336–337

Winding Stair, The: Francis Bacon, His Rise and Fall (du Maurier), **Supp. III**: 139

Windom's Way (Ambler), **Supp. IV**: 3

"Window, The" (Moore), **VI**: 93

Window in Thrums, A (Barrie), **V**: 392; **Supp. III**: 3

Windows (Galsworthy), **VI**: 269

"Windows, The" (Herbert), **Retro. Supp. II**: 176

Windows of Night (Williams, C. W. S.), **Supp. IX**: 274

"Wind's on the World, The" (Morris), **V**: 305

"Windscale" (Nicholson), **Supp. VI**: 218

Windsor Forest (Pope), **III**: 70, 77; **Retro. Supp. I**: 231

Wine, A Poem (Gay), **III**: 67

"Wine Fed Tree, The" (Powys), **VIII**: 251

Wine, Water and Song (Chesterton), **VI**: 340

Wine–Dark Sea, The (O'Brian), **Supp. XII**: 258–259

"Wingless" (Kincaid), **Supp. VII**: 220, 221, 226

"Wings of a Dove" (Brathwaite), **Supp. XII**: 44

Wings of the Dove, The (James), **VI**: 32, 55, **59–60**, 320; **Supp. IV**: 243

"Winkie" (Dunn), **Supp. X**: 77

Winkworth, Catherine, **V**: 149

Winnie–the–Pooh (Milne), **Supp. V**: 295, 303–307

"Winning of Etain, The" (Boland), **Supp. V**: 36

"Winnowers, The" (Bridges), **VI**: 78

Winslow Boy, The (Rattigan), **Supp. VII**: 307, 313–315

"Winter" (Blake), **Retro. Supp. I**: 34

"Winter" (Brontë), **V**: 107

"Winter" (Dunn), **Supp. X**: 69

"Winter" (Thomas), **Supp. XII**: 290

Winter (Thomson), **Supp. III**: 411, 412–413, 417, 418

Winter Apology (Bainbridge), **Supp. VI**: 22–23

"Winter Field" (Coppard), **VIII**: 98

Winter Fuel (Millais), **V**: 379

Winter Garden (Bainbridge), **Supp. VI:** 22–23, 24

Winter House and Other Poems, The (Cameron), **Supp. IX:** 17, 22–25

"Winter in Camp" (Fuller), **Supp. VII:** 70

"Winter in England" (Fuller), **Supp. VII:** 70

"Winter in July" (Lessing), **Supp. I:** 240

Winter in the Air (Warner), **Supp. VII:** 380

"Winter Landscape near Ely, A" (Davie), **Supp. VI:** 110

"Winter, My Secret" (Rossetti), **V:** 256

"Winter Night" (Fuller), **Supp. VII:** 72

Winter Pilgrimage, A (Haggard), **Supp. III:** 214

Winter Pollen: Occasional Prose (Hughes), **Retro. Supp. II:** 202

Winter Tales (Brown), **Supp. VI:** 68–70

"Winter with the Gulf Stream" (Hopkins), **V:** 361, 381

Winter Words, in Various Moods and Metres (Hardy), **VI:** 20

Winter Work (Fallon), **Supp. XII:** 106–108, 109, 114

"Winter Work" (Fallon), **Supp. XII:** 106

Wintering Out (Heaney), **Supp. II:** 268, 272–273; **Retro. Supp. I:** 125, 128

Winters, Yvor, **VI:** 219; **Supp. IV:** 256–257, 261; **Retro. Supp. I:** 335

"Winters and the Palmleys, The" (Hardy), **VI:** 22

"Winter's Talc, A" (Thomas), **Supp. I:** 177, 178

Winter's Tale, The (Chaucer), **I:** 25

Winter's Tale, The (Shakespeare), **I:** 166n, 302, 322–323, 327

"Winter's Talents" (Davie), **Supp. VI:** 112

"Winter–Saturday" (Crawford), **Supp. XI:** 70–71

Winterslow: Essays and Characters Written There (Hazlitt), **IV:** 140

Winterson, Jeanette, **Supp. IV: 541–559**

Winterwood and Other Hauntings (Roberts, K.), **Supp. X:** 273

"Wintry Manifesto, A" (Wallace–Crabbe), **VIII:** 313

"Wires" (Larkin), **Supp. I:** 278, 285

"Wisdom Literature", **Retro. Supp. II:** 304

Wisdom of Father Brown, The (Chesterton), **VI:** 338

"Wisdom of Gautama, The" (Caudwell), **Supp. IX:** 33

Wisdom of Solomon Paraphrased, The (Middleton), **II:** 2

Wisdom of the Ancients (Bacon), *see De sapientia veterum*

Wise, T. J., **V:** 150, 151

Wise Children (Carter), **Supp. III:** 90–91

Wise Virgins (Wilson), **Supp. VI:** 297, **301**, 303

Wise Wound, The (Redgrove), **Supp. VI:** 230, 233

"Wish, The" (Cowley), **II:** 195, 198

"Wish, The" (Dahl), **Supp. IV:** 206, 221

"Wish House, The" (Kipling), **VI:** 169, 193, 196, **197–199**

"Wish in Spring" (Warner), **Supp. VII:** 373

"Wishes to His (Supposed), Mistresse" (Crashaw), **II:** 180

Wit at Several Weapons, **II:** 21, 66

Wit Without Money (Fletcher), **II:** 66

Witch, The (Middleton), **II:** 3, 21; **IV:** 79

Witch, The (Williams, C. W. S.), **Supp. IX:** 276–277

Witch Hunt (Rankin), **Supp. X:** 245, 252

"Witch of Atlas, The" (Shelley), **IV:** 196, 204

Witch of Edmonton, The (Dekker, Ford, Rowley), **II:** 89, 100

"Witch of Fife, The" (Hogg), **Supp. X:** 106–108

Witchcraft (Williams, C. W. S.), **Supp. IX:** 284

Witches, The (Dahl), **Supp. IV:** 204, 213, 215, 225–226

Witches, The (film), **Supp. IV:** 203

"Witches' Corner, The" (Fallon), **Supp. XII:** 108–109

"Witches of Traquair, The" (Hogg), **Supp. X:** 110

Witch's Head, The (Haggard), **Supp. III:** 213

With My Little Eye (Fuller), **Supp. VII:** 70–71

"With my Sons at Boarhills" (Stevenson), **Supp. VI:** 260

"With Your Tongue Down My Throat" (Kureishi), **Supp. XI:** 158

Wither, George, **IV:** 81

"Withered Arm, The" (Hardy), **VI:** 22; **Retro. Supp. I:** 116

Within the Gates (O'Casey), **VII:** 7

Within the Tides: Tales (Conrad), **VI:** 148

"Without Benefit of Clergy" (Kipling), **VI:** 180–183

"Without Eyes" (Redgrove), **Supp. VI:** 235

"Without the Option" (Wodehouse), **Supp. III:** 456

Witlings, The (Burney), **Supp. III:** 64, 71, 72, 75

"Witness, The" (Lessing), **Supp. I: 244**

Witness for the Prosecution (Christie), **Supp. II:** 125, 134

Wit's Treasury (Meres), **I:** 296

Wittig, Monique, **Supp. IV:** 558

Wives and Daughters (Gaskell), **V:** xxiii, 1–4, 8, 11–13, 14, 15

Wizard of Oz, The (Baum), **Supp. IV:** 450

Wizard of Oz, The (film), **Supp. IV:** 434, 443, 448, 450, 455

Wizard of Oz, The (Rushdie), **Supp. IV:** 434

Wodehouse, P. G., **Supp. III: 447–464**

Wodwo (Hughes), **Supp. I:** 343, 346, **348–350**, 363; **Retro. Supp. II:** 205–206

Woefully Arrayed (Skelton), **I:** 84

Wog (Carey), **Supp. XII:** 52

Wolf and the Lamb, The (Henryson), **Supp. VII:** 136, 141

Wolf and the Wether, The (Henryson), **Supp. VII:** 136, 140–141

Wolf, Friedrich, **IV:** 316–317

Wolf, Lucien, **IV:** 293

Wolf Leader, The (Dumas *père*), **III:** 339

Wolf that gat the Nekhering throw the wrinkis of the Foxe that begylit the Cadgear, The (Henryson), see *Fox, the Wolf, and the Cadger, The*

Wolfe, Tom, **Supp. IV:** 454

Wolff, S. L., **I:** 164

"Wolfhound, The" (Murphy), **Supp. V:** 323

Wolfman (Rankin), **Supp. X:** 244, 246, 248, 250

Wolfwatching (Hughes), **Retro. Supp. II:** 214

Wollstonecraft, Mary, **Supp. III: 465–482**; **Retro. Supp. I:** 39

Wolves and the Lamb, The (Thackeray), **V:** 35

Woman (periodical), **VI:** 249

Woman, The (Bond), **Supp. I:** 423, 434, 435

"Woman, The Place, The Poet, The" (Boland), **Supp. V:** 35

Woman and Labour (Schreiner), **Supp. II:** 444, **454–456**

"Woman at the Shore, The" (Mansfield), **VII:** 173

Woman Beware Woman 231, 233–234, 235 236

Woman–Captain, The (Shadwell), **II:** 359

Woman Hater, The (Beaumont and Fletcher), **II:** 46, 65

Woman–Hater, The (Burney), **Supp. III:** 64

"Woman in His Life, The" (Kipling), **VI:** 193

Woman in Mind (Ayckbourn), **Supp. V:** 3, 6–7, 10, 11, 13, 15

Woman in the Moon, The (Lyly), **I:** 204–205

Woman in White, The (Collins), **III:** 340, 345; **Supp. VI:** 91–94, **95–97**, 100, 102–103

Woman Killed With Kindness, A (Heywood), **II:** 19

Woman of No Importance, A (Bennett), **VIII:** 27

Woman of No Importance, A (Wilde), **V:** xxvi, 414, 419; **Retro. Supp. II:** 369

"Woman of No Standing, A" (Behan), **Supp. II:** 66

"Woman of the House, The" (Murphy), **Supp. V:** 313, 318–319

Woman of the Inner Sea (Keneally), **Supp. IV:** 347, 348, 358–360

"Woman out of a Dream, A" (Warner), **Supp. VII:** 373

Woman Pleased (Fletcher), **II:** 45, 65

"Woman! When I behold thee flippant, vain" (Keats), **Retro. Supp. I:** 188–189

"Woman Who Rode Away, The" (Lawrence), **VII:** 87–88, 91, 115

Woman Who Walked into Doors, The (Doyle), **Supp. V:** 78, 88, 91–92

Womanhood, Wanton, Ye Want (Skelton), **I:** 83

"Womans constancy" (Donne), **Retro. Supp. II:** 89

"Woman's History, A" (Davies), **Supp. XI:** 99

"Woman's Last Word, A" (Browning), **IV:** 367; **Retro. Supp. II:** 24

Woman's Prize, The; or, The Tamer Tamed (Fletcher), **II:** 43, 45, 65

"Woman's Song" (Warner), **Supp. VII:** 373

Woman's World (periodical), **V:** 404

Womb of Space: The Cross–Cultural Imagination (Harris), **Supp. V:** 140, 146

"Women, The" (Boland), **Supp. V:** 50–51

"Women" (Smith, I. C.), **Supp. IX:** 218

"Women, The" (Stevenson), **Supp. VI:** 254

Women at Oxford: A Fragment of History, The (Brittain), **Supp. X:** 47

"Women at Geneva" (Brittain), **Supp. X:** 37

Women: Or, Pour et Contre (Maturin), **VIII:** 207

Women Beware Women (Middleton), **II:** 1, 3, 8, **10–14,** 19

Women Fly When Men Aren't Watching (Maitland), **Supp. XI:** 170, 174, 175, 176

Women in Love (Lawrence), **IV:** 119; **VI:** 276; **VII:** 87–88, 89, 91, 98, **101–104;** **Retro. Supp. II:** 228–229

Women's Work in Modern England (Brittain), **Supp. X:** 39

"Wonder" (Traherne), **II:** 191; **Supp. XI:** 266

Wonder of Women, The; or, The Tragedie of Sophonisba (Marston), **II:** 25, 30–31, 40, 305

"Wonderful Story of Henry Sugar, The" (Dahl), **Supp. IV:** 223

Wonderful Tennessee (Friel), **Supp. V:** 126–127

Wonderful Visit, The (Wells), **VI:** 226, 228, 230, 243

Wondrous Tale of Alroy, The (Disraeli), *see Alroy*

Wood, Anthony à, **II:** 185

Wood Beyond, The (Hill, R.), **Supp. IX:** 121

Wood Beyond the World, The (Morris), **V:** 306

"Wood Fire, The" (Hardy), **Retro. Supp. I:** 121

"Wooden Chair with Arms" (MacCaig), **Supp. VI:** 192

Woodhouse, Richard, **IV:** 230, 232, 233

Woodlanders, The (Hardy), **VI:** 1, 5, 7, 8, 9; **Retro. Supp. I:** 115

Woodman, Thomas, **Supp. IV:** 364

Woods, Helen Emily, *see* Kavan, Anna

"Woods of Westermain, The" (Meredith), **V:** 221

"Woodsman" (MacCaig), **Supp. VI:** 192

"Woodspurge, The" (Rossetti), **V:** 241, 242, 314–315

Woodstock (Scott), **IV:** xviii, 27, 39

Woodward, Benjamin, **V:** 178

Woolf, Leonard, **VI:** 415; **VII:** 17

Woolf, Virginia, **I:** 169; **IV:** 107, 320, 322; **V:** xxv, 226, 256, 260, 281, 290; **VI:** 243, 252, 275, 411; **VII:** xii, xiv–xv, **17–39; Supp. II:** 341–342, 487, 501–502;

Supp. III: 19, 41–42, 45, 49, 60, 103, 107, 108; **Supp. IV:** 231, 233, 246, 399, 407, 461, 542, 558; **Supp. V:** 36, 63; **Retro. Supp. I:** 59, **305–323**

"Wool–Gatherer, The" (Hogg), **Supp. X:** 111

Woolley, Hannah, **Supp. III:** 21

Woolley, Leonard, **Supp. II:** 284

"Word, The" (Hart), **Supp. XI:** 132

"Word, The" (E. Thomas), **Supp. III:** 406

"Word, The" (R.S. Thomas), **Supp. XII:** 290, 291

Word Child, A (Murdoch), **Supp. I:** 228

Word for the Navy, A (Swinburne), **V:** 332

Word over All (Day Lewis), **Supp. III:** 118, 128

Word–Links (Carroll), **V:** 274

"Words" (Gunn), **Supp. IV:** 267

Words and Music (Beckett), **Supp. I:** 53, 60

Words and Music (Coward), **Supp. II:** 152

"Words for Jazz Perhaps" (Longley), **VIII:** 167

Words of Advice (Weldon), **Supp. IV:** 536–537

Words upon the Window Pane, The (Yeats), **VI:** 219, 222

Wordsworth, Dorothy, **II:** 273; **IV:** 1–4, 10, 19, 49, 128, 143, 146

Wordsworth, William, **II:** 188–189; **III:** 174; **IV:** viii–xi, **1–26,** 33, 70, 73, 95–96, 111, 137, 178, 214, 215, 281, 311, 351, 352; **V:** 287, 311, 331, 351–352; **VI:** 1; and Coleridge, **IV:** 43–45, 50, 51, 54; **Retro. Supp. II:** 62, 63–64; and DeQuincey, **IV:** 141–143, 146, 154; and Hazlitt, **IV:** 126–130, 133–134, 137, 138; and Keats, **IV:** 214, 215, 225, 233; and Shelley, **IV:** 198, 203, 207; and Tennyson, **IV:** 326, 329, 336; literary style, **III:** 304, 338; **IV:** 95–96, 154, 336; verse forms, **II:** 200; **V:** 224; **Supp. II:** 269; **Supp. IV:** 230, 252, 558

"Wordsworth" (Pater), **V:** 351–352

"Wordsworth and Byron" (Swinburne), **V:** 332

"Wordsworth's Ethics" (Stephen), **V:** 287

"Work" (Lamb), **IV:** 83

Work in Hand (Cameron), **Supp. IX:** 26–27

Work in Progress (Cameron), **Supp. IX:** 17

Work in Progress (Lowry), **Supp. III:** 280

Work in Progress (Redgrove), **Supp. VI:** 231

Work in Regress (Reading), **VIII:** 273

"Work of Art, A" (Warner), **Supp. VII:** 380

"Work of My Own, A" (Winterson), **Supp. IV:** 558

"Work of Water, The" (Redgrove), **Supp. VI:** 235

Work Suspended (Waugh), **VII:** 298–299

Work, Wealth and Happiness of Mankind, The (Wells), **VI:** 225

"Work without Hope" (Coleridge), **Retro. Supp. II:** 65

Workers in the Dawn (Gissing), **V:** 424, 435, 437

Workes of Edmund Waller in This Parliament, The (Waller), **II:** 238

"Workhouse Clock, The," (Hood), **IV:** 261, 264

Workhouse Donkey, The (Arden), **Supp. II:** 28, 30

Workhouse Ward, The (Gregory), **VI:** 315, 316

Working Legs: A Two–Act Play for Disabled Performers (Gray, A.), Supp. **IX:** 89–90

Working Novelist, The (Pritchett), **VI:** 290

Working of Water, The (Redgrove), **Supp. VI:** 235–236

Working with Structuralism: Essays and Reviews on Nineteenth– and Twentieth–Century Literature (Lodge), **Supp. IV:** 365, 377

"Workmen" (Crawford), **Supp. XI:** 81

Works (Congreve), **II:** 348

Works (Cowley), **II:** 195

Works (Swift), **III:** 24

Works of Art and Artists in England (Waagen), **III:** 328

Works of Charles Lamb, The, **IV:** 73, 81, 85

Works of Henry Fielding, The (ed. Stephen), **V:** 290

Works of Henry Vaughan, The (Martin), **II:** 184

Works of Max Beerbohm, The (Beerbohm), **Supp. II:** 45, 46, 47

Works of Morris and Yeats in Relation to Early Saga Literature, The (Hoare), **V:** 299, 306

Works of Ossian (Macpherson), **VIII:** 189, 192

Works of Samuel Johnson, The, **III:** 108n, 121

Works of Sir John Vanbrugh, The (ed. Dobrée and Webb), **II:** 323n

Works of Sir Thomas Malory, The (ed. Vinavier), **I:** 70, 80

Works of the English Poets (Johnson), **Retro. Supp. I:** 143

Works of Thomas Lodge, The (Tyler), **VI:** 102

Works of Virgil, The (tr. Dryden), **II:** 304

Works of William Blake, The (ed. Yeats), **VI:** 222

World (periodical), **VI:** 103, 104

"World, The" (Vaughan), **II:** 185, 186, 188

World Authors: 1970–1975 (ed. Wakeman), **Supp. XI:** 246, 248, 249, 253

World Bank: A Prospect, The (Morris, J.), **Supp. X:** 175

World Crisis, The (Churchill), **VI:** 353–354

World I Breathe, The (Thomas), **Supp. I:** 176, 180–181

World in the Evening, The (Isherwood), **VII:** 309, 314–315

World of Charles Dickens, The (Wilson), **Supp. I:** 166

World of Difference, A (MacCaig), **Supp. VI:** 193–194

"World of Light, A" (Jennings), **Supp. V:** 210

World of Light, A (Sarton), **Supp. II:** 82

World of Light, The (Huxley), **VII:** 201

World of Love, A (Bowen), **Supp. II:** 77, 79, 81, 84, 94

World of Paul Slickey, The (Osborne), **Supp. I:** 333–334

World of Strangers, A (Gordimer), **Supp. II:** 227, 231, 232, 236, 243

"World of Women, The" (Fallon), **Supp. XII:** 111

World Set Free, The: A Story of Mankind (Wells), **VI:** 227, 244

World Within World (Spender), **Supp. II:** 482, 483, 484, 485, 486, 487, 488, 490

Worldliness (Moore), **VI:** 95, 98

Worlds, The (Bond), **Supp. I:** 423, 434

World's Desire, The (Haggard and Lang), **Supp. III:** 213, 222

"World's End, The" (Empson), **Supp. II:** 182

World's Room, The (MacCaig), **Supp. VI:** 192

"Worlds That Flourish" (Okri), **Supp. V:** 356

Worm and the Ring, The (Burgess), **Supp. I:** 186, 187, 188, 189

Worm of Spindlestonheugh, The (Swinburne), **V:** 333

Wormwood (Kinsella), **Supp. V:** 262–263

"Wormwood" (Kinsella), **Supp. V:** 262

Worst Fears (Weldon), **Supp. IV:** 538

"Worst of It, The" (Browning), **IV:** 369

"Worstward Ho" (Beckett), **Supp. I:** 62; **Retro. Supp. I:** 29–30

Worthies of England (Fuller), **II:** 45

Worthies of Westminster (Fuller), **Retro. Supp. I:** 152

Wotton, Sir Henry, **II:** 132, 133, 134, 138, 140, 141, 142, 166

Wotton, William, **III:** 23

Wotton Reinfred (Carlyle), **IV:** 250

Woty, W., **III:** 170n

"Wound, The" (Gunn), **Supp. IV:** 259

"Wound, The" (Hughes), **Supp. I:** 348

Wound in My Heart, The (Ngũgĩ), **VIII:** 222

"Wounds" (Longley), **VIII:** 171

"Wowing of the King quhen he wes in Dumfermeling, The" (Dunbar), **VIII:** 118

"Wreath for Tom Moore's Statue" (Kavanagh), **Supp. VII:** 193

"Wreaths" (Hill), **Supp. V:** 186

"Wreaths" (Longley), **VIII:** 173

"Wreck" (MacCaig), **Supp. VI:** 186

Wreck of the Archangel, The (Brown), **Supp. VI:** 71

"Wreck of the Deutschland, The" (Hopkins), **V:** 361, 362, **363–366**, 367, 369, 370, 375, 379, 380, 381; **Retro. Supp. II:** 189, 191–194

"Wreck of the Deutschland, The": A New Reading (Schneider), **V:** 366, 382

Wreck of the Mary Deare, The (film, Ambler), **Supp. IV:** 3

Wrecked Eggs (Hare), **Supp. IV:** 282, 293

Wrecker, The (Stevenson), **V:** 383, 387, 396

Wrens, The (Gregory), **VI:** 315–316

"Wrestling" (Rossetti), **V:** 260

Wretched of the Earth, The (Fanon), *see Les Damnés de la terre*

Wright, William Aldis, **IV:** 343, 353

Write On: Occasional Essays, '65–'85 (Lodge), **Supp. IV:** 366

Writer and the Absolute, The (Lewis), **VII:** xv, 71, 72, 73–74, 76

Writer in Disguise, The (Bennett), **VIII:** 27

Writers and Their Work series, **VII:** xi, xxii

Writer's Britain: Landscape in Literature, A (ed. Drabble), **Supp. IV:** 230, 252

Writer's Diary, A (Woolf), **V:** 226

"Writer's Friends, A" (Stead), **Supp. IV:** 461, 466

Writers in Politics (Ngũgĩ), **VIII:** 224

Writer's Ireland: Landscape in Literature, A (Trevor), **Supp. IV:** 514

Writer's Notebook, A (Maugham), **VI:** 365, 366

"Writers Take Sides, The" (Stead), **Supp. IV:** 463, 466

"Writing" (Auden), **Retro. Supp. I:** 13

"Writing" (Motion), **Supp. VII:** 256

"Writing as a Woman" (Stevenson), **Supp. VI:** 257

Writing Game: A Comedy, The (Lodge), **Supp. IV:** 366, 381

Writing in a State of Seige (Brink), **Supp. VI:** 47, 49

Writing Left Handed (Hare), **Supp. IV:** 282, 283

"Written After the Death of Charles Lamb" (Wordsworth), **IV:** 73

"Written in My Lady Speke's Singing Book" (Waller), **II:** 234

Written on the Body (Winterson), **Supp. IV:** 542, 547, 549–551, 552, 553, 555, 557

Wrong About Japan: A Father's Journey with His Son (Carey), **Supp. XII:** 54

Wrong Box, The (Stevenson and Osbourne), **V:** 387, 396

"Wrong Name, The" (Powys), **VIII:** 251

Wulf and Eadwacer, **Retro. Supp. II:** 305

Wulfstan, Archbishop, **Retro. Supp. II:** 298

Wurzel–Flummery (Milne), **Supp. V:** 298–299

Wuthering Heights (Brontë), **III:** 333, 338, 344, 345; **V:** xx, 113, 114, 127, 128, 131, 133–135, 140, **141–145,** 254; **Supp. III:** 144, 145; **Supp. IV:** 231, 452, 462, 513; **Retro. Supp. I:** 50, 52, 53, 54, 57–58

Wyatt, Sir Thomas, **I:** **97–112,** 113, 115

"Wyatt resteth here, that quick could never rest" (Surrey), **I:** 115

Wycherley, William, **II:** **307–322,** 343, 352, 360

Wycliffe, John, **I:** 375

Wyllard's Weird (Braddon), **VIII:** 49

Wymer, T. L., **V:** 324, 335

"Wyncote, Pennsylvania: A Gloss" (Kinsella), **Supp. V:** 274

Wyndham, Francis, **Supp. IV:** 159, 161, 304

Wyndham, John, **Supp. V:** 22

Wyndham Lewis: A Memoir (Eliot), **VII:** 77

Wyndham Lewis: His Theory of Art and Communication (McLuhan), **VII:** 71n

Xanadu (Armitage), **VIII:** 1

"XL. A Lake" (Beddoes), **Supp. XI:** 29

Xorandor (Brooke–Rose), **Supp. IV:** 100, 111

X/Self (Brathwaite), **Supp. XII:** 33, 41–42, 46

XVI Revelations of Divine Love, Shewed to a Devout Servant of Our Lord, Called Mother Juliana, an Anchorete of Norwich: Who Lived in the Dayes of King Edward the Third (Julian of Norwich), **Supp. XII:** 155

XX Poems (Larkin), **Supp. I:** 277

"XXII. Life a Glass Window" (Beddoes), **Supp. XI:** 29

"XXXVIII. Rain" (Beddoes), **Supp. XI:** 29

"Yaddo Letter, The" (Mahon), **Supp. VI:** 176

Yan Tan Tethera (Harrison), **Supp. V:** 150, 164

Yangtse Incident (film, Ambler), Supp. **IV:** 3

Yangtze Valley and Beyond, The (Bird), **Supp. X:** 31

Yard of Sun, A (Fry), **Supp. III:** 191, 194, 195, 204–205

"Yardley Oak" (Cowper), **III:** 218

"Yarrow" (Muldoon), **Supp. IV:** 429–432

Yarrow Revisited, and Other Poems (Wordsworth), **IV:** 25

Yates, Edmund, **V:** 20

Yates, Frances M., **I:** 237

"Ye happy youths, whose hearts are free" (Etherege), **II:** 267

Yealland, Lewis, **Supp. IV:** 58–59

Year of the Whale, The (Brown), **Supp. VI:** 71

Year In, Year Out (Milne), **Supp. V:** 309, 310–311

"Year of the Foxes, The" (Malouf), **Supp. XII:** 219

"Year of the Sloes, For Ishi, The" (Muldoon), **Supp. IV:** 414

Year to Remember: A Reminiscence of 1931, A (Waugh), **Supp. VI:** 273

Years, The (Woolf), **VII:** 18, 22, 24, 27, 28, 36, 38; **Retro. Supp. I:** 308

Year's Afternoon, The (Dunn), **Supp. X:** 81–83

Years Between, The (Kipling), **VI:** 204

"Years Later" (Murphy), **Supp. V:** 313, 320

Years of the Young Rebels, The (Spender), **Supp. II:** 493

"Years On" (Wallace–Crabbe), **VIII:** 323

Yeast (Kingsley), **V:** 4

"Yeats, Berkeley, and Romanticism" (Davie), **Supp. VI:** 107

Yeats, William Butler, **II:** 78; **III:** 21, 36, 184; **IV:** 196, 216, 323, 329; **V:** xxiii, xxv, xxvi, 301, 304, 306, 311, 318,